Lecture Notes in Computer Science 13099

More information about this subseries at https://link.springer.com/bookseries/7410

Mauro Conti · Marc Stevens ·
Stephan Krenn (Eds.)

Cryptology and Network Security

20th International Conference, CANS 2021
Vienna, Austria, December 13–15, 2021
Proceedings

 Springer

Editors
Mauro Conti 🆔
University of Padua
Padua, Italy

Marc Stevens 🆔
Centrum Wiskunde & Informatica
Amsterdam, The Netherlands

Stephan Krenn 🆔
AIT Austrian Institute of Technology
Vienna, Austria

ISSN 0302-9743   ISSN 1611-3349 (electronic)
Lecture Notes in Computer Science
ISBN 978-3-030-92547-5   ISBN 978-3-030-92548-2 (eBook)
https://doi.org/10.1007/978-3-030-92548-2

LNCS Sublibrary: SL4 – Security and Cryptology

This Springer imprint is published by the registered company Springer Nature Switzerland AG
The registered company address is: Gewerbestrasse 11, 6330 Cham, Switzerland

Preface

The 20th International Conference on Cryptology and Network Security (CANS 2021) was held during December 13–15, 2021. CANS 2021 was held in cooperation with the International Association for Cryptologic Research (IACR) and the AIT Austrian Institute of Technology. Due to the ongoing COVID-19 pandemic, CANS 2021 was held as a virtual conference, instead of at the intended venue in Vienna, Austria.

CANS is a recognized annual conference focusing on cryptology, computer and network security, and data security and privacy, attracting cutting-edge research findings from scientists around the world. Previous editions of CANS were held in Taipei (2001), San Francisco (2002), Miami (2003), Xiamen (2005), Suzhou (2006), Singapore (2007), Hong Kong (2008), Kanazawa (2009), Kuala Lumpur (2010), Sanya (2011), Darmstadt (2012), Parary (2013), Crete (2014), Marrakesh (2015), Milan (2016), Hong Kong (2017), Naples (2018), Fuzhou (2019), and virtually (2020).

In 2021, the conference received 85 valid submissions. The submission and review process were completed using the EasyChair Web-based software system. We were helped by 30 Program Committee members and 63 external reviewers. The submissions went through a double-blind review process and 28 papers were selected. This volume collates the revised versions of the accepted papers. The Best Paper Award was given to the paper "Subversion-Resistant Quasi-Adaptive NIZK and Applications to Modular zk-SNARKs" by Behzad Abdolmaleki and Daniel Slamanig.

We would like to thank the AIT Austrian Institute of Technology, as well as the H2020 initiative CyberSec4Europe, for their support during the planning of the conference. We would also like to thank Springer for their support with producing the proceedings. We heartily thank the authors of all submitted papers. Moreover, we are grateful to the members of the Program Committee and the external sub-reviewers for their diligent work, as well as all members of the Organizing Committee for their kind help. We would also like to acknowledge the Steering Committee for supporting us.

October 2021

Mauro Conti
Marc Stevens
Stephan Krenn

Organization

Steering Committee

Yvo G. Desmedt (Chair)	University of Texas at Dallas, USA
Juan A. Garay	Texas A&M University, USA
Amir Herzberg	Bar-Ilan University, Israel
Yi Mu	Fujian Normal University, China
Panos Papadimitratos	KTH Royal Institute of Technology, Sweden
David Pointcheval	CNRS and ENS Paris, France
Huaxiong Wang	Nanyang Technological University, Singapore

Program Committee Chairs

Mauro Conti	Università degli Studi di Padova, Italy
Marc Stevens	Centrum Wiskunde & Informatica (CWI), The Netherlands

General Chair

Stephan Krenn	AIT Austrian Institute of Technology, Austria

Organizing Committee

Alessandro Brighente	Università degli Studi di Padova, Italy
Manuela Kos	AIT Austrian Institute of Technology, Austria
Edgar Weippl	SBA Research and University of Vienna, Austria

Program Committee

Masayuki Abe	NTT, Japan
Cristina Alcaraz	University of Malaga, Spain
Lejla Batina	Radboud University, The Netherlands
Alastair Beresford	University of Cambridge, UK
Alessandro Brighente	University of Padua, Italy
Mauro Conti	University of Padua, Italy
Zekeriya Erkin	Delft University of Technology, The Netherlands
Peter Gaži	IOHK Research, Slovakia
Dieter Gollmann	Hamburg University of Technology, Germany
Sotiris Ioannidis	Technical University of Crete, Greece
Chhagan Lal	University of Padua, Italy
Riccardo Lazzeretti	Sapienza University of Rome, Italy

Eleonora Losiouk	University of Padua, Italy
Mark Manulis	University of Surrey, UK
Chris Mitchell	Royal Holloway, University of London, UK
Veelasha Moonsamy	Ruhr University Bochum, Germany
Gerardo Pelosi	Politecnico di Milano, Italy
Raphael C.-W. Phan	Monash University, Malaysia
Stjepan Picek	Delft University of Technology, The Netherlands
Sushmita Ruj	CSIRO, Data61, Australia
Dominique Schroeder	Friedrich-Alexander University Erlangen-Nürnberg, Germany
Angelo Spognardi	Sapienza University of Rome, Italy
Marc Stevens	Centrum Wiskunde & Informatica (CWI), The Netherlands
Thorsten Strufe	Karlsruhe Institute of Technology (KIT) and TU Dresden, Germany
Daniele Venturi	Sapienza University of Rome, Italy
Frederik Vercauteren	Katholieke Universiteit Leuven, Belgium
Damien Vergnaud	Université Pierre et Marie Curie and Institut Universitaire de France, France
Corrado Aaron Visaggio	University of Sannio, Italy
Edgar Weippl	University of Vienna, Austria
Chia-Mu Yu	National Chung Hsing University, Taiwan

Additional Reviewers

Hamza Abusalah
Kamalesh Acharya
Erdem Alkim
Miguel Ambrona
Francesco Antognazza
Fatih Balli
Ward Beullens
Tim Beyne
Sanjay Bhattacherjee
Hamid Bostani
George Christou
Sandro Coretti
Joan Daemen
F. W. Dekker
Cyprien Delpech de Saint Guilhem
Dominic Deuber
Sabyasachi Dey
Dimitris Deyannis
Michalis Diamantaris
Sabyasachi Dutta
Christoph Egger

Maryam Ehsanpour
Solane El Hirch
Francesco Felet
Danilo Francati
Jonathan Fuchs
Rafa Gálvez
Ankit Gangwal
Robert Granger
Bernhard Haslhofer
Ilia Iliashenko
Gulshan Kumar
Russell W. F. Lai
Eftychia Lakka
Mario Larangeira
Julia Len
Tianyu Li
Jia Liu
Philipp Markert
Subhra Mazumdar
Alireza Mehrdad
Konstantina Miteloudi

Vinod P. Nair
Miyako Ohkubo
Guillermo Pascual-Perez
Robi Pedersen
Hilder Vitor Lima Pereira
Nikolaos Petroulakis
Md Masoom Rabbani
Viktoria Ronge
Paul Rösler
Rahul Saha
Simona Samardjiska

Laltu Sardar
Sruthi Sekar
Vojtech Suchanek
Titouan Tanguy
Cihangir Tezcan
Sri Aravinda Krishnan Thyagarajan
Meltem Sonmez Turan
Michiel Van Beirendonck
Jelle Vos
Florian Weber

Contents

Encryption

Cross-Domain Attribute-Based Access Control Encryption

Mahdi Sedaghat[✉] and Bart Preneel

imec-COSIC, KU Leuven, Leuven, Belgium
{ssedagha,bart.preneel}@esat.kuleuven.be

Abstract. Logic access control enforces who can read and write data; the enforcement is typically performed by a fully trusted entity. At TCC 2016, Damgård et al. proposed Access Control Encryption (ACE) schemes where a predicate function decides whether or not users can read (decrypt) and write (encrypt) data, while the message secrecy and the users' anonymity are preserved against malicious parties. Subsequently, several ACE constructions with an arbitrary identity-based access policy have been proposed, but they have huge ciphertext and key sizes and/or rely on indistinguishability obfuscation. At IEEE S&P 2021, Wang and Chow proposed a Cross-Domain ACE scheme with constant-size ciphertext and arbitrary identity-based policy; the key generators are separated into two distinct parties, called Sender Authority and Receiver Authority. In this paper, we improve over their work with a novel construction that provides a more expressive access control policy based on attributes rather than on identities, the security of which relies on standard assumptions. Our generic construction combines Structure-Preserving Signatures, Non-Interactive Zero-Knowledge proofs, and Re-randomizable Ciphertext-Policy Attribute-Based Encryption schemes. Moreover, we propose an efficient scheme in which the sizes of ciphertexts and encryption and decryption keys are constant and thus independent of the number of receivers and their attributes. Our experiments demonstrate that not only is our system more flexible, but it also is more efficient and results in shorter decryption keys (reduced from about 100 to 47 bytes) and ciphertexts (reduced from about 1400 to 1047).

Keywords: Access Control Encryption · Ciphertext-Policy Attribute-Based Encryption · Structure-Preserving Signature · Non-Interactive Zero-Knowledge Proofs

1 Introduction

Information Flow Control (IFC) systems enforce which parts of the communication amongst the users are allowed to pass over the network [23,25]. As introduced in the seminal work of Bell and LaPadula [5], restrictions have to be imposed on who can receive a message (enforce the No-Read rule) and who

© Springer Nature Switzerland AG 2021
M. Conti et al. (Eds.): CANS 2021, LNCS 13099, pp. 3–23, 2021.
https://doi.org/10.1007/978-3-030-92548-2_1

can send a message (enforce the NO-WRITE rule). Although encryption guarantees users' privacy by limiting the set of recipients, we need more functionality to control who can write and transfer a ciphertext. Broadcasting of sensitive data by malicious senders is a serious threat for companies that handle highly sensitive data such as cryptocurrency wallets with access to signing keys [8].

Although some advanced cryptographical tools such as *Functional Encryption* provide fine-grained access to encrypted data, they do not allow to enforce the NO-WRITE rule, hence additional functionalities beyond these cryptographic primitives are required to protect against data leakage.

To achieve this aim, Damgård et al. [10] introduced a novel scheme called *Access Control Encryption (ACE)* to impose information flow control systems using cryptographic tools. They have defined two security notions for an ACE scheme: the NO-READ rule and the NO-WRITE rule. Unauthorized receivers cannot decrypt the ciphertext and unauthorized senders are not able to transmit data over the network. The model assumes that all the communications are transmitted through an honest-but-curious third party, called SANITIZER. The SANITIZER follows the protocol honestly but it is curious to find out more about the encrypted message and the identities of the users. The SANITIZER performs some operations on the received messages before transmitting them to the intended recipients without learning any information about the message itself or the identity of the users. More precisely, with a set of senders $\mathcal{S}$ and receivers $\mathcal{R}$, an ACE scheme determines via a hidden Boolean Predicate function $\text{PF} : \mathcal{S} \times \mathcal{R} \rightarrow \{0,1\}$ which group of senders (like $i \in \mathcal{S}$) are allowed to communicate with a certain group of receivers (like $j \in \mathcal{R}$): communication is allowed iff $\text{PF}(i,j) = 1$, else the request will be rejected.

Damgård et al. proposed two ACE constructions that support arbitrary policies. Their first construction takes a brute-force approach that is based on standard number-theoretic assumptions, while the size of the ciphertext grows exponentially in the number of receivers. The second scheme is more efficient: ciphertext length is poly-logarithmic in the number of the receivers, but it relies on the strong assumption of *indistinguishability obfuscation (iO)* [13]. In a subsequent work, Fuchsbauer et al. [12] proposed an ACE scheme for restricted classes of predicates including equality, comparisons, and interval membership. Although their scheme is secure under standard assumptions in groups with bilinear maps and asymptotically efficient (i.e., the length of the ciphertext is linear in the number of the receivers), the functionalities of their construction are restricted to a limited class of predicates. Tan et al. [31] proposed an ACE scheme based on the *Learning With Error* (LWE) assumption [24]. Since their construction follows the Damgård et al. approach, the ciphertexts in their construction also grow exponentially with the number of receivers. Recently, Wang et al. [34], proposed an efficient LWE-based ACE construction from group encryptions. Kim and Wu [20] proposed a generic ACE construction based on standard assumptions such that the ciphertext shrinks to poly-logarithmic size in the number of receivers and with arbitrary policies. Their construction requires Digital Signature, Predicate Encryption, and Functional Encryption schemes to obtain an ACE construction based on standard assumptions. Recently, Wang and Chow [33] proposed a new notion called Cross-Domain ACE in which the keys are generated by two distinct entities, the Receiver-Authority and the Sender-Authority. Structure Preserving Signatures, Non-Interactive Zero-Knowledge proofs, and Sanitizable Identity-Based Encryption schemes constitute the main ingredients in their construction. In [33], the length of the ciphertext is constant, but it fails to preserve the identity of the receivers and also the decryption key size grows linearly.

Our Contributions. In this paper, we propose a generic *Cross-Domain Attribute-Based Access Control Encryption* (CD-ABACE) scheme and then propose an efficient CD-ABACE scheme with a constant ciphertext size and constant key length. Next we explain our results in more detail.

This paper re-defines the way to conceive the predicate function in ACE constructions by considering users' attributes instead of their identities. Based on an *Attribute-Based* predicate function, $\mathrm{PF} : \Sigma_k \times \Sigma_c \to \{0,1\}$, the senders with a certain ciphertext index value in Σ_c are limited to transmit data only to restricted recipients with a key index Σ_k. In a nutshell, for an attribute space $\mathbb{U}$, s.t. $\Sigma_k, \Sigma_c \subseteq \mathbb{U}$, the sender who owns a secret encryption key for ciphertext index $\mathbb{P} \in \Sigma_c$ can transmit data to those receivers with private decryption key corresponding to key index $\mathbb{B} \in \Sigma_k$, iff $\mathrm{PF}(\mathbb{B}, \mathbb{P}) = 1$, otherwise, the SANITIZER bans the communication between them. One of the main differences between this approach and the identity-based one is that the anonymity of the receivers corresponds to the level of attribute hiding applied to the underlying *Attribute-Based Encryption (ABE)* scheme.

ABE schemes provide a powerful tool to enforce fine-grained access control over encrypted data; they have been used in several applications [26]. Goyal et al. in [16], proposed two complementary types of ABE schemes: *Key-Policy Attribute-Based Encryption* (KP-ABE) and *Ciphertext-Policy Attribute-Based Encryption* (CP-ABE) schemes. In CP-ABE, the sender embeds a (policy) function $f(\cdot)$ into ciphertext to describe which group of receivers can learn the encrypted message. In this approach, the ciphertext is labeled by an arbitrary function $f(\cdot)$, and secret keys are associated with attributes in the domain of $f(\cdot)$. The decryption algorithm yields the plaintext iff the receivers' attribute set $\mathbb{A}$ satisfies $f(\cdot)$, i.e., $f(\mathbb{A}) = 1$. Conversely, in KP-ABE the secret keys are labeled by the function $f(\cdot)$; this label is set in the setup phase and a ciphertext can only be decrypted with a key whose access structure is satisfied by the set of attributes. In KP-ABE, the access policy cannot be altered after setup phase, while in CP-ABE data owners can control the data access.

Hence, we utilize CP-ABE schemes to limit senders to transmit data to a specific ciphertext index $\mathbb{P}$. While CP-ABE schemes only enable fine-grained access to the encrypted data, they are not equipped to enforce policies for writing a message as well; thus we need additional functionalities to cover the latter by defining secret encryption keys. We utilize a Structure-Preserving Signature to guarantee the given encryption key is valid and one can only get access with a valid signature. A signature of this type allows selective re-randomization of a valid signature, and therefore efficiently proves the validity of this operation. Additionally, the CP-ABE scheme must also be re-randomizable in order to achieve the key-less sanitizability.

Based on realistic application scenarios for ACE constructions, the proposed scheme follows the Cross-Domain key generation method, proposed by Wang and Chow in [33]. In an ACE scheme, the users might belong to two distinct companies with different security levels, so one of them may not be able to grant access rights to the other. In this context, two entities referred to as Sender Authority and Receiver Authority locally generate secret keys for senders and receivers, respectively. Moreover, since users, including senders and receivers, may need to be added to the system later on, the setup phase will be carried out independently of the predicate function. Hence, our approach follows this setup method and we provide a generic construction of a *Cross-Domain Access Control Encryption* scheme based on *Attribute-Based Encryption* constructions.

We finally propose an efficient CD-ABACE construction with constant key and ciphertext sizes. To obtain a CD-ABACE scheme that is efficient both in the length of the parameters and the computational overhead, we propose a novel CP-ABE scheme with AND-gate circuits. More specifically, we say a Boolean AND-gate circuit is satisfied (i.e., the output is true) iff all the input gates are true. In particular, we say the set of attributes $\mathbb{B} \subset \mathbb{U}$ satisfies the AND-gate circuit with the set of input constraints $\mathbb{P} \subseteq \mathbb{U}$ iff $\mathbb{P}$ is a subset of $\mathbb{B}$, i.e., $\mathbb{P} \subseteq \mathbb{B}$. As a simple example, let $\mathbb{U} = \{U_1, U_2, U_3, U_4\}$, then the set of input wires $\mathbb{B} = \{U_1, U_3, U_4\}$ satisfies the circuit $\mathbb{P} = \{U_1, U_4\}$, because $\mathbb{P} \subseteq \mathbb{B}$. Identity-based encryptions are special cases of AND-gate ABE schemes with an attribute universe consisting of the users' identity and also $|\mathbb{B}| = 1$. Moreover, in this construction the SANITIZER only requires public parameters, but no secret or public keys. Our CD-ABACE scheme has the following properties:

– Predicate function takes as inputs user attributes instead of their identities.
– The length of the ciphertext remains constant regardless of the number of receivers and the number of attributes in the access policy.
– All users' secret keys for encryption and decryption consist of only one group element, regardless of the number of attributes of the users.
– As an additional result, we present an efficient CP-ABE scheme with constant size ciphertexts and keys.

Table 1 compares the efficiency of the proposed construction with related works. As illustrated, in our scheme the lengths of the ciphertext and the key are improved to a constant size. The computational overhead for decryption grows linearly with the number of attributes that a receiver owns, while the encryption cost is constant and completely independent of the number of intended recipients. Our experiments show that the time required to run the encryption and decryption algorithm is only $\sim$15 ms and $\sim$45 ms, respectively.

Road-map: The rest of the paper is organized as follows: In Sect. 2, we review the preliminaries and definitions and describe the system architecture. The formal definition of the CD-ABACE scheme and its security definitions are described in Sect. 3. In Sect. 4, we propose the generic construction of CD-ABACE schemes and discuss their security features. In Sect. 5 we present an efficient CD-ABACE construction based on a novel CP-ABE scheme. The performance of the proposed construction is compared in Sect. 6.

Table 1. Comparison of Efficiency and Functionality. n is the number of receivers and the total number of attributes in the system. $r \ll n$ indicates the maximum number of receivers that any sender is allowed to communicate with, and $s \ll n$ denotes the maximum number of senders that any receiver can receive a message from. $t \ll n$ indicates the maximum number of attributes that a sender can transmit data to. The maximum number of legitimate attributes that any recipients possesses to decrypt a ciphertext is denoted by $w \ll n$. SS, CD, PF, PE, IB, AB are short for Selectively Secure, Cross-Domain, Predicate Function, Predicate Encryption, Identity-Based and Attribute-Based, respectively.

Scheme	Ciph. size	Enc. key size	Dec. key size	San. key size	Enc. cost	Dec. cost	CD	PF	Assump.
[10, ‡ 3]	$O(2^n)$	$O(r)$	$O(1)$	$O(1)$	$O(n)$	$O(n)$	✓	IB	DDH/DCR
[10, ‡ 4]	$poly(n)$	$O(1)$	$O(1)$	$O(1)$	$O(1)$	$O(1)$	✗	IB	iO
[12]	$O(n)$	$O(1)$	$O(1)$	$O(1)$	$O(1)$	$O(1)$	✗	IB	SXDH
[20]	$poly(n)$	$O(1)$	$O(1)$	$O(1)$	$O(n)$	$O(n)$	✗	PE	DDH/LWE
[33] (SS)	$O(1)$	$O(1)$	$O(s)$	0	$O(1)$	$O(s)$	✓	IB	GBDP
Ours (SS)	$O(1)$	$O(1)$	$O(1)$	0	$O(1)$	$O(w)$	✓	AB	MSE-DDH

2 Preliminaries and Definitions

To detail the CD-ABACE schemes we need to review some preliminaries. Throu-ghout, we suppose the security parameter of the scheme is λ and $\mathsf{negl}(\lambda)$ denotes a negligible function. Let $\mathbb{U} = \{U_1, \ldots, U_n\} \in \mathbb{Z}_p^n$ be a set and for each subset $\mathbb{A} \subset \mathbb{U}$ we denote the ith component scalar of this subset by A_i. We use $Y \leftarrow_\$ F(X)$ to denote a probabilistic function F that on input X is uniformly sampled resulting in the output Y. Also, $[n]$ denotes the set of integers between 1 and n. The algorithms are randomized unless expressly stated. "PPT" refers to "Probabilistic Polynomial Time". Two computationally indistinguishable distributions A and B are shown with $A \approx_c B$. We assumed a prime order field $\mathbb{F}$ and denote by $\mathbb{F}_{<d}[X]$ the set of univariate polynomials with degree smaller than d. The ith coefficient of the univariate polynomial $f(x) \in \mathbb{F}_{<d}[X]$ is denoted by f_i and a polynomial with degree d has at most $d + 1$ coefficients. The set $\{1, X, X^2, \ldots, X^d\}$ forms the standard basis: it is trivial to show that the representation of the coefficients for a polynomial with degree d as the coefficients of powers X is unique. The vector of A is denoted by $\boldsymbol{A}$.

Definition 1 (Access Structure [4]). *For a given set of parties $\mathcal{P} = \{p_1, \ldots, p_n\}$, we say a collection $\mathbb{U} \subseteq 2^{\mathcal{P}}$ is monotone if, for all A, B, if $A \in \mathbb{U}$ and $A \subseteq B$ then $B \in \mathbb{U}$. Also, $a(n)$ (monotonic) access structure is a (monotone) collection $\mathbb{U} \subseteq 2^{\mathcal{P}} \setminus \{\emptyset\}$. We call the sets in $\mathbb{U}$ authorized sets and the sets that do not belong to $\mathbb{U}$ are called unauthorized.*

Definition 2 (Binary Representation of a subset). *For a given universe set $\mathbb{U}$ of size n, we can represent each subset $\mathbb{A}$ as a binary string of length n. Particularly, the ith the element of the binary string for the subset $\mathbb{A} \subseteq \mathbb{U}$ is equal to 1 (i.e., $a[i] = 1$) if $A_i = U_i$. We show a binary representation set as binary tuple $(a[1], \ldots, a[n]) \in \mathbb{Z}_2^n$.*

Definition 3 (Zero-polynomial). *For a finite set* $\mathbb{U} = \{k_1, \ldots, k_n\}$, *we define the zero-polynomial* $Z_{\mathbb{A}}(X)$ *for a nonempty subset of* $\mathbb{A} \subset \mathbb{U}$ *as* $Z_{\mathbb{A}}(X) := \prod_{i=1}^{n} (X - k_i)^{\overline{a[i]}}$, *where* $\overline{a[i]}$ *is the binary representation of the complement set* $\overline{\mathbb{A}}$. *In other words, this univariate polynomial vanishes on all the elements of the set* $\mathbb{U}$ *for which the binary representation of the subset* $\mathbb{A}$ *is zero.*

Definition 4 (Bilinear Groups [7]). *A Type-III[1] bilinear group generator* $\mathcal{BG}(\lambda)$ *returns a tuple* $(\mathbb{G}_1, \mathbb{G}_2, \mathbb{G}_T, \mathsf{p}, \hat{e})$, *such that* $\mathbb{G}_1$, $\mathbb{G}_2$ *and* $\mathbb{G}_T$ *are cyclic groups of the same prime order* p, *and* $\hat{e} : \mathbb{G}_1 \times \mathbb{G}_2 \to \mathbb{G}_T$ *such that* $\hat{e}(G, H) \neq 1$ *is an efficiently computable bilinear map with the following properties;*

- $\forall \, a, b \in \mathbb{Z}_{\mathsf{p}}, \, \hat{e}(G^a, H^b) = \hat{e}(G, H)^{ab} = \hat{e}(G^b, H^a)$,
- $\forall \, a, b \in \mathbb{Z}_{\mathsf{p}}, \, \hat{e}(G^{a+b}, H) = \hat{e}(G^a, H)\hat{e}(G^b, H)$.

We use the bracket notation: for randomly selected generators $G \in \mathbb{G}_1$ *and* $H \in \mathbb{G}_2$ *we denote* $x \cdot G \in \mathbb{G}_1$ *with* $[x]_1$, *and we write* $\hat{e}\left(G^a, H^b\right) = [a]_1 \bullet [b]_2$.

System Architecture. The proposed scheme's architecture is based on the Cross-Domain ACE technique described in [33]. In a Cross-Domain ACE setting, two distinct entities generate the keys to determine which group of senders can send data to a certain group of receivers and control which group of receivers can read this data. There are five entities in this system as follows:

Receiver Authority (RA) as a trusted third party generates and distributes system parameters and the secret decryption keys for the Receivers. For this aim, based on a certified predicate function $\mathrm{PF}(.,.)$, it authorizes the claimed attributes by the receivers and returns the corresponding secret decryption keys.

Sender Authority (SA) as a semi-trusted entity generates the pair of SA's public parameters and master secret keys; it publishes the former, while it keeps the latter secret. Moreover, it generates the secret encryption keys for the Senders based on a predicate function $\mathrm{PF}(.,.)$ and SA's master secret keys.

Sanitizer is an honest-but-curious party in the network that checks the validity of the communication links and acts based on the predicate function $\mathrm{PF}(.,.)$. If the sender does not allow to transmit a message to the recipients, then the SANITIZER bans the request, else it broadcasts the received ciphertexts. The SANITIZER is semi-honest which means that it follows the protocol honestly but tries to infer some sensitive information including the identities of the users (Senders and Receivers) or compromise the secrecy of a message.

Senders: to share a secret message among a group of receivers, they encrypt data and send the resulting ciphertext to the SANITIZER along with a proof to ensure that they possess a valid encryption key generated by the SA.

Receivers: by having access to the ciphertexts, they can recover the plaintexts using their own attributes and the corresponding secret key for decryption. Conversely, if the receiver does not satisfy the access policy then the ciphertext never reveals any meaningful information about the encrypted message.

---

[1] For the two distinct cyclic groups $\mathbb{G}_1 \neq \mathbb{G}_2$, there is neither efficient algorithm to compute a nontrivial homomorphism in both directions.

In a nutshell, RA sets up the global public parameters of the network and publishes them, while it securely stores its master secret key. After authorizing the receivers' attribute set, RA computes the decryption secret keys corresponding to their attribute sets. From the public parameters issued by RA, SA generates the rest of parameters required for authorization of the senders. Also, SA uses its master secret key to create the authorized secret encryption keys for the senders based on the predicate function $\mathrm{PF}(.,.)$. Since RA is generating the main parameters of the system, it can compromise the security requirements, so we assume this entity is fully-trusted. The sender who wants to share a message securely among a group of receivers re-randomizes the signature (to ensure sender anonymity), then encrypts the plaintext and proves the validity of the claimed hidden witness. The SANITIZER receives the sender's request, and checks the validity of the proof and the signature to decide on rejecting the unauthorized senders without learning their identities. Otherwise, if the sender – based on the predicate function – is authorized to communicate with the selected group of receivers, the SANITIZER re-randomizes the received ciphertext and then passes the sanitized ciphertext on the recipients. Finally, the receivers who are allowed to decrypt a ciphertext can run the decryption algorithm and retrieve the message, else they learn nothing about it. It is assumed the SANITIZER is honest-but-curious: while it follows the protocol honestly, it is unable to compromise the message secrecy and anonymity of the users.

3   Cross-Domain Attribute-Based ACE Scheme

Next we introduce the notion of *Cross-Domain Attribute-Based Access Control Encryption* (CD-ABACE) schemes. The high-level idea behind the definition of a CD-ABACE is that we can generalize the concept of Boolean relations in the plain CP-ABE schemes (see full version [28]) to the predicate function in an ACE construction. In this scenario, the encryption key generator allows the sender to talk to a restricted group of receivers based on a given predicate function. By contrast with the original approach of specifying the ciphertext access rights during the encryption phase, in the present approach, the Sender Authority declares the access right during the encryption key generation phase. Moreover, the generated encryption keys are signed by the SA, and no one can convincingly assert ownership unless they have a correct signature.

Definition 5 (CD-ABACE schemes). *A CD-ABACE scheme $\Psi_{\mathrm{CD\text{-}ABACE}}$ over the message space $\mathcal{M}$, the ciphertext space $\mathcal{C}$ and a predicate function $\mathrm{PF}: \Sigma_k \times \Sigma_c \to \{0,1\}$ has the following PPT algorithms:*

- $(\mathsf{pp}_{ra}, \mathsf{msk}_{ra}) \leftarrow \mathsf{RAgen}(\mathbb{U}, \lambda)$: *This randomized algorithm takes as inputs the security parameter λ and the universe attribute set $\mathbb{U}$, and outputs the public parameters pp_{ra} and master secret key msk_{ra}.*
- $(\mathsf{pp}_{sa}, \mathsf{msk}_{sa}) \leftarrow \mathsf{SAgen}(\lambda, \mathsf{pp}_{ra})$: *This randomized algorithm takes the security parameter λ and RA's public parameters pp_{ra} as inputs and generates the pair of SA's public parameters pp_{sa} and SA's master secret key msk_{sa}.*

- $(\mathsf{dk}_\mathbb{B}) \leftarrow \mathsf{DecKGen}(\mathsf{msk}_{ra}, \mathbb{B})$: *This randomized algorithm takes RA's master secret key* msk_{ra} *and the authorized set of attributes* $\mathbb{B} \in \Sigma_k$ *as inputs and outputs the corresponding private decryption key* $\mathsf{dk}_\mathbb{B}$.

- $(\mathsf{ek}_\mathbb{P}, \sigma, W) \leftarrow \mathsf{EncKGen}(\mathsf{pp}_{ra}, \mathsf{pp}_{sa}, \mathsf{msk}_{sa}, \mathbb{P}, \mathrm{PF})$: *This algorithm takes the public parameters* pp_{ra} *and* pp_{sa}, *the SA's master secret key* msk_{sa}, *authorized ciphertext index* $\mathbb{P} \in \Sigma_c$, *and predicate function* $\mathrm{PF}(.,.)$ *as inputs. It returns the secret encryption key* $\mathsf{ek}_\mathbb{P}$ *that enforces that only the sender can send a message to those receivers who satisfy* $\mathbb{P}$ *along with the signature* σ *and its underlying re-randomizing token* W.

- $(\pi, \mathsf{x}) \leftarrow \mathsf{Enc}(\mathsf{pp}_{ra}, \mathsf{pp}_{sa}, m, \mathsf{ek}_\mathbb{P}, \sigma, W)$: *This algorithm takes as inputs the public parameters, a message* $m \in \mathcal{M}$, *the encryption key corresponding to the attribute set of* $\mathbb{P}$, *a valid signature* σ *and the token* W. *It returns a request including a proof* π *along with its underlying public instance* x.

- $(\tilde{\mathsf{Ct}}, \bot) \leftarrow \mathsf{San}(\mathsf{pp}_{ra}, \mathsf{pp}_{sa}, \pi, \mathsf{x}, \mathrm{PF})$: *This algorithm takes as inputs the public parameters* pp_{ra} *and* pp_{sa}, *a ciphertext along with a proof* π *and its corresponding instance* x. *Afterwards, the algorithm either re-randomizes the ciphertext to* $\tilde{\mathsf{Ct}}$ *or rejects the request. To this end, it checks the validity of the proof and, if it allows this flow based on the predicate function* $\mathrm{PF}(.,.)$, *it transfers the ciphertext* $\tilde{\mathsf{Ct}} \in \mathcal{C}$ *to the receivers, else it returns* $\bot$.

- $(m', \bot) \leftarrow \mathsf{Dec}(\mathsf{pp}_{ra}, \mathsf{pp}_{sa}, \tilde{\mathsf{Ct}}, \mathsf{dk}_\mathbb{B})$: *The decryption algorithm takes as inputs the public parameters* pp_{ra} *and* pp_{sa}, *a re-randomized ciphertext* $\tilde{\mathsf{Ct}}$ *and the decryption key* $\mathsf{dk}_\mathbb{B}$. *If* $\mathrm{PF}(\mathbb{B}, \mathbb{P}) = 1$, *then it returns a message* $m' \in \mathcal{M}$, *otherwise it responds by* $\bot$. *In other words, a recipient with a wrong decryption key learns nothing from the output of this algorithm.*

3.1 Security Definitions

Next we present the required security properties for a CD-ABACE scheme under only CPA-based definitions, where $\mathcal{A}$ has access to encryption, encryption-key generation, and decryption-key generation oracles. Noted that the following security games are motivated by the notion of co-selective CPA security in [3], such that $\mathcal{A}$ has to declare q decryption key queries before the Initialization phase, while it can select the target challenge ciphertext, adaptively. We slightly modify the extended security notions introduced in [33] to adapt them to the CD-ABACE system model.

Definition 6 (Correctness). *For a given attribute universe* $\mathbb{U}$ *and predicate function* $\mathrm{PF} : \Sigma_k \times \Sigma_c \rightarrow \{0, 1\}$, *we say that* $\Psi_{\text{CD-ABACE}}$ *over message space* $\mathcal{M}$ *and ciphertext space* $\mathcal{C}$ *is correct if we have,*

$$\Pr\left[\mathsf{Dec}\left(\mathsf{dk}_\mathbb{B}, \mathsf{San}(\mathsf{Enc}(m, \mathsf{ek}_\mathbb{P}, \mathbb{P}))\right) = m : \mathrm{PF}(\mathbb{B}, \mathbb{P}) = 1\right] \approx_c 1$$

Correctness captures the feature that a sender with an encryption key $\mathsf{ek}_\mathbb{P}$ is able to deliver a message to those receivers for which the attribute set $\mathbb{B}$ satisfies $\mathrm{PF}(\mathbb{B}, \mathbb{P}) = 1$ with a high probability. In this case, the SANITIZER should pass the information on and a receiver with decryption key $\mathsf{dk}_\mathbb{B}$ should be able to retrieve the message correctly from a re-randomized ciphertext.

Definition 7 (No-Read Rule). *Consider $\Psi_{\text{CD-ABACE}}$ over the attribute universe $\mathbb{U}$, message space $\mathcal{M}$, a ciphertext space $\mathcal{C}$ and a predicate function $\text{PF} : \Sigma_k \times \Sigma_c \rightarrow \{0,1\}$. For a security parameter λ, we say that a PPT adversary $\mathcal{A}$ wins the defined* NO-READ *rule security game described in Fig. 1 with access to the oracles in the same table, if she guesses the random bit b better than by chance. It is assumed that for a challenge access structure $\mathbb{P}^*$, $\mathcal{A}$ would not request the decryption key for attribute set $\mathbb{B}_j$, such that $\text{PF}(\mathbb{B}_j, \mathbb{P}^*) = 1$. $\Psi_{\text{CD-ABACE}}$ satisfies the* NO-READ *rule if for all PPT adversaries $\mathcal{A}$ with advantage $Adv^{\text{No-Read}}_{\Psi_{\text{CD-ABACE}}, \mathcal{A}}(1^\lambda, b) = (\Pr[\mathcal{A} \text{ wins the} \text{ No-Read } \text{game}] - 1/2)$ we have,*

$$\left| Adv^{\text{No-Read}}_{\Psi_{\text{CD-ABACE}}, \mathcal{A}}(1^\lambda, b = 0) - Adv^{\text{No-Read}}_{\Psi_{\text{CD-ABACE}}, \mathcal{A}}(1^\lambda, b = 1) \right| \approx_c 0. \text{ When we call } \mathcal{A}, \text{ it}$$

wins the defined security game iff $b' == b$.

Similar to the ID-based ACE constructions, the NO-READ rule in an attribute-based model enforces that only eligible recipients who satisfy a certain access structure, should learn the message while the other participants learn nothing. In particular, not only should an unauthorized receiver be unable to read the messages, combining the decryption secret keys of a group of unauthorized receivers should not reveal any information about the message. Also, this property has to hold even if the recipients collude with the SANITIZER.

Definition 8 (Parameterized No-Write Rule). *Consider $\Psi_{\text{CD-ABACE}}$ over $\mathbb{U}$, a message space $\mathcal{M}$, ciphertext space $\mathcal{C}$ and a predicate function $\text{PF} : \Sigma_k \times \Sigma_c \rightarrow \{0,1\}$. We say a $\Psi_{\text{CD-ABACE}}$ scheme satisfies the Parameterized* NO-WRITE *rule, if no PPT adversary $\mathcal{A}$ with access to the oracles in Fig. 1 has a non-negligible advantage in winning the* NO-WRITE *game, i.e., under the advantage $Adv^{\text{No-Write}}_{\Psi_{\text{CD-ABACE}}, \mathcal{A}}(1^\lambda, b) = (\Pr[\mathcal{A} \text{ wins} \text{ No-Write}] - 1/2)$ we have,*

$$\left| Adv^{\text{No-Write}}_{\Psi_{\text{CD-ABACE}}, \mathcal{A}}(1^\lambda, b = 0) - Adv^{\text{No-Write}}_{\Psi_{\text{CD-ABACE}}, \mathcal{A}}(1^\lambda, b = 1) \right| \approx_c 0.$$

We say $\mathcal{A}$ wins the defined NO-WRITE *game iff $b' == b$ under the condition that for all queried secret encryption keys $\mathbb{P}_i \in \mathcal{Q}_{\mathcal{E}} \cup \{\mathbb{P}^*\}$ and all requested private decryption keys $\mathbb{B}_j \in \mathcal{Q}_{\mathcal{D}}$, along with the challenge access structure $\mathbb{P}^*$, we have $\text{PF}(\mathbb{B}_j, \mathbb{P}_i) = 0$. The function* fix(.) *accepts a ciphertext* Ct *as input and generates auxiliary information* aux *of* Ct *that is not sanitizable [33]. By seeding an encryption algorithm with this auxiliary information, the resulting ciphertext has also the same auxiliary information.*

Remark 1. With regard to the security definitions, the anonymity of the sender is guaranteed and the SANITIZER cannot deduce the identity of the sender while the receivers' anonymity relies on the CP-ABE construction. Note that the same type of property is known as weak attribute hiding in the context of ABE constructions [22]. Although an IND-CPA-secure CP-ABE satisfies the payload hiding property, a stronger security concept, called attribute-hiding CP-ABE, ensures that the set of attributes associated with each ciphertext is also obscured [19]. The latter increases the ciphertext size incrementally and the identity-based encryptions reveal the receivers' identity in plain.

$\text{No-Read}^{\mathcal{A}}_{\text{CD-ABACE}}(1^\lambda, \mathbb{U})$	$\text{No-Write}^{\mathcal{A}}_{\text{CD-ABACE}}(1^\lambda, \mathbb{U})$
1: $(\text{pp}_{ra}, \text{msk}_{ra}) \leftarrow \text{RAgen}(1^\lambda, \mathbb{U})$	1: $(\text{pp}_{ra}, \text{msk}_{ra}) \leftarrow \text{RAgen}(1^\lambda, \mathbb{U})$
2: $(\text{pp}_{sa}, \text{msk}_{sa}) \leftarrow \text{SAgen}(\text{pp}_{ra}, \mathbf{R_L})$	2: $(\text{pp}_{sa}, \text{msk}_{sa}) \leftarrow \text{SAgen}(\text{pp}_{ra}, \mathbf{R_L})$
3: $\mathbb{P}^* \leftarrow \mathcal{A}(\text{pp}_{ra}, \text{pp}_{sa})$	3: $(\pi^*, x^*, \mathbb{P}^*) \leftarrow \mathcal{A}^{\mathcal{O}}(\text{pp}_{ra}, \text{pp}_{sa})$
4: $(m_0, m_1) \leftarrow \mathcal{A}^{\mathcal{O}}(\text{pp}_{ra}, \text{pp}_{sa})$	4: $(\pi_0, x_0) := (\pi^*, x^*)$
5: $(\text{ek}_{\mathbb{P}^*}, \sigma^*, W^*) \leftarrow \text{EncKGen}(\mathbb{P}^*)$	5: $(\text{ek}_{\mathbb{P}^*}, \sigma^*, W^*) \leftarrow \text{EncKGen}(\mathbb{P}^*)$
6: $b \leftarrow\!\$\, \{0, 1\}$	6: $m^* \leftarrow\!\$\, \mathcal{M},\ \text{aux} \leftarrow \text{fix}(\text{Ct}_0)$
7: $(\pi_b, x_b) \leftarrow\!\$\, \text{Enc}(\text{pp}_{ra}, \text{pp}_{sa}, \text{ek}_{\mathbb{P}^*}, m_b)$	7: $(\pi_1, x_1) \leftarrow \text{Enc}(\text{ek}_{\mathbb{P}^*}, m^*, \text{aux})$
8: $b' \leftarrow\!\$\, \mathcal{A}^{\mathcal{O}}(\pi_b, x_b)$	8: $b \leftarrow\!\$\, \{0, 1\},\ \tilde{\text{Ct}}_b \leftarrow \text{San}(\pi_b, x_b)$
	9: $b' \leftarrow\!\$\, \mathcal{A}^{\mathcal{O}}(\tilde{\text{Ct}}_b)$
Oracle $\mathcal{O}_{\text{DecKGen}}(\mathbb{B}_j)$	**Oracle** $\mathcal{O}_{\text{Enc}}(m, \mathbb{P}_i)$
1: Initialize $\mathcal{Q}_{\mathcal{D}} = \{\emptyset\}$	1: $(\text{ek}_{\mathbb{P}_i}, \sigma_i, W_i) \leftarrow \text{EncKGen}(\mathbb{P}_i, \text{PF})$
2: **if** $\mathbb{B}_j \notin \mathcal{Q}_{\mathcal{D}}$:	2: $(\pi, x) \leftarrow \text{Enc}(\text{ek}_{\mathbb{P}_i}, m)$
3: $\quad \text{dk}_{\mathbb{B}_j} \leftarrow \text{DecKGen}(\mathbb{B}_j)$	3: **return** (π, x)
4: $\quad$ **return** $(\text{dk}_{\mathbb{B}_j}) \wedge \mathcal{Q}_{\mathcal{D}} = \mathcal{Q}_{\mathcal{D}} \cup \{\mathbb{B}_j\}$	
5: **else** : **return** $(\text{dk}_{\mathbb{B}_j})$	
Oracle $\mathcal{O}_{\text{EncKGen}}(\mathbb{P}_i)$	
1: Initialize $\mathcal{Q}_{\mathcal{E}} = \{\emptyset\}$	
2: **if** $\mathbb{P}_i \notin \mathcal{Q}_{\mathcal{E}}$:	
3: $\quad (\text{ek}_{\mathbb{P}_i}, \sigma_i, W_i) \leftarrow \text{EncKGen}(\mathbb{P}_i, \text{PF})$	
4: $\quad$ **return** $(\text{ek}_{\mathbb{P}_i}, \sigma_i, W_i) \wedge \mathcal{Q}_{\mathcal{E}} = \mathcal{Q}_{\mathcal{E}} \cup \{\mathbb{P}_i\}$	
5: **else** : **return** $(\text{ek}_{\mathbb{P}_i}, \sigma_i, W_i)$	

Fig. 1. No-Read and No-Write security games

4   Generic Construction

Our generic construction for a general predicate function and universal CP-ABE is built from following constructions:

1. An EUF-CMA-secure SPS construction, $\mathcal{SPS}.(\text{Pgen}, \text{KG}, \text{Sign}, \text{Randz}, \text{Vf})$ (see full version [28] for formal definition).
2. A computational Knowledge-Sound NIZK proof, $\mathcal{ZK}.(\text{K}_{\text{crs}}, \text{P}, \text{V}, \text{Sim})$ (see full version for formal definition [28]).
3. A publicly re-randomizable CP-ABE scheme, $r\mathcal{ABE}.(\text{Pgen}, \text{KGen}, \text{Col}, \text{Enc}, \text{Randz}, \text{Dec})$ (see full version for formal definition [28]).

For a given predicate function PF, message space $\mathcal{M}$ and ciphertext space $\mathcal{C}$, the generic construction consists of the following PPT algorithms:

- **RA setup** (RAgen($\mathbb{U}, \lambda$)): Takes the security parameter λ and an attribute universe $\mathbb{U}$, and runs the $r\mathcal{ABE}$.Pgen($\lambda, \mathbb{U}$) algorithm to generate the global and CP-ABE parameters. It outputs RA's master secret key set $\mathsf{msk}_{ra} = (\mathsf{msk}_{r\mathcal{ABE}})$ and RA's public parameters $\mathsf{pp}_{ra} = (\mathsf{pp}_{r\mathcal{ABE}})$.
- **SA setup** (SAgen($\mathsf{pp}_{ra}, \mathbf{R_L}$)): Takes RA's public parameters pp_{ra} and relation $\mathbf{R_L}$ as inputs and runs the $\mathcal{ZK}$.K$_{\mathsf{crs}}$($\mathbf{R_L}$), $\mathcal{SPS}$.Pgen(λ) and $\mathcal{SPS}$.KG(pp) algorithms and returns $\mathsf{pp}_{sa} = (\mathsf{pp}, \mathsf{vk}, \mathsf{crs})$ and $\mathsf{msk}_{sa} = (\mathsf{ts}, \mathsf{sk})$ as outputs. The underlying relation $\mathbf{R_L}$ is defined corresponding to the NP-language $\mathbf{L}$ for the statement $\mathsf{x} = (\sigma', \mathsf{vk}', \mathsf{ek}', \mathsf{Ct})$ and witness $\mathsf{w} = (\sigma, \mathsf{ek}, m, r, t)$.
- **Decryption KGen** (DecKGen($\mathsf{msk}_{ra}, \mathbb{B}$)): Takes as inputs RA's master secret key msk_{ra} and a key index $\mathbb{B} \in \Sigma_k$. It generates the private decryption key $\mathsf{dk}_\mathbb{B}$ by executing the algorithm $r\mathcal{ABE}$.KGen($\mathsf{msk}_{ra}, \mathbb{B}$).
- **Encryption KGen** (EncKGen($\mathsf{pp}_{ra}, \mathsf{msk}_{sa}, \mathbb{P}, \mathrm{PF}$)): Takes as inputs pp_{ra}, msk_{sa} and a ciphertext index $\mathbb{P} \in \Sigma_c$ that indicates to whom the sender is allowed to talk based on predicate function $\mathrm{PF}(.,.)$. It executes the collector algorithm $r\mathcal{ABE}$.Col($\mathsf{pp}_{ra}, \mathbb{P}$) to obtain the aggregated value $\mathsf{ek}_\mathbb{P}$ and then signs it by running the algorithm $\mathcal{SPS}$.Sign($\mathsf{sk}, \mathsf{ek}_\mathbb{P}$). It returns both the encryption key and the underlying signature to the sender.
- **Encryption** (Enc ($\mathsf{pp}_{sa}, \mathsf{pp}_{ra}, m, \mathsf{ek}_\mathbb{P}, \sigma, W$)): Takes as inouts the secret encryption key $\mathsf{ek}_\mathbb{P}$ and the underlying signature σ, the public parameters and a message $m \in \mathcal{M}$. It re-randomizes σ under an initial random string μ by running $\mathcal{SPS}$.Randz($\mathsf{pp}_{sa}, \mathsf{ek}_\mathbb{P}, \sigma, W; \mu$). Next it runs the re-randomizable CP-ABE encryption algorithm $r\mathcal{ABE}$.Enc($\mathsf{pp}_{ra}, m, \mathsf{ek}_\mathbb{P}$) and proves knowledge of hidden values by executing the $\mathcal{ZK}$.P($\mathbf{R_L}, \mathsf{crs}, \mathsf{w}, \mathsf{x}$) algorithm. It returns the instance and underlying proof (π, x) as outputs.
- **Sanitization** (San($\mathsf{pp}_{sa}, \mathsf{pp}_{ra}, \pi, \mathsf{x}$)): Takes as inputs the proof π and the instance x: if $\mathcal{SPS}$.Vf($\mathsf{pp}, \mathsf{vk}', \sigma', \mathsf{ek}'$) = 1 and $\mathcal{ZK}$.V($\mathbf{R_L}, \mathsf{crs}, \pi, \mathsf{x}$) = 1, it runs the algorithm $r\mathcal{ABE}$.Randz($\mathsf{pp}_{ra}, \mathsf{Ct}$) and returns the sanitized ciphertext $\tilde{\mathsf{Ct}}$ as output; otherwise it rejects the link and returns $\perp$.
- **Decryption** (Dec($\mathsf{pp}_{sa}, \mathsf{pp}_{ra}, \tilde{\mathsf{Ct}}, \mathsf{dk}_\mathbb{B}$)): Takes as inputs the public parameters, a sanitized ciphertext $\tilde{\mathsf{Ct}}$ and the decryption key $\mathsf{dk}_\mathbb{B}$. It returns the plaintext $m \in \mathcal{M}$ by executing $r\mathcal{ABE}$.Dec($\mathsf{pp}_{ra}, \tilde{\mathsf{Ct}}, \mathsf{dk}_\mathbb{B}$) algorithm if and only if $\mathrm{PF}(\mathbb{B}, \mathbb{P}) = 1$; otherwise this algorithm returns $\perp$.

Theorem 1. *The proposed generic* CD-ABACE *construction is correct.*

The proof can be found in the full version [28].

Theorem 2. *The proposed generic* CD-ABACE *scheme satisfies the* No-Read *rule of Definition 7.*

The proof can be found in the full version [28].

Theorem 3. *No PPT adversary $\mathcal{A}$ can win the* No-Write *security game of Definition 8 for the proposed* CD-ABACE *scheme under a fixed predicate function* $\mathrm{PF}(.,.)$.

The proof can be found in the full version [28].

5   An Efficient CD-ABACE Scheme

In this section, we propose a CD-ABACE scheme such that the key and cipher-text sizes are constant. It primarily comes from a novel CP-ABE scheme; we believe that this is a result that is valuable by itself. Following on from Sect. 4, there are three main cryptographic primitives that are listed below;

Structure-Preserving Signature (SPS): In this paper, we use a variant of the selectively re-randomizable SPS scheme of Abe et al. [1] (see full version [28]) as an efficient, unified and selectively re-randomizable SPS. Since in the proposed CD-ABACE construction the generator of the first cyclic group is hidden and the message is a second group element over the Type-III bilinear groups, we need to slightly modify this scheme with the following PPT algorithms:

- (pp) $\leftarrow \mathcal{SPS}$.Pgen(λ): This algorithm takes as input the security parameter λ and picks a random integer $\alpha \leftarrow_\$ \mathbb{Z}_p^*$ and a group generator $Y \leftarrow_\$ \mathbb{G}_2$. It returns the public parameters pp by running a Type-III bilinear group generator $\mathcal{BG}(\lambda) = (\mathbb{G}_1, \mathbb{G}_2, \mathbb{G}_T, \mathsf{p}, \hat{e})$ and publishes pp $= (\mathbb{G}_1, \mathbb{G}_2, \mathbb{G}_T, \mathsf{p}, \hat{e}, [\alpha^2]_1, Y)$, while it keeps α secret.
- (sk, vk) $\leftarrow \mathcal{SPS}$.KG(pp): Samples $v \leftarrow_\$ \mathbb{Z}_p$ and publishes the public verification key vk $= [v\alpha^2]_1$ while it securely stores the secret signing key sk $= v$.
- $(\sigma, W) \leftarrow \mathcal{SPS}$.Sign(pp, sk, m): The signing algorithm takes as inputs the public parameters pp, the secret key sk and a message $m \in \mathbb{G}_2$. It samples $r \leftarrow_\$ \mathbb{Z}_p^*$, computes $\sigma = (R, S, T) = \left([r\alpha^2]_1, m^{v/r}Y^{1/r}, S^{v/r}[1/r]_2\right)$, and outputs $(\sigma, W = [1/r]_2)$.
- $(\sigma', W') \leftarrow \mathcal{SPS}$.Randz(pp, σ, W): The re-randomizing algorithm takes as inputs the public parameters pp, a signature $\sigma \in \mathcal{S}$ along with W, picks a random integer $t \leftarrow_\$ \mathbb{Z}_p^*$ and computes the re-randomized signature as $\sigma' = (R', S', T') = (R^{1/t}, S^t, T^{t^2}W^{t(1-t)})$ and returns it along with a new token $W' = W^t$.
- $(0, 1) \leftarrow \mathcal{SPS}$.Vf(pp, vk, σ', m): The verification algorithm takes as inputs pp, either a plain signature σ or a re-randomized signature σ', a message m and the verification key vk. It first checks $m, S', T' \in \mathbb{G}_2$, $R' \in \mathbb{G}_1$ and then checks the pairing equations $R' \bullet S' = (\mathsf{vk} \bullet m)([\alpha^2]_1 \bullet Y)$ and $R' \bullet T' = (\mathsf{vk} \bullet S')([\alpha^2]_1 \bullet [1]_2)$. If both conditions hold, then it returns 1, otherwise it responds with 0 (rejecting the signature).

The proof of correctness is identical to that of Abe et al.'s SPS construction, where a message is part of the second rather than the first group. As the first group generator is hidden in the proposed CD-ABACE scheme, we need to take $[\alpha^2]_1$ instead of $[1]_1$ to generate and verify signatures.

Non-Interactive Zero-Knowledge (NIZK) Proofs: As discussed in full version [28], Zero-Knowledge proofs [15] allow a prover to convince the verifier about the validity of a statement without revealing any other information. We use a standard Schnorr proof [27] to prove the knowledge of exponents in the random oracle model. To convert an interactive protocol to a non-interactive framework, we utilize the Fiat-Shamir heuristic [11]. More precisely, the prover has access to a hash function, modeled as a random function $(\mathcal{O})$, to generate the challenges instead of receiving them from the verifier. For a given cyclic group $\mathbb{G}_i$ of order p with generator g_i, we denote by $\mathrm{PoK}\{(\mathsf{w}) : \mathbf{R_L}(\mathsf{x}, \mathsf{w}) = 1\}$, the proof of knowledge of a hidden witness w that satisfies a given relation $\mathbf{R_L}$. Figure 2 formalizes a NIZK in ROM for proof of exponentiation.

$\mathsf{K_{crs}}(\mathbf{R_L}, \lambda)$	$\mathrm{PROVE}(\mathbf{R_L}, \mathsf{x}, \mathsf{w})$	$\mathrm{VERIFIER}(\mathbf{R_L}, \pi, \mathsf{x})$
1 : **Instance**$(\mathsf{x}) : y \in \mathbb{G}_i$	1 : Parse $(\mathbf{R_L}, \mathsf{x}, \mathsf{w})$	1 : Parse $(\mathbf{R_L}, \pi, \mathsf{x})$
2 : **Witness**$(\mathsf{w}) : x \in \mathbb{Z}_p$	2 : $r \leftarrow_\$ \mathbb{Z}_p$	2 : Computes $c = \mathcal{O}(y, t)$
3 : **Statement:**	3 : $t := g_i^r$	3 : if $\{y, t \in \mathbb{G}_i \ \wedge \ z \in \mathbb{Z}_p$
4 : Knwl of $x := \log_{g_i} y$	4 : $c := \mathcal{O}(y, t)$	4 : $\wedge \, y^c t == g_i^z\}$:
5 : **return** (x, w)	5 : $z := cx + r \mod p$	5 : **return** (ACCEPT)
	6 : **return** $\pi = (t, z)$	6 : **else** : (REJECT)

Fig. 2. Proof of knowledge of exponents

An Efficient Re-randomizable CP-ABE: In what follows, we define a new IND-CPA-secure CP-ABE scheme with a constant key and ciphertext size. The Boolean function of this scheme is applied in AND-gate circuits. Although Guo et al. in [17] took a similar approach and presented a constant-key size CP-ABE scheme, the ciphertext size in their scheme increases linearly with the total number of attributes. The proposed re-randomizable CP-ABE scheme consists of the following algorithms:

- $(\mathsf{pp}, \mathsf{msk}) \leftarrow \mathcal{ABE}.\mathsf{Pgen}(\mathbb{U}, \lambda)$: Takes as inputs an attribute space $\mathbb{U}$ with size n along with the security parameter λ, and runs a Type-III bilinear group generator $\mathcal{BG}(\lambda) = (\mathbb{G}_1, \mathbb{G}_2, \mathbb{G}_T, \mathsf{p}, \hat{e})$. It also selects a standard collision-resistant hash function $\mathsf{H} \leftarrow_\$ \mathcal{H}$ that is modeled as a random oracle in the security proofs. For a randomly selected integer $\alpha \leftarrow_\$ \mathbb{Z}_p^*$, it computes $h_i = [\alpha^i]_2$ as the set of monomials in $\mathbb{G}_2$ and $g_2 = [\alpha^2]_1$. It returns the master secret key $\mathsf{msk} = ([1]_1, \alpha)$ and the system's public parameters $\mathsf{pp} = (\mathbb{G}_1, \mathbb{G}_2, \mathbb{G}_T, \mathsf{p}, \hat{e}, g_2, \{h_i\}_{i=0}^n, [\alpha]_T, \mathsf{H})$.
- $(\mathsf{dk}_\mathbb{B}) \leftarrow \mathcal{ABE}.\mathsf{KGen}(\mathsf{msk}, \mathbb{B})$: Takes as inputs msk and generates a secret decryption key corresponding to attribute set $\mathbb{B} \in \Sigma_k$, such that $|\mathbb{B}| < n - 1$. It first computes the Zero-Polynomial $Z_\mathbb{B}(x) = \prod_{i=1}^n (x - k_i)^{\overline{b[i]}}$ such that $k_i = \{\mathsf{H}(U_i)\}_{U_i \in \mathbb{U}}$. It returns the secret decryption key $\mathsf{dk}_\mathbb{B} = [1/Z_\mathbb{B}(\alpha)]_1$.
- $(\mathsf{Ct}) \leftarrow \mathcal{ABE}.\mathsf{Enc}(\mathsf{pp}, m, \mathbb{P})$: Takes as inputs the message $m \in \mathcal{M}$, the public parameters pp and an access structure $\mathbb{P} \in \Sigma_c$. It first samples $r \leftarrow_\$ \mathbb{Z}_p^*$, calculates $Z_\mathbb{P}(x) = \sum_{j=0}^n z_j x^j$ and returns the ciphertext as a tuple $\mathsf{Ct} = (\mathbb{P}, C, C_1, C_2) = (\mathbb{P}, m [r\alpha]_T, (\prod_{j=0}^n h_{j+1}^{z_j})^r = [r\alpha Z_\mathbb{P}(\alpha)]_2, g_2^{-r} = [-r\alpha^2]_1)$. We define the collector algorithm as $\mathsf{Col}(\mathsf{pp}, \mathbb{P}) = [\alpha Z_\mathbb{P}(\alpha)]_2$.

- $(m', \perp) \leftarrow \mathcal{ABE}.\mathsf{Dec}\,(\mathsf{pp}, \mathsf{Ct}, \mathsf{dk}_\mathbb{B})$: This algorithm takes as input the public parameters pp, a ciphertext Ct and a secret decryption key $\mathsf{dk}_\mathbb{B}$. If $\mathbb{P} \subseteq \mathbb{B}$, it computes, $F_{\mathbb{B},\mathbb{P}}(x) = \prod_{i=1}^{n} (x - k_i)^{c[i]} = \sum_{j=0}^{n} f_j x^j$ for $c[i] = b[i] - p[i]$ and returns $m' = C \cdot \left((C_2 \bullet \prod_{i=1}^{n} (h_{i-1})^{f_i}) \cdot (\mathsf{dk}_\mathbb{B} \bullet C_1) \right)^{\frac{-1}{f_0}}$; otherwise it responds with $\perp$.

In the full version [28], we evaluated the proposed CP-ABE scheme regarding its security properties including the correctness and IND-CPA.

Next we modify the re-randomizing phase of our CP-ABE scheme; the other algorithms are the same, except that the decryption algorithm can take either $\tilde{\mathsf{Ct}}$ or Ct as input.

- $(\tilde{\mathsf{Ct}}) \leftarrow r\mathcal{ABE}.\mathsf{Randz}(\mathsf{pp}, \mathsf{Ct})$: Takes as inputs pp and a ciphertext Ct under access structure $\mathbb{P} \in \Sigma_c$. To re-randomize the ciphertext $\mathsf{Ct} \in \mathcal{C}$, it samples an initial random integer $s \leftarrow_\$ \mathbb{Z}_p^*$ and computes the Zero-polynomial $Z_\mathbb{P}(x)$. Then it outputs $\tilde{\mathsf{Ct}} = (\tilde{C}, \tilde{C}_1, \tilde{C}_2) = (C \cdot [s\alpha]_T, C_1 \cdot [sZ_\mathbb{P}(\alpha)]_2, C_2 \cdot g_2^{-s})$.

Remark 2. The proposed construction guarantees that no PPT adversary can obtain the receiver's identity, deterministically. This is the same as the notion of "weak attribute-hiding" in the context of Attribute-Based Signatures [30]. Indeed, the access policy corresponding to a ciphertext only reveals the list of receivers who satisfy a specific set of attributes, even though it never leaks any information about the identity of the receivers. Under the assumption that there is more than one user who satisfies a set of certain attributes, the adversary is unable to deduce for which specific receiver the challenge ciphertext is intended.

Related Works: The first CP-ABE scheme, which allows the data owners to implement an arbitrary and fine-grained access policy in terms of any monotonic formula for each message was proposed by Bethencourt et al. at IEEE S&P 2007 in [6]; its security was proven in the *Generic Group Model* (GGM). In a subsequent work, Cheung et al. [9] constructed a CP-ABE scheme in the standard model, which is however restricted to a single AND-gate. Waters [35] introduced an asymptotically efficient CP-ABE scheme in the standard model, which is based on a *Linear Secret Sharing Scheme* (LSSS) to establish an arbitrary access policy. Lewko and Waters [21] introduced a secure construction based on LSSS in which the length of the ciphertext, the size of users' secret keys, and the number of required pairings to decrypt a ciphertext correspond to the size of the *Monotone Span Program* (MSP) that defines the access structure. Some recent works have extended the functionality of these schemes for various applications [18,29]. While these CP-ABE schemes allow to define in an effective way the right to access data, either the key or the ciphertext size grows linearly in the number of attributes. Therefore, CP-ABE schemes based on AND-gate circuits are considered promising candidates to address this downside. In this approach the sender defines a specific Boolean AND-gate circuit such that a recipient can learn the encrypted data iff they satisfy all the attributes, otherwise the decryption algorithm returns nothing. Considering AND-gate circuits

$(\mathsf{pp}_{ra}, \mathsf{msk}_{ra}) \leftarrow \mathsf{RAgen}(\mathbb{U}, \lambda)$	$(\mathsf{pp}_{sa}, \mathsf{msk}_{sa}) \leftarrow \mathsf{SAgen}(\lambda, \mathsf{pp}_{ra}, \mathbf{R_L})$

1: Run $\mathcal{BG}(\lambda) = (\mathbb{G}_1, \mathbb{G}_2, \mathbb{G}_T, \mathsf{p}, \hat{e})$ 1: Parse $(\mathcal{BG}(\lambda), \mathsf{pp}_{ra})$

2: $\mathsf{H} \leftarrow\!\$\,\mathcal{H}, \alpha \leftarrow\!\$\,\mathbb{Z}_p^*$ 2: $Y \leftarrow\!\$\,\mathbb{G}_2$

3: $h_i = \left[\alpha^i\right]_2$ 3: $\mathsf{sk} := v \leftarrow\!\$\,\mathbb{Z}_p$

4: $g_2 = \left[\alpha^2\right]_1$ 4: $\mathsf{vk} = g_2^v = \left[\alpha^2 v\right]_1$

5: $\mathsf{msk}_{ra} = ([1]_1, \alpha)$ 5: $(\mathbf{crs}, \mathbf{ts}) \leftarrow\!\$\,\mathcal{ZK}.\mathsf{K_{crs}}(\lambda, \mathbf{R_L})$

6: $\mathsf{pp}_{ra} = (g_2, \{h_i\}_{i=0}^n, [\alpha]_T, \mathsf{H})$ 6: $\mathsf{msk}_{sa} = (\mathsf{sk}, \mathbf{ts})$

7: return $(\mathsf{msk}_{ra}, \mathsf{pp}_{ra})$ 7: $\mathsf{pp}_{sa} = (\mathbf{R_L}, \mathbf{crs}, Y, \mathsf{vk})$

   8: return $(\mathsf{msk}_{sa}, \mathsf{pp}_{sa})$

$(\mathsf{dk}_\mathbb{B}) \leftarrow \mathsf{DecKGen}(\mathsf{msk}_{ra}, \mathbb{B})$	$(\mathsf{ek}_\mathbb{P}, \sigma, W) \leftarrow \mathsf{EncKGen}(\mathsf{pp}_{ra}, \mathsf{pp}_{sa}, \mathsf{msk}_{sa}, \mathbb{P}, \mathrm{PF})$

1: Parse $(\mathcal{BG}(\lambda), \mathsf{msk}_{ra})$ 1: Parse $(\mathcal{BG}(\lambda), \mathsf{pp}_{ra}, \mathsf{msk}_{sa})$

2: $Z_\mathbb{B}(x) = \prod_{i=1}^n (x - k_i)^{\overline{b[i]}}$ 2: $Z_\mathbb{P}(x) = \prod_{i=1}^n (x - k_i)^{\overline{p[i]}} = \sum_{j=0}^n z_i x^i$

3: $\mathsf{dk}_\mathbb{B} = [1/Z_\mathbb{B}(\alpha)]_1$ 3: $\mathsf{ek}_\mathbb{P} = \mathsf{Col}(\mathsf{pp}, \mathbb{P}) = \prod_{i=0}^n h_{i+1}^{z_i} = [\alpha Z_\mathbb{P}(\alpha)]_2$

4: return $(\mathsf{dk}_\mathbb{B})$ 4: $t_u \leftarrow\!\$\,\mathbb{Z}_p^*, W = [1/t_u]_2$

   5: $(R, S, T) = (g_2^{t_u}, \mathsf{ek}_\mathbb{P}^{\mathsf{sk}/t_u} Y^{1/t_u}, S^{\mathsf{sk}/t_u}[1/t_u]_2)$

   6: return $(\mathsf{ek}_\mathbb{P}, \sigma = (R, S, T), W)$

$(\pi, \mathsf{x}) \leftarrow \mathsf{Enc}(\mathsf{pp}_{sa}, \mathsf{pp}_{ra}, m, \mathsf{ek}_\mathbb{P}, \sigma, W)$	$(\tilde{\mathsf{Ct}}, \perp) \leftarrow \mathsf{San}(\mathsf{pp}_{sa}, \mathsf{pp}_{ra}, \pi, \mathsf{x})$

1: Parse $(\mathcal{BG}(\lambda), \mathsf{pp}_{ra}, \mathsf{pp}_{sa})$ 1: Parse $(\mathcal{BG}(\lambda), \mathsf{pp}_{ra}, \mathsf{pp}_{sa})$

2: $r, t \leftarrow\!\$\,\mathbb{Z}_p^*$ 2: if $\{R' \in \mathbb{G}_1 \wedge \mathsf{ek}_\mathbb{P}', S', T' \in \mathbb{G}_2 \wedge$

3: $(C, C_1, C_2) = (m[r\alpha]_T, \mathsf{ek}_\mathbb{P}^r, g_2^{-r})$ 3: $R' \bullet S' = (\mathsf{vk}' \bullet \mathsf{ek}_\mathbb{P}')(g_2 \bullet Y) \wedge$

4: $R' = R^{1/t}, S' = S^t, T' = T^{t^2} W^{t(1-t)}$ 4: $R' \bullet T' = (\mathsf{vk} \bullet S')(g_2 \bullet [1]_2) \wedge$

5: $\sigma' = (R', S', T')$ 5: $\mathcal{ZK}.\mathsf{V}(\mathbf{R_L}, \mathbf{crs}, \pi, \mathsf{x}) = 1\}$:

6: $\mathsf{vk}' = \mathsf{vk}^{1/t}, \mathsf{ek}_\mathbb{P}' = \mathsf{ek}_\mathbb{P}^t$ 6: $s \leftarrow\!\$\,\mathbb{Z}_p^*, \tilde{C} = C \cdot [s\alpha]_T$

7: $\mathsf{x} = (\sigma', \mathsf{vk}', \mathsf{ek}_\mathbb{P}', \mathsf{Ct} = (\mathbb{P}, C, C_1, C_2))$ 7: $\tilde{C}_1 = C_1 \cdot [s\alpha Z_\mathbb{P}(\alpha)]_2$

8: $\mathsf{w} = (\mathsf{ek}_\mathbb{P}, \sigma, m, r, t)$ 8: $\tilde{C}_2 = C_2 \cdot g_2^{-s}$

9: $\pi \leftarrow \mathsf{PoK}\{(\mathsf{w}) : \mathbf{R_L}(\mathsf{x}, \mathsf{w}) = 1\}$ 9: return $\tilde{\mathsf{Ct}} = (\mathbb{P}, \tilde{C}, \tilde{C}_1, \tilde{C}_2)$

10: return (π, x) 10: else : abort

$(m', \perp) \leftarrow \mathsf{Dec}(\mathsf{pp}_{sa}, \mathsf{pp}_{ra}, \tilde{\mathsf{Ct}}, \mathsf{dk}_\mathbb{B})$

1: Parse $(\mathcal{BG}(\lambda), \mathsf{pp}_{ra}, \mathsf{pp}_{sa})$

2: if $\mathbb{P} \subseteq \mathbb{B}$:

3: $c[i] = b[i] - p[i], F_{\mathbb{B}, \mathbb{P}}(x) = \prod_{i=1}^n (x - k_i)^{c[i]} = \sum_{j=0}^n f_j x^j$

4: return $m' = C\left(\left(C_2 \bullet \prod_{i=1}^n (h_{i-1})^{f_i}\right) \cdot (\mathsf{dk}_\mathbb{B} \bullet C_1)\right)^{-1/f_0}$

5: else : abort

Fig. 3. The proposed CD-ABACE scheme

provides a constant ciphertext length; several CP-ABE schemes are proposed based on this approach [17, 32].

The Proposed CD-ABACE Scheme: At this point, we can wrap up the construction described in Fig. 3 by taking a family of collision-resistant hash functions $\mathcal{H} : \{0, 1\}^* \rightarrow \mathbb{Z}_p^*$. Our CD-ABACE scheme is built under a CP-ABE scheme based on AND-gate circuits with constant key and ciphertext sizes. The primary motivation behind this circuit choice is to construct a fully constant ACE within the context of CD-ABACE schemes. Note that we can build more universal circuit levels using the generic model discussed in Sect. 4.

Remark 3. While the proposed CD-ABACE scheme achieves a weak notion of receiver anonymity, it improves Wang and Chow's weak point where recipients' identities are public. In order to resolve this issue we can use the existing CP-ABE schemes with a more universal circuit level, but this compromises the efficiency. For instance, according to Garg et al. [14], we can fully anonymize the receiver using our generic construction based on multilinear maps and iO assumptions. We specify in the full version [28] a CD-ABACE scheme, using Waters's CP-ABE [35], which is defined under Linear Secret Sharing Schemes; we compare it with our proposed CD-ABACE scheme in Sect. 6.

6   Performance Analysis

In this section, we examine how the performance of our proposed fully-constant CD-ABACE scheme compares to the selectively-secure ACE scheme of Wang and Chow [33], which is the only implemented ACE construction to date and a CD-ABACE variant of Waters's CP-ABE [35] that is described in detail in the full version [28].

We obtained the benchmarks for our proposed CD-ABACE scheme on Ubuntu 20.04.2 LTS with an Intel Core i7-9850H CPU @ 2.60 GHz with 16 GB of memory. We applied the Barreto-Naehrig (BN) curve, type F, $y^2 = x^3 + b$ over the field $\mathbb{F}_q$ of order p with embedding curve degree $k = 12$ and 1920-bit DLog security. For simplicity the bit-lengths of expressions of access policies and computations over $\mathbb{Z}_p$ are not taken into account. We implemented the proposed construction using the Charm-Crypto framework [2], a Python library for Pairing-based Cryptography[2]. Figure 4 consists of six graphs depicting the following relationships:

- *Total number of Attributes/Users versus RA Setup time*: The top left graph displays the relationship between the total number of attributes/users and time required to generate the parameter of the Receiver Authority. As can be seen, in our scheme and [33] scheme the time required to run this algorithm grows linearly with the total number of attributes/users, and for a generous consideration of 1 000 attributes, it only requires ∼200 milliseconds (ms) and ∼300 ms, respectively. However, for an ACE variation of Waters' CP-ABE [35] construction (see full version [28]) this time is constant and less than 30 ms.

---

[2] https://github.com/CDABACE.

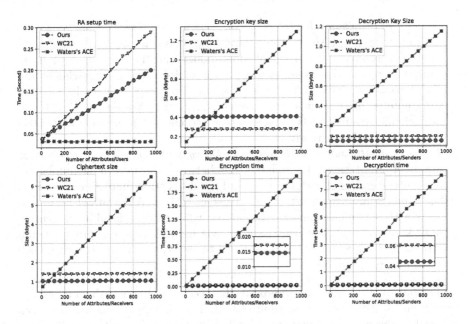

Fig. 4. Running time of attribute size dependence algorithms

- *Maximum number of Attributes/Receivers versus Encryption key size*: The top centre graph of Fig. 4 shows the relationship between the total number of attributes/receivers that a sender can send to them and the size of the stored encryption key. As can be seen, this relationship in Waters' ACE variant is linear, however the our proposed construction and [33] require a constant storage. Assuming 1 000 attributes/receivers to be the highest number used by a sender, the required memory for storing this key for [33], Waters' ACE variant and our scheme is ~300, ~1 200 and ~400 bytes, respectively.

- *Maximum number of Attributes/Senders versus Decryption key size*: The top right graph of Fig. 4 shows the relationship between maximum the number of attributes/senders for each receiver and the size of the decryption key. As can be seen, in Waters' ACE variant this relationship grows linearly with number of attributes while in both our scheme and [33] the requires storage is constant independent of the number of attributes/senders; for instance, this size for a user having 1 000 attributes/senders is equal to ~50, ~100 bytes, while Waters' ACE variant is equal to ~1.2 KB.

- *Number of Attributes/Receivers versus ciphertext size*: The bottom left graph of Fig. 4 depicts the relationship between the total number of attributes/receivers in the policy and the length of ciphertext. As can be seen, in Waters' ACE scheme this relationship is linear while our scheme and [33] achieve a constant ciphertext size. For instance, a ciphertext with 100 embedded attributes/receivers in the policy has a ciphertext of size ~1, ~1.4, ~7 KB in our scheme, [33] and Waters' ACE scheme.

- *Number of Attributes/Receivers versus Encryption time*: The bottom centre graph of Fig. 4 shows the relationship between the total number of attributes/receivers of in the embedded policy and the encryption time. As can be seen, the time required to encrypt a ciphertext in our scheme and [33] is constant, while in Waters's ACE variation it grows linearly with the total number of attributes. For example, a sender in Waters' ACE, [33] and our scheme requires $\sim$2 000, $\sim$18, $\sim$15 ms to encrypt a message with 1 000 embedded attributes/receivers.
- *Number of Attributes/Senders versus Decryption time*: The bottom right graph of Fig. 4 shows the relationship between the maximum number of attributes/senders of each receivers and the decryption time. As can be seen, the time required to decrypt a ciphertext in Waters' ACE variant grows linearly with maximum number of attributes, while this overhead in our scheme and [33] is constant. For instance, a receiver in [33,35] and our proposed construction requires $\sim$8 000, $\sim$60, $\sim$45 ms to decrypt a ciphertext with 1 000 attributes in the policy.

Overall, our scheme has improved the receivers' key length and privacy level from identity-based to attribute-based. The ciphertext size has also been reduced, along with the number of public parameters. Since the second group generator is hidden in [33], the SA has to choose a new generator to create the SPS parameters. In contrast, the proposed variant of Abe et al.'s SPS [1] requires no new generator for the second cyclic group, and the intended NIZK proof cuts out the need for a target group proof of exponentiation.

7   Conclusion

In this work, we proposed a generic and an efficient CD-ABACE scheme based on attribute-based predicate functions. In comparison with earlier works, the length of the secret decryption keys and the ciphertext size has been substantially reduced to less than $\sim$50 and $\sim$1000 bytes as compared to Wang and Chow scheme where the size was $\sim$100 and $\sim$1400 bytes, respectively. Moreover, the computational overhead of encryption and decryption is linear in the number of the policy attributes and user attributes, respectively. Also, it is formally proved that the proposed scheme satisfies the NO-READ and the NO-WRITE rules based on standard assumptions. We leave the construction of a CD-ABACE scheme based on a Boolean circuit instead of AND-gate circuits with the same performance as an interesting open problem. As we discussed, the main downside for AND-gate circuits is that the attribute sets in plain may reveal some meaningful information about the intended constraints and consequently, applying a Boolean circuit can result in stronger anonymity guarantees for the receivers.

Acknowledgements. We would like to thank Sherman S. M. Chow, Georg Fuchsbauer, Karim Baghery, Ward Beullens, Pavel Hubáček and anonymous reviewers for their helpful discussions and valuable comments. This work was supported by Flanders Innovation & Entrepreneurship through the Spearhead Cluster Flux50 ICON project

PrivateFlex. In addition, this work was supported in part by the Research Council KU Leuven C1 on Security and Privacy for Cyber-Physical Systems and the Internet of Things with contract number C16/15/058 and by CyberSecurity Research Flanders with reference number VR20192203.

References

1. Abe, M., Groth, J., Ohkubo, M., Tibouchi, M.: Unified, minimal and selectively randomizable structure-preserving signatures. In: Lindell, Y. (ed.) TCC 2014. LNCS, vol. 8349, pp. 688–712. Springer, Heidelberg (2014). https://doi.org/10.1007/978-3-642-54242-8_29

2. Akinyele, J.A., et al.: Charm: a framework for rapidly prototyping cryptosystems. J. Cryptogr. Eng. 3(2), 111–128 (2013). https://doi.org/10.1007/s13389-013-0057-3

3. Attrapadung, N., Libert, B.: Functional encryption for inner product: achieving constant-size ciphertexts with adaptive security or support for negation. In: Nguyen, P.Q., Pointcheval, D. (eds.) PKC 2010. LNCS, vol. 6056, pp. 384–402. Springer, Heidelberg (2010). https://doi.org/10.1007/978-3-642-13013-7_23

4. Beimel, A..: Secure schemes for secret sharing and key distribution. Faculty of Computer Science, Technion-Israel Institute of Technology (1996)

5. Bell, D.E., LaPadula, L.J.: Secure computer systems: mathematical foundations. Technical report, DTIC document (1973)

6. Bethencourt, J., Sahai, A., Waters, B.: Ciphertext-policy attribute-based encryption. In: 2007 IEEE Symposium on Security and Privacy, SP 2007, pp. 321–334. IEEE (2007)

7. Boneh, D., Franklin, M.: Identity-based encryption from the Weil pairing. In: Kilian, J. (ed.) CRYPTO 2001. LNCS, vol. 2139, pp. 213–229. Springer, Heidelberg (2001). https://doi.org/10.1007/3-540-44647-8_13

8. Brengel, M., Rossow, C.: Identifying key leakage of bitcoin users. In: Bailey, M., Holz, T., Stamatogiannakis, M., Ioannidis, S. (eds.) RAID 2018. LNCS, vol. 11050, pp. 623–643. Springer, Cham (2018). https://doi.org/10.1007/978-3-030-00470-5_29

9. Cheung, L., Newport, C.: Provably secure ciphertext policy ABE. In: Proceedings of the 14th ACM Conference on Computer and Communications Security, pp. 456–465 (2007)

10. Damgård, I., Haagh, H., Orlandi, C.: Access control encryption: enforcing information flow with cryptography. In: Hirt, M., Smith, A. (eds.) TCC 2016. LNCS, vol. 9986, pp. 547–576. Springer, Heidelberg (2016). https://doi.org/10.1007/978-3-662-53644-5_21

11. Fiat, A., Shamir, A.: How to prove yourself: practical solutions to identification and signature problems. In: Odlyzko, A.M. (ed.) CRYPTO 1986. LNCS, vol. 263, pp. 186–194. Springer, Heidelberg (1987). https://doi.org/10.1007/3-540-47721-7_12

12. Fuchsbauer, G., Gay, R., Kowalczyk, L., Orlandi, C.: Access control encryption for equality, comparison, and more. In: Fehr, S. (ed.) PKC 2017. LNCS, vol. 10175, pp. 88–118. Springer, Heidelberg (2017). https://doi.org/10.1007/978-3-662-54388-7_4

13. Garg, S., Gentry, C., Halevi, S., Raykova, M., Sahai, A., Waters, B.: Candidate indistinguishability obfuscation and functional encryption for all circuits. SIAM J. Comput. 45(3), 882–929 (2016)

14. Garg, S., Gentry, C., Halevi, S., Sahai, A., Waters, B.: Attribute-based encryption for circuits from multilinear maps. In: Canetti, R., Garay, J.A. (eds.) CRYPTO 2013. LNCS, vol. 8043, pp. 479–499. Springer, Heidelberg (2013). https://doi.org/10.1007/978-3-642-40084-1_27

15. Goldwasser, S., Micali, S., Rackoff, C.: The knowledge complexity of interactive proof systems. SIAM J. Comput. **18**(1), 186–208 (1989)

16. Goyal, V., Pandey, O., Sahai, A., Waters, B.: Attribute-based encryption for fine-grained access control of encrypted data. In: Proceedings of the 13th ACM Conference on Computer and Communications Security, pp. 89–98 (2006)

17. Guo, F., Mu, Y., Susilo, W., Wong, D.S., Varadharajan, V.: CP-ABE with constant-size keys for lightweight devices. IEEE Trans. Inf. Forensics Secur. **9**(5), 763–771 (2014)

18. Hong, H., Sun, Z.: An efficient and secure attribute based signcryption scheme with LSSS access structure. Springerplus **5**(1), 644 (2016)

19. Katz, J., Sahai, A., Waters, B.: Predicate encryption supporting disjunctions, polynomial equations, and inner products. In: Smart, N. (ed.) EUROCRYPT 2008. LNCS, vol. 4965, pp. 146–162. Springer, Heidelberg (2008). https://doi.org/10.1007/978-3-540-78967-3_9

20. Kim, S., Wu, D.J.: Access control encryption for general policies from standard assumptions. In: Takagi, T., Peyrin, T. (eds.) ASIACRYPT 2017. LNCS, vol. 10624, pp. 471–501. Springer, Cham (2017). https://doi.org/10.1007/978-3-319-70694-8_17

21. Lewko, A., Waters, B.: Decentralizing attribute-based encryption. In: Paterson, K.G. (ed.) EUROCRYPT 2011. LNCS, vol. 6632, pp. 568–588. Springer, Heidelberg (2011). https://doi.org/10.1007/978-3-642-20465-4_31

22. Okamoto, T., Takashima, K.: Adaptively attribute-hiding (hierarchical) inner product encryption. In: Pointcheval, D., Johansson, T. (eds.) EUROCRYPT 2012. LNCS, vol. 7237, pp. 591–608. Springer, Heidelberg (2012). https://doi.org/10.1007/978-3-642-29011-4_35

23. Osborn, S., Sandhu, R., Munawer, Q.: Configuring role-based access control to enforce mandatory and discretionary access control policies. ACM Trans. Inf. Syst. Secur. (TISSEC) **3**(2), 85–106 (2000)

24. Regev, O.: On lattices, learning with errors, random linear codes, and cryptography. J. ACM **56**(6), 1–40 (2009)

25. Sabelfeld, A., Myers, A.C.: Language-based information-flow security. IEEE J. Sel. Areas Commun. **21**(1), 5–19 (2003)

26. Sahai, A., Waters, B.: Fuzzy identity-based encryption. In: Cramer, R. (ed.) EUROCRYPT 2005. LNCS, vol. 3494, pp. 457–473. Springer, Heidelberg (2005). https://doi.org/10.1007/11426639_27

27. Schnorr, C.P.: Efficient identification and signatures for smart cards. In: Brassard, G. (ed.) CRYPTO 1989. LNCS, vol. 435, pp. 239–252. Springer, New York (1990). https://doi.org/10.1007/0-387-34805-0_22

28. Sedaghat, M., Preneel, B.: Cross-domain attribute-based access control encryption. Cryptology ePrint Archive, Report 2021/074 (2021). https://eprint.iacr.org/2021/074

29. Sedaghat, S.M., Ameri, M.H., Mohajeri, J., Aref, M.R.: An efficient and secure data sharing in Smart Grid: ciphertext-policy attribute-based signcryption. In: 2017 Iranian Conference on Electrical Engineering (ICEE), pp. 2003–2008. IEEE (2017)

30. Shahandashti, S.F., Safavi-Naini, R.: Threshold attribute-based signatures and their application to anonymous credential systems. In: Preneel, B. (ed.) AFRICACRYPT 2009. LNCS, vol. 5580, pp. 198–216. Springer, Heidelberg (2009). https://doi.org/10.1007/978-3-642-02384-2_13
31. Tan, G., Zhang, R., Ma, H., Tao, Y.: Access control encryption based on LWE. In: Proceedings of the 4th ACM International Workshop on ASIA Public-Key Cryptography, pp. 43–50. ACM (2017)
32. Tran, P.V.X., Dinh, T.N., Miyaji, A.: Efficient ciphertext-policy ABE with constant ciphertext length. In: 2012 7th International Conference on Computing and Convergence Technology (ICCCT), pp. 543–549. IEEE (2012)
33. Wang, X., Chow, S.M.: Cross-domain access control encryption: arbitrary-policy, constant-size, efficient. In: IEEE Symposium on Security and Privacy (SP), Los Alamitos, CA, USA, pp. 388–401. IEEE Computer Society (May 2021)
34. Wang, X., Wong, H.W.H., Chow, S.S.M.: Access control encryption from group encryption. In: Sako, K., Tippenhauer, N.O. (eds.) ACNS 2021. LNCS, vol. 12726, pp. 417–441. Springer, Cham (2021). https://doi.org/10.1007/978-3-030-78372-3_16
35. Waters, B.: Ciphertext-policy attribute-based encryption: an expressive, efficient, and provably secure realization. In: Catalano, D., Fazio, N., Gennaro, R., Nicolosi, A. (eds.) PKC 2011. LNCS, vol. 6571, pp. 53–70. Springer, Heidelberg (2011). https://doi.org/10.1007/978-3-642-19379-8_4

Grain-128AEADv2: Strengthening the Initialization Against Key Reconstruction

Martin Hell[1]([⊠]), Thomas Johansson[1], Alexander Maximov[2], Willi Meier[3], and Hirotaka Yoshida[4]

[1] Department of Electrical and Information Technology,
Lund University, Lund, Sweden
{martin,thomas}@eit.lth.se
[2] Ericsson AB, Lund, Sweden
alexander.maximov@ericsson.com
[3] FHNW, Windisch, Switzerland
willi.meier@fhnw.ch
[4] Cyber Physical Security Research Center (CPSEC), National Institute of Advanced Industrial Science and Technology (AIST), Tokyo, Japan
hirotaka.yoshida@aist.go.jp

Abstract. Properties of the Grain-128AEAD key re-introduction, as part of the cipher initialization, are analyzed and discussed. We consider and analyze several possible alternatives for key re-introduction and identify weaknesses, or potential weaknesses, in them. Our results show that it seems favorable to separate the state initialization, the key re-introduction, and the A/R register initialization into three separate phases. Based on this, we propose a new cipher initialization and update the cipher version to Grain-128AEADv2. It can be noted that previously reported and published analysis of the cipher remains valid also for this new version.

Keywords: Stream cipher · Grain · Initialization · Key reconstruction · Differentials

1 Introduction

Grain-128AEAD is a member of the Grain family of stream ciphers and was submitted to the NIST lightweight cryptography standardization process. In this process, NIST aims to standardize cryptographic algorithms that are suitable for constrained environments. Grain-128AEAD is a stream cipher supporting authenticated encryption with associated data [17] and was selected as one out of ten finalists from an initial pool of 57 algorithms. It has so far shown competitive performance in both hardware [18] and software [15].

The Grain family of stream ciphers has been extensively analyzed since its introduction in the eSTREAM process, where the 80-bit key variant Grain

© Springer Nature Switzerland AG 2021
M. Conti et al. (Eds.): CANS 2021, LNCS 13099, pp. 24–41, 2021.
https://doi.org/10.1007/978-3-030-92548-2_2

v1 [13], together with MICKEY 2.0 [4] and Trivium [6], was selected into the final portfolio of algorithms (hardware category). Since then, also Grain-128 [12] and Grain-128a [1], both with 128-bit key and the latter with optional message authentication, have been proposed. Grain-128 is considered broken by the dynamic cube attacks proposed in [7,8], and it has been shown that for Grain-128a without authentication, there are also attacks more efficient than brute force.

The design approach, combining one linear and one non-linear shift register, has inspired also other lightweight ciphers, aiming at resource constrained environments, e.g., Fruit-80 [2], Sprout [3] and its successor Plantlet [16], and Lizard [10].

Compared to the previous variants, Grain-128AEAD modifies the cipher initialization such that the key is re-introduced at the end of the initialization. The purpose of this key re-introduction is to not allow the secret key to be immediately reconstructed in case the states of the LFSR and NFSR are known. This is a feature inspired by the Lizard stream cipher [10].

Even though any stream cipher would be considered broken if the state can be recovered in less than 2^K computations, where K is the keysize, such additional precautions provide some practical security in certain cases since only the current instantiation is broken in case of a state recovery. For a lightweight cipher, it is important that this key re-introduction is very resource efficient.

Since a key-from-state recovery assumes an already broken cipher, it is not crucial that the key reconstruction requires 2^K computations, but a too efficient key reconstruction limits the value of this additional precaution.

In [5], Chang and Turan noted that with knowledge of the LFSR and NFSR states, a message tag, and the corresponding message, it is possible to reconstruct the secret key with complexity 2^{62}. This complexity is probably less than one would expect from a state-of-the-art cipher and it seems that the Grain-128AEAD key re-introduction does not provide much added security. Indeed, any state recovery attack would now only require an additional 2^{62} computational steps to reconstruct the key.

In this paper, we first briefly outline and discuss the analysis by Chang and Turan. After analyzing the main issue with the key re-introduction, we present and discuss a few different main strategies for protecting against key reconstruction from a known state. In addition to the strategy from [5], we also analyze differential biases that could be used to reconstruct the key. Our analysis shows that (1) the key re-introduction should be separated from the initialization of the authentication registers, denoted A and R, and (2) the existence of differentials in high initialization rounds requires an increased number of initialization clocks in order to prevent a key-from-state reconstruction. From this we conclude that an increased number of initialization steps is needed in order to avoid key information leakage, resulting in an updated algorithm specification, denoted Grain-128AEADv2.

The paper is outlined as follows. In Sect. 2 we specify the key and nonce initialization of Grain-128AEAD. Then, we outline the key reconstruction proposed by Chang and Turan in Sect. 3. In Sect. 4, we discuss several options for avoiding similar and more advanced key reconstruction algorithms and show that they are inadequate. Then, in Sect. 5 we provide a generic initialization approach and use the derived differentials in order to motivate suitable parameters for the initialization. These parameters are then derived in Sect. 6, before the paper is concluded in Sect. 7.

2   Grain-128AEAD Initialization

Similar to all previous versions, Grain-128AEAD uses three main functions together with an LFSR and an NFSR. If authentication is used, which is optional in Grain-128a and mandatory in Grain-128AEAD, there are also two additional registers for supporting this, denoted A and R. A schematic overview of the initializations is given in Fig. 1. We will adopt the notation as used in [5] for the shift register bits, i.e., let (B_t, S_t, A_t, R_t) be the full state of Grain-128AEAD at time t, where,

$$
\begin{aligned}
B_t &= (b_t, \ldots, b_{t+127}) \text{ denotes NFSR state at } t \geq 0, \\
S_t &= (s_t, \ldots, s_{t+127}) \text{ denotes LFSR state at } t \geq 0, \\
A_t &= (a_0^t, \ldots, a_{63}^t) \text{ denotes the Accumulator bits at } t \geq 384, \\
R_t &= (r_0^t, \ldots, r_{63}^t) \text{ denotes the Register bits at } t \geq 384.
\end{aligned}
$$

The functions for updating the LFSR and NFSR are given by

$$
\begin{aligned}
s_{t+128} &= s_t + s_{t+7} + s_{t+38} + s_{t+70} + s_{t+81} + s_{t+96} \\
&= s_t + f'(s_{t+7..t+96}), \tag{1} \\
b_{t+128} &= s_t + b_t + b_{t+26} + b_{t+56} + b_{t+91} + b_{t+96} + b_{t+3}b_{t+67} + b_{t+11}b_{t+13} \\
&\quad + b_{t+17}b_{t+18} + b_{t+27}b_{t+59} + b_{t+40}b_{t+48} + b_{t+61}b_{t+65} + b_{t+68}b_{t+84} \\
&\quad + b_{t+22}b_{t+24}b_{t+25} + b_{t+70}b_{t+78}b_{t+82} + b_{t+88}b_{t+92}b_{t+93}b_{t+95} \\
&= s_t + b_t + g'(b_{t+3..t+96}), \tag{2}
\end{aligned}
$$

where the functions $f'()$ and $g'()$ are introduced in order to simplify notation in our analysis in later sections. The output of Grain-128AEAD uses a nine-variable, degree three Boolean function h,

$$
h(x) = x_0x_1 + x_2x_3 + x_4x_5 + x_6x_7 + x_0x_4x_8, \tag{3}
$$

and is given by

$$
\begin{aligned}
y_t &= s_{t+93} + b_{t+2} + b_{t+15} + b_{t+36} + b_{t+45} + b_{t+64} + b_{t+73} + b_{t+89} \tag{4} \\
&\quad + h(b_{t+12}, s_{t+8}, s_{t+13}, s_{t+20}, b_{t+95}, s_{t+42}, s_{t+60}, s_{t+79}, s_{t+94}) \\
&= b_{t+2} + h'(b_{t+12..t+95}, s_{t+8..t+94}), \tag{5}
\end{aligned}
$$

where, again, $h'()$ is introduced for later convenience. The key and nonce (IV) are 128 and 96 bits respectively and we denote them as $k_0, \ldots, k_{127}$ and $IV_0, \ldots, IV_{95}$. To initialize the cipher, let

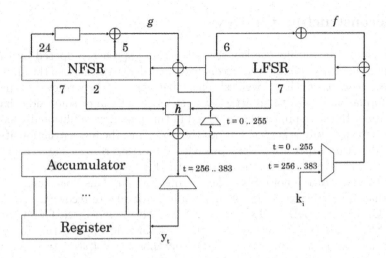

Fig. 1. Overview of the initialisation of Grain-128AEAD

$$B_0 = (k_0, \ldots, k_{127}), \tag{6}$$
$$S_0 = (IV_0, \ldots, IV_{95}, 1, 1, \ldots, 1, 0). \tag{7}$$

Then, for 256 clocks, the LFSR and NFSR are updated according to

$$s_{t+128} = s_t + f'(s_{t+7..t+96}) + y_t, \quad 0 \le t \le 255, \tag{8}$$
$$b_{t+128} = s_t + b_t + g'(b_{t+3..t+96}) + y_t, \quad 0 \le t \le 255. \tag{9}$$

Then, in the next 128 clocks, the key is re-introduced into the LFSR while the NFSR is updated as in regular keystream mode,

$$s_{t+128} = s_t + f'(s_{t+7..t+96}) + k_{t-256}, \quad 256 \le t \le 383, \tag{10}$$
$$b_{t+128} = s_t + b_t + g'(b_{t+3..t+96}), \quad 256 \le t \le 383. \tag{11}$$

In parallel to this key re-introduction, the A and R registers are initialized with the generated y_t. At the end of the initialization, we thus have

$$S_{384} = (s_{384}, \ldots, s_{511}),$$
$$B_{384} = (b_{384}, \ldots, b_{511}),$$
$$A_{384} = (y_{256}, \ldots, y_{319}),$$
$$R_{384} = (y_{320}, \ldots, y_{383}).$$

Note that this notation is slightly different from the design document, but consistent with [5]. Starting at $t = 384$, the generated y_t is used for encryption and message authentication. The details here are left out as we will only be considering the cipher initialization.

3 Reconstructing the Key

In this section, we outline the key reconstruction approach proposed by Chang and Turan in [5]. We use the term *reconstruct* in order to distinguish the approach from *key recovery*, which is a well established attack goal. Key recovery typically uses information known to an attacker, such as keystream or some side channel information. In the approaches considered in this paper, we additionally assume that the internal state is known, but not the key. Thus, the reconstruction attacks discussed in this paper are always preceded by a state recovery attack. This is implicit in the paper and, in this context, the key recovery attack consists of a state recovery attack followed by a key reconstruction. This does, however, *not* imply that all key recovery attacks must start with a state recovery.

For Grain-128AEAD (and similarly for the other ciphers in the Grain family), the LFSR/NFSR can always be clocked backward during the running phase ($t \geq 384$). Thus, if the state is recovered at any time $t \geq 384$, it is straightforward to obtain the state B_{384} and S_{384}. Thus, knowing one state, we can assume that the attacker has knowledge of $b_t, t \geq 384$ and $s_t, t \geq 384$. However, finding B_{383} and S_{383}, which includes b_{383} and s_{383} requires knowing the key bit k_{127}, as

$$s_{511} = s_{383} + s_{390} + s_{421} + s_{453} + s_{464} + s_{479} + k_{127}. \tag{12}$$

Thus, we have two unknowns. Combining this with the update for b_{511}, we have

$$
\begin{aligned}
b_{511} = {}& s_{383} + b_{383} + b_{409} + b_{439} + b_{474} + b_{479} + b_{386}b_{450} + b_{394}b_{396} \\
& + b_{400}b_{401} + b_{410}b_{442} + b_{423}b_{431} + b_{444}b_{448} + b_{451}b_{467} \\
& + b_{405}b_{407}b_{408} + b_{453}b_{461}b_{465} + b_{471}b_{475}b_{476}b_{478}.
\end{aligned}
\tag{13}
$$

Adding this equation gives another unknown, b_{383}. However, if we assume that also the register R is known at time $t = 384$, i.e., $R_{384} = [y_{320}, \ldots y_{383}]$ is known, then we can add the expression

$$
\begin{aligned}
y_{381} = {}& h(b_{393}, s_{389}, s_{394}, s_{401}, b_{476}, s_{423}, s_{441}, s_{460}, s_{475}) + s_{474} + b_{383} \\
& + b_{396} + b_{417} + b_{426} + b_{445} + b_{454} + b_{470},
\end{aligned}
\tag{14}
$$

which includes the unknown term b_{383}. Thus, we now have 3 equations and 3 unknown variables that are linearly added in this equation. All key bits can now be recovered by continuing to clock backwards. The pre-output bits in the accumulator

$$A_{384} = [y_{256}, y_{257}, \ldots, y_{319}]$$

can be computed as

$$A_{384} = T + \sum_{i=0}^{L-1} m_i \cdot R_{2i+384}, \tag{15}$$

where $m_0, m_1, \ldots, m_L$ is a known message with the corresponding authentication tag T. With both the state (S_{384} and B_{384}) and the register contents known, we can easily reconstruct the secret key. Since the keystream does not depend on the registers A and R, a state recovery attack is more likely to recover only the LFSR and NFSR states. Then, as y_{382} and y_{383} can be directly determined from S_{384} and B_{384}, a key reconstruction requires 2^{62} computational steps, i.e., guessing the bits $y_{320}, \ldots, y_{381}$.

4   Basic Attempts to Make the Key Re-introduction Stronger

In this section, we analyze alternative approaches for key re-introduction in parallel with the initialization of A/R registers while maintaining 384 clocks for initialization. We take a conservative approach and assume that the contents of all four registers (B, S, A, R) are known to an adversary at time $t = 384$. As will be shown, virtually any solution in this model fails to protect the key if the state is recovered.

4.1   Group 1: Push Key Bits into NFSR Instead of LFSR

There are a number of initialization options that fall into the same category, where the derivation of unknown bits is immediately possible without any extra effort.

Let us first consider what happens if we XOR the key bits into the NFSR instead of the LFSR, i.e., the updates given by Eqs. (10) and (11) are replaced by

$$s_{t+128} = s_t + f'(s_{t+7..t+96}), \tag{16}$$

$$b_{t+128} = s_t + b_t + g'(b_{t+3..t+96}) + k_{t-256}. \tag{17}$$

Considering the equations for computing the same bits as before (y_{381}, s_{511} and b_{511}), we have

$$s_{511} = s_{383} + f'(s_{390..479}), \tag{18}$$

$$b_{511} = s_{383} + b_{383} + g'(b_{386..479}) + k_{127}, \tag{19}$$

$$y_{381} = b_{383} + h'(b_{393..476}, s_{389..475}). \tag{20}$$

As seen, we end up in the same situation with three equations and three unknowns that can easily be solved explicitly.

Summary: Any initialization option that leads to a linearly independent system of 3 equations on 3 unknowns is easily broken.

4.2   Group 2: Push Key Bits into both NFSR and LFSR

Another approach could be to make the above vulnerable system of 3 equations linearly dependent. There are also several options in this category, but we give just one example where we XOR the key bits into *both* the LFSR and the NFSR, i.e., the update given by Eq. (11) is replaced by

$$b_{t+128} = s_t + b_t + g'(b_{t+3..t+96}) + k_{t-256}. \tag{21}$$

The corresponding expressions for y_{381}, s_{511} and b_{511} are then

$$s_{511} = s_{383} + k_{127} + f'(s_{390..479}), \tag{22}$$

$$b_{511} = s_{383} + b_{383} + k_{127} + g'(b_{386..479}), \tag{23}$$

$$y_{381} = b_{383} + h'(b_{393..476}, s_{389..475}), \tag{24}$$

which is a linearly dependent system of equations. At first glance, this seems to be a better key re-introduction, as it is not possible to determine both s_{383} and k_{127}, but only their sum $s_{383} + k_{127}$. However, this does leak information. It is possible to guess the value of s_{383} and verify this guess *in a time offset manner* as follows.

Let us first generalize Eqs. (22–24),

$$s_{t+128} = (s_t + k_{t-256}) + f'(s_{t+7..t+96}), \tag{25}$$

$$b_{t+128} = (s_t + k_{t-256}) + b_t + g'(b_{t+3..t+96}), \tag{26}$$

$$y_{t-8} = b_{t-6} + b_{t+4}s_t + e'(b_{t+4..t+87}, s_{t+5..t+86}), \tag{27}$$

where e' is the function h' without the $x_0 x_1$ term (here represented by $b_{t+4}s_t$). As for the key reconstruction algorithm, we will run a recursion starting from $t = 383$ and clocking the cipher backward. On each step of the recursion we assume that all values $s_{t+1..}, b_{t+1..}$ are known (or guessed), and we want to recover the three new bits of s_t, b_t, k_{t-256}.

From Eqs. (25–26) we can derive b_t and $(s_t + k_{t-256})$. Then, we can guess s_t and from that derive k_{t-256}. This guess can then be verified just only 6 recursion steps later at time $(t-6)$ by using Eq. (27) since it involves the guessed bit s_t, and the newly derived bit b_{t-6}, while y_{t-8} here serves as a known value taken from the A/R states and is used as the verification value for the guessing paths along the recursion. Note that the derived b_t is also correct only if all previous guesses of the involved bits were correct.

Summary: Re-introduction of the key bits such that the 3 equations become linearly dependent does not help, since the previous guesses may be verified at a later stage of a recursion backtracing algorithm.

4.3   Generic Recursive Backtracing Attack

An even simpler and generic backtracing recursion that covers attacks on any tweak from both groups listed above, would be to just guess the s_t in each step t, derive b_t, k_{t-256}, and simply compute the value of y_t and verify it against the known correct value taken from the A/R state. In this case, we do not even need to go deeper into the structure of the Boolean functions involved, and the recursion will automatically return one step backward once it detects that some previous guess was wrong. The complexity of the key reconstruction can be summarized in Theorem 1.

Theorem 1 (Backtracing complexity). *For all considered initializations from the groups 1 and 2, one can organize a recursion starting from $t = 383$ and going down to $t = 256$, where the expressions on b_{t+128}, s_{t+128} involve 3 unknowns s_t, b_t, k_{t-256}. At every step of recursion, the attacker guesses the value of s_t (or b_t depending on the initialization) and directly derives the other two unknowns, then clocks the cipher backward by 1 step and decrements the time instance t by 1.*

In the above recursion, if the guessed value s_t can be verified (against some other equation or a new constraint, e.g., y-values) only after the recursion depth d (i.e., in time $t - d$), then the overall backtracing complexity will be $O(2^d)$.

Proof. The depth of the recursion is 128, and if every guess would be correct, then the complexity of each node would be $O(1)$ resulting in $O(1)$ overall. However, in each node of the recursion, we have to make $O(2^d)$ other guesses before the current node can be verified and resolved. Therefore, the overall complexity is multiplied by $O(2^d)$.

Simulation Results. We implemented the above backtracing recursion algorithm and applied it on two different initialization options that belong to the second group of initializations (see Sect. 4.2). We were able to reconstruct the whole 128-bit key quite efficiently within some milliseconds, and the time complexity matched well the results of Theorem 1.

Summary: The main problem with these approaches is that the key is reintroduced while initializing the registers A and R. Thus, it is possible to use the values of y in these registers for verification in the reconstruction algorithm.

4.4 The Parallel Option: Parallel XOR of the Whole Key at the End of Initialization

A straightforward approach, and one that is inspired by [9], is to simply XOR all key bits into one of the registers as a final step in the initialization. This is also a tweak that was suggested in [5].

First of all, this has a significant drawback of adding to the hardware footprint, since, for 128 register cells, we need to add one XOR gate and one multiplexer, i.e., at least 256 new gates. This makes the hardware footprint much larger and we would still prefer to explore options where the key is serially inserted into one or both registers.

Secondly, this approach seems also vulnerable to the generic backtracing recursion or similar, since y-values stored in A/R can again be used for verification at some backward time instances of the recursion against the guessing paths. Moreover, the order of guessing in this scenario can be chosen freely by an attacker.

Conclusions: Any tweak where the A/R bits are initialized in parallel or before the key re-introduction can be broken. From this, we conclude that the initialization of the registers A and R must be done *after* the key re-introduction. In the next section, we will consider new approaches for initialization that are more resistant to key reconstruction when the state is known.

5 Re-introducing the Key Before A/R Register Initialization

Separating key re-introduction and A/R initialization removes the possibility to verify guesses against the A/R content. In this section, we will consider various options for a new tweak in initialization that meet these new requirements.

5.1 New Generic Initialization Steps

Considering the above analysis, it becomes clear that the initialization should consist of 3 clearly separated phases. We believe these phases should be as follows:

– C_n standard initialization clocks, like in Grain-128a, where the pre-output y_t is added to both LFSR and NFSR, i.e., for $t = [0, \ldots, C_n - 1]$:

$$s_{t+128} = s_t + f'(s_{t+7..t+96}) + y_t, \tag{28}$$

$$b_{t+128} = s_t + b_t + g'(b_{t+3..t+96}) + y_t; \tag{29}$$

– C_k clocks where the key is re-introduced (to be defined later);
– C_m clocks where the pre-output y_t is used to initialize the registers A/R, while the LFSR and NFSR are updated in the standard keystream mode, i.e., for $t = [C_n + C_k, \ldots, C_n + C_k + C_m - 1]$:

$$s_{t+128} = s_t + f'(s_{t+7..t+96}), \tag{30}$$

$$b_{t+128} = s_t + b_t + g'(b_{t+3..t+96}), \tag{31}$$

$$A/R \leftarrow y_t. \tag{32}$$

In a straightforward approach, one could select $C_k = 128$ to re-introduce the key bits serially in 128 clocks into either (or both) the LFSR and/or NFSR. However, we can compress this stage to $C_k = 64$ clocks by splitting the key into two parts, adding each part to one of the registers,

$$s_{t+128} = s_t + f'(s_{t+7..t+96}) + y_t + k_{t-C_n+64}, \tag{33}$$

$$b_{t+128} = s_t + b_t + g'(b_{t+3..t+96}) + y_t + k_{t-C_n}, \tag{34}$$

for 64 time instances $t = [C_n, \ldots, C_n + 63]$. This solution is efficient in both hardware and software. We fix the two initialization parameters to $C_k = 64$ and $C_m = 128$, and it remains to decide C_n, i.e., the duration of the initial phase.

5.2   An Attempt to Keep 384 Clocks in Total, $C_n = 192$

To keep the original 384 initialization clocks, we explore the possibility to re-introduce the key bits in clocks $[192, \ldots, 255]$. Assume a state recovery attack, where the state B_{384}, S_{384} after initialization is recovered. Since the key is introduced earlier, we can clock backward and recover B_{256}, S_{256}. The content of A/R can be recovered immediately since they are initialized at $256 \leq t \leq 383$ using $y_{256}, \ldots, y_{383}$. However, now these bits cannot be used for verification of the guessing paths. The last key bits, k_{63} and k_{127} are introduced through

$$s_{383} = s_{255} + f'(s_{262..351}) + y_{255} + k_{127}, \tag{35}$$

$$b_{383} = s_{255} + b_{255} + g'(b_{258..351}) + y_{255} + k_{63}, \tag{36}$$

where $s_{255}, b_{255}, k_{63}, k_{127}$ are unknowns, and other terms can be derived; therefore, the pre-outputs y_t in time $t \geq 256$ are now useless for key reconstruction (unlike the approaches in Sect. 4).

The only remaining possibility for an attacker to verify the guesses, or to recover key bits, is to link somehow the known state B_{256}, S_{256} to the initial state B_0, S_0, i.e., to the original Key, IV values.

Differential Analysis. We now show that if C_n is too small, then the initialization as defined by Eqs. (33) and (34) leaks key information through a differential attack. Consider the following sum of variables, denoted by z,

$$
\begin{aligned}
z_{t+128} &= b_{t+128} + s_{t+128} + g'(b_{t+3..t+96}) + f'(s_{t+7..t+96}) \\
&= (s_t + b_t + g'(b_{t+3..t+96}) + y_t + k_{t-192}) \\
&\quad + (s_t + f'(s_{t+7..t+96}) + y_t + k_{t-128}) \\
&\quad + g'(b_{t+3..t+96}) + f'(s_{t+7..t+96}) \\
&= b_t + k_{t-192} + k_{t-128}.
\end{aligned}
\tag{37}
$$

Since we know b_t and s_t for $t \geq 256$, we can compute z_{t+128} for $t \geq 253$ (since $t + 3$ is the lowest used index in the g' and f' functions). Thus, we can find a differential

$$\Delta z_{t+128} = \Delta(b_t + k_{t-256} + k_{t-192}) = \Delta b_t, \quad \text{for } t \geq 253. \tag{38}$$

A Possible Scenario for Key Bit Reconstruction with Conditional Differentials. In a simple scenario we would like to recover some key bit k_x, based on the conditional differential distributions $D_0 = (\Delta b_t | k_x = 0)$ and $D_1 = (\Delta b_t | k_x = 1)$, for some ΔIV. If these distributions have different biases, then by collecting many samples Δb_t, we can determine the key bit k_x. This way, we can recover one key bit. The differential should be introduced, ideally, by some ΔIV while keeping the same Key, and we would then collect r pairs of the form (Key, IV_i) and $(Key, IV_i + \Delta IV)$, for $i = 1, \ldots, r$, some fixed Key and random IV_is. Then, for each pair Δz_{t+128} (that is equal to Δb_t) is computed and the empirical distribution D is constructed. Finally, we compute the distances from D to both D_0 and D_1, and the shorter distance decides on the key bit value k_x.

Of course, the above procedure for recovering k_x requires applying a state recovery attack on $2r$ keystreams, recovering $2r$ states of (B_{256}, S_{256}). These states are used for collecting the z_{t+128} samples and the construction of the empirical distribution D. However, when, for example, the two key bits k_{63}, k_{127} are recovered, it is possible to clock further backward, and all those recovered states can be used to collect differential samples to recover some other key bit.

One approach could be to collect many samples with a number of differentials $\Delta IV_0, \ldots, \Delta IV_{127}$ – one for each key bit, not necessarily to be used at the same time instance t. Then, depending on the time instance t and the target key bit k_x, we could derive differential samples from one of the ith group of the recovered states. As soon as it becomes possible (i.e., when certain key bits are recovered), the attacker clocks all states backward by one or more clocks, which opens up for applying other Δ_is and thus to recover other key bits.

Differential Probabilistic Model. In order to study conditional and/or differential probabilities, we have adopted the following model for a binary signal x, where the signal x is associated with two probabilities:

$$p_x = \Pr\{x = 1\},$$
$$p_{\Delta x} = \Pr\{x \oplus x' = 1\},$$

where x' is the same signal but may have a different value, i.e., $\Delta x = x \oplus x'$.

For two *independent* signals x and y we derive expressions for the resulting probabilities of XOR and AND gates:

$$p_{x \oplus y} = p_x + p_y - 2p_x p_y,$$
$$p_{\Delta(x \oplus y)} = p_{\Delta x} + p_{\Delta y} - 2p_{\Delta x} p_{\Delta y},$$
$$p_{x \& y} = p_x p_y,$$
$$p_{\Delta(x \& y)} = p_{\Delta x} p_{\Delta y}(2(1 - p_x)(1 - p_y) - 1) + p_x p_{\Delta y} + p_y p_{\Delta x}.$$

By this, we can configure the initial state of Grain with these signals, where some of the signals will be random values, constants 0 or 1, or differential bits. Then we clock the cipher and derive probabilities for the resulting signals. In the end, we check if some bit of the state or its differential has a detectable bias and if yes then we can try to use it in an attack.

Note that this method is expected, in most cases, to give a *lower bound* for these biases since above we consider x and y as independent. In reality, many of those signals will be dependent. For example, $x = abc$ and $y = bcd$ are dependent as they share b and c signals. Also, if some term a is added in a Boolean expression twice then it should be canceled out, while in this model it will be treated as two different independent signals, thus making the resulting biases smaller than in reality. Therefore, this method is suitable for first searching statistical anomalies, but the actual bias can be verified and refined through, e.g., real simulations.

The state of Grain is thus initialized as follows:

$$\begin{aligned}
\text{Constant } 0 &\rightarrow p_0 = 0, \; p_{\Delta 0} = 0, \\
\text{Constant } 1 &\rightarrow p_1 = 1, \; p_{\Delta 1} = 0, \\
\text{Key bits} &\rightarrow p_k = 0.5, \; p_{\Delta k} = 0, \\
\text{Fixed random } IV \text{ bits} &\rightarrow p_{iv} = 0.5, \; p_{\Delta iv} = 0, \\
\text{Differential } \Delta\, IV \text{ bits} &\rightarrow p_{iv} = 0 \text{ or } 1, \; p_{\Delta iv} = 1.
\end{aligned}$$

Examples of Conditional Differentials. We have not managed to find a complete path for the sketched conditional differential attack, but we have found at least some examples where some of the key bits can be recovered by looking into $\Delta z_{255+128}$.

The best approach found is to initialize the cipher with a difference in a single IV-bit. If $\Pr(\Delta z_{383}) = \Pr(\Delta b_{255}) = 0.5(1+\varepsilon)$ we can distinguish the cipher from random using about ε^{-2} such samples. By utilizing the differential probabilistic model, we find that such a difference can be observed with a differential in IV_{56}, whenever all other Key and IV bits are random:

$$\begin{aligned}
\Delta IV_{56}|Key_{109} = 0 &\rightarrow \varepsilon(\Delta b_{255}) = 2^{-6.73}, \\
\Delta IV_{56}|Key_{109} = 1 &\rightarrow \varepsilon(\Delta b_{255}) = 0.
\end{aligned} \tag{39}$$

The above biases were refined through real simulations by collecting 2^{24} samples, resulting in:

$$\begin{aligned}
\Delta IV_{56}|Key_{109} = 0 &\rightarrow \varepsilon(\Delta b_{255}) = 2^{-3.23}, \\
\Delta IV_{56}|Key_{109} = 1 &\rightarrow \varepsilon(\Delta b_{255}) = 0.
\end{aligned} \tag{40}$$

It is hard to say exactly how these distributions will behave for a concrete fixed key, but let us assume that for all or most keys the above is true. Then, recovering k_{109} would proceed as follows. Collect differential samples Δz_{383} for ΔIV_{56}, i.e., the cipher is initialized with many random IV pairs where we flip only the bit IV_{56}. Then, based on the empirical distribution of Δz_{383} we can determine the value of k_{109}. This will require around $2 \cdot 2^{6.46} = 2^{7.46}$ initializations, each followed by a state recovery attack. Recovering all key bits in this way requires finding biases similar to Eq. (40) (where we can also utilize any other $t \geq 253$). While this might not be feasible for all key bits, recovering some key bits in this way could be followed by an exhaustive search for the rest. We stress that this requires a state recovery for each initialization and is thus always more expensive than a state recovery attack. Still, the relatively large biases found here question the suitability of re-introducing the key in this way as early as $t = 192$ since a state recovery attack gives information about the state already at $t = 256$.

Conclusion: In the presented example we only show that such a conditional differential exists to some extent. This approach for key reconstruction can be investigated further, and we leave it for future research. What is clear is that for $C_n = 192$ there is at least *some* leakage of information about the key, although the exact attack scenario is not easy to find.

Other Differentials Detected. The differential probabilistic model was also used to detect some other biases. For example, we were fixing the key to a random state and were running the model to see how far we can get a bias with that model. We found that in $\sim 9.4\%$ of random keys, where we also set $IV_{48..96} = 0$ while $IV_{0..47}$ are random, we get for ΔIV_{69} the differential Δb_{288} to have the bias around $2^{-9.9..-12.9}$.

Through real simulations, we collected 2^{30} samples for each random key, and received the refined bias in the range $2^{-9..-11}$, but with a higher success rate of $\sim 12.5\%$ for 2600 random keys tested. For these simulations we used a PRNG with high entropy. Simulation results are given in Fig. 2.

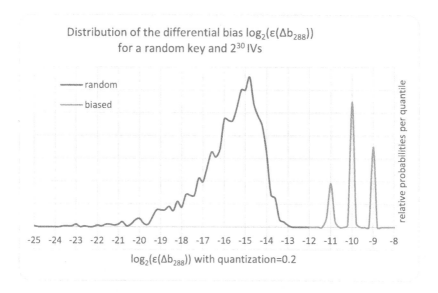

Fig. 2. Refining simulation results for the bias of Δb_{288}.

I.e., for about one key out of 8 random keys, we can distinguish $\Delta z_{288+128}$ from random by collecting around $2^{18..22}$ IV-differential samples. However, the result of the distinguisher may leak up to 5 bits of information about the key in connection to 4 possible answers: random, or one of the 3 biased peaks. To be more precise, reverse-engineering of the random keys led to the four different answers resulting in the following key information:

$$\text{if }\ \Delta b_{288}\ \text{ is biased } \textbf{then } k_{73} = k_{122} = 0, k_{109} = 1,$$
$$\text{if }\ \varepsilon(\Delta b_{288}) \approx 2^{-9}\ \text{ then } k_{77} = k_{112} = 0,$$
$$\text{if }\ \varepsilon(\Delta b_{288}) \approx 2^{-10}\ \text{ then } k_{77} + k_{112} = 1,$$
$$\text{if }\ \varepsilon(\Delta b_{288}) \approx 2^{-11}\ \text{ then } k_{77} = k_{112} = 1,$$

which means that Δz_{416} can be used to get some information about the key.

5.3   What Would Be the Minimum C_n?

From Differential Attacks Perspectives. Recall the previously derived expression for Δz_{t+128},

$$\Delta z_{t+128} = \Delta(b_{t+128} + s_{t+128} + g'(b_{t+3..t+96}) + f'(s_{t+7..t+96})) = \Delta b_t,$$

and the first (smallest) t for which the above differential is available, right after the set of state recovery attacks, is $t = C_n + C_k - 3$ (see Eq. (37)), where $C_k = 64$ but C_n is not yet known. Thus, if there is a weakness in Δb_t then the lower bound for C_n to mitigate such a weakness would be

$$C_n \geq t - 60.$$

In [14], the authors managed to recover 18 key bits after 169 clocks of initialization, but there they were looking at y_t values instead of the state bits. In a naïve approximation, this would translate to having some (differential) bias in at most s_{169+94}, b_{169+95} state bits, where $169 + 95 = 264$ is the highest index of the state bits involved in y_{169}. Thinking purely theoretically one could, perhaps, collect some statistics on up to Δb_{264}. This leads to the first lower bound $C_n \geq 204$. Clearly, $C_n = 192$ looks too low – the case we first considered in Sect. 5.2 in order to keep 384 clocks of initialization.

However, in our simulations, we were able to find highly biased differentials up to around Δb_{288} (see Sect. 5.2), which means that C_n must be at least $C_n \geq 228$ in order to prevent these differentials as well.

Finally, we would like to note that the mentioned paper [14] also provides a distinguishing attack after 195 initialization rounds, by again looking into y_t. Note that in the case of a state recovery attack a distinguishing attack is not relevant at all – if the attacker can recover the state of a given keystream then, certainly, we have a distinguisher. What only matters for this type of analysis is the possibility to reconstruct at least some key bits given available expressions and values. Nevertheless, if we could anyways get some biased conditional distribution on Δb_{195+95} then that assumption translates into the hardest lower bound $C_n \geq 230$.

Although we make here a very strong assumption that some key bits can still be recovered by looking at Δb_{290}, there is great uncertainty about how large the bias would be, and therefore how many samples one has to collect. The complexity of such an attack is then at least the number of samples needed multiplied by the complexity of a single state recovery attack. There is also uncertainty about how many and which key bits can be statistically detected, and whether this leads to any additional backward clocks of the collected states. The order of determining key bits is important for the backtracing ability.

Summary: Given the current state-of-the-art analysis of Grain, and making the most strict (and, perhaps, unrealistic) assumptions, we conclude that we have a lower bound $C_n \geq 230$. This means that we cannot really stay with 384 clocks for the initialization (starting to re-introduce the key at $t = 192$), but should increase it by at least 38 (plus some added margin), even if these strong attack models are hard to achieve.

Combining State Recovery, Guess-and-determine, and Distinguishing Attacks. Let us again consider the distinguishing attack in [14] using y-terms after 195 initialization clocks. This means that there could also exist a distinguisher on Δb_{195+95}, since y_{195} involves b_{195+95}. So, if $C_n = 229$ then we can sample $\Delta z_{418} = \Delta b_{290}$ and distinguish that from random. Though a pure distinguishing attack itself is not interesting in key reconstruction, such a distinguisher can be used for verifying guessed key bits.

Assume that, based on the previous discussion, we adopt $C_n = 256$. Then, we can collect r pairs of keystreams, each pair with one keystream generated with some random IV, and one using a differential $IV + \Delta IV$ for some fixed ΔIV. Then we apply a state recovery attack on each of the $2r$ keystreams, recovering r pairs of states $(B_{320}^{(i)}, S_{320}^{(i)})$ and $(B_{320}^{\prime(i)}, S_{320}^{\prime(i)})$, for $i = 1, \ldots, r$.

Then, by guessing the first 54 key bits, we can reverse 27 initialization steps, recovering $(B_{293}^{(i)}, S_{293}^{(i)})$ and $(B_{293}^{\prime(i)}, S_{293}^{\prime(i)})$. Thus, we reach $C_n = 229$. At this point, for each pair of states in time $t = 293$, we compute r samples $\Delta z_{290+128}^{(i)}$, i.e., $\Delta b_{290}^{(i)}$, see Eq. (38). With many states, we can use the empirical distribution for Δb_{290} and distinguish it from random. If the 54 key bits were correctly guessed, we get a biased empirical distribution, otherwise, the guess was incorrect. Note that, for every key guess we can use the same set of the recovered states for sampling.

Example. Let us give an example of the complexity of this attack. Assume that there is a ΔIV that makes Δb_{290} being biased with $\varepsilon = 2^{-10}$. With 2^{54} distributions, to distinguish the correct key guess, we need about $(54 \cdot 2 \ln 2) \cdot 2^{20} = 2^{26.2}$ samples, i.e., $2^{27.2}$ keystreams are needed [11]. If the state recovery attack has complexity 2^e then the total attack complexity would be $O(2^e \cdot 2^{27.2} + 2^{54} \cdot 2^{27.2}) = O(2^{e+27.2} + 2^{81.2})$. Note also, if the bias of Δb_{290} would be too small, the attacker can guess a few more key bits and reach a lower index of Δb_t where the bias is larger. For example, guessing 2 more key bits makes it possible to backtrace one more step.

Conclusion: The sketched attack is purely theoretical at the moment, and we leave further investigations for future research. However, to mitigate such kinds of more advanced attacks, the lower bound on C_n should be increased by 64, i.e., $C_n \geq 294$. In this case, all key bits need to be guessed in order to reach the time instance where one can collect biased samples and use them for verification. And, of course, future research might reveal biases in Δb_t with $t > 290$. For these reasons, $C_n = 256$ also looks too low in the context of key reconstruction from known states.

6   A Modified Key Re-introduction

From the analysis in the previous sections, we can conclude:

1. The key should not be re-introduced while also initializing the A and R register, or in parallel after;

2. Introducing the key as early as $t = 256$ is questionable due to rather large biases found in some differentials.

Based on our analysis done in the previous sections, we propose to increase the initialization by 128 extra clocks and to adopt $C_n = 320, C_k = 64, C_m = 128$ in the generic description given in Sect. 5.1. We believe that this tweak makes the key re-introduction secure against the attacks discussed in this paper. The cipher using this new initialization is denoted Grain-128AEADv2. To summarize the result of this new initialization, we highlight the following aspects.

- Both Grain-128a and Grain-128AEAD have 256 clocks of initialization, and no attack was found on that so far. In the proposed tweak we do $C_n = 320$ initialization clocks, in order to protect the key re-introduction phase in case the whole state is recovered from the keystream. After that we re-introduce the key, followed by the A/R initialization. This amounts to a total of 512 initialization steps, adding 33% to the 384 steps in Grain-128AEAD. In the proposed design we have security not worse than in the previous instances of Grain, which in turn were analyzed for many years;
- We use only 64 clocks for the key re-introduction phase, which is a compromise between a parallel XOR of the key (that is more expensive in hardware) and the introduction of the key bits in 128 clocks (that is more expensive in time). Moreover, we believe that serialized key re-introduction is more secure than the parallel, since then an attacker has much less freedom to exploit available Boolean expressions;
- The attacks on the key re-introduction, similar to the one in [5] are no longer possible. The three initialization phases are now clearly separated;
- With the proposed tweak we prevent key reconstruction from known states also with more advanced and comprehensive types of attacks, though some of them are currently theoretical and speculative, and also under strong assumptions.

As noted, we believe that the choice of $C_n = 320$ provides a good security margin against key reconstruction from conditional differentials.

7   Conclusions

The security property found in [5] of the key re-introduction of Grain-128AEAD shows that the key can be reconstructed with low complexity if the state is known. In this paper, we analyze the initialization, and in particular the key re-introduction further by considering several different possible approaches for key reconstruction. We also analyze these approaches, both in relation to a previously published reconstruction technique, but also by considering more sophisticated methods. As a result, we suggest a modification to the cipher initialization that is both more secure, but also maintains the validity of previous analysis of the initialization algorithm. The new cipher version is denoted Grain-128AEADv2.

Acknowledgements. This research was funded in part by the Swedish Foundation for Strategic Research, grant RIT17-0032 and in part by the ELLIIT project.

References

1. Ågren, M., Hell, M., Johansson, T., Meier, W.: Grain-128a: a new version of Grain-128 with optional authentication. Int. J. Wireless Mobile Comput. **5**(1), 48–59 (2011)
2. Amin Ghafari, V., Hu, H.: Fruit-80: a secure ultra-lightweight stream cipher for constrained environments. Entropy **20**(3) (2018). https://www.mdpi.com/1099-4300/20/3/180
3. Armknecht, F., Mikhalev, V.: On lightweight stream ciphers with shorter internal states. In: Leander, G. (ed.) FSE 2015. LNCS, vol. 9054, pp. 451–470. Springer, Heidelberg (2015). https://doi.org/10.1007/978-3-662-48116-5_22
4. Babbage, S., Dodd, M.: The stream cipher mickey 2.0. eSTREAM: the ECRYPT Stream Cipher Project (2006)
5. Chang, D., Turan, M.S.: Recovering the key from the internal state of grain-128aead. Cryptology ePrint Archive, Report 2021/439 (2021). https://eprint.iacr.org/2021/439
6. Cannière, C.: TRIVIUM: a stream cipher construction inspired by block cipher design principles. In: Katsikas, S.K., López, J., Backes, M., Gritzalis, S., Preneel, B. (eds.) ISC 2006. LNCS, vol. 4176, pp. 171–186. Springer, Heidelberg (2006). https://doi.org/10.1007/11836810_13
7. Dinur, I., Güneysu, T., Paar, C., Shamir, A., Zimmermann, R.: An experimentally verified attack on full grain-128 using dedicated reconfigurable hardware. In: Lee, D.H., Wang, X. (eds.) ASIACRYPT 2011. LNCS, vol. 7073, pp. 327–343. Springer, Heidelberg (2011). https://doi.org/10.1007/978-3-642-25385-0_18
8. Dinur, I., Shamir, A.: Breaking grain-128 with dynamic cube attacks. In: Joux, A. (ed.) FSE 2011. LNCS, vol. 6733, pp. 167–187. Springer, Heidelberg (2011). https://doi.org/10.1007/978-3-642-21702-9_10
9. Hamann, M., Krause, M.: On stream ciphers with provable beyond-the-birthday-bound security against time-memory-data tradeoff attacks. Cryptogr. Commun. **10**(5), 959–1012 (2018). https://doi.org/10.1007/s12095-018-0294-5
10. Hamann, M., Krause, M., Meier, W.: Lizard - a lightweight stream cipher for power-constrained devices. IACR Trans. Symmetric Cryptology **2017**(1), 45–79 (2017)
11. Hell, M., Johansson, T., Brynielsson, L.: An overview of distinguishing attacks on stream ciphers. Cryptogr. Commun. **1**(1), 71–94 (2009)
12. Hell, M., Johansson, T., Maximov, A., Meier, W.: A stream cipher proposal: Grain-128. In: 2006 IEEE International Symposium on Information Theory, pp. 1614–1618. IEEE (2006)
13. Hell, M., Johansson, T., Meier, W.: Grain: a stream cipher for constrained environments. Int. J. Wireless Mobile Comput. **2**(1), 86–93 (2007)
14. Ma, Z., Tian, T., Qi, W.F.: Conditional differential attacks on grain-128a stream cipher. IET Inf. Secur. **11**(3), 139–145 (2017)
15. Maximov, A., Hell, M.: Software evaluation of grain-128aead for embedded platforms. Cryptology ePrint Archive, Report 2020/659 (2020). https://eprint.iacr.org/2020/659
16. Mikhalev, V., Armknecht, F., Müller, C.: On ciphers that continuously access the non-volatile key. IACR Trans. Symmetric Cryptology **2016**(2), 52–79 (2017)

17. Rogaway, P.: Authenticated-encryption with associated-data. In: Proceedings of the 9th ACM Conference on Computer and Communications Security, CCS 2002, pp. 98–107. Association for Computing Machinery (2002)
18. Sönnerup, J., Hell, M., Sönnerup, M., Khattar, R.: Efficient hardware implementations of grain-128AEAD. In: Hao, F., Ruj, S., Sen Gupta, S. (eds.) INDOCRYPT 2019. LNCS, vol. 11898, pp. 495–513. Springer, Cham (2019). https://doi.org/10.1007/978-3-030-35423-7_25

Partition Oracles from Weak Key Forgeries

Marcel Armour[1]([envelope]) [ORCID] and Carlos Cid[1,2] [ORCID]

[1] Royal Holloway University of London, Egham, UK
{marcel.armour.2017,carlos.cid}@rhul.ac.uk
[2] Simula UiB, Bergen, Norway

Abstract. In this work, we show how weak key forgeries against polynomial hash based Authenticated Encryption (AE) schemes, such as AES-GCM, can be leveraged to launch partitioning oracle attacks. Partitioning oracle attacks were recently introduced by Len et al. (Usenix'21) as a new class of decryption error oracle which, conceptually, takes a ciphertext as input and outputs whether or not the decryption key belongs to some known subset of keys. Partitioning oracle attacks allow an adversary to query multiple keys simultaneously, leading to practical attacks against low entropy keys (e. g. those derived from passwords).

Weak key forgeries were given a systematic treatment in the work of Procter and Cid (FSE'13), who showed how to construct MAC forgeries that effectively test whether the decryption key is in some (arbitrary) set of target keys. Consequently, it would appear that weak key forgeries naturally lend themselves to constructing partition oracles; we show that this is indeed the case, and discuss some practical applications of such an attack. Our attack applies in settings where AE schemes are used with static session keys, and has the particular advantage that an attacker has full control over the underlying plaintexts, allowing any format checks on underlying plaintexts to be met – including those designed to mitigate against partitioning oracle attacks.

Prior work demonstrated that key commitment is an important security property of AE schemes, in particular settings. Our results suggest that resistance to weak key forgeries should be considered a related design goal. Lastly, our results reinforce the message that weak passwords should never be used to derive encryption keys.

Keywords: Authenticated Encryption · Partitioning oracles · Weak key forgeries · Polynomial hashing · GCM

1 Introduction

Authenticated Encryption (AE) schemes are designed to provide the core properties of confidentiality and message integrity against chosen-ciphertext attacks (CCA). A particularly important practical class of AE schemes offer Authenticated Encryption with Associated Data (AEAD); AEAD schemes are widely

M. Conti et al. (Eds.): CANS 2021, LNCS 13099, pp. 42–62, 2021.
https://doi.org/10.1007/978-3-030-92548-2_3

standardised and implemented due to their efficiency and security. As a result of their widespread adoption, AEAD schemes have in some cases been used in contexts that require additional properties beyond standard CCA security. One particular property that has attracted recent attention is key-commitment [3,18,24], also known as robustness [21], which (informally) states that a ciphertext will only decrypt under the key that was used to encrypt it.

A lack of key-commitment in particular AEAD schemes was exploited by Len et al., who introduced a new class of attack they call "partitioning oracle attacks" [31]. Conceptually, a partitioning oracle takes as input a ciphertext and outputs whether the decryption key belongs to some known subset of keys. Len et al. first construct so-called "splitting ciphertexts" for AES-GCM and ChaCha20Poly1305 that decrypt under every key in a set of target keys. This splitting ciphertext is submitted to a decryption oracle; on observing whether the ciphertext is accepted or rejected, the adversary learns whether or not the decryption key is in the set of target keys. As a result, the adversary is able to query multiple keys simultaneously, speeding up a brute force attack. Combining this with low entropy keys, such as those derived from passwords, results in practical attacks. Len et al. give a number of examples including against Shadowsocks [1], a censorship evasion tool, where the attack results in key recovery.

The concept of weak keys shares some similarities with that of partitioning oracles. Whilst there is no precise definition in the literature, the concept is intuitively clear; Handschuh and Preneel [25] describe a weak key as a key that results in an algorithm behaving in an unexpected way (that can easily be detected) – the idea is that a weak key can be tested for with less effort than brute force. Procter and Cid [36] give a framework that neatly captures weak key forgeries (forgeries that are valid if the key is "weak"), which generalised previous attacks against polynomial hash based message authentication codes (MACs) by Handschuh and Preneel [25] and Saarinen [37]. Procter and Cid's results showed that for these cases the term is a misnomer: in fact, for a polynomial hash based MAC, any set of keys can be considered weak using their forgery techniques.

Abstractly, weak key forgeries and splitting ciphertexts share the same structure: ciphertexts whose successful decryption is contingent on the user's key being in a set of target keys. This suggests that weak key forgeries are a good candidate to carry out partitioning oracle attacks; we show that this is indeed the case. We first generalise the attack formalisation of Len et al. to allow the adversary to act as a machine-in-the-middle, in a more realistic reflection of an attacker's capabilities. As a result we obtain a more abstract definition that encompasses weak key forgeries and splitting ciphertexts. We show how to carry out a partitioning oracle attack using weak key forgeries, and discuss some practical applications of the attack. An advantage of our attack is the control that an adversary obtains over underlying plaintexts, allowing for partitioning oracle attacks in settings that are resistant to the attack of [31], in particular where there are format requirements on underlying plaintexts – including format requirements that are designed to render schemes key-committing. Our results reinforce the conclusions of [31], especially on the danger of deriving encryption keys from user-generated passwords. Furthermore, our results suggest that resistance to weak key forgeries should be considered a related design goal to key-commitment, particularly in settings that are vulnerable to partitioning oracle attacks. Concretely, our results demonstrate – in contrast to the suggestions of prior work – that adding structure to underlying plaintexts (e.g. packet headers that prefix every plaintext message, or an appended block of all zeros) is not a sufficient mitigation against partitioning oracle attacks.

Related Work. Bellovin and Merritt introduced partition attacks against encrypted key exchange: trial decryption of intercepted traffic allowed multiple keys to be eliminated at once [11]. Other oracle attacks include padding oracles [16,38] or other format oracles [4,6,23]; these attacks are similar to but distinct from partitioning oracles as they recover information regarding plaintexts rather than secret keys. Subverted decryption oracles that reveal information about secret keys were considered in [8,9].

Structure. This paper is structured as follows. After describing our notation below, we provide the relevant background material on polynomial hash based schemes in Sect. 2. Partitioning Oracle Attacks are introduced in Sect. 3, and our extension based on Weak Key Forgeries in Sect. 4. Section 5 describes our experiments with Shadowsocks, as well as other protocols. We close the paper with our conclusions in Sect. 6.

1.1 Notation

We refer to an element $x \in \{0,1\}^*$ as a string, and denote its length by $|x|$; ε denotes the empty string. The set of strings of length ℓ is denoted $\{0,1\}^\ell$. In addition, we denote by $\perp \notin \{0,1\}^*$ a reserved special symbol. For two strings x, x' we denote by $x \parallel x'$ their concatenation. A block cipher E is a family of permutations on $\{0,1\}^n$, with each permutation indexed by a key $k \in K$, where the key space $K = \{0,1\}^\ell$ for some fixed key length ℓ. The application of a block cipher to input $x \in \{0,1\}^n$ using key k will be denoted by $\mathsf{E}_k(x)$. Arbitrary finite fields are denoted by $\mathbb{F}$, or when we specify its characteristic by $\mathbb{F}_{p^r}$, with p prime.

We use code-based notation for probability and security experiments. We write $\leftarrow$ for the assignment operator (that assigns a right-hand-side value to a left-hand-side variable). If S is a finite set, then $s \leftarrow_\$ S$ denotes choosing s uniformly at random from S. We use superscript notation to indicate when an algorithm (typically an adversary) is given access to specific oracles. If $\mathcal{A}$ is a randomised algorithm, we write $y \leftarrow_\$ \mathcal{A}(x)$ to indicate that it is invoked on input x (and fresh random coins), and the result is assigned to variable y. An experiment terminates with a "stop with x" instruction, where value x is understood as the outcome of the experiment. We write "win" ("lose") as shorthand for "stop with 1" ("stop with 0"). We write "require C", for a Boolean condition C, shorthand for "if not C: lose". (We use require clauses typically to abort a game when the adversary performs some disallowed action, e.g. one that would lead to a trivial win.) We use Iverson brackets $[\cdot]$ to derive bit values from Boolean conditions: For a condition C we have $[C] = 1$ if C holds; otherwise we have $[C] = 0$. In security games we write $\mathcal{A}^{\mathcal{O}_1,\ldots,\mathcal{O}_c} \Rightarrow 1$ to denote the event that the adversary outputs 1 after being given access to the c oracles.

2 Background: Polynomial Hashing

MACs are a symmetric cryptographic primitive that allows two parties sharing a secret key to communicate with the assurance that their messages have not been tampered with. Many popular MAC schemes are constructed from universal hash functions that are realised by polynomial evaluation; such MACs based on polynomial hashing are discussed in Sect. 2.1. They are often used to provide the authentication component for AEAD schemes, which are discussed in Sect. 2.2, where we give an overview of the two most widely used polynomial hash based AEAD constructions, McGrew and Viega's Galois/Counter Mode (GCM) [32] and Bernstein's ChaCha20-Poly1305 [12].

2.1 MACs from Polynomial Hashing

A polynomial hash based authentication scheme is built on a family of universal hash functions that are based on polynomial evaluation. It takes as input an authentication key H and message M (consisting of plaintext or ciphertext blocks depending on context). Let $M = M_1 \parallel \cdots \parallel M_p \parallel M_{p+1}$ with $M_{p+1} = \text{len}(M)$ and all M_i considered as elements of a field $\mathbb{F}$ (typically $\mathbb{F}_{2^n}$), and $g_M(x)$ be the polynomial in $\mathbb{F}[x]$ defined as $g_M(x) = \sum_{i=1}^{p+1} M_i x^{p+2-i}$. If we also consider $H \in \mathbb{F}$, the polynomial hash $h_H(M)$ of M is calculated by evaluating $g_M(x)$ at H, i.e.

$$h_H(M) := g_M(H) = \sum_{i=1}^{p+1} M_i H^{p+2-i} \in \mathbb{F}.$$

The hash value is usually encrypted with a pseudo-random one-time pad, to provide the output authentication tag.

The underlying properties of polynomials are inherited by the hash function and thus the authentication scheme; in particular, the fact that adding a zero valued polynomial will not change the value of the hash (which gives rise to "weak key" forgeries, discussed in Sect. 2.4) and the fact that it is possible to construct a polynomial that passes through a set of given points (giving rise to multi-key collisions, discussed in Sect. 2.3).

2.2 AEAD

Let AEAD = (AuthEnc, AuthDec) be an AEAD scheme, and let its key space be the set K. Encryption takes as input a key $k \in K$, together with a tuple of nonce, associated data and plaintext (N, D, P) and returns a ciphertext and authentication tag. We write $(C, T) \leftarrow \mathsf{AuthEnc}_k(N, D, P)$. Similarly, decryption takes as input a key $k \in K$ together with a tuple (N, D, C, T) of nonce, associated data, ciphertext and authentication tag and returns either a message or the error message $\perp$ to indicate that the decryption was not successful. Correctness requires that for all N, D, P not exceeding the scheme's length restrictions, $\mathsf{AuthDec}_k(N, D, C, T) = P$ with $(C, T) = \mathsf{AuthEnc}_k(N, D, P)$.

A common paradigm for constructing AEAD schemes is to use an Encrypt-then-MAC (EtM) construction with a stream cipher for encryption and an authentication component from a polynomial based universal hash function. We give a brief overview of the most widely adopted and standardised schemes: McGrew and Viega's AES Galois/Counter Mode (AES-GCM) [32] below and Bernstein's ChaCha20-Poly1305 [12, 35] in Appendix A.

AES-GCM. AES-GCM encryption takes as input: an AES key k, a nonce N, plaintext $P = P_1 \| \cdots \| P_p$ and associated data $D = D_1 \| \cdots \| D_d$. The key is 128, 192 or 256 bits long, the nonce N should preferably be 96 bits long although any length is supported. For each i, $|P_i| = |D_i| = 128$ except for perhaps a partial final block. With this input, AES-GCM returns a ciphertext $C = C_1 \| \cdots \| C_p$ (the same length as the plaintext) and an authentication tag T. From here on, we will omit associated data for simplicity. The plaintext is encrypted using an instance of the AES in counter mode, under key k with counter value starting at CTR_1. If the nonce is 96 bits long the initial counter value (CTR_0) is $N \| 0^{31}1$, otherwise it is a polynomial evaluation-based hash of N after zero padding (using the hash key described below). For each i, $\mathrm{CTR}_i = \mathrm{inc}(\mathrm{CTR}_{i-1})$, where $\mathrm{inc}(\cdot)$ increments the last 32 bits of its argument (modulo 2^{32}).

The authentication tag is computed from GHASH, a polynomial evaluation hash (in $\mathbb{F}_{2^{128}}$). The ciphertext C is parsed as 128-bit blocks (with partial final blocks zero padded) and each block is interpreted as an element of $\mathbb{F}_{2^{128}}$. We denote by L an encoding of the length of the (unpadded) ciphertext and additional data. The hash key H is derived from the AES block cipher key: $H = \mathsf{E}_k(0^{128})$. The hash function is then computed as:

$$h_H(C) = L \cdot H \oplus C_p^* \cdot H^2 \oplus C_{p-1} \cdot H^3 \oplus \cdots \oplus C_2 \cdot H^p \oplus C_1 \cdot H^{p+1}, \quad (1)$$

where all operations are in $\mathbb{F}_{2^{128}}$, and C_p^* denotes the zero-padded last block. The authentication tag is given by: $T = \mathsf{E}_k(\mathrm{CTR}_0) \oplus h_H(C)$.

2.3 Key Commitment

A committing AE scheme is one which satisfies the property of *key commitment*, which (informally) states that a ciphertext will only decrypt under the key that was used to encrypt it. Equivalently, for a committing AE scheme, it should be infeasible to find a ciphertext that will decrypt under two different keys. Security goals for committing AE were first formalised by Farshim et al. [21] under the name "robustness". Although key commitment is not part of the design goal of AE schemes, there are natural scenarios where a lack of key commitment results in security issues. Dodis et al. [18] and Grubbs et al. [24] show how to exploit non-committing AE schemes in the context of abuse reporting in Facebook Messenger. Albertini et al. [3] give some further practical examples where a lack of key commitment leads to practical attacks, e.g. in the setting of paywalled subscription material where a malicious publisher might prepare a ciphertext that decrypts to different content for different users.

The partitioning oracle attack of Len et al. [31] exploits the inherent lack of key commitment for polynomial hash based AEAD schemes. They construct a ciphertext $\hat{C}$ that decrypts under every key in a set of target keys $\mathbb{K}^* = \{k_1, \cdots, k_\ell\}$ by constructing a linear equation whose variables are the blocks of ciphertext; $\hat{C}$ is the solution to the equation. We describe the technique using AES-GCM for concreteness.

Given $\mathbb{K}^*$ and nonce N, first derive the associated GHASH key $H_i = \mathsf{E}_{k_i}(0^n)$ for each $k_i \in \mathbb{K}^*$. Then construct the linear equation

$$T = C_1 \cdot H_i^{p-1} \oplus \cdots \oplus C_{p-1} \cdot H_i^2 \oplus L \cdot H_i \oplus \mathsf{E}_{k_i}(N \parallel 0^{31}1),$$

which is arrived at by assigning H_i to H in Eq. (1) and substituting the result into the expression for the tag $T = h_H(C) \oplus \mathsf{E}_{k_i}(\mathrm{CTR}_0)$. The result is a system of ℓ equations in ℓ unknowns which can be solved; this can be done more efficiently using a clever trick (fixing T and adding one block of ciphertext as a new variable, giving a Vandermonde matrix). We refer the reader to [31] for further detail.

Generic AE solutions, the so-called *generic composition* constructions such as Encrypt-then-MAC, can provide key-commitment, as shown by Farshim et al. [21] who suggested using a keyed hash function such as HMAC [10] for authentication. However, if a key-committing scheme is required for security in some particular setting, then performance considerations may mean that switching to e.g. encrypt-then-HMAC is not practical. This is illustrated by the choice of Facebook Messenger to use AES-GCM to encrypt message attachments despite work showing that this was insecure. Albertini et al. [3] propose two generic fixes that minimise the changes needed to add key-commitment to widely deployed, highly efficient schemes such as AES-GCM:

1. **Padding Fix.** Prepend a constant string to messages before encrypting; check for the presence of the constant string after decrypting. This fix is also given in an early draft of an OPAQUE protocol RFC [30], and discussed in [31]. This solution – essentially adding redundancy to the message – is not generically secure and must be analysed per scheme. Albertini et al. [3] perform this analysis for AES-GCM and ChaCha20-Poly1305, showing that in both cases the resulting scheme is key-committing.
2. **Generic Fix.** From a given key k, derive an encryption key $k_{\mathrm{enc}} = F_{\mathrm{enc}}(k)$ and a commitment to the key $k_{\mathrm{com}} = F_{\mathrm{com}}(k)$. Here F_{enc} and F_{com} are collision resistant hash functions. Ciphertexts for the resulting key-committing scheme consist of a regular ciphertext (for the underlying AEAD scheme) together with the commitment to the key. Albertini et al. [3] show that this construction provides key-commitment, if the functions F_{enc} and F_{com} used to derive the encryption key and commitment are collision resistant pseudorandom functions.

2.4   Weak Key Forgeries

In symmetric cryptography, a class of keys is called a *weak key class* if the algorithm behaves in an unexpected way when operating under members of that class, and this behaviour is easy to detect. In addition, identifying that a key belongs to such a weak key class should require trying fewer than N keys by exhaustive search (or verification queries), where N is the size of the class [25]. In the context of polynomial hash based authentication schemes, e.g. the GCM mode, Handschuh and Preneel [25] and Saarinen [37] identified several weak key classes. In [36], Procter and Cid proposed a generic framework to mount forgery attacks against polynomial-based MAC schemes based on weak keys. Their framework encompasses the previous forgery attacks from [25] and [37], as well as the earlier Joux's Forbidden Attack [27], and is based on a malleability property present in polynomial-based MAC schemes.

If h_H is a polynomial hash under key H and M is a message input, let $h_H(M) = g_M(H)$, where $g_M(x) = \sum_{i=1}^{p+1} M_i x^{p+2-i} \in \mathbb{F}[x]$ and $H \in \mathbb{F}$ (as in Sect. 2.1). Now let $q(x) = \sum_{i=1}^{p+1} q_i x^{p+2-i} \in \mathbb{F}[x]$ be a polynomial with constant term zero, such that $q(H) = 0$. Then

$$h_H(M) = g_M(H) = g_M(H) + q(H) = g_{M+Q}(H) = h_H(M + Q),$$

where $Q = q_1 \parallel q_2 \parallel \ldots \parallel q_\ell$ and the addition $M + Q$ is done block-wise[1]. It follows that given a polynomial $q(x)$ satisfying these properties, it is straightforward to construct collisions for the hash function. In fact, we have that $q(x)$ is in the ideal $\langle x^2 - Hx \rangle$, and any polynomial in this ideal can be used to produce collisions. On the other hand, collisions in the hash function correspond to MAC forgeries, by substituting the original message for the one that yields a collision in the polynomial hash. Thus this method allows an adversary to create forgeries when they have seen a tuple of (nonce, message, tag), by simply modifying the message, as above. Saarinen's cycling attacks [37] are a special case of this attack. Forgeries for GCM and variants are presented in [36]. Later, an efficient method for constructing forgery polynomials which have disjoint sets of roots (i.e. keys) was proposed in [2].

3   Partitioning Oracle Attacks

Partitioning oracles, introduced by Len et al. [31] are a class of decryption error oracles which, conceptually, take a ciphertext and return whether the decryption key belongs to some known subset of keys. This allows an adversary to speed up an exhaustive search by querying multiple keys at once; in effect, partitioning the key space. The approach of [31] relies on two conditions: (1) the non-key committing property of polynomial hash based AE schemes is exploited to craft targeted "splitting" ciphertexts that will decrypt under multiple keys; and (2) a decryption oracle that reveals whether decryption (with the user's key) of such a splitting ciphertext succeeds or not.

---

[1] The shorter message is zero-padded if required.

Abstractly, a partitioning oracle will (in the optimal case) allow a binary search of the key space, giving a logarithmic improvement over naïve exhaustive search. This requires being able to query half the keys in the key space. In practice however, there is a limit to the number of keys that can be queried at once – e.g. for AES-GCM, messages are required to be less than approx. 64GB (2^{39} – 256 bits [20]), and applications may impose further restrictions depending on context. Nevertheless, as shown in [31], it is still possible to launch practical attacks by combining partitioning oracles with knowledge of non-uniform key distributions, which arise in particular when human memorable passwords are used to derive keys, and can be estimated from password breaches [33].

We note that the conditions for a partitioning oracle attack can be satisfied with weak key forgeries, following the work of Procter and Cid [36] (see Sect. 2.4). Weak key forgeries require a valid ciphertext to construct the forgery; a crucial difference to [31], which considers adversaries that only have access to a decryption oracle. In practice this is a limitation of the adversary that does not tally with observed adversarial strategies against censorship evasion [14,39]. We thus extend the model by allowing an adversary to obtain valid ciphertexts from chosen plaintexts, a standard adversarial model for AE. In fact, this assumption is stronger than required; as we later show, adversaries with only "machine-in-the-middle" capabilities can carry out effective partitioning oracle attacks using weak key forgeries. Known and chosen plaintext capabilities lead to more powerful attacks, as we briefly describe in Sect. 5.1.

Example: Generic Encryption. Consider a client and server communicating with end-to-end encryption, using an AEAD scheme and a shared key k derived from password pw. The client encrypts message P (together with any associated data D), using key k and nonce N to obtain a ciphertext tag pair $(C, T) \leftarrow$ $\mathsf{AuthEnc}_k(N, D, P)$. The conditions for a partitioning oracle attack are met if the server reveals whether or not decryption succeeds; it might for example output an observable error message, or reveal the information via a side-channel.

Example: Password-Authenticated Key Exchange. A Password Authenticated Key Exchange (PAKE) is a cryptographic key exchange protocol in which a client authenticates to a server using a password pw that the server has stored (as the equivalent of a hash). Len et al. show how to launch a partitioning oracle attack against OPAQUE, a modern PAKE protocol currently undergoing standardisation. OPAQUE uses an AEAD scheme as a component, and Len et al. show the necessity of the AEAD scheme being key-committing by considering deviations from the specification in some early prototype implementations. OPAQUE works by composing an oblivious PRF with an authenticated key exchange; Len et al. 's attack relies on the fact that the server sends a ciphertext C encrypted using the password during an execution of the protocol.

3.1   Attack Abstraction: Formal Definition of a Partitioning Oracle

Following [31], we consider settings in which an attacker targets AE and seeks to recover a user's key $k \in K$, where the key is deterministically derived from secret password $pw \in \mathcal{D}$. We write $K(\mathcal{D}) \subseteq K$ for the set of keys derived from passwords and $k(pw) \in K(\mathcal{D})$ to denote a key derived from password pw. The attacker is given access to an interface that takes as input ciphertext C, and outputs whether or not the ciphertext decrypts correctly (passing any format checks) under the user's key $k(pw)$. The attacker is further given access to an interface that will encrypt plaintexts of the attacker's choosing and return the ciphertext. This set-up represents a "partitioning oracle" if it is computationally tractable for the adversary, given any set $\mathbb{K} \subseteq K(\mathcal{D})$, to compute a value $\hat{C}$ that partitions $\mathbb{K}$ into two sets $\mathbb{K}^*$ and $\mathbb{K} \setminus \mathbb{K}^*$, with $|\mathbb{K}^*| \leq |\mathbb{K} \setminus \mathbb{K}^*|$, such that $\mathsf{AuthDec}_k(\hat{C}) \neq \bot$ for all $k \in \mathbb{K}^*$ and $\mathsf{AuthDec}_k(\hat{C}) = \bot$ for all $k \in \mathbb{K} \setminus \mathbb{K}^*$. We call such a $\hat{C}$ a *splitting ciphertext* and refer to $|\mathbb{K}^*|$ as the degree of $\hat{C}$. We distinguish between targeted splitting ciphertexts, where the adversary can select the secrets in $\mathbb{K}^*$, and untargeted attacks.

In general, the definition can be applied to arbitrary cryptographic functionalities by considering a Boolean function f that takes as input a string and a key, returning 1 if some cryptographic operation succeeds and 0 otherwise. The attacker has access to an interface that takes as input a bit string V, and uses it plus k to output the result of some Boolean function $f_k : \{0,1\}^* \to \{0,1\}$. Here f_k is an abstraction of some cryptographic operations that may succeed or fail depending on k and V; set $f_k(V) = 1$ for success and $f_k(V) = 0$ for failure. We note that partitioning oracles may output more than two possible outputs, for example if there are multiple distinguishable error messages, following [17].

3.2   Multi-Key Contingent Forgeries

Central to launching a partitioning oracle attack is the ability to craft splitting ciphertexts. This is formalised in the notion of "Targeted Multi-Key Contingent Forgeries", which quantifies an adversary's advantage in crafting splitting ciphertexts against a particular AEAD scheme, with oracle access to encryption. Our definition is a slight generalisation of the "Targeted Multi-Key Collision" notion from [31]; their notion can be obtained from ours by removing the adversary's encryption oracle.[2]

Targeted multi-key contingent forgery resistance (TMKCR) security is defined by the game given in Fig. 1 (left). It is parameterised by a scheme AEAD and a target key set $\mathbb{K}^* \subseteq K$. A possibly randomised adversary $\mathcal{A}$ is given input a target set $\mathbb{K}^*$ and must produce nonce N^*, associated data D^* and ciphertext C^* such that $\mathsf{AuthDec}_k(N^*, D^*, C^*) \neq \bot$ for all $k \in \mathbb{K}^*$. We define the advantage via

$$\mathsf{Adv}^{\text{tmk-cr}}_{\mathsf{AEAD}, \mathbb{K}^*}(\mathcal{A}) = \Pr\left[\mathrm{TMKCR}^{\mathcal{A}}_{\mathsf{AEAD}, \mathbb{K}^*} \Rightarrow 1\right] \tag{2}$$

---

[2] We hope the reader forgives our abuse of nomenclature; although we refer to both notions as TMKCR, ours is a (slight) generalisation of Len et al.'s, and we use the term "key contingent forgery" to encompass both.

where "$\mathsf{TMKCR}^{\mathcal{A}}_{\mathsf{AEAD},\mathbb{K}^*} \Rightarrow 1$" denotes the event that $\mathcal{A}$ succeeds in finding N^*, D^*, C^* that decrypt under all keys in $\mathbb{K}^*$. The event is defined over the coins used by $\mathcal{A}$.

We can define a similar untargeted multi-key contingent forgery resistance goal, called $\mathsf{MKCR}^{\mathcal{A}}_{\mathsf{AEAD},\kappa}$. The associated security game, given in Fig. 1 (right), is the same except that the adversary gets to output a set $\mathbb{K}^*$ of its choosing in addition to the nonce N^*, associated data D^*, and ciphertext C^*. The adversary wins if $|\mathbb{K}^*| \geq \kappa$ for some parameter $\kappa > 1$ and decryption of N^*, D^*, C^* succeeds for all $k \in \mathbb{K}^*$. We define the advantage via

$$\mathsf{Adv}^{\mathsf{mk\text{-}cr}}_{\mathsf{AEAD},\kappa}(\mathcal{A}) = \Pr\left[\mathsf{MKCR}^{\mathcal{A}}_{\mathsf{AEAD},\kappa} \Rightarrow 1\right] \qquad (3)$$

where "$\mathsf{MKCR}^{\mathcal{A}}_{\mathsf{AEAD},\kappa} \Rightarrow 1$" denotes the event that $\mathcal{A}$ succeeds in finding $\mathbb{K}^*$ and N^*, D^*, C^* that decrypt under all keys in $\mathbb{K}^*$. The event is defined over the coins used by $\mathcal{A}$.

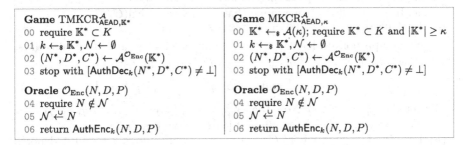

Fig. 1. Games modelling (targeted) multi-key contingent forgery resistance for an AEAD scheme. Note that in both cases, an adversary that can produce a ciphertext C^* that decrypts under every key in $\mathbb{K}^*$ will win the game with probability 1. **Left:** Targeted Multi-Key Collision Resistance. **Right:** Multi-key contingent forgery resistance, a weaker notion which lets the adversary choose the set of target keys $\mathbb{K}^*$.

4 Partitioning Oracle Attacks from Weak Key Forgeries

At a high level, our attack works as follows: Construct key-contingent forgeries from captured ciphertexts using weak-key forgery techniques and submit these to a decryption oracle; that is, an oracle that reveals whether a ciphertext is accepted or rejected. The weak key forgery ensures that the ciphertext will only be accepted if the user's key is in the set of weak keys.

More specifically: (1) In an offline phase, the adversary pre-computes a set of ciphertext masks. Each mask corresponds to a set of passwords to be tested. (2) In an online phase, the adversary intercepts a ciphertext and, using a ciphertext mask, constructs a key-contingent forgery which it forwards to the partitioning oracle. Observing whether or not the key-contingent forgery is accepted reveals whether or not the user's key is in the set of target keys corresponding to the ciphertext mask. Our attack relies on the ability of the adversary to act as a "machine-in-the-middle" between sender and receiver. We first give an abstract description of a key contingent forgery consisting of ℓ ciphertext blocks which encompasses two special cases: a targeted key-contingent forgery testing ℓ keys, (Sect. 4.1); and a targeted forgery passing format requirements on underlying plaintexts, (Sect. 4.2).

1. **Offline phase.** The attack takes a set of target keys $\mathbb{K}^* = \{K_1, \ldots, K_{\ell-1}\}$ as input and outputs a ciphertext mask. We note that one key is lost per ciphertext block that is not a free variable.
   (a) First derive the associated authentication (GHASH) keys by setting $\mathbb{H}^* = \{\mathsf{E}_k(0^{128}) | k \in \mathbb{K}^*\}$.
   (b) Set $q(x) = \displaystyle\sum_{i=1}^{\ell} q_i \cdot x^{\ell+1-i} = x \cdot \prod_{H \in \mathbb{H}^*} (x \oplus H)$.

2. **Online phase.** The online phase takes as further input a valid nonce, ciphertext, tag tuple (N, C, T) and outputs a key-contingent forgery consisting of tuple $(N, \hat{C}, T)$. The key-contingent forgery is forwarded to the partitioning oracle. In what follows, we assume that $\ell - 1 \geq p = \lceil \mathrm{len}(C/128) \rceil$
   (a) First parse the captured ciphertext as $C = C_1 \| \cdots \| C_p^*$, i.e., as blocks of the appropriate length. Let $\alpha = \mathrm{len}(C) \oplus \mathrm{len}(\hat{C})$ and β be constants. Now set $q'(x) = \sum_{i=1}^{\ell+1} q_i' \cdot x^{\ell+2-i} = (a \oplus bx) \cdot q(x)$, with

   $$a = \alpha \cdot q_\ell^{-1} \text{ and } b = \beta \cdot q_2^{-1} \oplus \alpha \cdot q_1 \cdot q_2^{-1} \cdot q_\ell^{-1}. \tag{4}$$

   Set $Q' = q_1' \| \cdots \| q_\ell'$. Note that $q_{\ell+1}' = q_\ell \cdot a = \alpha$ and $q_1' = a \cdot q_1 \oplus b \cdot q_2 = \beta$. This step can take place offline if $\mathrm{len}(C)$ is known in advance.
   (b) Let $\hat{C} = C^* \oplus Q'$, where $C^* = 0^{128} \| \cdots \| 0^{128} \| C_1 \| \cdots \| C_p^*$ denotes the ciphertext C padded (pre-pended) with blocks of zeros to match the length of Q'. As $\ell \geq p + 1$, at least one block of padding is pre-pended. Note that if the user key $k \in \mathbb{K}^* \cup \{K_\ell\} \cup \{0\}$, where $K_\ell = a \cdot b^{-1}$, then for $H = \mathsf{E}_k(0^{128})$,

   $$h_H(\hat{C}) = \mathrm{len}(\hat{C}) \cdot H \oplus \hat{C}_\ell^* \cdot H^2 \oplus \hat{C}_{\ell-1} \cdot H^3 \oplus \cdots \oplus \hat{C}_1 \cdot H^{\ell+1}$$
   $$= (\alpha \oplus \mathrm{len}(C)) \cdot H \oplus (C_p^* \oplus q_\ell') \cdot H^2 \oplus \cdots \oplus (0^{128} \oplus q_1') \cdot H^{\ell+1}$$
   $$= q'(H) \oplus h_H(C).$$

Consequently, the tag is a valid forgery and $\mathsf{AuthEnc}_k(N, \varepsilon, \hat{C}) \neq \perp$.

4.1   Targeted Key Contingent Forgery Testing ℓ keys

We first consider key contingent ciphertext forgeries that test ℓ keys with no restrictions on the format of the underlying plaintext. Setting $\beta = a \cdot q_2 \cdot H_\ell^{-1} \oplus a \cdot q_1$ in Eq. (4) for $H_\ell = \mathsf{E}_{K_\ell}(0^{128})$ gives $a = b \cdot H_\ell$. Thus,

$$q'(x) = b \cdot (x + H_\ell) \cdot x \cdot \prod_{H \in \mathbb{H}^*} (x \oplus H) = b \cdot x \cdot \prod_{H \in \mathbb{H}^* \cup \{H_\ell\}} (x \oplus H).$$

The ciphertext forgery $\hat{C}$ is a valid forgery if $k \in \mathbb{K}^* \cup K_\ell \cup \{0\}$. Thus, we are in effect able to test target key sets of size $|\mathbb{K}^*| + 1 = \ell$.

Performance. The attack description above is for a fixed set of target keys $\mathbb{K}^*$; in practice, an attacker would prepare a collection of ciphertext masks corresponding to disjoint target key sets $\{\mathbb{K}_i^*\}_{i \in I}$, such that $p_{i+1} \geq p_i$ for all i, where p_i denotes the aggregate success probability of target key set $\mathbb{K}_i^*$. Given $n = |\mathbb{K}^*|$ hashing keys, the coefficients of the polynomial $q(x)$ can be computed using $\mathcal{O}(n^2)$ time and $\mathcal{O}(n)$ space. We note that the offline phase need only occur once, allowing the adversary to amortise the upfront cost of pre-computation over multiple targets. This is especially useful in cases where generating target keys from passwords is particularly slow.

In the online phase, splitting ciphertexts are then submitted in order until a query is successful; we note that a negative result is returned immediately. For a successful query, we know that the key $k \in \mathbb{K}_i^*$ for some particular i. As our result relies on pre-computation to be practical, in order to perform a binary search on $\mathbb{K}_i^*$ appropriate forgery masks would have to be pre-computed – this would require $\mathcal{O}(n \log n)$ space. In most cases it is probably more efficient, once an adversary knows that $k \in \mathbb{K}_i^*$, to perform the first few iterations of a binary search (having precomputed the necessary values) before switching to trial decryption of C with each key in $\mathbb{K}_i^*$. We assume that the cost of querying a ciphertext is low and that either (1) there is a steady supply of ciphertexts to intercept or (2) it is possible to reuse the same nonce – the server may or may not enforce unique nonces depending on context. Regarding point (1), we note that a common adversarial model introduced by the BEAST attack [19] gives an attacker the ability to inject arbitrary plaintexts via client-side JavaScript in some window in the user's browser (see e. g. [5,6,15]).

Our attack is limited to scenarios where keys are deterministically derived from passwords; that is, if passwords are salted (using randomly generated salts) then pre-computation is no longer feasible. This highlights the fact that whilst salts are not secret values, they should be unpredictable when used to derive encryption keys from passwords, in a direct analogue to password storage. Better security in any case is obtained by using password authenticated key exchange protocols such as [26], rather than deriving session keys statically from passwords.

4.2   Targeted Key Contingent Forgery Passing Format Checks

The targeted multi-key contingent forgery attack from the previous section results in ciphertexts that decrypt under the user's key to plaintexts that are "garbage". This is a problem in cases where plaintexts are required to meet some format check. The most common form of format check will be a header field containing (for example) protocol data, sender and receiver addresses, serial numbers or integrity check values. The weak key forgery method of [36] allows full control over the underlying plaintext, with the caveat that the ciphertext forgery represents an (untargeted) multi-key contingent forgery – for every block of underlying plaintext that is part of the format check, the number of *targeted* keys being tested will decrease by one, with one extra untargeted key gained. In practice this will not make much difference: usually, the prefix is designed to be as short as possible, which means one or at most two blocks. We would typically expect splitting ciphertexts of degree ≈ 500 so that losing one or two blocks represents only a small fraction of the total.

Let us assume that the captured nonce, ciphertext, tag tuple (N, C, T) corresponds to some underlying plaintext matching the (known) required format. For concreteness, assume that the first block of plaintext (respectively, ciphertext) corresponds to the format to be checked. This means that we need to leave the first block of plaintext unchanged. We thus set $\beta = C_1 \oplus 0$ in Eq. (4) and note that the method may easily be adapted to "flip bits" in the underlying plaintext by using a suitable value of $\beta = C_1 \oplus \delta$; furthermore, it is straightforward to extend the method to deal with multiple blocks. By construction, $\hat{C}_1 = q_1' = \beta$, which gives $\hat{C} = C_1 \parallel \hat{C}_2 \parallel \cdots \parallel \hat{C}_\ell$, i.e., a ciphertext forgery $\hat{C}$ with the same first block of ciphertext (and thus underlying plaintext) as the original intercepted ciphertext C. Note that we gain $K_\ell = a \cdot b^{-1}$ as an untargeted key.

Len et al. [31] show how to craft (untargeted) multi-key collisions to pass format checks with fixed prefixes, however their method is impractical for prefixes longer than a couple of bytes; in contrast, our method can easily be applied to arbitary prefixes and is targeted. Lastly, we observe that this method circumvents the key committing "padding fix" discussed in Sect. 2.3, i.e., to prepend a constant string to messages before encrypting. The ability to control underlying plaintexts in this way allows an attacker to apply partitioning oracle attacks using weak key forgeries where attacks based on exploiting non-committment are infeasible.

5 Partitioning Oracle Attacks Against Shadowsocks

Originally written by a pseudonymous developer, Shadowsocks [1] is an encrypted proxy for TCP and UDP traffic, based on SOCKS5. Shadowsocks was first built to help evade censorship in China, and it underlies other tools such as Jigsaw's Outline VPN. To use Shadowsocks, a user first deploys the Shadowsocks proxy server on a remote machine, provisions it with a static password and chooses an encryption scheme to use for all connections. The most up-to-date implementations only support AEAD schemes for encryption, with the options consisting of AES-GCM (128-bit or 256-bit) or ChaCha20/Poly1305. Next the user configures the Shadowsocks client on their local machine, and can then forward TCP or UDP traffic from their machine to the Shadowsocks proxy server.

Len et al. [31] showed how to build a practical partitioning oracle attack against Shadowsocks proxy servers. At a high level, their attack exploited the non-key committing property of the AEAD schemes used, making it possible to craft ciphertexts which decrypt correctly under a set of target keys. Furthermore, the attack exploits the fact that the proxy server opens an ephemeral UDP port in response to a valid request (and otherwise does not) which reveals whether a ciphertext has been accepted or rejected. The attack depends on a particular configuration: password derived keys and UDP traffic. As a response to [31], users are advised to mitigate against the attack by generating good quality passwords and disabling UDP mode [7]. In this section, we first describe the Shadowsocks protocol and the partitioning oracle attack of Len et al. , before going on to describe how weak key forgeries can be used to launch a partitioning oracle attack. We note that whilst our attack is rendered impractical by the per-message salt used in the Shadowsocks protocol, a description of a hypothetical attack still offers a useful case study, which we describe below.

The Shadowsocks Protocol. The client starts by hashing the user password pw to obtain a key $k = h(pw)$. The client then samples a random sixteen-byte salt s and computes a session key $k_s \leftarrow \mathrm{HKDF}(k, s, info)$ using HKDF [29], where $info$ is the string ss-subkey. A new salt and session key are generated for every message. The client encrypts its plaintext payload P by computing $C \leftarrow \mathsf{AuthEnc}_{k_s}(Z, \varepsilon, flag \parallel ip \parallel port \parallel payload)$ where Z denotes a nonce set to a string of zero bytes (12 for AES-GCM); the value ε empty associated data; and $flag$ is a one-byte header indicating the format of ip with the following convention: $flag = 01$ indicates that ip is a 4-byte IPv4 address, $flag = 03$ indicates that ip consists of a one byte length and then hostname, and $flag = 04$ indicates that ip is a 16-byte IPv6 address. The port field $port$ is two bytes long. The client sends (s, C) to the server via UDP. If the client is using TCP, the process is the same except that the ciphertext is prefixed with a two-byte encrypted length (and authentication tag) before being sent to the server via TCP.

When the Shadowsocks server receives (s, C), it extracts the salt and uses it together with pw to re-derive the session key k_s. It decrypts the remainder of the ciphertext with k_s. If decryption fails, no error message is sent back to the client. If decryption succeeds, the plaintext's format is checked by verifying that its first byte is equal to a valid $flag$ value. If that check passes, the next bytes are interpreted as an appropriately encoded address ip, and two-byte port number $port$. Finally, the rest of the payload is sent to the remote server identified by ip and $port$. The proxy then listens on an ephemeral source UDP port assigned by the kernel networking stack for a reply from the remote server. When Shadowsocks receives a reply on the ephemeral port, the server generates a random salt and uses it with pw to generate a new session key. It then encrypts the response, and sends the resulting salt and ciphertext back to the client. The same encryption algorithm is used in both directions.

The Attack of Len et al. The proxy server opens an ephemeral UDP port in repsonse to a valid request (and otherwise not). One can view this as a remotely observable logical side-channel that reveals whether decryption succeeds. The attacker starts with knowledge of a password dictionary $\mathcal{D}$ and an estimate $\hat{p}$ of the probability distribution over keys in the dictionary. The attack has two steps, a pre-computation phase and an active querying phase.

In the pre-computation phase, the attacker chooses an arbitrary salt s and derives a set of session keys $\mathbb{K} = \mathbb{K}(\mathcal{D})$ by $k_s^i \leftarrow \mathrm{HKDF}(h(pw_i), s, \text{ss-subkey})$ for all $pw_i \in \mathcal{D}$; the nonce is set as a string of all zeroes. The adversary then outputs a ciphertext $\hat{C}$ of length 4093 (to meet the length restriction imposed by Shadowsocks servers) and a set $\mathbb{K}^*$ of 4091 keys such that $\hat{C}$ decrypts under every key in S to give a plaintext with first byte 01. We gloss over the details of how $\hat{C}$ is constructed and refer the reader to [31]; we note that the construction is not a targeted multi-key collision.

In the querying phase, the attacker then submits (s^*, C^*) to the proxy server. Should the user's key be in the set of target keys, $k(pw) \in \mathbb{K}^*$, the server will interpret the decrypted plaintext as a 01 byte followed by a random IPv4 address, destination port, and payload. The IPv4 and destination port will be accepted by the server's network protocol stack with high probability, and so the server will send the payload as a UDP packet and open a UDP source port to listen for a response, which the attacker can observe by port scanning.

5.1 Partitioning Oracles from Weak Key Forgeries

We now describe how to launch a partitioning oracle attack using weak key forgeries against Shadowsocks (in the same configuration as the attack of Len et al. described above). As noted above, our attack is impractical as session keys are salted on a per-message basis in the Shadowsocks protocol, making pre-computation of forgery masks infeasible. Nevertheless, a weak key forgery partitioning oracle attack against Shadowsocks is an instructive case study, demonstrating the feasibility of the approach and allowing us to point out some interesting features; in particular, we are able to construct targeted multi-key contingent forgeries that meet arbitrary format requirements as we explain below.

Basic Version. We separate the attack into two steps, a computation phase and an active querying phase. The attacker starts with knowledge of a password dictionary $\mathcal{D}$ and an estimate $\hat{p}$ of the probability distribution over keys in the dictionary and then intercepts a salt, ciphertext tuple (s, C).

In the computation phase, the attacker first chooses a set of passwords $\mathcal{D}^*$ with $|\mathcal{D}^*| = 4092$, such that the set has the maximum aggregate probability according to $\hat{p}$. The attacker then derives a set of session keys $\mathbb{K}^*$ from the salt s and set of passwords $\mathcal{D}^*$ by $k_s^i \leftarrow \mathsf{HKDF}(h(pw_i), s, \mathsf{ss\text{-}subkey})$; the nonce is set as a string of all zeroes. Using the weak key forgery method described in Sect. 4.2, the attacker outputs a ciphertext $\hat{C}$ of length 4093 (to meet the length restriction imposed by Shadowsocks servers) such that $\hat{C}$ decrypts under the users key k if $k \in \mathbb{K}^*$. Furthermore, the underlying plaintext $P \leftarrow \mathsf{AuthDec}_k(\hat{C})$ passes the format check.

In the querying phase, the attacker then submits (s, C^*) to the proxy server. Should the user's key be in the set of target keys, the server will interpret the decrypted plaintext as $\textit{flag} \parallel \textit{ip} \parallel \textit{port} \parallel \textit{payload}$; that is, an IP address, destination port and payload. Note that these are unchanged from the original plaintext that was sent by the user, so will be accepted by the server's network protocol stack. The server will send the payload as a UDP packet and open a UDP source port to listen for a response, which the attacker can observe by port scanning.

Extension 1: Redirection (Known Plaintext Attack). If the attacker knows the first 7 bytes of an underlying plaintext, which we write as *prefix*, then they can use the weak key forgery technique to redirect the user's payload to arbitrary destinations. In particular, the first 7 bytes can be modified to give $01 \parallel ip' \parallel port'$, with ip' a four-byte IPv4 address, and $port'$ a two-byte destination port. This is the idea behind Peng's "redirect attack" [22, 34], discovered in February 2020, which exploited the use of stream ciphers without integrity protection in the Shadowsocks protocol. Obtaining plaintexts with known *prefix* is relatively easy in the server to client direction, as many common server protocols start with the same bytes (e. g. HTTP/1. for HTTP). In the client to server direction, underlying plaintexts will be in the format [destination][payload], so that the adversary needs to know the target address (and its encoding), perhaps through injecting plaintexts via client-side JavaScript in some window in the user's browser [5, 6, 15, 19]. Note that if an adversary is able to launch chosen plaintext attacks, they could target the TCP configuration of Shadowsocks (the recommended option) by crafting plaintexts with the maximum length to overcome the fact that for TCP the length is sent encrypted together with the encrypted payload.

The adversary intercepts a ciphertext C from server to client, and using weak key forgery techniques modifies C to give a splitting ciphertext $\hat{C}$ whose underlying plaintext begins with $prefix' = 01 \parallel ip' \parallel port'$, i. e., an address that the adversary controls. The splitting ciphertext is then sent to the Shadowsocks server: if the splitting ciphertext is accepted, the payload is sent to the adversary, revealing that the user's key is in the set of target keys associated to $\hat{C}$. To produce $\hat{C}$, we modify the basic attack above as follows: when it comes to constructing the weak key forgery mask, following the technique outlined in Sect. 4.2, we use a non-zero value of β in Eq. (4); specifically, $\beta = prefix \oplus (01 \parallel ip' \parallel port')$, interpreted as an element of $\mathbb{F}_{2^{128}}$. The effect is to flip some bits in the 7-byte prefix *prefix*, so that we obtain the attacker's address *prefix'*.

We note that this attack allows the adversary to efficiently and reliably determine whether the ciphertext has been accepted; it is no longer necessary to scan the server for open ports, which is time consuming and not necessarily completely reliable. Furthermore, if the splitting ciphertext is accepted, the adversary receives the payload *payload* which means that it can efficiently test target keys against the ciphertext by encrypting one block of plaintext and checking whether it matches. Without this, the adversary would need to calculate the authentication tag of the captured ciphertext for each target key.

Extension 2: Bypassing the Padding Fix. As discussed in Sect. 2.3, prior work on non-key committing AEAD schemes showed that applying a "padding fix", that is prepending a fixed constant string to underlying plaintexts, transforms the scheme to be key-committing. Applying a padding fix is recommended by Len et al. as a way to mitigate against partitioning oracle attacks; however, a partitioning oracle attack using weak key forgeries will still be successful despite that mitigation. To see this, we simply modify the description of the "basic attack version" in the previous subsection to leave one further block unaltered, at the cost of testing one less key per ciphertext $\hat{C}$. We note that the reason that our attack impractical is due to the salting of passwords to derive per-message ephemeral keys, rather than because of the non-key committing property of the AEAD scheme used.

5.2   Other Proxy Servers (VPNs)

Virtual Private Networks (VPNs) are often used to achieve similar objectives to Shadowsocks (allowing a user to access the internet via a proxy server), although Shadowsocks was designed specifically to circumvent internet censorship, which is not part of the threat model for VPNs. VPNs allow users to interact with what appears to be a private network, despite the interaction taking place over a public network (typically, the internet). This is achieved by encrypting packets in transit so that the contents are hidden from the public network. VPNs have a number of applications, including enabling users to remotely access local resources, or allowing individuals to improve their anonymity and privacy online (by masking their IP and hiding their traffic). Users connect to a proxy server via an encrypted tunnel, and the proxy server acts as an intermediary for the client and the internet (or a portion thereof). The most widely used protocols for VPNs are TLS and the IPsec protocol

At a high level, IPsec works as follows: the user first composes a TLS packet that will be sent to the end destination. This is encapsulated in an IPsec Encapsulating Security Payload (ESP) packet in tunnelling mode, which essentially adds a header and encrypts the whole packet to give a ciphertext C. This encrypted packet C is sent to the proxy server, where it is decrypted to recover the underlying TLS packet. The proxy server now forwards the TLS packet to its intended destination. There are many configuration options for how the user and proxy server authenticate and/or encrypt the ESP packets, including to provision the user and proxy server with static keys [28]. This is known as "manual management", and is suited to small static environments. However, the standard does not allow AES-GCM (or ChaCha20-Poly1305) with manual keys, although they are available in other configurations, due to concerns over the brittleness when a nonce/key combination is reused. AES with HMAC is preferred, which happens to be both key-committing and not vulnerable to weak key forgeries. Similarly, OpenVPN disallows AEAD cipher mode with static keys to avoid the insecurity of potential nonce/key reuse. We have thus not been able to find any vulnerable applications "in the wild", but note that partitioning oracle attacks are theoretically possible against implementations incorrectly deviating from the specification.

6   Conclusions

Prior work demonstrated that key commitment is an important security property of AEAD schemes. Our results suggest that resistance to weak key forgeries should be considered a related design goal to key-commitment, particularly in settings that are vulnerable to partitioning oracle attacks. Concretely, our results demonstrate – in contrast to the suggestions of prior work – that structured underlying plaintexts (e.g. packet headers that prefix every plaintext message, or an appended block of all zeros) is not a sufficient mitigation against partitioning oracle attacks. Lastly, our results reinforce the message that weak passwords should never be used to derive encryption keys.

Acknowledgements. This research was supported by the EPSRC and the UK government as part of the Centre for Doctoral Training in Cyber Security at Royal Holloway, University of London (EP/P009301/1).

The authors would like to thank Kenny Paterson for the discussion and feedback on an early draft, as well as the anonymous reviewers.

A   ChaCha20-Poly1305 AEAD Scheme

Poly1305 is similar to GHASH, and to form AEAD schemes it is most commonly combined with the ChaCha20 stream cipher [13], although Poly1305-AES is also an option [12]. For concreteness, we will give a description of ChaCha20-Poly1305 and note that the differences are trivial.

ChaCha20-Poly1305 encryption takes as input: a 32-byte ChaCha20 key k, a 12-byte nonce N, plaintext P and additional data D. With this input, ChaCha20-Poly1305 returns a ciphertext C (the same length as the plaintext) and an authentication tag T of length 16 bytes. From here on, we will omit the associated data for simplicity. First, the plaintext is divided into 64 byte blocks, except perhaps for a partial final block, and encrypted using the ChaCha20 stream cipher, under key k.

The authentication tag is next computed from a polynomial evaluation hash in the finite field $\mathbb{F}_{2^{130}-5}$. The ciphertext to be hashed is divided into 16-byte blocks with any partial final block zero-padded to 16 bytes. We denote by L an encoding of the (unpadded) ciphertext and additional data. Each block is encoded as an integer modulo $2^{130} - 5$ by first appending 0x01 to each block, and interpreting the resulting block as a little-endian integer X_i.

The authentication tag is computed from a polynomial evaluation hash (in $\mathbb{F}_{2^{130}-5}$). First we derive the hashing key r and the pseudo-random one time pad s: the first 32 bytes of $H = E_k(N_0 \parallel N)$ is divided into two 16-byte strings $\tilde{r}$ and s. Here N_0 represents 0 encoded as a 4-btye little-endian integer.

The hashing key r is obtained from the string $\tilde{r}$ by setting some of the bits to zero in a process referred to as "clamping"; we gloss over the specific details. The hash function is then computed as

$$h_r(C) = L \cdot r \oplus C_p^* \cdot r^2 \oplus C_{p-1} \cdot r^3 \oplus \cdots \oplus C_2 \cdot r^p \oplus C_1 \cdot r^{p+1},$$

where all operations are in $\mathbb{F}_{2^{130}-5}$, and C_p^* denotes the last zero-padded block. The authentication tag is given by:

$$T = (s \oplus h_r(C)) \mod 2^{128},$$

where s and $h_r(C)$ are interpreted as elements of $\mathbb{F}_{2^{128}}$, and the result as an integer modulo 2^{128}.

References

1. Shadowsocks - a fast tunnel proxy that helps you bypass firewalls. https:// shadowsocks.org, Accessed May 2021
2. Abdelraheem, M.A., Beelen, P., Bogdanov, A., Tischhauser, E.: Twisted polynomials and forgery attacks on GCM. In: Oswald, E., Fischlin, M. (eds.) EUROCRYPT 2015. LNCS, vol. 9056, pp. 762–786. Springer, Heidelberg (2015). https://doi.org/ 10.1007/978-3-662-46800-5_29
3. Albertini, A., Duong, T., Gueron, S., Kölbl, S., Luykx, A., Schmieg, S.: How to abuse and fix authenticated encryption without key commitment. Cryptology ePrint Archive, Report 2020/1456 (2020). https://eprint.iacr.org/2020/1456
4. Albrecht, M.R., Paterson, K.G.: Lucky microseconds: a timing attack on amazon's s2n implementation of TLS. In: Fischlin, M., Coron, J.-S. (eds.) EUROCRYPT 2016. LNCS, vol. 9665, pp. 622–643. Springer, Heidelberg (2016). https://doi.org/ 10.1007/978-3-662-49890-3_24
5. AlFardan, N.J., Bernstein, D.J., Paterson, K.G., Poettering, B., Schuldt, J.C.N.: On the security of RC4 in TLS. In: King, S.T. (ed.) USENIX Security 2013: 22nd USENIX Security Symposium, pp. 305–320. USENIX Association (2013)
6. AlFardan, N.J., Paterson, K.G.: Lucky thirteen: breaking the TLS and DTLS record protocols. In: 2013 IEEE Symposium on Security and Privacy, pp. 526–540. IEEE Computer Society Press (2013). https://doi.org/10.1109/SP.2013.42
7. Anonymous, Anonymous, Anonymous, Fifield, D., Houmansadr, A.: A practical guide to defend against the GFW's latest active probing (2021). https://gfw. report/blog/ss_advise/en/, Accessed May 2021
8. Armour, M., Poettering, B.: Substitution attacks against message authentication. IACR Trans. Symm. Cryptol. **2019**(3), 152–168 (2019). https://doi.org/10.13154/ tosc.v2019.i3.152-168
9. Armour, M., Poettering, B.: Subverting decryption in AEAD. In: Albrecht, M. (ed.) IMACC 2019. LNCS, vol. 11929, pp. 22–41. Springer, Cham (2019). https:// doi.org/10.1007/978-3-030-35199-1_2
10. Bellare, M., Canetti, R., Krawczyk, H.: Keying hash functions for message authentication. In: Koblitz, N. (ed.) CRYPTO 1996. LNCS, vol. 1109, pp. 1–15. Springer, Heidelberg (1996). https://doi.org/10.1007/3-540-68697-5_1
11. Bellovin, S.M., Merritt, M.: Encrypted key exchange: Password-based protocols secure against dictionary attacks. In: 1992 IEEE Symposium on Security and Privacy, pp. 72–84. IEEE Computer Society Press (1992). https://doi.org/10.1109/ RISP.1992.213269
12. Bernstein, D.J.: The Poly1305-AES message-authentication code. In: Gilbert, H., Handschuh, H. (eds.) FSE 2005. LNCS, vol. 3557, pp. 32–49. Springer, Heidelberg (2005). https://doi.org/10.1007/11502760_3
13. Bernstein, D.J.: ChaCha, a variant of Salsa20. In: Workshop Record of SASC, vol. 8, pp. 3–5 (2008)
14. Beznazwy, J., Houmansadr, A.: How China detects and blocks shadowsocks. In: Proceedings of the ACM Internet Measurement Conference, pp. 111–124 (2020)

15. Bhargavan, K., Leurent, G.: On the practical (in-)security of 64-bit block ciphers: collision attacks on HTTP over TLS and OpenVPN. In: Weippl, E.R., Katzenbeisser, S., Kruegel, C., Myers, A.C., Halevi, S. (eds.) ACM CCS 2016: 23rd Conference on Computer and Communications Security, pp. 456–467. ACM Press (2016). https://doi.org/10.1145/2976749.2978423

16. Bleichenbacher, D.: Chosen ciphertext attacks against protocols based on the RSA encryption standard PKCS #1. In: Krawczyk, H. (ed.) CRYPTO 1998. LNCS, vol. 1462, pp. 1–12. Springer, Heidelberg (1998). https://doi.org/10.1007/BFb0055716

17. Boldyreva, A., Degabriele, J.P., Paterson, K.G., Stam, M.: On symmetric encryption with distinguishable decryption failures. In: Moriai, S. (ed.) FSE 2013. LNCS, vol. 8424, pp. 367–390. Springer, Heidelberg (2014). https://doi.org/10.1007/978-3-662-43933-3_19

18. Dodis, Y., Grubbs, P., Ristenpart, T., Woodage, J.: Fast message franking: from invisible salamanders to encryptment. In: Shacham, H., Boldyreva, A. (eds.) CRYPTO 2018. LNCS, vol. 10991, pp. 155–186. Springer, Cham (2018). https://doi.org/10.1007/978-3-319-96884-1_6

19. Duong, T., Rizzo, J.: Here come the $\oplus$ ninjas. Unpublished manuscript. https://tlseminar.github.io/docs/beast.pdf, Accessed May 2021

20. Dworkin, M.J.: SP 800–38D. recommendation for block cipher modes of operation: Galois/counter mode (GCM) and GMAC. Technical report (2007)

21. Farshim, P., Orlandi, C., Roşie, R.: Security of symmetric primitives under incorrect usage of keys. IACR Trans. Symm. Cryptol. **2017**(1), 449–473 (2017). https://doi.org/10.13154/tosc.v2017.i1.449-473

22. Fifield, D.: Decryption vulnerability in shadowsocks stream ciphers. https://github.com/net4people/bbs/issues/24, Accessed May 2021

23. Garman, C., Green, M., Kaptchuk, G., Miers, I., Rushanan, M.: Dancing on the lip of the volcano: chosen ciphertext attacks on apple iMessage. In: Holz, T., Savage, S. (eds.) USENIX Security 2016: 25th USENIX Security Symposium, pp. 655–672. USENIX Association (2016)

24. Grubbs, P., Lu, J., Ristenpart, T.: Message franking via committing authenticated encryption. In: Katz, J., Shacham, H. (eds.) CRYPTO 2017. LNCS, vol. 10403, pp. 66–97. Springer, Cham (2017). https://doi.org/10.1007/978-3-319-63697-9_3

25. Handschuh, H., Preneel, B.: Key-recovery attacks on universal hash function based MAC algorithms. In: Wagner, D. (ed.) CRYPTO 2008. LNCS, vol. 5157, pp. 144–161. Springer, Heidelberg (2008). https://doi.org/10.1007/978-3-540-85174-5_9

26. Jarecki, S., Krawczyk, H., Xu, J.: OPAQUE: an asymmetric PAKE protocol secure against pre-computation attacks. In: Nielsen, J.B., Rijmen, V. (eds.) EUROCRYPT 2018. LNCS, vol. 10822, pp. 456–486. Springer, Cham (2018). https://doi.org/10.1007/978-3-319-78372-7_15

27. Joux, A.: Authentication failures in NIST version of GCM. Technical report (2006)

28. Kent, S., Seo, K.: Security architecture for the internet protocol. RFC 4301, RFC Editor (2005). https://tools.ietf.org/html/rfc4301

29. Krawczyk, H.: Cryptographic extraction and key derivation: the HKDF scheme. In: Rabin, T. (ed.) CRYPTO 2010. LNCS, vol. 6223, pp. 631–648. Springer, Heidelberg (2010). https://doi.org/10.1007/978-3-642-14623-7_34

30. Krawczyk, H.: The opaque asymmetric PAKE protocol (draft). Technical report (2018), https://datatracker.ietf.org/doc/html/draft-krawczyk-cfrg-opaque-02

31. Len, J., Grubbs, P., Ristenpart, T.: Partitioning oracle attacks. In: 30th USENIX Security Symposium (USENIX Security 21), pp. 195–212. USENIX Association (2021). https://www.usenix.org/conference/usenixsecurity21/presentation/len

32. McGrew, D., Viega, J.: The galois/counter mode of operation (GCM). Technical report (2004). http://csrc.nist.gov/groups/ST/toolkit/BCM/documents/proposedmodes/gcm/gcm-revised-spec.pdf

33. Pal, B., Daniel, T., Chatterjee, R., Ristenpart, T.: Beyond credential stuffing: password similarity models using neural networks. In: 2019 IEEE Symposium on Security and Privacy, pp. 417–434. IEEE Computer Society Press (2019). https://doi.org/10.1109/SP.2019.00056

34. Peng, Z.: Redirect attack on shadowsocks stream ciphers. https://github.com/edwardz246003/shadowsocks, Accessed May 2020

35. Procter, G.: A security analysis of the composition of ChaCha20 and Poly1305. Cryptology ePrint Archive, Report 2014/613 (2014). https://eprint.iacr.org/2014/613

36. Procter, G., Cid, C.: On weak keys and forgery attacks against polynomial-based MAC schemes. In: Moriai, S. (ed.) FSE 2013. LNCS, vol. 8424, pp. 287–304. Springer, Heidelberg (2014). https://doi.org/10.1007/978-3-662-43933-3_15

37. Saarinen, M.-J.O.: Cycling attacks on GCM, GHASH and other polynomial MACs and hashes. In: Canteaut, A. (ed.) FSE 2012. LNCS, vol. 7549, pp. 216–225. Springer, Heidelberg (2012). https://doi.org/10.1007/978-3-642-34047-5_13

38. Vaudenay, S.: Security flaws induced by CBC padding — applications to SSL, IPSEC, WTLS... In: Knudsen, L.R. (ed.) EUROCRYPT 2002. LNCS, vol. 2332, pp. 534–545. Springer, Heidelberg (2002). https://doi.org/10.1007/3-540-46035-7_35

39. Winter, P., Lindskog, S.: How the great firewall of China is blocking Tor. In: Dingledine, R., Wright, J. (eds.) 2nd USENIX Workshop on Free and Open Communications on the Internet, FOCI '12, Bellevue, WA, USA, 6 August 2012. USENIX Association (2012). https://www.usenix.org/conference/foci12/workshop-program/presentation/winter

Practical Privacy-Preserving Face Identification Based on Function-Hiding Functional Encryption

Alberto Ibarrondo[1,2(✉)], Hervé Chabanne[1,3], and Melek Önen[2]

[1] IDEMIA, Courbevoie, France
[2] EURECOM, Biot, France
{ibarrond,onen}@eurecom.fr
[3] Telecom Paris, Paris, France
herve.chabanne@telecom-paristech.fr

Abstract. Leveraging on function-hiding Functional Encryption (FE) and inner-product-based matching, this work presents a practical privacy-preserving face identification system with two key novelties: switching functionalities of encryption and key generation algorithms of FE to optimize matching latency while maintaining its security guarantees, and identifying output leakage to later formalize two new attacks based on it with appropriate countermeasures. We validate our scheme in a realistic face matching scenario, attesting its applicability to pseudo real-time one-use face identification scenarios like passenger identification.

Keywords: Biometric matching · Face identification · Functional encryption · Privacy-preserving technologies

1 Introduction

The field of Biometrics studies physical and behavioral human characteristics to digitally identify a person. The most commonly used biometric traits are face, iris and fingerprint [16]. Biometrics are used in modern identification systems such as personal (mobile and laptop) authentication, identification for public administration, or border control/passenger identification in the travel industry.

However, biometric data acquisition and processing raises privacy concerns. Since biometric traits cannot be modified or re-issued, its protection is deemed indispensable. Furthermore, data protection regulations enforce strict limitations over usage and storage of biometrics data. While standard cryptography allows secure storage and transmission, secure processing requires advanced cryptographic techniques such as Fully Homomorphic Encryption (FHE) [9], Multiparty Computation (MPC) [17,19] and Functional Encryption (FE) [4].

This work uses FE to protect the biometric matching step with local output decryption. While FE is costly for arbitrary function evaluations, the inner product computed for a matching can be efficiently implemented using FE.

M. Conti et al. (Eds.): CANS 2021, LNCS 13099, pp. 63–71, 2021.
https://doi.org/10.1007/978-3-030-92548-2_4

We present a face identification solution built on FE-based private inner product matching, with the key novelties of optimizing matching latency by switching functionalities of encryption and key generation FE algorithms, and identifying two attacks based on inner product output leakage coupled with suitable countermeasures. The paper is outlined as follows. Section 2 describes the Biometric Matching and FE preliminaries. Section 3 details the proposed solution, architecture and characteristics. Section 4 covers a security analysis. Section 5 comprises implementation and experiments. Section 6 addresses previous work and positions our contribution.

2   Preliminaries

Biometric systems are pattern recognition systems that establish the authenticity of a specific physiological or behavioral user's characteristic. To do so, they scan and compress biometric traits into succinct representations called biometric templates, and perform comparisons between templates.

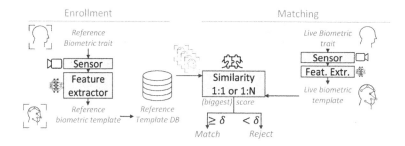

Fig. 1. Diagram of a standard biometric system

Biometric systems present two distinct phases, illustrated in Fig. 1. The *enrollment phase*, where reference templates are acquired and stored in a database, and the *matching phase*, when a live template is captured and matched with the reference templates yielding a positive result if the similarity score is higher than a fixed threshold δ. Depending on the number of reference templates, we can have two scenarios: *Verification* (a.k.a. Authentication) for 1:1 matching, and *Identification* for 1:N matchings. Receiving its input image from a capture sensor, the feature extractor component for face biometrics is nowadays based on Deep Learning models applied to Vision [2,7,8]. The resulting templates are normalized and matched using an inner product as similarity metric.

The face identification scenario we study on this work leads to two practical considerations. First, high numerical precision is paired with low error rates but privacy-preserving techniques support only integer operations. Secondly, N identities in the DB imply N similarity score computations for a matching, creating a natural bound to N so that an end-to-end identification be performed in pseudo real time, which we set to up to 5s. We exemplify the applicability of this work in a use-case of identification for transport boarding, requiring one-time-per-passenger identification of tens to low hundreds of individuals.

A **Functional Encryption** (FE) [4] scheme is a public-key encryption scheme where a "master" secret key msk is used to derive "functional" secret keys sk_k, allowing decryption for a certain function evaluation $F(k, x)$ on inputs x previously encrypted with public key pk without revealing anything else about them. Only a handful of functions F efficiently are supported by FE schemes. The inner dot product $\mathbf{x} \cdot \mathbf{y}$ between two vectors $\mathbf{x}, \mathbf{y} \in \mathbb{Z}_L^K$ is one of them [1].

We remark that there is no restriction to what the functional secret keys sk_k reveal about the function parameters k. For inner products where $F(k, \mathbf{x}) = \mathbf{x} \cdot \mathbf{y}_k$, sk_k reveal $\mathbf{y}_k$, one of the two biometric templates. We thus resort to *Function-Hiding* inner product encryption (FHIPE) schemes [12], which guarantees that sk_k hide the underlying vectors y_k. These are its four algorithms:

$pp, msk \leftarrow FE.setup(1^\lambda)$	generates public parameters pp and master secret key msk given security parameter λ
$sk_y \leftarrow FE.keygen(msk, \mathbf{y})$	generates functional secret keys sk_y for input y using master secret key msk
$c_x \leftarrow FE.encr(msk, \mathbf{x})$	encrypts message x with master secret key msk into ciphertext c
$z \leftarrow FE.decr(pp, sk_y, c_x)$	evaluates $z = \mathbf{x} \cdot \mathbf{y}$ from ciphertext c_x and functional secret key sk_y using pp

3 Our Solution

Security Goals. We begin by establishing the security goals of our solution:

- **Privacy of all templates.** The enrollment phase should store *reference templates* in a privacy preserving manner still allowing inner products. Likewise, extracted *live templates* should support the inner product computation while remaining private for any other use. This is a standard by-design security goal of FE, already covered by the FHIPE scheme [12] of our solution.
- **Protection against inner product leakage.** FE schemes do not treat the inherent leakage of the reference template when computing several inner product operations with it. We formalize the newly identified output leakage below, and develop two practical leakage-based attacks in Sect. 4: *full reference template extraction* and *brute-force impersonation*. Usually overlooked in the secure computation literature, we stress the importance of this leakage in our face identification scenario, where multiple inner products are computed over the same reference template. To protect against them, we establish a carefully selected limit to the total number of identification requests in our solution.

Definition 1 (Inner Product Leakage). *For a single call to* $\mathbf{x} \cdot \mathbf{y}$, *an inner product of two vectors in* $\mathbf{Z}_L^K$, *we define function leakage* ι *as the inverse of the minimum number* p *of calls required to unequivocally determine an unknown input* $\mathbf{y}$ *from known inputs* $\mathbf{x}_j$ *and known outputs* $z_j = \mathbf{x}_j \cdot \mathbf{y}$ $\forall j \in \mathbb{N}, j \leq p$. *As an extension, for* n *inner product calls we define accumulated leakage to be* $\breve{\iota} = n * \iota$. *With* $\breve{\iota} \geq 1$, *the unknown input* $\mathbf{y}$ *is revealed.*

Threat Model. We consider a semi-honest adversary corrupting the similarity score operation and all steps after that, seeking to obtain as much information as possible from the inputs but preserving their integrity. We consider the adversary to have oracle access to the matching phase, thus being able to submit chosen live biometric samples. Our system is built with trust on the enrollment and the capture modules, for they receive the *msk* which can decrypt any ciphertext.

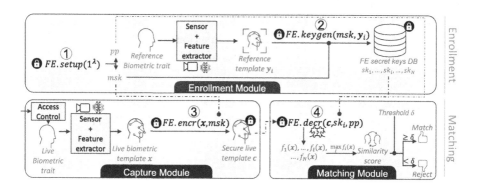

Fig. 2. Architecture of our secure face identification system based on FE

Swapping *FE.encr* with *FE.keygen*. The original FHIPE scheme (Sect. 5.1 of [12]) and posterior works based on it [11] use the function-hiding *FE.keygen* functionality to protect the live template (step 3 in Fig. 2), keeping *FE.encr* for the stored templates (step 2 in Fig. 2). We observe that, given the dual nature of the FHIPE scheme, the same security properties hold if we were to swap them. This observation is grounded on remark 3.4.5. of [5]: in the game-based IND-CPA security definition of FHIPE (Fig. 3.10 of [5] or definition 2.1) the adversary and the oracle follow a perfectly equivalent game. To optimize the matching latency we employ the fastest functionality for this phase, which happens to be *FE.encr* (see Sect. 5), thereby swapping *FE.encr* $\rightleftharpoons$ *FE.keygen* with respect to [11,12].

Limiting the Number of Requests. For templates with K l-bit elements in $\mathbb{Z}_L$ $(L \approx 2^{(l-1)})$, we limit the number N of identification requests of our solution to $N < K$, in order to prevent full reference template extraction due to output leakage (keeping $\breve{\iota} < 1$, detailed in Sect. 4). We enforce this limit via an *access control step* with open instantiation, which could materialize as an agent-controlled checkpoint or a one-time token generated in the enrollment. Furthermore, we add a security margin of 80 bits to hinder brute-force impersonation attacks identified in Sect. 4, leading to a final limit of $N < (K - 80/l)$ requests.

System Description. We display our solution in Fig. 2. In the *enrollment phase*, the enrollment module acts as trusted authority to generate msk & pp and protect N ref. templates by converting them into functional keys sk_i. msk is sent to the capture module, and all sk_i along with pp are sent to the matching module. The *matching phase* starts with the access control step. The capture module then gets a live template x and encrypts it into c using msk. Afterwards, the matching module takes sk_i and c, computes their privacy-preserving inner product $z_i = \mathbf{x} \cdot \mathbf{y_i}$, compares the highest score $max(z_i)$ to the threshold δ, and returns a match with the ID/index i of the highest score, or nothing if rejected.

The feature extractor outputs normalized templates $\mathbf{t} \in \mathbb{R}_{[-1,1]}^K$, easily projected into the FHIPE discrete space $\mathbb{Z}_{2^l}$ by scaling with factor 2^l and a truncation to l bits. The subsequent inner product is naturally up-scaled twice:

$$f(\mathbf{x}_{fix}, \mathbf{y}_{fix}) = \lfloor \mathbf{x}_{float} * 2^l \rfloor_l \cdot \lfloor \mathbf{y}_{float} * 2^l \rfloor_l \approx 2^{2l} * f(\mathbf{x}, \mathbf{y})$$

To compare against the threshold $\delta \in [0, 1]$ we upscale δ twice: $\delta_{fix} = \delta * 2^{2l}$, obtaining an equivalent comparison. This fixed-point translation imposes a minimum ring size of $2l$ bits to avoid overflows. The approximation impacts the accuracy, since more bits yield more precision, but at the cost of bigger primitives in the FE scheme and thus worse latency. We study this trade-off in Sect. 5.

4 Security Analysis

This section first covers the template privacy with FHIPE security, then identifies two novel attacks based on output leakage (Definition 1), proposing countermeasures.

Theorem 1. *Our system preserves the privacy of the live template and the reference templates while allowing the inner product similarity computation.*

Proof. The security of FE sits upon game-based definitions that prove Indistinguishability against Chosen Plaintext Attacks a.k.a. IND-CPA (*IND* [1,4])). The FHIPE scheme of our solution is proven to hold strong SIM-based security guarantees as per theorem 3.1 of [12], which implies IND-CPA secure in Remark 2.5 of [12]. This directly ensures the privacy of the biometric templates inside ciphertexts and functional secret keys of our solution. □

Protection Against Output Leakage. The inner product function, and by extension all IPE schemes, suffer from output leakage of $\iota = 1/K$, for input vectors of K elements. This leads to a **full reference template extraction attack**, where the attacker launches N chosen identification requests and uses the results to reconstruct a hidden reference template. Indeed the system of N linear equations $\{z_j = \sum_{i=1}^{K} \mathbf{x}_j^{[i]} * \mathbf{y}^{[i]}, j \in \{1, 2, ..., N\}\}$ for known z_j and $\mathbf{x}_j$ has a unique, non-trivial solution for the K unknown variables $\mathbf{y}^{[i]}$ when all the equations are linearly independent and $N \geq K$. In our system (Sect. 3) we propose the countermeasure of limiting the number N of calls to F to $N < K$, ensuring $\check{\iota} < 1$. This way, the above system of equations is underdetermined; for $\mathbf{y}^{[i]} \in \mathbb{Z}_L = \{-L, \cdots, -1, 0, 1, \cdots L\}$ there are exactly $(2*L+1)^{(K-N)}$ solutions.

In addition, IPE-based biometric matching schemes with up to $N < K$ requests can be subject to a **brute-force impersonation attack**, where a partially extracted ($\check{\iota} < 1$) reference template $\hat{\mathbf{y}}$ is used to impersonate its owner. The attacker first sets the remaining $K - N$ unknown values of $\hat{\mathbf{y}}$ to arbitrary values and launches several identification requests, so that the FHIPE result $z = \hat{\mathbf{y}} \cdot \mathbf{y}$ might yield $z \geq \delta$, thus matching positive for the identity of $\mathbf{y}$. Beyond this, the attacker could also resort to prior knowledge of the template space (obtainable from feature extractors with similar characteristics) and project the partially extracted template to it, further increasing the chances of a successful impersonation. To thwart these attacks, we set an additional security margin τ to the number N of calls to F in our solution (see Sect. 3), so that $N < (K - \tau)$. Seeking to increase the number of possible solutions of the above system of equations to 2^{80} (80 bits), we fix $\tau \approx 80/l$ for template values of l bits ($L \approx 2^{(l-1)}$).

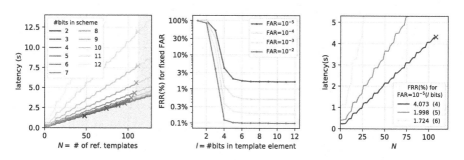

Fig. 3. Experimental results on Latency vs number N of identities (left), on precision vs template element size l (center), and practical trade-off between parameters (right).

Table 1. Latency (seconds) for single-core FE.decr with template elements of l bits.

l	2	4	6	8	10	12	14	16
FE.decrypt (s)	0.18	0.18	0.19	0.25	0.40	1.08	3.81	14.86

5 Experiments

We implement our Cython-based solution using the CiFEr [15] library, an Arc-Face based [7] feature extractor with templates of size $K = 128$. The experiments were run in an Intel(R) Core(TM) i7-7800X CPU and averaged over 10 runs. **Latency** optimization in the matching phase is essential to make our system practical. Using a single core, we measure $FE.setup$ (step 1) to take 0.35s, $FE.keygen$ (step 2) requires 0.19s per key, and $FE.encr$ (step 3) demands 0.082s; thus our proposed swapping reduces the latency of live template protection by 55%. As the only FE operation depending on the template element size, $FE.decr$ latency is recorded in Table 1. The feature extractor clocks 36 ± 1 ms. We disregard the latency of the access control step, as its instantiation is left open; and the max, the comparison with δ and the secure transmission for being negligible compared to the FE operations. Additionally, we analyze the matching module in the left Fig. 3 based on the number N of identities in our system for a one-time identification scenario. As per Sect. 4, N is limited to strictly less than the template vector length ($N < 128$) to avoid full leakage of the stored templates, and a red area marks the additional security margin to thwart brute-force attacks.

Precision is measured with face identification benchmarks using the Labeled Faces in the Wild (LFW) dataset [10] consisting of 13233 $112 \times 112px$ real face images of famous people. We employ the widespread False Acceptance Rate (FAR) and False Rejection Rate (FRR) as metrics[1]. Typically, robust identification systems enforce $FAR < 10^{-4}$, obtaining a corresponding higher FRR. In the central graph of Fig. 3, we remark that highly compressed templates maintain high precision, with little improvement beyond $l = 6$.
To close up, the right Fig. 3 presents the best trade-offs in two scenarios:

- **Higher precision**: Optimizing for low FRR, setting $l = 5$ bits per template element to support up to 70 identities, with slower matching of up to 5s.
- **Many identities**, optimizing for high N (up to 100 identities) by setting $l = 4$ bits, at the cost of $+2\%$ FRR but with faster matching (≈ 4 s).

6 Previous Work

The study of IPE started off with selective security in [1], already envisioning biometric use-cases, and reaching full security with [6,18]. The function-hiding properties for IPE were introduced in [12], applied to biometric authentication based on Hamming weight ($l = 1$). Further works in function-hiding approaches include [13] and [11]. [3] covers an overhaul of efficient techniques.

The use of FE for privacy-preserving biometrics has also been subject to intense scrutiny, from [20] for biometric authentication using threshold predicate encryption, to the extreme efficiency of [14]. Whereas these works employ Hamming-weight based matchings that do not require approximations (typical

---

[1] More info in https://en.wikipedia.org/wiki/Biometrics#Performance.

from fingerprint or iris), our work tackles the cosine-similarity based matching of face biometrics. [2] covers an exhaustive revision of face recognition, which includes the LFW dataset [10] and the foundations of our feature extractor [7].

Among the most recent works, [11] proposes a useful acceleration trick for the FE scheme of [12], by caching all the repetitive computation depending only of the stored templates, obtaining up to 30% speedups. Much like the original [12], their function-hiding approach uses $FE.encr$ for the stored templates and $FE.keygen$ for the live templates. Our function-hiding solution swaps $FE.encr \rightleftharpoons FE.keygen$ to optimize the latency of the system.

Finally, where all previous works focus on the privacy provided by FE, we identify and address the IPE output leakage, often overlooked and not covered by the security guarantees of FE schemes.

7   Conclusions

This work proposes an efficient, precise and privacy-preserving face identification system based on function-hiding functional encryption. We highlight the inherent leakage of inner product schemes and identify novel reference template extraction and brute force attacks. To counter them, we set a hard limit with a security margin to the number N of identities in the system, adding an access control step to enforce it. In addition, we optimize the matching phase latency by swapping $FE.encr$ and $FE.keygen$ usage, speeding up the live template protection by 55% while maintaining the FE security guarantees. Finally, we implemented this system, showing that 4/5 bits per template element are enough to obtain precise setups that compute matchings against a database of up to 100 identities in pseudo real-time, applicable to passenger identification use-cases.

Acknowledgements. The authors thank Vincent Despiegel for his valuable help towards giving birth to this work. Moreover, we express our gratitude to the willful guidance of Zekeriya Erkin. This work has also been partially supported by the 3IA Côte d'Azur program (reference number ANR19-P3IA-0002).

References

1. Abdalla, M., Bourse, F., De Caro, A., Pointcheval, D.: Simple functional encryption schemes for inner products. In: Katz, J. (ed.) PKC 2015. LNCS, vol. 9020, pp. 733–751. Springer, Heidelberg (2015). https://doi.org/10.1007/978-3-662-46447-2_33
2. Adjabi, I., Ouahabi, A., Benzaoui, A., Taleb-Ahmed, A.: Past, present, and future of face recognition: a review. Electronics 9(8), 1188 (2020)
3. Barbosa, M., Catalano, D., Soleimanian, A., Warinschi, B.: Efficient function-hiding functional encryption: from inner-products to orthogonality. In: Matsui, M. (ed.) CT-RSA 2019. LNCS, vol. 11405, pp. 127–148. Springer, Cham (2019). https://doi.org/10.1007/978-3-030-12612-4_7
4. Boneh, D., Sahai, A., Waters, B.: Functional encryption: definitions and challenges. In: Ishai, Y. (ed.) TCC 2011. LNCS, vol. 6597, pp. 253–273. Springer, Heidelberg (2011). https://doi.org/10.1007/978-3-642-19571-6_16

5. Bourse, F.: Functional encryption for inner-product evaluations. Ph.D. thesis, PSL Research University (2017)
6. Datta, P., Dutta, R., Mukhopadhyay, S.: Functional encryption for inner product with full function privacy. In: Cheng, C.-M., Chung, K.-M., Persiano, G., Yang, B.-Y. (eds.) PKC 2016. LNCS, vol. 9614, pp. 164–195. Springer, Heidelberg (2016). https://doi.org/10.1007/978-3-662-49384-7_7
7. Deng, J., Guo, J., Niannan, X., Zafeiriou, S.: Arcface: additive angular margin loss for deep face recognition. In: CVPR (2019)
8. Deng, J., Guo, J., Yuxiang, Z., Yu, J., Kotsia, I., Zafeiriou, S.: Retinaface: single-stage dense face localisation in the wild. In: arxiv (2019)
9. Gentry, C., et al.: A fully homomorphic encryption scheme, vol. 20. Stanford (2009)
10. Huang, G.B., Ramesh, M., Berg, T., Learned-Miller, E.: Labeled faces in the wild: A database for studying face recognition in unconstrained environments. Technical Report. 07–49, University of Massachusetts, Amherst (2007)
11. Jeon, S.Y., Lee, M.K.: Acceleration of inner-pairing product operation for secure biometric verification. Sensors 21(8), 2859 (2021)
12. Kim, S., Lewi, K., Mandal, A., Montgomery, H., Roy, A., Wu, D.J.: Function-hiding inner product encryption is practical. In: Catalano, D., De Prisco, R. (eds.) SCN 2018. LNCS, vol. 11035, pp. 544–562. Springer, Cham (2018). https://doi.org/10.1007/978-3-319-98113-0_29
13. Kim, S., Kim, J., Seo, J.H.: A new approach to practical function-private inner product encryption. Theor. Comput. Sci. 783, 22–40 (2019)
14. Lee, J., Kim, D., Kim, D., Song, Y., Shin, J., Cheon, J.H.: Instant privacy-preserving biometric authentication for hamming distance. IACR Cryptol. ePrint Arch. 2018, 1214 (2018)
15. Project, F.: Cifer: functional encryption library (2021). https://github.com/fentec-project/CiFEr
16. Sabhanayagam, T., Venkatesan, V.P., Senthamaraikannan, K.: A comprehensive survey on various biometric systems. Int. J. Appl. Eng. Res. 13(5), 2276–2297 (2018)
17. Shamir, A.: How to share a secret. Commun. ACM 22(11), 612–613 (1979)
18. Tomida, J., Abe, M., Okamoto, T.: Efficient functional encryption for inner-product values with full-hiding security. In: Bishop, M., Nascimento, A.C.A. (eds.) ISC 2016. LNCS, vol. 9866, pp. 408–425. Springer, Cham (2016). https://doi.org/10.1007/978-3-319-45871-7_24
19. Yao, A.C.C.: How to generate and exchange secrets. In: 27th Annual Symposium on Foundations of Computer Science (sfcs 1986), pp. 162–167. IEEE (1986)
20. Zhou, K., Ren, J.: Passbio: privacy-preserving user-centric biometric authentication. IEEE Trans. Inf. Forens. Secur. 13(12), 3050–3063 (2018)

The Matrix Reloaded: Multiplication Strategies in FrodoKEM

Joppe W. Bos[1], Maximilian Ofner[1,2], Joost Renes[1], Tobias Schneider[1(✉)], and Christine van Vredendaal[1]

[1] NXP Semiconductors, Eindhoven, The Netherlands
{joppe.bos,joost.renes,tobias.schneider,christine.cloostermans}@nxp.com
[2] Graz University of Technology, Graz, Austria
m.ofner@student.tugraz.at

Abstract. Lattice-based schemes are promising candidates to replace the current public-key cryptographic infrastructure in wake of the looming threat of quantum computers. One of the Round 3 candidates of the ongoing NIST post-quantum standardization effort is FrodoKEM. It was designed to provide conservative security, which comes with the caveat that implementations are often bigger and slower compared to alternative schemes. In particular, the most time-consuming arithmetic operation of FrodoKEM is the multiplication of matrices with entries in $\mathbb{Z}_q$.

In this work, we investigate the performance of different matrix multiplication approaches in the specific setting of FrodoKEM. We consider both optimized "naïve" matrix multiplication with cubic complexity, as well as the Strassen multiplication algorithm which has a lower asymptotic run-time complexity. Our results show that for the proposed parameter sets of FrodoKEM we can improve over the state-of-the-art implementation with a row-wise blocking and packing approach, denoted as RWCF in the following. For the matrix multiplication in FrodoKEM, this results in a factor two speed-up. The impact of these improvements on the full decapsulation operation is up to 22%. We additionally show that for batching use-cases, where many inputs are processed at once, the Strassen approach can be the best choice from batch size 8 upwards. For a practically-relevant batch size of 128 inputs the observed speed-up is in the range of 5 to 11% over using the efficient RWCF approach and this speed-up grows with the batch size.

Keywords: Post-quantum cryptography · Matrix multiplication · Software implementation · Strassen

1 Introduction

The security of nearly all our digital assets as well as our online activities relies on the hardness of the underlying cryptographic primitives. *Public-key cryptography*, most notably RSA [37] and Elliptic Curve Cryptography [27,30], is one of

M. Ofner—This work was performed while this author was an internship student at NXP Semiconductors.

M. Conti et al. (Eds.): CANS 2021, LNCS 13099, pp. 72–91, 2021.
https://doi.org/10.1007/978-3-030-92548-2_5

the fundamental components to establish a secure cryptographic infrastructure. With the steady progress in the development of quantum computers, the long-term security of this infrastructure, including encrypted information and digital signatures, is being threatened. When a full-scale quantum computer becomes available, all the currently standardized and widely-used public-key algorithms are vulnerable to polynomial-time attacks using a quantum computer [35,39].

As a reaction to this imminent threat on our currently deployed public-key infrastructure, the USA's National Institute of Standards and Technology (NIST) initiated a process to solicit, evaluate, and standardize one or more quantum-resistant public-key cryptographic algorithms in 2016 [32] where a new replacement standard is expected in 2024. These algorithms are known as *post-quantum* or *quantum-safe* algorithms. Arguably the most promising family of post-quantum secure cryptographic approaches are the *lattice-based* schemes. From its inception with Ajtai's seminal works [2,3], the field has grown to an active area of research (see e.g., [33] for a comprehensive overview).

Among the lattice-based family, the *learning with errors* (LWE) problem is a common foundation on which to construct practical and post-quantum secure schemes. It was first introduced by Regev in [36] and subsequently gained traction due to its hardness reduction proofs; the hardness of LWE (for certain parameterizations) can be reduced to the hardness of various worst-case lattice problems. To improve efficiency, multiple variants of the original LWE problem have been proposed. These use additional structures in the lattice to realize a faster and more compact version of LWE-based schemes. Notable examples are the Ring-LWE [29,34] and the Module-LWE [13,28] versions. While these variants indeed offer schemes with better performances, they are more removed from the original hardness proof of LWE.

In this paper, we focus on the NIST Round 3 candidate FrodoKEM [10,31]. It is derived from the base LWE problem and was designed to provide a practical post-quantum key exchange mechanism with conservative security. In particular, it is based on a carefully parameterized LWE problem, which is closely related to the conjectured-hard problems on *generic*, "algebraically unstructured" lattices. This makes it a very conservative and secure choice in practice.

The downside, of course, is that practical realizations of FrodoKEM are often bigger and slower compared to the algebraically structured alternatives, i.e., Kyber [11,38], NTRU [15], NTRU Prime [8,9] and Saber [17,18]. Still, the advance to the third round of the ongoing NIST standardization effort as well as being one of two post-quantum algorithms recommended by the German Federal Office for Information Security (BSI) as cryptographically suitable for long-term confidentiality [14] underline the practical relevance of FrodoKEM.

From a performance perspective, the most costly operations in FrodoKEM are the (pseudo-random) generation, multiplication and addition of large integer matrices. Hence, from an arithmetic point of view the main bottleneck and, therefore, focus of optimization is the implementation of the matrix multiplication. The main matrix used in these computations is a square integer matrix of dimension $n \in \{640, 976, 1344\}$ depending on the used parameter set of FrodoKEM. In the reference and optimized implementations of [31], this is achieved (if available) using the Advanced Vector Extensions (AVX) instructions on the x64 platform. For matrix dimensions n, the implementations of [31] use a naïve matrix multiplication approach, i.e. of asymptotic complexity $\mathcal{O}(n^3)$. This is motivated by "street wisdom" that the asymptotically faster matrix multiplication algorithms only provide benefits for much larger values of n than used in FrodoKEM. Examples of such algorithms are the Strassen algorithm [41] ($\mathcal{O}(n^{\log_2(7)}) = \mathcal{O}(n^{2.807355})$), the Coppersmith–Winograd algorithm [16] ($\mathcal{O}(n^{2.375477})$), and the most recent improvements by Alman and Williams [6] ($\mathcal{O}(n^{2.3728596})$).

The concept of *batch cryptography* was first introduced by Fiat in [19]. He proposed to perform multiple encryptions or signature generations simultaneously in order to reduce the total complexity. This is achieved by batching the operations instead of performing them one-by-one (see Sect. 4.2 for more details and references). For certain use cases, which require the rapid processing of a large number of cryptographic operations, this approach can be very beneficial, e.g., one of the recent emerging technologies with such requirements is vehicular communication [12]. In the setting of FrodoKEM, batching could be used to decapsulate multiple encapsulated keys with the same private key, e.g., a server processing a multitude of client requests. In effect, this batch decapsulation would increase one dimension of the multiplied matrices in function of the processed queries.

Contributions. In this work, we investigate the validity of this "street wisdom". This is motivated and in line with the results from Huang, Smith, Henry, and van de Geijn [22] where they dispel some of the preconceived notions regarding the practicality of the Strassen matrix multiplication algorithm. They introduce various implementation strategies to make Strassen a viable alternative to and even outperform the naïve $\mathcal{O}(n^3)$ approach for much smaller dimensions than previously assumed. We apply the learnings from [22] to the cryptographic setting of FrodoKEM: matrix multiplication where one of the inputs is significantly smaller (dimension $\bar{n} \times n = 8 \times n$) compared to the other (dimension $n \times n$ matrix) with the added aspect that one matrix can be generated *on-the-fly*.

To this end, we first implement FrodoKEM with various approaches for matrix multiplication. In particular, we explore variations of naïve matrix multiplication and Strassen matrix multiplication. We show that using a row-wise blocking and packing approach, denoted as RWCF, combined with on-the-fly generation of the FrodoKEM matrix outperforms the current FrodoKEM matrix multiplication implementation by almost a factor two. When the RWCF approach is used in FrodoKEM decapsulation, we show an improvement of up to 22%.

Furthermore, we investigate the viability of Strassen for the batching use case. To this end, we benchmark the performance of FrodoKEM when computing batch operations. We show that for batch sizes as small as 8 (for FrodoKEM-1344), using the Strassen algorithm can provide better performances than the naïve multiplication and even the RWCF approach. For batch sizes 128 and upward, we show that we can expect improvements in the range 19 to 35% compared to the FrodoKEM matrix-multiplication method and of 5 to 11% over the RWCF

Table 1. The relevant FrodoKEM parameters for matrix multiplication for the various security levels.

Parameter set	NIST security level	q	$\bar{n}$	n
FrodoKEM-640	1	2^{15}	8	640
FrodoKEM-976	3	2^{16}	8	976
FrodoKEM-1344	5	2^{16}	8	1344

approach. As expected, the benefit of using Strassen becomes more significant as the batch size increases.

Outline. The remainder of this paper is structured as follows. In Sect. 2, we provide the necessary background on FrodoKEM and recursive matrix multiplication, in particular the Strassen algorithm. In Sect. 3, we outline the application of the different matrix multiplication approaches in the context of FrodoKEM. These are then benchmarked for FrodoKEM and batched FrodoKEM in Sect. 4, and the paper is concluded in Sect. 5.

2 Preliminaries

In this section we outline the basics of the FrodoKEM algorithm [10,31], with a focus on the generation of the public matrix $\mathbf{A} \in \mathbb{Z}_q^{n \times n}$. We also recall the Strassen [41] matrix multiplication algorithm.

Notation. We denote the ring of integers modulo q with $\mathbb{Z}_q = \mathbb{Z}/q\mathbb{Z}$. Matrices are denoted with upper case boldface letters, e.g., $\mathbf{B} \in \mathbb{Z}_q^{m \times n}$, and its matrix element in the i-th row and j-th column as $\mathbf{B}_{i,j}$ (with $0 \leq i < m$ and $0 \leq j < n$).

2.1 The FrodoKEM Algorithm

FrodoKEM was derived from the Frodo key agreement protocol proposed in [10]. The security of Frodo reduces to the hardness of the standard Learning With Errors (LWE) problem with a short secret. In this section, we only recall the aspects of FrodoKEM relevant to our contribution. For further information, we refer the interested reader to the specification of FrodoKEM [31].

Table 1 contains the FrodoKEM parameters related to the matrix multiplication and their associated security levels. The NIST security levels 1, 3 and 5 correspond to the brute-force security of AES128, AES-192 and AES-256, respectively.

As can be seen from Table 1, the LWE integer modulus $q \leq 2^{16}$ is always a power of two in FrodoKEM. This was chosen for efficiency reasons: reduction modulo q is "for free" on modern computer architectures.

During the FrodoKEM key generation, secret and public keys are generated from an initial secret and public seeds. In particular, the *public* matrix $\mathbf{A} \in \mathbb{Z}_q^{n \times n}$

Algorithm 1. Frodo.Gen using AES128 (algorithm taken from [31]).

Input: Seed $\text{seed}_\mathbf{A} \in \{0,1\}^{\text{len}_{\text{seed}\mathbf{A}}}$.
Output: Matrix $\mathbf{A} \in \mathbb{Z}_q^{n \times n}$.

1: **for** $(i = 0; i < n; i \leftarrow i + 1)$ **do**
2:    **for** $(j = 0; j < n; j \leftarrow j + 8)$ **do**
3:       $\mathbf{b} \leftarrow \langle i \rangle \| \langle j \rangle \| 0 \cdots 0 \in \{0,1\}^{128}$ where $\langle i \rangle, \langle j \rangle \in \{0,1\}^{16}$
4:       $\langle c_{i,j} \rangle \| \langle c_{i,j+1} \rangle \| \cdots \| \langle c_{i,j+7} \rangle \leftarrow \text{AES128}_{\text{seed}\mathbf{A}}(\mathbf{b})$ where each $\langle c_{i,k} \rangle \in \{0,1\}^{16}$
5:       **for** $(k = 0; k < 8; k \leftarrow k + 1)$ **do**
6:          $\mathbf{A}_{i,j+k} \leftarrow c_{i,j+k} \bmod q$
7: **return** $\mathbf{A}$

---

is created by calling FrodoKEM.Gen ($\text{seed}_\mathbf{A}$) for the public seed $\text{seed}_\mathbf{A}$. Given $\mathbf{A}$ and the *secret* matrix $\mathbf{S} \in \mathbb{Z}_q^{n \times \bar{n}}$, a second *public* matrix $\mathbf{B} \in \mathbb{Z}_q^{n \times \bar{n}}$ is computed as

$$\mathbf{B} = \mathbf{A} \cdot \mathbf{S} + \mathbf{E},$$

where $\mathbf{E}$ is randomly drawn from a (small) distribution χ. FrodoKEM security in this context relies on the hardness of recovering $\mathbf{S}$ from $\mathbf{B}$ and $\mathbf{A}$. The public key pk is then derived from $\mathbf{B}$ and $\text{seed}_\mathbf{A}$, while the secret key sk further contains the secret seeds and matrices. Note that $\mathbf{A}$ is not part of any key and it is assumed to be always generated on-the-fly using $\text{seed}_\mathbf{A}$.

Apart from error sampling and calls to symmetric primitives (i.e., AES128 or SHAKE128), the main operations in FrodoKEM are matrix operations. In the remainder of this section we focus on these operations.

To perform encryption FrodoPKE.Enc with respect to the matrix $\mathbf{A}$ one generates a secret matrix $\mathbf{S}' \in \mathbb{Z}_q^{\bar{n} \times n}$ and computes $\mathbf{B}' \in \mathbb{Z}_q^{\bar{n} \times n}$ as

$$\mathbf{B}' = \mathbf{S}' \cdot \mathbf{A} + \mathbf{E}',$$

where $\mathbf{E}'$ is another matrix randomly drawn from a (small) distribution χ. Since encryption is a subroutine of both encapsulation and decapsulation, this matrix multiplication operation is also a critical component of FrodoKEM.Enc and FrodoKEM.Dec.

Generation of the Public Matrix A. To reduce the size of public keys and accelerate encryption, the public matrix $\mathbf{A} \in \mathbb{Z}_q^{n \times n}$ could be set to a fixed value. However, the designers of FrodoKEM chose to assign the public matrix $\mathbf{A}$ dynamically and pseudorandomly generate it for every generated key. Following previous work in this area [5,10], using dynamic matrices $\mathbf{A}$ helps to avoid the possibility of backdoors and all-for-the-price-of-one attacks [1].

Let us recall how the matrix is constructed following the FrodoKEM specification [31]. The algorithm FrodoKEM.Gen takes as input the modulus q, a seed $\text{seed}_\mathbf{A} \in \{0,1\}^{\text{len}_{\text{seed}\mathbf{A}}}$ and a dimension $n \in \mathbb{Z}$, and outputs a pseudorandom matrix $\mathbf{A} \in \mathbb{Z}_q^{n \times n}$. There are two options for instantiating FrodoKEM.Gen. The first method uses AES128; the second instead uses SHAKE128.

Algorithm 2. Frodo.Gen using SHAKE128 (algorithm taken from [31]).

Input: Seed $\text{seed}_A \in \{0,1\}^{\text{len}_{\text{seed}\,A}}$.
Output: Pseudorandom matrix $A \in \mathbb{Z}_q^{n \times n}$.

1: **for** $(i = 0; i < n; i \leftarrow i + 1)$ **do**
2:   $\langle c_{i,0}\rangle \| \langle c_{i,1}\rangle \| \cdots \| \langle c_{i,n-1}\rangle \leftarrow \text{SHAKE128}(\text{seed}_A, 16n, 2^8 + i)$ where each $\langle c_{i,j}\rangle \in \{0,1\}^{16}$.
3:   **for** $(j = 0; j < n; j \leftarrow j + 1)$ **do**
4:     $A_{i,j} \leftarrow c_{i,j} \mod q$
5: **return** A

When using AES128, the matrix $A \in \mathbb{Z}_q^{n \times n}$ is generated 8 elements at-a-time. For each row and each block of 8 elements (in different columns), the algorithm generates a 128-bit block of predefined input based on the location in the matrix. This input is encrypted using the seed_A as the AES128 key. This process is outlined in Algorithm 1. More specifically, the input blocks to AES128 are $\langle i\rangle \| \langle j\rangle \| 0 \| \cdots \| 0 \in \{0,1\}^{128}$, where i, j are encoded as 16-bit integers (see Line 3). It then splits the 128-bit AES128 output block into eight 16-bit elements, which it interprets as non-negative integers $c_{i,j+k}$ for $k = 0, 1, \ldots, 7$ (see Line 4). Finally, it sets $A_{i,j+k} = c_{i,j+k} \mod q$ for all k. This modular reduction is "for free" by dropping the most significant bits whenever $q < 2^{16}$.

The second method uses SHAKE128 instead of AES128 to generate the rows of the matrix $A \in \mathbb{Z}_q^{n \times n}$. This process is shown in Algorithm 2. In this case, each entire row is generated with a SHAKE128 call. Its input consists of seed_A and a customization value $2^8 + i$ to produce a $16n$-bit output (see Line 2). The output is then split into 16-bit integers $c_{i,j} \in \{0,1\}^{16}$ (for $j = 0, 1, \ldots, n-1$), and used to set the corresponding matrix entries $A_{i,j} = c_{i,j} \mod q$ in Line 4. Note that the offset of 2^8 in the customization value is used for domain separation where for details we refer to the specification [31] of FrodoKEM.

2.2 The Strassen Algorithm

In this section we consider the application of the Strassen algorithm to the FrodoKEM multiplication $B' = S'A + E'$, where $B', S', E' \in \mathbb{Z}_q^{\bar{n} \times n}$ and $A \in \mathbb{Z}_q^{n \times n}$. The schoolbook approach of computing this sum would be to compute

$$B'_{i,j} = E'_{i,j} + \sum_{k=0}^{n-1} S'_{i,k} A_{k,j},$$

for each $i = 0, 1, \ldots, \bar{n} - 1$ and $j = 0, 1, \ldots, n - 1$. This requires $\bar{n}n^2$ multiplications of coefficients in $\mathbb{Z}_q$, and therefore is of complexity $\mathcal{O}(\bar{n}n^2)$. In the remainder we will refer to this specific multiplication method as the *straightforward* approach, while we will refer to $\mathcal{O}(\bar{n}n^2)$ methods in general as *naïve* approaches.

In 1969, Strassen introduced an algorithm for matrix multiplication [41] asymptotically faster compared to the straightforward approach. The Strassen algorithm works as follows. First the matrices $\mathbf{S}', \mathbf{A}$ and $\mathbf{E}'$ are split into four sub-matrices of equal size:

$$\mathbf{S}' = \begin{pmatrix} \mathbf{S}'_{00} & \mathbf{S}'_{01} \\ \mathbf{S}'_{10} & \mathbf{S}'_{11} \end{pmatrix}, \quad \mathbf{A} = \begin{pmatrix} \mathbf{A}_{00} & \mathbf{A}_{01} \\ \mathbf{A}_{10} & \mathbf{A}_{11} \end{pmatrix}, \quad \mathbf{E}' = \begin{pmatrix} \mathbf{E}'_{00} & \mathbf{E}'_{01} \\ \mathbf{E}'_{10} & \mathbf{E}'_{11} \end{pmatrix},$$

where the sub-matrices of $\mathbf{S}'$ and $\mathbf{E}'$ are of dimension $\bar{n}/2 \times n/2$ and the sub-matrices of $\mathbf{A}$ of dimension $n/2 \times n/2$ each. The straightforward method would then be to compute

$$\mathbf{B}' = \begin{pmatrix} \mathbf{B}'_{00} & \mathbf{B}'_{01} \\ \mathbf{B}'_{10} & \mathbf{B}'_{11} \end{pmatrix},$$

where

$$\mathbf{B}'_{00} = \mathbf{E}'_{00} + \mathbf{S}'_{00} \cdot \mathbf{A}_{00} + \mathbf{S}'_{01} \cdot \mathbf{A}_{10},$$
$$\mathbf{B}'_{01} = \mathbf{E}'_{01} + \mathbf{S}'_{00} \cdot \mathbf{A}_{01} + \mathbf{S}'_{01} \cdot \mathbf{A}_{11},$$
$$\mathbf{B}'_{10} = \mathbf{E}'_{10} + \mathbf{S}'_{10} \cdot \mathbf{A}_{00} + \mathbf{S}'_{11} \cdot \mathbf{A}_{10},$$
$$\mathbf{B}'_{11} = \mathbf{E}'_{11} + \mathbf{S}'_{10} \cdot \mathbf{A}_{01} + \mathbf{S}'_{11} \cdot \mathbf{A}_{11}.$$

This split computation consists of eight products of dimension $\bar{n}/2 \times n/2$ sub-matrices with dimension $n/2 \times n/2$ sub-matrices, and does not decrease the overall number of multiplications compared to the straightforward approach. The idea by Strassen is to compute this instead as

$$\mathbf{M}_0 = (\mathbf{S}'_{00} + \mathbf{S}'_{11}) \cdot (\mathbf{A}_{00} + \mathbf{A}_{11}), \quad \mathbf{B}'_{00} = \mathbf{E}'_{00} + \mathbf{M}_0 + \mathbf{M}_3 - \mathbf{M}_4 + \mathbf{M}_6,$$
$$\mathbf{M}_1 = (\mathbf{S}'_{10} + \mathbf{S}'_{11}) \cdot \mathbf{A}_{00}, \quad \mathbf{B}'_{01} = \mathbf{E}'_{01} + \mathbf{M}_2 + \mathbf{M}_4,$$
$$\mathbf{M}_2 = \mathbf{S}'_{00} \cdot (\mathbf{A}_{01} - \mathbf{A}_{11}) \quad \mathbf{B}'_{10} = \mathbf{E}'_{10} + \mathbf{M}_1 + \mathbf{M}_3,$$
$$\mathbf{M}_3 = \mathbf{S}'_{11} \cdot (\mathbf{A}_{10} - \mathbf{A}_{00}), \quad \mathbf{B}'_{11} = \mathbf{E}'_{11} + \mathbf{M}_0 - \mathbf{M}_1 + \mathbf{M}_2 + \mathbf{M}_5.$$
$$\mathbf{M}_4 = (\mathbf{S}'_{00} + \mathbf{S}'_{01}) \cdot \mathbf{A}_{11},$$
$$\mathbf{M}_5 = (\mathbf{S}'_{10} - \mathbf{S}'_{00}) \cdot (\mathbf{A}_{00} + \mathbf{A}_{01}),$$
$$\mathbf{M}_6 = (\mathbf{S}'_{01} - \mathbf{S}'_{11}) \cdot (\mathbf{A}_{10} + \mathbf{A}_{11}),$$

This requires only seven multiplications of dimension $\bar{n}/2 \times n/2$ sub-matrices with dimension $n/2 \times n/2$ sub-matrices, but has an increased number of additions and subtractions compared to the naïve method. Strassen's algorithm applies this splitting recursively, which asymptotically outperforms the straightforward block-by-block computation. For example, applying the recursion $\log_2 \bar{n}$ times leads to a complexity of $\mathcal{O}(\bar{n}^{\log_2 7 - 2} \cdot n^2)$, which is asymptotically better than the complexity of $\mathcal{O}(\bar{n}n^2)$ of naïve methods. The optimal number of recursion levels will depend on the various parameters and the platform on which the algorithm is implemented. In [22] it was shown that different strategies can reduce the overhead of Strassen and that the algorithm can show good results for smaller dimensions than previously known.

3   Matrix Multiplication Strategies for Cryptography

In this section, we present different strategies to realize efficient and practical implementations of matrix multiplication algorithms. These methods have been studied extensively in the literature before and are not new. The cryptographic application to FrodoKEM, however, which comes with the different setting of integer matrices where one of the operands is generated on-the-fly, has as far as we are aware not been considered in detail before. We use the techniques as proposed in the BLAS-like Library Instantiation Software (BLIS) framework [42]. BLIS is a software framework and gives the infrastructure for instantiating Basic Linear Algebra Subprograms (BLAS) functionality. The core design idea of BLIS is that virtually all BLAS operations (such as matrix-vector and matrix-matrix multiplications) can be expressed and optimized in terms of very simple kernels. Moreover, we use and describe the optimizing strategies as summarized and studied in [40].

3.1   Matrix Multiplication for FrodoKEM

In the setting of FrodoKEM we are particularly interested in the matrix product with accumulation. That is, we consider the operations $\mathbf{B} = \mathbf{A} \cdot \mathbf{S} + \mathbf{E}$ and $\mathbf{B}' = \mathbf{S}' \cdot \mathbf{A} + \mathbf{E}'$ where $\mathbf{S}, \mathbf{E} \in \mathbb{Z}_q^{n \times \bar{n}}$ and $\mathbf{S}', \mathbf{E}' \in \mathbb{Z}_q^{\bar{n} \times n}$ are sampled from a rounded continuous Gaussian distribution and $\mathbf{A} \in \mathbb{Z}_q^{n \times n}$ is generated pseudorandomly from a seed $\mathsf{seed_A}$ according to Algorithm 1 or Algorithm 2. For simplicity, and as it is the case in which the approach of Sect. 3.3 has the most impact, we only focus on the generation of $\mathbf{A}$ with AES128 in this section. However, the application when using SHAKE128 is straightforward. In the proposed parameter sets in [31], one uses $\bar{n} = 8$ and $n \in \{640, 976, 1344\}$ (see Table 1) and therefore the public matrix $\mathbf{A}$ is quite large: 800, 1860 and 3528 kilobytes, respectively.

We begin with a brief discussion on the multiplication $\mathbf{B} = \mathbf{A} \cdot \mathbf{S} + \mathbf{E}$, which is the most straightforward. In the FrodoKEM submission this is performed with the naïve (schoolbook) matrix multiplication $\mathbf{B}_{i,j} = \sum_{k=0}^{n-1} \mathbf{A}_{i,k} \mathbf{S}_{k,j} + \mathbf{E}_{i,j}$. Note that this works particularly well with on-the-fly matrix generation: since each $\mathbf{B}_{i,j}$ only depends on the i-th row of $\mathbf{A}$, and since $\mathbf{A}$ is generated *row-wise* (see Sect. 2.1), one can generate a row of $\mathbf{A}$ and use it to generate all $\bar{n}$ elements in the same row of $\mathbf{B}$. This also sets itself up well for using 16-way SIMD 16-bit integer instructions (like AVX and AVX2 [23]), but hand-optimizing those results in only a one percent performance improvement due to the compiler being able to generate such optimized code very well [31, Sect. 3.2.1]. Hence, in this work we make no improvements to the multiplication $\mathbf{B} = \mathbf{A} \cdot \mathbf{S} + \mathbf{E}$.

Instead, we consider the matrix operation $\mathbf{B}' = \mathbf{S}' \cdot \mathbf{A} + \mathbf{E}'$. In this case, the naïve computation $\mathbf{B}'_{i,j} = \sum_{k=0}^{n-1} \mathbf{S}'_{i,k} \mathbf{A}_{k,j} + \mathbf{E}'_{i,j}$ relies on the j-th *column* of $\mathbf{A}$. This leads to a non-trivial problem for on-the-fly computation, as the matrix $\mathbf{A}$ is generated row by row. In the case of AES128 the situation is actually slightly simpler, as $\mathbf{A}$ is really only generated 8 row-elements at a time. However, we shall see that the choice of algorithm still has significant impact on performance.

In the remainder of this section we compare various algorithms to compute $\mathbf{B}' = \mathbf{S}' \cdot \mathbf{A} + \mathbf{E}'$.

3.2 The FrodoKEM Algorithm

The idea of FrodoKEM for computing $\mathbf{B}' = \mathbf{S}' \cdot \mathbf{A} + \mathbf{E}'$ is simple to describe: since elements of a row of $\mathbf{A}$ are generated 8 columns at a time, the elements of $\mathbf{B}'$ are also generated 8 columns at a time. That is, for a fixed j one generates

$$\mathbf{A}_{i,j} \| \mathbf{A}_{i,j+1} \| \cdots \| \mathbf{A}_{i,j+7} \leftarrow \text{AES128}_{\text{seed}_{\mathbf{A}}} (\langle i \rangle \| \langle j \rangle \| 0 \cdots \| 0)$$

for all $i = 0, 1, \ldots, n - 1$ according to Algorithm 1. These elements can then be used to compute $\mathbf{B}'_{k,j}, \ldots, \mathbf{B}'_{k,j+7}$ for $k = 0, 1, \ldots, \bar{n} - 1$.

The most straightforward way to implement this, which is done by FrodoKEM, is to store the input to AES128 as a sequence of n blocks of 128-bit each

$$\langle 0 \rangle \| \langle j \rangle \| 0 \| \cdots \| 0 \| \langle 1 \rangle \| \langle j \rangle \| 0 \| \cdots \| 0 \| \cdots \| 0 \| \langle n - 1 \rangle \| \langle j \rangle \| 0 \| \cdots \| 0 \,,$$

to which AES128 can be applied independently. As a result, the elements of the 8 columns of $\mathbf{A}$ are stored sequentially as

$$\mathbf{A}_{0,j} \| \cdots \| \mathbf{A}_{0,j+7} \| \mathbf{A}_{1,j} \| \cdots \| \mathbf{A}_{1,j+7} \| \cdots \| \mathbf{A}_{n-1,j} \| \cdots \| \mathbf{A}_{n-1,j+7} \,.$$

However, to compute $\mathbf{B}'_{0,j}$ one would need to access $\mathbf{A}_{0,j}, \mathbf{A}_{1,j}, \ldots, \mathbf{A}_{n-1,j}$ which are *not* stored sequentially in memory. To solve this, FrodoKEM explicitly converts the representation to

$$\mathbf{A}_{0,j} \| \cdots \| \mathbf{A}_{n-1,j} \| \mathbf{A}_{0,j+1} \| \cdots \| \mathbf{A}_{n-1,j+1} \| \cdots \| \mathbf{A}_{0,j+7} \| \cdots \| \mathbf{A}_{n-1,j+7} \,,$$

which is essentially a *transpose* of the columns of $\mathbf{A}$. We observe that this memory re-organization does have a significant impact on the efficiency of the algorithm (cf. Table 2 in Sect. 4). For completeness, we summarize the matrix multiplication algorithm of FrodoKEM in Algorithm 3, where the transposition is performed in Lines 12 to 14. The authors of FrodoKEM made an efficient implementation of Algorithm 3 available where the multiplications and additions of the matrix elements are computed using the 256-bit Advanced Vector Extensions (AVX) 16-way SIMD 16-bit integer instructions [4].

3.3 The RWCF Approach: Row-Wise Cache-Friendly Multiplication

In this paper we look at an alternative approach to implement the same straightforward matrix multiplication algorithm with asymptotic run-time $\mathcal{O}(n^2 \bar{n})$. We follow the blocking and packing approach as outlined in [20,42] which does not seem to have been considered for the FrodoKEM submission. Note that the multiplication with this complexity still falls under the naïve matrix multiplication methods. The idea is to avoid the expensive transposition in memory required by the FrodoKEM algorithm, which leads to an improvement in performance.

Algorithm 3. Matrix multiplication as implemented in the official FrodoKEM submission when using AES128. The temporary memory buffers used are $\mathbf{A}^{\mathrm{cols}}, \mathbf{T}$ and $\mathbf{AT}^{\mathrm{cols}}$ of $8n$ elements of $\mathbb{Z}_q$ each.

Input: Seed $\mathsf{seed}_\mathbf{A} \in \{0,1\}^{\mathsf{len}_{\mathsf{seed}}\mathbf{A}}$ and matrices $\mathbf{S}', \mathbf{E}' \in \mathbb{Z}_q^{\bar{n} \times n}$.
Output: $\mathbb{Z}_q^{\bar{n} \times n} \ni \mathsf{out} = \mathbf{S}' \cdot \mathbf{A} + \mathbf{E}'$.

```
1:  for i ← 0; i < n̄; i ← i + 1 do
2:      for j ← 0; j < n; j ← j + 1 do
3:          out_{i,j} ← E'_{i,j}
4:  Set T to all zeros
5:  aes_k ← AES128_load_key_schedule(seed_A)
6:  for i ← 0; i < n; i ← i + 1 do
7:      T[8i] ← i
8:  for k ← 0; k < n; k ← k + 8 do
9:      for i ← 0; i < n; i ← i + 1 do
10:         T[8i + 1] ← k
11:     A^cols ← AES128_ECB_{aes_k}(T)
12:     for i ← 0; i < n; i ← i + 1 do
13:         for j ← 0; j < 8; j ← j + 1 do
14:             AT^cols[j · n + i] ← A^cols[8i + j]          // Transpose
15:     for i ← 0; i < n̄; i ← i + 1 do
16:         for ℓ ← 0; ℓ < 8; ℓ ← ℓ + 1 do
17:             sum ← 0
18:             for j ← 0; j < n; j ← j + 1 do
19:                 sum ← sum + S'_{i,j} · AT^cols[ℓ · n + j]   // Access AT sequentially
20:             out_{i,k+ℓ} ← out_{i,k+ℓ} + sum
```

For this purpose, the elements of $\mathbf{A}$ are generated *row-wise* as opposed to column-wise. This is done 8 rows at a time in our benchmarked implementation, as this led to the best performance. However, doing fewer or more is possible as there is no dependency between different rows (as opposed to columns). For simplicity, we describe the approach for a single row, as using more rows can be deduced easily by doing them in parallel. We provide the full description for 8 rows in Algorithm 4.

For a fixed row k, the input to AES128 is generated (sequentially in memory) as

$$\langle k \rangle \| \langle 0 \rangle \| 0 \| \cdots \| 0 \| \langle k \rangle \| \langle 8 \rangle \| 0 \| \cdots \| 0 \| \cdots \| \langle k \rangle \| \langle n - 8 \rangle \| 0 \| \cdots \| 0,$$

to which we apply AES128 to obtain

$$\mathbf{A}_{k,0} \| \mathbf{A}_{k,1} \| \cdots \| \mathbf{A}_{k,n-1}.$$

We then initialize $\mathbf{B}'^{(-1)} = \mathbf{E}'$ and iteratively accumulate $\mathbf{B}'^{(k)}$ as

$$\mathbf{B}_{i,j}'^{(k)} = \mathbf{B}_{i,j}'^{(k-1)} + \mathbf{S}_{i,k}' \mathbf{A}_{k,j}, \tag{1}$$

Algorithm 4. Matrix multiplication in FrodoKEM with row-wise AES128 generation. The temporary memory buffers used are $\mathbf{A}^{\text{rows}}$ and $\mathbf{T}$ of $8n$ elements of $\mathbb{Z}_q$ each.

Input: Seed $\text{seed}_{\mathbf{A}} \in \{0,1\}^{\text{len}_{\text{seed}_{\mathbf{A}}}}$ and matrices $\mathbf{S}', \mathbf{E}' \in \mathbb{Z}_q^{\bar{n} \times n}$.
Output: $\mathbb{Z}_q^{\bar{n} \times n} \ni \mathbf{B}' = \mathbf{S}' \cdot \mathbf{A} + \mathbf{E}'$.

1: **for** $i \leftarrow 0;\ i < \bar{n};\ i \leftarrow i+1$ **do**
2:     **for** $j \leftarrow 0;\ j < n;\ j \leftarrow j+1$ **do**
3:         $\mathbf{B}'_{i,j} \leftarrow \mathbf{E}'_{i,j}$
4: Set $\mathbf{T}$ to all zeros
5: $\text{aes}_k \leftarrow \text{AES128\_load\_key\_schedule}(\text{seed}_{\mathbf{A}})$
6: **for** $i \leftarrow 0;\ i < n;\ i \leftarrow i+8$ **do**
7:     **for** $j \leftarrow 0;\ j < 8;\ j \leftarrow j+1$ **do**
8:         $\mathbf{T}[j \cdot n + i + 1] \leftarrow i$
9: **for** $i \leftarrow 0;\ i < n;\ i \leftarrow i+8$ **do**
10:     **for** $j \leftarrow 0;\ j < 8;\ j \leftarrow j+1$ **do**
11:         **for** $k \leftarrow 0;\ k < n;\ k \leftarrow k+8$ **do**
12:             $\mathbf{T}[j \cdot n + k] \leftarrow i + j$
13:         $\mathbf{A}^{\text{rows}} \leftarrow \text{AES128\_ECB}_{\text{aes}_k}(\mathbf{T})$
14:         **for** $j \leftarrow 0;\ j < \bar{n};\ j \leftarrow j+1$ **do**
15:             **for** $\ell \leftarrow 0;\ \ell < n;\ \ell \leftarrow \ell+1$ **do**
16:                 $\text{sum} = \mathbf{B}'_{j,\ell}$
17:                 **for** $k \leftarrow 0;\ k < 8;\ k \leftarrow k+1$ **do**
18:                     $\text{sum} = \text{sum} + \mathbf{S}'_{j,i+k} \cdot \mathbf{A}^{\text{rows}}[k \cdot n + \ell]$ // 16 in parallel (AVX2)
19:                 $\mathbf{B}'_{j,\ell} \leftarrow \text{sum}$

---

for all $i = 0, 1 \ldots, \bar{n} - 1$ and $j = 0, 1 \ldots, n - 1$. One sees that

$$\mathbf{B}'_{i,j} = \mathbf{B}'^{(n-1)}_{i,j} = \mathbf{E}'_{i,j} + \sum_{k=0}^{n-1} \mathbf{S}'_{i,k} \mathbf{A}_{k,j},$$

proving correctness of the algorithm. Moreover, the elements of $\mathbf{A}$ are accessed in the same order in which they are generated, making this algorithm very suitable to on-the-fly generation.

This approach can be combined very efficiently with the available SIMD extensions. Specifically, one can broadcast the (16-bit) value $\mathbf{S}'_{i,k}$ to the 16 SIMD slots. This broadcast is done using the AVX instruction $\_\text{mm256\_set1\_epi16}(\cdot)$ which puts the 16-bit integer a in all 16 slots of the returned 256-bit vector register. These values can be multiplied with 16 matrix elements $\mathbf{A}_{k,j} \| \cdots \| \mathbf{A}_{k,j+15}$ using a single instruction: $\_\text{mm256\_mullo\_epi16}(\cdot,\cdot)$. This computes the products $\mathbf{S}'_{i,k} \mathbf{A}_{k,j}, \ldots, \mathbf{S}'_{i,k} \mathbf{A}_{k,j+15}$, for the 16-bit integers $\mathbf{S}'_{i,k}$ and $\mathbf{A}_{k,j}, \ldots, \mathbf{A}_{k,j+15}$, and has the additional advantage that the obtained result is automatically reduced modulo q (or $2q$ when $q = 2^{15}$ is used). This can be applied in Line 18 of Algorithm 4. Note that $16 \mid n$ for all parameter sets of FrodoKEM, so generating 16 row elements of $\mathbf{A}$ at a time is not a problem.

It should be clear that the accumulation step in Eq. (1) can be computed for multiple rows at the same time by generating those rows simultaneously

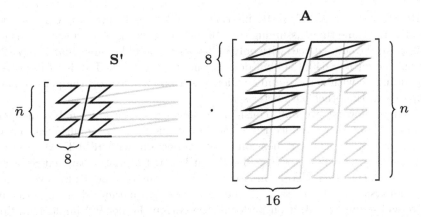

Fig. 1. Graphical representation of processing the elements. In gray the FrodoKEM approach, which for cache-friendly access requires transposing the blocks of columns from **A**, before multiplying with the rows of **S**. In black the RWCF approach, which does not require a transpose.

for various k. Although the number of multiplications and additions does not change in that case, it can be beneficial for the overall run-time by reducing the overall loads and stores of the $\mathbf{B}'_{i,j}$. This is especially true when loads and stores are performed to and from AVX registers. For example, in Line 16 and 19 of Algorithm 4 there is only a single load and store of $\mathbf{B}'_{j,\ell}$ for every 8 accumulations.

Note that for AES128-based version it is not actually necessary to generate a whole row of **A**: as we apply AES128 to 8 elements at a time, we can generate exactly those 8 elements (in the same row) on-the-fly (though 16 would be preferable for compatibility with AVX instructions). In that case we could consider another extreme version of the above algorithm where we process n rows simultaneously, generating 16 columns on-the-fly and multiplying and accumulating. This would reduce essentially to a column-based approach again, though the order of multiplications is different from FrodoKEM and a tranposition in memory is not necessary. However, since this algorithm is not compatible with SHAKE, which does generate whole rows from a single SHAKE call, we do not pursue this further here.

To illustrate the high-level difference in the order of accessing **A**, we present a simplified representation in Fig. 1. In gray, we see how the columns of **A** are processed, which require an additional memory transposition. In black the row-wise method is shown, which needs no explicit memory transformations.

3.4   FrodoKEM Multiplication Using Strassen

The last multiplication approach we discuss in the context of FrodoKEM is Strassen, which was already introduced in Sect. 2.2. In [22] it was shown that Strassen can also be implemented in a cache-friendly manner. The method presented there can be easily combined with the on-the-fly generation of **A**.

Recall that the AVX2 SIMD instructions allow us to process 16 16-bit elements at the same time, assuming that $16 \mid n$. To apply the same instructions for Strassen to the submatrices with only $n/2$ rows, we would require that $16 \mid (n/2)$. This is true for $n = 640, 1344$ but does not hold for $n = 976$. This is easily solved by padding $\mathbf{A}$ with zero columns which has a minor effect on the performance compared to the other parameter sets.

In the following, we only consider one-level Strassen and analyze its performance. That is, we reduce the matrix multiplication to 7 multiplications of half-size row and column dimensions that we perform with RWCF. More levels of recursion can of course be considered, but it is not a priori clear that Strassen will outperform other algorithms for the dimensions of FrodoKEM (even for a single recursion level), as its improvements are only guaranteed asymptotically. As we will see in Sect. 4, it outperforms the current FrodoKEM implementation but does not improve over RWCF itself. Nevertheless, even if Strassen does not scale fast enough to be relevant for single FrodoKEM, it can still be useful to explore its application for *batching*, as we show in Sect. 4.2.

4   Implementation and Benchmark Results

In this section we discuss the comparative performance for the different approaches of implementing the FrodoKEM matrix multiplication. The performance results have been obtained when running on a single core of the 12-core AMD Ryzen 9 3900XT running at a base clock of 3.8GHz. We consider both the setting where a single key exchange or encryption is performed, as well as their batched analogues where multiple keys are handled in parallel. For this section we focus on the results for AES128 only: as this is much faster on the selected platform, the significance of the matrix multiplication is higher and therefore so is the significance of our speed-ups. We expect speed-ups for SHAKE128 can be obtained on platforms with access to a hardware accelerator, but these are less significant given that this approach does not have the inefficiency of a matrix transposition. Both versions have been integrated into the reference implementation of the FrodoKEM submission.[1]

4.1   Performance Results

The performance measurements for all three FrodoKEM parameter sets are summarized in Table 2. This shows the performance in 10^3 cycles of the individual matrix multiplication routines $\mathbf{A} \cdot \mathbf{S} + \mathbf{E}$ (frodo_mul_add_as_plus_e) and $\mathbf{S}' \cdot \mathbf{A} + \mathbf{E}'$ (frodo_mul_add_sa_plus_e). These routines consist of two computationally significant steps: generation of the matrix elements of $\mathbf{A}$ using AES128 and multiplying the resulting matrix with $\mathbf{S}$ or $\mathbf{S}'$. Although a fresh $\mathbf{A}$ is generated for each IND-CPA encryption or key exchange, in a KEM setting where a static key pair is used one can pre-compute $\mathbf{A}$ and store for encapsulation and

---

[1] https://github.com/microsoft/PQCrypto-LWEKE commit 5c3123f.

decapsulation. Therefore we distinguish two separate cases: excluding (labeled "pre") and including the generation time of the matrix elements from $\mathbf{A}$ using AES128. Note that the algorithms described in Sect. 3 only impact the matrix *multiplication* step and not the *generation*, so have relatively more impact when $\mathbf{A}$ is not freshly generated. For completeness, we also include the total cost of key generation, encapsulation and decapsulation, which generate $\mathbf{A}$ on-the-fly to align with the reference implementation. Again, the impact on encapsulation and decapsulation is greater by storing $\mathbf{A}$ in advance.

Firstly, we highlight an interesting observation about the reference implementation (using AVX instructions) of FrodoKEM (the "x64" column in Table 2). When comparing the two matrix multiplication routines, we see that computing $\mathbf{A}\cdot\mathbf{S}+\mathbf{E}$ is up to 1.4 times faster than $\mathbf{S}'\cdot\mathbf{A}+\mathbf{E}'$ if the generation of $\mathbf{A}$ is included, and up to 1.9 times faster if $\mathbf{A}$ is pre-generated. The latter speed-up is almost fully determined by the matrix multiplication, but is surprisingly large since the dimensions of the multiplications are exactly the same (though transposed). Using the RWCF algorithm from Sect. 3.3 for $\mathbf{S}'\cdot\mathbf{A}+\mathbf{E}'$ leads to a speed-up of up to 1.4 times including generation of $\mathbf{A}$, or of up to 2.0 times excluding it, when compared to the reference implementation. Indeed, the RWCF approach reduces the cost of $\mathbf{S}'\cdot\mathbf{A}+\mathbf{E}'$ so that it is essentially equal to computing $\mathbf{A}\cdot\mathbf{S}+\mathbf{E}$, which should be expected for multiplications of equal dimensions. Overall, employing the RWCF approach leads to an up to 22% improvement in encapsulation or decapsulation when $\mathbf{A}$ is generated on-the-fly, while not affecting key generation since it only computes $\mathbf{A}\cdot\mathbf{S}+\mathbf{E}$.

Interestingly, the Strassen implementation also outperforms the ×64 implementation. This approach uses a single level of Strassen and then reverts to the RWCF approach for multiplying the smaller sub-matrices. This explains why Strassen outperforms x64 and not the RWCF approach. For the best overall performance one should use the RWCF approach. We expect that these results carry over to other approaches, compared to AES128, to generate the matrix elements. One such example is when using SHAKE128 as outlined in Sect. 2.1, but as noted before the relative impact of our method is less significant in this case.

4.2 Batching

Let us consider the setting of batch cryptography [19]. The main idea is to reduce the computational burden of an entity which receives multiple (i.e., a batch of) cryptographic operations. It might be possible to process this batch of computation and take advantage of some arithmetic or algorithmic advantages that increase the latency (compared to a single request) but also increase the overall throughput (the number of cryptographic operations per second) to ensure an overall increase of computation on this batch processing system. Many of such approaches have been proposed such as batch verification of RSA signatures [21], ECDSA batch signature verification [24–26] and batch Diffie-Hellman key agreement [7].

Table 2. Performance numbers of the matrix multiplication methods with and without ("pre") generation of the elements using AES128. In parentheses the relative performance against the reference implementation "×64". The numbers are reported in 10^3 cycles and an average over 1000 runs.

Function	×64	Strassen	RWCF
FrodoKEM-640			
frodo_mul_add_as_plus_e *(pre)*	208	212 (1.02)	212 (1.02)
frodo_mul_add_sa_plus_e *(pre)*	396	282 (0.71)	202 (0.51)
frodo_mul_add_as_plus_e	473	477 (1.01)	477 (1.01)
frodo_mul_add_sa_plus_e	661	547 (0.83)	467 (0.70)
crypto_kem_keypair	902	902 (1.00)	903 (1.00)
crypto_kem_enc	1 275	1 174 (0.92)	1 068 (0.84)
crypto_kem_dec	1 232	1 121 (0.91)	1 025 (0.83)
FrodoKEM-976			
frodo_mul_add_as_plus_e *(pre)*	507	508 (1.00)	501 (0.99)
frodo_mul_add_sa_plus_e *(pre)*	931	759 (0.82)	493 (0.53)
frodo_mul_add_as_plus_e	1 095	1 096 (1.00)	1 089 (0.99)
frodo_mul_add_sa_plus_e	1 519	1 347 (0.89)	1 081 (0.71)
crypto_kem_keypair	1 718	1 727 (1.01)	1 712 (1.00)
crypto_kem_enc	2 398	2 246 (0.94)	1 955 (0.82)
crypto_kem_dec	2 310	2 141 (0.93)	1 850 (0.80)
FrodoKEM-1344			
frodo_mul_add_as_plus_e *(pre)*	1 060	1 031 (0.97)	1 024 (0.97)
frodo_mul_add_sa_plus_e *(pre)*	1 888	1 412 (0.75)	1 012 (0.54)
frodo_mul_add_as_plus_e	2 140	2 111 (0.99)	2 104 (0.98)
frodo_mul_add_sa_plus_e	2 968	2 492 (0.84)	2 092 (0.70)
crypto_kem_keypair	3 070	3 023 (0.98)	3 017 (0.98)
crypto_kem_enc	4 279	3 777 (0.88)	3 363 (0.79)
crypto_kem_dec	4 130	3 634 (0.88)	3 221 (0.78)

In Frodo, the seed $\mathsf{seed_A}$ used to generate the large public matrix $\mathbf{A}$ (on-the-fly) is part of the *public-key*. This means that when Frodo is used as a public-key encryption scheme multiple devices or clients can encrypt messages to be sent to the same server which can then perform a *batch decryption* on all these ciphertexts which use the same matrix $\mathbf{A}$. Along similar lines multiple clients can start the key encapsulation mechanism (using FrodoKEM) with the same clients using the same $\mathsf{seed_A}$ and corresponding matrix $\mathbf{A}$. This allows for *batch decapsulation* on the server. This batching technique enables the server to use the same public matrix $\mathbf{A}$ for multiple requests and increase the dimension in the matrix multiplication $\mathbf{S} \cdot \mathbf{A}$ by considering multiple matrices $\mathbf{S}$ at once.

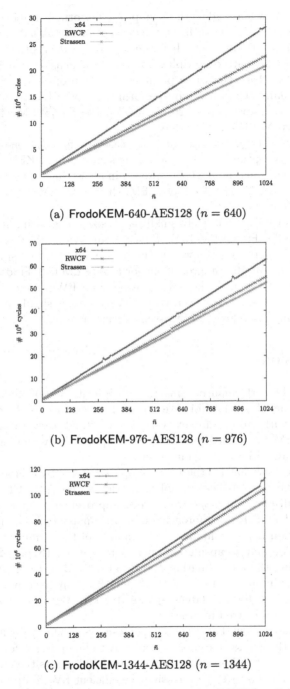

(a) FrodoKEM-640-AES128 ($n = 640$)

(b) FrodoKEM-976-AES128 ($n = 976$)

(c) FrodoKEM-1344-AES128 ($n = 1344$)

Fig. 2. The performance of the row-wise cache-friendly (RWCF) and Strassen matrix multiplication (dimensions $\bar{n} \times n$ with $n \times n$) when varying $\bar{n}$. Note that the dimension $\bar{n}$ in this case represents $\bar{n}/8$ batch computations.

We investigate when (and if) the asymptotic performance gain of the Strassen algorithm becomes visible in such a batch decryption or batch decapsulation approach. Performance results when batching up to 128 decryptions or decapsulations (and therefore matrix multiplications up to dimension $\bar{n} = 8 \cdot 128 = 1024$) are shown in Fig. 2 for the three parameters sets proposed in FrodoKEM. As expected eventually Strassen will outperform the FrodoKEM approach in all settings. We see an improvement of 26, 16 and 16% for FrodoKEM-640, FrodoKEM-976 and FrodoKEM-1344, respectively.

This shows that for the batching use case, performing one-level Strassen becomes a viable option for the parameter sizes of FrodoKEM. Strassen also eventually outperforms the RWCF approach in all settings. The cross-over point is at $\bar{n}$ equal to 120, 152, 64, for FrodoKEM-640, FrodoKEM-976 and FrodoKEM-1344, respectively.

This means that for relatively small batch sizes (e.g., using a batch of only 8 computations for FrodoKEM-1344) Strassen already starts to outperform the straightforward approaches. However, the maximum observed speed-up is relatively small: a 9, 5 or 10% improvement for FrodoKEM-640, FrodoKEM-976 and FrodoKEM-1344. Of course, the difference between RWCF and Strassen grows with the batch size used. For even larger batch sizes it should also be checked whether applying more levels of Strassen is even faster.

5   Conclusions

We evaluated the performance of matrix multiplication approaches in the cryptographic setting of FrodoKEM. We consider both optimized "naïve" matrix multiplication with cubic complexity (i.e., the straightforward algorithm used in the FrodoKEM submission and the RWCF approach) as well as the Strassen multiplication algorithm (using one level).

Our results show that for the proposed parameter sets of FrodoKEM we can improve over the state-of-the-art implementation with the RWCF approach. For the matrix multiplication alone we achieve improvements up to 30% over the straightforward FrodoKEM approach (and are almost twice as fast when the matrix generation is pre-computed). The impact of these improvements on the full encapsulation and decapsulation operations are slightly over 20%. Interestingly, performing the encapsulation and decapsulation with the Strassen approach also gains improvements over the FrodoKEM approach, with an improvement of up to 12% for the largest parameter set. We note that the RWCF approach is to be preferred in practice.

We additionally show that for batching use-cases, where many inputs are processed at once, the Strassen approach is already to be preferred for small batches of size 8. For a practically-relevant batch size of 128 inputs the observed speed-up is in the range of 5 to 11% over using the efficient RWCF approach, growing with the batch size. Over the current FrodoKEM approach the improvement is even in the range of 19 to 35%.

This work therefore both improves on the FrodoKEM multiplication approach, and shows that the Strassen method is relevant for FrodoKEM parameter in practice.

References

1. Adrian, D., et al.: Imperfect forward secrecy: how Diffie-Hellman fails in practice. In: Ray, I., Li, N., Kruegel, C. (eds.) ACM CCS 2015, pp. 5–17. ACM Press (2015). https://doi.org/10.1145/2810103.2813707

2. Ajtai, M.: Generating hard instances of lattice problems (extended abstract). In: 28th ACM STOC, pp. 99–108. ACM Press (1996). https://doi.org/10.1145/237814.237838

3. Ajtai, M., Dwork, C.: A public-key cryptosystem with worst-case/average-case equivalence. In: 29th ACM STOC, pp. 284–293. ACM Press (1997). https://doi.org/10.1145/258533.258604

4. Alkim, E., et al.: FrodoKEM: Learning with Errors Key Encapsulations (2021). https://github.com/microsoft/PQCrypto-LWEKE

5. Alkim, E., Ducas, L., Pöppelmann, T., Schwabe, P.: Post-quantum key exchange - a new hope. In: Holz, T., Savage, S. (eds.) USENIX Security 2016, pp. 327–343. USENIX Association (2016)

6. Alman, J., Williams, V.V.: A refined laser method and faster matrix multiplication. In: Marx, D. (ed.) Symposium on Discrete Algorithms - SODA, pp. 522–539. SIAM (2021). https://doi.org/10.1137/1.9781611976465.32

7. Beller, M.J., Yacobi, Y.: Batch Diffie-Hellman key agreement systems and their application to portable communications. In: Rueppel, R.A. (ed.) EUROCRYPT 1992. LNCS, vol. 658, pp. 208–220. Springer, Heidelberg (1993). https://doi.org/10.1007/3-540-47555-9_19

8. Bernstein, D.J., et al.: NTRU Prime. Technical report, National Institute of Standards and Technology (2020). https://csrc.nist.gov/projects/post-quantum-cryptography/round-3-submissions

9. Bernstein, D.J., Chuengsatiansup, C., Lange, T., van Vredendaal, C.: NTRU prime: reducing attack surface at low cost. In: Adams, C., Camenisch, J. (eds.) SAC 2017. LNCS, vol. 10719, pp. 235–260. Springer, Cham (2018). https://doi.org/10.1007/978-3-319-72565-9_12

10. Bos, J.W., et al.: Frodo: Take off the ring! Practical, quantum-secure key exchange from LWE. In: Weippl, E.R., Katzenbeisser, S., Kruegel, C., Myers, A.C., Halevi, S. (eds.) ACM CCS 2016, pp. 1006–1018. ACM Press (2016). https://doi.org/10.1145/2976749.2978425

11. Bos, J.W., et al.: CRYSTALS - kyber: a cca-secure module-lattice-based KEM. In: 2018 IEEE European Symposium on Security and Privacy - Euro S&P, pp. 353–367. IEEE (2018). https://doi.org/10.1109/EuroSP.2018.00032

12. Bottinelli, P., Lambert, R.: Accelerating V2X cryptography through batch operations. Cryptology ePrint Archive, Report 2019/887 (2019). https://eprint.iacr.org/2019/887

13. Brakerski, Z., Gentry, C., Vaikuntanathan, V.: (Leveled) fully homomorphic encryption without bootstrapping. In: Goldwasser, S. (ed.) ITCS 2012, pp. 309–325. ACM (2012). https://doi.org/10.1145/2090236.2090262

14. Bundesamt für Sicherheit in der Informationstechnik: Cryptographic mechanisms: Recommendations and key lengths. Bsi tr-02102-1, Federal Office for Information Security (2021). https://www.bsi.bund.de/SharedDocs/Downloads/EN/BSI/Publications/TechGuidelines/TG02102/BSI-TR-02102-1.pdf

15. Chen, C., et al.: NTRU. Technical report, National Institute of Standards and Technology (2020). https://csrc.nist.gov/projects/post-quantum-cryptography/round-3-submissions

16. Coppersmith, D., Winograd, S.: Matrix multiplication via arithmetic progressions. In: Aho, A. (ed.) 19th ACM STOC, pp. 1–6. ACM Press (1987). https://doi.org/10.1145/28395.28396

17. D'Anvers, J.-P., Karmakar, A., Sinha Roy, S., Vercauteren, F.: Saber: module-LWR based key exchange, CPA-secure encryption and CCA-secure KEM. In: Joux, A., Nitaj, A., Rachidi, T. (eds.) AFRICACRYPT 2018. LNCS, vol. 10831, pp. 282–305. Springer, Cham (2018). https://doi.org/10.1007/978-3-319-89339-6_16

18. D'Anvers, J.P., et al.: SABER. Technical report, National Institute of Standards and Technology (2020). https://csrc.nist.gov/projects/post-quantum-cryptography/round-3-submissions

19. Fiat, A.: Batch RSA. In: Brassard, G. (ed.) CRYPTO 1989. LNCS, vol. 435, pp. 175–185. Springer, New York (1990). https://doi.org/10.1007/0-387-34805-0_17

20. Goto, K., van de Geijn, R.A.: Anatomy of high-performance matrix multiplication. ACM Trans. Math. Softw. **34**(3) (2008). https://doi.org/10.1145/1356052.1356053

21. Harn, L.: Batch verifying multiple RSA digital signatures. Electron. Lett. **34**, 1219–1220 (1998)

22. Huang, J., Smith, T.M., Henry, G.M., van de Geijn, R.A.: Strassen's algorithm reloaded. In: West, J., Pancake, C.M. (eds.) International Conference for High Performance Computing, Networking, Storage and Analysis - SC, pp. 690–701. IEEE Computer Society (2016). https://doi.org/10.1109/SC.2016.58

23. Intel: Advanced vector extensions programming reference (2011). https://software.intel.com/content/dam/develop/external/us/en/documents/36945

24. Karati, S., Das, A.: Faster batch verification of standard ECDSA signatures using summation polynomials. In: Boureanu, I., Owesarski, P., Vaudenay, S. (eds.) ACNS 2014. LNCS, vol. 8479, pp. 438–456. Springer, Cham (2014). https://doi.org/10.1007/978-3-319-07536-5_26

25. Karati, S., Das, A., Roychowdhury, D., Bellur, B., Bhattacharya, D., Iyer, A.: Batch verification of ECDSA signatures. In: Mitrokotsa, A., Vaudenay, S. (eds.) AFRICACRYPT 2012. LNCS, vol. 7374, pp. 1–18. Springer, Heidelberg (2012). https://doi.org/10.1007/978-3-642-31410-0_1

26. Karati, S., Das, A., Roychowdhury, D., Bellur, B., Bhattacharya, D., Iyer, A.: New algorithms for batch verification of standard ECDSA signatures. J. Cryptogr. Eng. **4**(4), 237–258 (2014). https://doi.org/10.1007/s13389-014-0082-x

27. Koblitz, N.: Elliptic curve cryptosystems. Math. Comput. **48**, 203–209 (1987)

28. Langlois, A., Stehlé, D.: Worst-case to average-case reductions for module lattices. Des. Codes Cryptogr. **75**(3), 565–599 (2014). https://doi.org/10.1007/s10623-014-9938-4

29. Lyubashevsky, V., Peikert, C., Regev, O.: On ideal lattices and learning with errors over rings. In: Gilbert, H. (ed.) EUROCRYPT 2010. LNCS, vol. 6110, pp. 1–23. Springer, Heidelberg (2010). https://doi.org/10.1007/978-3-642-13190-5_1

30. Miller, V.S.: Use of elliptic curves in cryptography. In: Williams, H.C. (ed.) CRYPTO 1985. LNCS, vol. 218, pp. 417–426. Springer, Heidelberg (1986). https://doi.org/10.1007/3-540-39799-X_31

31. Naehrig, M., et al.: FrodoKEM. Technical report, National Institute of Standards and Technology (2020). https://csrc.nist.gov/projects/post-quantum-cryptography/round-3-submissions
32. National Institute of Standards and Technology: Post-quantum cryptography standardization. https://csrc.nist.gov/Projects/Post-Quantum-Cryptography/Post-Quantum-Cryptography-Standardization
33. Peikert, C.: A decade of lattice cryptography. Found. Trends Theor. Comput. Sci. **10**(4), 283–424 (2016). https://doi.org/10.1561/0400000074
34. Peikert, C., Regev, O., Stephens-Davidowitz, N.: Pseudorandomness of ring-LWE for any ring and modulus. In: Hatami, H., McKenzie, P., King, V. (eds.) 49th ACM STOC, pp. 461–473. ACM Press (2017). https://doi.org/10.1145/3055399.3055489
35. Proos, J., Zalka, C.: Shor's discrete logarithm quantum algorithm for elliptic curves. Quant. Inf. Comput. **3**, 317–344 (2003). https://cds.cern.ch/record/602816
36. Regev, O.: On lattices, learning with errors, random linear codes, and cryptography. In: Gabow, H.N., Fagin, R. (eds.) 37th ACM STOC, pp. 84–93. ACM Press (2005). https://doi.org/10.1145/1060590.1060603
37. Rivest, R.L., Shamir, A., Adleman, L.M.: A method for obtaining digital signatures and public-key cryptosystems. Commun. Assoc. Comput. Mach **21**(2), 120–126 (1978)
38. Schwabe, P., et al.: CRYSTALS-KYBER. Technical report, National Institute of Standards and Technology (2020). https://csrc.nist.gov/projects/post-quantum-cryptography/round-3-submissions
39. Shor, P.W.: Algorithms for quantum computation: discrete logarithms and factoring. In: 35th FOCS, pp. 124–134. IEEE Computer Society Press (1994). https://doi.org/10.1109/SFCS.1994.365700
40. Smith, T.M., van de Geijn, R.A., Smelyanskiy, M., Hammond, J.R., Van Zee, F.G.: Anatomy of high-performance many-threaded matrix multiplication. In: IEEE International Parallel and Distributed Processing Symposium, pp. 1049–1059. IEEE Computer Society (2014). https://doi.org/10.1109/IPDPS.2014.110
41. Strassen, V.: Gaussian elimination is not optimal. Numerische mathematik **13**(4), 354–356 (1969)
42. Van Zee, F.G., van de Geijn, R.A.: BLIS: A framework for rapidly instantiating BLAS functionality. ACM Trans. Math. Softw. **41**(3), 14:1-14:33 (2015). https://doi.org/10.1145/2764454

Signatures

BlindOR: an Efficient Lattice-Based Blind Signature Scheme from OR-Proofs

Nabil Alkeilani Alkadri$^{(\boxtimes)}$, Patrick Harasser, and Christian Janson

Technische Universität Darmstadt, Darmstadt, Germany
{nabil.alkadri,patrick.harasser,christian.janson}@tu-darmstadt.de

Abstract. An OR-proof is a protocol that enables a user to prove the possession of a witness for one of two (or more) statements, without revealing which one. Abe and Okamoto (CRYPTO 2000) used this technique to build a partially blind signature scheme whose security is based on the hardness of the discrete logarithm problem. Inspired by their approach, we present BlindOR, an efficient blind signature scheme from OR-proofs based on lattices over modules. Using OR-proofs allows us to reduce the security of our scheme from the MLWE and MSIS problems, yielding a much more efficient solution compared to previous works.

Keywords: Blind signatures · OR-proof · Lattice-based cryptography

1 Introduction

Blind signature schemes are a fundamental cryptographic primitive. First introduced by Chaum [9] in the context of an anonymous e-cash system, they have since become an essential building block in many applications such as anonymous credentials, e-voting, and blockchain protocols. They have been standardized as *ISO/IEC 18370*, and were deployed in real-life applications such as Microsoft's *U-Prove* technology and smart card devices produced by Gemalto.

In a blind signature scheme, a user holding a message m interacts with a signer to generate a blind signature on m under the signer's secret key. The scheme is required to satisfy two security properties called *blindness* and *one-more unforgeability* [16,19]. Informally, the first condition means that the signer gets no information about m during the signing process, while the latter ensures that the user cannot generate signatures without interacting with the signer.

In an effort to develop practical blind signature schemes from a diverse range of assumptions (in particular, those conjectured to be secure against quantum attacks), various schemes based on lattice problems have been proposed. The first such scheme by Rückert [20] can be seen as an important step in carrying the core design of classical constructions based on the discrete logarithm problem [19] over to the lattice setting. The same design principle was then adopted in subsequent works, *e.g.*, by Alkeilani Alkadri *et al.* [3,4], where the scheme BLAZE and its successor BLAZE$^+$ have been proposed and shown to be practical.

© Springer Nature Switzerland AG 2021
M. Conti et al. (Eds.): CANS 2021, LNCS 13099, pp. 95–115, 2021.
https://doi.org/10.1007/978-3-030-92548-2_6

Recently, Hauck *et al.* [15] pointed out that the proof of the one-more unforgeability property, originally by Pointcheval and Stern for a discrete logarithm based construction [19] and later reproposed by Rückert for his lattice-based scheme [20], has not been adapted correctly to this new setting. Indeed, the main idea of the reduction in [19] is to select a secret key sk and then run the forger with the related public key pk, which represents an instance of a computationally hard problem that admits more than one solution. In other words, pk is related to more than one sk, and the forger cannot distinguish which sk is used by the reduction. Note that it is crucial for the reduction to know a secret key because, unlike standard signature schemes, the signer cannot be simulated without one (otherwise the scheme would be universally forgeable [19]). After running the forger and obtaining an element z, the reduction rewinds the forger with the same random tape and partially different random oracle replies to obtain z'. The proof in [19] then uses a subtle argument to ensure that $z \neq z'$ with noticeable probability, which yields a solution to the underlying hard problem.

In lattice-based schemes, the hardness assumption underpinning security is usually the *Short Integer Solution* (SIS) problem or its ring variant RSIS. In this context, after obtaining z and z', the reduction simply returns $z - z'$ as a non-zero solution to (R)SIS. The problem, as discussed in [15], is that Rückert's argument is not sufficient to ensure that $z \neq z'$ with high probability, and further assumptions are required to guarantee that a transcript of the scheme with a given key sk can be preserved with high probability when switching to a different valid secret key. Based on this observation, Hauck *et al.* [15] extended the modular framework for blind signatures from linear functions given in [14] to the lattice setting, and provided a proof that covers the missing argument.

Unfortunately, as stated by the authors themselves, their work is mostly of theoretical interest. Indeed, the solution presented in [15] entails increasing the parameter sizes, so that their framework applies and yields a correct proof. In particular, the RSIS-based instantiation given in [15] has public and secret keys of size 443.75 KB and 4275 KB, respectively, and generates signatures of size 7915.52 KB. This leaves us in the regrettable position where all known (three-move) lattice-based blind signature schemes are either not backed by a correct security proof, or need impractically large parameters to achieve security.

Our Contributions. In this paper we make a significant progress towards constructing efficient and at the same time provably secure lattice-based blind signature schemes. We present BlindOR, a new blind signature scheme based on lattices over modules. Our scheme uses the OR-technique of Cramer *et al.* [10], a feature which allows us to sidestep the missing security argument pointed out in [15]. At a high level, an OR-proof is a Sigma protocol that proves the knowledge of a witness for one of two statements, without revealing which one. Therefore, the public key of our scheme consists of two statements (two instances of a hard lattice problem), and the secret key includes a witness for one of them. Consequently and for the first time, the hardness assumption underlying the public key does not have to "natively" admit multiple solutions, because the

OR-technique already forces there to be more than one (and thus simulation of signatures is still possible).

In particular, the public key of BlindOR consists of two instances of the *Module Learning with Errors* (MLWE) problem, which results in a much more efficient scheme. Signing is carried out by proving the possession of the witness included in the secret key. A user interacting with the signer blinds the two transcripts generated by the signer without being able to distinguish for which instance the signer holds a witness. We capture these blinding steps in a set of algorithms and show that BlindOR is statistically blind. The one-more unforgeability of our scheme is proven in the random oracle model (ROM) assuming the hardness of both MLWE and MSIS (the module version of SIS). The reduction creates one instance of the hard problem with a witness in order to simulate the signing oracle, and tries to solve the other instance, which is given to the reduction as input. That is, the reduction does not know a witness for its input. This is analogous to the security proof of standard lattice-based signature schemes, and hence no further conditions are required to ensure the correctness and success of the reduction with high probability. This is in contrast to previous lattice-based constructions of blind signatures, as observed in [15].

BlindOR uses techniques from prior works in order to reduce or even remove the number of restarts inherent in lattice-based schemes. More precisely, it uses the *partitioning and permutation* technique introduced in [3]. Given a hash function taking values in the challenge space of the underlying Sigma protocol, it allows to blind the hash values without having to carry out any security check or potential restart. Another advantage of this technique is that it can be used to construct OR-proofs based on lattice assumptions, because it allows to use a specified challenge space that has an abelian group structure, a crucial requirement for OR-proofs. This is in contrast to the typical challenge space used in current lattice-based schemes, which consists of polynomials from the ring $\mathbb{Z}[X]/\langle X^n+1\rangle$ with coefficients in $\{-1, 0, 1\}$ and a given Hamming weight. We also use the *trees of commitments* technique from [4] to remove the restarts induced by the user when blinding the signature generated by the signer. We extend this technique in BlindOR to reduce the potential restarts induced by the signer when computing signatures, which must be distributed independently from the secret key.

To demonstrate the efficiency of our scheme, we propose concrete parameters for BlindOR targeting 128 bits of security. The related key and signature sizes, the communication cost, and a comparison with the corresponding metrics for the scheme proposed by Hauck *et al.* [15] are given in Table 1. In summary, although our scheme requires twice as many public key and signature parts, which is inherent to using OR-proofs, it yields smaller sizes compared to the provably secure construction from [15], resulting in a more efficient scheme overall.

We remark that the security of our scheme can easily be extended to the stronger security notions of *selective failure blindness* [8] and *honest-user unforgeability* [21]. This is established by signing a commitment to the message instead of the message itself [12,21]. However, and similar to [15], it is still unclear how to prove the blindness property under a maliciously generated key pair [11].

Table 1. A comparison between BlindOR and the scheme introduced in [15] in terms of key and signature sizes and communication cost. Numbers are given in kilobytes (KB). The related parameters are given in Table 3 and [15, Figure 9].

Scheme	Public key	Secret key	Signature	Communication
BlindOR	10.3	1.7	17.2	375.6
[15]	443.75	4275	7915.52	34037.25

Related Work. Our construction is inspired by the work of Abe and Okamoto [1], who used OR-proofs to build partially blind signatures with security based on the hardness of the discrete logarithm problem. Observe that we cannot simply convert their scheme to the lattice setting, as this would force us to use MSIS (instead of MLWE) and result in an inefficient scheme. The change to MLWE is possible because there is no common information to consider in our case.

Hauck *et al.* [15] showed that all lattice-based constructions of blind signatures from Sigma protocols (or canonical identification schemes) prior to their framework, such as [3,20], do not have a valid security argument. Furthermore, Alkeilani Alkadri *et al.* [3] showed that all two-round lattice-based blind signature schemes based on preimage sampleable trapdoor functions are insecure.

Recently, Agrawal *et al.* [2] made a step towards practical two-round lattice-based blind signatures. They improved the two-round construction of Garg *et al.* [13] which is based on general complexity assumptions, and *degraded* it to rely on the ROM. This allows them to avoid complexity leveraging, the main source of inefficiency in [13]. However, as pointed out by the authors, there are some challenges left before this approach becomes practical. For instance, the scheme requires the homomorphic evaluation of a specific signing algorithm that relies on the ROM. In practice, this must be instantiated with a cryptographic hash function that can be evaluated homomorphically. Finding such a function is still an open problem. We refer to [2, Section 6.3] for more details and discussions on the limitations of their construction.

2   Preliminaries

Notation. We denote by $\mathbb{N}$, $\mathbb{Z}$, and $\mathbb{R}$ the sets of natural numbers, integers, and real numbers, respectively. If $k \in \mathbb{N}$, we let $[k] := \{1, \ldots, k\}$. For $q \in \mathbb{N}$, we write $\mathbb{Z}_q$ to denote the ring of integers modulo q with representatives in $\left[-\frac{q}{2}, \frac{q}{2}\right) \cap \mathbb{Z}$. If n is a fixed power of 2, we define the ring $R := \mathbb{Z}[X]/\langle X^n + 1\rangle$ and its quotient $R_q := R/qR$. Elements in R and R_q are denoted by regular font letters. Column vectors with coefficients in R or R_q are denoted by bold lower-case letters, while bold upper-case letters are matrices. We let $\mathbf{I}_k$ denote the identity matrix of dimension k, and $\mathbb{T}_\kappa^n$ the subset of R_q containing all polynomials with coefficients in $\{-1, 0, 1\}$ and Hamming weight κ. The ℓ_2 and ℓ_∞

norms of an element $a = \sum_{i=0}^{n-1} a_i X^i \in R$ are defined by $\|a\| := (\sum_{i=0}^{n-1} |a_i|^2)^{1/2}$ and $\|a\|_\infty := \max_i |a_i|$, respectively. Similarly, for $\mathbf{b} = (b_1, \ldots, b_k)^t \in R^k$, we let $\|\mathbf{b}\| := (\sum_{i=1}^{k} \|b_i\|^2)^{1/2}$ and $\|\mathbf{b}\|_\infty := \max_i \|b_i\|_\infty$. All logarithms are to base 2.

If D is a distribution, we write $x \leftarrow_\$ D$ to denote that x is sampled according to D. For a finite set S, we also write $x \leftarrow_\$ S$ if x is chosen from the uniform distribution over S. The *statistical distance* between two distributions X and Y over a countable set S is defined by $\Delta(X, Y) := \frac{1}{2} \sum_{s \in S} |\Pr[X = s] - \Pr[Y = s]|$. For $\varepsilon > 0$ we say that X and Y are ε-*statistically close* if $\Delta(X, Y) \leq \varepsilon$.

We denote the security parameter by $\lambda \in \mathbb{N}$, and abbreviate probabilistic polynomial-time by PPT and deterministic polynomial-time by DPT. For a probabilistic algorithm A, we write $y \leftarrow_\$ \mathsf{A}^O(x)$ to denote that A returns y when run on input x with access to oracle O, and $y \in \mathsf{A}^O(x)$ if y is a possible output of $\mathsf{A}^O(x)$. To make the randomness $r \in \mathcal{RS}_\mathsf{A}$ on which A is run explicit, we use the notation $y \leftarrow \mathsf{A}^O(x; r)$. If A and B are interactive algorithms, we write $(x, y) \leftarrow_\$ \langle \mathsf{A}(a), \mathsf{B}(b) \rangle$ to denote the joint execution of A and B in an interactive protocol with private inputs a for A and b for B, as well as private outputs x for A and y for B. Accordingly, we write $\mathsf{A}^{\langle \cdot, \mathsf{B}(b) \rangle^k}(a)$ if A can invoke up to k executions of the protocol with B.

The *random oracle model* (ROM) [7] is a model of computation where all occurrences of a hash function are replaced by a *random oracle* H, *i.e.*, a function chosen at random from the space of all functions $\{0, 1\}^* \to \{0, 1\}^{\ell_\mathsf{H}}$ for some $\ell_\mathsf{H} \in \mathbb{N}$, to which all involved parties have oracle access. This means that, for every new oracle query, H returns a truly random response from $\{0, 1\}^{\ell_\mathsf{H}}$, and every repeated query consistently yields the same output.

Relations, Sigma Protocols, and OR-Proofs

Definition 1. *A* relation *is a tuple* $\mathcal{R} = (\mathcal{R}.\mathsf{PGen}, \mathcal{R}.\mathsf{RSet}, \mathcal{R}.\mathsf{Gen})$, *where:*

$\mathcal{R}.\mathsf{PGen}$ *is the* parameter generation algorithm *which, on input the security parameter* $\lambda \in \mathbb{N}$, *returns public parameters* pp.

$\mathcal{R}.\mathsf{RSet}$ *is the* relation set, *a collection of sets indexed by* $pp \in \mathcal{R}.\mathsf{PGen}(1^\lambda)$.

$\mathcal{R}.\mathsf{Gen}$ *is the* instance generator algorithm *which, on input* $pp \in \mathcal{R}.\mathsf{PGen}(1^\lambda)$ *and* $b \in \{0, 1\}$, *returns a pair* $(x, w) \in \mathcal{R}.\mathsf{RSet}(pp)$ *if* $b = 1$ *(where* x *is called a* yes-instance *for* $\mathcal{R}$ *w.r.t.* pp *and* w *a corresponding* witness*), and an element* x *if* $b = 0$ *(called a* no-instance *for* $\mathcal{R}$ *w.r.t.* pp*).*

We now define the OR-relation $\mathcal{R}_{\mathsf{OR}}$ on a relation $\mathcal{R}$. Informally, for $\lambda \in \mathbb{N}$ and public parameters $pp \in \mathcal{R}.\mathsf{PGen}(1^\lambda)$, a yes-instance for $\mathcal{R}_{\mathsf{OR}}$ w.r.t. pp is a pair of values (x_0, x_1), each a yes-instance for $\mathcal{R}$ w.r.t. pp. A witness for such an instance is a witness for one of the two coordinates, *i.e.* a pair (d, w) with $d \in \{0, 1\}$ and w a witness for x_d. In contrast, a no-instance for $\mathcal{R}_{\mathsf{OR}}$ consists of a pair (x_0, x_1), where at least one coordinate is a no-instance for $\mathcal{R}$ w.r.t. pp.

Definition 2. *Let* $\mathcal{R}$ *be a relation. The* OR-relation on $\mathcal{R}$ *is the relation* $\mathcal{R}_{\mathsf{OR}}$ *whose parameter generation algorithm is* $\mathcal{R}_{\mathsf{OR}}.\mathsf{PGen} := \mathcal{R}.\mathsf{PGen}$, *whose relation set is* $\mathcal{R}_{\mathsf{OR}}.\mathsf{RSet}(pp) := \{((x_0, x_1), (d, w)) \mid (x_d, w), (x_{1-d}, \cdot) \in \mathcal{R}.\mathsf{Gen}(pp, 1)\}$, *and whose instance generator* $\mathcal{R}_{\mathsf{OR}}.\mathsf{Gen}$ *is given in Fig. 1.*

$\mathcal{R}_{\mathsf{OR}}.\mathsf{Gen}(pp, b)$:

11: **if** $b = 0$ **then**

12:    $d, d' \leftarrow\!\!\!\text{\$} \{0, 1\}$

13:    $x_d \leftarrow\!\!\!\text{\$} \mathcal{R}.\mathsf{Gen}(pp, 0), \quad x_{1-d} \leftarrow\!\!\!\text{\$} \mathcal{R}.\mathsf{Gen}(pp, d')$

14:    **return** (x_0, x_1)

15: **else**

16:    $d \leftarrow\!\!\!\text{\$} \{0, 1\}$

17:    $(x_0, w_0) \leftarrow\!\!\!\text{\$} \mathcal{R}.\mathsf{Gen}(pp, 1), \quad (x_1, w_1) \leftarrow\!\!\!\text{\$} \mathcal{R}.\mathsf{Gen}(pp, 1)$

18:    $w \leftarrow w_d$

19:    **return** $((x_0, x_1), (d, w))$

Fig. 1. Definition of the instance generator $\mathcal{R}_{\mathsf{OR}}.\mathsf{Gen}$ of the OR-relation on $\mathcal{R}$. Note that in line 13 we slightly abuse notation: If $d' = 1$, we only consider the first component of the output, and ignore the witness in the second coordinate.

Definition 3. *Let $\mathcal{R}$ be a relation. A* Sigma protocol *for $\mathcal{R}$ is a tuple of algorithms $\Sigma = (\Sigma.\mathsf{P}, \Sigma.\mathsf{V}, \Sigma.\mathsf{Sim}, \Sigma.\mathsf{Ext}, \Sigma.\mathsf{ComRec})$, where:*

$\Sigma.\mathsf{P}$ *is an interactive algorithm, called* prover, *that consists of two algorithms $\Sigma.\mathsf{P} = (\Sigma.\mathsf{P}_1, \Sigma.\mathsf{P}_2)$, where:*
- *$\Sigma.\mathsf{P}_1$ is a PPT algorithm which, on input a set of public parameters pp and an instance-witness pair (x, w), returns a message cm, called the* commitment, *and a state $st_{\Sigma.\mathsf{P}}$.*
- *$\Sigma.\mathsf{P}_2$ is a DPT algorithm which, on input a set of public parameters pp, an instance-witness pair (x, w), the state information $st_{\Sigma.\mathsf{P}}$, and a verifier message ch, outputs a message rp, called the* response.

$\Sigma.\mathsf{V}$ *is an interactive algorithm, called* verifier, *that consists of two algorithms $\Sigma.\mathsf{V} = (\Sigma.\mathsf{V}_1, \Sigma.\mathsf{V}_2)$, where:*
- *$\Sigma.\mathsf{V}_1$ is a PPT algorithm which, on input a set of public parameters pp, an instance x, and a prover message cm, returns a message ch (called the* challenge*) sampled uniformly at random from a finite abelian group $\mathcal{C}(pp)$ (called the* challenge space*), as well as a state $st_{\Sigma.\mathsf{V}} = (cm, ch)$ consisting only of the received message and the sampled challenge.*
- *$\Sigma.\mathsf{V}_2$ is a DPT algorithm which, on input a set of public parameters pp, an instance x, the state information $st_{\Sigma.\mathsf{V}} = (cm, ch)$, and a prover message rp, outputs a pair (b, int) with $b \in \{0, 1\}$ and $int \in \mathbb{Z}$. We say that the verifier accepts the transcript if $b = 1$, and that it rejects if $b = 0$.*

$\Sigma.\mathsf{Sim}$ *is a PPT algorithm, called* simulator. *On input a set of public parameters pp, an instance x, and a challenge ch, it outputs a pair of messages (cm, rp).*

$\Sigma.\mathsf{Ext}$ *is a DPT algorithm, called* extractor. *On input a set of public parameters pp, an instance x, and two transcripts (cm, ch, rp) and (cm, ch', rp') such that $ch \neq ch'$ and $\Sigma.\mathsf{V}_2$ returns the same output $(1, int)$ in both cases, $\Sigma.\mathsf{Ext}$ outputs a string w such that $(x, w) \in \mathcal{R}.\mathsf{RSet}(pp)$.*

Σ.ComRec *is a DPT algorithm, called* commitment recovering *algorithm. On input a set of public parameters pp, an instance x, a challenge ch, and a response rp, it returns a message cm.*

If $\mathcal{R}$ is a relation, the Sigma protocols for $\mathcal{R}$ we consider must satisfy a few properties which we briefly describe in the following. The first one is correctness, saying that an honest protocol execution is likely to be accepted by the verifier. Next, there is a variant of the zero-knowledge property, where we require that on input an instance x and a randomly chosen challenge ch, the simulator be able to provide an authentic-looking transcript. Finally, we have soundness, saying that if the commitment recovering algorithm succeeds in finding a commitment, this commitment verifies for the given challenge and response.

We now consider the OR-combination of two Sigma protocols (*OR-proof*). It enables a prover P to show that it knows the witness of one of several statements, or that one out of many statements is true. Here, we restrict ourselves to the case where a prover holds two statements (x_0, x_1) and one witness w for x_d, with $d \in \{0,1\}$. The prover's goal is to convince the verifier that it holds a witness for one of the two statements, without revealing which one. This problem was first solved by Cramer *et al.* [10], and we now recall their construction.

Let $\mathcal{R}$ be a relation and Σ_0, Σ_1 be two Sigma protocols for $\mathcal{R}$. The construction of [10] allows to combine Σ_0 and Σ_1 into a new Sigma protocol $\Sigma_{\mathsf{OR}} = \mathsf{OR}[\Sigma_0, \Sigma_1]$ for the relation $\mathcal{R}_{\mathsf{OR}}$. The key idea of the construction is that the prover Σ_{OR}.P splits the challenge ch received by Σ_{OR}.V into two random parts $ch = ch_0 + ch_1$, and is able to provide accepting transcripts for both statements x_0 and x_1 for the respective challenge share. In more detail, for a given security parameter $\lambda \in \mathbb{N}$, public parameters $pp \in \mathcal{R}.\mathsf{PGen}(1^\lambda)$, and instance-witness pair $((x_0, x_1), (d, w)) \in \mathcal{R}_{\mathsf{OR}}.\mathsf{Gen}(pp, 1)$, the execution of Σ_{OR} proceeds as follows:

(a) The prover Σ_{OR}.P$_1$ starts with computing $(cm_d, st_{\Sigma_d.\mathsf{P}}) \leftarrow\!\!{\scriptstyle\$}\ \Sigma_d.\mathsf{P}_1(pp, x_d, w)$ and samples a challenge $ch_{1-d} \leftarrow\!\!{\scriptstyle\$}\ \mathcal{C}(pp)$. Next, it runs $(cm_{1-d}, rp_{1-d}) \leftarrow\!\!{\scriptstyle\$}$ $\Sigma_{1-d}.\mathsf{Sim}(pp, x_{1-d}, ch_{1-d})$ to complete the transcript of x_{1-d}. In case the simulation fails $(i.e.(cm_{1-d}, rp_{1-d}) = (\bot, \bot))$, the prover re-runs the simulator. Finally, it sets $st_{\Sigma_{\mathsf{OR}}.\mathsf{P}} \leftarrow (st_{\Sigma_d.\mathsf{P}}, ch_{1-d}, rp_{1-d})$ and sends (cm_0, cm_1) to the verifier Σ_{OR}.V$_1$.

(b) Upon receiving the commitments (cm_0, cm_1), Σ_{OR}.V$_1$ samples a random challenge from the challenge space, $i.e.ch \leftarrow\!\!{\scriptstyle\$}\ \mathcal{C}(pp)$, and sends it to Σ_{OR}.P$_2$. Finally, it sets its state to $st_{\Sigma_{\mathsf{OR}}.\mathsf{V}} \leftarrow (cm_0, cm_1, ch)$.

(c) After receiving the challenge ch, Σ_{OR}.P$_2$ sets $ch_d \leftarrow ch - ch_{1-d}$ and computes a response for x_d as $rp_d \leftarrow \Sigma_d.\mathsf{P}_2(pp, x_d, w, st_{\Sigma_d.\mathsf{P}}, ch_d)$. In case this computation fails $(i.e.rp_d = \bot)$, it also sets $rp_{1-d} \leftarrow \bot$. Otherwise, the prover sends the split challenges and responses to the verifier.

(d) After receiving (ch_0, ch_1, rp_0, rp_1) from the prover, Σ_{OR}.V$_2$ accepts if and only if the shares satisfy $ch = ch_0 + ch_1$ and both transcripts verify correctly.

For the remainder of the paper, we are interested in the situation where a Sigma protocol is combined with itself, *i.e.*, we obtain a new Sigma protocol $\Sigma_{\mathsf{OR}} = \mathsf{OR}[\Sigma, \Sigma]$ for the relation $\mathcal{R}_{\mathsf{OR}}$. One can show that this protocol inherits many properties of Σ, such as correctness and special honest-verifier zero-knowledge. An important property of Σ_{OR} is that it is witness indistinguishable, meaning that the verifier does not learn which particular witness was used to generate the proof.

Blind Signatures. We define blind signatures following the exposition of Hauck *et al.* [15], where the interaction between signer and user consists of three moves.

Definition 4. *A* blind signature scheme *is a tuple of polynomial-time algorithms* $\mathsf{BS} = (\mathsf{BS.PGen}, \mathsf{BS.KGen}, \mathsf{BS.S}, \mathsf{BS.U}, \mathsf{BS.Verify})$ *where:*

$\mathsf{BS.PGen}$ *is a PPT parameter generation algorithm that, on input the security parameter* $\lambda \in \mathbb{N}$, *returns a set of public parameters pp. We assume that the set pp identifies the message space* $\mathcal{M}(pp)$ *of the scheme.*

$\mathsf{BS.KGen}$ *is a PPT key generation algorithm that, on input a set of public parameters* $pp \in \mathsf{BS.PGen}(1^\lambda)$, *returns a public/secret key pair* (pk, sk).

$\mathsf{BS.S}$ *is an interactive algorithm, called* signer, *that consists of two algorithms:*
  – *The PPT algorithm* $\mathsf{BS.S_1}$ *takes as input a set of public parameters* pp *and a key pair* (pk, sk), *and returns the signer message* s_1 *and a state* st_S.
  – *The DPT algorithm* $\mathsf{BS.S_2}$ *takes as input a set of public parameters* pp, *a key pair* (pk, sk), *the state information* st_S, *and the user message* u_1, *and returns the next signer message* s_2.

$\mathsf{BS.U}$ *is an interactive algorithm, called* user, *that consists of two algorithms:*
  – *The PPT algorithm* $\mathsf{BS.U_1}$ *takes as input a set of public parameters* pp, *a public key* pk, *a message* $m \in \mathcal{M}(pp)$, *and a signer message* s_1, *and returns a user message* u_1 *and a state* st_U.
  – *The DPT algorithm* $\mathsf{BS.U_2}$ *takes as input a set of public parameters* pp, *a public key* pk, *a message* m, *a user state* st_U, *and a signer message* s_2, *and outputs a signature* sig. *We let* $sig = \bot$ *denote failure.*

$\mathsf{BS.Verify}$ *is a DPT verification algorithm that, upon receiving a set of public parameters* pp, *a public key* pk, *a message* m, *and a signature* sig *as input, outputs 1 if the signature is valid and 0 otherwise.*

Let $pp \in \mathsf{BS.PGen}(1^\lambda)$. We say that BS is $\mathsf{corr_{BS}}$-*correct* w.r.t. pp if $\mathsf{BS.Verify}$ validates honestly signed messages under honestly created keys with probability at least $1 - \mathsf{corr_{BS}}$. The security of blind signatures is defined by the notions blindness and one-more unforgeability [16,19].

Definition 5. *Let* BS *be a blind signature scheme,* $\lambda \in \mathbb{N}$ *and* $pp \in \mathsf{BS.PGen}(1^\lambda)$. *We say that* BS *is* (t, ε)-*blind w.r.t. pp if, for every adversarial signer* S^* *running in time at most* t *and working in modes* find, issue, *and* guess, *we have* $\mathbf{Adv}_{\mathsf{BS},\mathsf{S}^*}^{\mathrm{Blind}}(pp) := 2 \cdot |\Pr[\mathbf{Exp}_{\mathsf{BS},\mathsf{S}^*}^{\mathrm{Blind}}(pp) = 1] - \frac{1}{2}| \le \varepsilon$, *where the game* $\mathbf{Exp}_{\mathsf{BS},\mathsf{S}^*}^{\mathrm{Blind}}$ *is depicted in Fig. 2.* BS *is* ε-*statistically blind if it is* (t, ε)-*blind for every* t.

Definition 6. *Let* BS *be a blind signature scheme,* $\lambda \in \mathbb{N}$ *and* $pp \in \mathsf{BS.PGen}(1^\lambda)$. *We say that* BS *is* $(t, q_{\mathsf{Sign}}, \varepsilon)$-*one-more unforgeable w.r.t. pp if, for every adversarial user* U^* *running in time at most* t *and making at most* q_{Sign} *signing queries, we have* $\mathbf{Adv}_{\mathsf{BS},\mathsf{U}^*}^{\mathrm{OMUF}}(pp) := \Pr[\mathbf{Exp}_{\mathsf{BS},\mathsf{U}^*}^{\mathrm{OMUF}}(pp) = 1] \le \varepsilon$, *where the game* $\mathbf{Exp}_{\mathsf{BS},\mathsf{U}^*}^{\mathrm{OMUF}}$ *is depicted in Fig. 2.*

$\mathbf{Exp}_{\mathsf{BS},\mathsf{S}^*}^{\mathrm{Blind}}(pp)$:	$\mathbf{Exp}_{\mathsf{BS},\mathsf{U}^*}^{\mathrm{OMUF}}(pp)$:
11: $b \leftarrow_\$ \{0,1\}$	31: $(pk, sk) \leftarrow_\$ \mathsf{BS.KGen}(pp)$
12: $(pk, sk) \leftarrow_\$ \mathsf{BS.KGen}(pp)$	32: $((m_1, sig_1), \ldots, (m_l, sig_l)) \leftarrow_\$$
13: $(m_0, m_1, st_{\mathsf{find}}) \leftarrow_\$ \mathsf{S}^*(\mathsf{find}, pp, pk, sk)$	$\leftarrow_\$ \mathsf{U}^{*\langle \mathsf{BS.S}(pp,pk,sk),\cdot\rangle^\infty}(pp, pk)$
$\langle \cdot, \mathsf{BS.U}(pp,pk,m_b)\rangle^1,$	33: $k \leftarrow$ No. successful signing invocations
14: $st_{\mathsf{issue}} \leftarrow_\$ \mathsf{S}^{*\langle \cdot, \mathsf{BS.U}(pp,pk,m_{1-b})\rangle^1}(\mathsf{issue}, st_{\mathsf{find}})$	34: if $\forall i, j \in [l], \ i \neq j :$
15: $sig_b \leftarrow \mathsf{BS.U}(pp, pk, m_b)$	$(m_i \neq m_j) \wedge$
16: $sig_{1-b} \leftarrow \mathsf{BS.U}(pp, pk, m_{1-b})$	$(\mathsf{BS.Verify}(pp, pk, m_i, sig_i) = 1) \wedge$
17: if $(sig_0 = \perp) \vee (sig_1 = \perp)$ then	$(k + 1 = l)$ then
18: $(sig_0, sig_1) \leftarrow (\perp, \perp)$	35: return 1
19: $b^* \leftarrow_\$ \mathsf{S}^*(\mathsf{guess}, sig_0, sig_1, st_{\mathsf{issue}})$	36: return 0
20: if $b = b^*$ then	
21: return 1	
22: return 0	

Fig. 2. Definition of the experiments $\mathbf{Exp}_{\mathsf{BS},\mathsf{S}^*}^{\mathrm{Blind}}$ and $\mathbf{Exp}_{\mathsf{BS},\mathsf{U}^*}^{\mathrm{OMUF}}$.

Lattices and Gaussians

Definition 7. *Let $\mathcal{L} \subset \mathbb{R}^m$ be a lattice, $\sigma \in \mathbb{R}_{>0}$, and $\mathbf{c} \in \mathbb{R}^m$. The discrete Gaussian distribution over $\mathcal{L}$ with standard deviation σ and center $\mathbf{c}$ is the probability distribution $D_{\mathcal{L},\sigma,\mathbf{c}}$ which assigns to every $\mathbf{x} \in \mathcal{L}$ the probability of occurrence given by $D_{\mathcal{L},\sigma,\mathbf{c}}(\mathbf{x}) := \rho_{\sigma,\mathbf{c}}(\mathbf{x})/\rho_{\sigma,\mathbf{c}}(\mathcal{L})$, where $\rho_{\sigma,\mathbf{c}}(\mathbf{x}) := \exp(-\frac{\|\mathbf{x}-\mathbf{c}\|^2}{2\sigma^2})$ and $\rho_{\sigma,\mathbf{c}}(\mathcal{L}) := \sum_{\mathbf{x}\in\mathcal{L}} \rho_{\sigma,\mathbf{c}}(\mathbf{x})$. We will omit the subscript $\mathbf{c}$ when $\mathbf{c} = \mathbf{0}$.*

Next we recall a special version of the rejection sampling lemma related to the discrete Gaussian distribution [18, Theorem 4.6].

Lemma 8. *Let $T \in \mathbb{R}_{>0}$, and define $V := \{\mathbf{v} \in \mathbb{Z}^m \mid \|\mathbf{v}\| \leq T\}$. Let $\sigma := \alpha T$ for some $\alpha \in \mathbb{R}_{>0}$, and let $h\colon V \to \mathbb{R}$ be a probability distribution. Then there exists a constant $M \in \mathbb{R}_{>0}$ such that $\exp(\frac{12}{\alpha} + \frac{1}{2\alpha^2}) \leq M$, and such that the following two algorithms are within statistical distance of at most $2^{-100}/M$:*

(a) $\mathbf{v} \leftarrow_\$ h$, $\mathbf{z} \leftarrow_\$ D_{\mathbb{Z}^m,\sigma,\mathbf{v}}$, output $(\mathbf{z}, \mathbf{v})$ with probability $\frac{D_{\mathbb{Z}^m,\sigma}(\mathbf{z})}{M \cdot D_{\mathbb{Z}^m,\sigma,\mathbf{v}}(\mathbf{z})}$, and $\perp$ otherwise.

(b) $\mathbf{v} \leftarrow_\$ h$, $\mathbf{z} \leftarrow_\$ D_{\mathbb{Z}^m,\sigma}$, output $(\mathbf{z}, \mathbf{v})$ with probability $1/M$, and $\perp$ otherwise.

Moreover, the probability that the first algorithm returns a value different from $\perp$ is at least $\frac{1-2^{-100}}{M}$.

We let Rej denote an algorithm that carries out rejection sampling on $\mathbf{z}$, where $\mathbf{z} \leftarrow_\$ D_{\mathbb{Z}^m,\sigma,\mathbf{v}}$, with $\mathbf{v} \in \mathbb{Z}^m$ such that $\|\mathbf{v}\| \leq T$, and $\sigma = \alpha T$. It outputs 1 if $\mathbf{z}$ is accepted and 0 if rejected.

Finally, we recall the definitions of the two lattice problems relevant to our work, the Module Short Integer Solution (MSIS) and the decisional Module Learning With Errors (D-MLWE) problems. In both cases, we assume that there is an algorithm that, on input 1^λ, generates a set of public parameters pp. Note that D-MLWE can be defined w.r.t. an arbitrary distribution; here we only focus on the case where the witness is sampled from the Gaussian distribution.

$\mathbf{Exp}_{\mathsf{A}^*}^{\mathsf{MSIS}}(pp)$:	$\mathbf{Exp}_{\mathsf{D}^*}^{\mathsf{D\text{-}MLWE}}(pp)$:
11: **parse** $pp = (n, q, k_1, k_2, \beta)$	21: **parse** $pp = (n, q, k_1, k_2, \sigma, \mathbf{A})$
12: $\mathbf{A} \leftarrow_\$ R_q^{k_1 \times k_2}$	22: $b \leftarrow_\$ \{0, 1\}$, $\mathbf{b} \leftarrow_\$ R_q^{k_1}$
13: $\mathbf{x} \leftarrow_\$ \mathsf{A}^*(pp, \mathbf{A})$	23: **if** $b = 1$ **then**
14: **if** $(\mathbf{x} \in R^{k_1+k_2}) \wedge$	24: $\quad \mathbf{s} \leftarrow_\$ D_{\mathbb{Z}^n, \sigma}^{k_1+k_2}$, $\mathbf{b} \leftarrow [\mathbf{I}_{k_1} \mid \mathbf{A}] \cdot \mathbf{s} \pmod{q}$
$\quad (\mathbf{0} = [\mathbf{I}_{k_1} \mid \mathbf{A}] \cdot \mathbf{x} \pmod{q}) \wedge$	25: $b^* \leftarrow_\$ \mathsf{D}^*(pp, \mathbf{b})$
$\quad (\mathbf{x} \neq \mathbf{0}) \wedge (\|\mathbf{x}\| \leq \beta)$ **then**	26: **if** $b = b^*$ **then**
15: $\quad$ **return** 1	27: $\quad$ **return** 1
16: **return** 0	28: **return** 0

Fig. 3. Definition of the experiments $\mathbf{Exp}_{\mathsf{A}^*}^{\mathsf{MSIS}}$ and $\mathbf{Exp}_{\mathsf{D}^*}^{\mathsf{D\text{-}MLWE}}$.

Definition 9. *Let* $pp = (n, q, k_1, k_2, \beta)$, *where* $n, q, k_1, k_2 \in \mathbb{Z}_{>0}$, *and* $\beta \in \mathbb{R}_{>0}$. *We say that the Hermite normal form of the module short integer solution problem (MSIS) is* (t, ε)-*hard w.r.t.* pp *if, for every algorithm* A^* *running in time at most* t, *we have* $\mathbf{Adv}_{\mathsf{A}^*}^{\mathsf{MSIS}}(pp) := \Pr[\mathbf{Exp}_{\mathsf{A}^*}^{\mathsf{MSIS}}(pp) = 1] \leq \varepsilon$, *where the game* $\mathbf{Exp}_{\mathsf{A}^*}^{\mathsf{MSIS}}$ *is depicted in Fig. 3.*

Definition 10. *Let* $pp = (n, q, k_1, k_2, \sigma, \mathbf{A})$, *where* $n, q, k_1, k_2 \in \mathbb{Z}_{>0}$, $\sigma \in \mathbb{R}_{>0}$, *and* $\mathbf{A} \leftarrow_\$ R_q^{k_1 \times k_2}$. *We say that the decisional module learning with errors problem (D-MLWE) is* (t, ε)-*hard w.r.t.* pp *if, for every algorithm* A^* *running in time at most* t, *we have* $\mathbf{Adv}_{\mathsf{A}^*}^{\mathsf{D\text{-}MLWE}}(pp) := 2 \cdot |\Pr[\mathbf{Exp}_{\mathsf{A}^*}^{\mathsf{D\text{-}MLWE}}(pp) = 1] - \frac{1}{2}| \leq \varepsilon$, *where the game* $\mathbf{Exp}_{\mathsf{A}^*}^{\mathsf{D\text{-}MLWE}}$ *is depicted in Fig. 3.*

Additional Preliminaries. In the full version of this paper [5] we provide a description of the partitioning and permutation technique [3], trees of commitments technique [4], and a minor modified version of the general forking lemma [6], which is used in the security proof of BlindOR. Here, we only give the required definitions.

We define by $\mathbb{T} := \{(-1)^b \cdot X^i \mid b \in \{0, 1\}, \ i \in \mathbb{Z}\}$ the set of signed permutation polynomials, which represent a rotation multiplied by a sign. The set $\mathbb{T}$ has an abelian group structure with respect to multiplication in R. The inverse of any $p = (-1)^b \cdot X^i \in \mathbb{T}$ is given by $p^{-1} = (-1)^{1-b} \cdot X^{n-i} \in \mathbb{T}$. When constructing OR-proofs, we will use the abelian group $\mathbb{T}^\kappa$ as the challenge space rather than $\mathbb{T}_\kappa^n$, since the latter does not have a group structure.

Let $\mathsf{F}: \{0, 1\}^* \to \{0, 1\}^{\ell_\mathsf{F}}$ be a cryptographic hash function, where $\ell_\mathsf{F} \geq 2\lambda$ for F to be collision resistant. We consider the following algorithms:

HashTree is an algorithm that computes an (unbalanced) binary hash tree of height $h \geq 1$. On input $\ell \leq 2^h$ strings $v_0, \ldots, v_{\ell-1}$, it returns a pair $(root, tree)$, where $root$ is the root of the hash tree whose leaves are hashes of $v_0, \ldots, v_{\ell-1}$, and $tree$ is the sequence of all the other nodes in the tree.

BuildAuth is an algorithm that, on input an index $0 \leq k \leq \ell - 1$, a sequence of nodes $tree$, and a height h, returns the authentication path $auth$ for k.

RootCalc is an algorithm that computes the root of a hash tree given a leaf and its authentication path.

3   BlindOR: a New Blind Signature Scheme

Sigma Protocol. In lattice-based cryptography, it is common to prove in zero-knowledge the possession of a witness s with small entries such that $b = As$, given a matrix A and a vector b over some ring (typically $\mathbb{Z}_q$ or R_q). One approach to do so is the so-called *Fiat-Shamir with Aborts* technique [17]. However, rather than proving knowledge of s itself, this method allows to prove knowledge of a pair $(\bar{s}, \bar{c})$ satisfying $b\bar{c} = A\bar{s}$, where the entries of $\bar{s}$ are still small but slightly larger than those of s, and $\bar{c}$ is small as well. More precisely, the Fiat-Shamir with Aborts technique allows to prove possession of a witness of the form $(\bar{s}, \bar{c}) \in B_1 \times B_2$, where B_1 and B_2 are some predefined sets, even though the prover actually holds a witness of the form $(s, 1) \in B_1' \times B_2$, where $B_1' \subseteq B_1$. This relaxation is known to be sufficient for many cryptographic applications, *e.g.*, digital signatures [18]. Here we extend this line of applications to blind signatures.

BlindOR is built on a variant of the Sigma protocol introduced in [17], so we briefly recall this construction before presenting our modified protocol. Given a public matrix $A \in R_q^{k_1 \times k_2}$ and an instance $b \in R_q^{k_1}$, the prover holds a witness $(s, 1) \in B_1' \times B_2 \subseteq R^{k_1+k_2} \times R_q$ such that $b = [I_{k_1} \,|\, A] \cdot s \pmod{q}$. An execution of the protocol allows him to prove knowledge of a witness $(\bar{s}, \bar{c}) \in B_1 \times B_2$, with $B_1' \subseteq B_1 \subseteq R^{k_1+k_2}$, such that $b\bar{c} = [I_{k_1} \,|\, A] \cdot \bar{s} \pmod{q}$. The commitment message is given by $v = [I_{k_1} \,|\, A] \cdot y \pmod{q}$, where y is a masking vector with small entries. Upon receiving a challenge $c \in \mathbb{T}_\kappa^n$, the response is computed as $z = y + sc$, and is sent to the verifier only if it follows a specified distribution, typically the Gaussian distribution $D_{\mathbb{Z}^n, \sigma}^{k_1+k_2}$ for some $\sigma > 0$ or the uniform distribution over a small subset of $R^{k_1+k_2}$. This ensures that y masks the secret-related term sc and that z is independently distributed from s. If z does not follow the target distribution, the prover restarts the protocol with a fresh y. The verifier accepts if $v = [I_{k_1} \,|\, A] \cdot z - bc \pmod{q}$ and if $\|z\|_p$ is bounded by some predefined value. Note that $p \in \{2, \infty\}$, depending on the distribution of z.

We now turn our attention to our modified Sigma protocol, built on top of the protocol recalled above, and start by introducing the relation $\mathcal{R}$ it is associated to. The algorithm $\mathcal{R}.\mathsf{PGen}$ generates a set of public parameters of the form

$$pp = (1^\lambda, n, k_1, k_2, q, \omega, \kappa, \sigma', \sigma^*, S, B_s, B_{z^*}, B_z, \delta^*, A) \leftarrow_\$ \mathcal{R}.\mathsf{PGen}(1^\lambda) \,,$$

subject to the constraints given in Table 2, where the matrix $A \in R_q^{k_1 \times k_2}$ follows the uniform distribution. In Table 3 we propose a concrete tuple of such parameters targeting 128 bits of security. The relation set is then given by

$$\mathcal{R}.\mathsf{RSet}(pp) := \Big\{ (b, (\bar{s}, \bar{c})) \in R_q^{k_1} \times (R^{k_1+k_2} \times R_q^\kappa) \,\Big|\, (b\bar{c} = [I_{k_1} \,|\, A] \cdot \bar{s} \pmod{q})$$

$$\wedge \, (\bar{c} = (\bar{c}_1, \dots, \bar{c}_\kappa) \in \overline{\mathcal{C}}) \wedge (\bar{c} = \sum_{j=1}^\kappa \bar{c}_j) \wedge (\|\bar{s}\| \leq 2B_z) \Big\} \,, \quad (1)$$

where $\overline{C} = \{\mathbf{c} - \mathbf{c}' = (c_1 - c'_1, \ldots, c_\kappa - c'_\kappa) \mid \mathbf{c}, \mathbf{c}' \in \mathbb{T}^\kappa, \ \mathbf{c} \neq \mathbf{c}'\}$, and the instance generator is given in Fig. 4. The actual witness the prover possesses is of the form $(\mathbf{s}, 1)$, where $\|\mathbf{s}\| \leq B_s < B_z$ and $\mathbf{b} = [\mathbf{I}_{k_1} \mid \mathbf{A}] \cdot \mathbf{s} \pmod{q}$. The challenge space of the protocol is $\mathbb{T}^\kappa$, and its other algorithms are given in Fig. 4.

At a high level, the protocol can be seen as a generalized version of the one given in [17] and briefly recalled above. In particular, it is optimized to work for BlindOR. Rather than computing only one commitment to a masking vector in $\Sigma.\mathsf{P}_1$, the prover computes commitments to $\omega \geq 1$ such vectors and sends them to the verifier all at once. Choosing $\omega > 1$ allows to reduce the number of restarts, since the chance of masking the secret-related term without restarting the protocol is increased. More concretely, increasing ω allows to compute a response such that there is no need to trigger a protocol restart with some fixed probability. The masking vectors are chosen according to the Gaussian distribution $D_{\mathbb{Z}^n, \sigma^*}^{k_1 + k_2}$. Upon receiving the challenge $\mathbf{c} \in \mathbb{T}^\kappa$, the prover sends the first response $\mathbf{z}$ for which rejection sampling accepts, i.e., for the masking vector $\mathbf{y}^{(i)}$ such that $\mathsf{Rej}(pp, \mathbf{z}) = 1$ and i is chosen from the uniform distribution over the set $T \subseteq \{0, \ldots, \omega-1\}$. The random choice of the index i ensures that the simulator $\Sigma.\mathsf{Sim}$ returns $(\mathbf{v}, \mathbf{z}) \neq (\perp, \perp)$ with the same probability as the prover. Note that each of the ω commitments consists of κ components, where κ defines the challenge space $\mathbb{T}^\kappa$. This allows to use the partitioning and permutation technique in BlindOR. To verify a transcript $(\mathbf{v}, \mathbf{c}, \mathbf{z})$, the verifier first finds out which of the ω commitments is related to the response. The index i of the corresponding commitment is part of the verifier's output.

Theorem 11. *Given the parameters in Table 2, the protocol depicted in Fig. 4 is a Sigma protocol for relation $\mathcal{R}$ given in Eq. (1).*

The proof is provided in the full version of this paper [5]. We remark that when constructing the Sigma protocol $\Sigma_{\mathsf{OR}} = \mathsf{OR}[\Sigma, \Sigma]$, where Σ is the protocol introduced above, we must consider the group operation defined on the challenge space $\mathbb{T}^\kappa$. More precisely, $\Sigma_{\mathsf{OR}}.\mathsf{P}_1$ samples $\mathbf{c}_{1-d} = (c_{1,1-d}, \ldots, c_{\kappa,1-d}) \xleftarrow{\$} \mathbb{T}^\kappa$ and then runs $\Sigma_{1-d}.\mathsf{Sim}$ on $\mathbf{c}_{1-d}$. Upon receiving a challenge $\mathbf{c} = (c_1, \ldots, c_\kappa)$ from $\Sigma_{\mathsf{OR}}.\mathsf{V}_1$, $\Sigma_{\mathsf{OR}}.\mathsf{P}_2$ computes $\mathbf{c}_d = (c_1 c_{1,1-d}^{-1}, \ldots, c_\kappa c_{\kappa,1-d}^{-1})$ and runs $\Sigma_d.\mathsf{P}_2$ on $\mathbf{c}_d$. Therefore, we have $\mathbf{c} = \mathbf{c}_d \cdot \mathbf{c}_{1-d} = (c_{1,d} c_{1,1-d}, \ldots, c_{\kappa,d} c_{\kappa,1-d})$.

Description of BlindOR. Let BS be a blind signature scheme as defined in Sect. 2. Recall how signing and verification of such a scheme works. The signer computes and sends a commitment cm^* to the user. The user blinds cm^* to obtain a blind commitment cm and computes a challenge ch, which is generated by evaluating a hash function H on input (cm, m), i.e. $ch = \mathsf{H}(cm, m)$ with m being a message. After that, the user unblinds ch to obtain a challenge ch^* and sends it to the signer. The signer computes a response rp^* and sends it back to the user. Finally, the user blinds rp^* to obtain a blind response rp and outputs $sig = (ch, rp)$. Verifying the validity of sig is established by computing a commitment cm corresponding to ch and rp, and then checking if ch matches $\mathsf{H}(cm, m)$. Observe that while the steps carried out by the signer are actually what a prover in a Sigma protocol does when proving the possession of

$\mathcal{R}.\mathsf{Gen}(pp, b)$:

101: **if** $b = 0$ **then**
102:    $\mathbf{b} \leftarrow_\$ R_q^{k_1}$
103:    **return** $\mathbf{b}$
104: **if** $b = 1$ **then**
105:    **repeat** $\mathbf{s} \leftarrow_\$ D_{\mathbb{Z}^n,\sigma'}^{k_1+k_2}$ **until** $\|\mathbf{s}\| \leq B_s$
106:    $\mathbf{b} \leftarrow [\mathbf{I}_{k_1} \mid \mathbf{A}] \cdot \mathbf{s} \pmod{q}$
107:    **return** $(\mathbf{b}, \mathbf{s})$

$\Sigma.\mathsf{P}_1(pp, \mathbf{b}, \mathbf{s})$:

111: **for** $i = 0$ **to** $\omega - 1$ **do**
112:    **for** $j = 1$ **to** κ **do**
113:       $\mathbf{y}_j \leftarrow_\$ D_{\mathbb{Z}^n,\sigma^*}^{k_1+k_2}$
114:       $\mathbf{v}_j \leftarrow [\mathbf{I}_{k_1} \mid \mathbf{A}] \cdot \mathbf{y}_j \pmod{q}$
115:    $\mathbf{v}^{(i)} \leftarrow (\mathbf{v}_1, \dots, \mathbf{v}_\kappa)$
116:    $\mathbf{y}^{(i)} \leftarrow (\mathbf{y}_1, \dots, \mathbf{y}_\kappa)$
117: $\mathbf{v} \leftarrow (\mathbf{v}^{(0)}, \dots, \mathbf{v}^{(\omega-1)})$
118: $st_{\Sigma.\mathsf{P}} \leftarrow (\mathbf{y}^{(0)}, \dots, \mathbf{y}^{(\omega-1)})$
119: **return** $(\mathbf{v}, st_{\Sigma.\mathsf{P}})$

$\Sigma.\mathsf{V}_1(pp, \mathbf{b}, \mathbf{v})$:

121: $\mathbf{c} = (c_1, \dots, c_\kappa) \leftarrow_\$ \mathbb{T}^\kappa$
122: $st_{\Sigma.\mathsf{V}} \leftarrow (\mathbf{v}, \mathbf{c})$
123: **return** $(\mathbf{c}, st_{\Sigma.\mathsf{V}})$

$\Sigma.\mathsf{P}_2(pp, \mathbf{b}, \mathbf{s}, st_{\Sigma.\mathsf{P}}, \mathbf{c})$:

131: **parse** $st_{\Sigma.\mathsf{P}} = (\mathbf{y}^{(0)}, \dots, \mathbf{y}^{(\omega-1)})$
132: **parse** $\mathbf{c} = (c_1, \dots, c_\kappa)$
133: $T := \{0, \dots, \omega - 1\}$
134: **while** $T \neq \emptyset$ **do**
135:    $i \leftarrow_\$ T, \; T \leftarrow T \setminus \{i\}$
136:    **parse** $\mathbf{y}^{(i)} = (\mathbf{y}_1, \dots, \mathbf{y}_\kappa)$
137:    **for** $j = 1$ **to** κ **do**
138:       $\mathbf{z}_j \leftarrow \mathbf{y}_j + \mathbf{s}c_j$
139:    $\mathbf{z} \leftarrow (\mathbf{z}_1, \dots, \mathbf{z}_\kappa)$
140:    **if** $\mathsf{Rej}(pp, \mathbf{z}) = 1$ **then**
141:       **return** $\mathbf{z}$
142: **return** $\perp$

$\Sigma.\mathsf{Ext}(pp, \mathbf{b}, (\mathbf{v}, \mathbf{c}, \mathbf{z}), (\mathbf{v}, \mathbf{c}', \mathbf{z}'))$:

191: **parse** $\mathbf{z} = (\mathbf{z}_1, \dots, \mathbf{z}_\kappa)$
192: **parse** $\mathbf{z}' = (\mathbf{z}'_1, \dots, \mathbf{z}'_\kappa)$
193: $\bar{\mathbf{s}} \leftarrow \sum_{j=1}^{\kappa} (\mathbf{z}_j - \mathbf{z}'_j)$
194: $\bar{\mathbf{c}} \leftarrow \mathbf{c} - \mathbf{c}'$
195: **return** $(\bar{\mathbf{s}}, \bar{\mathbf{c}})$

$\Sigma.\mathsf{V}_2(pp, \mathbf{b}, st_{\Sigma.\mathsf{V}}, \mathbf{z})$:

151: **if** $\|\mathbf{z}\| > B_z$ **then**
152:    **return** $(0, -1)$
153: **parse** $st_{\Sigma.\mathsf{V}} = (\mathbf{v}, \mathbf{c})$
154: **parse** $\mathbf{v} = (\mathbf{v}^{(0)}, \dots, \mathbf{v}^{(\omega-1)})$
155: **parse** $\mathbf{c} = (c_1, \dots, c_\kappa)$
156: **parse** $\mathbf{z} = (\mathbf{z}_1, \dots, \mathbf{z}_\kappa)$
157: **for** $j = 1$ **to** κ **do**
158:    $\mathbf{w}_j \leftarrow [\mathbf{I}_{k_1} \mid \mathbf{A}] \cdot \mathbf{z}_j - \mathbf{b}c_j \pmod{q}$
159: **for** $i = 0$ **to** $\omega - 1$ **do**
160:    $int \leftarrow 0$
161:    **parse** $\mathbf{v}^{(i)} = (\mathbf{v}_1, \dots, \mathbf{v}_\kappa)$
162:    **for** $j = 1$ **to** κ **do**
163:       **if** $\mathbf{w}_j = \mathbf{v}_j$ **then**
164:          $int = int + 1$
165:    **if** $int = \kappa$ **then**
166:       **return** $(1, i)$
167: **return** $(0, -1)$

$\Sigma.\mathsf{Sim}(pp, \mathbf{b}, \mathbf{c})$:

171: **return** $(\perp, \perp)$ with probability δ^*
172: **parse** $\mathbf{c} = (c_1, \dots, c_\kappa)$
173: $i \leftarrow_\$ \{0, \dots, \omega - 1\}$
174: **for** $j = 1$ **to** κ **do**
175:    $\mathbf{z}_j \leftarrow_\$ D_{\mathbb{Z}^n,\sigma^*}^{k_1+k_2}$
176:    $\mathbf{v}_j \leftarrow [\mathbf{I}_{k_1} \mid \mathbf{A}] \cdot \mathbf{z}_j - \mathbf{b}c_j \pmod{q}$
177: $\mathbf{z} \leftarrow (\mathbf{z}_1, \dots, \mathbf{z}_\kappa), \; \mathbf{v}^{(i)} \leftarrow (\mathbf{v}_1, \dots, \mathbf{v}_\kappa)$
178: **for** $k = 0$ **to** $\omega - 1$ **do**
179:    **if** $k = i$ **then**
180:       **continue**
181:    **for** $j = 1$ **to** κ **do**
182:       $\mathbf{y}_j \leftarrow_\$ D_{\mathbb{Z}^n,\sigma^*}^{k_1+k_2}$
183:       $\mathbf{v}_j \leftarrow [\mathbf{I}_{k_1} \mid \mathbf{A}] \cdot \mathbf{y}_j \pmod{q}$
184:    $\mathbf{v}^{(k)} \leftarrow (\mathbf{v}_1, \dots, \mathbf{v}_\kappa)$
185: $\mathbf{v} \leftarrow (\mathbf{v}^{(0)}, \dots, \mathbf{v}^{(\omega-1)})$
186: **return** $(\mathbf{v}, \mathbf{z})$

$\Sigma.\mathsf{ComRec}(pp, \mathbf{b}, \mathbf{c}, \mathbf{z})$:

201: **if** $\|\mathbf{z}\| > B_z$ **then**
202:    **return** $\perp$
203: **parse** $\mathbf{c} = (c_1, \dots, c_\kappa), \; \mathbf{z} = (\mathbf{z}_1, \dots, \mathbf{z}_\kappa)$
204: **for** $j = 1$ **to** κ **do**
205:    $\mathbf{v}_j \leftarrow [\mathbf{I}_{k_1} \mid \mathbf{A}] \cdot \mathbf{z}_j - \mathbf{b}c_j \pmod{q}$
206: $\mathbf{v}^{(0)} \leftarrow (\mathbf{v}_1, \dots, \mathbf{v}_\kappa)$
207: **for** $i = 1$ **to** $\omega - 1$ **do**
208:    $\mathbf{v}^{(i)} \leftarrow (\mathbf{0}, \dots, \mathbf{0}) \in (R_q^{k_1})^\kappa$
209: $\mathbf{v} \leftarrow (\mathbf{v}^{(0)}, \dots, \mathbf{v}^{(\omega-1)})$
210: **return** $\mathbf{v}$

Fig. 4. The Sigma protocol underlying BlindOR. Prover restarts Σ if $\Sigma.\mathsf{P}_2$ returns $\perp$.

a witness for a statement, the steps performed by the user consist of blinding the transcript (cm^*, ch^*, rp^*) during interaction. In BlindOR, we capture these blinding steps by algorithms Com, Cha, and Rsp, which we describe next.

For the remainder of this section we let Σ be the Sigma protocol depicted in Fig. 4. Furthermore, let $h = \lceil \log(\omega \ell) \rceil$ and define the bijective mapping IntIdx: $\{0, \ldots, \omega - 1\} \times \{0, \ldots, \ell - 1\} \to \{0, \ldots, \omega \ell - 1\}$, $(i, k) \mapsto k + i\ell$. IntIdx converts the pair (i, k) to a unique positive integer. This is used in BlindOR to build authentication paths via the algorithm BuildAuth. Let pp be a set of public parameters for BlindOR and $x = \mathbf{b} \in R_q^{k_1}$ be an instance for $\mathcal{R}$. We define the following algorithms, which are formally described in Fig. 5:

Com is a PPT algorithm that, on input pp, x, and a commitment $cm^* = \mathbf{v}^*$ generated by $\Sigma.\mathsf{P}_1$, returns a blind commitment $cm = root$ and a state $(\mathbf{p}, tree, \mathbf{e})$.

Cha is a DPT algorithm that, on input pp, a randomness $\mathbf{p} \in \mathbb{T}^\kappa$, a challenge $ch^* = \mathbf{c}^* \in \mathbb{T}^\kappa$, and an auxiliary bit $b \in \{0, 1\}$, returns a challenge $ch = \mathbf{c} \in \mathbb{T}^\kappa$. Observe that b determines if $\mathbf{c}^*$ will be blinded using $\mathbf{p}$ or using its inverse with respect to the group operation defined on $\mathbb{T}^\kappa$.

Rsp is a DPT algorithm that, on input pp, a state $(\mathbf{p}, tree, \mathbf{e})$, a response $rp^* = \mathbf{z}^*$ generated by $\Sigma.\mathsf{P}_2$, and an integer $i \in \{0, \ldots, \omega - 1\}$, returns a blind response $rp = (\mathbf{z}, auth)$, where $rp = (\perp, \perp)$ is possible.

Rec is a DPT algorithm that, on input pp, the statement x, a challenge ch, and a response rp, returns a commitment cm, where $cm = \perp$ is possible.

Note that the blinding algorithms depicted in Fig. 5 can be seen as a generalized version of the blinding steps implicitly presented in the lattice-based blind signature scheme BLAZE$^+$ [4]. Unlike BLAZE$^+$, the algorithms shown in Fig. 5 are defined for lattices over modules rather than over rings. This complies with the module structure of Σ and allows for more flexibility when choosing concrete parameters. Furthermore, these blinding algorithms employ the partitioning and permutation technique, which allows to use the abelian group $\mathbb{T}^\kappa$ as a challenge space rather than the set $\mathbb{T}_\kappa^n$, which does not have a group structure. Moreover, the algorithm Com blinds ω commitments $\mathbf{v}^{*(0)}, \ldots, \mathbf{v}^{*(\omega-1)}$ rather than only one commitment generated by $\Sigma.\mathsf{P}_1$. More precisely, the trees of commitments technique employed in BLAZE$^+$ is extended to further include ω commitments created by the prover. These ω commitments are then combined with ℓ commitments generated within Com to compute the root related to a tree of $\omega \ell$ commitments. We require ℓ to be chosen large enough so that Rsp returns a blind response $(\mathbf{z}, auth) = (\perp, \perp)$ with probability close to zero, e.g., 2^{-80}. This is crucial for BlindOR since otherwise, we would need an extra move between the signer and user, which would allow the user to request a restart of the signing protocol in case the algorithm IterateRej returns $(\perp, \perp)$. This extra move would increase the communication complexity and force the signer to carry out almost all computations performed by the user before triggering a protocol restart. Moreover, this extra move would not allow the use of Gaussian distributed masking vectors $\mathbf{e}$ since a blind signature could be correctly verified even if rejection sampling does not accept. This would enable the user to request a protocol restart

---

$\mathsf{Com}(pp, \mathbf{b}, \mathbf{v}^*)$:

11: **parse** $\mathbf{v}^* = (\mathbf{v}^{*(0)}, \ldots, \mathbf{v}^{*(\omega-1)})$

12: $\mathbf{p} = (p_1, \ldots, p_\kappa) \leftarrow_\$ \mathbb{T}^\kappa$

13: **for** $i = 0$ **to** $\omega - 1$ **do**

14:     **parse** $\mathbf{v}^{*(i)} = (\mathbf{v}_1^*, \ldots, \mathbf{v}_\kappa^*)$

15:     $\mathbf{v}'^{(i)} \leftarrow \sum_{j=1}^{\kappa} \mathbf{v}_j^* p_j \pmod{q}$

16:     **for** $k = 0$ **to** $\ell - 1$ **do**

17:        $\mathbf{e}^{(k)} \leftarrow_\$ D_{\mathbb{Z}^n, \sigma}^{k_1 + k_2}$

18:        $\mathbf{v}^{(i,k)} \leftarrow [\mathbf{I}_{k_1} \mid \mathbf{A}] \cdot \mathbf{e}^{(k)} +$
              $+ \mathbf{v}'^{(i)} \pmod{q}$

19: $(root, tree) \leftarrow$
     $\leftarrow \mathsf{HashTree}(\mathbf{v}^{(0,0)}, \ldots, \mathbf{v}^{(\omega-1,\ell-1)})$

20: $\mathbf{e} \leftarrow (\mathbf{e}^{(0)}, \ldots, \mathbf{e}^{(\ell-1)})$

21: **return** $(root, (\mathbf{p}, tree, \mathbf{e}))$

$\mathsf{Cha}(pp, \mathbf{p}, \mathbf{c}^*, b)$:

31: **parse** $\mathbf{p} = (p_1, \ldots, p_\kappa)$

32: **parse** $\mathbf{c}^* = (c_1^*, \ldots, c_\kappa^*)$

33: **if** $b = 0$ **then**

34:     $\mathbf{c} \leftarrow (c_1^* p_1^{-1}, \ldots, c_\kappa^* p_\kappa^{-1})$

35: **else**

36:     $\mathbf{c} \leftarrow (c_1^* p_1, \ldots, c_\kappa^* p_\kappa)$

37: **return** $\mathbf{c}$

$\mathsf{Rsp}(pp, (\mathbf{p}, tree, \mathbf{e}), \mathbf{z}^*, i)$:

41: **parse** $\mathbf{p} = (p_1, \ldots, p_\kappa)$, $\mathbf{z}^* = (\mathbf{z}_1^*, \ldots, \mathbf{z}_\kappa^*)$

42: $\mathbf{z}' \leftarrow \sum_{j=1}^{\kappa} \mathbf{z}_j^* p_j$

43: $(\mathbf{z}, k) \leftarrow \mathsf{IterateRej}(pp, \mathbf{e}, \mathbf{z}')$

44: **if** $(\mathbf{z}, k) = (\bot, \bot)$ **then**

45:     **return** $(\bot, \bot)$

46: $auth \leftarrow \mathsf{BuildAuth}(\mathsf{IntIdx}(i, k), tree, h)$

47: **return** $(\mathbf{z}, auth)$

$\mathsf{IterateRej}(pp, \mathbf{e}, \mathbf{z}')$:

51: **parse** $\mathbf{e} = (\mathbf{e}^{(0)}, \ldots, \mathbf{e}^{(\ell-1)})$

52: **for** $k = 0$ **to** $\ell - 1$ **do**

53:     $\mathbf{z} \leftarrow \mathbf{e}^{(k)} + \mathbf{z}'$

54:     **if** $\mathsf{Rej}(pp, \mathbf{z}) = 1$ **then**

55:        **return** $(\mathbf{z}, k)$

56: **return** $(\bot, \bot)$

$\mathsf{Rec}(pp, \mathbf{b}, \mathbf{c}, \mathbf{z}, auth)$:

61: **if** $\|\mathbf{z}\| > B_z$ **then**

62:     **return** $\bot$

63: **parse** $\mathbf{c} = (c_1, \ldots, c_\kappa)$

64: $c \leftarrow \sum_{j=1}^{\kappa} c_j$

65: $\mathbf{w} \leftarrow [\mathbf{I}_{k_1} \mid \mathbf{A}] \cdot \mathbf{z} - \mathbf{b}c \pmod{q}$

66: $root \leftarrow \mathsf{RootCalc}(\mathbf{w}, auth)$

67: **return** $root$

Fig. 5. A formal description of algorithms Com, Cha, Rsp, and Rec.

and obtain two different signatures. The advantage of using the Gaussian distribution for masking is that it allows to generate blind signatures with a size smaller than signatures generated using masking vectors that are uniformly distributed over a small subset of R.

Next, we describe BlindOR. Let $\Sigma_{\mathsf{OR}} = \mathsf{OR}[\Sigma, \Sigma]$ and $\mathsf{F} : \{0,1\}^* \to \{0,1\}^{\ell_\mathsf{F}}$, $\mathsf{H} : \{0,1\}^* \to \mathbb{T}^\kappa$ be hash functions, where $\ell_\mathsf{F} \geq 2\lambda$ and $\mathbb{T}^\kappa$ is the challenge space of Σ. The algorithm $\mathsf{BS.PGen}$ generates and returns a set of public parameters $pp = (1^\lambda, n, k_1, k_2, q, \omega, \ell, h, \kappa, \sigma', \sigma^*, \sigma, S, M, B_s, B_{z^*}, B_z, \ell_\mathsf{F}, \mathbf{A})$. The description of the parameters is summarized in Table 2. The matrix $\mathbf{A}$ is chosen from the uniform distribution over $R_q^{k_1 \times k_2}$. We remark that pp includes the public parameters of the relation $\mathcal{R}$ for which Σ is defined, *i.e.*, $\mathsf{BS.PGen}$ may first run $\mathcal{R}.\mathsf{PGen}(1^\lambda)$ and then generates the remaining parameters of the scheme. For simplicity, the input of the algorithms of Σ includes pp. The remaining algorithms of BlindOR are formalized in Fig. 6.

In Table 3, we propose concrete parameters for BlindOR targeting 128 bits of security. Next, we state the correctness, blindness, and one-more unforgeability

```
BS.KGen(pp):                                    BS.U₂(pp, pk, m, st_U, c₀*, c₁*, z₀*, z₁*):

11:  ((b₀, b₁), (d, s)) ←$ R_OR.Gen(pp, 1)      51:  parse pk = (b₀, b₁)
12:  pk ← (b₀, b₁),  sk ← (d, s)                52:  parse st_U = (p₀, p₁, tree₀, tree₁, e₀, e₁,
13:  return (pk, sk)                                       st_Σ_OR.V)
                                                53:  (b, (i₀, i₁)) ← Σ_OR.V₂(pp, (b₀, b₁),
                                                          st_Σ_OR.V, c₀*, c₁*, z₀*, z₁*)
BS.S₁(pp, pk, sk):                              54:  if b = 0 then
                                                55:     return ⊥
21:  parse pk = (b₀, b₁),  sk = (d, s)          56:  c₀ ← Cha(pp, p₀, c₀*, 1)
22:  (v₀*, v₁*, st_S) ←$                         57:  c₁ ← Cha(pp, p₁, c₁*, 1)
        ←$ Σ_OR.P₁(pp, (b₀, b₁), (d, s))        58:  (z₀, auth₀) ←
23:  return (v₀*, v₁*, st_S)                             ← Rsp(pp, (p₀, tree₀, e₀), z₀*, i₀)
                                                59:  (z₁, auth₁) ←
                                                        ← Rsp(pp, (p₁, tree₁, e₁), z₁*, i₁)
BS.U₁(pp, pk, m, v₀*, v₁*):                     60:  if (z₀ = ⊥) ∨ (z₁ = ⊥) then
                                                61:     return ⊥
31:  parse pk = (b₀, b₁)                         62:  sig ← (c₀, c₁, z₀, z₁, auth₀, auth₁)
32:  (root₀, (p₀, tree₀, e₀)) ←$ Com(pp, b₀, v₀*) 63:  return (m, sig)
33:  (root₁, (p₁, tree₁, e₁)) ←$ Com(pp, b₁, v₁*)
34:  c ← H(root₀, root₁, m)
35:  c* ← Cha(pp, p₀ · p₁, c, 0)
36:  st_Σ_OR.V ← (v₀*, v₁*, c*)                 BS.Verify(pp, pk, m, sig):
37:  st_U ← (p₀, p₁, tree₀, tree₁, e₀, e₁, st_Σ_OR.V)
38:  return (c*, st_U)                           71:  parse pk = (b₀, b₁)
                                                72:  parse sig = (c₀, c₁, z₀, z₁, auth₀, auth₁)
                                                73:  root₀ ← Rec(pp, b₀, c₀, z₀, auth₀)
BS.S₂(pp, pk, sk, st_S, c*):                    74:  root₁ ← Rec(pp, b₁, c₁, z₁, auth₁)
                                                75:  if (root₀ = ⊥) ∨ (root₁ = ⊥) then
41:  parse pk = (b₀, b₁),  sk = (d, s)          76:     return 0
42:  (c₀*, c₁*, z₀*, z₁*) ←                      77:  c ← H(root₀, root₁, m)
        ← Σ_OR.P₂(pp, (b₀, b₁), (d, s), st_S, c*) 78:  if c ≠ c₀ · c₁ then
43:  if (z₀*, z₁*) = (⊥, ⊥) then                 79:     return 0
44:     return ⊥                                 80:  return 1
45:  return (c₀*, c₁*, z₀*, z₁*)
```

Fig. 6. A formal description of BlindOR. Signer restarts the protocol if $(z_0^*, z_1^*) = (\bot, \bot)$.

of BlindOR. We provide the description of the parameter selection as well as the proof of correctness in the full version of this paper [5].

Theorem 12. *Given the parameters in Table 2,* BlindOR *is* corr_{BS}-*correct w.r.t.* pp, *where* $\mathsf{corr}_{BS} = \delta^* + 2\varepsilon^* + 2\delta + 2\varepsilon$, δ^* *is the probability that algorithm* $\Sigma_{OR}.P_2$ *returns* $\bot$, ε^* *is the probability that algorithm* $\Sigma.V_2$ *returns* $(0, i)$, δ *is the probability that algorithm* Rsp *returns* $\bot$, *and* ε *is the probability that* Rec *returns* $\bot$.

Theorem 13. *Let* $\mathsf{F}: \{0,1\}^* \to \{0,1\}^{\ell_F}$ *and* $\mathsf{H}: \{0,1\}^* \to \mathbb{T}^\kappa$ *be two hash functions modeled as random oracles. Given the parameters in Table 2,* BlindOR *is* ε-*statistically blind w.r.t.* pp *in the ROM, where* $\varepsilon = \max\{*\}(2n)^{-\kappa}, 2^{-100}/U$.

Proof. Let S^* be an adversarial signer in the blindness experiment $\mathbf{Exp}_{BS,S^*}^{Blind}$ defined in Fig. 2. Then, S^* selects two messages m_0, m_1 and interacts with the honest user twice. The goal is to show that after both interactions, the messages

Table 2. A review of the parameters of BlindOR.

Parameter	Description	Bounds
n, k_1, k_2	Dimension	$n = 2^{n'}$, $n', k_1, k_2 \in \mathbb{Z}_{\geq 1}$
q	Modulus	prime, $q = 2p + 1 \pmod{4p}$, $n \geq p > 1$, $p = 2^{p'}$, $p' \in \mathbb{Z}_{\geq 1}$, $q^{1/p} > 2\kappa$
ω, ℓ	No. masking vectors	$\omega, \ell \in \mathbb{Z}_{\geq 1}$
h	Tree height	$h = \lceil \log(\omega \ell) \rceil$
κ	Specifies the set $\mathbb{T}^\kappa$	$|\mathbb{T}^\kappa| = (2n)^\kappa \geq 2^\lambda$
σ'	Standard deviation of in sk	$\sigma' > 0$
σ^*	Standard deviation in Σ	$\sigma^* = \alpha^* \sqrt{\kappa} B_s$, $S = \exp(\frac{12}{\alpha^*} + \frac{1}{2\alpha^{*2}})$, $(1 - \frac{1 - 2^{-100}}{S})^\omega \leq \delta^*$, $\delta^* > 0$
σ	Standard deviation in BS.U	$\sigma = \alpha \eta \frac{B_{z^*}}{\eta^*}$, $U = \exp(\frac{12}{\alpha} + \frac{1}{2\alpha^2})$, $(1 - \frac{1 - 2^{-100}}{U})^\ell \leq \delta$, $\delta > 0$
M	No. restarts of BS.S	$M = 1/(1 - \delta^*)$
B_s	Bound of $\|\mathbf{s}\|$ in sk	$B_s = \eta' \sigma' \sqrt{(k_1 + k_2)n}$, $\eta' > 0$
B_{z^*}	Bound of $\|\mathbf{z}\|$ in Σ	$B_{z^*} = \eta^* \sigma^* \sqrt{(k_1 + k_2)\kappa n}$, $\eta^* > 0$
B_z	Bound of $\|\mathbf{z}\|$ in BS.U	$B_z = \eta \sigma \sqrt{(k_1 + k_2)n}$, $\eta > 0$
ℓ_F	Output length of F	$\ell_\mathsf{F} \geq 2\lambda$

Table 3. Concrete parameters of BlindOR targeting 128 bits of security.

n	k_1	k_2	q	ω	ℓ	h	κ	σ'	α^*	σ^*	α	σ	M	ℓ_F
256	5	4	$\approx 2^{33}$	1	8	3	15	4	11	8344	41	71230016	3	384

output by the user, *i.e.*, two blind challenges of the form $\mathbf{c}^* \in \mathbb{T}^\kappa$ together with two blind signatures of the form $sig = (\mathbf{c}_0, \mathbf{c}_1, \mathbf{z}_0, \mathbf{z}_1, auth_0, auth_1)$, are independently distributed and do not leak any information about the signed messages and the respective interaction.

The authentication paths $auth_0$, $auth_1$ include hash values that are uniformly distributed over $\{0, 1\}^{\ell_\mathsf{F}}$. The challenge $\mathbf{c}^*$ as well as the signature part $(\mathbf{c}_0, \mathbf{c}_1)$ are uniformly distributed over $\mathbb{T}^\kappa$, and hence they do not leak any information. Moreover, [3, Lemma 4] ensures that $\mathbf{c}^*$ is independently distributed from $\mathbf{c} = \mathbf{c}_0 \cdot \mathbf{c}_1$, and S^* can link $\mathbf{c}$ to the correct $\mathbf{c}^*$ only with probability $(2n)^{-\kappa}$ over guessing. The blind vectors $\mathbf{z}_0, \mathbf{z}_1$ have the form $\mathbf{z} = \mathbf{e} + \sum_{j=1}^\kappa \mathbf{z}_j^* p_j$ (see Fig. 5). By Lemma 8, both vectors completely mask $\sum_{j=1}^\kappa \mathbf{z}_j^* p_j$ and are independently distributed within statistical distance of $2^{-100}/U$ from $D_{\mathbb{Z}^n, \sigma}^{k_1 + k_2}$.

Finally, if a protocol restart is triggered by S^*, then BS.U generates fresh random elements. Therefore, the protocol restarts are independent of each other, and hence S^* does not get any information about the message being signed. □

Theorem 14. *Let* $\mathsf{F}: \{0, 1\}^* \to \{0, 1\}^{\ell_\mathsf{F}}$ *and* $\mathsf{H}: \{0, 1\}^* \to \mathbb{T}^\kappa$ *be two hash functions modeled as random oracles. Given the parameters in Table 2,* BlindOR *is* $(t, q_\mathsf{Sign}, q_\mathsf{F}, q_\mathsf{H}, \varepsilon)$*-one-more unforgeable w.r.t.* pp *in the ROM if* D-MLWE *is* (t', ε')*-hard w.r.t.* $pp_\mathsf{MLWE} = (n, q, k_1, k_2, \sigma', \mathbf{A})$ *and* MSIS *is* (t'', ε'')*-hard w.r.t.* $pp_\mathsf{MSIS} = (n, q, k_1, k_2 + 1, 2\sqrt{B_z^2 + \kappa^2})$. *More precisely, if there exists a forger* A^*

against BlindOR *w.r.t. pp that returns* $q_{\mathsf{Sign}} + 1$ *blind signatures in time t and with probability* ε, *and after making* $q_{\mathsf{F}}, q_{\mathsf{H}}$ *queries to* F, H, *respectively, then* A* *can be used to solve* D-MLWE *w.r.t.* pp_{MLWE} *in time* $t' \approx t$ *and advantage* $\varepsilon' \approx \varepsilon$, *or* A* *can be used to solve* MSIS *w.r.t.* pp_{MSIS} *in time* $t'' \approx 2t$ *and probability*

$$\varepsilon'' \approx \left(\frac{1}{2} - \varepsilon'\right) \cdot \left(\frac{1}{q_{\mathsf{Sign}} + 1}\right) \cdot acc \cdot \left(\frac{acc}{(q_{\mathsf{Sign}} + 1)\omega\ell} - \frac{1}{|\mathbb{T}^\kappa|}\right),$$

where $acc = \left(\varepsilon - \frac{q_{\mathsf{F}}^2 + q_{\mathsf{F}}}{2^{\ell_{\mathsf{F}}}} - \frac{q_{\mathsf{Sign}} + 1}{|\mathbb{T}^\kappa|}\right) \Big/ q_{\mathsf{H}}^{q_{\mathsf{Sign}} + 1}$.

Proof. First we observe that the hardness of D-MLWE is required to protect against key recovery attacks, *i.e.*, being able to determine the yes-instance of MLWE included in the public key $pk = (\mathbf{b}_0, \mathbf{b}_1)$ allows to compute the secret key, and hence forgeries. Therefore, in what follows we assume the hardness of D-MLWE w.r.t. pp_{MLWE}, and construct a reduction algorithm R that solves MSIS w.r.t. pp_{MSIS} as given in the theorem statement.

Given pp_{MSIS} and a matrix $\mathbf{A}' \in R_q^{k_1 \times (k_2+1)}$, R chooses a bit $d \leftarrow_\$ \{0, 1\}$, and writes $\mathbf{A}' = [\mathbf{A} \mid \mathbf{b}_{1-d}] \in R_q^{k_1 \times k_2} \times R_q^{k_1}$. Then, it generates the remaining public parameters pp of BlindOR, and sets $C = \{\mathbf{c}_1, \ldots, \mathbf{c}_{q_{\mathsf{H}}}\}$, where $\mathbf{c}_1, \ldots, \mathbf{c}_{q_{\mathsf{H}}} \leftarrow_\$ \mathbb{T}^\kappa$. Afterwards, R runs $\mathcal{R}.\mathsf{Gen}(pp, 1)$ to obtain $(\mathbf{b}_d, \mathbf{s})$. Then, R sets $pk = (\mathbf{b}_0, \mathbf{b}_1)$, $sk = (d, \mathbf{s})$, and runs A* on input (pp, pk). The random oracle and signing queries that A* make are answered by R as follows:

Random Oracle Query. R maintains a list L_{H} initialized by the empty set. It stores pairs of queries to H and their answers. If H was previously queried on some input, then R looks up its entry in L_{H} and returns its answer $\mathbf{c}$. Otherwise, it picks the first unused $\mathbf{c} \in C$ and updates the list. Furthermore, R initializes an empty list L_{F} to store pairs of queries to F and their answers. The queries to F are answered in a way that excludes collisions and chains. Excluding collisions rules out queries $\mathbf{x} \neq \mathbf{x}'$ such that $\mathsf{F}(\mathbf{x}) = \mathsf{F}(\mathbf{x}')$, and excluding chains guarantees that the query $\mathsf{F}(\mathsf{F}(\mathbf{x}))$ will not be made before the query $\mathsf{F}(\mathbf{x})$. This ensures that each node output by HashTree has a unique preimage, and prevents spanning hash trees with cycles. Simulating F this way is within statistical distance of at most $\frac{q_{\mathsf{F}}^2 + q_{\mathsf{F}}}{2^{\ell_{\mathsf{F}}}}$ from an oracle that allows collisions and chains.

Signature Query. Upon receiving a signature query from A*, R runs the signing protocol of BlindOR. Furthermore, R updates both lists L_{H} and L_{F} accordingly.

After q_{Sign} successful invocations, A* returns $q_{\mathsf{Sign}} + 1$ pairs of distinct messages and their signatures, where one of these pairs is not generated during the interaction. If H was not programmed or queried during invocation of A*, then A* produces a $\mathbf{c} \in \mathbb{T}^\kappa$ that validates correctly with probability $1/|\mathbb{T}^\kappa|$. Therefore, the probability that A* succeeds in a forgery such that all $q_{\mathsf{Sign}} + 1$ signatures correspond to random oracle queries made by A* is at least $\varepsilon - \frac{q_{\mathsf{Sign}} + 1}{|\mathbb{T}^\kappa|}$.

Afterwards, R guesses an index $i^* \in [q_{\mathsf{Sign}} + 1]$ such that $\mathbf{c}_{i^*} = \mathbf{c}_{j^*}$ for some $j^* \in [q_{\mathsf{H}}]$. Then, R records the pair $(m_{i^*}, sig_{i^*} =$

$(\mathbf{c}_0, \mathbf{c}_1, \mathbf{z}_0, \mathbf{z}_1, auth_0, auth_1))$ and invokes A^* again with the same random tape and the random oracle queries $C' = \{\mathbf{c}_1, \ldots, \mathbf{c}_{j^*-1}, \mathbf{c}'_{j^*}, \ldots, \mathbf{c}'_{q_H}\}$, where $\mathbf{c}'_{j^*}, \ldots, \mathbf{c}'_{q_H} \in \mathbb{T}^\kappa$ are freshly generated by R. After rewinding, A^* returns $q_{\mathsf{Sign}} + 1$ pairs of distinct messages and their valid signatures. The potential two valid forgeries (before and after rewinding) output by A^* at index i^* have the form

$$(m, (\mathbf{c}_0, \mathbf{c}_1, \mathbf{z}_0, \mathbf{z}_1, auth_0, auth_1)) \text{ and } (m', (*)\mathbf{c}'_0, \mathbf{c}'_1, \mathbf{z}'_0, \mathbf{z}'_1, auth'_0, auth'_1) \,,$$

where $\mathbf{c}_i = (c_{1,i}, \ldots, c_{\kappa,i})$ and $\mathbf{c}'_i = (*)c'_{1,i}, \ldots, c'_{\kappa,i}, i \in \{0,1\}$. By the verification algorithm we obtain

$$\mathbf{w}_{1-d} = [\mathbf{I}_{k_1} \mid \mathbf{A}] \cdot \mathbf{z}_{1-d} - \mathbf{b}_{1-d}c_{1-d} \pmod{q} \,,$$
$$\mathbf{w}'_{1-d} = [\mathbf{I}_{k_1} \mid \mathbf{A}] \cdot \mathbf{z}'_{1-d} - \mathbf{b}_{1-d}c'_{1-d} \pmod{q} \,,$$
$$root_{1-d} = \mathsf{RootCalc}(\mathbf{w}_{1-d}, auth_{1-d}), \ root'_{1-d} = \mathsf{RootCalc}(\mathbf{w}'_{1-d}, auth'_{1-d}) \,,$$
$$\mathbf{c}_0 \cdot \mathbf{c}_1 = \mathbf{c} = \mathsf{H}(root_0, root_1, m), \ \mathbf{c}'_0 \cdot \mathbf{c}'_1 = \mathbf{c}' = \mathsf{H}(root'_0, root'_1, m') \,,$$

By the forking lemma (see the full version [5]) we have $root_0 = root'_0$, $root_1 = root'_1$, $m = m'$, $\mathbf{c} \neq \mathbf{c}'$, and $k_{1-d} = k'_{1-d}$, where $k_{1-d}, k'_{1-d} \in \{0, \ldots, \omega\ell - 1\}$ are the indices included in $auth_{1-d}, auth'_{1-d}$, respectively. Observe that simulating the hash queries to F as described above ensures that both $auth_{1-d}, auth'_{1-d}$ include the same sequence of hash values, and hence $auth_{1-d} = auth'_{1-d}$ and $\mathbf{w}_{1-d} = \mathbf{w}'_{1-d}$. If $\mathbf{c}_{1-d} \neq \mathbf{c}'_{1-d}$, then we have

$$[\mathbf{I}_{k_1} \mid \mathbf{A}] \cdot \mathbf{z}_{1-d} - \mathbf{b}_{1-d}c_{1-d} = [\mathbf{I}_{k_1} \mid \mathbf{A}] \cdot \mathbf{z}'_{1-d} - \mathbf{b}_{1-d}c'_{1-d} \pmod{q},$$

where $c_{1-d} = \sum_{j=1}^\kappa c_{j,1-d}$ and $c'_{1-d} = \sum_{j=1}^\kappa c'_{j,1-d}$. In this case, R runs $\Sigma.\mathsf{Ext}$ on input $(pp, \mathbf{b}_{1-d}, (\mathbf{v}, \mathbf{c}, \mathbf{z}), (\mathbf{v}, \mathbf{c}', \mathbf{z}'))$, where

$$\mathbf{v} = (\mathbf{v}^{(0)}, \ldots, \mathbf{v}^{(\omega-1)}), \ \mathbf{v}^{(0)} = (\mathbf{w}_{1-d}, 0, \ldots, 0) \in (R_q^{k_1})^\kappa,$$
$$\mathbf{v}^{(i)} = (0, \ldots, 0) \in (R_q^{k_1})^\kappa \text{ for all } i \in [\omega - 1], \ \mathbf{z} = (\mathbf{z}_{1-d}, 0, \ldots, 0) \in (R_q^{k_1})^\kappa,$$
$$\mathbf{z}' = (\mathbf{z}'_{1-d}, 0, \ldots, 0) \in (R_q^{k_1})^\kappa, \ \|\mathbf{z}_{1-d}\| \leq B_z, \ \|\mathbf{z}'_{1-d}\| \leq B_z.$$

The output of $\Sigma.\mathsf{Ext}$ is the pair $(\mathbf{z}_{1-d} - \mathbf{z}'_{1-d}, c_{1-d} - c'_{1-d})$, which gives the nontrivial solution $[\mathbf{z}_{1-d} - \mathbf{z}'_{1-d} \mid c'_{1-d} - c_{1-d}]^\top$ to MSIS w.r.t. pp_{MSIS} and the matrix $[\mathbf{I}_{k_1} \mid \mathbf{A} \mid \mathbf{b}_{1-d}] = [\mathbf{I}_{k_1} \mid \mathbf{A}']$.

Next, we analyze the success probability of R. The probability that R answers the correct sequence of $q_{\mathsf{Sign}} + 1$ random oracle queries to H that are used by A^* in the forgery is at least $1/q_H^{q_{\mathsf{Sign}}+1}$. Since one of the $q_{\mathsf{Sign}} + 1$ pairs output by A^* is by assumption not generated during the interaction with R, the probability of correctly guessing the index i^* corresponding to this pair is $1/(q_{\mathsf{Sign}} + 1)$. The success probability of the forking is given by $frk \geq acc \cdot \left(\frac{acc}{(q_{\mathsf{Sign}}+1)\omega\ell} - \frac{1}{|\mathbb{T}^\kappa|} \right)$, where $acc = \left(\varepsilon - \frac{q_F^2 + q_F}{2^{\ell_F}} - \frac{q_{\mathsf{Sign}}+1}{|\mathbb{T}^\kappa|} \right) / q_H^{q_{\mathsf{Sign}}+1}$. By Lemma 15, the probability that $\mathbf{c}_{1-d} \neq \mathbf{c}'_{1-d}$ is given by $\frac{1}{2} - \varepsilon'$. This deduces the probability ε'' that is given in the theorem statement. □

Lemma 15. *Assume that after rewinding the forger* A^* *by the reduction* R *given in Theorem 14, the two forgeries output by* A^* *satisfy* $c_{1-d} = c'_{1-d}$ *with probability* $1/2 + \varepsilon'$, *where* d *corresponds to the yes-instance of* MLWE *included in the public key and* ε' *is noticeably greater than 0. Then, there exists a distinguisher* D^* *that uses* A^* *to win the experiment* $\mathbf{Exp}_{D^*}^{D\text{-}MLWE}$ *with the advantage* ε'.

The proof is provided in the full version of this paper [5].

Acknowledgments. We thank Marc Fischlin for helpful discussions. This work was funded by the Deutsche Forschungsgemeinschaft (DFG, German Research Foundation) – SFB 1119 – 236615297.

References

1. Abe, M., Okamoto, T.: Provably secure partially blind signatures. In: Bellare, M. (ed.) CRYPTO 2000. LNCS, vol. 1880, pp. 271–286. Springer, Heidelberg (2000). https://doi.org/10.1007/3-540-44598-6_17
2. Agrawal, S., Yadav, A.L.: Towards practical and round-optimal lattice-based threshold and blind signatures. Cryptology ePrint Archive, Report 2021/381
3. Alkeilani Alkadri, N., El Bansarkhani, R., Buchmann, J.: BLAZE: practical lattice-based blind signatures for privacy-preserving applications. In: Bonneau, J., Heninger, N. (eds.) FC 2020. LNCS, vol. 12059, pp. 484–502. Springer, Cham (2020). https://doi.org/10.1007/978-3-030-51280-4_26
4. Alkeilani Alkadri, N., El Bansarkhani, R., Buchmann, J.: On lattice-based interactive protocols: an approach with less or no aborts. In: Liu, J.K., Cui, H. (eds.) ACISP 2020. LNCS, vol. 12248, pp. 41–61. Springer, Cham (2020). https://doi.org/10.1007/978-3-030-55304-3_3
5. Alkeilani Alkadri, N., Harasser, P., Janson, C.: BlindOR: an efficient lattice-based blind signature scheme from or-proofs. Cryptology ePrint Archive, Report 2021/1385
6. Bellare, M., Neven, G.: Multi-signatures in the plain public-key model and a general forking lemma. In: ACM CCS 2006
7. Bellare, M., Rogaway, P.: Random oracles are practical: a paradigm for designing efficient protocols. In: ACM CCS 93
8. Camenisch, J., Neven, G., Shelat: Simulatable adaptive oblivious transfer. In: Naor, M. (ed.) EUROCRYPT 2007. LNCS, vol. 4515, pp. 573–590. Springer, Heidelberg (2007). https://doi.org/10.1007/978-3-540-72540-4_33
9. Chaum, D.: Blind signatures for untraceable payments. In: Chaum, D., Rivest, R.L., Sherman, A.T. (eds.) Advances in Cryptology. LNCS, pp. 199–203. Springer, Boston, MA (1983). https://doi.org/10.1007/978-1-4757-0602-4_18
10. Cramer, R., Damgård, I., Schoenmakers, B.: Proofs of partial knowledge and simplified design of witness hiding protocols. In: Desmedt, Y.G. (ed.) CRYPTO 1994. LNCS, vol. 839, pp. 174–187. Springer, Heidelberg (1994). https://doi.org/10.1007/3-540-48658-5_19
11. Fischlin, M.: Round-optimal composable blind signatures in the common reference string model. In: Dwork, C. (ed.) CRYPTO 2006. LNCS, vol. 4117, pp. 60–77. Springer, Heidelberg (2006). https://doi.org/10.1007/11818175_4
12. Fischlin, M., Schröder, D.: Security of blind signatures under aborts. In: Jarecki, S., Tsudik, G. (eds.) PKC 2009. LNCS, vol. 5443, pp. 297–316. Springer, Heidelberg (2009). https://doi.org/10.1007/978-3-642-00468-1_17

13. Garg, S., Rao, V., Sahai, A., Schröder, D., Unruh, D.: Round optimal blind signatures. In: Rogaway, P. (ed.) CRYPTO 2011. LNCS, vol. 6841, pp. 630–648. Springer, Heidelberg (2011). https://doi.org/10.1007/978-3-642-22792-9_36
14. Hauck, E., Kiltz, E., Loss, J.: A modular treatment of blind signatures from identification schemes. In: Ishai, Y., Rijmen, V. (eds.) EUROCRYPT 2019. LNCS, vol. 11478, pp. 345–375. Springer, Cham (2019). https://doi.org/10.1007/978-3-030-17659-4_12
15. Rückert, M.: Lattice-based blind signatures. In: Abe, M. (ed.) ASIACRYPT 2010. LNCS, vol. 6477, pp. 413–430. Springer, Heidelberg (2010). https://doi.org/10.1007/978-3-642-17373-8_24
16. Juels, A., Luby, M., Ostrovsky, R.: Security of blind digital signatures (extended abstract). In: Kaliski, B.S. (ed.) CRYPTO 1997. LNCS, vol. 1294, pp. 150–164. Springer, Heidelberg (1997). https://doi.org/10.1007/BFb0052233
17. Lyubashevsky, V.: Fiat-shamir with aborts: applications to lattice and factoring-based signatures. In: Matsui, M. (ed.) ASIACRYPT 2009. LNCS, vol. 5912, pp. 598–616. Springer, Heidelberg (2009). https://doi.org/10.1007/978-3-642-10366-7_35
18. Lyubashevsky, V.: Lattice signatures without trapdoors. In: Pointcheval, D., Johansson, T. (eds.) EUROCRYPT 2012. LNCS, vol. 7237, pp. 738–755. Springer, Heidelberg (2012). https://doi.org/10.1007/978-3-642-29011-4_43
19. Pointcheval, D., Stern, J.: Security arguments for digital signatures and blind signatures. J. Cryptology 13(3), 361–396 (2000)
20. Rückert, M.: Lattice-based blind signatures. In: Abe, M. (ed.) ASIACRYPT 2010. LNCS, vol. 6477, pp. 413–430. Springer, Heidelberg (2010). https://doi.org/10.1007/978-3-642-17373-8_24
21. Schröder, D., Unruh, D.: Security of blind signatures revisited. J. Cryptology, 30(2), 470–494 (2017)

Efficient Threshold-Optimal ECDSA

Michaella Pettit[(✉)]

nChain AG, Zug, Switzerland
m.pettit@nchain.com

Abstract. This paper proposes a threshold-optimal ECDSA scheme based on the first threshold signature scheme by Gennaro et al. with efficient non-interactive signing for any $t + 1$ signers in the group, provided the total group size is more than twice the threshold t. The scheme does not require any homomorphic encryption or zero-knowledge proofs and is proven to be robust and unforgeable with identifiable aborts tolerating at most t corrupted participants. The security of the scheme is proven in a simulation-based definition, assuming DDH and that ECDSA is existentially unforgeable under chosen message attack. To evaluate the performance of the protocol, it has been implemented in C++ and the results demonstrate the non-interactive signing phase takes 0.12 ms on average meaning over 8000 signatures can be created per second. With pre-signing phase, it takes 3.35 ms in total, which is over 144 times faster than the current state of the art.

Keywords: ECDSA · Multiparty computation · Threshold signatures

1 Introduction

A (t, N) threshold signature scheme is a method for a group of N participants to generate a signature on a message, without any individual participant having knowledge of the private key. A valid signature cannot be created by less than $t + 1$ participants. A benefit of using a threshold signature scheme is that the private key never exists at any point in time. There is no single point of failure, which mitigates against attack or loss of a private key.

One of the first threshold ECDSA schemes was proposed by Gennaro, Jarecki, Krawczyk, and Rabin [1]. A private key with threshold t is split between participants such that a subset of $2t + 1$ participants are required to create a signature. This protocol is fast during signing, in which a participant can compute their share of the signature upon request without knowledge of other signers. This absence of back-and-forth communication is known as non-interactive signing.

The drawback of [1] is that the threshold of participants required to create a signature is $2t$, which is twice that of computing the private key. The multiplication of two shared secrets, each with threshold t, requires $2t + 1$ participants. In the context of [1] the shared secrets are the private and ephemeral key.

Further work focused on achieving threshold-optimality in which the private key and signing threshold are the same, initially for two signers [2–5]. In 2016,

© Springer Nature Switzerland AG 2021
M. Conti et al. (Eds.): CANS 2021, LNCS 13099, pp. 116–135, 2021.
https://doi.org/10.1007/978-3-030-92548-2_7

a scheme by Gennaro et al. [6] was the first to achieve threshold-optimality for any threshold t and group size N in theory. It required a distributed generation of an RSA modulus, which cannot efficiently involve more than two parties. As a consequence, [6] cannot achieve more than $(1, N)$ in practice.

The first practical (t, N) threshold-optimal scheme for any threshold t and group size N was published in 2018 by Gennaro and Goldfeder [7]. This scheme was based on [6] and achieves optimality by turning multiplication of two secrets into an addition of secrets using homomorphic encryption, along with zero-knowledge proofs to ensure security of the scheme. This leads to multiple rounds of communication and an increase in computation, particularly during signing. The signing protocol requires one-to-one communication with every other signing participant, limiting the scaling capability of the scheme. If a participant drops offline during signing, the signing protocol must be restarted.

Recently, there have been many (t, N) threshold-optimal schemes proposed [8–12]. Their use of homomorphic encryption and zero-knowledge proofs means that they still require expensive computation and interactive signing.

In 2020, Canetti et al. [13] and Gennaro and Goldfeder [14] each proposed a non-interactive threshold-optimal scheme, with the latter including identifiable abort. However, both schemes still rely on homomorphic encryption and zero-knowledge proofs. Another property of these schemes is that the participants who must collaborate during the non-interactive signing process is predetermined.

In spite of recent advances in threshold ECDSA, to the best of the author's knowledge, current schemes have only achieved threshold-optimality with expensive computation such as homomorphic encryption and zero-knowledge proofs. Additionally, the signing must be interactive or involve a set of participants that is decided before the message has been received, and either case results in a large number of communication rounds and a high demand on overall computation.

Contributions. This paper proposes an efficient threshold-optimal ECDSA scheme.

- *Low computational complexity:* this is the first scheme to achieve threshold optimality without expensive computation like homomorphic encryption or zero-knowledge proofs on discrete logarithms, ranges of discrete logarithms, or others. Results show that it is over 144 times faster than [14] and almost 240 times faster than [13].
- *Low number of communication rounds:* the scheme requires four rounds in the signing protocol with identifiable abort where only the first requires secure one-to-one communication, equivalent to [1]. This is the same number of rounds as[13] and three rounds fewer than the protocol with identifiable abort in [14]. There are two rounds of communication in key generation which one round fewer than [14] and [13].
- *Non-interactive threshold-optimal signing:* the scheme is split into a pre-signing phase and a non-interactive signing phase once the message is known, similar to [14] and [13]. The signers are not predetermined in the signing step,

unlike [14] and [13]. Therefore, any failures by less than $N - t$ participants does not affect the ability to complete the final round.

- *Identifiable corrupted participants*: participants that deviate from the protocol can be identified, in line with the recent proposal in [14].
- *Provably secure*: a simulation-based security proof is provided to show that the scheme is robust and unforgeable.

2   Preliminaries

2.1   Decisional Diffie-Hellman Assumption

Decisional Diffie-Hellman. Let $\mathcal{G}$ be a cyclic group of prime order n generated by G. The following are computationally indistinguishable: (aG, bG, abG) with $a, b \in_R \mathbb{Z}_n$ and (aG, bG, cG) with $a, b, c \in_R \mathbb{Z}_n$.

2.2   ECDSA

The Digital Signature Algorithm is a digital signature scheme proposed by Kravitz [15] in 1991.[1] The public parameters PP in the scheme are an elliptic curve group $\mathcal{G}$ with points over the field $\mathbb{F}_p$, generator G, and order n.

- DSKeyGen: On input of a security parameter 1^l, this outputs a random private key $a \xleftarrow{\$} \mathbb{Z}_n^*$ and the corresponding public key $P = aG$ where aG is notation for point multiplication on an elliptic curve.
- DSSign: In order to calculate the signature on a message m using the private key a, the following steps are taken.
    1. Calculate the hash of the message $e \leftarrow hash(m)$.
    2. Randomly generate an ephemeral key $k \xleftarrow{\$} \mathbb{Z}_n^*$.
    3. Calculate $(x, y) \leftarrow kG$ then $r \leftarrow x \mod n$. If $r = 0$ return to Step 2.
    4. Calculate $s \leftarrow k^{-1}(e + ar) \mod n$. If $s = 0$ return to Step 2, otherwise output the signature as (r, s).
- DSVerify: In order to verify a signature (r, s) on a message m with a given public key P, the following steps are taken.
    1. Calculate the hash of the message $e \leftarrow hash(m)$.
    2. Calculate $(x', y') \leftarrow s^{-1}(eG + rP)$.
    3. Check if $r \overset{?}{=} x' \mod n$.

2.3   Threshold Signature Scheme

A threshold signature scheme is a tuple of protocols.

---

[1] The method can be applied to elliptic curve groups as given here, but it is understood that it may be applied to generic cyclic groups used in the standard DSA.

- TSKeyGen: The key generation algorithm takes public parameters PP as input. The output is composed of private outputs a_i known only to participant i for $i = 1, \ldots, N$, forming a (t, N) shared secret scheme corresponding to shared private key a, and a public output known to all participants which is the public key P corresponding to the shared private key.
- TSSign: The signing algorithm takes private key shares a_i and a message m in the message space $\mathcal{M}$ and outputs a signature sig.
- TSVerify: The verification algorithm has the public key P, signature sig, and message m as input, and outputs 1 if the signature is valid, or 0 otherwise.

2.4   Communication Model

In a scheme with N participants, it is assumed that they are connected by one-to-one secure communication channels and a broadcast channel. If participant i broadcasts a message, it is identifiable as being from that participant.

2.5   Adversary Model

It is assumed that an adversary can corrupt at most t participants in a threshold signature scheme, where $t + 1$ shares are required to reconstruct the private key. It is also assumed that the adversary has computational power that can be modelled by a probabilistic polynomial time (PPT) machine. There are three subtypes of adversaries:

- *Eavesdropping adversary:* this is a passive adversary that learns all information stored at corrupted nodes and all broadcasted messages.
- *Halting adversary:* this is an active adversary that is eavesdropping and may also stop corrupted participants from sending messages at each step.
- *Malicious adversary:* this is an active adversary that may cause any corrupted participant to deviate from the protocol.

A halting or malicious adversary may also be a *rushing adversary*, which is one that ensures corrupted participants speak last in any rounds of communication and may reorder any messages that are sent.

Definition 1. *As defined in* [1], *the view of the adversary is the knowledge of the adversary in a protocol. That is, the computational history of all corrupted participants and public communications, including the output of the protocol.*

The definitions of unforgeability and robustness are now given. These will enable a secure threshold signature scheme to be defined.

Definition 2. *A (t, N) threshold signature scheme is unforgeable if no malicious PPT adversary can produce a valid signature on a previously unsigned message m with non-negligible probability, where the adversary has knowledge of the following: the output of the key generation protocol $a_1, \ldots, a_t$ and P, and the output of the signature generation protocol $sig_1, \ldots, sig_\nu$ on messages $m_1, \ldots, m_\nu$, which the adversary chose.*

Definition 3. *A* threshold signature scheme *is* robust *if* TSKeyGen *and* TSSign *produce the expected outputs even in the presence of a halting or malicious adversary. An expected output of* TSKeyGen *is one in which* a_i *for* $i = 1, \ldots, N$ *are shares of a* (t, N) *shared secret that corresponds to the public output* P. *For* TSSign, *an expected output is one that is accepted by verification using* TSVerify.

For robustness, it does not matter if more than t participants are corrupted by an eavesdropping adversary, the protocol will still produce an expected output.

Definition 4. *A* (t, N) threshold signature scheme *is* secure *if it is robust and unforgeable in the presence of an adversary who corrupts at most* t *participants.*

In order to prove the unforgeability of the threshold scheme, it is necessary to be able to simulate the scheme. This is the definition from [1].

Definition 5. *A* threshold signature scheme *is* simulatable *if:*

1. *The key generation protocol* TSKeyGen *is simulatable. That is, there exists a simulator that can simulate the view of an adversary in an execution of* TSKeyGen *given the input of the public key and the public output generated by an execution of* TSKeyGen.
2. *The signing protocol* TSSign *is simulatable. That is, there exists a simulator that can simulate the view of the adversary on an execution of* TSSign *that takes the public key, message, t shares of a shared private key, and the signature on the message as input, and generates sig as an output.*

The security is proven by comparing the view of the adversary in the protocols TSKeyGen and TSSign to an ideal setting. This ideal setting is a simulation that is secure by definition. Therefore, showing that the view is indistinguishable to the attacker proves that the protocols TSKeyGen and TSSign are secure.

2.6   Verifiable Random Secret Sharing [16]

The TSKeyGen and TSSign protocols require a (t, N) secret sharing protocol, which has been chosen to be the scheme in [16] and has two rounds of communication.

- VRSS: This is the shared secret generation algorithm that takes the index i of each participant and the threshold t as input and outputs a share a_i of a shared secret for each participant i.
  1. Each participant i randomly generates integers $a_{il}, b_{il} \overset{\$}{\leftarrow} \mathbb{Z}_n$ for $l = 0, \ldots, t$, where a_{il}, b_{il} are the coefficients for the degree-l term in the polynomials $f_i(x)$ and $f_i'(x)$, respectively. Each participant i computes and broadcasts $C_{il} = a_{il}G + b_{il}H$ for each l, where H is a generator of the group and it is assumed an adversary cannot compute $log_G H$. Each participant i sends $f_i(j)$, $f_i'(j)$ via a one-to-one communication channel to participant j for each $j \neq i$.

2. Each participant j verifies if $f_i(j)G + f_i'(j)H \overset{?}{=} \sum_{l=0}^{t}(j)^l C_{il}$, for all $i \neq j$. If any i fails, participant j broadcasts a complaint against participant i.

3. Each participant i who was the subject of a complaint in the previous step broadcasts the values $f_i(j)$, $f_i'(j)$ satisfying the equation in Step 2.

4. The set of non-disqualified parties Q are those that received t or fewer complaints in Step 2, or answered the complaints with correct values.

5. Each participant $i \in Q$ calculates their secret share $a_i \leftarrow \sum_{j \in Q} f_j(i)$.

6. Each participant $i \in Q$ calculates and broadcasts $a_{il}G$ for each l.

7. Each participant j verifies if $f_i(j)G \overset{?}{=} \sum_{l=0}^{t}(j)^l(a_{il}G)$, for all $i \neq j$. If any i that passed the check in Step 2 fails this verification, participant j broadcasts a complaint against that participant by sharing the values $f_i(j)$, $f_i'(j)$ they received.

8. Each participant i reconstructs the values a_{j0} and $a_{j0}G$ for each participant j who receives a valid complaint, that is, those values that satisfy the equation in Step 2 and not in Step 7. Each participant constructs $P \leftarrow \sum_{i \in Q} a_{i0}G$.

Shares a_i allow operations on the shared secret values to be computed whilst keeping the value of the shared secrets hidden, even to the participants of the scheme. That is, the shared secret values never exist and cannot be computed by any participant unless the threshold is passed. Note in Feldman's verifiable secret sharing scheme [17], an adversary can change the distribution of the public key. Therefore, it can be used for shared secrets in which the corresponding public key is fixed or not used, or if the corrupted participants are eavesdropping only.

2.7 Verifiable Zero Secret Sharing [1]

It will be required to create shares of zero, using (t, N) verifiable zero secret sharing VZSS. This uses Feldman's verifiable secret sharing scheme [17] as the corresponding public key is fixed, so an adversary cannot change the distribution.

- VZSS: This is the shared secret generation algorithm that takes the index i of each participant and the threshold t as input and outputs a share a_i of a zero-valued shared secret for each participant i.

  1. Each participant i randomly generates integers $a_{il} \overset{\$}{\leftarrow} \mathbb{Z}_n$ for $l = 1, \ldots, t$ and sets $a_{i0} \leftarrow 0$, where a_{il} is the coefficient for the term of degree l in the polynomial $f_i(x)$. Each participant i sends $f_i(j)$ via a one-to-one communication channel to participant j for each $j \neq i$.
  2. Each participant i calculates their secret share $a_i \leftarrow \sum_{j=1}^{N} f_j(i)$.
  3. Each participant i calculates and broadcasts their obfuscated coefficients $a_{il}G$ for each $l = 1, \ldots, t$.
  4. Each participant j calculates $f_i(j)G$ using the value received in Step 2 and verifies if $f_i(j)G \overset{?}{=} \sum_{l=1}^{t}(j)^l(a_{il}G)$, for all $i \neq j$. Participant j broadcasts a complaint for any i whose values do not satisfy the equation.

By adding zero-shares to computations with shared secrets, a randomization of the shares is achieved without changing the result of the computation.

2.8   Operations on Shared Secrets

Given multiple shared secrets where the shares are points on a polynomial, it is possible to directly compute operations such as addition of secrets, multiplication of secrets, multiplication by a constant, or a combination of these simultaneously, provided enough shares of each shared secret are available. The shares k_i^{-1} that correspond to the inverse of a (t, N) shared secret with shares k_i are computed using the following protocol as given in [1].

- SSInverse: This takes shares k_i for $i = 1, \ldots, N$ as input and outputs the corresponding inverse shares k_i^{-1} for each i.
  1. All participants execute a (t, N) shared secret scheme, where the share of participant i is denoted by α_i.
  2. Each participant i computes $\mu_i \leftarrow \alpha_i k_i$ and broadcasts the result.
  3. All participants calculate $\mu \leftarrow interpolate(\mu_1, \ldots, \mu_{2t+1})$, where the notation $interpolate(\ldots)$ is Lagrange interpolation evaluated at $x = 0$ over shares $\mu_1, \ldots, \mu_{2t+1}$.
  4. Each participant i calculates their inverse share $k_i^{-1} \leftarrow \mu^{-1}\alpha_i$.

3   Efficient Threshold-Optimal Scheme

Threshold ECDSA signature generation involves the multiplication of two shared secrets, each with a threshold of t. The present scheme illustrates that it is possible to precalculate all multiplications prior to receiving a message without the use of expensive computation. The signature generation on the message is threshold-optimal and non-interactive, with no restriction on the $t + 1$ participants that sign. While the number of participants required to calculate the multiplication in precalculation is $2t + 1$, the signature threshold during the non-interactive signing phase is now the same as the threshold t of the private key.

Observe that a signature in ECDSA has the form (r, s), where

$$s = k^{-1}e + k^{-1}ar. \tag{1}$$

Here, e is the hash of the message, a is the private key, and r is derived from the public key corresponding to the ephemeral key k. The second term is independent of the message, meaning that it can be calculated prior to receiving a message in a pre-signing phase. However, if the value $k^{-1}a$ itself is known, as soon as the signature is calculated it is trivial to calculate the private key a. To secure the result $k^{-1}a$, another (t, N) shared secret β is added into this computation.

Explicitly, the signature is

$$s = k^{-1}e + r(\sigma - \beta), \tag{2}$$

where $\sigma = k^{-1}a + \beta$ is precalculated. The signature is now an addition of k^{-1} and β which are both (t, N) shared secrets, therefore only $t + 1$ shares are required.

While at least $2t+1$ participants are required to execute the full scheme, during the final step once the message is known the number of participants required

$t + 1$ is the same as the number required to calculate the private key and this may be any subset of the group. Therefore, threshold-optimality is achieved in the non-interactive signing phase without requiring expensive computations like homomorphic encryption or zero-knowledge proofs. Due to the absence of these expensive computations, it is feasible for multiple k, σ, and corresponding r values to be precalculated in parallel and stored until required. Benchmarking shows an average time of this pre-computation in a scheme with three participants, 2 of which are required to compute a signature, is 3.22 ms before any parallelisation, meaning that over 310 values could be calculated per second. One of these precalculated values is used with each signature and then discarded.

If optimised, the rounds of communication may be as low as three prior to receiving the message and there will be only one round during signature generation. Similarly, after the initial round during VRSS, which has one-to-one communication, the remaining rounds are broadcasts, including signature generation. The implication of this is that the scheme is easily scalable.

3.1 Distributed Key Generation

The following protocol is a known result. TSKeyGen takes the public parameters PP as input and outputs a secret share a_i only known to participant i that corresponds to a share of a (t, N) shared private key a and a public output that is the public key P. The protocol has two rounds of communication since it uses VRSS. Assume all participants have agreed on each other's unique, non-zero integer i, usually chosen to be $i = 1, \ldots, N$.

TSKeyGen
Input: public parameters PP, index i for $i = 1, \ldots, N$, threshold t
Output: shares a_i for $i = 1, \ldots, N$, public key P

1. All participants execute a (t, N) shared key generation VRSS where participant i obtains the secret output a_i and public output P.

At the end of this protocol, each participant i stores a share a_i and the public key P where $P = aG$ is the same for all participants.

3.2 Signature Generation

The signature generation protocol TSSign allows for precalculation which has 3 rounds of communication. The participants compute all the possible values that are independent of the message and store until it is required to calculate a signature on a message m in the final round.

TSSign
Input: private key shares a_i for $i = 1, \ldots, N$, message m
Output: signature (r, s)

1. All participants calculate the ephemeral key shares and corresponding public key using a (t, N) execution of VRSS, where participant i's share is k_i and the public key is $(x, y) \leftarrow \sum_{i=1}^{N} k_{i0}G$. All participants calculate $r \leftarrow x \mod n$.
2. All participants create two (t, N) shared secrets using two instances of VRSS with resulting shares denoted by α_i and β_i corresponding to participant i. Each participant i also calculates the commitment of α_j and β_j

$$\alpha_j G \leftarrow \sum_{l=1}^{N} \sum_{m=0}^{t} j^m (\alpha_{lm}G) , \tag{3}$$

$$\beta_j G \leftarrow \sum_{l=1}^{N} \sum_{m=0}^{t} j^m (\beta_{lm}G) , \tag{4}$$

for each participant $j \neq i$, where $\alpha_{lm}G$ and $\beta_{lm}G$ are received during Step 6 of VRSS, and stores $\alpha_j G$ and $\beta_j G$.
3. All participants create a zero-valued $(2t, N)$ shared secret with shares denoted by κ_i for participant i using VZSS.
4. Each participant i calculates $\mu_i \leftarrow \alpha_i k_i + \kappa_i$ and $\lambda_i \leftarrow \alpha_i a_i + \beta_i$, and $\alpha_i(kG)$, $(\alpha_i P + \beta_i G)$ and broadcasts these.
5. Each participant i verifies

$$interpolate(\mu_i, \ldots, \mu_{i'})G \stackrel{?}{=} interpolate(\alpha_i(kG), \ldots, \alpha_{j'}(kG)) , \tag{5}$$

$$interpolate(\lambda_i, \ldots, \lambda_{i'})G \stackrel{?}{=} interpolate((\alpha_i P + \beta_i G), \ldots, (\alpha_{j'} P + \beta_{j'}G)) , \tag{6}$$

where $i' = (i + 2t + 1)$ and $j' = (i + t + 1)$. If the index i' is larger than N, the values wrap around to index 1 again. If any of these are found to be different, the adversaries are identified by interpolating over all possible sets of shares and all sets which result in the same values contain only honest participants. Corrupted participants are identified as those not contained in these sets.
6. If the equalities hold for all participants, each participant i sets

$$\mu \leftarrow interpolate(\mu_1, \ldots, \mu_{2t+1}) \quad (= \alpha k) , \tag{7}$$

$$\lambda \leftarrow interpolate(\lambda_1, \ldots, \lambda_{2t+1}) \quad (= \alpha a + \beta) . \tag{8}$$

7. Each participant i calculates their inverse shares $k_i^{-1} \leftarrow \mu^{-1}\alpha_i$ of the shared ephemeral key and their precalculated shares $\sigma_i \leftarrow r\mu^{-1}(\lambda - \beta_i)$.
8. Each participant i stores (r, k_i^{-1}, σ_i) for use in the signature computation and $(\alpha_j G, \beta_j G)$ for all participants j for verification of the signature.

The pre-signing phase can be executed prior to receiving any message. The non-interactive signing phase takes the message m and precalculated values (r, k_i^{-1}, σ_i) as input and output the signature (r, s).

9. At least $t + 1$ participants compute the hash the message $e = hash(m)$, calculate their signature share $s_i \leftarrow k_i^{-1}e + \sigma_i$, and broadcast.

10. Participants set $s \leftarrow interpolate(s_1, \ldots, s_{t+1})$ and the signature is (r, s).

A signature has been computed using only $t+1$ shares after precalculation. Note that TSVerify is the same as DSVerify described in Sect. 2.2 and is not repeated here. If the signature is found to be incorrect using TSVerify, the corrupted participants are identified using CorruptID.

3.3 Identifiable Abort

If the signature generated with TSSign is found to be incorrect, the following protocol is executed. Assume the participants that have signed are those with indices $i = 1, \ldots, t+1$, without loss of generality.

CorruptID
Input: obfuscated shares $\alpha_i G, \beta_i G$ for $i = 1, \ldots, t+1$
Output: identity of corrupted participants j

1. Each participant i calculates $k_j^{-1}G \leftarrow (k\alpha)^{-1}\alpha_j G$ and $\sigma_j G \leftarrow r\mu^{-1}(\lambda G - \beta_j G)$ for each participant j who executed Step 9 to 10 in TSSign.
2. Each participant then checks $s_j G \overset{?}{=} e(k_j^{-1}G) + (\sigma_j G)$ for each j. If this does not hold for a given j, that share is incorrect.

3.4 Discussion

In TSSign, a signature has been created with the same threshold as that of the shared private key, after the precalculation steps have been completed. The s value of the signature can be written as

$$s = \mu^{-1}\alpha e + r\mu^{-1}(\lambda - \beta) , \qquad (9)$$

where α and β are (t, N) shared secrets, and $\mu = \alpha k$ and $\lambda = \alpha a + \beta$ are precalculated. By replacing μ and λ, this becomes $s = k^{-1}(e + ar)$, as required.

The computation of λ may be considered a method to calculate the multiplication of two shared secrets whilst hiding the result. With each shared secret having a threshold t, the computation of λ requires $2t + 1$ shares. Interpolation over $t + 1$ shares of σ_i will result in $k^{-1}a$ as the β terms will cancel. This share σ_i may be seen as a share of $k^{-1}a$ with a threshold of t. Therefore, after Step 6 the threshold of the multiplication of the two shared secrets is reduced to t.

While $2t + 1$ participants are required until Step 8 of TSSign, after this only $t + 1$ of the N participants are required. There may be multiple parallelized computations running up to Step 8, at which point these σ_i, k_i^{-1}, r values may be stored until required for use. Once a value is used for signing, these are not to be used again.

No expensive computation such as homomorphic encryption or zero-knowledge proofs are required as in all previous threshold-optimal constructions [6–14, 18]. Instead of homomorphic encryption and zero-knowledge proofs, this protocol has three additional executions of VRSS compared to other threshold-optimal protocols, however it will be shown to be 144 times faster than [14] which also proposes precomputation. Additionally, by not using homomorphic encryption and zero-knowledge proofs, the proposed scheme has fewer communication rounds even with additional VRSS and VZSS executions compared to other schemes. Although $2t + 1$ participants are required for precomputation, with all these other efficiency improvements it is still more practical than previous schemes.

Verification of $\alpha_i(kG)$ and $(\alpha_i P + \beta_i G)$ in Steps 4 and 5 ensure robustness. Without these, it is possible for an unidentifiable corrupted participant j to send incorrect values for μ_j or λ_j, which would prevent a signature from being created. If a corrupted participant attempts to send an incorrect value for the multiplication of shares, there is no value that will pass the verifications aside from the correct value. This is because every participant is interpolating over a different set of shares and knows that all participants receive the same broadcasted values. The same logic is applied to the verification of λ_i and $\alpha_i P$.

Note that in the non-interactive signing phase of the scheme, the signature is calculated assuming the participants are honest, but the result is verified for correctness. If the signature is found to be invalid, the shares are checked individually to identify the incorrect share. This does not require any further rounds of communication, since all participants already have enough knowledge to verify shares. While this could be executed prior to calculating the signature, it would slow down those rounds which are executed correctly and is therefore more efficient to perform these verification steps only if necessary.

4   Security Proof

In this section, the following theorem is proven, assuming it is infeasible to forge a signature in ECDSA [19].

Theorem 1. *The threshold signature scheme in Sect. 3 is secure in the presence of d participants corrupted by an eavesdropping adversary and h participants corrupted by a halting or malicious adversary, if the total number of participants is $N > 2t + h$ and number of corrupted participants is $d + h \leq t$.*

The proof is split into proving robustness and then unforgeability.

Lemma 1. *The threshold signature scheme in Sect. 3 is robust, if the number of participants in the scheme is $N > 2t + h$ where h is the number of participants corrupted by a halting (or malicious) adversary.*

Proof. The scheme will be shown to be robust in the presence of $2t + 1$ participants who do not deviate from the protocol, such that the signature that is generated will always be accepted by an execution of TSVerify. Note that these participants may include d eavesdropping participants. Shares that belong to participants who do not deviate from the protocol will be referred to as correct shares. Specifically, the requirement of $2t + 1$ correct shares is due to the multiplications of (t, N) shared secrets in Step 4 of TSSign. After this point, only $t + 1$ correct shares are required to be robust.

There are three rounds of communication in which there is scope for participants to send values that deviate from the protocol. Each of these rounds are followed by verifications and it is these steps that identify correct shares.

- Step 2 and Step 7 of VRSS executed in TSKeyGen and TSSign: if shares of any $f_i(j)$ are not received or invalid before Step 4, all shares of that private polynomial are removed from the calculation. The values that do not validate correctly in Step 7 are recovered by the honest participants using the values received in Step 1 to compute the public key corresponding to the shares. There will be at most h private polynomials removed, with at least $2t + 1$ remaining. Therefore, there will still be at least $2t + 1$ shares a_i output from VRSS due to the requirement of $N > 2t + h$.
- Step 5 of TSSign: there must be $2t + 1$ shares of μ or λ, since they are a multiplication of (t, N) shared secrets. This is the case as there are at least $2t + 1$ participants who do not deviate from the protocol. These shares can be detected as those which are contained in sets that find the equalities in this step hold. Therefore, enough correct shares exist and can be identified. The calculations of μ and λ use these correct shares.
- Steps 1 and 2 in CorruptID: the shares s_i which agree with the obfuscated shares calculated from the execution of VRSS are used in the computation of the signature. Since there are at least $2t + 1$ participants that do not deviate from the protocol, and there are $t + 1$ required for this calculation, there will always enough shares to calculate the signature. These shares can be detected using CorruptID.

It has been illustrated that incorrect shares can always be detected and there will always be enough correct shares remaining for each computation. Hence, TSKeyGen and TSSign will produce expected outputs given $N > 2t + h$ and the scheme described in Sect. 3 is robust.   □

The proof of unforgeability is given by proving each protocol can be simulated in a way which the adversary cannot distinguish the simulation from the real protocol. In order to prove that TSSign is indistinguishable from its simulation, it is necessary to generate an elliptic curve point (x, y) from the r value in a signature such that the point appears uniformly random among the set of all candidates of (x, y). Recall that r in a signature (r, s) is an x value of an elliptic curve point modulo n and the elliptic curve is defined over $\mathbb{F}_p$.

ECPointDerivation
Input: r
Output: $\hat{k}G$

1. To calculate the x value
   - If $n \geq p$, set $x \leftarrow r$.

– If $n < p$ and
  - $r \geq (p - n)$, set $x \leftarrow r$.
  - $r < (p - n)$, calculate $(r + n) \mod p$. Check which of r and $(r + n)$ correspond to x values on the elliptic curve.
    * If only one is an x value on the elliptic curve, set that to x.
    * If both are x values, randomly choose one to set to x.
2. Calculate a y' value corresponding to x according to the elliptic curve equation. If there is only one unique y' value, set $y \leftarrow y'$, otherwise calculate $-y'$ and randomly select $y \leftarrow y'$ or $y \leftarrow -y'$.
3. Set the point to be $\hat{k}G \leftarrow (x, y)$.

This derivation ensures that the distribution of points kG remains uniform when derived from r. The point that r was derived from does not need to be the same as the point that is found with this method.

Each protocol in the scheme described in Sect. 3 is now shown to be simulatable and indistinguishable from that simulation. In each step of the simulations, the action in the brackets describe the steps the adversary takes. It is assumed that the adversary generates the values corresponding to the corrupted participants. This is stronger than assuming that the adversary only learns the shares of the corrupted participants and so subsumes this case. Note that to ensure the steps in the simulation coincide with the steps in the protocol, some of simulation steps require that the simulator wait for the adversary to execute computations. These steps are written as 'go to next step', or 'end protocol' if it is the last step in the protocol.

VRSS is proven to be secure in [16], which is used in both the key generation simulation and in the signature generation simulation, denoted VRSS-sim. The input to the simulation is the public key P, indices i, and threshold t.

Lemma 2. *The* TSKeyGen *protocol described in Sect. 3.1 is simulatable and is indistinguishable from its simulation from the point of view of the adversary.*

Proof. Assume that the indices i of participants have been generated already and, without loss of generality, that the adversary has corrupted participants $i = 1, \ldots, t$. The steps in the following simulation coincide with the steps in the protocol in Sect. 3.1.

TSKeyGen-sim
Input: public key P, index i for $i = 1, \ldots, N$, threshold t
Output: shares $\hat{a}_i$ for $i = 1, \ldots, N$, public key P

1. The simulator invokes VRSS-sim outputting a_i for $i = t + 1, \ldots, N$ and P. (The adversary executes VRSS to calculate a_i for $i = 1, \ldots, t$ and P.)

It has been shown in [16] that VRSS is indistinguishable from VRSS-sim. The signature that is to be generated can be verified against this public key and the verification will be accepted. These steps are therefore indistinguishable to the adversary from TSKeyGen.   □

In order to simulate TSKeyGen, VZSS is first shown to be unforgeable.

Lemma 3. *The* VZSS *protocol described in Sect. 2.7 is simulatable and is indistinguishable from its simulation from the point of view of the adversary.*

Proof. The simulation of VZSS is given below.

VZSS-sim
Input: index i, threshold t
Output: shares $\hat{a}_i$ for $i = 1, \ldots, N$

1. The simulator generates uniformly random values $\eta_{ji} \in \mathbb{Z}_n^*$ for $j = t+1, \ldots, N$ and $i = 1, \ldots, t$ and shares $\hat{f}_j(i) \leftarrow \eta_{ji}$ with the adversary and receives $\hat{f}_i(j)$ for $j = t+1, \ldots, N$. (The adversary generates coefficients $\hat{a}_{il}$ of $\hat{f}_i(x)$ for $i, l = 1, \ldots, t$, shares $\hat{f}_i(j)$ and receives $\hat{f}_j(i)$ from the simulator for $j = t+1, \ldots, N$.)
2. Go to next step. (The adversary calculates $\hat{a}_i$ for $i = 1, \ldots, t$.)
3. The simulator calculates

$$\hat{f}_j(x) \leftarrow \sum_{l=1}^{t} \hat{f}_j(l) \prod_{\substack{1 \leq j \leq t+1, \\ j \neq i}} (x-j)(l-j)^{-1} \mod n, \tag{10}$$

that satisfy the above values. The simulator uses these values to calculate $\hat{a}_j$, $\hat{a}_{jl}G$ for $j = t+1, \ldots, N$ and stores $\hat{a}_j$. The simulator shares $\hat{a}_{jl}G$ and receives $\hat{a}_{il}G$ from the adversary. (The adversary shares $\hat{a}_{il}G$ and receives $\hat{a}_{jl}G$ from the simulator.)
4. End protocol. (The adversary verifies $f_i(j)$.)

In Step 1 above, the adversary receives shares $\hat{f}_i(j)$ from the simulator which are randomly generated and therefore uniformly distributed. Compare this to VZSS, where the adversary receives shares $f_i(j)$ which are calculated from the addition of values which are uniformly distributed. To an adversary, these sets of values are indistinguishable.

Similarly, in Step 3 of VZSS-sim, the adversary receives coefficients $\hat{a}_{jl}G$ which are calculated from the addition of randomly generated values η_{ji}, hence are uniformly distributed across the set. This ensures they are indistinguishable from the values $a_{jl}G$ that are received in VZSS.

Finally, the verifications in Step 4 will be accepted by the adversary due to the way that the coefficients are generated in Step 3 of the simulation.   □

Lemma 4. *The* TSSign *protocol described in Sect. 3.2 is simulatable and is indistinguishable from its simulation from the point of view of the adversary.*

Proof. The steps in the following simulation coincide with those in the protocol in Sect. 3.2.

TSSign-sim
Input: shares $\hat{a}_1, \ldots, \hat{a}_t$, public key P, message m, signature (r, s)
Output: $\bot$

1. The simulator executes ECPointDerivation that outputs $\hat{k}G \leftarrow (x, y)$ with r as input. The simulator invokes VRSS-sim using input $\hat{k}G$, outputting $\hat{k}_i$ for $i = 1, \ldots, t$. (The adversary executes VRSS to obtain $\hat{k}_i$, $\hat{k}G$ and computes r.)

2. The simulator randomly generates $\hat{\alpha}$, $\hat{\beta}$, $\hat{\mu}$ and calculates $\hat{\lambda} \leftarrow r^{-1}(\hat{\mu}s - \hat{\alpha}e + \hat{\beta}r) \mod n$, where $e = hash(m)$. The simulator executes two instances of VRSS-sim to calculate $\hat{\alpha}_i$ and $\hat{\beta}_i$ for $j = 1, \ldots, N$, using $\hat{\alpha}$ and $\hat{\beta}$ as input. (Adversary calculates $\hat{\alpha}_i$ and $\hat{\beta}_i$ for $i = 1, \ldots, t$ using two instances of VRSS, $\hat{\alpha}_j G, \hat{\beta}_j G$ and stores.)

3. The simulator executes VZSS-sim outputting $\hat{\kappa}_i$ for $i = 1, \ldots, t$. (The adversary calculates $\hat{\kappa}_i$ using VZSS for $i = 1, \ldots, t$.)

4. The simulator takes the following steps.
   - Calculate $\hat{\mu}_i \leftarrow \hat{\alpha}_i \hat{k}_i + \hat{\kappa}_i$ for $i = 1, \ldots, t$. Calculate $\hat{\mu}_i$ for $i = t+1, \ldots, 2t$ such that $\hat{\mu}_i$ for $i = 1, \ldots, 2t$ defines a polynomial $\hat{f}(x)$ such that $\hat{f}(0) = \hat{\mu}$. Calculate $\hat{\mu}_i \leftarrow \hat{f}(i)$ for $i = 2t+1, \ldots, N$.
   - Calculate $\hat{\lambda}_i \leftarrow \hat{\alpha}_i \hat{a}_i + \hat{\beta}_i$ for $i = 1, \ldots, t$. Calculate share $\hat{\lambda}_i$ for $i = t+1, \ldots 2t$ such that $\hat{\lambda}_i$ for $i = 1, \ldots, 2t$ define a polynomial $\hat{g}(x)$ such that $\hat{g}(0) = \hat{\lambda}$. Calculate $\hat{\lambda}_i \leftarrow \hat{g}(i)$ for $i = 2t+1, \ldots, N$.
   - Calculate $\hat{\alpha}_i(\hat{k}G)$, and $(\hat{\alpha}_i P + \hat{\beta}_i G)$ for $i = 1, \ldots, t$, and calculate $\hat{\mu}G$ and $\hat{\lambda}G$. Compute

$$\hat{\alpha}_j(\hat{k}G) \leftarrow interpolate(\hat{\mu}G, \hat{\alpha}_1(\hat{k}G), \ldots, \hat{\alpha}_t(\hat{k}G)), \tag{11}$$

$$(\hat{\alpha}_j P + \hat{\beta}G) \leftarrow interpolate(\hat{\lambda}G, (\hat{\alpha}_1 P + \hat{\beta}_1 G), \ldots, (\hat{\alpha}_t P + \hat{\beta}_t G)), \tag{12}$$

   for $j = t+1, \ldots, N$ and where $\hat{\mu}G$ and $\hat{\lambda}G$ are the points at $x = 0$.
   - The simulator broadcasts $\hat{\mu}_i$, $\hat{\lambda}_i$, $\hat{\alpha}_i(\hat{k}G)$, and $(\hat{\alpha}_i P + \hat{\beta}_i G)$ for each $i = t+1, \ldots, N$ and receives values for $i = 1, \ldots, t$. (The adversary calculates $\hat{\mu}_i$, $\hat{\lambda}_i$, $\hat{\alpha}_i(\hat{k}G)$, and $(\hat{\alpha}_i P + \hat{\beta}_i G)$ and broadcasts.)

5. Go to next step. (The adversary verifies $\hat{\mu}_i$, $\hat{\lambda}_i$ and $\hat{\alpha}_i(\hat{k}G)$, $(\hat{\alpha}_i P + \hat{\beta}_i G)$ interpolate to the same result.)

6. Go to next step. (The adversary sets values $\hat{\mu}, \hat{\lambda}$.)

7. Calculate $\hat{k}_i^{-1} \leftarrow \hat{\mu}^{-1} \hat{\alpha}_i$ and $\hat{\sigma}_i \leftarrow r\hat{\mu}^{-1}(\hat{\lambda} - \hat{\beta}_i)$ for all $i = t+1, \ldots, N$ given $\hat{\alpha}_i$, $\hat{\beta}_i$ calculated in Step 2. (The adversary calculates $\hat{k}_i^{-1}$ and $\hat{\sigma}_i$ for $i = 1, \ldots, t$.)

8. Go to next step. (The adversary stores values.)

9. The simulator calculates $\hat{s}_i \leftarrow \hat{k}_i^{-1} e + \hat{\sigma}_i$ for $t+1$ randomly selected values of i within the range $i = t+1, \ldots, N$ and shares these values. (The adversary calculates $\hat{s}_i$ for $i = 1, \ldots, t$.)

10. End protocol. (The adversary calculates (r, s).)

While the signature (r, s) will be accepted if verified with the public key, the adversary can still ensure the shares generated by the simulator are also correct.

CorruptID-sim
Input: shares $\hat{s}_1, \ldots, \hat{s}_{t+1}$, message m
Output: $\perp$

1. Go to next step. (The adversary calculates $\hat{k}_j^{-1}G$ and $\hat{\sigma}_jG$ for each participant j that took part in the signature.)
2. End protocol. (The adversary verifies that these obfuscated values were used to generate the signature shares $\hat{s}_i$ by comparing to $\hat{s}_iG$.)

In Step 1 to 3, the simulation of VRSS is used multiple times. It has been already shown that the simulation is indistinguishable from VRSS itself in [16]. Moreover, the public key $\hat{k}G$ that is calculated by the adversary in Step 1 is uniformly distributed across the set of elliptic curve points as it uses ECPoint-Derivation. Therefore, the first three steps are indistinguishable to the adversary from the first three steps in TSSign.

The values $\hat{\mu}$, $\hat{\alpha}$, $\hat{\beta}$ are randomly generated from a uniformly distributed set of values. All values in Step 4 of the simulation are derived from these, including $\hat{\mu}_i$, $\hat{\lambda}_i$, $\hat{\alpha}_i(\hat{k}G)$, and $(\hat{\alpha}_iP + \hat{\beta}_iG)$, which the adversary receives. Therefore, the values that the adversary receives also appear uniformly distributed. On the other hand, in TSSign, the corresponding values μ_i, λ_i, $\alpha_i(kG)$, and $(\alpha_iP + \beta_iG)$ that an adversary receives are similarly uniformly distributed, by the same reasoning. Therefore, an adversary will not be able to distinguish between the two sets.

Note that the values $\hat{\mu}$ and $\hat{\lambda}-\hat{\beta}$ are not equivalent to $\hat{a}\hat{k}$ and $\hat{a}a$. If they were, a and $\hat{k}$ could be revealed, since the values $\hat{\alpha}$, $\hat{\beta}$ must be known to ensure that $\hat{s}_i$ are accepted in CorruptID-sim. This contradicts the assumption that ECDSA is unforgeable. As a result of this, the DDH assumption is required as described in Sect. 2.1, similar to [1]. However, due to the construction of the values, the verifications by the adversary are still accepted in the simulation.

In Step 5 to 9, the adversary is executing their own calculations. In Step 10 the simulator shares the values $\hat{s}_i$. Since $\hat{s}_i$ are calculated from values that are uniformly distributed themselves, the result is that the set of signature shares are also uniformly distributed. Again, this is the same as the protocol TSSign and so the adversary will have the same view within the two protocols. The calculations executed by the simulator in Step 4 ensure that the shares will result in the correct signature. Step 4 also ensures that the signature shares will individually pass the checks in CorruptID-sim, as stated previously.

As a result, the calculations executed by the adversary will be accepted and have the same probability distribution. Therefore, the adversary will not be able to identify that it is in the simulation. □

Lemma 5. *The view of an adversary in the protocol described in Sect. 3 is indistinguishable from the view of the adversary in a simulation from the point of view of the adversary.*

Proof. It has been shown that both TSKeyGen and TSSign are simulatable and indistinguishable from their simulation in Lemma 2 and Lemma 4. Therefore, the view of the adversary in the scheme described in Sect. 3 is indistinguishable from the simulation from the point of view of the adversary. □

Lemma 6. *The threshold signature scheme described in Sect. 3 is unforgeable if the total number of participants is $N > 2t + h$ and there are number of corrupted* participants is $d + h \leq t$, where d and h are the number of participants corrupted by an eavesdropping adversary and by a halting (or malicious) adversary, respectively.

Proof. If the total number of corrupted participants is more than t, that the (t, N) shared secret can be calculated and therefore also a signature. On the other hand, by assuming that $d + h \leq t$, the shared private key, and therefore signature, cannot be calculated. This has been shown in that the view of the adversary in TSKeyGen and TSSign is indistinguishable from their simulations. Since the simulations are unforgeable by definition, this means that TSKeyGen and TSSign are also unforgeable. □

5   Benchmarking

TSKeyGen and TSSign have been implemented assuming there are only eavesdropping adversaries in TSSign. That is, it uses Feldman secret sharing as in [17] and excludes Step 5 of TSSign and CorruptID. The implementation is compared data given for schemes [14] and [13] which are also non-interactive. The implementation was written in C++ and was run on a 2018 MacBook Pro with a 2.6 GHz Intel Core i7 processor and 32GB RAM. Participants were run as separate processes on a single machine using a single core. In practice, calculation by different participants is executed in parallel and so the timings will be reduced further. The data for [14] is chosen to be the scheme without identifiable abort to compare fairly with the implementation of the scheme in Sect. 3. The data for [13] was only available for precalculation of the signature and up to $t = 8$.

The scheme was run 20 times for each threshold and group size up to $t = 9$ and $N = 20$ in line with [14] and [13]. TSSign was split to measure the average time for the precalculation in Step 1 to 8, and the average time for the non-interactive signing in Step 9 to 10. Even if there are failures by at most t participants, this does not impact the progression of the protocol.

While the main benefit of this scheme is lost if precalculation is executed after the message has been received, in the effort of fair comparison, the whole TSSign protocol is compared to other schemes. It was found that the majority of time is taken with precalculation, as expected, and so the time to run TSSign from Sect. 3 was roughly constant even as the threshold increased for the same group size. This is expected because all participants are required in precalculation for any threshold. Choosing the group sizes to be $N = 2t + 1$ for Sect. 3, the comparison with [14] and [13] are shown in Fig. 1.

All data excludes network latency time for equal comparison with [14] and [13], since the connection speed is independent of the protocol. Table 1 compares rounds of communication in the three schemes. Since Sect. 3 has fewer communication rounds, it will be even faster than [14] and [13], when including network latency. By avoiding use of complex protocols such as homomorphic encryption and zero-knowledge proofs, the communication rounds have been reduced.

Figure 2 shows the speed of signing after precalculation for the scheme presented in Sect. 3. That is, Step 9 to 10 in TSSign, taking $N = 2t + 1$ for each t.

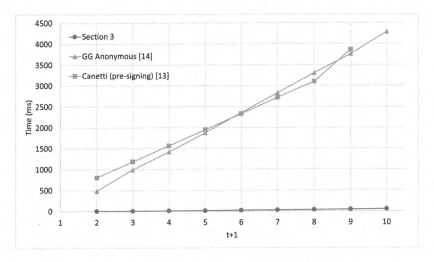

Fig. 1. Comparison of signing timings (including precalculation) of Sect. 3 with [14] and [13] for t up to 9. [13] includes only precalculation and t up to 8.

Table 1. Table showing the number of rounds of communication in key generation and signing comparing Sect. 3 in the presence of eavesdropping adversaries, [14], and [13].

Communication rounds	Sect. 3	[14]	[13]
Key generation	2	3	3
Signing protocol	4	6	4

Given a non-interactive signing time of 0.12ms for $t = 1$, the number of signatures that can be generated per second with this scheme is over 8000.

Finally, the size of communications is compared in Fig. 3. The data is given in kB and compared to precalculation in [13] (the data is not available in [14]). The size of communications given for Sect. 3 includes both precalculation and the non-interactive signing step.

The communication size in [13] increases linearly in the group size, whilst the data for Sect. 3 increases quadratically with the group size. This is because all participants are required during precalculation steps in signing for the scheme in Sect. 3. This impacts the precalculation stage but has the benefit that any participant can execute the non-interactive phase. In the non-interactive phase, the communication in Sect. 3 increases linearly with the number of signers.

There is also timing and communication size in [13] for part of the key generation algorithm, which has a significant overhead. The data is for generating Pallier keys (required in both [14] and [13]), which are not needed for the scheme in Sect. 3, and therefore not comparable. This is additional time and computational complexity in [14] and [13] that is not in the scheme in Sect. 3.

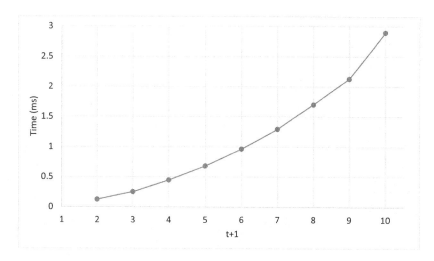

Fig. 2. Time taken to create a signature after precalculation given in milliseconds (ms) for Sect. 3.

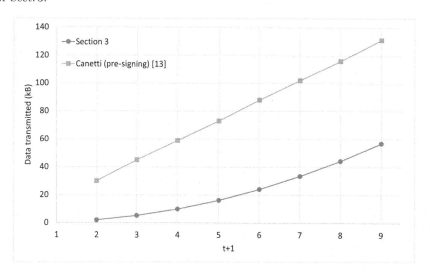

Fig. 3. Size of communication transmitted in kilobytes (kB). The data in [13] is the precalculated data only, and the data for Sect. 3 includes data for the whole signing protocol.

Acknowledgements. The author thanks Owen Vaughan, Wei Zhang, Mehmet Sabir Kiraz, and Katharine Molloy for useful comments on the paper. The author also thanks John Murphy and Josie Wilden for implementing the scheme.

References

1. Gennaro, R., Jarecki, S., Krawczyk, H., Rabin, T.: Robust threshold DSS signatures. In: Maurer, U. (ed.) EUROCRYPT 1996. LNCS, vol. 1070, pp. 354–371. Springer, Heidelberg (1996). https://doi.org/10.1007/3-540-68339-9_31

2. MacKenzie, P., Reiter, M.K.: Two-party generation of DSA signatures. Int. J. Inf. Secur. **2**(3–4), 218–239 (2004)
3. Lindell, Y.: Fast secure two-party ECDSA signing. In: Katz, J., Shacham, H. (eds.) CRYPTO 2017. LNCS, vol. 10402, pp. 613–644. Springer, Cham (2017). https://doi.org/10.1007/978-3-319-63715-0_21
4. Doerner, J., Kondi, Y., Lee, E., Shelat, A.: Secure two-party threshold ecdsa from ecdsa assumptions. In: 2018 IEEE Symposium on Security and Privacy (SP), pp. 980–997. IEEE (2018)
5. Castagnos, G., Catalano, D., Laguillaumie, F., Savasta, F., Tucker, I.: Two-party ECDSA from hash proof systems and efficient instantiations. In: Boldyreva, A., Micciancio, D. (eds.) CRYPTO 2019. LNCS, vol. 11694, pp. 191–221. Springer, Cham (2019). https://doi.org/10.1007/978-3-030-26954-8_7
6. Gennaro, R., Goldfeder, S., Narayanan, A.: Threshold-optimal DSA/ECDSA signatures and an application to bitcoin wallet security. In: Manulis, M., Sadeghi, A.-R., Schneider, S. (eds.) ACNS 2016. LNCS, vol. 9696, pp. 156–174. Springer, Cham (2016). https://doi.org/10.1007/978-3-319-39555-5_9
7. Gennaro, R., Goldfeder, S.: Fast multiparty threshold ecdsa with fast trustless setup. In: Proceedings of the 2018 ACM SIGSAC Conference on Computer and Communications Security, pp. 1179–1194 (2018)
8. Lindell, Y., Nof, A.: Fast secure multiparty ecdsa with practical distributed key generation and applications to cryptocurrency custody. In: Proceedings of the 2018 ACM SIGSAC Conference on Computer and Communications Security, pp. 1837–1854 (2018)
9. Doerner, J., Kondi, Y., Lee, E., Shelat, A.: Threshold ecdsa from ecdsa assumptions: the multiparty case. In: 2019 IEEE Symposium on Security and Privacy (SP), pp. 1051–1066. IEEE (2019)
10. Castagnos, G., Catalano, D., Laguillaumie, F., Savasta, F., Tucker, I.: Bandwidth-efficient threshold EC-DSA. In: Kiayias, A., Kohlweiss, M., Wallden, P., Zikas, V. (eds.) PKC 2020. LNCS, vol. 12111, pp. 266–296. Springer, Cham (2020). https://doi.org/10.1007/978-3-030-45388-6_10
11. Battagliola, M., Longo, R., Meneghetti, A., Sala, M.: Threshold ecdsa with an offline recovery party. arXiv preprint arXiv:2007.04036 (2020)
12. Gagol, A., Straszak, D.: Threshold ecdsa for decentralized asset custody (2020)
13. Canetti, R., Makriyannis, N., Peled, U.: Uc non-interactive, proactive, threshold ecdsa. IACR Cryptol. ePrint Arch. **2020**, 492 (2020)
14. Gennaro, R., Goldfeder, S.: One round threshold ecdsa with identifiable abort. IACR Cryptol. ePrint Arch. **2020**, 540 (2020)
15. Kravitz, D.W.: Digital signature algorithm (Jul 27 1993), uS Patent 5,231,668
16. Gennaro, R., Jarecki, S., Krawczyk, H., Rabin, T.: Secure distributed key generation for discrete-log based cryptosystems. J. Cryptology **20**(1), 51–83 (2007)
17. Feldman, P.: A practical scheme for non-interactive verifiable secret sharing. In: 28th Annual Symposium on Foundations of Computer Science (sfcs 1987), pp. 427–438. IEEE (1987)
18. Damgård, I., Jakobsen, T.P., Nielsen, J.B., Pagter, J.I., Østergård, M.B.: Fast threshold ecdsa with honest majority. IACR Cryptol. ePrint Arch. **2020**, 501 (2020)
19. Goldwasser, S., Micali, S., Rivest, R.L.: A digital signature scheme secure against adaptive chosen-message attacks. SIAM J. Comput. **17**(2), 281–308 (1988)

GM^{MT}: A Revocable Group Merkle Multi-tree Signature Scheme

Mahmoud Yehia, Riham AlTawy$^{(\boxtimes)}$, and T. Aaron Gulliver

Department of Electrical and Computer Engineering, University of Victoria,
Victoria, BC, Canada
raltawy@uvic.ca

Abstract. G-Merkle (GM) (PQCrypto 2018) is the first hash-based group signature scheme where it was stated that multi-tree approaches are not applicable, thus limiting the maximum number of supported signatures to 2^{20}. DGM (ESORICS 2019) is a dynamic and revocable GM-based group signature scheme that utilizes a computationally expensive puncturable encryption for revocation and requires interaction between verifiers and the group manager for signature verification. In this paper, we propose GM^{MT}, a hash-based group signature scheme that provides solutions to the aforementioned challenges of the two schemes. GM^{MT} builds on GM and adopts a multi-tree construction that constructs new GM trees for new signing leaves assignment while keeping the group public key unchanged, Compared to a single GM instance which enables 2^{20} signature, GM^{MT} allows growing the multi-tree structure adaptively to support 2^{64} signatures under the same public key. Moreover, GM^{MT} has a revocation mechanism that attains linkable anonymity of revoked signatures and has a logarithmic verification computational complexity compared to the linear complexity of DGM. The group manager in GM^{MT} requires storage that is linear in the number of members while the corresponding storage in DGM is linear in the number of signatures supported by the system. Concretely, for a system that supports 2^{64} signatures with 2^{15} members and provides 256-bit security, the required storage of the group manager is 1 MB (resp. $10^{8.7}$ TB) in GM^{MT}(resp. DGM).

Keywords: Digital signatures · Hash-based signature schemes · Group signature schemes · Post-quantum cryptography · Merkle trees

1 Introduction

A Group Signature Scheme (GSS) is a signature scheme where N members share one public key and any member is allowed to sign anonymously on behalf of the whole group [19]. Such a scheme designates a group manager that is responsible for setup, revealing the signer's identity when needed, and revoking the membership of group members when required. Group signature schemes are usually adopted by applications in which the signer's identity is required to

© Springer Nature Switzerland AG 2021
M. Conti et al. (Eds.): CANS 2021, LNCS 13099, pp. 136–157, 2021.
https://doi.org/10.1007/978-3-030-92548-2_8

be maintained private while attaining accountability when required. Relevant applications include vehicle safety communication systems in which authorized vehicles share their status information with other nearby vehicles while keeping their identity private in order to prevent tracking [31]. Remote attestation protocols benefit from group signatures where the identities of the attested platforms should be kept private to thwart dedicated platform vulnerability-based attacks[13]. Other applications of group signatures include e-voting and privacy preserving applications on blockchains [4,13]. Several group signature schemes have been proposed [11,13,17,18,29,30]. However, the security of most of these algorithms rely on the hardness of finding discrete logarithms and factoring in finite groups which are solved by Shor's algorithm in polynomial time and thus, they are not post quantum secure [36].

In 2010, Gordon *et al.* proposed the first post quantum (PQ) lattice-based group signature scheme [23]. Later, several theoretical lattice-based constructions were developed [26–28,32,33]. In 2018, the first lattice-based group signature scheme with an experimental implementation was proposed [20]. Although lattice-based signature scheme candidates have been deemed suitable in the current NIST post-quantum cryptography standardization competition (PQC) [34], their group signature constructions are not efficient [40]. Code-based group signature schemes were introduced as a quantum resilient alternative [2,3,22], but they have much larger signature sizes on the order of Megabytes [7]. Moreover, the size of the associated public keys and signatures increases with the number of group members.

Hash-based group signature schemes [14,21] have recently attracted research interest due to recent advances in the design of stateless hash-based signature schemes and the confidence in their PQ security [1,6,9,10]. In 2018, El Bansarkhani and Misoczki introduced Group Merkle (GM), the first post-quantum stateful hash-based group signature scheme [21]. GM is a one-layer Merkle tree construction which limits the maximum achievable tree height and thus restricts the maximum number of signatures that can be issued by the group under one public key. The authors claimed that multi-tree approaches are not applicable for group hash-based schemes without justification and stated that the required storage for each member is a limiting factor. Dynamic Group Merkle (DGM) is a recent hash-based group signature scheme where the group manager can assign signing keys to group members who have used all their keys and add new group members after the group public key has been generated [14]. Additionally, the group manager stores the indexes of the assigned leaves for each user in order to reveal their identity and revoke their membership when required. Challenges to the practical adoption of DGM such as the fact that a verifier needs to interact with the group manager to ensure the validity of the signature were discussed. Moreover, the revocation mechanism utilizes a puncturable encryption algorithm [37] for membership verification with a computational cost that is linear in the number of revoked signatures of the members. The authors of DGM claim that anonymity of revoked signatures is maintained. However, linkability of revoked signatures is possible if the adversary have two subsequent states of the revocation list. Privacy-preserving group membership revocation for PQ schemes is still an open research problem. The works in [38,39] enable members revocation without compromising their anonymity or requiring a trusted third party. However, the protocols either have linear proving complexity in the number of revocations or rely on history-dependent accumulators through updated certificates. Camenisch et al. proposed member revocation by periodically updating member credentials in which a specific attribute encodes a validity period [16]. Unfortunately, the technique would place extra effort on the group manager who would be essentially running a periodic updates setup phase. All the aforementioned works are also not quantum secure as they rely on noninteractive discrete logarithm based zero knowledge (zk) proofs. The adoption of zk-based revocation schemes in PQ group signature schemes may be attainable if research on generic PQ zk proofs enable their practical implementation.

Our Contributions . The contributions of this work are as follows.

- We propose GM^{MT}, a hash-based group signature scheme that enables 2^{64} signatures per group public key. It utilizes an adaptively growing multi-tree Merkle approach which periodically creates a new GM tree. Consequently, GM^{MT} enables the group members to renew their signing leaves without changing the group public key.
- We introduce a revocation algorithm that maintains the anonymity of revoked members while enabling the linkability of their revoked signatures. GM^{MT} relies on symmetric encryption and hashing such that the membership verification cost is logarithmic in the number of revoked signatures and the required storage at the group manager is linear in the number of members.
- We provide detailed comparisons between GM^{MT} and both GM and DGM. To demonstrate the validity of GM^{MT}, we implement its procedures using the C language and present the performance in terms of the number of clock cycles.

2   Preliminaries

A Group Signature Scheme (GSS) is a tuple of five polynomial-time algorithms $\mathcal{GS} = (GKGen, GSign, GVerify, GRevoke, GOpen)$, which are given as follows.

- $GKGen(1^n, N)$: The group key generation Alg. takes as inputs the security parameter n and the number of the group members N. It outputs the group public key GPK, the group members secret keys sk_i for $1 \leq i \leq N$, and the group manager secret key sk_{gm} that is used to reveal signer identities.
- $GSign(M, sk_i)$: The group signing Alg. takes as inputs a message M and a group member secret key sk_i. It outputs the signature Σ of the message.
- $GVerify(M, \Sigma, GPK, RevList)$: The group verification Alg. is a deterministic algorithm that takes as inputs a message M and the corresponding signature Σ, the group public key GPK, and the revocation list $RevList$. It outputs 1 for a valid signature and 0 otherwise.
- $GRevoke$: The revocation Alg. updates the revocation list based on the revoked members/signatures to revoke their ability to generate valid signature.

– $GOpen(\Sigma, sk_{gm})$: The open Alg. takes as input the signature Σ and the group manager secret key sk_{gm}, and outputs the identity of the signer.

In what follows, we provide definitions of the standard security notions for analyzing group signature schemes.

Definition 1 *(Correctness).* *A group signature scheme* $\mathcal{GS}$ *with a group public key* GPK *achieves correctness if for an honest signer with a secret key* sk_i

$$\Pr[GVerify(GSign(M, sk_i), M, GPK) = 0] < negl(n)$$

Other notions that capture the required GSS security include unforgeability, anonymity, unlinkability, collusion resistance, exculpability, and framing resistance. It was shown in [8] that full-anonymity and full-traceability ensures that a given GSS achieves all the aforementioned security requirements. The notion of full-anonymity [8] is very strong as it assumes that an adversary has access to the secret keys of all members and the group manager. Camenisch and Groth introduced a relaxed type of anonymity in which an adversary cannot corrupt the group manger and at least two group members, i.e., challenge identities in the anonymity experiment in Fig. 1. In our scheme, we follow the anonymity notion introduced by Camenisch and Groth [15] because in our scheme, only secret keys of the group manager are used to reveal signer identities, and knowledge of the signing keys along with the associated signatures also uncovers the corresponding identities. Such a security notion is formally defined in $Exp_{\mathcal{GS},\mathcal{A}}^{Anon-b}(n, N)$ in Fig. 1. Hence in our analysis, we focus on the anonymity and full-traceability security definitions. In their security experiments, we assume an adversary is allowed a training phase where they can call the following oracles.

– $Corrupt(id_i)$: The adversary $\mathcal{A}$ has access to all secret keys of member id_i.
– $chal_b(id_0, id_1, M)$: The oracle returns the signature of message M for a randomly chosen group member id_b for $b \in \{0, 1\}$.
– $Sign(M, id_i)$: The oracle returns the signature of a message M for a randomly chosen group member id_i where $1 \leq i \leq N$.
– $Open(\Sigma, GPK, M)$: The oracle returns the identity id_i of the member who issued the valid signature Σ of message M.

Following [14,21], we present the security definitions and analysis in the classical setting, i.e., PPT adversaries. For quantum security we consider the Quantum Accessible Random Oracle Model (QROM) [12], where all legitimate users and oracles perform classical computations while adversaries have quantum capabilities. Given that the security of GM^{MT} relies on the standard assumptions of hash functions, it is assumed that Grover's search algorithm is used to accelerate exhaustive search in an unstructured space. In such a case, a QPT adversary achieves a maximum of quadratic speed over the considered PPT adversary. The work in [25] gives more details on the generic security of hash function security notions with respect to QPT adversaries in QROM.

Anonymity. In the security experiment Exp^{Anon-b} in Fig. 1, the adversary $\mathcal{A}$ is allowed a training phase, train, with unrestricted access to both the signing and opening oracles and they have the ability to corrupt some of the group members. At the end, $\mathcal{A}$ returns an un-queried random message, M and the identities of two uncorrupted members, id_0 and id_1. Then in the challenge phase, challange, $\mathcal{A}$ calls $chal_b(id_0, id_1, M)$ which return the signature on M signed by one of two uncorrupted users i_0 or i_1. $\mathcal{A}$ wins if they are able to identify the signer's identity with a non-negligible advantage.

Definition 2 *(Anonymity [15]). A group signature scheme $\mathcal{GS}$ achieves anonymity if a probabilistic polynomial time (ppt) adversary $\mathcal{A}$ who is not the group manager but has access to the signing and opening oracles and is able to corrupt all but two group members i_0 and i_1, is not able to reveal the identity of the signer when challenged with a signature of a message that is signed by either i_0 or i_1. $\mathcal{A}$ has a negligible advantage in the experiment $Exp_{\mathcal{GS}}^{Anon-b}$, where $b = \{0, 1\}$ denotes the index of the identity of the signer.*

$$Adv_{\mathcal{GS},\mathcal{A}}^{Anon-b}(n, N) = |\Pr[Exp_{\mathcal{GS},\mathcal{A}}^{Anon-0}(n, N) = 1] - \Pr[Exp_{\mathcal{GS},\mathcal{A}}^{Anon-1}(n, N) = 1]| \leq negl(n)$$

$Exp_{\mathcal{GS},\mathcal{A}}^{Anon-b}(n, N)$
- $b \in \{0, 1\}$
- $(GPK, sk_{gm}, sk_*) \leftarrow GKGen(1^n, N)$
- $(id_0, id_1, M) \leftarrow \mathcal{A}^{Sign(\cdot, id_i), Corrupt(\cdot), Open(\cdot, sk_{gm})}(\text{train}, GPK)$
- $b \leftarrow \mathcal{A}^{chal_b(id_0, id_1, M)}(\text{challenge}, GPK)$
- **Return** b

Fig. 1. Anonymity experiment

Full-traceability. This security notion requires that the group manager is always able to reveal the identity of a signer of a valid signature and trace back every signature to the corresponding signer. Moreover, full-traceability ensures that even if an adversary is capable of corrupting some group members, they are not able to generate a valid signature which is traced by the group manager to an uncorrupted member.

Definition 3 *(Full-traceability [8]). A group signature scheme $\mathcal{GS}$ satisfies full-traceability if a ppt adversary $\mathcal{A}$ that is given unrestricted access to the signing and opening oracles and is able to corrupt some of the group members is not able to generate a valid signature which cannot be opened or traced back by the group manager to an uncorrupted member. $\mathcal{A}$ has a negligible advantage in the experiment $Exp_{\mathcal{GS},\mathcal{A}}^{Full-Trace}$ as defined in Fig. 2*

$$Adv_{\mathcal{GS},\mathcal{A}}^{Full-Trace}(n, N) = |\Pr[Exp_{\mathcal{GS},\mathcal{A}}^{Full-Trace}(n, N) = 1]| \leq negl(n)$$

3 GM^{MT} Hash-Based Group Signature Scheme

GM^{MT} is a revocable hash-based group signature scheme that is constructed using a multi-tree approach and utilizes a One Time Signing Scheme (OTS) as

$$Exp_{GS,A}^{Full-Trace}(n, N)$$
- $(GPK, sk_{gm}, sk_*) \leftarrow GKGen(1^n, N)$
- $(\Sigma', M') \leftarrow \mathcal{A}^{Sign(\cdot, id_i), Corrupt(\cdot), Open(\cdot, sk_{gm})}(GPK)$
- **Return** $GVerify(\Sigma', M', gpk) == 1 \wedge GOpen(\Sigma') = \perp$
  or id_j(non corrupted id_j)

Fig. 2. Full-traceability experiment

the underlying signing scheme. It is designed as a generic construction such that any stateful hash-based Merkle signing scheme with an OTS leaves can be used. However, we recommend instantiating GM^{MT} with XMSS-T [25], to mitigate multi-target and path attacks. For more details on the security analysis of hash-based group signature schemes instantiated by XMSS-T, the reader is referred to [41]. GM^{MT} provides a flexible setup phase where the group manager generates the group public key independent of the parameters of the group members (OTS public keys and their indexes). Figure 3 shows that GM^{MT} can be regarded as a hybrid construction that encompasses several Group Merkle (GM) signature trees (denoted by clusters) at layer 0, and one stateful hash-based signature scheme consuming all higher layers, i.e., layers 1 to $d-1$. Each GM tree at layer 0 contains a subset of the OTSs of all group members while the multi-tree stateful hash-based signature scheme is used by the group manager to sign the roots of the GM trees at layer 0. The group public key, GPK, is the root of the top layer tree which is generated using the group manager's secret key. Such a construction allows layer 0 GM trees to be constructed adaptively as the signing leaves are used up. Specifically, all group members signing leaves are clustered into GM trees where each GM tree has a subset of the signing leaves of all members. This allows the group manager to manage leaf assignment for all members in a clustered manner. Hence, the scheme enables a practical setup phase with less storage requirements for each group member compared to GM [21] because not all the signing leaves for each group member have to be assigned upfront, and a member can reuse the storage that was allocated to their used leaves. In the following, we give detailed specifications of the setup, signing ,verifying, membership revocation, and opening procedures in GM^{MT}. An algorithmic description of these procedures is provided in Algorithm 1. Table 1 gives the parameters and notation used in the specification of GM^{MT}.

3.1   Setup Phase and Key Generation

The setup phase is an interactive procedure that involves communication between the group members and group manager for signing leaves assignment. However, since GM^{MT} is a multi-tree structure, the group public key is computed by the group manager independent of the inputs from members. Hence, the setup phase is divided into two procedures, group public key generation and signing leaves assignment. The former is performed once during initial group setup while the latter is repeated periodically with the addition of new cluster trees at layer 0.

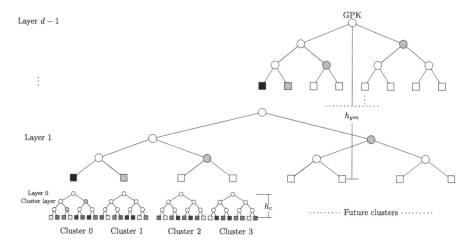

Fig. 3. A simplified Ex. of the GM^{MT} initial setup phase. The gray nodes and the first red node in cluster 0 are the auth. path for signing with the first yellow leaf in cluster 0, while the black leaves are the group manager signing leaves. (Color figure online)

Table 1. GM^{MT} parameters and notation.

n	Security parameter
N	Initial number of group members
B	Initial number of signing indexes for each group member
BC_{max}	Maximum number of signing leaves for a member in a GM tree (cluster)
Bu_{max}	Maximum number of signing leaves for a member in the scheme
d	Number of tree layers
h	Maximum tree height
h_c	GM/cluster tree height
h_{gm}	Group manager tree height, $h_{gm} = h - h_c$
w	Winternitz parameter of the used OTS
l	Number of elements, each of length n bits, in the OTS signature
GPK	Group public key which is the root of the top layer tree

Key Generation Algorithm . The algorithm randomly samples the secret keys $SK = (sk.enc_{gm}, sk.seed_{gm}) \in \{0,1\}^n \times \{0,1\}^n$, where $sk.enc_{gm}$ is the group manager encryption secret key that is used to reveal the signer identity and $sk.seed_{gm}$ is used to generate the trees of the multi-tree signing scheme, e.g., XMSS-T scheme [25], at layers 1 to $d-1$ (the top layer). Each tree has height $h_{gm}/(d-1)$. In an actual instantiation, $sk.seed_{gm}$ may be used in a manner similar to the random secret seed in [25]. The root of the top layer tree is the group public key GPK.

Signing Leaves Assignment . This procedure adds a new GM cluster tree containing a subset of the signing leaves of all N members to the construction. The trees at layer 0 are GM trees, each of height $h_c = h - h_{gm}$, and the first tree (cluster 0), contains B signing leaves of each group members so there are $NB = 2^{h_c}$ signing leaves in total. Note that each cluster tree contains an equal number of signing leaves for each member. However, GM^{MT} allows revocation and h_c is a constant, so the number of leaves assigned per member in the i-th cluster, $0 < i < 2^{h_{gm}}$, B, may increase because N may decrease. The assignment procedure is the interactive part of the setup phase and involves the following three steps.

- *Label Assignment.* The group manager sets the maximum number of leaves that can be assigned to a member for the lifetime of the scheme, and assigns to each member a sequence of numbers corresponding to their identity, denoted as labels. Specifically, let $BC_{max} > B$ be the maximum number of leaves that can be assigned to a group member in a cluster, so the maximum number of signatures that a group member can sign is $Bu_{max} = 2^{h_{gm}} \times BC_{max}$. Consequently, the i-th group member is assigned Bu_{max} labels denoted by $b_{0,i}, b_{1,i}, \ldots, b_{Bu_{max}-1,i} = iBu_{max}, iBu_{max}+1, \ldots, iBu_{max}+Bu_{max}-1$ where $0 \le i \le N-1$. Since GM^{MT} provides member revocation, BC_{max} is chosen to be greater than B to simplify label assignment, so all labels dedicated to a member may not be assigned. Hence, we use the term label to differentiate from a cluster signing leaf index because unlike indexes, not all labels may be assigned. However, each cluster leaf signing index assigned to a member is associated with a label in the dedicated range. Finally, the group manager stores the last assigned label for each group member in the users list, $UList$. Henceforth, the last assigned label of the i-th member is denoted by $la = UList[i]$ and it is used to evaluate their identity by $\lfloor UList[i]/Bu_{max} \rfloor = i$. When a new cluster is being generated, the group manager retrieves the last assigned label, $la = UList[i]$, for each group member, i, and a new range of labels, B, is dedicated to their new cluster signing leaves starting from the next value from the last stored label. More precisely, for a new cluster, the i-th member is given B labels $b_{0,i}, b_{1,i}, \ldots, b_{B-1,i} = UList[i] + 1, UList[i] + 2, \ldots, UList[i] + B$. The group manager then updates the stored label in $UList$ with the last label in the new range, i.e., $UList[i] = UList[i] + B$.
- *Signing keys generation.* Each group member, i, generates B OTS public keys $(pk_{0,i}, pk_{1,i}, \ldots, pk_{B-1,i})$ using their own secret key sk_i, and sends them to the group manager, where $pk_{j,i}$ denotes the j-th public key of the i-th group member within a cluster for $0 \le i \le N-1$ and $0 \le j \le B-1$.
- *Shuffling and clustering.* The group manager retrieves the last assigned label for each group member and assigns the next set of labels to their public keys (the cluster leaves), in ascending order i.e. $(pk_{0,0}, b_{0,0}), (pk_{1,0}, b_{1,0}), \ldots, (pk_{B-1,0}, b_{B-1,0}), \ldots \ldots, (pk_{0,N-1}, b_{0,N-1}),$ $(pk_{1,N-1}, b_{1,N-1}), \ldots, (pk_{B-1,N-1}, b_{B-1,N-1})$, where $pk_{j,i}$ is the j-th public key of group member i, and $b_{j,i}$ is the corresponding label for $0 \le i \le N-1$

and $0 \leq j \leq B - 1$. The group manager then updates the last assigned label for each member.

Let $E(k, M)$ denote a symmetric encryption of a plaintext M using the key k. The group manager encrypts the labels assigned to the members by $sk.enc_{gm}$ and generates the corresponding encrypted labels $(Eb_{0,0}, \ldots, Eb_{B-1,0}), \ldots \ldots, (Eb_{0,N-1}, \ldots, Eb_{B-1,N-1})$, where $Eb_{j,i} = E(sk.enc_{gm}, b_{j,i})$. The group manager then generates the cluster leaves, $L_{0,0}, L_{1,0}, \ldots, L_{B-1,0}, \ldots \ldots, L_{0,N-1}, L_{1,N-1}, \ldots, L_{B-1,N-1}$, by hashing the concatenation of each group member public key and its corresponding encrypted label, i.e. $L_{j,i} = H(pk_{j,i} \| Eb_{j,i})$ is the j-th leaf node of group member i. Next, the group manager permutes the group members leaves by reordering their encrypted labels in ascending order. Then, the group manager builds the cluster tree, and signs its root, $root_c$, by the corresponding upper tree leaf node and this continues until the top layer. Finally, the group manager broadcasts to the group members 2^{h_c} tuples of the encrypted labels, cluster tree leaves, and the corresponding signature of its root. Each member, i, identifies their leaf nodes using their public keys, the corresponding encrypted labels, and authentication paths, all of which are referred to by group member parameters, $param_i$.

After a specific time determined by the group manager, by which the group members are expected to have used up almost all their current cluster leaves, the signing leaves assignment procedure is repeated and a new cluster is generated. This is continued until the last cluster is constructed. Figure 3 depicts a simplified example of the initial setup phase. It shows a d layer GM^{MT} with 4 clusters in the bottom layer. It is assumed that the group has $N = 4$ members and each member has two signing leaves colored blue, green, yellow, and red in each cluster. $Cluster_1$ is generated after some time period (when the $Cluster_0$ leaves are almost all used up), to provide new signing leaves to the members.

3.2 Signing Algorithm

The signing algorithm takes as input a message M of arbitrary length, the signer's secret key (sk_i), which contains the state of the signer (i-th member), which is the signing index t. The algorithm outputs the signature Σ that contains the OTS signature $\sigma_{OTS,0}$ of the message M and the corresponding authentication path $Auth_0 = (Eb, A_{0,0}, A_{0,1}, \ldots, A_{0,h_c-1})$ from the cluster tree in layer 0. Moreover, Σ contains the signature of the group manager on the cluster root, $\sigma_{root_c} = \sigma_{OTS,1}, Auth_1, \ldots, \sigma_{OTS,d-1}, Auth_{d-1}$, where $\sigma_{OTS,j}$ is the OTS signature of the lower layer tree root, $root_{j-1}$, and $Auth_j$ is the corresponding authentication path $Auth_j = (A_{j,0}, A_{j,1}, \ldots, A_{j, \frac{h_{gm}}{d-1} - 1})$. The GM^{MT} signature is then given by $\Sigma = \sigma_{OTS,0}, Auth_0, \ldots, \sigma_{OTS,d-1}, Auth_{d-1}$.

3.3 Verification Algorithm

The verification algorithm takes as input the message M, the signature Σ, the public key GPK, and the revocation list $RevList$. It first checks if the received signature has been revoked (see Sect. 3.4). If the signature has not been revoked, the algorithm continues with verification by calculating the OTS public key, pk', from the message digest and the signature element $\sigma_{OTS,0}$ Next, the leaf node is calculated by hashing the concatenation of this OTS public key and the signature element Eb of $Auth_0$, i.e., $L' = H(pk'||Eb)$. Then, the leaf node, L', leaf index, and $(A_{0,0}, A_{0,1}, \ldots, A_{0,h_c-1})$ from $Auth_0$ are used by the Root Computation Algorithm, RCA, (cf. Algorithm 1 in [25] for details) to calculate the cluster root that is used with $\sigma_{OTS,1}$ to get the OTS public key at layer 1. Next, this public key and its index along with the authentication path $Auth_1$ are used to calculate the tree root at layer 1 using RCA. This procedure is repeated until the top layer tree root is calculated, GPK'. If it is equal to the public root, $GPK' = GPK$, the algorithm outputs 1 for a valid signature, and 0 otherwise.

Algorithm 1 GM^{MT} Algorithm. Red (resp. blue) denotes the procedures which are performed by the group manager (resp. member).

Setup Phase
Input: $n, N, d, h_{gm}, h_c, BC_{max}$
$(sk.seed_{gm}, sk.enc_{gm}, GPK) \leftarrow GKGen(1^n)$
$Bu_{max} = h_{gm} \times BC_{max}$
for $0 \leq i \leq N - 1$ do
   $UList[i] = (i \times Bu_{max}) - 1$
end for
  for $0 \leq i \leq N - 1$ do
     $id_i : sk_i \xleftarrow{R} \{0,1\}^n$
  end for
  Return: $sk.seed_{gm}, sk.enc_{gm}, GPK, UList$

Cluster Generation
Input: $N, h_c, UList, sk.enc_{gm},$ and Bu_{max}
for $0 \leq i \leq N - 1$ do
   $id_i : (pk_{i,0}, \ldots, pk_{i,B-1}) \leftarrow OTS.KGen(1^n, sk_i)$
end for
for $0 \leq i \leq N - 1$ do
   $b = UList[i] + 1$
   for $0 \leq j \leq B - 1$ do
      $Eb_{i,j} \leftarrow E(sk.enc_{gm}, b + j)$
      $TupleList[iB + j, 0] = (pk_{i,j})$
      $TupleList[iB + j, 1] = (Eb_{i,j})$
   end for
   $UList[i] = b + B - 1$
end for
$SortedList \leftarrow sort(TupleList)$
for $0 \leq p < NB$ do
   $leaf[p] = H(SortedList[p, 0]||SortedList[p, 1])$
end for
  $root_c \leftarrow MerkleTree(leaf)$
  $\sigma_{root_c} \leftarrow Sign(root_c, sk.seed_{gm})$
for $0 \leq i < N$ do
  for $0 \leq j < B$ do
    $p = 0$
    while $p < NB$ do
      if $pk_{i,j} = SortedList[p, 0]$ then
        $param1_i[j, 0] = p$
        $param1_i[j, 1] = SortedList[p, 1] = Eb_{i,j}$
        $param1_i[j, 2] = Auth$
        Break
      end if
    end while
  end for
  $param2_i = \sigma_{root_c}$
end for

Signing Algorithm
Input: $M, param1_i, param2_i, sk_i, state_i$
$\sigma_{OTS,0} \leftarrow OTS.Sign(M, sk_i, state_i)$
$GM^{\text{MT}}.\Sigma = M, indx, \sigma_{OTS,0}, Eb, Auth_0, param2_i$
$state_i = state_i + 1$
Return: $GM^{\text{MT}}.\Sigma$

Verification Algorithm
Input: $M, GPK, \Sigma, RevList$
if $Eb \in RevList$ then
  Return 0
else
  $pk' \leftarrow OTS.Verify(\sigma_{OTS,0})$
  $L'_{indx} \leftarrow H(pk'||Eb)$
  $root'_c \leftarrow RCA(indx, L', Auth_0)$
  for $1 \leq i \leq d - 1$ do
    $L' \leftarrow OTS.Verify(root'_{i-1}, \sigma_{OTS,i})$
    $root'_i \leftarrow RCA(indx, L', Auth_i)$
  end for
  if $root'_{d-1} = GPK$ then
    Return 1
  else
    Return 0
  end if
end if

Revocation Algorithm
Input: $UList, Bu_{max}, RevList, sk.enc_{gm}, i$
$j = UList[i]$
while $j \geq i \times Bu_{max}$ do
  Add $E(sk.enc_{gm}, j)$ to $RevList$
  $j--$
end while
$RevList \leftarrow sort(RevList)$
Return $RevList$

Opening Algorithm
Input: $\Sigma, sk.enc_{gm}, Bu_{max}, N, UList$
$b' \leftarrow D(sk.enc_{gm}, Eb)$
if $b' \geq N \cdot Bu_{max} \vee b' > Ulist[\lfloor b'/Bu_{max} \rfloor]$ then
  return $\perp$
else
  Return $\lfloor b'/Bu_{max} \rfloor$
end if

3.4   Revocation Algorithm

The group manager retrieves the last assigned label of the revoked i-th member, $la = UList[i]$, and then regenerates all the encrypted labels which were assigned to that member, i.e., for the i-th member, the manager generates $E(sk.enc_{gm}, iBu_{max}), E(sk.enc_{gm}, iBu_{max} + 1), \ldots, E(sk.enc_{gm}, l_a)$. The generated encrypted labels are added to the revocation list, $RevList$, which is then permuted using a sorting algorithm so that successive entries in the revocation list are not grouped by members.

Revocation Check: The verifier checks if the received signature is revoked or not by first extracting the encrypted label, Eb, from the signature and checking if it exists in the revocation list, $RevList$. If $Eb \in RevList$, then the received signature has been revoked, otherwise the verifier continues the verification steps.

3.5   Opening Algorithm

The opening algorithm takes as input a message M, a signature Σ, and the group manager secret key $sk.enc_{gm}$, and outputs the identity of the signer i. The algorithm first decrypts the signature element Eb to recover the label $b = D(sk.enc_{gm}, Eb)$. Next, the manager calculates the member's identity $i = \lfloor b/Bu_{max} \rfloor$ and checks that b is less than the last assigned label to the i-th group member, $b \le Ulist[i]$, if not it aborts.

3.6   Recommended Parameters

GM^{MT} parameterization follows the NIST PQC requirements which state that a given signing key pair should produce up to 2^{64} signatures while maintaining the claimed security [35]. Thus, we recommend that GM^{MT} be instantiated with a four layer ($d = 4$) XMSS-T where the tree height in the bottom layer (clusters), h_c, has three possible values, $h_c = \{16, 18, 20\}$, depending on the number of group members and their signing requirements and storage capabilities. The height of the group manager trees in layers 1 to 3 is 16. The GM^{MT} signature size depends on the required security level. More precisely, the GM^{MT} signature size is $d \times l + h + 2$ elements, each of length n bits, where n is the security parameter, $n = \{128, 192, 256\}$, and l is the number of OTS signature elements, i.e., XMSS-T utilizes WOTS, then $l = \{35, 51, 67\}$ for the respective aforementioned security parameters [25]. Table 2 gives our recommended parameters for GM^{MT} such that it supports at least 2^{64} signatures under the same group public key and the corresponding signature size in bytes (B).

Table 2. GM^{MT} recommended parameters and signature sizes.

Instance	Bit security	d	h	h_c	h_{gm}	N	B	l	w	Signature (B)
GM^{MT}-128a	128	4	64	16	48	$2 < N \le 2^6$	$2^{10} < B \le 2^{15}$	35	16	3296
GM^{MT}-128b	128	4	66	18	48	$2^6 < N \le 2^{10}$	$2^8 < B \le 2^{12}$	35	16	3328
GM^{MT}-128c	128	4	68	20	48	$2^{10} < N \le 2^{16}$	$2^4 < B \le 2^{10}$	35	16	3360
GM^{MT}-192a	192	4	64	16	48	$2 < N \le 2^6$	$2^{10} < B \le 2^{15}$	51	16	6480
GM^{MT}-192b	192	4	66	18	48	$2^6 < N \le 2^{10}$	$2^8 < B \le 2^{12}$	51	16	6528
GM^{MT}-192c	192	4	68	20	48	$2^{10} < N \le 2^{16}$	$2^4 < B \le 2^{10}$	51	16	6576
GM^{MT}-256a	256	4	64	16	48	$2 < N \le 2^6$	$2^{10} < B \le 2^{15}$	67	16	10688
GM^{MT}-256b	256	4	66	18	48	$2^6 < N \le 2^{10}$	$2^8 < B \le 2^{12}$	67	16	10752
GM^{MT}-256c	256	4	68	20	48	$2^{10} < N \le 2^{16}$	$2^4 < B \le 2^{10}$	67	16	10816

4 Security Analysis

In this section we show that GM^{MT} satisfies the security requirements of correctness, anonymity [15], and full-traceability [8]. We also analyze the security of the proposed revocation mechanism and discuss the drawbacks of adopting a dynamic approach.

Theorem 1 (Correctness). *Let GM^{MT} be the multi-tree group Merkle signature algorithm described in Sect. 3. Then GM^{MT} achieves correctness as defined in Definition 1.*

Proof (Sketch). GM^{MT} utilizes a multi-tree Merkle signing scheme for generating signatures and only uses extra shuffling and clustering procedures to assign the signing leaves to different members. Thus, the correctness of GM^{MT} is achieved by the correctness of the underling Merkle signature scheme.

Theorem 2 (Anonymity). *Let GM^{MT} be the multi-tree group Merkle signature algorithm provided in Sect. 3 with secure hash function H and encryption algorithm E. Then GM^{MT} achieves anonymity for each cluster as defined in Definition 2.*

Proof. We adopt the $Exp_{\mathcal{GS},\mathcal{A}}^{Anon-b}$ game (see Fig. 1) on the group members. The proof follows the strategy in [21]. Assume that each group member is assigned B signing leaves in each cluster, i.e., each group member is assigned a total of $B \times 2^{h_{gm}}$ signing leaves over all clusters. An adversary $\mathcal{A}$ is given access to the signing and opening oracles, and can corrupt some group members. Assume there are only two members i_0 and i_1 that are uncorrupted. Moreover, $\mathcal{A}$ queries the signing and opening oracles for a maximum of $2^{h_{gm}} \times (B - 1)$ messages for each uncorrupted member such that the signing oracle replies with $B - 1$ signatures from each cluster for the two members, i.e., each member has the ability to sign at least one more message with a leaf from any cluster of the $2^{h_{gm}}$ clusters. Recall that the opening oracle when queried by a signature Σ replies with the decryption of the encrypted label Eb in the signature, $b = D(sk.enc_{gm}, Eb)$, which directly reveals the signing identity i. Thus, $\mathcal{A}$ has $B - 1$ labels and their corresponding ciphertext pairs (b_{j,i_g}, Eb_{j,i_g}) for each group member i_g from each cluster where $g = \{0,1\}$ and $Eb_{j,i_g} = E(sk.enc_{gm}, b_{j,i_g})$, $0 \le j \le B - 2$.

$\mathcal{A}$ queries the signing oracle with an arbitrary message M of their choice such that the signing oracle replies with the signature for either i_0 or i_1. From this signature, $\mathcal{A}$ retrieves the encrypted label Eb_{B-1,i_g}. Moreover, they are able to determine the signing cluster, and thus the corresponding $B - 1$ label-encrypted label pairs (b_{j,i_g}, Eb_{j,i_g}), $0 \le j \le B - 2$, for each group member i_g collected in the query phase. Then, $\mathcal{A}$ is required to correctly guess the identity of the signer. Since the labels for each group member are set sequentially, and $\mathcal{A}$ knows the first $B - 1$ labels for each group member, then $\mathcal{A}$ knows with certainty the B-th labels for both group members, i.e., b_{B-1,i_0} and b_{B-1,i_1}. Accordingly, $\mathcal{A}$ must determine which label is the plaintext corresponding to the encrypted label Eb_{B-1,i_g} received in the queried signature. In other words, the adversary needs to win a distinguishability game that distinguishes the encryption of different plaintexts. As the encryption algorithm used is semantically secure, $\mathcal{A}$ has a negligible advantage in winning the $Exp_{\mathcal{GS},\mathcal{A}}^{Anon-b}$ game.

Theorem 3 (Full-traceability). *Let* GM^{MT} *be the multi-tree group Merkle signature algorithm specified in Sect. 3 with secure hash function H, encryption algorithm E, and an underlying existentially unforgeable Merkle signing scheme. Then, GM^{MT} achieves full-traceability as in Definition 3.*

Proof. Recall that the group manager opens a signature by decrypting the encrypted label Eb in the signature. Assume that an adversary $\mathcal{A}$ collects all the signatures from all clusters. i.e., $\mathcal{A}$ knows (Eb_t, pk_t) where pk_t is the OTS public key at leaf index t for $0 \le t \le 2^h - 1$. Assuming $\mathcal{A}$ corrupts a set of members $\mathcal{C}$, then $\mathcal{A}$ wins the traceability game $Exp_{\mathcal{GS},\mathcal{A}}^{Full-Trace}$ in Fig. 2 if they are successful in either of the following scenarios.

- $\mathcal{A}$ generates a valid signature of the i-th member where $i \in N \wedge i \notin \mathcal{C}$. Since opening a signature depends on the signature element Eb, then $\mathcal{A}$ should include in the signature an element $Eb^\star$ from one of the signatures of any of the uncorrupted members so that it decrypts to a valid label assigned to an uncorrupted member. Furthermore, $\mathcal{A}$ should pair $Eb^\star$ with one of the OTS public keys of a corrupted member so that they can sign using the corresponding secret key. More precisely, $\mathcal{A}$ must find a pair $(pk_{j,i_c}, Eb^\star)$ that is a second preimage of the pair (pk_{j,i_c}, Eb_{j,i_c}), i.e., $H(pk_{j,i_c}||Eb^\star) = H(pk_{j,i_c}||Eb_{j,i_c})$ where pk_{j,i_c} is the j-th OTS public key of a corrupted member i_c and Eb_{j,i_c} is the corresponding encrypted label. The existence of such an adversary contradicts the assumption of a secure hash function. Conversely, $\mathcal{A}$ does not use any of the OTS public keys of the corrupted members, but rather uses some $Eb^\star$ with a forged signature of the underlying Merkle signature scheme such that it passes verification and then decrypts to a valid assigned label. However, this contradicts the existential unforgeability assumption of the underlying signature scheme.
- $\mathcal{A}$ generates a valid signature which the group manager cannot open. In this case, $\mathcal{A}$ includes in the signature an encrypted label Eb' that is not equal to

any of the valid encrypted labels which were collected in the query phase. Then following the steps in the previous scenario, $\mathcal{A}$ needs to either pair Eb' with an OTS public key of a corrupted member, or include it with a forgery of the underlying signature scheme. In both cases, the existence of $\mathcal{A}$ contradicts the assumptions of a secure hash function and an existentially unforgeable signing scheme.

4.1 Revocation Security

For revoking a member with identity i, our revocation mechanism updates a revocation list, *Revlist*, by adding the member's encrypted labels that were assigned to their signing leaves, i.e., $Eb_{0,i}, Eb_{1,i}, \ldots, Eb_{la-iBu_{max},i} = E(sk.enc_{gm}, iBu_{max}), E(sk.enc_{gm}, iBu_{max}+1), \ldots, E(sk.enc_{gm}, la)$, where $la = Ulist[i]$ denotes the last assigned label. Each of these encrypted labels is part of a signature. Hence, an adversary $\mathcal{A}$ is able to recover the new set of encrypted labels that is added to *Revlist* with updates by comparing the contents of *Revlist* before and after the update. If $\mathcal{A}$ has collected signatures generated by the system before an update of the revocation list, then $\mathcal{A}$ can check if the encrypted labels in some of the collected signatures are in the newly revoked set. Accordingly, if such a set belongs to one revoked member, then $\mathcal{A}$ is able to link these signatures to the same revoked member. Otherwise, the signatures are for more than one revoked member and $\mathcal{A}$ is required to distinguishes the signatures over a small anonymity set (the newly revoked members). In all cases, only the encrypted labels of the revoked members are added to the revocation list, hence, it is infeasible to reveal the identities associated with these labels because they are encrypted. Note that if $\mathcal{A}$ is given only the last updated revocation list, then $\mathcal{A}$ cannot distinguish the newly revoked signatures from the old ones, and hence cannot link a set of signatures to one signer.

Theorem 4 (Revocation). *Let GM^{MT} be the multi-tree Merkle group signature algorithm provided in Sect. 3 with secure hash function H and encryption algorithm E. Then, GM^{MT} maintains the anonymity of revoked members and linkability of their signatures.*

Proof. Assume an adversary $\mathcal{A}$ has the previous and current states of the revocation list, and a set of signatures that has been collected between two updates of the revocation list. Then, $\mathcal{A}$ is able to recover the set of newly revoked signatures by running the revocation check on the collected signatures against the previous and current states of *Revlist*. If the update of *Revlist* corresponds to revoking one member, then $\mathcal{A}$ is able to link these revoked signatures to this member without revealing their identity. However, if the current states are updated by revoking more than one member, then we adopt an anonymity game for the revoked members which can be seen as a variant of the $Exp_{\mathcal{GS},\mathcal{A}}^{Anon-b}$ game that allows $\mathcal{A}$ to be challenged with a set of revoked encrypted labels instead of a signature of their choice. $\mathcal{A}$ wins the game if they are able to attribute a subset of the challenge set to a given revoked signer out of two possible revoked signers.

Precisely, $\mathcal{A}$ is given access to the opening algorithm for $B - 1$ signatures from each cluster signed by each of two newly revoked members, i.e., $\mathcal{A}$ gets $B - 1$ (label, encrypted label) pairs from each cluster for each revoked member. Then, they are challenged with the B-th encrypted label from each cluster for each revoked member and are required to determine which encrypted label belongs to which set of $B - 1$ (label-encrypted label) pairs. If $\mathcal{A}$ is able to attribute the challenge encrypted labels to a given signer, then they can build another adversary that is able to distinguish between ciphertexts corresponding to a given plaintext, which contradicts the assumption of a secure encryption algorithm.

4.2   Security of Dynamic $\mathbf{GM^{MT}}$

Our scheme can be adapted to allow adding new members at each cluster generation. In this case, the number of leaves assigned to each group member decreases because the maximum number of leaves in a cluster is 2^{20} and the number of group members is increased. A drawback of dynamic $\mathrm{GM^{MT}}$ is that the anonymity game cannot be played on all clusters. More precisely, if the two challenge identities in $Exp_{\mathcal{GS},\mathcal{A}}^{Anon-b}$ given in Fig. 1 are for a newly joined member and an older member, then the game must be played on the clusters which contain signing leaves for both members. This is because if $\mathcal{A}$ is given a signature from clusters created before the new member has joined the group, then $\mathcal{A}$ can determine that this signature is signed by the older member. On the other hand, if the signature comes from clusters created with both members, the anonymity security is the same as that for static group construction given in Theorem 2.

5   Comparison with GM and DGM

In this section, we compare $\mathrm{GM^{MT}}$ with the hash-based group signature schemes GM [21] and DGM [14]. Due to the multi-tree construction, $\mathrm{GM^{MT}}$ has a larger signature size than either that of GM or DGM, for example, for 256-bit security, the signature size of $\mathrm{GM^{MT}}$ instance of largest signature size, $\mathrm{GM^{MT}}$-256c, is 10.816 KB whereas that of GM (resp. DGM) is 2.88 KB (resp. 2.72 KB).

5.1 $\mathbf{GM^{MT}}$ and GM

Unlike GM, $\mathrm{GM^{MT}}$ provides a revocation algorithm and is a multi-tree Merkle construction. Both schemes require comparable computations from the group manager for the opening and setup phase. Hence, we focus on their maximum number of signing leaves and the storage requirements for each group member.

Maximum Number of Signing Leaves. GM is a one layer tree with a static group construction and the maximum number of signing leaves has been stated to be 2^{20} [21]. On the other hand, $\mathrm{GM^{MT}}$ allows the multi-tree structure to grow once the initial signing leaves are consumed by repeating the last two steps of the setup phase. Thus, the group members renew their signing keys each time a new cluster is generated while keeping the group public key unchanged. For a 4-layer GM^{MT} construction, up to 2^{64} signing leaves are created for the group depending on the tree height h.

Member Storage Requirements. In GM, the storage required for each group member is reported to be $B(1 + \log N)$ nodes [21]. Note that since the first node of each authentication path and each leaf node contains an OTS public key and an AES-256 ciphertext, the required storage is in fact $B(3 + \log N)$ n-bit elements. In GM^{MT}, for a cluster of N members, the required storage is $B(2 + \log N) + (d - 1)l + h_{gm}$ n-bit elements. More precisely, a member stores the B nodes at the $(\log N)$-th level, each of which is n bits, and $B(1 + \log N)$ n-bit elements for the authentication paths. Note that in GM, a group member stores 3 n-bit values per leaf node, while in GM^{MT} a group member stores 2 n-bit values for each leaf node. Additionally, in GM^{MT} each group member needs to store the signature of the group manager for the cluster tree root, which is composed of $d - 1$ OTS signatures, along with the corresponding authentication paths. Table 3 gives the required storage for each group member in GM and GM^{MT}. We compare GM^{MT} and GM when the total number of supported signatures is 2^{20} for the GM tree and GM^{MT} cluster, which is the maximum number of signatures for GM, and with $N = 2^{10}$ group members, so the number of signing leaves for each member is $B = 2^{10}$. We choose GM^{MT}-256 instances for the comparison as it has the highest storage requirements among all instances. The results show that GM^{MT}-256c saves at least 5.8% of the required storage compared to GM-256. Note that the values in Table 3 are for 256-bit security where $l = 67$. Thus, the above percentages will increase for lower bit security requirements, i.e., for 128 and 192 bit security with $l = 35$ and 51, respectively. Given the recommended parameters in Table 2, the total required storage for each group member in GM^{MT} is $B(2 + \log N) + 3l + 48$ n-bit elements.

Table 3. Group member storage for GM and GM^{MT} with $N = B = 2^{10}$.

Algorithm	$B = N = 2^{10}$	
	Required storage (number of n-bit elements)	
GM	$B(3 + \log N)$	$2^{10} \cdot 13 = 13312$
GM^{MT}-256c	$B(2 + \log N) + 3l^{\dagger} + 48$	$2^{10} \times 12 + 3l + 48 = 12537$

† The values are for $l = 67$ and 256-bit security.

5.2 GM^{MT} and DGM

Both DGM and GM^{MT} are revocable GSSs, but DGM is a dynamic GSS that allows new members to be added to the group after the group public key is generated. Unlike GM^{MT}, DGM requires interaction between verifiers and the group manager to validate the authentication path for each signature verification. Moreover, the group manager in DGM generates the signing keys for the members and thus can sign on their behalf, so it does not satisfy exculpability [5]. A limitation of our scheme is that all group members simultaneously renew their signing keys periodically. Thus, a group member who has used all their signing leaves cannot renew them before a specific time as they need to wait until the new cluster generation occurs. On the other hand, DGM allows new leaves to be assigned on request. In what follows, we compare GM^{MT} with DGM with respect to the efficiency of the revocation mechanism.

Revocation Efficiency. DGM utilizes symmetric puncturable encryption [37] in its revocation mechanism. With each new revoked member, the group manager punctures the encrypted indexes of the signing leaves of all revoked members. Hence, the group manager is required to store all the indexes assigned to all members. In GM^{MT}, the corresponding storage required is for the last assigned label of each member because all the encrypted labels assigned to a member can be regenerated from this label. For example, consider a GM^{MT}-256c instance which has 2^{15} members, supports 2^{64} signatures, and provides 256-bit security. The required storage in GM^{MT} (resp. DGM) is $2^{15} \times 2^8 = 1$ MB (resp. $2^{64} \times 2^8 \approx 10^{8.7}$ TB). Both schemes have equal sized revocation lists and the revocation computational complexity of the group managers are comparable (linear in the size of the revocation list). However, for a revocation check in DGM, the verifier invokes a hash function for 3 times the number of revoked positions in the revocation list [37]. On the other hand, in GM^{MT}, the verifier must search for an n-bit signature element (the encrypted label, Eb) in a sorted revocation list, $RevList$, which has logarithmic complexity. Hence, our revocation algorithm reduces the computational complexity for verification compared to DGM. Nevertheless, the revocation list is large, so in Appendix A we provide an alternative revocation mechanism where the size of the revocation list is linear in the number of revoked members. The alternative mechanism is equivalent to traditional revocation by key, and may be suitable for some applications that do not require anonymity of the revoked members.

6   Implementation

In this section, we provide an unoptimized implementation of the main procedures of GM^{MT} for the purposes of performance evaluation. This C language implementation uses the $XMSS^{MT}$/WOTS standard implementation given in RFC 8391 [24], [25] employing SHA2-256 as a hash function, and AES256 for encryption. Shuffling the signing of leaf nodes is done by reordering the leaf nodes in ascending order using the sorting algorithm for 256 bit integers.

Table 4 provides the performance in kilocycles and the corresponding milliseconds when the code is executed on an Intel(R) Core(TM) i5-5200U CPU at 2.20 GHz. The values in the table are the average of 100 runs. This table gives the performance for group public key generation, group member OTS public keys generation, (cluster) label encryption, leaf shuffling, cluster root generation, cluster root signing, signature opening, message signing, and signature verification. The reported numbers are for the three instances GM^{MT}-256a with $(h_c, N, B) = (16, 2^6, 2^{10})$, GM^{MT}-256b with $(h_c, N, B) = (18, 2^8, 2^{10})$, and GM^{MT}-256c with$(h_c, N, B) = (20, 2^{10}, 2^{10})$. Other parameters are possible according to the application and member storage capabilities. A process is performed by a user (U) or the group manager (GM).

Table 4. GM^{MT} Performance results in kilocycles (kc) and millisecond (ms).

Process	GM^{MT}-256a $(h_c, N, B) = (16, 2^6, 2^{10})$	GM^{MT}-256b $(h_c, N, B) = (18, 2^8, 2^{10})$	GM^{MT}-256c $(h_c, N, B) = (20, 2^{10}, 2^{10})$
Public key gen. (GM)	1,245,539,484 kc - 566,154.3 ms		
OTS public keys gen. (U)	6,147,667 kc - 2,794.4 ms		
Label encryption (GM)	170,471 kc - 77.5 ms	680,758 kc - 309.5 ms	2,721,486 kc - 1,237.1 ms
Shuffling (GM)	48,436 kc - 22.1 ms	205,428 kc - 93.4 ms	854,614 kc - 388.5 ms
Cluster root gen. [†] (GM)	3,364,756 kc - 1,529 ms	13,450,764 kc - 6,113 ms	53,427,148 kc - 24,285 ms
Cluster root signing (GM)	33,064 kc - 15.1 ms		
Message signing (U)	2,957 kc - 1.4 ms		
Signature verification (U)	12,174 kc - 5.6 ms	15,124 kc - 6.9 ms	19,326 kc - 8.8 ms
Signature opening (GM)	46 kc - 0.03 ms		

[†] The Merkle tree is constructed after the leaf nodes have been computed.

7   Conclusion

We proposed GM^{MT}, a revocable hash-based group signature scheme that addresses some of the challenges identified by the designers of the GM and DGM hash-based group signature schemes. Unlike GM, GM^{MT} is a multi-tree construction that allows up to 2^{64} signatures under one group public key. It was shown that GM^{MT} saves at least 5.8% of the required storage for each group member compared to GM for an GM^{MT}-256c instance with 2^{10} group members each assigned 2^{10} signing leaves. Unlike DGM, GM^{MT} verification procedures do not require interaction with the group manager. Moreover, the required storage for the group manager in GM^{MT} is linear in the number of members, while in DGM it is linear in the total number of signatures supported by the scheme. GM^{MT} also reduces the computation complexity of checking revocations from linear in DGM to logarithmic in the size of the revocation list. An analysis of GM^{MT} with respect to anonymity [15] and full traceability [8] was given which shows that its security relies on the standard security assumptions of hash functions and symmetric encryption, and the existential unforgeability of the underlying signing scheme. Finally, we compared GM^{MT} to both GM and DGM, and presented the performance of its procedures using an unoptimized C implementation.

Acknowledgment. The authors would like to thank the anonymous reviewers for their valuable comments that helped improve the quality of the paper.

A   Alternative Solution for a Large Revocation List

In this section, we provide a solution for the large revocation list of GM^{MT} which is suitable for some applications that do not require anonymity of revoked members. We propose the following modification to the leaf generation procedure.

- The group manager generates a secret key sk_i^* for each group member, for $0 \leq i \leq N-1$. This key is different from the group member secret key sk_i that is used to generate the WOTS signing keys.
- The encrypted label in GM^{MT} is replaced by the output of hashing the concatenation of the corresponding $WOTS.pk$ and the group member key $A^* = H(WOTS.pk||sk_i^*)$.

The remaining procedures are the same as in GM^{MT} with the following three differences in the revocation, verification and opening procedures.

- To revoke the j-th member, the group manager adds their key sk_j^* to the revocation list, $RevList$.
- In the verification process, the verifier checks if the calculated WOTS from the signature and keys in the revocation list gives the value A^* in the received signature (which means that the signature has been revoked), if not the verifier continues with the verification.
- In the opening process, the group manager checks which group member's secret key sk_i^* gives the value A^* in the signature $A^* = H(WOTS.pk||sk_i^*)$ for $0 \leq i \leq N-1$.

Applying the above modification has the following consequences.

- The revocation list size is linear in the number of revoked members, while in GM^{MT} it is linear in the number of revoked leaves.
- Revocation does not maintain the anonymity of revoked members.
- The verification complexity is linear in the number of revoked members, while GM^{MT} verification has logarithmic computational complexity with respect to the number of revoked leaves.
- The opening complexity is linear in the number of members, while GM^{MT} has a constant opening complexity, i.e., one decryption operation.

References

1. Alagic, G., et al.: Nistir 8309 status report on the second round of the NIST post-quantum cryptography standardization process. US Department of Commerce, National Institute of Standards and Technology (NIST) (2020)
2. Alamélou, Q., Blazy, O., Cauchie, S., Gaborit, P.: A practical group signature scheme based on rank metric. In: Duquesne, S., Petkova-Nikova, S. (eds.) WAIFI 2016. LNCS, vol. 10064, pp. 258–275. Springer, Cham (2016). https://doi.org/10.1007/978-3-319-55227-9_18
3. Alamélou, Q., Blazy, O., Cauchie, S., Gaborit, P.: A code-based group signature scheme. Des. Codes Crypt. **82**(1–2), 469–493 (2017)

4. AlTawy, R., Gong, G.: Mesh: a supply chain solution with locally private blockchain transactions. Proc. Priv. Enhancing Technol. **2019**(3), 149–169 (2019)

5. Ateniese, G., Tsudik, G.: Some open issues and new directions in group signatures. In: Franklin, M. (ed.) FC 1999. LNCS, vol. 1648, pp. 196–211. Springer, Heidelberg (1999). https://doi.org/10.1007/3-540-48390-X_15

6. Aumasson, J.-P., Endignoux, G.: Improving stateless hash-based signatures. In: Smart, N.P. (ed.) CT-RSA 2018. LNCS, vol. 10808, pp. 219–242. Springer, Cham (2018). https://doi.org/10.1007/978-3-319-76953-0_12

7. Ayebie, B.E., Assidi, H., Souidi, E.M.: A new dynamic code-based group signature scheme. In: El Hajji, S., Nitaj, A., Souidi, E.M. (eds.) C2SI 2017. LNCS, vol. 10194, pp. 346–364. Springer, Cham (2017). https://doi.org/10.1007/978-3-319-55589-8_23

8. Bellare, M., Micciancio, D., Warinschi, B.: Foundations of group signatures: formal definitions, simplified requirements, and a construction based on general assumptions. In: Biham, E. (ed.) EUROCRYPT 2003. LNCS, vol. 2656, pp. 614–629. Springer, Heidelberg (2003). https://doi.org/10.1007/3-540-39200-9_38

9. Bernstein, D.J., et al.: SPHINCS: practical stateless hash-based signatures. In: Oswald, E., Fischlin, M. (eds.) EUROCRYPT 2015. LNCS, vol. 9056, pp. 368–397. Springer, Heidelberg (2015). https://doi.org/10.1007/978-3-662-46800-5_15

10. Bernstein, D. J., Hülsing, A., Kölbl, S., Niederhagen, R., Rijneveld, J., Schwabe, P.: The sphincs+ signature framework. In: ACM SIGSAC CCS (2019), pp. 2129–2146

11. Boneh, D., Boyen, X., Shacham, H.: Short group signatures. In: Franklin, M. (ed.) CRYPTO 2004. LNCS, vol. 3152, pp. 41–55. Springer, Heidelberg (2004). https://doi.org/10.1007/978-3-540-28628-8_3

12. Boneh, D., Dagdelen, Ö., Fischlin, M., Lehmann, A., Schaffner, C., Zhandry, M.: Random oracles in a quantum world. In: Lee, D.H., Wang, X. (eds.) ASIACRYPT 2011. LNCS, vol. 7073, pp. 41–69. Springer, Heidelberg (2011). https://doi.org/10.1007/978-3-642-25385-0_3

13. Boneh, D., Shacham, H.: Group signatures with verifier-local revocation. In: ACM CCS, pp. 168–177 (2004)

14. Buser, M., Liu, J.K., Steinfeld, R., Sakzad, A., Sun, S.-F.: DGM: a dynamic and revocable group merkle signature. In: Sako, K., Schneider, S., Ryan, P.Y.A. (eds.) ESORICS 2019. LNCS, vol. 11735, pp. 194–214. Springer, Cham (2019). https://doi.org/10.1007/978-3-030-29959-0_10

15. Camenisch, J., Groth, J.: Group signatures: better efficiency and new theoretical aspects. In: Blundo, C., Cimato, S. (eds.) SCN 2004. LNCS, vol. 3352, pp. 120–133. Springer, Heidelberg (2005). https://doi.org/10.1007/978-3-540-30598-9_9

16. Camenisch, J., Kohlweiss, M., Soriente, C.: Solving revocation with efficient update of anonymous credentials. In: Garay, J.A., De Prisco, R. (eds.) SCN 2010. LNCS, vol. 6280, pp. 454–471. Springer, Heidelberg (2010). https://doi.org/10.1007/978-3-642-15317-4_28

17. Camenisch, J., Lysyanskaya, A.: Dynamic accumulators and application to efficient revocation of anonymous credentials. In: Yung, M. (ed.) CRYPTO 2002. LNCS, vol. 2442, pp. 61–76. Springer, Heidelberg (2002). https://doi.org/10.1007/3-540-45708-9_5

18. Camenisch, J., Lysyanskaya, A.: Signature schemes and anonymous credentials from bilinear maps. In: Franklin, M. (ed.) CRYPTO 2004. LNCS, vol. 3152, pp. 56–72. Springer, Heidelberg (2004). https://doi.org/10.1007/978-3-540-28628-8_4

19. Chaum, D., van Heyst, E.: Group signatures. In: Davies, D.W. (ed.) EUROCRYPT 1991. LNCS, vol. 547, pp. 257–265. Springer, Heidelberg (1991). https://doi.org/10.1007/3-540-46416-6_22

20. Del Pino, R., Lyubashevsky, V., Seiler, G.: Lattice-based group signatures and zero-knowledge proofs of automorphism stability. In: ACM SIGSAC CCS, pp. 574–591 (2018)

21. El Bansarkhani, R., Misoczki, R.: G-Merkle: a hash-based group signature scheme from standard assumptions. In: Lange, T., Steinwandt, R. (eds.) PQCrypto 2018. LNCS, vol. 10786, pp. 441–463. Springer, Cham (2018). https://doi.org/10.1007/978-3-319-79063-3_21

22. Ezerman, M.F., Lee, H.T., Ling, S., Nguyen, K., Wang, H.: Provably secure group signature schemes from code-based assumptions. IEEE Trans. Inf. Theory **66**(9), 5754–5773 (2020)

23. Gordon, S.D., Katz, J., Vaikuntanathan, V.: A group signature scheme from lattice assumptions. In: Abe, M. (ed.) ASIACRYPT 2010. LNCS, vol. 6477, pp. 395–412. Springer, Heidelberg (2010). https://doi.org/10.1007/978-3-642-17373-8_23

24. Hülsing, A., Butin, D., Gazdag, S.-L., Rijneveld, J., Mohaisen, A.: Xmss: extended merkle signature scheme. In: RFC 8391. IRTF (2018)

25. Hülsing, A., Rijneveld, J., Song, F.: Mitigating multi-target attacks in hash-based signatures. In: Cheng, C.-M., Chung, K.-M., Persiano, G., Yang, B.-Y. (eds.) PKC 2016. LNCS, vol. 9614, pp. 387–416. Springer, Heidelberg (2016). https://doi.org/10.1007/978-3-662-49384-7_15

26. Laguillaumie, F., Langlois, A., Libert, B., Stehlé, D.: Lattice-based group signatures with logarithmic signature size. In: Sako, K., Sarkar, P. (eds.) ASIACRYPT 2013. LNCS, vol. 8270, pp. 41–61. Springer, Heidelberg (2013). https://doi.org/10.1007/978-3-642-42045-0_3

27. Langlois, A., Ling, S., Nguyen, K., Wang, H.: Lattice-based group signature scheme with verifier-local revocation. In: Krawczyk, H. (ed.) PKC 2014. LNCS, vol. 8383, pp. 345–361. Springer, Heidelberg (2014). https://doi.org/10.1007/978-3-642-54631-0_20

28. Libert, B., Ling, S., Mouhartem, F., Nguyen, K., Wang, H.: Signature schemes with efficient protocols and dynamic group signatures from lattice assumptions. In: Cheon, J.H., Takagi, T. (eds.) ASIACRYPT 2016. LNCS, vol. 10032, pp. 373–403. Springer, Heidelberg (2016). https://doi.org/10.1007/978-3-662-53890-6_13

29. Libert, B., Peters, T., Yung, M.: Group signatures with almost-for-free revocation. In: Safavi-Naini, R., Canetti, R. (eds.) CRYPTO 2012. LNCS, vol. 7417, pp. 571–589. Springer, Heidelberg (2012). https://doi.org/10.1007/978-3-642-32009-5_34

30. Libert, B., Peters, T., Yung, M.: Scalable group signatures with revocation. In: Pointcheval, D., Johansson, T. (eds.) EUROCRYPT 2012. LNCS, vol. 7237, pp. 609–627. Springer, Heidelberg (2012). https://doi.org/10.1007/978-3-642-29011-4_36

31. Lin, X., Sun, X., Ho, P.-H., Shen, X.: GSIS: a secure and privacy-preserving protocol for vehicular communications. IEEE Trans. Veh. Technol **56**(6), 3442–3456 (2007)

32. Ling, S., Nguyen, K., Wang, H.: Group signatures from lattices: simpler, tighter, shorter, ring-based. In: Katz, J. (ed.) PKC 2015. LNCS, vol. 9020, pp. 427–449. Springer, Heidelberg (2015). https://doi.org/10.1007/978-3-662-46447-2_19

33. Nguyen, P.Q., Zhang, J., Zhang, Z.: Simpler efficient group signatures from lattices. In: Katz, J. (ed.) PKC 2015. LNCS, vol. 9020, pp. 401–426. Springer, Heidelberg (2015). https://doi.org/10.1007/978-3-662-46447-2_18

34. NIST. Post quantum crypto project. http://csrc.nist.gov/groups/ST/post-quantum-crypto

35. NIST. Submission requirements and evaluation criteria for the post-quantum cryptography standardization process. https://csrc.nist.gov/Projects/post-quantum-cryptography/post-quantum-cryptography-standardization/Call-for-Proposals
36. Shor, P.W.: Algorithms for quantum computation: discrete logarithms and factoring. In: IEEE SFCS, pp. 124–134. IEEE (1994)
37. Sun, S.-F., et al.: Practical backward-secure searchable encryption from symmetric puncturable encryption. In: ACM SIGSAC CCS, pp. 763–780 (2018)
38. Tsang, P.P., Au, M.H., Kapadia, A., Smith, S.W.: Blacklistable anonymous credentials: Blocking misbehaving users without ttps. In: CCS, CCS '07, pp. 72–81. ACM (2007)
39. Tsang, P.P., Au, M.H., Kapadia, A., Smith, S.W.: PEREA: towards practical TTP-free revocation in anonymous authentication. In CCS, CCS '08, pp. 333–344. ACM (2008)
40. Yang, R., Au, M.H., Zhang, Z., Xu, Q., Yu, Z., Whyte, W.: Efficient lattice-based zero-knowledge arguments with standard soundness: construction and applications. In: Boldyreva, A., Micciancio, D. (eds.) CRYPTO 2019. LNCS, vol. 11692, pp. 147–175. Springer, Cham (2019). https://doi.org/10.1007/978-3-030-26948-7_6
41. Yehia, M., AlTawy, R., Gulliver, T.A.: Security analysis of DGM and GM group signature schemes instantiated with XMSS-T. In: Insecrypt. Springer, Heidelberg (2021). https://doi.org/10.1007/978-3-030-88323-2_4

Issuer-Hiding Attribute-Based Credentials

Jan Bobolz[1], Fabian Eidens[1], Stephan Krenn[2(✉)], Sebastian Ramacher[2], and Kai Samelin[3]

[1] Paderborn University, Paderborn, Germany
{jan.bobolz,fabian.eidens}@uni-paderborn.de
[2] AIT Austrian Institute of Technology, Vienna, Austria
{stephan.krenn,sebastian.ramacher}@ait.ac.at
[3] Heidelberg, Germany

Abstract. Attribute-based credential systems enable users to authenticate in a privacy-preserving manner. However, in such schemes verifying a user's credential requires knowledge of the issuer's public key, which by itself might already reveal private information about the user.

In this paper, we tackle this problem by introducing the notion of *issuer-hiding* attribute-based credential systems. In such a system, the verifier can define a set of acceptable issuers in an ad-hoc manner, and the user can then prove that her credential was issued by one of the accepted issuers – without revealing which one. We then provide a generic construction, as well as a concrete instantiation based on Groth's structure preserving signature scheme (ASIACRYPT'15) and simulation-sound extractable NIZK, for which we also provide concrete benchmarks in order to prove its practicability.

The online complexity of all constructions is independent of the number of acceptable verifiers, which makes it also suitable for highly federated scenarios.

Keywords: Cryptographic protocols · Issuer-hiding ·
Privacy-preserving · Anonymous credentials · Authentication

1 Introduction

Anonymous credential systems and their attribute-based extensions (ABCs) allow *users* to receive digital certificates (*credentials*) certifying certain pieces of personal information (*attributes*) from *issuers*. A user can then present her credential to a *verifier* in a way that respects the user's privacy while giving high authenticity guarantees to the verifier. That is, the user can decide, on a fine-granular basis, which information about her attributes she wants to disclose to the verifier, while no further information, including metadata, is revealed. In

---

K. Samelin—Independent.

M. Conti et al. (Eds.): CANS 2021, LNCS 13099, pp. 158–178, 2021.
https://doi.org/10.1007/978-3-030-92548-2_9

particular, different actions of the same user can only be linked through the disclosed information. In the most general case, the verifier can publish arbitrary predicates (Boolean formulas) over attribute values that users need to satisfy for authentication (e.g., a user is older than 21, comes from a specific country, or has a certain name), and receives cryptographic evidence that such attribute values were certified by the given issuer. Anonymous credential systems were first envisioned by Chaum [24,25]. Besides well-known systems like Microsoft's U-Prove [11,43] and IBM's Identity Mixer [18–20,22], a large body of work with different optimizations and functionalities can be found in the literature, e.g. [7,8,15–17,27,37,44].

All of the aforementioned ABC systems have in common that the privacy guarantees only hold with respect to a single issuer key: whilst not being able to link actions of a single user, a verifier learns the public key of the issuer of the underlying credential. Even though this seems to be a natural property at first glance, it turns out that this approach leads to a tradeoff between scalability and user privacy. As an example, consider a state-wide electronic identity system with millions of users. In order to give users the highest level of privacy, all citizens' personal credentials need to be issued under the same public key. In case of a compromise of the secret key, all previously issued keys need to be invalidated, potentially requiring millions of certificates to be re-issued under a new key. Alternatively, different keys could be used for groups of citizens, e.g., randomly, per time period, or per administrative region. However, as the issuer's public key is revealed upon presentation, this approach dramatically reduces the size of the anonymity set of a specific user.

Furthermore, many scenarios would benefit from a dynamic and ad-hoc definition of a set of issuer keys accepted by a verifier. For instance, universities may issue electronic student IDs to their students. Depending on the concrete scenario, students may need to prove that they are enrolled at a specific university (e.g., to enter the campus), or that they are enrolled at any university without needing to reveal the university (e.g., to be granted an online student discount). Similarly, citizens may receive electronic identities from their nation state, which they can then use to prove that they are eligible, e.g., for participation in opinion polls in their country. However, they might want to use the same credential to also prove that they are living in any country of a specific region (e.g., the European Union) for cross-country citizen engagement processes which do not require to reveal the specific citizenship.

In vehicular ad-hoc networks (VANETs) [32] or vehicle-to-infrastructure networks (V2I), such a solution allows each car manufacturer to use their own secret keys (e.g., per model), while avoiding to reveal unnecessary information (e.g., the model) when authenticating towards other parties.

Finally, Cloudflare recently announced a replacement of CAPTCHAs by cryptographic attestation of personhood using, e.g., FIDO tokens.[1] The idea is that instead of solving a puzzle, users click a physical button on an accepted hardware token, which responds to a cryptographic challenge. However, as pointed

---

[1] https://blog.cloudflare.com/introducing-cryptographic-attestation-of-personhood/.

out by Cloudflare, a user's key "looks like all other keys in the batch", meaning that the anonymity set of a user shrinks to the number of devices in a batch. It would thus be desirable to dynamically add additional batches to this anonymity set, without users needing to obtain new credentials for their existing devices.

Related Work. Different mitigation strategies for these challenges exists. For instance, approaches for decentralizing the issuer have been proposed, e.g., by fully avoiding the need for a trusted issuer leveraging public append-only ledgers [33,48], or by deploying threshold cryptography to require multiple issuers to contribute to the credential issuance process [14,41,47]. While such approaches reduce the risk of compromised issuer keys, they do not directly allow to dynamically adjust the set of issuers among which a user should remain private.

Delegatable credentials [4,7,13,23,27] offer an alternative solution, where users can issue credentials derived from their own credentials to other users. All credentials eventually trace back to a root authority's public key, yet the verifier does not learn the precise issuer within the delegation "tree". While delegatable credentials are a valuable tool, e.g., for managing privileges within organizations, they do not solve the issues addressed in this paper as they assume a single root authority, which will typically not exist in the federated scenarios sketched above. They also do not allow for ad-hoc definitions of accepted issuers. Furthermore, revocation of sub-issuers within the delegation tree is computationally expensive, while it can be achieved for free in our construction.

Closely related to anonymous credentials, also in self-sovereign identity (SSI) systems multiple issuers will participate. In such systems, e.g., [2,3,38], users can join by presenting some form of credential to one or multiple verification nodes. In eSSIF[2], which is the European Union's attempt to build a large scale SSI system, these credentials are issued by national authorities run by each member state. If the credential is accepted by the nodes, they record their decision on a distributed ledger. Even if these systems are not built from ABCs, they can be designed to mimic some of their functionalities. Indeed, whenever the user wants to present attributes included in their credential to a service provider, a presentation of some of the attributes can be computed with respect to the information stored on the ledger. Due to the trust put into the distributed ledger and the verification nodes, it is thereby not necessary to show the issuer public key to the verifier. Hence, this additional layer, i.e. the ledger and verification nodes, provides some level of mitigation against identification attempts based on the issuer. Yet, the issuer is known to the verification nodes responsible for the initial joining of the system. Especially when the system is built from a public ledger, a service provider could also run such a node and therefore information on the issuers could potentially be gathered. Also, the authenticity guarantees are no longer end-to-end, but partially rely on the verification nodes and the consensus mechanism employed for the distributed ledger.

---

[2] https://decentralized-id.com/government/europe/eSSIF/.

Our Contributions. In this paper we address the discussed challenges by presenting an *issuer-hiding* attribute-based credential system. That is, our system allows a user to hide the issuer of her credential among a set of issuers. More specifically, the verifier may issue a *policy* defining the issuers he is willing to accept for a certain presentation session, and the user may then prove that she indeed owns a credential issued by one of those issuers.

Firstly, this approach allows a user to use her credential in various contexts, as described in the examples above. Secondly, the revocation of issuers becomes efficient in the sense that credentials issued by a specific issuer can be revoked by simply no longer including this issuer in the policy. Finally, additional issuers can be added in a seamless fashion by adding them to the policy.

Overview of Our Approach. To explain the technicalities of our construction let us first solve the hiding of public keys during authentication straightforwardly. As already mentioned, a user's credential on attributes $m = [$age, name, state, reputation$]$ by issuer I_j is a signature *cred* on the message vector m valid under the issuer's public key ipk_j. To authenticate at a verifier V_k the user U proves validity of *cred* under the public key ipk_j. More formally, U sends a non-interactive proof $NIZK[(x = ipk_j, w = \{m, cred\}): \mathsf{Verify}(ipk_j, cred, m)]$. Public common input to the NIZK is ipk_j. The witness, hence private input by the user are *cred* and m. The NIZK deals with the privacy of the witness, but ipk_j is publicly known. As a feature this lets verifiers interpret attributes and credentials with respect to the issuer, e.g. reputation has potentially more weight if ipk_j belongs to a government agency. In other cases, this is a detriment to user privacy, e.g. the attribute state certified in *cred* is never revealed by the user, nonetheless the verifier may learn state implicitly by looking at ipk_j.

An idea to hide ipk_j in the above NIZK is to build a structure reminiscent of ring signatures. For authentication, the user collects an appropriate set of issuer public keys $PK := \{ipk_1, \ldots, ipk_j, \ldots, ipk_n\}$. Then we change the NIZK statement to $NIZK[(x = PK, w = \{ipk_j, m, cred\}): \bigvee_{i=1}^n \mathsf{Verify}(ipk_i, cred, m)]$. We solved our problem, the or-statement in the NIZK hides under which ipk the user's credential is valid.

The downside is that naively the proof size and verification cost is now linear in $n := |PK|$ which limits the practicability of this approach. Hence, the next essential step is to avoid the or-statement in the NIZK.

This can be achieved by letting the verifier sign the public keys of the accepted issuers, by computing $\sigma_j \xleftarrow{\$} \mathsf{Sign}(vsk, ipk_j)$ for all $ipk_j \in PK$, where (vsk, vpk) is the verifier's key pair. Instead of performing an or-proof, the user can now show that she knows a signature, issued by the verifier, on the public key of the issuer that issued the user's credential. That is, the user can now send $NIZK[(x = vpk, w = (\sigma, ipk, cred, m): \mathsf{Verify}(ipk, cred, m) \land \mathsf{Verify}(vpk, \sigma, ipk)]$, which is independent of the number of accepted issuers, i.e., $|PK|$.

A remaining technicality is now that the same verifier may accept different issuers for different scenarios, which is why every σ_j needs to be bound to the specific scenario. Using ephemeral signature keys (vpk, vsk) in each presentation session would require linear computation for computing and verifying

$\mathbf{Exp}_{\mathsf{Adv}}^{\mathsf{EUF-CMA}}(\lambda)$

$\quad pp \xleftarrow{\$} \Sigma.\mathsf{ParGen}(1^\lambda)$ where:

$\quad (sk, pk) \xleftarrow{\$} \Sigma.\mathsf{KGen}(pp)$ $\mathcal{O}_{\mathtt{sign}}(m)$:

$\quad \mathcal{Q} \leftarrow \emptyset$ $\quad \sigma \xleftarrow{\$} \Sigma.\mathsf{Sign}(pp, sk, m)$

$\quad (m^*, \sigma^*) \xleftarrow{\$} \mathsf{Adv}^{\mathcal{O}_{\mathtt{sign}}}(pk)$ $\quad \mathcal{Q} \leftarrow \mathcal{Q} \cup \{m\}$

$\quad$ return 0, if $m^* \in \mathcal{Q}$ $\quad$ return σ

$\quad$ return 1, if $\Sigma.\mathsf{Verify}(pp, pk, \sigma^*, m^*) = 1$

$\quad$ return 0

Exp. 1: EUF-CMA experiment for digital signatures.

the signatures; alternatively, a unique key pair per verifier could be used, and $\sigma_j \xleftarrow{\$} (vsk, (ipk_j, \mathsf{domain}))$ could be bound to a specific application domain. We finally opted for a combination, where the verifier is still key-less, yet signatures on public keys can be reused. This is done by letting the verifier define *policies* where a policy consists of signatures on all *ipk*'s for a specific domain, but different signing keys are used for different domains, and thus the respective signing keys can be discarded after publishing a policy.

We formalize the above intuition through a generic construction, for which we provide formal security proofs. We then give a concrete instantiation based on Groth's structure preserving signature scheme [36]. To ease readability, our basic construction focuses on the core functionality of anonymous credential systems; however, we finally also discuss how to achieve advances functionalities including non-frameability, revocation of credentials, and fine-granular linkability.

2   Preliminaries

We denote the main security parameter by λ. We write $a \xleftarrow{\$} \mathsf{A}$ to denote that a is the output of a potentially randomized algorithm A and $v \xleftarrow{\$} \mathcal{S}$ to denote that v is uniformly sampled at random from a set $\mathcal{S}$. If not explicitly stated otherwise, all algorithms are assumed to be polynomial-time (PPT).

Digital Signatures. A digital signature scheme consists of four algorithms:

- $pp \xleftarrow{\$} \Sigma.\mathsf{ParGen}(1^\lambda)$ generates public parameters pp.
- $(sk, pk) \xleftarrow{\$} \Sigma.\mathsf{KGen}(pp)$ generates a secret key sk and a public key pk.
- $\sigma \xleftarrow{\$} \Sigma.\mathsf{Sign}(pp, sk, m)$ creates a signature σ on message m.
- $b \leftarrow \Sigma.\mathsf{Verify}(pp, pk, \sigma, m)$ verifies the signature.

Following Goldwasser et al. [34], we require a digital signature scheme to be existentially unforgeable, meaning that no adversary can efficiently come up with a valid signature on a new message of the adversary's choice, even if it is given access to a signing oracle that may sign an arbitrary number of messages chosen by the adversary:

Definition 1. *A digital signature scheme is* EUF-CMA *secure if and only if for every PPT adversary* Adv *there exists a negligible function* negl *such that:*

$$\Pr\left[\mathbf{Exp}_{\mathsf{Adv}}^{\mathsf{EUF-CMA}}(\lambda) = 1\right] \leq \mathsf{negl}(\lambda),$$

where the experiment is as defined in Experiment 1.

Structure-Preserving Signatures. We recall the randomizable structure-preserving signature scheme by Groth [36]. While the scheme is able to sign matrices of group elements, we only require it to sign a single group element. Similar to Camenisch et al. [13], we consider the scheme in two variants: Groth_1 signs elements of $\mathbb{G}_1$ (and its public keys live in $\mathbb{G}_2$), and $\mathsf{Groth}2$, which signs elements of $\mathbb{G}_2$ (with public keys in $\mathbb{G}_1$). We describe Groth_1. The other scheme, Groth_2, can be obtained easily by switching the roles of $\mathbb{G}_1$ and $\mathbb{G}_2$.

- $\mathsf{Groth}_1.\mathsf{ParGen}(1^\lambda)$ generates public parameters pp consisting of a bilinear group $(\mathbb{G}_1, \mathbb{G}_2, \mathbb{G}_T, e, p, G, \tilde{G})$ of prime order p with generators $G \in \mathbb{G}_1, \tilde{G} \in \mathbb{G}_2$, and a random element $Y \xleftarrow{\$} \mathbb{G}_1$.
- $\mathsf{Groth}_1.\mathsf{KGen}(pp)$ generates a secret key $sk_{\mathsf{sps}} = v \xleftarrow{\$} \mathbb{Z}_p^*$ and the corresponding public key $pk_{\mathsf{sps}} = \tilde{V} = \tilde{G}^v$.
- $\mathsf{Groth}_1.\mathsf{Sign}(pp, sk_{\mathsf{sps}}, M)$ chooses $r \xleftarrow{\$} \mathbb{Z}_p^*$ and outputs the signature $\sigma = (\tilde{R}, S, T) = (\tilde{G}^r, (Y \cdot G^v)^{1/r}, (Y^v \cdot M)^{1/r})$.
- $\mathsf{Groth}_1.\mathsf{Rand}(pp, \sigma)$ chooses $r' \xleftarrow{\$} \mathbb{Z}_p^*$ and outputs $\sigma' = (\tilde{R}', S', T') = (\tilde{R}^r, S^{1/r}, T^{1/r})$.
- $\mathsf{Groth}_1.\mathsf{Verify}(pp, pk_{\mathsf{sps}}, \sigma, M)$ checks that $e(S, \tilde{R}) = e(Y, \tilde{G}) \cdot e(G, \tilde{V})$ and $e(T, \tilde{R}) = e(Y, \tilde{V}) \cdot e(M, \tilde{G})$.

This construction is EUF-CMA secure in the generic group model [36].

Zero-Knowledge Proofs. A non-interactive zero-knowledge proof of knowledge (NIZK) allows a prover to generate a cryptographic proof that he knows a secret witness w such that $(x, w) \in \mathcal{R}$ for some binary relation $\mathcal{R}$ and a public statement x, without revealing any additional information about w than what is already revealed by x. We denote the language associated with $\mathcal{R}$ by L.

Formally, a NIZK consists of three algorithms:

- $pp \xleftarrow{\$} \Pi.\mathsf{ParGen}(1^\lambda)$ generates the public parameters pp.
- $\pi \xleftarrow{\$} \Pi.\mathsf{Prove}(pp, x, w, \mathsf{ctx})$ generates a non-interactive zero-knowledge proof of knowledge π of w such that $(x, w) \in \mathcal{R}$ bound to ctx.
- $b \leftarrow \Pi.\mathsf{Verify}(pp, x, \mathsf{ctx}, \pi)$ verifies a proof π.

Besides correctness, we will require zero-knowledge and simulation-sound extractability from all NIZKs.

Informally, the zero-knowledge property ensures that the receiver of a NIZK does not learn anything beyond what is already revealed by the statement itself.

$\mathbf{Exp}_{\mathsf{Adv}}^{\mathsf{zero-knowledge}}(\lambda)$

$\quad (pp, \tau) \xleftarrow{\$} \mathsf{Sim}_1(1^\lambda)$

$\quad b \xleftarrow{\$} \{0, 1\}$

$\quad b^* \xleftarrow{\$} \mathsf{Adv}^{\mathcal{O}_b}(pp)$

$\quad$ return 1, if $b = b^*$

$\quad$ return 0

where:

$\quad \mathcal{O}_0(x, w, \mathsf{ctx})$:

$\qquad$ return $\pi \xleftarrow{\$} \Pi.\mathsf{Prove}(pp, x, w, \mathsf{ctx})$, if $(x, w) \in \mathcal{R}$

$\qquad$ return $\bot$

$\quad \mathcal{O}_1(x, w, \mathsf{ctx})$:

$\qquad$ return $\pi \xleftarrow{\$} \mathsf{Sim}_2(pp, \tau, x, \mathsf{ctx})$, if $(x, w) \in \mathcal{R}$

$\qquad$ return $\bot$

Exp. 2: Zero-knowledge experiment for NIZKs.

$\mathbf{Exp}_{\mathsf{Adv}}^{\mathsf{SimSoundExt}}(\lambda)$

$\quad (pp, \tau, \zeta) \xleftarrow{\$} \mathsf{Ext}_1(1^\lambda)$

$\quad Q \leftarrow \emptyset$

$\quad (x^*, \mathsf{ctx}^*, \pi^*) \xleftarrow{\$} \mathsf{Adv}^{\mathcal{O}_{\mathsf{SIM}}}(pp)$

$\quad w^* \xleftarrow{\$} \mathsf{Ext}_2(pp, \zeta, x^*, \mathsf{ctx}^*, \pi^*)$

$\quad$ return 1, if:

$\qquad \Pi.\mathsf{Verify}(pp, x^*, \mathsf{ctx}^*, \pi^*) = 1$,

$\qquad (x^*, w^*) \notin \mathcal{R}$, and

$\qquad (x^*, \mathsf{ctx}^*) \notin Q$

$\quad$ return 0

where:

$\quad \mathcal{O}_{\mathsf{SIM}}(x, \mathsf{ctx})$:

$\qquad \pi \xleftarrow{\$} \mathsf{Sim}_2(pp, \tau, x, \mathsf{ctx})$

$\qquad Q \leftarrow Q \cup \{(x, \mathsf{ctx})\}$

$\qquad$ return π

Exp. 3: Simulation-sound extractability experiment for NIZKs.

Definition 2. *A non-interactive proof system Π satisfies* zero-knowledge *for a relation $\mathcal{R}$, if and only if for every PPT adversary Adv there exists a PPT simulator $\mathsf{Sim} = (\mathsf{Sim}_1, \mathsf{Sim}_2)$ such that there exists negligible functions negl_1 and negl_2 such that:*

$$\left| \Pr\left[\mathsf{Adv}(pp) = 1 : pp \xleftarrow{\$} \Pi.\mathsf{ParGen}(1^\lambda) \right] \right.$$

$$\left. - \Pr\left[\mathsf{Adv}(pp) = 1 : (pp, \tau) \xleftarrow{\$} \mathsf{Sim}_1(1^\lambda) \right] \right| \leq \mathsf{negl}_1(\lambda),$$

and

$$\left| \Pr\left[\mathbf{Exp}_{\mathsf{Adv}}^{\mathsf{zero-knowledge}}(\lambda) = 1 \right] - \frac{1}{2} \right| \leq \mathsf{negl}_2(\lambda),$$

where the experiment is as defined in Experiment 2.

Intuitively, simulation-sound extractability requires that any adversary that can generate a valid proof must also know a valid witness for this statement, even if it has previously seen arbitrarily many (simulated) proofs of potentially false statements. Note that the original definition of Groth [35], combining simulation-soundness [45] and proofs of knowledge [28], is stronger than ours in the sense that the adversary also gets access to the extraction trapdoor; however, similar to previous work [1,29,30] the following slightly weaker definition is sufficient for our purposes. Furthermore, the inclusion of a context ctx essentially makes the NIZK a *signature* of knowledge [23].

Definition 3. *A zero-knowledge non-interactive proof system Π satisfies simulation-sound extractability for a relation $\mathcal{R}$, if and only if for every PPT adversary* Adv *there exists a PPT extractor* Ext $= (\mathsf{Ext}_1, \mathsf{Ext}_2)$ *such that there exists a negligible function* negl *such that:*

$$\left| \Pr\left[\mathsf{Adv}(pp, \tau) = 1 : (pp, \tau) \xleftarrow{\$} \mathsf{Sim}_1(1^\lambda) \right] \right.$$

$$\left. - \Pr\left[\mathsf{Adv}(pp, \tau) = 1 : (pp, \tau, \zeta) \xleftarrow{\$} \mathsf{Ext}_1(1^\lambda) \right] \right| = 0,$$

and

$$\Pr\left[\mathbf{Exp}_{\mathsf{Adv}}^{\mathsf{SimSoundExt}}(\lambda) = 1 \right] \leq \mathsf{negl}(\lambda),$$

where the experiment is as defined in Experiment 3 and Sim $= (\mathsf{Sim}_1, \mathsf{Sim}_2)$ *is as in Definition 2.*

For notational convenience, we use the following notation for NIZKs, initially introduced by Camenisch and Stadler [21]. In this notation, a statement like

$$\mathrm{NIZK}\left[(\alpha, \beta, \gamma) : y_1 = g_1^\alpha g_2^\beta \wedge y_2 = g_1^\alpha g_3^\gamma \wedge \alpha \geq \gamma \right] (\mathsf{ctx})$$

denotes a non-interactive zero-knowledge proof of knowledge, bound to the context ctx, of values α, β, γ such that the relation on the right hand side is satisfied. We also omit the public proof parameters pp.

3 Framework for Issuer-Hiding ABCs

We next define the syntax for issuer-hiding attribute-based credential systems, and then formalize the security properties required from such a system.

3.1 Syntax

An issuer-hiding ABC system is specified by eight algorithms. Initially, the parameters are generated by ParGen. Having generated a key pair using IKGen, an issuer can then issue credentials on attributes to a user by means of Issue; users can verify the received credential locally by VfCred in order to detect malformed credentials. To define the set of accepted issuers, a verifier generates a policy using PresPolicy, which can be checked for well-formedness using VfPolicy by everyone. Finally, holding a credential from an issuer and a policy from the verifier, a user uses Present to derive a presentation token, which is verified by Verify. The inputs and outputs of the algorithms are introduced in the following:

Parameter Generation. The public parameters are generated as:

$$pp \xleftarrow{\$} \mathsf{ParGen}(1^\lambda).$$

The public parameters are assumed to be implicit input to all algorithms presented in the following. We assume pp in particular specifies the number L of attributes that may be certified per credential, as well as the attribute space $\mathbb{A}$.

Key Generation. Issuers compute their respective private and public keys as:

$$(isk, ipk) \xleftarrow{\$} \mathsf{IKGen}(pp).$$

Issuance. The issuer creates a credential *cred* on attributes $\vec{a}$ as follows:

$$cred \xleftarrow{\$} \mathsf{Issue}(isk, \vec{a}).$$

For the sake of simplicity, this process is modeled as a non-interactive algorithm as opposed an interactive protocol between the issuer and the user.

Credential Verification. The validity of a credential can be checked as follows:

$$b \xleftarrow{\$} \mathsf{VfCred}(cred, \vec{a}, ipk).$$

Presentation Policies. Verifiers can define presentation policies defining sets of issuers they are willing to accept for certain presentation sessions:

$$pol \xleftarrow{\$} \mathsf{PresPolicy}(\{ipk_i\}).$$

Note that *pol* only defines the sets of issuers accepted by a verifier, but not, e.g., which attributes a verifier needs to disclose. By this, *pol* can be reused for multiple contexts, reducing the number of policies.

Policy Verification. Presentation policies can be checked for validity as follows:

$$b \leftarrow \mathsf{VfPolicy}(pol, \{ipk_i\}).$$

Presentation. For practical reasons, we only focus on non-interactive presentation protocols. Having agreed on a presentation policy which has been verified by the user, she computes a presentation token:

$$pt \xleftarrow{\$} \mathsf{Present}(ipk, cred, \phi, \vec{a}, pol, \mathsf{ctx}).$$

The verifier then validates the token as:

$$b \leftarrow \mathsf{Verify}(pt, \phi, pol, \mathsf{ctx}).$$

Here, $\phi : \mathbb{A}^L \rightarrow \{0, 1\}$ is a predicate over the user's attributes that needs to be satisfied in order to pass verification, i.e., verification only passes if $\phi(\vec{a}) = 1$. For instance, ϕ might require that some a_i equals some previously agreed value, corresponding to the disclosure of this attribute, or that $a_i \in [l, r]$ for some bounds l and r. Finally, the purpose of ctx is to define a context in which the presentation token is accepted, e.g., a session identifier or a random nonce to avoid replay attacks or similar.

Policies will typically be long-lived, and it thus not necessary for a user to verify the policy every time before computing a presentation token. We thus do not consider these computational costs as part of the verification algorithm.

3.2   Security Definitions

We next define necessary security properties for an issuer-hiding ABC system.

Correctness. We omit a formal definition here, as the requirements are what one would expect: if all parties follow the protocol specifications during all phases, any presentation token computed by the user will be accepted by the verifier.

Unforgeability. Unforgeability requires that it is infeasible for an adversary to generate a valid presentation token, if it has not previously received a credential on attributes satisfying ϕ from one of the accepted issuers, or a presentation token for the same (ctx, ϕ, pol).

In the following definition, note that while the challenge policy pol^* may only include honest issuers' keys, the adversary may request presentation tokens for arbitrary sets of ipk's from the presentation oracle $\mathcal{O}_{\mathrm{present}}$, covering the case of adversarial issuers.

$\mathbf{Exp}_{\mathrm{Adv}}^{\mathrm{Unforgeability}}(\lambda, n_\mathrm{I})$

$\quad pp \xleftarrow{\$} \mathsf{ParGen}(1^\lambda)$

$\quad Q_{\mathrm{issue}} \leftarrow \emptyset, Q_{\mathrm{present}} \leftarrow \emptyset, Q_{\mathrm{reveal}} \leftarrow \emptyset$

$\quad (isk_i, ipk_i) \xleftarrow{\$} \mathsf{IKGen}(pp) \text{ for } i = 1, \ldots, n_\mathrm{I}$

$\quad (I^*, st) \xleftarrow{\$} \mathsf{Adv}^{\mathcal{O}_{\mathrm{issue}}, \mathcal{O}_{\mathrm{present}}, \mathcal{O}_{\mathrm{reveal}}}(pp, \{ipk_i\}_{i=1}^{n_\mathrm{I}})$

$\quad pol^* \xleftarrow{\$} \mathsf{PresPolicy}(I^*)$

$\quad (pt^*, \phi^*, \mathsf{ctx}^*) \xleftarrow{\$} \mathsf{Adv}^{\mathcal{O}_{\mathrm{issue}}, \mathcal{O}_{\mathrm{present}}, \mathcal{O}_{\mathrm{reveal}}}(st, pol^*)$

$\qquad$ where the oracles are defined as follows:

$\qquad \mathcal{O}_{\mathrm{issue}}(i_j, \vec{a}_j)$

$\qquad\qquad cred_j \xleftarrow{\$} \mathsf{Issue}(isk_{i_j}, \vec{a}_j)$

$\qquad\qquad \text{add } (i_j, \vec{a}_j) \text{ to } Q_{\mathrm{issue}}$

$\qquad \mathcal{O}_{\mathrm{present}}(j, pol, \phi, \mathsf{ctx})$

$\qquad\qquad \text{add } (pol, \phi, \mathsf{ctx}) \text{ to } Q_{\mathrm{present}}$

$\qquad\qquad \text{return } pt \xleftarrow{\$} \mathsf{Present}(cred_j, ipk_{i_j}, \vec{a}_j, \phi, pol, \mathsf{ctx})$

$\qquad \mathcal{O}_{\mathrm{reveal}}(j)$

$\qquad\qquad \text{add } (i_j, \vec{a}_j) \text{ to } Q_{\mathrm{reveal}}$

$\qquad\qquad \text{return } cred_j$

$\quad \text{return 1 if:}$

$\qquad I^* \subseteq \{ipk_i\}_{i=1}^{n_\mathrm{I}}$

$\qquad \mathsf{Verify}(pt^*, pol^*, \phi^*, \mathsf{ctx}^*) = 1$

$\qquad (pol^*, \phi^*, \mathsf{ctx}^*) \notin Q_{\mathrm{present}}$

$\qquad \nexists (i_j, \vec{a}_j) \in Q_{\mathrm{reveal}} \text{ such that } \phi^*(\vec{a}_j) = 1 \text{ and } ipk_{i_j} \in I^*$

$\quad \text{return 0}$

Exp. 4: Unforgeability experiment

Definition 4. *An issuer-hiding ABC system satisfies* unforgeability, *if and only if for every PPT adversary* Adv *and every number of issuers* n_I *there exists a negligible function* negl *such that:*

$$\Pr\left[\mathbf{Exp}_{\mathrm{Adv}}^{\mathrm{Unforgeability}}(\lambda, n_\mathrm{I}) = 1\right] \leq \mathsf{negl}(\lambda),$$

where the experiment is as defined in Experiment 4.

$\mathbf{Exp}_{\mathsf{Adv}}^{\mathsf{Unlinkability}}(\lambda)$

    $b \xleftarrow{\$} \{0,1\}$

    $pp \xleftarrow{\$} \mathsf{ParGen}(1^\lambda)$

    $(\{cred_l, \vec{a}_l, i_l\}_{l=0}^{1}, pol, \phi, \{ipk_i\}, \mathsf{ctx}, st) \xleftarrow{\$} \mathsf{Adv}(pp)$

    $pt^* \xleftarrow{\$} \mathsf{Present}(\{ipk_i\}, cred_b, \phi, \vec{a}_b, pol, \mathsf{ctx})$

    $b^* \xleftarrow{\$} \mathsf{Adv}(pt^*, st)$

    return 1 if and only if:

        $b = b^*,$

        $\mathsf{VfCred}(cred_l, \vec{a}_l, ipk_{i_l}) = 1$ for $l \in \{0,1\}$,

        $\phi(\vec{a}_l) = 1$ for $l \in \{0,1\}$, and

        $\mathsf{VfPolicy}(pol, \{ipk_i\}) = 1$

    return $b' \xleftarrow{\$} \{0,1\}$

Exp. 5: Unlinkability experiment

Unlinkability. Unlinkability requires that no two user actions can be linked by an adversary. This even needs to hold if the adversary has full control over verifiers, issuers, and the user's credential. In the experiment (cf. Experiment 5), we thus let the adversary output two sets of credentials, attributes, and respective issuers, as well as a presentation policy *pol*, a predicate ϕ, and the issuers' public keys. Upon receiving a presentation token derived from one of the two credentials, the adversary must not be able to decide which underlying credential was used, as long as both credentials are valid and consistent with ϕ.

Definition 5. *An issuer-hiding ABC system satisfies* unlinkability, *if and only if for every PPT adversary* Adv *there exists a negligible function* negl *such that:*

$$\left| \Pr\left[\mathbf{Exp}_{\mathsf{Adv}}^{\mathsf{Unlinkability}}(\lambda) = 1 \right] - \frac{1}{2} \right| \leq \mathsf{negl}(\lambda),$$

where the experiment is as defined in Experiment 5.

4   A Generic Construction

The following section describes a generic construction of issuer-hiding attribute-based credentials, and gives a formal security analysis of its security.

4.1   Construction

Let $\Sigma_{\mathsf{I}} = (\Sigma.\mathsf{ParGen}, \Sigma_{\mathsf{I}}.\mathsf{KGen}, \Sigma_{\mathsf{I}}.\mathsf{Sign}, \Sigma_{\mathsf{I}}.\mathsf{Verify})$ and $\Sigma_{\mathsf{V}} = (\Sigma.\mathsf{ParGen}, \Sigma_{\mathsf{V}}.\mathsf{KGen},$ $\Sigma_{\mathsf{V}}.\mathsf{Sign}, \Sigma_{\mathsf{V}}.\mathsf{Verify})$ be digital signature schemes (cf. Sect. 2) with a common parameter generation algorithm.

Our generic construction is now depicted in Construction 1. We refer to Sect. 1 for a detailed description of the intuition underlying this construction.

$\underline{\mathsf{ParGen}(1^\lambda).}$ Return $pp \overset{\$}{\leftarrow} \Sigma.\mathsf{ParGen}(1^\lambda)$.

$\underline{\mathsf{IKGen}(pp).}$ Return $(isk, ipk) \overset{\$}{\leftarrow} \Sigma_\mathsf{I}.\mathsf{KGen}(pp)$.

$\underline{\mathsf{Issue}(isk, \vec{a}).}$ Return $cred \overset{\$}{\leftarrow} \Sigma_\mathsf{I}.\mathsf{Sign}(pp, isk, \vec{a})$.

$\underline{\mathsf{VfCred}(cred, \vec{a}, ipk).}$ Return 1 if $\Sigma_\mathsf{I}.\mathsf{Verify}(pp, ipk, cred, \vec{a}) = 1$. Otherwise, return 0.

$\underline{\mathsf{PresPolicy}(\{ipk_i\}).}$ Generate a signature key pair $(vsk, vpk) \overset{\$}{\leftarrow} \Sigma_\mathsf{V}.\mathsf{KGen}(pp)$ and compute the signature $\sigma_i \overset{\$}{\leftarrow} \Sigma_\mathsf{V}.\mathsf{Sign}(pp, vsk, ipk_i)$. Return

$$pol = (vpk, \{(ipk_i, \sigma_i)\}).$$

$\underline{\mathsf{VfPolicy}(pol, \{ipk_i\}).}$ Parse pol as $(vpk, \{(ipk_i, \sigma_i)\})$. Return 1 if and only if

$$\Sigma_\mathsf{V}.\mathsf{Verify}(pp, vpk, \sigma_i, ipk_i) = 1 \text{ for all } i.$$

Otherwise, return 0.

$\underline{\mathsf{Present}(cred, ipk, \vec{a}, \phi, pol, \mathsf{ctx}).}$ Parse pol as $(vpk, \{(ipk_i, \sigma_i)\})$. Set j such that $ipk_j = ipk$. Return a presentation token pt as follows:

$$
\begin{aligned}
pt \overset{\$}{\leftarrow} \mathsf{NIZK}[(\sigma_j, ipk_j, cred, \vec{a}) : &\Sigma_\mathsf{V}.\mathsf{Verify}(pp, vpk, \sigma_j, ipk_j) = 1 \ \wedge \qquad (1)\\
&\Sigma_\mathsf{I}.\mathsf{Verify}(pp, ipk_j, cred, \vec{a}) = 1 \ \wedge \\
&\phi(\vec{a}) = 1](pol, \phi, \mathsf{ctx})
\end{aligned}
$$

$\underline{\mathsf{Verify}(pt, pol, \phi).}$ Return 1 if and only if pt verifies correctly. Otherwise, return 0.

Construction 1: Generic construction of issuer-hiding ABCs.

4.2 Security Analysis

Theorem 1. *If Σ_I and Σ_V are EUF-CMA secure and the NIZK is zero-knowledge and simulation-sound extractable, then Construction 1 is unforgeable.*

Intuitively, the adversary has two potential ways of breaking unforgeability: (1) he can forge a Σ_V signature on his own public key ipk' (that is not part of the challenge policy pol^*), or (2) he can forge a credential by forging a Σ_I signature w.r.t. some honest issuer's public key ipk_i.

Proof. Let Adv be a PPT adversary. We first modify the unforgeability game by simulating all NIZK pt output by $\mathcal{O}_{\mathsf{present}}$. Because the NIZK is zero-knowledge, this increases the winning probability by at most a negligible amount. In the following, we argue that Adv's winning probability in the modified game is negligible.

In the (modified) unforgeability game, Adv outputs pol^* and (pt^*, ϕ^*). If Adv wins, we can apply the NIZK extractor to pt^* to extract a witness $(\sigma, ipk, cred, \vec{a})$. Let extractfail be the event that Adv wins but the extractor fails to output a valid witness. Let polforge be the event that Adv wins, the extractor does not fail, and the extracted ipk is not any honest issuer's public key, i.e. $ipk \notin \{ipk_i\}$. Let credforge be the event that Adv wins, the extractor does not fail, and the extracted ipk *is* one of the honest issuer's public keys, i.e. $ipk \in \{ipk_i\}$.

It holds that $\Pr[\mathsf{Adv\ wins}] \leq \Pr[\mathsf{Adv\ wins} \wedge \neg\mathsf{extractfail}] + \Pr[\mathsf{extractfail}] = \Pr[\mathsf{polforge}] + \Pr[\mathsf{credforge}] + \Pr[\mathsf{extractfail}]$. Because the NIZK is simulation-sound extractable, $\Pr[\mathsf{extractfail}]$ is negligible. We now show that both $\Pr[\mathsf{polforge}]$ and $\Pr[\mathsf{credforge}]$ are negligible, which will conclude this proof.

Type 1 Adversaries. We construct an adversary B against Σ_V's EUF-CMA security.

- B gets pp, pk as input and access to a signing oracle $\mathcal{O}_\mathtt{sign}$.
- B generates $(isk_i, ipk_i) \overset{\$}{\leftarrow} \mathsf{IKGen}(pp)$ for $i = 1, \ldots, n_\mathsf{I}$ and runs $(I^*, st) \overset{\$}{\leftarrow} \mathsf{Adv}^{\mathcal{O}_\mathtt{issue}, \mathcal{O}_\mathtt{present}, \mathcal{O}_\mathtt{reveal}}(pp, \{ipk_i\}_{i=1}^{n_\mathsf{I}})$. It answers oracle queries honestly using $\{isk_i\}$.
- B queries $\mathcal{O}_\mathtt{sign}$ for signatures σ_i on $ipk_i \in I^*$. It sets $pol^* = (pk, \{(ipk_i, \sigma_i)\})$ and runs $(pt^*, \phi^*, \mathsf{ctx}^*) \overset{\$}{\leftarrow} \mathsf{Adv}^{\mathcal{O}_\mathtt{issue}, \mathcal{O}_\mathtt{present}, \mathcal{O}_\mathtt{reveal}}(st, pol^*)$.
- If Adv's winning condition is not fulfilled, B aborts.
- Otherwise, B extracts a witness $(\sigma, ipk, cred, \vec{a})$ from pt^*.
- If $ipk \notin \{ipk_i\}$, B, it outputs (ipk, σ) as a forgery.

By construction, $\Pr[\mathsf{B\ wins}] = \Pr[\mathsf{polforge}]$ (note that if polforge occurs, B has not queried for a signature on ipk). Because Σ_V is EUF-CMA secure, $\Pr[\mathsf{polforge}]$ is negligible.

Type 2 Adversaries. We construct an adversary B against Σ_I's EUF-CMA security.

- B gets pp, pk as input and access to a signing oracle $\mathcal{O}_\mathtt{sign}$.
- B chooses a random $k \overset{\$}{\leftarrow} \{1, \ldots, n_\mathsf{I}\}$.
- B sets $ipk_k = pk$ and generates $(isk_i, ipk_i) \overset{\$}{\leftarrow} \mathsf{IKGen}(pp)$ for $i \in \{1, \ldots, n_\mathsf{I}\} \setminus \{k\}$. It runs $(I^*, st) \overset{\$}{\leftarrow} \mathsf{Adv}^{\mathcal{O}_\mathtt{issue}, \mathcal{O}_\mathtt{present}, \mathcal{O}_\mathtt{reveal}}(pp, \{ipk_i\}_{i=1}^{n_\mathsf{I}})$.
  - It answers $\mathcal{O}_\mathtt{issue}(i_j, \vec{a}_j)$ by adding $(i_j, \vec{a}_j)$ to $Q_\mathtt{issue}$ (but not generating a credential).
  - It answers $\mathcal{O}_\mathtt{present}(j, pol, \phi, \mathsf{ctx})$ by creating a simulated NIZK pt (unless $\phi(\vec{a}_j) = 0$).
  - It answers $\mathcal{O}_\mathtt{reveal}(j)$ with $cred_j$ as follows: if $i_j = k$, it queries $cred_j \overset{\$}{\leftarrow} \mathcal{O}_\mathtt{sign}(\vec{a}_j)$. Otherwise, it computes $cred_j \overset{\$}{\leftarrow} \Sigma_\mathsf{I}.\mathsf{Sign}(pp, isk_{i_j}, \vec{a}_j)$. Repeat reveal queries for j are answered with the same value $cred_j$ every time.
- B generates $pol^* \overset{\$}{\leftarrow} \mathsf{PresPolicy}(I^*)$. Afterwards, it runs $(pt^*, \phi^*, \mathsf{ctx}^*) \overset{\$}{\leftarrow} \mathsf{Adv}^{\mathcal{O}_\mathtt{issue}, \mathcal{O}_\mathtt{present}, \mathcal{O}_\mathtt{reveal}}(st, pol^*)$.
  - B answers oracle queries as above.
- If Adv's winning condition is not fulfilled, B aborts.
- Otherwise, B extracts a witness $(\sigma, ipk, cred, \vec{a})$ from pt^*.
- If $ipk = pk$, B outputs $(\vec{a}, \sigma)$ as a forgery.

Note that the way B answers oracle queries is consistent with the way the (modified) unforgeability experiment does so.

If credforge $\wedge$ $ipk = pk$, then $(\vec{a}, \sigma)$ is a valid forgery. σ is a valid signature on $\vec{a}$ by guarantee of the NIZK extractor. Furthermore, B has not queried for a signature on $\vec{a}$ (because $\phi^*(\vec{a}) = 1$ by guarantee of the extractor, but the winning condition guarantees that $\phi^*(\vec{a}') = 0$ for all signatures revealed through $\mathcal{O}_{\text{reveal}}$). Hence $\Pr[\text{B wins}] \geq \Pr[\text{credforge} \wedge ipk = pk] = \frac{1}{n_\mathsf{I}} \cdot \Pr[\text{credforge}]$. Because Σ_I is EUF-CMA secure, $\Pr[\text{credforge}]$ is negligible. □

Theorem 2. *If* NIZK *is zero-knowledge, then Construction 1 is unlinkable.*

Proof. Because the property follows almost immediately from the zero-knowledge property, we omit a full proof. Note that the unlinkability experiment ensures that the witnesses used when computing pt^* are valid for both $b = 0$ and $b = 1$ (for cases where the adversary does not output valid values, the experiment ends up outputting a random bit, not providing any advantage to the adversary). This means that the unlinkability experiment is computationally indistinguishable from one where pt^* is created by the NIZK simulator. In the latter, the view of Adv is independent of b. □

5 Concrete Instantiation

One possible instantiation of Construction 1 in Sect. 4 is with Groth's structure-preserving signatures (Sect. 2). This instantiation is inspired by delegatable credentials [13] where the issue of proving knowledge of a hidden signature on the hidden public key of another hidden signature also comes up (though in a different scenario).

Concretely, in this instantiation, the issuer signs attributes using hash-then-sign with the Pedersen hash $H(\vec{a}) = \prod_{i=1}^{L} H_i^{a_i}$ and the structure-preserving signature scheme Groth$_1$. The verifier signs valid issuer public keys using Groth$_2$. A presentation token is a Schnorr-style proof of knowledge [46] turned non-interactive using the Fiat-Shamir heuristic [31] which gives us a simulation-sound extractable NIZK. We assume that the statement and public values are included in the computation of the challenge in order to avoid malleability issues [6].

With these choices, the scheme works as specified in Construction 2.

5.1 Security Analysis

Theorem 3. *If* Groth$_1$ *and* Groth$_2$ *are EUF-CMA secure and the* NIZK *is zero-knowledge and simulation-sound extractable, then the concrete instantiation in Construction 2 is unforgeable and unlinkable.*

Unforgeability and unlinkability follow from the generic construction's unforgeability and unlinkability, which we're instantiating.

If Groth$_1$ is EUF-CMA secure, then also the hash-then-sign version of it (which is what we are effectively using in the concrete construction) is EUF-CMA

ParGen(1^λ). For $e : \mathbb{G}_1 \times \mathbb{G}_2 \to \mathbb{G}_T$ as in Groth$_1$.ParGen, choose $Y, H_i \overset{\$}{\leftarrow} \mathbb{G}_1$ and $\tilde{Y} \overset{\$}{\leftarrow} \mathbb{G}_2$. Define the hash function $H : \mathbb{Z}_p^L \to \mathbb{G}_1$, $H(\vec{a}) = \prod_{i=1}^L H_i^{a_i}$. Return $pp = (\mathbb{G}_1, \mathbb{G}_2, \mathbb{G}_T, e, p, G, \tilde{G}, Y, \tilde{Y}, (H_i)_{i=1}^L)$.

IKGen(pp). Generate a Groth$_1$ key pair $(isk, ipk) = (v, \tilde{V}) \overset{\$}{\leftarrow}$ Groth$_1$.KGen(pp).

Issue($isk, \vec{a}$). Return $cred = (\tilde{R}, S, T) \overset{\$}{\leftarrow}$ Groth$_1$.Sign($pp, v, H(\vec{a})$).

VfCred($cred, \vec{a}, ipk$). Return whatever Groth$_1$.Verify($pp, \tilde{V}, cred, H(\vec{a})$) returns.

PresPolicy($\{ipk_i\}$). Generate $(vsk, vpk) = (u, U) \overset{\$}{\leftarrow}$ Groth$_2$.KGen(pp) and $\sigma_i = (R_i, \tilde{S}_i, \tilde{T}_i) \overset{\$}{\leftarrow}$ Groth$_2$.Sign(pp, u, ipk_i). Return $pol = (U, \{(ipk_i, \sigma_i)\})$.

VfPolicy($pol, \{ipk_i\}$). Parse pol as $(vpk, \{(ipk_i, \sigma_i)\})$. Return 1 if Groth$_2$.Verify($pp, vpk, \sigma_i, ipk_i$) = 1 for all i. Otherwise, return 0.

Present($cred, ipk, \vec{a}, \phi, pol, \mathsf{ctx}$). Parse pol as $(vpk, \{(ipk_i, \sigma_i)\})$. Let j be the index of the credential's issuer's public key, i.e., $ipk_j = ipk$. Randomize $cred$ and σ_j as

$$(\tilde{R}, S, T) \overset{\$}{\leftarrow} \text{Groth}_1.\text{Rand}(pp, cred) \quad \text{and} \quad (R_j, \tilde{S}_j, \tilde{T}_j) \overset{\$}{\leftarrow} \text{Groth}_2.\text{Rand}(pp, \sigma_j).$$

Choose random blinding values $\alpha, \beta, \gamma, \delta \overset{\$}{\leftarrow} \mathbb{Z}_p^*$ and compute
- the blinded credential $(\tilde{R}, S', T') := (\tilde{R}, S^{1/\alpha}, T^{1/\beta})$ on $H(\vec{a})$ under the issuer's key ipk_j
- the issuer's blinded key $ipk_j' := ipk_j^{1/\gamma}$
- the blinded policy signature $(R_j, \tilde{S}_j, \tilde{T}_j') := (R_j, \tilde{S}_j, \tilde{T}_j^{1/\delta})$ on V_j under the verifier's public key vpk

Compute a Schnorr-style proof π:

$$\pi \overset{\$}{\leftarrow} \text{NIZK}[(\alpha, \beta, \gamma, \delta, \vec{a}) :$$

Groth$_1$ credential check: $e(S', \tilde{R})^\alpha = e(Y, \tilde{G}) \cdot e(G, ipk_j')^\gamma \ \wedge$

Groth$_1$ credential check: $e(T', \tilde{R})^\beta = e(Y, ipk_j')^\gamma \cdot e(\prod_{i=1}^L H_i^{a_i}, \tilde{G}) \ \wedge$

Groth$_2$ policy check: $e(R_j, \tilde{S}_j) = e(G, \tilde{Y}) \cdot e(vpk, \tilde{G}) \ \wedge$

Groth$_2$ policy check: $e(R_j, \tilde{T}_j')^\delta = e(vpk, \tilde{Y}) \cdot e(G, ipk_j')^\gamma \ \wedge$

Attribute check: $\phi(\vec{a}) = 1](pol, \phi, \mathsf{ctx})$

Finally, return $pt = ((\tilde{R}, S', T'), ipk_j', (R_j, \tilde{S}_j, \tilde{T}_j'), \pi)$.

Verify(pt, pol, ϕ). Return 1 if and only if pt verifies correctly. Otherwise, return 0.

Construction 2: Concrete instantiation of our generic construction.

secure (under the discrete logarithm assumption, which is implied by security of Groth$_1$, the hash function H is collision-resistant). It remains to argue that Present is a good instantiation of the NIZK specified in the generic construction.

For the zero-knowledge property, $pt = ((\tilde{R}, S', T'), ipk_j', (R_j, \tilde{S}_j, \tilde{T}_j'), \pi)$ can be simulated by choosing random $S', T', ipk_j' \overset{\$}{\leftarrow} \mathbb{G}_1$ and $\tilde{R}, \tilde{T}_j' \overset{\$}{\leftarrow} \mathbb{G}_2$, setting

$(R_j, \tilde{S}_j) = (R_1^r, \tilde{S}_1^{1/r})$ for random $r \xleftarrow{\$} \mathbb{Z}_p^*$ (where $(R_1, \tilde{S}_1, \cdot) = ipk_1$), and then simulating a corresponding π using the NIZK simulator.

For the proof of knowledge property, note that from π one can extract $\alpha, \beta, \gamma, \delta, \vec{a}$ with properties that guarantee that $cred := (\tilde{R}, (S')^\alpha, (T')^\beta)$ is a valid Groth_1 signature on $H(\vec{a})$ under $ipk_j := (ipk_j')^\gamma$ and that $\sigma_j := (R_j, \tilde{S}_j, (\tilde{T}_j')^\delta)$ is a valid Groth_2 signature on ipk_j under vpk, and that $\phi(\vec{a}) = 1$. This means that we can extract a valid witness $\sigma_j, ipk_j, cred, \vec{a}$ from pt, as required.

Table 1. Performance of Construction 2 on a Macbook Pro (i9-9980HK) with BN254 as the bilinear group. Other columns show the (device-independent) number of group operations (multiply and square operations, including those happening within exponentiations) and pairings performed.

	Runtime	$\mathbb{G}_1$	$\mathbb{G}_2$	$\mathbb{G}_T$	Pairings
PresPolicy (10 issuers)	14 ms	3 027	11 448	0	100
PresPolicy (100 issuers)	115 ms	27 666	115 430	0	0
VfPolicy (10 issuers)	3 ms	0	0	20	60
VfPolicy (100 issuers)	27 ms	0	0	200	600
Issue	2 ms	1 684	278	0	0
Present	4 ms	3 327	1 206	4	7
Verify	3 ms	2 398	0	901	12

Table 2. Number of group elements for the different keys and tokens in Construction 2, where I is the number of issuer keys accepted by a verifier, and L is the number of attributes certified in the credential.

	$\mathbb{G}_1$	$\mathbb{G}_2$	$\mathbb{G}_T$	$\mathbb{Z}_p$
Issuer secret key (isk)	–	–	–	1
Issuer public key (ipk)	–	1	–	–
Credential ($cred$)	2	1	–	–
Presentation policy (pol)	$I+1$	$3I$	–	–
Presentation token (pt)	3	4	–	$L+5$

5.2   Performance Evaluation

To practically evaluate our construction, we have implemented[3] a benchmarking prototype of Construction 2 using the Cryptimeleon library [9]. The results are shown in Table 1. For credentials, we are considering $L = 10$ random attributes,

---

[3] Code available at https://github.com/cryptimeleon/issuer-hiding-cred.

none of which are disclosed during presentation (which is the most expensive case of partial attribute disclosure). The policy consists of 10 or 100 valid issuers. This does not affect token verification, which is independent of policy size. Overall, performance is practical, especially given that VfPolicy only has to be run once for each new policy and can be delegated to a trusted party.

The sizes of all keys and tokens can be found in Table 2.

6   Extensions

To simplify presentation, our main construction only focuses on the key functionality of an issuer-hiding ABC system. In the following, we discuss in detail how to achieve non-frameability and anonymity revocation, controlled linkability and pseudonyms, and credential revocation. Further extensions like updating of credentials [8] or advanced predicates over attributes [5,40] are omitted here because of space limitations.

Anonymity Revocation and Non-frameability. While ABCs are important to protect the users' privacy and related fundamental rights, the high anonymity guarantees may lead to misuse of credentials and associated rights. In order to prevent such misuse, anonymity revocation (or inspection) is an important advanced functionality. Anonymity revocation allows a predefined opener (or inspector) to identify the originator of a given presentation token pt [12,18]. Closely related to this is the notion of non-frameability, which guarantees that even if issuers and the opener collude, it is infeasible for them to convince any third party that a specific user computed a given pt unless she indeed did so. This notion is closely related to non-frameability for group signatures [10,26,39].

This feature is achieved by letting the user generate a secret private key $(upk, usk) \xleftarrow{\$} \mathsf{UKGen}(pp)$, and the opener a key pair $(opk, osk) \xleftarrow{\$} \Gamma.\mathsf{KGen}(pp)$ for an encryption scheme Γ. Upon issuance, the user would now embed upk as an additional attribute which is signed by the issuer. When computing a presentation token, the user would treat upk as an undisclosed attribute, yet still prove that she knows the corresponding usk. Furthermore, she would encrypt upk under the opener's key as $enc \xleftarrow{\$} \Gamma.\mathsf{Enc}(upk, opk)$, and prove that enc contains the same upk which is also certified in the credential.

Controlled Linkability. In the case of stateful applications, for instance, users may wish to be recognized yet not identified by a verifier. This can be achieved by using scope-exclusive pseudonyms [16], in which pseudonyms can be linked within a given scope, but not across different scopes. For a pseudonym system Ψ with user secret key usk, the users' public key would be $upk \leftarrow \Psi.\mathsf{Gen}(usk, \varepsilon)$, which similar to before is embedded into the credential. For a given scope sc, the user now shares $nym = \Psi.\mathsf{Gen}(usk, \mathsf{sc})$ with the verifier, and proves that this is consistent with the (undisclosed) upk.

Revocation. In case of misuse, loss of privileges, or compromise of a credential, it may become necessary to invalidate an issued credential. Many approaches for revocation of anonymous credentials can be found in the literature. In the following we show how to incorporate an approach along the lines of Nakanishi et al. [42] into our solution. Their work follows a black-listing approach, where each credential contains a revocation handle rh which is never disclosed upon presentation. The revocation authority, holding a signature key pair (rpk, rsk), issues intervals $[a_i, b_i]$ of currently still valid revocation handles, together with signatures $\alpha_i \xleftarrow{\$} \Sigma_R.\mathsf{Sign}(pp, rsk, a_i)$ and $\beta_i \xleftarrow{\$} \Sigma_R.\mathsf{Sign}(pp, rsk, b_i)$. When computing a presentation token, the user now proves that the revocation handle embedded in her credential lies in some interval $[a_i, b_i]$ for which she knows corresponding signatures α_i and β_i. However, it may be the case that multiple revocation authorities, e.g., one per issuer, exist in our setting. We thus not only embed the rh but also the revocation authority's public key rpk as attributes in our credentials, and the user shows that the known signatures on the interval boundaries verify under this (undisclosed) signature key.

7 Conclusion and Future Work

We introduced the notion of issuer-hiding anonymous credential system, which allows for a dynamic and ad-hoc definition of sets of issuers among whose credentials a user may stay anonymous during presentation—a feature with various application domains, ranging from student identities over national eIDs to remote attestation. We provided a generic construction where the communication and computational complexity during presentation is independent of the number of issuers, as well as an efficient instantiation.

Nevertheless, we identified some open research questions. While our construction requires a minor joint setup across different issuers to define some group generators and the number of attributes L, in real applications, e.g., different nation states may wish to include different numbers of attributes in their credentials, vary the order of attributes, or use alternative generators for security reasons. It would be interesting to see whether this can be achieved more efficiently than via the generic or-composition discussed in Sect. 1. Also, the size of verifier policies is currently linear in the number of accepted issuers. One approach to overcome this limitation could be to add the accepted public keys to an accumulator, for which users, knowing all accumulated values, could compute the witnesses themselves, resulting in constant-size policies if the ipk's are assumed to be known. Instead of proving knowledge of a signature from the verifier, users would now prove that they know a witness for the public key that issued the credential. However, we are not aware of any accumulator and compatible signature scheme allowing for an efficient instantiation.

Acknowledgments. This work was in parts supported by the European Union's Horizon 2020 research and innovation programme under grant agreement No 871473 (KRAKEN) and 830929 (CyberSec4Europe), and by the German Research

Foundation (DFG) within the Collaborative Research Centre On-The-Fly Computing (GZ: SFB 901/3) under the project number 160364472.

References

1. Abe, M., David, B., Kohlweiss, M., Nishimaki, R., Ohkubo, M.: Tagged one-time signatures: tight security and optimal tag size. In: Kurosawa, K., Hanaoka, G. (eds.) PKC 2013. LNCS, vol. 7778, pp. 312–331. Springer, Heidelberg (2013). https://doi.org/10.1007/978-3-642-36362-7_20
2. Abraham, A., Hörandner, F., Omolola, O., Ramacher, S.: Privacy-preserving eID derivation for self-sovereign identity systems. In: Zhou, J., Luo, X., Shen, Q., Xu, Z. (eds.) ICICS 2019. LNCS, vol. 11999, pp. 307–323. Springer, Cham (2020). https://doi.org/10.1007/978-3-030-41579-2_18
3. Abraham, A., Theuermann, K., Kirchengast, E.: Qualified eID derivation into a distributed ledger based iDM system. In: TrustCom/BigDataSE (2018)
4. Belenkiy, M., Camenisch, J., Chase, M., Kohlweiss, M., Lysyanskaya, A., Shacham, H.: Randomizable proofs and delegatable anonymous credentials. In: Halevi, S. (ed.) CRYPTO 2009. LNCS, vol. 5677, pp. 108–125. Springer, Heidelberg (2009). https://doi.org/10.1007/978-3-642-03356-8_7
5. Bemmann, K., et al.: Fully-featured anonymous credentials with reputation system. In: ARES (2018)
6. Bernhard, D., Pereira, O., Warinschi, B.: How not to prove yourself: pitfalls of the Fiat-Shamir heuristic and applications to Helios. In: Wang, X., Sako, K. (eds.) ASIACRYPT 2012. LNCS, vol. 7658, pp. 626–643. Springer, Heidelberg (2012). https://doi.org/10.1007/978-3-642-34961-4_38
7. Blömer, J., Bobolz, J.: Delegatable attribute-based anonymous credentials from dynamically malleable signatures. In: Preneel, B., Vercauteren, F. (eds.) ACNS 2018. LNCS, vol. 10892, pp. 221–239. Springer, Cham (2018). https://doi.org/10.1007/978-3-319-93387-0_12
8. Blömer, J., Bobolz, J., Diemert, D., Eidens, F.: Updatable anonymous credentials and applications to incentive systems. In: ACM CCS 2019 (2019)
9. Bobolz, J., Eidens, F., Heitjohann, R., Fell, J.: Cryptimeleon: a library for fast prototyping of privacy-preserving cryptographic schemes. IACR ePrint (2021)
10. Bootle, J., Cerulli, A., Chaidos, P., Ghadafi, E., Groth, J.: Foundations of fully dynamic group signatures. In: Manulis, M., Sadeghi, A.-R., Schneider, S. (eds.) ACNS 2016. LNCS, vol. 9696, pp. 117–136. Springer, Cham (2016). https://doi.org/10.1007/978-3-319-39555-5_7
11. Brands, S.: Rethinking public key infrastructure and digital certificates - building in privacy. Ph.D. thesis, Eindhoven Institute of Technology (1999)
12. Camenisch, J.: Concepts around privacy-preserving attribute-based credentials. In: Hansen, M., Hoepman, J.-H., Leenes, R., Whitehouse, D. (eds.) Privacy and Identity 2013. IAICT, vol. 421, pp. 53–63. Springer, Heidelberg (2014). https://doi.org/10.1007/978-3-642-55137-6_4
13. Camenisch, J., Drijvers, M., Dubovitskaya, M.: Practical UC-secure delegatable credentials with attributes and their application to blockchain. In: ACM CCS 2017 (2017)
14. Camenisch, J., Drijvers, M., Lehmann, A., Neven, G., Towa, P.: Short threshold dynamic group signatures. In: Galdi, C., Kolesnikov, V. (eds.) SCN 2020. LNCS, vol. 12238, pp. 401–423. Springer, Cham (2020). https://doi.org/10.1007/978-3-030-57990-6_20

15. Camenisch, J., Dubovitskaya, M., Haralambiev, K., Kohlweiss, M.: Composable and modular anonymous credentials: definitions and practical constructions. In: Iwata, T., Cheon, J.H. (eds.) ASIACRYPT 2015. LNCS, vol. 9453, pp. 262–288. Springer, Heidelberg (2015). https://doi.org/10.1007/978-3-662-48800-3_11

16. Camenisch, J., Krenn, S., Lehmann, A., Mikkelsen, G.L., Neven, G., Pedersen, M.Ø.: Formal treatment of privacy-enhancing credential systems. In: Dunkelman, O., Keliher, L. (eds.) SAC 2015. LNCS, vol. 9566, pp. 3–24. Springer, Cham (2016). https://doi.org/10.1007/978-3-319-31301-6_1

17. Camenisch, J., Lehmann, A., Neven, G., Rial, A.: Privacy-preserving auditing for attribute-based credentials. In: Kutyłowski, M., Vaidya, J. (eds.) ESORICS 2014. LNCS, vol. 8713, pp. 109–127. Springer, Cham (2014). https://doi.org/10.1007/978-3-319-11212-1_7

18. Camenisch, J., Lysyanskaya, A.: An efficient system for non-transferable anonymous credentials with optional anonymity revocation. In: Pfitzmann, B. (ed.) EUROCRYPT 2001. LNCS, vol. 2045, pp. 93–118. Springer, Heidelberg (2001). https://doi.org/10.1007/3-540-44987-6_7

19. Camenisch, J., Lysyanskaya, A.: A signature scheme with efficient protocols. In: Cimato, S., Persiano, G., Galdi, C. (eds.) SCN 2002. LNCS, vol. 2576, pp. 268–289. Springer, Heidelberg (2003). https://doi.org/10.1007/3-540-36413-7_20

20. Camenisch, J., Lysyanskaya, A.: Signature schemes and anonymous credentials from bilinear maps. In: Franklin, M. (ed.) CRYPTO 2004. LNCS, vol. 3152, pp. 56–72. Springer, Heidelberg (2004). https://doi.org/10.1007/978-3-540-28628-8_4

21. Camenisch, J., Stadler, M.: Efficient group signature schemes for large groups. In: Kaliski, B.S. (ed.) CRYPTO 1997. LNCS, vol. 1294, pp. 410–424. Springer, Heidelberg (1997). https://doi.org/10.1007/BFb0052252

22. Camenisch, J., Van Herreweghen, E.: Design and implementation of the idemix anonymous credential system. In: ACM CCS 2002 (2002)

23. Chase, M., Lysyanskaya, A.: On signatures of knowledge. In: Dwork, C. (ed.) CRYPTO 2006. LNCS, vol. 4117, pp. 78–96. Springer, Heidelberg (2006). https://doi.org/10.1007/11818175_5

24. Chaum, D.: Untraceable electronic mail, return addresses, and digital pseudonyms. Commun. ACM 24(2), 84–88 (1981)

25. Chaum, D.: Security without identification: transaction systems to make big brother obsolete. Commun. ACM 28(10), 1030–1044 (1985)

26. Chen, L., Pedersen, T.P.: New group signature schemes. In: De Santis, A. (ed.) EUROCRYPT 1994. LNCS, vol. 950, pp. 171–181. Springer, Heidelberg (1995). https://doi.org/10.1007/BFb0053433

27. Crites, E.C., Lysyanskaya, A.: Delegatable anonymous credentials from mercurial signatures. In: Matsui, M. (ed.) CT-RSA 2019. LNCS, vol. 11405, pp. 535–555. Springer, Cham (2019). https://doi.org/10.1007/978-3-030-12612-4_27

28. De Santis, A., Persiano, G.: Zero-knowledge proofs of knowledge without interaction (extended abstract). In: 33rd FOCS (1992)

29. Derler, D., Krenn, S., Samelin, K., Slamanig, D.: Fully collision-resistant chameleon-hashes from simpler and post-quantum assumptions. In: Galdi, C., Kolesnikov, V. (eds.) SCN 2020. LNCS, vol. 12238, pp. 427–447. Springer, Cham (2020). https://doi.org/10.1007/978-3-030-57990-6_21

30. Dodis, Y., Haralambiev, K., López-Alt, A., Wichs, D.: Efficient public-key cryptography in the presence of key leakage. In: Abe, M. (ed.) ASIACRYPT 2010. LNCS, vol. 6477, pp. 613–631. Springer, Heidelberg (2010). https://doi.org/10.1007/978-3-642-17373-8_35

31. Fiat, A., Shamir, A.: How to prove yourself: practical solutions to identification and signature problems. In: Odlyzko, A.M. (ed.) CRYPTO 1986. LNCS, vol. 263, pp. 186–194. Springer, Heidelberg (1987). https://doi.org/10.1007/3-540-47721-7_12
32. de Fuentes, J.M., González-Manzano, L., Serna-Olvera, J., Veseli, F.: Assessment of attribute-based credentials for privacy-preserving road traffic services in smart cities. Pers. Ubiquitous Comput. **21**(5), 869–891 (2017)
33. Garman, C., Green, M., Miers, I.: Decentralized anonymous credentials. In: NDSS 2014 (2014)
34. Goldwasser, S., Micali, S., Rivest, R.L.: A digital signature scheme secure against adaptive chosen-message attacks. SIAM J. Comput. **17**(2), 281–308 (1988)
35. Groth, J.: Simulation-sound NIZK proofs for a practical language and constant size group signatures. In: Lai, X., Chen, K. (eds.) ASIACRYPT 2006. LNCS, vol. 4284, pp. 444–459. Springer, Heidelberg (2006). https://doi.org/10.1007/11935230_29
36. Groth, J.: Efficient fully structure-preserving signatures for large messages. In: Iwata, T., Cheon, J.H. (eds.) ASIACRYPT 2015. LNCS, vol. 9452, pp. 239–259. Springer, Heidelberg (2015). https://doi.org/10.1007/978-3-662-48797-6_11
37. Haböck, U., Krenn, S.: Breaking and fixing anonymous credentials for the cloud. In: Mu, Y., Deng, R.H., Huang, X. (eds.) CANS 2019. LNCS, vol. 11829, pp. 249–269. Springer, Cham (2019). https://doi.org/10.1007/978-3-030-31578-8_14
38. Khovratovich, D., Law, J.: Sovrin: digital signatures in the blockchain area (2016). https://sovrin.org/wp-content/uploads/AnonCred-RWC.pdf
39. Krenn, S., Samelin, K., Striecks, C.: Practical group-signatures with privacy-friendly openings. In: ARES (2019)
40. Lipmaa, H.: On Diophantine complexity and statistical zero-knowledge arguments. In: Laih, C.-S. (ed.) ASIACRYPT 2003. LNCS, vol. 2894, pp. 398–415. Springer, Heidelberg (2003). https://doi.org/10.1007/978-3-540-40061-5_26
41. Moreno, R.T., et al.: The OLYMPUS architecture - oblivious identity management for private user-friendly services. Sensors **20**(3), 945 (2020)
42. Nakanishi, T., Fujii, H., Hira, Y., Funabiki, N.: Revocable group signature schemes with constant costs for signing and verifying. In: Jarecki, S., Tsudik, G. (eds.) PKC 2009. LNCS, vol. 5443, pp. 463–480. Springer, Heidelberg (2009). https://doi.org/10.1007/978-3-642-00468-1_26
43. Paquin, C., Zaverucha, G.: U-prove cryptographic specification v1.1 (revision2). Technical report, Microsoft Corporation (2013)
44. Ringers, S., Verheul, E., Hoepman, J.-H.: An efficient self-blindable attribute-based credential scheme. In: Kiayias, A. (ed.) FC 2017. LNCS, vol. 10322, pp. 3–20. Springer, Cham (2017). https://doi.org/10.1007/978-3-319-70972-7_1
45. Sahai, A.: Non-malleable non-interactive zero knowledge and adaptive chosen-ciphertext security. In: 40th FOCS (1999)
46. Schnorr, C.P.: Efficient signature generation by smart cards. J. Cryptol. **4**(3), 161–174 (1991)
47. Sonnino, A., Al-Bassam, M., Bano, S., Meiklejohn, S., Danezis, G.: Coconut: threshold issuance selective disclosure credentials with applications to distributed ledgers. In: NDSS 2019 (2019)
48. Yang, R., Au, M.H., Xu, Q., Yu, Z.: Decentralized blacklistable anonymous credentials with reputation. In: Susilo, W., Yang, G. (eds.) ACISP 2018. LNCS, vol. 10946, pp. 720–738. Springer, Cham (2018). https://doi.org/10.1007/978-3-319-93638-3_41

Report and Trace Ring Signatures

Ashley Fraser[1,2]($\boxtimes$) and Elizabeth A. Quaglia[1]

[1] Information Security Group, Royal Holloway, University of London, Egham, UK
Elizabeth.Quaglia@rhul.ac.uk
[2] Department of Computer Science, University of Surrey, Guildford, UK
a.fraser@surrey.ac.uk

Abstract. We introduce *report and trace* ring signature schemes, balancing the desire for signer anonymity with the ability to report malicious behaviour and subsequently revoke anonymity. We contribute a formal security model for report and trace ring signatures that incorporates established properties of anonymity, unforgeability and traceability, and captures a new notion of reporter anonymity. We present a construction of a report and trace ring signature scheme, proving its security and analysing its efficiency, comparing with the state of the art in the accountable ring signatures literature. Our analysis demonstrates that our report and trace scheme is efficient, particularly for the choice of cryptographic primitives that we use to instantiate our construction.

Keywords: Ring signatures · Accountability · Security model · Construction

1 Introduction

Group signatures [8] and ring signatures [21] provide signers with anonymity within a set of users. Anonymity is a sought-after property, yet, under certain circumstances, it is also desirable to provide a guarantee of *traceability*, which means that anonymity can be revoked. This presents an interesting problem: how does a group or ring signature guarantee anonymity *and* traceability?

Group signatures rely on a trusted group manager to achieve these conflicting aims. The group manager determines the members of the group and issues key pairs to group members. Signers are anonymous within the group, but the group manager can learn the identity of signers and revoke anonymity. On the other hand, ring signatures do not rely on a trusted manager. In fact, signers generate their key pairs and select the group of users, known as the ring, within which the

---

A. Fraser—The author conducted the majority of this work at Royal Holloway, University of London and was supported by the EPSRC and the UK government as part of the Centre for Doctoral Training in Cyber Security at Royal Holloway under grant number EP/P009301/1. This work was also partly supported by the EPSRC Next Stage Digital Economy Centre in the Decentralised Digital Economy (DECaDE) under grant number EP/T022485/1.

M. Conti et al. (Eds.): CANS 2021, LNCS 13099, pp. 179–199, 2021.
https://doi.org/10.1007/978-3-030-92548-2_10

signer is anonymous. The solution to achieving anonymous and traceable ring signatures is *accountable* ring signatures [6,26], which define a designated tracer who can identify signers. Accountable ring signatures retain the versatility of ring signatures, allowing signers to generate their keys and select the anonymity ring, and additionally allow signer anonymity to be revoked.

In practice, to begin the tracing process, the designated tracer in an accountable ring signature will often receive a report of malicious behaviour from a reporter. However, the reporter is outside the scope of the syntax and security model of accountable ring signatures. Consequently, it is implicit that the tracer must be trusted not to revoke anonymity without first receiving a report. Moreover, by omitting the role of the reporter from the security model, it is not possible to make any formal statements about the privacy of the reporter.

To address this, we introduce *report and trace* ring signatures. The underlying idea of report and trace is that a designated tracer can revoke anonymity of a signer if and only if a report of malicious behaviour is made by a user. In other words, a user reports a malicious message to the tracer, and the tracer must receive a report to revoke anonymity of the signer. Accordingly, report and trace achieves the balance between anonymity and traceability of accountable ring signatures, ensuring that the anonymity of a signer is preserved until tracing is complete. Additionally, report and trace incorporates a reporting system that preserves the anonymity of the signer *and* the reporter.

1.1   Related Work

Group signatures were introduced in [8], and the first security models were presented in [2,3]. Generally, the group manager can revoke the anonymity of a signer and must be trusted to preserve signer anonymity in the absence of malicious behaviour. Several variants of group signatures have been proposed to limit trust in the group manager. For example, accountable tracing signatures [16] require that the group manager produce a proof of correct tracing and, if tracing occurred, a proof denying tracing cannot be produced. Traceable signatures [15] define a designated authority that can trace all signatures produced by a particular signer if the group manager provides the authority with a tracing token for that signer. Furthermore, group signatures with message dependent opening (MDO signatures) [22] allow the group manager to revoke the anonymity of all signers that produced a signature for a particular message if and only if a reporter first produces a report related to that message. Our report and trace ring signature provides a similar distributed tracing function, but, in our setting, the report is attached to a signature rather than a message. Additionally, MDO signatures define the reporter to be a fixed entity with a secret key generated during setup. Report and trace ring signatures, on the other hand, model reporters as system users, and our security model ensures anonymity of the reporter. Finally, we note that report and trace is a variation of a *ring* signature and, as such, does not rely upon a trusted group manager to issue key pairs to users and allows users to select their anonymity ring.

Ring signatures were first formally defined in [21] and a security model was presented in [4]. Following this, numerous variations of ring signatures have appeared (see, for example, [25] for a survey of some of these variations), a number of which offer some notion of traceability. For instance, linkable [18] and traceable [12] ring signatures provide limited tracing functionality, allowing two signatures generated by the same signer to be linked. Moreover, accountable ring signatures, introduced in [26] and formalised in [6], allow revocation of signer anonymity by a designated tracer and are, as a result, most closely related to our work. In fact, report and trace ring signatures can be viewed as an extension of accountable ring signatures, where the role of the tracer is distributed and the reporter is modelled as an anonymous system user.

A closely related line of work is purpose-built reporting systems [1,17,20]. Analogously to our work, these systems allow a user to report another user and subsequently allow revocation of anonymity by a designated tracer. However, unlike our report and trace scheme, these systems are stand-alone reporting systems. Specifically, their design allows a user to identify an individual that has, for example, harassed or assaulted the user, hiding the identity of the accused and reporter until a threshold of reports related to the accused are submitted, at which point a tracer reveals the identity of the accused and the reporter(s). We note that, critically, these systems require a *threshold* of reports to revoke anonymity of the accused. This design decision empowers reporters, allowing them to submit accusations with the confidence that they will remain anonymous unless (or until) a number of other reporters have come forward. Finally, in [24], a report and trace scheme was introduced in the context of end-to-end encrypted messaging. In such systems, a message receiver can report a malicious message to a designated tracer, and the tracer can revoke anonymity of the sender. The tracer learns nothing about the sender unless a report is provided by the recipient of that message, and the identity of the reporter is revealed only to the tracer, albeit the reporter's identity is known to the tracer before tracing is complete.

1.2 Our Contributions

We define syntax and a security model for report and trace (R&T) ring signatures (Sect. 2). Our syntax defines a reporting user who provides the tracer with a reporter token, recovered from a signature, and a designated tracer who uses the reporter token to revoke anonymity of the signer. Our security model extends the generic definitions of correctness, anonymity and unforgeability for ring signatures defined in [4] to capture ring signatures with a report and trace functionality. Furthermore, we define *traceability*, adapting the security properties of an accountable ring signature to our setting. We complete our security model with a new definition of *reporter anonymity* for report and trace ring signatures, which ensures that the reporter is anonymous even *after* tracing is complete.

We demonstrate feasibility of report and trace by providing a construction of an R&T ring signature scheme that relies on standard cryptographic primitives (Sect. 3). Briefly, the signer provably encrypts their identity under the tracer's public key for a public-key encryption scheme and then encrypts the resulting ciphertext using a one-time key-pair for a public-key encryption scheme. Additionally, the signer provably encrypts the one-time decryption key (which we call the reporter token) to all potential reporters. Then, the reporter decrypts their token, and the tracer requires the reporter token to recover the signer's identity. Our construction is based on the accountable ring signature of [6] in which the signer provable encrypts their identity under the tracer's public key and the tracer can revoke the signer's anonymity by decrypting the resulting ciphertext. We choose this construction due to its efficiency and because its security relies upon standard, well-understood cryptographic hardness assumptions (namely, the decisional Diffie-Hellman assumption). We provide a sketch proof that our construction satisfies our security model. Our full proof of security, which we present in the full version of this paper [11], relies on standard notions of security for the cryptographic primitives used in our construction.

We analyse the efficiency of our construction (Sect. 3.3), summarising the computational and communication costs associated with signing, reporting and tracing for our scheme. We provide an instantiation of our construction (Sect. 3.2), which demonstrates that it can be implemented efficiently. In fact, for the cryptographic primitives we select, our construction performs favourably to the accountable ring signature of [6], and the additional cost of reporting is small.

Finally, we extend our construction to support multiple reporters (Sect. 4) using threshold publicly verifiable secret sharing [23]. We provide each potential reporter with a share of the reporter token, and a threshold of shares are required to recover the reporter token. We conclude with an efficiency analysis for our multiple reporter construction.

1.3   Contextualising R&T Ring Signatures

In this paper, we introduce a new primitive, an R&T ring signature, and provide a way to achieve it. We are also interested in placing this primitive in the context of related schemes and in highlighting the advantages it brings. We explore this next and summarise our findings in Table 1.

Revoking Anonymity of the Accused. All primitives with tracing functionality discussed so far [1,6,15–17,20,22,24,26] hide the identity of the accused (i.e., the signer in an R&T ring signature schemes) until tracing is complete, at which point, anonymity of the accused is revoked. We note that [1,17,20,24] reveal the identity of the accused only to the tracer. However, for accountable ring signatures schemes [6,26], group signature variants [15,16] and our R&T ring signature, anonymity of the accused is *publicly* revoked to allow for public verification of the tracing process. Accordingly, the tracer is *accountable* for their actions and can only (provably) revoke the anonymity of a real accused user.

Entities Revoking Anonymity. Every primitive we consider [1,6,15–17,20,22, 24,26] requires a designated tracer. In some systems, e.g., [1,17,26], the tracer is distributed. Whilst our R&T ring signature construction (Sect. 3), and our multiple reporter construction (Sect. 4), model the tracer as a single entity, we remark that we can also distribute the tracer, thus distributing trust amongst a set of tracers. Trust in the tracer can be further reduced by requiring a reporter. Our R&T ring signature and [1,17,20,22,24] define a reporter such that the reporter and tracer must cooperate to revoke anonymity. Additionally, purpose-built tracing systems [1,17,20] require a *threshold* of reports to trigger the tracing process. We provide both options: our R&T ring signature construction (Sect. 3) requires a single report; our multiple reporter construction (Sect. 4) requires a threshold of reports.

Anonymity of the Reporter. Our (single reporter) R&T scheme ensures that the reporter is anonymous even *after* tracing. This is not true of MDO signatures [22], where the reporter is a fixed, publicly-known, entity. Also, for end-to-end encrypted messaging [24], the tracer learns the identity of the reporter *before* starting the tracing process. Moreover, purpose-build reporting systems [1,17,20] intentionally reveal the identity of reporters after tracing. Recall that reporting systems allow reporters to communicate the identity of an accused person (e.g., a person accused of assault or illegal activity). Therefore, to follow up on allegations, revealing the reporter's identity is necessary. As the tracer in our R&T scheme does not require the identity of the reporter to follow up on an allegation (in fact, the allegation is that the message signed by the accused is malicious, and the message is public), we can protect the reporter's anonymity even after tracing.

Table 1. Contextualising R&T ring signatures.

	Publicly verifiable tracing	Entities revoking anonymity	Reporter Anonymity	Integrated functionality
Group signature variants [15,16]	✓	Tracer	N/A	Signature
Group signature with message dependent opening [22]	✗	Reporter Tracer	✗	Signature
Accountable ring signatures [6,26]	✓	Tracer	N/A	Signature
Traceable E2E encrypted messaging [24]	✗	Reporter Tracer	✗	Encryption
Reporting systems [1,17,20]	✗	Reporter (threshold) Tracer	✓*	None
R&T ring signatures (This work)	✓	Reporter Tracer	✓	Signature
R&T ring signatures (multiple reporters) (This work)	✓	Reporter (threshold) Tracer	✗	Signature

* denotes anonymity only holds until tracing is complete.

Application. We describe a potential application of report and trace. Consider a forum platform and a set of registered users that can post messages to the forum. Users may wish to post messages anonymously, while also providing a signature proving that they are a registered user. Moreover, if a user posts a malicious message, the platform may wish to hold the signer accountable. Standard group and ring signature facilitate the ability of a user to sign a message anonymously. Furthermore, group signatures and accountable ring signatures balance anonymity and traceability. However, we believe that R&T ring signatures provide a unique solution to this scenario. Firstly, R&T ring signatures (and group signatures with message dependent opening) do not rely solely on a designated tracer to revoke anonymity and, as such, provide additional protection for the signer's identity above that provided by accountable ring signatures and group signatures. Moreover, distributing the tracing function reduces the burden on the tracer to check for malicious messages. Indeed, the tracer need only check messages for which the tracer receives a report. Additionally, our R&T signature allows the tracer to revoke anonymity only for the reported signature. That is, the signer preserves their anonymity with respect to all other signatures and no other signer who posts the same message will be de-anonymised. In our forum scenario, it may not be desirable to revoke anonymity for all signatures produced by the signer of a single malicious message. Moreover, it may be the case that a signed message is malicious in the context of which it is reported, but may be entirely innocuous in a different context. Consequently, R&T ring signatures are more appropriate than traceable signatures or MDO signatures for this setting. Finally, R&T ring signatures retain the versatility of ring signatures and define the reporter to be a system user, which can foster a sense of community responsibility for forum content, and provide a unique guarantee of anonymity for the reporter which can empower users to report malicious behaviour without fear of repercussions.

2   Syntax and Security

We introduce the syntax of a *report and trace* (R&T) ring signature scheme and accompanying security model. In a standard ring signature, users digitally sign messages with respect to a set of users, known as a ring. Ring signatures ensure that the signer cannot be identified; any ring member is equally likely to have produced the signature. R&T ring signatures extend this notion, allowing a signer to be identified if an anonymous report is made to a designated tracer, who then traces the signer. Alongside a set of users $\mathcal{U}$, an R&T ring signature scheme involves the following entities. A *reporter* produces a report. Within our syntax and security model, reporters are ring members, though this need not be the case. A *designated tracer*, denoted T, revokes the signer's anonymity if the tracer received a report for the signature in question. Anybody can verify the correctness of the report and trace by running a public verification algorithm. Formally, we define an R&T ring signature in Definition 1.

Definition 1 (R&T ring signature). *An* R&T *ring signature scheme is a tuple of algorithms (*Setup, T.KGen, U.KGen, Sign, Verify, Report, Trace, VerTrace*) such that*

- Setup(1^λ): On input security parameter 1^λ, Setup outputs public parameters *pp*.

- T.KGen(pp): On input pp, T.KGen outputs a tracer key pair (pk_T, sk_T). We write that $pk_T \leftarrow$ T.KGen($pp; sk_T$).
- U.KGen(pp): On input pp, U.KGen outputs a user key pair (pk_U, sk_U). We write that $pk_U \leftarrow$ U.KGen($pp; sk_U$).
- Sign(pp, sk_U, pk_T, m, R): On input pp, sk_U, pk_T, message m and ring R, Sign outputs a signature σ.
- Verify(pp, pk_T, m, R, σ): On input pp, pk_T, m, R and σ, Verify outputs 1 if σ is a valid signature on m with respect to R, and 0 otherwise.
- Report($pp, pk_T, sk_U, m, R, \sigma$): On input pp, pk_T, sk_U, m, R and σ, Report outputs a reporter token Rep.
- Trace($pp, sk_T, m, R, \sigma, \text{Rep}$): On input pp, sk_T, m, R, σ and Rep, Trace outputs the signer's identity pk_U, auxiliary information Tr consisting of the reporter token, and a proof of correct trace ρ_t.
- VerTrace($pp, pk_T, m, R, \sigma, pk_U, \text{Tr}, \rho_t$): On input pp, pk_T, m, R, σ, pk_U, Tr and ρ_t, VerTrace outputs 1 if the trace is valid, and 0 otherwise.

We define correctness for our syntax as the property that honestly generated signatures are verifiable.

Definition 2 (Correctness). *An* R&T *ring signature is correct if, for any* $n = \text{poly}(\lambda)$, $j \in [n]$ *and message* m, *there exists a negligible function* negl *such that,*

$$\Pr \left[\begin{array}{l} pp \leftarrow \text{Setup}(1^\lambda); \\ (pk_T, sk_T) \leftarrow \text{T.KGen}(pp); \\ \text{for } i = 1,...,n : (pk_{U_i}, sk_{U_i}) \leftarrow \text{U.KGen}(pp); \\ R = \{pk_{U_1},...,pk_{U_n}\}; \\ \sigma \leftarrow \text{Sign}(pp, sk_{U_j}, pk_T, m, R); \\ b \leftarrow \text{Verify}(pp, pk_T, m, R, \sigma) \end{array} : b = 1 \right] \geq 1 - \text{negl}(\lambda).$$

2.1 Security Model

We present a security model for our syntax that incorporates accepted security properties from the ring signature literature. Firstly, we extend well-established definitions of anonymity and unforgeability for standard ring signature schemes, presented in [4], to our setting. Then, we cast the security requirements of an accountable ring signature into our syntax. Namely, we define traceability, which captures notions of trace correctness, non-frameability and tracing soundness defined in [6]. Finally, we present a definition of reporter anonymity, a new security property for our report and trace setting.

In Fig. 1, we define a number of oracles for our security experiments. We write $\mathcal{O}X_{(y_1,...,y_n)}(z_1, \ldots, z_n)$ to denote oracle X that has access to parameters and sets $y_1, \ldots, y_n$ and takes as input $z_1, \ldots, z_n$. Oracles $\mathcal{O}$reg, $\mathcal{O}$corrupt and $\mathcal{O}$sign operate as expected: they model registration of users, corruption of users, and signature generation respectively. Moreover, $\mathcal{O}$report is called to obtain a reporter token for a message and $\mathcal{O}$trace is called to trace the signer of a message.

Our security model considers entities (i.e., users, reporters and tracers) that are honest, corrupt, or under the attacker's control. In detail, honest entities do not provide an attacker with secret keys; corrupt entities generate their keys honestly, but may later provide the attacker with their secret keys; the attacker can generate keys on behalf of controlled entities. An attacker with credentials of users, reporters or tracers can generate signatures, reports or traces respectively.

$\mathcal{O}\text{reg}_{(pp,\mathcal{Q}\text{reg},L)}()$	$\mathcal{O}\text{corrupt}_{(L,\mathcal{Q}\text{corr})}(pk_U)$	$\mathcal{O}\text{sign}_{(pp,L,\mathcal{Q}\text{sign})}(pk_U, pk_T, m, R)$
$(pk_U, sk_U) \leftarrow \text{U.KGen}(pp)$	if $(pk_U, \cdot) \notin L$ return $\perp$	if $(pk_U, \cdot) \notin L$ return $\perp$
$\mathcal{Q}\text{reg} \leftarrow \mathcal{Q}\text{reg} \cup \{pk_U\}$	$\mathcal{Q}\text{corr} \leftarrow \mathcal{Q}\text{corr} \cup \{pk_U\}$	$\sigma \leftarrow \text{Sign}(pp, sk_U, pk_T, m, R \cup \{pk_U\})$
$L \leftarrow L \cup \{(pk_U, sk_U)\}$	return sk_U	$\mathcal{Q}\text{sign} \leftarrow \mathcal{Q}\text{sign} \cup \{(pk_T, pk_U, m, R, \sigma)\}$
return pk_U		return σ

$\mathcal{O}\text{report}_{(pp,pk_T,L,\mathcal{Q}\text{report})}(pk_U, m, R, \sigma)$	$\mathcal{O}\text{trace}_{(pp,sk_T,\mathcal{Q}\text{trace})}(m, R, \sigma, \text{Rep})$
if $pk_U \notin R \vee (pk_U, \cdot) \notin L$ return $\perp$	$(pk_U, \text{Tr}, \rho_t) \leftarrow \text{Trace}(pp, sk_T, m, R, \sigma, \text{Rep})$
$\text{Rep} \leftarrow \text{Report}(pp, pk_T, sk_U, m, R, \sigma)$	$\mathcal{Q}\text{trace} \leftarrow \mathcal{Q}\text{trace} \cup \{(m, R, \sigma)\}$
$\mathcal{Q}\text{report} \leftarrow \mathcal{Q}\text{report} \cup \{(pk_U, m, R, \sigma)\}$	return $(pk_U, \text{Tr}, \rho_t)$
return Rep	

Fig. 1. Oracles used in the experiments for anonymity, unforgeability, traceability and reporter anonymity of an R&T ring signature scheme.

Anonymity. Anonymity is the property that a signature does not reveal the identity of the signer *unless* the signature is reported and the signer traced. Our formal definition of anonymity captures anonymity against adversarially generated keys as defined in [4]. As such, we assume that the adversary can corrupt and control users and reporters, but that the tracer is honest. We require that the adversary, when provided with a challenge signature, cannot determine which of two potential honest signers generated the signature, on the condition that the adversary does not obtain a trace for the challenge signature.

Definition 3 (Anonymity). *An R&T ring signature is anonymous with respect to adversarially generated keys if, for any probabilistic, polynomial-time (PPT) adversary* $\mathcal{A} = (\mathcal{A}_1, \mathcal{A}_2)$, *there exists a negligible function* negl *such that,*

$$\Pr \left[\begin{array}{l} pp \leftarrow \text{Setup}(1^\lambda); \\ L, \mathcal{Q}\text{reg}, \mathcal{Q}\text{corr}, \mathcal{Q}\text{sign}, \mathcal{Q}\text{report}, \mathcal{Q}\text{trace} \leftarrow \emptyset; \\ (pk_T, sk_T) \leftarrow \text{T.KGen}(pp); \\ (m, R, pk_{U_0}, pk_{U_1}, st) \leftarrow \mathcal{A}_1^{\mathcal{O}}(pp, pk_T); \\ b \leftarrow \{0,1\}; \\ \sigma \leftarrow \text{Sign}(pp, sk_{U_b}, pk_T, m, R \cup \{pk_{U_0}, pk_{U_1}\}); \\ b' \leftarrow \mathcal{A}_2^{\mathcal{O}}(\sigma, st) \end{array} : \begin{array}{l} b' = b \wedge (m, R, \sigma) \notin \mathcal{Q}\text{trace} \\ \wedge \{pk_{U_0}, pk_{U_1}\} \subseteq \mathcal{Q}\text{reg} \setminus \mathcal{Q}\text{corr} \end{array} \right]$$
$$\leq \frac{1}{2} + \text{negl}(\lambda)$$

where $\mathcal{O} = \{\mathcal{O}\text{reg}, \mathcal{O}\text{corrupt}, \mathcal{O}\text{sign}, \mathcal{O}\text{report}, \mathcal{O}\text{trace}\}$ *are the oracles defined in Fig. 1.*

Unforgeability. We require that signatures are unforgeable. That is, an attacker cannot output a valid signature on behalf of an honest user, even if an attacker can trace the identity of honest signers through the report and trace functionality. Formally, we consider an unforgeability definition similar to that presented in [4]. Thus, in our unforgeability experiment, we assume that the adversary controls the tracer and can corrupt and control users and reporters. We require that the adversary cannot output a valid signature for a ring of honest users, where the signature is not the output of the signing oracle.

Definition 4 (Unforgeability). *An* R&T *ring signature scheme is* unforgeable *if, for any PPT adversary $\mathcal{A}$, there exists a negligible function* negl *such that,*

$$
\Pr\left[\begin{array}{l} pp \leftarrow \mathsf{Setup}(1^\lambda); \\ L,\ \mathcal{Q}\mathsf{reg},\ \mathcal{Q}\mathsf{corr},\ \mathcal{Q}\mathsf{sign},\ \mathcal{Q}\mathsf{report} \leftarrow \emptyset;\ : \\ (pk_\mathsf{T},m,R,\sigma) \leftarrow \mathcal{A}^\mathcal{O}(pp) \end{array}\middle| \begin{array}{l} \mathsf{Verify}(pp,pk_\mathsf{T},m,R,\sigma) = 1 \\ \wedge\ R \subseteq \mathcal{Q}\mathsf{reg}\backslash\mathcal{Q}\mathsf{corr} \\ \wedge\ (pk_\mathsf{T},\cdot,m,R,\sigma) \notin \mathcal{Q}\mathsf{sign} \end{array}\right] \leq \mathsf{negl}\,(\lambda)
$$

where $\mathcal{O} = \{\mathcal{O}\mathsf{reg}, \mathcal{O}\mathsf{corrupt}, \mathcal{O}\mathsf{sign}, \mathcal{O}\mathsf{report}\}$ are the oracles defined in Fig. 1.

Traceability. R&T signatures must satisfy *traceability.* In other words, it must be possible to identify the signer of a message. Traceability comprises three conditions: trace correctness, non-frameability and trace soundness. *Trace correctness* requires that an honestly generated signature must be traceable to the correct signer. Accordingly, any trace output by the tracer must be valid. We capture trace correctness in an experiment that requires an honestly generated report and trace for an honestly generated signature to verify. *Non-frameability* states that a report and trace mechanism cannot identify a non-signer as the signer. To this end, our non-frameability definition requires that the adversary, with control of the tracer and a subset of users, cannot output a valid trace such that the trace identifies a non-signer. Finally, *trace soundness,* defined in [6], stipulates that the signer identified by the report and trace mechanism is unique. That is, it is not possible to verifiably identify two users as the signer of a single message. The trace soundness definition in [6], which we cast into our syntax, considers an adversary that controls the tracer and can corrupt and control users and reporters. Trace soundness requires that the adversary cannot output two valid traces that identify two different signers for the same message.

Definition 5 (Traceability). *An* R&T *ring signature satisfies* traceability *if the following conditions are satisfied:*

1. Trace correctness: *for any $n = \mathsf{poly}(\lambda)$, $j,k \in [n]$ where $j \neq k$, and message m, there exists a negligible function* negl *such that,*

$$
\Pr\left[\begin{array}{l} pp \leftarrow \mathsf{Setup}(1^\lambda); \\ (pk_\mathsf{T},sk_\mathsf{T}) \leftarrow \mathsf{T.KGen}(pp); \\ \text{for } i = 1,\dots,n\ :\ (pk_{\mathsf{U}_i},sk_{\mathsf{U}_i}) \leftarrow \mathsf{U.KGen}(pp); \\ R = \{pk_{\mathsf{U}_1},\dots,pk_{\mathsf{U}_n}\}; \\ \sigma \leftarrow \mathsf{Sign}(pp,sk_{\mathsf{U}_j},pk_\mathsf{T},m,R); \\ \mathsf{Rep} \leftarrow \mathsf{Report}(pp,pk_\mathsf{T},sk_{\mathsf{U}_k},m,R,\sigma); \\ (pk_\mathsf{U},\mathsf{Tr},\rho_t) \leftarrow \mathsf{Trace}(pp,sk_\mathsf{T},m,R,\sigma,\mathsf{Rep}); \\ b \leftarrow \mathsf{VerTrace}(pp,pk_\mathsf{T},m,R,\sigma,pk_\mathsf{U},\mathsf{Tr},\rho_t) \end{array}\ :\ b = 1\right] \geq 1 - \mathsf{negl}\,(\lambda).
$$

2. Non-frameability; *for any PPT adversary $\mathcal{A}$, there exists a negligible function* negl *such that,*

$$\Pr\left[\begin{array}{l} pp \leftarrow \mathsf{Setup}(1^\lambda); \\ L,\ \mathcal{Q}\mathrm{reg},\ \mathcal{Q}\mathrm{corr},\ \mathcal{Q}\mathrm{sign},\ \mathcal{Q}\mathrm{report} \leftarrow \emptyset; \\ (pk_\mathsf{T},m,R,\sigma,pk_\mathsf{U},\mathsf{Tr},\rho_t) \leftarrow \mathcal{A}^{\mathcal{O}}(pp); \\ b \leftarrow \mathsf{VerTrace}(pp,pk_\mathsf{T},m,R,\sigma,pk_\mathsf{U},\mathsf{Tr},\rho_t) \end{array} : \begin{array}{l} b = 1 \wedge pk_\mathsf{U} \in \mathcal{Q}\mathrm{reg}\backslash\mathcal{Q}\mathrm{corr} \\ \wedge\ \mathsf{Verify}(pp,pk_\mathsf{T},m,R,\sigma) = 1 \\ \wedge\ (pk_\mathsf{T},pk_\mathsf{U},m,R,\sigma) \notin \mathcal{Q}\mathrm{sign} \end{array}\right] \leq \mathsf{negl}\,(\lambda)$$

3. Trace soundness: *for any PPT adversary $\mathcal{A}$, there exists a negligible function* negl *such that,*

$$\Pr\left[\begin{array}{l} pp \leftarrow \mathsf{Setup}(1^\lambda); \\ L,\ \mathcal{Q}\mathrm{reg},\ \mathcal{Q}\mathrm{corr},\ \mathcal{Q}\mathrm{sign},\ \mathcal{Q}\mathrm{report} \leftarrow \emptyset; \\ (pk_\mathsf{T},m,R,\sigma,pk_{\mathsf{U}_i},\mathsf{Tr}_i,\rho_{t_i},pk_{\mathsf{U}_j},\mathsf{Tr}_j,\rho_{t_j}) \leftarrow \mathcal{A}^{\mathcal{O}}(pp) \\ b_1 \leftarrow \mathsf{VerTrace}(pp,pk_\mathsf{T},m,R,\sigma,pk_{\mathsf{U}_i},\mathsf{Tr}_i,\rho_{t_i}); \\ b_2 \leftarrow \mathsf{VerTrace}(pp,pk_\mathsf{T},m,R,\sigma,pk_{\mathsf{U}_j},\mathsf{Tr}_j,\rho_{t_j}) \end{array} : \begin{array}{l} b_1 = 1 \wedge b_2 = 1 \\ \wedge\ pk_{\mathsf{U}_i} \neq pk_{\mathsf{U}_j} \end{array}\right] \leq \mathsf{negl}\,(\lambda)$$

where $\mathcal{O} = \{\mathcal{O}\mathrm{reg}, \mathcal{O}\mathrm{corrupt}, \mathcal{O}\mathrm{sign}, \mathcal{O}\mathrm{report}\}$ are the oracles defined in Fig. 1.

Reporter Anonymity. We define *reporter anonymity*, a new property that requires that a report does not reveal the ring member that produced it. We formally define reporter anonymity as the property that an adversary, when provided with a report for a signature, cannot determine which of two potential reporters produced the report. Our definition captures an adversary that can corrupt and control users and reporters, and controls the tracer. We require that the adversary does not corrupt either of the potential reporters and does not obtain a report through access to oracles.

Definition 6 (Reporter anonymity). *An* R&T *ring signature is* reporter anonymous *if, for any PPT adversary $\mathcal{A} = (\mathcal{A}_1, \mathcal{A}_2)$, there exists a negligible function* negl *such that,*

$$\Pr\left[\begin{array}{l} pp \leftarrow \mathsf{Setup}(1^\lambda); \\ L,\ \mathcal{Q}\mathrm{reg},\ \mathcal{Q}\mathrm{corr},\ \mathcal{Q}\mathrm{sign},\ \mathcal{Q}\mathrm{report} \leftarrow \emptyset; \\ (pk_\mathsf{T},m,R,\sigma,pk_{\mathsf{U}_0},pk_{\mathsf{U}_1},st) \leftarrow \mathcal{A}_1^{\mathcal{O}}(pp); \\ b \leftarrow \{0,1\}; \\ \mathsf{Rep} \leftarrow \mathsf{Report}(pp,pk_\mathsf{T},sk_{\mathsf{U}_b},m,R,\sigma); \\ b' \leftarrow \mathcal{A}_2^{\mathcal{O}}(\sigma,st) \end{array} : \begin{array}{l} b' = b \\ \wedge\{pk_{\mathsf{U}_0},pk_{\mathsf{U}_1}\} \subseteq (R \cap \mathcal{Q}\mathrm{reg})\backslash\mathcal{Q}\mathrm{corr} \\ \wedge\ (m,R,\sigma,pk_{\mathsf{U}_0}) \notin \mathcal{Q}\mathrm{report} \\ \wedge\ (m,R,\sigma,pk_{\mathsf{U}_1}) \notin \mathcal{Q}\mathrm{report} \end{array}\right]$$

$$\leq \tfrac{1}{2} + \mathsf{negl}\,(\lambda)$$

where $\mathcal{O} = \{\mathcal{O}\mathrm{reg}, \mathcal{O}\mathrm{corrupt}, \mathcal{O}\mathrm{sign}, \mathcal{O}\mathrm{report}\}$ are the oracles defined in Fig. 1.

3 A Report and Trace Ring Signature Construction

We present an R&T ring signature construction, formally defined in Fig. 2. Our construction requires a one-way function $f : X \rightarrow Y$ such that, given $y = f(x)$, it is hard to compute x, and a standard public key encryption scheme $\mathsf{PKE} = (\mathsf{PKE.KGen}, \mathsf{PKE.Enc}, \mathsf{PKE.Dec})$ that is secure against chosen plaintext attacks (IND-CPA) [13]. We require a zero-knowledge proof system $\mathsf{NIZK} = (\mathsf{NIZK.Setup}, \mathsf{NIZK.Prove}, \mathsf{NIZK.Verify})$ that satisfies completeness, knowledge soundness and zero-knowledge where such security definitions are drawn from [14]. Finally, we utilise a signature of knowledge $\mathsf{SOK} =$

(SoK.Setup, SoK.Sign, SoK.Verify) [7], that satisfies correctness, simulatability and extractability, all of which are defined in [6].

The idea behind our construction is as follows. The tracer and users obtain a key pair for a PKE scheme. The signer generates a fresh key pair for a PKE scheme, and the freshly generated decryption key (known as the reporter token in our construction) is encrypted to all members of the ring using a PKE scheme. The signer then uses a double layer of encryption to encrypt their public identity, which is generated via one-way function f. That is, the signer encrypts their public identity under the public key of the tracer, and encrypts the resulting ciphertext under the freshly generated encryption key. In this way, a reporter *and* the tracer are required to recover the identity of the signer. Indeed, any ring member can decrypt the reporter token, and the tracer requires the reporter token, along with their own decryption key, to remove the double-layer of encryption and revoke anonymity of the signer. Our construction additionally employs NIZK proofs and an SOK to ensure that operations are performed correctly, i.e., that the signer encrypts the correct public identity and reporter token, and that the reporter and tracer identify the correct signer.

Our construction is similar to the construction in [6], which provides an efficient accountable ring signature scheme that allows a designated tracer to revoke signer anonymity. In [6], the signer uses a PKE scheme to encrypt their public identity under the tracer's public key, and the tracer recovers the signer's identity by decrypting the ciphertext. This construction also relies on an SOK that allows the signer to prove that they have encrypted a public identity for which they know a corresponding secret, and a NIZK proof such that the tracer can prove correct decryption, i.e., that they traced the correct signer. Our R&T construction differs from [6] in the following way. We require the encryption of a token to a set of reporters and provide a NIZK proof of correct encryption. Additionally, we use a double-layer of encryption, which is crucial to ensuring that the tracer cannot decrypt the signer's identity without a reporter token.

3.1 Description of Our Construction

We now describe the details of our construction. A trusted third party runs Setup, performing setup for the PKE, NIZK and SOK schemes. We assume that the public parameters generated for each scheme defines the public/secret key, randomness and message spaces (which we denote respectively as PK, SK, Rand and M) as appropriate. T.KGen generates a tracer key pair for a PKE scheme, and U.KGen is run to generate user key pairs. In particular, users generate a signing/verification key pair (pk_{RS}, sk_{RS}) using one-way function f, and a key pair (pk_{PKE}, sk_{PKE}) for a PKE scheme.

To sign a message m with respect to a ring R, the signer runs algorithm Sign. The signer generates a key pair (pk_{Sign}, sk_{Sign}) for a PKE scheme and encrypts the reporter token sk_{Sign} to each ring member (i.e., encrypts sk_{Sign} under the public encryption key of each ring member). The signer proves that each PKE ciphertext encrypt the reporter token sk_{Sign} associated with pk_{Sign}, which is included in the signature. That is, the signer provides a NIZK proof for the following relation:

$$\mathcal{R}_{\mathsf{Enc}} = \left\{ \begin{array}{l} (pp,(pk_{\mathsf{Sign}},pk_{\mathsf{PKE}_i},\mathbf{c_1}),(r_{1,1},...,r_{1,|R|},sk_{\mathsf{Sign}})) \; : \; pk_{\mathsf{Sign}} := \mathsf{PKE.KGen}(pp_{\mathsf{PKE}};sk_{\mathsf{Sign}}) \\ \qquad \wedge \left\{ \forall \; i \in 1,...,|R| \; : \; c_{1,i} := \mathsf{PKE.Enc}(pp_{\mathsf{PKE}},pk_{\mathsf{PKE}_i},sk_{\mathsf{Sign}};r_{1,i}) \right\} \end{array} \right\} \quad (1)$$

Then, the signer's verification key pk_{RS} is encrypted under the tracer's public key, resulting in ciphertext c_2, which is then encrypted under the freshly generated public key pk_{Sign}, giving ciphertext c_3. Finally, the signer produces a signature of knowledge, which proves that c_3 encrypts a verification key in the ring such that the signer knows the associated signing key. The signature of knowledge is associated with the following relation:

$$\mathcal{R}_{\mathsf{SOK}} = \left\{ \begin{array}{l} (pp,(pk_{\mathsf{T}},pk_{\mathsf{Sign}},R,c_3),(r_2,r_3,sk_{\mathsf{RS}}),m) \; : \; c_3 := \mathsf{PKE.Enc}(pp_{\mathsf{PKE}},pk_{\mathsf{Sign}},c_2;r_3) \\ \qquad \wedge \; c_2 := \mathsf{PKE.Enc}(pp_{\mathsf{PKE}},pk_{\mathsf{T}},pk;r_2) \; \wedge \; pk := f(sk_{\mathsf{RS}}) \in R \end{array} \right\} \quad (2)$$

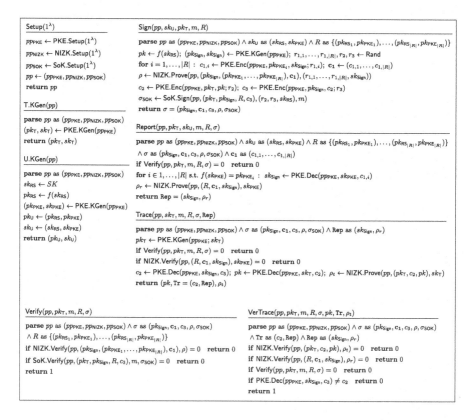

Fig. 2. Our R&T ring signature construction.

To report a message, a ring member runs Report to decrypt the reporter token. The reporter also provides a proof of correct decryption, without revealing which member of the ring decrypted the token. This is given by the following relation:

$$\mathcal{R}_{\mathsf{Dec}_r} = \left\{ \begin{matrix} (pp,(R,\mathbf{c_1},sk_{\mathsf{Sign}}),sk_{\mathsf{PKE}}) \;:\; sk_{\mathsf{Sign}} := \mathsf{PKE.Dec}(pp_{\mathsf{PKE}},sk_{\mathsf{PKE}},c_{1,i}) \\ \wedge \; c_{1,i} \in \mathbf{c_1} \wedge pk_{\mathsf{PKE}} := \mathsf{PKE.KGen}(pp_{\mathsf{PKE}};sk_{\mathsf{PKE}}) \in R \end{matrix} \right\} \quad (3)$$

On receipt of a report, the tracer runs Trace to decrypt ciphertexts c_3 and c_2 and reveal the signer's verification key. As sk_{Sign} is included in the report, anyone can decrypt c_3, hence checking correct decryption directly. As such, the tracer need only prove correct decryption of c_2, which is given by the following relation:

$$\mathcal{R}_{\mathsf{Dec}_t} = \left\{ \begin{matrix} (pp,(pk_{\mathsf{T}},c_2,pk_{\mathsf{RS}}),sk_{\mathsf{T}}) \;:\; pk := \mathsf{PKE.Dec}(pp_{\mathsf{PKE}},sk_{\mathsf{T}},c_2) \\ \wedge \; pk_{\mathsf{T}} := \mathsf{PKE.KGen}(pp_{\mathsf{PKE}};sk_{\mathsf{T}}) \end{matrix} \right\} \quad (4)$$

Our construction additionally provides a public signing verification algorithm Verify, which ensures that the signer provides an encryption of their own public key, enabling tracing if the message is malicious. Moreover, a public trace verification algorithm VerTrace ensures that the correct signer is traced.

We prove that our construction satisfies correctness, anonymity, unforgeability, traceability and reporter anonymity as defined in Sect. 2. We obtain Theorem 1, which we formally prove in [11] and provide a proof sketch here.

Theorem 1. *The construction in Fig. 2 satisfies correctness, anonymity, unforgeability, traceability and reporter anonymity as defined in Definitions 2– 6.*

Proof (Sketch). Correctness and tracing correctness of our construction follows trivially from the correctness of the building blocks. Unforgeability follows from extractability of the SOK and the fact that f is a one-way function. In fact, if our construction is not unforgeable, the adversary can break the one-wayness of function f, or can be used to construct an adversary against the extractability property. To prove non-frameability, we show that, if our construction is not unforgeable, the adversary can be used to construct an adversary against the soundness property of the NIZK scheme or the extractability property of the SOK. Else, the construction does not satisfy unforgeability. Soundness is proven by showing that, if the construction is not sound, then the adversary can be used to construct an adversary against the soundness of the NIZK scheme.

To prove anonymity and reporter anonymity, we proceed via a series of game hops, demonstrating that each hop is indistinguishable to the adversary. Our final game hop result in a game for which the view of the adversary is identical for $\beta = 0$ and $\beta = 1$ and the proof holds. In our anonymity proof, we simulate the setup and proofs for the NIZK and SOK systems, which is an indistinguishable game hop if the NIZK scheme satisfies the zero-knowledge property and the SOK satisfies simulatability. Then, we extract the plaintext from the ciphertexts, rather than running the decryption algorithm. By the knowledge extractability property of the NIZK and extractability of the SOK, this hop is also indistinguishable. Finally, we encrypt the identity of the same signer, regardless of β, which is indistinguishable by the IND-CPA property of the PKE scheme. Our proof of reporter anonymity is similar. We simulate the setup and proofs for the NIZK proof system and then extract the plaintext from the ciphertexts, rather than running the decryption algorithm when generating a reporter token. These game hops are indistinguishable if the NIZK scheme satisfies the zero-knowledge and knowledge extractability properties.

3.2 Instantiating Our Construction

We instantiate our construction with ElGamal encryption and the signature of knowledge of [6], modified to account for the double layer of encryption of the signer's identity. Additionally, we instantiate our NIZK protocols for signing, reporting and tracing with various Σ-protocols. For our choice of primitives, our instantiation is secure. We provide full details of our instantiation and a sketch proof of its security in [11]. Here, we present an overview of our instantiation.

Setup and Key Generation. We let $pp_{\mathsf{PKE}} = pp_{\mathsf{NIZK}} = (\mathbb{G}, g, q)$ where $\mathbb{G}$ is a cyclic group of order q with generator g. Moreover, $pp_{\mathsf{SOK}} = (ek, ck)$ where ek is an ElGamal encryption key and ck is a key for a commitment scheme. We define one-way function f to perform group exponentiation such that $f(x) = g^x$ for some $x \in \mathbb{Z}_q$. We write $pp = (pp_{\mathsf{PKE}}, pp_{\mathsf{SOK}})$ as the output of algorithm Setup. We write the key pair for the tracer as $(pk_{\mathsf{T}} = g^{sk_{\mathsf{T}}}, sk_{\mathsf{T}})$ and the key pair for the user as $(pk_{\mathsf{U}}, sk_{\mathsf{U}}) = ((g^{sk_{\mathsf{RS}}}, g^{sk_{\mathsf{PKE}}}), (sk_{\mathsf{RS}}, sk_{\mathsf{PKE}}))$ where $sk_{\mathsf{T}}, sk_{\mathsf{RS}}, sk_{\mathsf{PKE}} \in \mathbb{Z}_q$.

Sign. We use a standard ElGamal encryption scheme to generate ciphertext c_1 and to double-encrypt the signer's identity in algorithm Sign. That is, we define ciphertexts $c_2 = (A_2, B_2) = (g^{r_2}, pk_{\mathsf{T}}^{r_2} \cdot pk)$ and $c_3 = (A_2, A_3, B_3) = (g^{r_2}, g^{r_3}, pk_{\mathsf{Sign}}^{r_3} \cdot pk_{\mathsf{T}}^{r_2} \cdot pk)$. To generate proof ρ for the relation in Eq. 1, we use the Σ-protocol of [23], which shows that c_1 encrypts the discrete log of a public element pk_{Sign} and can be transformed into a NIZK proof using the Fiat-Shamir transform [10]. Finally, we modify the SOK of [6] to generate σ_{SOK}, which proves that the signer knows sk_{RS} such that $pk_{\mathsf{RS}} = g^{sk_{\mathsf{RS}}}$ is an element of the ring. Our modification accounts for the double-layer of encryption used in our construction, rather than the single ElGamal encryption required in the accountable ring signature construction of [6].

Report and Trace. The reporter runs PKE.Dec to generate sk_{Sign}. For our instantiation, the reporter need not generate a proof of knowledge of correct decryption for the relation in Eq. 3. In fact, as $\mathbb{G}$ is a cyclic group, $g^i = g^j$ if $i = j \mod q$. Therefore, pk_{Sign} is uniquely defined by $g^{sk_{\mathsf{Sign}}}$. The tracer (and any public verifier) can trivially check correct decryption of the reporter token by computing a single group exponentiation, i.e., check $g^{sk_{\mathsf{Sign}}} = pk_{\mathsf{Sign}}$ where sk_{Sign} is returned by the reporter and pk_{Sign} is included in the signature. The tracer decrypts the signer's identity by computing $B_3/(A_2^{sk_{\mathsf{T}}} A_3^{sk_{\mathsf{Sign}}})$ for $c_3 = (A_2, A_3, B_3)$. The tracer proves correct decryption of c_2 using a standard Σ-protocol as in [6].

3.3 Efficiency of Our Construction

Here, we discuss the efficiency of our construction, showing that it incurs reasonable costs with respect to the functionality provided and that our proposed

Table 2. Computation (comp.) and communication (comm.) costs of generic constructions. We write (enc) and (dec) to indicate a proof of correct encryption or decryption respectively. For our multiple reporters construction, we provide costs relative to a ring of size $|R|$ and a threshold of t.

		Accountable ring signature [6]	Our R&T construction (Fig. 3)	R&T with multiple reporters (Sect. 5)
Sign	Comp.	1 PKE.Enc 1 SoK.Sign	$\|R\| + 2$ PKE.Enc 1 NIZK.Prove ($\|R\|$ enc) 1 SoK.Sign	$\|R\| + 2$ PKE.Enc $\|R\|$ NIZK.Prove (enc) 1 SoK.Sign $\|R\|$ public share gen
	Comm.	1 PKE ciphertext 1 SOK	$\|R\| + 1$ PKE ciphertext 1 NIZK proof ($\|R\|$ enc) 1 SOK 1 element pk_{Sign}	$\|R\| + 1$ PKE ciphertext $\|R\|$ NIZK proof (enc) 1 SOK $\|R\|$ PVSS public shares 1 element S
Verify	Comp.	1 SoK.Verify	1 SoK.Verify 1 NIZK.Verify ($\|R\|$ enc)	1 SoK.Verify $\|R\|$ NIZK.Verify (enc) 1 SS.Verify
	Comm.	N/A	N/A	N/A
Report	Comp.	N/A	1 PKE.Dec 1 NIZK.Prove(dec)	1 PKE.Dec 1 NIZK.Prove(dec)
	Comm.	N/A	1 token sk_{Sign} 1 NIZK proof (dec)	1 sub-token s_i 1 NIZK proof (dec)
Trace	Comp.	1 PKE.Dec 1 NIZK.Prove (dec)	2 PKE.Dec 1 NIZK.Prove (dec) 1 NIZK.Verify(dec)	2 PKE.Dec 1 NIZK.Prove (dec) t NIZK.Verify(dec) 1 SS.Combine
	Comm.	1 pk of signer 1 NIZK proof (dec)	1 pk of signer 1 token sk_{Sign} 1 PKE ciphertext 2 NIZK proof (dec)	1 pk of signer t sub-tokens $s_1, \ldots, s_t$ 1 PKE ciphertext 2 NIZK proof (dec)
VerTrace	Comp.	1 NIZK.Verify (dec)	2 NIZK.Verify (PKE dec) 1 PKE.Dec	$t + 1$ NIZK.Verify (dec) 1 PKE.Dec 1 SS.Combine
	Comm.	N/A	N/A	N/A

instantiation is practical. We also highlight the additional costs associated with our report and trace functionality by comparing with the accountable ring signature in [6]. We show that our construction compares favourably to the accountable ring signature construction of [6]: we require additional computation, but these computations are minimal considering the extra functionality provided by our R&T construction. We summarise the computation and communication costs of our generic construction and instantiation in Tables 2 and 3, respectively. We now briefly describe the costs incurred by the signer, reporter, tracer and verifier.

Signer. The signer's computation costs are dominated by the SOK and PKE computations, both of which grow linearly in the size of the ring. In comparison to the accountable ring signature of [6], we see that encrypting a reporter token doubles the computation costs for the signer. Moreover, the size of the signature also increases, requiring the communication of a number of group and field

Table 3. Computation (comp.) and communication (comm.) costs of instantiations. We present costs relative to a ring of size $|R|$. Our computation costs are given in terms of the number of group exponentiations required, and our communication costs are presented in terms of the number of group elements from $\mathbb{G}$ and field elements from $\mathbb{Z}_q$.

		Accountable ring signature [6]	Our R&T instantiation (Sect. 3.2)
Sign	Comp	$4|R| + 14$	$8|R| + 19$
	Comm.	$14\mathbb{G} + (|R| + 7)\mathbb{Z}_q$	$(3|R| + 19)\mathbb{G} + (2|R| + 7)\mathbb{Z}_q$
Verify	Comp	$3|R| + 19$	$6|R| + 23$
	Comm.	N/A	N/A
Report	Comp	N/A	1
	Comm.	N/A	$1\mathbb{Z}_q$
Trace	Comp	3	5
	Comm.	$3\mathbb{G} + 1\mathbb{Z}_q$	$5\mathbb{G} + 2\mathbb{Z}_q$
VerTrace	Comp	4	6
	Comm.	N/A	N/A

elements that grow linearly in the size of the ring (whereas the accountable ring signature communicates a constant number of group elements).

Reporter. The computation and communication costs incurred by the reporter, which is unique to our construction, are minimal. In fact, for our instantiation, the reporter need only perform a single decryption (i.e., 1 group exponentiation) and a report consists of a single field element. This demonstrates that, though our generic construction allows for a reporter who proves correct decryption, by using cyclic group operations, it is possible to provide an efficient instantiation in which the computation costs of the reporter are minimised.

Tracer. The tracer's costs are small and compare favourably to accountable ring signatures. Indeed, computation of the trace requires a constant number of group exponentiations, calling for only 2 additional group exponentiation when compared to accountable ring signatures. In particular, to verify correct decryption of the reporter token, the tracer need only perform a single group exponentiation, rather than verifying a NIZK proof (cf. Sect. 3.2). Furthermore, the size of a trace is constant and requires only 1 extra field element and 2 extra group elements, when compared to accountable ring signatures.

Verifier. As for signature generation, signature verification costs are dominated by the SOK and PKE scheme. Specifically, our PKE computations require computation costs similar to those required to verify the SOK, which means verification of an R&T ring signature incurs double the computational costs of an accountable ring signature. On the other hand, verification of the trace requires only 6 group exponentiations, only 2 more than accountable ring signatures.

Potential Efficiency Improvements. Our instantiation builds upon the accountable ring signature of [6] but techniques from group signature literature (e.g.,

[15,16,22]) could be used to provide a more efficient construction. We opt to build upon the construction of [6] to clearly demonstrate the additional costs associated with reporting. Indeed, our instantiation presents worst-case efficiency results and can perform reasonably for a small ring.

Our instantiation could use a broadcast encryption (BE) scheme [9] to encrypt the reporter token to all members of the ring. Potentially, by using a BE scheme that is based on bilinear maps (as, for example, [5] and subsequent works), our costs would be similar to those of the accountable ring signature construction [6]. Our reasons for not following this approach are twofold. First, in contrast with BE schemes based on bilinear maps, our construction does not require an interactive key generation protocol. Accordingly, our instantiation retains the benefit of ring signatures with respect to non-interactive key generation. Second, NIZK proofs of correct encryption for schemes based on bilinear maps are currently unknown [19]. Our construction, on the other hand, requires Σ-protocols to prove correct encryption and decryption of the reporter token. Moreover, by relying on cyclic groups, our instantiation does not require a proof of correct decryption for the reporter token, and the tracer can efficiently verify correct decryption.

We note two further modifications that lead to a more efficient, yet more limited, protocol. Firstly, during setup, the signer could choose a *static* set of possible reporters that share a secret key for a PKE scheme. Then, the reporter share is encrypted under the corresponding public key. Though this approach is more efficient, we opt to allow the signer to *dynamically* choose the reporter set, fostering a sense of user empowerment and capturing the functionality of a user posting entries in different fora. Secondly, if reporter anonymity is not a concern and a proof of correct decryption is required by the reporter, the reporter can produce a proof that indicates which reporter decrypted the token, which would decrease the computation costs incurred by the reporter. However, we opt to provide a construction that meets a strong security model, ensuring that reporters can produce reports without the concern of their identity being leaked.

4   Extending R&T to Multiple Reporters

In our construction, we assume that the reporter and tracer do not collude and, hence, if a reported message is not malicious, the tracer does not reveal the identity of the signer. We can further mitigate against a malicious reporter by requiring that the tracer receive *multiple* reports to trigger the tracing process. We describe an extension of our construction to multiple reporters that requires a (t, n)-publicly verifiable secret sharing scheme PVSS = (SS.Gen, SS.Verify, SS.Combine), with syntax drawn from [23], where $n = |R|$ is the size of the ring and t is the number of shares required to reconstruct the secret. The PVSS scheme is used to generate $|R|$ shares of the reporter token, i.e., reporter token $s = (s_1, \ldots, s_{|R|})$. Each share is encrypted under a ring member's public key for a PKE scheme, rather than encrypting a single reporter token to all members of the ring. This extension requires minimal changes to our construction, which we outline here.

$\mathsf{Sign}(pp, sk_U, pk_T, m, R)$

---

parse pp as $(pp_{\mathsf{PKE}}, pp_{\mathsf{NIZK}}, pp_{\mathsf{SOK}}) \land sk_U$ as $(sk_{\mathsf{RS}}, sk_{\mathsf{PKE}})$

$\land R$ as $\{(pk_{\mathsf{RS}_1}, pk_{\mathsf{PKE}_1}), \ldots, (pk_{\mathsf{RS}_{|R|}}, pk_{\mathsf{PKE}_{|R|}})\}$

$pk \leftarrow f(sk_{\mathsf{RS}}); \quad s \leftarrow SK; \quad r_{1,1}, \ldots, r_{1,|R|}, r_2, r_3 \leftarrow \mathsf{Rand}$

$(\{s_1, \ldots, s_{|R|}\}, \{S_1, \ldots, S_{|R|}\}, S) \leftarrow \mathsf{SS.Gen}(s, t, |R|)$

for $i = 1, \ldots, |R|$

  $c_{1,i} \leftarrow \mathsf{PKE.Enc}(pp_{\mathsf{PKE}}, pk_{\mathsf{PKE}_i}, s_i; r_{1,i})$

  $\rho_i \leftarrow \mathsf{NIZK.Prove}(pp, (S_i, pk_{\mathsf{PKE}_i}, c_{1,i}), (r_{1,i}, s_i)); \quad \mathsf{Share}_i \leftarrow (S_i, c_{1,i}, \rho_{1,i})$

$c_2 \leftarrow \mathsf{PKE.Enc}(pp_{\mathsf{PKE}}, pk_T, pk; r_2); \quad c_3 \leftarrow \mathsf{PKE.Enc}(pp_{\mathsf{PKE}}, S, c_2; r_3)$

$\sigma_{\mathsf{SOK}} \leftarrow \mathsf{SoK.Sign}(pp, (pk_T, S, R, c_3), (r_2, r_3, sk_{\mathsf{RS}}), m)$

return $\sigma = (S, (\mathsf{Share}_1, \ldots, \mathsf{Share}_{|R|}), c_3, \sigma_{\mathsf{SOK}})$

Fig. 3. Algorithm Sign for our construction with multiple reporters.

To sign a message, the signer uses the PVSS scheme to produce $|R|$ reporter sub-tokens. Each sub-token s_i is encrypted under the public key of a ring member and accompanied with a NIZK proof of correct encryption and a public version of the sub-token, S_i. For clarity, we outline the changes to the signing algorithm in Fig. 3. As before, our construction provides public verification algorithm Verify, which additionally requires that the verifier run algorithm SS.Verify to verify the secret sharing operations. A ring member reports a message by decrypting their sub-token and sending the sub-token to the tracer, accompanied with a proof of correct decryption. Once the tracer has received a threshold number of sub-tokens, the tracer runs algorithm SS.Combine to recover the reporter token, then decrypts the signer's identity as per the original construction.

Anonymity of Reporters. In our multiple reporter construction, each reporter produces a unique sub-token, and public versions of each sub-token are published to verify correctness of the PVSS scheme. In this way, when a reporter produces a report, i.e., their sub-token, anyone can check which share (denoted Share) this belongs to. Thus, it is possible to determine the reporter's identity. For this reason, reporter sub-tokens should be treated carefully by the tracer *before* tracing. That is, the sub-tokens should not be revealed by the tracer until tracing is completed. In this way, the identities of reporters are known to the tracer before tracing but are not made public until after tracing.

Efficiency of Multiple Reporters. Our construction with multiple reporters is less efficient than our generic construction with a single reporter, where the communication and computation costs are outlined in Table 2. Specifically, producing a signature requires the additional computation and communication of $|R|$ reporter sub-tokens, and the computation and communication costs of the tracer grow linearly in the size of the threshold. Moreover, the computation costs associated with signature and trace verification grow linearly in the size of the ring and threshold, respectively. However, these costs can be minimised. In particular, secret share generation and combination, for efficient PVSS schemes (e.g., [23]), simply requires the computation of group exponentiations and the addition of field elements respectively [23]. Additionally, the NIZK proofs associated with these extra costs can be instantiated with efficient primitives, as in our single reporter construction. That being said, we note that the size and computation costs of a report are identical to our single reporter construction, consisting of a single reporter sub-token, and requiring a single decryption of a PKE ciphertext.

5   Conclusion

We introduced and defined report and trace ring signatures, and presented an accompanying security model. We presented an R&T ring signature construction that satisfies our security model, and extended our construction to the multiple reporter setting. Additionally, we provided an instantiation of our single reporter construction and compared its efficiency with accountable ring signatures [6], demonstrating the additional costs associated with our report and trace functionality, and showing that our proposed instantiation is practical. Though our construction can be efficiently instantiated, the costs incurred by the signer and the verifier grow linearly in the size of the ring. An interesting area of future research is to define an efficient, yet (efficiently) verifiable, broadcast encryption scheme that can be used to instantiate our construction. Moreover, our multiple reporter setting could be formalised by extending our existing security model to capture multiple reporters.

References

1. Arun, V., Kate, A., Garg, D., Druschel, P., Bhattacharjee, B.: Finding safety in numbers with secure allegation escrows. In: NDSS'20. Internet Society (2020)
2. Bellare, M., Micciancio, D., Warinschi, B.: Foundations of group signatures: formal definitions, simplified requirements, and a construction based on general assumptions. In: Biham, E. (ed.) EUROCRYPT 2003. LNCS, vol. 2656, pp. 614–629. Springer, Heidelberg (2003). https://doi.org/10.1007/3-540-39200-9_38
3. Bellare, M., Shi, H., Zhang, C.: Foundations of group signatures: the case of dynamic groups. In: Menezes, A. (ed.) CT-RSA 2005. LNCS, vol. 3376, pp. 136–153. Springer, Heidelberg (2005). https://doi.org/10.1007/978-3-540-30574-3_11
4. Bender, A., Katz, J., Morselli, R.: Ring signatures: stronger definitions, and constructions without random oracles. In: Halevi, S., Rabin, T. (eds.) TCC 2006. LNCS, vol. 3876, pp. 60–79. Springer, Heidelberg (2006). https://doi.org/10.1007/11681878_4
5. Boneh, D., Gentry, C., Waters, B.: Collusion resistant broadcast encryption with short ciphertexts and private keys. In: Shoup, V. (ed.) CRYPTO 2005. LNCS, vol. 3621, pp. 258–275. Springer, Heidelberg (2005). https://doi.org/10.1007/11535218_16
6. Bootle, J., Cerulli, A., Chaidos, P., Ghadafi, E., Groth, J., Petit, C.: Short accountable ring signatures based on DDH. In: Pernul, G., Ryan, P.Y.A., Weippl, E. (eds.) ESORICS 2015. LNCS, vol. 9326, pp. 243–265. Springer, Cham (2015). https://doi.org/10.1007/978-3-319-24174-6_13

7. Camenisch, J., Stadler, M.: Efficient group signature schemes for large groups. In: Kaliski, B.S. (ed.) CRYPTO 1997. LNCS, vol. 1294, pp. 410–424. Springer, Heidelberg (1997). https://doi.org/10.1007/BFb0052252

8. Chaum, D., van Heyst, E.: Group signatures. In: Davies, D.W. (ed.) EUROCRYPT 1991. LNCS, vol. 547, pp. 257–265. Springer, Heidelberg (1991). https://doi.org/10.1007/3-540-46416-6_22

9. Fiat, A., Naor, M.: Broadcast encryption. In: Stinson, D.R. (ed.) CRYPTO 1993. LNCS, vol. 773, pp. 480–491. Springer, Heidelberg (1994). https://doi.org/10.1007/3-540-48329-2_40

10. Fiat, A., Shamir, A.: How To prove yourself: practical solutions to identification and signature problems. In: Odlyzko, A.M. (ed.) CRYPTO 1986. LNCS, vol. 263, pp. 186–194. Springer, Heidelberg (1987). https://doi.org/10.1007/3-540-47721-7_12

11. Fraser, A., Quaglia, E.A.: Report and trace ring signatures. In: IACR ePrint Archive Report (2021)

12. Fujisaki, E., Suzuki, K.: Traceable ring signature. In: Okamoto, T., Wang, X. (eds.) PKC 2007. LNCS, vol. 4450, pp. 181–200. Springer, Heidelberg (2007). https://doi.org/10.1007/978-3-540-71677-8_13

13. Goldwasser, S., Micali, S.: Probabilistic encryption. J. Comput. Syst. Sci. **28**(2), 270–299 (1984)

14. Groth, J., Ostrovsky, R., Sahai, A.: Perfect non-interactive zero knowledge for NP. In: Vaudenay, S. (ed.) EUROCRYPT 2006. LNCS, vol. 4004, pp. 339–358. Springer, Heidelberg (2006). https://doi.org/10.1007/11761679_21

15. Kiayias, A., Tsiounis, Y., Yung, M.: Traceable signatures. In: Cachin, C., Camenisch, J.L. (eds.) EUROCRYPT 2004. LNCS, vol. 3027, pp. 571–589. Springer, Heidelberg (2004). https://doi.org/10.1007/978-3-540-24676-3_34

16. Kohlweiss, M., Miers, I.: Accountable metadata-hiding escrow: a group signature case study. PoPETs **2015**(2), 206–221 (2015)

17. Kuykendall, B., Krawczyk, H., Rabin, T.: Cryptography for #metoo. PoPETs **2019**(3), 409–429 (2019)

18. Liu, J.K., Wei, V.K., Wong, D.S.: Linkable spontaneous anonymous group signature for ad hoc groups. In: Wang, H., Pieprzyk, J., Varadharajan, V. (eds.) ACISP 2004. LNCS, vol. 3108, pp. 325–335. Springer, Heidelberg (2004). https://doi.org/10.1007/978-3-540-27800-9_28

19. Phan, D.-H., Pointcheval, D., Shahandashti, S.F., Strefler, M.: Adaptive CCA broadcast encryption with constant-size secret keys and ciphertexts. Int. J. Inf. Secur. **12**(4), 251–265 (2013)

20. Rajan, A., Qin, L., Archer, D.W., Boneh, D., Lepoint, T., Varia, M.: Callisto: a cryptographic approach to detecting serial perpetrators of sexual misconduct. In: COMPASS'18, pp. 1–4. Association for Computing Machinery (2018)

21. Rivest, R.L., Shamir, A., Tauman, Y.: How to leak a secret. In: Boyd, C. (ed.) ASIACRYPT 2001. LNCS, vol. 2248, pp. 552–565. Springer, Heidelberg (2001). https://doi.org/10.1007/3-540-45682-1_32

22. Sakai, Y., Emura, K., Hanaoka, G., Kawai, Y., Matsuda, T., Omote, K.: Group signatures with message-dependent opening. In: Abdalla, M., Lange, T. (eds.) Pairing 2012. LNCS, vol. 7708, pp. 270–294. Springer, Heidelberg (2013). https://doi.org/10.1007/978-3-642-36334-4_18

23. Stadler, M.: Publicly verifiable secret sharing. In: Maurer, U. (ed.) EUROCRYPT 1996. LNCS, vol. 1070, pp. 190–199. Springer, Heidelberg (1996). https://doi.org/10.1007/3-540-68339-9_17

24. Tyagi, N., Miers, I., Ristenpart, T.: Traceback for end-to-end encrypted messaging. In: CCS'19, pp. 413–430. Association for Computing Machinery (2019)

25. Wang, L., Zhang, G., Ma, C.: A survey of ring signature. Front. Electric. Electron. Eng. China **3**(1), 10–19 (2008)
26. Xu, S., Yung, M.: Accountable ring signatures: a smart card approach. In: Quisquater, J.-J., Paradinas, P., Deswarte, Y., El Kalam, A.A. (eds.) CARDIS 2004. IIFIP, vol. 153, pp. 271–286. Springer, Boston, MA (2004). https://doi.org/10.1007/1-4020-8147-2_18

Selectively Linkable Group Signatures—Stronger Security and Preserved Verifiability

Ashley Fraser[1], Lydia Garms[2,3](✉), and Anja Lehmann[4]

[1] University of Surrey, Guildford, UK
a.fraser@surrey.ac.uk
[2] Royal Holloway, University of London, Egham, UK
[3] IMDEA Software Institute, Madrid, Spain
lydia.garms@imdea.org
[4] Hasso-Plattner-Institute, University of Potsdam, Potsdam, Germany
anja.lehmann@hpi.de

Abstract. Group signatures allow group members to sign on behalf of the group anonymously. They are therefore well suited to storing data in a way that preserves the users' privacy, while guaranteeing its authenticity. Garms and Lehmann (PKC'19) introduced a new type of group signatures that balance privacy with utility by allowing to selectively link subsets of the group signatures via an oblivious entity, the converter. The conversion takes a batch of group signatures and blindly transforms signatures originating from the same user into a consistent representation. Their scheme essentially targets a setting where the entity receiving fully unlinkable signatures and the converted ones is the same: only pseudonyms but not full signatures are converted, and the input to the converter is assumed to be well-formed. Thus, the converted outputs are merely linkable pseudonyms but no longer signatures.

In this work we extend and strengthen such convertibly linkable group signatures. Conversion can now be triggered by malicious entities too, and the converted outputs can be publicly verified. This preserves the authentication of data during the conversion process. We define the security of this scheme and give a provably secure instantiation. Our scheme makes use of controlled-malleable NIZKs, which allow proofs to be mauled in a controlled manner. This allows signatures to be blinded, while still ensuring they can be verified during conversions.

A. Fraser—The author was supported by the EPSRC Next Stage Digital Economy Centre in the Decentralised Digital Economy (DECaDE) under grant number EP/T022485/1.

L. Garms—The author was supported by the EPSRC and the UK government as part of the Centre for Doctoral Training in Cyber Security at Royal Holloway, University of London (EP/K035584/1) and by the InnovateUK funded project AQuaSec, as well as by a research grant from Nomadic Labs and the Tezos Foundation.

M. Conti et al. (Eds.): CANS 2021, LNCS 13099, pp. 200–221, 2021.
https://doi.org/10.1007/978-3-030-92548-2_11

1   Introduction

Group signatures allow members of a group to sign messages anonymously [4, 7,8,13,18,30,37]. A valid group signature attests that it was signed by a group member, without revealing the signer's identity, or whether signatures stem from the same user. They are therefore useful when data is collected that should be authenticated while preserving the privacy of the data sources. However, full anonymity might be undesirable. It may be necessary to know the correlation among *some* data events. For instance, several high value blood pressure measurements might not be critical unless they originate from a single user.

To address the balance between privacy and utility, several linkability mechanisms have been introduced. Standard group signatures [4,5,7,8,18,37] have an opening mechanism, that allows a trusted opener to de-anonymise signatures. Less privacy invasive forms exist, where the opener no longer fully de-anonymises users, but merely tests whether two signatures stem from the same one [20,32–34,40]. Another line of work avoids the trusted entity for opening and rather supports *pseudonymous* group signatures where users can choose to sign either with a fresh, and unlinkable pseudonym or re-use an established one, making all signatures under the same pseudonym publicly linkable [6,9–11,14,23,24].

Group Signatures with Selective Linkability. Garms and Lehmann [28] argue that none of these schemes provides the flexibility and privacy needed in practice, as they either require the user to decide upon the desired linkability when signatures are computed, or the usage of the linkability gradually erodes the users' privacy.

To overcome these limitations, they proposed a more flexible variant of linkability in the form of the CLS scheme [28]. While all group signatures therein are fully unlinkable per default, i.e. each pseudonym is fresh, certain subsets can be converted into a linked representation. The conversion is performed obliviously by a trusted converter that blindly transforms a batch of pseudonyms, mapping different pseudonyms stemming from the same user into the same one. To avoid the erosion of privacy, due to a user's signatures gradually being linked together as a result of successive convert queries, converted pseudonyms obtained through *different* queries remain unlinkable, i.e., conversions are strictly non-transitive.

Trusted Data Lakes and Data Processors. However, [28] assumes the party receiving/verifying fully unlinkable signatures (the data lake) and the one obtaining the converted linked ones (the data processor) to be the same entity, or belong to the same trust domain. In their scheme the data lake only inputs pseudonyms to the converter but not the actual signatures, the authenticity of data gets lost in the conversion process. Therefore, a data processor only receives converted pseudonyms from the converter and must trust the data lake that converted data originates from actual user data. It also assumes inputs from the data lake to the converter to be well-formed. The security guarantees only hold when "valid" pseudonyms are converted for which correct group signatures exist. As the converter in [28] receives *blinded* pseudonyms and no signatures, this assumption is impossible to enforce other than by considering honest requests only.

For many applications, this assumption may not be realisable and security from a malicious data lake is vital. For example, in the US the Regional Health Information Organization (a data processor) has the role of integrating the medical records of many hospitals. In practise, this data is often stored by a third party (a data lake) that is not trusted by the hospitals or research organisations that process the data [19]. As discussed above, correlation of data by user can provide additional insights to the data processor in terms of medical analysis. However, to protect the user's privacy, correlated data should not be revealed to the data lake. Additionally, the data processor will want assurances that the data processed is authentic user data. Also, Google (a data lake) has been collecting anonymised location data during the COVID-19 pandemic to monitor social distancing [1]. In this case the correlation of data by user is valuable for analysis, such as to gain insights into how behaviour changes based on restrictions. However, this comes with a threat to the user's privacy. Ideally, data should be stored anonymously to preserve the users' privacy, but data processors, such as a governmental public health organisation, might be allowed to request to blindly link the data, for example, to provide insight into distances travelled which is only possible if data is correlated by user. Such data processors may not fully trust Google as a data lake. Therefore, the data processor may want assurance that security and privacy holds even if the data lake acts maliciously.

Our Contributions. In this work we strengthen the concept of convertibly linkable group signatures (CLS+) to capture the scenario that the data lake and data processor do not belong to the same trust domain. That is, we guarantee the desired security even when conversion is triggered by malicious data lakes. Further, we leverage the trusted converter to not only blindly transform the pseudonyms but also blindly re-authenticate the associated messages, preserving the authenticity of the data during conversions. We start by lifting the security and privacy definition given in [28] to this stronger setting. Our security model grants the adversary the power to request conversions of arbitrary and blinded inputs. We propose a construction that provably satisfies the desired properties.

Our CLS+ Construction. In the CLS+ model, an issuer joins users to the group. A data lake holds a set of users' (message, pseudonym, signature) tuples. They blind a subset of these to the converter for conversion with respect to the intended data processor's public key. The resulting *converted* (message, pseudonym, signature) tuples are output to the data processor for unblinding. After unblinding the pseudonyms should be consistent, i.e. pseudonyms from the same conversion and from the same user should be the same. As conversions should be non-transitive, pseudonyms should be unlinkable by user across conversion queries.

A user's and issuer's key pair is that of an automorphic signature scheme [26], a structure–preserving signature scheme [2] where the verification keys lie within the message space. When joining the group, the issuer signs the user's verification key, yielding the user's membership credential. During signing, the user encrypts its verification key under an encryption public key held by the converter to form the pseudonym, and proves knowledge of a valid automorphic signature on the message with respect to this verification key, and of a valid credential for this key. In order to blind signatures yet still allow verification during conversions, we use zero-knowledge proofs (NIZKs) that are controlled malleable [16], which can be realised with Groth-Sahai proofs [31]. This allows to encrypt the pseudonym and message under an encryption public key held by the data processor (the blinding public key), and transform the proof accordingly. Because the malleability is controlled, this does not affect the unforgeability of the signatures.

The converter then removes the layer of encryption under the converter's encryption public key. The resulting pseudonym is re-randomised under the blinding public key and then transformed under a random value r. This value is chosen fresh for every conversion query to ensure non-transitive conversions, but re-used within this query to ensure the resulting pseudonyms are consistent. The converter signs the converted pseudonym and message to attest that they originate from a valid query containing verifiable signatures. As we assume the converter is at most honest-but-curious, the authentication of converted signatures is carried over from that of the blinded signatures. During unblinding, the data processor decrypts the message and converted pseudonym under the blinding secret key. The original output of the converter is included in the signature, along with a proof of correct unblinding. We prove that our construction is secure, assuming the security of the automorphic signatures, standard digital signatures and the controlled malleable NIZKs, as well as the SXDH assumption.

Other Related Work. In [35] group signatures can be converted into standard signatures, but all of a user's signatures are de-anonymised. In [36,38], the power of the opener is reduced. In [36], they avoid the need for an opener, by allowing users to prove or deny authorship of a signature. The opener can also prove that two signatures originate from the same user without revealing user identities. In [38], another entity is introduced, the admitter. They have the power to specify messages, so that only signatures on those messages can be opened.

2   Syntax and Security Model for CLS+

We define the syntax and security model for CLS+ signatures, an extension of the CLS model [28] that no longer requires the assumption that conversion of signatures is triggered by *honest* verifiers. Whereas CLS only converts pseudonyms, our CLS+ scheme preserves the validity of the associated signatures.

As in CLS, our CLS+ scheme assumes an issuer $\mathcal{I}$, a set of users $\mathcal{U} = \{uid_i\}$, and a converter $\mathcal{C}$. The issuer $\mathcal{I}$ joins new users to the group, who can sign pseudonymously. While signatures are fully unlinkable by default, they can be linked in a controlled manner by the converter $\mathcal{C}$, who blindly converts pseudonym-message-signature tuples into a consistent (now) authenticated form.

In contrast to CLS, we split the verifier role into a data lake $\mathcal{L}$ and data processor $\mathcal{P}$. The data lake (or *any* verifier) can collect and verify the unlinkable signatures w.r.t the group's public key. Additionally, the data lake can request conversions by blinding signatures for a particular data processor $\mathcal{P}$ in a conversion request to the converter. The data processor can **unblind** and verify the converted signatures output by the converter. Once unblinded, *any* verifier can check the validity of the converted signature. In this way, we capture the setting where a data processor (in a separate trust domain from the data lake) can verify converted group signatures, whereas, CLS assumed that unlinkable and converted signatures are used by the same entity (or within the same trust domain). Any verifier can take the data lake role, as there are no dedicated keys.

2.1 Syntax of CLS+

We closely follow the notation from the framework for CLS [28], but extend the blinding, conversion and unblinding procedures to transform signatures, as well as pseudonyms. Verification is extended to also handle transformed and linkable signatures. More precisely, a convertibly linkable group signature scheme with preserved verifiability CLS+ consists of the following algorithms:

Setup and Key Generation. Each central entity generates their individual key pair.

CLS+.Setup$(1^\tau) \rightarrow$ pp: on input a security parameter, outputs the public parameters pp.

CLS+.IKGen(pp) $\rightarrow (ipk, isk)$: performed by the issuer $\mathcal{I}$, outputs the issuer secret key isk, and the issuer public key ipk.

CLS+.CKGen(pp) $\rightarrow (cpk, csk)$: performed by the converter $\mathcal{C}$, outputs the converter secret key csk, and the converter public key cpk.

CLS+.BKGen(pp) $\rightarrow (bpk, bsk)$: performed by the data processor $\mathcal{P}$, outputs the blinding public key bpk and blinding private key bsk.

We write the group public key gpk to refer to (pp, ipk, cpk) and $\mathcal{BK}$ to denote the public/private key space induced by CLS+.BKGen.

Join, Sign and Verify. A user must join the group via an interactive protocol with the issuer, as is standard in group signatures [5]. Our construction requires that the user already specifies the data processor's key bpk when creating signatures, and thus we reflect this in the syntax. While this limits the flexibility of the data lake (it has to adhere to the choice of the user) it gives the users strong control over the usage of their data, as only they can choose who can unblind the converted (linkable) signatures. Signers still do not need to decide which data should be linked, but only which data processors they trust to process their data.

CLS+.Verify takes as input $type = \{\texttt{tier-1}, \texttt{tier-2}\}$ that indicates the type of signature. We denote standard, fully unlinkable signatures produced by CLS+.Sign as tier-1 signatures, and converted ones (from processing a tier-1 signature with CLS+.Blind − CLS+.Convert − CLS+.Unblind introduced below) as tier-2 signatures.

$\langle$CLS+.Join(gpk), CLS+.Issue$(isk, gpk)\rangle$: an interactive protocol performed by the joining user uid and the issuer $\mathcal{I}$, who perform CLS+.Join and CLS+.Issue respectively. If successful, CLS+.Join outputs $\mathbf{gsk}[uid]$. During the protocol, each algorithm inputs a state and an incoming message, and outputs an updated state, an outgoing message, and a decision cont/accept/reject.

CLS+.Sign$(gpk, bpk, \mathbf{gsk}[uid], m) \rightarrow (\mu, \sigma)$: performed by user uid for a data processor with key bpk, outputs pseudonym μ and signature σ. For ease of expression we treat the pseudonym μ as a dedicated part of the signature.

CLS+.Verify$(type, gpk, bpk, m, \mu, \sigma) \rightarrow \{0, 1\}$: performed by the data lake (or any verifier), outputs 1 if σ is a valid $\{\texttt{tier-1}, \texttt{tier-2}\}$-signature.

Blind Conversion. As in the CLS model, to allow for blind conversions of signatures, there are the CLS+.Blind, CLS+.Convert and CLS+.Unblind algorithms for the data lake, converter and data processor respectively. The CLS+.Convert algorithm, on input blinded unlinkable pseudonyms, outputs converted pseudonyms that after unblinding are identical when from the same user. Now, all three of these algorithms are extended to handle the signatures as inputs and outputs.

CLS+.Blind$(gpk, bpk, (\mu, \sigma, m)) \rightarrow (c\mu, c\sigma, c)$: performed by the data lake, outputs a blinded pseudonym, signature and message.

CLS+.Convert$(gpk, bpk, csk, \{(c\mu_i, c\sigma_i, c_i)\}_k) \rightarrow \{(\overline{c\mu}_i, \overline{c\sigma}_i, \overline{c}_i)\}_k$: performed by the converter, on input k blinded tuples, outputs k converted tuples.

CLS+.Unblind$(bsk, (\overline{c\mu}, \overline{c\sigma}, \overline{c})) \rightarrow (\overline{\mu}, \overline{\sigma}, m)$: performed by the data processor, outputs an unblinded, converted (tier-2) tuple.

2.2 Security Properties of CLS+

We need the CLS+ model to capture (roughly) the same security properties as the CLS model, without the assumption that conversion is triggered by honest parties and such that converted data is verifiable. We describe the properties that CLS+ schemes must satisfy in the table below. The first three constitute the privacy related properties and the final three constitute the unforgeability properties. We no longer include the *join anonymity* requirement from the CLS model, which ensures the corrupted issuer and converter cannot trace signatures to a user's join session. As the converter is corrupted, this requirement only offers weak privacy guarantees, and so we believe this requirement is less important than the positives of a simple modular construction. In all experiments the key generation stage is performed honestly, as standard for group signatures [5].

Our CLS+ schemes still rely on the converter being honest-but-curious. We believe this is an acceptable assumption in practice, as the converter is a central entity that can undergo more scrutiny than the many verifiers and data lakes. In Sect. 6 of the full version [25], we discuss how our work could be adapted to achieve security with respect to a fully malicious converter.

Requirement	Corrupted entities	Overview
Anonymity	Issuer, Data Lake, Data Processor	Group signatures which have not been linked through a conversion request should not leak any information about the signer's identity
Non-transitivity	Issuer, Data Lake, Data Processor	While conversion guarantees linkability *within* a batch of converted signatures, the data processor(s) should not be able to link the outputs of *different* convert queries
Conversion blindness	Issuer, Converter, Data Lake	The converter should learn no information about the blinded messages and pseudonyms that are input to a conversion
Traceability	Converter, Data Lake, Data Processor	An adversary should not be able to create more (blinded) tier-1 signatures that remain unlinkable in an (honest) conversion than they control corrupt users. We show in the full version [25] this implies the same for tier-1 signatures that are not blinded
Conversion unforgeability	Issuer, Data Lake, Data Processor	All valid tier-2 signatures should originate from an honest conversion
Non-frameability	Issuer, Converter, Data Lake, Data Processor	An adversary should not be able to output a (blinded) tier-1 signature that would be linked to the signature of an honest user. We show in the full version [25] this implies the same for tier-1 signatures that are not blinded

Oracles and State. As in the CLS model, our security requirements make use of oracles which keep joint state. We follow the notation of [4,5] and give the adversary oracle access to honest users, the issuer and the converter (depending on the corruption setting in each game). All oracles have access to the following maintained as global state: a list HUL of *uid*s of honest users, a list CUL of *uid*s of corrupt users (where the issuer is honest), a list SL of requests to the SIGN oracle, and a list UBL containing inputs to the CONVERT oracle and the corresponding unblinded, converted pseudonyms/messages. We provide an overview of all oracles below.

ADDU (join of honest user & honest issuer) Creates an honest user *uid*, by internally running a join protocol between the honest user and honest issuer. As a result, the oracle stores the secret key **gsk**[*uid*] for later use.

SNDU (Send to User) (join of honest user & corrupt issuer) Creates an honest user *uid*, by running the join protocol on behalf of the honest user with the corrupt issuer. If the join session is successful, the oracle stores the user's secret key **gsk**[*uid*] for later use.

SNDI (Send to Issuer) (join of corrupt user & honest issuer) Creates a corrupt user *uid*, by running the join protocol on behalf of the honest issuer with the corrupt user.

SIGN Outputs signatures on behalf of honest users that have successfully joined (via ADDU or SNDU, depending on whether the issuer is corrupt).

CONVERT The oracle returns a set of converted signatures. In the CLS+ model, the CONVERT oracle is input blinded pseudonym, signature, message tuples instead of tier-1 tuples that must be verified and honestly blinded in the oracle. This is because we no longer assume honest inputs from the data verifier. The adversary must input the blinding secret key, which is necessary for our privacy-related security notions, e.g., to ensure that the adversary does not input a re-randomisation of the challenge signature.

Aside from the CONVERT oracle, the oracles are minor adaptations of the oracles in the CLS model. The full description is deferred to the full version [25].

Helper Algorithms. In the CLS model, helper algorithms allow for notational simplicity when defining security. Indeed, the algorithms Identify and UnLink respectively test whether a signature originated from a particular user secret key and determine whether signatures would be linked upon conversion. We adapt the helper algorithms for the CLS+ model. These now take as input signatures, because they make use of CLS+.Convert. Identify tests whether a blinded signature belongs to a certain user *uid*, by creating a second signature for $\mathbf{gsk}[uid]$ and using the converter's secret key to test whether both signatures are linked. This algorithm uses our second helper algorithm UnLink internally, which takes a list of blinded pseudonym-message-signatures pairs and returns 1 only if they are all unlinkable after being converted and unblinded. The tier-2 signatures output as a result of the linking are also now verified. Full details are given in the full version [25].

Adapting Our Unforgeability Requirements to the CLS+ Setting. As well as tier-1 signatures, we now must ensure our unforgeability guarantees for tier-2 signatures, as well as signatures input to and output from conversions. We introduce conversion unforgeability, a new security property that ensures all valid tier-2 signatures stem from an honest conversion. In doing so, our unforgeability guarantees carry over to tier-2 signatures, under the assumption of an honest-but-curious converter. Moreover, in the CLS traceability and non-frameability requirements, the adversary outputs tier-1 signatures, which are then verified and blinded honestly. We update these requirements for the CLS+ setting, so that *blinded* tier-1 signatures are output by the adversary. In the case that conversions are honest, the traceability and non-frameability guarantees carry through to tier-2 signatures. When the converter is corrupted no unforgeability guarantees hold for tier-2 signatures anyway.

We need to ensure that our traceability and non-frameability requirements ensure the CLS definitions, meaning that our unforgeability guarantees hold for tier-1 signatures. In the full version of this paper [25], we give reductions that show this is the case. For traceability, we show that if an adversary can output more valid tier-1 signatures that are unlinkable after conversion than they control corrupt users then, by blinding these tier-1 signatures, we can win in our CLS+ traceability game. For non-frameability, we show that if an adversary can output a tier-1 signature that links to that of an honest user in a conversion then, by blinding this signature, we can win in our CLS+ non-frameability game.

To make several of our requirements realisable, we require that the adversary outputs the blinding secret key. We do this for notational simplicity, but alternatively we could add a mechanism for the *bsk* to be extracted from the *bpk*. Due to the fact that the adversary outputs blinded tier-1 signatures in our traceability and non-frameability requirements, this is necessary to determine whether signatures are linked. Even if the adversary was to output tier-2 signatures, then the blinding secret key would still be necessary to enforce that the tier-2 signatures originate from an honest conversion.

Correctness and Consistency. As in CLS, correctness consists of *correctness of sign*, which ensures that signatures generated honestly will be valid, and *correctness of conversion*, which ensures that honest blinding, conversion and unblinding will result in valid and consistent messages, pseudonyms and signatures.

As in CLS, we require *consistency*, which for CLS+ we relabel *consistency of linking*. This ensures that linking is consistent across multiple convert queries, i.e. if after conversion $c\mu_1$ and $c\mu_2$ are linked, and after conversion $c\mu_2$ and $c\mu_3$ are linked, then $c\mu_1$ and $c\mu_3$ are also linked after conversion. We additionally introduce *consistency of verification*. This is necessary as the verifiability of signatures is now preserved throughout the conversion process. This requirement ensures that a set of valid tier-1 signatures will result in valid tier-2 signatures for the same set of messages after blinding, conversion and unblinding.

We give the full correctness and consistency definitions in the full version [25].

We now provide an overview of all CLS+ security requirements. We present these in full in the full version [25].

Anonymity. This requirement ensures that an adversary that has corrupted the issuer, data lake and data processor, while the converter remains honest, cannot link an honest user's signatures or trace them to their join session. The adversary outputs two honest users uid_0^* and uid_1^*, a message m^*, and a blinding public key bpk^* (as this is fixed in signing), and must guess which user authored the resulting tier-1 signature.

The adversary has access to the SNDU and SIGN oracles to create honest users and obtain their signatures, as well as the CONVERT oracle. The CLS notion assumed the data lake to be honest, and so the conversion oracle only took unblinded tuples as input, allowing the oracle to check the validity of the input, before blinding and converting them. The adversary was prevented from submitting the challenge signature along with a signature authored by user uid_0^* or uid_1^*, which would allow them to trivially win.

Here we enable the data lake to ask for the conversion of blinded tuples. To prevent trivial wins, we still must be able to detect whether the adversary tries to convert the challenge signature. As signatures will be re-randomisable to satisfy non-transitivity, we opt for an RCCA-style of definition [15]. The CONVERT oracle checks whether any of the blinded signature-tuples would link via Identify to either of the challenge users and match the challenge message m^*. To do so, we require the adversary to input the blinding *secret* key to the oracle. This key is used to check whether the inputs can be traced to a challenge user, but there are no checks that enforce that the inputs are well-formed.

As in CLS, our privacy related requirements do not yield forward anonymity, because the secret keys of honest users cannot be corrupted. It seems difficult to achieve this whilst also ensuring the non-transitivity of conversions [28].

Non-transitivity. Non-transitivity ensures that the outputs of separate convert queries cannot be linked together across multiple queries, further than what is already possible due to the messages queried. Otherwise, data processor(s) could gradually re-recover the linkability among all signatures. This must hold when the issuer, data lake and processor can be fully corrupt.

As in the CLS model, our non-transitivity definition follows a simulation-based approach, where the adversary must distinguish between the real and ideal world. As the issuer is corrupted, the adversary has access to the SNDU and SIGN oracles for honest users. In the real world, the adversary interacts with the CONVERT oracle, which converts the blinded message-pseudonym-signature tuples that are input. In the ideal world, they interact with the CONVSIM oracle which, for inputs that originate from honest users, uses a simulator SIM that outputs converted pseudonyms/signatures. SIM only learns which blinded messages belong to the same honest users, without learning the pseudonyms/signatures input. As in CLS, the CONVSIM oracle generates converted pseudonyms/signatures for corrupt users normally via CLS+.Convert.

In contrast to the original CLS model, we now allow the data lake to trigger conversions on *blinded* inputs. Similarly to the anonymity game, the adversary must also input the blinding (secret) key with each query to the conversion oracle. Here the key is used to internally unblind the inputs and determine the correlation among the signatures. This is necessary to obtain a security definition that is realisable, as the CONVSIM oracle is still expected to provide consistently transformed outputs *within* a query. Further, the ideal CONVSIM oracle first internally runs the real conversion algorithm and aborts if it fails. This is again necessary to avoid trivial wins where the adversary might input malformed tuples—which the simulator never gets and thus cannot verify.

Conversion Blindness. In the original CLS model, conversion blindness ensures that the converter learns nothing about the pseudonyms and messages it converts. In the CLS+ model, the converter now receives and outputs signatures, which must also be converted obliviously. This must hold when all the entities, except for the data processor, can be fully corrupt. The adversary outputs two pseudonym-message-signature tuples and receives a blinded version of one of them. They must guess which tuple was blinded. We must ensure the adversary's outputs are valid to avoid trivial wins. In the CLS model, no oracles are required because blinding is a public-key operation. However, CLS+.Unblind now outputs a tier-2 signature, and so we must ensure that this does not leak anything that might allow for the unblinding of other converted signatures. We therefore give the adversary access to an UNBLIND oracle that blinds, converts and unblinds signatures. We stress that this requirement only provides CPA–level security as in CLS, because the oracle both blinds and unblinds signatures.

Conversion Unforgeability. As converted data is authenticated in the CLS+ model, we introduce the conversion unforgeability requirement. This ensures that all valid tier-2 signatures originate from an honest conversion when all entities other than the converter are corrupt. This carries over the traceability and non-frameability guarantees for blinded tier-1 signatures, ensuring that both properties hold for tier-2 signatures, provided the converter remains honest-but-curious.

We do not differentiate between honest and corrupt users in this requirement, so the adversary only has access to the CONVERT oracle. The adversary must output a valid tier-2 signature that does not originate from the CONVERT oracle. In order to check whether the tier-2 signature output by the adversary stems from an honest conversion, the adversary must input the blinding secret key to the conversion oracle. The oracle can then unblind all converted outputs and store tier-2 pseudonyms/messages in the UBL list, to compare with the adversary's output.

Traceability. This requirement formalises that an adversary cannot output more unlinkable signatures that the number of corrupted users, when the issuer is honest but the converter, data lake, data processor and some users are corrupt.

As the issuer is honest, the adversary has access to the ADDU and SNDI oracles to create honest and corrupt users respectively, and the SIGN oracle. To lift the CLS traceability notion to the setting where malicious parties can trigger conversions, the adversary outputs a list of *blinded* signatures. As we still assume the converter to be honest-but-curious, the signatures are then *honestly* converted and unblinded by the challenger. For the traceability requirement to be achievable we must ensure that all signatures originate from the same convert query, due to the non-transitivity property. Therefore, it is natural to require the adversary to output a set of blinded tier-1 signatures, that are honestly converted. The blinding secret key must then be output by the adversary to determine whether signatures are linked.

In the CLS model, the adversary needed to output more unlinkable tier-1 signatures than the number of corrupted users. As the adversary now outputs blinded signatures, we can no longer check if they originate from the signing oracle. Instead, we allow the adversary to output the signatures of honest users. However, for each honest user that could have authored a message, we increase by 1 the number of unlinkable signatures the adversary is required to output. The adversary wins if they output more unlinkable signatures than the number of corrupted users plus the number of signing queries for distinct users.

Our traceability guarantee carries forward to tier-2 signatures when the converter is honest. This is because, conversion unforgeability ensures that all valid `tier`-2 signatures originate from a blinded `tier`-1 signature that is input to the honest converter, even when the data processor is corrupted. With a corrupted converter, no guarantees can be made for `tier`-2 signatures anyway.

Non-frameability. This notion prevents the impersonation of an honest user, whereby an adversary generates signatures that will link to those of this user, when the issuer, converter, data lake and data processor are corrupt.

As the issuer is corrupt, the adversary has access to the SNDU and SIGN oracles to create honest users and obtain their signatures. The adversary outputs a blinded message-pseudonym-signature tuple, along with a blinding public and secret key. As in the CLS model, we use the Identify algorithm to check whether signatures stem from an honest user. On input a blinded `tier`-1 signature, this creates a second blinded `tier`-1 signature, and converts and unblinds both, checking if they are linked. Identify now checks the validity of the `tier`-2 signature which is necessary for a framing attack to occur.

When defining the non-frameability of `tier`-2 signatures, firstly consider that the converter is corrupted. As the security guarantees for `tier`-2 signatures depend on the converter being honest-but-curious, in this case the adversary can trivially forge tier-2 signatures and so we can only prevent framing attacks via blinded `tier`-1 signatures. If the converter remains honest, the conversion unforgeability requirement ensures that an adversary can only impersonate an honest user via a blinded signature that is honestly converted and unblinded. Therefore, both cases are captured by the adversary outputting a blinded signature that is converted honestly in the experiment, as in our requirement.

The blinding secret key must be output by the adversary to determine the linkage between signatures. Although in our requirement unblinding is honest, the conversion unforgeability requirement ensures that all valid `tier`-2 signature can be traced to a conversion assuming the converter is honest. Even if the requirement was formulated so that `tier`-2 signatures were output, the blinding secret key would still need to be output by the adversary to check that this signature originated from an honest conversion. Therefore, the adversary must output the blinding secret key for our definition to be realisable.

As in the CLS model, we must prevent trivial wins via the signing oracle. Due to the re-randomisability of CLS+ signatures to allow for non-transitivity, instead of not allowing signatures output by SIGN, we consider whether the attached message was input to the signing oracle. As the adversary outputs a blinded tuple, we must convert and unblind their output to obtain this message.

3   Preliminaries

We now present the building blocks required in this work.

Bilinear Maps. Let $\mathbb{G}_1$, $\mathbb{G}_2$, $\mathbb{G}_T$ be cyclic multiplicative groups with prime order p. A bilinear map $e : \mathbb{G}_1 \times \mathbb{G}_2 \to \mathbb{G}_T$ must satisfy: *bilinearity*, i.e., $e(g_1^x, g_2^y) = e(g_1, g_2)^{xy}$; *non-degeneracy*, i.e., for generators $g_1 \in \mathbb{G}_1$ and $g_2 \in \mathbb{G}_2$, $e(g_1, g_2)$

generates $\mathbb{G}_T$; and *efficiency*, i.e., there exists efficient algorithms $\mathcal{G}(1^\tau)$ that outputs a bilinear group $(p, \mathbb{G}_1, \mathbb{G}_2, \mathbb{G}_T, e, g_1, g_2)$ and to compute $e(a, b)$ for all $a \in \mathbb{G}_1$, $b \in \mathbb{G}_2$. We use type-3 pairings in this work and do not assume $\mathbb{G}_1 = \mathbb{G}_2$ or an efficiently computable isomorphism between groups [27]. Type-3 pairings benefit from the most efficient curves, when balancing the cost of pairings and group operations, the size of the representation of an element of $\mathbb{G}_2$ and the flexibility of parameter choice [17,27].

Standard and Automorphic Signatures. We use digital signatures which satisfy Existential Unforgeability against Chosen Message Attacks (EUF-CMA), consisting of: SIG.Setup outputs the parameters $\mathsf{pp}_{\mathsf{sig}}$, SIG.KeyGen($\mathsf{pp}_{\mathsf{sig}}$) outputs the signing and verification keys (sk, vk), SIG.Sign(sk, m) outputs a signature Ω, SIG.Ver(Ω, vk, m) checks the signature is valid.

An *automorphic signature* [26] over a bilinear group is an EUF-CMA secure signature whose verification keys are contained in the message space. Moreover, the messages and signatures consist of elements of $\mathbb{G}_1$ and $\mathbb{G}_2$, and the verification predicate is a conjunction of pairing-product equations over the verification key, the message and the signature. They consist of the following algorithms: ASetup(1^τ) outputs the parameters $\mathsf{pp}_{\mathsf{auto}}$; AKeyGen($\mathsf{pp}_{\mathsf{auto}}$) outputs the signing and verification keys, (apk, ask); ASign(ask, m) outputs a signature Ω; and AVerify(Ω, apk, m) checks that Ω is a valid signature.

ElGamal Encryption. We use the ElGamal encryption scheme [22], which is chosen-plaintext secure under the DDH assumption. We will use the *homomorphic* property of ElGamal, i.e., if $C_1 \in \mathsf{Enc}(pk, m_1)$, and $C_2 \in \mathsf{Enc}(pk, m_2)$, then $C_1 \odot C_2 \in \mathsf{Enc}(pk, m_1 \cdot m_2)$. ElGamal ciphertexts $c = \mathsf{Enc}(pk, m)$ are *publicly re-randomisable* in the sense that a re-randomised version c' of c looks indistinguishable from a fresh encryption of the plaintext m.

Proof Protocols. When referring to zero-knowledge proofs of knowledge of discrete logarithms, $\mathsf{PK}\{(a, b, c) : y = g^a h^b \wedge \tilde{y} = \tilde{g}^a \tilde{h}^c\}$ denotes a proof of knowledge of integers a, b and c such that $y = g^a h^b$ and $\tilde{y} = \tilde{g}^a \tilde{h}^c$ hold, as in the notation of [12]. SPK denotes a signature proof of knowledge, a non-interactive transformation of a proof PK. We require the proof system to be *sound* and *zero-knowledge*.

Controlled Malleable NIZKs. A controlled malleable proof [16] for a relation $\mathcal{R}$ and transformation class $\mathcal{T}$ consists of three algorithms constituting a regular non-interactive proof. CRSSetup(1^τ) generates a common reference string σ_{crs}; $\mathcal{P}(\sigma_{\mathsf{crs}}, x, w)$: takes as input σ_{crs}, a statement x and a witness such that $(x, w) \in \mathcal{R}$, and outputs a proof π; $\mathcal{V}(\sigma_{\mathsf{crs}}, x, \pi)$ outputs 1 if π is valid for statement x. Such a proof is called zero knowledge (NIZK) if there exists a PPT simulator (S_1, S_2) such that an adversary cannot distinguish between proofs formed by the prover and simulator, and a proof of knowledge (NIZKPoK) if there exists a PPT extractor (E_1, E_2) that can produce a valid witness from any valid proof.

The fourth algorithm, specific to malleable proof systems, is: ZKEval $(\sigma_{\text{crs}}, T, x, \pi)$: which on input σ_{crs}, a transformation $T = (T_{\text{inst}}, T_{\text{wit}})$ (in transformation class $\mathcal{T}$), an instance x, and a proof π, outputs a mauled proof π' for instance $T_{\text{inst}}(x)$.

The controlled-malleable simulation-sound extractability requirement reconciles malleability with simulation-sound extractability [21,29]. It requires that, for any instance x, if an adversary can produce a valid proof π that $x \in \mathcal{R}$ then an extractor can extract from π either a witness w such that $(x, w) \in \mathcal{R}$ or a previously proved instance x' and transformation $T \in \mathcal{T}$ such that $x = T_{\text{inst}}(x')$. This guarantees that any proof that the adversary produces is either generated from scratch using a valid witness, or formed by applying a transformation from the class $\mathcal{T}$ to an existing proof. The full definition is detailed in the full version [25].

In [16] strong derivation privacy for such proofs is also defined. This ensures simulated proofs are indistinguishable from those formed via a transformation, as defined formally in the full version [25]. Putting this together, a cm-NIZK is a proof system that is CM-SSE, strongly derivation private, and zero knowledge.

4   Our CLS+ Construction

Our CLS+ construction uses automorphic signatures, ElGamal encryption, controlled malleable NIZKs, a digital signature scheme, and a signature proof of knowledge as building blocks. Automorphic signatures are structure-preserving signatures, for which the verification key lies within the message space. Controlled-malleable NIZKs allow proofs to be mauled to blind signatures, but because the malleability is controlled the unforgeability properties are still satisfied.

High-Level Idea. We now present a high-level overview of our CLS+ construction, demonstrating how our construction differs from the CLS scheme presented in [28]. The issuer's key pair is that of an automorphic signature [26] as recalled in Sect. 3. The converter's key pair is an ElGamal encryption key pair and a key pair for a signature scheme. The blinding key pair, held by the data processor, is an ElGamal encryption key pair. Unlike [28], when joining, a user generates a key pair of an automorphic signature as their secret and public key (usk, upk). The issuer signs the user's public key to form a credential, which is possible due to the automorphic property. An automorphic signature is used, instead of a BBS+ signature in [28], to generate credentials, for compatibility with the cm-NIZK proofs, which are necessary to allow signatures to be blinded.

When a user signs a message m, as in [28] they encrypt their public key upk under the converter public key to form a pseudonym, and must prove knowledge of a secret key relating to a valid credential. In the CLS+ scheme to do so, they "normally" sign the message using the automorphic signature. The latter is never revealed, but is only used to generate a cm-NIZK, which proves knowledge of a signature of m under its public key, an issuer's credential on its public key and correctness of the pseudonym. To ensure that conversion queries cannot be used to de-anonymise honest users' signatures, we include upk' as witness such that $e(g_1, upk) = e(upk', g_2)$. The blinding public key must be fixed in signing, as it must be part of the statement proved by the cm-NIZK. This allows for the proof to be transformed in blinding, because cm-NIZKs are defined for relations that are closed under all allowable transformations. However, this allows users to have control when signing over the data processors that can use their data.

Blinding proceeds as in [28] for the pseudonym and message. The pseudonym is re-randomised, and an extra layer of encryption under the blinding public key is added. The message is encrypted under the blinding public key. In the CLS+ model, we need to use the malleability of the cm-NIZK to update the signature. This ensures that the new traceability and non–frameability requirements are satisfied, where the adversary outputs blinded signatures. The mauled proofs still ensure that the user holds a valid secret key corresponding to the public key that is encrypted in the pseudonym to provide non–frameability, and a valid credential on this public key to provide traceability. The strong derivation privacy of the cm-NIZK ensures that the modified conversion blindness requirement holds.

During conversions, each blinded pseudonym, message and now signature is verified. Like [28], the encryption is re-randomised on the message and pseudonym. The converter decrypts the pseudonym using the converter secret key and raises the resulting pseudonym to the power of r which is chosen afresh in every convert query, but used consistently within. Unlike [28], the resulting pseudonym is transformed to the target group to prevent anonymity attacks, and the converter now outputs a standard signature on the converted pseudonym and message.

During unblinding, as in [28], the tier-2 pseudonyms and messages are retrieved, by decrypting under the blinding secret key. In the CLS+ scheme, tier-2 pseudonyms are of the form $e(g_1, upk)^r$, and so signatures can be linked by author. The final tier-2 signature is the blindly signed tuple from the converter and a proof of correct unblinding by the data processor, which can both be publicly verified. This ensures that our new requirement conversion unforgeability is satisfied. To ensure that the converter only blindly signs messages that were authenticated via a group signature, we use that mauled cm-NIZKs can be verified. As the converter is assumed to be honest-but-curious, this transmits the authentication guarantees from the original group signatures to converted ones.

Additional Structural Assumptions of Automorphic Signatures. We make the following assumptions satisfied by our instantiation in Sect. 5. The automorphic signature scheme can be simplified so either messages are elements of $\mathbb{G}_1$ and the verification key is an element of $\mathbb{G}_2$ ($\mathsf{ASetup}_1, \mathsf{AKeyGen}_1, \mathsf{ASign}_1, \mathsf{AVerify}_1$), or messages are elements of $\mathbb{G}_2$ and the verification key is an element of $\mathbb{G}_1$ ($\mathsf{ASetup}_2, \mathsf{AKeyGen}_2, \mathsf{ASign}_2, \mathsf{AVerify}_2$). We assume our automorphic signatures are in the type-3 setting, ASetup is input the bilinear group, and the signing key and verification key are of the form $sk \in \mathbb{Z}_p^*$ and $vk = g_j^{sk}$ when $vk \in \mathbb{G}_j$.

4.1 Detailed Description of CLS–CM

Setup and Key Generation. In CLS+.Setup, parameters for all building blocks are generated. The issuing keypair is the keypair of an automorphic signature. The converter's keypair is an ElGamal key pair in $\mathbb{G}_2$ and a keypair for a signature scheme. The blinding keypair is an ElGamal key pair in both $\mathbb{G}_1$ and $\mathbb{G}_2$.

CLS+.Setup(1^τ)

$(p, \mathbb{G}_1, \mathbb{G}_2, \mathbb{G}_T, e, g_1, g_2) \leftarrow \mathcal{G}(1^\tau)$
$\mathsf{pp}_{\mathsf{auto1}} \leftarrow \mathsf{ASetup}_1(p, \mathbb{G}_1, \mathbb{G}_2, \mathbb{G}_T, e, g_1, g_2), \mathsf{pp}_{\mathsf{auto2}} \leftarrow \mathsf{ASetup}_2(p, \mathbb{G}_1, \mathbb{G}_2, \mathbb{G}_T, e, g_1, g_2)$
$g \leftarrow\!\!\$ \, \mathbb{G}_1, \hat{g} \leftarrow\!\!\$ \, \mathbb{G}_2, \sigma_{\mathsf{crs}} \leftarrow \mathsf{CRSSetup}(1^\tau), \mathsf{pp}_{\mathsf{sig}} \leftarrow \mathsf{SIG}.\mathsf{Setup}(1^\tau)$
return $((p, \mathbb{G}_1, \mathbb{G}_2, \mathbb{G}_T, e, g_1, g_2), \mathsf{pp}_{\mathsf{auto1}}, \mathsf{pp}_{\mathsf{auto2}}, g, \hat{g}, \sigma_{\mathsf{crs}}, \mathsf{pp}_{\mathsf{sig}})$

CLS+.IKGen(pp)	CLS+.BKGen(pp)	CLS+.CKGen(pp)
$(ipk, isk) \leftarrow \mathsf{AKeyGen}_2(\mathsf{pp}_{\mathsf{auto2}})$	$bsk_1, bsk_2 \leftarrow\!\!\$ \, \mathbb{Z}_p^*$	$csk_1 \leftarrow\!\!\$ \, \mathbb{Z}_p^*, cpk_1 \leftarrow \hat{g}^{csk_1}$
return (ipk, isk)	$bpk_1 \leftarrow g^{bsk_1}, bpk_2 \leftarrow \hat{g}^{bsk_2}$	$(cpk_2, csk_2) \leftarrow \mathsf{SIG}.\mathsf{KeyGen}(\mathsf{pp}_{\mathsf{sig}})$
	return $((bpk_1, bpk_2), (bsk_1, bsk_2))$	**return** $((cpk_1, cpk_2), (csk_1, csk_2))$

Join. We give the join protocol of our CLS–CM construction in Fig. 1. When joining, the users generate a key pair (usk, upk) for an automorphic signature and obtain the issuer's signature on their public key. They also compute $upk' = g_1^{usk}$.

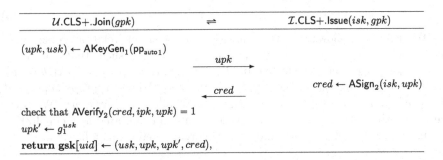

Fig. 1. Join protocol of our CLS–CM construction.

Sign and Verication of tier-1 Signatures. When signing, the user's public key is encrypted under the converter public key to form the pseudonym $\mu = (\hat{g}^\alpha, 1 \in \mathbb{G}_2, upk \cdot cpk_1^\alpha)$. The pseudonym can also be seen as an encryption under the blinding key with encryption randomness 0. The ciphertext encrypting m under the blinding key with encryption randomness 0, is of the form $(1 \in \mathbb{G}_1, m)$. This means that blinding encryption can be added by re-randomising both ciphertexts in CLS+.Blind, while maintaining the ability to update the associated proof.

The user then signs m with their user secret key to output Ω. The signature Ω is never output, but instead a cm-NIZK is computed which proves that μ is an encryption of upk, c is an "encryption" of m (with randomness 0), and knowledge of a correct Ω. The latter comprises showing that Ω is a valid signature on m under upk, and it knows a credential $cred$ that is a valid signature on upk under ipk. We also prove knowledge of upk' such that $e(upk', g_2) = e(g_1, upk)$ to prevent attacks on anonymity via conversion queries. This is because usk can no longer be included as a witness as in [28], as it is not a group element. Instead we include upk', which due to the DDH assumption in $\mathbb{G}_2$ and the pairing setting, is hard to derive from upk. This prevents the following attack against anonymity: the adversary uses the upk of an honest user uid to create a new signature with user public key upk^a using a known $a \in \mathbb{Z}_p^*$. They could then test whether another signature belongs to this honest user uid by submitting it alongside the signature they created to the converter. If any of the tier-2 pseudonyms are of the form P, P^a for any P, then they know the signature belongs to uid. The final signature simply consists of the cm-NIZK.

More formally we define the relation R such that $((cpk_1, bpk_1, bpk_2, ipk, \mu, c),$ $(upk', upk, cred, \Omega, g_1^\alpha, g_1^\beta, g_2^\gamma, m)) \in R$ if and only if:

$$e(g_1, \mu_1) = e(g_1^\alpha, \hat{g}), \quad e(g_1, \mu_2) = e(g_1^\beta, \hat{g}), \quad \text{and} \tag{1}$$

$$e(g_1, \mu_3) = e(g_1, upk)e(g_1^\alpha, cpk_1)e(g_1^\beta, bpk_2), \quad \text{and} \tag{2}$$

$$\mathsf{AVerify}_1(\Omega, upk, m) = 1, \quad \mathsf{AVerify}_2(cred, ipk, upk) = 1, \quad \text{and} \tag{3}$$

$$e(c_1, g_2) = e(g, g_2^\gamma), \quad e(c_2, g_2) = e(m, g_2)e(bpk_1, g_2^\gamma), \quad \text{and} \tag{4}$$

$$e(upk', g_2) = e(g_1, upk). \tag{5}$$

We define the allowable set of transformations for this relation to be:
$\mathcal{T} = \{(r_{enc1}, r_{enc2}, r_{enc3}) : r_{enc1}, r_{enc2}, r_{enc3} \in \mathbb{Z}_p^*\}$, such that for $T = (r_{enc1}, r_{enc2}, r_{enc3})$, the transformation $T_{inst}(cpk_1, bpk, ipk, \mu, c) = (cpk_1, bpk, ipk, (\mu_1 \hat{g}^{r_{enc1}}, \mu_2 \hat{g}^{r_{enc2}}, \mu_3 \cdot cpk_1^{r_{enc1}} bpk_2^{r_{enc2}}), (c_1 g^{r_{enc3}}, c_2 bpk_1^{r_{enc3}}))$ and $T_{wit}(upk', upk, cred, \Omega, g_1^\alpha, g_1^\beta, g_2^\gamma, m) = (upk', upk, cred, \Omega, g_1^\alpha g_1^{r_{enc1}}, g_1^\beta g_1^{r_{enc2}}, g_2^\gamma g_2^{r_{enc3}}, m)$. We show later that this relation and transformation can be instantiated as a cm-NIZK.

In more detail, CLS+.Sign and CLS+.Verify are defined as follows:

CLS+.Sign$(gpk, bpk, \mathbf{gsk}[uid], m)$

---

parse $\mathbf{gsk}[uid] = (usk, upk, upk', cred)$, $\alpha \leftarrow_\$ \mathbb{Z}_p^*$, $\mu \leftarrow (\hat{g}^\alpha, 1, upk \cdot cpk_1^\alpha)$

$\beta \leftarrow 0, \gamma \leftarrow 0, c \leftarrow (1, m), \Omega \leftarrow \mathsf{ASign}_1(usk, m)$

$\sigma \leftarrow$ cm-NIZK$\{(upk', upk, cred, \Omega, g_1^\alpha, g_1^\beta, g_2^\gamma, m) : e(g_1, \mu_1) = e(g_1^\alpha, \hat{g}) \quad e(g_1, \mu_2) = e(g_1^\beta, \hat{g})$

$e(g_1, \mu_3) = e(g_1, upk)e(g_1^\alpha, cpk_1)e(g_1^\beta, bpk_2) \quad \mathsf{AVerify}_1(\Omega, upk, m) = 1$

$\mathsf{AVerify}_2(cred, ipk, upk) = 1 \quad e(c_1, g_2) = e(g, g_2^\gamma) \quad e(c_2, g_2) = e(m, g_2)e(bpk_1, g_2^\gamma)$

$e(upk', g_2) = e(g_1, upk)\}$

return (μ, σ)

CLS+.Verify$(\texttt{tier-1}, gpk, bpk, m, \mu, \sigma)$

Check $\mu_2 = 1$, Verify σ with respect to $(cpk_1, bpk, ipk, \mu, (1, m))$

Blind Conversions. During blinding, the pseudonym and message are encrypted under the blinding public key, and the encryption under the converter public key is re-randomised. The cm-NIZK is transformed with ZKEval so that it is consistent with the blinded pseudonym, and message, which also re-randomises the proof due to the derivation privacy.

In CLS+.Convert, blinded signatures are now input and verified, leveraging the fact that even fully blinded inputs can be checked for their correctness. The pseudonyms, and blinded messages are re-randomised to ensure non-transitivity. The encryption under the converter public key is then removed from the pseudonyms and they are converted by raising them to the power of r and transforming them into the target group, to ensure non-transitivity. The converted signature is simply a digital signature on the blinded converted pseudonym and message, with respect to the converter's verification key.

In CLS+.Unblind the converted pseudonym and ciphertext are now decrypted under the blinding secret key. The blinded then converted pseudonym, message and signature are output, along with a proof that the unblinding has been done correctly. During tier-2 verification, the converter's signature on the blinded values and the proof of unblinding are verified.

CLS+.Blind$(gpk, bpk, (m, \mu, \sigma))$

---

if CLS+.Verify(tier-1, $gpk, bpk, m, \mu, \sigma) = 0$ return $\perp$

$\alpha', \beta', \gamma' \leftarrow\!\!\$ \, \mathbb{Z}_p^*, c\mu \leftarrow (\mu_1 \hat{g}^{\alpha'}, \mu_2 \hat{g}^{\beta'}, \mu_3 cpk_1^{\alpha'} bpk_2^{\beta'})$

$c \leftarrow (g^{\gamma'}, m \cdot bpk_1^{\gamma'}), c\sigma \leftarrow \mathsf{ZKEval}(\sigma_{\mathsf{crs}}, (\alpha', \beta', \gamma'), (cpk_1, bpk, ipk, \mu, (1, m)), \sigma)$

return $(c, c\mu, c\sigma)$

CLS+.Convert$(gpk, bpk, csk, \{(c\mu_i, c\sigma_i, c_i)\}_k)$

$r \leftarrow\!\!\$ \, \mathbb{Z}_p^*, \mathbf{for}\ i = 1, \ldots k:$ Verify $c\sigma_i$ with respect to $c\mu_i, c_i, gpk$ and bpk

$\quad \alpha', \beta', \gamma' \leftarrow\!\!\$ \, \mathbb{Z}_p^*, c\mu_i' \leftarrow (c\mu_{i,1} \hat{g}^{\alpha'}, c\mu_{i,2} \hat{g}^{\beta'}, c\mu_{i,3} cpk_1^{\alpha'} bpk_2^{\beta'}), c_i' \leftarrow (c_{i,1} g^{\gamma'}, c_{i,2} bpk_1^{\gamma'})$

$\quad c\mu_i'' \leftarrow (c\mu_{i,2}', c\mu_{i,3}' \cdot c\mu_{i,1}'^{\,csk_1}), c\mu_{i,1}''' \leftarrow e(g_1, c\mu_{i,1}'')^r, c\mu_{i,2}''' \leftarrow e(g_1, c\mu_{i,2}'')^r$

$\quad \sigma_i' \leftarrow \mathsf{SIG.Sign}(csk_2, (c_i', c\mu_i''', bpk))$

choose random permutation $\Pi, \mathbf{for}\ i = 1, \ldots, k: (\overline{c\mu}_i, \overline{c}_i, \overline{c\sigma}_i) \leftarrow (c\mu_{\Pi(i)}''', c_{\Pi(i)}', \sigma_{\Pi(i)}')$

return $((\overline{c\mu}_1, \overline{c}_1, \overline{c\sigma}_1)), \ldots, (\overline{c\mu}_k, \overline{c}_k, \overline{c\sigma}_k)))$

CLS+.Unblind$(bsk, (\overline{c\mu}, \overline{c\sigma}, \overline{c}))$

$\overline{\mu} \leftarrow \overline{c\mu}_2 \cdot \overline{c\mu}_1^{\,bsk_2}, m \leftarrow \overline{c}_2 \overline{c}_1^{\,bsk_1}$

$\pi_{\mathsf{ub}} \leftarrow \mathsf{SPK}\{(bsk_1, bsk_2): \overline{\mu} = \overline{c\mu}_2 \cdot \overline{c\mu}_1^{\,bsk_2} \quad m = \overline{c}_2 \overline{c}_1^{\,bsk_1} \quad bpk_1 = g^{bsk_1} \quad bpk_2 = \hat{g}^{bsk_2}\}$

$\overline{\sigma} \leftarrow (\overline{c\mu}, \overline{c\sigma}, \overline{c}, \pi_{\mathsf{ub}})$ return $(\overline{\mu}, m, \overline{\sigma})$

CLS+.Verify(tier-2, $gpk, bpk, \overline{m}, \overline{\mu}, \overline{\sigma})$

---

parse $\overline{\sigma} = (\overline{c\mu}, \overline{c\sigma}, \overline{c}, \pi_{\mathsf{ub}})$, Verify π_{ub} holds for $\overline{c\mu}, \overline{\mu}, \overline{c}, \overline{m}, bpk$

if SIG.Ver$((\overline{c\mu}, \overline{c}, bpk), cpk_2, \overline{c\sigma}) = 1$ return 1   else return $\perp$

4.2 Security of CLS–CM.

In the full version [25], we show that our scheme satisfies all security properties defined in Sect. 2. More precisely, we show that the following theorem holds.

Theorem 1. *The CLS–CM construction presented in Sect. 4.1 is a secure CLS+ as defined in Sect. 2 if: the automorphic signatures schemes are EUF-CMA secure and satisfy the additional structural assumptions given in Sect. 4; the cm-NIZK is zero knowledge, strongly derivation private and controlled-malleable simulation-sound extractable (cm-SSE); the SPK is a sound zero-knowledge proof; the DDH assumption holds in $\mathbb{G}_1$ and $\mathbb{G}_2$; and the SIG is EUF-CMA secure.*

5 Concrete Instantiation of CLS–CM construction

We show the building blocks of our CLS–CM construction can be instantiated.

Automorphic Signatures and Standard Signatures. An instantiation of automorphic signatures that is EUF-CMA secure based on the Asymmetric Double Hidden SDH (ADHSDH) assumption is given in [26]. It is easy to see that this scheme satisfies the additional structural assumptions needed for our construction. For the digital signature scheme, we will make use of Schnorr signatures [39].

Controlled Malleable NIZKs. We demonstrate that cm-NIZKs for the relation $\mathcal{R}$, and set of allowable transformations $\mathcal{T}$ defined above can be instantiated. It is shown in Theorem 4.5 in [16] that cm-NIZKS for $(\mathcal{R}, \mathcal{T})$ can be instantiated if $(\mathcal{R}, \mathcal{T})$ are CM-friendly, which we show in the full version [25]. This instantiation makes use of Groth Sahai proofs [31] to build malleable NIWIPOKs and structure preserving signatures (SPS) based on the DLIN assumption. However for our instantiation, we make use of Groth Sahai proofs [31] in the type-3 setting based on the SXDH assumption, that the DDH assumption holds in both groups $\mathbb{G}_1$ and $\mathbb{G}_2$. We make use of a different Structure Preserving Signature scheme [3] in the type 3 setting, with better efficiency and based on the SXDH assumption.

Instantiating the Proof of Unblinding. For transforming interactive into non-interactive zero-knowledge proofs we rely on the Fiat-Shamir heuristic that ensures security in the random oracle model.

Efficiency. We compare the computational cost of our construction to that of [28] in Fig. 2. We denote k exponentiations in group $\mathbb{G}_i$ by $k\mathsf{exp}_{\mathbb{G}_i}$, k pairing operations by $k\mathsf{pair}$, and k exponentiations in $\mathbb{Z}_{n^2}^*$ by $k\mathsf{exp}_{\mathbb{Z}_{n^2}^*}$. In Fig. 3, we compare the combined sizes of pseudonyms and signatures in terms of the amount of group elements to [28]. We denote the length required to represent k elements in $\mathbb{G}_i$ as $k\mathbb{G}_i$, k elements in $\mathbb{Z}_p$ as $k\mathbb{Z}_p$ and k elements in $\mathbb{Z}_{n^2}^*$ as $k\mathbb{Z}_{n^2}^*$. Our construction is significantly less efficient than that of [28], particularly in terms of the signing, verification and size of tier-1 signatures. However, we demonstrate that stronger security can be achieved and the assumption of trusted data lakes can be avoided.

Algorithm	Computational cost [28]	Computational cost (this work)
Sign	$16\mathrm{exp}_{G_1} + 15\mathrm{exp}_{Z_{n^2}}$	$668\mathrm{exp}_{G_1} + 703\mathrm{exp}_{G_2}$
Verify(tier-1)	$12\mathrm{exp}_{G_1} + 11\mathrm{exp}_{Z_{n^2}} + 2\mathrm{pair}$	$1548\mathrm{pair}$
Verify(tier-2)	-	$6\mathrm{exp}_{G_1} + 2\mathrm{exp}_{G_2} + 2\mathrm{exp}_{G_T}$
Blind	$6\mathrm{exp}_{G_1}$	$2\mathrm{exp}_{G_1} + 4\mathrm{exp}_{G_2}$
Unblind	$2\mathrm{exp}_{G_1}$	$3\mathrm{exp}_{G_1} + 1\mathrm{exp}_{G_2} + 2\mathrm{exp}_{G_T}$
Convert (k pseudonyms input)	$7k\mathrm{exp}_{G_1}$	$k(3\mathrm{exp}_{G_1} + 7\mathrm{exp}_{G_2} + 2\mathrm{pair})$

Fig. 2. Computational costs.

	tier-1 (μ, σ)	Blinded $(c\mu, c\sigma)$	Converted $(\overline{c\mu}, \overline{c\sigma})$	tier-2 $(\overline{\mu}, \overline{\sigma})$
Size [28]	$5G_1\ 7Z_p\ 6Z^*_{n^2}$	$3G_1$	$2G_1$	$1G_1$
Size (this work)	$446G_1\ 541G_2$	$446G_1\ 541G_2$	$2G_T\ 2Z_p$	$3G_T\ 2G_1\ 5Z_p$

Fig. 3. Sizes of pseudonyms and signatures.

References

1. Helping public health officials combat covid-19. https://blog.google/technology/health/covid-19-community-mobility-reports/
2. Abe, M., Fuchsbauer, G., Groth, J., Haralambiev, K., Ohkubo, M.: Structure-preserving signatures and commitments to group elements. In: Rabin, T. (ed.) CRYPTO 2010. LNCS, vol. 6223, pp. 209–236. Springer, Heidelberg (2010). https://doi.org/10.1007/978-3-642-14623-7_12
3. Abe, M., Hofheinz, D., Nishimaki, R., Ohkubo, M., Pan, J.: Compact structure-preserving signatures with almost tight security. In: Katz, J., Shacham, H. (eds.) CRYPTO 2017. LNCS, vol. 10402, pp. 548–580. Springer, Cham (2017). https://doi.org/10.1007/978-3-319-63715-0_19
4. Bellare, M., Micciancio, D., Warinschi, B.: Foundations of group signatures: formal definitions, simplified requirements, and a construction based on general assumptions. In: Biham, E. (ed.) EUROCRYPT 2003. LNCS, vol. 2656, pp. 614–629. Springer, Heidelberg (2003). https://doi.org/10.1007/3-540-39200-9_38
5. Bellare, M., Shi, H., Zhang, C.: Foundations of group signatures: the case of dynamic groups. In: Menezes, A. (ed.) CT-RSA 2005. LNCS, vol. 3376, pp. 136–153. Springer, Heidelberg (2005). https://doi.org/10.1007/978-3-540-30574-3_11
6. Bernhard, D., Fuchsbauer, G., Ghadafi, E., Smart, N.P., Warinschi, B.: Anonymous attestation with user-controlled linkability. Int. J. Inf. Secur. **12**(3), 219–249 (2013). https://doi.org/10.1007/s10207-013-0191-z
7. Boneh, D., Boyen, X., Shacham, H.: Short group signatures. In: Franklin, M. (ed.) CRYPTO 2004. LNCS, vol. 3152, pp. 41–55. Springer, Heidelberg (2004). https://doi.org/10.1007/978-3-540-28628-8_3
8. Bootle, J., Cerulli, A., Chaidos, P., Ghadafi, E., Groth, J.: Foundations of fully dynamic group signatures. In: Manulis, M., Sadeghi, A.-R., Schneider, S. (eds.) ACNS 2016. LNCS, vol. 9696, pp. 117–136. Springer, Cham (2016). https://doi.org/10.1007/978-3-319-39555-5_7
9. Brickell, E., Camenisch, J., Chen, L.: Direct anonymous attestation. In: ACM CCS (2004)

10. Camenisch, J., Drijvers, M., Lehmann, A.: Anonymous attestation using the strong Diffie Hellman assumption revisited. In: Franz, M., Papadimitratos, P. (eds.) Trust 2016. LNCS, vol. 9824, pp. 1–20. Springer, Cham (2016). https://doi.org/10.1007/978-3-319-45572-3_1

11. Camenisch, J., Drijvers, M., Lehmann, A.: Universally composable direct anonymous attestation. In: Cheng, C.-M., Chung, K.-M., Persiano, G., Yang, B.-Y. (eds.) PKC 2016. LNCS, vol. 9615, pp. 234–264. Springer, Heidelberg (2016). https://doi.org/10.1007/978-3-662-49387-8_10

12. Camenisch, J., Kiayias, A., Yung, M.: On the portability of generalized Schnorr proofs. In: Joux, A. (ed.) EUROCRYPT 2009. LNCS, vol. 5479, pp. 425–442. Springer, Heidelberg (2009). https://doi.org/10.1007/978-3-642-01001-9_25

13. Camenisch, J., Stadler, M.: Efficient group signature schemes for large groups. In: Kaliski, B.S. (ed.) CRYPTO 1997. LNCS, vol. 1294, pp. 410–424. Springer, Heidelberg (1997). https://doi.org/10.1007/BFb0052252

14. Canard, S., Schoenmakers, B., Stam, M., Traoré, J.: List signature schemes. Discrete Appl. Math. 154(2), 189–201 (2006)

15. Canetti, R., Krawczyk, H., Nielsen, J.B.: Relaxing chosen-ciphertext security. In: Boneh, D. (ed.) CRYPTO 2003. LNCS, vol. 2729, pp. 565–582. Springer, Heidelberg (2003). https://doi.org/10.1007/978-3-540-45146-4_33

16. Chase, M., Kohlweiss, M., Lysyanskaya, A., Meiklejohn, S.: Malleable proof systems and applications. In: Pointcheval, D., Johansson, T. (eds.) EUROCRYPT 2012. LNCS, vol. 7237, pp. 281–300. Springer, Heidelberg (2012). https://doi.org/10.1007/978-3-642-29011-4_18

17. Chatterjee, S., Menezes, A.: On cryptographic protocols employing asymmetric pairings- the role of ψ revisited. Discrete Appl. Math. 159(13), 1311–1322 (2011)

18. Chaum, D., van Heyst, E.: Group signatures. In: Davies, D.W. (ed.) EUROCRYPT 1991. LNCS, vol. 547, pp. 257–265. Springer, Heidelberg (1991). https://doi.org/10.1007/3-540-46416-6_22

19. Chow, S., Lee, J., Subramanian, L.: Two-party computation model for privacy-preserving queries over distributed databases. In: NDSS (2009)

20. Chow, S.S.M., Susilo, W., Yuen, T.H.: Escrowed linkability of ring signatures and its applications. In: Nguyen, P.Q. (ed.) VIETCRYPT 2006. LNCS, vol. 4341, pp. 175–192. Springer, Heidelberg (2006). https://doi.org/10.1007/11958239_12

21. De Santis, A., Di Crescenzo, G., Ostrovsky, R., Persiano, G., Sahai, A.: Robust non-interactive zero knowledge. In: Kilian, J. (ed.) CRYPTO 2001. LNCS, vol. 2139, pp. 566–598. Springer, Heidelberg (2001). https://doi.org/10.1007/3-540-44647-8_33

22. ElGamal, T.: A public key cryptosystem and a signature scheme based on discrete logarithms. IEEE Trans. Inf. Theory 31(4), 469–472 (1985)

23. Emura, K., Hayashi, T.: Road-to-vehicle communications with time-dependent anonymity: a lightweight construction and its experimental results. IEEE Trans. Veh. Technol. 67(2), 1582–1597 (2017)

24. Franklin, M., Zhang, H.: Unique group signatures. In: Foresti, S., Yung, M., Martinelli, F. (eds.) ESORICS 2012. LNCS, vol. 7459, pp. 643–660. Springer, Heidelberg (2012). https://doi.org/10.1007/978-3-642-33167-1_37

25. Fraser, A., Garms, L., Lehmann, A.: Selectively linkable group signatures - stronger security and preserved verifiability. Cryptology ePrint Archive 2021/1312 (2021). https://eprint.iacr.org/2021/1312.pdf

26. Fuchsbauer, G.: Automorphic signatures in bilinear groups and an application to round-optimal blind signatures. Cryptology ePrint Archive 2009/320 (2009)

27. Galbraith, S.D., Paterson, K.G., Smart, N.P.: Pairings for cryptographers. Discrete Appl. Math. 156(16), 3113–3121 (2008)

28. Garms, L., Lehmann, A.: Group signatures with selective linkability. In: Lin, D., Sako, K. (eds.) PKC 2019. LNCS, vol. 11442, pp. 190–220. Springer, Cham (2019). https://doi.org/10.1007/978-3-030-17253-4_7

29. Groth, J.: Simulation-sound NIZK proofs for a practical language and constant size group signatures. In: Lai, X., Chen, K. (eds.) ASIACRYPT 2006. LNCS, vol. 4284, pp. 444–459. Springer, Heidelberg (2006). https://doi.org/10.1007/11935230_29

30. Groth, J.: Fully anonymous group signatures without random oracles. In: Kurosawa, K. (ed.) ASIACRYPT 2007. LNCS, vol. 4833, pp. 164–180. Springer, Heidelberg (2007). https://doi.org/10.1007/978-3-540-76900-2_10

31. Groth, J., Sahai, A.: Efficient non-interactive proof systems for bilinear groups. In: Smart, N. (ed.) EUROCRYPT 2008. LNCS, vol. 4965, pp. 415–432. Springer, Heidelberg (2008). https://doi.org/10.1007/978-3-540-78967-3_24

32. Hwang, J.Y., Lee, S., Chung, B.H., Cho, H.S., Nyang, D.: Short group signatures with controllable linkability. In: Workshop on Lightweight Security & Privacy: (LightSec) (2011)

33. Hwang, J.Y., Lee, S., Chung, B.H., Cho, H.S., Nyang, D.: Group signatures with controllable linkability for dynamic membership. Inf. Sci. **222**, 761–778 (2013)

34. Kiayias, A., Tsiounis, Y., Yung, M.: Traceable signatures. In: Cachin, C., Camenisch, J.L. (eds.) EUROCRYPT 2004. LNCS, vol. 3027, pp. 571–589. Springer, Heidelberg (2004). https://doi.org/10.1007/978-3-540-24676-3_34

35. Kim, S.J., Park, S.J., Won, D.H.: Convertible group signatures. In: Kim, K., Matsumoto, T. (eds.) ASIACRYPT 1996. LNCS, vol. 1163, pp. 311–321. Springer, Heidelberg (1996). https://doi.org/10.1007/BFb0034857

36. Krenn, S., Samelin, K., Striecks, C.: Practical group-signatures with privacy-friendly openings. In: ARES (2019)

37. Libert, B., Peters, T., Yung, M.: Scalable group signatures with revocation. In: Pointcheval, D., Johansson, T. (eds.) EUROCRYPT 2012. LNCS, vol. 7237, pp. 609–627. Springer, Heidelberg (2012). https://doi.org/10.1007/978-3-642-29011-4_36

38. Sakai, Y., Emura, K., Hanaoka, G., Kawai, Y., Matsuda, T., Omote, K.: Group signatures with message-dependent opening. In: Abdalla, M., Lange, T. (eds.) Pairing 2012. LNCS, vol. 7708, pp. 270–294. Springer, Heidelberg (2013). https://doi.org/10.1007/978-3-642-36334-4_18

39. Schnorr, C.P.: Efficient identification and signatures for smart cards. In: Quisquater, J.-J., Vandewalle, J. (eds.) EUROCRYPT 1989. LNCS, vol. 434, pp. 688–689. Springer, Heidelberg (1990). https://doi.org/10.1007/3-540-46885-4_68

40. Slamanig, D., Spreitzer, R., Unterluggauer, T.: Adding controllable linkability to pairing-based group signatures for free. In: Chow, S.S.M., Camenisch, J., Hui, L.C.K., Yiu, S.M. (eds.) ISC 2014. LNCS, vol. 8783, pp. 388–400. Springer, Cham (2014). https://doi.org/10.1007/978-3-319-13257-0_23

Cryptographic Schemes and Protocols

FO-like Combiners and Hybrid Post-Quantum Cryptography

Loïs Huguenin-Dumittan$^{(\boxtimes)}$ and Serge Vaudenay$^{(\boxtimes)}$

EPFL, Lausanne, Switzerland
{lois.huguenin-dumittan,serge.vaudenay}@epfl.ch

Abstract. Combining several primitives together to offer greater security is an old idea in cryptography. Recently, this concept has resurfaced as it could be used to improve trust in new Post-Quantum (PQ) schemes and smooth the transition to PQ cryptography. In particular, several ways to combine key exchange mechanisms (KEMs) into a secure hybrid KEM have been proposed. In this work, we observe that most PQ KEMs are built using a variant of the Fujisaki-Okamoto (FO) transform. Thus, we propose several efficient combiners that take OW-CPA public-key encryption schemes (PKEs) and directly build hybrid IND-CCA KEMs. Our constructions are secure in the ROM and QROM and can be seen as generalizations of the FO transform. We also study how the hash functions (ROs) used in our transforms can be combined in order to improve efficiency and security. In a second part, we implement a hybrid KEM using one of our combiners as a proof-of-concept and benchmark it. More precisely, we build a hybrid IND-CCA KEM from the CPA-secure versions of HQC and LAC, two NIST Round 2 PQ proposals. We show that the resulting KEM offers comparable performances to HQC, thus improving security at a small cost. Finally, we discuss which PQ schemes should be combined in order to offer the best efficiency/security trade-off.

Keywords: Hybrid cryptography · Combiners · Fujisaki-Okamoto transform

1 Introduction

Redundancy is one of the most important concepts of computer science, mostly used to prevent the failure of one component affecting the whole system. In cryptography, the same idea has been used under different terms and in different forms. For instance, increasing the security of DES by performing multiple encryptions was studied by Merkle and Hellman in 1981 [16] and in 2005, Herzberg [12] studied so-called *tolerant* encryption schemes, which remain secure even if one or several of their components are broken. However, the topic became popular in the last few years, following the launch of the post-quantum (PQ) standardization process.

As promising developments have been made in the development of quantum computers, the need for secure post-quantum public-key cryptography (PKC)

© Springer Nature Switzerland AG 2021
M. Conti et al. (Eds.): CANS 2021, LNCS 13099, pp. 225–244, 2021.
https://doi.org/10.1007/978-3-030-92548-2_12

primitives is pressing. This led the US National Institute of Standards and Technology (NIST) to launch a post-quantum standardization process for public-key encryption (PKE), key-exchange mechanisms (KEMs) and signatures in 2017. In the second round, 26 proposals were retained and only 7 have been selected for the third round of this process (+8 "alternate candidates").

Most of the assumptions the PQ schemes are based on (e.g. learning with errors, syndrome decoding) have been less extensively studied than their classical counterparts (e.g. factorization, discrete logarithm). Thus, combining several of these schemes into one is considered a sound idea. For example, one could combine both a standard PKE/KEM scheme with a PQ one, and ideally the resulting cryptosystem should be secure as long as one of the underlying schemes is secure. Such systems have been popularized under the term *hybrid* schemes and the way the underlying systems are combined is called a *combiner*. Moreover, if the resulting hybrid scheme is secure as long as one of the underlying systems is secure, the *combiner* is said to be *robust*.

When it comes to PQ cryptography, hybrid schemes have many advantages, such as:

1. Guaranteeing security as long as practical quantum computers do not exist as discussed above.
2. Fulfilling the standards requirement by combining a standardized scheme with another one which is not. This possibility is actively considered by NIST[1].
3. Allowing a smooth transition between classical and PQ cryptography in practice. Hybrid cryptography would allow support of both classical and PQ schemes, allowing compatibility between older and newer systems.
4. Combining multiple PQ schemes together might offer better confidence as most of the problems/assumptions are newer and less studied. Such hybrid schemes would come at the cost of efficiency, however combining two efficient schemes might result in a more efficient scheme than one inefficient one. Such ideas and issues were briefly discussed on the NIST PQ forum[2]. We focus mostly on this application of hybrid systems in this work.

Unfortunately, hybrid schemes do not offer much improvement in terms of theoretical security. Indeed, if both underlying schemes require 2^λ operations to be broken, the hybrid system would be broken in $2^{\lambda+1}$ operations (i.e. we gain only 1 bit of security). In practice however, the security gain might be better, depending on the underlying schemes. Indeed, one might reasonably argue that the probability of a major breakthrough in two different problems believed to be hard by the community is lower than the probability of one (but even more devastating) breakthrough. In any case, while the practical security offered by hybrid cryptosystems obviously depends on many parameters, we think that such schemes offer a greater security boost than what can be deduced from the theoretical bounds only.

---

[1] https://csrc.nist.gov/Projects/post-quantum-cryptography/faqs.

[2] https://groups.google.com/a/list.nist.gov/forum/#!topic/pqc-forum/msRrR13muS4.

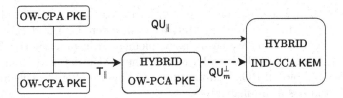

Fig. 1. Solid arrows indicate results implied by our combiners, bold arrows indicate QROM security. The dashed arrow indicates results from Hofheinz et al. [13].

Our Contributions

Several authors have considered KEM or signature combiners targeting post-quantum systems in recent years [3,4,10]. However, all the combiners introduced in these papers work in a black-box manner on IND-CCA KEMs. That is, combiners that take two KEMs (or signature schemes) as inputs and output the hybrid construction. Yet, most PQ KEM proposals share a very similar structure: an OW/IND-CPA secure PKE is introduced and then the Fujisaki-Okamoto (FO) transform or a variant (e.g. [8,9,13,19]) is applied to give an IND-CCA KEM. Therefore, one could try to directly combine the IND-CPA schemes to give an IND-CCA KEM, hopefully getting better performances. Therefore, we present in this report several hybrid FO-like transforms which combine two OW-CPA PKEs into one IND-CCA KEM. We also generalize these constructions to n schemes (i.e. n PKEs are combined into one KEM).

Compared to previous work, our combiners are simpler as they do not require extra primitives such as special types of PRFs or MACs. As a result, they are slightly more efficient by removing calls to these primitives and by optimizing the use of hash functions. Finally, our combiners follow a different paradigm as they replace FO transforms. Thus, they would likely be implemented in cryptographic libraries directly, whereas previous combiners would likely be implemented in applications/protocol libraries (e.g. openssl). Hence, our constructions offer another approach that might be useful to implementors, for example for optimization or security purposes.

The main disadvantage of FO transforms is that they are only secure in the random oracle model (ROM) and we prove the security of our FO-like hybrid combiner in the ROM as well. However, as all PQ IND-CCA KEM submitted to the NIST process are only proven secure in the ROM, it does not add an extra assumption. We also prove that one of our combiners is secure in the Quantum Random Oracle Model (QROM). The results are summarized in Fig. 1.

At a high level, our combiners share the same structure as a system that would apply a robust PKE combiner (e.g. concatenating ciphertexts) followed by a FO-like transform to get a KEM. However, having one scheme for the whole process allows a fine-grained control over the way key derivation and de-randomization are performed, in turn offering better flexibility. For instance, we study how one can combine hash functions (i.e. random oracles) s.t. our main FO-like combiner is more efficient or secure. More precisely, we define the properties the functions g (used to derive random coins in our construction) and h (used to derive the shared key) should have in order for our construction to be secure. Such theoretical analysis is important, as it was demonstrated that Random Oracles in FO transforms are easily misimplemented in practice [1]. Therefore, by presenting generic n-PKEs-to-KEM combiners with detailed security proofs and several examples of ROs combinations, we hope to offer clear flexibility and security guarantees to implementors.

As a proof of concept, we implemented a hybrid KEM based on the IND-CPA version of HQC and LAC, two round 2 proposals to the NIST PQ standardisation process. We call this hybrid KEM hqc_lac_128 and we report and analyse how this scheme compares to the other round 2 proposals[3]. In particular, we show that the performance of the hybrid scheme is comparable to the performance of the least efficient underlying scheme (i.e. HQC in this case). Moreover, as our combiner is highly parallelizable, our tests show that a parallelized version of hqc_lac_128 is as efficient as HQC in term of speed, excluding a negligible overhead (mainly due to the creation of an additional thread). We think this demonstrates that using a hybrid PQ system in place of a single PQ scheme may increase significantly the security at a small cost.

Finally, we compute the theoretical performance (based on the data from eBACS [2]) of every possible hybrid scheme based on two PQ IND-CPA schemes that are based on assumptions of a different type (e.g. a lattice-based scheme with a code-based scheme). We discuss the performance of the most efficient ones in two metrics, namely public key/ciphertext size and encapsulation/decapsulation speed. This analysis shows that a given hybrid scheme struggles to perform as well as an efficient non-hybrid one in both metrics. Due to space constraint, we defer this analysis to the full version of the paper [14].

Related Work

Many authors have considered robust combiners for different primitives, like combiners for PKE [5,20], hash functions [6,7], commitment schemes [12], PQ signatures [4], AEAD [17]. Recently, robust combiners for KEM have also been considered by Giacon et al. in [10]. In that work, they propose various robust combiners in the standard model and in the random oracle model that take two IND-CCA KEM and output another IND-CCA KEM. Similarly, Bindel et al. [3] propose similar robust KEM combiners which are secure against quantum adversaries. Our combiners differ from these as we aim at building a monolithic IND-CCA KEM based on several IND-CPA (or OW-CPA) PKEs. In a way, we bypass the intermediate KEM constructions, as many KEMs are based on FO-transformed IND-CPA schemes.

Another related line of work is the construction of Fujisaki-Okamoto (FO)-like transforms [8,9], which have been a hot topic these last years. Several variants meant to be secure in the quantum random oracle (QROM) have been proposed along with tighter security proofs [13,15,18,19]. Our combiner can be seen as a generalization of a FO-like transform as it takes multiples CPA-secure PKEs and outputs a robust IND-CCA KEM.

---

[3] At the time of the tests, round 3 proposals were not announced.

2   Notation

Let $\mathcal{A}$ be a randomized algorithm, then we write $b \leftarrow_\$ \mathcal{A}$ to indicate b is assigned the value output by $\mathcal{A}$. Similarly, if Ψ (resp. $\mathcal{X}$) is a distribution (resp. a set), then $x \leftarrow_\$ \Psi$ (resp. $x \leftarrow_\$ \mathcal{X}$) means that x is sampled uniformly at random from Ψ (resp. $\mathcal{X}$). We denote by 1_P the indicator function which returns 1 if the predicate P is fulfilled and 0 otherwise. We write $[n]$ the set $\{0, 1, \ldots, n-1\}$.

Let $\mathcal{A}$ be an algorithm. Then, we write $\mathcal{A} \Rightarrow b$ to denote the event $\mathcal{A}$ *outputs* b. Finally, in an algorithm (or game) **abort** means the algorithm is stopped and "**output** b" means the algorithm is stopped and b is returned.

3   PKC and KEM

We recall several standard definitions in Public-Key Cryptography, namely PKE and KEM.

3.1   Public-Key Encryption Scheme

Definition 1 (Public-Key Encryption). *A Public-Key Encryption scheme is composed of four algorithms* setup, gen, enc, dec*:*

- pp $\leftarrow_\$$ setup(1^λ)*: The setup algorithm randomly generates the public parameters* pp *according to a security parameter* λ.
- (pk, sk) $\leftarrow_\$$ gen(pp)*: The key generation algorithm takes the public parameters as inputs and outputs the public key* pk *and the secret key* sk.
- ct $\leftarrow_\$$ enc(pp, pk, pt)*: The encryption algorithm takes as inputs the public parameters* pp*, the public key* pk *and a plaintext* pt $\in \mathcal{M}$ *and it outputs a ciphertext* ct.
- pt$'$ $\leftarrow$ dec(pp, sk, ct)*: The decryption procedure takes as inputs the public parameters* pp*, the secret key* sk *and the ciphertext* ct $\in \mathcal{C}$ *and it outputs a plaintext* pt$'$ $\in \mathcal{M} \cup \{\perp\}$.

The setup*,* gen *and* enc *are probabilistic algorithms that can be made deterministic by adding random coins as inputs. The decryption procedure is deterministic. Finally, for the sake of simplicity, we omit the public parameters in the inputs from now on.*

Correctness. We define the $\delta(q_H)$-correctness in the random oracle model (ROM) as in [13], using the game CORR defined in Fig. 2. We say a PKE scheme is $\delta(q_H)$ correct if for any ppt adversary $\mathcal{A}$ making at most q_H adversary to the random oracle H, we have

$$\Pr[\text{CORR}_{\text{PKE}}(\mathcal{A}) \Rightarrow 1] \leq \delta(q_H, \lambda)$$

where λ is the security parameter, we omit it from now on for the sake of simplicity. That is, no adversary can find with probability greater than $\delta(q_H)$ a plaintext such that its encryption does not decrypt to the original plaintext. The correctness δ might depend on the number of queries to the RO, thus it is represented as a function of q_H. The correctness in the standard model is the same except δ is fixed.

$$\text{CORR}_{\mathsf{PKE}}(\mathcal{A})$$

pp $\leftarrow$$ \mathsf{setup}(1^\lambda)$
(pk, sk) $\leftarrow$$ \mathsf{gen}(\mathsf{pp})$
pt $\leftarrow \mathcal{A}^H(\mathsf{pk}, \mathsf{sk})$
ct $\leftarrow$$ \mathsf{enc}(\mathsf{pk}, \mathsf{pt})$
return $1_{\mathsf{dec}(\mathsf{sk},\mathsf{ct}) \neq \mathsf{pt}}$

Fig. 2. Correctness game.

$$\text{IND-ATK}_{\mathsf{PKE}}^b(\mathcal{A}) \qquad\qquad \textbf{Oracle } \mathcal{O}^{\mathsf{Dec}}(\mathsf{ct})$$

pp $\leftarrow$$ \mathsf{setup}(1^\lambda)$	1 : **if** ct $=$ ct* : **return** $\perp$
(pk, sk) $\leftarrow$$ \mathsf{gen}(\mathsf{pp})$	2 : pt$'$ $\leftarrow \mathsf{dec}(\mathsf{pp}, \mathsf{sk}, \mathsf{ct})$
define ct$^* \leftarrow \emptyset$	3 : **return** pt$'$
pt$_0$, pt$_1 \leftarrow \mathcal{A}^{\mathcal{O}^{\mathsf{ATK1}}}(\mathsf{pk})$	
ct$^* \leftarrow$$ \mathsf{enc}(\mathsf{pk}, \mathsf{pt}_b)$	
$b' \leftarrow \mathcal{A}^{\mathcal{O}^{\mathsf{ATK2}}}(\mathsf{pk}, \mathsf{ct}^*)$	
return b'	

Fig. 3. Indistinguishability games.

Definition 2 (IND-CPA/CCA/CCA1). *We consider the game defined in Fig. 3, where the oracles given in each game are defined as in the left of Table 1. A PKE scheme* PKE $=$ (setup, gen, enc, dec) *is IND-ATK for* ATK $\in$ {*CPA, CCA, CCA1*} *if for any ppt adversary $\mathcal{A}$ we have*

$$\mathsf{Adv}_{\mathcal{A},\mathsf{PKE}}^{\mathsf{ind}\text{-}\mathsf{atk}} = \left| \Pr\left[\text{IND-ATK}_{\mathsf{PKE}}^1(\mathcal{A}) \Rightarrow 1\right] - \Pr\left[\text{IND-ATK}_{\mathsf{PKE}}^0(\mathcal{A}) \Rightarrow 1\right]\right| = \mathsf{negl}(\lambda)$$

where $\Pr\left[\text{IND-ATK}_{\mathsf{PKE}}^b(\mathcal{A}) \Rightarrow 1\right]$ *is the probability that $\mathcal{A}$ wins the IND-ATK$_{\mathsf{PKE}}^b(\mathcal{A})$ game defined in Fig. 3.*

Plaintext and Validity Checking. We also recall three less common security definitions: One-Wayness under Plaintext-Checking Attacks (OW-PCA)/Validity Checking Attacks (OW-VA)/Plaintext and Validity Checking Attacks (OW-PVCA). These notions are useful when proving the security of FO-like transforms, as shown by Hofheinz et al. [13]. All these notions are weaker than IND-CCA but they model the concept of *reaction attacks*, that is when an adversary can observe whether a decryption is successful or not.

Definition 3 (One-Wayness and Plaintext/Validity Checking). *Let $\mathcal{M}$ be the message space,* PKE *a PKE scheme and we consider the games defined in Fig. 4 with the different oracles as defined on the right in Table 1. Then,* PKE *is OW-ATK, for* ATK $\in$ {*CPA, PCA, VCA, PVCA*}*, if for any ppt adversary $\mathcal{A}$ we have*

$$\mathsf{Adv}_{\mathsf{PKE}}^{\mathsf{ow}\text{-}\mathsf{atk}}(\mathcal{A}) = \Pr\left[\text{OW-ATK}_{\mathsf{PKE}}(\mathcal{A}) \Rightarrow 1\right] = \mathsf{negl}(\lambda)$$

Table 1. Oracles for IND and OW games.

ATK	CPA	CCA1	CCA
$\mathcal{O}^{\text{ATK1}}$	$\perp$	$\mathcal{O}^{\text{Dec}}$	$\mathcal{O}^{\text{Dec}}$
$\mathcal{O}^{\text{ATK2}}$	$\perp$	$\perp$	$\mathcal{O}^{\text{Dec}}$

ATK	CPA	PCA	VCA	PVCA
$\mathcal{O}^{\text{ATK}}$	$\perp$	$\mathcal{O}^{\text{PCO}}$	$\mathcal{O}^{\text{VCO}}$	$\mathcal{O}^{\text{PCO}}, \mathcal{O}^{\text{VCO}}$

OW-ATK$_{\text{PKE}}(\mathcal{A})$

pp $\leftarrow_\$ \text{setup}(1^\lambda)$
(pk, sk) $\leftarrow_\$ \text{gen}(\text{pp})$
pt$^* \leftarrow_\$ \mathcal{M}$
ct$^* \leftarrow \text{enc}(\text{pk}, \text{pt}^*)$
pt$' \leftarrow \mathcal{A}^{\mathcal{O}^{\text{ATK}}}(\text{pk}, \text{ct}^*)$
return $1_{\text{pt}'=\text{pt}^*}$

Oracle $\mathcal{O}^{\text{PCO}}(\text{pt}, \text{ct})$

1 : pt$' \leftarrow \text{dec}(\text{pp}, \text{sk}, \text{ct})$
2 : **return** $1_{\text{pt}'=\text{pt}}$

Oracle $\mathcal{O}^{\text{VCO}}(\text{ct} \neq \text{ct}^*)$

1 : pt$' \leftarrow \text{dec}(\text{pp}, \text{sk}, \text{ct})$
2 : **return** $1_{\text{pt}' \in \mathcal{M}}$

Fig. 4. One-Wayness games.

where $\Pr\left[\text{OW-ATK}_{\text{PKE}}(\mathcal{A}) \Rightarrow 1\right]$ *is the probability that the adversary wins the* OW-ATK *game.*

3.2 Key Encapsulation Mechanism (KEM)

Definition 4 (Key Encapsulation Mechanism). *A KEM is a tuple of four algorithms* setup, gen, encaps, decaps:

- pp $\leftarrow_\$ \text{setup}(1^\lambda)$: *The setup algorithm takes the security parameter* λ *as input and outputs the public parameters* pp.
- (pk, sk) $\leftarrow_\$ \text{gen}(\text{pp})$: *The key generation algorithm takes as inputs the public parameters and it outputs the public key* pk *and the secret key* sk.
- ct, $K \leftarrow_\$ \text{encaps}(\text{pp}, \text{pk})$: *The encapsulation algorithm takes as inputs the public parameters* pp, *the public key* pk *and it outputs a ciphertext* ct $\in \mathcal{C}$ *and a key* $K \in \mathcal{K}$.
- $K' \leftarrow \text{decaps}(\text{pp}, \text{sk}, \text{ct})$: *The decapsulation procedure takes as inputs the public parameters* pp, *the secret key* sk *and the ciphertext* ct $\in \mathcal{C}$ *and it outputs a key* K. *If the KEM allows explicit rejection, the output is a key* $K \in \mathcal{K}$ *or the rejection symbol* $\perp$. *If the rejection is implicit, the output is always a key* $K \in \mathcal{K}$.

The setup, gen *and* encaps *are probabilistic algorithms that can be made deterministic by adding random coins as inputs. The decapsulation function is deterministic. For the sake of simplicity, we omit the public parameters in the inputs from now on.*

IND-ATK$_{\mathsf{KEM}}(\mathcal{A})$	Oracle $\mathcal{O}^{\mathsf{Dec}}(\mathsf{ct})$
$\mathsf{pp} \leftarrow_\$ \mathsf{setup}(1^\lambda)$	1 : if $\mathsf{ct} = \mathsf{ct}^*$ then return $\perp$
$(\mathsf{pk}, \mathsf{sk}) \leftarrow_\$ \mathsf{gen}(\mathsf{pp})$	2 : $K' \leftarrow \mathsf{decaps}(\mathsf{pp}, \mathsf{sk}, \mathsf{ct})$
$st \leftarrow \mathcal{A}^{\mathcal{O}^{\mathsf{ATK1}}}(\mathsf{pk})$	3 : return K'
$b \leftarrow_\$ \{0, 1\}$	
$\mathsf{ct}^*, K_0 \leftarrow_\$ \mathsf{encaps}(\mathsf{pk})$	
$K_1 \leftarrow_\$ \mathcal{K}$	
$b' \leftarrow \mathcal{A}^{\mathcal{O}^{\mathsf{ATK2}}}(st, \mathsf{pk}, \mathsf{ct}^*, K_b)$	
return $1_{b'=b}$	

Fig. 5. Indistinguishability games.

Definition 5. *We consider the games defined in Fig. 5. The oracles the adversary has access to are defined on the left in Table 1 and $\mathcal{K}$ is the key space. A KEM scheme $\mathsf{KEM} = (\mathsf{setup}, \mathsf{gen}, \mathsf{encaps}, \mathsf{decaps})$ is IND-ATK if for any ppt adversary $\mathcal{A}$ we have*

$$\mathsf{Adv}_{\mathsf{KEM}}^{\mathsf{ind\text{-}atk}}(\mathcal{A}) = \left| \Pr\left[\mathrm{IND} - \mathrm{ATK}_{\mathsf{KEM}}(\mathcal{A}) \Rightarrow 1\right] - \frac{1}{2} \right| = \mathsf{negl}(\lambda)$$

where $\Pr\left[\mathrm{IND\text{-}ATK}_{\mathsf{KEM}}(\mathcal{A}) \Rightarrow 1\right]$ is the probability that $\mathcal{A}$ wins the IND-ATK$_{\mathsf{KEM}}(\mathcal{A})$ game defined in Fig. 5.

4   FO-like Combiners

We wish to design constructions that take two (or more) IND/OW-CPA schemes instead of one and output an IND-CCA KEM. Compared to black-box combiners, this approach allows for lower-level combiners, which in turn can be more efficient. As more precise examples, we consider KEM combiners proposed by Bindel et al. [3]. These 3 constructions, namely XtM, dualPRF and N are based on special kinds of MAC and PRF. In the XtM combiner, the keys must be split and a tag on the ciphertexts is computed. Similarly, in the dualPRF and N combiners, multiple passes on the keys and ciphertext must be performed to derive the key (see Bindel et al. [3] for more details). All these operations add complexity and/or increase the ciphertext length while being redundant if the underlying KEMs are built using a FO-like transform. Thus, one could hope to remove several superfluous computations and primitives by looking at the actual implementation of the underlying KEMs. We apply this idea to construct several new combiners, which we call *FO-like combiners*. In addition of not being black-box, these combiners differ from other proposals in the fact that they take several PKEs as inputs and output a KEM.

gen()	enc(pk, (pt_1, pt_2))	dec(sk, (ct_1, ct_2))
$(pk_1, sk_1) \leftarrow\!\!{\scriptstyle\$}\ gen_1$	parse $(pk_1, pk_2) \leftarrow pk$	parse $(sk_1, sk_2) \leftarrow sk$
$(pk_2, sk_2) \leftarrow\!\!{\scriptstyle\$}\ gen_2$	$ct_1 \leftarrow enc_1(pk_1, pt_1; G(pt_1))$	$pt_1' \leftarrow dec_1(sk_1, ct_1)$
$pk \leftarrow (pk_1, pk_2)$	$ct_2 \leftarrow enc_2(pk_2, pt_2; G(pt_2))$	$pt_2' \leftarrow dec_2(sk_2, ct_2)$
$sk \leftarrow (sk_1, sk_2)$	return (ct_1, ct_2)	if $enc_1(pk_1, pt_1'; G(pt_1')) \neq ct_1$:
return (pk, sk)		return $\perp$
		if $enc_2(pk_2, pt_2'; G(pt_2')) \neq ct_2$:
		return $\perp$
		return (pt_1', pt_2')

Fig. 6. $T_\parallel$ combiner.

gen()	encaps(pk)	decaps(sk, ct)
$(pk, sk) \leftarrow\!\!{\scriptstyle\$}\ gen_1$	$pt \leftarrow\!\!{\scriptstyle\$}\ \mathcal{M}$	parse $sk, s \leftarrow sk$ // $U^{\not\perp}$
$s \leftarrow\!\!{\scriptstyle\$}\ \mathcal{M}$ // $U^{\not\perp}$	$ct \leftarrow enc(pk, pt)$	$pt' \leftarrow dec(sk, ct)$
$sk \leftarrow (sk, s)$ // $U^{\not\perp}$	$K \leftarrow H(pt, ct)$	if $pt' = \perp$ return $\perp$ // $U^\perp$
return (pk, sk)	return ct, K	if $pt' = \perp$ return $H(s, ct)$ // $U^{\not\perp}$
		return $H(pt', ct)$

Fig. 7. $U^\perp$ and $U^{\not\perp}$ transforms of [13].

4.1 $T_\parallel$ Combiner

For our first construction, the idea is to apply twice the T transform of Hofheinz et al. [13] to obtain an OW-PCA PKE from two OW-CPA PKEs $PKE_i = (setup_i, gen_i, enc_i, dec_i)$, $i \in \{1, 2\}$. We call this FO-like combiner $T_\parallel$ and we present it in Fig. 6 (we omit the setup algorithm, which is trivial). Then, one can apply the $U^{\not\perp}$ transform (see Fig. 7) and Theorem 3.4 of Hofheinz et al. [13] to obtain an IND-CCA KEM. The message space $\mathcal{M}$ of the resulting PKE is $\mathcal{M}_1 \times \mathcal{M}_2$ (i.e. the space product of the two message spaces). This construction is actually a useful intermediary step towards a more general OW-CPA to KEM IND-CCA combiner we present in the next section.

The following theorem shows that $T_\parallel$ is a robust combiner (as long as one of the two underlying PKEs is OW-CPA, the resulting PKE is OW-PCA).

Theorem 1. *Let* PKE *be the PKE resulting from applying* $T_\parallel$ *on* PKE_1 *and* PKE_2, *which are respectively* δ_1 *and* δ_2 *correct. In addition, let* G *be a hash function modelled as a random oracle. Then, for all ppt OW-PCA adversary* $\mathcal{A}$ *making at most* q_G *queries to* G *and* q_P *queries to the plaintext-checking oracle, there exists adversaries* $\mathcal{B}_1$ *and* $\mathcal{B}_2$ *such that*

$$\mathsf{Adv}_{\mathsf{PKE}}^{\mathrm{ow-pca}}(\mathcal{A}) \leq (q_G + q_P) \cdot (\delta_1 + \delta_2) + (q_G + 1) \cdot \min\{\mathsf{Adv}_{\mathsf{PKE}_1}^{\mathrm{ow-cpa}}(\mathcal{B}_1), \mathsf{Adv}_{\mathsf{PKE}_2}^{\mathrm{ow-cpa}}(\mathcal{B}_2)\}$$

where $\mathcal{B}_1$ *and* $\mathcal{B}_2$ *run in about the same time as* $\mathcal{A}$.

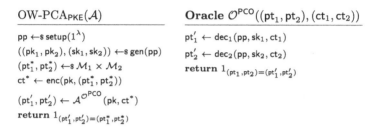

Fig. 8. Trivial PKE combiner C.

$$\text{OW-PCA}_{\text{PKE}}(\mathcal{A})$$

$\text{pp} \leftarrow\!\!\text{\$ setup}(1^\lambda)$

$((\text{pk}_1, \text{pk}_2), (\text{sk}_1, \text{sk}_2)) \leftarrow\!\!\text{\$ gen(pp)}$

$(\text{pt}_1^*, \text{pt}_2^*) \leftarrow\!\!\text{\$} \mathcal{M}_1 \times \mathcal{M}_2$

$\text{ct}^* \leftarrow \text{enc}(\text{pk}, (\text{pt}_1^*, \text{pt}_2^*))$

$(\text{pt}_1', \text{pt}_2') \leftarrow \mathcal{A}^{\mathcal{O}^{\text{PCO}}}(\text{pk}, \text{ct}^*)$

$\text{return } 1_{(\text{pt}_1', \text{pt}_2') = (\text{pt}_1^*, \text{pt}_2^*)}$

$$\textbf{Oracle } \mathcal{O}^{\text{PCO}}((\text{pt}_1, \text{pt}_2), (\text{ct}_1, \text{ct}_2))$$

$\text{pt}_1' \leftarrow \text{dec}_1(\text{pp}, \text{sk}_1, \text{ct}_1)$

$\text{pt}_2' \leftarrow \text{dec}_2(\text{pp}, \text{sk}_2, \text{ct}_2)$

$\text{return } 1_{(\text{pt}_1, \text{pt}_2) = (\text{pt}_1', \text{pt}_2')}$

Fig. 9. OW-PCA game against PKE for the proof of Theorem 1.

Proof. We first show that the trivial PKE combiner C in Fig. 8 is a robust OW-PCA combiner. Let $\text{PKE} = \text{C}(\text{PKE}_1, \text{PKE}_2)$ be the PKE resulting from applying C on two PKEs PKE_1 and PKE_2. We show w.l.o.g. that the OW-PCA security of PKE reduces to the OW-PCA security of PKE_1. The OW-PCA game against PKE is presented in Fig. 9. One can see that the plaintext-checking oracle can easily be simulated by an adversary having access to a plaintext-checking oracle for PKE_1 and holding the secret key sk_2. Thus, we can easily build an adversary $\mathcal{B}$ against the OW-PCA security of PKE_1. This adversary generates itself $\text{pk}_2, \text{sk}_2, \text{ct}_2^*$, runs $\mathcal{A}$ and simulates perfectly the PCO oracle with its own oracle and sk_2. When $\mathcal{A}$ returns $(\text{pt}_1', \text{pt}_2')$, $\mathcal{B}$ returns pt_1' and wins with at least the same advantage as $\mathcal{A}$. Hence,

$$\text{Adv}_{\text{PKE}}^{\text{ow-pca}}(\mathcal{A}) \leq \min\{\text{Adv}_{\text{PKE}_1}^{\text{ow-pca}}(\mathcal{B}_1), \text{Adv}_{\text{PKE}_2}^{\text{ow-pca}}(\mathcal{B}_2)\} .$$

To conclude the proof, one can just observe that $\text{T}_\|(\text{PKE}_1, \text{PKE}_2) = \text{C}(\text{T}(\text{PKE}_1), \text{T}(\text{PKE}_2))$, where T is the OW-CPA to OW-PCA transform from Hofheinz et al. [13]. $\qquad\square$

Corollary 1. *Let* KEM *be the KEM resulting from applying* $\text{U}^{\not\perp} \circ \text{T}_\|$ *onto two PKE schemes* PKE_1 *and* PKE_2, *which are* δ_1-correct *and* δ_2-correct, *respectively. Then, for any IND-CCA adversary* $\mathcal{A}$ *making at most* q_H *and* q_G *queries to the ROs* H *and* G, *respectively, and* q_D *queries to the decapsulation oracle, there exists OW-CPA adversaries* $\mathcal{B}_1$ *and* $\mathcal{B}_2$ *such that*

$$\text{Adv}_{\text{KEM}}^{\text{ind-cca}}(\mathcal{A}) \leq \frac{q_H}{|\mathcal{M}_1||\mathcal{M}_2|} + (q_G + q_D) \cdot (\delta_1 + \delta_2)$$
$$+ (q_G + 1) \cdot \min\{\text{Adv}_{\text{PKE}_1}^{\text{ow-cpa}}(\mathcal{B}_1), \text{Adv}_{\text{PKE}_2}^{\text{ow-cpa}}(\mathcal{B}_2)\}$$

$\mathcal{B}_1^{\mathcal{A},\mathcal{O}^{PCO_1}}(\mathsf{pk}_1,\mathsf{ct}_1^*)$	**Oracle** $\mathcal{O}^{PCO}((\mathsf{pt}_1,\mathsf{pt}_2),(\mathsf{ct}_1,\mathsf{ct}_2))$
$\mathsf{pp}_2 \leftarrow\!\!{}_\$ \mathsf{setup}_2(1^\lambda)$	$r \leftarrow \mathcal{O}^{PCO_1}(\mathsf{pt}_1,\mathsf{ct}_1)$
$(\mathsf{pk}_2,\mathsf{sk}_2) \leftarrow\!\!{}_\$ \mathsf{gen}_2(\mathsf{pp}_2)$	$\mathsf{pt}_2' \leftarrow \mathsf{dec}_2(\mathsf{pp},\mathsf{sk}_2,\mathsf{ct}_2)$
$\mathsf{pt}_2^* \leftarrow\!\!{}_\$ \mathcal{M}_2$	**return** $1_{r=1 \wedge \mathsf{pt}_2 = \mathsf{pt}_2'}$
$\mathsf{ct}_2^* \leftarrow \mathsf{enc}_2(\mathsf{pk},\mathsf{pt}_2^*)$	
$(\mathsf{pt}_1',\mathsf{pt}_2') \leftarrow \mathcal{A}^{\mathcal{O}^{PCO}}((\mathsf{pk}_1,\mathsf{pk}_2),(\mathsf{ct}_1^*,\mathsf{ct}_2^*))$	
return pt_1'	

Fig. 10. OW-CPA adversary for the proof of Theorem 1.

where $\mathcal{M}_i$ is the message space of PKE$_i$ *and $\mathcal{B}_i$ runs in about the same time as $\mathcal{A}$ (Fig. 10).*

Proof. This is a simple consequence of Theorem 3.4 of Hofheinz et al. [13] and Theorem 1. □

Discussion. Let $\mathsf{UT}_{\parallel}^{\not\perp}$ be the combiner resulting from composing $\mathsf{U}^{\not\perp}$ and $\mathsf{T}_{\parallel}$. One could wonder whether combining two PKEs in a trivial way (i.e. encrypting $\mathsf{pt}_1,\mathsf{pt}_2$ as $(\mathsf{enc}_1(\mathsf{pt}_1),\mathsf{enc}_2(\mathsf{pt}_2))$ and decrypting both ciphertexts independently) and then applying a FO-like transform would hold a robust IND-CCA KEM. In fact, this would give a combiner similar to $\mathsf{UT}_{\parallel}^{\not\perp}$, except the random coins would be split into two parts $(G(\mathsf{pt}_1,\mathsf{pt}_2))_{\lambda_1}$ and $(G(\mathsf{pt}_1,\mathsf{pt}_2))_{\lambda_2}$ for each encryption procedure, where λ_i is the number of coins needed by the encryption of PKE$_i$. As G is a RO, both shares would be independent and the result would be similar to the coins $G(\mathsf{pt}_i)$ in our $\mathsf{UT}_{\parallel}^{\not\perp}$ transform. We preferred the latter solution as it is possible to compute the coins in parallel and we think it makes the separation between both sets of coins clear. One could also wonder whether setting the coins to $G(\mathsf{pt}_1,\mathsf{pt}_2)$ would work. This, in turn, creates a correlation between both ciphertexts, which cannot be dealt with in the security proof.

The choice of computing the deterministic coins for ct_i based on σ_i only (instead of σ_1 and σ_2) has positive and negative impacts on the resulting scheme.

Efficiency: Both ciphertexts are totally independent and can be computed in parallel. In turn, this would allow to keep a key share static for a period of time while varying the other one. This could improve consequently the efficiency of hybrid schemes in protocols.

Malleability and Misuse Resistance: The ciphertexts of the resulting KEM $\mathsf{ct}^* = (\mathsf{ct}_1^*,\mathsf{ct}_2^*)$ are somewhat malleable. Indeed, it is easy to modify a ciphertext into another one s.t. the decryption is valid. For instance, $\mathsf{ct}' = (\mathsf{ct}_1^*,\mathsf{ct}_2')$, for a valid ct_2', will decapsulate properly to the key $H(\sigma_1^*,\sigma_2',\mathsf{ct}')$. This has no consequence in the ROM as the RO hides perfectly σ_1^*, but this does not necessarily seem a desired property. In particular, due to this malleability effect, the key must be derived as $H(\sigma_1,\sigma_2,\ldots)$ and other KDFs that would seem intuitive lead to security flaw. For instance, computing the key as $H(\sigma_1) \oplus H(\sigma_2)$ in the transform makes a trivial IND-CCA attack possible.

gen()	encaps(pk)	decaps(sk, (ct$_1$, ct$_2$))
$(pk_1, sk_1) \leftarrow\!\!{\scriptstyle\$} \, gen_1$	parse $(pk_1, pk_2) \leftarrow pk$	parse $(sk_1, sk_2) \leftarrow sk$
$(pk_2, sk_2) \leftarrow\!\!{\scriptstyle\$} \, gen_2$	$(\sigma_1, \sigma_2) \leftarrow\!\!{\scriptstyle\$} \, \mathcal{M}_1 \times \mathcal{M}_2$	$\sigma_1' \leftarrow dec_1(sk_1, ct_1)$
$pk \leftarrow (pk_1, pk_2)$	$ct_1 \leftarrow enc_1(pk_1, \sigma_1; G(1, \sigma_1, \sigma_2))$	$\sigma_2' \leftarrow dec_2(sk_2, ct_2)$
$sk \leftarrow (sk_1, sk_2)$	$ct_2 \leftarrow enc_2(pk_2, \sigma_2; G(2, \sigma_1, \sigma_2))$	if $enc_1(pk_1, \sigma_1'; G(1, \sigma_1', \sigma_2')) \neq ct_1$:
return (pk, sk)	$K \leftarrow H(\sigma_1 \oplus \sigma_2)$	return $\perp$
	return $(ct_1, ct_2), K$	if $enc_2(pk_2, \sigma_2'; G(2, \sigma_1', \sigma_2')) \neq ct_2$:
		return $\perp$
		return $H(\sigma_1' \oplus \sigma_2')$

Fig. 11. $UT_{\|}$ combiner.

Efficiency. One can see that the main cost of the combiner is to compute two hash values on the two plaintexts (i.e. seeds) and then a hash on the two plaintexts and ciphertexts. This already seems slightly more efficient than the XtM (XOR-then-MAC) combiner proposed by Bindel et al. [3]. Indeed, XtM doubles the size of the keys returned by the underlying KEMs, split them and compute a MAC on the ciphertexts using two halves of the keys.

Now, as the ciphertexts in post-quantum cryptography can be large (usually a few kilobytes), computing a hash on two ciphertexts can be an expensive operation. Our combiner presented in the next section fixes this drawback.

4.2 $UT_{\|}$

We now propose an FO-like combiner similar to $T_{\|}$ that combines two OW-CPA PKEs into an IND-CCA KEM. In a way, we skip the $U^{\not\perp}$ transform to get directly a KEM. The idea is to encrypt two seeds (i.e. plaintexts) σ_1, σ_2 using the PKE resulting from $T_{\|}$ and then compute the key as $H(\sigma_1 \oplus \sigma_2)$. However, in order to avoid the malleability issue described in the previous section, the deterministic coins are computed as $G(i, \sigma_1, \sigma_2)$. This links both ciphertexts together and makes tampering one of the two more difficult. Note that in order to compute the XOR, we assume that the seeds σ_i are binary strings or that there exists an efficient and unique encoding of these objects as binary strings. Alternatively, one can take the hash of a plaintext to get a binary seed. All these options are compatible with our combiner and the choice of an approach depends on the underlying PKEs. We present the combiner in Fig. 11.

Now, the following theorem formally states the security of the $UT_{\|}$ combiner.

Theorem 2. *Let* KEM *be the KEM resulting from applying* $UT_{\|}$ *on* PKE$_1$ *and* PKE$_2$, *which are respectively* δ_1 *and* δ_2 *correct, and* γ_1 *and* γ_2-*spread. In addition, let* G *and* H *be hash functions modelled as a random oracle. Then, for all ppt IND-CCA adversary* $\mathcal{A}$ *making at most* q_G, q_H *and* q_D *queries to* G, H *and* $\mathcal{O}^{Dec}$, *respectively, there exists adversaries* $\mathcal{B}_1$ *and* $\mathcal{B}_2$ *such that*

$$\mathsf{Adv}_{\mathsf{KEM}}^{\mathrm{ind-cca}}(\mathcal{A}) \leq (q_D + q_G + 1) \cdot (\delta_1 + \delta_2) + q_D \cdot (2^{-\gamma_1} + 2^{-\gamma_2})$$
$$+ (q_G + q_H) \cdot \min\{\mathsf{Adv}_{\mathsf{PKE}_1}^{\mathrm{ow-cpa}}(\mathcal{B}_1), \mathsf{Adv}_{\mathsf{PKE}_2}^{\mathrm{ow-cpa}}(\mathcal{B}_2)\}$$

where $\mathcal{B}_1$ and $\mathcal{B}_2$ run in about the same time as $\mathcal{A}$ and make the same number of queries.

Proof. Due to space constraint, the proof is deferred to the full version of the paper [14].

Generalisation to n PKEs. While the $\mathsf{UT}_\|$ combiner presented in Fig. 11 takes two PKEs as input, it is straightforward to generalise it to n PKEs. Each of the n ciphertexts will simply be computed as $\mathsf{enc}_i(\mathsf{pk}_i, \sigma_i; G(i, \sigma_1, \ldots, \sigma_n))$ and the key as $H(\oplus_i^n \sigma_i)$. Then, the security of such a combiner (we call it $\mathsf{UT}_\|^n$) can be stated in the following Theorem, which is a generalization of Theorem 2.

Theorem 3. *Let* KEM *be the* KEM *resulting from applying* $\mathsf{UT}_\|^n$ *on* $\mathsf{PKE}_1, \ldots, \mathsf{PKE}_n$, *which are respectively* $\delta_1, \ldots, \delta_n$ *correct, and* $\gamma_1, \ldots, \gamma_n$-*spread. In addition, let* G *and* H *be hash functions modelled as a random oracle. Then, for all ppt IND-CCA adversary* $\mathcal{A}$ *making at most* q_G, q_H *and* q_D *queries to* G, H *and* $\mathcal{O}^{\mathsf{Dec}}$, *respectively, there exists adversaries* $\mathcal{B}_1, \ldots, \mathcal{B}_n$ *such that*

$$\mathsf{Adv}_{\mathsf{KEM}}^{\mathrm{ind-cca}}(\mathcal{A}) \leq (q_D + q_G + 1) \cdot \sum_{i=1}^{n} \delta_i + q_D \cdot \sum_{i=1}^{n} 2^{-\gamma_i}$$
$$+ (q_G + q_H) \cdot \min\{\mathsf{Adv}_{\mathsf{PKE}_1}^{\mathrm{ow-cpa}}(\mathcal{B}_1), \ldots, \mathsf{Adv}_{\mathsf{PKE}_n}^{\mathrm{ow-cpa}}(\mathcal{B}_n)\}$$

where $\mathcal{B}_1, \ldots, \mathcal{B}_n$ run in about the same time as $\mathcal{A}$ and make the same number of queries.

Proof Idea. The proof is exactly the same as the one for the security of $\mathsf{UT}_\|$ with two PKEs except we consider n schemes. In particular, the probability of having a correctness or spreadness error in some query is upper bounded by $\sum_{i=1}^{n} \delta_i$ and $\sum_{i=1}^{n} 2^{-\gamma_i}$, respectively. Also, the reductions $\mathcal{B}_i$ from the OW-CPA of the PKEs still work the same, as an adversary $\mathcal{B}_i$ picks all σ_j^* s.t. $j \neq i$. That is, if $(i, \sigma_1^*, \ldots, \sigma_n^*)$ is queried, $\mathcal{B}_i$ can recover σ_i^*, otherwise we can replace the deterministic coins by random ones. Similarly, if $\sigma^* = \oplus_j^n \sigma_j^*$ is queried by the adversary to H, $\mathcal{B}_i$ can recover σ_i^* by computing $\sigma^* \oplus_{j \neq i} \sigma_j^*$. $\quad\square$

Security in the Quantum Random Oracle Model (QROM). We discuss the security of combiners in the QROM in the full version of the paper [14]. In particular, the security of the $\mathsf{T}_\|$ combiner follows from the QROM security of the T transform.

4.3 Other Combiners

It has been shown that the implementation of ROs in FO-like transforms, in particular in the de-randomization step (i.e. computation of the deterministic coins), is particularly vulnerable to implementation mistakes [1]. Thus, it is of interest to study how these coins can be computed without compromising the security of the resulting scheme. We show in this section how hash functions (i.e. ROs) can be combined s.t. the de-randomization step is secure and efficient. Many combinations of hash functions are possible and we propose a few of those below, offering flexibility to implementors. Finally, we consider using different hash functions to increase the security at no (or very small) cost. This relates to the notion of hash combiner [6,7], which constructs a hash function that fulfils certain security properties as long as one of the underlying hash functions has this property. In our case, we want the hash functions to behave as random oracles, thus we can combine two different functions to make the whole scheme secure as long as *one* of the hash functions is indistinguishable from a RO.

How to Combine Hash Functions. From now on, in order to distinguish (random) functions from random oracles, we denote a function by a small letter and a RO by a capital letter (e.g. $g(x)$ is a function evaluated on x and $G(x)$ is a RO queried on x). Note that in our case, the functions are defined using random oracles (e.g. $g(x) := G(1, x) \oplus G(2, x)$). We consider replacing the RO G in our combiners by such a random function g (but still in the ROM).

One can see from the proofs of security of both $\mathsf{T}_\parallel$ and $\mathsf{UT}_\parallel$ that we want the deterministic coins to be indistinguishable from random ones until we can recover the seeds (or plaintexts) from the list of queries. In addition to this property, one also wants the values $g(i, \sigma_1, \sigma_2)$ to be close to uniform. Indeed, in the proof of Theorem 2, we extensively use the fact that the correctness and spreadness property hold with probability at least δ and $2^{-\gamma}$, respectively, even when the coins are not random but computed as $g(i, \sigma_1, \sigma_2)$. Obviously, if the values $g(1, \sigma_1, \sigma_2)$ are not sampled uniformly at random, this may not hold anymore. In other words, we want $g(i, \sigma_1, \sigma_2)$ to be either computable by the adversary using its queries to G or distributed uniformly at random. We developed formal definitions (called *Extractable Random Function (ERF)* and *Indistinguishable unless Queried (IUQ)*) capturing these properties, they are presented in the full version of the paper [14]. We give two examples of such functions g satisfying these properties in Table 2. Note that these are based on a RO G.

Replacing H. As we did for G, one can also replace the key derivation function H by another random function h. The function $h(\sigma_1, \sigma_2) = H(\sigma_1) \oplus H(\sigma_2)$ is one example. More details can be found in the full version [14].

Then, one can show the following theorem.

Theorem 4 (Informal). *Let g be a function from Table 2. Let $h(\sigma_1, \sigma_2) := H(\sigma_1, \sigma_2)$ or $h(\sigma_1, \sigma_2) := H(\sigma_1) \oplus H(\sigma_2)$. Then, the $\mathsf{UT}_\parallel$ transform where the deterministic coins for encrypting the seed σ_i are computed as $g(i, \sigma_1, \sigma_2)$ instead of $G(i, \sigma_1, \sigma_2)$ and the key is derived as $h(\sigma_1, \sigma_2)$, is still a robust combiner.*

A formal version of this result is stated in the full version of the paper [14].

Table 2. Different g functions, where G, G_i are ROs.

$g(i, \sigma_1, \sigma_2)$
$G(\sigma_1 \oplus \sigma_2) \oplus G(i, \sigma_i)$
$G_1(i, \sigma_1) \oplus G_2(i, \sigma_2)$

Hash Combiners. As some of the proposed functions g use more than one hash functions, these functions are themselves hash combiners. Thus, it is of interest to study the robustness of such constructions. That is, if one of the underlying hash functions is broken (i.e. shown not to behave as a RO), is the g function (thus the whole FO-like combiner) still secure? As one of the main security concerns of the use of FO-like transforms is that the proofs are in the ROM, using robust hash combiners may improve the trust in such constructions.

The last function g in Table 2 is actually a robust combiner with respect to the RO property and one of the seeds. That is, $G_1(i, \sigma_1) \oplus G_2(i, \sigma_2)$ is indistinguishable from a RO, even if G_1 (or G_2) is any function. Hence, if we take both $g(i, \sigma_1, \sigma_2) = G_1(i, \sigma_1) \oplus G_2(i, \sigma_2)$ and $h(\sigma_1, \sigma_2) = H_1(\sigma_1) \oplus H_2(\sigma_2)$ in the FO-like combiner, we will obtain a secure KEM as long as G_i **and** H_i **and** PKE_i are secure for some $i \in [2]$.

Proposition 1 (Informal). *Let* $g(i, \sigma_1, \sigma_2) = G_1(i, \sigma_1) \oplus G_2(i, \sigma_2)$ *and* $h(\sigma_1, \sigma_2) = H_1(\sigma_1) \oplus H_2(\sigma_2)$. *We call a tuple* $(G_i, H_i, \mathsf{PKE}_i)$ *secure if* G_i, H_i *are ROs and* PKE_i *is OW-CPA. Let* KEM *be the hybrid KEM resulting from applying* $\mathsf{UT}_{\|}$ *on* PKE_1 *and* PKE_2 *with* g *and* h *to derive the deterministic coins and key, respectively. Then,* KEM *is IND-CCA if* $(G_1, H_1, \mathsf{PKE}_1)$ *or* $(G_2, H_2, \mathsf{PKE}_2)$ *(or both) is secure.*

Proof Sketch. We assume w.l.o.g. that the tuple $(G_1, H_1, \mathsf{PKE}_1)$ is secure and G_2, H_2 can be any functions and PKE_2 might not be OW-CPA. In addition, we assume G_1, H_1, G_2, H_2 are mutually independent functions (e.g. this can be implemented by RO separation). The result follows simply from the fact that in the IND-CCA game against KEM, as long as G_1 is a RO, the coins $G_1(i, \sigma_1) \oplus G_2(i, \sigma_2)$ are indistinguishable from uniform unless (i, σ_1) is queried, irrespectively of the value $G_2(i, \sigma_2)$. But in turn such a query would break the OW-CPA assumption on PKE_1 (or happens with negligible probability). The same argument for $h(\sigma_1, \sigma_2) = H_1(\sigma_1) \oplus H_2(\sigma_2)$ holds that the key will always be indistinguishable from uniform if H_1 is a RO and PKE_1 is OW-CPA. $\square$

5 Implementation

As a proof of concept, we implemented a fully PQ hybrid KEM using two IND-CPA proposals that passed to the Round 2 of the standardization process and our combiner. As the main goal of our combiner is to increase the security while still offering good performances, we chose HQC and LAC since

1. LAC is one of the most efficient schemes in term of speed and public-key/ciphertext size but it has been attacked recently in [11]. More generally, it seems LAC is more vulnerable to failure attacks than other schemes and that led this scheme to be dropped for Round 3. Thus, using it along another cryptosystem does not imply a large overhead while preventing a failure attack alone against LAC to break the whole scheme.

2. HQC is a code-based scheme that offers good performance, although the hardness assumption it is based on has not been extensively studied as of yet. Thus, combining it with another efficient scheme might provide more confidence in this scheme at the expense of a small overhead.

3. HQC is code-based while LAC is lattice-based. Therefore, one can hope that any progress in breaking the assumption of one does not lead to a better cryptanalysis of the other.

5.1 Design Choices

We used the reference IND-CPA implementations provided by the authors in the second round for both schemes. Then, we applied our $UT_{\parallel}$ combiner. In practice we implemented $G(1, \cdot, \cdot)$ as SHA256($\cdot$), $G(2, \cdot, \cdot)$ as the AES-based expansion function provided by the NIST and $H(\cdot)$ as SHA512($\cdot$). These choices made the implementation easier as we could stick to most of the author's choices. For example, HQC encryption function in the original FO transform is using a seed output by the AES-based expander and our choice of $G(2, \sigma_1, \sigma_2)$ makes the reuse of most of the code possible.

We implemented two versions of the hybrid cryptosystem, a standard version that we are calling hqc_lac128 and a parallel version denoted by hqc_lac128_par, both using the Level 1 (i.e. aiming at 128 bits of classical security) reference implementations of LAC and HQC. The parallel implementation uses the pthread library and is implemented without any other optimization. In particular, only the encryption of the seeds is parallelized in the encapsulation function (i.e. the encryption functions of LAC and HQC are called in different threads) and only the decryption and reencryption is parallelized in the decapsulation procedure.

5.2 Results and Efficiency

We tested both our hybrid schemes on a laptop running Ubuntu 14.04 with an Intel(R) Core(TM) i7-3520M CPU @ 2.90GHz. The results for our hybrid schemes, the original schemes and reference implementations of two other popular lattice-based schemes (Frodo and Kyber) are reported in Table 3. The sizes are in bytes and the times are given in microseconds (10^{-6}s) and are averaged over 10000 runs. Obviously, the size of the public/secret key and ciphertext are the addition of the corresponding ones in LAC and HQC, except for the ciphertext, which is a bit smaller. This follows from the fact that the ciphertext in HQC contains a confirmation hash that we omit in our FO-like combiner. One can see that compared to a proposal with large keys and ciphertexts (i.e. Frodo), our

Table 3. Performance of hqc_lac128 and hqc_lac128_par compared to other schemes. The size of the public/secret key and ciphertext are in bytes. The time for key generation, encapsulation, decapsulation is in microseconds.

Scheme	SK (B)	PK (B)	CT (B)	KeyGen (μs)	Encaps (μs)	Decaps (μs)
frodo640	19888	9616	9720	847.553	4650.037	4602.284
hqc128	3165	3125	6234	144.166	298.120	528.624
kyber512	1632	800	736	154.077	210.857	263.194
lac128	1056	544	712	115.308	199.776	311.709
hqc_lac128	4221	3669	6882	260.032	484.969	813.452
hqc_lac128_par	4221	3669	6882	162.502	315.137	549.516

hybrid compares well. In addition, as LAC produces small outputs, the increase compared to HQC is small. That is, the size of the secret key, public key and ciphertext is increased by roughly 33%, 17% and 10%, respectively.

Considering the speed, the non-optimized hybrid hqc_lac128 performs slightly better than both LAC and HQC run one after the other. However, all procedures are still much faster than the ones of a slower scheme, like Frodo. On the other hand, the parallelized hybrid hqc_lac128_par offers very good performance as one could expect from such a parallelizable design. In particular, we observe only a 13%, 6% and 4% increase of latency compared to HQC, for key generation, encapsulation and decapsulation, respectively. Therefore, hqc_lac128_par can perform nearly as good as HQC on systems that offers efficient parallelization, such as laptops or any machine with regularly idle processors.

We give on Fig. 12 a visualisation of the performance of hqc_lac128 compared to other round 2 candidates with security Level 1. Most of the data comes from the SUPERCOP [2] benchmarking system (we picked the results of a test performed on a 2018 Intel Core i7-8809G). All round 2 proposals are represented, except for BIKE, Round 5 and LEDACrypt, which did not have an IND-CCA version benchmarked at the time of the test. We still added the keys and ciphertext sizes of BIKE as they are similar to the ones of HQC.

For the hybrid scheme hqc_lac128, we computed the cycles needed for key generation, encapsulation and decapsulation as the sum of the corresponding cycles needed by LAC and HQC. Note that this is a pessimistic approximation as the hybrid system requires less instructions than the sum of both underlying schemes (e.g. we apply some hash functions only once), this is confirmed in practice by the results shown in Table 3. We do not plot the parallelized version hqc_lac128_par as the sizes are the same as in hqc_lac128 and the time is upper bounded by the latter as well.

Analysis. From all three graphs in Fig. 12, we can deduce that our hybrid does not perform particularly well compared to other schemes in these metrics. However, one can see that the bottleneck is the use of HQC here. In particular, hqc_lac128 performs nearly as well as HQC in the metrics considered. This confirm what we wanted to show, that is boosting security by combining a very

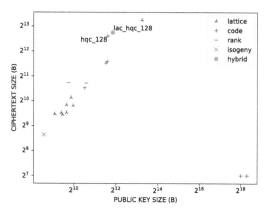

(a) Public Key size vs Cipertext size.

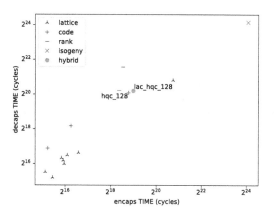

(b) Encapsulation time vs Decapsulation time.

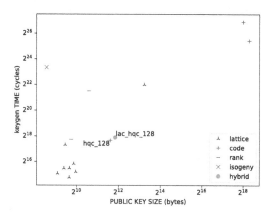

(c) Public Key size vs Key Generation time.

Fig. 12. Visualisation of the performance of `hqc_lac128` compared to several Level 1 implementation of NIST round 2 proposals.

efficient scheme with one that is less so does not worsen much the performance of the latter one. In other words, if one is willing to use HQC, one can as well use the hybrid hqc_lac128 for a very small overhead but arguably much better security.

Finally, one can wonder what is the speedup of our combiners compared to existing ones. We take as an example the XtM combiner from Bindel et al. [3], which applies a special kind of MAC to the ciphertexts and keys. It is proposed to implement this primitive as the concatenation (or the XOR) of two standard MACs. This computation is the main overhead compared to our construction and we simulated it as two calls to SHA256 on both ciphertexts and keys. This takes approximately $40\,\mu s$ on our setup, hence the speedup when considering hqc_lac128_par is slightly over 10% for encapsulation. This obviously depends on many factors like hardware, hash functions, parallelization and the underlying schemes. For example, for small ciphertexts the speedup will be negligible while for large ones it will be more important. Finally, we note that PQ schemes are not optimized thus the gain might be more noticeable in the future.

Acknowledgements. Loïs Huguenin-Dumittan is supported by a grant (project N° 192364) of the Swiss National Science Foundation (SNSF).

References

1. Bellare, M., Davis, H., Günther, F.: Separate your domains: NIST PQC KEMs, Oracle cloning and read-only indifferentiability. In: Canteaut, A., Ishai, Y. (eds.) EUROCRYPT 2020. LNCS, vol. 12106, pp. 3–32. Springer, Cham (2020). https://doi.org/10.1007/978-3-030-45724-2_1

2. Bernstein, D.J., (editors), T.L.: eBACS: ECRYPT benchmarking of cryptographic systems. https://bench.cr.yp.to. Accessed 14 May 2020

3. Bindel, N., Brendel, J., Fischlin, M., Goncalves, B., Stebila, D.: Hybrid key encapsulation mechanisms and authenticated key exchange. In: Ding, J., Steinwandt, R. (eds.) PQCrypto 2019. LNCS, vol. 11505, pp. 206–226. Springer, Cham (2019). https://doi.org/10.1007/978-3-030-25510-7_12

4. Bindel, N., Herath, U., McKague, M., Stebila, D.: Transitioning to a quantum-resistant public key infrastructure. Cryptology ePrint Archive, Report 2017/460 (2017). https://eprint.iacr.org/2017/460

5. Dodis, Y., Katz, J.: Chosen-ciphertext security of multiple encryption. In: Kilian, J. (ed.) TCC 2005. LNCS, vol. 3378, pp. 188–209. Springer, Heidelberg (2005). https://doi.org/10.1007/978-3-540-30576-7_11

6. Fischlin, M., Lehmann, A.: Multi-property preserving combiners for hash functions. In: Canetti, R. (ed.) TCC 2008. LNCS, vol. 4948, pp. 375–392. Springer, Heidelberg (2008). https://doi.org/10.1007/978-3-540-78524-8_21

7. Fischlin, M., Lehmann, A., Pietrzak, K.: Robust multi-property combiners for hash functions revisited. In: Aceto, L., Damgård, I., Goldberg, L.A., Halldórsson, M.M., Ingólfsdóttir, A., Walukiewicz, I. (eds.) ICALP 2008. LNCS, vol. 5126, pp. 655–666. Springer, Heidelberg (2008). https://doi.org/10.1007/978-3-540-70583-3_53

8. Fujisaki, E., Okamoto, T.: Secure integration of asymmetric and symmetric encryption schemes. In: Wiener, M. (ed.) CRYPTO 1999. LNCS, vol. 1666, pp. 537–554. Springer, Heidelberg (1999). https://doi.org/10.1007/3-540-48405-1_34

9. Fujisaki, E., Okamoto, T.: Secure integration of asymmetric and symmetric encryption schemes. J.Cryptology **26**(1), 80–101 (2013). https://doi.org/10.1007/s00145-011-9114-1

10. Giacon, F., Heuer, F., Poettering, B.: KEM Combiners. Cryptology ePrint Archive, Report 2018/024 (2018). https://eprint.iacr.org/2018/024

11. Guo, Q., Johansson, T., Yang, J.: A novel CCA attack using decryption errors against LAC. In: Galbraith, S.D., Moriai, S. (eds.) ASIACRYPT 2019. LNCS, vol. 11921, pp. 82–111. Springer, Cham (2019). https://doi.org/10.1007/978-3-030-34578-5_4

12. Herzberg, A.: On tolerant cryptographic constructions. In: Menezes, A. (ed.) CT-RSA 2005. LNCS, vol. 3376, pp. 172–190. Springer, Heidelberg (2005). https://doi.org/10.1007/978-3-540-30574-3_13

13. Hofheinz, D., Hövelmanns, K., Kiltz, E.: A modular analysis of the fujisaki-okamoto transformation. In: Kalai, Y., Reyzin, L. (eds.) TCC 2017. LNCS, vol. 10677, pp. 341–371. Springer, Cham (2017). https://doi.org/10.1007/978-3-319-70500-2_12

14. Huguenin-Dumittan, L., Vaudenay, S.: FO-like combiners and hybrid post-quantum cryptography. Cryptology ePrint Archive, Report 2021/1288 (2021). https://ia.cr/2021/1288

15. Kuchta, V., Sakzad, A., Stehlé, D., Steinfeld, R., Sun, S.-F.: Measure-rewind-measure: tighter quantum random oracle model proofs for one-way to hiding and CCA security. In: Canteaut, A., Ishai, Y. (eds.) EUROCRYPT 2020. LNCS, vol. 12107, pp. 703–728. Springer, Cham (2020). https://doi.org/10.1007/978-3-030-45727-3_24

16. Merkle, R.C., Hellman, M.E.: On the security of multiple encryption. Commun. ACM **24**(7), 465–467 (1981). https://doi.org/10.1145/358699.358718

17. Poettering, B., Rösler, P.: Combiners for aead. IACR Trans. Symmetric Cryptology, 121–143 (2020)

18. Saito, T., Xagawa, K., Yamakawa, T.: Tightly-secure key-encapsulation mechanism in the quantum random Oracle model. In: Nielsen, J.B., Rijmen, V. (eds.) EUROCRYPT 2018. LNCS, vol. 10822, pp. 520–551. Springer, Cham (2018). https://doi.org/10.1007/978-3-319-78372-7_17

19. Targhi, E.E., Unruh, D.: Post-quantum security of the Fujisaki-Okamoto and OAEP transforms. In: Hirt, M., Smith, A. (eds.) TCC 2016. LNCS, vol. 9986, pp. 192–216. Springer, Heidelberg (2016). https://doi.org/10.1007/978-3-662-53644-5_8

20. Zhang, C., Cash, D., Wang, X., Yu, X., Chow, S.S.M.: Combiners for chosen-ciphertext security. In: Dinh, T.N., Thai, M.T. (eds.) COCOON 2016. LNCS, vol. 9797, pp. 257–268. Springer, Cham (2016). https://doi.org/10.1007/978-3-319-42634-1_21

Linear-Time Oblivious Permutations for SPDZ

Peeter Laud[(✉)]

Cybernetica AS, Tartu, Estonia
peeter.laud@cyber.ee

Abstract. In this paper, we present a secure multiparty computation (MPC) subroutine for obliviously permuting elements in a private vector. The subroutine makes use of the private data representations used in the SPDZ protocol set; it can be composed with other privacy-preserving operations in this set and it also provides active security with abort. The online computation and communication complexity of the subroutine is linear in the length of the permuted vector.

1 Introduction

Large secure multiparty computation (MPC) protocols are constructed on top of MPC frameworks supporting a small number of primitive operations with private data—input, output, addition, multiplication, conversions between integers and bit-strings. These operations do not hide, which memory locations they access, thus only supporting *data-oblivious* computations.

Certain frameworks support *oblivious permutations* that shuffle a vector of private values in a manner that keeps the reordering private as well. Efficient oblivious permutations are a useful subroutine for certain non-data-oblivious algorithms, in particular the fast algorithms for sorting [6,11], as well as for the declassification of certain values without leaking their location in memory [1,5].

Currently, truly efficient oblivious permutations (number of primitive operations being linear in the length of the vector, with small multiplicative overhead) are supported only by MPC protocol sets with passive security and honest majority [16]. In this short paper, we show how to add them to the well-known SPDZ [10] protocol set, which supports dishonest majority, as well as fail-stop security (active attacks are detected). In SPDZ, the computation is split into input-independent offline and efficient online phases. We describe the online phase of oblivious permutations, state which offline precomputations our protocol requires, and discuss the possible implementations of the offline phase. We state the security properties of both the online and offline phase, and argue the security of our protocol.

State of the Art. Applying a sorting network to a random vector is the folk method for random permutations. Laur et al. [16] gave the most widely used

© Springer Nature Switzerland AG 2021
M. Conti et al. (Eds.): CANS 2021, LNCS 13099, pp. 245–252, 2021.
https://doi.org/10.1007/978-3-030-92548-2_13

permutation protocol for passively secure MPC; it's (communication) complexity is $O(m) \cdot 2^{O(n)}$ (elements of vectors), where m is the length of the vector and n the number of parties in the MPC protocol. The protocol is very efficient for a small n. Asharov et al. [2] gave a protocol with $O(m \log m)$ complexity, based on techniques used for ORAM.

Oblivious (extended) permutations are needed for private function evaluation. Mohassel et al. [17] achieve active security through a combination of MPC and Mix-nets. Laud et al. [14] obtain it through post-execution verification, using precomputed *permutation tuples*. Such tuples form one half of our solution.

Encodings of RAM computations for zero-knowledge proofs requires stating that certain vectors describing memory accesses are permutations of each other. Here, besides the earlier permutation network based solutions [4], Bootle et al. [7] proposed a linear-time construction based on showing the equality of polynomials that have the elements of one of the vectors as its roots [18]. Such polynomial equality checking forms the second half of our solution.

Our approach is also an instance of first performing the computations with passive security (but with privacy also against active attackers), and then verifying the results using an actively secure protocol [12,15].

Notation. The elements of a vector $\vec{v}$ are denoted $v_1, v_2, \ldots$. Given a vector $\vec{v}$ of length m, and a permutation $\pi \in S_m$ (where S_m is the *symmetric group* of all permutations on m elements), we let $\pi(\vec{v})$ denote the vector $(v_{\pi(1)}, v_{\pi(2)}, \ldots, v_{\pi(m)})$. We write $\vec{w} \leftarrow \vec{u} + \vec{v}$ to denote that $\vec{w}$ is the pointwise sum of $\vec{u}$ and $\vec{v}$; other operations may be used similarly. We use $[m]$ to denote the set $\{1, \ldots, m\}$.

SPDZ [10] is an MPC protocol for n parties, tolerating up to $(n-1)$ static active corruptions, and providing fail-stop security, i.e. misbehaviour by a corrupted party is detected, but the party is not ousted. Also, the misbehaviour does not impact the privacy of honest parties. The protocol executes an arithmetic circuit over a large finite field $\mathbb{F}$, with all values secret-shared among the parties. The protocol works has offline (input-independent) and online phases; in the offline phase each party P_i has selected a private value α_i (denote $\alpha = \alpha_1 + \cdots + \alpha_n$), and parties have executed "heavyweight" protocols to generate correlated values usable for linearizing all operations of the arithmetic circuit. In online phase, the private representation $[\![x]\!]$ of a value x is a tuple of random values $(([\![x]\!]_1, \gamma(x)_1), \ldots, ([\![x]\!]_n, \gamma(x)_n))$, with the i-th party knowing $[\![x]\!]_i$ and $\gamma(x)_i$, and with the values satisfying $[\![x]\!]_1 + \cdots + [\![x]\!]_n = x$ and $\gamma(x)_1 + \cdots + \gamma(x)_n = \alpha \cdot x$ (this is called the "MAC of $[\![x]\!]$"). Linear computations with private values can be done locally by parties. Multiplication triples generated during the offline phase are used for multiplication; the opening of values creates obligations to check that the MAC of the opened value is correct. MAC checks can be done without revealing α. Several MAC checks cost the same as one.

2 Offline Phase

In Fig. 1 we present our additions to the ideal functionality $\mathcal{F}_{\text{PREP}}$ for the offline phase of SPDZ. They allow each pair of parties to obtain additive shares of a

On input $\mathbf{Shuffle}(m, P_j, P_k, \pi)$ from P_j and $\mathbf{Shuffle}(m, P_j, P_k)$ from P_k:

0. Ignore the query, if both P_j and P_k are corrupted
1. Pick random vectors $\vec{x}, \vec{y} \in \mathbb{F}^m$. Put $\vec{z} = \pi(\vec{x}) - \vec{y}$
2. Set $X_j = \langle \pi, \vec{z} \rangle$ and $X_k = \langle \vec{x}, \vec{y} \rangle$
3. If P_c is corrupted and P_h is honest ($\{c, h\} = \{j, k\}$), then
   - Output X_c to P_c and the adversary
   - Get the description of a polynomial-time algorithm $\mathcal{A}$ from the adversary
   - Output $\mathcal{A}(X_h)$ to P_h
4. Otherwise (both P_j and P_k are honest), output X_j to P_j and X_k to P_k

Fig. 1. Addition to the ideal functionality $\mathcal{F}_{\mathrm{PREP}}$ of the offline phase

permutation of a vector, with the first party providing the permutation $\pi \in S_m$ and the second party also learning the vector. The correctness of the outputs is not guaranteed if the parties are corrupt, but privacy still is. We call $(\pi, \vec{z}; \vec{x}, \vec{y})$ a *permutation tuple*. A possible corresponding real implementation Π_{PREP} is discussed by Chase et al. [8] under the name *Permute-and-Share*, including the trade-offs for executing the protocol several times in parallel with the same π.

3   Online Phase

In the online phase, when evaluating an arithmetic circuit, we want to take a number of already computed values, treat them as a vector, apply an oblivious permutation to them, and continue computations with the permuted values. Existing algorithms [11,13] use oblivious permutations in a couple of different ways. The operations we present below as additions to the SPDZ protocol set Π_{ONLINE} cover all these ways.

3.1   Randomly Permuting a Vector

There is a private vector $[\![\vec{v}]\!]$ of length m, the elements of which we want to permute, with no party, or a coalition of up to $(n-1)$ parties learning anything about the permutation. The protocol for this operation is given in Fig. 2.

We see that during the i-th iteration of the main loop, the current share of each party P_j ($j \neq i$) gets permuted with π_i and then additively shared between P_i and P_j. Here the share of P_j is $\vec{y}_1^{(i,j)}$ (for the "value itself") and $\vec{y}_2^{(i,j)}$ (for the MAC), while the share for P_i is $\vec{r}_{ij}$ and $\vec{s}_{ij}$ [14]. Having obtained such shares from every other party, P_i defines his share for the next round be adding them all up (step 1.3). In step (1.1.1), P_j sends his current shares to P_i, but they are masked with random vectors $\vec{x}_k^{(i,j)}$, hence there is no leakage. All parties contribute to the resulting permutation $\pi = \pi_1 \circ \cdots \circ \pi_n$, hence it stays private. After the n-th iteration, parties obtain the shares of the output vector $[\![\vec{v}^{(n)}]\!]$.

In steps (2)–(3), the parties verify that $\vec{v}^{(n)}$ is indeed a permutation of $\vec{v}^{(0)}$. For any vector $\vec{u} \in \mathbb{F}^m$, define the polynomial $f_{\vec{u}}(X) \in \mathbb{F}[X]$ by $f_{\vec{u}}(X) =$

Input: private vector $[\![\vec{v}^{(0)}]\!]$ of length m.
Output: private vector $[\![\vec{v}^{(n)}]\!]$, such that $\vec{v}^{(n)}$ is a permutation of $\vec{v}^{(0)}$
Offline:
(1) Each party P_i selects a random permutation π_i of length m.
(2) Each pair of parties P_i, P_j runs two instances of $\mathcal{F}_{\text{PREP}}$.Shuffle, with P_i providing the input π_i. Let the result of k-th instance be $\vec{z}_k^{(i,j)}$ for P_i and $\vec{x}_k^{(i,j)}, \vec{y}_k^{(i,j)}$ for P_j
Online:
(1) For i going from 1 to n, do the following:
(1.1) For each j different from i, do the following:
(1.1.1) P_j sends $\vec{w}_1^{(i,j)} \leftarrow [\![\vec{v}^{(i-1)}]\!]_j - \vec{x}_1^{(i,j)}$ and $\vec{w}_2^{(i,j)} \leftarrow \gamma(\vec{v}^{(i-1)})_j - \vec{x}_2^{(i,j)}$ to P_i
(1.1.2) P_i computes $\vec{r}_{ij} \leftarrow \pi_i(\vec{w}_1^{(i,j)}) + \vec{z}_1^{(i,j)}$ and $\vec{s}_{ij} \leftarrow \pi_i(\vec{w}_2^{(i,j)}) + \vec{z}_2^{(i,j)}$
(1.1.3) P_j defines shares of the next round: $[\![\vec{v}^{(i)}]\!]_j = \vec{y}_1^{(i,j)}$ and $\gamma(\vec{v}^{(i)})_j = \vec{y}_2^{(i,j)}$.
(1.2) P_i computes $\vec{r}_{ii} \leftarrow \pi_i([\![\vec{v}^{(i-1)}]\!]_i)$ and $\vec{s}_{ii} \leftarrow \pi_i(\gamma(\vec{v}^{(i-1)})_i)$
(1.3) P_i defines shares of the next round: $[\![\vec{v}^{(i)}]\!]_i = \sum_j \vec{r}_{ij}$ and $\gamma(\vec{v}^{(i)})_i = \sum_j \vec{s}_{ij}$.
(2) Parties pick fresh random $[\![r]\!], [\![r']\!] \in \mathbb{F}$, and **Reveal** r // SPDZ supports this
(3) Parties check whether **Reveal**$([\![r']\!] \cdot (\prod_{i=1}^m (r - [\![v_i^{(n)}]\!]) - \prod_{i=1}^m (r - [\![v_i^{(0)}]\!]))) = 0$

Fig. 2. Obliviously shuffling a private vector

$\prod_{i=1}^m (X - u_i)$. Two polynomials $f_{\vec{u}}, f_{\vec{u}'}$ are equal if $\vec{u}$ and $\vec{u}'$ are permutations of each other [18]. In steps (2)–(3), this polynomial equality is tested by evaluating $f_{\vec{v}^{(0)}}$ and $f_{\vec{v}^{(n)}}$ at a random point r and making sure that their difference is 0 (masking the result with r' before opening it). We know that if the polynomial $f_{\vec{v}^{(n)}} - f_{\vec{v}^{(0)}}$ is non-zero, then it has at most m roots, hence the probability of test (2)–(3) falsely accepting is at most $m/|\mathbb{F}|$.

The equality check for polynomials involves a number of multiplications, whose implementation includes the check of MACs on the multiplicands. Obviously, all these MAC checks have to pass before the value $f_{\vec{v}^{(n)}}(r) - f_{\vec{v}^{(0)}}(r)$ is revealed in the equality check.

Complexity. With n computing parties and a vector of length m, the round complexity (of the online phase) of the protocol is $O(n + \log m)$. Here $O(n)$ comes from the loop (1) and $O(\log m)$ comes from the computation of the products of length m in (3). The $\log m$ term can be removed at the cost increasing the number of (binary) multiplications several times [3].

The communication complexity of the online phase is $O(n^2 m)$, when we consider the elements of $\mathbb{F}$ to have constant size. This holds, because at each iteration of the loop (1), one party exchanges $O(m)$ elements of $\mathbb{F}$ with every other party. The communication complexity of the offline phase is somewhat larger than $O(n^2 m)$, because an implementation of a single invocation of $\mathcal{F}_{\text{PREP}}$.**Shuffle** needs somewhat more than $O(m)$ communication [8].

3.2 Creating a Random Permutation and Applying It

We may also want to "create and store" a random oblivious permutation, such that it can be applied to several vectors during the later steps of the computation.

For the creation, we pick a vector $\vec{u}^{(0)} \in \mathbb{F}^m$, where all elements are different, classify it, and apply the protocol in Fig. 2 to it. To represent this permutation π, each party stores his π_i. Also, the protocol stores both $[\![\vec{u}^{(0)}]\!]$ and $[\![\vec{u}^{(n)}]\!]$.

Input: private vector $[\![\vec{v}^{(0)}]\!]$ of length m, and private vectors $[\![\vec{u}^{(0)}]\!]$, $[\![\vec{u}^{(n)}]\!]$ representing a private permutation π. Each party P_i also has π_i such that $\pi_1 \circ \cdots \circ \pi_n = \pi$.
Output: private vector $[\![\vec{v}^{(n)}]\!]$, such that $v_i^{(n)} = v_{\pi(i)}^{(0)}$ for all $i \in [m]$.
Offline:
Each pair of parties P_i, P_j runs two instances of $\mathcal{F}_{\text{PREP}}$.Shuffle, with P_i providing the input π_i. Let the result of k-th instance be $\vec{z}_k^{(i,j)}$ for P_i and $\vec{x}_k^{(i,j)}, \vec{y}_k^{(i,j)}$ for P_j
Online:
Apply the steps (1) of the online phase of Fig. 2, obtaining $[\![\vec{v}^{(n)}]\!]$
(2) Parties pick fresh random $[\![r]\!], [\![r']\!], [\![s]\!] \in \mathbb{F}$ and **Reveal** r, s
(3) Parties evaluate the following expression, open it, and check that it is 0

$$[\![r']\!] \cdot \left(\prod_{i=1}^{m}(r - [\![v_i^{(n)}]\!] - s \cdot [\![u_i^{(n)}]\!]) - \prod_{i=1}^{m}(r - [\![v_i^{(0)}]\!] - s \cdot [\![u_i^{(0)}]\!]) \right)$$

Fig. 3. Applying a private permutation to a private vector

The protocol for applying a stored π to a private vector $[\![\vec{v}^{(0)}]\!]$ is given in Fig. 3. It assumes that the identity of the permutation we want to apply is already known during the offline phase. This is a natural assumption, if, during the offline phase, we already know the computation that we want to do once we have the data. Even if the assumption does not hold, the protocol in Fig. 3 can still be used, because a permutation tuple $(\rho, \vec{z}; \vec{x}, \vec{y})$ for parties P_i, P_j with a *random* permutation ρ can easily be converted to another permutation tuple with an arbitrary permutation τ known to P_i by P_i sending $\rho^{-1} \circ \tau$ to P_j, which the parties then apply to $\vec{z}$ and $\vec{y}$. If ρ is a random permutation then it is a sufficient mask for that message, preserving the privacy of τ from P_j.

The functionality and privacy arguments of this protocol are the same as for the protocol in Fig. 2. For the correctness check, consider the bivariate polynomial $g_{\vec{u},\vec{v}} \in \mathbb{F}[X, Y]$ for $\vec{u}, \vec{v} \in \mathbb{F}^m$, defined by $g_{\vec{u},\vec{v}}(X, Y) = \prod_{i=1}^{m}(X - v_i - u_i Y)$. By our arguments in Sect. 3.1, two polynomials $g_{\vec{u},\vec{v}}$ and $g_{\vec{u}',\vec{v}'}$ are equal iff the vector of polynomials $(v_1 + u_1 Y, \ldots, v_m + u_m Y)$ is a permutation of the vector $(v_1' + u_1' Y, \ldots, v_m' + u_m' Y)$. But this is only possible if $\vec{u}'$ is a permutation of $\vec{u}$, and $\vec{v}'$ is the same permutation of $\vec{v}$. In Fig. 3, we check the equality of $g_{\vec{u}^{(n)},\vec{v}^{(n)}}$ and $g_{\vec{u}^{(0)},\vec{v}^{(0)}}$ by evaluating their difference at a random point (r, s) and checking that it is zero (again masking with r'). We thus obtain that the permutation that brings $\vec{v}^{(0)}$ into $\vec{v}^{(n)}$ is the same that brought $\vec{u}^{(0)}$ into $\vec{u}^{(n)}$.

3.3 Applying the Inverse of a Random Permutation

After creating and storing the representation $[\![\vec{u}^{(0)}]\!]$, $[\![\vec{u}^{(n)}]\!]$ of a random permutation π, we may want to apply π^{-1} to a private vector $[\![\vec{v}^{(0)}]\!]$ [13]. The protocol for this application is basically the same as the one given in Fig. 3, with the following differences: (a) the offline phase is executed with inputs $\pi_1^{-1}, \ldots, \pi_n^{-1}$, (b) the main loop (iterations indexed by i) runs from n down to 1, and (c) the test in step (3) swaps $[\![v_i^{(n)}]\!]$ and $[\![v_i^{(0)}]\!]$.

3.4 Optimizations

As remarked by Chase et al. [8], running in parallel several instantiations of the implementation of $\mathcal{F}_{\mathrm{PREP}}$.**Shuffle** with the same permutation π may have better communication complexity than running them independently. Our online phase requires several permutation tuples with the same permutation, if the overlaying privacy-preserving computation invokes the protocol in Fig. 3 many times, hence the parallel execution is a natural fit.

In the offline phase, we generate permutation tuples of the form $(\pi, \vec{z}; \vec{x}, \vec{y})$. When applying the inverse of a permutation, we need permutation tuples that contain π^{-1}. We can anticipate that need and create these tuples separately. However, we can also transform the tuple $(\pi, \vec{z}; \vec{x}, \vec{y})$ into the permutation tuple $(\pi^{-1}, \pi^{-1}(-\vec{z}); \vec{y}, \vec{x})$ with no interaction between the parties.

4   Security Analysis

In previous section, we presented our additions to the protocol Π_{ONLINE}. The extended Π_{ONLINE} is required to be at least as secure as the extended ideal functionality $\mathcal{F}_{\mathrm{ONLINE}}$. The extensions to latter consist of idealized versions to permute a vector, make a random permutation, and apply it, all working with *handles* to private values, and all abortable by the adversary. For space reasons, we omit precise descriptions.

Security is proved by giving a simulator between $\mathcal{F}_{\mathrm{ONLINE}}$ and Π_{ONLINE}. The simulator runs a copy of the real protocol inside, using real inputs of corrupted parties (which the adversary gave to the machines implementing the protocol on behalf of those parties), and dummy inputs for honest parties. The adversary cannot tell the difference between Π_{ONLINE} and $\mathcal{F}_{\mathrm{ONLINE}} \| \mathcal{S}_{\mathrm{ONLINE}}$, because all messages the honest parties send to corrupted parties are uniformly random. Whenever a value y is revealed, which may happen at the end of the protocol, or at other steps of the overlaying algorithm (e.g. after comparisons in a non-data-oblivious sorting algorithm), $\mathcal{F}_{\mathrm{ONLINE}}$ tells $\mathcal{S}_{\mathrm{ONLINE}}$, what the value of y is. The simulator then obtains the shares of corrupted parties from the adversary, and adjusts the shares of the honest parties, such that they add up to y. The same additive correction is applied to honest parties' shares of $\gamma(y)$ (the simulator knows α). If the subsequent MAC check between the simulator and the adversary fails, then the simulator tells $\mathcal{F}_{\mathrm{ONLINE}}$ to stop.

The evaluation of the check in step (3) of Figs. 2, 3 does not involve $\mathcal{F}_{\mathrm{ONLINE}}$. It is performed by $\mathcal{S}_{\mathrm{ONLINE}}$ and the adversary. If it fails (the MACs do not pass the check, or the computed difference is non-zero), then $\mathcal{S}_{\mathrm{ONLINE}}$ tells $\mathcal{F}_{\mathrm{ONLINE}}$ to stop. Again, the view of the adversary during this check consists of uniformly randomly distributed values in $\mathbb{F}$.

5 Conclusions

This paper gives the first presentation of an efficient permutation protocol for secure MPC, with security against active adversaries, and with compatibility towards the well-known SPDZ protocol set. Both the communication complexity and the round complexity of the online phase of the protocol are highly attractive in the context of a small number of computing parties, which is expected to be the most frequent use-case. This opens up a large body of efficient algorithms, built on top of passively secure, honest-majority MPC systems, for conversion onto systems with active security.

Our future work involves the choice of implementation details for both the online and offline phases of our protocols. It is also worthwhile to study, to which extent our protocols are adaptable to other rings, similarly to SPDZ [9].

Acknowledgements. This work has been supported by Estonian Research Council, grant no. PRG920, and by European Regional Development Fund through the ICT Centre of Excellence EXCITE.

References

1. Abidin, A., Aly, A., Cleemput, S., Mustafa, M.A.: An MPC-based privacy-preserving protocol for a local electricity trading market. In: Foresti, S., Persiano, G. (eds.) CANS 2016. LNCS, vol. 10052, pp. 615–625. Springer, Cham (2016). https://doi.org/10.1007/978-3-319-48965-0_40
2. Asharov, G., Chan, T.H., Nayak, K., Pass, R., Ren, L., Shi, E.: Bucket oblivious sort: an extremely simple oblivious sort. In: Farach-Colton, M., Gørtz, I.L. (eds.) 3rd Symposium on Simplicity in Algorithms, SOSA 2020, Salt Lake City, UT, USA, 6–7 January 2020, pp. 8–14. SIAM (2020)
3. Bar-Ilan, J., Beaver, D.: Non-cryptographic fault-tolerant computing in constant number of rounds of interaction. In: Rudnicki, P. (ed.) Proceedings of the Eighth Annual ACM Symposium on Principles of Distributed Computing, Edmonton, Alberta, Canada, 14–16 August 1989, pp. 201–209. ACM (1989)
4. Ben-Sasson, E., Chiesa, A., Genkin, D., Tromer, E.: Fast reductions from RAMs to delegatable succinct constraint satisfaction problems: extended abstract. In: Kleinberg, R.D. (ed.) Innovations in Theoretical Computer Science, ITCS 2013, Berkeley, CA, USA, 9–12 January 2013, pp. 401–414. ACM (2013)
5. Bogdanov, D., Kamm, L., Laur, S., Sokk, V.: Rmind: a tool for cryptographically secure statistical analysis. IEEE Trans. Dependable Secur. Comput. **15**(3), 481–495 (2018)
6. Bogdanov, D., Laur, S., Talviste, R.: A practical analysis of oblivious sorting algorithms for secure multi-party computation. In: Bernsmed, K., Fischer-Hübner, S. (eds.) NordSec 2014. LNCS, vol. 8788, pp. 59–74. Springer, Cham (2014). https://doi.org/10.1007/978-3-319-11599-3_4
7. Bootle, J., Cerulli, A., Groth, J., Jakobsen, S., Maller, M.: Arya: nearly linear-time zero-knowledge proofs for correct program execution. In: Peyrin, T., Galbraith, S. (eds.) ASIACRYPT 2018. LNCS, vol. 11272, pp. 595–626. Springer, Cham (2018). https://doi.org/10.1007/978-3-030-03326-2_20

8. Chase, M., Ghosh, E., Poburinnaya, O.: Secret-shared shuffle. In: Moriai, S., Wang, H. (eds.) ASIACRYPT 2020. LNCS, vol. 12493, pp. 342–372. Springer, Cham (2020). https://doi.org/10.1007/978-3-030-64840-4_12

9. Cramer, R., Damgård, I., Escudero, D., Scholl, P., Xing, C.: SPD$\mathbb{Z}_{2^k}$: efficient MPC mod 2^k for dishonest majority. In: Shacham, H., Boldyreva, A. (eds.) CRYPTO 2018. LNCS, vol. 10992, pp. 769–798. Springer, Cham (2018). https://doi.org/10.1007/978-3-319-96881-0_26

10. Damgård, I., Keller, M., Larraia, E., Pastro, V., Scholl, P., Smart, N.P.: Practical covertly secure MPC for dishonest majority – or: breaking the SPDZ limits. In: Crampton, J., Jajodia, S., Mayes, K. (eds.) ESORICS 2013. LNCS, vol. 8134, pp. 1–18. Springer, Heidelberg (2013). https://doi.org/10.1007/978-3-642-40203-6_1

11. Hamada, K., Kikuchi, R., Ikarashi, D., Chida, K., Takahashi, K.: Practically efficient multi-party sorting protocols from comparison sort algorithms. In: Kwon, T., Lee, M.-K., Kwon, D. (eds.) ICISC 2012. LNCS, vol. 7839, pp. 202–216. Springer, Heidelberg (2013). https://doi.org/10.1007/978-3-642-37682-5_15

12. de Hoogh, S., Schoenmakers, B., Veeningen, M.: Certificate validation in secure computation and its use in verifiable linear programming. In: Pointcheval, D., Nitaj, A., Rachidi, T. (eds.) AFRICACRYPT 2016. LNCS, vol. 9646, pp. 265–284. Springer, Cham (2016). https://doi.org/10.1007/978-3-319-31517-1_14

13. Laud, P.: Parallel oblivious array access for secure multiparty computation and privacy-preserving minimum spanning trees. Proc. Priv. Enhancing Technol. **2015**(2), 188–205 (2015)

14. Laud, P., Pankova, A., Jagomägis, R.: Preprocessing based verification of multiparty protocols with honest majority. Proc. Priv. Enhancing Technol. **2017**(4), 23–76 (2017)

15. Laud, P., Pettai, M.: Secure multiparty sorting protocols with covert privacy. In: Brumley, B.B., Röning, J. (eds.) NordSec 2016. LNCS, vol. 10014, pp. 216–231. Springer, Cham (2016). https://doi.org/10.1007/978-3-319-47560-8_14

16. Laur, S., Willemson, J., Zhang, B.: Round-efficient oblivious database manipulation. In: Lai, X., Zhou, J., Li, H. (eds.) ISC 2011. LNCS, vol. 7001, pp. 262–277. Springer, Heidelberg (2011). https://doi.org/10.1007/978-3-642-24861-0_18

17. Mohassel, P., Sadeghian, S., Smart, N.P.: Actively secure private function evaluation. In: Sarkar, P., Iwata, T. (eds.) ASIACRYPT 2014. LNCS, vol. 8874, pp. 486–505. Springer, Heidelberg (2014). https://doi.org/10.1007/978-3-662-45608-8_26

18. Neff, C.A.: A verifiable secret shuffle and its application to e-voting. In: Reiter, M.K., Samarati, P. (eds.) CCS 2001, Proceedings of the 8th ACM Conference on Computer and Communications Security, Philadelphia, Pennsylvania, USA, 6–8 November 2001, pp. 116–125. ACM (2001)

On the Higher-Bit Version
of Approximate Inhomogeneous Short
Integer Solution Problem

Anaëlle Le Dévéhat[(✉)], Hiroki Shizuya, and Shingo Hasegawa

Tohoku University, Sendai, Japan
anaelle.le.devehat.s8@dc.tohoku.ac.jp

Abstract. We explore a bitwise modification in Ajtai's one-way function. Our main contribution is to define the higher-bit approximate inhomogeneous short integer solution (ISIS) problem and prove its reduction to the ISIS problem. In this new instance, our main idea is to discard low-weighted bits to gain compactness.

As an application, we construct a bitwise version of a hash-and-sign signature in the random oracle model whose security relies on the (Ring)-LWE and (Ring)-ISIS assumptions. Our scheme is built from the hash-and-sign digital signature scheme based on the relaxed notion of approximate trapdoors introduced by Chen, Genise and Mukherjee (2019). Their work can be interpreted as a bitwise optimization of the work of Micciancio and Peikert (2012). We extend this idea and apply our technique to the scheme by discarding low-weighted bits in the public key. Our modification brings improvement in the public key size but also in the signature size when used in the right setting.

However, constructions based on the higher-bit approximate ISIS save memory space at the expense of loosening security. Parameters must be set in regards with this trade-off.

1 Introduction

1.1 Background

Since Peter Shor's breakthrough work in 1994 [25], it became clear that quantum computers are able to break usual cryptographic primitives based on number theory assumptions. For instance, a quantum computer can break factoring-based cryptography in polynomial time of the security parameter. This results threaten usual cryptography and reveal a need for efficient post-quantum secure cryptography. In 2017, NIST launched its still ongoing post-quantum cryptography (PQC) standardization process [22]. It illustrates the necessity of finding efficient and realistic post-quantum secure cryptographic constructions in order to guarantee the confidentiality and integrity of digital communications.

One high potential candidate for PQC is lattice-based cryptography. It has been an active area of research since Ajtai's groundbreaking work in 1996 which

© Springer Nature Switzerland AG 2021
M. Conti et al. (Eds.): CANS 2021, LNCS 13099, pp. 253–272, 2021.
https://doi.org/10.1007/978-3-030-92548-2_14

demonstrates strong worst-case to average-case reductions on lattices problems [2,3]. Worst-case to average-case hardness is very important in cryptographic constructions since it needs to be hard to attack a construction for random instances. Moreover, underlying lattice problems provide strong security even for quantum adversaries (no polynomial attack is known).

The attractiveness of lattice-based cryptography comes from its elegant constructions and efficiency improvements obtained using lattices with algebraic structure [14,20]. It also enjoys great versatility afforded by the learning with errors (LWE) problem [24]. A lot of lattice-based cryptographic primitives has been studied such as fully homomorphic encryption schemes [12], public-key encryption [14,15] but also attribute-based encryption and (hierarchical) identity-based encryption [1,7].

In this work, we focus on lattice-based signatures among lattice-based cryptographic schemes. Even if there has been early attempts at lattice-based digital signatures, it is only in 2008 that the first direct constructions of lattice-based signatures appeared. A "hash-and-sign" signature scheme was constructed by Gentry, Peikert and Vaikuntanathan [13]. At the same time, a provably secure one-time signature using ideal lattices was constructed by Lyubashevsky and Micciancio [17]. Both schemes enjoys security based on the hardness of worst-case lattice problems. Even if both schemes achieved short signatures, they still had several disadvantages. These constructions led the way to two lines of research. First, Lyubashevsky used the Fiat-Shamir transform to improve the one-time signature [17] in several subsequent works [16]. Several of the best candidates in NIST PQC standardization procedure are based on the rejection sampling method [4,10,22]. On the other hand, the GPV "hash-and-sign" signature scheme [13] is not very practical. In their work, Gentry, Peikert and Vaikuntanathan show how to sample solutions following a distribution simulatable without knowing the secret to avoid any information leakage. In order to do so, they use a gaussian sampler which leads to various difficulties and complexity. A more satisfactory solution to this problem was given by Micciancio and Peikert [21]. Their work brought several improvements both for security and efficiency in GPV scheme line of work.

1.2   Related Work

In this work, we study constructions based on Ajtai's one-way function and trapdoor [3]. In lattice-based hash-and-sign GPV signature [13], a signer is assigned a uniformly random public matrix $A \in \mathbb{Z}_q^{n \times m}$ along with a trapdoor $S \in \mathbb{Z}_q^{m \times m}$ which verifies $AS = 0 \pmod{q}$. The trapdoor S is usually a basis of short lattice vectors solution to the SIS problem with regards to A. Thus, using S, one can find short preimages for the Ajtai's function defined by A and sign a message. The resulting signature's norm depends on the norms of the columns in S. In order to further optimize and improve this kind of digital signature, it is highly relevant to improve the algorithms for trapdoor and key generation.

At first, improvements of Ajtai's trapdoor generation algorithm [5,23] were rather complex and inefficient. Only in 2012, the introduction by Micciancio and Peikert of their elegant G-trapdoor construction [21] enabled faster and shorter signatures. However, even using the G-trapdoor construction, hash-and-sign signature based on Ajtai's function is still impractical due to large keys and signatures sizes. For instance, when compared to lattice-based signatures candidates of NIST PQC standardization process [4,10,11], the hash-and-sign signature instantiated with G-trapdoors has about six times larger public keys and signatures sizes for a same level of security.

In order to reduce this difference, Chen, Genise and Mukherjee constructed a F-trapdoor [9] from the G-trapdoor [21]. The innovation in their work is the definition of the approximate ISIS problem which reduces to the ISIS problem. It allows a certain error when sampling a preimage for Ajtai's function. By allowing a little error, the G-trapdoor is reduced to an approximate version called F-trapdoor. The hash-and-sign signature instantiated with F-trapdoors enjoys sEU-CMA security and much smaller public keys and signatures sizes than the one with G-trapdoors. However, these sizes are still too large when compared with state-of-the-art digital signatures based on NTRU lattices [11] or on the rejection sampling approach [4,10].

1.3 Contributions

Our main contribution is the definition of the higher-bit approximate ISIS problem along with its reduction to the ISIS problem. This newly defined problem permits improvements in constructions based on the ISIS problem. It is based on discarding low-weighted bits of coefficients in the matrix A which defines Ajtai's function. As an application of the higher-bit approximate ISIS problem, we adapt the hash-and-sign signature by Chen, Genise and Mukherjee [9]: we construct a sEU-CMA secure hash-and-sign digital signature along with adapted trapdoor generation and preimage sampling algorithms.

In our application, the public key A is constructed from the high-weighted bits of the public key in [9]. This idea fits in the approximate setting. Furthermore, with the right parameters setting, discarding low-weighted bits in the public key allows for a possible similar optimization of the signature. Our construction seems like a natural following of the F-trapdoor signature scheme [9]. Indeed, the gadget matrix F is basically defined as the gadget matrix G [21] but without low-weighted bits entries.

With our modification, the public key belongs to $\mathbb{Z}_{\frac{q}{b^d}}^{n \times m}$ rather than $\mathbb{Z}_q^{n \times m}$ (where $q = b^k, d < k$). This is a direct consequence of using the higher-bit approximate ISIS problem as the underlying hardness problem. Moreover, the signature is in $\mathbb{Z}_{\frac{q}{b^d}}^m$ rather than $\mathbb{Z}_q^m$. Applying our technique to the F-trapdoor signature scheme allows to save $n \times m \times d\lceil \log_2 b \rceil$ bits in the public key and $m \times d\lceil \log_2 b \rceil$ bits in the signature.

However, this setting implies a trade-off between security and memory space. This trade-off is due to the reduction loss when using the higher-bit approximate ISIS rather than the approximate ISIS. In order to assess this trade-off, we give some concrete parameters and results. We expect our construction to reduce the public key size by about half and significantly reduce the signature size at the expense of a reasonable drop in the security level. Moreover, providing a higher security parameter, we estimate 140-bit security level rather than 88-bit security as given in [9] for about the same key sizes. We may note that optimization based on discarding low-weighted bits can be seen in the lattice-based signature CRYSTALS-Dilithium [10].

We note that our hash-and-sign signature construction in the random oracle model can translate to the Ring setting under Ring-LWE and Ring-SIS assumptions [18].

1.4 Organization

In Sect. 3, we define and study the higher-bit approximate ISIS problem and its reduction to the ISIS problem. In Sect. 4, we introduce our main idea for a new construction based on the higher-bit approximate ISIS. In Sect. 5, we construct new trapdoor generation and preimage sampling algorithms and study the resulting distributions. Finally, in Sect. 6, we instantiate a sEU-CMA secure hash-and-sign signature using our algorithms.

2 Preliminaries

2.1 Notations and Linear Algebra

We denote the set of real numbers by $\mathbb{R}$, the set of integers by $\mathbb{Z}$ and the set of positive integers by $\mathbb{N}$. Denote $\mathbb{Z}/q\mathbb{Z}$ by $\mathbb{Z}_q$. We use the notation $x \leftarrow U(S)$ when a variable x is drawn uniformly at random from the set S. Moreover, we use $\approx_s$ as the abbreviation for statistically close. A vector v is always in column form and represented in lower-case bold letters. A matrix A is always represented in upper-case bold letters. For a vector v, we denote the ith component of v as v_i. We do the same for a matrix A and denote the ith component of the jth column of A as $a_{i,j}$. We denote the l_p-norm of a vector v as $\|v\|_p := (\sum v_i^p)^{\frac{1}{p}}$. The norm of a matrix is the norm of its longest column: $\|A\|_p := max_i\|a_i\|_p$. By default we use l_2-norm. A short vector is a vector whose norm is small but not necessarily its dimension.

If a symmetric matrix $\Sigma \in \mathbb{R}^{n \times n}$ verifies that for all $x \in \mathbb{R}^n$, $x^t \Sigma x > 0$ (≥ 0) then Σ is positive (semi-)definite. For two positive (semi-)definite matrices Σ_1 and Σ_2, we note $\Sigma_1 > \Sigma_2$ ($\geq$) if $\Sigma_1 - \Sigma_2$ is positive (semi-)definite. $\sqrt{\Sigma}$ designates any full rank matrix T such that $\Sigma = TT^t$.

2.2 Lattices Background

A m-dimensional lattice Λ of rank $k \leq m$ is a discrete additive subgroup of $\mathbb{R}^m$. It is generated by all linear combinations with integers coefficients of k linearly independent basis vectors $B = \{b_1, ..., b_k\}$.

In many cryptographic work, we use q-ary integer lattices. For some positive integers $m, n \in \mathbb{N}$, $q \geq 2$, $\boldsymbol{u} \in \mathbb{Z}_q^n$ and $\boldsymbol{A} \in \mathbb{Z}_q^{n \times m}$ we can define the following m-dimensional full rank q-ary lattices :

$$\Lambda^{\perp}(\boldsymbol{A}) = \Lambda_q^{\perp}(\boldsymbol{A}) := \{\boldsymbol{x} \in \mathbb{Z}^m : \boldsymbol{A}.\boldsymbol{x} = \boldsymbol{0} \pmod q\};$$
$$\Lambda_{\boldsymbol{u}}^{\perp}(\boldsymbol{A}) := \{\boldsymbol{x} \in \mathbb{Z}^m : \boldsymbol{A}.\boldsymbol{x} = \boldsymbol{u} \pmod q\}.$$

In this work, we study vectors distributions obtained when sampling in q-ary lattices. To do so, we first need to define what is a discrete Gaussian distribution over a lattice Λ.

Definition 1 (Gaussian function on $\mathbb{R}^n$ with parameter s: ρ_s [9]). *For any $s > 0$,*

$$\forall \boldsymbol{x} \in \mathbb{R}^n, \quad \rho_s(\boldsymbol{x}) = e^{-\pi \|\boldsymbol{x}\|^2 / s^2}$$

Definition 2 (Discrete Gaussian distribution $D_{\Lambda+c,s}$ [9]). *For any $\boldsymbol{c} \in \mathbb{R}^n$, real $s > 0$, and n-dimensional lattice Λ,*

$$\forall \boldsymbol{x} \in \Lambda + \boldsymbol{c}, \quad D_{\Lambda+c,s}(\boldsymbol{x}) = \frac{\rho_s(\boldsymbol{x})}{\sum_{\boldsymbol{a} \in \Lambda+c} \rho_s(\boldsymbol{a})}$$

When omitted, s and $\boldsymbol{c}$ are taken to be 1 and 0 respectively.

This definition of discrete Gaussian distribution can be extended to non-spherical Gaussians [9]. However we do not make use of this definition in our work, thus we omit it here.

Moreover, in this work, some conditions on the parameters are set in regards with the smoothing parameter. We recall its definition.

Definition 3 (Smoothing parameter [19]). *For any lattice Λ and positive real $\epsilon > 0$, the smoothing parameter $\eta_\epsilon(\Lambda)$ is the smallest real $s > 0$ such that $\rho_{1/s}(\Lambda^*\{\boldsymbol{0}\}) \leq \epsilon$.*

Definition 4 ([9]). *For a positive semi-definite $\boldsymbol{\Sigma} = \boldsymbol{T}\boldsymbol{T}^t$, $\epsilon > 0$, and lattice Λ with $span(\Lambda) \subseteq span(\boldsymbol{\Sigma})$, we say $\eta_\epsilon(\Lambda) \leq \sqrt{\boldsymbol{\Sigma}}$ if $\eta_\epsilon(\boldsymbol{T}^+\Lambda) \leq 1$.*

2.3   LWE, SIS, ISIS and Approximate ISIS

First we recall the definition of the learning with errors problem.

Definition 5 (Decisional learning with errors [24]). *For $n, m \in \mathbb{N}$ and modulus $q \geq 2$, distributions $\theta, \pi, \chi \subseteq \mathbb{Z}_q$. An LWE sample is obtained from sampling secret vector $\boldsymbol{s} \leftarrow \theta^n$, public matrix $\boldsymbol{A} \leftarrow \pi^{n \times m}$, and error vector $\boldsymbol{e} \leftarrow \chi^m$, and outputting $(\boldsymbol{A}, \boldsymbol{y}^t := \boldsymbol{s}^t \boldsymbol{A} + \boldsymbol{e}^t \pmod q)$.*

We say that an algorithm solves $LWE_{n,m,q,\theta,\pi,\chi}$ if it distinguishes the LWE sample from a random sample distributed as $\pi^{n \times m} \times U(\mathbb{Z}_q^m)$ with probability greater than $1/2$ plus non-negligible.

Lemma 1 ([6]). *For n, m, q, s chosen as LWE hardness is based on GapSVP and SIVP,*
$LWE_{n,m',q,D_{\mathbb{Z},s},U(\mathbb{Z}_q),D_{\mathbb{Z},s}}$ *is as hard as* $LWE_{n,m,q,U(\mathbb{Z}_q),U(\mathbb{Z}_q),D_{\mathbb{Z},s}}$ *for* $m' \leq m - (16n + 4 \log \log q)$.

Now we recall the SIS and ISIS problems.

Definition 6 (SIS [2]**).** *For any $n, m \in \mathbb{N}$, $q \in \mathbb{Z}$ and $\beta \in \mathbb{R}$, define the short integer solution problem $SIS_{n,m,q,\beta}$ as follows: Given $\mathbf{A} \in \mathbb{Z}_q^{n \times m}$, find a non-zero vector $\mathbf{x} \in \mathbb{Z}^m$ such that $\|\mathbf{x}\| \leq \beta$, and*

$$\mathbf{Ax} = \mathbf{0} \pmod{q}$$

Definition 7 (ISIS). *For any $n, m \in \mathbb{N}$, $q \in \mathbb{Z}$ and $\beta \in \mathbb{R}$, define the inhomogeneous short integer solution problem $ISIS_{n,m,q,\beta}$ as follows: Given $\mathbf{A} \in \mathbb{Z}_q^{n \times m}$, $\mathbf{y} \in \mathbb{Z}_q^n$, find a vector $\mathbf{x} \in \mathbb{Z}^m$ such that $\|\mathbf{x}\| \leq \beta$, and*

$$\mathbf{Ax} = \mathbf{y} \pmod{q}$$

In their work, Chen, Genise and Mukherjee introduce a relaxed notion of the ISIS problem. We will be using their approximate setting in our work.

Definition 8 (Approx.ISIS [9]**).** *For any $n, m \in \mathbb{N}$, $q \in \mathbb{Z}$ and $\alpha, \beta \in \mathbb{R}$, define the approximate inhomogeneous short integer solution problem $Approx.ISIS_{n,m,q,\alpha,\beta}$ as follows: Given $\mathbf{A} \in \mathbb{Z}_q^{n \times m}$, $\mathbf{y} \in \mathbb{Z}_q^n$, find a vector $\mathbf{x} \in \mathbb{Z}^m$ such that $\|\mathbf{x}\| \leq \beta$, and there is a vector $\mathbf{z} \in \mathbb{Z}^n$ satisfying*

$$\|\mathbf{z}\| \leq \alpha \quad and \quad \mathbf{Ax} = \mathbf{y} + \mathbf{z} \pmod{q}$$

With the right parameters, we have the following reductions [9]:

- $LWE_{n,m,q,\theta,U(\mathbb{Z}_q),\chi} \leq_p Approx.ISIS_{n,m,q,\alpha,\beta}$
- $ISIS_{n,n+m,q,\beta} \geq_p Approx.ISIS_{n,m,q,\alpha+\beta,\beta}$
- $ISIS_{n,n+m,q,\alpha+\beta} \leq_p Approx.ISIS_{n,m,q,\alpha,\beta}$

An *approximate trapdoor* for a public matrix $\mathbf{A} \in \mathbb{Z}_q^{n \times m}$ is a string that allows one to solve efficiently the Approx.ISIS and LWE problems w.r.t $\mathbf{A}$.

2.4 Recall: F-Trapdoors [9]

The work of Chen, Genise and Mukherjee is itself based on the gadget-based trapdoor generation and preimage sampling algorithms of Micciancio and Peikert [21]. In their work on approximate trapdoors, Chen, Genise and Mukherjee create a new gadget matrix $\mathbf{F}$ which is an adaptation of the $\mathbf{G}$-gadget matrix from [21] where the l lower-orders entries are dropped.

The integer $b \geq 2$ defines the base for the $\mathbf{F}$-lattice and q the modulus ($k = \lceil \log_b q \rceil$).

The gadget matrix $\mathbf{F}$ is chosen such that it is easy to sample a short approximate preimage from $\Lambda_u^\perp(\mathbf{F})$. To do so, the approximate gadget-vector is set as

$f^t := (b^l, b^{l+1}, ..., b^{k-1})^t \in \mathbb{Z}_q^{(k-l)}$. Let $w = n(k-l)$ be the number of columns of the approximate gadget matrix $F := I_n \otimes f^t \in \mathbb{Z}_q^{(n \times w)}$. The numbers of columns of A as defined below is $m := 2n + w$. (To sample approximately from $\Lambda_u^{\perp}(F)$, we first sample from $\Lambda_u^{\perp}(G)$ as described in [21].)

Recall that the public matrix A is defined as:

$$A = [\bar{A}|F - \bar{A}R] \in \mathbb{Z}_q^{n \times m} \quad \text{with} \quad \bar{A} = [I_n, \hat{A}] \in \mathbb{Z}_q^{n \times 2n}$$

where R is a secret, trapdoor matrix with small random entries. R is sampled from the distribution $\chi^{2n \times w}$ where $\chi \subseteq \mathbb{Z}$ is chosen to be a distribution such that $LWE_{n,n,q,\chi,U(\mathbb{Z}_q),\chi}$ is hard. $\hat{A}$ is sampled from $U(\mathbb{Z}_q^{n \times n})$. Doing so, A is pseudorandom.

In order to sample a short approximate preimage of u, we use the trapdoor R to map short approximate coset representatives of $\Lambda^{\perp}(F)$ to short approximate coset representatives of $\Lambda^{\perp}(A)$ by the relation

$$A \begin{bmatrix} R \\ I \end{bmatrix} = F$$

However, using this relation alone would leak information about the secret trapdoor R. To avoid this, the perturbation-based Gaussian sampler technique of [21] is used. The covariance of the perturbation p is defined as the positive definite matrix $\Sigma_p := s^2 I_m - \sigma^2 \begin{bmatrix} RR^t & R \\ R^t & I \end{bmatrix}$ where σ is at least $\eta_\epsilon(\Lambda^{\perp}(G))$ and s is a parameter. This perturbation can be computed offline as $p \leftarrow D_{\mathbb{Z}^m, \sqrt{\Sigma_p}}$.

To approximately sample from $\Lambda_u^{\perp}(A)$, first define $v = u - Ap$ and sample a vector z following the distribution $D_{\Lambda_v^{\perp}(F),\sigma}$ as described in [21]. Finally, the approximate preimage is set to be:

$$y := p + \begin{bmatrix} R \\ I \end{bmatrix} z.$$

3   Hardness of Higher-Bit Version Problems

In this work, we aim at optimizing the memory space used to store elements in cryptographic constructions based on Ajtai's function upon some slight approximation. Our main idea is to use the base decomposition of elements in $\mathbb{Z}_q$. Using this decomposition, we discard low-weighted bits and only keep high-weighted ones.

To create such bitwise setting, we define the higher-bit approximate inhomogeneous short integer problem as well as the higher-bit near collision resistance of Ajtai's function. These instances are defined in regard to a higher-bit version of Ajtai's function.

3.1 Notations - High/Low Order Bits Functions

Let $b \geq 2$ be the base used in decomposition and $q \in \mathbb{Z}$ ($k = \lceil \log_b q \rceil$). Let d be an integer s.t $0 \leq d < k$. d is chosen as the turning point exponent between high order and low order bits.

Definition 9 (Decomposition in base b). *For $z \in \mathbb{Z}_q$, define the decomposition in base b of z as the elements $\{\alpha_{z,r}\}_{r=0}^{k-1}$ in $[|0, b-1|]$ s.t :*

$$z = \sum_{r=0}^{k-1} \alpha_{z,r} b^r$$

Definition 10 (HighBits and LowBits functions). *For $z \in \mathbb{Z}_q$,*

$$HighBits_d(z) = \sum_{r=d}^{k-1} \alpha_{z,r} b^r$$

$$LowBits_d(z) = \sum_{r=0}^{d-1} \alpha_{z,r} b^r$$

In introducing these definitions, our goal is to apply them to matrices in $\mathbb{Z}_q^{n \times m}$ and vectors in $\mathbb{Z}_q^m$ ($n, m \in \mathbb{N}$). Thus, we extend these definitions as in the following.

Definition 11. *For $\boldsymbol{y} \in \mathbb{Z}_q^n$,*

$$\boldsymbol{y}^H = (HighBits_d(y_i))_{0 \leq i < n} \quad and \quad \boldsymbol{y}^L = (LowBits_d(y_i))_{0 \leq i < n}$$

For $\boldsymbol{A} \in \mathbb{Z}_q^{n \times m}$,

$$\boldsymbol{A}^H = (HighBits_d(a_{i,j}))_{0 \leq i < n; 0 \leq j < m} \quad and \quad \boldsymbol{A}^L = (LowBits_d(a_{i,j}))_{0 \leq i < n; 0 \leq j < m}$$

3.2 Hardness of Higher-Bit Approximate ISIS

Let $b \geq 2$ be the base used in decomposition.

Definition 12. *For any $n, m \in \mathbb{N}$, $q \in \mathbb{Z}$, $\alpha, \beta \in \mathbb{R}$ and $d \in \mathbb{N}$ ($d < \lceil \log_b q \rceil$), define the higher-bit approximate inhomogeneous short integer solution problem $H.Approx.ISIS_{n,m,q,d,\alpha,\beta}$ as follows :*
Given $\boldsymbol{A} \in \mathbb{Z}_q^{n \times m}$, $\boldsymbol{y} \in \mathbb{Z}_q^n$, find a vector $\boldsymbol{x} \in \mathbb{Z}^m$ such that $\|\boldsymbol{x}\| \leq \beta$ and there is a vector $\boldsymbol{z} \in \mathbb{Z}^n$ satisfying :

$$\|\boldsymbol{z}\| \leq \alpha \quad and \quad b^d \boldsymbol{A} \boldsymbol{x} = \boldsymbol{y} + \boldsymbol{z} \pmod{q}.$$

We show that the higher-bit approximate ISIS problem is as hard as the standard ISIS. We know that the approximate ISIS is as hard as the standard ISIS under the right parameters setting (see Sect. 2). Thus, we only need to show the reductions between the higher-bit approximate ISIS and the approximate ISIS.

Lemma 2.

$$Approx.ISIS_{n,m,q,\alpha,\beta} \geq_p H.Approx.ISIS_{n,m,q,d,\alpha,\beta};$$
$$H.Approx.ISIS_{n,m,q,d,\alpha,\beta} \geq_p Approx.ISIS_{n,m,q,\alpha+\sqrt{n}b^d\beta,\beta}.$$

Proof. The first reduction is straightforward.

Suppose there is a polynomial time algorithm $\mathcal{A}$ that solves H.Approx. $ISIS_{n,m,q,d,\alpha,\beta}$, we build a polynomial time algorithm $\mathcal{B}$ that solves Approx.ISIS$_{n,m,q,\alpha+\sqrt{n}b^d\beta,\beta}$. Given an Approx.ISIS instance $(\boldsymbol{A} \in \mathbb{Z}_q^{n\times m}$, $\boldsymbol{y} \in \mathbb{Z}_q^n)$, $\mathcal{B}$ passes $(\frac{\boldsymbol{A}^H}{b^d} \in \mathbb{Z}_{\frac{q}{b^d}}^{n\times m}$, $\boldsymbol{y})$ to $\mathcal{A}$ and get $\boldsymbol{x} \in \mathbb{Z}_q^m$ such that:

$$\boldsymbol{A}^H\boldsymbol{x} = \boldsymbol{y} + \boldsymbol{z} \pmod{q} \quad \text{with} \quad \|\boldsymbol{x}\| \leq \beta, \|\boldsymbol{z}\| \leq \alpha.$$

We do :

$$\boldsymbol{A}\boldsymbol{x} = \boldsymbol{y} + \boldsymbol{z} + \boldsymbol{A}^L\boldsymbol{x} \pmod{q}$$

Moreover,

$$\|\boldsymbol{z} + \boldsymbol{A}^L\boldsymbol{x}\| \leq \|\boldsymbol{z}\| + \|\boldsymbol{A}^L\boldsymbol{x}\|$$
$$\leq \alpha + \|\boldsymbol{A}^L\|\|\boldsymbol{x}\|$$
$$\leq \alpha + \sqrt{n}b^d\beta$$

since all coefficients in $\boldsymbol{A}^L$ are less than b^d.

So $\boldsymbol{x}$ is a valid solution to Approx.ISIS$_{n,m,q,\alpha+\sqrt{n}b^d\beta,\beta}$. $\qquad\square$

Theorem 1.

$$ISIS_{n,n+m,q,\beta} \geq_p H.Approx.ISIS_{n,m,q,d,\alpha+\beta,\beta};$$
$$H.Approx.ISIS_{n,m,q,d,\alpha,\beta} \geq_p ISIS_{n,n+m,q,\alpha+(\sqrt{n}b^d+1)\beta}.$$

Proof. We can prove this Theorem by using both Lemma 2 above and reductions from [9] (see Sect. 2). $\qquad\square$

3.3   The Near Collision Resistance of Higher-Bit Ajtai's Function

Let $b \geq 2$ be the base used in decomposition.

Lemma 3. (The near-collision-resistance of Ajtai's function [9]**).** *For any* $n, m, q \in \mathbb{N}$ *and* $\alpha, \beta \in \mathbb{R}$,
   If *there is an efficient adversary* $\mathcal{A}$ *that given* $\boldsymbol{A} \leftarrow U(\mathbb{Z}_q^{n \times m})$, *finds* $\boldsymbol{x}_1 \neq \boldsymbol{x}_2 \in \mathbb{Z}^m$ *such that:*

$$\|\boldsymbol{x}_1\| \leq \beta \quad and \quad \|\boldsymbol{x}_2\| \leq \beta \quad and \quad \|\boldsymbol{A}\boldsymbol{x}_1 - \boldsymbol{A}\boldsymbol{x}_2 \pmod{q}\| \leq 2\alpha$$

   Then *there is an efficient adversary* $\mathcal{B}$ *that solves* $SIS_{n,n+m,q,2(\alpha+\beta)}$.

Lemma 4. *For any* $n, m, q \in \mathbb{N}$, $\alpha, \beta \in \mathbb{R}$ *and* $d \in \mathbb{N}$ *(d* $< \lceil \log_b q \rceil)$,
   If *there is an efficient adversary* $\mathcal{A}$ *that given* $\boldsymbol{A} \leftarrow U(\mathbb{Z}_{\frac{q}{b^d}}^{n \times m})$, *finds* $\boldsymbol{x}_1 \neq \boldsymbol{x}_2 \in \mathbb{Z}^m$ *such that:*

$$\|\boldsymbol{x}_1\| \leq \beta \quad and \quad \|\boldsymbol{x}_2\| \leq \beta \quad and \quad \|b^d \boldsymbol{A}\boldsymbol{x}_1 - b^d \boldsymbol{A}\boldsymbol{x}_2 \pmod{q}\| \leq 2\alpha$$

   Then *there is an efficient adversary* $\mathcal{B}$ *that given* $\boldsymbol{A} \leftarrow U(\mathbb{Z}_q^{n \times m})$, *finds* $\boldsymbol{x}_1 \neq \boldsymbol{x}_2 \in \mathbb{Z}^m$ *such that:*

$$\|\boldsymbol{x}_1\| \leq \beta \quad and \quad \|\boldsymbol{x}_2\| \leq \beta \quad and \quad \|\boldsymbol{A}\boldsymbol{x}_1 - \boldsymbol{A}\boldsymbol{x}_2 \pmod{q}\| \leq 2(\alpha + \sqrt{n}b^d\beta)$$

Proof. Suppose $\mathcal{B}$ gets $\boldsymbol{A} \in \mathbb{Z}_q^{n \times m}$. $\mathcal{B}$ sends $\frac{\boldsymbol{A}^H}{b^d}$ to $\mathcal{A}$ and gets back $\boldsymbol{x}_1 \neq \boldsymbol{x}_2 \in \mathbb{Z}^m$ such that:

$$\|\boldsymbol{x}_1\| \leq \beta \quad and \quad \|\boldsymbol{x}_2\| \leq \beta \quad and \quad \|\boldsymbol{A}^H \boldsymbol{x}_1 - \boldsymbol{A}^H \boldsymbol{x}_2 \pmod{q}\| \leq 2\alpha$$

We define $\boldsymbol{z} = \boldsymbol{A}^H \boldsymbol{x}_1 - \boldsymbol{A}^H \boldsymbol{x}_2 \pmod{q}$,

$$\boldsymbol{A}\boldsymbol{x}_1 - \boldsymbol{A}\boldsymbol{x}_2 = \boldsymbol{z} + \boldsymbol{A}^L \boldsymbol{x}_1 - \boldsymbol{A}^L \boldsymbol{x}_2 \pmod{q}$$

Thus ,

$$\begin{aligned}
\|\boldsymbol{A}\boldsymbol{x}_1 - \boldsymbol{A}\boldsymbol{x}_2 \pmod{q}\| &\leq \|\boldsymbol{z}\| + \|\boldsymbol{A}^L \boldsymbol{x}_1\| + \|\boldsymbol{A}^L \boldsymbol{x}_2\| \\
&\leq 2(\alpha + \sqrt{n}b^d\beta)
\end{aligned}$$

$\square$

Theorem 2. (The near collision resistance of higher-bit Ajtai's function). *For any* $n, m, q \in \mathbb{N}$, $\alpha, \beta \in \mathbb{R}$ *and* $d \in \mathbb{N}$ *(d* $< \lceil \log_b q \rceil)$,
   If *there is an efficient adversary* $\mathcal{A}$ *that given* $\boldsymbol{A} \leftarrow U(\mathbb{Z}_{\frac{q}{b^d}}^{n \times m})$, *finds* $\boldsymbol{x}_1 \neq \boldsymbol{x}_2 \in \mathbb{Z}^m$ *such that:*

$$\|\boldsymbol{x}_1\| \leq \beta \quad and \quad \|\boldsymbol{x}_2\| \leq \beta \quad and \quad \|b^d \boldsymbol{A}\boldsymbol{x}_1 - b^d \boldsymbol{A}\boldsymbol{x}_2 \pmod{q}\| \leq 2\alpha$$

   Then *there is an efficient adversary* $\mathcal{B}$ *that solves* $SIS_{n,n+m,q,2[\alpha+(\sqrt{n}b^d+1)\beta]}$

Proof. We can prove this Theorem using both Lemma 3 [9] and Lemma 4 above.

$\square$

4   New Construction - Main Idea

We construct an application of the higher-bit approximate ISIS problem. Our goal is to reduce the sizes of both the matrix $A \in \mathbb{Z}_q^{n \times m}$ generated with an approximate trapdoor as in the algorithms of [9], and of the sampled approximate preimage $y \in \mathbb{Z}_q^m$ by Ajtai's Function defined by A.

Let b be the base for the matrix F of [9] with parameter l. As mentioned above, we will be using the decomposition in base b ($k = \lceil \log_b q \rceil$). Let d be an integer s.t $0 \leq d \leq l$.

4.1   Modification in the Public Matrix A

Modification in the Construction
We recall that in [9], the public matrix A is defined as:

$$A := [\bar{A}|F - \bar{A}R] \in \mathbb{Z}_q^{n \times m}$$

where F is the public approximate gadget matrix and R is the approximate trapdoor associated with the Ajtai's Function defined by A (see Sect. 2.4).

The selected modification on A is straightforward. We construct $A^{new} \in \mathbb{Z}_{\frac{q}{b^d}}^{n \times m}$ by doing the same as above and applying the HighBits function on A.

$$A^{new} = \frac{A^H}{b^d} \quad \text{where} \quad A^H = [\bar{A}^H|(F - \bar{A}R)^H]$$

In the following work, we need to isolate F. We observe that F is already in a higher-bit form since $F = I_n \otimes (b^l, b^{l+1}, ..., b^{k-1})^t$ and $d \leq l$.

We use this property to express A^H while keeping F untouched:

$$A^H = [\bar{A}^H|F + (-\bar{A}R)^H]$$

It is easy to see that $A^{new} \in \mathbb{Z}_{\frac{q}{b^d}}^{n \times m}$.

Optimization in the Public Matrix Size. Using this modification, we save $n \times m \times d\lceil \log_2 b \rceil$ bits in the public matrix A^{new} memory space.

4.2   Repercussion on the Security and Underlying Problem

This change in the public matrix A implies a modification in the hardness of the underlying problem. In this construction, security relies on the higher-bit approximate $\text{ISIS}_{n,m,q,d,\alpha,\beta}$ problem. As seen in Theorem 1, there is a reduction from this problem to the $\text{SIS}_{n,m,q,\alpha+\sqrt{n}b^d\beta}$ problem. For same α and β as in the original construction from [9], we need to deal with an additional $\sqrt{n}b^d$ factor in the SIS problem solution length.

5   New Construction - Algorithms

Let n, m, q, k and d be defined as in Sect. 4.

In the following section, we present our compact approximate trapdoor generation algorithm and approximate preimage sampling algorithm. Our algorithms use those from [9]. Our method generates a pseudorandom $\boldsymbol{A} \in \mathbb{Z}_{\frac{q}{b^d}}^{n \times m}$ along with an approximate trapdoor $\boldsymbol{R}$ which allows to sample an approximate preimage $\boldsymbol{y} \in \mathbb{Z}_{\frac{q}{b^d}}^{m}$ for higher-bit Ajtai's function defined by $\boldsymbol{A}$.

5.1   The Higher-Bit Version Algorithms

We consider that HIGHBITS and LOWBITS are two functions implemented as described in Sect. 3.1.

Algorithm 1: HIGHBITS.APPROX.TRAPGEN$_\chi$

Input: Security parameter λ.
Output: Matrix-approximate trapdoor pair $(\boldsymbol{A}, \boldsymbol{R}) \in \mathbb{Z}_{\frac{q}{b^d}}^{n \times m} \times \mathbb{Z}^{2n \times w}$;
      matrix $\boldsymbol{A}_0^L \in \mathbb{Z}_{b^d}^{n \times m}$
1   $(\boldsymbol{A}_0, \boldsymbol{R})$= APPROX.TRAPGEN$_\chi(\lambda)$ // Algorithm from [9]
2   $\boldsymbol{A}_0^H, \boldsymbol{A}_0^L = HIGHBITS(\boldsymbol{A}_0, d), LOWBITS(\boldsymbol{A}_0, d)$
3   $\boldsymbol{A} = \frac{\boldsymbol{A}_0^H}{b^d}$
4   **return** $((\boldsymbol{A}, \boldsymbol{R}), \boldsymbol{A}_0^L)$

Algorithm 2: HIGHBITS.APPROX.SAMPLEPRE

Input: $(\boldsymbol{A}, \boldsymbol{A}_0^L, \boldsymbol{R}, \boldsymbol{u}, \text{s})$.
Output: An approximate preimage of $\boldsymbol{u} \in \mathbb{Z}_q^n$ for $b^d \boldsymbol{A} : \boldsymbol{y} \in \mathbb{Z}_{\frac{q}{b^d}}^m$
1   $\boldsymbol{y}_0$= APPROX.SAMPLEPRE$(b^d \boldsymbol{A} + \boldsymbol{A}_0^L, \boldsymbol{R}, \boldsymbol{u}, \text{s})$ // $\boldsymbol{A}_0 = b^d \boldsymbol{A} + \boldsymbol{A}_0^L$;
                                              // Algorithm from [9]
2   $\boldsymbol{y} = LOWBITS(\boldsymbol{y}_0, k - d)$
3   **return** $\boldsymbol{y}$

Fig. 1. Pseudocode for the higher-bit version approximate trapdoor generation and approximate preimage sampling algorithms. The distribution χ is chosen so that LWE$_{n,n,q,\chi,U(\mathbb{Z}_q),\chi}$ is hard. For the sake of optimization in Algorithm 2, we need to set $q = b^k$.

Algorithm 1. This algorithm is instantiated such as described in Sect. 4. The overall goal is to use only the high-weighted bits of the previous public matrix $\boldsymbol{A}_0$ as our new public key. Doing so, we induce a b^d-approximation on every coefficient of the resulting public key $\boldsymbol{A}$ when compared to $\boldsymbol{A}_0$.

One should note that this algorithm does not only generate a matrix-approximate trapdoor pair. It also returns the low-weighted bits of the original matrix $\boldsymbol{A}_0$. This information is given to the approximate preimage sampling algorithm. We should notice that information on A_0^L leaks through the error distribution. However this is not a problem because it does not leak information on the secret trapdoor R since A_0^L is pseudorandom as we will see in Subsect. 5.2.

Algorithm 2. This algorithm samples an approximate preimage $y \in \mathbb{Z}_{\frac{q}{b^d}}^m$ of $u \in \mathbb{Z}_q^n$ by the higher-bit Ajtai's function $A \in \mathbb{Z}_{\frac{q}{b^d}}^{n \times m}$.

First, we sample an approximate preimage $y_0 \in \mathbb{Z}_q^m$ of the Ajtai's function defined by A_0 using the algorithm from [9].

Secondly, in order to reduce the signature size, we use a little trick. It relies on the following lemma:

Lemma 5. *For $z \in \mathbb{Z}_q$, $q = b^k$, and integers d, j such that $j \geq d$,*

$$b^j z = b^j LowBits_{k-d}(z) \pmod{q}$$

Proof.

$$b^j z = b^{j-d} \sum_{r=d}^{k-1} \alpha_{z, r-d} b^r \pmod{q} = b^j \sum_{r=0}^{k-1-d} \alpha_{z,r} b^r \pmod{q}$$

$\square$

Using Lemma 5 and the fact that $b^d A$ is in a higher-bit form, we see that the d highest bits of y_0 have no impact on the product $b^d A y_0$.

Theorem 3. *For $A \in \mathbb{Z}_{\frac{q}{b^d}}^{n \times m}$ and $y_0 \in \mathbb{Z}^m$, $q = b^k$,*

$$b^d A y = b^d A y_0 \pmod{q} \quad where \quad y = LowBits_{k-d}(y_0)$$

Therefore, our modification in the public key A allows for an optimization in the approximate preimage.

Remark 1. The norm of the approximate preimage is decreased by this modification. Thus, if y_0 is short then y is too.

Remark 2. This optimization needs the additional condition $q = b^k$. If this condition is not met, we should use the approximate preimage y_0 from [9].

Optimization in the Preimage Size. Using this modification, we save $m \times d \lceil \log_2 b \rceil$ bits in the approximate preimage memory space.

Remark 3. An idea to optimize the preimage size even more would be to apply the HighBits function on y in the same way as for A. However, doing so would increase a lot more the error term and thus impact security. We decide not to add such modification as a trade-off between size and security.

Error Term. We define the error $e \in \mathbb{Z}_q^n$ as $e = u - b^d A y \pmod{q}$. e_0 defines the error term induced by y_0 i.e. $e_0 = u - A_0 y_0 \pmod{q}$.

The error term e can be expressed as:

$$\boxed{e = e_0 + e_{new} \pmod{q}} \quad \text{where} \quad e_{new} = A_0^L y_0 \pmod{q}$$

Proof.

$$e = u - b^d A y \pmod{q}$$
$$= u - A_0^H y_0 \pmod{q} \quad \textit{Theorem 3}$$
$$= u - (A_0 - A_0^L) y_0 \pmod{q}$$
$$= \underbrace{u - A_0 y_0}_{e_0} + \underbrace{A_0^L y_0}_{e_{new}} \pmod{q}$$

$\square$

Remark 4. If we had chosen to calculate y_0 with regard to $b^d A$ rather than A_0, the error term e would be $e = e_0 + A_0^L \begin{bmatrix} R \\ I \end{bmatrix} z$ (z is an approximate preimage for F). We observe that $A_0^L \begin{bmatrix} R \\ I \end{bmatrix} = \bar{A}^L R + (-\bar{A}R)^L + F$. Thus, information on the secret R would leak from the distribution of e. Even though the norm of e is decreased by this method, the security is compromised.

5.2   Study of the Resulting Distributions

The results of this subsection are summarized in the following Theorem.

Theorem 4. *There exist probabilistic, polynomial time algorithms HIGHBITS. APPROX.TRAPGEN$_\chi$ and HIGHBITS.APPROX.SAMPLEPRE satisfying the following :*

1. *HIGHBITS.APPROX.TRAPGEN$_\chi(\lambda)$ returns a matrix-approximate trap-door pair $(A,R) \in \mathbb{Z}_{\frac{q}{b^d}}^{n \times m} \times \mathbb{Z}^{2n \times n(k-l)}$ along with a matrix $A_0^L \in \mathbb{Z}_{b^d}^{n \times m}$.*

   The matrices A and A_0^L are pseudorandom assuming the hardness of $LWE_{n,n,q,\chi,U(\mathbb{Z}_q),\chi}$.

2. *Let $((A,R),A_0^L)$ be generated by HIGHBITS.APPROX.TRAPGEN$_\chi(\lambda)$. The following two distributions are statistically indistinguishable:*

$$\{(A,y,u,e) : u \leftarrow U(\mathbb{Z}_q^n),$$
$$y \leftarrow HIGHBITS.APPROX.SAMPLEPRE(A, A_0^L, R, u, s),$$
$$e = u - b^d A y \pmod{q}\}$$

and

$$\{(A, y, u, e) : y_0 \leftarrow D_{\mathbb{Z}^m, s}, e_0 \leftarrow D_{\mathbb{Z}^n, \sigma\sqrt{(b^{2l}-1)/(b^2-1)}} \pmod{q},$$

$$y = LowBits_{k-d}(y_0), e = e_0 + A_0^L y_0 \pmod{q},$$

$$u = b^d A y + e \pmod{q}\}$$

for any $\sigma \geq \sqrt{b^2 + 1}.w(\sqrt{\log n})$ and $s \gtrsim \sqrt{b^2 + 1}\frac{s_1^2(R)}{s_{2n}(R)}\eta_\epsilon(\mathbb{Z}^{nk})$.

Proof. The proof is described in the end of this section. We use the distributions study results in Theorem 4 from [9]. □

Distributions of A and A_0^L.

Lemma 6. *For any matrix M with distribution $U(\mathbb{Z}_q^{n\times m})$,*

$\frac{M^H}{b^d}$ follows the distribution $U(\mathbb{Z}_{\frac{q}{b^d}}^{n\times m})$ and M^L follows the distribution

$U(\mathbb{Z}_{b^d}^{n\times m})$. The distributions of $\frac{M^H}{b^d}$ and M^L are independent.

Proof. Let i,j be two integers s.t $0 \leq i \leq n$ and $0 \leq j \leq m$. Let x be an integer in $[[0, \frac{q}{b^d} - 1]]$.

$$\mathbb{P}\left(\frac{m_{i,j}^H}{b^d} = x \pmod{\frac{q}{b^d}}\right) = \mathbb{P}(HighBits_d(m_{i,j}) = b^d x \pmod{q})$$

$$= \sum_{l_0 \in [[0, b^d-1]]} \mathbb{P}(m_{i,j} = b^d x + l_0 \pmod{q})$$

$$= \sum_{l_0 \in [[0, b^d-1]]} \frac{1}{q} = \frac{b^d}{q} = \frac{1}{\frac{q}{b^d}}$$

Using the same kind of reasoning, we can find that for any $x \in [[0, b^d - 1]]$, $\mathbb{P}(m_{i,j}^L = x \pmod{b^d}) = \frac{1}{b^d}$

M^H and M^L do not share any random sources thus their distributions are independent.

□

We know that A_0 is computationally indistinguishable from random assuming $LWE_{n,n,q,\chi,U(\mathbb{Z}_q),\chi}$ [9].

Thus, using Lemma 6, we deduce that $A \approx_s U(\mathbb{Z}_{\frac{q}{b^d}}^{n\times m})$ and $A_0^L \approx_s U(\mathbb{Z}_{b^d}^{n\times m})$.

Distribution of y. We know that the distribution of $y_0 \leftarrow APPROX.$ $SAMPLEPRE(A_0, R, u, s)$ is statistically indistinguishable from $y_0 \leftarrow D_{\mathbb{Z}^m, s}$ for a random target. Since $y = LowBits_{k-d}(y_0)$, we can say that the distribution of y is statistically indistinguishable from $\{y_0 \leftarrow D_{\mathbb{Z}^m, s}, y = LowBits_{k-d}(y_0)\}$ for a random target.

Thus, the distribution of $\boldsymbol{y}$ is simulatable without knowing the secret $\boldsymbol{R}$ nor the public key $\boldsymbol{A}$.

Distribution of e. We know that the distribution of $\{\boldsymbol{y}_0 \leftarrow APPROX.$ $SAMPLEPRE(\boldsymbol{A}_0, \boldsymbol{R}, \boldsymbol{u}, s), \boldsymbol{e}_0 = \boldsymbol{u} - \boldsymbol{A}_0\boldsymbol{y}_0\}$ is statistically indistinguishable from $\{\boldsymbol{y}_0 \leftarrow D_{\mathbb{Z}^m, s}, \boldsymbol{e}_0 \leftarrow D_{\mathbb{Z}^n, \sigma\sqrt{(b^{2l}-1)/(b^2-1)}} \pmod q\}$ for a random target $\boldsymbol{u}$. Since $\boldsymbol{e} = \boldsymbol{e}_0 + \boldsymbol{A}_0^L\boldsymbol{y}_0 \pmod q$, we can say that the distribution of $\boldsymbol{e}$ is statistically indistinguishable from $\{\boldsymbol{y}_0 \leftarrow D_{\mathbb{Z}^m, s}, \boldsymbol{e}_0 \leftarrow D_{\mathbb{Z}^n, \sigma\sqrt{(b^{2l}-1)/(b^2-1)}}$ $\pmod q, \boldsymbol{e} = \boldsymbol{e}_0 + \boldsymbol{A}_0^L\boldsymbol{y}_0 \pmod q\}$ for a random target.

Thus, the distribution of $\boldsymbol{e}$ is simulatable without knowing the secret $\boldsymbol{R}$. Compared to [9], we need to know $\boldsymbol{A}_0^L$ to simulate $\boldsymbol{e}$. However, as seen in 5.2, $\boldsymbol{A}_0^L$ is computationally indistinguishable from random and thus do not leak information about $\boldsymbol{R}$.

6   Hash-and-Sign Signature

This section is dedicated to the construction of a sEU-CMA secure [9] hash-and-sign signature scheme instantiated with the algorithms and parameters from Fig. 1. Let $\sigma, s \in \mathbb{R}^+$ be the discrete Gaussian widths of the distributions over the cosets of $\Lambda_q^\perp(\boldsymbol{G})$ [21] and approximate $\Lambda_q^\perp(\boldsymbol{A}_0)$ [9] respectively. We choose a distribution χ to sample $\boldsymbol{R}$ so that $\mathrm{LWE}_{n,n,q,\chi,U(\mathbb{Z}_q),\chi}$ is hard.

6.1   Construction of a Hash-and-sign Signature

The following construction is written in the same way as the one in Sect. 5 from [9]. This shows how it is adjusted to fit the "higher-bit setting".

Construction 1. *Given the algorithms from Theorem 4, a hash function $H = \{H_\lambda : \{0,1\}^* \to \mathbb{Z}_q^n\}$ modeled as a random oracle, we build a signature scheme as follows.*

- *Gen(1^λ): The key-generation algorithm samples $\boldsymbol{A} \in \mathbb{Z}_{\frac{q}{b^d}}^{n \times m}$ together with its (α, β)-approximate trapdoor $\boldsymbol{R}$ and the matrix $\boldsymbol{A}_0^L \in \mathbb{Z}_{b^d}^{n \times m}$ from HIGHBITS.APPROX.TRAPGEN$_\chi(\lambda)$. It outputs $\boldsymbol{A}$ as the verification key, keeps $\boldsymbol{R}$ as the secret signing key and gives $\boldsymbol{A}_0^L$ to the signing algorithm.*
- *Sig($\boldsymbol{R}, \boldsymbol{m}$): The signing algorithm checks if the message-signature pair $(\boldsymbol{m}, \boldsymbol{x}_m)$ has been produced before. If so, it outputs $\boldsymbol{x}_m$ as the signature of $\boldsymbol{m}$; if not, it computes $\boldsymbol{u} = H(\boldsymbol{m})$, and samples an approximate preimage $\boldsymbol{x}_m \leftarrow HIGHBITS.APPROX.SAMPLEPRE(\boldsymbol{A}, \boldsymbol{A}_0^L, \boldsymbol{R}, \boldsymbol{u}, s)$. It outputs $\boldsymbol{x}_m$ as the signature and stores $(\boldsymbol{m}, \boldsymbol{x}_m)$ in the list.*
- *Ver($\boldsymbol{A}, \boldsymbol{m}, \boldsymbol{x}$): The verification algorithm checks if $\|\boldsymbol{x}\| \leq \beta$ and $\|b^d \boldsymbol{A}\boldsymbol{x} - H(\boldsymbol{m})\| \leq \alpha$. If so, it outputs accept; otherwise, it outputs reject.*

6.2   Correctness

It is straightforward to verify that construction 1 is correct with overwhelming probability by the settings of the parameters and definitions of our algorithms.

6.3   Proof of Security

For a random target, the preimage and error term are simulatable from distributions without knowing the secret key R (see Theorem 4). We denote these distributions by D_{pre} and D_{err}. To prove that our construction satisfies sEU-CMA security, we rely on Theorem 2 about "higher-bit near-collision-resistance" property for Ajtai's function. We use the same definition for sEU-CMA security as defined in [9].

Theorem 5. *Construction 1 is strongly existentially unforgeable under a chosen-message attack in the random oracle model assuming the hardness of $SIS_{n,n+m,q,2[\alpha+(\sqrt{n}b^d+1)\beta]}$ and $LWE_{n,n,q,\chi,U(\mathbb{Z}_q),\chi}$.*

Proof. Assume that there is an adversary $\mathcal{A}$ which breaks the sEU-CMA security of construction 1 in polynomial time. We describe a polynomial time adversary $\mathcal{B}$ invoking $\mathcal{A}$ that breaks the higher-bit near-collision-resistance of Ajtai's function, which is as hard as $SIS_{n,n+m,q,2[\alpha+(\sqrt{n}b^d+1)\beta]}$ (Theorem 2).

$\mathcal{B}$ receives the matrix A as a challenge for "the higher-bit near-collision-resistance of Ajtai's function". $\mathcal{B}$ runs $\mathcal{A}$ on input pk A. $\mathcal{B}$ answers hash queries to random oracle H and signing queries as follows. We note that its answers are indistinguishable from the real ones due to the properties of D_{pre} and D_{err}, and that a real public key is indistinguishable from random under $LWE_{n,n,q,\chi,U(\mathbb{Z}_q),\chi}$.

Simulation of Hash Queries. We assume that $\mathcal{B}$ has chosen a random A_0^L to calculate D_{err}. $\mathcal{A}$'s hash query $H(m)$ on a message m is answered by $\mathcal{B}$ as follows : $\mathcal{B}$ samples $x \leftarrow D_{pre}$, gives $u := b^d Ax + D_{err} \pmod{q}$ to $\mathcal{A}$ as $H(m)$.

$\mathcal{B}$ stores (m,u) in the random oracle storage, (m,x) in the message-signature pair storage.

Simulation of Signing Queries. Assume that on $\mathcal{A}$'s signature query m, m has been queried to the random oracle before. $\mathcal{B}$ generates the signature x by finding (m,x) in the message-signature pair storage.

Forgery. Generality is equivalent to assumption that before $\mathcal{A}$'s attempt to forge a signature on m^*, $\mathcal{A}$ has queried H on m^*. We denote (m^*,u^*) and (m^*,x^*) as the pairs prepared by $\mathcal{B}$ in the random oracle storage and message-signature pair storage respectively. $\mathcal{A}$ forges a signature x on m^*. By the definition of a correct signature, we have $\|b^d A(x - x^*) \pmod{q}\| \leq 2\alpha$.

In the case where m^* has been queried to the signing oracle, $x \neq x^*$ by the definition of a successful forgery. Otherwise, we know that $D_{\mathbb{Z}^m,s}$ is set with high min-entropy. Thus, D_{pre} is also with high min-entropy since D_{pre} means compressing b^d points to one point when using $D_{\mathbb{Z}^m,s}$. So, $x \neq x^*$ with overwhelming probability. □

6.4   Implementation and Analysis

The results in Theorem 4 induce the following length bounds on the signature x and error term e: $\|x\| \leq s$ and $\|e\| \leq b^l \sigma + \sqrt{n} b^d s$.

We need to respect these bounds to set the parameters α and β of the underlying security problem. Thus, combining with the results in Theorem 5, we observe a trade-off between security and memory space. This trade-off is due to the increase in the norm of a solution to the SIS problem. It is summarized in Fig. 2 for the matrix setting.

	F-trapdoor [9]	This work
Norm of a short solution in the underlying SIS problem	$2(s + b^l \sigma)$	$2(s + b^l \sigma) + 4\sqrt{n}b^d s$
Signature size (in bits)	$m \times k \times log_2(b)$	$m \times (k - d) \times log_2(b)$
Public key size (in bits)	$m \times n \times k \times log_2(b)$	$m \times n \times (k - d) \times log_2(b)$

Fig. 2. The parameters are for a fixed lattice dimension n, vector dimension m, a base b, a modulus q where $k = \lceil log_b q \rceil$. Parameters l, s and σ are the same as in [9].

Proof-of-Concept Implementation. Due to this trade-off, we need to analyse the benefits of our construction for different parameters sets. To do so, we implement our construction for different concrete parameters. The code used in this implementation is provided by Dr. Chen [8]. We get our security assuming the hardness of Ring-LWE and Ring-SIS. Our goal in doing this implementation is to compare our construction for different parameters choices with the two best reference implementations from [9]. In Fig. 3, we list three groups of parameters.

	F-trapdoor [9]	F-trapdoor [9]	This work	This work	This work
n	512	1024	512	1024	1024
$k = \lceil log_b q \rceil$	8	9	8	9	8
b	4	4	4	4	4
l	4	5	4	5	3
d	-	-	4	5	3
τ	2.6	2.8	2.6	2.8	2.8
s	2505.6	3733.1	2496.3	3741.7	4306.1
m	3072	6144	3072	6144	7168
$||x||_2$	138326.9	296473.0	8175.1	11495.9	50023.6
$||x||_\infty$	10144	13647	255	255	1023
$||e||_2$	19793.8	1502259.7	431768.4	2452040.3	594441.7
PK	5.12	11.52	2.56	5.12	7.68
LWE	104.7	192.7	104.7	192.7	192.7
AISIS	87.8	183.7	75.0	140.5	153.9

Fig. 3. Some concrete parameters. The size of PK is measured in kB. LWE and AISIS refers to the security levels of breaking the associated problems. $||x||$ and $||e||$ are the norms of the preimage and error term. τ is the gaussian width of R.

Figure 3 shows that for a same security parameter n, we can expect our construction to reduce the public key size to half and significantly reduce the signature size at the expense of a reasonable drop in the security level. Thus, our modification allows us to find interesting results for achieving different levels of security than those given by the original construction from [9]. Our implementation shows that an estimation of 75-bit security could be achieved for a public key size of 2.56 kB, and an estimation of 140-bit security could be achieved for a public key size of 5.12 kB.

Moreover, it is noteworthy to observe that if we increase the security parameter n compared to [9], we might obtain a better security while keeping somewhat equivalent public key size and better preimage norm. For example, we obtain an estimation of 140-bit security for about the same key sizes than the 88-bit security reference implementation of [8]. However, the security parameter n is doubled in our construction which can lead to bigger algorithms running times.

Acknowledgments. We would like to thank Yilei Chen, Nicholas Genise and Pratyay Mukherjee for kindly sharing with us their implementation of Hash-and-Sign signature based on F-trapdoors. We are especially grateful to Yilei Chen for his invaluable advice to our work.

References

1. Agrawal, S., Boneh, D., Boyen, X.: Efficient lattice (H)IBE in the standard model. In: Gilbert, H. (ed.) EUROCRYPT 2010. LNCS, vol. 6110, pp. 553–572. Springer, Heidelberg (2010). https://doi.org/10.1007/978-3-642-13190-5_28

2. Ajtai, M.: Generating hard instances of lattice problems (extended abstract). In: STOC 1996. ACM, New York (1996). https://doi.org/10.1145/237814.237838

3. Ajtai, M.: Generating hard instances of the short basis problem. In: Wiedermann, J., van Emde Boas, P., Nielsen, M. (eds.) ICALP 1999. LNCS, vol. 1644, pp. 1–9. Springer, Heidelberg (1999). https://doi.org/10.1007/3-540-48523-6_1

4. Alkim, E., Barreto, P.S.L.M., Bindel, N., Krämer, J., Longa, P., Ricardini, J.E.: The lattice-based digital signature scheme qTESLA. In: Conti, M., Zhou, J., Casalicchio, E., Spognardi, A. (eds.) ACNS 2020. LNCS, vol. 12146, pp. 441–460. Springer, Cham (2020). https://doi.org/10.1007/978-3-030-57808-4_22

5. Alwen, J., Peikert, C.: Generating shorter bases for hard random lattices. Theor. Comp. Sys. **48**(3), 535–553 (2010). https://doi.org/10.1007/s00224-010-9278-3

6. Brakerski, Z., Langlois, A., Peikert, C., Regev, O., Stehlé, D.: Classical hardness of learning with errors. In: STOC 2013. ACM, New York (2013). https://doi.org/10.1145/2488608.2488680

7. Cash, D., Hofheinz, D., Kiltz, E., Peikert, C.: Bonsai trees, or how to delegate a lattice basis. J. Cryptol. **25**(4), 601–639 (2011). https://doi.org/10.1007/s00145-011-9105-2

8. Chen, Y.: Private communication (2021)

9. Chen, Y., Genise, N., Mukherjee, P.: Approximate trapdoors for lattices and smaller hash-and-sign signatures. In: Galbraith, S.D., Moriai, S. (eds.) ASIACRYPT 2019. LNCS, vol. 11923, pp. 3–32. Springer, Cham (2019). https://doi.org/10.1007/978-3-030-34618-8_1

10. Ducas, L., et al.: CRYSTALS-Dilithium: a lattice-based digital signature scheme. IACR Trans. Cryptographic Hardware Embedded Syst. (1), 238–268 (2018). https://doi.org/10.13154/tches.v2018.i1.238-268

11. Fouque, P.-A., e.a.: Falcon: fast-Fourier lattice-based compact signatures over NTRU (2018). https://falcon-sign.info/
12. Gentry, C.: Fully homomorphic encryption using ideal lattices. In: STOC 2009. ACM (2009). https://doi.org/10.1145/1536414.1536440
13. Gentry, C., Peikert, C., Vaikuntanathan, V.: Trapdoors for hard lattices and new cryptographic constructions. In: STOC 2008. ACM (2008). https://doi.org/10.1145/1374376.1374407
14. Hoffstein, J., Pipher, J., Silverman, J.H.: NTRU: a ring-based public key cryptosystem. In: Buhler, J.P. (ed.) ANTS 1998. LNCS, vol. 1423, pp. 267–288. Springer, Heidelberg (1998). https://doi.org/10.1007/BFb0054868
15. Lindner, R., Peikert, C.: Better key sizes (and attacks) for LWE-based encryption. In: Kiayias, A. (ed.) CT-RSA 2011. LNCS, vol. 6558, pp. 319–339. Springer, Heidelberg (2011). https://doi.org/10.1007/978-3-642-19074-2_21
16. Lyubashevsky, V.: Lattice signatures without trapdoors. In: Pointcheval, D., Johansson, T. (eds.) EUROCRYPT 2012. LNCS, vol. 7237, pp. 738–755. Springer, Heidelberg (2012). https://doi.org/10.1007/978-3-642-29011-4_43
17. Lyubashevsky, V., Micciancio, D.: Asymptotically efficient lattice-based digital signatures. In: Canetti, R. (ed.) TCC 2008. LNCS, vol. 4948, pp. 37–54. Springer, Heidelberg (2008). https://doi.org/10.1007/978-3-540-78524-8_3
18. Lyubashevsky, V., Peikert, C., Regev, O.: On ideal lattices and learning with errors over rings. In: Gilbert, H. (ed.) EUROCRYPT 2010. LNCS, vol. 6110, pp. 1–23. Springer, Heidelberg (2010). https://doi.org/10.1007/978-3-642-13190-5_1
19. Micciancio, D., Regev, O.: Worst-case to average-case reductions based on Gaussian measures. In: 45th IEEE Symposium on FOCS, pp. 372–381 (2004). https://doi.org/10.1109/FOCS.2004.72
20. Micciancio, D.: Generalized compact knapsacks, cyclic lattices, and efficient one-way functions from worst-case complexity assumptions. In: FOCS 2002. IEEE (2002). https://doi.org/10.1109/SFCS.2002.1181960
21. Micciancio, D., Peikert, C.: Trapdoors for lattices: simpler, tighter, faster, smaller. In: Pointcheval, D., Johansson, T. (eds.) EUROCRYPT 2012. LNCS, vol. 7237, pp. 700–718. Springer, Heidelberg (2012). https://doi.org/10.1007/978-3-642-29011-4_41
22. Moody, D., et al.: Status report on the second round of the NIST post-quantum cryptography standardization process (2020). https://doi.org/10.6028/NIST.IR.8309
23. Peikert, C.: An efficient and parallel Gaussian sampler for lattices. In: Rabin, T. (ed.) CRYPTO 2010. LNCS, vol. 6223, pp. 80–97. Springer, Heidelberg (2010). https://doi.org/10.1007/978-3-642-14623-7_5
24. Regev, O.: On lattices, learning with errors, random linear codes, and cryptography. J. ACM 56(6) (2009). https://doi.org/10.1145/1568318.1568324
25. Shor, P.W.: Algorithms for quantum computation: discrete logarithms and factoring. In: SFCS 1994. IEEE Computer Society (1994). https://doi.org/10.1109/SFCS.1994.365700

Practical Continuously Non-malleable Randomness Encoders in the Random Oracle Model

Antonio Faonio[✉]

EURECOM, Biot, France
antonio.faonio@eurecom.fr

Abstract. A randomness encoder is a generalization of encoding schemes with an efficient procedure for encoding *uniformly random strings*. In this paper we continue the study of randomness encoders that additionally have the property of being continuous non-malleable. The beautiful notion of non-malleability for encoding schemes, introduced by Dziembowski, Pietrzak and Wichs (ICS'10), states that tampering with the codeword can either keep the encoded message identical or produce an uncorrelated message. Continuous non-malleability extends the security notion to a setting where the adversary can tamper the codeword polynomially many times and where we assume a self-destruction mechanism in place in case of decoding errors. Our contributions are: (1) two practical constructions of continuous non-malleable randomness encoders in the random oracle model, and (2) a new compiler from continuous non-malleable randomness encoders to continuous non-malleable codes, and (3) a study of lower bounds for continuous non-malleability in the random oracle model.

1 Introduction

Non-malleable codes (Dziembowski, Pietrzak and Wichs [18]) find applications to cryptography, for example, for protecting arbitrary cryptographic primitives against related-key attacks [18] and commitments (Agrawal *et al.* [4]). Limitations on the nature of the tampering functions must be imposed, as otherwise NMCs are impossible to achieve [18]. One of the most studied settings for which NMCs are achievable is the split-state model [2,9,17], see also [3,14,27,29,30]. In this model we assume that the codeword is divided into two pieces, and that the tampering functions can alter the two pieces independently.

Continuous Non-malleability. In the definition of non-malleable codes, the property is guaranteed as long as a *single* tampering function is applied to a target codeword. In particular, no security is guaranteed if an adversary can tamper multiple times with the target codeword. Faust *et al.* [22] introduced a natural extension of non-malleable codes where the adversary is allowed to tamper a target codeword by specifying polynomially-many tampering functions;

© Springer Nature Switzerland AG 2021
M. Conti et al. (Eds.): CANS 2021, LNCS 13099, pp. 273–291, 2021.
https://doi.org/10.1007/978-3-030-92548-2_15

As argued in [22], such *continuously* non-malleable codes allow to overcome several limitations of one-time non-malleable codes, and further led to new applications where continuous non-malleability is essential [10,12]. Continuous non-malleability requires a special "self-destruct" capability that instructs the decoding algorithm to always output the symbol ⊥ (meaning "decoding error") after the first invalid codeword is decoded, otherwise generic attacks are possible [22,24].

Randomness Encoders. A randomness encoder consists of an encoding procedure which can produce a codeword for a random message and the relative decoding algorithm. Kanukurthi, Obbattu and Sekar [25] introduced the concept of non-malleable randomness encoders (NMREs) as a relaxation of NMCs. As shown by [25], NMREs are already sufficient for many of the applications of NMCs. For example, in the typical application of NMCs to tamper-resilient cryptography, the encoded messages are randomly generated secret keys. Moreover, they gave a construction of a NMC from a NMRE and (one-time) authenticated secret key encryption.

1.1   Our Contributions

As our main contribution, we present two practical CNMREs in the random oracle model. Our randomness encoders can encode random messages of size λ bits, where λ is the security parameter. The size of the codewords in the first randomness encoder is approximately 12λ bits, and the decoding function computes two cryptographic hash evaluations and an inner product between two vectors in $\mathbb{Z}_p^4$ for a prime $p \geq 2^\lambda$. The second randomness encoder has shorter codewords (the size of the codewords is approximately 8λ bits), but it has a more expensive decoding function which consists of four cryptographic hash evaluations and an inner product between two vectors in $\mathbb{Z}_p^4$. Compared to the state-of-art for CNMC (the construction of Ostrovsky *et al.* [30]) both our randomness encoders are thousands of times more efficient. Comparing with state-of-art for practical NMC (the construction of Fehr, Karpman and Mennink [23]), our randomness encoders are comparably similarly efficient both in terms of sizes of the codewords and in terms of the computational complexities of the algorithms. (We give more details in the next section.)

As second contribution, we show how to construct CNMCs from CNMREs, thus extending the result of [25] to the continuous setting. We consider the compiler of Coretti, Faonio and Venturi [11]. Although our compiler and their compiler are similar, their analysis does not apply directly to our setting (we elaborate further in the next section). As third contribution, we extend the lower bounds of [22] to the case of continuous non-malleability in the random oracle model. We show that we can have information-theoretic security, as long as the number of random oracle queries made by the adversary is bounded.

1.2   Technical Overview

In the continuous non-malleability experiment, the adversary receives two messages μ_0, μ_1 and gets oracle access to a target codeword (c_0, c_1) for the message μ_b with the goal of guessing the bit b. The adversary can submit tampering functions (f_0, f_1) receiving back the value $\mathsf{Dec}(f_0(c_0), f_1(c_1))$. If the output of the decoding algorithm is $\bot$ then the adversary loses access to the tampering oracle. In the very same vein, in the continuous non-malleability experiment for randomness encoders, the adversary gets input two uniformly random keys κ_0 and κ_1 (one of which is sampled using the randomness encoder) and gets oracle access to a target codeword (c_0, c_1). We proceed in two steps to construct our CNMREs. In the first step we reduce continuous non-malleability to leakage resilience. In particular for this step, we first define the notion of noisy leakage-resilient randomness encoders (LRREs, for short), then we show an efficient compiler from LRREs to CNMREs. In the second step, we give constructions of leakage-resilient randomness encoders. In the security game for the notion of LRREs the adversary has access to a leakage oracle to the codeword. The adversary can submit queries of the form (g_0, g_1) receiving back the values $g_0(c_0), g_1(c_1)$. In our definition we consider the so-called noisy-leakage model [5] where the leakage is measured as the drop of min-entropy of the codeword.

The compiler from LRREs to CNMREs is very similar to the original construction of CNMC of [22], and its proof of security follows a proof technique similar to [11,20,21]. Our LRREs are inspired by the leakage-resilient storage of Davi, Dziembowski and Venturi [15] based on the inner-product extractor (see also Dziembowski and Faust [16]). In more detail, let $\Pi' = (\mathsf{REncode}', \mathsf{Dec}')$ be a LRRE and let RO be a random oracle, we construct a CNMRE $\Pi = (\mathsf{REncode}, \mathsf{Dec})$ where the encoding function samples a codeword c_0', c_1' from $\mathsf{REncode}'$ and then outputs $(c_0', h_1), (c_1', h_0)$ where $h_\beta = \mathsf{RO}(\beta \| c_\beta')$. The decoding function on input a codeword $(c_0', h_1), (c_1', h_0)$ first checks that the hash values match, namely that $h_\beta = \mathsf{RO}(\beta \| c_\beta')$ for $\beta \in \{0, 1\}$, and if so it decodes the codeword using Dec'. The main idea behind the security of the scheme is that if an adversary can tamper, let say c_0', in a non-trivial way obtaining a value $\tilde{c}_0'$ then it must already know the tampered value $\tilde{c}_0'$, as otherwise the adversary would not be able to compute correctly $\mathsf{RO}(0 \| \tilde{c}_0')$. (Recall that the adversary can only tamper c_0' and h_0 independently, as they are in two different shares.) The latter implies that the output of the tampering oracle is predictable, and therefore we can simulate it using a leakage function that does not decrease the (average conditional) min-entropy of the target codeword.

The second step is to construct practical LRREs. Our first leakage-resilient randomness encoder encodes a random message by sampling two random vectors from a field with large enough cardinality, the decoding function outputs the inner product between the two vectors. Previous works considered the encoding scheme where, on input a message μ, the two vectors were sampled conditioned on their inner product being equal to μ. The proofs of security in the previous works relied on (1) the fact that the inner product is a two-source extractor and then (2) a complexity leveraging argument to break the dependence between the two vectors. By downgrading to randomness encoders, our proof of security does not need the complexity leveraging argument. This simple observation allows a significant gain in the concrete parameters of the scheme. The second scheme exploits the power of the random oracle. In fact, instead of sampling two vectors, we could sample two seeds which fed to the random oracle would produce the required vectors. By setting the parameters properly, the second randomness encoder has more compact codewords then our first one.

Compiler from Randomness-Encoders to Codes. Similar to [1,11,25], the idea for our compiler is to encode a random key for an authenticated secret key encryption scheme using a CNMRE and then to encrypt the message we want to encode, thus obtaining a ciphertext γ. As proposed by [11], we store the resulting ciphertext in both sides of the codeword and check for equality of the two copies of the ciphertext when decoding. The proof of security of [11] relies on the leakage resilience of the inner CNMC. We show that leakage resilience is not necessary. In fact, any adversarially generated codeword $(\tilde{c}_0\|\tilde{\gamma}_0, \tilde{c}_1\|\tilde{\gamma}_1)$ (for the compiled code) that successfully decodes must have $\tilde{\gamma}_0 = \tilde{\gamma}_1$. Our novel idea is to use this correlated information to synchronize the tampering functions performed by the reduction and to extract the adversarially generated ciphertext. In more detail, when reducing to the continuous non-malleability of the CNMRE, we additionally sample two valid codewords for two distinct keys κ_0, κ_1. Upon a tampering query for the compiled code, suppose that the tampered codeword is $(\tilde{c}_0\|\tilde{\gamma}, \tilde{c}_1\|\tilde{\gamma})$, we first extract, bit-by-bit, the ciphertext $\tilde{\gamma}$ by sending tampering queries that output either κ_0 or κ_1 according to the bits of $\tilde{\gamma}$, and then we send an extra query that allows to decode $\tilde{c}_0, \tilde{c}_1$, thus obtaining the secret key for the chipertext $\tilde{\gamma}$.

Lower Bounds on Continuous Non-malleability in the ROM. Very roughly speaking, the proof of the impossibility result of [22] shows that any CNMC musts have (at least) two special codewords. The strategy is to hardwire such codewords in their adversary and to use them to extract, bit-by-bit, all the information about the target codeword. However, in the random oracle model, the codeword space is a random variable that depends on the random oracle. Thus an adversary cannot simply have hardwired these two specials codewords, but it needs first to compute them. In other words, the complexity of the generic attack of [22], in our framework, depends on the random-oracle-query complexity of finding such two special codewords. Additionally, we show that, even if these two special codewords do not exist, we can still break continuous non-malleability when the adversary can query the random oracle enough time and de-randomize the full codeword space.

Lastly, we give a lower bound specific to our CNMRE construction. The number of random oracle queries that an adversary needs in order to break the security of our construction depends both on the random-oracle query complexity of the inner leakage-resilient randomness encoder and on the classical birthday-paradox lower bound.

1.3 Related Work

In the Table 1 we compare our results with the most relevant related works. We compare with the work of Kiayias, Liu and Tselekounis [26] (resp. the work of Fehr, Karpman and Mennink [23]) which showed a *practical* construction of NMC in the CRS model (resp. plain model), the work of Dachman-Soled and Kulkarni [13] which showed a construction of CNMRE in the CRS model and a general compiler from CNMREs to 1-bit messages CNMCs, and the work of Ostrovsky, Persiano, Visconti and Venturi [30] which showed a construction of CNMC in the standard model. The result of [30] makes use of a statistically binding commitment scheme and of the leakage-resilient (one-time) non-malleable code of Aggarwal *et al.* [3]. While, we could implement very efficiently the former ingredient in the random oracle model (by hashing the message together with some randomness), the latter ingredient is the bottleneck of their construction. In fact, the codeword size needs to be at least $O(\lambda^7)$ to encode a message of size λ. Without diving into the details, if we don't consider the cryptographic hash computations, for both our and their scheme the computational complexity of the decoding function is at least super-linear in the size of the codeword, which implies that our schemes are asymptotically faster than [30] of at least 7 orders of magnitude. We could obtain such a speed up because our schemes rely on the random-oracle methodology, on the other hand, the scheme of Ostrovsky *et al.* is in the standard model. We stress that the goal of this paper is, indeed, to construct very efficient schemes which could be already used in practice. Dachman-Soled and Kulkarni [13] give a compiler from CNMRE to CNMC. The idea of their compiler is to sample from the encoding procedure of the CNMRE until we obtain a valid codeword of the message to be encoded. The scheme $DK19_2$ in Table 1 is the result of applying their compiler to their scheme $DK19_1$. The codeword size is approx. $14\lambda^2$ while the codeword size of $DK19_1$ is approx. $14\lambda^3$. The reason is that the compiler works only for 1-bit messages. This limitation is due to the complexity-leveraging argument needed to prove the security of their compiler and the computational security of their scheme $DK19_1$. We notice that a natural extension to multi-bit messages of their compiler would work when applied to our scheme Π_1^* because our scheme is secure against unbounded adversaries in the random oracle model. However, the size of the codeword would have a multiplicative blow up in the security parameter[1]. On the other hand, our compiler has only an additive security loss, thus the resulting scheme is more efficient. Additionally, in terms of assumptions, Π_3^* is computationally secure when k, the length of the message, is such that $k > \lambda$, however, it can be information-theoretically secure when $k \leq \lambda/2$.

Non-malleability *in the multi-tampering* [8, 28] model is related to the notion of continuous non-malleability. In the former notion, the number of tampering queries is a priori bounded, however there is no need for self-destruct mechanisms.

---

[1] The proof of security would work through a complexity-leveraging argument.

2   Preliminaries

We use standard notations for strings, sampling from sets, randomized algorithms, negligible functions and noticeable functions. We denote with $\lambda \in \mathbb{N}$ the security parameter. Throughout the paper, if not differently specified, we let RO be a uniformly random function from $\{0,1\}^*$ to $\{0,1\}^{2\lambda}$. The min-entropy of a random variable X over a set $\mathcal{X}$ is denoted with $\mathbb{H}_\infty(X) := -\log \max_{x \in \mathcal{X}} \mathbb{P}[X = x]$, the conditional average min-entropy of a random variable X given a random variable $Z \in \mathcal{Z}$ is denoted as $\widetilde{\mathbb{H}}_\infty(X|Z) := -\log \mathbb{E}_{z \in \mathcal{Z}} \max_{x \in \mathcal{X}} \mathbb{P}[X = x|Z = z]$.

Table 1. Comparison with related work. In the table λ is the security parameter and k is the length of the message; R stands for randomness encoders and E for encoding schemes; inj. OWF stands for injective one-way functions, Ext-HF stands for extractable hash functions, LR-PRP (resp. RK-PRP) stands for leakage-resilient (resp. related-key secure) pseudorandom permutation. OWF stands for one-way functions.

Scheme	Non-Malleability	Codeword Size	Type	Model	Assumption
[13] DK19$_1$	continuous	$\approx 14\lambda^3$	R	CRS	inj. OWF
Π_1^*	continuous	6λ	R	ROM	-
Π_2^*	continuous	4λ	R	ROM	-
[23] FKM18	one-time	$2\lambda + k$	E	-	LR-PRP, RK-PRP
[26] KLT16	one-time	$9\lambda + 2\log^2 \lambda + k$	E	CRS	Ext-HF
[30] OPVV18	continuous	$\Omega(\lambda^6 k)$	E	-	inj. OWF
[13] DK19$_2$	continuous	$\approx 14\lambda^2$	E	CRS	inj. OWF
Π_3^*	continuous	$8\lambda + k$	E	ROM	OWF

2.1   Split-State Codes and Randomness-Encoders in the ROM

Definition 1 (Split-State Encoding Scheme in the ROM, [11]). *Let* $k(\lambda) = k \in \mathbb{N}$ *and* $n(\lambda) = n \in \mathbb{N}$ *be functions of the security parameter* $\lambda \in \mathbb{N}$. *A* (k, n)-*split-state-code is a tuple of algorithms* $\Sigma = (\mathsf{Enc}^{\mathsf{RO}}, \mathsf{Dec}^{\mathsf{RO}})$ *specified as follows: (1) The randomized algorithm* $\mathsf{Enc}^{\mathsf{RO}}$ *takes as input a value* $s \in \{0,1\}^k$, *and outputs a codeword* $(c_0, c_1) \in \{0,1\}^{2n}$; *(2) The deterministic decoding algorithm* $\mathsf{Dec}^{\mathsf{RO}}$ *takes as input a codeword* $(c_0, c_1) \in \{0,1\}^{2n}$, *and outputs a value* $s \in \{0,1\}^k \cup \{\bot\}$ *(where* $\bot$ *denotes an invalid codeword).*

We say that Σ satisfies correctness if for all values $s \in \{0,1\}^k$, $\mathbb{P}\left[\mathsf{Dec}^{\mathsf{RO}}\right.$
$\left(\mathsf{Enc}^{\mathsf{RO}}(s)\right) = s\right] = 1$.

We introduce the notion of split-state randomness-encoders in the ROM.

Definition 2 (Split-State Randomness Encoders in the ROM). *Let*
$n(\lambda) = n \in \mathbb{N}$ be functions of the security parameter $\lambda \in \mathbb{N}$. A n-split-
state-randomness-encoder is a tuple of algorithms $\Pi = (\mathsf{REncode}^{\mathsf{RO}}, \mathsf{Dec}^{\mathsf{RO}})$
specified as follows: (1) The randomized algorithm $\mathsf{REncode}^{\mathsf{RO}}$ (with the only
input the security parameter) outputs a value $\kappa \in \{0,1\}^\lambda$ and a codeword
$(c_0, c_1) \in \{0,1\}^{2n}$; (2) The deterministic decoding algorithm $\mathsf{Dec}^{\mathsf{RO}}$ takes as
input a codeword $(c_0, c_1) \in \{0,1\}^{2n}$, and outputs a value $\kappa \in \{0,1\}^\lambda \cup \{\bot\}$
(where $\bot$ denotes an invalid codeword). We say that Σ satisfies correctness if
for all λ the following holds:

$$\mathbb{P}\left[\kappa = \kappa' \wedge (\kappa, c) \leftarrow_{\$} \mathsf{REncode}^{\mathsf{RO}}(1^\lambda) \wedge \kappa' \leftarrow \mathsf{Dec}^{\mathsf{RO}}(c)\right] = 1.$$

The contributions of this paper focus on split-state encoding schemes and split-state randomness encoders. To avoid redundancy, we therefore omit the adjective "split-state" whenever it is clear from the context. Many of the algorithms described in this paper make use of a random oracle, we avoid to upper script them with the oracle RO whenever it is clear from the context.

2.2 Continuous Non-malleability in the ROM

Because we consider schemes in the random oracle model, we enlarge the class of possible tampering functions considering functions that additionally can query the random oracle RO. Consider the following class of tampering functions parameterized by two values $n(\lambda), q(\lambda)$:

$$\mathcal{F}_{n,q} = \left\{ (f_0, f_1) | \forall b : \begin{array}{l} f_b : \{0,1\}^{n(\lambda)} \to \{0,1\}^{n(\lambda)} \\ f_b \text{ makes at most } q(\lambda) \text{ RO queries} \end{array}, \lambda \in \mathbb{N} \right\}$$

Definition 3 (Continuously non-malleable codes and randomness encoders in the ROM). *Let $k(\lambda), n(\lambda), q(\lambda), q_T(\lambda), q_{\mathsf{RO}}(\lambda) \in \mathbb{N}$ and let*
$\epsilon(\lambda) \in \mathbb{R}$.

Let $\Sigma = (\mathsf{Enc}, \mathsf{Dec})$ be a (k,n)-encoding scheme. We say that Σ is $(\epsilon, q, q_{\mathsf{RO}})$-
continuously non-malleable code, $(\epsilon, q, q_{\mathsf{RO}})$-CNMC for short, if for all messages
μ_0, μ_1, for all $q_T = \mathsf{poly}(\lambda)$, and for all unbounded adversaries A making up to
q_T tampering oracle queries from the class of tampering functions $\mathcal{F}_{n,q}$ and up to
q_{RO} random oracle queries, we have:

$$\mathbf{Adv}^{\mathsf{cnmc}}_{\Sigma,\mathsf{A}}(\lambda) := |\mathbb{P}\left[\mathbf{G}^{\mathsf{cnmc}}_{\Sigma,\mathsf{A}}(\lambda, \mu_0, \mu_1) = 1\right] - 1/2| \leq \epsilon(\lambda). \tag{1}$$

Let $\Pi = (\mathsf{REncode}, \mathsf{Dec})$ be a n-randomness encoder. We say that Π is
$(\epsilon, q, q_{\mathsf{RO}})$-continuously non-malleable randomness encoder, $(\epsilon, q, q_{\mathsf{RO}})$-CNMRE

$\mathbf{G}_{\Sigma,\mathsf{A}}^{\mathsf{cnmc}}(\lambda, \mu_0, \mu_1):$
$b \leftarrow\!\!\$ \{0,1\}; (c_0, c_1) \leftarrow\!\!\$ \mathsf{Enc}(\mu_b)$
$\mathcal{M} := \{\mu_0, \mu_1\}$
$\mathbf{stop} \leftarrow 0$
$b' \leftarrow \mathsf{A}^{\mathcal{O}_{\mathsf{tamp}}(\cdot,\cdot)}(1^\lambda, \mu_0, \mu_1)$
Return $b \overset{?}{=} b'$

$\mathbf{G}_{\Pi,\mathsf{A}}^{\mathsf{cnmre}}(\lambda):$
$(\kappa, (c_0, c_1)) \leftarrow\!\!\$ \mathsf{REncode}(1^\lambda)$
$b \leftarrow\!\!\$ \{0,1\}; \kappa_b \leftarrow \kappa, \kappa_{1-b} \leftarrow\!\!\$ \{0,1\}^\lambda$
$\mathcal{M} := \{\kappa_0, \kappa_1\}$
$\mathbf{stop} \leftarrow 0$
$b' \leftarrow \mathsf{A}^{\mathcal{O}_{\mathsf{tamp}}(\cdot,\cdot)}(\kappa_0, \kappa_1)$
Return $b \overset{?}{=} b'$

$\mathbf{G}_{\Pi,\mathsf{A}}^{\mathsf{lrre}}(\lambda):$
$(c_0, c_1) \leftarrow\!\!\$ \mathsf{REncode}(1^\lambda)$
$\kappa_b \leftarrow \mathsf{Dec}(c_0, c_1), \kappa_{1-b} \leftarrow\!\!\$ \{0,1\}^\lambda$
$b' \leftarrow \mathsf{A}^{\mathcal{O}_{\mathsf{leak}}(\cdot,\cdot)}(\kappa_0, \kappa_1)$
Return $b \overset{?}{=} b'$

Oracle $\mathcal{O}_{\mathsf{tamp}}(f_0, f_1):$
If $\mathbf{stop} = 1$
    Return $\perp$
Else
    $(\tilde{c}_0, \tilde{c}_1) = (f_0(c_0), f_1(c_1))$
    $\tilde{\mu} = \mathsf{Dec}(\tilde{c}_0, \tilde{c}_1)$
    If $\tilde{\mu} \in \mathcal{M}$ Return $\diamond$
    If $\tilde{\mu} = \perp$ Return $\perp$ and $\mathbf{stop} \leftarrow 1$
    Else return $\tilde{\mu}$

Oracle $\mathcal{O}_{\mathsf{leak}}(g_0, g_1):$
    Return $(g_0(c_0), g_1(c_1))$

Fig. 1. Experiment defining continuously non-malleable codes and randomness-encoders in the split-state model, and leakage-resilient randomness encoders. The tampering oracle $\mathcal{O}_{\mathsf{tamp}}$ is implicitly parameterized by the flag $\mathbf{stop}$, the codeword c_0, c_1 and the set $\mathcal{M}$. Similarly, the leakage oracle is implicitly parameterized by the codeword c_0, c_1. If Π (resp. Σ) is in the random oracle model, then all the procedures and functions (including the adversary A, the leakage functions g_0, g_1 and the tampering functions f_0, f_1) implicitly have oracle access to RO.

for short, if for all $q_T = \mathtt{poly}(\lambda)$, and for all (possibly unbounded) adversaries A making up to q_T tampering oracle queries from the class of tampering functions $\mathcal{F}_{n,q}$ and up to q_{RO} random oracle queries, we have:

$$\mathbf{Adv}_{\Pi,\mathsf{A}}^{\mathsf{cnmre}}(\lambda) := |\mathbb{P}\left[\mathbf{G}_{\Sigma,\mathsf{A}}^{\mathsf{cnmre}}(\lambda) = 1\right] - 1/2| \leq \epsilon(\lambda). \tag{2}$$

The experiments $\mathbf{G}_{\Sigma,\mathsf{A}}^{\mathsf{cnmc}}(\lambda)$ and $\mathbf{G}_{\Sigma,\mathsf{A}}^{\mathsf{cnmc}}(\lambda, \mu_0, \mu_1)$ are described in Fig. 1.

Remark 1 (On the choice of q_T). We could prove security of our constructions even when $q_T = \Omega(2^\lambda)$. However, in the definitions above we limit the number of tampering queries to be a polynomial in the security parameter. The reason is that for each tampering query there is an associated call to the decoding algorithm of the attacked device. We can assume that the attacked device runs in polynomial time.

2.3 Noisy-leakage Resilient Randomness Encoders

As in previous works [6,11,20,21], we use the notion of *admissibility* to define noisy-leakage resilience. We extend this notion to the ROM.

Definition 4 (Admissible adversaries for randomness encoders). *Let $n(\lambda), \ell(\lambda), q_{\mathsf{RO}}(\lambda) \in \mathbb{N}$ such that $\ell(\lambda) \leq n(\lambda)$, let $\Pi = (\mathsf{REncode}, \mathsf{Dec})$ be a n-randomness-encoder. An adversary A is (ℓ, q_{RO})-admissible for Π if it outputs a sequences of (adaptively-chosen) leakage functions that can make random oracle queries $(g_0^{(i)}, g_1^{(i)})_{i\in[q]}$ for $q \in \mathbb{N}$ and it outputs a sequences of (adaptively-chosen) random oracle queries $(x_i)_{i\in[q_{\mathsf{RO}}]}$, such that:*

$$\widetilde{\mathbb{H}}_\infty\left(c_\beta | c_{1-\beta}, (g_\beta^{(i)}(c_\beta))_{i\in[q]}, (x_i, \mathsf{RO}(x_i))_{i\in[q_{\mathsf{RO}}]}\right) \geq \widetilde{\mathbb{H}}_\infty(c_\beta | c_{1-\beta}, \mathsf{RO}) - \ell \qquad (3)$$

where (c_0, c_1) is the joint random variable corresponding to $\mathsf{REncode}(1^\lambda)$ and RO is a shortcut for $(\mathsf{RO}(x))_{x\in\{0,1\}^*}$.

Definition 5 (noisy-leakage resilient randomness encoders). *Let $n(\lambda)$, $\ell(\lambda), q_{\mathsf{RO}}(\lambda) \in \mathbb{N}$ and $\epsilon(\lambda) \in \mathbb{R}$, and let $\Pi = (\mathsf{REncode}, \mathsf{Dec})$ be a n-randomness encoder. We say that Π is $(\epsilon, \ell, q_{\mathsf{RO}})$-noisy-leakage resilient randomness encoder in the ROM, $(\epsilon, \ell, q_{\mathsf{RO}})$-LRRE for short, if for all (ℓ, q_{RO})-admissible adversaries A, we have that:*

$$\mathbf{Adv}_{\Pi,\mathsf{A}}^{\mathsf{lrs}}(\lambda) := \left|\mathbb{P}\left[\mathbf{G}_{\Sigma,\mathsf{A}}^{\mathsf{lrre}}(\lambda) = 1\right] - 1/2\right| \leq \epsilon(\lambda), \qquad (4)$$

where experiment $\mathbf{G}_{\Sigma,\mathsf{A}}^{\mathsf{lrre}}(\lambda)$ is depicted in Fig. 1.

3 Our Continuous Non-malleable Randomness Encoder

Let $\Pi = (\mathsf{REncode}, \mathsf{Dec})$ be a n'-randomness-encoder, and let RO be a random oracle. Consider the following construction of a n-randomness-encoder $\Pi^* = (\mathsf{REncode}^*, \mathsf{Dec}^*)$ where $n := n' + 2\lambda$:

$\mathsf{REncode}^*(1^\lambda)$: Sample $\kappa, (c_0, c_1) \leftarrow_\$ \mathsf{REncode}(1^\lambda)$, compute $h_\beta \leftarrow \mathsf{RO}(\beta\|c_\beta)$ and set the codeword $c_\beta^* := (c_\beta, h_{1-\beta})$ for $i \in \{0,1\}$. Return $\kappa, (c_0^*, c_1^*)$.

$\mathsf{Dec}^*(c_0^*, c_1^*)$: Execute the following steps:
1. For $\beta \in \{0,1\}$, parse c_β^* as $(c_\beta, h_{1-\beta})$;
2. **(Hash Values Check.)** If $h_0 \neq \mathsf{RO}(0\|c_0)$ or $h_1 \neq \mathsf{RO}(1\|c_1)$ output $\bot$;
3. Else output $\mathsf{Dec}(c_0, c_1)$.

We give the following definition to simplify the notation in the statement of the theorem.

Definition 6. *Let Π be a n-randomness encoder, we define with $\alpha_\Pi(\lambda) := \min_\beta\{\mathbb{H}_\infty(c_\beta) - \widetilde{\mathbb{H}}_\infty(c_\beta|c_{1-\beta}, \mathsf{RO})\}$ where $c_0, c_1 \leftarrow_\$ \mathsf{REncode}(1^\lambda)$.*

Theorem 1 (LRREs $\Rightarrow$ CNMREs in ROM). *For any $q_T := q_T(\lambda), q := q(\lambda)$, and for any adversary A that does up to q_T tampering oracle queries from the class of tampering functions $\mathcal{F}_{n,q}$ and up to $q_{RO} := q_{RO}(\lambda)$ random oracle queries there exists a (ℓ, q_{RO})-admissible adversary B where $\ell = 2 \log q_{RO} + \log q_T$ such that:*

$$\mathbf{Adv}_{\Pi^*,A}^{\mathsf{cnmre}}(\lambda) \leq \mathbf{Adv}_{\Pi,B}^{\mathsf{lrs}}(\lambda) + \frac{q_T}{2^{2\lambda}} + \frac{(q_{RO} + q \cdot q_T)^2}{2^{2\lambda}} + \frac{(q_{RO} + q \cdot q_T)\lambda q_T}{2^{\alpha_\Pi(\lambda) - 1}}.$$

If Π is $(\mathsf{negl}(\lambda), O(\lambda), \mathsf{poly}(\lambda))$-LRRE then Π^* is $(\mathsf{negl}(\lambda), \mathsf{poly}(\lambda), \mathsf{poly}(\lambda))$-CNMRE.

Proof. We give a reduction to the noisy-leakage resilience of Π. Before describing the reduction we introduce a sub-routine.

Procedure LEAK(g_0, g_1)
- Let $g_{\beta,i}$ be the restriction of the function g_β to the i-th bit.
- For $i \in [\lambda]$ send the leakage oracle query $(g_{0,i}, g_{1,i})$:
    - let $z_{0,i}, z_{1,i}$ be the output of the oracle,
    - if $z_{0,i} \neq z_{1,i}$ output $\perp$,
    - if $z_{0,i} = z_{1,i} = \diamond$ output $\diamond$.
- Output $z = z_{0,0}, \ldots, z_{0,l}$.

We are now ready to describe an adversary for Π [2]

We will keep track of the random oracle queries made by the adversary and by the tampering functions. We denote with $\mathcal{Q}_A, \mathcal{Q}_0, \mathcal{Q}_1$ the lexicographically ordered set of tuple $x, \mathsf{RO}(x)$, and with $\bar{\mathcal{Q}}_A, \bar{\mathcal{Q}}_0, \bar{\mathcal{Q}}_1$ the lexicographically ordered set of oracle queries (i.e., the inputs to the RO without the outputs).

Adversary B(κ_0, κ_1)
1. **Hash values h_0, h_1.** Sample $h_\beta \leftarrow_\$ \{0,1\}^{2\lambda}$ for $\beta \in \{0,1\}$.
2. Run the adversary A with input (κ_0, κ_1).
3. **Random oracle queries.** Whenever A sends a query x to the random oracle, forward the query to random oracle RO. Add the query $(x, \mathsf{RO}(x))$ in the set $\mathcal{Q}_A$.
4. **Tampering oracle queries.** When the adversary A sends its j-th tampering query $(f_0^{(j)}, f_1^{(j)})$, if the flag stop $= 1$ return $\perp$, else run the sub-routine LEAK($g_0^{(j)}, g_1^{(j)}$), where the leakage functions $g_\beta^{(j)}$ is described below:
   Leakage function $g_\beta^{(j)}(c_\beta)$:
   (a) Compile the set $\mathcal{Q}_\beta$ of random oracle query made by the previous tampering functions by running $f_\beta^{(j')}(c_\beta, h_{1-\beta})$ for any $j' < j$ and collecting the queries. Whenever one of the tampering functions calls RO on $(\beta \| c_\beta)$ answer with h_β.

---

[2] Notice that Π might be a randomness encoder in the standard model (i.e. no random oracle), whilst our reduction makes random oracle queries. In this case we could assume that RO is a lazy-sampled, locally-stored random function, therefore B would be a standard-model adversary for Π.

(b) Compute $(\tilde{c}_\beta, \tilde{h}_{1-\beta}) \leftarrow f_\beta^{(j)}(c_\beta, h_{1-\beta})$ and forward all the RO queries made by $f_\beta^{(j)}$ to the RO (but whenever the tampering function calls RO on $\beta \| c_\beta$ answer with h_β, instead of querying the RO).

(c) If $(\tilde{c}_\beta, \tilde{h}_{1-\beta}) = (c_\beta, h_{1-\beta})$ then output $\diamond$.

(d) If there is a tuple $(1 - \beta \| c_{1-\beta}^\star, \tilde{h}_{1-\beta}) \in \mathcal{Q}_A \cup \mathcal{Q}_\beta$,
   - if $\beta = 0$ then output $\mathsf{Dec}(\tilde{c}_0, c_1^\star)$,
   - if $\beta = 1$ then output $\mathsf{Dec}(c_0^\star, \tilde{c}_1)$,
   else output $\bot$.

Let $\tilde{\mu}$ be the output of the LEAK procedure, if $\tilde{\mu} = \bot$ then set the flag stop $\leftarrow 1$. Return $\tilde{\mu}$.

5. Eventually the adversary returns a bit b'. Output b'.

Claim. The adversary B is $(\log \lambda + \log q_T + 1, q_{\mathsf{RO}})$-admissible.

The proof of the lemma follows an argument almost identical to [6,21] and can be found in the full version [19].

We now analyze the advantage of B. First notice that by the claim above and taking an union bound over the elements in $\bar{\mathcal{Q}}_A \cup \bar{\mathcal{Q}}_{1-\beta}$ we have that for $\beta \in \{0,1\}$:

$$\mathbb{P}\left[c_\beta \in \bar{\mathcal{Q}}_A \cup \bar{\mathcal{Q}}_{1-\beta}\right] \le (q_{\mathsf{RO}} + q \cdot q_T)2^{-\alpha_\Pi(\lambda) + \log \lambda + \log q_T + 1}.$$

We condition on the event that $\forall \beta : c_\beta \notin \bar{\mathcal{Q}}_A \cup \bar{\mathcal{Q}}_{1-\beta}$. Under this condition the distributions of $(h_\beta)_{\beta \in \{0,1\}}$ and $(\mathsf{RO}(c_\beta))_{\beta \in \{0,1\}}$, given the full view of the adversary, are exactly the same, because the adversary could query c_β to the random oracle only inside the tampering functions $(f_\beta^{(j)})_{j \in [q_T]}$, but in this case the reduction would answer with h_β.

We further condition on the event that no collisions are found in RO on an execution of B. Notice that the probability of finding a collision is upper bounded by $\frac{(q_{\mathsf{RO}} + q \cdot q_T)^2}{2^{2\lambda}}$.

The adversary B simulates almost perfectly the experiment to A. Indeed, if the adversary B returns a message $\tilde{\mu} \ne \bot$ to A at the j-th tampering query then, since we assumed that there aren't collisions in the RO, it musts be that $c_\beta^\star = \tilde{c}_\beta$, where the former is computed by the leakage function $g_\beta^{(j)}$ and the latter is computed by the leakage function $g_{1-\beta}^{(j)}$.

The only difference between the simulation of B and the real experiment is that, at step 4 it could happen that B returns $\bot$ but the tampering query in the real experiment would output a message different than $\bot$. Let j be the index when this event happens for the first time. If B returns $\bot$ then either the procedure LEAK finds two mismatching outputs from the leakage oracle or $\exists \beta$ s.t. the leakage function $g_\beta^{(j)}$ outputs $\bot$.

The first case reduces to the event of finding a collision in the RO which we assumed that cannot happen, in fact, $\mathsf{Dec}(\tilde{c}_0, c_1^\star) \ne \mathsf{Dec}(c_0^\star, \tilde{c}_1)$ but $\mathsf{RO}(\beta \| \tilde{c}_\beta) = \mathsf{RO}(\beta \| c_\beta^\star)$ for $\beta \in \{0,1\}$. The second case instead is more interesting. In fact,

$\mathcal{Q}_A \cup \mathcal{Q}_\beta$ might not cover the full set of random oracle queries that the adversary A can do through the tampering queries, thus, in principle, it could happen that the reduction cannot find a tuple $(1-\beta\|c^\star_{1-\beta}, \tilde{h}_{1-\beta}) \in \mathcal{Q}_A \cup \mathcal{Q}_\beta$ but, nevertheless, the adversary queried $\tilde{c}_{1-\beta} = c^\star_{1-\beta}$ to the random oracle in one of the tampering queries $f^{(j')}_{1-\beta}$ for $j' \le j$, i.e., $(1-\beta\|\tilde{c}_{1-\beta}) \in \bar{\mathcal{Q}}_{1-\beta}$. We show that the adversary cannot guess, using the tampering query $f^{(j)}_\beta$, the valid value for $\tilde{h}_{1-\beta}$ that would make pass the consistency check of the decoding algorithm $\mathsf{Dec}^\star$. Recall that we condition on j being the first index where the bad event described before could happen. Thus we have that for all $j' < j$ the output of the leakage functions $g^{(j')}_0$ and the output of $g^{(j')}_1$ agree. Also, as just said above, we condition on $(1-\beta\|\tilde{c}_{1-\beta}) \in \bar{\mathcal{Q}}_{1-\beta} \wedge (1-\beta\|c^\star_{1-\beta}, \tilde{h}_{1-\beta})) \notin \mathcal{Q}_\beta \cup \mathcal{Q}_A$, and we want to compute the probability that $\tilde{h}_{1-\beta} = \mathsf{RO}(1-\beta\|\tilde{c}_{1-\beta})$.

We compute the average conditional min-entropy of $\mathsf{RO}(1-\beta\|\tilde{c}_{1-\beta})$ given the full view of the j-th leakage function $g^{(j)}_\beta$:

$$\widetilde{\mathbb{H}}_\infty(\mathsf{RO}(1-\beta\|\tilde{c}_{1-\beta})|\mathcal{Q}_A, \mathcal{Q}_\beta, (\tilde{\mu}^{(j')})_{j'<j}, c_\beta, h_{1-\beta})$$
$$= \widetilde{\mathbb{H}}_\infty(\mathsf{RO}(1-\beta\|\tilde{c}_{1-\beta})|\mathcal{Q}_A, \mathcal{Q}_\beta, c_\beta, h_{1-\beta})$$
$$= \widetilde{\mathbb{H}}_\infty(\mathsf{RO}(1-\beta\|\tilde{c}_{1-\beta})|c_\beta, h_{1-\beta}) = 2\lambda.$$

First we notice that the tuple $(\mathcal{Q}_A, \mathcal{Q}_\beta, (\tilde{\mu}^{(j')})_{j'<j}, c_\beta, h_{1-\beta})$ is indeed the full view of the leakage function $g^{(j)}_\beta$, as all the randomness in the experiment comes from the random oracle queries, the challenge codeword and, possibly, the outputs of the leakage oracle. In the derivation above, the first equation holds because $(\tilde{\mu}^{(j')})_{j'<j}$ can be computed as deterministic function of $\mathcal{Q}_A, \mathcal{Q}_\beta, c_\beta, h_{1-\beta}$, the second equation holds because we assumed that $(1-\beta\|c^\star_{1-\beta}, \tilde{h}_{1-\beta}) \notin \mathcal{Q}_A \cup \mathcal{Q}_\beta$. This shows that the probability that $g^{(j)}_\beta$ computes $\tilde{h}_{1-\beta}$ at the j-th query equal to $\mathsf{RO}(1-\beta\|\tilde{c}_{1-\beta})$ is $2^{-2\lambda}$, even when $(1-\beta\|\tilde{c}_{1-\beta}) \in \bar{\mathcal{Q}}_{1-\beta}$. We can prove that the same holds when $(1-\beta\|\tilde{c}_{1-\beta}) \notin \mathcal{Q}_{1-\beta}$, in this case the value was never queried to the RO, thus the adversary can guess it with probability $2^{-2\lambda}$. Taking an union bound over all the tampering oracle queries made by A the probability that B outputs $\perp$ but the real experiment would have not is bounded by $q_T 2^{-2\lambda}$.

Putting all together, we can conclude that the advantage of B is bigger or equal to

$$\mathbf{Adv}^{\mathsf{cnmre}}_{\Pi^*,A}(\lambda) - \frac{q_T}{2^{2\lambda}} + \frac{(q_{\mathsf{RO}}+q\cdot q_T)^2}{2^{2\lambda}}.$$

We can easily show that B is $(2\lambda + 2\log q_{\mathsf{RO}} + \log q_T, q_{\mathsf{RO}})$-admissible. See the full version [19] for the details. □

Remark 2. Similarly to [25,26,30], we do not consider leakage resilience for our continuous non-malleable randomness encoder. Nevertheless, our reduction can easily handle leakage functions by hardcoding the hash values h_0, h_1 and forwarding the leakage queries to its own oracle. However, there is a catch: the leakage queries sent by the adversary cannot have access to the random oracle. In fact, an attacker could forward leakage functions that make random-oracle queries on behalf of the adversary. These *obfuscated* random oracle queries could not be seen by our reduction thus invalidating our observability-based argument.

The Theorem 1 gives an upper bound to the advantage of any adversary against the continuous non-malleability of Π^*. To give a full picture, in Sect. 6 (Corollary 1) we give a lower bound based on the random-oracle query complexity and randomness complexity of the underlying randomness encoder Π. Informally, the theorem states the existence of an adversary whose random-oracle query complexity is $\Omega(2^\lambda)$, tampering-oracle complexity is $O(n)$ and advantage is at least $(1/e)^8$.

4   Compiler from Randomness Encoders to Code Schemes

In this section we recall the compiler of Coretti, Faonio and Venturi [11]. The compiler makes use of an authenticated encryption scheme. A (k, m)-SKE scheme Ω encrypts k-bit messages and outputs ciphertexts of size m. We consider the standard security property of *authenticity* whose security game is denoted by $\mathbf{G}_\Omega^{\text{auth}}$, and the standard security property of *indistinghuishability* which security game is denoted by $\mathbf{G}_\Omega^{\text{ind}}$. Let $\Pi = (\text{REncode}, \text{Dec})$ be a n-randomness-encoder, and $\Omega = (\text{AEnc}, \text{ADec})$ be a (k, m)-SKE scheme. Consider the following construction of a (k, n')-code $\Sigma' = (\text{Enc}', \text{Dec}')$, where $n' := m + n$.

$\text{Enc}'(s)$: Upon input a value $s \in \{0, 1\}^k$, compute $c_0, c_1 \leftarrow_\$ \text{REncode}(1^\lambda)$, let $\kappa \leftarrow \text{Dec}(c_0, c_1)$, and compute $\gamma \leftarrow_\$ \text{AEnc}(\kappa, s)$; return c_0', c_1' where $c_\beta' = (c_\beta, \gamma)$ for $\beta \in \{0, 1\}$.

$\text{Dec}'(c_0', c_1')$: Parse $c_\beta' := (c_\beta, \gamma_\beta)$ for $\beta \in \{0, 1\}$. If $\gamma_0 \neq \gamma_1$, return $\perp$ and self destruct; else let $\tilde{\kappa} = \text{Dec}(c_0, c_1)$. If $\tilde{\kappa} = \perp$, return $\perp$ and self destruct; else return the same as $\text{ADec}(\tilde{\kappa}, \gamma_0)$.

The difference between the compiler Σ described above and the compiler of [11] is that our compiler starts from a CNMRE, while their construction starts from a noisy-leakage-resilient CNMC. A similar strategy to ours was recently used by Brian, Faonio and Venturi in the context of continuous non-malleable secret sharing schemes [7].

Theorem 2. *For any adversary* A *which makes at most* $q_T := q_T(\lambda)$ *tampering oracle queries there exist adversaries* B *which makes at most* $(m + 1) \cdot q_T$ *tampering oracle queries, and adversaries* B' *and* B'' *such that* $\mathbf{Adv}_{\Sigma, \mathsf{A}}^{\text{cnmc}}(\lambda) \leq 2\mathbf{Adv}_{\Pi, \mathsf{B}}^{\text{cnmre}}(\lambda) + q_T \cdot \mathbf{Adv}_{\Omega, \mathsf{B}'}^{\text{auth}}(\lambda) + \mathbf{Adv}_{\Omega, \mathsf{B}''}^{\text{ind}}(\lambda)$.

5   Our Leakage-Resilient Randomness Encoders

We give two constructions Π_1 and Π_2 of LRREs, due to space constraints the proofs of security of Π_1 and Π_2 appear in the full version [19]. Notably the randomness encoder Π_2 has optimal leakage parameter, namely the leakage parameter is only λ bits smaller than the size of the codeword.

Let p be a prime such that $p \geq 2^\lambda$ and let $m \in \mathbb{N}$. Consider the following $(m \log p)$-randomness-encoder $\Pi_1 = (\mathsf{REncode}_1, \mathsf{Dec}_1)$:

$\mathsf{REncode}_1(1^\lambda)$: Sample column vectors $\boldsymbol{x}_0, \boldsymbol{x}_1 \leftarrow_\$ \mathbb{Z}_p^m$. Output c_0, c_1 where c_β is the binary representation of $\boldsymbol{x}_\beta$

$\mathsf{Dec}_1(c_0, c_1)$: Parse c_β as a vector $\boldsymbol{x}_\beta \in \mathbb{Z}_p^m$. Return the binary representation of $\boldsymbol{x}_0^T \cdot \boldsymbol{x}_1 \in \mathbb{Z}_p$.

Theorem 3. *Let $\ell \leq m \log p$, for any q, the Π_1 scheme is $(O(2^{-\lambda}), \ell, q)$-noisy-leakage resilient for $\ell \leq (m+1) \log p / 2 - 2\lambda$. In more detail, for any (ℓ, q)-admissible adversary* A: $\mathbf{Adv}_{\Pi_1, A}^{\mathsf{lrs}}(\lambda) \leq 2^{-(m-1) \log p / 2 + \ell}$.

Let $(m-1) \log p / 2 \geq n$ and let RO be a random oracle[3] with output $\mathbb{Z}_p^m$. Consider the following n-randomness-encoder $\Pi_2 = (\mathsf{REncode}_2, \mathsf{Dec}_2)$.

$\mathsf{REncode}(1^\lambda)$: Sample and output $c_0, c_1 \leftarrow_\$ \{0, 1\}^n$.
$\mathsf{Dec}(c_0, c_1)$: Compute $\boldsymbol{x}_i \leftarrow \mathsf{RO}(c_i)$ for $i \in \{0, 1\}$ and return the binary representation of $\boldsymbol{x}_0^T \cdot \boldsymbol{x}_1$.

Theorem 4. *Let $\ell + \lambda \leq n$, for any $q_{\mathsf{RO}}(\lambda) \in \mathbb{N}$, the encoding scheme Π_2 is $(O(2^{-\lambda} q_{\mathsf{RO}}), \ell, q_{\mathsf{RO}})$-noisy-leakage resilient. In more detail, for any (ℓ, q_{RO})-admissible adversary* A: $\mathbf{Adv}_{\Pi_2, A}^{\mathsf{lrs}}(\lambda) \leq 2^{\ell - n}(2q_{\mathsf{RO}} + 2)$.

The idea for the proof is that the adversary can either leak from c_i or directly from $\mathsf{RO}(c_i)$. The former kind of leakage cannot give any advantage to the adversary, since the adversary should be able to guess $n - \ell \geq \lambda$ bits to obtain any information about $\mathsf{RO}(c_i)$, the latter form of leakage is protected by the same argument of the leakage resilience of Π_1.

5.1   Instantiations

We present two instantiations for our continuous non-malleable randomness encoders. By joining together the results of Theorem 1 and Theorem 3 we obtain a $(m \log p + 2\lambda)$-randomness-encoders scheme Π_1^* with concrete security being:

$$\max_A \mathbf{Adv}_{\Pi_1^*, A}^{\mathsf{cnmre}}(\lambda) \leq \exp(-(m-1) \log p / 2 + \log \lambda + \log q_T + 1)$$

$$+ \frac{q_T + (q_{\mathsf{RO}} + q \cdot q_T)^2}{2^{2\lambda}} + \frac{(q_{\mathsf{RO}} + q \cdot q_T)\lambda q_T}{2^{m \log p - 1}}.$$

For concreteness, suppose that an adversary can make $q_{\mathsf{RO}} + q \cdot q_T = 2^{40}$ random-oracle queries and $q_T = 2^{20}$ tampering-oracle queries, then to have ≈ 128-bits of security we need to set $(m-1) \log p \geq 312$ and $p \geq 2^{128}$, for example we can set we $m = 2$ and $p \geq 2^{312}$. Instantiating the random oracle using SHA256 then the codeword size would be approximately 2×880 bits. The time complexity of the decoding algorithm would be approximately the same as two SHA256 functions plus an inner-product between two vectors in $\mathbb{Z}_p^m$. Our second instantiation is

---

[3] It can be easily realized using a RO' with codomain $\{0, 1\}^{2\lambda}$.

derived by joining together the results of Theorem 1 and Theorem 4. We obtain a $n + \lambda$-randomness-encoders scheme Π_2^* with concrete security being:

$$\max_{A} \mathbf{Adv}_{\Pi_2^*,A}^{\mathsf{cnmre}}(\lambda) \leq \exp(-n + \log \lambda + \log q_T + \log q_{RO} + 2)$$

$$+ \frac{q_T + (q_{RO} + q \cdot q_T)^2}{2^{2\lambda}} + \frac{(q_{RO} + q \cdot q_T)\lambda q_T}{2^{m \log p - 1}}.$$

Assuming the same setup of before, to get $\approx$128-bits of security we need to set $n \geq 128 + 69$. Using SHA256 the codeword size would be approximately 2×453 bits. The time complexity of the decoding algorithm would be the same of 8 SHA256 functions. In particular, the size of the codeword is in total only ≈ 7 times bigger than the size of the derived key.

6   Lower Bounds for CNMREs in the ROM

Definition 7. *Given a n-randomness encoder Π, an algorithm A is a (ϵ, q_{RO})-finder for Π if $A(1^\lambda)$ makes at most $q_{RO}(\lambda)$ random oracle queries and if:*

$$\mathbb{P}\left[\begin{array}{c} \perp \neq \mathsf{Dec}(c_0, c_1) \neq \mathsf{Dec}(c_0, c_1') \neq \perp \\ (c_0 = c_0') \vee (c_1 = c_1') \end{array} : (c_0, c_1, c_0', c_1') \leftarrow A^{\mathsf{RO}}(1^\lambda) \right] \geq \epsilon(\lambda)$$

In the next theorem first we show that the existence of a finder is sufficient to break continuous non-malleability, then we show that even if there is no finder, we still can break continuous non-malleability given enough random oracle queries.

Theorem 5. *Let $n(\lambda) \in \mathbb{N}$ and let Π be a n-randomness encoder:*

1. *If there exists a (ϵ, q_{RO})-finder for Π then for any $\frac{\epsilon}{2} \geq \delta > 0$, Π is not a $(\frac{\epsilon}{2} - \delta, 0, q_{RO})$-CNMRE. Namely, there exists an adversary A' making up to q_{RO} random oracle queries and $n + 1$ tampering queries from $\mathcal{F}_{n,0}$, such that $\frac{\epsilon}{2} \leq \mathbf{Adv}_{\Pi,A'}^{\mathsf{cnmre}}(1^\lambda)$.*
2. *Suppose that $\mathsf{Enc}(1^\lambda)$ makes at most $q_{RO}^{\mathsf{Enc}}(\lambda)$ random oracle queries and uses $r(\lambda)$ random bits. If for any ϵ, q_{RO}', there does not exist a (ϵ, q_{RO}')-finder then for any $\delta > 0$ any q_{RO}, q such that $q_{RO} + q \geq 2^r \cdot q_{RO}^{\mathsf{Enc}}$ the scheme Π is not a $(1/2 - \delta, q, q_{RO})$-CNMRE. Namely, there exists an adversary A' making up to q_{RO} random oracle queries and 1 tampering query from $\mathcal{F}_{n,q}$ such that $\mathbf{Adv}_{\Pi,A'}^{\mathsf{cnmre}}(1^\lambda) = 1/2$.*

Proof (Sketch). For the first part of the theorem let the adversary A' first run the finder algorithm. For simplicity, let us assume that the finder outputs a tuple (c_0, c_1, c_0', c_1') where $c_0 = c_0'$. If the output of the finder is not valid then the adversary A' outputs a random bit. Else, for $i = 0, \ldots, n - 1$ sends the tampering query $(f_0^{(i)}, f_1^{(i)})$ where $f_0^{(i)}$ returns c_0 and $f_1^{(i)}(c^*)$ returns either c_1 or to c_1' depending on the on the i-th bit of c_1^*. After this process, the adversary can extract in full the value c_1^* of the target codeword, thus it can send a last tampering query that breaks non-malleability. It is clear that the adversary wins the game $\mathbf{G}^{\mathsf{cnmre}}$ with probability at least $\epsilon + (1 - \epsilon)\frac{1}{2}$.

For the second part of the theorem, for simplicity we consider first the case where $q = 0$. Since no finder exists, then for any c_0 there exists unique c_1 such that $(c_0, c_1) \in \{\mathsf{Enc}(1^\lambda; \rho) : \rho \in \{0, 1\}^r\}$. Thus the adversary A' can compile a bijection L_0 such that $L_0(c_0) = c_1$, also let L_1 be the inverse of L_0. To compile such bijections the adversary A' needs at most $2^r \cdot q_{\mathsf{RO}}^{\mathsf{Enc}}$ random oracle queries. Then given such bijections, the adversary sends the tampering queries f_0, f_1 where $f_\beta(c_\beta)$ computes $c_{1-\beta} \leftarrow L_\beta(c_\beta)$, decodes $\kappa \leftarrow \mathsf{Dec}(c_0, c_1)$, and if $\kappa = \kappa_0$ sets the codeword to $\bot$, else leaves the codeword untouched. It is clear that the adversary wins the game $\mathbf{G}^{\mathsf{cnmre}}$ with probability 1.

For the case $q > 0$, we can consider an adversary that computes first partially the bijection L_0 using the budget of random-oracle queries q_{RO} and then finishes to computes the bijection L_0 using the budget of random-oracle queries that the tampering function can use.

Corollary 1. *Let $\Pi = (\mathsf{REncode}, \mathsf{Dec})$ be a randomness-encoder where $\mathsf{REncode}(1^\lambda)$ makes up to $q_{\mathsf{RO}}^{\mathsf{REncode}}(\lambda)$ queries to the random oracle and uses at most $r(\lambda)$ bits of randomness, and Dec makes up to $q_{\mathsf{RO}}^{\mathsf{Dec}}(\lambda)$ queries to the random oracle. Also, let Π be a $(\epsilon, \ell, 2^r(q_{\mathsf{RO}}^{\mathsf{REncode}} + q_{\mathsf{RO}}^{\mathsf{Dec}}))$-noisy leakage resilient in the ROM, for any ϵ, ℓ where $\ell \geq 2$.*

Consider Π^* be our CNMRE from Sect. 3 instantiated with the randomness encoder Π. There exists an adversary A that makes up to $2^r(q_{\mathsf{RO}}^{\mathsf{REncode}} + q_{\mathsf{RO}}^{\mathsf{Dec}}) + 2^\lambda$ random oracle queries and up to $n+1$ tampering oracle queries from $\mathcal{F}_{n+2\lambda,0}$ such that: $(1/e)^{((\frac{1}{2} - \epsilon)2^\lambda - 1)^2/2^{2\lambda - 1}} \leq \mathbf{Adv}_{\Pi^*, \mathsf{A}}^{\mathsf{cnmre}}(\lambda)$. In particular, when $\epsilon(\lambda) \in \mathtt{negl}(\lambda)$ then $(1/e)^8 \leq \mathbf{Adv}_{\Pi^*, \mathsf{A}}^{\mathsf{cnmre}}(\lambda)$.

Proof. We describe an $((1/e)^{((\frac{1}{2} - \epsilon)2^\lambda - 1)^2/2^{2\lambda - 1}}, 2^r(q_{\mathsf{RO}}^{\mathsf{REncode}} + q_{\mathsf{RO}}^{\mathsf{Dec}}) + 2^\lambda)$-finder for Π^*.

> Finder $\mathsf{F}^{\mathsf{RO}}(1^\lambda)$:
> 1. Compute for any c_0 the set $\mathcal{E}(c_0) = \{c_1 | \exists \rho : (c_0, c_1) = \Pi.\mathsf{Enc}^{\mathsf{RO}}(1^\lambda; \rho)\}$;
> 2. Compute for any c_0 the set $\mathcal{M}(c_0) = \{\Pi.\mathsf{Dec}(c_0, c_1) | c_1 \in \mathcal{E}(c_0)\}$;
> 3. Find c_0^* such that $|\mathcal{M}(c_0^*)| = \max_{c_0} |\mathcal{M}(c_0)|$;
> 4. Find $c_1^{(1)}, c_1^{(2)} \in \mathcal{E}(c_0^*)$ s.t. $\mathsf{RO}(c_1^{(1)}) = \mathsf{RO}(c_2^{(2)})$ and $\Pi.\mathsf{Dec}(c_0^*, c_1^{(1)}) \neq \Pi.\mathsf{Dec}(c_0^*, c_1^{(2)})$.
> 5. If such tuple does not exist output $\bot$,
>   else output $(\bar{c}_0, \bar{c}_1, \bar{c}'_0, \bar{c}'_1)$ such that:
>
> $$\bar{c}_0 = \bar{c}'_0 := (c_0^*, \mathsf{RO}(c_1^{(1)})) \quad \bar{c}_1 := (c_1^{(1)}, \mathsf{RO}(c_0^*)) \quad \bar{c}'_1 := (c_1^{(2)}, \mathsf{RO}(c_0^*)).$$

Claim. For any $\epsilon(\lambda) \in \mathbb{R}, \ell(\lambda) \in \mathbb{N}$, if Π is a $(\epsilon, \ell, 2^r(q_{\mathsf{RO}}^{\mathsf{REncode}} + q_{\mathsf{RO}}^{\mathsf{Dec}}))$-noisy-leakage resilient randomness encoder then $|\mathcal{M}(c_0^*)| \geq (\frac{1}{2} - \epsilon)2^\lambda$.

Proof (of the Claim). Suppose that for any c_0 we have $|\mathcal{M}(c_0)| < (\frac{1}{2} - \epsilon)2^\lambda$. Consider the following attacker against noisy-leakage resilience.

Adversary $\mathsf{B}(\kappa_0, \kappa_1)$:
1. Send the leakage function that on input c_0 outputs:
   - 1 if $\kappa_1 \in \mathcal{M}(c_0)$ but $\kappa_0 \notin \mathcal{M}(c_0)$,
   - 0 if $\kappa_0 \in \mathcal{M}(c_0)$ but $\kappa_1 \notin \mathcal{M}(c_0)$,
   - $\bot$ if $\kappa_0 \in \mathcal{M}(c_0)$ and $\kappa_1 \in \mathcal{M}(c_0)$.
   let b' be the output of the leakage function;
2. If $b' = \bot$ output a random bit, else output b'.

Let b be the challenge bit, the probability of $\kappa_{1-b} \in \mathcal{M}(c_0)$ is strictly smaller than $(\frac{1}{2} - \epsilon)2^\lambda/2^\lambda$. Notice that $\kappa_b \in \mathcal{M}(c_0)$, thus the adversary B successfully guesses the challenge bit whenever the output of the second leakage function is not $\bot$. We can conclude that the advantage of B is strictly greater then ϵ.

By the claim above there exists at least $(\frac{1}{2} - \epsilon)2^\lambda$ different values c_1 that decodes correctly with c_0^* and whose decoded messages are pairwise different. Thus applying the birthday-paradox bound the probability that the finder successfully outputs a valid tuple is at least $(1/e)^{((\frac{1}{2}-\epsilon)2^\lambda-1)^2/2^{2\lambda-1}}$. Finally, notice that the number of random oracle queries made by F are:

- $2^r(q_{\mathsf{RO}}^{\mathsf{Enc}} + q_{\mathsf{RO}}^{\mathsf{Dec}})$ to compute the sets $\mathcal{E}(c_0)$ for any c_0;
- At most 2^λ to compute the step 4.

By applying Theorem 5 point 1 we have the statement of the theorem.

References

1. Aggarwal, D., Agrawal, S., Gupta, D., Maji, H.K., Pandey, O., Prabhakaran, M.: Optimal computational split-state non-malleable codes. In: Kushilevitz, E., Malkin, T. (eds.) TCC 2016, Part II. LNCS, vol. 9563, pp. 393–417. Springer, Heidelberg (2016). https://doi.org/10.1007/978-3-662-49099-0_15
2. Aggarwal, D., Dodis, Y., Lovett, S.: Non-malleable codes from additive combinatorics. In: ACM STOC, pp. 774–783 (2014)
3. Aggarwal, D., Dziembowski, S., Kazana, T., Obremski, M.: Leakage-resilient non-malleable codes. In: Dodis, Y., Nielsen, J.B. (eds.) TCC 2015, Part I. LNCS, vol. 9014, pp. 398–426. Springer, Heidelberg (2015). https://doi.org/10.1007/978-3-662-46494-6_17
4. Agrawal, S., Gupta, D., Maji, H.K., Pandey, O., Prabhakaran, M.: Explicit non-malleable codes against bit-wise tampering and permutations. In: Gennaro, R., Robshaw, M. (eds.) CRYPTO 2015. LNCS, vol. 9215, pp. 538–557. Springer, Heidelberg (2015). https://doi.org/10.1007/978-3-662-47989-6_26
5. Alwen, J., Dodis, Y., Naor, M., Segev, G., Walfish, S., Wichs, D.: Public-key encryption in the bounded-retrieval model. In: Gilbert, H. (ed.) EUROCRYPT 2010. LNCS, vol. 6110, pp. 113–134. Springer, Heidelberg (2010). https://doi.org/10.1007/978-3-642-13190-5_6
6. Brian, G., Faonio, A., Venturi, D.: Continuously non-malleable secret sharing for general access structures. In: Hofheinz, D., Rosen, A. (eds.) TCC 2019, Part II. LNCS, vol. 11892, pp. 211–232. Springer, Cham (2019). https://doi.org/10.1007/978-3-030-36033-7_8

7. Brian, G., Faonio, A., Venturi, D.: Continuously non-malleable secret sharing: joint tampering, plain model and capacity. Cryptology ePrint Archive, Report 2021/1128 (2021). https://ia.cr/2021/1128

8. Chattopadhyay, E., Goyal, V., Li, X.: Non-malleable extractors and codes, with their many tampered extensions. In: 48th ACM STOC (2016)

9. Cheraghchi, M., Guruswami, V.: Non-malleable coding against bit-wise and split-state tampering. In: Lindell, Y. (ed.) TCC 2014. LNCS, vol. 8349, pp. 440–464. Springer, Heidelberg (2014). https://doi.org/10.1007/978-3-642-54242-8_19

10. Coretti, S., Dodis, Y., Tackmann, B., Venturi, D.: Non-malleable encryption: simpler, shorter, stronger. In: Kushilevitz, E., Malkin, T. (eds.) TCC 2016. LNCS, vol. 9562, pp. 306–335. Springer, Heidelberg (2016). https://doi.org/10.1007/978-3-662-49096-9_13

11. Coretti, S., Faonio, A., Venturi, D.: Rate-optimizing compilers for continuously non-malleable codes. In: Deng, R.H., Gauthier-Umaña, V., Ochoa, M., Yung, M. (eds.) ACNS 2019. LNCS, vol. 11464, pp. 3–23. Springer, Cham (2019). https://doi.org/10.1007/978-3-030-21568-2_1

12. Coretti, S., Maurer, U., Tackmann, B., Venturi, D.: From single-bit to multi-bit public-key encryption via non-malleable codes. In: Dodis, Y., Nielsen, J.B. (eds.) TCC 2015. LNCS, vol. 9014, pp. 532–560. Springer, Heidelberg (2015). https://doi.org/10.1007/978-3-662-46494-6_22

13. Dachman-Soled, D., Kulkarni, M.: Upper and lower bounds for continuous non-malleable codes. In: Lin, D., Sako, K. (eds.) PKC 2019, Part I. LNCS, vol. 11442, pp. 519–548. Springer, Cham (2019). https://doi.org/10.1007/978-3-030-17253-4_18

14. Dachman-Soled, D., Liu, F.-H., Shi, E., Zhou, H.-S.: Locally decodable and updatable non-malleable codes and their applications. In: Dodis, Y., Nielsen, J.B. (eds.) TCC 2015. LNCS, vol. 9014, pp. 427–450. Springer, Heidelberg (2015). https://doi.org/10.1007/978-3-662-46494-6_18

15. Davì, F., Dziembowski, S., Venturi, D.: Leakage-resilient storage. In: Garay, J.A., De Prisco, R. (eds.) SCN 2010. LNCS, vol. 6280, pp. 121–137. Springer, Heidelberg (2010). https://doi.org/10.1007/978-3-642-15317-4_9

16. Dziembowski, S., Faust, S.: Leakage-resilient cryptography from the inner-product extractor. In: Lee, D.H., Wang, X. (eds.) ASIACRYPT 2011. LNCS, vol. 7073, pp. 702–721. Springer, Heidelberg (2011). https://doi.org/10.1007/978-3-642-25385-0_38

17. Dziembowski, S., Kazana, T., Obremski, M.: Non-malleable codes from two-source extractors. In: Canetti, R., Garay, J.A. (eds.) CRYPTO 2013. LNCS, vol. 8043, pp. 239–257. Springer, Heidelberg (2013). https://doi.org/10.1007/978-3-642-40084-1_14

18. Dziembowski, S., Pietrzak, K., Wichs, D.: Non-malleable codes. In: ICS 2010 (2010)

19. Faonio, A.: Practical continuously non-malleable randomness encoders in the random oracle model. Cryptology ePrint Archive. https://ia.cr/2021/1269

20. Faonio, A., Nielsen, J.B., Simkin, M., Venturi, D.: Continuously non-malleable codes with split-state refresh. In: Preneel, B., Vercauteren, F. (eds.) ACNS 2018. LNCS, vol. 10892, pp. 121–139. Springer, Cham (2018). https://doi.org/10.1007/978-3-319-93387-0_7

21. Faonio, A., Venturi, D.: Non-malleable secret sharing in the computational setting: adaptive tampering, noisy-leakage resilience, and improved rate. In: Boldyreva, A., Micciancio, D. (eds.) CRYPTO 2019, Part II. LNCS, vol. 11693, pp. 448–479. Springer, Cham (2019). https://doi.org/10.1007/978-3-030-26951-7_16

22. Faust, S., Mukherjee, P., Nielsen, J.B., Venturi, D.: Continuous non-malleable codes. In: Lindell, Y. (ed.) TCC 2014. LNCS, vol. 8349, pp. 465–488. Springer, Heidelberg (2014). https://doi.org/10.1007/978-3-642-54242-8_20
23. Fehr, S., Karpman, P., Mennink, B.: Short non-malleable codes from related-key secure block ciphers. IACR Trans. Symm. Cryptol. (1) (2018)
24. Gennaro, R., Lysyanskaya, A., Malkin, T., Micali, S., Rabin, T.: Algorithmic Tamper-Proof (ATP) security: theoretical foundations for security against hardware tampering. In: Naor, M. (ed.) TCC 2004. LNCS, vol. 2951, pp. 258–277. Springer, Heidelberg (2004). https://doi.org/10.1007/978-3-540-24638-1_15
25. Kanukurthi, B., Obbattu, S.L.B., Sekar, S.: Non-malleable randomness encoders and their applications. In: Nielsen, J.B., Rijmen, V. (eds.) EUROCRYPT 2018. LNCS, vol. 10822, pp. 589–617. Springer, Cham (2018). https://doi.org/10.1007/978-3-319-78372-7_19
26. Kiayias, A., Liu, F.-H., Tselekounis, Y.: Practical non-malleable codes from l-more extractable hash functions. In: ACM CCS 2016 (2016)
27. Li, X.: Improved non-malleable extractors, non-malleable codes and independent source extractors. In: ACM STOC, pp. 1144–1156 (2017)
28. Li, X.: Improved non-malleable extractors, non-malleable codes and independent source extractors. In: 49th ACM STOC (2017)
29. Liu, F.-H., Lysyanskaya, A.: Tamper and leakage resilience in the split-state model. In: Safavi-Naini, R., Canetti, R. (eds.) CRYPTO 2012. LNCS, vol. 7417, pp. 517–532. Springer, Heidelberg (2012). https://doi.org/10.1007/978-3-642-32009-5_30
30. Ostrovsky, R., Persiano, G., Venturi, D., Visconti, I.: Continuously non-malleable codes in the split-state model from minimal assumptions. In: Shacham, H., Boldyreva, A. (eds.) CRYPTO 2018, Part III. LNCS, vol. 10993, pp. 608–639. Springer, Cham (2018). https://doi.org/10.1007/978-3-319-96878-0_21

Attacks and Counter-Measures

Countermeasures Against Backdoor Attacks Towards Malware Detectors

Shintaro Narisada[1]([✉]), Yuki Matsumoto[2], Seira Hidano[1],
Toshihiro Uchibayashi[3], Takuo Suganuma[4], Masahiro Hiji[5],
and Shinsaku Kiyomoto[1]

[1] KDDI Research, Inc., Fujimino, Japan
{sh-narisada,se-hidano,kiyomoto}@kddi-research.jp
[2] Graduate School of Information Sciences, Tohoku University, Sendai, Japan
matsumoto@ci.cc.tohoku.ac.jp
[3] Research Institute for Information Technology, Kyushu University, Fukuoka, Japan
uchibayashi.toshihiro.143@m.kyushu-u.ac.jp
[4] Cyberscience Center, Tohoku University, Sendai, Japan
suganuma@tohoku.ac.jp
[5] Graduate School of Economics and Management, Tohoku University, Sendai, Japan
hiji@tohoku.ac.jp

Abstract. Attacks on machine learning systems have been systematized as *adversarial machine learning*, and a variety of attack algorithms have been studied until today. In the malware classification problem, several papers have suggested the possibility of real-world attacks against machine learning-based malware classification models. A *data poisoning attack* is an attack technique in which an attacker mixes poisoned data into the training data, and the model learns from the poisoned training data to cause misclassification of specific (or unspecified) data. Although various poisoning attacks that inject poison into the *feature space* of malware classification models have been proposed, Severi *et al.* proposed the first backdoor poisoning attack in the *input space* towards malware detectors by injecting poison into the actual binary files in the data accumulation phase. They achieved an attack success rate of more than 90% by adding only 1% of the poison data to approximately 2% of the entire features with a backdoor. To the best of our knowledge, no fundamental countermeasure against these attacks has been proposed. In this paper, we propose the first countermeasure based on autoencoders in a realistic threat model such that a defender is available for the contaminated training data only. We replaced all potentially attackable dimensions with surrogate data generated by autoencoders instead of using autoencoders as anomaly detectors. The results of our experiments show that we succeeded in significantly reducing the attack success rate while maintaining the high prediction accuracy of the clean data using replacement with the autoencoder. Our results suggest a new possibility of autoencoders as a countermeasure against poisoning attacks.

Keywords: Backdoor poisoning attack · Malware detection · Autoencoder

© Springer Nature Switzerland AG 2021
M. Conti et al. (Eds.): CANS 2021, LNCS 13099, pp. 295–314, 2021.
https://doi.org/10.1007/978-3-030-92548-2_16

1 Introduction

In order to detect unknown malware that cannot be detected by conventional pattern-matching-based malware detection techniques, research on malware detection using machine learning is progressing. The malware classification task can be divided into two major categories: *dynamic analysis* and *static analysis* [13]. Dynamic analysis builds malware detection models by learning execution log files obtained by the behavior of malware and benign software [7,9,14,22]. In static analysis, machine learning models learn the features extracted by analyzing the software's binary itself [14,25]. There are two main techniques for extracting features from binaries: heuristic methods parsing general file information such as header information and byte histograms [1,24], and automatically extracting features from binaries using neural networks [21]. As an alternative to simple linear classifiers such as SVMs, highly accurate DNN-based malware detectors are also emerging [24,28,31].

While machine learning enables highly accurate classification, machine learning systems are also exposed to a variety of security risks from attackers. Attacks on machine learning systems are known as *adversarial machine learning* and have been shown to be possible under a variety of circumstances [12]. *Adversarial examples* are a type of attack in the test phase that aims to cause misclassification by adding small noises to the test data [3]. *Poisoning attacks* are stronger attacks during the learning phase that aim to create a model that misclassifies the attacker's data by mixing poisoned data into the training data [4]. Poisoning attacks towards image classification problems [19,34] and malware detection problems [19] against neural networks have been proposed. Recently, poisoning attacks on multi-task learning (MTL) [35] and graph neural networks (GNN) [5] have been also studied. *Model inversion attacks* recover private training data by exploiting information obtained from the middle layer of a trained model [8]. *Model extraction attacks* steal a the model's structure using the confidence values of the targeted model [29].

There have been various studies on countermeasures against these threats. For adversarial examples, reducing the feature dimension has been shown to be effective in decreasing the attack success rate [2]. On the other hand, there is a trade-off between the number of reduced dimensions and the classification accuracy. Principal component analysis (PCA) is also used to detect adversarial inputs [11]. For poisoning attacks, studies on extracting poison triggers by solving a loss minimization problem for the output of the model [32] or reducing neurons that are activated only by poisoned data [16] have been performed.

To address the malware classification problem, strong backdoor attacks have recently been proposed by Severi *et al.* [26]. *Backdoor attacks* inject poisoning data using a trigger called a backdoor into the training data, causing the prediction model to misclassify only the backdoored data. The unique aspect of their algorithms is that the backdoor is not injected in the *feature space* but rather in the *input file* (binary) itself so the attacker can plant poisoning data during the data accumulation phase. As a result, only the contaminated training data are available to the defender, and he must take countermeasures based on them. To the best of our knowledge, there is no effective countermeasure for these attacks.

1.1 Related Works

We will introduce several countermeasures relevant to this paper.

Mitigation of Backdoor Attacks. Isolation Forest [15] is a standard unsupervised learning method for anomaly detection, and can also be used for backdoor detection. Decision trees constructed from the feature values of a contaminated dataset are used to detect outliers. The spectral signatures proposed by Tran *et al.* [30] detect outliers by performing SVD on latent representations for the last layers in a (poisoned) neural network. In Severi's paper, these mitigation techniques were applied to backdoor attacks but were not shown to be effective against all attack algorithms.

Defenses by Generative Networks. Autoencoders, which are mainly used for dimensionality reduction, are used as anomaly detectors. Madani *et al.* [18] applied autoencoders as anomaly detectors for label contamination attacks. Their algorithm outperforms conventional PCA-based detectors in terms of the detection rate. There are also defenses using generative adversarial networks (GANs) to disable adversarial examples [23]. In their method, test data is replaced before input to the prediction model by surrogate data generated by a GAN. They show that adversarial noise can be sanitized by filtering through a GAN, thereby reducing the attack success rate. Note that the data used to generate the GAN needed to be clean.

1.2 Contributions

In this paper, we first consider effective countermeasures against backdoor poisoning attacks towards the malware classifier proposed by Severi *et al.* in the realistic threat model. Our defensive method is based on autoencoders not as anomaly detectors but as surrogate data generator to eliminate backdoors. We show that autoencoders are very effective at sanitizing backdoor attacks, even in attacker-favorable situations where the defender can only obtain contaminated training data. To the best of our knowledge, this is the first attempt to achieve this, especially in the following two points:

1. We applied autoencoders as *pseudodata generators* for defenses against backdoor attacks and showed that backdoors are actually removed by passing them through an autoencoder.
2. We show that even autoencoders generated from *contaminated* datasets are effective at sanitizing poisoned data. In other words, there is no need to assume the existence of a clean dataset as in existing supervised anomaly detection.

The experimental results show that our proposed method significantly reduces the attack success rate of the two backdoor attacks proposed by Severi *et al.* and the stronger variant combining the label flip attack and fast gradient sign method proposed in this work. In addition, we confirmed that the prediction accuracy of the surrogate model did not degrade much compared to the original model.

2 Preliminaries

2.1 Notation

We consider a binary classification from an (normalized) input $x \in \mathcal{X} = [-1, 1]$ to an output $y \in \mathcal{Y} = \{0, 1\}$. The goal of the binary classification is to learn a classifier f that maps $f : \mathcal{X} \mapsto \mathcal{Y}$. Let ℓ be a loss function. In this paper, we assume that the model is a neural network, and ℓ is the binary cross entropy loss. We denote the training data set as $\mathcal{D}_{tr}$ and the validation set as $\mathcal{D}_{val}$.

2.2 Threat Model

In this paper, we consider a general malware classification task using machine learning based on static analysis. First, binary files are aggregated on threat intelligence platforms. Honeypots and sensors are being used to collect malware/benign files. Users (including attackers) can also provide binary files to the platform. The aggregated binary files are automatically labeled through dynamic analysis using existing antivirus engines. In this way, a pretraining dataset $\mathcal{D}_{pre} = \{(b_i, y_i)\}_{i=1}^{n}$ consisting of a binary file b_i and its label y_i is generated. We assume the existence of an attacker with either of the following capabilities: (1) modify only the binary file $b_i \rightarrow \hat{b}_i$ (*clean label attacks*) or (2) modify both the binary file and the label $(b_i, y_i) \rightarrow (\hat{b}_i, \hat{y}_i)$ (*label flipping attacks*). Then, the attacker mixes an attacker's dataset $\mathcal{A}_{pre} = \{(\hat{b}_i, \hat{y}_i)\}_{i=1}^{p}$ consisting of p poisoned data into the pretraining dataset: $\hat{\mathcal{D}}_{pre} = \mathcal{D}_{pre} \cup \mathcal{A}_{pre}$. For the (poisoned) pretraining dataset, some feature extraction algorithms are applied to the binary files. In this paper, we use the EMBER feature extractor, which is commonly used for feature extraction in malware classification. Each binary file b is transformed into a 2351-dimensional feature vector v by EMBER. A model is trained on a (poisoned) dataset $\hat{\mathcal{D}}_{tr}$ consisting of a pair of feature vectors and labels (v, y), and it will classify the feature vectors extracted from the unknown binary file.

We assume that the attack is *targeted* since the attacker's objective is to misclassify the specific malware as benign software. As for the attack algorithm, we consider backdoor poisoning attacks as described in previous research. A *backdoor* (also called a trigger or watermark) is inserted into the input space (binary) of the attacker's pretraining data so that some dimension of the feature vector v changes to a certain value. Then, the poisoned model misclassifies the backdoored malware as goodware in the testing phase. In order to consider stronger defensive methods against the attacks, the attacker is assumed to have knowledge of all the feature extraction algorithms, the structure of the model, the learning algorithm, and a part of the pretraining dataset (*white box attacks*).

3   Backdoor Attacks Towards Malware Classifier

Backdoor attacks on malware classifier differ from the usual feature space-based attacks in that they assume the injection of a backdoor in the input space (binary file). The attacker's objective is to construct a poisoned classifier $\hat{f}$ that differs from a clean classifier f by injecting backdoored binary $\hat{b}$ into the training dataset. For binaries b with no backdoor inserted, f and $\hat{f}$ output the same prediction; whereas for backdoor binaries $\hat{b}$, the prediction of $\hat{f}$ is the targeted label $y_{target} = 0$ (benign software):

$$f(v) = \hat{f}(v), f(\hat{v}) = y, \hat{f}(\hat{v}) = y_{target} \neq y, \tag{1}$$

where $v \leftarrow \text{Feat}(b)$ and $\hat{v} \leftarrow \text{Feat}(\hat{b})$ for some feature extraction function Feat. In backdoor generation, the optimal backdoor value is first calculated in the feature space. Then, it is projected into the binary space through the inverse function Feat^{-1}. In the following, the term backdoor is used to denote a backdoor in the feature space. A backdoor is denoted by a pair of two lists (F, V) of length N. For $1 \leq i \leq N$, $F[i]$ denotes the i-th backdoor dimension and $V[i]$ denotes the backdoor value for $F[i]$. Namely, for a clean feature vector v, the i-th backdoor is generated by $v[F[i]] = V[i]$. The key of the backdoor generation algorithm is the choice of F and V and how to project the backdoor in input space.

3.1   Clean Label Backdoor Attacks [26]

Severi *et al.* used a model explanation technique called SHAP (SHapley Additive exPlanations) [17] for backdoor generation. SHAP can quantify the contribution of an input (feature vector) to the output of machine learning models by building a surrogate explanation model. Let g be an explanation model. For the original prediction model f and its input v, g approximates $f(v)$ as follows:

$$g(z) = \phi_0 + \sum_{i=1}^{n} \phi_i z_i, \tag{2}$$

where $z_i \in \{0, 1\}$ and $\phi_i \in \mathbb{R}$. ϕ_i represents the contribution of the i-th feature of the input v to $f(v)$ and $f(v) \approx \sum_{i=1}^{n} \phi_i$ is satisfied. $z = (z_1, \cdots, z_n)$ is a simplified input of v. $z_i = 1$ means that v_i is used for the prediction of f, and $z_i = 0$ means that v_i is not used for the prediction. In malware classification, $\phi_i < 0$ means that v_i contributes to the direction of benign software, and $\phi_i > 0$ means that v_i contributes to the malware. The magnitude of the contribution for v_i is obtained by $|\phi_i|$. Originally, SHAP is used to quantify the contribution of a specific feature of the input to the output, but it can also be used for feature vectors by constructing an explainable model g with a feature vector as input of g. Hereafter, we introduce two backdoor generation algorithms using the ϕ_i proposed by Severi *et al.*.

Independent Selection. First, we construct the list F consisting of the dimensions of the backdoor. For prediction model f, the SHAP values of the training data $\mathcal{D}_{tr}$ are computed. Namely, a SHAP matrix S is generated such that $S[i,j] = \phi_i^{(j)}$, where $\phi_i^{(j)} \hat{=} (v^{(j)}, y^{(j)}) \in \mathcal{D}_{tr}$. In the independent selection, the sum of the absolute values of the SHAP values is computed by $S_{abs}[i] = \sum_{j=1}^n |S[i,j]|$ for each dimension i. This allows us to obtain the magnitude of the contribution to the prediction for each dimension. Then, the first backdoor dimension is computed by $F[1] = \arg\max_i S_{abs}$. By taking the maximum, the most important dimension for the prediction is extracted, ignoring the directionality. The entire F is constructed by computing the second to N-th backdoor dimensions in the same way.

Regarding the value selection algorithms, one of the their algorithms inserts backdoor points in sparse and weak-confidence areas, aiming for the backdoor points to gain high leverage in the prediction. To do so, the value with the lowest frequency of occurrence in dimension $F[i]$ is chosen as the backdoor value, *i.e.*, $V[i] = \arg\max_a (1/c_a)$ for $a \in A = \{v_{F[i]} \mid \forall(v,y) \in \mathcal{D}_{tr}\}$, where c_a is the frequency of occurrence of the value a. Finally, for a randomly selected feature vector v of a benign software $(v, y = 0) \in \mathcal{D}_{tr}$, a backdoor is inserted into the binary file in the input space so that $v[F[i]] = V[i]$ is satisfied in the feature space using the inversion Feat^{-1}. The details of the inversion will be described later. In the testing phase, the same backdoor (F, V) is inserted into the malware, causing it to be predicted as benign.

Greedy Combined Selection. Another strategy is to choose the dimension with the highest contribution to the benign direction as F and choose the most benign value in F as V. For the SHAP matrix S, greedy combined selection computes the sum of the SHAP values $S_{sum}[i] = \sum_{j=1}^n S[i,j]$ for each dimension i. Then, the first backdoor dimension is determined by taking the minimum for S_{sum}, *i.e.*, $F[1] = \arg\min_i S_{sum}$. The first backdoor value $V[1]$ is obtained by $V[1] = \arg\min_a (1/c_a) + \sum_{j \in J} S[i][j]$ for $a \in A = \{v_{F[1]} \mid \forall(v,y) \in \mathcal{D}_{tr}\}$, where j is the index of the training data satisfying $v_{F[1]} = a$. In order to blend the backdoor with background benign data, the frequency terms are combined in the equation to choose high frequency values. When considering $(F[2], V[2])$, we exclude the training data that do not satisfy $v[F[1]] = V[1]$ from the candidates. This is repeated until the N-th backdoor is reached. This method guarantees that there is at least one background point with the backdoor in the training data. This causes poisoning data with backdoors to be easily mixed in with the training data. The backdoor injection scheme is the same as the independent selection algorithm.

Inversion from Feature Space to Input Space. Once the backdoor (F, V) in the feature space is ready, we want to project (F, V) into the input space (binary file) considering the inversion of the feature extraction algorithm. Although the inversion method varies for feature extraction algorithms, Severi *et al.* showed that it is indeed possible in several dimensions for the EMBER feature extractor.

They identified that 35 out of 2351 dimensions in EMBER are invertible and directly manipulable. In these dimensions, either *values* or *counts* of specific bit strings in the binary file are directly extracted. For instance, the 2240 dimension of EMBER is major_operating_system_version, where the OS version is stored as an integer. 2349 is urls, which stores the number of strings that may contain URLs. Thus, the location to be edited in the binary is identified and can be modified directly so that the corresponding feature vector has the backdoor value. Furthermore, they confirmed that the result of labeling the backdoored binary via dynamic analysis is identical to the original label. However, they stated that it is difficult to perform the inversion for the remaining 2316 dimensions due to the feature hashing function used in the EMBER extractor.

3.2   Stronger Label Flip Backdoor Attacks

Severi's backdoor attacks are practical but assume some limitations for an attacker: the attacker cannot modify labels, and the backdoor must be selected from the values present in the training dataset. However, assuming a stronger backdoor attack without these constraints is important from the defender's perspective to validate the upper limit (worst case) of the defense performance. If an attacker has the capability to manipulate labels besides the data itself, we can consider a label-flip variant of the backdoor attacks as in the standard poisoning attacks. We propose a new backdoor attack based on Severi's attacking scheme, which combines the Fast Gradient Sign Method (FGSM) [10], a type of adversarial examples; and the label flip attack. In our method, the initial poisoning data are malware randomly selected from the training data as in the conventional poisoning attacks. Its label is flipped to 0 (goodware). In feature selection, N dimensions with the highest contribution to the goodware are stored in F as in the greedy combined selection. The value of backdoor $V[i]$ is obtained by the following equation for $1 \leq i \leq N$:

$$V[i] = v[F[i]] - \varepsilon \operatorname{sign}(\nabla_v \ell(f(v), l_{\text{target}})[F[i]]), \tag{3}$$

where ε is a weight parameter and $l_{\text{target}} = 0$. In our experiments, we used the MSE loss for the loss function ℓ. Since the attack is targeted, v is updated so that the loss of l_{target} decreases for the backdoor dimension $F[i]$. Note that V is dependent on the backdoored initial vector v. Finally, the malware binary b and its label $y = 1$ are modified in the input space as $(\hat{b}, \bar{y} = 0)$ using the backdoor (F, V) and injected into the training data $\mathcal{D}_{\text{tr}}$. The difference between the proposed algorithm and the standard FGSM is that the FGSM adds adversarial noise to all feature dimensions at the testing phase. On the other hand, our algorithm adds adversarial noise to only the backdoor dimension during the training phase. In addition, to increase the probability that backdoor malware is misclassified as goodware during the testing phase, we flipped the label of backdoor malware in the training data to 0.

4   Defenses Against Malware Classification Models

As mentioned in the threat model, the training data in malware classification may be contaminated with poison since binary files are collected from public resources. However, many existing countermeasures against backdoor attacks assume the availability of clean training data for anomaly detection models. Previous research has shown that unsupervised anomaly detection is not always effective against backdoor attacks [26]. Our goal is to devise a comprehensive countermeasure against backdoor attacks under the assumption that the training data are contaminated. We focused on the fact that an attacker injects a backdoor into the input space (the actual binary) rather than the feature space in malware classification. Then, we verify the invertibility of each dimension for the feature extractor and investigate the possibility of attacks on each dimension of the feature space from the input space. We prevent attacks by applying countermeasures to the dimensions that are potentially attackable.

4.1   Invertibility of Backdoor

We extend the discussion between the feature space and the input space in Sect. 3.1 in terms of backdoor invertibility. In the EMBER extractor, a feature hashing function is used for 1708 out of 2351 dimensions (for details, see [1] or the implementation of the EMBER). In these dimensions, the LIEF parser [27] directly extracts the value or count of a particular bit string from a binary file as a dictionary. The extracted dictionary $\{name : x\}$ with $name$ associated with the some name on the binary file (function name, etc.) and value x is transformed into feature vector $\boldsymbol{v}$ of length m using the feature hashing function as follows:

$$\boldsymbol{v}[i] = \begin{cases} +x & (h_s \bmod 2 = 0) \\ -x & (h_s \bmod 2 = 1), \end{cases} \tag{4}$$

where $i = h \bmod m$ for a hashing function $h = hash(name)$ and a sign hash function $h_s = hash_s(name)$ for the feature name. Since the attacker has knowledge of the feature extraction algorithm, he can obtain both $\{name : x\}$ and the hash function. Thus, an attacker has the ability to invert the backdoor into the input space for these dimensions. For example, we assume that an attacker wants to modify the value x of a feature vector $\boldsymbol{v}[i]$ to $\boldsymbol{v}[i] = a$. The attacker's purpose is to obtain $name$ in order to modify binary strings associated to $name$ in the input space. If the attacker has knowledge about the feature extraction algorithm, he should also know the set of $name$ to be extracted by the algorithm (*e.g.*, by viewing the source code of the extractor). Then, he can identify the $name$ associated with i by checking $i = hash(name) \bmod m$ for each $name$. For the remaining 608 dimensions, except for the 35 dimensions shown in Sect. 3.1, the statistics of the entire file, such as histograms, are used. Therefore, it is physically impossible to modify the dimensions to arbitrary values without affecting the binary functionality or the other feature vectors for these dimensions. Based on the above discussion, Table 1 summarizes the results for each dimension along

Table 1. Invertibility of the backdoor for the EMBER extractor.

Dimension	Feature group	Directly manipulable	Feature hashed	Invertible
1–256	ByteHistogram	×	×	×
257–512	ByteEntropyHistogram	×	×	×
513–767	SectionFileInfo	✓	✓	✓
768–2047	ImportsInfo	×	✓	✓
2048–2175	ExportsInfo	×	✓	✓
2176–2185	GeneralFileInfo	✓	×	✓
2186–2247	HeaderFileInfo	✓	✓	✓
2248–2351	StringExtractor	✓	✓	✓

with feature groups regarding the possibility of the invertibility of the backdoor. We determined the attackable dimension of a feature vector to be a dimension that satisfies at least one of the following three conditions: (1) it can be directly manipulated from the input space, (2) it is extracted by using a feature hashing function, and (3) it is invertible to the input space. Table 1 shows that there is a possibility of inversion in the 513–2351 dimensions of EMBER. Although we focus on the EMBER extractor here, it is also plausible that an attacker is incapable of controlling all feature space if the input space and the feature space are separated for other domains. We are now ready to develop countermeasures against these potentially attackable dimensions.

4.2 Countermeasures Against Input-Space Backdoor Attacks

For a clean dataset $\mathcal{D}_{tr} = \{(v_i, y_i)\}_{i=1}^{n}$ and an attacker's dataset $\mathcal{A}_{tr} = \{(\hat{v}_i, \hat{y}_i)\}_{i=1}^{p}$ consisting of p backdoored points, the dataset available to the defender is only the poisoned dataset $\hat{\mathcal{D}}_{tr} = \mathcal{D}_{tr} \cup \mathcal{A}_{tr}$. Suppose a feature vector is represented as $v = (s, x)$ with uncontrollable feature vector s and controllable vector x. The uncontrollable feature vector s is a vector that cannot be modified to desired value by an attacker through a backdoor attack. In this paper, we define s to be a vector that does not satisfy all of the following conditions: (1) it can be manipulated directly from the input space, (2) it is generated by a feature hashing function, and (3) it is invertible to the input space. The definition of the controllable feature vector x is the complement of the definition of s. Then, we assume that the attacker manipulates the invertible vector x and/or its label y in the input space. Thus, the defender should apply countermeasures to the vector x. We propose the following defense algorithms based on data transformation on x.

Dimensionality Reduction. The naivest method to prevent the attack is to not use the vector x itself for model training. That is, we set the feature vector $v = s$. This approach reduces the success rate of attacks by data modification except for label flipping to zero. However, the prediction accuracy of the model for correct data also decreases by discarding the feature vectors necessary for training. In [20], the prediction accuracy decreased by 24.6% when only ByteHistogram (1–256 dimensions) was used to train the lightGBM model. This increases the false negative rate of the malware, which may lead to misclassification of the backdoored malware. The prediction model is trained on the reduced dataset $\{(s_i, y_i)\}_{i=1}^{n+p}$, and the input in the testing phase is also reduced to s.

Surrogate Data Generation by Autoencoder. Another approach is to replace the vector x with surrogate one x', aiming for a trade-off between the prediction accuracy and the attack success rate. To generate surrogate data, GANs are used in the field of privacy for fair data generation [6,33] and as anomaly detection against adversarial examples [23]. Autoencoders are also used as anomaly detectors [18]. The drawbacks of these methods are that they assume GAN or autoencoders generated from a clean dataset. However, the size of the backdoor is very small compared to the entire feature vector and can be regarded as noise. We expected that the autoencoder could learn the clean data distribution while ignoring the backdoor from the poisoned dataset by setting hyperparameters such as the compression ratio and batch size appropriately.

We construct an autoencoder as a surrogate data generator for the vector x. An autoencoder consists of two neural networks: Enc with an n-dimensional input and m-dimensional output, and Dec with an m-dimensional input and n-dimensional output. The dimensionality of the input x is reduced by $Enc(x)$, and the compression ratio is denoted by m/n. $Dec(Enc(x))$ recovers the encoded data $Enc(x)$ to the original feature space. The training parameter of our autoencoder θ_{AE} is learned so that the reconstructed input is close to the original input for the controllable feature in the poisoned dataset:

$$\theta_{AE} := \arg\min_{\theta_{AE}} \frac{1}{|\hat{\mathcal{D}}_{tr}|} \sum_{(s,x)\in\hat{\mathcal{D}}_{tr}} \|Dec(Enc(x)) - x\|_2^2. \tag{5}$$

Note that θ_{AE} is learned in a different way than the usual autoencoder where the objective function is $\sum_{(s,x)\in\hat{\mathcal{D}}_{tr}} \|Dec(Enc(s,x)) - (s,x)\|_2^2$. After the construction of the autoencoder, each x in the poisoned training dataset is replaced by $x' = Dec(Enc(x))$ using the autoencoder, and the surrogate training point becomes (s, x', y). Although setting $x' = Enc(x)$ without the decoder may seem to be appropriate from the viewpoint of reducing the computational costs, our experimental results show that the success rate of the attack is reduced more when the decoder is used. The prediction model is trained on the reconstructed dataset $\{(s, x', y)\}_{i=1}^{n+p}$. In the testing phase, it was observed that replacing x with x' is more effective for reducing the attack success rate than using x as is.

Table 2. Hyperparameters for our networks.

Model	Learning rate	Epochs	Batch size
linearNN	0.1	100	512
surrogateNN	0.01	300	512
reducedNN	0.01	300	512
autoencoder	0.1	50	128

5 Experiments

We evaluated the effectiveness of backdoor attacks and their countermeasures against a neural network-based malware detector. We compared the defense performances of proposed methods against three backdoor poisoning algorithms in terms of attack success rate and prediction accuracy. In addition, we analyzed how the surrogate feature vectors generated from the contaminated autoencoder affect their contribution to the prediction and the distribution of values.

5.1 Setup

Dataset. We used part of the EMBER dataset, which consists of 2351-dimensional features extracted from 1.1 million PE (Portable Executable) files. We sampled 10000 data points from the entire EMBER dataset so that the numbers of goodware and malware items were evenly split and randomly divided them into the training and test dataset at a ratio of 8 : 2. That is, the training dataset consists of 4000 malware and goodware, the test dataset consists of 1000 malware and goodware. The attacker's validation data is 1000 malware randomly chosen from the EMBER dataset, and the attack success rate is the percentage classified as goodware. The uncontrollable features of the attacker in the EMBER dataset are the ByteHistgram and the ByteEntropyHistgram from the analysis in Sect. 4, and the attacker chooses backdoor features between 513–2351 dimensions. Since our goal is to establish countermeasures supposing a stronger attacker, we do not consider inverting the backdoor into the input space, and the attacker is assumed to be capable of inserting a backdoor into the controllable features. The initial data of the attacker's dataset is randomly selected goodware from the training data for the independent selection and greedy selection attacks and malware for our FGSM-based attack. All values in feature vectors are normalized to the range $[-1, 1]$.

Implementation Details. For the malware classifier, we implemented a linear neural network model (linearNN) similar to the EmberNN model in previous research [26]. Our neural network consists of four 2351-dimensional densely connected linear layers. For the activation function, we used the ReLU for the first three layers and the sigmoid for the last layer. Batch normalization and dropout were also applied between the linear layers to improve the prediction

Table 3. Accuracy, false-positive rate and false-negative rate of each model trained on the clean training data.

Model	Accuracy	False-positive	False-negative
linearNN	0.968	0.029	0.035
surrogateNN	0.943	0.048	0.065
reducedNN	0.915	0.071	0.099

accuracy. The dropout ratio is fixed at 0.5. The network used to train the surrogate data generated by the autoencoder (surrogateNN) has the same network as the linearNN. The network for dimensionality reduction (reducedNN) is the same as linearNN except that the dimensionality is reduced from 2351 to 512. The architecture of the autoencoder to sanitize the backdoor and generate the surrogate data is composed of an encoder and decoder with two linear layers. Dropout is applied after the last layer of the encoder to prevent overfitting. We set the compression ratio to 44% (1024/2351). We show the hyperparameters used in our models in Table 2. These parameters were calculated using the grid search. Our algorithms were implemented in Python with PyTorch.[1] All experiments were conducted in Ubuntu 18.04 with an NVIDIA Tesla P100 GPU (CUDA Version: 11.2).

5.2   Results

First, we measured the prediction accuracy of each model trained on the clean training data. The results are shown in Table 3. The false positive rate is the percentage of goodware misclassified as malware, and the false negative rate is the percentage of malware that was not detected. Note that the attack success rate is the false negative rate against the attacker's validation dataset. For all metrics, the results of the linearNN are the highest since the model learned the entire feature vector. The accuracy of the surrogateNN, which learned feature vectors with 512–2351 dimensions replaced by surrogate data from the autoencoder, is 2.5% less than that of the linearNN. However, the accuracy of the surrogateNN is 2.8% higher than that of the reducedNN, where the corresponding dimension is completely removed.

In the following, we will examine the prediction accuracy and the attack success rate of these models constructed on the poisoned training data with backdoor produced by each backdoor generation algorithm. We varied the number of backdoored dimension N and the number of poisoning point p between 4 $(0.17\%) \leq N \leq 64$ (2.7%) and $0 \leq p \leq 1600$ (20%) to observe the effect of contamination on the accuracy and the success rate. When varying N, we fix $p = 80$ (1%) and fix $N = 8$ when we vary p. Note that $p = 0$ corresponds to the *evasion attack* (adversarial example) since we do not modify the training data

---

[1] Our implementation is available on https://github.com/mlearning-security/countermeasures-against-backdoor-attacks.

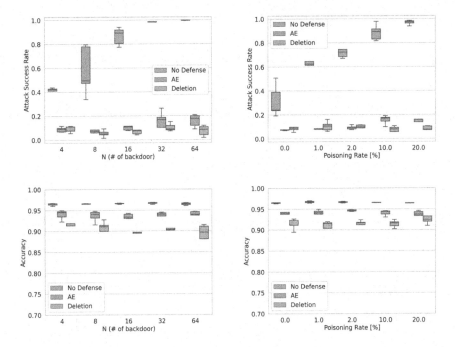

Fig. 1. The attack success rate (top) and the prediction accuracy (bottom) for each countermeasure against the independent selection attack.

itself but we inject N backdoor into the attacker's validation data at the testing phase. We are interested in how the attack success rate behaves with respect to variations in p when we consider backdoor attacks to be a generalization of evasion attacks.

Independent Selection. We show the results in Fig. 1. The attack success rate for the attacker's validation data increases as N and p increase when the defender has no countermeasures (No Defense in Fig. 1, 2 and 3). This is similar to the Severi's previous result. However, we found that the attack succeeded even though $p = 0$. This indicates that the backdoor attack can work as an evasion attacks when the training data is not contaminated with poisoning data. Furthermore, the prediction accuracy for the base network linearNN did not change.

When we use the reducedNN (Deletion in Fig. 1, 2 and 3) or surrogateNN (AE in Fig. 1, 2 and 3), the attack success rate is drastically reduced to approximately 10%. In the case of the reducedNN, the attack success rate is just the false negative rate of the malware since the backdoor has been completely removed via the dimensionality reduction. As for the surrogateNN, the attack success rate is reduced almost as much as that of the reducedNN, although the model was trained on the surrogate data from the autoencoder generated by the poisoned training data. The accuracy is almost the same as that of the clean dataset,

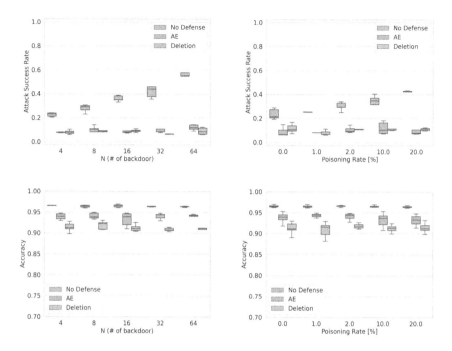

Fig. 2. The attack success rate and the prediction accuracy for each countermeasure against the greedy combined selection.

regardless of the size of N and p. Therefore, the `surrogateNN` has an advantage over the `reducedNN` in terms of the attack success rate and the accuracy.

Greedy Combined Selection. The results are given in Fig. 2. The attack success rate for the `linearNN` is lower than that of the independent selection. This is due to the constraint of the algorithm: there must be a background point in the training data that has the same value as the backdoor. In contrast, it was shown that existing countermeasures were ineffective against the algorithm because it is hard to distinguish the well blended backdoor points [26]. Against such advanced attacks, the `surrogateNN` can reduce the attack success rate as with the `reducedNN`. The prediction accuracies for the three models were almost the same as that of independent selection.

FGSM-Based Attack. Figure 3 shows the results of our FGSM-based attack. In our experiment, we set the weight parameter for gradients $\varepsilon = 1.5$. The attack success rate for the `linearNN` is saturated to 100% at $N = 16$ or $p = 10\%$. It is much higher than that of independent or greedy selection for the same parameter. This is because the algorithm has no constraints on the value of the backdoor (except for selecting a value from the feasible range $[-1, 1]$). Another reason is that the attacker has the capability to modify the label added to the data. There

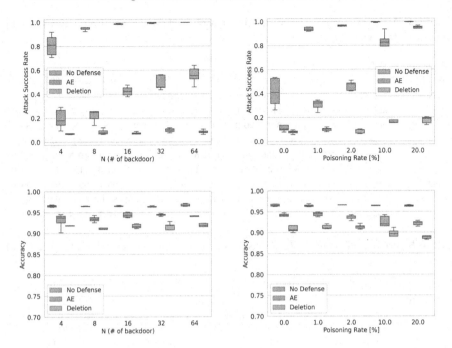

Fig. 3. The attack success rate and the prediction accuracy for each countermeasure against the FGSM-based label flip attack.

is a trade-off between the attack success rate and attacker capability. Even when $p = 0$ and $N = 8$, the attack succeeded by approximately 40%. Considering that the FGSM was originally proposed as a adversarial example, this result is plausible.

For the defender, the `surrogateNN` is still effective in decreasing the attack success rate. However, the protection performance drops sharply as the poisoning rate grows. The false negative rate for the `reducedNN` also increases as p increases due to the label-flipping of the training data. The prediction accuracy is stable as N varies but slightly decreases as p increases since neither the `surrogateNN` nor the `reducedNN` consider whether the labels are flipped. It is necessary to study how to defend against stronger backdoor attacks that combine label flip attacks.

Table 4 and Table 5 show the average attack success rate and the prediction accuracy for each backdoor generation algorithm and defensive strategy. We also show the results for large p (30% and 40%). From Table 4, we can observe a slight increase of the attack success rate of the `surrogateNN` for $p = 30\%$ and 40%. From Table 5, it is clear that there is no significant effect between the increase of p or N and the prediction accuracy of the clean data.

Table 4. Attack success rate (averaged) for each backdoor generation algorithm and defensive strategy.

Backdoor algorithm	Defensive strategy	N					p						
		4	8	16	32	64	0%	1%	2%	10%	20%	30%	40%
Independent	NoDefense	41.1	57.6	86.6	98.0	99.7	31.4	64.5	73.4	88.6	96.8	97.3	97.4
	AE	8.8	8.0	11.3	16.4	15.8	**7.4**	**8.3**	9.2	15.5	14.7	23.6	18.8
	Deletion	**8.6**	**5.3**	**8.3**	**10.2**	7.4	8.2	10.4	**9.1**	**7.8**	**8.5**	**12.9**	**8.4**
Greedy	NoDefense	22.4	27.8	36.0	44.7	56.9	23.4	29.7	30.2	35.1	42.5	52.5	54.6
	AE	**7.7**	10.3	10.2	10.3	11.2	**8.7**	8.0	10.6	12.0	**10.5**	23.9	10.4
	Deletion	7.9	**8.8**	**9.2**	**7.3**	**8.9**	11.5	**7.9**	**10.3**	**11.3**	11.0	**16.6**	**11.3**
FGSM	NoDefense	80.9	94.5	98.7	99.5	99.8	41.0	93.7	96.8	99.4	99.7	99.7	99.8
	AE	19.5	21.1	42.6	49.4	55.7	12.1	30.3	46.3	81.0	94.0	95.7	97.2
	Deletion	**7.2**	**8.4**	**7.1**	**9.7**	**8.3**	**7.7**	**9.9**	**8.4**	**16.7**	**17.4**	**8.45**	**11.5**

Table 5. Prediction accuracy (averaged) for each backdoor generation algorithm and defensive strategy.

Backdoor Algorithm	Defensive Strategy	N					p						
		4	8	16	32	64	0%	1%	2%	10%	20%	30%	40%
Ind.	NoDefense	96.5	96.5	96.6	96.7	96.4	96.4	96.7	96.6	96.4	96.5	96.4	96.6
	AE	**94.0**	**93.6**	**93.5**	**93.6**	**93.7**	**94.3**	**93.9**	**94.6**	**94.0**	**93.6**	**94.1**	**92.3**
	Deletion	91.6	87.4	88.1	90.3	85.9	91.5	89.6	91.2	91.3	92.3	90.0	91.7
Greedy	NoDefense	96.5	96.3	96.5	96.5	96.3	96.6	96.5	96.5	96.6	96.6	96.6	96.5
	AE	**93.9**	**94.1**	**93.2**	**94.0**	**94.2**	**93.0**	**94.4**	**94.5**	**93.1**	**94.1**	**92.7**	**93.3**
	Deletion	91.3	91.9	91.2	90.8	91.0	90.7	91.2	91.8	91.5	91.5	88.7	90.6
FGSM	NoDefense	96.5	96.4	96.5	96.4	96.7	96.5	96.4	96.8	96.4	96.4	96.2	96.5
	AE	**93.0**	**93.4**	**94.4**	**94.4**	**94.1**	**93.4**	**94.4**	**93.5**	88.1	**92.2**	**92.4**	**93.7**
	Deletion	91.4	91.1	91.7	91.1	91.5	90.9	91.2	91.3	**89.2**	89.0	88.4	88.6

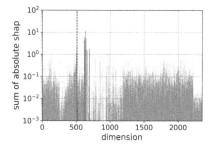
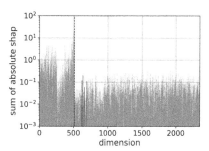

Fig. 4. Comparison of the sum of the absolute SHAP values for the training data (left) and the surrogate data (right).

Analysis. The above experimental results show that the autoencoder can weaken the power of the backdoor generated by using SHAP even if the autoencoder is learned from the poisoned dataset. To verify why this is possible, we conducted additional experiments on the surrogate data generated by the poisoned autoencoder. First, we compared the contribution of the true feature vector to the original model `linearNN` and that of the pseudo feature vector to the

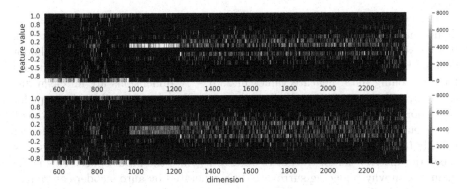

Fig. 5. Heatmap of histograms for the distribution in the clean training dataset (top) and the surrogate dataset (bottom) in 513–2351 dimensions.

surrogate model `surrogateNN`. If the autoencoder has not learned the backdoor, then backdoor dimensions should not contribute much to the prediction of the `surrogateNN`.

Figure 4 compares the contributions of true vectors and surrogate vectors to the prediction of the each model. In the experiment, we summed the absolute SHAP values in the training dataset for each dimension. The `linearNN` and the clean training dataset were used to create the left graph. The `surrogateNN` and surrogate training dataset were used to create the right graph. The purple lines show the backdoor dimensions chosen by the independent selection for $N = 8$. The backdoored dimensions are 637, 618, 642, 621, 692, 622, 641 and 658 (ordered by the sum of absolute SHAP values). The dotted line represents the 512 dimension. From the left figure, the backdoor is chosen from the dimensions whose contribution is very high. However, after the data replacement by the autoencoder, the contribution of the backdoor to the `surrogateNN` is reduced by approximately 100 times. Examining all dimensions, the contribution in 1–512 dimensions increases, where no data replacement occurred. Furthermore, the contribution in the remaining dimensions appears to be evenly distributed at approximately 10^{-1}. Therefore, we consider that autoencoders have the ability to equalize the contribution, and the incorrect contribution caused by the backdoor may be absorbed by the correct dimensions.

Finally, we compared the distribution of the true data and that of the surrogate data generated by the autoencoder and found that our autoencoder has the ability to remove noise (including the backdoor). Figure 5 compares the histograms for the distribution of feature vectors computed from clean dataset and surrogate dataset as heatmaps. The higher the brightness of the heatmap, the greater the frequency of feature vectors with values in the range. The y-axis represents the feature value. The number of bins = 16. It seems that the autoencoder learns by ignoring infrequent values or equates them with other frequent values since the purple bins in the upper figure disappear in the lower figure. In fact, we have confirmed that the autoencoder reconstructs a clean distributed point from a backdoored point for several backdoor dimensions.

Discussing from the point of view of the structure of the autoencoder, we found that the backdoor noise generated by the Severi's backdoor attacks can be removed by setting an appropriate compression ratio. In the Severi's backdoor attacks, backdoor is inserted in the N dimensions out of 2351 feature dimensions for p poisoning data. Feature values in $2351 - N$ dimensions are all clean distributed, and the remaining N dimensions are also clean distributed except for the p poisoning data. Therefore, when dimensionality is appropriately reduced by the encoding, the distribution that is considered as noise for the autoencoder is likely to be removed in the latent space. Then, the decoder decompresses only the major distribution of the entire dataset $\hat{\mathcal{D}}_{tr}$ into the input space. This is the main reason why replacing surrogate data generated by autoencoder can reduce the attack success rate. In our experiments, the higher the compression ratio, the greater the effect of removing backdoor noise and reducing the success rate of attacks. However, at the same time, the classification accuracy also decreased for too high compression ratio, so we needed to search an appropriate compression ratio.

6   Conclusion

In this work, we propose the first countermeasures against backdoor poisoning attacks towards the malware classifier presented by Severi *et al.* in a realistic threat model. In their attacks, an attacker injects a backdoor into the input space (binary file) during the data accumulation phase, and a defender is available only for the poisoned training dataset. In this favorable attack situation, we exploit the irreversibility between the input space and the feature space and identify the feature dimensions over which the attacker has no control. Then, we sanitize the backdoor for potentially attackable dimensions using the dimensionality reduction and an autoencoder as a pseudodata generator. In our experiments, our autoencoder generated from the contaminated dataset drastically reduced the attack success rate while retaining the high prediction accuracy of the clean data. For future works, analysis on the network structures of contaminated autoencoders and concrete comparison to the existing nonsupervised anomaly detection are needed. It is also necessary to verify the existence of adaptive backdoor attacks that are effective against the proposed countermeasures.

References

1. Anderson, H.S., Roth, P.: EMBER: an open dataset for training static PE malware machine learning models. arXiv preprint arXiv:1804.04637 (2018)
2. Bhagoji, A.N., Cullina, D., Mittal, P.: Dimensionality reduction as a defense against evasion attacks on machine learning classifiers. arXiv preprint arXiv:1704.02654 2 (2017)
3. Biggio, B., et al.: Evasion attacks against machine learning at test time. In: Blockeel, H., Kersting, K., Nijssen, S., Železný, F. (eds.) ECML PKDD 2013. LNCS (LNAI), vol. 8190, pp. 387–402. Springer, Heidelberg (2013). https://doi.org/10.1007/978-3-642-40994-3_25

4. Biggio, B., Nelson, B., Laskov, P.: Poisoning attacks against support vector machines. arXiv preprint arXiv:1206.6389 (2012)
5. Chang, H., et al.: A restricted black-box adversarial framework towards attacking graph embedding models. In: Proceedings of the AAAI Conference on Artificial Intelligence, vol. 34, pp. 3389–3396 (2020)
6. Choi, E., Biswal, S., Malin, B., Duke, J., Stewart, W.F., Sun, J.: Generating multi-label discrete patient records using generative adversarial networks. In: Machine Learning for Healthcare Conference, pp. 286–305. PMLR (2017)
7. Christodorescu, M., Jha, S., Kruegel, C.: Mining specifications of malicious behavior. In: Proceedings of the the 6th Joint Meeting of the European Software Engineering Conference and the ACM SIGSOFT Symposium on the Foundations of Software Engineering, pp. 5–14 (2007)
8. Fredrikson, M., Jha, S., Ristenpart, T.: Model inversion attacks that exploit confidence information and basic countermeasures. In: Proceedings of the 22nd ACM SIGSAC Conference on Computer and Communications Security, pp. 1322–1333 (2015)
9. Gavriluţ, D., Cimpoeşu, M., Anton, D., Ciortuz, L.: Malware detection using machine learning. In: 2009 International Multiconference on Computer Science and Information Technology, pp. 735–741. IEEE (2009)
10. Goodfellow, I.J., Shlens, J., Szegedy, C.: Explaining and harnessing adversarial examples. arXiv preprint arXiv:1412.6572 (2014)
11. Hendrycks, D., Gimpel, K.: Early methods for detecting adversarial images. arXiv preprint arXiv:1608.00530 (2016)
12. Huang, L., Joseph, A.D., Nelson, B., Rubinstein, B.I., Tygar, J.D.: Adversarial machine learning. In: Proceedings of the 4th ACM Workshop on Security and Artificial Intelligence, pp. 43–58 (2011)
13. Idika, N., Mathur, A.P.: A survey of malware detection techniques. Purdue University **48** (2007)
14. Ijaz, M., Durad, M.H., Ismail, M.: Static and dynamic malware analysis using machine learning. In: 2019 16th International Bhurban Conference on Applied Sciences and Technology (IBCAST), pp. 687–691. IEEE (2019)
15. Liu, F.T., Ting, K.M., Zhou, Z.H.: Isolation forest. In: 2008 Eighth IEEE International Conference on Data Mining, pp. 413–422. IEEE (2008)
16. Liu, K., Dolan-Gavitt, B., Garg, S.: Fine-pruning: defending against backdooring attacks on deep neural networks. In: Bailey, M., Holz, T., Stamatogiannakis, M., Ioannidis, S. (eds.) RAID 2018. LNCS, vol. 11050, pp. 273–294. Springer, Cham (2018). https://doi.org/10.1007/978-3-030-00470-5_13
17. Lundberg, S.M., Lee, S.I.: A unified approach to interpreting model predictions. In: Guyon, I., et al. (eds.) Advances in Neural Information Processing Systems 30, pp. 4765–4774. Curran Associates, Inc. (2017)
18. Madani, P., Vlajic, N.: Robustness of deep autoencoder in intrusion detection under adversarial contamination. In: Proceedings of the 5th Annual Symposium and Bootcamp on Hot Topics in the Science of Security, pp. 1–8 (2018)
19. Muñoz-González, L., et al.: Towards poisoning of deep learning algorithms with back-gradient optimization. In: Proceedings of the 10th ACM Workshop on Artificial Intelligence and Security, pp. 27–38 (2017)
20. Oyama, Y., Miyashita, T., Kokubo, H.: Identifying useful features for malware detection in the ember dataset. In: 2019 Seventh International Symposium on Computing and Networking Workshops (CANDARW), pp. 360–366. IEEE (2019)
21. Raff, E., Barker, J., Sylvester, J., Brandon, R., Catanzaro, B., Nicholas, C.: Malware detection by eating a whole exe. arXiv preprint arXiv:1710.09435 (2017)

22. Rieck, K., Trinius, P., Willems, C., Holz, T.: Automatic analysis of malware behavior using machine learning. J. Comput. Secur. **19**(4), 639–668 (2011)
23. Samangouei, P., Kabkab, M., Chellappa, R.: Defense-GAN: protecting classifiers against adversarial attacks using generative models. arXiv preprint arXiv:1805.06605 (2018)
24. Saxe, J., Berlin, K.: Deep neural network based malware detection using two dimensional binary program features. In: 2015 10th International Conference on Malicious and Unwanted Software (MALWARE), pp. 11–20. IEEE (2015)
25. Schmidt, A.D., et al.: Static analysis of executables for collaborative malware detection on android. In: 2009 IEEE International Conference on Communications, pp. 1–5. IEEE (2009)
26. Severi, G., Meyer, J., Coull, S., Oprea, A.: Explanation-guided backdoor poisoning attacks against malware classifiers. In: 30th USENIX Security Symposium (USENIX Security 21) (2021)
27. Thomas, R.: LIEF: Library to instrument executable formats (2017)
28. Tobiyama, S., Yamaguchi, Y., Shimada, H., Ikuse, T., Yagi, T.: Malware detection with deep neural network using process behavior. In: 2016 IEEE 40th Annual Computer Software and Applications Conference (COMPSAC), vol. 2, pp. 577–582. IEEE (2016)
29. Tramèr, F., Zhang, F., Juels, A., Reiter, M.K., Ristenpart, T.: Stealing machine learning models via prediction APIs. In: 25th USENIX Security Symposium (USENIX Security 16), pp. 601–618 (2016)
30. Tran, B., Li, J., Madry, A.: Spectral signatures in backdoor attacks. In: Advances in Neural Information Processing Systems, pp. 8000–8010 (2018)
31. Vinayakumar, R., Soman, K.: DeepMalNet: evaluating shallow and deep networks for static PE malware detection. ICT Express **4**(4), 255–258 (2018)
32. Wang, B., et al.: Neural cleanse: identifying and mitigating backdoor attacks in neural networks. In: 2019 IEEE Symposium on Security and Privacy (SP), pp. 707–723. IEEE (2019)
33. Xu, D., Yuan, S., Zhang, L., Wu, X.: FairGAN: fairness-aware generative adversarial networks. In: 2018 IEEE International Conference on Big Data (Big Data), pp. 570–575. IEEE (2018)
34. Yang, C., Wu, Q., Li, H., Chen, Y.: Generative poisoning attack method against neural networks. arXiv preprint arXiv:1703.01340 (2017)
35. Zhao, M., An, B., Yu, Y., Liu, S., Pan, S.: Data poisoning attacks on multi-task relationship learning. In: Proceedings of the AAAI Conference on Artificial Intelligence, vol. 32 (2018)

Free by Design: On the Feasibility of Free-Riding Attacks Against Zero-Rated Services

Julian Fietkau$^{(\boxtimes)}$, David Pascal Runge, and Jean-Pierre Seifert

Berlin Institute of Technology, Berlin, Germany
{fietkau,david.p.runge,jpseifert}@tu-berlin.de

Abstract. With free-riding attacks against zero-rated services, an attacker can avoid expenses by transmitting wrongly labeled zero-rated network traffic. When applied on large scale, these attacks impact network quality and revenue of network operators. Hence, various solutions are proposed to protect networks against this growing threat. While these protections cure some of the symptoms, they do not solve the underlying issue. In this paper, we argue that secure web services with high bandwidth requirements will increase the chances of free-riding attacks, when services are zero-rated by network operators. Therefore we show how tunnel-based free-riding attacks can be designed and implemented for secure services, such as instant messaging, cloud storage, and video chats. Furthermore, we evaluate these tunnels in terms of usability and performance and judge their feasibility. In addition, we also discuss the existing countermeasures and how they can be improved. As part of our work, we want to point out that free-riding attacks are a self-imposed problem created by Internet Service Providers that try to create artificial walls within a system that is free and open by design, such as the Internet. To tackle this issue, we publish the created tools to support those that are opposed to any form of zero-rating, censorship, and other forms of traffic discrimination.

1 Introduction

Internet access is a crucial aspect of modern life. Consequently, mobile Internet access is established in many parts of the world, and infrastructure costs are shared among users depending on how much everyone is using. Zero-rating is the practice of Internet Service Providers (ISPs) to either exclude traffic of specific applications from the user's data plan or even offer specific applications for free [15]. Various types and business models have become established in recent years. These can range from self-sponsored zero-rating, where an ISP independently decides to zero-rate a service, up to compound zero-rating, where multiple Content Providers (CPs) bundle their services into one zero-rated product of an ISP [3]. However, each practice of zero-rating is in heavy conflict with the idea of net neutrality [26]. As defined by the EU, the idea of net neutrality is to ensure equal and nondiscriminatory Internet access among all Internet users. This way,

© Springer Nature Switzerland AG 2021
M. Conti et al. (Eds.): CANS 2021, LNCS 13099, pp. 315–333, 2021.
https://doi.org/10.1007/978-3-030-92548-2_17

innovation without obstacles can be preserved, and discrimination by the ISPs can be prevented. Without net neutrality, a Content Provider (CP) could pay an ISP to prioritize its traffic to gain an advantage over its competitors.

One of the most prominent examples for zero-rating is the *Free Basics* initiative by Facebook [10]. This service aims to connect the world with essential online services, especially those who can not afford internet access so far. As of April 2018, 100 million people were using internet.org [10]. While the goal of the *Free Basics service* appears to be noble, the freely accessible service is very limited to a specific set of services and does not include Facebook's competitors. The initiative drew much criticism for this, and the Indian telecom regulator has even banned the service, seeing it as digital colonialism [24]. Moreover, other examples are not too different. For instance, Deutsche Telekom has offered its *Stream On* service until the EU court (EuGH) classified this practice as illegal [19]. Today, the debate about net neutrality is still not settled and will keep us busy for some years to come also, because traffic prioritization is now even part of 5G, the next generation of mobile networks [26].

Another way to think about zero-rating services is to use zero-rated traffic to enable free and unlimited Internet access via free-riding attacks. As the name suggests, the goal of a free-riding attack is to avoid the billing of Internet traffic by ISPs. In the context of zero-rating, an attacker tries to trick the ISP to zero-rate traffic that would be charged otherwise. Recent works on free-riding attacks against zero-rated services show that numerous attack approaches exist [11,15,20,22]. Furthermore, the damages by some of these attacks have already reached a critical level. For example, with a single free-riding attack against a Chinese ISP, damage of half a million US dollars loss has been created by creating 71 TB of wrongly labeled traffic [15]. These numbers show that free-riding attacks are real threats that ISPs and CPs should consider. As we see i) free-riding attacks are a real threat that is growing ii) they cause financial damage to network and content providers and impair network quality; and iii) the next generation of mobile networks will amplify this evolution by standardizing traffic prioritization

This work will explain how zero-rated services work and present a threat model for free-riding attacks. Based on that, we analyze the different types of zero-rated services to implement our free-riding attacks. This includes attacks via instant messaging, cloud storage, and VoIP services. Afterward, we evaluate the different approaches with respect to usability and performance. According to that, we will discuss existing countermeasures and their effectiveness. In summary, this paper makes the following **contributions**:

- We demonstrate the feasibility of tunnel-based free-riding attacks against three secure Internet services.
- We evaluate the presented free-riding attacks with respect to usability and performance with real-world applications.
- We discuss the effectiveness of existing countermeasures against free-riding attacks and explain why they fail.

- We point out how the concurrent adoption of zero-rating and secure web services with large bandwidth requirements can amplify free-riding attacks.
- We make our research tools and data accessible via: https://bit.ly/freebydesign

2 Background

This section introduces the necessary knowledge about free-riding attacks, zero-rating services, net neutrality and introduces the most related work in this field.

2.1 Zero Rating Services

Zero-rating is "a practice that exempts Internet traffic generated through certain applications or access to certain websites from usage charges" as defined by the European Commission [1]. Technically, this is realized by excluding the zero-rated traffic from the customer's data plan. In some cases, zero-rating will even "allow users to access content without having subscribed to a data plan at all" [1]. The various types of zero-rating are largely discussed in two publications by the European Commission [1] and in the work of Carillo [3]:

- Single-Service Zero-Rating: The ISP offers free access to one site or service. The CP has a contract with at least one ISP, e.g., Facebook Zero [6] or Wikipedia Zero [27].
- Sponsored Zero-Rating: The CP pays the ISP to offer its services at no charge, e.g., T-Mobile's Music Freedom, where some music streaming services are zero-rated [25].
- Compound Zero-Rating: A CP bundles services with an ISP, payments are not automatically implied, e.g., the Free Basics Service by Facebook, which includes Facebook, healthcare, news, and weather services [10].
- Faux/Non-Selective Zero-Rating: The CP partners the ISPs to exclude specific action from the user data volume, e.g., download specific apps, advertisements, or order a specific product such as data volume.

2.2 Net Neutrality

Net neutrality describes the idea to ensure equal and nondiscriminatory treatment of all Internet traffic. Accordingly, ISPs should treat every communication equally and not discriminate "based on IP addresses, domain name, cookie information, TCP port, and others" [28]. One can summarize net neutrality as the idea of treating every packet equally [23]. Without it, an ISP can throttle, prioritize or charge connections arbitrarily. Net neutrality is a fundamental property for fair competition and innovation. When not enforced, wealthy CPs can pay ISPs to prioritize or charge their traffic differently than a competitor's traffic. This will, above all, harm new CPs with new and alternative services. On the other hand, net neutrality is in the way of efficient traffic management and can even create inequality between customers and their different data demands [12]. In the end, net neutrality and zero-rating contradict themselves because the ISP treats the traffic differently in terms of costs, bandwidth, or latency.

2.3   Free-Riding Attacks

Free-riding attacks try to avoid the billing of Phone and Internet traffic. The first Free-riding attacks date back to the 1950s when phones were manipulated to enable free long-distance calls. Back then, the first attacks replayed 2600 Hz tone or the sound of dropping coins to avoid charging. Later on, the term "Phreaking" was coined [13], and after becoming too popular, countermeasures were implemented.

Today's networks are very different and more complex, but the underlying issues are still the same. Internet traffic is billed on a volume basis and has a limited data allowance; hence attacks try to avoid these limits. For example, DNS tunnelings allow a user to get free internet access via Wifi-Hotspots of Deutsche Telekom [22] and some US network providers as shown by Peng et al. [20]. The traffic will be encapsulated in DNS messages, and sent to a tunnel endpoint with unlimited Internet access. The endpoint resolves the tunneled request and sends the answer back via DNS messages. Besides this technique, many other ways to attack ISPs are known, e.g., spoofed TCP retransmission headers [7] or manipulated VoLTE signaling messages [14].

The first attack against zero-rated services was built for T-Mobile's *BingeOn* service and used manipulated HOST headers [11]. Based on this work, Liu et al. have developed more ways to do the same, for instance, by spoofing the *Server Name Indication* field [15]. As we see, various free-riding attacks have been built to establish free internet access by abusing the protocols that underlie those network services.

2.4   Countermeasures

With zero-rated services becoming more popular in recent years, free-riding attacks also got more attention; hence, industry and academia created several countermeasures.

One of the most recent solutions is ZFree, published by Liu et al. [15]. The solution proposes the cooperation of the CP, ISP, and an ISP assistant. Initially, the CP and the ISP assistant will establish a secure connection between each other. To check the network traffic for free-riding traffic, the CP will hash each network packet and send a message to the ISP over the origin network connection. In parallel, a hash of each packet is sent from the ISP to the ISP assistant. To verify the validity of the traffic, the ISP assistant compares the received hashes. As these hashes are generated at different places and sent over different channels, the packet's integrity is considered protected by Liu et al. The authors claim to prevent each known injection attacks that are used for free-riding attacks and state that "ZFree is formally verified and secure against free-riding attacks [15]".

Another work of Dusi et al. [5] focuses on the detection of tunnel-based free-riding attacks. The paper describes a traffic fingerprinting mechanism to identify tunnels in network traffic. The core idea is to integrate a statistical characterization mechanism at the IP layer to characterize traffic by observing network packets' length and inter-arrival time. In their evaluation, the approach achieves a detection rate of almost 100% by analyzing HTTP and SSH traffic [5]. Since their approach works without DPI, it can be used by ISPs and CPs.

The presented frameworks propose to secure zero-rating against free-riding attacks. However, in Sect. 6 we will point out the fundamental misconception of these solutions when applied in the context of secure Internet services.

3   The Threat of Free-Riding Attacks

To built upon previous research, we have adopted the threat model created by Liu et al., describing mainly three parties and how they interact [15]:

- The **user** accessing the Internet and specific applications that are zero-rated. A user can profit if she avoids costs by exploiting zero-rated services with free-riding attacks.
- The **ISP** providing the Internet access and facilitating zero-rating on a technical level. The ISP profits if no user can execute a free-riding attack and they have to pay their bills. Thus, ISPs want to mitigate all free-riding attacks and increase their profits.
- The **CP** providing a zero-rated service that wants to improve its performance to profit from a growing user base. A CP is interested in zero-rating to outperform its competitors but needs protection from free-riding attacks.

In reality, things can be quite different, e.g., ISP and CP can be the same entity, or in other cases, ISP and CP do not want to protect each other. Hence, motivational aspects of establishing zero-rating practices play an essential role when looking at each party's willingness to secure a service. With respect to the user role, several use cases can be conceived to substantiate the user's motivation to execute an attack, e.g., when we imagine the following scenarios:

- A user in a developing country without mobile Internet access has zero-rated Facebook access via Free Basics [6].
- A user abroad downloads a large file over a limited data connection but has zero-rated access to a cloud service provider.
- A user on an airplane wants to browse the web but only has limited access to instant messaging service.
- A user in China cannot access foreign internet contents but has unrestricted access to a secure instant messaging service.
- A user has limited or restricted Internet access at work but unrestricted access to a VoIP call service.

As we see, various use cases for free-riding attacks can be conceived and might resonate with some of our own experiences. Moreover, free-riding attacks do not only exist to avoid billing but also due to political and economic restrictions.

4   Building Free-Riding Tunnels

This section will explain how tunneling can be utilized to build free-riding attacks via secure Internet services. We explain how tunneling works in general, what devices are used for a real attack setup, and how we implemented the tunnel for messaging, cloud storage, and VoIP services.

4.1   General Tunneling Technique

The core idea of tunneling is to encapsulate application traffic into another application's traffic. This way, the tunneled application can be hidden from controlling network devices between the tunnel entry and endpoint. While only a specific protocol is allowed for the tunnel entry, the tunnel endpoint needs unrestricted or less limited Internet access.

To draw a more concrete picture, we can imagine a user accessing a WIFI hotspot. Without paying the hotspot provider, the HTTP traffic will be blocked. Nevertheless, DNS messages can be exchanged because they are necessary to establish communication. Hence, the real traffic can be encapsulated and sent to a self-hosted DNS service with unrestricted Internet access using DNS messages. This endpoint resolves the tunneled requests and sends the response to the user within a DNS response message.

This idea of tunneling data through other layers can also be applied to create unrestricted Internet access in mobile networks via zero-rated services. Like a DNS tunnel, the solution requires a specific setup that needs preparation.

4.2   Attack Setup

The attacker needs at least one device with some form of zero-rated access and a tunnel endpoint device, e.g., at home, with unrestricted Internet access. For our attacks, we used the following devices and services:

- 1x Samsung Galaxy S3 mini running Android 4.1.2.
- 2x HP Elitebook 840 (Intel Core i5-6300 (2.40 GHz), 16 GB DDR4 RAM, 256 GB SSD, Ubuntu 18.04.5 LTS)
- 1x pre-paid sim card with zero-rating options
- 1 × 8 Mbit unrestricted DSL connection "at home"

These components will be arranged as depicted in Fig. 1. In our setup, all devices are located in our office. The mobile device has full 4G connectivity, and the home client is connected via cable to a 1 Gbit internet connection. Depending on the targeted service, a specific mobile network must be selected, and a SIM card must be available. In our case, we have chosen a Portuguese network provider that offers five zero-rating packages called: Video, Social, Music, Messaging, and Cloud. Moreover, the provider also zero-rate its own cloud, TV, and navigation services free of charge. To book one of the packages, the user needs to i) access a specific website of the network service provider, ii) enter his mobile

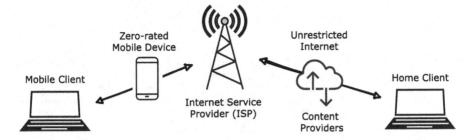

Fig. 1. A basic setup for a free-riding attack against a zero-rated service.

phone number, and iii) select a package. In our case, we selected the Messaging package for €4.99 per month, which includes 12 different messaging services, e.g., Skype, WhatsApp, Telegram, WeChat, etc. In addition, we booked the Cloud package for €4.99 per month, including Google Drive, Microsoft OneDrive, and Apple iCloud. In comparison, a general data plan costs €9.99 for 1 GB or €14.99 for 5 GB useable within a month. As requested by the network provider, we will not publish the name of the affected company.

4.3   Free-Riding via Instant Messaging

In the following, we explain how to build a free-riding attack via a zero-rated instant messaging service. We use the Telegram chat in our example, which we chose for its open and simple API. To establish the communication via Telegram we used the TDLib (Telegram Database Library), a cross-platform library to automate Telegram clients. Based on the Telegram chat, we built a document-based HTTP proxy that can transport even large files of up to 1.5 GB. A general overview of our implementation is depicted in Fig. 2.

Tunnel Entry Point. The tunnel entry point is built out of two components: an HTTP proxy and a server application to send and receive messages over the tunnel. The HTTP proxy allows a user to access the tunnel. A user only needs to add a proxy to the browser configuration; after the tunnel is initiated, and the communication is routed automatically through the zero-rated tunnel. We implemented the proxy using the Python Flask framework [18]. The tunnel interface is implemented using the python modul **python-pytun** [17]. The user provides credentials for two user accounts of the corresponding tunnel entry and endpoint to initiate the tunnel. The login will be verified with the registered mobile device. Afterward, the tunnel interface will be assigned to a static IP. To connect the tunnel interface to the unrestricted Internet, the tunnel entry-point has to route the traffic accordingly. Usually, the default route goes to the tunnel interface and IP of the tunnel endpoint, which acts as a gateway. Additionally, another route needs to be added to pass the Telegram traffic through the regular connection. From this point on, all packets received at the tunnel interface are

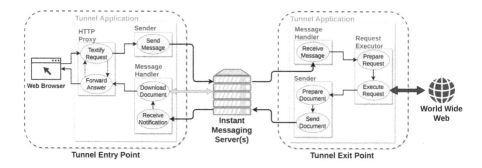

Fig. 2. HTTP tunnel through a zero-rated instant messaging service.

sent to the sender. The sender encodes each message with Base64 and sends the instant messages via `send_message()` to the tunnel endpoint.

After a message is sent, the message handler waits for the corresponding answer. To receive a message, the message handler needs to be registered to `TDlib`. The handler is called every time a new notification arrives via Telegram. This includes messages and notifications of other users' online status or the creation of new chats. The implemented message handler filters all the relevant messages decodes them and passes them back to the tunnel entry.

To receive a message, the message handler is registered to `TDlib` as well and will be called whenever a new notification arrives. At one point in time, a notification is pushed to the message handler by the instant messaging servers. In our case, the notification includes a caption and ID of the new message that needs to be fetched by the message handler of `TDlib` using the `downloadFile()` function and the corresponding ID. When receiving the file, the message handler delivers the caption and document back to the HTTP proxy. The caption contains the HTTP response string, headers, and the document containing the payload of the HTTP response. In the end, the HTTP proxy compiles the valid HTTP response from this and pass it to the tunnel entry point.

Tunnel End Point. The tunnel endpoint components appear similar to the entry point. Instead of the HTTP proxy, it uses a request executor that forwards each HTTP request received from the tunnel interface. The execution is implemented using the Pythons `requests` module.

Based on the presented approach, any HTTP request can be passed between tunnel entry and endpoint to allow web browsing via a zero-rated Telegram chat. For our proof-of-concept implementation, we only support the HTTP `GET` method. Furthermore parallel, and out-of-order execution is not considered. To lower the number of requests over the tunnel, the request executor can resolve all external page elements of a website on its own. To do this, we request and merge all website elements into a single HTML file using the Python module `webpage2html`.

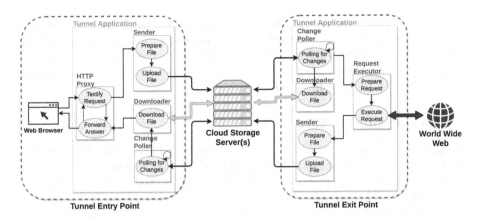

Fig. 3. HTTP tunnel through a zero-rated cloud storage service.

4.4 Free-Riding via Cloud Storage

Another example for free-riding attacks against zero-rated services can be created via cloud storage services such as Google Drive. To build a tunnel, the Google Drive API needs to be automated, e.g., by using a dedicated Python library such as `google-api-python-client` [8]. To initiate the Google Drive API, a Google Cloud project has to be created. In this project, we activated the Google Drive API to retrieve our personal API key. The API is limited to one billion queries per day and 10 queries per second for each project user. Instead of sending direct messages, like in the previous solution, the two devices will communicate by up- and downloading files through the cloud storage service. Hence, a shared storage location for the two user devices has to be created. We decided to use two separate accounts and two shared folders to reduce the risk of reaching the API limits. Each folder is assigned to one tunnel point and hence appears like a unidirectional communication channel. To send messages, a file is uploaded to the respective folder connected to the tunnel entry or endpoint. To receive messages, each tunnel point will regularly poll its respective folder for new content. Each new file that appears is considered as an incoming message. Thus, a simple communication through the cloud storage service has been established.

The implemented modules and how their interaction can be seen in Fig. 3. In general, we have refactored large parts of our Telegram solution since both solutions are very similar. The main differences are an additional pull mechanism and adopting the new API functions and limits for the cloud storage service. For example, to send files, the files need to be prepared and created on the cloud storage beforehand, using `files().create()`. Like the HTTP proxy and request executor, other components did not change and work like described in the previous solution. The polling mechanism is implemented on both sides. It will send out eight requests per second, which is closely below the API limits and can be adjusted by the user. On occurring changes, the polling mechanism will notify and forward a file ID to a downloading component. It will download the file with the `files().get_media()` function. Depending on which side of the tunnel, the file will be forwarded to the request executor or passed to the HTTP proxy. Similar to the previous solution, the created tunnel can be used for HTTP communication, but also allows the user to download large media files through the zero-rated connection.

4.5   Free-Riding via VoIP Calls

In our third free-riding attack, we create a tunnel using the UDP payloads of a VoIP call service without modifying the VoIP client. As requested by the service provider, we can not publish the name of the affected product and company.

In general, VoIP calls will be executed via peer-to-peer connections. However, when the user devices are behind a NAT service, a so-called TURN server will relay the communication between the two parties. For our attack, we use this communication to pass through the traffic by rewriting the contents of the sent packets. The created application flow is shown in Fig. 4.

The biggest challenge when creating the tunnel setup is to enable the two endpoints to rewrite the package contents in an automated way, since both ends need to know the IP and UDP port of the established connection. To do this, we extract the connection details from the SIP messages exchanged during the call establishment. On the caller side, the REMOTE_ADDRESS attribute of the STUN messages is extracted, while for the callee, the X-MAPPED-ADDRESS attribute from the Allocate Success Response message is used. This procedure can be different when using another service provider. To extract these details we use the Python scapy package [21]. After collecting the required session details, the injecting devices can manipulate parts of the UDP data stream and tunnel the traffic through the VoIP connection. To differentiate between the modified and the unmodified UDP packets, a 4-byte magic number is added to the payload. Using iptables, the injecting devices can filter the network packets to find the manipulated ones.

The tunnel entry and endpoints are very different from those of the previous two approaches. The sender receives the packet from a tunnel interface and forges a UDP packet with the corresponding TURN server IP, port, the magic number, and the packet contents. Afterward, the sender sends the packet to the TURN server. To improve the performance of the components, a raw socket is used to send the packets, while scapy provides the packet forging template. To receive packets, the receiver uses a socket as well. This socket is bound directly to the network interface with a Berkeley Packet Filter (BPF). The BPF checks for the appropriate IP addresses, ports, and identifier sequence. This way, the injected traffic can be filtered. The BPF is implemented in assembly based on an example created by Allan Boll [2]. Overall, the created interface allows very efficient packet injections into the active VoIP connection to arbitrary tunnel data through a zero-rated VoIP connection. Since VoIP applications need to be robust, we assume that the manipulated packets are simply ignored and dropped by the VoIP clients. However, even if the packets get validated by the client, our tool supports a feature to manipulate only the media contents of a data stream.

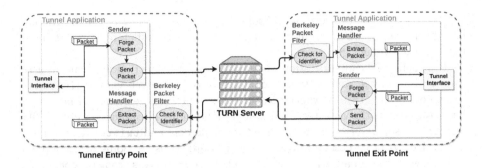

Fig. 4. Layer 3 tunnel through a zero-rated VoIP service.

When establishing the tunnel interfaces, an application can be configured to use the created communication link. To implement this, we used QUICHE, an open QUIC implementation with a low-level API that already provides an easy-to-use example for our use case [4]. For the sake of comparability, we hosted a QUIC HTTP server on our home client that runs HTTP via UDP and can be accessed through the proxy with any compatible browser, such as Chromium.

5 Evaluation

After we presented how free-riding attacks against zero-rated services can be implemented, we now evaluate how the tunnels perform in terms of usability and performance.

For all experiments, we used the setup as defined in Sect. 4.2. However, the measurements will also depend on other factors, like network connectivity, devices, network stacks, ISP provider, communication distance, etc. Hence, the presented results can only give a limited impression of the tunnel performance. Another setup might cause other results. Nevertheless, the measurements allow us to compare the different approaches of the tunnel with each other and understand their limitations. The experiments described here took place between January and mid-February 2021.

5.1 Usability

This work discusses three HTTP tunnels for three different service types: instant messaging, cloud storage, and VoIP. First, we will discuss the usability of the tunnels and, secondly, measure their performance. To examine the usability, the Alexa top 50 websites of the United States and their basic functionality are tested using the implemented HTTP proxy. Without any optimization, the total loading time of a website was very high due to the high number of requests. To improve this, merging the contents before transmission through the tunnel is recommended. Another way to reduce the load time is to disable JavaScript. Of course, this will remove a lot of functionality, but also reduce the amount of third-party content. Concerning the paper's goal, we will focus on the results that have been created when loading and merging the website before transmitting it through the tunnel.

In general, we can state, that the most basic web functionality can be used through the tunnel, such as `wikipedia.org` or online search via `google.com` or `bing.com`. Some of the advanced features like search suggestions did not work, but besides that, the websites are usable. Furthermore, e-commerce websites like `amazon.de`, social media networks like `facebook.com`, and `twitter.com` or news media like `nytimes.com` and `cnn.com` are working as usual. Some other popular services we tested in addition, such as `youtube.com` or `maps.google.com`, could not be loaded successfully, most probably due to their heavy use of JavaScript.

We measured an average load time for the top 50 websites of 12.65 s using an automated browsing session. This load time will vary depending on various factors such as content size, connection setup, user location, etc. The average load time for the 50 websites without an active tunnel though the same mobile connection was 1.83 s, which is approx. $\frac{1}{10}$ of the time required by a tunneled connection.

Besides web browsing, the HTTP tunnels can also be used to download large files. We successfully downloaded a Linux image (650 MB) and a set of MP3 files (52 MB in total) for our usability test. For each case, the download time increased by a multiple of the non-tunneled download duration. Compared to the non-tunneled test, the Google Drive tunnel took approx. 3× as long, while the Telegram and VoIP chat took approx. 2.2× as long when using the same mobile connection. The long delays result from the fact that each file has to be downloaded by the tunnel endpoint first, and only then will it be available for transmission through the tunnel. Nevertheless, while the data transfer takes more time, it is free of charge and hence represents a practical application considering the use cases from Sect. 3.

5.2 Performance

Since the created tunnels underly different properties, we want to figure out the technical limits of each tunnel.

First, we will analyze the Google Cloud tunnel. To evaluate its performance, we created 1000 random files of 1 KB and sent them through the tunnel. Thereby we measured upload, notification, and download time. The results of these measurements are shown in Fig. 5. As we see, the notification time is the bottleneck of this approach due to the polling every 125ms. On the right-hand side, the average time to download a file through the tunnel is shown. Downloading is much quicker than uploading, which stays roughly below 1 s. In total, the average overhead to transfer a 1KB message is around two seconds. In summary, the Google Drive tunnel does not allow low latency communication but allows parallel file transfer and is well suited for large data transmissions.

We can not create such a detailed measurement for Telegram and the VoIP tunnel because we do not control the individual components. For Telegram, the used `TDLib` library will handle the file transfer on its own. Hence, as shown

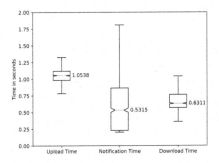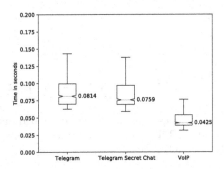

Fig. 5. Measuring the transmission time of 1000 random 1KB messages through the Google Drive (left), Telegram and VoIP tunnel (right). Whisker lengths for the Google Drive case are $Q3 + 1.5 * IQR$ (upper) and $Q1 - 1.5 * IQR$ (lower). Whisker lengths for the Telegram and VoIP case are $Q3 + 1.5 * IQR$ (upper) and $Q1 - 1.5 * IQR$ (lower).

in Fig. 5, we can only measure the full transmission time, which starts when a message is sent and stops when the other end is notified. As shown in Fig. 5, the transmission time is on average beneath 100 ms. Since we can disable the secret chat option, we tried, in addition, to measure what difference this makes. Interestingly, the secret chat results are slightly lower than those of the default chat. However, this difference should not be overrated because network properties represent the most dominant factor.

Likewise, we measured the full transmission time of the VoIP tunnel. As we see in Fig. 5, the VoIP latency is even lower compared to the Telegram tunnel and approx. 400 times smaller compared to the Google Drive case. When comparing the cloud service, we can observe that the time overhead is measurable higher than the other two services. This confirms our expected performance difference. As it was mentioned, instant messaging and VoIP services are built to deliver content very quickly and with low latency. Unlike the other approaches, the VoIP tunnel does not induce a remarkable overhead because packets are sent and immediately forwarded by the TURN server without further processing. Moreover, the TURN server is optimized for fast packet forwarding to enable low latency for seamless VoIP connections. Hence, the VoIP tunnel has the lowest latency among all tunnel approaches.

We evaluated the download speed for the Google Drive, Telegram, and VoIP tunnels with another measurement. We created 10 random files with a size of 100 MB on a remote web server. Afterward, we requested each of the files from the mobile user device through the tunnels. During the measurement, all other network connectivity was disabled.

As we can see in Fig. 6, we can approximate that a file download takes more than twice as long as it will take to download the file directly. In some cases, it will even take roughly 3 × as long compared to a non-tunneled setup. This result depends on the setup since our Lab is connected to a 10 Gbit Internet connection. This allows us to up- and download files to the tunnel end device very fast. Hence,

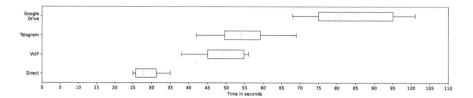

Fig. 6. Measurements for the download duration through each of the tunnels for a set of 100 MB files with random file contents. At $t = 0$ the download has been initiated by the mobile client.

in our case, the bottleneck is the download speed of the mobile network. With another setup, the upload speed of the tunnel end device might impair the results much more than it has done in our setup. This is because Internet connections at home are often asynchronous (download $>>$ upload speed) which impairs the file transfer. However, the task of up-and downloading files via zero-rated tunnels is an excellent use-case for the presented attacks when assuming the tunnel end device is connected to a high-speed internet connection.

6   Discussion

In the following, we will discuss and interpret our findings. We discuss the limitations and also elaborate on some advanced ideas.

6.1   All Tunnels are Different but Useful

Given the results from the previous section, we can see that each of the free-riding attacks enables Internet connectivity, but also comes with specific limitations and features. One of the easiest setups appears to be the Telegram tunnel; however, download file size and latency are only mediocre. The best solution to download large files via zero-rated connections seems to be the Cloud Storage approach. However, it suffers from the highest latency compared to all other solutions. The VoIP tunnel appears to be a universal solution; however, there are various obstacles to overcome, and much expertise is required to create and maintain the setup. Overall, the presented tunnels are maybe not the most novel, innovative or robust solutions, but they exist to prove a point. Secured Internet services combined with zero-rating can be used to smuggle arbitrary data, allowing cheap and unrestricted mobile communication. With just a little effort and some future developments, e.g., 5G networks, the presented solutions can be leveraged into many applications and enable people to get unrestricted internet access.

6.2   Countermeasures

During our experiments, we have not experienced any substantial impairment by the ISP or CP. Therefore, we either assume that there are no countermeasures in place, or they are not effective. Moreover, the affected provider does not answer our questions if countermeasures are in place to mitigate free-riding attacks like presented. Nevertheless, we want to describe how countermeasures, such as API limits, bandwidth limits, and traffic fingerprinting techniques, can be established to mitigate the proposed attacks.

API limits ensure that a user can make only a fixed number of requests in a specific time frame to the API. The limits are created to limit the number of resources used through the API, but also to mitigate risk, e.g., prevent denial-of-service attacks. In many cases, these limits will enforce a boundary on the tunnel's efficiency and render various tunnel approaches unreasonable. Hence, we designed the tunnels to stay slightly beneath the limits. For the VoIP tunnel those API limits do not exist, but other sanitation mechanisms can be in place. In conclusion, API limits can provide a very useful measurement against the effectiveness of tunnels, but they can not mitigate them entirely.

Bandwidth limits can be established by the ISP and the CP to enforce a maximum throughput on the zero-rated connection. Nevertheless, just like API limits, they can limit the tunnels' effectiveness while also creating issues for benign operations. For example, VoIP audio calls require way less bandwidth than VoIP. Hence, when strictly enforcing appropriate bandwidth limitations can easily protect some implementations. On the other hand, VoIP video services with high-quality demands are good targets since bandwidth requirements are very high.

Traffic fingerprinting is the process of analyzing the application traffic of each user to identify fraudulent patterns or anomalies to detect malicious users. For our research, we had a closer look at two solutions, introduced in Sect. 2.4.

The first solution, called Tunnel Hunter, is proposed by Dusi et al. [5]. The authors claim to identify tunnels using a statistical fingerprinting mechanism at the IP layer that will analyze the inter-arrival time of network packets [5]. Since their approach works without DPI, it can be used by ISPs as well as CPs. Given the proposed attacks, we see two major disadvantages with this approach. First, Tunnel Hunter will bind many resources and cannot deal with long-living sessions in real-time. Secondly, the communication is cryptographically secured; hence packet contents will be padded to mitigate side-channel attacks. This will greatly impair any traffic analysis and hence blind the Tunnel Hunter analysis as well.

Another solution is called ZFree and has been introduced by Liu et al. [15]. In summary, ZFree will try to find tunnels by fingerprinting the transferred traffic between ISP and CP. While this integrity check allows to detect attacks that rewrite packet contents, such as the request masquerading and response modification attacks, it can not mitigate tunnels via secured Internet services. The application traffic does not change on its route through the network and is only de- and encapsulated on the user's end devices.

In summary, the proposed countermeasures can not be effective since they typically rely on the detection of malformed traffic. They assume exploitation of lower-level protocols, while free-riding attacks via secure services will keep the integrity of the application traffic and use features on a higher level, which are in most cases confidential.

6.3   Effective Protection Against Secured Free-Riding Attacks

As diverse as the presented tunnels are, as diverse the mitigations have to be designed to prevent free-riding attacks. For some specific types of zero-rating services, a collaboration between ISP and CPs can be considered to detect malicious traffic. One example is the Google Drive tunnel because the CP has the right and possibility to examine the user's content. However, such a countermeasure will be in great conflict with the user trust, privacy, and goals of secure Internet services. Furthermore, this implies that the CP wants to collaborate with the ISP, which is not always the case. However, the ISP can enforce rules or policies that force CPs to mitigate free-riding attacks as best as they can. We think one of the best solutions will be to implement certain thresholds and limits for each user to render most free-riding attacks useless. Based on this, the affected vendor has already implemented the volume for each zero-rating package to a maximum amount of 10 GB. However, the zero-rated volume is still cheaper than the general data volume, and the cloud services of the ISP itself are still available without any limitation.

Maybe, mitigations alone will not solve the underlying issue. New ways will be found to create similar attacks, as we have learned from the times of Phreaking. In the future, new attacks will be executed by injecting data into video streams or into 5G high-bandwidth channels dedicated to special functions, such as car-to-car communications or emergency services. Hence, another solution to counter the growing thread of free-riding attacks can be found on an economic and political level. Mobile communication networks should not be restricted by artificial paywalls that only exist for monetary interest. Just like the flat-pricing models have become the default for cabled Internet connections, a similar model should be implemented for mobile networks. The ISPs can still profit from the volume-based tariffs, ensuring an equal distribution of costs to all users.

7   Conclusion

On our route to overcome the zero-rating practice of ISPs, we have evaluated several free-riding attacks. These attacks are intended to provide a technical argument against the growing adoption of zero-rating services. As we see, the large diversity of Internet services create various ways to bypass and exploit zero-rating offers to get unlimited Internet access for little money.

The extensive adoption of cryptography has further exaggerated this problem because countermeasures that maybe worked so far are now rendered ineffective. When the communication between the user device and the CP is secure, the ISP alone can not detect and defend against zero-rating attacks that are driven through the application layer. The only way to identify such an attack will be to cooperate with the CP if he is willing to help. However, for many applications, such as messaging services or VoIP applications, the communication will even be end-to-end encrypted, making the detection very difficult. As we see, the concurrent adoption of zero-rating services and secure web services with large bandwidth requirements can heavily amplify free-riding attacks and make them almost inevitable.

With our work, we don't want to discuss the presented attacks only; we want to shed light on the general conflict between zero-rating practices and secure Internet services. In our opinion, the best solution to this problem is not on a technical level. When net neutrality policies are enforced, the ISP cannot treat Internet traffic differently, which keeps the freedom of information exchange and fosters competition and innovation. This was essential for the growth of the Internet, and it will be necessary for its future. Likewise, this problem should not be imported into the future generation of networks, like 5G network slicing, which allows the creation of isolated networks with different priorities. A paying client can dynamically allocate the virtual slices to improve their service. In the end, prioritizing one application also means another one will be deprioritized [16]. We assume that free-riding attacks, as implemented in this work, can be used to abuse features, such as network slicing, to drive traffic through virtual high-speed networks. As we see, the issue is already adopted into the next generation of mobile networks and might create just another way for free-riding attacks.

The underlying reason why free-riding attacks exist is not only due to vulnerable protocols. It is a self-imposed issue created by Internet Service Providers that try to create artificial walls within a system that is free and open by design, such as the Internet.

Acknowledgement. The authors want to thank the Review Committee for the valuable feedback and comments. The project has received funding from the European Union's Horizon 2020 research and innovation program under grant agreement No 952684. Opinions, views, and conclusions are those of the authors and do not reflect the views of anyone else.

References

1. Aetha, DotEcon Ltd, European Commission, Directorate-General for Competition, Oswell Vahida: Zero-Rating Practices in Broadband Markets: Final Report (2017). http://dx.publications.europa.eu/10.2763/002126
2. Allan Riordan Boll: Allan's Blog: Raw sockets with BPF in Python (2011). http://allanrbo.blogspot.com/2011/12/raw-sockets-with-bpf-in-python.html
3. Carrillo, A.J.: Having Your Cake and Eating it Too? Zero-Rating, Net Neutrality and International Law (2016). https://papers.ssrn.com/abstract=2746447
4. Cloudflare Inc.: QUICHE an implementation of the quic transport protocol and http/3 as specified by the IETF. https://github.com/cloudflare/quiche
5. Dusi, M., Crotti, M., Gringoli, F., Salgarelli, L.: Tunnel Hunter: Detecting application-layer tunnels with statistical fingerprinting 53(1), 81–97 (2009). https://doi.org/10.1016/j.comnet.2008.09.010. http://www.sciencedirect.com/science/article/pii/S1389128608003071

6. Facebook: Fast and Free Facebook Mobile Access with 0.facebook.com (2010). https://web.archive.org/web/20140116060937/, http://www.facebook.com/notes/facebook/fast-and-free-facebook-mobile-access-with-0facebookcom/391295167130

7. Go, Y., Jeong, E., Won, J., Kim, Y., Kune, D.F., Park, K.: Gaining Control of Cellular Traffic Accounting by Spurious TCP Retransmission. In: NDSS Symposium 2014 (2014). https://doi.org/10.14722/ndss.2014.23118

8. Google: Googleapis/google-api-python-client (2020). https://github.com/googleapis/google-api-python-client

9. Internet.org: Free Basics by Facebook - Apps on Google Play (2020). https://play.google.com/store/apps/details?id=com.freebasics&hl=en

10. Internet.org: Internet.org - Our Mission (2020). https://info.internet.org/en/mission/

11. Kakhki, A.M., Li, F., Choffnes, D., Katz-Bassett, E., Mislove, A.: BingeOn under the microscope: understanding T-mobiles zero-rating implementation. In: Proceedings of the 2016 Workshop on QoE-Based Analysis and Management of Data Communication Networks, Internet-QoE 2016, pp. 43–48. Association for Computing Machinery (2016). https://doi.org/10.1145/2940136.2940140

12. Kraemer, J., Wiewiorra, L., Weinhardt, C.: Net neutrality: A progress report 37(9), 794–813. https://doi.org/10.1016/j.telpol.2012.08.005, http://www.sciencedirect.com/science/article/pii/S0308596112001450

13. Lapsley, P.: Exploding the Phone. Grove Press (2014)

14. Li, C.Y., et al.: Insecurity of voice solution VoLTE in LTE mobile networks. In: Proceedings of the 22nd ACM SIGSAC Conference on Computer and Communications Security, CCS 2015, pp. 316–327. Association for Computing Machinery. https://doi.org/10.1145/2810103.2813618

15. Liu, Z., Zhang, Z., Cao, Y., Xi, Z., Jing, S., Roche, H.L.: Towards a Secure Zero-rating Framework with Three Parties, pp. 711–728 (2018). https://www.usenix.org/node/217562

16. Lohninger, T.: 5G and Net Neutrality (2019). https://media.ccc.de/v/36c3-10711-5g_neutrality

17. montag451: Montag451/pytun (2020). https://github.com/montag451/pytun

18. Online, H.: Eugh: Zero rating verletzt netzneutralitaet (2020). https://www.heise.de/news/EuGH-Zero-Rating-verletzt-Netzneutralitaet-4894216.html

19. pallets: The python micro framework for building web applications (2020). https://github.com/pallets/flask

20. Peng, C., Li, C.y., Tu, G.H., Lu, S., Zhang, L.: Mobile data charging: New attacks and countermeasures. In: Proceedings of the 2012 ACM Conference on Computer and Communications Security, CCS 2012, pp. 195–204. Association for Computing Machinery. https://doi.org/10.1145/2382196.2382220

21. Philippe Biondi: Secdev/scapy (2020). https://github.com/secdev/scapy

22. ProSec GmbH: Die schwachstelle in fast allen hotspots!—prosec (2017). https://www.prosec-networks.com/blog/nach-wannacry-prosec-wannasurf/

23. Service, C.R.: The Net Neutrality Debate: Access to Broadband Networks. CreateSpace Independent Publishing Platform, crs report r40616–2018 edition edn

24. Solon, O.: 'It's digital colonialism': How Facebook's free internet service has failed its users (2017). https://www.theguardian.com/technology/2017/jul/27/facebook-free-basics-developing-markets

25. T-Mobile: Free Unlimited Streaming — Music Freedom Simple Choice Plan — T-Mobile (2020). https://www.t-mobile.com/offers/free-music-streaming

26. Lohninger, T., et al.: Report: The Net Neutrality Situation in the EU (2019). https://epicenter.works/sites/default/files/2019_eu-epicenter.works-r1.pdf
27. Wikimedia Foundation: Wikipedia Zero - Wikimedia Foundation Governance Wiki (2018). https://foundation.wikimedia.org/wiki/Wikipedia_Zero
28. Wu, T.: Network Neutrality, Broadband Discrimination (2003). https://scholarship.law.columbia.edu/faculty_scholarship/1281

Function-Private Conditional Disclosure of Secrets and Multi-evaluation Threshold Distributed Point Functions

Nolan Miranda[1,3], Foo Yee Yeo[2], and Vipin Singh Sehrawat[1(✉)]

[1] Seagate Technology, Fremont, CA, USA
[2] Seagate Technology, Singapore, Singapore
[3] Stanford University, Stanford, USA

Abstract. Conditional disclosure of secrets (CDS) allows multiple parties to reveal a secret to a third party if and only if some pre-decided condition is satisfied. In this work, we bolster the privacy guarantees of CDS by introducing function-private CDS wherein the pre-decided condition is never revealed to the third party. We also derive a function secret sharing scheme from our function-private CDS solution. The second problem that we consider concerns threshold distributed point functions, which allow one to split a point function such that at least a threshold number of shares are required to evaluate it at any given input. We consider a setting wherein a point function is split among a set of parties such that multiple evaluations do not leak non-negligible information about it.

1 Introduction

In 1994, De Santis et al. [1] introduced the concept of function secret sharing (FSS) as a special case of secret sharing [2,3] wherein a class $\mathcal{F}$ of efficiently computable and succinctly described functions $f_i : \{0,1\}^\ell \longrightarrow \mathbb{G}$, where $\mathbb{G}$ is a group, is shared among a set of parties. FSS allows a dealer to randomly split an arbitrary function $f \in \mathcal{F}$ into $n \geq 2$ shares $\{f_i\}_{i=1}^n$ such that only authorized subsets of shares can be combined to evaluate or to reconstruct f. In 2014, Gilboa and Ishai [4] considered a specialization of FSS called distributed point functions (DPF), which is an FSS scheme for a family of point functions $\mathcal{P}(A, B) = \{p_{a,b} : a \in A, b \in B\}$, whose members are defined as:

$$p_{a,b}(x) = \begin{cases} b & x = a, \\ 0 & \text{otherwise.} \end{cases}$$

A DPF scheme is said to be threshold if for some fixed $t \leq n$, all subsets of function shares $\{p_i\}_{i=1}^n$ with cardinality at least t can be used to reconstruct $p_{a,b}$. DPF has found applications in privacy-preserving primitives such as private information retrieval [4] and private contact tracing [5].

© Springer Nature Switzerland AG 2021
M. Conti et al. (Eds.): CANS 2021, LNCS 13099, pp. 334–354, 2021.
https://doi.org/10.1007/978-3-030-92548-2_18

The second topic whose existing solutions we improve upon is called conditional disclosure of secrets (CDS) [6], which allows two or more parties, holding some input, to share a secret s with an external party Carol such that s is revealed only if some fixed condition holds on the joint input and shared randomness of the parties. The condition is often encoded as some Boolean condition function $h : \mathcal{C} \to \{0, 1\}$. The parties are allowed to send a single message to Carol which may depend on their "shares" and shared randomness. CDS has found multiple applications in cryptography, including private information retrieval [6], attribute-based encryption [7], priced oblivious transfer [8] and secret sharing for uniform/general/forbidden/graph access structures [9–13].

1.1 Our Contributions

Function-Private CDS. Content-based filtering is a tried and tested subroutine used in generating content recommendations. It generates the intended information for users by comparing representations of information search to those of the contents extracted from user profiles, indicating users' interests. Recently, streaming services have been establishing collaborations wherein they provide services and content recommendations based on their combined data. For instance, Spotify, Hulu and Showtime announced such a collaboration in 2018 [14]. Moreover, almost all major streaming services have migrated to the cloud [15–17]. We know from [18–20] that it is possible for these streaming services to encode their content recommendations generating content-based filtering as Boolean functions, which reveal the recommendations for various demographics only when the function evaluates to "true". Since multiple collaborating service providers use the same cloud for their data and recommendations' generation, the third-party cloud service provider serves as Carol in these settings. Hence, CDS fits well in such settings. However, with their services outsourced to the cloud, the service provides may want to hide information about their recommendations suggesting algorithms. Hence, it is desirable to have a CDS scheme that hides the condition function(s) from Carol, even after the secret, i.e., recommendations for the target demographic, are revealed.

We address this requirement by introducing function-private CDS, which we define as follows: let h belong to a family $\mathcal{H} : \mathcal{C} \to \{0, 1\}$ of Boolean condition functions, then a function-private CDS scheme satisfies the following conditions:

1. Correctness: for every $c \in \mathcal{C}$, if it holds that $h(c) = 1$, then the correct secret s is revealed to Carol with probability 1. Else, if $h(c) = 0$, then Carol rejects with probability 1.
2. Secrecy: for any $c \in \mathcal{C}$ such that $h(c) = 0$, it holds that Carol cannot gain any information about the secret.
3. Function privacy: for certain conditions on the parties' inputs, it holds that no party has any non-negligible advantage in distinguishing the Boolean condition function $h \in \mathcal{H}$ from every $h' \in \mathcal{H}$, where $h'(c) = h(c)$.
4. Input privacy: for any $c, c' \in \mathcal{C}$ such that $h(c) = h(c')$, it holds that Carol has no non-negligible advantage in distinguishing between c and c'.

Function privacy has been studied in the context of functional encryption [21–26] but ours is the first scheme to achieve it for CDS. For an introduction to functional encryption, we refer the interested reader to [27].

Function-Private CDS to FSS. Given a function-private CDS scheme for k parties $P_1, \ldots, P_k$ (excluding Carol) for the family of Boolean condition functions $\mathcal{H}$, secret domain $\mathcal{S}$, and randomness r, we prove that there exists a k-out-of-k function secret sharing scheme for the family $\mathcal{H}$. To the best of our knowledge, this is the first derivation of FSS from CDS.

Multi-evaluation Threshold DPF. In an example in [28], Beimel et al. introduced threshold function secret sharing of a family of point functions $\mathcal{P}(A, B)$. We identify a weakness in that example. Specifically, their example approach leaks information about the point function $p_{a,b} \in \mathcal{P}(A, B)$ if multiple evaluations are performed. We rectify this issue by extending their solution such that repeated evaluations do not leak non-negligible information about $p_{a,b}$. Our scheme, called multi-evaluation threshold DPF, uses a key-homomorphic pseudorandom function (PRF) family.

Key-Homomorphic PRF: In a PRF family [29], each function is specified by a key such that it can be evaluated deterministically given the key whereas it behaves like a random function without the key. For a PRF F_k, the index k is called its key/seed. A PRF family F is called key-homomorphic if the set of keys has a group structure and if there is an efficient algorithm that, given $F_{k_1}(x)$ and $F_{k_2}(x)$, outputs $F_{k_1 \oplus k_2}(x)$, where $\oplus$ is the group operation [30].

Organization. The remaining text is organized as follows: Sect. 2 recalls the concepts required for the rest of the paper. In Sect. 3, we present our multi-evaluation threshold DPF scheme. In Sect. 4, we define function-private CDS and introduce the first scheme to realize it. In the same section, we provide a mechanism to extend any function-private CDS scheme into an FSS scheme.

2   Preliminaries

Definition 1 (Negligible Function). For security parameter λ, a function $\epsilon(\lambda)$ is called *negligible* if for all $c > 0$, there exists a λ_0 such that $\epsilon(\lambda) < 1/\lambda^c$ for all $\lambda > \lambda_0$.

Definition 2 (Computational Indistinguishability [31]). Let $X = \{X_\lambda\}_{\lambda \in \mathbb{N}}$ and $Y = \{Y_\lambda\}_{\lambda \in \mathbb{N}}$ be ensembles, where X_λ's and Y_λ's are probability distributions over $\{0, 1\}^{\kappa(\lambda)}$ for $\lambda \in \mathbb{N}$ and some polynomial $\kappa(\lambda)$. We say that $\{X_\lambda\}_{\lambda \in \mathbb{N}}$ and $\{Y_\lambda\}_{\lambda \in \mathbb{N}}$ are polynomially/computationally indistinguishable if the following holds for every (probabilistic) polynomial-time algorithm $\mathcal{D}$ and all $\lambda \in \mathbb{N}$:

$$\left| \Pr[t \leftarrow X_\lambda : \mathcal{D}(t) = 1] - \Pr[t \leftarrow Y_\lambda : \mathcal{D}(t) = 1] \right| \leq \epsilon(\lambda),$$

where ϵ is a negligible function.

Remark 1 (Perfect Indistinguishability). We say that $\{X_\lambda\}_{\lambda \in \mathbb{N}}$ and $\{Y_\lambda\}_{\lambda \in \mathbb{N}}$ are perfectly indistinguishable if the following holds for all t:

$$\Pr[t \leftarrow X_\lambda] = \Pr[t \leftarrow Y_\lambda].$$

Consider adversaries interacting as part of probabilistic games. For an adversary $\mathcal{A}$ and two games $\mathfrak{G}_0, \mathfrak{G}_1$ with which it can interact, $\mathcal{A}'s$ distinguishing advantage is: $Adv_{\mathfrak{G}_0, \mathfrak{G}_1}(\mathcal{A}) := \left| \Pr[\mathcal{A} \text{ accepts in } \mathfrak{G}_0] - \Pr[\mathcal{A} \text{ accepts in } \mathfrak{G}_1] \right|$. For security parameter λ and a negligible function ϵ, the two games are said to be computationally indistinguishable if it holds that: $Adv_{\mathfrak{G}_0, \mathfrak{G}_1}(\mathcal{A}) \leq \epsilon(\lambda)$.

Definition 3 (PRF). Let A and B be finite sets, and let $\mathcal{F} = \{F_k : A \to B\}$ be a function family, endowed with an efficiently sampleable distribution (more precisely, $\mathcal{F}$, A and B are all indexed by the security parameter λ). We say that $\mathcal{F}$ is a PRF family if the following two games are computationally indistinguishable:

1. Choose $F_k \in \mathcal{F}$ and give the adversary adaptive oracle access to $F_k(\cdot)$.
2. Choose a uniformly random function $U : A \to B$ and give the adversary adaptive oracle access to $U(\cdot)$.

Numerous PRF families with various useful properties have been constructed [30, 32–43]. For a detailed introduction to PRFs and review of the noteworthy results, we refer the interested reader to [44].

3   Multi-evaluation Threshold DPF

In this section, we introduce multi-evaluation threshold DPFs, and present a scheme to realize it.

Definition 4. Given a string $a \in \{0,1\}^\ell$ and a value $\alpha \in \mathbb{F}$, a computational multi-evaluation distributed point function scheme for a t-out-of-n threshold structure is defined as a collection of three algorithms (Gen, Eval, Rec) such that:

- A randomized algorithm Gen takes three inputs, $a \in \{0,1\}^\ell$, $\alpha \in \mathbb{F}$ and a security parameter $\lambda \in \mathbb{Z}^+$, and generates n keys $\{f_i\}_{i=1}^n$, representing secret shares of a dimension-2^ℓ vector $\mathbf{v}$ that has value $\alpha \in \mathbb{F}$ only at the a-th position and is zero at every other position.
- A deterministic algorithm Eval that takes three inputs, a key f_i ($i \in [n]$), $x \in \{0,1\}^\ell$ and some $r \in R$, and outputs a share s_i.
- A deterministic algorithm Rec that takes the outputs of Eval from t parties and outputs an element of $\mathbb{F}$.

These algorithms satisfy the following three conditions:

- *Computational Correctness:* for all strings $a \in \{0,1\}^{\ell}$, output values $\alpha \in \mathbb{F}$, $\lambda \in \mathbb{Z}^+$, $r \in R$, keys $\{f_i\}_{i=1}^n \leftarrow \mathsf{Gen}(a, \alpha, \lambda)$ and subsets $T \subseteq [n]$ of size t, it holds that: $\Pr\left[\mathsf{Rec}\left(\{\mathsf{Eval}(f_i, a, r)\}_{i \in T}\right) = \alpha\right] = 1$, and for all strings $x \in \{0,1\}^l$ such that $x \neq a$, $\Pr\left[\mathsf{Rec}\left(\{\mathsf{Eval}(f_i, x, r)\}_{i \in T}\right) = 0\right] > 1 - \mathsf{negl}(\lambda)$.
- *Perfect Secrecy:* for all strings $a, b \in \{0,1\}^{\ell}$, output values $\alpha, \beta \in \mathbb{F}$, $\lambda \in \mathbb{Z}^+$, keys $\{f_i\}_{i=1}^n \leftarrow \mathsf{Gen}(a, \alpha, \lambda)$ and $\{f_i'\}_{i=1}^n \leftarrow \mathsf{Gen}(b, \beta, \lambda)$ and subset $S \subset [n]$ of size $< t$, it holds that $\{f_i\}_{i \in S}$ and $\{f_i'\}_{i \in S}$ are perfectly indistinguishable.
- *Computational Multi-evaluation:* for all strings $a, b \in \{0,1\}^{\ell}$, output values $\alpha, \beta \in \mathbb{F}$, $\lambda \in \mathbb{Z}^+$, keys $\{f_i\}_{i=1}^n \leftarrow \mathsf{Gen}(a, \alpha, \lambda)$ and $\{f_i'\}_{i=1}^n \leftarrow \mathsf{Gen}(b, \beta, \lambda)$, it holds for all strings $x_1, x_2, \ldots, x_m \neq a, b$ and $r_1, r_2, \ldots, r_m \in R$ distinct, and subset $S \subset [n]$ of size $< t$, that:

$$\left(\{f_i\}_{i \in S}, \{\mathsf{Eval}(f_i, x_h, r_h)\}_{i \in [n], h \in [m]}\right), \left(\{f_i'\}_{i \in S}, \{\mathsf{Eval}(f_i', x_h, r_h)\}_{i \in [n], h \in [m]}\right)$$

are computationally indistinguishable w.r.t λ.

3.1 n-out-of-n Multi-evaluation DPF

Here, we describe an n-out-of-n computational multi-evaluation DPF for the class of point functions $\mathcal{P}\left(\{0,1\}^{\ell}, \mathbb{F}\right)$, where $\mathbb{F} = \mathbb{F}_q$ is the finite field with cardinality q. Let $\mathcal{F} = \{F^{(\lambda)} : \mathcal{K}^{(\lambda)} \times R \to \mathbb{F}^{2\ell + \lambda + 1}\}$ be a family of key-homomorphic PRFs such that the advantage of any polynomial-time adversary in distinguishing $F^{(\lambda)}$ from random is negligible in λ, and such that $F^{(\lambda)}(k_1 + k_2, r) = F^{(\lambda)}(k_1, r) + F^{(\lambda)}(k_2, r)$ for all $k_1, k_2 \in \mathcal{K}^{(\lambda)}$ and $r \in R$. Write $F^{(\lambda)} = (F_1^{(\lambda)}, F_2^{(\lambda)})$ with $F_1^{(\lambda)} : \mathcal{K}^{(\lambda)} \times R \to \mathbb{F}^{2\ell + \lambda}$ and $F_2^{(\lambda)} : \mathcal{K}^{(\lambda)} \times R \to \mathbb{F}$. For conciseness, we write F for $F^{(\lambda)}$ (and F_k for $F_k^{(\lambda)}$, $\mathcal{K}$ for $\mathcal{K}^{(\lambda)}$) when λ is clear from context.

We make the assumption that $\mathcal{K}^{(\lambda)}$ is an abelian group and that the order of any element in $\mathcal{K}^{(\lambda)}$ is bounded by some polynomial $\gamma(\lambda)$. (This is often the case; in particular, this holds when $\mathcal{K}^{(\lambda)} = (\mathbb{Z}/h(\lambda)\mathbb{Z})^{g(\lambda)}$, where $g(\lambda)$ is an arbitrary function of λ and $h(\lambda)$ is polynomially bounded.) Since $|\mathcal{K}^{(\lambda)}|$ is superpolynomial in λ, if the above conditions hold, then there exists λ_0 such that $\frac{\gamma(\lambda)^{2\ell n}}{|\mathcal{K}^{(\lambda)}|} < 1 - \frac{1}{\lambda}$ for all $\lambda \geq \lambda_0$. Hence, by replacing λ by a larger λ' if needed and truncating the output, we may assume that $\frac{\gamma(\lambda)^{2\ell n}}{|\mathcal{K}^{(\lambda)}|} < 1 - \frac{1}{\lambda}$ holds for all λ.

Remark 2. If $\mathbb{F}$ has characteristic p, then for any $k \in p\mathcal{K}$, $r \in R$,

$$F(k, r) = F(pk', r) = pF(k', r) = 0.$$

Thus, any key $k \in p\mathcal{K}$ is a "weak key", and since F is a secure PRF, $|\mathcal{K}/p\mathcal{K}|^{-1}$ must be a negligible function of λ. By the fundamental theorem of finite abelian groups, we can write

$$\mathcal{K} \cong \mathbb{Z}/(p_1^{n_1}\mathbb{Z}) \times \mathbb{Z}/(p_2^{n_2}\mathbb{Z}) \times \cdots \times \mathbb{Z}/(p_l^{n_l}\mathbb{Z})$$

where $p_1, \ldots, p_l$ are (not necessarily distinct) primes. Assume $p_i = p$ for $1 \le i \le l'$ and that $p_i \ne p$ for $l' < i \le l$. Then $\mathcal{K}/p\mathcal{K} \cong (\mathbb{Z}/p\mathbb{Z})^{l'}$ and thus $|\mathcal{K}/p\mathcal{K}|^{-1} = 1/p^{l'}$ must be a negligible function of λ.

Our scheme is a collection of three algorithms, $(\mathsf{Gen}(a, \alpha, \lambda),\ \mathsf{Eval}(f_i, x, r),\ \mathsf{Rec}(s_1, \ldots, s_n))$, which are defined as:

$\mathsf{Gen}(a, \alpha, \lambda)$

1. Choose 2ℓ random vectors $v_0, v_1, v_2, \ldots, v_{2\ell-1}$ from $\mathbb{F}^{2\ell+\lambda}$.
2. Choose $2\ell n$ random vectors $v_{i,j} \in \mathbb{F}^{2\ell+\lambda}$ $(1 \le i \le n,\ 0 \le j \le 2\ell - 1)$ subject to the condition $v_j = \sum_{i=0}^{n} v_{i,j}$ for all j.
3. Let $a = a_1 a_2 \ldots a_\ell$ and compute $\theta = \sum_{j=0}^{\ell-1} v_{2j+a_j}$. This sum includes either v_{2j} or v_{2j+1} depending on whether the j-th bit of a is 0 or 1 respectively.
4. Choose 2ℓ random elements $\alpha_0, \alpha_1, \ldots, \alpha_{2\ell-1} \in \mathbb{F}$ subject to the condition $\alpha = \sum_{j=0}^{\ell-1} \alpha_{2j+a_j}$.
5. Choose $2\ell n$ random elements $\alpha_{i,j} \in \mathbb{F}$ $(1 \le i \le n,\ 0 \le j \le 2\ell - 1)$ subject to the condition that $\alpha_j = \sum_{i=1}^{n} \alpha_{i,j}$ for all j.
6. Choose $2\ell n$ linearly independent keys $k_{i,j}$ $(1 \le i \le n,\ 0 \le j \le 2\ell - 1)$.
7. Compute $k = \sum_{i=1}^{n} \sum_{j=0}^{\ell-1} k_{i,2j+a_j}$.
8. Output $f_i = (v_{i,0}, \ldots, v_{i,2\ell-1}, \theta, \alpha_{i,0}, \ldots, \alpha_{i,2\ell-1}, k_{i,0}, \ldots, k_{i,2\ell-1}, k)$.

$\mathsf{Eval}(f_i, x, r)$

1. Parse f_i as $(v_{i,0}, \ldots, v_{i,2\ell-1}, \theta, \alpha_{i,0}, \ldots, \alpha_{i,2\ell-1}, k_{i,0}, \ldots, k_{i,2\ell-1}, k)$.
2. Let $x = x_1 x_2 \ldots x_\ell$. Compute $s_{i,0} = \sum_{j=0}^{\ell-1} \left(v_{i,2j+x_j} + F_1(k_{i,2j+x_j}, r) \right)$.
3. Compute $s_{i,1} = \sum_{j=0}^{\ell-1} \left(\alpha_{i,2j+x_j} + F_2(k_{i,2j+x_j}, r) \right)$.
4. Output $s_i = (s_{i,0}, s_{i,1}, r, \theta, k)$.

$\mathsf{Rec}(s_1, \ldots, s_n)$

1. Parse s_i as $(s_{i,0}, s_{i,1}, r, \theta, k)$.
2. Compute $\sum_{i=0}^{n} s_{i,0}$. If this equals $\theta + F_1(k, r)$, output $\sum_{i=0}^{n} s_{i,1} - F_2(k, r)$ else output 0.

Remark 3. In the above scheme, each party has a share size of

$$(4\ell^2 + 2\lambda\ell + 4\ell + \lambda) \log |\mathbb{F}| + (2\ell + 1) \log |\mathcal{K}|,$$

and the output of Eval for each party has size

$$(4\ell + 2\lambda + 1) \log |\mathbb{F}| + \log |\mathcal{K}| + \log |R|,$$

both of which are independent of the number of parties.

Theorem 1. *The above scheme is an n-out-of-n computational multi-evaluation DPF scheme for sharing the class of point functions* $\mathcal{P}\left(\{0,1\}^\ell, \mathbb{F}\right)$.

Proof. Computational Correctness: We first prove that evaluation at $x = a$ gives the correct result with probability 1, i.e., $\mathsf{Rec}\left(\{\mathsf{Eval}(f_i, a, r)\}_{i \in [n]}\right) = \alpha$. Note that:

$$
\begin{aligned}
\sum_{i=0}^{n} s_{i,0} &= \sum_{i=0}^{n} \sum_{j=0}^{\ell-1} \left(v_{i,2j+a_j} + F_1(k_{i,2j+a_j}, r)\right) \\
&= \sum_{j=0}^{\ell-1} \sum_{i=0}^{n} v_{i,2j+a_j} + \sum_{i=0}^{n} \sum_{j=0}^{\ell-1} F_1\left(k_{i,2j+a_j}, r\right) \\
&= \sum_{j=0}^{\ell-1} v_{2j+a_j} + F_1\left(\sum_{i=0}^{n} \sum_{j=0}^{\ell-1} k_{i,2j+a_j}, r\right) = \theta + F_1(k, r),
\end{aligned}
$$

hence, the output of Rec is:

$$
\begin{aligned}
\sum_{i=0}^{n} s_{i,1} - F_2(k, r) &= \sum_{i=0}^{n} \sum_{j=0}^{\ell-1} \left(\alpha_{i,2j+a_j} + F_2(k_{i,2j+a_j}, r)\right) - F_2(k, r) \\
&= \sum_{j=0}^{\ell-1} \sum_{i=0}^{n} \alpha_{i,2j+a_j} + \sum_{i=0}^{n} \sum_{j=0}^{\ell-1} F_2(k_{i,2j+a_j}, r) - F_2(k, r) \\
&= \sum_{j=0}^{\ell-1} \alpha_{2j+a_j} + F_2\left(\sum_{i=0}^{n} \sum_{j=0}^{\ell-1} k_{i,2j+a_j}, r\right) - F_2(k, r) \\
&= \alpha + F_2(k, r) - F_2(k, r) = \alpha.
\end{aligned}
$$

Next, we prove that evaluation at $x \neq a$ is correct except with probability negligible in λ. Let $u_j = v_j + F_1(k_j, r)$ for $j = 0, \dots, 2\ell-1$, where $k_j = \sum_{i=1}^{n} k_{i,j}$. A simple calculation shows that:

$$
\sum_{j=0}^{\ell} u_{2j+a_j} = \sum_{j=0}^{\ell-1} \left(v_{2j+a_j} + F_1(k_{2j+a_j}, r)\right) = \theta + F_1(k, r).
$$

Since F_1 is a PRF and $k_0, k_1, \dots, k_{2\ell-1}$ are linearly independent, the vectors $u_0, u_1, \dots, u_{2\ell-1}$ cannot be distinguished from random vectors in $\mathbb{F}^{2\ell+\lambda}$ except with probability negligible in λ. The probability that 2ℓ random vectors are linearly independent in $\mathbb{F}^{2\ell+\lambda}$ is:

$$
\begin{aligned}
\prod_{j=0}^{2\ell-1} \left(\frac{q^{2\ell+\lambda} - q^j}{q^{2\ell+\lambda}}\right) &= \prod_{j=0}^{2\ell-1} \left(1 - \frac{q^j}{q^{2\ell+\lambda}}\right) > 1 - \sum_{j=0}^{2\ell-1} \left(\frac{q^j}{q^{2\ell+\lambda}}\right) \\
&= 1 - \frac{1}{q^{2\ell+\lambda}} \left(\frac{q^{2\ell} - 1}{q - 1}\right) > 1 - \frac{1}{q^\lambda} = 1 - \mathrm{negl}(\lambda).
\end{aligned}
$$

If the vectors $u_0, u_1, \dots, u_{2\ell-1}$ are linearly independent, then there is no other linear combination of the u_j's that result in $\theta + F_1(k, r)$, and thus, Rec outputs 0 when given as inputs the outputs of Eval evaluated at $x \neq a$. Therefore, the output of Rec is 0 except with probability negligible in λ.

Perfect Secrecy: Recall that $\mathsf{Gen}(a, \alpha, \lambda)$ outputs $(f_1, f_2, \dots, f_n)$, where:

$$
f_i = (v_{i,0}, \dots, v_{i,2\ell-1}, \theta, \alpha_{i,0}, \dots, \alpha_{i,2\ell-1}, k_{i,0}, \dots, k_{i,2\ell-1}, k).
$$

For f_i's supplied by $n-1$ parties, which we assume, without loss of generality, to be the first $n-1$ parties, note that $v_{i,j}$ $(1 \leq i \leq n-1, 0 \leq j \leq 2\ell-1)$ and θ are independent elements (in the probabilistic sense) from the uniform distribution on $\mathbb{F}^{2\ell+\lambda}$, $\alpha_{i,j}$ $(1 \leq i \leq n-1, 0 \leq j \leq 2\ell-1)$ are independent elements from the uniform distribution on $\mathbb{F}$, while $k_{i,j}$ $(1 \leq i \leq n-1, 0 \leq j \leq 2\ell-1)$ and k are $2\ell(n-1)+1$ linearly independent elements picked uniformly at random from $\mathcal{K}$. Thus, $(f_1, \ldots, f_{n-1})$ has the same distribution regardless of the value of $a \in \{0,1\}^\ell$ and $\alpha \in \mathbb{F}$.

Computational Multi-evaluation: Let $S \subset [n]$ such that $|S| < n$. We have already established that $\{f_i\}_{i \in S}$ has the same distribution for all $a \in \{0,1\}^\ell$ and $\alpha \in \mathbb{F}$. Assume that $x_1, x_2, \ldots, x_m \neq a$ and $r_1, r_2, \ldots, r_m \in R$ are distinct. Then, we get

$$\mathsf{Eval}(f_i, x_h, r_h) = \left(\sum_{j=0}^{\ell-1} \left(v_{i,2j+x_{h,j}} + F_1(k_{i,2j+x_{h,j}}, r_h) \right), \right.$$

$$\left. \sum_{j=0}^{\ell-1} \left(\alpha_{i,2j+x_{h,j}} + F_2(k_{i,2j+x_{h,j}}, r_h) \right), r_h, \theta, k \right)$$

$$= \left(\sum_{j=0}^{\ell-1} v_{i,2j+x_{h,j}} + F_1 \left(\sum_{j=0}^{\ell-1} k_{i,2j+x_{h,j}}, r_h \right), \right.$$

$$\left. \sum_{j=0}^{\ell-1} \alpha_{i,2j+x_{h,j}} + F_2 \left(\sum_{j=0}^{\ell-1} k_{i,2j+x_{h,j}}, r_h \right), r_h, \theta, k \right).$$

Since $\{f_i\}_{i \in S}$ has the same distribution regardless of the choice of a and α, the same holds for $\left(\{f_i\}_{i \in S}, \{\mathsf{Eval}(f_i, x_h, r_h)\}_{i \in S, h \in [m]} \right)$.

We observe that, since $x_h \neq a$ for all $1 \leq h \leq m$, for any fixed h, the set

$$\{k_{i,j} : i \in S, \ 0 \leq j \leq 2\ell - 1\} \cup \{k\} \cup \{\textstyle\sum_{j=0}^{\ell-1} k_{i,2j+x_{h,j}} : i \notin S\}$$

is a set of random linearly independent elements in $\mathcal{K}$. Hence, any non-zero linear combination of $\{\sum_{j=0}^{\ell-1} k_{i,2j+x_{h,j}} : i \notin S\}$ is a uniformly random element in $\mathcal{K}$ that lies outside the span of $\{k\} \cup \{k_{i,j} : i \in S, \ 0 \leq j \leq 2\ell - 1\}$.

Since, by assumption, any element in $\mathcal{K}$ has order at most $\gamma(\lambda)$, the span of $2\ell(n-1) + 1$ elements has size at most $\gamma(\lambda)^{2\ell(n-1)+1} < \gamma(\lambda)^{2\ell n}$. By our assumption, $\frac{\gamma(\lambda)^{2\ell n}}{|\mathcal{K}(\lambda)|} < 1 - \frac{1}{\lambda}$, so the advantage of an adversary in distinguishing the PRF F from random when the key is selected from outside the span of $\{k\} \cup \{k_{i,j} : i \in T, \ 0 \leq j \leq 2\ell - 1\}$ is increased by a factor of at most λ, and hence this advantage is still negligible in λ.

Hence, given $\{f_i\}_{i \in S}$, the set $\{F(\sum_{j=0}^{\ell-1} k_{i,2j+x_{h,j}}, r_h)\}_{i \notin S, h \in [m]}$ cannot be distinguished from uniformly random except with negligible probability. It follows that for all $i \notin S$ and $h \in [m]$, $\sum_{j=0}^{\ell-1} v_{i,2j+x_{h,j}} + F_1 \left(\sum_{j=0}^{\ell-1} k_{i,2j+x_{h,j}}, r_h \right)$ and $\sum_{j=0}^{\ell-1} \alpha_{i,2j+x_{h,j}} + F_2 \left(\sum_{j=0}^{\ell-1} k_{i,2j+x_{h,j}}, r_h \right)$ are indistinguishable from independent uniform random elements of $\mathbb{F}^{2\ell+\lambda}$ and $\mathbb{F}$ respectively, except with probability negligible in λ. ∎

3.2 t-out-of-n Multi-evaluation DPF

In this section, we introduce the idea of an $\mathbb{F}$-key-homomorphic PRF. By assuming the existence of such PRFs, we extend the n-out-of-n scheme in the previous subsection to a t-out-of-n computational multi-evaluation threshold DPF scheme.

Definition 5 (F-key-homomorphic PRF). Let $\mathbb{F}$ be a field, $\mathcal{K}$ and $\mathbb{L}$ be extension fields of $\mathbb{F}$, and $F : \mathcal{K} \times \mathcal{X} \to \mathbb{L}^m$ be an efficiently computable function. We say that F is an $\mathbb{F}$-key-homomorphic PRF if the following properties hold:

1. F is a secure PRF,
2. $\forall k_1, k_2 \in \mathcal{K}, x \in \mathcal{X} : F_{k_1+k_2}(x) = F_{k_1}(x) + F_{k_2}(x)$,
3. $\forall c \in \mathbb{F}, k \in \mathcal{K}, x \in \mathcal{X} : F_{ck}(x) = c \cdot F_k(x)$.

Remark 4. Note that if $\mathcal{K}$ and $\mathbb{L}$ are fields with the same prime subfield $\mathbb{F}_p$, then a key-homomorphic PRF $F : \mathcal{K} \times \mathcal{X} \to \mathbb{L}^m$ satisfying (2) is always $\mathbb{F}_p$-key-homomorphic. Furthermore, since $\mathcal{K}$ is a finite field, we know that $(\mathcal{K}, +) \cong \mathbb{F}_{p'}^l$ for some prime p'. Then, it follows from Remark 2 that:

$$|\mathcal{K}/p\mathcal{K}|^{-1} = \begin{cases} 1/p^l & \text{if } p = p', \\ 1 & \text{otherwise.} \end{cases}$$

Since F is a secure PRF, $|\mathcal{K}/p\mathcal{K}|^{-1}$ is a negligible function of λ, thus it must be the case that $p' = p$, i.e. char($\mathcal{K}$) must be equal to char($\mathbb{L}$).

We will use an $\mathbb{F}$-key-homomorphic PRF family to produce a computational multi-evaluation threshold DPF scheme for the class of point functions $\mathcal{P}(\{0,1\}^\ell, \mathbb{L})$, where $\mathbb{L} = \mathbb{F}_q$ is the finite field with cardinality q. Assume $|\mathbb{F}| \geq n + 1$, and fix an injection $\iota : \{0, 1, \dots, n\} \to \mathbb{F}$. We will use this injection to identity elements in $\{0, 1, \dots, n\}$ with elements of $\mathbb{F}$. Note that this injection need not be a homomorphism. Let $\mathcal{F} = \{F^{(\lambda)} : \mathcal{K}^{(\lambda)} \times R \to \mathbb{L}^{2\ell+\lambda+1}\}$ be a family of $\mathbb{F}$-key-homomorphic PRFs such that the advantage of any polynomial-time adversary in distinguishing $F^{(\lambda)}$ from random is negligible in λ. As above, we write $F^{(\lambda)} = (F_1^{(\lambda)}, F_2^{(\lambda)})$.

Again, we will make the assumption that the order of any element in $\mathcal{K}^{(\lambda)}$ is bounded by some polynomial $\gamma(\lambda)$, from which it follows, without loss of generality, that $\frac{\gamma(\lambda)^{2\ell n}}{|\mathcal{K}^{(\lambda)}|} < 1 - \frac{1}{\lambda}$ holds for all λ. Our scheme is a collection of three algorithms, $(\mathsf{Gen}(a, \alpha, \lambda), \mathsf{Eval}(f_i, x, r), \mathsf{Rec}(\{s_i : i \in T\}))$, which are defined as:

$\mathsf{Gen}(a, \alpha, \lambda)$

1. Choose 2ℓ random vectors $v_0, v_1, v_2, \dots, v_{2\ell-1}$ from $\mathbb{L}^{2\ell+\lambda}$.
2. Compute Shamir shares $v_{i,j} \in \mathbb{L}^{2\ell+\lambda}$ ($1 \leq i \leq n$, $0 \leq j \leq 2\ell-1$) for v_i. To be precise, for each $0 \leq j \leq 2\ell-1$, randomly choose polynomials $r_{j,h}(X) \in \mathbb{L}[X]$ ($1 \leq h \leq 2\ell+\lambda$), each of degree $\leq t-1$, such that $r_{j,h}(0)$ is equal to the h-th coordinate of v_j, and let the h-th coordinate of $v_{i,j}$ be $r_{j,h}(i)$.
3. Let $a = a_1 a_2 \dots a_\ell$ and compute $\theta = \sum_{j=0}^{\ell-1} v_{2j+a_j}$.
4. Choose 2ℓ random elements $\alpha_0, \alpha_1, \dots, \alpha_{2\ell-1} \in \mathbb{L}$ subject to the condition $\alpha = \sum_{j=0}^{\ell-1} \alpha_{2j+a_j}$.
5. Compute Shamir shares $\alpha_{i,j} \in \mathbb{L}$ ($1 \leq i \leq n$, $0 \leq j \leq 2\ell-1$) for α_j, as in Step 2 above.
6. Choose $2\ell n$ linearly independent keys $k_{i,j}$ ($1 \leq i \leq n$, $0 \leq j \leq 2\ell-1$).

7. Choose random polynomials $p_{i,j}(X) \in \mathcal{K}[X]$ $(1 \leq i \leq n, 0 \leq j \leq 2\ell-1)$, each of degree $\leq t-1$ such that $p_{i,j}(0) = k_{i,j}$, and let $k_{i,j,l} = p_{i,j}(l)$ $(1 \leq l \leq n)$. Let $k^{(l)} = \{(i,j,k_{i,j,l}) : 1 \leq i \leq n, \ 0 \leq j \leq 2\ell - 1\}$.
8. Compute $k = \sum_{i=1}^{n} \sum_{j=0}^{\ell-1} k_{i,2j+a_j}$.
9. Output $f_i = (i, v_{i,0}, \ldots, v_{i,2\ell-1}, \theta, \alpha_{i,0}, \ldots, \alpha_{i,2\ell-1}, k_{i,0}, \ldots, k_{i,2\ell-1}, k^{(i)}, k)$.

Eval(f_i, x, r)

1. Parse f_i as $(i, v_{i,0}, \ldots, v_{i,2\ell-1}, \theta, \alpha_{i,0}, \ldots, \alpha_{i,2\ell-1}, k_{i,0}, \ldots, k_{i,2\ell-1}, k^{(i)}, k)$.
2. Let $x = x_1 x_2 \ldots x_\ell$. Compute $s_{i,0} = \sum_{j=0}^{\ell-1} \left(v_{i,2j+x_j} + \sum_{l=1}^{n} F_1(k_{l,2j+x_j,i}, r) \right)$.
3. Compute $s_{i,1} = \sum_{j=0}^{\ell-1} \left(\alpha_{i,2j+x_j} + \sum_{l=1}^{n} F_2(k_{l,2j+x_j,i}, r) \right)$.
4. Output $s_i = (i, s_{i,0}, s_{i,1}, r, \theta, k)$

Rec($\{s_i : i \in T\}$)

1. Parse s_i as $(i, s_{i,0}, s_{i,1}, r, \theta, k)$.
2. Compute $S_{0,1}(X), \ldots, S_{0,2\ell+\lambda}(X)$ and $S_1(X)$, polynomials of degree $\leq t-1$ such that $S_{0,h}(i)$ is equal to the h-th coordinate of $s_{i,0}$ and $S_1(i) = s_{i,1}$ for all $i \in T$.
3. If $(S_{0,1}(0), \ldots, S_{0,2\ell+\lambda}(0))$ equals $\theta + F_1(k,r)$, output $S_1(0) - F_2(k,r)$ else output 0.

Remark 5. Each party has a share size of

$$\log n + (4\ell^2 + 2\lambda\ell + 4\ell + \lambda)\log|\mathbb{L}| + (2\ell n + 2\ell + 1)\log|\mathcal{K}|$$

(assuming we fix an ordering for the elements in $k^{(l)}$, and replace $(i,j,k_{i,j,l})$ by $k_{i,j,l}$) and the output of Eval has size

$$\log n + (4\ell + 2\lambda + 1)\log|\mathbb{L}| + \log|\mathcal{K}| + \log|R|.$$

Theorem 2. *The above scheme is an t-out-of-n computational multi-evaluation DPF scheme for sharing the class of point functions $\mathcal{P}\left(\{0,1\}^\ell, \mathbb{L}\right)$.*

Before proving the above theorem, we prove two useful lemmas:

Lemma 1. *Let $x_0, x_1, \ldots, x_t \in \mathbb{F}$ be distinct, $\mathcal{K}$ be an extension field of $\mathbb{F}$ and let $p(X) \in \mathcal{K}[X]$ be a polynomial of degree $\leq t-1$. Then there exists $c_1, c_2, \ldots, c_t \in \mathbb{F}$ such that*

$$p(x_0) = c_1 p(x_1) + \cdots + c_t p(x_t).$$

Proof. By Lagrange interpolation,

$$p(X) = p(x_1) \cdot \frac{\prod_{i\neq 1}(X - x_i)}{\prod_{i\neq 1}(x_1 - x_i)} + \cdots + p(x_t) \cdot \frac{\prod_{i\neq t}(X - x_i)}{\prod_{i\neq t}(x_t - x_i)},$$

so

$$p(x_0) = p(x_1) \cdot \frac{\prod_{i\neq 1}(x_0 - x_i)}{\prod_{i\neq 1}(x_1 - x_i)} + \cdots + p(x_t) \cdot \frac{\prod_{i\neq t}(x_0 - x_i)}{\prod_{i\neq t}(x_t - x_i)}.$$

It is clear that $c_j = \frac{\prod_{i\neq j}(x_0 - x_i)}{\prod_{i\neq j}(x_j - x_i)}$ lies in the subfield $\mathbb{F}$ since $x_0, x_1, \ldots, x_t \in \mathbb{F}$. ∎

Lemma 2. *Let $F : \mathcal{K} \times X \to \mathbb{L}$ be an $\mathbb{F}$-key-homomorphic PRF, $x_0, x_1, \ldots, x_t \in \mathbb{F}$ be distinct, and $p(X) \in \mathcal{K}[X]$ be a polynomial of degree $\leq t - 1$. Then*

(a) $F(p(x_0), r)$ is an $\mathbb{F}$-linear combination of $F(p(x_i), r)$ $(1 \leq i \leq t)$,
(b) there exists a polynomial $\delta(X) \in \mathbb{L}[X]$ of degree $\leq t - 1$ such that $\delta(x_i) = F(p(x_i), r)$ for all $0 \leq i \leq t$.

Proof.(a) Since F is $\mathbb{F}$-key-homomorphic,

$$F(p(x_0), r) = c_1 \cdot F(p(x_1), r) + \cdots + c_t \cdot F(p(x_t), r),$$

where $c_1, \ldots c_t \in \mathbb{F}$ are as in Lemma 1.
(b) Let $\delta(X)$ be the polynomial

$$\delta(X) = F(p(x_1), r) \cdot \frac{\prod_{i \neq 1}(X - x_i)}{\prod_{i \neq 1}(x_1 - x_i)} + \cdots + F(p(x_t), r) \cdot \frac{\prod_{i \neq t}(X - x_i)}{\prod_{i \neq t}(x_t - x_i)}.$$

It is clear that $\delta(x_i) = F(p(x_i), r)$ for $1 \leq i \leq t$. And, by the proof of (a),

$$F(p(x_0), r) = F(p(x_1), r) \cdot \frac{\prod_{i \neq 1}(x_0 - x_i)}{\prod_{i \neq 1}(x_1 - x_i)} + \cdots + F(p(x_t), r) \cdot \frac{\prod_{i \neq t}(x_0 - x_i)}{\prod_{i \neq t}(x_t - x_i)}$$

$$= \delta(x_0).$$

∎

Proof (of Theorem 2) Computational Correctness: Let T be a subset of $[n]$ of size t. Without loss of generality, let us assume $T = [t]$. We start by proving that

$$\mathsf{Rec}\left(\{\mathsf{Eval}(f_i, a, r)\}_{i \in T}\right) = \alpha.$$

Note that for all $1 \leq i \leq t$ and $1 \leq h \leq 2\ell + \lambda$,

$$S_{0,h}(i) = s_{i,0}[h] = \sum_{j=0}^{\ell-1} \left(v_{i,2j+a_j}[h] + \sum_{l=1}^{n} F_1(k_{l,2j+a_j,i}, r)[h]\right)$$

$$= \sum_{j=0}^{\ell-1} r_{2j+a_j,h}(i) + \sum_{j=0}^{\ell-1}\sum_{l=1}^{n} F_1(p_{l,2j+a_j}(i), r)[h]$$

$$= \sum_{j=0}^{\ell-1} r_{2j+a_j,h}(i) + F_1\left(\sum_{j=0}^{\ell-1}\sum_{l=1}^{n} p_{l,2j+a_j}(i), r\right)[h].$$

Let $p(X) = \sum_{j=0}^{\ell-1}\sum_{l=1}^{n} p_{l,2j+a_j}(X)$, a polynomial of degree $\leq t - 1$. By Lemma 2(b), there exists a polynomial $\delta_h(X) \in \mathbb{L}[X]$ of degree $\leq t-1$, such that $\delta_h(i) = F_1(p(i), r)[h]$ for all $0 \leq i \leq t$. Since $S_{0,h}(X)$ agrees with $\sum_{j=0}^{\ell-1} r_{2j+a_j,h}(X) + \delta_h(X)$ at the t points $X = 1, 2, \ldots, t$, and both of them are polynomials of degree $\leq t-1$, they must be identical, i.e. $S_{0,h}(X) = \sum_{j=0}^{\ell-1} r_{2j+a_j,h}(X) + \delta_h(X)$. Therefore,

$$S_{0,h}(0) = \sum_{j=0}^{\ell-1} r_{2j+a_j,h}(0) + \delta_h(0)$$

$$= \sum_{j=0}^{\ell-1} v_{2j+a_j}[h] + F_1(p(0), r)[h]$$

$$= \sum_{j=0}^{\ell-1} v_{2j+a_j}[h] + F_1\left(\sum_{j=0}^{\ell-1}\sum_{l=1}^{n} p_{l,2j+a_j}(0), r\right)[h]$$

$$= \theta[h] + F_1\left(\sum_{j=0}^{\ell-1}\sum_{l=1}^{n} k_{l,2j+a_j}, r\right)[h]$$

$$= \theta[h] + F_1(k, r)[h],$$

i.e., $(S_{0,1}(0), \ldots, S_{0,2\ell+\lambda}(0)) = \theta + F_1(k, r)$. The output of Rec is thus $S_1(0) - F_2(k, r)$, which, by a similar argument as above, is equal to:

$$(\textstyle\sum_{j=0}^{\ell-1} \alpha_{2j+a_j} + F_2(k, r)) - F_2(k, r) = \textstyle\sum_{j=0}^{\ell-1} \alpha_{2j+a_j} = \alpha.$$

Next, we prove that evaluation at $x \neq a$ is correct except with probability negligible in λ. Let $u_j = v_j + F_1(k_j, r)$ for $j = 0, \ldots, 2\ell - 1$, where $k_j = \sum_{i=1}^n k_{i,j}$. Again, by a similar argument as above,

$$\textstyle\sum_{j=0}^{\ell-1} u_{2j+a_j} = \textstyle\sum_{j=0}^{\ell-1} \left(v_{2j+a_j} + F_1(\textstyle\sum_{l=1}^n k_{l,2j+a_j}, r) \right) = \theta + F_1(k, r),$$

and evaluation at $x \neq a$ gives:

$$(S_{0,1}(0), \ldots, S_{0,2\ell+\lambda}(0)) = \textstyle\sum_{j=0}^{\ell-1} \left(v_{2j+x_j} + F_1(\textstyle\sum_{l=1}^n k_{l,2j+x_j}, r) \right) = \textstyle\sum_{j=0}^{\ell-1} u_{2j+x_j}.$$

The result now follows by following the proof for computational correctness in Theorem 1.

Perfect Secrecy: $\mathsf{Gen}(a, \alpha, \lambda)$ outputs $(f_1, f_2, \ldots, f_n)$, where

$$f_i = (i, v_{i,0}, \ldots, v_{i,2\ell-1}, \theta, \alpha_{i,0}, \ldots, \alpha_{i,2\ell-1}, k_{i,0}, \ldots, k_{i,2\ell-1}, k^{(i)}, k)$$

and $k^{(i)} = \{(i', j', k_{i',j',i}) : 1 \leq i' \leq n, \ 0 \leq j' \leq 2\ell - 1\}$.

Suppose we are given f_i from $t - 1$ parties, which we will assume, without loss of generality, to be the first $t - 1$ parties. Any $t - 1$ Shamir shares of a t-out-of-n threshold scheme are independently and uniformly distributed. Thus, $v_{i,j}$ ($1 \leq i \leq t - 1, \ 0 \leq j \leq 2\ell - 1$) and θ are independently and uniformly distributed. The same holds for $\alpha_{i,j}$ ($1 \leq i \leq t - 1, \ 0 \leq j \leq 2\ell - 1$). $k_{i,j}$ ($1 \leq i \leq t-1, 0 \leq j \leq 2\ell-1$) and k are $2\ell(t-1)+1$ linearly independent elements picked uniformly at random from $\mathcal{K}$, while $k_{i',j',i}$ ($1 \leq i' \leq n, 0 \leq j' \leq 2\ell - 1$, $1 \leq i \leq t-1$) are independently and uniformly distributed. Thus, the distribution of $(f_1, \ldots, f_{t-1})$ does not depend on a or α.

Computational Multi-evaluation: Let $S \subset [n]$ such that $|S| < t$. Assume $x_1, x_2, \ldots, x_m \neq a$, and $r_1, r_2, \ldots, r_m \in R$ are distinct. We get

$$\mathsf{Eval}(f_i, x_h, r_h) = \left(i, \textstyle\sum_{j=0}^{\ell-1} \left(v_{i,2j+x_{h,j}} + \textstyle\sum_{l=1}^n F_1(k_{l,2j+x_{h,j},i}, r_h) \right), \right.$$
$$\left. \textstyle\sum_{j=0}^{\ell-1} \left(\alpha_{i,2j+x_{h,j}} + \textstyle\sum_{l=1}^n F_2(k_{l,2j+x_{h,j},i}, r_h) \right), r_h, \theta, k \right)$$
$$= \left(i, \textstyle\sum_{j=0}^{\ell-1} v_{i,2j+x_{h,j}} + F_1(\textstyle\sum_{j=0}^{\ell-1}\textstyle\sum_{l=1}^n k_{l,2j+x_{h,j},i}, r_h), \right.$$
$$\left. \textstyle\sum_{j=0}^{\ell-1} \alpha_{i,2j+x_{h,j}} + F_2(\textstyle\sum_{j=0}^{\ell-1}\textstyle\sum_{l=1}^n k_{l,2j+x_{h,j},i}, r_h), r_h, \theta, k \right).$$

Let $S \subseteq U \subseteq [n]$. We shall prove by induction on $|U|$ that the distribution of $(\{f_i\}_{i \in S}, \{\mathsf{Eval}(f_i, x_h, r_h)\}_{i \in U, h \in [m]})$ is computationally indistinguishable regardless of the choice of a and α. The base case simply follows from perfect secrecy; since the distribution of $\{f_i\}_{i \in S}$ is independent of the choice of a and α, so is the distribution of $(\{f_i\}_{i \in S}, \{\mathsf{Eval}(f_i, x_h, r_h)\}_{i \in S, h \in [m]})$.

Suppose, for some $S \subseteq U' \subset [n]$, that $\left(\{f_i\}_{i \in S}, \{\mathsf{Eval}(f_i, x_h, r_h)\}_{i \in U', h \in [m]}\right)$ is computationally indistinguishable regardless of the choice of a and α. Let $u \notin U'$, and let $U^* = U' \cup \{u\}$. We consider the following three cases.

Case 1: $|U'| < t - 1$, i.e. $|U^*| < t$. It follows from perfect secrecy that the distribution of $\left(\{f_i\}_{i \in S}, \{\mathsf{Eval}(f_i, x_h, r_h)\}_{i \in U^*, h \in [m]}\right)$ is independent of a and α.

Case 2: $|U'| = t - 1$, i.e. $|U^*| = t$. Assume we are given:

$$\left(\{f_i\}_{i \in U'}, \{\mathsf{Eval}(f_i, x_h, r_h)\}_{i \in U', h \in [m]}\right),$$

whose distribution is independent of a and α by perfect secrecy.

Fix some $h \in [m]$. Note that $\sum_{j=0}^{\ell-1}\sum_{l=1}^{n} k_{l,2j+x_{h,j},i}$ ($i \in U^*$) are Shamir shares of $\sum_{j=0}^{\ell-1}\sum_{l=1}^{n} k_{l,2j+x_{h,j}}$, which is randomly and uniformly distributed as an element of $\mathcal{K}$ outside the span of $\{k_{i,j} : i \in U', 0 \leq j \leq 2\ell-1\} \cup \{k\}$. It follows that the advantage of an adversary in distinguishing $F(\sum_{j=0}^{\ell-1}\sum_{l=1}^{n} k_{l,2j+x_{h,j}}, r)$ from random is negligible in λ, thus the same holds for $F(\sum_{j=0}^{\ell-1}\sum_{l=1}^{n} k_{l,2j+x_{h,j},u}, r)$ (which, by Lemma 2(a), is an $\mathbb{F}$-linear combination of $F(\sum_{j=0}^{\ell-1}\sum_{l=1}^{n} k_{l,2j+x_{h,j}}, r)$ and $F(\sum_{j=0}^{\ell-1}\sum_{l=1}^{n} k_{l,2j+x_{h,j},i}, r)$ for $i \in U'$).

Thus, even with knowledge of $\left(\{f_i\}_{i \in U'}, \{\mathsf{Eval}(f_i, x_h, r_h)\}_{i \in U', h \in [m]}\right)$, both the distribution of $\sum_{j=0}^{\ell-1} v_{u,2j+x_{h,j}} + F_1(\sum_{j=0}^{\ell-1}\sum_{l=1}^{n} k_{l,2j+x_{h,j},u}, r_h)$ and the distribution of $\sum_{j=0}^{\ell-1} \alpha_{u,2j+x_{h,j}} + F_2(\sum_{j=0}^{\ell-1}\sum_{l=1}^{n} k_{l,2j+x_{h,j},u}, r_h)$ are indistinguishable from uniformly random, except with probability negligible in λ.

Case 3: $|U'| \geq t$, i.e. $|U^*| > t$. Assume we are given:

$$\left(\{f_i\}_{i \in S}, \{\mathsf{Eval}(f_i, x_h, r_h)\}_{i \in U', h \in [m]}\right),$$

whose distribution is computationally independent of a and α by the induction hypothesis. Since $\sum_{j=0}^{\ell-1} v_{i,2j+x_{h,j}} + F_1(\sum_{j=0}^{\ell-1}\sum_{l=1}^{n} k_{l,2j+x_{h,j},i}, r_h)$ are Shamir shares of $\sum_{j=0}^{\ell-1} v_{2j+x_{h,j}} + F_1(\sum_{j=0}^{\ell-1}\sum_{l=1}^{n} k_{l,2j+x_{h,j}}, r_h)$, by Lemma 1, for any $u_1, \ldots, u_t \in U'$, there exists $c_1, \ldots, c_t \in \mathbb{F}$ such that

$$\sum_{j=0}^{\ell-1} v_{u,2j+x_{h,j}} + F_1(\sum_{j=0}^{\ell-1}\sum_{l=1}^{n} k_{l,2j+x_{h,j},u}, r_h)$$
$$= c_1 \cdot \left(\sum_{j=0}^{\ell-1} v_{u_1,2j+x_{h,j}} + F_1(\sum_{j=0}^{\ell-1}\sum_{l=1}^{n} k_{l,2j+x_{h,j},u_1}, r_h)\right)$$
$$+ \cdots + c_t \cdot \left(\sum_{j=0}^{\ell-1} v_{u_t,2j+x_{h,j}} + F_1(\sum_{j=0}^{\ell-1}\sum_{l=1}^{n} k_{l,2j+x_{h,j},u_t}, r_h)\right).$$

A similar argument shows that $\sum_{j=0}^{\ell-1} \alpha_{u,2j+x_{h,j}} + F_2(\sum_{j=0}^{\ell-1}\sum_{l=1}^{n} k_{l,2j+x_{h,j},u}, r_h)$ (i.e., $\mathsf{Eval}(f_u, x_h, r_h)$) is determined by $\left(\{f_i\}_{i \in S}, \{\mathsf{Eval}(f_i, x_h, r_h)\}_{i \in U', h \in [m]}\right)$. ∎

4   Function-Private CDS

In this section, we introduce the concept of a *function-private* CDS (FPCDS) scheme. We start with an informal description. Suppose we have k parties $P_1, \ldots, P_k$. Let $h : \mathcal{C} \to \{0, 1\}$, where $\mathcal{C} = \mathcal{C}_1 \times \mathcal{C}_2 \times \ldots \times \mathcal{C}_k$, be a Boolean condition function that lies in a family of Boolean condition functions $\mathcal{H}$. An FPCDS scheme for $h \in \mathcal{H}$ with secret domain $\mathcal{S}$ consists of a dealer $\mathcal{D}$, k parties $P_1, \ldots, P_k$ and a third party, called Carol, which possesses an algorithm, Carol.

The dealer runs a randomized Gen algorithm with the inputs h and s, and obtains $w_1, w_2, \ldots, w_k$. For $1 \leq j \leq k$, $\mathcal{D}$ sends P_j the output portion w_j. Then, each player P_j chooses some $c_j \in \mathcal{C}_j$ as their portion of the condition. Next, P_j sends some message m_j to Carol where $m_j = P_j(c_j, w_j)$ is the output of some party-specific algorithm run on their part c_j of the input c and their part w_j of the Gen output. Upon receiving the messages m_j, Carol runs $\mathsf{Carol}(m_1, m_2, \ldots, m_k)$; it accepts (and outputs the secret) or rejects based on the output of its Carol algorithm. This scheme satisfies certain correctness, privacy and secrecy properties, as detailed in the following definition:

Definition 6. Let $\mathcal{H}$ be a family of Boolean condition functions, where each $h \in \mathcal{H}$ is a function from $\mathcal{C} = \mathcal{C}_1 \times \cdots \times \mathcal{C}_k$ to $\{0,1\}$. A function-private CDS scheme for the family $\mathcal{H}$ of condition functions and secret domain $\mathcal{S}$ is defined as a collection of algorithms $(\mathsf{Gen}, P_1, \ldots, P_k, \mathsf{Carol})$ such that:

- Gen is a randomized algorithm that takes two inputs, $h \in \mathcal{H}$ and $s \in \mathcal{S}$, and generates k shares $\{w_i\}_{i=1}^k$.
- For each $i \in [k]$, P_i is a deterministic algorithm that takes two inputs, a share w_i and $c_i \in \mathcal{C}_i$, and outputs a message m_i.
- Carol is a deterministic algorithm that takes as inputs $m_1, \ldots, m_k$ and outputs either an element of $\mathcal{S}$ or $\perp$.

These algorithms satisfy the following four conditions:

- *Perfect Correctness:* For every $h \in \mathcal{H}$, $s \in \mathcal{S}$, and $c = (c_1, c_2, \ldots, c_k) \in \mathcal{C}$, when $\mathsf{Gen}(h, s) = (w_1, w_2, \ldots, w_k)$ and $m_j = P_j(c_j, w_j)$,

$$\mathsf{Carol}(m_1, m_2, \ldots, m_k) = \begin{cases} s & \text{if } h(c) = 1, \\ \perp & \text{if } h(c) = 0. \end{cases}$$

- *Perfect Secrecy:* Fix $h \in \mathcal{H}$. For every $c = (c_1, c_2, \ldots, c_k) \in \mathcal{C}$, and any pair of secrets $s, s' \in \mathcal{S}$, let $\mathsf{Gen}(h, s) = (w_1^{(s)}, w_2^{(s)}, \ldots, w_k^{(s)})$, $\mathsf{Gen}(h, s') = (w_1^{(s')}, w_2^{(s')}, \ldots, w_k^{(s')})$, $m_j^{(s)} = P_j(c_j, w_j^{(s)})$ and $m_j^{(s')} = P_j(c_j, w_j^{(s')})$. If $h(c) = 0$, then $(m_1^{(s)}, m_2^{(s)}, \ldots, m_k^{(s)})$ and $(m_1^{(s')}, m_2^{(s')}, \ldots, m_k^{(s')})$ are perfectly indistinguishable.
- *Perfect Input Privacy:* Let $h \in \mathcal{H}$ and $s \in \mathcal{S}$. Let $c = (c_1, c_2, \ldots, c_k) \in \mathcal{C}$ and $c' = (c_1', c_2', \ldots, c_k') \in \mathcal{C}$. Let $\mathsf{Gen}(h, s) = (w_1, w_2, \ldots, w_k)$, $m_j = P_j(c_j, w_j)$ and $m_j' = P_j(c_j', w_j)$. If $h(c) = h(c')$, then $(m_1, \ldots, m_k)$ and $(m_1', \ldots, m_k')$ are perfectly indistinguishable.
- *Perfect Function Privacy:* Fix $c = (c_1, c_2, \ldots, c_k) \in \mathcal{C}$, $s \in \mathcal{S}$ and $i \in [k]$. Let $h, h' \in \mathcal{H}$ such that $h(c) = h'(c)$ and such that for every $c_i' \in \mathcal{C}_i$,

$$\{h(c_1', c_2', \ldots, c_k') : c_j' \in \mathcal{C}_j \text{ for } j \neq i\} = \{h'(c_1', c_2', \ldots, c_k') : c_j' \in \mathcal{C}_j \text{ for } j \neq i\}.$$

Let $\mathsf{Gen}(h, s) = (w_1^{(h)}, w_2^{(h)}, \ldots, w_k^{(h)})$ and $\mathsf{Gen}(h', s) = (w_1^{(h')}, w_2^{(h')}, \ldots, w_k^{(h')})$. For all $j = 1, \ldots, k$, let $m_j^{(h)} = \mathsf{P}_j(c_j, w_j^{(h)})$ and $m_j^{(h')} = \mathsf{P}_j(c_j, w_j^{(h')})$. Then, $(c_i, s, w_i^{(h)}, m_1^{(h)}, \ldots, m_k^{(h)})$ and $(c_i, s, w_i^{(h')}, m_1^{(h')}, \ldots, m_k^{(h')})$ are perfectly indistinguishable.

4.1   A Simple FPCDS Scheme

In this section, we present the first FPCDS scheme. Our scheme works with the family $\mathcal{H} = \{h_{(a,b)} : a, b \in \{0,1\}^n\}$ of Boolean condition functions, where $h_{(a,b)} : \{0,1\}^{2n} \to \{0,1\}$ is defined as:

$$h_{(a,b)}(\alpha, \beta) = \begin{cases} 1 & \text{if } (\alpha, \beta) = (a, b), \\ 0 & \text{otherwise,} \end{cases}$$

and with secret domain $\mathcal{S} = \mathbb{G}$ where $\mathbb{G}$ is a finite Abelian group. Let $m_i[j]$ be the jth element of m_i with index starting at 0.

1. $\mathcal{D}$ chooses a secret element $s \in \mathbb{G}$ and runs $\mathsf{Gen}(h_{(a,b)}, s)$. To do so, $\mathcal{D}$ samples six random elements $t, r_1, r_2, u, v_1, v_2 \leftarrow \mathbb{G}$ such that u, v_1, v_2 are distinct. $\mathcal{D}$ sends $w_1 = (a, s, t, r_1, u, v_1)$ to P_1 and $w_2 = (b, s, t, r_2, u, v_2)$ to P_2.
2. P_1 chooses $\alpha \in \{0,1\}^n$. If $\alpha = a$, then P_1 sends $m_1 = (u, s \oplus t)$ to Carol; otherwise, it sends $m_1 = (v_1, r_1)$. P_2 chooses β in $\{0,1\}^n$. If $\beta = b$, then P_2 sends $m_2 = (u, t)$ to Carol; otherwise, it sends $m_2 = (v_2, r_2)$.
3. Carol rejects if $m_1[0] \neq m_2[0]$; else it returns $g = \mathsf{Carol}(m_1, m_2) = m_1[1] \oplus m_2[1]$.

Remark 6. The communication complexity between the dealer and party P_j is $|w_j| = n + 5|s|$, while the communication complexity between any party P_j and Carol is $|m_j| = 2|s|$.

Theorem 3. *The above scheme is a function-private CDS scheme.*

Proof. We prove that the scheme satisfies Definition 6 for FPCDS.

Perfect Correctness: Suppose the dealer chooses a secret $s \in \mathbb{G}$ and computes $\mathsf{Gen}(h_{(a,b)}, s) = (w_1, w_2)$, where $w_1 = (a, s, t, r_1, u, v_1)$ and $w_2 = (b, s, t, r_2, u, v_2)$. Suppose further that P_1 chooses $\alpha \in \{0,1\}^n$ and P_2 chooses $\beta \in \{0,1\}^n$. Let $m_1 = \mathsf{P}_1(\alpha, w_1)$ and $m_2 = \mathsf{P}_2(\beta, w_2)$. Suppose $h_{(a,b)}(\alpha, \beta) = 1$, i.e., $(\alpha, \beta) = (a, b)$. Then, $m_1 = (u, s \oplus t)$ and $m_2 = (u, t)$. Since $m_1[0] = u = m_2[0]$, Carol outputs:

$$g = m_1[1] \oplus m_2[1] = s \oplus t \oplus t = s.$$

Else, suppose $h_{(a,b)}(\alpha, \beta) = 0$, i.e., $(\alpha, \beta) \neq (a, b)$. Then,

$$(m_1[0], m_2[0]) = (u, v_2), \ (v_1, u) \text{ or } (v_1, v_2).$$

By the choice of u, v_1, and v_2, all three elements are distinct. Hence, Carol rejects in all three cases.

Perfect Secrecy: Let $s, s' \in \mathbb{G}$, $\mathsf{Gen}(h_{(a,b)}, s) = (w_1, w_2)$ and $\mathsf{Gen}(h_{(a,b)}, s') = (w'_1, w'_2)$, where $w_1 = (a, s, t, r_1, u, v_1)$, $w_2 = (b, s, t, r_2, u, v_2)$, $w'_1 = (a, s', t', r'_1, u, v_1)$ and $w'_2 = (b, s', t', r'_2, u', v'_2)$. For $\alpha, \beta \in \{0,1\}^n$, let $m_1 = \mathsf{P}_1(\alpha, w_1)$, $m_2 = \mathsf{P}_2(\beta, w_2)$, $m'_1 = \mathsf{P}_1(\alpha, w'_1)$ and $m'_2 = \mathsf{P}_2(\beta, w'_2)$. Suppose $h_{(a,b)}(\alpha, \beta) = 0$, i.e., $(\alpha, \beta) \neq (a, b)$. We show that (m_1, m_2) and (m'_1, m'_2) are perfectly indistinguishable. For the first case, suppose $\alpha = a$ and $\beta \neq b$. Then $(m_1, m_2) = ((u, s \oplus t), (v_2, r_2))$ and $(m'_1, m'_2) = ((u', s' \oplus t'), (v'_2, r'_2))$. In this case, since u, u', t, t', r_2, r'_2 are drawn uniformly, and v_2, v'_2 are drawn uniformly to be not equal to u, u', respectively, (m_1, m_2) and (m'_1, m'_2) are both indistinguishable from $((\gamma, \delta), (\zeta, \eta))$, where $\gamma, \delta, \zeta, \eta \xleftarrow{\$} \mathbb{G}$ such that $\gamma \neq \zeta$. The case where $\alpha \neq a$ and $\beta = b$ is analogous to this case.

For the final case, suppose $\alpha \neq a$ and $\beta \neq b$. Then, it follows that $(m_1, m_2) = ((v_1, r_1), (v_2, r_2))$ and $(m'_1, m'_2) = ((v'_1, r'_1), (v'_2, r'_2))$. Again, (m_1, m_2) and (m'_1, m'_2) are both indistinguishable from $((\gamma, \delta), (\zeta, \eta))$, where $\gamma, \delta, \zeta, \eta \xleftarrow{\$} \mathbb{G}$ such that $\gamma \neq \zeta$.

Perfect Input Privacy: Let $s \in \mathbb{G}$ and $\mathsf{Gen}(h_{(a,b)}, s) = (w_1, w_2)$ with $w_1 = (a, s, t, r_1, u, v_1)$ and $w_2 = (b, s, t, r_2, u, v_2)$. Suppose $\alpha, \alpha', \beta, \beta' \in \{0,1\}^n$ satisfy the condition that $h_{(a,b)}(\alpha, \beta) = h_{(a,b)}(\alpha', \beta')$. Let $m_1 = \mathsf{P}_1(\alpha, w_1)$, $m'_1 = \mathsf{P}_1(\alpha', w_1)$, $m_2 = \mathsf{P}_2(\beta, w_2)$ and $m'_2 = \mathsf{P}_2(\beta', w_2)$. We wish to show that (m_1, m_2) and (m'_1, m'_2) are indistinguishable. The only case where $h_{(a,b)}(\alpha, \beta) = 1 = h_{(a,b)}(\alpha', \beta')$ is when $(a, b) = (\alpha, \beta) = (\alpha', \beta')$, so this case is trivial. We now consider $h_{(a,b)}(\alpha, \beta) = 0 = h_{(a,b)}(\alpha', \beta')$. For the first case, suppose $\alpha = \alpha' = a$. Then, $\beta \neq b \neq \beta'$, and hence $m_1 = m'_1 = (u, s \oplus t)$ with $m_2 = m'_2 = (v_2, r_2)$. Thus, (m_1, m_2) and (m'_1, m'_2) are identical.

For the second case, suppose $\alpha = a$ and $\alpha' \neq a$ while $\beta \neq b$ and $\beta' = b$. Then, $(m_1, m_2) = ((u, s \oplus t), (v_2, r_2))$ while $(m'_1, m'_2) = ((v_1, r_1), (u, t))$. Since u, t, v_1, v_2, r_1, and r_2 are all drawn uniformly, both (m_1, m_2) and (m'_1, m'_2) are indistinguishable from $((\gamma, \delta), (\zeta, \eta))$, where $\gamma, \delta, \zeta, \eta \xleftarrow{\$} \mathbb{G}$ such that $\gamma \neq \zeta$. The rest of the cases are similar, and therefore the scheme satisfies perfect input privacy.

Perfect Function Privacy: Let $s \in \mathbb{G}$ and $\alpha, \beta \in \{0,1\}^n$. Let $h = h_{(a,b)}$ and $h' = h_{(c,d)} \in \mathcal{H}$ be point functions such that $h(\alpha, \beta) = h'(\alpha, \beta)$ and such that for every $c_1 \in \{0,1\}^n$, $\{h(c_1, c_2) : c_2 \in C_2\} = \{h'(c_1, c_2) : c_2 \in C_2\}$. Let $\mathsf{Gen}(h, s) = (w_1, w_2)$, $\mathsf{Gen}(h', s) = (w'_1, w'_2)$ where $w_1 = (a, s, t, u, r_1, v_1)$, $w_2 = (b, s, t, u, r_2, v_2)$, $w'_1 = (c, s, t', u', r'_1, v'_1)$ and $w'_2 = (d, s, t', u', r'_2, v'_2)$. Let $m_1 = \mathsf{P}_1(h, w_1)$, $m_2 = \mathsf{P}_2(h, w_2)$, $m'_1 = \mathsf{P}_1(h', w'_1)$ and $m'_2 = \mathsf{P}_2(h', w'_2)$. We wish to show that $(\alpha, s, w_1, m_1, m_2)$ and $(\alpha, s, w'_1, m'_1, m'_2)$ are indistinguishable. If $h(\alpha, \beta) = h'(\alpha, \beta) = 1$, then the functions are identical point functions. Thus, suppose $h(\alpha, \beta) = h'(\alpha, \beta) = 0$ so that $(a, b) \neq (\alpha, \beta) \neq (c, d)$. The condition that $\{h(c_1, c_2) : c_2 \in C_2\} = \{h'(c_1, c_2) : c_2 \in C_2\}$ for all $c_1 \in \{0,1\}^n$ means that $a = c$.

First, suppose $a \neq \alpha \neq c$ and $b \neq \beta \neq d$. Then, $(m_1, m_2) = ((v_1, r_1), (v_2, r_2))$ and $(m'_1, m'_2) = ((v'_1, r'_1), (v'_2, r'_2))$. Since $u, v_1, v_2, r_1, r_2, u', v'_1, v'_2, r'_1, r'_2$ are all drawn uniformly from $\mathbb{G}$ subject to the restrictions that u, v_1, v_2 and u',

v_1, v_2' are distinct, respectively, it follows that both $(\alpha, s, (a, s, t, u, r_1, v_1),$ $(v_1, r_1), (v_2, r_2))$ and $(\alpha, s, (a, s, t', u', r_1', v_1'), (v_1', r_1'), (v_2', r_2'))$ are indistinguishable from $(\alpha, s, (a, s, \theta, \lambda, \delta, \gamma), (\gamma, \delta), (\zeta, \eta))$, where $\gamma, \delta, \zeta, \eta, \theta, \lambda \xleftarrow{\$} \mathbb{G}$ such that γ, ζ and λ are distinct.

Next, suppose $a \neq \alpha \neq c$ and $b = \beta \neq d$. This gives $(m_1, m_2) = ((v_1, r_1), (u, t))$ and $(m_1', m_2') = ((v_1', r_1'), (v_2', r_2'))$. This case is similar to the one discussed above.

Finally, suppose $a = \alpha = c$ and $b \neq \beta \neq d$. In this case, $(m_1, m_2) = ((u, s \oplus t), (v_2, r_2))$ and $(m_1', m_2') = ((u', s \oplus t'), (v_2', r_2'))$. Then, both $(\alpha, s, (a, s, t, u, r_1, v_1), (u, s \oplus t), (v_2, r_2))$ and $(\alpha, s, (a, s, t', u', r_1', v_1'), (u', s \oplus t'), (v_2', r_2'))$ are indistinguishable from $(\alpha, s, (a, s, \delta, \gamma, \theta, \lambda), (\gamma, s \oplus \delta), (\zeta, \eta))$, where $\gamma, \delta, \zeta, \eta, \theta, \lambda \xleftarrow{\$} \mathbb{G}$ such that γ, ζ and λ are distinct.   ∎

Remark 7. In the above scheme, secrecy, input privacy and function privacy may no longer hold if P_1 and P_2 repeat Step 2 of the protocol with the same shares w_1 and w_2. However, we can remove this limitation if we allow P_1 and P_2 to "refresh" their shares.

To do so, we fix a PRF $F : \mathcal{K} \times \mathbb{G} \to \mathbb{G}$, a PRP $P : \mathcal{K} \times \mathbb{G} \to \mathbb{G}$ and a PRF $F' : \mathcal{K}' \times \{0,1\}^\ell \to \mathcal{K}$, and assume that the dealer $\mathcal{D}$ deals a common key $k' \in \mathcal{K}'$ to both parties P_1 and P_2. Each of the parties also keeps a counter c of the number of times Step 2 of the protocol has been performed. After each run of Step 2, P_i updates the share w_i by doing the following:

1. Compute $k_{1,i} = F'(k', c||1||i)$ and $k_j = F'(k', c||j)$ for $j = 2, 3$.
2. Replace r_i, t, v_i and u by $F(k_{1,i}, r_i)$, $F(k_2, t)$, $P(k_3, v_i)$ and $P(k_3, u)$, respectively.
3. Increment c.

Note that the keys $k_{1,1}$, $k_{1,2}$, k_2 and k_3 are unique to each run of the protocol. This is necessary as otherwise, if $|\mathbb{G}|$ is small, the elements r_i, t, v_i and u could end up in a cycle, repeating after a limited number of runs.

4.2   From FPCDS to FSS

Let there be an FPCDS scheme for k parties $P_1, \ldots, P_k$ for the family of Boolean condition functions $\mathcal{H}$, condition domain $\mathcal{C} = \mathcal{C}_1 \times \ldots \times \mathcal{C}_k$, and secret domain $\mathcal{S}$. Let $\mathcal{D}$ be the dealer for the FPCDS scheme and Gen be the randomized algorithm from the FPCDS scheme. We demonstrate that there exists a k-out-of-k FSS scheme for the family of functions $\mathcal{H}$. Let $\mathcal{D}'$ be the dealer and $P_1', \ldots, P_k'$ be the k parties for the FSS scheme. Our scheme is defined as a collection of three algorithms (KeyGen(h), Eval(k_j), Rec($m_1, \ldots, m_k$)), which are defined as:

KeyGen(h)

1. For the chosen condition function $h \in \mathcal{H}$, $\mathcal{D}'$ samples a random secret $s \in \mathcal{S}$ and runs Gen(h, s) to generate the tuple $(w_1, w_2, \ldots, w_k)$.

2. $\mathcal{D}'$ distributes to each P'_j the key $k_j = w_j$.

Eval(k_j)

1. Each party P'_j, given $k_j = w_j$, chooses an input $c_j \in \mathcal{C}_j$.
2. Each P'_j runs the party algorithm $m_j = \mathsf{P}_j(c_j, w_j)$ from the FPCDS scheme.

Rec($m_1, \ldots, m_k$)

1. The k parties publish the messages $m_1, m_2, \ldots, m_k$.
2. The k parties simulate Carol and compute $\mathsf{Carol}(m_1, m_2, \ldots, m_k)$. If the Carol algorithm rejects, then the parties output 0; otherwise, if the Carol algorithm outputs the correct secret, s, the parties output 1.

Correctness and Privacy. Our scheme satisfies the correctness and function privacy requirements for an FSS scheme.

Perfect Correctness: For the chosen condition function $h \in \mathcal{H}$, suppose $\mathcal{D}'$ samples $s \in \mathcal{S}$ and runs $\mathsf{Gen}(h, s) = (w_1, w_2, \ldots, w_k)$. Then, each P'_j chooses $c_j \in \mathcal{C}_j$ so that $m_j = \mathsf{P}_j(c_j, w_j)$. Now, if $h(c_1, c_2, \ldots, c_k) = 1$, then by perfect correctness of FPCDS, $\mathsf{Carol}(m_1, m_2, \ldots, m_k)$ returns the correct secret s. Hence, the parties output 1 during the reconstruction step. Similarly, when $h(c_1, c_2, \ldots, c_k) = 0$, $\mathsf{Carol}(m_1, m_2, \ldots, m_k)$ always rejects, and hence the parties output 0.

Function Privacy: Fix $c = (c_1, c_2, \ldots, c_k) \in \mathcal{C}$ and $i \in [k]$. Let $h, h' \in \mathcal{H}$ such that for every $c'_i \in \mathcal{C}_i$, the sets $\{h(c'_1, c'_2, \ldots, c'_k) : c'_j \in \mathcal{C}_j \text{ for } j \neq i\}$ and $\{h'(c'_1, c'_2, \ldots, c'_k) : c'_j \in \mathcal{C}_j \text{ for } j \neq i\}$ are equal. Select $s \in \mathcal{S}$, and let $\mathsf{Gen}(h, s) = (w_1, w_2, \ldots, w_k)$, $\mathsf{Gen}(h', s) = (w'_1, w'_2, \ldots, w'_k)$. Suppose $m_i = \mathsf{P}_i(c_i, w_i)$ and $m'_i = \mathsf{P}_i(c_i, w'_i)$. During evaluation and reconstruction, P'_i can observe $(c_i, w_i, m_1, m_2, \ldots, m_k)$ and $(c_i, w'_i, m'_1, m'_2, \ldots, m'_k)$, which are perfectly indistinguishable by the function privacy property of the FPCDS scheme.

Note that the given procedure is an FSS scheme for $\mathcal{H}$ with the following two caveats:

1. The input c_i must remain private to party P'_i.
2. For each party P'_i, function privacy only holds for $h, h' \in \mathcal{H}$ such that:

$$\{h(c'_1, c'_2, \ldots, c'_k) : c'_j \in \mathcal{C}_j \text{ for } j \neq i\} = \{h'(c'_1, c'_2, \ldots, c'_k) : c'_j \in \mathcal{C}_j \text{ for } j \neq i\}$$

for every $c'_i \in \mathcal{C}_i$.

References

1. De Santis, A., Desmedt, Y., Frankel, Y., Yung, M.: How to share a function securely. In: STOC, pp. 522–533 (1994)
2. Shamir, A.: How to share a secret. Commun. ACM **22**, 612–613 (1979)

3. Blakley, G.R.: Safeguarding cryptographic keys. Am. Feder. Inf. Process. **48**, 313–318 (1979)
4. Gilboa, N., Ishai, Y.: Distributed point functions and their applications. In: Nguyen, P.Q., Oswald, E. (eds.) EUROCRYPT 2014. LNCS, vol. 8441, pp. 640–658. Springer, Heidelberg (2014). https://doi.org/10.1007/978-3-642-55220-5_35
5. Dittmer, S., et al.: Function secret sharing for psi-ca:with applications to private contact tracing (2020)
6. Gertner, Y., Ishai, Y., Kushilevitz, E., Malkin, T.G.: Protecting data privacy in private information retrieval schemes. In: STOC (1998)
7. Gay, R., Kerenidis, I., Wee, H.: Communication complexity of conditional disclosure of secrets and attribute-based encryption. In: Gennaro, R., Robshaw, M. (eds.) CRYPTO 2015. LNCS, vol. 9216, pp. 485–502. Springer, Heidelberg (2015). https://doi.org/10.1007/978-3-662-48000-7_24
8. Aiello, B., Ishai, Y., Reingold, O.: Priced oblivious transfer: how to sell digital goods. In: Pfitzmann, B. (ed.) EUROCRYPT 2001. LNCS, vol. 2045, pp. 119–135. Springer, Heidelberg (2001). https://doi.org/10.1007/3-540-44987-6_8
9. Beimel, A., Farràs, O., Mintz, Y., Peter, N.: Linear secret-sharing schemes for forbidden graph access structures. Cryptology ePrint Archive, Report 2017/940 (2017). Accessed 2020, https://eprint.iacr.org/2017/940
10. Beimel, A., Farràs, O., Mintz, Y., Peter, N.: Linear secret-sharing schemes for forbidden graph access structures. In: Kalai, Y., Reyzin, L. (eds.) TCC 2017. LNCS, vol. 10678, pp. 394–423. Springer, Cham (2017). https://doi.org/10.1007/978-3-319-70503-3_13
11. Applebaum, B., Beimel, A., Farràs, O., Nir, O., Peter, N.: Secret-sharing schemes for general and uniform access structures. In: Ishai, Y., Rijmen, V. (eds.) EUROCRYPT 2019. LNCS, vol. 11478, pp. 441–471. Springer, Cham (2019). https://doi.org/10.1007/978-3-030-17659-4_15
12. Liu, T., Vaikuntanathan, V., Wee, H.: Towards breaking the exponential barrier for general secret sharing. In: Nielsen, J.B., Rijmen, V. (eds.) EUROCRYPT 2018. LNCS, vol. 10820, pp. 567–596. Springer, Cham (2018). https://doi.org/10.1007/978-3-319-78381-9_21
13. Applebaum, B., Beimel, A., Nir, O., Peter, N.: Better secret sharing via robust conditional disclosure of secrets. In: STOC, pp. 280–293 (2020)
14. Spotify expands its $4.99 per month student bundle with Hulu to include showtime (2018). https://tcrn.ch/2Pik9j4
15. Spotify: The future of audio. putting data to work, one listener at a time. https://cloud.google.com/customers/spotify
16. Completing the Netflix cloud migration. https://about.netflix.com/en/news/completing-the-netflix-cloud-migration
17. Hulu's move into live television makes amazon a surprise winner. https://fortune.com/2017/08/15/hulu-live-tv-amazon-aws/
18. Anick, P.G., Brennan, J.D., Flynn, R.A., Hanssen, D.R., Alvey, B., Robbins, J.M.: A direct manipulation interface for boolean information retrieval via natural language query. In: ACM SIGIR, pp. 135–150 (1989)
19. Lee, J.H., Kim, M.H., Lee, Y.J.: Ranking documents in thesaurus-based boolean retrieval systems. Inf. Process. Manag. **30**(1), 79–91 (1994)
20. Verhoeff, J., Goffman, W., Belzer, J.: Inefficiency of the use of boolean functions for information retrieval systems. Commun. ACM **4**(12), 557–558 (1961)
21. Agrawal, S., et al.: Functional encryption and property preserving encryption: New definitions and positive results. Cryptology ePrint Archive, Report 2013/744 (2013). https://eprint.iacr.org/2013/744

22. Boneh, D., Raghunathan, A., Segev, G.: Function-private identity-based encryption: hiding the function in functional encryption. In: Canetti, R., Garay, J.A. (eds.) CRYPTO 2013. LNCS, vol. 8043, pp. 461–478. Springer, Heidelberg (2013). https://doi.org/10.1007/978-3-642-40084-1_26

23. Boneh, D., Raghunathan, A., Segev, G.: Function-private subspace-membership encryption and its applications. In: Sako, K., Sarkar, P. (eds.) ASIACRYPT 2013. LNCS, vol. 8269, pp. 255–275. Springer, Heidelberg (2013). https://doi.org/10.1007/978-3-642-42033-7_14

24. Brakerski, Z., Segev, G.: Function-private functional encryption in the private-key setting. In: Dodis, Y., Nielsen, J.B. (eds.) TCC 2015. LNCS, vol. 9015, pp. 306–324. Springer, Heidelberg (2015). https://doi.org/10.1007/978-3-662-46497-7_12

25. Fan, X., Tang, Q.: Making public key functional encryption function private, distributively. In: Abdalla, M., Dahab, R. (eds.) PKC 2018. LNCS, vol. 10770, pp. 218–244. Springer, Cham (2018). https://doi.org/10.1007/978-3-319-76581-5_8

26. Abdalla, M., Pointcheval, D., Soleimanian, A.: 2-step multi-client quadratic functional encryption from decentralized function-hiding inner-product. Cryptology ePrint Archive, Report 2021/001 (2021). https://eprint.iacr.org/2021/001

27. Ahmad, K.A.B., Ahmad, K., Dulhare, U.N. (eds.): Functional Encryption. EICC, Springer, Cham (2021). https://doi.org/10.1007/978-3-030-60890-3

28. Beimel, A., Burmester, M., Desmedt, Y., Kushilevitz, E.: Computing functions of a shared secret. SIAM J. Discret. Math. **13**(3), 324–345 (2000)

29. Goldreich, O., Goldwasser, S., Micali, S.: How to construct random functions. JACM **33**, 792–807 (1986)

30. Naor, M., Pinkas, B., Reingold, O.: Distributed pseudo-random functions and KDCs. In: Stern, J. (ed.) EUROCRYPT 1999. LNCS, vol. 1592, pp. 327–346. Springer, Heidelberg (1999). https://doi.org/10.1007/3-540-48910-X_23

31. Goldwasser, S., Micali, S.M.: Probabilistic encryption & how to play mental poker keeping secret all partial information. In: STOC, pp. 365–377 (1982)

32. Boneh, D., Lewi, K., Montgomery, H., Raghunathan, A.: Key homomorphic PRFs and their applications. In: Canetti, R., Garay, J.A. (eds.) CRYPTO 2013. LNCS, vol. 8042, pp. 410–428. Springer, Heidelberg (2013). https://doi.org/10.1007/978-3-642-40041-4_23

33. Banerjee, A., Peikert, C.: New and improved key-homomorphic pseudorandom functions. In: Garay, J.A., Gennaro, R. (eds.) CRYPTO 2014. LNCS, vol. 8616, pp. 353–370. Springer, Heidelberg (2014). https://doi.org/10.1007/978-3-662-44371-2_20

34. Parra, J.R., Chan, T., Ho, S.-W.: A noiseless key-homomorphic PRF: application on distributed storage systems. In: Liu, J.K., Steinfeld, R. (eds.) ACISP 2016. LNCS, vol. 9723, pp. 505–513. Springer, Cham (2016). https://doi.org/10.1007/978-3-319-40367-0_34

35. Kim, S.: Key-homomorphic pseudorandom functions from LWE with small modulus. In: Canteaut, A., Ishai, Y. (eds.) EUROCRYPT 2020. LNCS, vol. 12106, pp. 576–607. Springer, Cham (2020). https://doi.org/10.1007/978-3-030-45724-2_20

36. Sehrawat, V.S., Desmedt, Y.: Bi-homomorphic lattice-based PRFs and unidirectional updatable encryption. In: Mu, Y., Deng, R.H., Huang, X. (eds.) CANS 2019. LNCS, vol. 11829, pp. 3–23. Springer, Cham (2019). https://doi.org/10.1007/978-3-030-31578-8_1

37. Brakerski, Z., Vaikuntanathan, V.: Constrained key-homomorphic PRFs from standard lattice assumptions. In: Dodis, Y., Nielsen, J.B. (eds.) TCC 2015. LNCS, vol. 9015, pp. 1–30. Springer, Heidelberg (2015). https://doi.org/10.1007/978-3-662-46497-7_1

38. Boneh, D., Kim, S., Montgomery, H.: Private puncturable PRFs from standard lattice assumptions. In: Coron, J.-S., Nielsen, J.B. (eds.) EUROCRYPT 2017. LNCS, vol. 10210, pp. 415–445. Springer, Cham (2017). https://doi.org/10.1007/978-3-319-56620-7_15

39. Brakerski, Z., Tsabary, R., Vaikuntanathan, V., Wee, H.: Private constrained PRFs (and more) from LWE. In: Kalai, Y., Reyzin, L. (eds.) TCC 2017. LNCS, vol. 10677, pp. 264–302. Springer, Cham (2017). https://doi.org/10.1007/978-3-319-70500-2_10

40. Canetti, R., Chen, Y.: Constraint-hiding constrained PRFs for NC^1 from LWE. In: Coron, J.-S., Nielsen, J.B. (eds.) EUROCRYPT 2017. LNCS, vol. 10210, pp. 446–476. Springer, Cham (2017). https://doi.org/10.1007/978-3-319-56620-7_16

41. Kim, S., Wu, D.J.: Watermarking cryptographic functionalities from standard lattice assumptions. In: Katz, J., Shacham, H. (eds.) CRYPTO 2017. LNCS, vol. 10401, pp. 503–536. Springer, Cham (2017). https://doi.org/10.1007/978-3-319-63688-7_17

42. Kim, S., Wu, D.J.: Watermarking PRFs from lattices: stronger security via extractable PRFs. In: Boldyreva, A., Micciancio, D. (eds.) CRYPTO 2019. LNCS, vol. 11694, pp. 335–366. Springer, Cham (2019). https://doi.org/10.1007/978-3-030-26954-8_11

43. Quach, W., Wichs, D., Zirdelis, G.: Watermarking PRFs under standard assumptions: public marking and security with extraction queries. In: Beimel, A., Dziembowski, S. (eds.) TCC 2018. LNCS, vol. 11240, pp. 669–698. Springer, Cham (2018). https://doi.org/10.1007/978-3-030-03810-6_24

44. Bogdanov, A., Rosen, A.: Pseudorandom functions: three decades later. In: Tutorials on the Foundations of Cryptography. ISC, pp. 79–158. Springer, Cham (2017). https://doi.org/10.1007/978-3-319-57048-8_3

How Distance-Bounding Can Detect Internet Traffic Hijacking

Ghada Arfaoui[1], Gildas Avoine[3], Olivier Gimenez[2,3](✉), and Jacques Traoré[2]

[1] Orange Labs, 4 rue du Clos Courtel, 35510 Cesson Sévigné, France
ghada.arfaoui@orange.com
[2] Orange Labs, 42 rue des Coutures, 14000 Caen, France
{olivier.gimenez,jacques.traore}@orange.com
[3] INSA Rennes, University of Rennes, IRISA, CNRS, Rennes, France
gildas.avoine@irisa.fr

Abstract. We propose a two-party cryptographic protocol for detecting traffic hijacking over the Internet. Our proposal relies on a distance-bounding mechanism that measures the round-trip time of packets to decide whether an attack is ongoing. The protocol requires only two cryptographic operations per execution which leads to very few additional workload for the users. We demonstrate the efficiency of the protocol using large-scale experiments and we discuss the choice of the decision function w.r.t. the false positive and negative cases.

1 Introduction

Hijacking attacks on Internet consist in deviating the traffic on a given route to make it travel through unexpected nodes. Two main motivations could justify this kind of attack. The first one is *denial of service*: the attacker stops the communication for some reason and prevents packets to reach their recipient. This attack can be quickly detected and may be due to a routing error. The second one is *relay attack*: the attacker aims to spy on industries, governments or individuals by forcing a flow of data to change its legitimate path and take a new one, involving nodes he owns or being under his control, hence, enabling him to have a capture of this flow. Such attacks may also have a political or ideological dimension.

Many instances of hijacking attacks occurred since the 2000s. On February 2008, Youtube became unreachable for two hours after Pakistan Telecom falsely claimed being the better route for joining it[1]. On April 2010, China Telecom advertised wrong traffic routes in the same fashion. For approximately 20 min, no less than 15% of the Internet traffic adopted those routes, including some traffic of the US government, military sites and commercial sites like Yahoo!

---

[1] https://www.ripe.net/publications/news/industry-developments/youtube-hijacking-a-ripe-ncc-ris-case-study.

© Springer Nature Switzerland AG 2021
M. Conti et al. (Eds.): CANS 2021, LNCS 13099, pp. 355–371, 2021.
https://doi.org/10.1007/978-3-030-92548-2_19

and IBM[2]. More recently, in June 2019, the same kind of incident with China Telecom occurred for about 2 h[3]. Although a portion of these attacks are perhaps caused by human mistakes and do not bear a malicious purpose, the fact remains that, such attacks do not come without consequences, from important slowdowns to potential leaks of sensitive information. Denial of services attacks are inconvenient for the victim, but they are, by nature, instantly detected. To the contrary, relay attacks may be established by a stealth attacker in the long term. If, nowadays, an overwhelming portion of communications is secured through TLS protocol, such an attacker still is able to gather potentially critical metadata.

For instance, Apostolaki, Zohar, and Vanbever showed in [1] that hijacking bitcoin messages can lead to severe impact on the bitcoin system, i.e., isolating parts of the network or delaying block propagation, entailing financial losses. Furthermore, for a government or an industry, allowing this kind of control from another structure is somehow an admission of weakness. In other words, this is also (and some might say mainly) the geopolitical and economical reputation which is at stake.

A large vector to lead this kind of attack lies on a major flaw of the *Border Gateway Protocol* (BGP) inherent to its construction. In a nutshell, this protocol is the backbone of the Internet routing, it allows macro-networks called *Autonomous Systems* (AS) to communicate with one another by announcing which set of IP adresses they can directly reach. By advertising and spreading those announcements to their neighbors, any connected device is able to reach any other one from all over the world. The issue with that procedure is that it fully relies on trust. Hence, a malicious AS could as well be lying on the set of machines it can reach, resulting in a modified path traveled by all the packets sent to this set.

Since July 1994, when BGP-4 was first described [13], a lot of proposals tried to enhance the protocol [8,9,15,16]. All these contributions aimed to strengthen BGP by working on the possibility to authenticate and authorize BGP updates between ASes. The *Internet Engineering Task Force* (IETF) initiated the BGPSec standardization project [10] based on Secure-BGP [9]. The key idea is to use the RPKI public-key infrastructure to certify ASes signatures. Hence a BGPSec update will contain the reachable set of IP addresses along with the list of all the ASes that received the update where all participating AS signed its own pre-path. Other attempts using techniques for anomaly detection, localization, and mitigation are to be found with different levels of efficiency [7,12,14], searching for strategies like alternative routes creation, or hijacked BGP routes announcement analyses. According to [11], these attempts target only specific subproblems and does not provide a complete detection.

---

[2] https://arstechnica.com/information-technology/2010/11/how-china-swallowed-15-of-net-traffic-for-18-minutes/.

[3] https://arstechnica.com/information-technology/2019/06/bgp-mishap-sends-european-mobile-traffic-through-china-telecom-for-2-hours/.

We address the hijacking attack in this article without relying on the routing protocol specificities. Instead, we propose an original application-layer approach that relies on a two-party cryptographic-based anomaly detection protocol, which measures the communication time between users. It performs statistical analysis upon these measurements and a trusted sample. Our protocol accurately distinguishes an hijacked set of packets with a genuine one. We believe our solution to be practical, because it is independent of the routing protocol in use and requires minimal involvements from the end-points. Our protocol is applicable in stable environments as it relies on time measurements stability, and between close collaborators frequently exchanging data flows. To the best of our knowledge, our protocol is the first to detect routing anomalies using time measurements. Previous works on specific protocols like BGP would become obsolete if the classical routing procedures were to drastically change. To the contrary, our protocol relies uniquely on the stability of the measures, and would still be useable whatever the protocol in use.

The remaining of the paper is organized as follows. In Sect. 2, we present the necessary background for our construction. Then we describe our protocol in Sect. 3, where we also elaborate on the protocol security. We also introduce a statistical decision function in Sect. 3.3, that can be used to detect traffic hijacking. We finally provide experimental results in Sect. 4, and conclude on the efficiency of our approach.

2 Preliminaries

In this section, we introduce the background that will be used in the paper.

2.1 Time Measurement

We distinguish two ways for measuring the time between two machines. The *One Way Transit Time* (OWTT) represents the time measured between the sending of a packets and the arrival to the destination. This approach attempts to capture the real time separating two endpoints but demands a precise clock synchronisation of those points and to send the timestamp along with the measured packet. The *Round Trip Time* (RTT) is measuring the time between the sending and the reception of a response. As this is a one-sided measure, there is no need of a clock synchronisation. The approximation $OWTT = \frac{RTT}{2}$ is often made but there is no insurance that the transit times in both directions are comparable. It is then preferable to consider RTT as a stand-alone metric rather than a way to measure OWTT.

2.2 Distance-Bounding Protocols

To the best of our knowledge, the strongest example of countermeasure to *relay attacks* using time measurements are the distance-bounding protocols, a.k.a. proximity checks. They have been massively studied [2] in the context of Radio

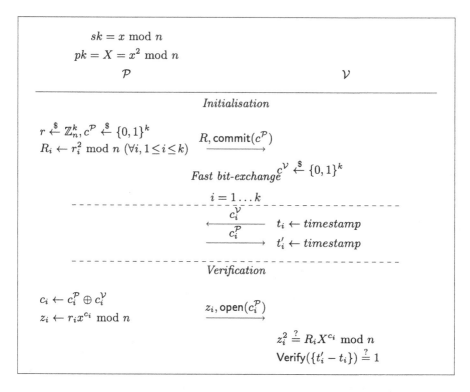

Fig. 1. Brands and Chaum's distance-bounding protocol based on the Fiat-Shamir zero-knowledge authentication

Frequency IDentification (RFID), and they are implemented in some contactless smartcards, e.g., Mifare Plus[4] and Mifare DESfire[5]. Given that the signal propagation cannot be faster than the speed of light, a verifier considers that there is no relaying adversary if the RTTs between the verifier and the prover are below a given upper bound.

A well-known relay attack is the *mafia fraud* introduced by Desmedt, Goutier and Bengio in 1987 [4], and applied to the Fiat-Shamir Zero-Knowledge authentication protocol [5]. This protocol is based on the complexity of the quadratic residuosity problem and allows to prove the knowledge of a number x such that $x^2 = X \mod n$, where X and n are public, with $n = p_1 p_2$ and p_1, p_2 two large and distinct primes. The attack name comes from Shamir's claim that Fiat-Shamir protocol remains secure even in a scenario where the prover is a mafia-owned store, which is contradicted by [4]. The mafia fraud actually allows the attacker to get authenticated by simply relaying the exchange between the genuine prover and the verifying device. Such an attack especially makes sense in contactless authentication that needs the prover (card, transit pass, or else)

---

[4] https://www.nxp.com/docs/en/data-sheet/MF1P(H)x2_SDS.pdf.
[5] https://www.nxp.com/docs/en/data-sheet/MF3DHx3_SDS.pdf.

to be in the proximity of the verifying device. Brands and Chaum introduced in 1994 [3] a countermeasure to this fraud. They indeed added to the Fiat-Shamir protocol a feature to bound the distance from which is standing the genuine prover and to dismiss the authentication if it concludes that the prover is standing further than a given distance. This countermeasure is so-called a *distance-bounding protocol*, and it uses a series of rapid bit-exchanges to measure the round trip time between the prover and the verifier, and so the distance, using the speed of light as an upper bound. We illustrate the protocol of Brands and Chaum in Fig. 1. In this protocol, $\mathcal{P}$ proves to $\mathcal{V}$ that he knows x such that $x^2 = X \bmod n$ in three steps:

- *Initialisation*: $\mathcal{P}$ picks k nonces r_i, computes their squares $R_i = r_i^2 \bmod n$, then picks k random bits $c_i^{\mathcal{P}}$. He then sends the R_i's and a commitment (typically a hash) of the $c_i^{\mathcal{P}}$s. The prover $\mathcal{V}$ then also computes k random bits $c_i^{\mathcal{V}}$.
- *Fast bit-exchange*: for $i = 1 \ldots k$, $\mathcal{V}$ creates a timestamp t_i, sends $c_i^{\mathcal{V}}$, receives the responses $c_i^{\mathcal{P}}$ and immediately creates another timestamp t_i', and stores $(t_i' - t_i)$.
- *Verification*: $\mathcal{P}$ computes all the $c_i = c_i^{\mathcal{P}} \oplus c_i^{\mathcal{V}}$, $z_i = r_i x^{c_i} \bmod n$ and sends z_i to $\mathcal{V}$. The latter checks (i) if the commited $c_i^{\mathcal{P}}$s in the initialisation phase are the same than those he received in the fast bit-exchange phase, (ii) computes the c_i similarly, (iii) checks if z_i^2 is equal to $R_i X^{c_i}$ and (iv) checks if $\max(\{t_i' - t_i\})$ is below a given upper bound.

Brands and Chaum's seminal work paved the way to many other distance-bounding protocols. One could for example cite Hancke and Kuhn's protocol [6] that uses only symmetric-key cryptography. Although describing the body of literature related to distance-bouding protocols is out of the scope of this article, interested readers will find a complete analysis of distance-bounding protocols in [2]. It is worth noting that these protocols are well suited for RFID authentication because communications are end-to-end (from the physical layer perspective) and the computations performed by the RFID tag are lightweight, which implies that the RTTs are very stable. However, it is important to raise that distance-bounding protocols does actually not detect relays: they detect abnormally long RTTs, and guess that this is due to a relay attack. However, a fast enough relay attack might remain undetected if the technology to perform the relay is faster than the technology to measure the RTTs.

The key difference between Internet communications and RF communications is that the former involve physical relays, namely routers, and routes dynamically evolve over time. In spite of that, RTTs are pretty stable as showed later in this article. Consequently, instead of comparing RTTs with a reference time bound as done with RF communications, our protocol compares RTTs with a reference profile defined during a learning phase.

3 Our Protocol to Detect Traffic Hijacking

3.1 Description

Our protocol, described in Fig. 2, runs between a sender $\mathcal{S}$ and a receiver $\mathcal{R}$. A full run of a protocol allows $\mathcal{S}$ to gather one sample of k RTTs, k being a public parameter. To do so, when a run is initiated, $\mathcal{S}$ marks k upcoming[6] packets p_i by a random bit s_i, creates a timestamp t_i and sends $p_i\|s_i$ to $\mathcal{R}$. In each marked round, $\mathcal{R}$ responds with a random bit r_i. Upon reception of r_i, $\mathcal{S}$ creates a new timestamp t'_i. The RTT of the current round is actually the time difference $t'_i - t_i$.

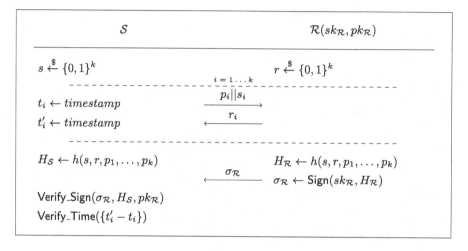

Fig. 2. Distance-bounding protocol to detect Internet traffic hijacking

Once the k rounds have been performed, $\mathcal{R}$ signs the hash of the p_i's along with the s_i's and the r_i's; this hash is denoted $H_\mathcal{R}$ and the signature $\sigma_\mathcal{R}$. Finally, $\mathcal{S}$ verifies that $\sigma_\mathcal{R}$ is a valid signature on $H_\mathcal{S}$ and let the collected sample of RTTs be analyzed by a decision function called Verify_Time. Our protocol differs from RFID Distance Bounding in the manner this RTT sample will be analyzed. As stated in Sect. 2.2, the Internet does not fit accurate distance computation, hence Verify_Time must work differently on the time analysis. This function can be seen as an interchangeable black box for this protocol, although we propose in Sect. 3.3 a suitable example of decision function that is based on a statistical analysis to decide whether some traffic is trustworthy or not. It is worth noting that the collected RTTs should be gathered from similar experiences in order to minimize latency effects. We analyze in Sect. 4 the impact of different factors such as the time of the day, day of the week, or packet size. Also the protocol can either be applied as so upon a punctual exchange or upon a data stream by repeating sequentially the protocol every k measures.

---

[6] For the sake of clarity, we assume that the k packets are consecutive, but this assumption is actually not necessary.

3.2   Security Analysis

Our protocol is called secure if it detects any hijacking attack. We call a successful hijacking attack, an attacker who deviates the routing path of an exchange between two end users S and R without raising an alarm from our protocol.

Threat Model. We assume that the attacker A is able to punctually change the path taken by any packet traveling from S to R and from R to S so that this packet gets to its destination through a node owned by A. This implies that, A is also able to drop or modify these packets. Finally, he can precisely deduce when to send a packet to a specific destination so that this packet arrives at an accurate target time

Attacker Strategies. An attacker A aims at relaying messages between S and R over the course of one run of the protocol without being detected. To do so, he can send to S his own responses $\tilde{r}_i$ at the right time to match the accepting results of Verify_Time. As R signs his view of the exchange at the end, the attacker will have to guess correctly the r_i's that R intends to use, otherwise, when S will verify the signature of R, the verification will fail, and the attacker will be detected. A can guess the correct r_i's with a $\frac{1}{2^k}$ probability, hence k should be chosen greater than 80. The attacker could also try to gather the true r_i's by playing the protocol in advance with R, but then, he will have to guess with the same probability the s_i's.

3.3   Decision Function

We describe in this section a statistical decision function, Verify_Time, that decides whether an hijacking attack is ongoing. For that, the function compares a sample of RTTs, denoted *samp* and collected during an execution of the protocol between two parties R and S, with a reference sample denoted *ref* also collected between R and S during a learning phase. This reference sample contains a large amount of measures that have been collected under trusted circumstances and can be seen as a fingerprint of the expected RTT behaviour.

Notations. We use the following notations throughout the next sections.

- Given a sample *samp* of integer values, we refer to its mean by the notation μ_{samp}./ and to its ith centile by the notation $q_i(samp)$.
- We call $p\%$-density interval the smallest interval containing $p\%$ of the values of *samp* by the notation $I_p(samp)$.
- Given an interval of integers I bounded between a and b ($a < b$), we refer to its length by the notation $len(I) = b - a$

Reference Sample. The reference sample ref consists of a large set of measures gathered in advance during a learning phase performed between $\mathcal{R}$ and $\mathcal{S}$. It represents the standard values one can expect when measuring RTTs between $\mathcal{R}$ and $\mathcal{S}$. It is worth noting that the learning phase should take place when there is no ongoing attack, that is, when the route taken by the packets during the measurements has not been altered by a malicious party.

The reference sample should be updated when the genuine RTTs deviate from their reference due, for example, to modifications in the network topology. Experiments presented in Sect. 4.2 show, though, that RTTs are quite stable even over long periods, e.g., several months.

In environments where RTTs are not stable, dynamically updating the reference sample may improve the reliability of the protocol. For example, any new execution of the protocol provides 256 fresh RTTs that can be concatenated to ref while the 256 oldest ones can be removed from ref. Automatic updates should be monitored, though, because an attacker would be able to slightly delay packets in every run of the protocol to stay undetected by the decision function, hence accepting a slightly modified sample and updating the reference sample. By repeating this process, the attacker gets to a point where the reference sample has been sufficiently poisoned to make the decision function accept relayed packets.

Statistical Test. To select an efficient decision function, we considered 5 different statistical tests and we performed about 500 protocol executions: 250 genuine executions and 250 executions while a relay was ongoing[7]. We then analyzed the results for each test, i.e., the rate of false negatives and false positives, and we selected the most convincing one[8].

Given a sample $samp$ to be tested, a reference sample ref, we denote μ_{samp} (resp. μ_{ref}) the average RTT of the tested sample (resp. reference sample). The selected statistical test is as follows:

Compute the difference $\Delta = |\mu_{samp} - \mu_{ref}|$.
Compute the 80%-density interval $I_{80}(ref)$.
If $\Delta < len(I_{80}(ref))$:
    Return 1
Else:
    Return 0

The use of the mean is justified by the overall stability of RTTs for a genuine sample and the impact of the presence of an intermediary node on the path over it. We choose the threshold value to be the length of the 80%-density interval of ref which allows the test to ignore the extreme values.

---

[7] We elaborate on how a relay node was implemented on Sect. 4.

[8] We describe the four other tests in Appendix A and we show how they perform in Appendix B.

4   Experimental Results

We present in this section the results of our experiments, and provide figures to evaluate the efficiency of our protocol to detect internet traffic hijacking.

4.1   Setup

We measured RTTs for UDP traffic between two parties, S the Sender and R the Receiver, sometimes relayed by A the attacker. We used four nodes connected on the Internet, under different Internet Service Providers and in the same country, this implies that we had no control over the route between S and R. For this reason, we simulate the presence of a relay by sending directly the packets from S to A then from A to R. This simulation of relay attack may obviously differ from what happens in reality, however it seems fair to assume that the presence of a relay implies a raise of the measured times. The more impacting factor in RTT evaluation lies in the processing delay of every router the packets will encounter. We used the traceroute command to estimate the numbers of hops separating each nodes[9] on our setup, we also used Wireshark to observe the Time To Live of our UDP packets at arrival. Table 1 shows the route length with A, B, C and D denoting these four nodes. We want to emphasis that these routes length are only stated to bring a more reliable sense of distance between our nodes than geographical distance, as our protocol does not use this information.

Table 1. Number of traversed routers obtained with traceroute command

Receiver	Sender			
	A	B	C	D
A	–	13	13	13
B	14	–	7	14
C	12	9	–	14
D	15	14	16	–

All the following measures have been collected by making S send random char strings of specified length and waiting for a constant length response then computing the RTT value before sending the next char string. The date and hour of the exchange, the size of packets, and the locations of the two end points are readable on every figure. To simulate a relay attack performed by A on the communication, we made S directly send packets to A. To reduce the delay to its minimum, A does not apply any kind of treatment to the relayed message, he does not print neither he stores it. He immediately transfers it to the original receiver R and wait his response which he will transfer in the exact same fashion.

---

[9] Note that traceroute can only deliver a probable and punctual estimation of the route between two points, such a route can change over time.

For all our experiments, the Sender, Receiver, and Attacker always belong to this set $\{A, B, C, D\}$.

4.2 Observation

Our experimental studies aim to give a neat view of the global behavior of RTTs for UDP packets. We focus our experiments, which have been performed over several months, on four main indicators: (1) behavior of RTT during a fast exchange, (2) Behavior of RTT over several days, (3) Impact of the packet size over RTT, (4) Impact of the presence of an intermediary party relaying the messages. The next figures show standard and compelling examples of all our observations, which consists in several thousands samples collected.

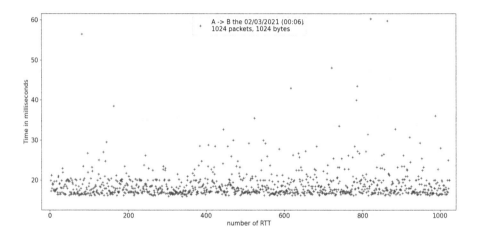

Fig. 3. A single sample of RTT

Figure 3 shows a sample, collected between A and B, containing 1024 RTTs for packets of size 1024 bytes. We observe that the majority of the measures stands around 17.5 ms and very few values goes higher than 21 ms. Figure 4 shows 3 samples collected in December 2020, January 2021, and March 2021 at different hours of the day between parties A and C. It illustrates that, even though the measures are separated from several weeks, the RTTs remain on the same interval, which seems to indicate a stability over a long period of time. These observations gives credit to the use of a static reference sample, as discussed in Sect. 3.3. Figure 5 shows two genuine samples of 256 RTTs between parties A and B, gathered 1 hour apart, and suffering from a time difference of about 10 ms. Indeed, it is fair to highlight that samples collected in a very short time can provide significantly different RTTs. This difference is likely caused by internal route management like load-balancing, multi-path, etc. Hopefully, even these alternative behaviours remain highly distinguishable from the latencies caused by an hijacking attack. Figure 6 displays two collected samples, whose

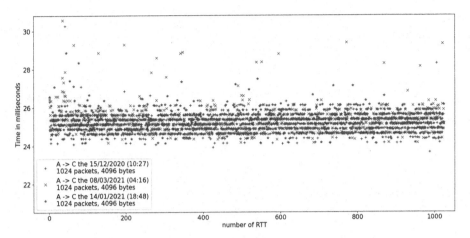

Fig. 4. Evolution of RTTs between two parties over several months

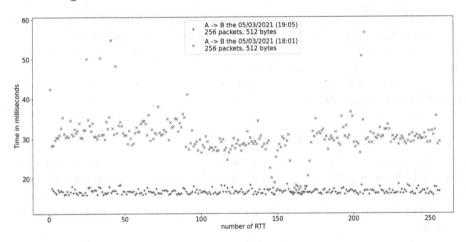

Fig. 5. Two samples a few minutes apart

one matches an hijacked traffic. The intermediary party is in this case C, and we can observe a large gap of more than 30 ms between the hijacked traffic and the genuine one. Figure 7 shows the RTTs measured in relation to the size of the packets sent. We so sent packets of every byte size by increasing it successively by 1 byte at each sending. This shows an impact on the RTT, with a variation of about 5 ms between a 1 byte message and a 4096 bytes message. This results indicates that applying our protocol while ignoring the size of the packets to be measured could reduce the precision of our statistical test. Figure 8 finally compares a sample gathered from an exchange between C and B using packets of random sizes in [896; 1152] and another with length fixed to 1024. The random size sample appears to be a little more spread out but stable enough to be efficiently analyzed by our function.

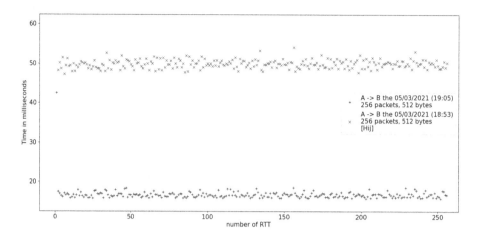

Fig. 6. Two samples: one genuine, the other issued from a relay

To conclude, the key point of these results is that the highest possible perturbations over RTTs occur only when a relay is ongoing, and the difference between a genuine traffic and an hijacked one is significant. To confirm that this difference can be exploited by our protocol, we present in the next part the results of our statistical tests.

4.3   Testing the Decision Function

In this section, we experimentally challenge the decision function described in Sect. 3.3. We define the false positive rate to be the percentage of genuine samples identified by the decision function as being hijacked samples, and the false negative to be the percentage of hijacked samples detected as being genuine samples.

Methodology. We define below the key points of our experiments.

- *Parties.* Tests are realized between two pairs of parties, being (D, C) with measures gathered on D's side, and (A, B) with measures gathered on A's side. The number of routing equipments on the route provided by traceroute command is summarized in Table 1.
- *Hijacked traffic.* When the traffic is hijacked, the traffic between A and B (resp. C and D) is deviated through C (resp. B).
- *Reference Sample.* As reference samples, we used about 10 samples of 256 measures that we concatenated for each category. These 10 samples were collected over one single day at different time of the day.
- *Packet size.* We tested the cases of both fixed and variable sizes for the packets sent to see if the tests did better on one category or the other. For the fixed size we choosed 512 bytes, and for variable size, between 480 and 544 (i.e., 512 ± 32) bytes. The collected samples are all made of 256 measures.

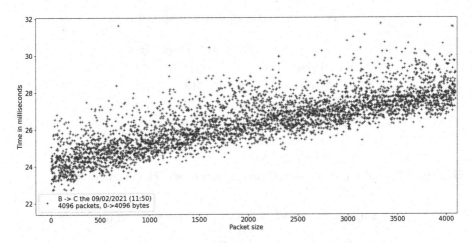

Fig. 7. Evolution of RTT for packets of size 1 to 4096 bytes

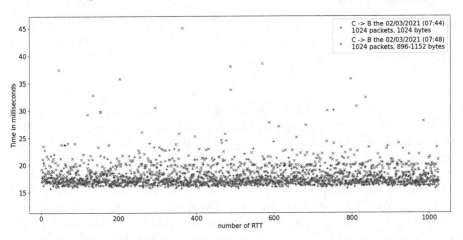

Fig. 8. Evolution of RTT for packets of size between 896 to 1152

We collected a large amount of samples to be tested (detailed in Table 2). All of them were collected over 4 to 5 consecutive days. About half of them being genuine, the rest being issued from a simulated relay.

Table 2. Number of analysed samples

	Genuine	Relayed	Total
(A, B) const. size	240	238	478
(A, B) var. size	190	188	378
(D, C) const. size	286	286	572
(D, C) var. size	249	251	500

Results. Table 3 gives the overall success rates for each category.

Table 3. Results of the test for our decision function

	False positive rate (%)	False negative rate (%)	Accuracy (%)
(A, B) const. size	0	0	100
(A, B) var. size	0.526	0	99.735
(D, C) const. size	3.846	0	98.077
(D, C) var. size	2.008	0	99.0

We can first observe that no false negative appear during the tests. As stated earlier, the impact of a relay over the sample is high and very perceptible. Though we emphasize on the false positive rate which shows inequal results in the two categories (almost none for A to B and actually none for the constant size experiment, and about 3% for D to C). This disparity might be caused by a difference of representativity of the reference samples. Hence we recommend to choose even larger reference samples. Based on these results the users can expect the protocol to raise an alarm any time a significative path change occurs, allowing them to check if that change is legitimate or not. One could argue that the protocol is likely to detect any kind of time-impacting routing anomaly, even if not issued from a relay attack. However, our experimental results showed that the occurrence of an attack is characterized by an extreme RTT raise. A punctual routing anomaly, if consistent enough, will indeed create a false positive but we believe such an event to be rare enough to be dealt with manually. Finally the function shows slightly better results when the samples are created from constant size packets, but keep an acceptable rate of false rejection otherwise, which makes our protocol suitable to realistic contexts.

5 Conclusion

We introduce in this article an innovative approach to detects internet traffic hijacking. Our protocol is based on a distance-bounding mechanism that detects abnormally long round trip times. Up to our knowledge, this is the first time such an approach is used in this context. We experimentally showed that our protocol was able to detect all deviated traffic. The false positive rate is low, and it could be made still lower by tightly tuning the decision function. This requires to perform large-scale experiments, what we expect to setup in the short future. It is worth noting that our protocol can be easily deployed: application-oriented, it does not require any update of the routers and it can be used by partners without following a long standardization process.

A   Description of Other Candidates for the Decision Function

We initially selected 4 other candidates for potential decision function. We did identical experiments to decide which one was the most efficient. Some test showed acceptable results but none was as precise as the one presented in Sect. 3.3. We present here the tests and their results.

A.1   Average Position

This test computes the mean of $samp$ μ_{samp} and computes the 80%-density interval $I_80(ref)$ of ref. It returns 1 if $\mu_{samp} \in I_{80}(ref)$, 0 otherwise.

A.2   10%-Minimum Overlap

This test computes the first decile of the both samples $q_{10}(samp)$, $q_{10}(ref)$ and consider the intervals $I = [min(samp), q_{10}(samp)]$ and $I' = [min(ref), q_{10}(ref)]$. It returns 1 if at least 50% of I overlaps I', that is to say if: $\frac{len(I \cap I')}{len(I)} > 0.5$. It returns 0 otherwise.

A.3   50%-Minimum Overlap

This test computes the median of the both samples $q_{50}(samp)$, $q_{50}(ref)$ and consider the intervals $I = [min(samp), q_{50}(samp)]$ and $I' = [min(ref), q_{50}(ref)]$. It returns 1 if at least 50% of I overlaps I', that is to say if: $\frac{len(I \cap I')}{len(I)} > 0.5$. It returns 0 otherwise.

A.4   Density Match

This test computes 80%-density interval $I_{80}(ref)$ and checks the proportion p of elements of $samp$ being in this interval. It returns 1 if $p > 0.5$, 0 otherwise

B   Experiments for all the Tests

(See Tables 4, 5, 6 and 7)

Table 4. Tests results between A and B for constant length

	False positive rate (%)	False negative rate (%)	Success rate (%)
Average pos.	2.5	0	98.745
10%-Min overlap	34.583	0	82.636
50%-Min overlap.	2.419	0	98.536
Density match	1.25	0	99.372

Table 5. Tests results between A and B for variable length

	False positive rate (%)	False negative rate (%)	Success rate (%)
Average pos.	3.684	0	98.148
10%-Min overlap	44.211	0	77.778
50%-Min overlap.	1.053	0	99.47
Density match	1.053	0	99.47

Table 6. Tests results between D and C for constant length

	False positive rate (%)	False negative rate (%)	Success rate (%)
Average pos.	7.343	0	96.329
10%-Min overlap	0.699	0	99.65
50%-Min overlap.	0.35	0	99.825
Density match	0.35	0	99.825

Table 7. Tests results between D and C for variable length

	False positive rate (%)	False negative rate (%)	Success rate (%)
Average pos.	4.016	0	98
10%-Min overlap	0.803	0	99.6
50%-Min overlap.	0.402	0	99.8
Density match	0.401	0	99.8

References

1. Apostolaki, M., Zohar, A., Vanbever, L.: Hijacking bitcoin: routing attacks on cryptocurrencies. In: 2017 IEEE Symposium on Security and Privacy (SP), pp. 375–392. IEEE (2017)

2. Avoine, G., et al.: Security of distance-bounding: a survey. ACM Comput. Surv. (CSUR) **51**(5), 1–33 (2018)

3. Brands, S., Chaum, D.: Distance-bounding protocols. In: Helleseth, T. (ed.) EURO-CRYPT 1993. LNCS, vol. 765, pp. 344–359. Springer, Heidelberg (1994). https://doi.org/10.1007/3-540-48285-7_30

4. Desmedt, Y., Goutier, C., Bengio, S.: Special uses and abuses of the Fiat-Shamir passport protocol (extended abstract). In: Pomerance, C. (ed.) CRYPTO 1987. LNCS, vol. 293, pp. 21–39. Springer, Heidelberg (1988). https://doi.org/10.1007/3-540-48184-2_3

5. Fiat, A., Shamir, A.: How to prove yourself: practical solutions to identification and signature problems. In: Odlyzko, A.M. (ed.) CRYPTO 1986. LNCS, vol. 263, pp. 186–194. Springer, Heidelberg (1987). https://doi.org/10.1007/3-540-47721-7_12

6. Hancke, G.P., Kuhn, M.G.: An RFID distance bounding protocol. In: 1st International Conference on Security and Privacy for Emerging Areas in Communications Networks, SECURECOMM 2005, pp. 67–73 (2005)

7. Holterbach, T., Vissicchio, S., Dainotti, A., Vanbever, L.: SWIFT: predictive fast reroute. In: . SIGCOMM 2017, pp. 460–473, Association for Computing Machinery, New York (2017). https://doi.org/10.1145/3098822.3098856

8. Karlin, J., Forrest, S., Rexford, J.: Pretty good BGP: improving BGP by cautiously adopting routes. In: ICNP, pp. 290–299 (December 2006). https://doi.org/10.1109/ICNP.2006.320179

9. Kent, S., Lynn, C., Seo, K.: Secure border gateway protocol (S-BGP). IEEE J. Sel. Areas Commun. **18**(4), 582–592 (2000)

10. Lepinski, M., Sriram, K.: BGPsec Protocol Specification. RFC 8205 (September 2017). https://doi.org/10.17487/RFC8205. https://rfc-editor.org/rfc/rfc8205.txt

11. Mitseva, A., Panchenko, A., Engel, T.: The state of affairs in BGP security: a survey of attacks and defenses. Comput. Commun. **124**, 45–60 (2018)

12. Qiu, T., Ji, L., Pei, D., Wang, J., Xu, J.: TowerDefense: deployment strategies for battling against IP prefix hijacking. In: The 18th IEEE International Conference on Network Protocols, pp. 134–143 (2010). https://doi.org/10.1109/ICNP.2010.5762762

13. Rekhter, Y., Li, T., Hares, S., et al.: A border gateway protocol 4 (BGP-4) (1994)

14. Sermpezis, P., et al.: ARTEMIS: neutralizing BGP hijacking within a minute. IEEE/ACM Trans. Netw. **26**(6), 2471–2486 (2018)

15. Wan, T., Kranakis, E., van Oorschot, P.C.: Pretty secure BGP, psBGP. In: NDSS. Citeseer (2005)

16. White, R.: Securing BGP through secure origin BGP (soBGP). Bus. Commun. Rev. **33**(5), 47 (2003)

SoK: Secure Memory Allocation

Bojan Novković$^{(\boxtimes)}$ (iD) and Marin Golub (iD)

Faculty of Electrical Engineering and Computing,
University of Zagreb, Zagreb, Croatia
{bojan.novkovic,marin.golub}@fer.hr

Abstract. Heap-related memory corruption vulnerabilities are a severe threat that continues to wreak havoc in widespread software despite a few decades of research. Research in hardening memory allocation yielded several proposed designs and a large number of techniques designed to mitigate common heap-related vulnerabilities. However, rigid performance requirements imposed by the majority of vulnerable workloads are a severe hindrance to the practical use of secure memory allocation techniques and systems.

This paper aims to systematically analyze and classify all secure heap allocation techniques and systems implementing them which emerged in the last two decades, and compare their performance to conventional systems. We provide a concise overview of heap-related vulnerabilities and construct a threat model to identify previously overlooked and unmitigated threats.

We analyze the root causes of performance overheads observed in the existing literature and identify practical issues hindering the adoption of secure memory allocation systems in practice. We conduct fine-grained and coarse-grained benchmarks on real-life workloads and well-known benchmark suites to compare and analyze the overall performance of secure memory allocation systems to conventional ones.

Using the aforementioned benchmark results, we compare different designs of secure memory allocation systems and provide guidelines for striking a balance between security and performance in future designs.

Keywords: Memory allocation · Systems security · Memory safety

1 Introduction

Although less popular than their stack-based counterparts, heap-related memory corruption bugs are a severe threat and have caused many catastrophic vulnerabilities over the past two decades [1,18]. Over the last couple of years, the number of heap-related vulnerabilities encountered in the wild is steadily growing. We support this claim with an extensive survey of memory corruption vulnerabilities reported through the last couple of years. We classify publicly available data provided by MITRE [9] based on the type of heap-related memory corruption vulnerabilites. Figure 1 represents the result of our classification and indicates

© Springer Nature Switzerland AG 2021
M. Conti et al. (Eds.): CANS 2021, LNCS 13099, pp. 372–391, 2021.
https://doi.org/10.1007/978-3-030-92548-2_20

a steady growth of heap-related memory corruption vulnerabilites throughout the years. Moreover, we found that a large number of heap-related vulnerabilities were found in widespread software written in **C/C++** such as the *Chrome* web browser and the *Linux* kernel. This steady increase can be attributed to increased use of active vulnerability discovery techniques and platforms (e.g., OSS-Fuzz) and an increasing number of mitigations for other attack vectors.

The majority of these vulnerabilities stem from human errors in languages without memory safety mechanisms. Their exploitation can lead to a wide range of misbehaviors and security risks, from denial of service to arbitrary code execution and information leaks [18]. Their exploitation is often made possible or facilitated by the deterministic behavior exhibited by conventional or performance-oriented memory allocation systems. This deterministic behavior is often a crucial part of larger exploit chains and is leveraged in few payload delivery techniques [17]. However, memory allocation systems are not the only part of the computing environment that has an impact on heap safety. Many tools aiming to harden the heap have been introduced throughout the whole computing stack, ranging from new hardware-based techniques and architectures (e.g. CHERI) to programming languages designed with memory safety in mind (e.g. Rust). However, they can often be unavailable or impractical to apply to legacy and modern applications written in C/C++ due to a variety of reasons (e.g. missing source code). Due to this, memory allocation systems are often the only practical way to retrofit heap safety to unsafe applications.

Many secure heap memory allocation techniques and systems have been proposed throughout the years. Although most of these systems aim to harden all aspects of memory allocation, some proposed systems focused on preventing specific types of heap-based vulnerability exploitation. However, these systems and techniques often impose non-negligible performance and memory overheads that hinder their adoption despite the security benefits they provide [15].

With a recent resurgence of interest in secure heap memory allocation research [1,3,19,20], this paper aims to provide the following contributions:

- a systematic analysis of existing secure heap memory allocation systems and techniques along with practical issues hindering their adoption
- an extended threat model identifying threats and vulnerabilities which are unmitigated in state-of-the-art systems
- a detailed coarse-grained and fine-grained performance analysis on real-life workloads, compared with conventional memory allocation systems and suggestions for future work
- a comparison of different secure memory allocation system designs with guidelines for future designs

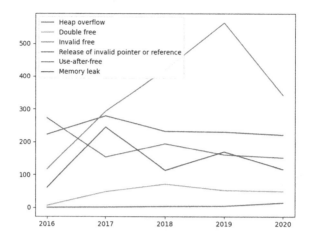

Fig. 1. Number of registered heap-related vulnerabilities per year.

2   Conventional Memory Allocation

The primary task of a memory allocation system is to partition the available free memory space and serve chunks of requested sizes in a timely manner while aiming to minimize internal and external fragmentation [13]. Memory allocation systems are usually rated by several important criteria: execution time, fragmentation rates, multithreaded scalability, and data locality. The most common approaches used for partitioning free space are:

– Binning,
– Coalescing.

The *binning* technique partitions the available space into fixed-size blocks while *coalescing* dynamically joins and splits memory regions depending on the requested chunk size. The free space management aspect can be further broken down as most memory allocation systems manage "small" and "large" memory chunks differently.

Each memory allocation system must maintain a certain amount of metadata describing the state of the memory pool. Based on the way free memory is tracked, conventional dynamic memory allocation systems fall into several categories:

– Freelist allocators,
– Bitmap allocators.

Freelist allocators utilize linked lists (*freelists*) to manage and track freed and currently used objects of varying sizes, often embedding metadata before the actual chunk or inside unused chunks to facilitate memory tracking and increase allocation performance. The second type of free memory management utilizes *bitmaps* to track states of fixed-size chunks in the memory pool. Although easily conflated with *binning*, this approach can be used with the *coalescing* technique. Multiple fixed-size chunks tracked by the *bitmap* can be merged into a larger chunk, depending on the requested chunk size (e.g., *buddy allocator*). This approach is more memory efficient, but its main drawback is slower chunk allocation since the bitmap needs to be sequentially scanned [13].

Traditionally, the heap is treated as a contiguous region of virtual memory, which is expanded through system calls such as brk, sbrk, and mmap. This view of the heap serves as a basis for various memory allocation algorithms utilizing binning or coalescing for managing free space (e.g., first-fit). However, the so-called *Big Bag Of Pages (BiBOP)* approach employs a non-sequential allocation approach using several pages as a "bag," which holds multiple objects of the same size [13]. Free space within each bag is managed using freelists or bitmaps and is grown on demand, usually by fetching additional pages from the kernel.

A ubiquitous conventional memory allocation system is ptmalloc [4], used as the default allocator in the GNU C library [8]. The system tracks memory chunks using inline metadata and manages free space using several "bins", each of which implements one or more free space management techniques.

3 Vulnerabilities

Programmer-induced errors in memory-unsafe programming languages cause heap-based memory corruption vulnerabilities. A lot of research has been devoted to detecting or preventing these vulnerabilities before any significant damage can occur [18]. However, security analyses often overlook the potential risk stemming from the memory allocation system. Since memory allocation systems run as a part of the executed program, they contribute to the resulting attack surface, albeit harder to exploit due to the constrained nature of memory allocation systems. Therefore, heap-related vulnerabilities fall into two main categories, memory-corruption vulnerabilities caused by user memory mismanagement and vulnerabilities present in the memory allocation system itself.

3.1 Heap-Based Memory Corruption Vulnerabilities

One of the most common heap-based memory corruption vulnerabilities is the heap-based buffer overflow caused by spatial memory safety violations. Attackers can exploit this vulnerability to overwrite an adjacent heap object, leading to unexpected program behavior, abrupt program termination, or in the most severe cases to arbitrary code execution. Heap-based buffer overreads are a similar and equally dangerous vulnerability as they enable the attacker to leak potentially sensitive memory contents, leading to the compromise of the entire system.

Another common vulnerability is the *Use-After-Free (UAF)* [13] vulnerability. It is caused by temporal memory safety violations, usually through *dangling* pointers, which point to a previously freed memory chunk. Referencing freed memory can cause various misbehaviors in the vulnerable program, ranging from unexpected crashes to code execution.

Interaction with uninitialized memory due to a lack of explicit initialization of allocated memory can lead to various vulnerabilities ranging from information leaks to code execution.

Another class of heap-related vulnerabilities tied to the underlying memory allocation system are *invalid* and *double* free vulnerabilities. The scope and impact of these vulnerabilities greatly depend on the implementation of the underlying memory allocation system and the robustness of mechanisms used to detect invalid `free` operations. Failure to detect *invalid* and *double* freeing results leads to inconsistencies in memory management metadata. The attacker can abuse this to reuse memory chunks he controls or use to perform arbitrary memory writes.

3.2   Allocator Vulnerabilities

Vulnerabilities in memory allocation systems can be exploited as standalone vulnerabilities or used as a means of facilitating or enabling the exploitation of another memory corruption vulnerability present in the program. They are primarily caused by abusing allocator-specific metadata used to track free memory space, causing the system to misbehave.

Although highly efficient, this approach is extremely susceptible to malicious manipulation via heap-based spatial and temporal memory violations as embedded metadata can be conveniently overwritten, leading to unwanted behavior. Malicious metadata manipulation is often paired with subtle implementation errors found while calculating chunk offsets and coalescing. These miscalculations can be used to create overlapping chunks, even with very restricted off-by-one miscalculations.

BiBOP-style allocator designs improve allocation security by dealing with metadata differently. Contrary to the freelist-based approach, metadata for allocated objects is stored in a separate area. While isolating the metadata from the objects enhances security, some implementations of *BiBOP*-style allocators store metadata at the beginning of each page, leaving room for spatial memory violations via adjacent objects [13].

Additionally, the historical record of vulnerabilities discovered in memory allocation systems utilizing the *coalescing* technique [20] indicates the approach itself is very error-prone.

Aside from vulnerabilities caused by erroneous implementations, the deterministic workflow of conventional memory allocation systems can often result in predictable behavior, which can be used to mount attacks on programs with heap-based memory corruption vulnerabilities.

The earliest attack technique leveraging deterministic memory allocation is known as *heap-spraying* [13]. A malicious actor with the ability to freely interact with the memory management system can allocate a significant number of chunks containing a malicious payload. These chunks can subsequently be used after other memory corruption vulnerabilities present in the program have been exploited. This approach facilitates the exploitation of other memory-corruption vulnerabilities by raising the likelihood of encountering the payload at a random heap address, thus removing the need to place the payload at fixed memory locations. Additionally, this technique can help circumvent modern defenses against memory-corruption attacks utilizing randomization, such as ASLR.

Another frequently encountered technique that leverages deterministic behavior, known as *heap feng shui* [17], takes a different approach. This technique relies on the fact that an attacker who can allocate and free memory has a significant influence on the state and layout of the heap. Sotirov [17] showed that this fact is sufficient to coerce the memory allocation system to behave predictably. For instance, if we observe a hypothetical memory allocation system that uses a freelist-based approach to track free memory chunks, an attacker can allocate an arbitrary chunk of memory, populate it with malicious data, and free the chunk. The subsequent allocation request of the same size is then guaranteed to return the block previously used by the attacker. When paired with memory-corruption vulnerabilities caused by uninitialized variables, this approach can have devastating consequences.

3.3 Threat Model

To thoroughly compare and evaluate various secure memory allocation techniques, we evaluate common exploitation scenarios found in real-life exploits and form a corresponding threat model.

To remain consistent with most threat models various authors used for security evaluations of their systems [7,13,15], we assume that the attacker can freely interact with the vulnerable program and launch successive attacks through a domain-specific channel (e.g., via network requests for web-facing services). For example, a network-facing service that stores and processes user-provided data on the heap is potentially vulnerable as the attacker indirectly controls some heap allocations. Moreover, to account for potential vulnerabilities in the memory allocation system, we assume that the attacker also can invoke an arbitrary number of memory management calls (malloc, free). Although highly dependent on the functionality of the vulnerable program, this assumption is necessary to account for attack vectors in various web browsers. In this scenario, the attacker controls all memory allocations through the browser's scripting engine and can trigger various vulnerabilities present in the browser itself. A prime example of this attack scenario among many real-life cases is CVE-2020-6449 [11], a *use-after-free* vulnerability in the *Chromium* browser which allowed the attacker to execute arbitrary code via a specially crafted web page. This particular vulnerability is especially relevant as its exploitation was paired with improper chunk freeing in a partitioning memory allocation system used to allocate objects in the browser's audio subsystem.

We assume that the underlying operating system is trusted. The attacker cannot leak or manipulate the metadata of memory allocation systems through channels other than malloc and free. We assume the possible presence of all previously enumerated heap-based memory corruption vulnerabilities and vulnerabilities present in the memory allocation system.

However, we found that existing models fail to consider certain threats stemming from improper memory management. More specifically, we form a stricter model by including abuse of memory leak bugs into the list of possible vulnerabilities. Commonly overlooked or unnoticed, memory leak bugs are a common occurrence whose abuse can seriously harm the availability of network services. One of many reported examples of an abusable memory leak vulnerability is CVE-2020-27753 [10], where several memory leak bugs were found in *ImageMagick*, a widely used image manipulation library. Using a specially crafted header in an image file, an attacker could abuse the memory leak to cause a denial of service.

Although existing research yielded sanitizers [16] and garbage-collection techniques [5] as a means of finding and preventing memory leak bugs, these measures are enforced in the development process or as a part of the programming environment and may not be applicable in some case. Thus, memory allocation systems represent a final safeguard and should incorporate some form of memory leak detection or mitigation. Moreover, Ainsworth et al. [1] demonstrated that tracking techniques similar to those found in garbage collection algorithms can be successfully used to combat temporal safety violations. We believe that, with further research, this model could be extended or adapted to provide a feasible mitigation against denial of service attacks caused by memory leaks.

4   Secure Memory Allocation Techniques

4.1   Metadata Segregation

Malicious metadata manipulation can be prevented by moving all metadata into a separate area, away from user-controlled data [13]. While this dramatically increases the security of the memory allocation system, a new issue must be carefully considered to retain or minimize potential performance impacts, the issue of mapping metadata to chunks. It should be noted that this approach increases cache pressure as the often-used metadata blocks are no longer adjacent to the allocated blocks, possibly leading to a drop in performance. A common approach used for mapping metadata utilizes a hash map to track allocated chunks.

Moreover, the metadata memory space should be protected from potential memory leaks as a single leaked pointer can circumvent all security guarantees provided by this technique. Most modern secure memory allocation systems rely on ASLR combined with the mmap system call to avoid predictable memory addresses when requesting additional pages from the underlying operating system [12,14].

4.2   Randomized Allocation

Randomized allocation features in *BiBOP*-style memory allocation systems or those using the *binning* technique can be augmented by incorporating a degree of redundancy. This usually means that the corresponding memory pool must be adaptively grown to maintain a fixed redundancy rate. All prior research evaluated this feature by using the *allocation entropy* metric defined as $\log_2(i)$, where i denotes the number of chunks available for allocation in a specific memory pool or bag. This approach can significantly improve the security properties of a given memory allocation system or even provide guarantees about *allocation entropy* values [13,15].

The performance impact of increased system calls required for fetching additional memory pages can be minimized through acquiring larger batches of pages or caching unused pages. However, the latter optimization can potentially lead to chunk reuse, thereby reducing randomization guarantees.

4.3   Overprovisioning

The overprovisioning technique augments overflow protection through the selective use of allocated memory chunks. A certain amount of allocated memory chunks are marked and never considered for future allocations and deallocations. Depending on the rate of unused chunks, there is a significant chance that most overflows will corrupt unused chunks and will have no impact on the underlying program. However, this approach comes with a significant memory overhead since a potentially large number of memory chunks are never considered for allocation, which can be detrimental for systems with constrained memory resources [7].

4.4   Delayed Reuse

Delaying reuse of freed chunks is a technique used for thwarting *use-after-free* attacks. It can be realized through randomized chunk selection during allocation [13,15], or explicit "quarantining" or tracking recently freed chunks [1]. A notable approach called *Fast-Forward Allocation* was conceived by Wickman et al. [19], explicitly aimed at preventing *use-after-free* attacks by never reusing freed memory.

4.5   Overflow Mitigation

Guard Pages: Memory allocation systems can leverage the paging memory model to enhance overflow mitigation. Placing unmapped pages around the target chunk ensures that every overflowed memory access generates a page fault, provides a valuable detection mechanism, and mitigates information leaks by preventing overreads. However, this approach comes with a significant performance overhead due to the system call required to place such pages and must be used sparsely to maintain acceptable performance [7]. Existing secure memory allocation systems utilize guard pages by placing them randomly within a memory range using a fixed ratio [14,15] or deferring their placement until a memory pool has to be expanded [7].

Canaries: This staple technique for overflow detection places random *canary* values on the boundaries of allocated chunks [13,15]. These values are usually checked upon freeing an allocated memory chunk, similar to the widespread *stack canary* technique.

Canary management also plays a key role in secure memory allocation systems. Depending on their mutability, *canary* values can be *dynamic* or *static*. Static *canary* values offer increased protection against overflows and incur a negligible performance overhead. However, fixed *canary* values enable an attacker to completely circumvent overflow detection through a single leaked pointer. Dynamic *canary* values circumvent this issue but require more complex handling and careful design to avoid performance and memory overhead.

It should be noted that *canary* values tend to increase internal memory fragmentation in *BiBOP*-style systems as the memory allocation system adds additional bytes to the requested chunk size [7]. This can cause the allocation request to be served from the next bag, which manages objects of the following size class, resulting in wasted memory.

4.6   Invalid Pointer Detection

Proper detection of invalid pointers passed to `free` calls must be enforced to prevent metadata injection through forged chunks [7]. Memory allocation systems can enforce invalid pointer detection on several levels of granularity:

- Detecting addresses which do not point inside the heap,
- Detecting unallocated addresses,
- Detecting unallocated addresses inside a specific size class.

The first level of granularity is present in most memory allocation systems. However, subsequent finely granulated levels are either not present in memory allocation systems or produce false positives and fail to detect some invalid pointers [14].

4.7   Information Leak Prevention

Performance-oriented memory allocation systems often reuse freed memory chunks to avoid the relatively expensive metadata traversal. However, contents of freed memory chunks are usually not sanitized (destroyed) by the memory allocation system as this can harm performance, leaving the sanitization to the programmer. Memory sanitization can be incorporated into a memory allocation system by overwriting chunk data with a predefined value when it is freed [13]. However, this is usually left as an optional feature that is not enabled by default, due to a significant performance impact [14].

5 Overview of existing Secure Memory Allocation Systems

When comparing different secure memory allocation systems designed in the last decade, a set of core design criteria, in addition to those found in conventional memory allocation systems, can be identified. The clash between a strong focus on mitigating well-known vulnerabilities and stark performance demands rewards simpler designs. All designs focus on mitigating common heap-related vulnerabilities while increasing randomization and removing deterministic behavior.

As a result, a few notable "tried-and-true" traits shared among all systems listed in Table 1 have emerged. First off, each reviewed system "physically" segregates metadata from the memory chunks which are passed to the user, that is, avoids the use of chunk-adjacent metadata. Furthermore, none of the reviewed systems use the *coalescing* technique for free space management. Combined with the track record of vulnerabilities found in conventional memory allocation caused by faulty *coalescing* implementations, this technique's implementation is much more error-prone and thus unfit for security-oriented memory allocation systems.

A condensed comparison of existing secure memory allocation systems obtained through existing literature and source code analysis can be found in Table 1. The first part of the table tracks free space management and metadata techniques, while the second part tracks the implementation of several secure memory allocation techniques.

It should be noted that, as seen in Table 1, not all systems implement all previously described secure memory allocation techniques. Several systems [1,19] have focused on preventing a specific class of heap-based memory corruption vulnerabilities. However, none of the reviewed systems implement memory leak detection, apart from *MarkUs* [1] which can be configured to track allocations due to the design of the prototype system.

Dieharder: Novark et al. [13] conducted the first formal analysis of memory allocation system designs and their security. Taking all shortcomings and issues of existing systems unearthed by their analysis into account, they proposed a new memory allocator dubbed *DieHarder* [13]. The proposed design is one of the first memory allocation systems with strong spatial and temporal randomization guarantees and mitigations for heap-related memory corruption vulnerabilities. However, *DieHarder* was later criticized for omitting specific protective mechanisms and imposing a non-negligible performance overhead using the bitmap chunk management approach, and overuse of system calls [14].

FreeGuard/Guarder: Silvestro et al. [14] conducted a detailed analysis of contemporary memory allocation systems found in commodity operating systems, analyzing their security features, flaws, and properties. Their proposed design, named *FreeGuard* [14], aims to balance performance and security by incorporating a majority of existing security features, excluding those which incur a significant performance overhead. This is accomplished by reducing the number of memory-related system calls, adopting freelist-based chunk management, and utilizing memory shadowing [14]. *FreeGuard*'s design was subsequently improved with the introduction of a novel allocator design named *Guarder* [15], which increased randomization guarantees and gave users the ability to configure the system to their desired level of security, adjusting to available resources [15].

MarkUs: Ainsworth et al. [1] developed a memory allocation system that focuses on preventing the exploitation of *use-after-free* vulnerabilities through the use of explicit memory chunk tracking and delayed chunk freeing instead of the common non-deterministic allocation approach. Freed chunks are placed in a *quarantine list* and are deallocated when no existing pointers point to those chunks. A traversal of several process memory regions is periodically performed during process execution to find memory chunks that are in use. Due to similarities with garbage collection systems, the Boehm-Demers-Weiser garbage collector was used as a basis for a prototype implementation of *MarkUs*.

OpenBSD Ottomalloc: The default memory allocation system used in OpenBSD's implementation of the C library, `ottomalloc` [12], was one of the first widespread, default memory allocation systems, which was designed with security in mind. Its design primarily focused on removing predictable allocation behavior while maintaining performance similar to conventional memory allocation systems. It was also one of the first memory allocation systems to fully segregate metadata from memory chunks, using a hash table to track addresses of allocated chunks and the corresponding metadata.

FFmalloc: Wickman et al. [19] proposed a novel memory allocation system, called *FFMalloc*, designed to prevent *use-after-free* vulnerabilities by revisiting the concept of *one-time-allocation*. Although eliminating memory reuse prevents *use-after-free* attacks, a naive approach would run into severe performance issues due to an increased need for new memory. The authors implemented and evaluated several possible approaches for eliminating this issue with a detailed experimental overview of various options used for acquiring and releasing memory. *FFMalloc* deals with these issues through lazy memory freeing using the `madvise` system call.

SlimGuard: Liu et al. [7] proposed *SlimGuard*, a comprehensive memory allocation system that tackles the problem of unacceptable memory overhead in state-of-the-art secure memory allocation systems. Due to the observed increase in memory fragmentation caused by power-of-two size classes, *SlimGuard* features many fine-grained size classes to deal with this problem. Its memory footprint is further reduced by using on-demand creation of data and metadata and combining randomized allocation and overprovisioning into a single feature.

Table 1. Classification of existing secure memory allocation systems

Feature	DieHarder	Guarder	MarkUs	ottomalloc	FFmalloc	SlimGuard
Coalescing	✗	✗	✗	✗	✗	✗
Binning	✓	✓	✓	✓	✓	✓
Freelists	✗	✓	✗	✗	✓	✓
Bitmaps	✓	✗	✓	✓	✓	✓
BiBOP	✓	✓	✗	✓	✗	✗
Multithreaded design	✗	✓	✓	✓	✓	✓
Metadata segregation	✓	✓	✓	✓	✓	✓
Overprovisioning	✓	✓	✗	✗	✗	✓
Randomized allocation	✓	✓	✗	✓	✗	✓
Delayed reuse	✓	✓	✓	✓	✓	✓
Overflow detection	✓	✓	✗	✓	✗	✓
Invalid pointer detection	✓	✓	✓	✓	✓	✓
Memory sanitization	✧	✧	✓	✧	✗	✧
Memory leak detection	✗	✗	✧	✗	✗	✗

✓ Present ✗ Not implemented ✧ Optional, disabled by default

6 Benchmarking

Although various authors have performed detailed evaluations of their proposed systems [7,13,15], there is a lack of a broader, more general performance evaluation of state-of-the-art secure memory allocation systems.

To provide insight into the viability of secure memory allocation techniques and proposed designs of such systems, we compare the performance of well-known and state-of-the-art secure memory allocation systems to ptmalloc. We place a strong emphasis on using real-life scenarios for each identified workload. In addition to high-level, workload-specific benchmarks, which usually rate systems using a single metric (e.g., throughput, number of operations per second), we collect several low-level hardware and kernel events during the execution of macro-benchmarks. This enables us to gain insight into the performance of different secure memory allocation systems. Additionally, we track several metrics related to the runtime state of the tested systems to verify various non-security-related guarantees offered by these systems.

Through these benchmarks, we investigate the following questions:

– Are existing secure memory allocation systems viable for the most vulnerable workloads?
– What are the root causes of previously observed performance overheads?
– How do different designs of secure memory allocation systems fare in comparison to each other?

6.1 Macro-benchmarks

We extend our initial classification of heap-related vulnerabilities to determine the most vulnerable and performance-sensitive workloads. The identified workloads serve as a basis for evaluating the performance of existing secure memory allocation systems.

The analysis identified browsers, scripting language interpreters, web servers, and media manipulation workloads as the workloads most affected by heap-related memory corruption vulnerabilities. A suitable benchmark resembling real-life scenarios as close as possible was selected for each identified workload, as listed in Table 2. We considered popular benchmarks for the domain of each workload and selected one of them based on the intensity of heap allocations.

However, web browsers were left out from the benchmark due to many consistent misbehaviors and crashes during preliminary testing. Most of the crashes were caused by triggering various mitigation or detection mechanisms present in the tested systems, for instance, a caught attempt to free invalid pointers when using *Guarder* with the *Chromium* web browser. We made no efforts to ascertain the cause and validity of these crashes as the misbehaving software is far too complex. Instead, we took a crucial component used in many web browsers, the V8 JavaScript engine, and used it as a standalone program for benchmarking browser performance. We use the *Octane* JavaScript benchmarking suite[1] to compare web browser performance for different memory allocation systems.

We use the `nginx` webserver to serve static content of increasing sizes for the webserver benchmark, using only one worker process. We use the `wrk`[2] tool to simulate 400 concurrent connections. The multimedia manipulation benchmark uses the `ffmpeg` tool to encode a video file from the HD `h.264` format to the `NTSC DV` format. It measures the time required for the encoding process to finish. The scripting language benchmark uses a suite of tests to evaluate the performance of the `php` language interpreter. The benchmark result is an abstract score, with higher values indicating better performance.

Table 2. Selected benchmarks

Workload	Selected benchmark	Benchmark metric
Web browsers	Octane JavaScript benchmark[1]	Abstract score
Web servers	Nginx static webpage	Request throughput
Language interpreters	Phoronix `phpbench` [6]	Abstract score
Media manipulation	Phoronix `ffmpeg` [6]	Execution time

6.2 Micro-benchmarks

Given the vital role memory allocation systems play during the runtime of user-space processes and a lack of detailed profiling analyses, we conduct a detailed

---

[1] https://chromium.github.io/octane/.
[2] https://github.com/wg/wrk.

analysis of low-level hardware and kernel events generated during the execution of each secure memory allocation system to gain insight into the root causes of the performance overhead of these systems previously observed by several authors. We track several low-level events generated by each `malloc` and `free` call and compare them to the values generated by the standard GNU `libc` memory allocation system, `ptmalloc`. We use the well-defined workloads in the PARSEC benchmarking suite [2] for profiling individual secure memory allocation systems. We use two specific tests from the "data-parallel" and "pipeline" category, `blackscholes` and `ferret` [2]. Moreover, we track each system's memory overhead during runtime to determine metadata size using the `pidstat` tool.

6.3 Experimental Setup

We conduct the evaluation of previously listed secure memory allocation systems on a system featuring an Intel Core i5-8265U CPU and 16 GB of DDR4 RAM, running the *Manjaro* Linux operating system with Linux v5.10. We used the 2.32 version of the GNU C library [8].

We evaluate all systems enumerated in Table 1, using the authors' latest publicly available source code. Additionally, we modify the default OpenBSD userspace memory allocation system, *ottomalloc* [12], for use with the GNU/Linux environment. Individual secure memory allocation systems were compiled as ELF shared libraries and loaded before execution using weak symbols and the `LD_PRELOAD` environment variable. Additionally, we gather low-level hardware and kernel events using a small shared library built for intercepting memory allocation calls and low-level event data gathering via the `perf` Linux kernel subsystem.

7 Results

Although most of these systems are not production-ready, it should be noted that there were few consistent misbehaviors of the tested systems, ranging from outright crashes upon the first allocation request to various runtime misbehaviors. For instance, both *SlimGuard* and *Guarder* failed to execute the `nginx` benchmark due to failed allocation requests and had to be left out from the benchmarking results.

As seen in Table 3, the worst performing system overall is *DieHarder*, with the worst score on the `phpbench` benchmark and second-worst score on the `ffmpeg` benchmark. However, it fares reasonably well on the `nginx` benchmark, as seen in Table 4.

However, the most interesting result for the `phpbench` benchmark is *Guarder*'s and *ottomalloc*'s performance. These systems achieved scores very similar to *ptmalloc*'s in the *phpbench* benchmark, demonstrating that secure memory allocation systems can match conventional memory allocation systems for some workloads. The link between the workload type and system performance also manifests in the `ffmpeg` benchmark, with *ottomalloc* demonstrating the performance difference between different workloads.

The `nginx` benchmark results show significant dispersion for the 1kB file size test, as shown in Fig. 2 and Table 4. This is where the differences in the design of various memory allocation systems show, with *MarkUs* serving as a prime example of the detrimental effect of overly complex designs. Similar to the `phpbench` results, the `nginx` benchmark results show that some systems can match `ptmalloc`'s performance for this workload. However, the results converge to similar values as the file size increases, especially in the 100 kB file size test where the time required for I/O operations dominates the total execution time.

The overall performance of secure memory allocation systems on the *Octane* benchmark (Table 3) was somewhat lower than other workloads with the best performing system, *Guarder*, coming in at ~96% of `ptmalloc`'s score.

Table 3. Macrobenchmark results for the `phpbench`, `ffmpeg` and `Octane` tests. A cross denotes a crash.

	phpbench (avg. score)	ffmpeg (seconds)	Octane (avg. score)
ptmalloc	546092.18	8.86	36710.7
ffmalloc	536603.64	9.16	34621.4
MarkUs	539101.64	✗	31725.0
SlimGuard	533577.45	✗	✗
Guarder	542540.64	9.29	35396.7
ottomalloc	540195.00	14.010	35042.9
DieHarder	422306.00	11.22	✗

Table 4. Averaged macrobenchmark results for the `nginx` tests. A cross denotes a crash.

	Request size		
	1 kB	10 kB	100 kB
ptmalloc	71871.69	10942.62	1128.87
ffmalloc	68754.68	10943.65	1128.89
MarkUs	47795.66	10836.04	1128.20
ottomalloc	69060.45	10942.31	1128.48
DieHarder	67607.20	10930.23	1128.79

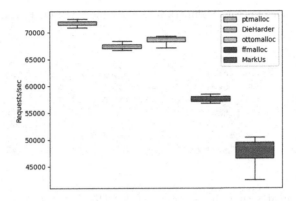

Fig. 2. Averaged macrobenchmark results for the **nginx** test with 1 kB file size.

As seen in Table 5, the average cycle count for a single `malloc` or `free` call is similar for all tested systems, except for *Guarder* which has the highest average cycle count for `malloc` calls and the lowest average cycle count for `free` calls. Increased cycle counts for the `ferret` test are accompanied by a high rate of page faults, `mmap` system calls, and high miss rates for some hardware caches.

However, results for the data-parallel `blackscholes` test (Table 6) show that average cycle counts are no longer uniform and vary greatly. Due to the parallel nature of the `blackscholes` test and increased memory consumption, there is a higher rate of hardware cache misses as well as higher rates of page faults and memory-related system calls for all tested systems.

Table 5. Averaged microbenchmark results for the PARSEC `ferret` test.

| | Memory usage (MB) | | malloc | | | | | free | | | |
	Virtual	Physical	Cycles	Page faults	mmap syscalls	dTLB miss rate	LL cache miss rate	Cycles	Page faults	dTLB miss rate	LL cache miss rate
ffmalloc	1195.66	125.24	7.04e+3	2.65e-4	1.76e-2	9.55e-6	3.2e-2	7.16e+3	0.e+0	1.33e-2	5.58e-2
ptmalloc	508.61	95.11	7.12e+3	2.73e-2	3.50e-5	5.3e-6	1.79e-2	6.96e+3	5.4e-3	1.95e-2	1.35e-1
SlimGuard	1295060.08	142.69	7.51e+3	3.51e-2	1.70e-3	6.12e-5	5.96e-2	7.52e+3	2.27e-2	3.87e-4	1.84e-1
DieHarder	182.89	129.80	7.29e+3	9.01e-4	9.92e-4	1.81e-5	1.89e-2	7.38e+3	0.e+0	2.26e-2	1.98e-2
OpenBSD	137.84	96.21	7.19e+3	1.49e-3	3.3e-2	5.23e-6	1.57e-2	7.36e+3	0.e+0	6.53e-6	9.09e-3
Guarder	16983210.26	237.24	2.11e+5	2.76e-2	8.78e-6	5.89e-5	1.10e-1	1.34e+3	4.06e-4	9.23e-6	5.86e-2
MarkUs	194.96	121.02	7.8e+3	1.32e-1	5.16e-2	1.63e-4	6.92e-2	7.06e+3	0.e+0	9.89e-6	5.36e-2

The multithreaded workload clearly outlined the differences in approaches used for managing metadata as overly complex or non-scalable systems (*MarkUs* and *DieHarder*) had a significantly higher average cycle count when compared to the rest of the tested systems (seen in Table 6).

However, *DieHarder*'s result is somewhat anomalous and, at first glance, inexplicable as it has the highest average CPU cycle count despite average scores for other metrics, as seen in Table 6. Combined with the fact that the tests in Table 3 are multithreaded and that the `nginx` test is performed using a single

Table 6. Averaged microbencghmark results for the PARSEC `blackscholes` test.

	Memory usage (MB)		malloc					free			
	Virtual	Physical	Cycles	Page faults	mmap syscalls	dTLB miss rate	LL cache miss rate	Cycles	Page faults	dTLB miss rate	LL cache miss rate
ffmalloc	1658.18	604.72	8.09e+3	6.20e-2	5.17e-3	6.23e-4	2.17e-1	5.63e+4	1.36e-3	8.25e-5	5.16e-1
ptmalloc	598.25	568.61	7.98e+3	1.95e-2	5.19e-3	2.67e-4	1.51e-1	5.60e+4	0.e+0	5.87e-5	5.28e-1
SlimGuard	40306.80	596.56	1.02e+4	1.65e-1	6.74e-2	1.22e-3	2.95e-1	7.29e+4	9.73e-1	8.89e-4	4.3e-1
DieHarder	605.29	574.32	7.68e+5	1.22e+0	4.67e+0	4.72e-5	1.56e-2	8.06e+5	0.e+0	5.88e-5	3.88e-2
OpenBSD	598.25	568.56	8.92e+3	1.69e-2	2.98e-2	8.60e-4	2.10e-1	5.74e+4	1.36e-3	9.51e-5	5.12e-1
Guarder	16983678.98	570.96	2.69e+4	7.29e+0	5.17e-3	1.69e-3	3.72e-1	5.78e+4	1.23e-2	2.27e-4	5.17e-1
MarkUs	626.69	591.07	8.14e+5	2.04e+2	2.07e-1	1.54e-3	5.48e-1	4.78e+4	1.21e-1	4.65e-5	1.96e-1

thread, this indicates that the main culprit for *DieHarder*'s low scores is its lack of multithreaded design, as noted in Table 1. This can once again be found in the microbenchmark tests, seeing as its average CPU cycle count in Table 5 is somewhat lower due to the single-threaded nature of the `ferret` benchmark [2].

There is also a clear link between stronger randomization guarantees, virtual memory usage, and increased data TLB miss rates. Results for *Guarder* and *SlimGuard* in Tables 5 and 6 show high virtual memory usage and a high rate of dTLB misses. This can be attributed to the randomized allocation and over-provisioning techniques, namely, the lack of constraints on the available virtual address ranges, leading to increased misses due to frequent access to previously uncached areas.

Large amounts of metadata and increased randomization guarantees have a negative impact on the total cycle count, as evidenced by *Guarder*'s result in Table 5. Moreover, the high LL cache miss rate indicates that a larger amount of metadata increases cache pressure, probably due to polluting the cache state of the workload interacting with the memory allocation system.

Furthermore, both microbenchmark results indicate another major factor contributing to higher cycle counts, a high rate of page faults per call. This can be observed in both microbenchmark test results and especially in the multithreaded `blackscholes` test and is accompanied by a high rate of physical memory usage. Thus, the page fault rate metric can be interpreted as an indicator for complex or large metadata structures or increased memory fragmentation. The case of increased memory fragmentation in *BiBOP*-style memory allocation systems was observed by Liu et al. [7] and *SlimGuard*'s results in Table 5 show that its primary design goal - reducing memory fragmentation, succeeded. Of course, avoiding kernel execution as much as possible has its apparent benefits, and a high rate of `mmap` system calls directly contributes to a higher average cycle count.

A general cycle count analysis of the microbenchmark results leads to an important observation - systems with lower miss rates for hardware caches tend to have a lower cycle count. Moreover, if the microbenchmark and macrobenchmark results are compared, a link between the former statement and higher performance can be observed. This leads to an important property that can be formulated as a design principle - all memory allocation systems should be designed to minimize their cache footprint, as cache pollution causes significant performance issues for the invoking program.

However, a significant issue that can potentially invalidate all security benefits provided by secure memory allocation systems exists in some workloads due to a common practice of implementing custom memory allocation systems in performance-critical applications. Although crucial for performance, this practice can degrade or completely invalidate all security features provided by secure memory allocation systems.

8   Conclusion

This paper presented a systematic overview of deficiencies present in conventional memory allocation systems and techniques to increase their security and mitigate common heap-related memory corruption vulnerabilities.

A systematic performance evaluation of several state-of-the-art secure memory allocation systems outlined several important factors which play a key in building performant, secure memory allocation systems. We found that some systems suffered performance overheads due to complex designs, a lack of explicit multithreaded design, and overuse of system calls. Furthermore, we have shown that systems with a smaller hardware cache footprint fared better in terms of performance overall. Strong randomized allocation guarantees coupled with a high overprovisioning rate can be detrimental to memory usage and overall performance as they increase hardware cache pressure.

A systematic analysis of existing secure memory allocation systems found that no existing system offers mitigation against memory leaks. We believe that this attack vector should not be overlooked as it can cause severe availability issues and that its detection should be addressed through future research. The analysis also unearthed the practice of application built-in custom memory allocation algorithms as a significant hindrance to the adoption of secure memory allocation techniques and systems.

Tests on vulnerable, real-life workloads have shown that most systems have a reasonably low performance overhead compared to conventional memory allocation systems, with some secure memory allocation systems closing the performance gap. Our findings indicate that secure memory allocation systems are a viable method for securing user programs and that state-of-the-art systems are ready to be deployed in real-life workloads.

Existing research has split up into two viable paths for improving the overall safety of memory allocation systems: using memory allocation systems that implement secure memory allocation techniques and autonomous exploration and uncovering vulnerabilities in conventional memory allocation systems [3, 20].

The former path can combat specific vulnerabilities or provide a comprehensive secure memory allocation system. As we have shown through a set of benchmarking tests, some of these systems have an acceptable performance overhead while providing an all-around secure allocation system. However, only a few of these systems have seen relatively widespread use and critical evaluation. Furthermore, their adoption is hindered as some workloads cannot benefit from the increased security guarantees offered by existing secure memory allocation systems. Thus, reconciling the common practice of custom, in-program memory allocation algorithms with secure memory allocation techniques is a crucial step towards eliminating the exploitability of heap-related memory corruption vulnerabilities.

Although the latter path seems more practical given its very low or nonexistent performance impact and overall labor required, it still cannot address the problems which arise from the deterministic behavior of conventional memory allocation systems.

Acknowledgment. This work has been carried out within the *AIPD2, Digital platform for personal data lifecycle management protection* project, funded by the European Regional Development Fund.

References

1. Ainsworth, S., Jones, T.M.: Markus: drop-in use-after-free prevention for low-level languages. In: 2020 IEEE Symposium on Security and Privacy (SP), pp. 860–860 (2020)
2. Bienia, C.: Benchmarking Modern Multiprocessors. Ph.D. thesis, Princeton University (2011)
3. Eckert, M., Bianchi, A., Wang, R., Shoshitaishvili, Y., Kruegel, C., Vigna, G.: Heaphopper: bringing bounded model checking to heap implementation security. In: 27th USENIX Security Symposium (USENIX Security 18), pp. 99–116. USENIX Association, Baltimore (2018). https://www.usenix.org/conference/usenixsecurity18/presentation/eckert
4. Gloger, W.: ptmalloc: a memory allocator 2006 (2006). http://malloc.de/en/
5. Jump, M., McKinley, K.S.: Cork: dynamic memory leak detection for garbage-collected languages. In: Proceedings of the 34th Annual ACM SIGPLAN-SIGACT Symposium on Principles of Programming Languages, pp. 31–38 (2007)
6. Larabel, M., Tippett, M.: Phoronix test suite. Phoronix Media (2011). https://www.phoronix-test-suite.com/, Accessed Feb 2020
7. Liu, B., Olivier, P., Ravindran, B.: Slimguard: a secure and memory-efficient heap allocator. In: Proceedings of the 20th International Middleware Conference, pp. 1–13 (2019)
8. Loosemore, S., Stallman, R., McGrath, R., Oram, A., Drepper, U.: The GNU C Library Reference Manual, for version 2.32. Free Software Foundation. https://www.gnu.org/software/libc/manual/html_node/The-GNU-Allocator.html
9. Mitre: Common vulnerabilities and exposures (2020). https://cve.mitre.org/data/downloads/index.html
10. Mitre: Cve-2020-27753 (2020). https://cve.mitre.org/cgi-bin/cvename.cgi?name=CVE-2020-27753
11. Mitre: Cve-2020-6449 (2020). https://cve.mitre.org/cgi-bin/cvename.cgi?name=CVE-2020-6449
12. Moerbeek, O.: A new malloc (3) for openbsd. In: Proceedings of the 2009 European BSD Conference, EuroBSDCon, vol. 9 (2009)
13. Novark, G., Berger, E.D.: Dieharder: securing the heap. In: Proceedings of the 17th ACM Conference on Computer and Communications Security, pp. 573–584 (2010)

14. Silvestro, S., Liu, H., Crosser, C., Lin, Z., Liu, T.: Freeguard: a faster secure heap allocator. In: Proceedings of the 2017 ACM SIGSAC Conference on Computer and Communications Security, pp. 2389–2403 (2017)

15. Silvestro, S., Liu, H., Liu, T., Lin, Z., Liu, T.: Guarder: a tunable secure allocator. In: 27th {USENIX} Security Symposium ({USENIX} Security 18), pp. 117–133 (2018)

16. Song, D., et al.: Sok: sanitizing for security. In: 2019 IEEE Symposium on Security and Privacy (SP), pp. 1275–1295. IEEE (2019)

17. Sotirov, A.: Heap feng shui in javascript. Black Hat Eur. **2007**, 11–20 (2007)

18. Szekeres, L., Payer, M., Wei, T., Sekar, R.: Eternal war in memory. IEEE Secur. Priv. **12**(3), 45–53 (2014)

19. Wickman, B., Hu, H., Jang, I.Y.D., Kashyap, J.L.S., Kim, T.: Preventing use-after-free attacks with fast forward allocation (2020)

20. Yun, I., Kapil, D., Kim, T.: Automatic techniques to systematically discover new heap exploitation primitives. In: 29th {USENIX} Security Symposium ({USENIX} Security 20), pp. 1111–1128 (2020)

Toward Learning Robust Detectors from Imbalanced Datasets Leveraging Weighted Adversarial Training

Kento Hasegawa[1]([⊠]), Seira Hidano[1], Shinsaku Kiyomoto[1],
and Nozomu Togawa[2]

[1] KDDI Research, Inc, 2-1-15 Ohara, Fujimino, Saitama, Japan
{kt-hasegawa,se-hidano,kiyomoto}@kddi-research.jp
[2] Waseda University, 3-4-1 Okubo, Shinjuku, Tokyo, Japan
ntogawa@waseda.jp

Abstract. Machine learning is an attractive technique in the security field to automate anomaly detection and to detect unknown threats. Most of the real-world training samples to learn with neural networks are imbalanced from the viewpoint of their distribution and importance priority on each class. In particular, datasets for security problems are imbalanced in most cases. Learning from an imbalanced dataset may cause the degradation of a classifier's performance, especially in the minority but important classes. We thus propose a new robust learning method for imbalanced datasets using adversarial training. Our proposed method leverages adversarial training to expand classification areas of minority classes. Specifically, we design *weighted adversarial training*, where the perturbation size of adversarial examples is weighted according to the number of samples in each class. We conducted experiments with real-world datasets, and the results demonstrate that our proposed method increases classification performance in both binary and multiclass classifications. Namely, our proposed method makes classifiers more robust even if the dataset is imbalanced, which is useful for us to apply machine learning to security tasks.

Keywords: Neural networks · Adversarial training · Imbalanced datasets · Detection

1 Introduction

Machine learning is an attractive technique in the security field to automate anomaly detection and to detect unknown threats. They also provide us with a significant benefit in various applications, such as complex classification tasks, object recognition, and speech recognition. Toward the real-world applications leveraging machine learning techniques, how to collect high-quality training datasets is a serious concern. For example, the datasets of security-related tasks are imbalanced in most cases [13]. Carefully dealing with such an imbalanced dataset

M. Conti et al. (Eds.): CANS 2021, LNCS 13099, pp. 392–411, 2021.
https://doi.org/10.1007/978-3-030-92548-2_21

is difficult. Although evaluation of a deep neural network and its generalization are performed with balanced datasets, imbalanced datasets must be well considered for real-world applications.

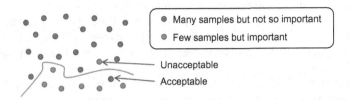

Fig. 1. An example of misclassification of an imbalanced dataset.

In the real-world application of machine learning, collecting a large number of samples to sufficiently train a classifier is essential in the practical use of machine learning. MNIST and CIFAR-10 datasets are well known to evaluate a classifier, in which the numbers of samples in each class are nearly even. However, collecting samples as the numbers of samples in each class become nearly even in the real world is quite difficult. As an example of an intrusion detection system (IDS), malicious traffic rarely appears in an ordinary situation. Moreover, malicious traffic is more remarkable than regular traffic because detecting all malicious traffic is the most important task for the IDS. In this case, we must avoid missing malicious traffics during classification. Figure 1 shows an example of misclassification. As shown in Fig. 1, we consider that misclassifying minority class samples is unacceptable. As exemplified above, considering the importance of each class is needed to classify imbalanced samples.

The existing study [12] investigates how to deal with imbalanced datasets and provides categories of the methods to learn imbalanced datasets. Sampling-based methods [4,11] and cost-sensitive learning methods [6,16] are the major approaches to tackle the imbalanced learning problem. Although several learning algorithms for imbalanced datasets have been developed, most of them focus on specific datasets and situations. Here, we study how to learn imbalanced datasets in order to apply machine learning techniques effectively to security tasks. Specifically, we aim to catch attacked samples as much as possible while keeping the total accuracy high enough.

In this paper, we leverage adversarial training [8,22] that is a defense learning method against adversarial examples. This method makes a classifier robust by replacing a part of training samples with adversarial examples. Adversarial examples, which are crafted by adding perturbation to original samples, are used to alter decision boundaries to desirable shapes. Although this concept can be applied to overcome the issues on imbalanced datasets, there is no detailed discussion on combining adversarial training with imbalanced datasets in the security field. Therefore, we propose a new method leveraging adversarial training for imbalanced datasets and evaluate its effectiveness empirically. The contributions of this paper are summarized as follows:

1. We design *weighted adversarial training* to expand classification areas of minority classes in a given imbalanced dataset. It is based on adversarial training [17] and performed with the distribution of perturbation weights. Our proposed method optimizes the perturbation weights on the basis of the number of training samples of each minority class.
2. Our proposed method takes two approaches, called the *untargeted* and *targeted adversarial training*. We apply both approaches to binary and multiclass classifications and discuss the difference between them based on the experimental results.
3. We applied weighted adversarial training to an IDS using a traffic flow dataset, which is a security-related task. The experimental results demonstrate that our proposed method successfully works for both binary and multiclass classification tasks.
4. We further analyze the classification results by visualizing the classification area using the t-SNE algorithm.

This paper is organized as follows: Sect. 2 shows some of the related works with our study. Section 3 describes preliminary definitions and equations. Section 4 proposes a robust learning algorithm for imbalanced datasets leveraging weighted adversarial training. Section 5 shows the experiments and their results of our proposed method. Section 6 gives concluding remarks.

2   Related Works

Machine learning is now being leveraged in the security field for various purposes, such as malware detection and abnormal traffic detection. In order to effectively apply a machine learning technique to such an anomaly detection system, collecting high-quality and high-quantity training samples is important. In general, we rarely obtain abnormal samples in the real world, except for the large volume of an attack such as a distributed denial-of-service (DDoS) attack. When we try to collect attack samples from network traffic in an ordinal way, only a few attacked samples might exist. Therefore, the samples collected from the real world could be imbalanced. To effectively leverage machine learning techniques for security, we should carefully deal with such an imbalanced dataset.

How to deal with imbalanced datasets for machine learning has been discussed in recent studies. There are mainly two approaches in training imbalanced datasets: 1) a data-level approach and 2) an algorithm-level approach [12]. A data-level approach balances the number of samples in each class by over- or under-sampling the datasets. The Synthetic Minority Over-sampling TEchnique (SMOTE) method [4], ADAptive SYNthetic Sampling (ADASYN) method [11], and their improved variety of methods have often been adopted to imbalanced learning problems. In the over-sampling methods, new samples are generated next to the original samples that are likely to be classified mistakenly. However, effectively choosing the samples, which would be mistakenly classified, is difficult. Recently, generative adversarial networks (GANs) have been often used for sample generation [5,18,20]. An algorithm-level approach often utilizes a loss function that considers the weights of each class in a dataset [6,16]. Some cost-sensitive methods are also leveraged to learn imbalanced datasets [14]. Margin-based methods have also been proposed in recent years [3,10].

Although the sampling-based approach is a simple way to learn imbalanced datasets, there are several drawbacks. In an over-sampled training approach, the generated samples might be redundant to improve classification performance. In an under-sampled training approach, the distribution of the dataset might be altered by sampling, which might lose potential representation. When we use a sampling-based approach, we should take care of the problems above.

Adversarial training is one of the approaches to make a classifier robust. This approach is essentially to enhance the robustness against adversarial examples [22]. Adversarial example images look natural for humans, but unsophisticated classifiers may misclassify them. The empirical description of adversarial examples is introduced by [8]. Recent attack methods such as Fast Gradient Sign Method (FSGM) [8] and Projected Gradient Descent (PGD) [17] have enabled to generate deceptive adversarial examples. Adversarial examples may become severe threats against physical world systems such as autonomous vehicles and robot vision [1]. In order to tackle the problem of adversarial example attacks, the first defense method has been proposed by [8]. PGD-based adversarial training [17] is one of the methods to defeat adversarial examples by learning them. The PGD-based method makes a classifier robust against adversarial examples by training adversarial examples generated during a training iteration. Other adversarial training methods, such as [24] and [25], have recently been proposed. Due to the detailed investigation of adversarial examples, the mechanism of deep neural networks has been well studied and becomes clarified. That will improve performance and enhance the robustness of deep neural networks [9].

As mentioned above, adversarial training helps us to improve the robustness of a classifier. As a result, that should enhance the classification performance as well as defend the classifier against adversarial attacks. From the perspective of improving classification performance, adversarial training is one of the promising approaches. Recently, as a new approach, adversarial training has been used for an imbalanced classification task [23]. The authors have proposed a new algorithm, the Wasserstein PGD (WPGD) model, which deals with the imbalanced dataset and manages the trade-off between the accuracy and robustness of the classifier. The WPGD model utilizes a Wasserstein distance to evaluate the difference between the genuine and predicted class. Based on the idea, the WPGD model introduces the Wasserstein loss function when generating perturbation. However, the WPGD model could not consider the borderline between the neighbor classes, particularly in multiclass classification. Another study [15] addresses the imbalanced classification task by translating some majority class samples to the target minority class. The translation of majority class samples is performed by adding a small noise to the majority class samples toward the target minority class, and the translated samples are re-labeled as the target minority class. From the recent studies, adversarial training is one of the promising approaches to cope with imbalanced classification.

In this paper, we proposed a new method addressing imbalanced classification with a PGD-based approach.

3   Preliminaries

This section introduces the backgrounds and notations necessary for our proposed method.

3.1   Machine Learning

Let $\mathbf{x} \in \mathbb{R}^d$ be a d-dimensional feature vector, and let $\mathbf{y} = [y_1, \ldots, y_s] \in \{0, 1\}^s$ be a one-hot vector that indicates the class of the feature vector $\mathbf{x}$. If $\mathbf{x}$ belongs to a class $i \in [s]$, $y_i = 1$, otherwise $y_i = 0$. We denote by $\mathcal{D}$ a training dataset consisting of N pairs of a feature vector $\mathbf{x}$ and the class label $\mathbf{y}$. In supervised learning, an s-class classifier $F : \mathbb{R}^d \rightarrow \mathbb{R}^s$ is generated from a training dataset $\mathcal{D}$. The classifier F is parameterized by θ, and θ is chosen to minimize an expected loss function $\mathcal{L}_\theta(\mathcal{D})$ of the training dataset $\mathcal{D}$. Given a loss function $l_\theta(\mathbf{x}, \mathbf{y})$ of a training sample $(\mathbf{x}, \mathbf{y}) \in \mathcal{D}$, $\mathcal{L}_\theta(\mathcal{D})$ can be written as $\mathcal{L}_\theta(\mathcal{D}) = \frac{1}{N} \sum_{(\mathbf{x}, \mathbf{y}) \in \mathcal{D}} l_\theta(\mathbf{x}, \mathbf{y})$. In this paper, we especially focus on a deep neural network whose final layer has a softmax function. Let $o(\cdot)$ denote the output of the last layer before the softmax layer. The model's output is expressed as $F(\mathbf{x}) = \mathrm{softmax}(o(\mathbf{x}))$. When the number of samples in a training dataset $\mathcal{D}$ is greatly different for each class, we call $\mathcal{D}$ an *imbalanced dataset*. We also call learning a robust classifier F from an imbalanced dataset *imbalanced learning*.

3.2   Adversarial Examples

Adversarial examples are used to deceive a classifier and induce misclassification. Let $\mathbf{r} \in \mathbb{R}^d$ be a small perturbation. Given a sample $\mathbf{x}$, an adversarial example $\mathbf{x}'$ is generated by $\mathbf{x}' = \mathbf{x} + \mathbf{r}$. However, optimizing the perturbation $\mathbf{r}$ is a difficult problem in terms of computational complexity. Thus the focus of interest of early studies was to generate adversarial examples effectively.

The *PGD* [17] method is a well-known solution for generating adversarial examples. This method is optimized for the L_∞ norm of the perturbation. The perturbation is iteratively updated K times. Let α be the step size of the perturbation at each iteration, and let ϵ be the maximum size of the perturbation. Given a sample $(\mathbf{x}, \mathbf{y})$, the PGD method generates the adversarial example with the following update function:

$$\begin{cases} \mathbf{x}'^{(0)} & = \mathbf{x} \\ \mathbf{x}'^{(t+1)} & = \mathrm{clip}_{\mathbf{x}, \epsilon} \left[\mathbf{x}'^{(t)} + \alpha \, \mathrm{sign}(\nabla_{\mathbf{x}'^{(t)}} l_\theta(\mathbf{x}'^{(t)}, \mathbf{y})) \right], \end{cases} \qquad (1)$$

where $\mathrm{clip}_{\mathbf{x}, \epsilon}[\mathbf{a}]$ projects each element $a_i \in \mathbf{a}$ onto the range $[x_i - \epsilon, x_i + \epsilon]$.

If it is required to misclassify a sample with a label $i \in [s]$ to a specific class $j \in [s] \setminus i$, the update function at t-th iteration can be written as follows:

$$\mathbf{x}'^{(t+1)} = \mathrm{clip}_{\mathbf{x}, \epsilon} \left[\mathbf{x}'^{(t)} - \alpha \, \mathrm{sign}(\nabla_{\mathbf{x}'^{(t)}} l_\theta(\mathbf{x}'^{(t)}, \mathbf{y}_j)) \right], \qquad (2)$$

where $\mathbf{y}_j$ is a vector that indicates a class j. We call the method with the Eq. (1) (resp. the Eq. (2)) the *untargeted* (resp. *targeted*) PGD method.

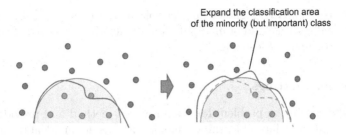

Fig. 2. The concept of the proposed method. (Color figure online)

3.3   Adversarial Training

The basic idea of *adversarial training* is to inject adversarial examples themselves into the training dataset to make the model robust to adversarial examples. For instance, the expected loss function $\mathcal{L}_\theta(\mathcal{D})$ for adversarial training using the untargeted PGD method can be written as follows:

$$\mathcal{L}_\theta(\mathcal{D}) = \frac{1}{N} \sum_{(\mathbf{x},\mathbf{y}) \in \mathcal{D}} \left[l_\theta(\mathbf{x}, \mathbf{y}) + \max_{\mathbf{r} \in \mathcal{S}(\mathbf{x})} l_\theta(\mathbf{x} + \mathbf{r}, \mathbf{y}) \right], \tag{3}$$

where $\mathcal{S}(\mathbf{x})$ is the perturbation constraint for a given sample $\mathbf{x}$. In contrast, different loss functions can be defined for adversarial training with the targeted PGD method based on the purpose. We thus design a special loss function to imbalanced learning in Sect. 4.2. Hereinafter, we call adversarial training with the untargeted (resp. targeted) PGD method the *untargeted* (resp. *targeted*) *adversarial training*.

4   Method

In this section, we propose a robust learning method for imbalanced datasets leveraging adversarial training.

4.1   Overview

Our proposed method aims to expand the classification area of the minority but important classes as much as possible. Figure 2 illustrates how to determine a decision boundary between the majority and the minority classes in binary classification. In Fig. 2, the blue samples belong to the majority class, while the green samples belong to the minority class. The red line is the decision boundary formed by a classifier. The green shaded area shows the ideal distribution of the minority class samples. In the left figure, while the orange sample originally belongs to the minority class, it is outside the red line; therefore, the classifier misclassifies it as the majority class. We thus consider expanding the decision boundary towards the majority class in order to avoid such misclassification.

The right figure in Fig. 2 shows an example of the expansion. Our proposed method actualizes this kind of manipulation by introducing *weighted adversarial training* to imbalanced learning.

4.2   Problem Settings

We formally define the problem for our proposed method and provide the loss function for our imbalanced learning. Here let us consider an ideal training dataset $\mathcal{D}^*$. Let $\mathcal{D}_i^*$ be the set of training samples $(\mathbf{x}^*, \mathbf{y}) \in \mathcal{D}^*$ such that $\mathbf{y}$ indicates a class $i \in [s]$. Given an imbalanced training dataset $\mathcal{D}$, we assume that $\mathcal{D}_i^* \approx \{(\mathbf{x}^*, \mathbf{y}) \mid \|\mathbf{x}^* - \mathbf{x}\|_\infty \le \epsilon_i', (\mathbf{x}, \mathbf{y}) \in \mathcal{D}_i\}$, where $\mathcal{D}_i$ is the set of training samples $(\mathbf{x}, \mathbf{y}) \in \mathcal{D}$ such that $\mathbf{y}$ indicates the class i, and ϵ_i' is the perturbation size for the class i. $\|\cdot\|_\infty$ is the L_∞ norm. In other words, we assume that any ideal training sample $(\mathbf{x}^*, \mathbf{y}) \in \mathcal{D}^*$ can be represented by adding an appropriate d-dimensional perturbation $\mathbf{r}$ satisfying $\|\mathbf{r}\|_\infty \le \epsilon_i'$ to a training sample $\mathbf{x}$ in an imbalanced dataset.

However, in order to generate the ideal training dataset $\mathcal{D}^*$ from a given training dataset $\mathcal{D}$, the maximum perturbation size ϵ_i' should be optimized for each class i. The values of ϵ_i' for minor classes will be larger than those for majority classes. To simplify the problem, we thus assume that ϵ_i' can be represented as a function g of the number of training samples for each class i, $n_i = |\mathcal{D}_i|$, i.e., $\epsilon_i' = \xi \cdot g(n_i)$, where ξ is a positive parameter. Examples of the function g are given in Sect. 5.1. In addition, it is difficult to involve all samples in $\mathcal{D}^*$ in the training of a classifier F, as the number of feature vectors $\mathbf{x}^*$ satisfying $\|\mathbf{x}^* - \mathbf{x}\|_\infty$ for a given sample $\mathbf{x}$ is exponentially large. We thus suggest adding only samples that change the shape of the decision boundary. The classification area expanded with such samples will cover many other samples that are not included in a training dataset $\mathcal{D}$ and are inside the added samples. We finally define an expected loss function for a given imbalanced dataset $\mathcal{D}$ as follows:

$$\mathcal{L}_\theta(\mathcal{D}) = \frac{1}{N} \sum_{i \in [s]} \sum_{(\mathbf{x}, \mathbf{y}) \in \mathcal{D}_i} \{l_\theta(\mathbf{x}, \mathbf{y}) + \max_{\mathbf{r}} l_\theta(\mathbf{x} + \mathbf{r}, \mathbf{y})\}, \tag{4}$$

$$\text{s.t. } \|\mathbf{r}\|_\infty \le \xi \cdot g(n_i). \tag{5}$$

The Eq. (5) is formulated as untargeted adversarial training. It should be noted that untargeted adversarial training might cause *label leaking* effect [17]. Because of this effect, we expect that untargeted adversarial training will expand more classification area than targeted adversarial training. Therefore, untargeted adversarial training gains better classification performance in terms of recall.

Our proposed learning method generates a classifier F that minimizes the loss function $\mathcal{L}_\theta$ while optimizing the parameter ξ. This optimization problem is similar to the problem for adversarial training shown by the Eq. (3). The key differences are that (1) the maximum size of perturbation, $\epsilon_i' (= \xi \cdot g(n_i))$, is different between classes, and that (2) it is required to find out the optimal values of ϵ_i' that improve the accuracy of minority classes while keeping that of majority classes. Since the perturbation for adversarial examples should be sufficiently small for avoiding detection, a fixed small value of ϵ is used for adversarial training. However, in imbalanced learning, it is preferable to enlarge the classification area as much as possible. Therefore, our proposed method optimizes the values of ϵ_i' by exploring an optimal solution of ξ.

Application to Multiclass Classification. In imbalanced learning for multiclass classification, the classification area of each minority class should be expanded in the directions of multiple neighbor classes. However, there is a possibility that training only a single adversarial example for a training sample cannot realize this purpose due to the inappropriate structure of classification areas. We thus suggest generating multiple adversarial examples for a training sample. Each adversarial example is used for expanding the classification area towards the corresponding neighbor class. In Sect. 5.3, we show through experiments that imbalanced learning with multiple adversarial examples has higher performance than that with a single adversarial example. The loss function for multiclass classification can be written as follows:

$$\mathcal{L}_\theta(\mathcal{D}) = \frac{1}{N} \sum_{i \in [s]} \sum_{(\mathbf{x},\mathbf{y}) \in \mathcal{D}_i} \{l_\theta(\mathbf{x},\mathbf{y}) + \sum_{j \in [s] \setminus i} \max_{\mathbf{r}_j} -l_\theta(\mathbf{x}+\mathbf{r}_j, \mathbf{y}_j)\},$$
$$\text{s.t. } \|\mathbf{r}_j\|_\infty \leq \xi \cdot g(n_i), \tag{6}$$

where $\mathbf{y}_j$ is a vector that indicates a class j, and $\mathbf{r}_j$ is a perturbation for the class j.

Unlike the Eq. (5), the Eq. (6) is formulated as targeted adversarial training. This is because untargeted adversarial training cannot generate multiple different adversarial examples for a training sample. Our proposed learning method for multiclass classification seeks the optimal multiple perturbations $\mathbf{r}_j$ that minimize the Eq. (6).

4.3 Algorithm

We then consider an algorithm to solve θ minimizing the Eq. (5) with fixed values of ϵ_i'. Our proposed algorithm is based on the PGD method shown in Sect. 3. While the PGD method uses the non-weighted parameters α and ϵ for all classes, we introduce weight vectors $\boldsymbol{\alpha}' \in \mathbb{R}^s$ and $\boldsymbol{\epsilon}' \in \mathbb{R}^s$. In the PGD method, α is used to control the perturbation size at each iteration, and ϵ indicates the maximum perturbation size. $\boldsymbol{\alpha}'$ and $\boldsymbol{\epsilon}'$ have nearly the same meanings as α and ϵ, yet both of the parameters consider the weights of the corresponding classes. $\boldsymbol{\alpha}'^T\mathbf{y}$ obtains the perturbation size at an iteration corresponding to a class $i \in [s]$. Similarly, $\boldsymbol{\epsilon}'^T\mathbf{y}$ obtains the maximum perturbation size corresponding to the class i. Therefore, given a training sample $(\mathbf{x},\mathbf{y})$, the update function of the weighted adversarial training is expressed as follows:

$$\left\{ \begin{array}{l} \mathbf{x}'^{(0)} = \mathbf{x} \\ \mathbf{x}'^{(t+1)} = \\ \quad \text{clip}_{\mathbf{x},\boldsymbol{\epsilon}'^T\mathbf{y}} \left\{ \mathbf{x}'^{(t)} + \boldsymbol{\alpha}'^T\mathbf{y} \, \text{sign}(\nabla_{\mathbf{x}'^{(t)}} \mathcal{L}_\theta(\mathbf{x}'^{(t)}, \mathbf{y})) \right\}. \end{array} \right. \tag{7}$$

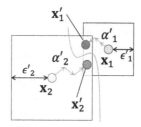

Fig. 3. An example of the weighted adversarial training. (Color figure online)

Algorithm 1. Imbalanced leaning by weighted adversarial training

---

Inputs: Classifier F, training dataset $\mathcal{D}$, minibatch size m, number of iterations of generating adversarial examples K, and ratio of trained adversarial examples p.

1: Initialize the classifier F.
2: **repeat**
3:    Obtain m samples from a training dataset $\mathcal{D}$ so that the number of samples of each class is even, and store them as a minibatch B.
4:    Iterate adversarial training steps according to the Eq. (7) for K times, and generate adversarial examples.
5:    Replace $p\%$ of the samples in B with the generated adversarial examples and store them as a minibatch B'.
6:    Perform one training step of the classifier F using the minibatch B'.
7: **until** training converged.

Figure 3 depicts the proposed method. The blue sample $\mathbf{x}_1$ belongs to the majority class, and the green sample $\mathbf{x}_2$ belongs to the minority class. Here, we define weight vectors $\boldsymbol{\alpha}'$ and $\boldsymbol{\epsilon}'$ as $\boldsymbol{\epsilon}' = (\epsilon'_1, \epsilon'_2) \in \mathbb{R}^2$, and $\boldsymbol{\alpha}' = (\alpha'_1, \alpha'_2) \in \mathbb{R}^2$, where the first class is the majority class and the second class is the minority class. Since we regard that the minority class is more important than the majority class, we set variables as $\epsilon'_1 < \epsilon'_2$ and $\alpha'_1 < \alpha'_2$. Then, the distribution of the perturbation is illustrated as the blue and green shaded areas shown in Fig. 3. Based on the PGD-based adversarial example generation and training, the adversarial examples are generated as $\mathbf{x}'_1$ and $\mathbf{x}'_2$. As a result, the decision boundary can be described as the orange curve in Fig. 3. Since the classification area for the minority class is expanded, the classification performance of the minority class is expected to be improved by the proposed method. Note that, in case of a multiclass classification problem, we define $\boldsymbol{\epsilon}' = (\epsilon'_1, \cdots, \epsilon'_s) \in \mathbb{R}^s$ and $\boldsymbol{\alpha}' = (\alpha'_1, \cdots, \alpha'_s) \in \mathbb{R}^s$.

The entire learning process is described in Algorithm 1. To balance the learning dataset during the training epoch, we draw the samples from the training dataset so that the number of samples in each class is even in the minibatch. In order to further enhance the classification performance for imbalanced datasets, the perturbation of the generated adversarial examples in the proposed method is weighted based on $\boldsymbol{\alpha}'$ and $\boldsymbol{\epsilon}'$ as shown in the Eq. (7).

5   Experiments

In this section, we evaluate the effectiveness of our proposed method through experiments with real-world datasets related to security tasks. We compare with well-known sampling methods for imbalanced learning and show that our proposed method improves the classification performance of minority classes.

5.1   Setup

Dataset. We use multiple datasets included in CICIDS2017 [21], which is designed to evaluate network-based IDSs. CICIDS2017 has benign and attacked network traffic samples. Each record consists of the statistics of network traffics. In the experiments, we perform both binary and multiclass classification with the datasets.

Specifically, CICIDS2017 contains seven datasets for a machine-learning purpose. Each dataset includes statistical samples of network packets with different times and different attacks. Some datasets have binary-class labels that show benign or attacked, and others have multiclass labels that show benign or one of the attack types. In order to deal with the imbalanced classification, we use the five datasets: **Bot, Infiltration, DoS, Patataor**, and **WebAttacks**, out of the seven ones in CICIDS2017. In the selected five datasets, the 'Benign' class is the largest (i.e., it is the majority class), and the other attacked classes are smaller than the 'Benign' class (i.e., they are the minority classes). The two datasets **Bot** and **Infiltration** contain binary-class labels, and the other three datasets **DoS**, **Patataor**, and **WebAttacks** contain multiclass labels. Table 1 summarizes the contents of the datasets we use in this paper. Each sample consists of 78 feature values and a label. The feature values represent the statistical characteristics of the packet flow, such as a destination port, the total length of the packets, the flow packets per second. The label shows the attack types, including benign.

In the experiments, we standardize the dataset so that the mean of each column is 0 and the variance of that is 1. Note that we replace 'NaN' and infinity values with 0 in the pre-processing phase because they appear in the 'Flows per second' and 'Packets per second' columns at '0' duration time.

After the standardization, we use 80% of the dataset as training samples and the rest as test samples.

Models. To evaluate the classification performance, we perform experiments with several models. The model used in this paper is summarized as follows:

1. **Normal:** A normal classifier with a cross-entropy without any balancing methods is used.
2. **B.B.** (Balanced mini-Batch): The 'Normal' model is used, but the trainer draws the training samples so that the number of samples in each class is equal in a minibatch (only the third step in Algorithm 1).
3. **SMOTE:** The training samples are over-sampled by the SMOTE [4] method beforehand.

Table 1. Contents of CICIDS 2017 Dataset.

File names	Classes	Samples
Patator: Tuesday-WorkingHours.pcap_ISCX.csv		
	Benign	432,074
	FTP-Patator	7,938
	SSH-Patator	5,897
DoS: Wednesday-workingHours.pcap_ISCX.csv		
	Benign	440,031
	DoS Hulk	231,073
	DoS GoldenEye	10,293
	DoS slowloris	5,796
	DoS Slowhttptest	5,499
	Heartbleed	11
WebAttacks: Thursday-WorkingHours-Morning-WebAttacks.pcap_ISCX.csv		
	Benign	168,186
	Web Attack Brute Force	1,507
	Web Attack XSS	652
	Web Attack Sql Injection	21
Infiltration: Thursday-WorkingHours-Afternoon-Infilteration.pcap_ISCX.csv		
	Benign	288,566
	Infiltration	36
Bot: Friday-WorkingHours-Morning.pcap_ISCX.csv		
	Benign	189,067
	Bot	1,966

4. **ADASYN:** The training samples are over-sampled by the ADASYN [11] method beforehand.
5. **WPGD:** A robust classification method employing a Wasserstein loss [23].
6. **UT-wPGD:** Our proposed method is applied to the classifier with UnTargeted Weighted PGD-based perturbation. The perturbation is generated with the untargeted adversarial training. Its amount is weighted based on the cardinality of the class where the sample belongs.
7. **T-wPGD:** Our proposed method is applied to the classifier with Targeted Weighted PGD-based perturbation. The perturbation is generated with the targeted adversarial training toward another class. Its amount is weighted based on the cardinality of the class where the sample belongs.

We use a multi-layer perceptron model to train and classify the dataset. The structure and hyper-parameters of the multi-layer perceptron are the same in all the models above. The model has three middle layers with $[64, 32, 32]$ units. We use sigmoid activation functions in the middle layers and a soft-max function in the output layer. The optimization method is Adam. We train a model for 50 epochs with a minibatch size of 256.

We tune the hyper-parameters of the PGD models by changing them. The weighting functions determine the weighting values with the cardinality of each class as an argument. Here, we set the maximum size of the perturbation vector

Table 2. Weighting function. $n_{\max} = \max_i n_i$ in the dataset $\mathcal{D}$.

Name	Function
ln	$g_{\ln}(n_i) = \ln(n_{\max})/ln(n_i)$
lnm	$g_{\mathsf{lnm}}(n_i) = \ln(n_{\max}/n_i)$
sqrt	$g_{\mathsf{sqrt}}(n_i) = \sqrt{n_{\max}/n_i}$
4thr	$g_{\mathsf{4thr}}(n_i) = \sqrt[4]{n_{\max}/n_i}$

ϵ' as $k \cdot \alpha'$ and the number of iteration K as $3/2 \cdot k$ so that $\epsilon' = k \cdot \alpha'$ will clip too large perturbation generated by $K \cdot \alpha'$. In the experiments, we set $k = 10$. As shown in Sect. 4.2, the weight of the i-th class ϵ'_i can be represented as a function g with the cardinality of the class $n_i = |\mathcal{D}_i|$, i.e., $\epsilon'_i = \xi \cdot g(n_i)$. In the experiments, we set ξ to 0.001, 0.005, 0.01, and 0.05. Also, for comparison, we set the weights of the Wasserstein matrix according to $g(n_i)$. Table 2 describes the weighting functions used in the experiments.

5.2 Evaluation Metrics

In the experiments, we evaluate the experimental results with several metrics.

In the evaluation, we focus on not missing any attacked samples. In other words, our top priority is to catch attacked samples as much as possible while keeping the total accuracy high enough. We introduce the evaluation metrics from the viewpoint of this priority.

A classifier classifies the samples in a training dataset as either a majority class or a minority class in binary classification. Let $\mathcal{D}_-$ be a set of majority class samples, and $\mathcal{D}_+$ be a set of minority class samples in a dataset. Then, the classifier classifies the two-class dataset $\mathcal{D} = \mathcal{D}_- \cup \mathcal{D}_+$ as either the majority or minority class. We denote by $\mathcal{E}_-$ a dataset classified as the majority class and denote by $\mathcal{E}_+$ a dataset classified as the minority class by the classifier. To see the overall classification performance, we can use the accuracy. However, the accuracy puts weight to the majority class. Therefore, we also refer to the recall to evaluate whether we have detected a minority class of attacked samples. Then, the accuracy and recall values are expressed as follows:

$$\text{Accuracy} = \frac{|\mathcal{D}_- \cap \mathcal{E}_-| + |\mathcal{D}_+ \cap \mathcal{E}_+|}{|\mathcal{D}|} \tag{8}$$

$$\text{Recall} = \frac{|\mathcal{D}_+ \cap \mathcal{E}_+|}{|\mathcal{D}_+|} \tag{9}$$

where $|\cdot|$ is a cardinality of a class.

In multiclass classification, we obtain the average score for each class. Here, let $\mathcal{E}_i$ be the dataset labeled as the i-th class by the classifier. Then, we define the overall accuracy, Accuracy_M as follows:

$$\text{Accuracy}_M = \frac{\sum_{i \in [s]} |\mathcal{D}_i \cap \mathcal{E}_i|}{|\mathcal{D}|} \tag{10}$$

Table 3. CICIDS2017 binary classification results.

Dataset	Model	Parameters	Accuracy	**Recall**
Bot				
	Normal		0.996	0.648
	B.B.		0.984	0.988
	SMOTE		0.978	0.990
	ADASYN		0.984	0.990
	WPGD	$g_{\lg}, \xi = 0.01$	0.981	0.990
	UT-wPGD	$g_{\lg m}, \xi = 0.01$	0.974	**0.995**
	T-wPGD	$g_{\lg}, \xi = 0.05$	0.981	0.993
Infiltration				
	Normal		1.000	0.778
	B.B.		0.996	0.778
	SMOTE		1.000	0.889
	ADASYN		1.000	0.889
	WPGD	$g_{\lg}, \xi = 0.01$	0.996	0.778
	UT-wPGD	$g_{\lg m}, \xi = 0.01$	0.996	**1.000**
	T-wPGD	$g_{\text{4thr}}, \xi = 0.005$	0.998	0.889

There are two averaging methods in terms of the recall score: micro-averaging and macro-averaging [7]. The micro-averaging is an average weighted by the class distribution, and it is equivalent to the overall accuracy. The macro-averaging is an arithmetic mean of the recall score for each class, and it would consider the recall of each class fairly. In this paper, we use the macro-averaged recall score for evaluation. The recall Recall_M used for evaluating multiclass classification are expressed as follows:

$$\text{Recall}_M = \frac{1}{s} \sum_{i \in [s]} \text{Recall}_i \qquad (11)$$

where $\text{Recall}_i = |\mathcal{D}_i \cap \mathcal{E}_i| / |\mathcal{D}_i|$. Note that the Recall_M score is also known as the *balanced accuracy* [2].

In the following section, we evaluate the classification results based on accuracy and recall scores. When evaluating imbalanced datasets, the accuracy tends to become high enough because the classifier may classify most of the samples as a majority class. If the samples in minority classes are misclassified, it does not affect the accuracy significantly. As mentioned at the top of this section, our goal is to classify the minority-class samples correctly. In this sense, we use the recall scores to see how many samples a model correctly classifies as their original classes.

5.3   Experimental Results

First, we explore the weighting function and parameter ξ with which we can obtain the best classification performance for each model. Then, we pick up the best classification results over the explored parameters for each model.

Table 4. CICIDS2017 multiclass classification results.

Dataset	Model	Parameters	Accuracy$_M$	Recall$_M$
DoS				
	Normal		0.997	0.961
	B.B.		0.998	0.964
	SMOTE		0.998	0.964
	ADASYN		0.995	0.994
	WPGD	$g_{\ln}, \xi = 0.01$	0.997	0.964
	UT-wPGD	$g_{\ln m}, \xi = 0.05$	0.997	**0.997**
	T-wPGD	$g_{4thr}, \xi = 0.01$	0.996	**0.997**
Patator				
	Normal		0.999	0.992
	B.B.		0.999	**0.997**
	SMOTE		0.999	0.996
	ADASYN		0.992	0.867
	WPGD	$g_{\ln}, \xi = 0.01$	0.999	**0.997**
	UT-wPGD	$g_{sqrt}, \xi = 0.05$	0.997	**0.997**
	T-wPGD	$g_{4thr}, \xi = 0.05$	0.998	**0.997**
WebAttack				
	Normal		0.994	0.502
	B.B.		0.992	0.709
	SMOTE		0.991	0.758
	ADASYN		0.990	0.721
	WPGD	$g_{\ln}, \xi = 0.01$	0.992	0.723
	UT-wPGD	$g_{\ln}, \xi = 0.005$	0.978	0.774
	T-wPGD	$g_{4thr}, \xi = 0.005$	0.989	**0.775**

Binary Classification Results. Table 3 shows the parameters and results of binary classification. The 'Parameters' column shows the weighting function (see Table 2) and the parameter ξ used for each PGD model. We show the two metrics: Accuracy and Recall as shown in the Eqs. (8) and (9) for binary classification. As shown in Table 3, we use Bot and Infiltration datasets to evaluate binary classification. They contain benign and attacked samples, and attacked samples are in the minority class. From the results in Table 3, the Normal model obtains the best accuracy in all the models in both Bot and Infiltration datasets. However, a high accuracy score in imbalanced classification means that a classifier correctly classifies most of the majority class samples, not the minority class samples. Actually, the recall scores of both Bot and Infiltration datasets are the lowest in all the models. In contrast, our proposed method, the **UT-wPGD** and **T-wPGD** models obtain the first and second highest recall scores in all the models for each dataset. It should be noted that the **B.B.** model itself improves the recall score compared to the Normal model. Combining the **B.B.** model and weighted PGD-based perturbation could further improve the recall score. Our proposed method successfully works in the two datasets.

Multiclass Classification Results. Table 4 shows the results of multiclass classification. The evaluation metrics used in this table are as shown in the Eqs. (10) and (11). To see the detailed classification results in each dataset, Table 5 shows the number of correctly classified samples for each class. In multiclass classification, we evaluate the classification results based on the $Accuracy_M$ and $Recall_M$ scores. In the multiclass classification, we aim to maximize the recall scores of the minority classes; therefore a high $Recall_M$ score is the desired result.

In the DoS dataset, the **UT-wPGD** and the **T-wPGD** models obtain the highest $Recall_M$ scores. As shown in Table 5, the **UT-wPGD** and **T-wPGD** models correctly classify more samples of DoS GoldenEye, DoS Slowhttptest, DoS slowloris, and Heartbleed classes than the Normal model. These classes include fewer samples than the other classes. From the viewpoint of classifying minority class samples (especially the bottom three classes), the **T-wPGD** model outperforms the other models.

In the Patator dataset, the difference between the models is slight. However, our proposed models successfully obtain equal to or better classification results than the existing methods.

In the WebAttack dataset, the **T-wPGD** model outperforms other models. This is because the **T-wPGD** model successfully classifies the minority classes with good balance. In particular, the 'Web Attack Brute Force' and 'Web Attack XSS' classes have similar features, and most of the classifiers are prone to misclassify them. A recent study [19] has also shown that the accuracy and recall score of 'Web Attack XSS' is not so high when those of 'Web Attack Brute Force.' Moreover, detecting 'Web Attack Sql Injection' is also difficult because it contains a tiny number of samples. In this paper, as shown in Table 5, the numbers of correctly classified samples in the 'Web Attack Brute Force' and 'Web Attack XSS' classes are unstable. Actually, the 'Web Attack Brute Force' class contains 293 test samples, and the 'Web Attack XSS' class contains 128 test samples. The Normal model could not consider the class distribution, and therefore classification borderline is not well constructed. The **UT-wPGD** model adds perturbation toward the direction where the loss is most increased. In other words, the model cannot control the direction of the perturbation directly. Consequently, the perturbed sample might invade another smaller class, whereas we expect to invade a larger class. In contrast, the **T-wPGD** model controls the direction of the perturbation directly, decreasing the loss as much as possible, as mentioned in Sect. 4.2 with the Eq. (6). As a result, the perturbed samples would not invade another class any more than necessary. Therefore, the **T-wPGD** model successfully classifies them considering class weights, and the $Recall_M$ score becomes the best in all the models.

In conclusion, the **UT-wPGD** and **T-wPGD** models successfully classify the real-world imbalanced datasets. When the dataset is a binary-class set, the **UT-wPGD** model would be more effective due to the label leaking effect. Otherwise, the **T-wPGD** model would effectively work considering the class weights.

Table 5. CICIDS2017 correctly classified samples.

Dataset	Class	Normal	UT-wPGD	T-wPGD
DoS				
	Benign	87,714	87,760	87,594
	DoS Hulk	46,120	46,059	46,094
	DoS GoldenEye	2,008	2,024	2,023
	DoS slowloris	1,141	1,148	1,148
	DoS Slowhttptest	1,109	1,112	1,114
	Heartbleed	4	5	5
Patator				
	Benign	86,305	86,097	86,144
	FTP-Patator	1,585	1,588	1,588
	SSH-Patator	1,235	1,254	1,255
WebAttacks				
	Benign	33,569	33,163	33,466
	Web Attack Brute Force	291	35	122
	Web Attack XSS	2	127	114
	Web Attack Sql Injection	0	5	4

t-SNE Analysis. In order to analyze the class distribution obtained by the classifier, we visualize the test samples and their classes with the t-distributed Stochastic Neighbor Embedding (t-SNE) method. The t-SNE method is commonly used to reduce the dimension of the dataset. Specifically, it is useful to visualize the distribution of high-dimensional data as a two-dimensional scatter plot. Using the scatter plot obtained with the t-SNE method, we visually analyze the data distribution calculated by the classifier.

To visualize the classification results of binary classification, Fig. 4 shows the t-SNE plots of the results using the Infiltration dataset. The plot area has been enlarged to make it easy to see the notable areas. The blue points belong to the 'Benign' class (the majority class), and the red points belong to the 'Bot' class (the minority class). The depth of the color shows the probability of being classified into the color's class, with a deep color indicating a high probability.

Figure 4(a) illustrates the distribution of each class in the training dataset. As shown in the figure, there are quite a few attacked samples, and the samples are intricately distributed, with some majority and minority class samples overlapping. Figure 4(b) illustrates the distribution of each class in the test dataset. There are fewer red points (= minority class samples) compared to the training dataset. Figures 4(c)–(f) illustrate the classification results of the test dataset. Figure 4(c) illustrates the classification result by the Normal model. In the figure, the sample circled in red in (b) is misclassified as the majority class. Figure 4(d) is obtained by ADASYN. Compared to the Normal model, minority class samples are correctly classified. Figure 4(e) is obtained by the **UT-wPGD** classifier. Due to the small perturbation of our proposed method, the classification area of

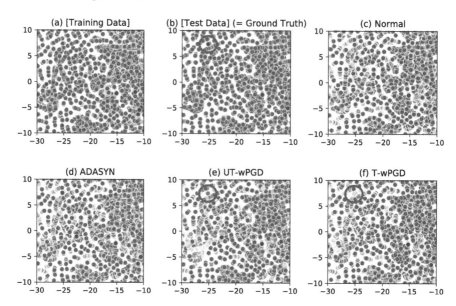

Fig. 4. The t-SNE plots of the classification results (Infiltration dataset). The blue points are the majority class samples, and the red ones are the minority class samples. (Color figure online)

the minority class is expanded. However, more majority class samples are misclassified as the minority class. The misclassified samples are distributed around the minority class samples in the training dataset. Therefore, the **UT-wPGD** classifier expands the classification area of the minority class, but it seems too large. Figure 4(f) is obtained by the **T-wPGD** classifier. Because the perturbation direction is targeted toward the other class, the classification area is not expanded compared to the **UT-wPGD** classifier. However, the sample circled in red is misclassified as the majority class, whereas the **UT-wPGD** classifier successfully classifies. From the results above, our proposed models **UT-wPGD** and **T-wPGD** successfully work for the binary classification. In particular, the **UT-wPGD** model expands more classification area than the **T-wPGD**. As mentioned in Sect. 4.2, untargeted adversarial training would cause *label leaking* effect [17]. We can observe this effect from the results, and the **UT-wPGD** model performs more effectively.

To visualize the classification results of multiclass classification, we select the WebAttack dataset. This dataset is difficult to classify, as shown in Table 5, because the samples of the Brute Force and XSS classes have similar features. Figure 5 shows the t-SNE plots of the results using the WebAttack dataset. There are four colors: blue, orange, green, and red. Different from Fig. 4, the depth of the face color is fixed. The blue points are the majority class, and the others are the minority classes. The green (resp. yellow or red) samples correspond to the Brute Force class (resp. XSS or Sql Injection). The number of red samples is quite small compared to the other classes. It should be noted that the green

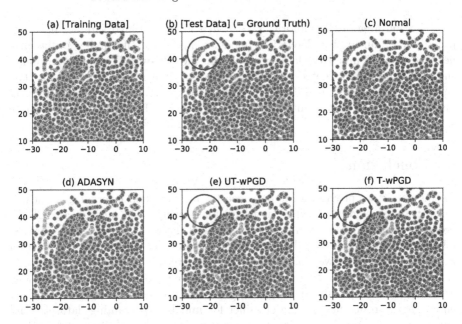

Fig. 5. The t-SNE plots of the classification results (WebAttack dataset). (Color figure online)

and yellow class samples are overlapped because their features are quite similar. In the figures, green samples are on top of yellow samples.

Similar to Fig. 4, Fig. 5(a) illustrates the distribution of the training dataset, and Fig. 5(b) illustrates the distribution of the test dataset. Figures 5(c)–(f) illustrate the classification results of the test dataset. Figure 5(c) illustrates the classification result by the Normal model, which fails to classify red class samples. Figure 5(d) is obtained by the ADASYN method. Compared to the Normal model, minority class samples are correctly classified, and it seems to have a similar distribution to the test dataset. Figure 5(e) is obtained by the **UT-wPGD** classifier. Although the classification areas of the minority classes are successfully expanded, some samples in the red circle are misclassified. Figure 5(f) is obtained by the **T-wPGD** classifier. Ideally, green and yellow samples should be distributed in the plot area. However, ADASYN and the **UT-wPGD** model could not classify green samples. In contrast, the **T-wPGD** classifier successfully classifies several green samples, as shown in the red circle in the figure.

From the discussion in this section, we find out the following results. Firstly, balancing class distribution in a minibatch successfully expands the classification area of the minority class. Secondly, our proposed method outperforms conventional over-sampling methods such as SMOTE and ADASYN. The SMOTE and ADASYN models can certainly contribute to improving the recall score of the minority class. However, those models might strongly misclassify the majority class samples in the neighborhood of the minority class. Compared to the SMOTE and ADASYN models, the **UT-wPGD** and **T-wPGD** expand the classification area of the minority class, but the misclassified samples have low probability. Thirdly, the **T-wPGD** model tends to classify higher probability near the genuine minority-class samples than the **UT-wPGD** model. Although the targeted and untargeted perturbation have similar meanings in binary classification, they result in different classification areas. While the **UT-wPGD** model obtains the best results in the experiment, the **T-wPGD** model is more stable in classification.

6 Conclusion

In this paper, we propose an imbalanced training method leveraging an adversarial training algorithm, which is useful for security tasks such as an IDS. In order to realize robust learning for imbalanced datasets, we leverage weighted adversarial training that makes it possible to spread or shrink the classification area according to the weighting vector that is determined by the importance of each class. We perform several experiments with real-world imbalanced datasets. The experimental results demonstrate that our proposed method successfully enhances the robustness of the classifier for imbalanced training datasets, and effectively increases the classification performance for a security task. Furthermore, we visually analyze the classification area of our proposed method.

While our proposed method gives a significant contribution to imbalanced learning, some points are still remained to be further considered. In order to appropriately set the maximum perturbation size ϵ_i' for each class i, optimizing the function $g(x)$ is one of the most challenging problems, and this will be our future work.

References

1. Akhtar, N., Mian, A.: Threat of adversarial attacks on deep learning in computer vision: a survey. IEEE Access **6**(AUGUST), 14410–14430 (2018)
2. Brodersen, K.H., Ong, C.S., Stephan, K.E., Buhmann, J.M.: The balanced accuracy and its posterior distribution. In: International Conference on Pattern Recognition (ICPR), pp. 3121–3124 (2010)
3. Cao, K., Wei, C., Gaidon, A., Aréchiga, N., Ma, T.: Learning imbalanced datasets with label-distribution-aware margin loss. In: Neural Information Processing Systems, pp. 1565–1576 (2019)
4. Chawla, N.V., Bowyer, K.W., Hall, L.O., Kegelmeyer, W.P.: SMOTE: synthetic minority over-sampling technique. J. Artif. Intell. Res. **16**, 321–357 (2002)
5. Douzas, G., Bação, F.: Effective data generation for imbalanced learning using conditional generative adversarial networks. Expert Syst. Appl. **91**, 464–471 (2018)
6. Elkan, C.: The foundations of cost-sensitive learning. In: International Joint Conference on Artificial Intelligence, pp. 973–978 (2001)
7. Forman, G.: An extensive empirical study of feature selection metrics for text classification. J. Mach. Learn. Res. **3**(Mar), 1289–1305 (2003)
8. Goodfellow, I.J., Shlens, J., Szegedy, C.: Explaining and harnessing adversarial examples. In: International Conference on Learning Representations (ICLR) (2015)

9. Goswami, G., Ratha, N., Agarwal, A., Singh, R., Vatsa, M.: Unravelling robustness of deep learning based face recognition against adversarial attacks. In: Proceedings of the Thirty-Second AAAI Conference on Artificial Intelligence, pp. 6829–6836 (2018)

10. Hayat, M., Khan, S., Zamir, W., Shen, J., Shao, L.: Max-margin class imbalanced learning with gaussian affinity (2019). http://arxiv.org/abs/1901.07711v1

11. He, H., Bai, Y., Garcia, E.A., Li, S.: ADASYN: adaptive synthetic sampling approach for imbalanced learning. In: 2008 IEEE International Joint Conference on Neural Networks (IEEE World Congress on Computational Intelligence), pp. 1322–1328 (2008)

12. He, H., Garcia, E.A.: Learning from imbalanced data. IEEE Trans. Knowl. Data Eng. 21(9), 1263–1284 (2009)

13. Kaur, H., Pannu, H.S., Malhi, A.K.: A systematic review on imbalanced data challenges in machine learning - applications and solutions. ACM Comput. Surv. 52(4), 79:1–79:36 (2019)

14. Khan, S.H., Hayat, M., Bennamoun, M., Sohel, F., Togneri, R.: Cost-sensitive learning of deep feature representations from imbalanced data. IEEE Trans. Neural Netw. Learn. Syst. 29(8), 3573–3587 (2017)

15. Kim, J., Jeong, J., Shin, J.: M2m: imbalanced classification via major-to-minor translation. In: Proceedings of the IEEE/CVF Conference on Computer Vision and Pattern Recognition (CVPR), pp. 13893–13902 (2020)

16. Kukar, M., Kononenko, I.: Cost-sensitive learning with neural networks. In: Proceedings of the 13th European Conference on Artificial Intelligence, pp. 445–449 (1998)

17. Kurakin, A., Goodfellow, I., Bengio, S.: Adversarial machine learning at scale. In: International Conference on Learning Representations (ICLR) (2017)

18. Lee, J., Park, K.: Gan-based imbalanced data intrusion detection system. Personal Ubiquit. Comput. 25(1), 121–128 (2021)

19. Maseer, Z.K., Yusof, R., Bahaman, N., Mostafa, S.A., Foozy, C.F.M.: Benchmarking of machine learning for anomaly based intrusion detection systems in the CICIDS2017 dataset. IEEE Access 9, 22351–22370 (2021)

20. Montahaei, E., Ghorbani, M., Baghshah, M.S., Rabiee, H.R.: Adversarial classifier for imbalanced problems (2018). http://arxiv.org/abs/1811.08812v1

21. Sharafaldin, I., Lashkari, A.H., Ghorbani, A.A.: Toward generating a new intrusion detection dataset and intrusion traffic characterization. In: International Conference on Information Systems Security and Privacy (ICISSP), pp. 108–116 (2018)

22. Szegedy, C., et al.: Intriguing properties of neural networks. In: International Conference on Learning Representations (ICLR) (2014)

23. Terzi, M., Susto, G.A., Chaudhari, P.: Directional adversarial training for cost sensitive deep learning classification applications. Eng. Appl. Artif. Intell. 91, 103550 (2020)

24. Tramèr, F., Kurakin, A., Papernot, N., Goodfellow, I., Boneh, D., McDaniel, P.: Ensemble adversarial training: attacks and defenses. In: International Conference on Learning Representations (ICLR) (2018)

25. Vivek, B.S., Mopuri, K.R., Babu, R.V.: Gray-box adversarial training. In: Proceedings of the European Conference on Computer Vision (ECCV), pp. 213–228 (2018)

Towards Quantum Large-Scale Password Guessing on Real-World Distributions

Markus Dürmuth[1], Maximilian Golla[2], Philipp Markert[1], Alexander May[1], and Lars Schlieper[1(✉)]

[1] Ruhr University Bochum, Bochum, Germany
{markus.duermuth,philipp.markert,alex.may,lars.schlieper}@rub.de
[2] Max Planck Institute for Security and Privacy, Bochum, Germany
maximilian.golla@csp.mpg.de

Abstract. Password-based authentication is a central tool for end-user security. As part of this, password hashing is used to ensure the security of passwords at rest. If quantum computers become available at sufficient size, they are able to significantly speed up the computation of preimages of hash functions. Using Grover's algorithm, at most, a square-root speedup can be achieved, and thus it is expected that quantum password guessing also admits a square-root speedup. However, password inputs are not uniformly distributed but highly biased. Moreover, typical password attacks do not only compromise a random user's password but address a large fraction of all users' passwords within a database of millions of users.

In this work, we study those quantum large-scale password guessing attacks for the first time. In comparison to classical attacks, we still gain a square-root speedup in the quantum setting when attacking a constant fraction of all passwords, even considering strongly biased password distributions as they appear in real-world password breaches. We verify the accuracy of our theoretical predictions using the LinkedIn leak and derive specific recommendations for password hashing and password security for a quantum computer era.

Keywords: Passwords · Quantum computing · Hash function · ZIPF.

1 Introduction

Despite its significant weaknesses, password-based authentication continues to be widely used. An average user may have hundreds of password-protected online accounts [38,51], needs to enter a password for decrypting and booting the computer, or accessing the Wi-Fi and VPN. Reasons for the continued use of passwords include their intuitive and simple usage and an "ecosystem" of coping strategies (such as password reuse [16,21,37] and choosing passwords with predictable patterns [45–47]) to work around limitations of passwords.

Password hashing is a central building block for ensuring the security of passwords at rest: for passwords stored in databases or hard disk encryption, it is recommended to use a salted, iterated, and memory-hard cryptographic hash

© Springer Nature Switzerland AG 2021
M. Conti et al. (Eds.): CANS 2021, LNCS 13099, pp. 412–431, 2021.
https://doi.org/10.1007/978-3-030-92548-2_22

function [4]. Hashed passwords can be attacked by an offline guessing attack: an attacker generates password candidates that a human user likely chooses, in decreasing order of likelihood. Then, the attacker hashes the password candidates and compares them against the stored password hash, revealing if the tested password candidate matches the real password [19,34]. Considering the heavily skewed distribution of human password choice, consumer-grade hardware such as gaming GPUs can already pose a threat for password security [15,23], except for very slow password hashes such as Argon2i [3].

With the availability of quantum computers, many cryptographic primitives are at high risk [26,29,32,33,39,40]. Specifically, popular public-key cryptography that is in use today and based on the factorization or discrete logarithm problem, such as the RSA cryptosystem, can be broken by Shor's algorithm [43]. In symmetric cryptography, the situation is different. For many symmetric ciphers, it is assumed that the only impact in a quantum setting is the Grover square-root speedup, which can be countered by doubling the key length. Similarly, Grover's algorithm gives a square-root speedup for finding preimages of cryptographic hash functions. A straight-forward application of Grover's algorithm to *uniformly distributed* N passwords displays a similar speedup: quantum computers can find preimages for hashed passwords faster (in $\sqrt{N}$ steps) than traditional computers [12]. For more realistic *human-chosen* passwords that are not uniformly distributed but highly skewed, it is unknown if a square-root speedup can also be realized.

Our Contribution. In this work, we investigate the impact of quantum computers on password guessing. To the best of our knowledge, our work is the first to consider realistic (non-uniform) password distributions, as well as quantum attackers guessing passwords for more than a single password hash. Our contribution is three-fold:

1. We investigate how an attacker equipped with a quantum computer (of sufficient size) can use Grover's algorithm to guess non-uniformly distributed *human-chosen* passwords. We realize square-root speedups in two different attack scenarios: targeting a single (fixed) user and large-scale attacks targeting a whole password database at once. Both scenarios are commonly found in password research and password security practice.
2. As a central tool, we use a ZIPF distribution to model human password choices. We provide analytic bounds for the required number of evaluations of the password hashing function that holds both in the classical and the quantum world, which may be of independent interest.
3. We use the well-known LinkedIn password leak to check the accuracy of our ZIPF model, verifying the applicability of our results. We then discuss the implications and consequences for real-world practices. Even though quantum computers of the required size for our attack might not yet be available today, we discuss the possible consequences of our results on the required increase in password strength. Moreover, we address possible solutions based on alternative password hash functions.

Overall, we believe that our work allows for a better understanding of the long-term impact of quantum computers on the security of password hashing and provides a first step in taking appropriate steps to mitigate problems.

Related Work. A first step towards modeling user-chosen password distributions with ZIPF's law has been done by Malone and Maher [35]. They conclude that ZIPF's law may not allow for an exact yet good approximation of the frequencies in which users choose passwords. Bonneau [6] and Wang et al. [49] came to a similar conclusion. The latter also refined accuracy by independently modeling less and more frequent passwords. A subsequent work by Wang et al. [48] revised the approach even further, also utilizing it to measure password dataset security.

Corrigan-Gibs et al. [12] discussed how the security of hashed passwords changes in the presence of quantum computers. For this purpose, they assume a 10-character password that is randomly chosen from the space of all 95 printable ASCII characters. By applying Grover's algorithm [25], the security of such a password reduces from $95^{10} \approx 2^{66}$ to only $\sqrt{95^{10}} \approx \sqrt{2^{66}} = 2^{33}$. Hence, Corrigan-Gibs et al. conclude that quantum computers would put hashed passwords at risk, which are currently perceived as secure.

Moreover, the quantum scenario also allows for identity authentication protocols with improved privacy and security properties [13]. However, these protocols require all communicating parties to have quantum computer access, which is not the scenario we are considering.

2 Password Guessing

In the following section, we provide a brief introduction to password guessing and the real-world password datasets we are using. Moreover, we describe how human password choice can be approximated by ZIPF's law and introduce our overall attack setting.

2.1 Threat Model

Passwords are typically stored in salted hashed form, i.e., instead of storing the password *pwd* in plain text, one stores $(s, h(pwd|s))$ for a hash function h and a random salt s. Due to the strong bias and the resulting low entropy of human-chosen passwords, effective attacks against such password hashes are *guessing attacks*. Here an attacker enumerates password candidates by their likelihood, and for each candidate tests if it is the correct password. In an *online guessing attack*, the attacker tests potential password candidates directly with the service provider. These attacks can be reasonably mitigated on the server-side, e.g., by rate-limiting. A more pronounced threat is *offline guessing attacks*, where the attacker is in possession of the database with the password hashes and is thus only limited by the available computational resources, as the correctness of the passwords can be tested locally. This offline scenario is the threat model we consider in the remainder of this work.

In order to minimize the number of hashing operations for the guessing attack, an attacker will try to guess the most frequent passwords first. For our work, we consider the strongest threat model possible in form of a *perfect knowledge attacker* that uses the actual password distribution and guesses passwords in order of decreasing probability.

We distinguish between the following two attack scenarios:

Scenario A: Fixed User Attack. This is the simplest attack scenario, where the attacker targets a *certain fixed password hash* by testing a list of common passwords in decreasing probability. A typical example for Scenario A is when an attacker is interested in a single user in a password file (e. g., law enforcement). Another important use case is (software-based) *hard disk encryption*, where the content of the disk is encrypted using a symmetric key. This key needs to be stored on the hard disk as well (unless supported by specialized hardware), protected by a password. To this end, the password is the input to a key derivation function (KDF), which typically uses hash functions (e. g., PBKDF2) or similar cryptographic constructions to derive a cryptographic key from the password. This key is not directly used to encrypt the hard disk but to encrypt a keystore, which facilitates key management, e. g., to allow for changing the password or for multiple users. Such a keystore construction enables the attacker to verify a password candidate by feeding the candidate password through the KDF, decrypting the keystore, and testing if it has the correct form.

Scenario B: Large-Scale Attack. An often even more relevant attack scenario is when an attacker tries to recover *a certain fraction of all of the password hashes* from a large number of accounts. A typical example for this Scenario B are breached databases, like the one from LinkedIn (as described in Sect. 2.2), of which 98 % of the passwords were recovered as they were hashed using SHA-1 and no salt [23]. In order to optimize the attack, the attacker will guess passwords based on decreasing likelihood and test each password for all hashes before continuing with the next guess. The recovered passwords can then be used in a variety of ways: they can be further weaponized in a *credential stuffing* attack [36,37], in a targeted password guessing attack [50], they can be monetized on black markets [17], or used for further illegal activities such as sending spam emails. Moreover, they can be of interest for password security research [4,16,20,35,47] or for enthusiasts that crack passwords out of fun or as a sort of competition [14,23].

2.2 Password Datasets

When analyzing human-chosen passwords, one must consider that password choice is contextual and influenced by many factors [2,18,38]. While it is difficult to adjust for all factors, we will analyze the impact of these influencing factors and describe our used comparison metrics in Sect. 2.3.

An overview of our used datasets that are described in the following is given in Table 1. We selected the datasets to allow for easy verification and to generate reproducible results based on publicly available data.

Table 1. Evaluated password datasets

Name	Service	Year	Policy	# Accounts
LinkedIn	Social network	2012	6+	160.8 million
RockYou	Social games	2009	5+	32.6 million
000Webhost	Web hosting	2016	6+ [a–Z][0–9]	15.3 million

To reason about the strength of a password distribution considering a *perfect knowledge* attacker, we use the partial guessing entropy (α-guesswork) G_α for $\alpha = 0.25$ as described by Bonneau [6]. Our datasets are:

- **LinkedIn:** The social networking website LinkedIn was hacked in June 2012. It consists of a database dump of approx. 163 million unsalted SHA-1 hashes. We use a 98.68 % recovered plaintext version of the leak, as we expect the bias introduced by ignoring 1.32 % of (presumably strong) passwords to be low. We include LinkedIn because we consider those passwords to be a reasonable candidate for *medium*-strong passwords ($\tilde{G}_{0.25} = 19$ bits).
- **RockYou:** This is a well-established leak used extensively in previous work. The 32 million plaintext passwords leaked from the RockYou web service in December 2009 via an SQL injection attack. Its passwords are considered relatively *weak* ($\tilde{G}_{0.25} = 16$ bits).
- **000Webhost:** This leak occurred in October 2015 and contains 15 million plaintext passwords from a free web space provider. We include this leak because of its enforcement of a stricter password composition policy, which results in a different password distribution containing relatively *strong* passwords ($\tilde{G}_{0.25} = 21$ bits).

2.3 Approximating Human Password Choice by a Zipf Distribution

Real-world datasets allow researchers to study human password choice, and it has been realized that real-world distributions $\mathcal{D}_{\text{Pw}}$ typically follow a ZIPF distribution. The ZIPF distribution was originally formulated in the context of quantitative linguistics based on the frequency of words in English text [53] but has since been shown to be a good model for human password choice as well. It is well documented that real-world password distributions (roughly) follow a ZIPF distribution (cf. Wang et al. [48,49], Malone and Maher [35], and Bonneau [6]).

Let $P = \{pwd_1, \ldots, pwd_N\}$ be an ordered set of N passwords, and let $s \geq 0$. We define the generalized harmonic number as

$$H_s(N) := \sum_{i=1}^{N} \frac{1}{i^s} \, .$$

Let X be a ZIPF$_{N,s}$-distributed random variable over P with *steepness parameter* s (the larger s, the steeper). Then

$$p_i := \mathbb{P}[X = pwd_i] = \frac{1}{H_s(N)} \cdot \frac{1}{i^s} \, ,$$

where $H_s(N)$ normalizes the distribution. Throughout the paper, we use that partial sums of ZIPF probabilities can be easily expressed as

$$\sum_{i=1}^{k} p_i = \frac{1}{H_s(N)} \sum_{i=1}^{k} \frac{1}{i^s} = \frac{H_s(k)}{H_s(N)}. \tag{1}$$

Notice that for $s = 0$ we have $H_0(N) = N$ and $p_i = \mathbb{P}[X = pwd_i] = \frac{1}{N}$. Thus, $\text{ZIPF}_{N,0}$ is the uniform distribution on all passwords. For $0 \leq s < 1$, the following lemma shows that $H_s(N) \leq N^{1-s}$, and therefore $p_1 \geq N^{s-1}$.

For example, for steepness $s = \frac{3}{4}$ the most likely password pwd_1 has probability $p_1 \geq N^{-\frac{1}{4}} \gg N^{-1}$. This already implies that on expectation we can identify a user with password pwd_1 with at most $N^{\frac{1}{4}}$ tries.

Lemma 1. *For $0 \leq s < 1$ we have*

$$\frac{N^{1-s}}{1-s} - \frac{1}{1-s} < H_s(N) \leq \frac{N^{1-s}}{1-s}.$$

In particular, $H_s(N) = \Theta(N^{1-s})$.

Proof.

$$\frac{N^{1-s}}{1-s} - \frac{1}{1-s} = \int_1^N i^{-s} \, di < \sum_{x=1}^{N} \frac{1}{i^s} = H_s(N)$$

$$\leq 1 + \int_1^N i^{-s} \, di = 1 + \frac{N^{1-s}}{1-s} - \frac{1}{1-s} \leq \frac{N^{1-s}}{1-s}. \qquad \square$$

In order to determine typical steepness values s in practical settings, let us provide an explicit approximation using the ZIPF distribution. As a first example, we take the LinkedIn database [23], with roughly $160 \cdot 10^6 \sim 2^{27}$ users and $N \sim 60 \cdot 10^6 \sim 2^{26}$ different passwords $P = \{pwd_1, \ldots, pwd_N\}$. We choose s so that $\text{ZIPF}_{N,s}$ is the best approximation of the password-distribution $\mathcal{D}_{Pw}$ of the database. For this, we use the coefficient of determination R^2 from Definition 1 between $\text{ZIPF}_{N,s}$ and the password distribution of the database, and select s so that R^2 is maximized. This is the case for $s \sim 0.777$ with a coefficient of determination of $R^2 = 0.781$. A log/log-scaled plot of a $\text{ZIPF}_{N,0.777}$ distribution and $\mathcal{D}_{Pw}$ can be seen in Fig. 1a. The results of analog calculations for the Rock-You and 000Webhost leak are shown in Fig. 1b and 1c. In the following, we will use the LinkedIn leak as our main dataset, since it is by far the largest publicly available dataset that includes *medium*-strong passwords ($\tilde{G}_{0.25} = 19$ bits).

Definition 1 (Coefficient of Determination (R^2)). *We define the coefficient of determination between two datasets $D = \{y_1, \ldots, y_n\}$ and $\hat{D} = \{\hat{y}_1, \ldots, \hat{y}_n\}$ as*

$$R^2 = 1 - \frac{\sum_{i=1}^{n} (y_i - \hat{y}_i)^2}{\sum_{i=1}^{n} (y_i - \overline{y})^2},$$

where $\overline{y} = \frac{1}{n} \sum_{i=1}^{n} y_i$ is the mean of the dataset D.

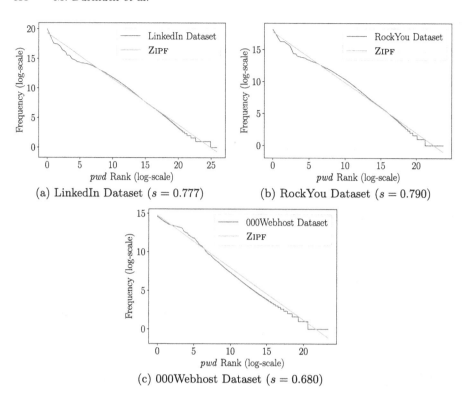

(a) LinkedIn Dataset ($s = 0.777$)   (b) RockYou Dataset ($s = 0.790$)

(c) 000Webhost Dataset ($s = 0.680$)

Fig. 1. Approximation of password leaks by the ZIPF distribution.

In the following, we show that the complexity of password guessing attacks in the fixed user case can be described by a random variable X distributed according to some ZIPF distribution. Therefore, we are interested in the expectation of X. The following Lemma 2 shows that the expectation is linear in the number N of passwords.

Lemma 2. *Let X be a $\mathrm{ZIPF}_{N,s}$ distributed random variable with $0 \leq s < 1$. Then*

$$\mathbb{E}[X] = \frac{1-s}{2-s} \cdot N \left(1 \pm o\left(1\right)\right) .$$

Proof. By definition of expectation, we have

$$\mathbb{E}[X] = \sum_{i=1}^{N} i \cdot \mathbb{P}[X = pwd_i] = \sum_{i=1}^{N} i \cdot \frac{1}{H_s(N)} \cdot \frac{1}{i^s} = \frac{1}{H_s(N)} \sum_{i=1}^{N} \frac{1}{i^{s-1}} = \frac{H_{s-1}(N)}{H_s(N)} .$$

Using Lemma 1, we show the upper and lower bound for $\mathbb{E}[X]$, starting with the upper bound.

$$\mathbb{E}[X] = \frac{H_{s-1}(N)}{H_s(N)} \le \frac{\frac{N^{2-s}}{2-s}}{\frac{N^{1-s}}{1-s} - \frac{1}{1-s}} = \frac{1-s}{2-s} \cdot N \cdot \left(\frac{N^{1-s}}{N^{1-s} - 1}\right)$$

$$= \frac{1-s}{2-s} \cdot N \cdot \left(1 + \frac{1}{N^{1-s} - 1}\right) = \frac{1-s}{2-s} \cdot N \cdot (1 + o(1)) \ .$$

Analogously, we derive the lower bound

$$\mathbb{E}[X] = \frac{H_{s-1}(N)}{H_s(N)} \ge \frac{\frac{N^{2-s}}{2-s} - \frac{1}{2-s}}{\frac{N^{1-s}}{1-s}} = \frac{1-s}{2-s} \cdot N \cdot \left(\frac{N^{1-s} - 1}{N^{1-s}}\right)$$

$$= \frac{1-s}{2-s} \cdot N \cdot \left(1 - \frac{1}{N^{1-s}}\right) = \frac{1-s}{2-s} \cdot N \cdot (1 - o(1)) \ .$$

$\square$

2.4   Password Guessing Scenario

Let $U = \{u_1, \ldots, u_w\}$ be a set of w users and $P = \{pwd_1, \ldots, pwd_N\}$ a set of N passwords. We denote by $g : U \mapsto \{1, \ldots, N\}$ a function that maps each $u \in U$ to its password index, i.e., u has password $pwd_{g(u)}$. Further, we define for each user u a random salt s_u.

We denote by L a leaked database of $|U|$ triples $(u, s_u, h(pwd_{g(u)}|s_u))$, where h is a cryptographic hash function. In other words, the leaked database L reveals for each user u its salt s_u and a salted hash of its password.

As in the previous Sect. 2.3, the set of password follows a $\text{ZIPF}_{N,s}$ distribution. Hence, a uniformly random user $u \in U$ has $pwd_i \in P$ with probability

$$p_i := \mathbb{P}_{u \in U}[g(u) = i] = \frac{1}{H_s(N)} \cdot \frac{1}{i^s} \ .$$

Let us define a *password verification function* $V : L \times P \mapsto \{0, 1\}$ as

$$V_{u, s_u, h(pwd_{g(u)}|s_u)}(pwd) := \begin{cases} 1 & \text{if } h(pwd_{g(u)}|s_u) = h(pwd|s_u), \\ 0 & \text{else} \end{cases} \qquad (2)$$

By the definition of V, a password guess pwd is correctly linked to user u with entry $(u, s_u, h(pwd_{f(u)}|s_u)) \in L$ if pwd has the correct salted hash value. We call every user for which our guesser finds a correctly linked password *compromised*.

We check the correctness of our password guesses via function evaluation of V. Notice that each evaluation requires a hash evaluation of h, which is our unit cost measure. Thus, we define the *average cost* of password guessing as

$$C := \frac{\#\text{Evaluations of } h}{\#\text{Compromised Users}} \ . \qquad (3)$$

Notice that our cost measure is independent of the underlying hash function. In Sect. 6.2, we discuss the effects of taking the run time of hash function evaluations into account.

In the following, we show that for both scenarios described in Sect. 2.1 (i.e., attacking a fixed user or large-scale attacks), the average cost of a quantum attacker is only the square-root of the average cost of a classical attacker.

2.5   Quantum Password Guessing

While previous applications of quantum algorithms to the problem of password guessing considered uniform password distribution [12], we generalize to a ZIPF distribution, which more accurately captures real-world password distributions. As in previous work [12], we consider error-free quantum computations [1, 10, 31].

When attacking a fixed user u (Scenario A), the key advantage of quantum computations is that we check the correctness of *all passwords* on u in a parallel superposition. In the large-scale Scenario B, first studied quantumly in our work, the key advantage of quantum computation is that we can check the correctness of a single password on *all users* in parallel.

Grover's Algorithm. The key to many square-root speedups in quantum computation is Grover's algorithm [25] and its generalizations [7, 8].

Theorem 1 (Grover [7, 8, 25]). *Let Ω be a finite search space with solutions $T \subseteq \Omega$. Let $f : \Omega \mapsto \{0, 1\}$ be an efficiently computable target function with $f(x) = 1$ iff $x \in T$.*

1. *In the single solution case $|T| \leq 1$, Grover's algorithm computes the unique solution $x \in T$ with $c \cdot \sqrt{|\Omega|}$ f-queries, where $c = \frac{\pi}{4} \cdot \left(1 + o\left(\frac{|T|}{|\Omega|}\right)\right) \sim 0.785$, or outputs FAIL if $|T| = 0$.*
2. *In the general case, Grover's algorithm computes a random solution $x \in T$ after $\mathcal{O}\left(\sqrt{\frac{|\Omega|}{|T|}}\right)$ f-queries, or outputs FAIL if $|T| = 0$.*

For illustrative purposes, let us first consider the case of uniformly distributed passwords.

Fixed User Attack. Let L be our database with entries $\ell_u = (u, s_u, h(pwd_{f(u)}|s_u))$. Consider some fixed ℓ_u, and take our password verification function
$V : L \times P \to \{0, 1\}$ from Eq. (2). We define the Grover target function

$$f_{\ell_u} : P \to \{0, 1\}, \quad pwd \mapsto V(\ell_u, pwd). \tag{4}$$

Since a unique password $pwd \in P$ verifies correctly for user u (unless we find collisions in h), we are in the single solution case $|T| = 1$ of Theorem 1. Thus, Grover's algorithm recovers the correct password with $c \cdot \sqrt{|P|} \sim 0.785 \cdot \sqrt{N}$ hash evaluations.

Large-Scale Attack. We check for all users in $U = \{u_1, \dots u_w\}$ the correctness of a single fixed password pwd. To this end, define the Grover function

$$f_{pwd} : U \to \{0, 1\}, \quad u \to V(\ell_u, pwd). \tag{5}$$

Since many users may use the same password pwd, we are in the general case of Theorem 1. Let $T \subseteq U$ be the number of users that share pwd. Then Grover's algorithm recovers a random user $u \in T$ within $\mathcal{O}(\sqrt{\frac{|U|}{|T|}})$ hash evaluations. In the following sections, we also take the effects of our ZIPF distribution into account.

3   Scenario A: Fixed User Attack

Classical. First, we study how the ZIPF distribution affects an optimal classical attacker targeting a fixed user u with leaked data $\ell_u = (u, s_u, h(pwd_{f(u)}|s_u)) \in L$.

A classical attacker's optimal strategy is to try passwords $pwd_1, pwd_2, \dots$ in order of decreasing probability. Let X be a random variable for the number of hash evaluation. Then the attacker succeeds with a single hash evaluation with probability $\mathbb{P}[X = 1] = p_1 = \mathbb{P}[u$ has password $pwd_1]$. In general, X is $\text{ZIPF}_{N,s}$-distributed. By Lemma 2 and neglecting low order terms, the expected number of hash evaluations is

$$\mathbb{E}[X] = \sum_{i=1}^{N} i \cdot p_i = \frac{1-s}{2-s} \cdot N. \tag{6}$$

This implies that for the uniform distribution with $s = 0$, we need to test on expectation half of the passwords. For the typical value of $s = \frac{3}{4}$ from Figs. 1a and 1b, on expectation it suffices to try only $\frac{1}{5}N$ passwords.

Quantum. In the quantum setting, we use Grover's theorem (Theorem 1) with target function $f_{\ell_u} : P \to \{0,1\}$, $f_{\ell_u}(pwd) := V(\ell, pwd)$ from Eq. (4). Moreover, we split our search space P at the mean $\mu := \mathbb{E}[X]$ of our $\text{ZIPF}_{N,s}$ distribution from Eq. (6). Our quantum attack first checks whether our desired password is in $P_1 = \{pwd_1, \dots, pwd_\mu\}$. By Theorem (1), this first check can be performed with $c\sqrt{\mu}$ hash evaluations and succeeds with probability

$$p_1 + \dots + p_\mu = \frac{1}{H_s(N)} \sum_{i=1}^{\mu} \frac{1}{i^s} = \frac{H_s(\mu)}{H_s(N)}.$$

Using Lemma 2, we have to perform the second check on the remaining search space $P \setminus P_1$ with probability at most $1 - \frac{H_s(\mu)}{H_s(N)} \leq \sqrt{1-s}$. In total the number of hash evaluations is upper bounded by

$$c\left(\sqrt{\mu} + \sqrt{1-s} \cdot \sqrt{N-\mu}\right) = 2c\sqrt{\mathbb{E}[X]}.$$

Thus, up to a factor of at most $2c \leq 1.6$ our quantum algorithm achieves the square-root cost of the optimal classical cost from Eq. (6).

Remark 1. A result of similar quality can be achieved by using the *Amplitude Amplification* technique of Brassard et al. [8]. However, our Grover-based approach benefits from its simplicity, since in Amplitude Amplification, we have to create a superposition over all passwords weighted by their $\text{ZIPF}_{N,s}$-distribution. This creates some technical difficulties and unnecessary overhead.

4   Scenario B: Large-Scale Attack

Let us now look at the scenario where an attacker wants to compromise just a single user with a weak password. In some attack scenarios, this may already provide an attacker access to an infrastructure, e.g., in a company.

4.1   Scenario B.1: Attacking a Single (and All) Weakest User(s)

Classical. To identify a single weakest user, the optimal classical approach is to try the most likely password pwd_1 with success probability p_1 on random users. This takes expected running time $\frac{1}{p_1}$. If our passwords followed a uniform distribution, then this attack still takes expected time $\frac{1}{p_1} = N$. However, in the more general case of a $\text{ZIPF}_{N,s}$ distribution by Lemma 1 we have

$$\frac{1}{p_1} = H_s(N) \leq \frac{N^{1-s}}{1-s}.$$

This implies, for our typical value $s = \frac{3}{4}$ from Figs. 1a and 1b, that an attacker finds a user with a weakest password in time with at most $4N^{\frac{1}{4}}$ hash evaluations.

Quantum. In the quantum setting, we use Grover's algorithm over a superposition of *all users* to identify a user with password pwd_1.

Let $U = \{u_1, \ldots, u_w\}$ be the user set, and L be a our leaked database with entry ℓ_u for user u. We use the Grover function $f_{pwd_1} : U \rightarrow \{0,1\}$, $u \rightarrow V(\ell_u, pwd_1)$, as defined in Eq. (5).

Let T be the set of users with weakest password pwd_1. Then on expectation $|T| = p_1|U|$. An application of Theorem 1 shows that we find a random user from T in time

$$\mathcal{O}\left(\sqrt{\frac{|U|}{|T|}}\right) = \mathcal{O}\left(\sqrt{\frac{1}{p_1}}\right) = \mathcal{O}(\sqrt{H_s(N)}) = \mathcal{O}(N^{\frac{1-s}{2}}).$$

For $s = \frac{3}{4}$, this implies that we quantumly compromise a user with the weakest password within only $\mathcal{O}(N^{\frac{1}{8}})$ hash function evaluations.

Using our cost function from Eq. (3), we obtain average classical cost $\mathcal{O}(N^{1-s})$ respectively quantum cost $\mathcal{O}(N^{\frac{1-s}{2}})$ for compromising a single user with weakest password. In the following, we show that with the same average cost per user, we can also compromise all users with password pwd_1.

All Weakest Users. Classically, we simply test for all $|U|$ users the validity of password pwd_1, resulting in expected $|T| = p_1|U|$ compromised users. This implies average cost $C = \frac{|U|}{p_1|U|} = H_s(N) = \mathcal{O}(N^{1-s})$.

Quantumly, we use the aforementioned Grover algorithm until we find $|T| = p_1|U|$ different users with password pwd_1. Using coupon collector, this takes $|T| \cdot \ln|T|$ runs of the above algorithm. Omitting the low order $\ln|T|$-term, we obtain average cost

$$\frac{|T| \cdot \mathcal{O}\left(\sqrt{\frac{|U|}{|T|}}\right)}{|T|} = \mathcal{O}\left(\sqrt{\frac{1}{p_1}}\right) = \mathcal{O}(N^{\frac{1-s}{2}}),$$

giving us again the desired square-root speedup.

4.2   Scenario B.2: Attacking a Constant Fraction of All Users

Finally, we want to generalize the techniques from the previous Sect. 4.1 to large-scale adversaries that try to recover a constant fraction c of all users. As an illustrating example, we use $c = 10\%$ respectively $c = 50\%$ of the users. In a nutshell, in both the classical and quantum setting an attacker recovers those users that use the k weakest passwords $pwd_1, \ldots, pwd_k$ with probabilities $p_1, \ldots, p_k$. We set k such that we obtain the desired c-fraction of all users. Using Eq. (1) and Lemma 1 we obtain

$$\sum_{i=1}^{k} p_i = \frac{H_s(k)}{H_s(N)} \approx \left(\frac{k}{N}\right)^{1-s} \stackrel{!}{=} c,$$

where $\approx$ suppresses an $(1 + o(1))$-factor. This means we can solve the above relation in k by setting

$$k = c^{\frac{1}{1-s}} N. \tag{7}$$

Classical. Consider an attacker that in a first pass tries on all $|U|$ users password pwd_1, thereby recovering $p_1|U|$ users. In a second pass, the attacker tries on all remaining $|U| - p_1|U|$ users pwd_2, recovering $p_2|U|$ users, etc. The attacker stops on identifying at least $c|U|$ many user passwords.

The amount of hash function evaluations per pass is clearly upper bounded by $|U|$, and lower bounded by $(1 - c)|U| = \Omega(|U|)$. Thus, the attacker recovers $c|U|$ passwords in total time $k \cdot \Theta(|U|) = \Theta(c^{\frac{1}{1-s}} N|U|)$. This gives us an average cost per password of

$$C = \frac{\Theta(c^{\frac{1}{1-s}} N|U|)}{c|U|} = \Theta\left(c^{\frac{s}{1-s}} N\right). \tag{8}$$

Let us briefly ignore the small constant hidden in the Θ-notion. For the uniform distribution with $s = 0$, the average cost per password is N, as one would expect. For the typical value $s = \frac{3}{4}$, we obtain the average cost $c^3 N$. This means that $\text{ZIPF}_{N,\frac{3}{4}}$ gives us a speedup of factor c^{-3} per compromised password. Thus, for $c = 0.5$ we obtain a speedup of 8, and for $c = 0.1$ we even obtain a speedup factor of 1000 over the uniform distribution.

Quantum. From Sect. 4.1 we know that we can quantumly recover all $p_i|U|$ users with password pwd_i in time $\mathcal{O}(p_i|U| \cdot \sqrt{\frac{|U|}{p_i|U|}}) = \mathcal{O}(\sqrt{p_i}|U|)$. Hence, for all k passwords $pwd_1, \ldots, pwd_k$ we need a total time of

$$\mathcal{O}\left(\sum_{i=1}^{k} \sqrt{p_i}|U|\right) = \mathcal{O}\left(\frac{1}{H_s(N)} \sum_{i=1}^{k} i^{-\frac{s}{2}}|U|\right) = \mathcal{O}\left(N^{\frac{s-1}{2}} \cdot k^{1-\frac{s}{2}} \cdot |U|\right)$$

$$= \mathcal{O}\left(N^{\frac{s-1}{2}} \cdot (c^{\frac{1}{1-s}} N)^{1-\frac{s}{2}} \cdot |U|\right) = \mathcal{O}\left(c^{1+\frac{s}{2(1-s)}} N^{\frac{1}{2}} \cdot |U|\right).$$

Since we recover $c|U|$ passwords, this implies an average cost per password of

$$\mathcal{O}\left(\sqrt{c^{\frac{s}{1-s}}N}\right),$$

i. e., the square-root of the classical cost from Eq. (8).

5   Real-World Impact

Let us now check the accuracy of our theoretical predictions for the ZIPF distribution from Sects. 3 and 4, when applied to a real-world password leak distribution $\mathcal{D}_{\mathrm{Pw}}$. As described in Sect. 2.2, we take the LinkedIn database for this purpose because it is a good example for a medium-strong real-world distribution.

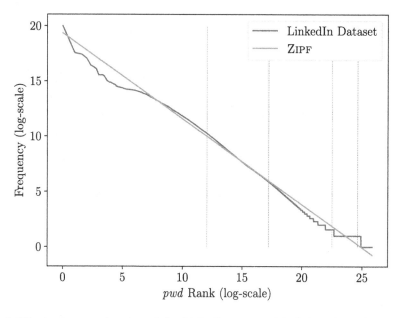

Fig. 2. The best approximation of the LinkedIn password leak by a ZIPF distribution ($s = 0.777$). The dotted lines correspond to a fraction of 10 %, 25 %, 50 %, and 75 % of all users.

Notice that we only take the distribution from LinkedIn, see also Fig. 2, but otherwise stay in our attack model with *salted hashes* (which is not the case for the LinkedIn dataset).

Scenario A: Fixed User Attack. Table 2 provides an overview of our results of the real-world Scenario A. We see that $\mathrm{ZIPF}_{N,0.777}$ quite accurately approximates the number of required hash evaluations for the real-world distribution $\mathcal{D}_{\mathrm{Pw}}$ – within a factor of 1.3 classically and $1.15 \approx \sqrt{1.3}$ quantumly.

Table 2. Scenario A: fixed user attack. Required hash evaluations for finding a fixed user's password (using the approaches of Sect. 3 and Grover with $c = 1$)).

Distribution	Required hash evaluations	
	Classical	Quantum
Uniform $\sim \text{ZIPF}_{N,0}$	30 000 000	7 750
$\text{ZIPF}_{N,0.777}$	11 100 000	5 560
LinkedIn $\mathcal{D}_{\text{Pw}}$	14 600 000	6 430

Compared to a quantum attacker for the *uniform distribution* ($\text{ZIPF}_{N,0}$), our new quantum attacker with knowledge of the *human-chosen password distribution* ($\mathcal{D}_{\text{Pw}}$) only requires 83 % of the hash evaluations.

It is also worth stressing the absolute numbers for $\mathcal{D}_{\text{Pw}}$. While the classical attacker needs almost 15 million hash evaluations, the quantum attacker succeeds with roughly 6400 hash evaluations.

Table 3. Attack scenario B: large-scale attack. Required number of hash evaluations *per user* for compromising a constant fraction of all users (using the approaches of Sect. 4 and Grover with $c = 1$.

Setting	Distribution	Required hash evaluations per User				
		10 %	25 %	50 %	75 %	100 %
Classical	Uniform $\sim \text{ZIPF}_{N,0}$	57 100 000	52 600 000	45 100 000	37 500 000	30 000 000
	$\text{ZIPF}_{N,0.777}$	33 300	473 000	3 430 000	8 800 000	11 100 000
	LinkedIn $\mathcal{D}_{\text{Pw}}$	38 700	482 000	6 820 000	14 300 000	14 600 000
Quantum	Uniform $\sim \text{ZIPF}_{N,0}$	7 750	7 750	7 750	7 750	7 750
	$\text{ZIPF}_{N,0.777}$	158	613	1 880	3 710	6 030
	LinkedIn $\mathcal{D}_{\text{Pw}}$	181	622	2 520	4 640	6 380

Scenario B: Large-Scale Attack. Table 3 provides an overview of our results for large-scale attackers, when compromising a total user fraction of 10 %, 25 %, 50 %, 75 %, and 100 %.

The values predicted by the $\text{ZIPF}_{N,0.777}$ distribution differ only by a factor of at most 2 from the values for the LinkedIn distribution $\mathcal{D}_{\text{Pw}}$, again validating the accuracy of ZIPF.

Notice that in comparison to Scenario A, the reduction of the absolute numbers through the quantum square-root speedup is even more significant in this large-scale scenario. Within the weakest 10 % of the users, we require only about 180 hash evaluations per user on average. When attacking 50 % of the users, we still require just 2500 evaluations per user. Only if we address the full database, the average grows to 6400, matching the analysis from Scenario A.

Let us put the 10 % weakest user scenario into perspective. Assume that, both classically and quantumly, a hash evaluation takes about 1 s [3]. Then quantumly we would require only 180 s, i.e. 3 min, whereas a classical attacker would need, on average, about 10 h per user.

6   Discussion

In light of our new results for the quantum setting, we now discuss recommendations for increasing password security in a post-quantum world.

6.1   Password Strength

A square-root speedup seems moderate from a cryptographic perspective and merely means doubling the cryptographic keys' length to achieve the same security level. However, from a user's perspective, this is much more dramatic. To bring this into perspective, let us consider an 8 character password *randomly* chosen from the alphabet of all 95 printable ASCII characters (lowercase, uppercase, digits, symbols) as the minimal level of security. If we want to achieve the same security in the quantum setting, users would need to remember 16 instead of 8 characters due to the square-root speedup-up from Grover's algorithm. While assigning random passwords to users is not recommendable from a usability perspective, studies showed that users are potentially able to remember random 8 character passwords [28,52,54]. Increasing this to 16 random characters crosses a threshold where we cannot expect users to be able to memorize such a password. This is the situation for randomly chosen passwords; let us now focus on human password choice.

As described earlier, users struggle and often fail to create secure passwords, resulting in a highly skewed distribution. This worsens the situation because we demonstrated in Sect. 5 that an attacker with knowledge of the password distribution is much more effective in guessing the passwords. Hence, if we want to achieve the security level as described above, users would need to increase the length of their password beyond 16 characters. While increasing the password length is recommended by current best practice policies, among others, NIST [24], they do not require more than 16 characters. This limit ensures that the created passwords are not only secure but also memorable [41,42,44]. Hence, we argue that for both random and user-chosen passwords, we are going to face the problem that we as humans simply can no longer memorize the passwords for all our accounts.

If we insist on solving the problem by increasing the password length, this seems only possible with password managers. Using them is already recommended nowadays, but their advantage of generating and storing a long, random string for each and every account becomes even more apparent in the quantum setting. Nevertheless, considering their low adoption rates and the goal in mind not to burden users, it is important to look at alternative solutions.

6.2   Password Hash Functions

So far, our cost measure used the number of hash function evaluations but ignored their individual run times. We did this to provide results independently from actual implementations. Still, for recommendations that tend to increase security, we remark on the importance of choosing suitable and future-proof password hashing functions. Currently widely deployed hash functions such as bcrypt, PBKDF2, or iterated versions of SHA-256 and SHA-512 [9,22], are based on the idea that the computing power of an adversary is limited. This also holds for attackers in the quantum setting.

Currently, the biggest limitations of quantum computers are the number of qubits that can be implemented as well as the time span they can keep their entangled states, i.e., their information. As of June 2021, the technology scales up to around 65 qubits [11], with predictions of multiple hundred in the foreseeable future. Thus, a short-term solution could be the use of an unusually long salt that does not add complexity but exploits the shortage of available qubits in a quantum computer. However, a far better approach is *memory-hard* password hashes [3,5], which require large amounts of memory to be efficiently computed. While memory-hard password hashes were originally intended to counter the massive computing power of ASICs, FPGAs, and GPUs, we believe that they are also effective in countering quantum computer-based attacks. Still, further research is necessary to focus on the quantum-hardness of memory-hard password hash functions.

6.3   Encrypted Passwords and Secret Salts

As an additional layer of protection NIST [24] recommends that service operators should "perform an additional iteration of a KDF using a salt value that is secret and known only to the verifier." This *secret salt*, sometimes also called *pepper*, needs to be stored separately from the password hashes and should ideally reside in a hardware security module (HSM) or similar protected device. Likewise, passwords could also be encrypted using a quantum-resistant authenticated encryption scheme like NTRU [27]. In both cases, the attacker would need to obtain or attack (using Grover's algorithm) the secret salt/encryption key first. Thus, these protection mechanisms are only applicable to scenarios where a remote device or rate-limited hardware component like a trusted platform module could be utilized to store the required high entropy key material.

In cases where an HSM is not available, one could use a different notion of a secret salt in the form of a random value that is not stored but needs to be rediscovered every time it is needed [30]. However, since the server itself has to brute-force this value for every authentication attempt, it has to be chosen from a smaller set than a stored salt. Hence, this countermeasure is only effective against a large-scale attacker that targets multiple hashes because the slowdown becomes significant if the individual but negligible brute-force attempts add up. Finally, a randomly chosen salt only gives a probabilistic guarantee, whereas iterated hash functions, as described in Sect. 6.2, ensure a fixed slowdown.

7   Conclusion

Motivated by the recent advancements in the field of quantum computers, we analyzed the potential impact of quantum computing on securely stored human-chosen passwords. We showed how a quantum computer-equipped attacker can take advantage of the bias in real-world password distributions and still gains a square-root speedup in the quantum world. We validated our theoretical ZIPF modeling with a real-world distribution from LinkedIn. Our quantum speedup on real-world data leads to an already small number of 6400 hash evaluations for attacking a fixed user (Scenario A) and to a frightening number of less than 200 hash evaluations per user among the 10 % users with weakest passwords (Scenario B). Our results underline the necessity of new password protection mechanisms in a quantum world.

Acknowledgments. This research was supported by the research training group "Human Centered Systems Security" sponsored by the state of North Rhine-Westphalia and funded by the Deutsche Forschungsgemeinschaft (DFG, German Research Foundation) under Germany's Excellence Strategy - EXC 2092 CASA – 390781972.

References

1. Aharonov, D., Ben-Or, M.: Fault-tolerant quantum computation with constant error rate. SIAM J. Comput. **38**(4), 1207–1282 (2008)
2. Bailey, D.V., Dürmuth, M., Paar, C.: Statistics on password re-use and adaptive strength for financial accounts. In: Abdalla, M., De Prisco, R. (eds.) SCN 2014. LNCS, vol. 8642, pp. 218–235. Springer, Cham (2014). https://doi.org/10.1007/978-3-319-10879-7_13
3. Biryukov, A., Dinu, D., Khovratovich, D., Josefsson, S.: Argon2 Memory-Hard Function for Password Hashing and Proof-of-Work Applications. RFC 9106, RFC Editor, September 2021. https://tools.ietf.org/html/rfc9106
4. Blocki, J., Harsha, B., Zhou, S.: On the economics of offline password cracking. In: IEEE Symposium on Security and Privacy. SP 2018, pp. 35–53. IEEE, San Francisco, California, USA, May 2018
5. Boneh, D., Corrigan-Gibbs, H., Schechter, S.: Balloon hashing: a memory-hard function providing provable protection against sequential attacks. In: Cheon, J.H., Takagi, T. (eds.) ASIACRYPT 2016. LNCS, vol. 10031, pp. 220–248. Springer, Heidelberg (2016). https://doi.org/10.1007/978-3-662-53887-6_8
6. Bonneau, J.: The Science of guessing: analyzing an anonymized corpus of 70 million passwords. In: IEEE Symposium on Security and Privacy. SP 2012, pp. 538–552. IEEE, San Jose, California, USA, May 2012
7. Boyer, M., Brassard, G., Høyer, P., Tapp, A.: Tight bounds on quantum searching. In: Workshop on Physics and Computation. PhysComp 1996, pp. 493–506, Elsevier, Boston, Massachusetts, USA, November 1996
8. Brassard, G., Høyer, P., Mosca, M., Tapp, A.: Quantum amplitude amplification and estimation. Contemporary Math. **305**, 53–74 (2002)
9. Brewster, T.: Why You Shouldn't Panic About Dropbox Leaking 68 Million Passwords, August 2016. https://www.forbes.com/sites/thomasbrewster/2016/08/31/dropbox-hacked-but-its-not-that-bad/, as of 2021/11/20 18:59:40

10. Campbell, E.T., Terhal, B.M., Vuillot, C.: Roads towards fault-tolerant universal quantum computation. Nature **549**(7671), 172–179 (2017)
11. Cho, A.: IBM Promises 1000-Qubit Quantum Computer by 2023, September 2020. https://www.sciencemag.org/news/2020/09/ibm-promises-1000-qubit-quantum-computer-milestone-2023, as of 2021/11/20 18:59:40
12. Corrigan-Gibbs, H., Wu, D.J., Boneh, D.: Quantum operating systems. In: Workshop on Hot Topics in Operating Systems. HotOS 2017, pp. 76–81. ACM, Vancouver, British Columbia, Canada, May 2017
13. Crawford, H., Atkin, S.: Quantum authentication: current and future research directions. In: Who Are You?! Adventures in Authentication Workshop. WAY 2019, pp. 1–5, USENIX, Santa Clara, California, USA, August 2019
14. Croley ("Chick3nman"), S.: Abusing Password Reuse at Scale: Bcrypt and Beyond, August 2018. https://www.youtube.com/watch?v=5su3_Py8iMQ, as of 2021/11/20 18:59:40
15. Croley ("Chick3nman"), S.: NVIDIA GeForce RTX 3090 Hashcat Benchmarks, November 2020. https://gist.github.com/Chick3nman/e4fcee00cb6d82874dace721 06d73fef, as of 2021/11/20 18:59:40
16. Das, A., Bonneau, J., Caesar, M., Borisov, N., Wang, X.: The tangled web of password reuse. In: Symposium on Network and Distributed System Security. NDSS 2014, ISOC, San Diego, California, USA, February 2014
17. Digital Shadows Ltd: From Exposure to Takeover: The 15 Billion Stolen Credentials Allowing Account Takeover, July 2020. https://resources.digitalshadows.com/whitepapers-and-reports/from-exposure-to-takeover, as of 2021/11/20 18:59:40
18. Florêncio, D., Herley, C.: A large-scale study of web password habits. In: The World Wide Web Conference. WWW 2007, pp. 657–666. ACM, Banff, Alberta, Canada, May 2007
19. Florêncio, D., Herley, C., Van Oorschot, P.C.: An administrator's guide to internet password research. In: Large Installation System Administration Conference, pp. 44–61. LISA 2014, USENIX, Seattle, Washington, USA, November 2014
20. Golla, M., Dürmuth, M.: On the accuracy of password strength meters. In: ACM Conference on Computer and Communications Security. CCS 2018, pp. 1567–1582. ACM, Toronto, Ontario, Canada, October 2018
21. Golla, M., et al.: What was that site doing with my Facebook password? Designing password-reuse notifications. In: ACM Conference on Computer and Communications Security, pp. 1549–1566. ACM. CCS 2018, Toronto, Ontario, Canada, October 2018
22. Goodin, D.: Once Seen as Bulletproof, 11 Million+ Ashley Madison Passwords Already Cracked, September 2015. https://arstechnica.com/information-technology/2015/09/once-seen-as-bulletproof-11-million-ashley-madison-passwords-already-cracked/, as of 2021/11/20 18:59:40
23. Gosney ("epixoip"), J.M.: How LinkedIn's Password Sloppiness Hurts Us All, June 2016. https://arstechnica.com/information-technology/2016/06/how-linkedins-password-sloppiness-hurts-us-all/, as of 2021/11/20 18:59:40
24. Grassi, P.A., Fenton, J.L., Burr, W.E.: Digital Identity Guidelines - Authentication and Lifecycle Management: NIST Special Publication 800–63B, Jun 2017
25. Grover, L.K.: A fast quantum mechanical algorithm for database search. In: ACM Symposium on Theory of Computing. STOC 1996, pp. 212–219. ACM, Philadelphia, Pennsylvania, USA, May 1996
26. Häner, T., Roetteler, M., Svore, K.M.: Factoring using $2n + 2$ qubits with Toffoli based modular multiplication. Quantum Inf. Comput. **17**(7–8), 673–684 (2017)

27. Hoffstein, J., Pipher, J., Silverman, J.H.: NTRU: a ring-based public key cryptosystem. In: Buhler, J.P. (ed.) ANTS 1998. LNCS, vol. 1423, pp. 267–288. Springer, Heidelberg (1998). https://doi.org/10.1007/BFb0054868

28. Huh, J.H., Kim, H., Bobba, R.B., Bashir, M.N., Beznosov, K.: On the memorability of system-generated PINs: can chunking help? In: Symposium on Usable Privacy and Security, pp. 197–209. SOUPS 2015, USENIX, Ottawa, Canada, July 2015

29. Kaplan, M., Leurent, G., Leverrier, A., Naya-Plasencia, M.: Breaking symmetric cryptosystems using quantum period finding. In: Robshaw, M., Katz, J. (eds.) CRYPTO 2016. LNCS, vol. 9815, pp. 207–237. Springer, Heidelberg (2016). https://doi.org/10.1007/978-3-662-53008-5_8

30. Kedem, G., Ishihara, Y.: Brute force attack on UNIX passwords with SIMD computer. In: USENIX Security Symposium. SSYM 1999, pp. 93–98, USENIX, Washington, District of Columbia, USA, August 1999

31. Knill, E., Laflamme, R., Zurek, W.H.: Resilient quantum computation: error models and thresholds. Proc. Royal Soc. A: Math. Phys. Eng. Sci. **454**(1969), 365–384 (1998)

32. Kuwakado, H., Morii, M.: Security on the quantum-type even-Mansour cipher. In: International Symposium on Information Theory and Its Applications. ISITA 2012, pp. 312–316. IEEE, Honolulu, Hawaii, USA, October 2012

33. Leander, G., May, A.: Grover meets Simon – quantumly attacking the FX-construction. In: Takagi, T., Peyrin, T. (eds.) ASIACRYPT 2017. LNCS, vol. 10625, pp. 161–178. Springer, Cham (2017). https://doi.org/10.1007/978-3-319-70697-9_6

34. Liu, E., Nakanishi, A., Golla, M., Cash, D., Ur, B.: reasoning analytically about password-cracking software. In: IEEE Symposium on Security and Privacy. SP 2019, pp. 380–397. IEEE, San Francisco, California, USA, May 2019

35. Malone, D., Maher, K.: Investigating the distribution of password choices. In: The World Wide Web Conference. WWW 2012, pp. 301–310. ACM, Lyon, France, April 2012

36. Mirian, A., DeBlasio, J., Savage, S., Voelker, G.M., Thomas, K.: Hack for hire: exploring the emerging market for account hijacking. In: The World Wide Web Conference. WWW 2019, pp. 1279–1289. ACM, San Francisco, California, USA, May 2019

37. Pal, B., Daniel, T., Chatterjee, R., Ristenpart, T.: Beyond credential stuffing: password similarity models using neural networks. In: IEEE Symposium on Security and Privacy. SP 2019, pp. 866–883. IEEE, San Francisco, California, USA, May 2019

38. Pearman, S., et al.: Let's go in for a closer look: observing passwords in their natural habitat. In: ACM Conference on Computer and Communications Security. CCS 2017, pp. 295–310. ACM, Dallas, Texas, USA, Oct 2017

39. Roetteler, M., Naehrig, M., Svore, K.M., Lauter, K.: Quantum resource estimates for computing elliptic curve discrete logarithms. In: Takagi, T., Peyrin, T. (eds.) ASIACRYPT 2017. LNCS, vol. 10625, pp. 241–270. Springer, Cham (2017). https://doi.org/10.1007/978-3-319-70697-9_9

40. Roetteler, M., Svore, K.M.: Quantum computing: codebreaking and beyond. IEEE Secur. Privacy **16**(5), 22–36 (2018)

41. Shay, R., et al.: A spoonful of sugar?: The impact of guidance and feedback on password-creation behavior. In: ACM Conference on Human Factors in Computing Systems. CHI 2015, pp. 2903–2912. ACM, Seoul, Republic of Korea, April 2015

42. Shay, R., et al.: Can long passwords be secure and usable? In: ACM Conference on Human Factors in Computing Systems. CHI 2014, pp. 2927–2936. ACM, Toronto, Ontario, Canada, April 2014
43. Shor, P.W.: Algorithms for quantum computation: discrete logarithms and factoring. In: IEEE Annual Symposium on Foundations of Computer Science. FOCS 1994, pp. 124–134. IEEE, Santa Fe, New Mexico, USA, November 1994
44. Tan, J., Bauer, L., Christin, N., Cranor, L.F.: Definitive recommendations for stronger, more usable passwords combining minimum-strength, minimum-length, and blacklist requirements. In: ACM Conference on Computer and Communications Security. CCS 2020, pp. 1407–1426. ACM, Virtual Event, USA, November 2020
45. Ur, B., Bees, J., Segreti, S.M., Bauer, L., Christin, N., Cranor, L.F.: Do users' perceptions of password security match reality? In: ACM Conference on Human Factors in Computing Systems. CHI 2016, pp. 3748–3760. ACM, Santa Clara, California, USA, May 2016
46. Ur, B., et al.: "I Added '!' at the end to make it secure": observing password creation in the lab. In: Symposium on Usable Privacy and Security, pp. 123–140. SOUPS 2015, USENIX, Ottawa, Ontario, Canada, July 2015
47. Veras, R., Collins, C., Thorpe, J.: On the semantic patterns of passwords and their security impact. In: Symposium on Network and Distributed System Security. NDSS 2014, ISOC, San Diego, California, USA, February 2014
48. Wang, D., Cheng, H., Wang, P., Huang, X., Jian, G.: Zipf's law in passwords. IEEE Trans. Inf. Forensics Secur. **12**(11), 2776–2791 (2017)
49. Wang, D., Wang, P.: On the implications of Zipf's law in passwords. In: Askoxylakis, I., Ioannidis, S., Katsikas, S., Meadows, C. (eds.) ESORICS 2016. LNCS, vol. 9878, pp. 111–131. Springer, Cham (2016). https://doi.org/10.1007/978-3-319-45744-4_6
50. Wang, D., Zhang, Z., Wang, P., Yan, J., Huang, X.: Targeted online password guessing: an underestimated threat. In: ACM Conference on Computer and Communications Security. CCS 2016, pp. 1242–1254. ACM, Vienna, Austria, October 2016
51. Wash, R., Radar, E., Berman, R., Wellmer, Z.: Understanding password choices: how frequently entered passwords are re-used across websites. In: Symposium on Usable Privacy and Security, pp. 175–188. SOUPS 2016, USENIX, Denver, Colorado, USA, July 2016
52. Yan, J., Blackwell, A., Anderson, R., Grant, A.: Password memorability and security: empirical results. IEEE Secur. Privacy **2**(5), 25–31 (2004)
53. Zipf, G.K.: Human Behavior and the Principle of Least Effort: An Introduction to Human Ecology. Addison-Wesley Press, Cambridge (1949)
54. Zviran, M., Haga, W.J.: A comparison of password techniques for multilevel authentication mechanisms. Comput. J. **36**(3), 227–237 (1993)

Attestation and Verification

Anonymous Transactions with Revocation and Auditing in Hyperledger Fabric

Dmytro Bogatov[1]([✉])([iD]), Angelo De Caro[2], Kaoutar Elkhiyaoui[2], and Björn Tackmann[3]

[1] Boston University, Boston, USA
dmytro@bu.edu
[2] IBM Research, Zürich, Switzerland
{adc,kao}@zurich.ibm.com
[3] DFINITY, Zürich, Switzerland
bjoern@dfinity.org

Abstract. In permissioned blockchain systems, participants are admitted to the network by receiving a credential from a certification authority. Each transaction processed by the network is required to be authorized by a valid participant who authenticates via her credential. Use case settings where privacy is a concern thus require proper privacy-preserving authentication and authorization mechanisms.

Anonymous credential schemes allow a user to authenticate while showing only those attributes necessary in a given setting. This makes them a great tool for authorizing transactions in permissioned blockchain systems based on the user's attributes. In most setups, there is one distinct certification authority for each organization in the network. Consequently, the use of plain anonymous credential schemes still leaks the association of a user to the organization that issued her credentials. Camenisch, Drijvers and Dubovitskaya (CCS 2017) therefore suggest the use of a delegatable anonymous credential scheme to also hide that remaining piece of information.

In this paper, we propose the revocation and auditability—two functionalities that are necessary for real-world adoption—and integrate them into the scheme. We present a complete protocol, its security definition and the proof, and provide its open-source implementation. Our distributed-setting performance measurements show that the integration of the scheme with Hyperledger Fabric, while incurring an overhead in comparison to the less privacy-preserving solutions, is practical for settings with stringent privacy requirements.

Keywords: Blockchain security and privacy · Anonymity & pseudonymity · Anonymous credentials · Applied cryptography

1 Introduction

Blockchain systems allow two or more mutually distrustful parties to perform transactions by appending them to a shared ledger without the need to rely on

© Springer Nature Switzerland AG 2021
M. Conti et al. (Eds.): CANS 2021, LNCS 13099, pp. 435–459, 2021.
https://doi.org/10.1007/978-3-030-92548-2_23

a trusted third party. The first and still most prominent use of blockchains is in the area of cryptocurrencies where each transaction transfers fungible tokens between two or more parties. Blockchain systems used for cryptocurrencies are usually *permissionless*, meaning that joining the system does not require the parties to register their identity; everyone can participate.

Many other application scenarios for blockchains, however, require the participants to be registered, and access to the blockchain system to be *permissioned*. For instance, use cases in the financial domain are restricted by know-your-customer (KYC) or anti-money-laundering (AML) regulations. Elections require the set of eligible voters to be known in order to prevent illegitimate voters from submitting votes or any voter from double-voting. Enterprise blockchain systems accelerate processing of transactions in business networks with known participants. All aforementioned use cases require the transactions to be properly authorized by a member of the network. Note that *permissioned* does not mean *centralized*: the trust is still distributed among the participants of the network, the difference with permissionless networks is that joining the network becomes an explicit operation. For example, instead of a centralized certification authority for all participants, a permissioned blockchain network uses multiple such authorities, one per organization, resulting in a *federated model*.

Use cases that call for a transaction authorization often still require the identity of the transaction origin to be hidden. The most salient example is elections, where re-voting (as a measure against coercion [1]) inherently requires voters to be anonymous. Financial use cases where the transaction history of a user can leak sensitive personal information through usage patterns, are another good example. In such cases, the use of anonymous credential systems like Identity Mixer [16] allows participants to submit transactions while revealing only the attributes necessary to authorize that particular transaction (such as being a registered voter or having passed KYC checks), and keeping all other attributes (such as name, address or age) hidden.

Unfortunately, even the use of anonymous credentials can be insufficient. The reason is that each organization has its own certificate authority, and anonymity is only guaranteed relative to that authority. In other words, the particular certificate authority that issued a user's credential still will be leaked from the authorized transactions. In certain use cases even this leakage is not acceptable, for example, the leakage of a patient being treated in a particular hospital department. A naïve approach to tackle this is to have one global certificate authority issuing anonymous credentials. This, however, means that all credentials are issued by the same central entity, essentially eliminating the federated management model that permissioned blockchains are supposed to bring.

As first observed in [14], this is where *delegatable credentials* come in handy: in a delegatable credential scheme, a root authority delegates issuance of credentials to intermediate authorities in a way that using the credentials only reveals the root authority. In particular, the issuance of credentials for each organization can be delegated to a different certification authority. This helps keeping the management largely decentralized, while at the same time hides the particular authority that issued a given credential.

In this paper, we design practical extensions for revocation and auditing, and integrate the system into Hyperledger Fabric [2]. Our contributions are three-fold:

- We propose mechanisms for credentials revocation and authorizations auditing, compatible with a scheme of [14]. The new extensions are efficient as they are based solely on ElGamal encryption [22] and Schnorr proofs [34]. We also provide a security definition for delegatable anonymous credentials with revocation and auditing in the UC framework, and prove the full scheme secure.
- We enable auditable and private transactions via delegatable anonymous credentials in Hyperledger Fabric. This includes both the design of the relevant protocol parts and their implementation.
- We present comprehensive benchmarks and evaluation of the scheme and the proposed extensions. Namely, we design a Fabric prototype that measures the incurred computational overhead, the gains from our optimizations, and network usage. Our prototype runs in a fully distributed setting faithfully executing all parts of the protocol. We open-source the implementation of the optimized core protocol and our extensions in Go [11].

2   Related Work

The most immediately related work is [14], which our paper builds on. That paper presents an instantiation of delegatable anonymous credentials, proves its security, and provides initial performance numbers. It also discusses, but only on a general and conceptual level, the use of anonymous credentials in permissioned blockchains. Our paper extends [14] in three main directions: (a) we design and evaluate practically-relevant functionalities such as revocation and auditing; (b) we integrate anonymous credentials in the Hyperledger Fabric protocols, which in fact requires a different approach than described in [14] (for example, ensuring that the *creator* of the transaction is the one who generates a signature while maintaining anonymity); (c) we provide an extensive set of benchmarks and a production-grade implementation, which includes multiple performance optimizations ([14] implemented just enough to run a simple performance test).

After the publication of [14], two further papers on delegatable credentials were published, namely [10] and [19]. Both claim stronger security properties compared to [14] by also supporting an anonymous delegation phase; this feature is however not required in our setting where the user and the intermediate authority know each other. On the flip side, the scheme in [10] supports only a fixed number of attributes that is determined during setup, whereas we want to be able to dynamically add attributes per intermediate authority. Furthermore, the paper does not describe a full instantiation of the protocol, which when instantiated, appears to be less efficient than the one in [14]. The scheme in [19] does not support attributes, which makes it unsuitable for our application.

Sovrin [37] also combines anonymous credentials with a permissioned blockchain system. While we use anonymous credentials to authorize transactions on a blockchain, the Sovrin platform instead leverages the blockchain to produce anonymous credentials, in the vein of previous work on decentralized anonymous credentials of [23]. The two approaches thus serve two different purposes. In the context of Sovrin, there is also an implementation of [14] in Rust [26], which appears to be in its earlier stages.

A growing segment of the research literature on blockchain systems aims to improve the confidentiality of transactions using techniques such as zero-knowledge proofs (e.g. [4,8,24,33,39]), different types of state channels (e.g. [3, 21]) or multi-party computation (e.g. [9]). While the underlying cryptographic machinery, particularly in the work on zero-knowledge proofs, is similar to what we use here, achieving confidentiality of transactions is orthogonal to achieving privacy of participants, and eventually privacy-friendly permissioned blockchain systems will have to combine both.

3   Background: Blockchain and Fabric

The purpose of a blockchain is to implement an immutable append-only ledger that is maintained by a network of mutually distrustful parties. As a data structure, the ledger is a chain of blocks such that each block refers to its predecessor by including its hash, enforcing thus a total order on the blocks. The parties continuously extend the chain by running a consensus mechanism (e.g., proof of work or PBFT) to decide on the respective next block. Blocks contain transactions that have been submitted by clients for inclusion in the ledger.

Blockchains are either *permissionless* or *permissioned*. In a permissionless blockchain such as Bitcoin [31] or Ethereum [38], anyone can run a peer that joins the network, participates in consensus and validates transactions. Clients can submit their transactions anonymously (or rather: pseudonymously). Trust in such networks is established via consensus mechanisms that are based on proofs of work (e.g., [31,38]) or proofs of stake (e.g., [18,29]), which penalize misbehaving parties either by requiring them to expend a lot of computational power in the case of proof of work or losing their money in the case of proof of stake.

Permissioned blockchains, on the other hand, leverage identity management to counter misbehavior, foster trust and aid governance. Most permissioned blockchain systems (e.g., [25,36]) build on variants of the well-studied and efficient PBFT [17] to reach consensus. Permissioned blockchains are particularly well-suited for applications where participant identities are required either inherently or by regulation, or those with high performance requirements. This includes enterprise applications in logistics and supply-chain management, but also use cases in the financial and governmental domains. Examples of prominent permissioned blockchain platforms include Quorum [27] and Hyperledger Fabric [2]. We have chosen the latter as the permissioned blockchain to integrate our protocol into. We refer to the original paper [2] for a detailed description of the Fabric's complete protocol and system. We also provide concise description of the relevant Fabric components in [13, Section III].

3.1 Authentication, Authorization and Identity Mixer in Fabric

The default Fabric *membership service provider* (MSP) is based on X.509 certificates—an identity is an X.509 certificate and its validation/revocation follows the X.509 standard. This approach is efficient, flexible and scalable—organizations may have hierarchical CAs which translate to hierarchical MSPs. Each transaction (as a data structure) has two specific fields for transaction authorization: the *Creator* (i.e., identity of the client invoking the transaction) and the *Signature* (i.e., authorization of the transaction). As each transaction carries the identity of its origin as a certificate and a signature, the X.509 implementation compromises the anonymity and the privacy of clients.

To remedy this issue, Fabric uses Identity Mixer (idemix for short), an anonymous credentials scheme based on the protocols in [15]. The idemix-based MSP protocol enables clients to sign transactions anonymously. Instead of an X.509 certificate, an idemix MSP issues a special credential containing a set of attributes. To sign a transaction, the holder of an idemix identity generates a non-interactive zero-knowledge (NIZK) proof that she received a credential from idemix that certifies her attributes. More specifically, if *Alice* is a member of an organization *Org* whose members are authorized to submit certain transactions, then *Alice* proves that she possesses an idemix credential from her MSP that attests that she is a member of *Org*.

As discussed in the introduction, even the use of anonymous credentials is sometimes not sufficient from a privacy perspective. Namely, the current implementation of idemix leaks the identity of the MSP that issued the anonymous credential. To mitigate this leakage, we provide a Fabric-tailored implementation of delegatable anonymous credentials based on the work of [14]. This implementation ensures that the only information leaked by a transaction is the root CA common to all network participants. Additionally, the implementation supports efficient revocation and comes with auditing capabilities that allow authorized parties to trace the transactions back to their authors achieving some level of accountability.

We provide a brief background on delegatable anonymous credential schemes in [13, Section IV].

3.2 Notation

Let $\mathbb{Z}_q$ be the set of natural numbers in $[0; q)$ where q is a large prime. Let $\mathbb{G}_1$, $\mathbb{G}_2$ and $\mathbb{G}_T$ be three groups of order q, such that there exists an efficient bilinear pairing $e : \mathbb{G}_1 \times \mathbb{G}_2 \to \mathbb{G}_T$. Let g_i be a random generator for $\mathbb{G}_i$ for $i \in \{1, 2\}$. Let FEXP and $\hat{t}$ be the final exponentiation and Miller's loop operations respectively, such that $e = \text{FEXP} \circ \hat{t}$. Let $\leftarrow\!\!\$$ describe the operation of random sampling. Let sp denote the public parameters available to all algorithms in the system. These include the description of the bilinear groups and hash functions. Let NIZK$\{w : x\}$ denote a non-interactive zero-knowledge proof for statement x and witness w (i.e., private input).

4   Auditability and Revocation

Revocation. Classical mechanisms for revocation are at odds with anonymous credentials, whereas privacy-friendly alternatives—such as as zero-knowledge sets [30] or accumulators combined with zero-knowledge proofs [6]—are too computationally prohibitive to be integrated into the blockchain.

To enable *efficient* and *privacy-preserving* revocation we couple *epoch-based whitelisting* with signatures in a way that yields efficient proofs of *non-revocation*. Namely, we divide the timeline into *epochs* that define the validity periods of the credentials. For each epoch, a non-revoked participant is issued an *epoch handle* (a signature) that binds her public key to the epoch. When a participant presents her credentials, she provides along with them a proof of non-revocation that consists of proving in zero-knowledge that she holds a signature linking her public key to the current epoch. Credentials that are valid for a certain epoch are automatically revoked the moment the epoch expires. An epoch expires either naturally (epoch elapses) or manually (authorized parties advance the epoch by putting a special message on the ledger).

We define epochs in terms of blockchain height, which ensures that transactions of revoked parties are going to be rejected by the verifiers in the blockchain.

For ease of exposition, we assume that only the credentials of users are revoked (i.e. *Level-L* credentials). We contend that such an assumption is fair as organizations in a permissioned blockchain will not be revoked as frequently as users, who, on the other hand, may have their authorization to submit transactions denied at any moment (e.g., a failure to pay a monthly subscription, an employee leaving her company, etc.). We note though that the proposed mechanisms can be generalized to accommodate settings in which intermediate authorities are also revoked.

Audit. To enable auditing, the transaction author embeds her identifier (the public key) encrypted under the auditor's public key into the transaction using a semantically secure encryption. For this solution to be viable, it must ensure that the user **(1)** encrypts her own public key and **(2)** uses the public key of the authorized auditor Zero-knowledge proofs such as [34] coupled with ElGamal encryption [22] allow us to address these challenges relatively efficiently.

For the sake of simplicity, we only focus on settings where just a single auditor is present for all the users in the system. The proposed solution could be easily enhanced to support scenarios with multiple auditors. Namely, users will have their auditor's public key as an attribute and the proof of correct encryption will show that the correct public key is being used.

4.1   Security Definition

We define the security of our extended scheme based on the functionality $\mathcal{F}_{\text{dac}}$ from [14]. We model revocation by introducing a message ADVANCE that can be input by a special party $\mathcal{T}$, and that effects in all last-level delegations as well as generated proofs becoming invalid. This input models an epoch switch.

We model audit by providing an input AUDIT to an auditor $\mathcal{AU}$, which upon input of a credential proof $\mathfrak{p}$ outputs the party $\mathcal{P}$ that presented $\mathfrak{p}$. Properly modeling audit also requires to account for the case where $\mathcal{AU}$ is corrupted. This is achieved by allowing $\mathcal{A}$ to input the parameters pp' so that Present can include the identity of the origin of each proof $\mathfrak{p}$, which is necessary since a corrupt auditor will be able to decrypt this information anyway. The complete functionality $\mathcal{F}_{\text{dac}+}$ is specified in Fig. 1.

4.2   Revocation

We describe two alternative solutions that differ in their generality. The first one is straightforward but requires revocations being handled by the same authorities that issue user credentials. The second is more complex but allows revocations and credentials to be handled by different authorities. See Sect. 6 for performance analysis of the latter approach.

Epoch as an Attribute. We implement revocation using delegatable credentials in such a way that users in the last level of delegation have epoch identifiers as attributes. A user thus needs to request new delegatable credentials from her issuer every time an epoch expires to be able to submit transactions. The proof of non-revocation in this case uses the proof generation depicted in [13, Algorithm 6] such that one of the disclosed attributes is the identifier of the current epoch. Note that in this case only the last-level credentials are being regenerated in each epoch.

Explicit Proof of Non-revocation. The solution above requires no additional cryptographic implementation, however, it suffers from the limitation that the credential issuer must always be the same as the revocation authority. To accommodate settings where credential issuers are different from revocation authorities, we decouple the credentials for user attributes from epoch credentials. To obtain authorization for the current epoch, a user contacts the *revocation authority* with a proof of her public key possession. The revocation authority in turn responds with a Groth signature of the user's public key and the epoch identifier. When the user wishes to submit a transaction, she generates a proof of non-revocation that shows the knowledge of an epoch handle and the associated secret key. Verifiers in the blockchain check the non-revocation proof and if valid, verify the user's signature on the transaction content. In more formal terms, we augment the protocol in [14] with the following.

Let g denote a generator of the bilinear group in which the public keys of users (i.e., public keys associated with *Level-L* credentials) reside, and let f denote a generator of the other bilinear group.

Revocation Setup. The revocation authority computes its pair of Groth secret and public keys $(\mathsf{rsk}, \mathsf{rpk} = f^{\mathsf{rsk}}) \leftarrow_\$ \text{GROTH.KEYGEN}(\Lambda^\star)$ and publishes rpk.

Generation of Non-revocation Credentials. Upon receipt of a credential request for public key cpk and current epoch, revocation authority verifies that the requestor knows the secret key matching cpk, and computes

$$\varepsilon := g^{\text{HASH(epoch)}}$$
$$\sigma \leftarrow\!\$ \ \text{GROTH.SIGN}(\text{rsk}; \varepsilon, \text{cpk})$$

and returns non-revocation credentials (σ, cpk).

Proof Generation. A user signs a message m and proves that she is not revoked during the current epoch by outputting a tuple $(m, \langle a_{i,j} \rangle_{(i,j) \in D}, \mathfrak{P})$ such that:

$$\mathfrak{P} \leftarrow\!\$ \ \text{NIZK}\{(\sigma_{1,\dots,L}, \text{cpk}_{1,\dots,L}, \langle a_{i,j} \rangle_{(i,j) \notin D}, \sigma_m, \sigma) :$$

$$\bigwedge_{i=2,4,\dots}^{L} \text{GROTH}_1.\text{VERIFY}(\text{cpk}_{i-1}; \sigma_i; \text{cpk}_i, a_{i,1}, \dots, a_{i,n_i})$$

$$\bigwedge_{i=1,3,\dots}^{L} \text{GROTH}_2.\text{VERIFY}(\text{cpk}_{i-1}; \sigma_i; \text{cpk}_i, a_{i,1}, \dots, a_{i,n_i})$$

$$\wedge \text{SCHNORR.VERIFY}(\text{cpk}_L; \sigma_m; m)$$
$$\wedge \text{GROTH.VERIFY}(\text{rpk}; \sigma; \varepsilon, \text{cpk}_L)\}$$

4.3 Audit

Our auditable anonymous delegatable credentials extension adds an *Audit setup* step and enhances the credential presentation with verifiable encryption.

Audit Setup. The authorized auditor computes a pair of ElGamal secret and public keys $(\text{ask}, \text{apk} = g^{\text{ask}})$ and then announces apk. We assume there are mechanisms in place to verify that the auditor is legitimate and knows the secret key ask.

Proof Generation. A user signs a message m in an auditable manner and outputs a tuple $(m, \langle a_{i,j} \rangle_{(i,j) \in D}, \text{enc}, \mathfrak{P})$ such that:

$$\mathfrak{P} \leftarrow\!\$ \ \text{NIZK}\{(\sigma_{1,\dots,L}, \text{cpk}_{1,\dots,L}, \langle a_{i,j} \rangle_{(i,j) \notin D}, \sigma_m, \sigma, \rho) :$$

$$\bigwedge_{i=2,4,\dots}^{L} \text{GROTH}_1.\text{VERIFY}(\text{cpk}_{i-1}; \sigma_i; \text{cpk}_i, a_{i,1}, \dots, a_{i,n_i})$$

$$\bigwedge_{i=1,3,\dots}^{L} \text{GROTH}_2.\text{VERIFY}(\text{cpk}_{i-1}; \sigma_i; \text{cpk}_i, a_{i,1}, \dots, a_{i,n_i})$$

$$\wedge \text{SCHNORR.VERIFY}(\text{cpk}_L; \sigma_m; m)$$
$$\wedge \text{GROTH.VERIFY}(\text{rpk}; \sigma; \varepsilon, \text{cpk}_L)$$
$$\wedge \text{enc} = (\text{cpk}_L \cdot \text{apk}^\rho, g^\rho)\}$$

If the auditor decides to learn the identity of the origin of a message m, all she needs to do is to decrypt ciphertext enc. This process is guaranteed to succeed and correctly yield the right public key thanks to the soundness of $\mathfrak{P}$.

Details on the implementation of this extension are provided in Algorithms 2 to 4 in Appendix A. Algorithm 1 puts all the components together and includes elements of the integration with Hyperledger Fabric.

4.4 Security Statement

In Appendix A, we prove that our extended protocol realizes the functionality specified in Fig. 1.

Delegatable credentials protocol $\Pi_{\text{dac}+}$ securely realizes $\mathcal{F}_{\text{dac}+}$ in the $(\mathcal{F}_{\text{smt}}, \mathcal{F}_{\text{ca}}, \mathcal{F}_{\text{crs}}, \mathcal{F}_{\text{clock}})$-hybrid model, provided that

- SignNym (Algorithm 2) is a strongly unforgeable signature,
- the auditing encryption is semantically secure,
- NIZK is a simulation-sound extractable non-interactive zero-knowledge proof.

Our instantiated protocol is covered by the security statement since both Schnorr (used in binding the pseudonym) and Groth signatures are existentially unforgeable, ElGamal encryption is semantically secure, and Schnorr proofs are simulation-sound extractable.

The full proof of the theorem could be found in Appendix A.

Let $sid = (\mathcal{R}, \mathcal{AU}, \mathcal{T}, L, \text{Param}, sid')$ be the session identifier.

1. **Setup.** On input (SETUP, $\langle n_i \rangle_i$) from root $\mathcal{R}$.
   - Output (SETUP, $\langle n_i \rangle_i$) to $\mathcal{A}$ and wait for response (SETUP, pp', Present, Verify, $\langle \mathbb{A}_i \rangle_i$) from $\mathcal{A}$.
   - Store algorithms Present and Verify and parameters $\langle \mathbb{A}_i \rangle_i, \langle n_i \rangle_i$, initialize $\mathcal{L}_{\text{de}}, \mathcal{L}_{\text{p}}, \mathcal{L}_{\text{au}} \leftarrow \emptyset$. If $\mathcal{AU}$ is corrupt set $pp \leftarrow pp'$, else set $pp \leftarrow$ Param().
   - Output SETUPDONE to $\mathcal{R}$. On input SETUP from $\mathcal{AU}$, output (SETUP, $\mathcal{AU}$) to $\mathcal{A}$, wait for response; output SETUPDONE to $\mathcal{AU}$.

2. **Advance.** On input ADVANCE from $\mathcal{T}$, set $\mathcal{L}_{\text{p}} \leftarrow \emptyset$, $\mathcal{L}_{\text{de}} \leftarrow \{ \langle \mathcal{P}_i, \vec{a}_1, \ldots, \vec{a}_l \rangle \in \mathcal{L}_{\text{de}} : l < L \}$.

3. **Delegate.** On input (DELEGATE, $ssid, \vec{a}_1, \ldots, \vec{a}_l, \mathcal{P}_j$) from some party $\mathcal{P}_i$, with $l \leq L$ and $\vec{a}_l \in \mathbb{A}_l^{n_l}$.
   - If $l = 1$: check $sid = (\mathcal{P}_i, \mathcal{AU}, \mathcal{T}, L, sid')$, else abort.
   - If $l > 1$, check that $\langle \mathcal{P}_i, \vec{a}_1, \ldots, \vec{a}_{l-1} \rangle \in \mathcal{L}_{\text{de}}$, else abort.
   - Output (ALLOWDEL, $ssid, \mathcal{P}_i, \mathcal{P}_j, l$) to $\mathcal{A}$; wait for input (ALLOWDEL, $ssid$) from $\mathcal{A}$.
   - Add an entry $\langle \mathcal{P}_j, \vec{a}_1, \ldots, \vec{a}_l \rangle$ to $\mathcal{L}_{\text{de}}$.
   - Output (DELEGATE, $ssid, \vec{a}_1, \ldots, \vec{a}_l, \mathcal{P}_i$) to $\mathcal{P}_j$.

4. **Present.** On input (PRESENT, $m, \vec{a}_1, \ldots, \vec{a}_L$) from some party $\mathcal{P}_i$, with $\vec{a}_i \in (\mathbb{A}_i \cup \{\bot\})^{n_i}$ for $i = 1, \ldots, L$.
   - Check that an entry $\langle \mathcal{P}_i, \vec{a}'_1, \ldots, \vec{a}'_L \rangle$ exists in $\mathcal{L}_{\text{de}}$ such that $\vec{a}_i \preceq \vec{a}'_i$ for $i = 1, \ldots, L$.
   - If $\mathcal{AU}$ honest, set $\text{p} \leftarrow$ Present$(pp, m, \vec{a}_1, \ldots, \vec{a}_L; \bot)$, else $\text{p} \leftarrow$ Present$(pp, m, \vec{a}_1, \ldots, \vec{a}_L; \mathcal{P}_i)$. Abort if Verify$(pp, \text{p}, m, \vec{a}_1, \ldots, \vec{a}_L) = 0$.
   - Store $\langle m, \vec{a}_1, \ldots, \vec{a}_L, \text{p} \rangle$ in $\mathcal{L}_{\text{p}}$ and $\langle \text{p}, \mathcal{P}_i \rangle$ in $\mathcal{L}_{\text{au}}$.
   - Output (PROOF, p) to $\mathcal{P}_i$.

5. **Verify.** On input (VERIFY, $\text{p}, m, \vec{a}_1, \ldots, \vec{a}_L$) from $\mathcal{P}_i$.
   - If $\langle m, \vec{a}_1, \ldots, \vec{a}_L, \text{p} \rangle \notin \mathcal{L}_{\text{p}}$, $\mathcal{R}$ is honest, and for $i = 1, \ldots, L$, there is no corrupt $\mathcal{P}_j$ with $\langle \mathcal{P}_j, \vec{a}'_1, \ldots, \vec{a}'_i \rangle \in \mathcal{L}_{\text{de}}$ and $\vec{a}_j \preceq \vec{a}'_j$ for $j = 1, \ldots, i$, set $f \leftarrow 0$.
   - Else, output (VERIFY, p) to $\mathcal{A}$; expect response (VERIFY, $\mathcal{P}$). Set $f \leftarrow$ Verify$(pp, \text{p}, m, \vec{a}_1, \ldots, \vec{a}_L)$. If $\mathcal{P}$ corrupt $\wedge f$ then add $\langle \text{p}, \mathcal{P} \rangle$ to $\mathcal{L}_{\text{au}}$.
   - Output (VERIFIED, f) to $\mathcal{P}_i$.

6. **Audit.** On input (AUDIT, p) from $\mathcal{AU}$, if $\langle \text{p}, \mathcal{P} \rangle \notin \mathcal{L}_{\text{au}}$, output (AUDIT, p) to $\mathcal{A}$. Upon obtaining (AUDIT, $\mathcal{P}$) from $\mathcal{A}$, where $\mathcal{P}$ is corrupted, store $\langle \text{p}, \mathcal{P} \rangle$ in $\mathcal{L}_{\text{au}}$. If now there is a valid record $\langle \text{p}, \mathcal{P} \rangle$ in $\mathcal{L}_{\text{au}}$, then output (RESULT, $\mathcal{P}$) to $\mathcal{AU}$. Else, output $\bot$ to $\mathcal{AU}$.

Fig. 1. Extended credentials functionality $\mathcal{F}_{\text{dac}+}$

4.5   Optimized Implementation

While implementing our extended protocol, we discovered several enhancements and optimizations over the scheme in [14]. This section presents our improvements of the base scheme.

Parallelization. We have noticed that the heaviest operation in the code is the computation of commitments. Moreover, we have found that commitments can be computed independently of one another, and therefore can be easily parallelized. Instead of computing the commitments eagerly, our program schedules the computation and puts it in a queue. Before hashing the commitments, the program waits for the last computation to finish, signaling that the commitment set is computed. We find this task granularity optimal in this scenario as the computation takes long enough to neglect a cost of spawning an extra thread and is small enough that the system can uniformly disperse its load among available resources.

Miller's Loop and Final Exponentiation. [14] mention that when computing a product of pairings it makes sense to compute Miller's loop first on some pairs, multiply them and only then apply final exponentiation. However, the authors used this tactic only on a fraction of computations. We have discovered a way to extend this optimization and apply it globally.

The idea is to convert every pairing product to a set of Miller's loops and apply final exponentiation once per such a product. The trick is to use bilinearity of Miller's loop to put exponents inside the pairings. For example, the following computations are equivalent:

$$\prod_i e\left(a_i, b_i\right)^{c_i} = \text{FEXP}\left(\prod_i \hat{t}(a_i^{c_i}, b_i)\right) = \text{FEXP}\left(\prod_i \hat{t}(a_i, b_i^{c_i})\right)$$

Since exponentiations are cheaper in $\mathbb{G}_1$ than in $\mathbb{G}_2$ (specifically, when using AMCL library [35]), we decided to exponentiate elements in $\mathbb{G}_1$.

5   Integration with Hyperledger Fabric

This section presents our protocol and explains how the building blocks defined earlier work together within Fabric. We assume that all parties have access to system parameters sp and public key cpk_0 of the root authority, and that they have generated their pairs of secret and public keys. The keys are always generated as $\text{sk} \leftarrow_\$ \mathbb{Z}_q$ and $\text{pk} := g^{\text{sk}}$ where g is a group generator of either $\mathbb{G}_1$ or $\mathbb{G}_2$ depending on the delegation level.

5.1   Including Pseudonyms in Proof

In Fabric, a transaction has two special fields that are used in tandem to establish its authenticity. A *Creator* field that contains the identity of the transaction

Algorithm 1. $\Pi_{\text{dac+}}$: delegation, revocation, auditing and transaction submission protocols

1:	*Level-i* **CA**	*Level-*$(i+1)$ **CA**
	.... Repeated for L rounds of delegation (from the Root CA to Intermediate CAs to the User)	
2:	$\text{csk}_i \leftarrow\!\!\$\, \mathbb{Z}_q, \text{cpk}_i := g^{\text{csk}_i}$	$\text{csk}_{i+1} \leftarrow\!\!\$\, \mathbb{Z}_q, \text{cpk}_{i+1} := f^{\text{csk}_{i+1}}$
3:	$\text{nonce} \leftarrow\!\!\$\, \{0,1\}^\lambda \qquad \xrightarrow{\ \ \text{nonce}\ \ }$	$\mathfrak{P}_{\text{pk}} \leftarrow\!\!\$\, \text{PROVEPK}(\text{csk}_{i+1}, \text{cpk}_{i+1}, \text{nonce})$
4:	$\text{VERIFYPK}(\mathfrak{P}_{\text{pk}}, \text{cpk}_{i+1}, \text{nonce}) \quad \xleftarrow{\ \ \mathfrak{P}_{\text{pk}}, \text{cpk}_{i+1}\ \ }$	
5:	$\sigma_{i+1} \leftarrow\!\!\$\, \text{GROTH.SIGN}(\text{csk}_i; \text{cpk}_{i+1}, a_{i+1}) \quad \xrightarrow{\ \ \sigma_{i+1}\ \ }$	$\text{cred}_{i+1} := (\sigma_{i+1}, a_{i+1}, \text{cpk}_{i+1})$
6:	**Revocation authority**	**User**
	................................On each epoch, user requests a non-revocation handle....................................	
7:	$\text{rsk} \leftarrow\!\!\$\, \mathbb{Z}_q, \text{rpk} := g^{\text{rsk}}$	$\text{csk} \leftarrow\!\!\$\, \mathbb{Z}_q, \text{cpk} := g^{\text{csk}}$
8:	$\text{nonce} \leftarrow\!\!\$\, \{0,1\}^\lambda \qquad \xrightarrow{\ \ \text{nonce}\ \ }$	$\mathfrak{P}_{\text{pk}} \leftarrow\!\!\$\, \text{PROVEPK}(\text{csk}, \text{cpk}, \text{nonce})$
9:	$\text{VERIFYPK}(\mathfrak{P}_{\text{pk}}, \text{cpk}, \text{nonce}) \quad \xleftarrow{\ \ \mathfrak{P}_{\text{pk}}, \text{cpk}\ \ }$	
10:	$\sigma \leftarrow\!\!\$\, \text{NRSIGN}(\text{rsk}; \text{cpk}, \text{epoch}) \quad \xrightarrow{\ \ \sigma\ \ }$	σ, epoch
11:	**Verifier**	**User**
12:	(from the delegation stage)	$\text{cred} := (\langle \sigma_j, a_j, \text{cpk}_j \rangle_{j=1}^{L})$
	.... User submits a transaction	
13:		$\text{enc}, \rho := \text{AUDITENC}(\text{apk}, \text{cpk})$
14:		$\text{sk}_{\text{nym}}, \text{pk}_{\text{nym}} \leftarrow\!\!\$\, \text{MAKENYM}(\text{csk})$
15:		$\mathfrak{P}_{\text{rev}} \leftarrow\!\!\$\, \text{NRPROVE}(\sigma, \text{csk}, \text{sk}_{\text{nym}}, \text{epoch})$
16:		$\mathfrak{P}_{\text{audit}} \leftarrow\!\!\$\, \text{AUDITPROVE}(\text{enc}, \rho, \text{csk}, \text{cpk}, \text{pk}_{\text{nym}}, \text{sk}_{\text{nym}})$
17:	(no need to sign a message)	$\mathfrak{P}_{\text{cred}} \leftarrow\!\!\$\, \text{CREDPROVE}(\text{cred}, D, \text{sk}_{\text{nym}}, \text{csk}, \perp)$
18:		$\sigma_{\text{nym}} \leftarrow\!\!\$\, \text{SIGNNYM}(\text{pk}_{\text{nym}}, \text{sk}_{\text{nym}}, \text{csk}, \text{tx})$
19:	$(\mathfrak{P}_{\text{cred}}, \mathfrak{P}_{\text{rev}}, \mathfrak{P}_{\text{audit}}, \text{enc}, \text{tx}, \text{pk}_{\text{nym}}) := m \quad \xleftarrow{\ \ m, \sigma_{\text{nym}}\ \ }$	$m := (\mathfrak{P}_{\text{cred}}, \mathfrak{P}_{\text{rev}}, \mathfrak{P}_{\text{audit}}, \text{enc}, \text{tx}, \text{pk}_{\text{nym}})$
20:	$\text{VERIFYNYM}(\text{pk}_{\text{nym}}, \text{tx}, \sigma_{\text{nym}})$	
21:	$\text{NRVERIFY}(\mathfrak{P}_{\text{rev}}, \text{pk}_{\text{nym}}, \text{epoch})$	
22:	$\text{AUDITVERIFY}(\mathfrak{P}_{\text{audit}}, \text{enc}, \text{pk}_{\text{nym}})$	
23:	$\text{CREDVERIFY}(\mathfrak{P}_{\text{cred}}, D, \text{pk}_{\text{nym}}, \perp)$	

author, and a *Signature* field that holds a signature of the rest of the transaction by its author. Fabric specifications require that *Creator* and *Signature* be validated individually. Integrating delegatable credentials directly introduces two security flaws: namely, if *Creator* is a NIZK of the credential validity and *Signature* is a regular signature with the author's secret key, then **(1)** there is no guarantee that the keys used to generate the NIZK and the signature are the same, and **(2)** the regular signature itself would leak the identity of the signer by going through all users' public keys and testing whether the signature verifies.

To solve the above problems, we generate a *Pedersen commitment* (called pseudonym) to the secret key and place it in both fields. This pseudonym ensures that the same secret key is used to produce *Creator* and *Signature* fields. Notably, *Creator* contains a modified NIZK proof that shows that the prover knows the secret key used to construct the pseudonym and that it is the same secret key underlying the credentials. *Signature*, on the other hand, is a Schnorr-like proof of knowledge that leverages the content of the transaction to compute the challenge and shows knowledge of the secret key committed in the pseudonym.

The verifier first checks whether *Creator* and *Signature* include the same pseudonym. If so, it verifies the validity of the content of those fields independently; otherwise it rejects. See Algorithm 2 for more details.

5.2 Submitting Transactions

A user authorizes the execution of a chaincode by providing a NIZK proof and a linked signature on the proposal, as described in Sect. 5.1. During this process, the user can decide to selectively disclose attributes, which are made available to the chaincode so access control can be implemented as needed by the application. The protocol has the following global stages (see Algorithm 1).

At the **setup** stage (line 2), the parties generate their secret and public keys.

The **delegation** stage starts by a *credential request* from the delegatee to the delegator where the former proves that she knows the secret key corresponding to her public key, using a classical non-interactive Schnorr proof (see Algorithm 2). To ensure the freshness of the proof the delegator (i.e., verifier) provides a nonce that would be used to compute the challenge in the proof. If the provided proof is valid, then the delegator signs, using Groth, the public key and the attributes of the delegatee. We note that it is up to the delegator to determine the delegatee's valid attributes. This process of credential issuance can be repeated an arbitrary number of times increasing the length of the credential chain. In more concrete terms, the first level of the delegation corresponds to the root authority issuing credentials to intermediate authorities that in turn delegate the credentials further down the hierarchy (lines 2–5). On the last level of the credential chain, we find users who submit transactions to Fabric.

The **transaction** stage (lines 13–23) has the user generate randomized proofs and signatures to authenticate the content of her transactions anonymously. Namely, the user generates a pseudonym (i.e., Pedersen commitment) to commit to her secret key (see Sect. 5.1). Then she generates a proof in which she discloses her attributes as needed and shows the following: **(1)** the user knows valid credentials, and **(2)** the pseudonym commits to the secret key matching the credentials. As part of the transaction the user also includes the proof of possessing a non-revocation handle (line 15) and an encryption of her public key under auditor's key, along with the proof of its correctness (lines 13 and 16). If the user does not have a non-revocation handle for the current epoch, she requests it from the authority (lines 8–10). Finally, she signs the content of the transaction with the secret key in the pseudonym (lines 14 and 18).

Verifiers consequently validate the transaction by checking that the proofs and signatures refer to the same pseudonym and that they are valid with respect to the disclosed attributes (lines 20 and 23).

6   Experimental Evaluation

We provide a generic implementation of improved DAC scheme and our extensions. The scheme produces valid credentials and proofs for any number of levels and attributes for both groups: $\mathbb{G}_1$ and $\mathbb{G}_2$, for odd and even levels.

The project is tested with over 470 tests and they cover 100% of the code. We note that this is a significant improvement over the original code, which was only a prototype computing a single hard-coded credential. We also note that the original code is not open-sourced.

All benchmarks (unless otherwise specified) were run on `c2-standard-60` GCE VM running Ubuntu 18.04 (60 vCPUs, Intel Cascade Lake 3.1 GHz, 240 GB RAM). We have used Apache Milagro Cryptographic Library (AMCL) [35] with a 254-bit Barreto-Naehrig curve [7] for low-level operations such as pairings, exponentiations and PRG operations.

We design our experiments to answer the following questions:

Question-1 What is the performance benefit of our optimizations?

Question-2 How does the improved core DAC scheme scale with the number of levels and attributes?

Question-3 What overhead do our extensions impose?

Question-4 How does the system compare to the old non-delegatable idemix?

Question-5 How practical is maintaining a single and possibly distributed revocation authority that we designed?

Question-6 What is the efficacy of the entire blockchain stack using our protocol? How efficiently does it use the network? How does it scale with the number of users, peers and endorsers?

Table 1. Optimizations benchmark for $L = 2$ and $n = 2$ (small) and $L = 5$ and $n = 3$ (big). The values are in milliseconds.

e-product	Parallelization	CREDPROVE Big	CREDPROVE Small	CREDVERIFY Big	CREDVERIFY Small
Disabled	Disabled	2873	843	1523	948
Enabled	Disabled	1312	341	853	372
Disabled	**Enabled**	1480	357	890	352
Enabled	**Enabled**	890	191	391	197
Improvement ($\approx$ times)		3.2	4.4	3.9	**4.8**

Comparing to [14]. We stress that our evaluation results differ from the ones in [14]. First, the implementations are written in different languages and run on different processors. These differences are significant when benchmarking cryptographic primitives, which mostly involve bit manipulations. Second, we have obtained the original code of [14] and we have noticed distinctions in benchmark methodologies. The code in [14] pre-computes some values (pairings) during the signature phase, and therefore this time is not included in the proof generation and verification stages. Our benchmarks involve no pre-computations to produce most fair results. Third, our scheme includes pseudonym commitments, which add noticeable overhead for small values of L and n. Overall, given that our code is production-ready, generic and open-sourced, we want our benchmarks to be treated independently of the previous work.

In the following, L stands for the number of delegation levels, n stands for the number of attributes per level, which we set to be the same for every level for simplicity. All benchmarked operations were run 100 times. Note that the most sensitive overhead is due to verification, since it is the operation that will be run by the entire Fabric network. In Fabric, having $L = 2$ and $n = 2$ covers most use-cases. We noticed that the overhead value is very sensible, thus for fairness we present the results with the highest overhead.

Question-1: Optimizations. First of all, we wanted to demonstrate the improvement due to our optimizations. We have run the benchmarks with all combinations of e-product and parallelization optimizations (see Table 1). Results show that for the most commonly-used parameter values the improvement is almost fivefold.

Table 2. Parameters benchmark. In each cell from top to bottom: a proof generation overhead, a proof verification overhead and the proof size.

L	n				
	0	1	2	3	4
	41 ms	51 ms	63 ms	72 ms	82 ms
1	89 ms	110 ms	116 ms	153 ms	173 ms
	398 B	534 B	670 B	806 B	942 B
	94 ms	138 ms	192 ms	255 ms	315 ms
2	124 ms	158 ms	198 ms	262 ms	310 ms
	801 B	1.2 kB	1.6 kB	2.0 kB	2.4 kB
	173 ms	273 ms	367 ms	516 ms	616 ms
3	188 ms	249 ms	329 ms	387 ms	427 ms
	1.2 kB	1.7 kB	2.3 kB	2.8 kB	3.3 kB
	333 ms	542 ms	661 ms	891 ms	1146 ms
5	276 ms	342 ms	391 ms	500 ms	648 ms
	2.0 kB	2.9 kB	3.9 kB	4.8 kB	5.7 kB
	822 ms	1177 ms	1652 ms	2115 ms	2666 ms
10	457 ms	638 ms	860 ms	1053 ms	1234 ms
	4.0 kB	6 kB	8 kB	10 kB	12 kB

Question-2: Different Parameters. With optimizations enabled we have run the operations for multiple combinations of levels and attributes. In Table 2 we put the proof generation and verification times along with the generated proof size for $L \in \{1, 2, 3, 5, 10\}$ and $n \in [0; 4]$. In all cases all attributes are hidden—the overhead difference when all attributes are revealed is minimal. We can confirm that the overhead and proof size grow linearly with L and n.

Question-3: Extensions. Table 3 depicts the performance results for the helper methods. Each method was run in both $\mathbb{G}_1$ and $\mathbb{G}_2$ (judged by the number of operations in a group). Note that operations in $\mathbb{G}_2$ are considerably slower in AMCL and that revocation routines are relatively slower due to the use of pairing in proofs. Our future work is to apply the optimizations we used with delegatable credentials scheme to this procedure as well. Also note that adding pseudonyms, enabling auditing and proving possession of the secret key incur little overhead relative to the cost of credential proof generation.

Table 3. Running time of extensions in milliseconds.

Procedure	Time		Procedure	Time	
	$\mathbb{G}_1$	$\mathbb{G}_2$		$\mathbb{G}_1$	$\mathbb{G}_2$
GROTH.KEYGEN	1.6	4.7	GROTH.SIGN	16	41
GROTH.RANDOMIZE	11	23	GROTH.VERIFY	53	62
SCHNORR.SIGN	1.6	4.8	SCHNORR.VERIFY	2	9.6
AUDITENCRYPT	3	9.4	NRSIGN	14	30
AUDITPROVE	5.8	24	NRPROVE	66	88
AUDITVERIFY	9.2	39	NRVERIFY	127	149
MAKENYM	2.1	9.4	PROVEPK	3.1	9.4
SIGNNYM	2.2	9.9	VERIFYPK	2	9.5
VERIFYNYM	3.5	14	KEYGEN	1.5	4.2

Question-4: Against Older Idemix. We have run the benchmarks against the non-delegatable idemix implementation currently in Fabric and against the Fabric MSP with no anonymity (see Sect. 3.1). The default (non-idemix) Fabric MSP simply uses X.509 certificates and ECDSA algorithms [32] for signatures and verifications. The current idemix implementation in Fabric [15] uses BBS+ signatures [5]. A user in this construction proves the knowledge of a signature on her attributes. This mechanism however, does not support delegation.

We have run a simple workload—generating secrets, signing and verifying identities—for all three mechanisms. For the default MSP we have run ECDSA algorithms available in Go `crypto` module using the P-384 curve—the most secure option available in Fabric. For the Fabric idemix MSP we have run the entire workload against the actual Go code in the official Fabric repository using five attributes. Lastly, we have run the workload with our solution using a single level and five attributes.

Experimental results show the relative costs of using more privacy-preserving solutions. Default MSP takes 21 ms, idemix MSP in Fabric takes 108 ms and our solution takes 210 ms. Reasonably, the more anonymity a solution offers, the more expensive it is. We believe that this overhead is acceptable, given that privacy-preserving MSP operations are tailored for applications that see value in trading gains in performance for gains in privacy.

Question-5: Revocation Authority Overhead. The revocation functionality requires a single (possibly distributed) revocation authority. A legitimate concern is that the revocation authority could become a bottleneck in a real-world deployment, as at the beginning of each epoch users need to update their revocation credentials to be able to submit transactions. We contend that in most cases this will not be an issue for the following reasons. First, since the users require the handle to submit transactions, we can safely assume that they will only request it when they are about to submit a transaction. Therefore, the load is more likely to be distributed, especially for long epochs. For short epochs a user may not even need the handle if she does not wish to submit a transaction. Second, the overhead of issuing the non-revocation handle is 15 ms to 30 ms, which is much smaller than the time it takes to process an anonymous transaction. This means that a faster revocation authority does not necessarily result in any improvement on the perceived performance of the network (i.e., transaction latency and throughput).

To validate our intuition, we have designed a minimalistic server in Go that uses our library to process requests for non-revocation handles. We observed a stable 200 requests per second throughput on our testing machine. We note that the real deployment will likely use a replicated horizontally scalable service.

Question-6: Blockchain Prototype. We have built a standalone Hyperledger Fabric prototype to empirically assess the computation and network overhead of our implementation (open-sourced [12])

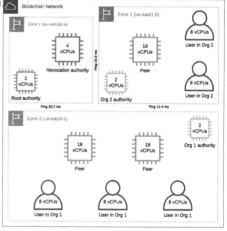

We note that although our prototype faithfully mimics the processing and network components of Fabric, it is still an idealized version of the latter. Thus, the numbers we present here are a lower bound of the expected integration cost.

Our prototype integrates the cryptographic protocols of credentials delegation and transaction processing (recall Algorithm 1). In the *transaction* phase, all users submit a configured number of transactions—sequentially for a single user but in parallel among all users. We wait for all peers to validate a transaction, not for 50%+1. We model the chaincode

Fig. 2. Network architecture

execution by waiting 50 ms—average time to execute the simplest chaincode. In the *auditing* phase, an auditor goes over all transactions decrypting the user public keys.

The components (authorities, users and peers) are running each on its own VM and they transfer the objects over the real network. Experiments were run on n1-standard GCE VMs running Ubuntu 18.04 (Intel Broadwell 2.2 GHz) and talking among each other through RPCs. To mimic realistic deployment we have used three geographically different regions for different components. See Fig. 2 for the details of the setup, including the sizes and regions of the parties' VMs, and interzone pings.

Local Simulator. On top of the distributed simulator, we have also built a local version that runs on a single machine, simulates the transactions and reports a precise network log. We delineate the setup and discussion in [13, Section VIII Question-6] and report here the main observation that the use of our revocation extension does not result in network bottlenecks even for short epochs.

Results. Our default setting is 2 organizations, 5 users, 3 peers, 2 required endorsements and revocation with auditing enabled (see Fig. 2). In all experiments the users submit 100 transactions each.

In the *distributed* setting, we started with a hypothetical best-case scenario: a single user and a single peer. The time it takes to generate, validate and commit a single transaction is below a second on average (855 ms). Disabling auditing and revocation saves additional 256 ms, see Fig. 3 *minimal* category. Out of this, 164 ms is spent on endorsement, whereas validation takes 432 ms. The rest is taken by user's actions: credential proof generation, signing, collecting and verifying endorsements, etc.

Auditing takes 4574 ms, which corresponds to the decryption of the ElGamal ciphertexts (500 decryptions, about 9 ms per decryption).

We have run the default experiment (5 users, 3 peers, 2 endorsements, 20 s epochs and both extensions enabled) and have studied the effects of changing the settings on the transaction processing overhead. The default experiment involves 500 transactions and takes 1555 ms per

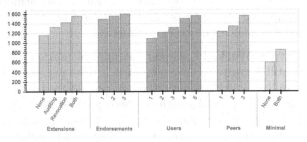

Fig. 3. Distributed experiments results. Average transaction overhead is reported in milliseconds.

transaction. The first group of experiments examines the overheads of extensions. Disabling revocation saves 15%, disabling auditing saves another 8%, see Fig. 3 *extensions.*

We have found that the number of required endorsements does not significantly affect the overhead, see Fig. 3 *endorsements* category. This is expected since endorsements are processed in parallel and take a small fraction of transaction processing time.

The number of users influences the overhead substantially, see Fig. 3 *users* category. Each new user increases the number of transactions validated by a single peer at a time. Since each peer eventually validates all transactions, the number of users is linearly correlated with the overhead regardless of the number of peers. Figure 3 indeed depicts linear relationship with a difference between 3 and 4 users attributed to different ping times between zones (recall Fig. 2).

Finally, we have found that the number of peers is also positively correlated with the overhead, see Fig. 3 *peers* category. This is also expected since a transaction is completed when the *last* peer validates it, and each new peer increases the variance in validation overhead. The difference between 2 and 3 peers is also attributed to interzone ping time.

7   Conclusion

The possibility to perform transactions privately and anonymously is crucial to the use of blockchain technology in many financial and governmental use cases, as well as all use cases that involve personal data. Anonymous transaction authorization, as achieved through our implementation and extensions, is a key enabler for blockchain technology in privacy-sensitive use cases.

The enhanced privacy guarantees incur a price in terms of computational complexity in the transaction generation and achievable throughput. For this reason, we identified points for optimization to make the performance of delegatable credentials closer to practical.

Future Work. In our current implementation, the root certificate authority is still a central party. Although it does not play an active role in the online protocols and does not issue any certificates to users, we plan to implement a threshold protocol in which the organizations participating in the blockchain system jointly produce the first-level signatures, further distributing the trust.

In Fabric, every transaction is executed (endorsed) only by a subset of the peers, which allows parallel execution and addresses potential non-determinism. A flexible endorsement policy specifies which peers, or how many of them, need to vouch for the correct execution of a given smart contract. Currently, the endorsement policy reveals the identity of the involved peers. A future line of work would be to remove this leakage. The idea is to equip the peers with idemix credentials and use commitments to obfuscate the endorsement policy. Consequently, after collecting all the required endorsements, the client can prove in zero-knowledge the knowledge of valid signatures that satisfy the obfuscated endorsement policy.

Acknowledgments. This work has been supported in part by the European Union's Horizon 2020 research and innovation programme under grant agreement No. 780477 PRIViLEDGE. We thank the authors of [14] for giving us access to their source code. We also thank the program committees of CANS 2021 for the thorough reviews. Finally, we thank George Kollios, Leonid Reyzin, Daria Bogatova and Oleksandr Narykov for their early feedback.

A Security Analysis

Let $sid = (\mathcal{R}, \mathcal{AU}, \mathcal{T}, L, \mathsf{Param}, sid')$ be the session identifier.

1. **Setup.** On input $(\mathsf{SETUP}, \langle n_i \rangle_i)$ from root $\mathcal{R}$.
   - Output $(\mathsf{SETUP}, \langle n_i \rangle_i)$ to $\mathcal{A}$ and wait for response $(\mathsf{SETUP}, pp', \mathsf{Present}, \mathsf{Verify}, \langle A_i \rangle_i)$ from $\mathcal{A}$.
   - Store algorithms Present and Verify and parameters $\langle A_i \rangle_i, \langle n_i \rangle_i$, initialize $\mathcal{L}_{\mathrm{de}}, \mathcal{L}_{\mathfrak{p}}, \mathcal{L}_{\mathrm{au}} \leftarrow \emptyset$. If $\mathcal{AU}$ is corrupt set $pp \leftarrow pp'$, else set $pp \leftarrow \mathsf{Param}()$.
   - Output SETUPDONE to $\mathcal{R}$.
   On input SETUP from $\mathcal{AU}$, output $(\mathsf{SETUP}, \mathcal{AU})$ to $\mathcal{A}$, wait for response; output SETUPDONE to $\mathcal{AU}$.
2. **Advance.** On input ADVANCE from $\mathcal{T}$, set $\mathcal{L}_{\mathfrak{p}} \leftarrow \emptyset$, $\mathcal{L}_{\mathrm{de}} \leftarrow \{\langle \mathcal{P}_i, \vec{a}_1, \dots, \vec{a}_l \rangle \in \mathcal{L}_{\mathrm{de}} : l < L\}$.
3. **Delegate.** On input $(\mathsf{DELEGATE}, ssid, \vec{a}_1, \dots, \vec{a}_l, \mathcal{P}_j)$ from some party $\mathcal{P}_i$, with $l \leq L$ and $\vec{a}_l \in A_l^{n_l}$.
   - If $l = 1$: check $sid = (\mathcal{P}_i, \mathcal{AU}, \mathcal{T}, L, sid')$, else abort.
   - If $l > 1$, check that $\langle \mathcal{P}_i, \vec{a}_1, \dots, \vec{a}_{l-1} \rangle \in \mathcal{L}_{\mathrm{de}}$, else abort.
   - Output $(\mathsf{ALLOWDEL}, ssid, \mathcal{P}_i, \mathcal{P}_j, l)$ to $\mathcal{A}$; wait for input $(\mathsf{ALLOWDEL}, ssid)$ from $\mathcal{A}$.
   - Add an entry $\langle \mathcal{P}_j, \vec{a}_1, \dots, \vec{a}_l \rangle$ to $\mathcal{L}_{\mathrm{de}}$.
   - Output $(\mathsf{DELEGATE}, ssid, \vec{a}_1, \dots, \vec{a}_l, \mathcal{P}_i)$ to $\mathcal{P}_j$.

4. **Present.** On input $(\mathsf{PRESENT}, m, \vec{a}_1, \dots, \vec{a}_L)$ from some party $\mathcal{P}_i$, with $\vec{a}_i \in (A_i \cup \{\perp\})^{n_i}$ for $i = 1, \dots, L$.
   - Check that an entry $\langle \mathcal{P}_i, \vec{a}'_1, \dots, \vec{a}'_L \rangle$ exists in $\mathcal{L}_{\mathrm{de}}$ such that $\vec{a}_i \preceq \vec{a}'_i$ for $i = 1, \dots, L$.
   - If $\mathcal{AU}$ honest, set $\mathfrak{p} \leftarrow \mathsf{Present}(pp, m, \vec{a}_1, \dots, \vec{a}_L; \perp)$, else $\mathfrak{p} \leftarrow \mathsf{Present}(pp, m, \vec{a}_1, \dots, \vec{a}_L; \mathcal{P}_i)$. Abort if $\mathsf{Verify}(pp, \mathfrak{p}, m, \vec{a}_1, \dots, \vec{a}_L) = 0$.
   - Store $\langle m, \vec{a}_1, \dots, \vec{a}_L, \mathfrak{p} \rangle$ in $\mathcal{L}_{\mathfrak{p}}$ and $\langle \mathfrak{p}, \mathcal{P}_i \rangle$ in $\mathcal{L}_{\mathrm{au}}$.
   - Output $(\mathsf{PROOF}, \mathfrak{p})$ to $\mathcal{P}_i$.
5. **Verify.** On input $(\mathsf{VERIFY}, \mathfrak{p}, m, \vec{a}_1, \dots, \vec{a}_L)$ from $\mathcal{P}_i$.
   - If $\langle m, \vec{a}_1, \dots, \vec{a}_L, \mathfrak{p} \rangle \notin \mathcal{L}_{\mathfrak{p}}$, $\mathcal{R}$ is honest, and for $i = 1, \dots, L$, there is no corrupt $\mathcal{P}_j$ with $\langle \mathcal{P}_j, \vec{a}'_1, \dots, \vec{a}'_i \rangle \in \mathcal{L}_{\mathrm{de}}$ and $\vec{a}_j \preceq \vec{a}'_j$ for $j = 1, \dots, i$, set $f \leftarrow 0$.
   - Else, output $(\mathsf{VERIFY}, \mathfrak{p})$ to $\mathcal{A}$; expect response $(\mathsf{VERIFY}, \mathcal{P})$. Set $f \leftarrow \mathsf{Verify}(pp, \mathfrak{p}, m, \vec{a}_1, \dots, \vec{a}_L)$. If $\mathcal{P}$ corrupt $\wedge f$ then add $\langle \mathfrak{p}, \mathcal{P} \rangle$ to $\mathcal{L}_{\mathrm{au}}$.
   - Output $(\mathsf{VERIFIED}, f)$ to $\mathcal{P}_i$.
6. **Audit.** On input $(\mathsf{AUDIT}, \mathfrak{p})$ from $\mathcal{AU}$, if $\langle \mathfrak{p}, \mathcal{P} \rangle \notin \mathcal{L}_{\mathrm{au}}$, output $(\mathsf{AUDIT}, \mathfrak{p})$ to $\mathcal{A}$. Upon obtaining $(\mathsf{AUDIT}, \mathcal{P})$ from $\mathcal{A}$, where $\mathcal{P}$ is corrupted, store $\langle \mathfrak{p}, \mathcal{P} \rangle$ in $\mathcal{L}_{\mathrm{au}}$. If now there is a valid record $\langle \mathfrak{p}, \mathcal{P} \rangle$ in $\mathcal{L}_{\mathrm{au}}$, then output $(\mathsf{RESULT}, \mathcal{P})$ to $\mathcal{AU}$. Else, output $\perp$ to $\mathcal{AU}$.

Fig. 4. Extended credentials functionality $\mathcal{F}_{\mathrm{dac}+}$ (restated Fig. 1)

Our theorem proving the security of the extended protocol builds directly on the proof of the core protocol from [14] and extended by [20]. Our extensions that cover revocation and auditability are as follows. **(1)** We construct the scheme as a combination of standard signatures and NIZK, instead of sibling signatures and NIZK as used in [14,20]. This is possible as we restrict ourselves to the case where the length of each delegation chain is fixed. **(2)** We need the NIZK to be non-malleable, as otherwise $\mathcal{F}_{\mathrm{dac}+}$ cannot identify the correct credential owner during an auditing query. This, however, is already implied by simulation-sound extractability. (3) We use a clock functionality [28] to model the advancement of epochs for the revocation scheme. We skip the parts of the description of the protocol $\Pi_{\text{dac+}}$ and the proof that are identical to [14], and only discuss the differences that appear due to the revocation and auditing features (Fig. 4).

Setup. In addition to root authority $\mathcal{R}$, auditor $\mathcal{AU}$ creates a Diffie-Hellman key pair and registers the public key. The auditor also registers a proof-of-knowledge of the private key like root authority $\mathcal{R}$, at functionality $\mathcal{F}_{\text{ca}}$. We use the same scheme for $\mathcal{AU}$ as [14] uses for $\mathcal{R}$, so that we also achieve online extractability.

Advance. Upon input, the epoch counter $\mathcal{T}$ provides an input to $\mathcal{F}_{\text{clock}}$, which advances the epoch.[1]

Delegate. Delegation is almost the same, except for the last delegation step (the one to the end user) where the delegator includes as one attribute the current epoch obtained from $\mathcal{F}_{\text{clock}}$. In this step, the delegator also deposits the delegate's public key with $\mathcal{AU}$.

Present. There are three modifications during presentation. The first is that the user generates a new pseudonym and proves consistency. The second is that a credential proof is only generated if a relevant credential exists *for the present epoch*, and the attribute that encodes the current epoch is always disclosed. The third one is that, as explained in Sect. 4.3, the user encrypts their public key under the auditor's public key using AUDITENC and then proves consistent encryption using AUDITPROVE.

Verify. The changes are dual to the above ones. The receiver, in addition to the standard credential validation, checks the consistency of the pseudonym, that the epoch attribute in the credential proof is valid, and the consistency of the auditing proof.

Audit. Given a credential proof, the auditor first checks its validity. If the credential proof is valid, the auditor then extracts the ciphertext that encrypts the user's key and decrypts it.

Delegatable credentials protocol $\Pi_{\text{dac+}}$ securely realizes $\mathcal{F}_{\text{dac+}}$ in the $(\mathcal{F}_{\text{smt}}, \mathcal{F}_{\text{ca}}, \mathcal{F}_{\text{crs}}, \mathcal{F}_{\text{clock}})$-hybrid model, provided that

- SIGNNYM (Algorithm 2) is a strongly unforgeable signature,
- the auditing encryption is semantically secure,
- NIZK is a simulation-sound extractable non-interactive zero-knowledge proof.

The proof holds for static corruption of $\mathcal{AU}$.

Proof. We extend the proof of [14] to the functionality we added to the scheme. In Setup, the additional setup phase of auditor $\mathcal{AU}$ is proved analogously to that of the root authority. This includes the extraction of the private key if $\mathcal{AU}$ is

---

[1] Other parties interact with $\mathcal{F}_{\text{clock}}$ to read the epoch. They technically also provide input to $\mathcal{F}_{\text{clock}}$, which is required for modeling a synchrony assumption such as epochs in the otherwise asynchronous UC framework [28].

corrupt; in that case the simulator sets pp to include the auditor's public key as well as public keys for all parties. If $\mathcal{AU}$ is honest, algorithm Param provides a fresh random key. Advance in $\mathcal{F}_{\mathrm{dac+}}$ means that all issued credential proofs become invalid, and that the last-level delegations are deleted from $\mathcal{L}_{\mathrm{de}}$. The same effect appears in the protocol, where the epoch advanced and inputs with old credential proofs to VERIFY will fail, as will the presentation of credentials that have been issued in an earlier epoch. Delegate behaves the same as before.

In the presentation phase, the credential proof $\mathfrak{p}$ returned by the functionality contains multiple additional elements (which in $\mathcal{F}_{\mathrm{dac+}}$ are generated by the algorithm Present). The first two are $\mathsf{pk}_{\mathsf{nym}}$ and σ_{nym}, the pseudonym generated for this presentation and the signature on m. The next two are enc and $\mathfrak{P}_{\mathsf{audit}}$, the encryption of the user's public key pk under the auditor's public key apk, and the NIZK proving the correctness of this encryption. Algorithm Present generates the credential proof by building a fresh delegation chain with fresh keys and only the specified attributes; the only exception is that if $\mathcal{AU}$ is corrupt, then the correct user's public key, as indicated by the additional argument to Present, is chosen from pp and encrypted under the auditor's key. If $\mathcal{AU}$ is honest, then Present includes an encryption of a random message under the simulated auditor's public key in $\mathfrak{p}$. Present sets the additional values as follows: $\mathsf{pk}_{\mathsf{nym}}$ and σ_{nym} are set to a fresh pseudonym and a signature relative to $\mathsf{pk}_{\mathsf{nym}}$ and the also fresh user public key. If $\mathcal{AU}$ is corrupt then the encryption of the user public key under apk and the corresponding zero-knowledge proof are computed as in the scheme using the values from pp. If $\mathcal{AU}$ is honest, then (as discussed) a random encryption is chosen and the proof is simulated. This simulation requires that the encryption scheme is semantically secure and the NIZK is zero-knowledge to ensure that the consistency proof for the encryption is indistinguishable from a real proof, and that as in [14] fresh delegations are indistinguishable from the real world where the same delegations are used for multiple presentations.

In the verification phase, in both the real and the ideal cases, the verification algorithm is used to verify $\mathfrak{p}$. While in the ideal case with honest auditor the auditing proof is simulated, this will also successfully verify in Verify. The main difference is that $\mathcal{F}_{\mathrm{dac+}}$ prevents forgeries ideally whereas the protocol merely relies on the verification of the zero-knowledge proofs. The functionality also ensures that, for credential proofs that are accepted, their holders are known, therefore auditing will succeed. In the ideal world, the simulator knows the private key of $\mathcal{AU}$ (since it is chosen by the simulator if $\mathcal{AU}$ is honest, or extracted if $\mathcal{AU}$ is corrupt), and can therefore obtain the public key of the credential holder. This difference is indistinguishable by the simulation-sound extractability of the zero-knowledge proofs and the unforgeability of the signature scheme. Note that, in contrast with [14], we allow verification to succeed only for credential proofs $\mathfrak{p}$ that have either been generated by $\mathcal{F}_{\mathrm{dac+}}$ or are valid for corrupt parties. This in particular means that credential proofs are non-malleable, but non-malleability is already implied by simulation-sound extractability.

When honest $\mathcal{AU}$ inputs a credential proof $\mathfrak{p}$, the embedded ciphertext is decrypted. For credential proofs generated by an honest $\mathcal{P}_i$ this will always succeed. For those not generated by an honest $\mathcal{P}_i$, the functionality lets the adversary decide on the identity of the holder; the adversary can choose any corrupted party. The simulator can decrypt the auditing field of the credential proofs using the secret key of the auditor (which in case of a dishonest auditor has been extracted during setup). Indistinguishability again follows by the zero-knowledge property of the NIZK.

B   Algorithms

Algorithm 2. Pseudonym and public key possession proof algorithms

---

1: **procedure** MAKENYM(csk)
2:     $\mathsf{sk_{nym}} \leftarrow\!\!\$\ \mathbb{Z}_q$
3:     $\mathsf{pk_{nym}} := g^{\mathsf{csk}} h^{\mathsf{sk_{nym}}}$
4:     **return** $\mathsf{sk_{nym}}, \mathsf{pk_{nym}}$
5: **procedure** SIGNNYM($\mathsf{pk_{nym}}, \mathsf{sk_{nym}}, \mathsf{csk}, m$)
6:     $\rho_1, \rho_2 \leftarrow\!\!\$\ \mathbb{Z}_q$
7:     $\mathsf{com} := g^{\rho_1} h^{\rho_2}$
8:     $c := \text{HASH}(\mathsf{com}, \mathsf{pk_{nym}}, m)$
9:     $\mathfrak{p}_{\mathsf{csk}} := \rho_1 + c \cdot \mathsf{csk}$
10:    $\mathfrak{p}_{\mathsf{skNym}} := \rho_2 + c \cdot \mathsf{sk_{nym}}$
11:    **return** $c, \mathfrak{p}_{\mathsf{csk}}, \mathfrak{p}_{\mathsf{skNym}}$

12: **procedure**   VERIFYNYM($\mathsf{pk_{nym}}, m, c, \mathfrak{p}_{\mathsf{csk}},$ $\mathfrak{p}_{\mathsf{skNym}}$)
13:    $\mathsf{com} = g^{\mathfrak{p}_{\mathsf{csk}}} h^{\mathfrak{p}_{\mathsf{skNym}}} \mathsf{pk}_{\mathsf{nym}}^{-c}$
14:    **return** $c = \text{HASH}(\mathsf{com}, \mathsf{pk_{nym}}, m)$
15: **procedure** PROVEPK(csk, cpk, nonce)
16:    $\rho \leftarrow\!\!\$\ \mathbb{Z}_q$
17:    $\mathsf{com} := g^{\rho}$
18:    $c := \text{HASH}(\mathsf{com}, \mathsf{cpk}, \mathsf{nonce})$
19:    $\mathfrak{p} := \rho + c \cdot \mathsf{csk}$
20:    **return** $c, \mathfrak{p}$
21: **procedure** VERIFYPK($c, \mathfrak{p}$, cpk, nonce)
22:    $\mathsf{com} = g^{\mathfrak{p}} \mathsf{cpk}^{-c}$
23:    **return** $c = \text{HASH}(\mathsf{com}, \mathsf{cpk}, \mathsf{nonce})$

Algorithm 3. Non-revocation proof generation and verification algorithms

---

1: **procedure** NRPROVE(σ, csk, $\mathsf{sk_{nym}}$, epoch)
2:     $(r', s', t'_1, t'_2) \leftarrow\!\!\$\ \text{GROTH.RANDOMIZE}(\sigma)$
3:     $\langle \rho \rangle_{1\ldots4} \leftarrow\!\!\$\ \mathbb{Z}_q$
4:     $\mathsf{com}_1 := e\left(r', g_2^{\rho_1}\right) \cdot e\left(g_1^{-1}, g_2^{\rho_2}\right)$
5:     $\mathsf{com}_2 := e\left(r', g_2^{\rho_3}\right)$
6:     $\mathsf{com}_3 := g_1^{\rho_2} h^{\rho_4}$
7:     $c := \text{HASH}(r', s', \mathsf{com}_1, \mathsf{com}_2, \mathsf{com}_3, \text{epoch})$
8:     $\mathfrak{p}_1 := g_2^{\rho_1} t_1^{\prime\,c}$
9:     $\mathfrak{p}_2 := \rho_2 + \mathsf{csk} \cdot c$
10:    $\mathfrak{p}_3 := g_2^{\rho_3} t_2^{\prime\,c}$
11:    $\mathfrak{p}_4 := \rho_4 + \mathsf{sk_{nym}} \cdot c$
12:    **return** $c, \langle \mathfrak{p} \rangle_{1\ldots4}, r', s'$

13: **procedure** NRSIGN(rsk, cpk, epoch)
14:    $\varepsilon := \text{HASH}(\text{epoch})$
15:    **return** GROTH.SIGN(rsk; cpk, g^{ε})
16: **procedure**   NRVERIFY($c, \langle \mathfrak{p} \rangle_{1\ldots4}, r', s',$ $\mathsf{pk_{nym}}$, epoch)
17:    **if** $e\left(r', s'\right) \neq e\left(g_1, y_1\right) \cdot e\left(\mathsf{rpk}, g_2\right)$ **then**
18:        **return** false
19:    $\varepsilon := \text{HASH}(\text{epoch})$
20:    $\mathsf{com}_1 := e\left(r', \mathfrak{p}_1\right) \cdot e\left(g_1^{-1}, g_2\right)^{\mathfrak{p}_2} \cdot$ $e\left(\mathsf{rpk}, y_1\right)^{-c}$
21:    $\mathsf{com}_2 := e\left(r', \mathfrak{p}_3\right) \cdot e\left(\mathsf{rpk}, y_2\right)^{-c} \cdot$ $e\left(g_1, g_2^{\varepsilon}\right)^{-c}$
22:    $\mathsf{com}_3 := g_1^{\mathfrak{p}_2} h^{\mathfrak{p}_4} \mathsf{pk}_{\mathsf{nym}}^{-c}$
23:    $c' := \text{HASH}(r', s', \mathsf{com}_1, \mathsf{com}_2, \mathsf{com}_3, \text{epoch})$
24:    **return** $c = c'$

Algorithm 4. Auditing proof generation and verification algorithms

1: **procedure** AUDITPROVE(enc, ρ, cpk, csk, pk$_{nym}$, sk$_{nym}$)
2:     $\langle \rho \rangle_{1\ldots3} \leftarrow\!\!\$\, \mathbb{Z}_q$
3:     com$_1$:= g^{ρ_1}apk$^{\rho_2}$
4:     com$_2$:= g^{ρ_2}
5:     com$_3$:= $g^{\rho_1}h^{\rho_3}$
6:     c := HASH(com$_1$, com$_2$, com$_3$, enc, pk$_{nym}$)
7:     $\mathfrak{p}_1$:= $\rho_1 + c \cdot$ csk
8:     $\mathfrak{p}_2$:= $\rho_2 + c \cdot \rho$
9:     $\mathfrak{p}_3$:= $\rho_3 + c \cdot$ sk$_{nym}$
10:     **return** $c, \langle \mathfrak{p} \rangle_{1\ldots3}$

11: **procedure** AUDITENC(apk, cpk)   ▷ ELGAMAL
12:     $\rho \leftarrow\!\!\$\, \mathbb{Z}_q$
13:     enc := (enc$_1$, enc$_2$) := (cpk $\cdot$ apk$^\rho$, g^ρ)
14:     **return** enc, ρ
15: **procedure** AUDITVERIFY(c, enc, $\langle \mathfrak{p} \rangle_{1\ldots3}$, pk$_{nym}$)
16:     com$_1$:= $g^{\mathfrak{p}_1}$apk$^{\mathfrak{p}_2}$enc$_1^{-c}$
17:     com$_2$:= $g^{\mathfrak{p}_2}$enc$_2^{-c}$
18:     com$_3$:= $g^{\mathfrak{p}_1}h^{\mathfrak{p}_3}pk_{nym}^{-c}$
19:     c' := HASH(com$_1$, com$_2$, com$_3$, enc, pk$_{nym}$)
20:     **return** $c = c'$

References

1. Achenbach, D., Kempka, C., Löwe, B., Müller-Quade, J.: Improved coercion-resistant electronic elections through deniable re-voting. In: JETS 2015 (2015)
2. Androulaki, E., et al.: Hyperledger fabric: a distributed operating system for permissioned blockchains. In: Proceedings of the 13th EuroSys Conference, EuroSys 2018, pp. 30:1–30:15 (2018)
3. Androulaki, E., Cachin, C., De Caro, A., Kokoris-Kogias, E.: Channels: horizontal scaling and confidentiality on permissioned blockchains. In: Lopez, J., Zhou, J., Soriano, M. (eds.) ESORICS 2018. LNCS, vol. 11098, pp. 111–131. Springer, Cham (2018). https://doi.org/10.1007/978-3-319-99073-6_6
4. Androulaki, E., Camenisch, J., Caro, A.D., Dubovitskaya, M., Elkhiyaoui, K., Tackmann, B.: Privacy-preserving auditable token payments in a permissioned blockchain system. Cryptology ePrint Report 2019/1058 (November 2019)
5. Au, M.H., Susilo, W., Mu, Y.: Constant-size dynamic k-TAA. In: De Prisco, R., Yung, M. (eds.) SCN 2006. LNCS, vol. 4116, pp. 111–125. Springer, Heidelberg (2006). https://doi.org/10.1007/11832072_8
6. Baldimtsi, F., et al.: Accumulators with applications to anonymity-preserving revocation. In: 2017 IEEE European Symposium on Security and Privacy, EuroS&P 2017, Paris, France, 26–28 April 2017, pp. 301–315 (2017)
7. Barreto, P.S.L.M., Naehrig, M.: Pairing-friendly elliptic curves of prime order. In: Preneel, B., Tavares, S. (eds.) SAC 2005. LNCS, vol. 3897, pp. 319–331. Springer, Heidelberg (2006). https://doi.org/10.1007/11693383_22
8. Ben-Sasson, E., et al.: Zerocash: decentralized anonymous payments from Bitcoin. In: IEEE Symposium on Security and Privacy, pp. 459–474. IEEE (2014)
9. Benhamouda, F., et al.: Initial public offering (IPO) on permissioned blockchain using secure multiparty computation. In: IEEE Blockchain. IEEE (2019)
10. Blömer, J., Bobolz, J.: Delegatable attribute-based anonymous credentials from dynamically malleable signatures. In: Preneel, B., Vercauteren, F. (eds.) ACNS 2018. LNCS, vol. 10892, pp. 221–239. Springer, Cham (2018). https://doi.org/10.1007/978-3-319-93387-0_12
11. Bogatov, D.: Delegatable anonymous credentials library (2021). https://github.com/dbogatov/dac-lib
12. Bogatov, D.: Fabric network and crypto simulator (2021). https://github.com/dbogatov/fabric-simulator

13. Bogatov, D., Caro, A.D., Elkhiyaoui, K., Tackmann, B.: Anonymous transactions with revocation and auditing in hyperledger fabric. Cryptology ePrint Archive, Report 2019/1097 (2019). https://ia.cr/2019/1097
14. Camenisch, J., Drijvers, M., Dubovitskaya, M.: Practical UC-secure delegatable credentials with attributes and their application to blockchain. In: Proceedings of the 2017 ACM SIGSAC Conference on Computer and Communications Security, pp. 683–699. ACM (2017)
15. Camenisch, J., Drijvers, M., Lehmann, A.: Anonymous attestation using the strong Diffie Hellman assumption revisited. In: Franz, M., Papadimitratos, P. (eds.) Trust 2016. LNCS, vol. 9824, pp. 1–20. Springer, Cham (2016). https://doi.org/10.1007/978-3-319-45572-3_1
16. Camenisch, J., van Heerweeghen, E.: Design and implementation of the idemix anonymous credential system. In: ACM Conference on Computer and Communication Security, pp. 21–30. ACM (2002)
17. Castro, M., Liskov, B.: Practical Byzantine fault tolerance. In: 3rd Symposium on Operating Systems Design and Implementation (1999)
18. Chen, J., Micali, S.: Algorand: a secure and efficient distributed ledger. Theoret. Comput. Sci. **777**, 155–183 (2019)
19. Crites, E.C., Lysyanskaya, A.: Delegatable anonymous credentials from mercurial signatures. In: Matsui, M. (ed.) CT-RSA 2019. LNCS, vol. 11405, pp. 535–555. Springer, Cham (2019). https://doi.org/10.1007/978-3-030-12612-4_27
20. Drijvers, M.: Composable anonymous credentials from global random oracles. Ph.D. thesis, ETH Zürich, Zürich, Switzerland (2018)
21. Dziembowski, S., Eckey, L., Faust, S., Hesse, J., Hostáková, K.: Multi-party virtual state channels. In: Ishai, Y., Rijmen, V. (eds.) EUROCRYPT 2019. LNCS, vol. 11476, pp. 625–656. Springer, Cham (2019). https://doi.org/10.1007/978-3-030-17653-2_21
22. ElGamal, T.: A public key cryptosystem and a signature scheme based on discrete logarithms. IEEE Trans. Inf. Theor. **31**(4), 469–472 (1985)
23. Garman, C., Green, M., Miers, I.: Decentralized anonymous credentials. In: NDSS. Internet Society (2014)
24. Garman, C., Green, M., Miers, I.: Accountable privacy for decentralized anonymous payments. In: Grossklags, J., Preneel, B. (eds.) FC 2016. LNCS, vol. 9603, pp. 81–98. Springer, Heidelberg (2017). https://doi.org/10.1007/978-3-662-54970-4_5
25. Golan-Gueta, G., et al.: SBFT: a scalable and decentralized trust infrastructure. In: DSN, pp. 568–580 (2019)
26. Harchandani, L.: Delegatable anonymous credentials in rust (September 2019). https://github.com/lovesh/signature-schemes/tree/delegatable/delg_cred_cdd
27. Harris, O.: Quorum (2020). https://www.goquorum.com/
28. Katz, J., Maurer, U., Tackmann, B., Zikas, V.: Universally composable synchronous computation. In: Sahai, A. (ed.) TCC 2013. LNCS, vol. 7785, pp. 477–498. Springer, Heidelberg (2013). https://doi.org/10.1007/978-3-642-36594-2_27
29. Kiayias, A., Russell, A., David, B., Oliynykov, R.: Ouroboros: a provably secure proof-of-stake blockchain protocol. In: Katz, J., Shacham, H. (eds.) CRYPTO 2017. LNCS, vol. 10401, pp. 357–388. Springer, Cham (2017). https://doi.org/10.1007/978-3-319-63688-7_12
30. Micali, S., Rabin, M., Kilian, J.: Zero-knowledge sets. In: 44th Annual IEEE Symposium on Foundations of Computer Science, pp. 80–91 (10 2003)
31. Nakamoto, S.: Bitcoin: a peer-to-peer electronic cash system (2009)
32. National Institute of Standards and Technology: FIPS PUB 186-4: Digital Signature Standard. National Institute for Standards and Technology (July 2013)

33. Poelstra, A., Back, A., Friedenbach, M., Maxwell, G., Wuille, P.: Confidential assets. In: Zohar, A., et al. (eds.) FC 2018. LNCS, vol. 10958, pp. 43–63. Springer, Heidelberg (2019). https://doi.org/10.1007/978-3-662-58820-8_4
34. Schnorr, C.P.: Efficient identification and signatures for smart cards. In: Brassard, G. (ed.) CRYPTO 1989. LNCS, vol. 435, pp. 239–252. Springer, New York (1990). https://doi.org/10.1007/0-387-34805-0_22
35. Scott, M.: The Apache Milagro Crypto Library
36. Stathakopoulou, C., David, T., Vukolić, M.: Mir-BFT: high-throughput BFT for blockchains. arXiv:1906.05552 (June 2019)
37. Windley, P.J.: Sovrin (2020). https://sovrin.org/
38. Wood, G.: Ethereum: a secure decentralised generalised transaction ledger (2020)
39. Wüst, K., Kostiainen, K., Capkun, V., Capkun, S.: PRCash: fast, private and regulated transactions for digital currencies. Cryptology archive: 2018/412 (May 2018)

Attestation Waves:
Platform Trust via Remote
Power Analysis

Ignacio M. Delgado-Lozano[1]([⊠]) [iD], Macarena C. Martínez-Rodríguez[2] [iD],
Alexandros Bakas[1] [iD], Billy Bob Brumley[1] [iD], and Antonis Michalas[1] [iD]

[1] Tampere University, Tampere, Finland
{ignacio.delgadolozano,alexandros.bakas}@tuni.fi
[2] Instituto de Microelectrónica de Sevilla, CSIC/Universidad de Sevilla,
Sevilla, Spain
macarena@imse-cnm.csic.es

Abstract. Attestation is a strong tool to verify the integrity of an untrusted system. However, in recent years, different attacks have appeared that are able to mislead the attestation process with treacherous practices as memory copy, proxy, and rootkit attacks, just to name a few. A successful attack leads to systems that are considered trusted by a verifier system, while the prover has bypassed the challenge. To mitigate these attacks against attestation methods and protocols, some proposals have considered the use of side-channel information that can be measured externally, as it is the case of electromagnetic (EM) emanation. Nonetheless, these methods require the physical proximity of an external setup to capture the EM radiation.

In this paper, we present the possibility of performing attestation by using the side-channel information captured by a sensor or peripheral that lives in the same System-on-Chip (SoC) than the processor system (PS) which executes the operation that we aim to attest, by only sharing the Power Distribution Network (PDN). In our case, an analog-to-digital converter (ADC) that captures the voltage fluctuations at its input terminal while a certain operation is taking place is suitable to characterize itself and to distinguish it from other binaries. The resultant power traces are enough to clearly identify a given operation without the requirement of physical proximity.

Keywords: Attestation · Remote power analysis · Side channels · ADC · Secure protocols · Secure communications

1 Introduction

In our current network and interconnected world, establishing platform trust for execution of different security-critical operations is a need in diverse fields: examples include manufacturing, automation, communications, transport, work,

© Springer Nature Switzerland AG 2021
M. Conti et al. (Eds.): CANS 2021, LNCS 13099, pp. 460–482, 2021.
https://doi.org/10.1007/978-3-030-92548-2_24

and finance [5]. One approach is to use attestation mechanisms, which are suitable to verify the integrity of several elements such as application binaries, data, or other internal platform state. Attestation normally consists of presenting a challenge by a verifier system that is already trusted to a prover system.

Attestation is a powerful concept to verify the integrity of untrusted systems. Recently, different attacks have appeared that aid in circumventing attestation by making a copy of the code that generates the checksum expected by the verifier (memory copy attack) [3, 29, 30], forwarding the challenge to another device that is able to compute the checksum properly (proxy attack) [15], or using return oriented programming gadgets to transiently hide the malicious code in parts of memory where the verifier cannot find it (rootkit attack) [2]. As a result, what we get are systems that are considered trusted by a verifier system, while the prover has bypassed the challenge.

To harden against these attacks on attestation methods and protocols, some proposals have considered the use of side-channel information that can be measured externally. For example, Sehatbakhsh et al. [28] recently utilized electromagnetic (EM) emanation to verify honest checksum computation. Nonetheless, these methods require proximity: a local external testbed set up near the prover in such a way that a carefully-placed probe can capture the EM radiation (traces) of the prover's device. Furthermore, this testbed itself must be secured and trusted. The physical proximity requirement directly contradicts with the goals of remote attestation, not to mention failure to scale.

Recent trends in offensive cryptanalytic side-channel analysis are towards *remote power analysis* [19]. These techniques allow attackers to utilize pre-existing sensors or peripherals living in the same System-on-Chip (SoC) to procure traces. Regarding cryptanalytic side-channel attacks, this removes the physical proximity requirement from the threat model. In practice, these traces feature granularity reduced by several orders of magnitude when compared to traces captured with traditional high sampling rate oscilloscopes (e.g. 1MSPS in Sect. 3 vs. 40GSPS in [17]). Hence, remote power analysis trades this relaxed threat model for lower quality and higher quantity of traces. Section 2 contains more background on both remote power analysis and attestation.

In this paper, we propose utilizing remote power analysis for remote dynamic attestation, eliminating the physical proximity requirement of previous EM-based attestation proposals. Section 3 describes our testbed, with an application processor (AP) that executes the binary we aim to attest, by only sharing the Power Distribution Network (PDN) with the sensor that captures the traces. In our case, an analog-to-digital converter (ADC) captures the voltage fluctuations at its input terminal during attestation. Section 4 proposes an attestation protocol to establish secure communication between prover and verifier systems in a platform-agnostic way. Section 5 characterizes the degree to which the resulting traces captured from ADC vary over different binaries, with the goal of accurately matching traces to a priori applications with signal processing techniques via templating. In particular, we show that with a sufficient (yet small) number of traces, parameterized (in part) by various error rates, we are able to achieve excellent security levels and also understand the limitations of attestation in this novel setting. We conclude in Sect. 6.

2   Background

In a typical software-based attestation, a verifier is able to establish the absence of malware in a prover system with no physical access to its memory. This is possible because the verifier proposes a challenge to the prover, in which it must compute a checksum of its memory content. This challenge can only be correctly replied to if the memory content is not tampered, since the result of the checksum is only correct if the memory content within the prover system is exactly as expected by the verifier. For this, the verifier system needs to know several critical data about the prover, such as the clock speed, the instruction set architecture, the memory architecture of its microcontroller, and the size of its memories. This way, if in any moment a malicious prover aims to alter its memory, it is detectable by the verifier because the prover will present a wrong checksum result or a delay in the response [31]. This means that the integrity of the prover is verified, not only matching the checksum result with the expected result ($Response_{prover} = Response_{expected}$), but also through a parameter known as the request-to-response time ($t_{response} < t_{expected}$).

Numerous works focus on software-based attestation [3,29,30]. To threaten these attestation processes, several attacks have appeared during the last fifteen years that aim to break this attestation method. Attackers normally attempt to forge the response with a checksum computed in a different region of the prover memory that duplicates the code. This allows them to generate the expected response, which is known as a memory copy attack [3,29,30]. Another possibility is to forward the challenge to another device that is able to compute the checksum, then send it back to the verifier while satisfying the request-to-response time requirement, leading to proxy attacks. Li et al. [15] extensively describe proxy attacks and present attestation protocols to prevent them. The last option consists of storing the malicious code previous to the checksum calculation, by hiding it in other parts of the memory, allowing the prover to compute the correct checksum while the verifier is not able to detect the parts of the code that have been hidden, called a rootkit attack [2].

Along with software-based attestation processes, hardware-supported Trusted Execution Environments (TEE) are frequently used to ensure that the response of the computation is not tampered. Abera et al. [1] allow remote control-flow path attestation of an application without needing the code. They utilize ARM's TrustZone (TZ) in order to avoid memory corruption attacks. Clercq et al. [4] present a Control Flow Integrity (CFI) mechanism, guarding against code injection and code reuse attacks. They also present Software Integrity (SI) by storing precomputed MACs of instructions and comparing them with the MAC of the run-time execution. Moreover, Dessouky et al. [6] monitor every branch, a mitigation leveraging un-instrumented control-flow instructions.

Besides classical attestation, several recent works have used the EM emanations generated by a monitored system as a consequence of a certain execution within it, to detect malware in IoT devices. An example of this is EDDIE [21], a method that studies the spikes on the EM spectrum generated during a program execution and compares them to other peaks previously learned during a training stage. Significant differences in the spikes of EM spectrum allow to infer the introduction of malware in the studied program. Han et al. [13] give a similar approach, presenting ZEUS. This is a contactless embedded controller security monitor that is able to ensure the integrity of certain operations, by leveraging the EM emission produced during their execution, with no additional hardware support or software modifications. Yang et al. [32] and Liu and Vasserman [18] present very similar studies. The latter additionally considers the problem in terms of participants of an attestation protocol, namely, verifier and prover systems, although they do not develop a complete protocol itself. Msgna et al. [20] give another proposal that uses side-channel signals to check the integrity of program executions, where the use of power consumption templates is suitable to verify the integrity of code without previous knowledge about it. However, Sehatbakhsh et al. [28] propose the first attestation protocol based on EM signals with EMMA. The authors observe that execution time is only one of the multiple examples of using measurable side-channel information to gain knowledge about a specific computation, providing in many cases much finer-grain information than a unique temporal parameter. To develop this idea, they design a new attestation method based on the EM emanations generated by the prover while computing the checksum challenge proposed by the verifier, instead of the request-to-response time. After this, they show the implementation of this design, and consider and evaluate different attacks on EMMA. On the negative side, and opposed to classical attestation, this method requires physical proximity to the setup that captures the emanation, namely, a probe connected to an oscilloscope or external Software Defined Radio (SDR).

On a separate issue, several recent studies consider the possibility of attacking cryptosystems by using the side-channel information provided by mixed-signal components, such as ADCs [8,22], or other sensors such as ring oscillators (ROs) [11,25,33] and time-to-digital converters (TDCs) [9,12,26,27]. In real-world devices, these components are already placed in the same FPGA or SoC as a certain cryptographic module that is running some operations with secret parameters, or available through some interfaces present in processors, e.g. Intel Running Average Power Limit (RAPL) [16]. However, to the best of our knowledge, no study exists aiming to perform an attestation process by using the side-channel information captured by said components, leading to what we call *remote power analysis for attestation*. This technique features the benefits of the EM side channel (finer-grain information) without the negative sides (external setup with physical proximity).

3 Remote Power Analysis for Attestation

3.1 System Description and Measurements

As mentioned in the previous section, the goal of this work is to attest an operation run in a system by using the power leakage caused by the operation itself. In this context, where the power consumption traces can be acquired remotely, they can be used to attest an operation, because the procurement process can be automated. Generally, the voltage fluctuations caused by the operation can be captured by any mixed-signal component, that could be an ADC, a sensor implemented on the programmable logic (PL), or any power supply monitor.

Figure 1 gives an overview of our system. It contains an AP where the operation (prover) and attestation (verifier) processes are run. Additionally, it contains the mixed-signal component that measures the supply voltage via ADC with Direct Memory Access (DMA) while the operation is run. The verification process saves the power trace captured by the mixed-signal component as binary data. Since we are using this side-channel trace data as evidence, the data must be trustworthy. Therefore, in our system, the ADC is inside the trust perimeter. Exactly how this happens in practice depends on the TEE technology. For example, on a platform that supports virtualization, this might be accomplished by a two-stage Memory Management Unit (MMU), where the hypervisor (or TEE) removes access from the untrusted High Level Operating System (HLOS) by simply not mapping the second-stage translation that would allow access to the ADC's physical address space or the memory where it stores its data. This is indeed the scenario that Fig. 1 depicts. On ARM-based SoCs this could also be accomplished with a Memory Protection Unit (MPU) that would be configured by a TZ-based TEE. The analogous upcoming technology for RISC-V would be Physical Memory Protection (PMP) [14]. So while the concrete protection mechanism on a given architecture depends on the TEE implementation, in this work we generically use the Linux kernel to simulate the TEE in terms of trust, and the kernel gates all userspace access to the ADC with traditional MMU-based access control.

Specifically, in this paper we conduct our experiments on a PYNQ-Z1 board. We programmed the FPGA of its Zynq 7000 chip to activate the ADC present on it, and capture the voltage fluctuations produced due to the execution of different operations inside the ARM Cortex-A9 processor. With this approach, we aim to carry out the attestation process of an execution performed within the processor, simply with the side-channel information, given by the voltage fluctuations at the input of the ADC. This is present in the PL, and totally isolated from the AP core, having only a shared PDN as a common element.

The XADC module is a hard macro available in the FPGA of the Zynq 7000 chip. This module is not only an ADC converter of the analog data connected to the input channel, but it can also be configured to monitor the supply voltages and temperature. The XADC module supports multichannel, however we configure it with a single channel that monitors the internal core supply voltage. The output data size of this module is 16-bit data, with 12-bit precision. The

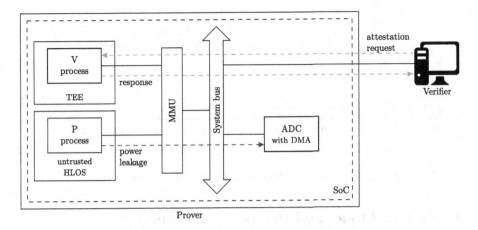

Fig. 1. Block diagram of the attestation process while running the operation.

sample rate is 1MSPS. The 32-bit AXI streaming output of the XADC is used to transfer as many samples as possible to the AP. The XADC outputs samples on the AXI Stream for each of its channels when it is enabled, in this case, only one channel. We use DMA transfer from the PL to the AP to move XADC samples into the AP memory, and we use an AXI GPIO to set the size of the transfer. Since the width of the AXI stream is double the output data size, there are two measurements at each memory position.

During the attestation process, first the number of power measurements to be captured is set: that is, the buffer size. Just before running the operation, the DMA is enabled, then we run a trigger operation to indicate in the signal the beginning of the operation to be attested, then the operation itself is run, and finally, another trigger operation indicates that it has ended. The XADC is capturing power data until the DMA transfer is completed. The AP reads the part of the memory where the measurements are stored and processes it as needed.

We summarize our procurement process as follows, that saves the power traces as binary data used in the attestation protocol. (i) Set the buffer size; (ii) enable the DMA engine; (iii) send the start trigger; (iv) execute the target binary; (v) send the end trigger; (vi) wait for the DMA to complete; (vii) process the resulting binary data (trace). In practice, the (untrusted) HLOS executes step (iv) and the TEE executes all other steps.

Figure 2 shows a power trace captured with the XADC while an operation is run. The two trigger operations are shown at the beginning and the end of the operation, determining the operation area. The rest of the trace is the value of the supply voltage after the operation is finished. This trace is subsequently processed in the protocol to attest the operation.

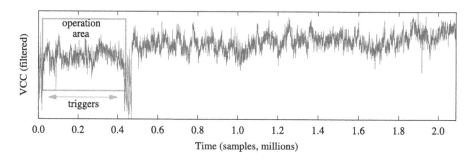

Fig. 2. Example of a power trace captured with the XADC.

4   System Model and Protocol Construction

In this section, we demonstrate how our attestation technique can be applied and used in real-life deployments and not remain just a lab-concept. To this end, we present a detailed protocol showing the communication and all the messages exchanged between the involved entities. Our protocol description includes the definition of the underlying system model, as well as the presentation of all the involved entities and their specifications. Finally, we construct our threat model and show our protocol's resistance against a powerful malicious adversary $\mathcal{ADV}$. While this is not the core contribution of this work, we consider it an important part since it tackles a problem so far only dealt with at a high level in other similar works (e.g. [28]). We believe our approach can provide an impetus towards paving the way for the integration of our, or similar, techniques in existing services.

4.1   System Model

We assume the existence of the following components:

Verifier ($\mathcal{V}$): Here, verifier is a user who wishes to execute a piece of software on an untrusted platform. Prior to exchanging the data with the untrusted platform, the user needs to verify its trustworthiness.

Prover ($\mathcal{P}$): The prover is an untrusted platform that needs to convince a verifier of its trustworthiness. It consists of an untrusted application and a TEE.

1. Untrusted application: The application handles the communication between the verifier and the untrusted platform. After proving its trustworthiness, the application will be responsible for executing software specified by the user.
2. Trusted Execution Environment: We assume the existence of a TEE residing either on the untrusted platform or in a remote location. The TEE is invoked by the untrusted application upon receiving an attestation request by a verifier. TEE's main responsibility is to measure the power consumption of the untrusted part of $\mathcal{P}$, while running an application requested by $\mathcal{V}$. (Here we recall that the TEE also hosts the component that takes the measurements.)

Measurements Tray (MT): MT is an entity residing in the cloud. Its main responsibility is to store templates and compare them with traces that are received by $\mathcal{V}$. There are two separate reasons that led us to have MT as an independent component and not as a part of $\mathcal{V}$. (i) MT residing on $\mathcal{V}$'s side would result in higher local storage costs, as $\mathcal{V}$ would have to keep a copy of each template locally. (ii) Assuming that MT is an independent cloud component, all MT updates are executed centrally. This eliminates the need for separate updates.

4.2   Attestation Protocol

Having defined our system model, we can now proceed to describe our attestation protocol. Our construction is divided into three phases: the *Setup Phase*, the *Trusted Launch Phase* (Fig. 3), and the *Computations Phase* (Fig. 4). For the rest of this paper, we assume the existence [10] of an IND-CCA2 secure public key cryptosystem, EUF-CMA secure signature scheme, and a first and second preimage resistant hash function $H(\cdot)$.

Setup Phase: During this phase, each entity receives a public/private key pair. More specifically:

- $(\mathsf{pk}_\mathcal{V}, \mathsf{sk}_\mathcal{V})$ - Verifier $\mathcal{V}$'s public/private key pair.
- $(\mathsf{pk}_\mathcal{P}, \mathsf{sk}_\mathcal{P})$ - Prover $\mathcal{P}$'s public/private key pair.
- $(\mathsf{pk}_{\mathsf{MT}}, \mathsf{sk}_{\mathsf{MT}})$ - MT's public/private key pair.

Trusted Launch Phase: In this phase, $\mathcal{V}$ wishes to launch a TEE on the untrusted platform. The TEE will be responsible for measuring the power consumption while $\mathcal{P}$ executes applications of $\mathcal{V}$'s choice. To facilitate $\mathcal{V}$, we assume the existence of a setup function F_s, responsible for setting up the TEE[1]. Finally, we further assume that the setup function F_s is publicly known.

This phase commences with the verifier $\mathcal{V}$ generating a random number r_1 and sending $m_1 = \langle r_1, A \rangle$ to $\mathcal{P}$, where A is the unique identifier of the application that $\mathcal{V}$ wishes to execute on the TEE. Moreover, $\mathcal{V}$ captures the current time t_1. Upon reception, $\mathcal{P}$ calculates checksum(r_1, F_s), and gets the result res. After the successful execution of F_s, a new TEE is launched on the untrusted platform. Upon its creation, the TEE also obtains a public/private key pair $(\mathsf{pk}_{\mathsf{TEE}}, \mathsf{sk}_{\mathsf{TEE}})$ (sealing/unsealing keys). The result of the checksum will be then sent back to $\mathcal{V}$ along with the launched TEE's public key. More precisely, $\mathcal{P}$ sends the following message to $\mathcal{V}$: $m_2 = \langle r_2, \mathsf{Enc}_{\mathsf{pk}_\mathcal{V}}(\mathcal{P}, \mathsf{res}, \mathsf{pk}_{\mathsf{TEE}}), \sigma_\mathcal{P}(H_1) \rangle$, where $H_1 = H(r_2 || \mathcal{P} || \mathsf{res} || \mathsf{pk}_{\mathsf{TEE}})$. Upon reception, $\mathcal{V}$ captures the time t_2 and calculates $\Delta t = t_2 - t_1$ (possible because $\mathcal{V}$ also knows the function F_s). If Δt is as expected, then $\mathcal{V}$ knows that there is a TEE residing on the untrusted platform. Figure 3 illustrates this phase.

---

[1] The specifications of F_s will be TEE-dependent. However, it must be designed in such a way that any manipulation will create a noticeable time increase in the computation of the checksum.

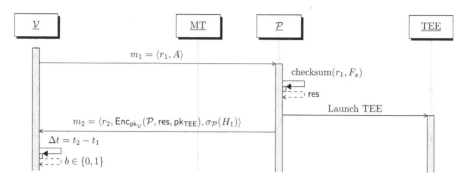

Fig. 3. Trusted launch phase.

Computations Phase: After the successful execution of the Trusted Launch Phase, $\mathcal{V}$ is convinced that a newly launched TEE is residing on the untrusted platform. $\mathcal{V}$ wishes to run an executable application A on the untrusted part of $\mathcal{P}$. To ensure that the results will be accurate, $\mathcal{V}$ first decides the number of required traces. This decision depends on the statistical results described later (Sect. 5). After deciding the number of runs n, $\mathcal{V}$ initiates the protocol. To this end, $\mathcal{V}$ first generates a token τ and a fresh random number r_3, and contacts $\mathcal{P}$ by sending $m_3 = \langle r_3, n, \tau, A, \sigma_{\mathcal{V}}(H_2)\rangle$, where $H_2 = H(r_3||\tau||A||n)$ and A is the unique identifier of the application that $\mathcal{V}$ wishes to execute on $\mathcal{P}$. Upon reception, $\mathcal{P}$ starts running application A n times with τ as input, and produces an output out, and a fingerprint $H(\tau, A)$. Simultaneously, the TEE measures the power consumption of the untrusted part of $\mathcal{P}$ to get a sequence of traces $\{tr\}_{i=1}^{n}$ (one for each execution of A). As soon as $\mathcal{P}$ outputs out, it sends an acknowledgement ack to the TEE. Upon reception, the TEE will reply to $\mathcal{P}$ with $m_4 = \langle r_4, \mathsf{Enc}_{pk_{\mathcal{V}}}(\{tr\}_{i=1}^{n}), \sigma_{TEE}(H_3)\rangle$, where $H_3 = H(r_4||tr_1||\ldots||tr_n)$. $\mathcal{P}$ will finally send $m_5 = \langle r_5, m_4, H(\tau, A), \mathsf{out}, \sigma_{\mathcal{P}}(H_4)\rangle$, where $H_4 = H(r_5||m_4||\mathsf{out})$. Upon receiving m_5, $\mathcal{V}$ verifies the signatures of the TEE and $\mathcal{P}$, and the freshness of both m_4 and m_5 messages. After the first successful execution of the protocol, $\mathcal{V}$ commences a fresh run, until she gathers all the required traces. When $\mathcal{V}$ gets the desired number of traces, she generates $m_6 = \langle r_6, \mathsf{Enc}_{pk_{MT}}(\tau, \mathsf{out}, A, \{tr_i\}_{i=1}^{n}), \sigma_{\mathcal{V}}(H_3)\rangle$, where $H_3 = H(r_6||\tau||A||\mathsf{out}||\{tr_i\}_{i=1}^{n})$ and sends it to MT. MT can then check the trust level of $\mathcal{P}$ by comparing out and each tr_i against its pre-computed list of measurements. Finally, MT outputs a bit $b \in \{0, 1\}$ and sends $m_7 = \langle r_7, \mathsf{Enc}_{pk_{\mathcal{V}}}(b), \sigma_{MT}(H_4)\rangle$, where $H_4 = H(r_7||b)$ to $\mathcal{V}$. Figure 4 depicts the Computations Phase.

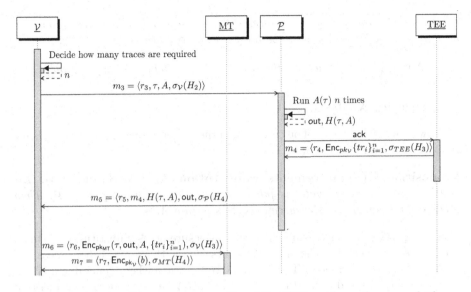

Fig. 4. Computations Phase: we assume $\mathcal{P}$ and the TEE reside on the same platform.

4.3   Threat Model

Our threat model is based on the Dolev-Yao adversarial model [7]. Furthermore, we assume that $\mathcal{ADV}$ can load programs of her choice in the enclaves and observe their output. This assumption significantly strengthens $\mathcal{ADV}$ since we need to ensure that such an attack will not be detectable from $\mathcal{V}$'s point of view. Finally, we extend the above threat model by defining a set of attacks available to $\mathcal{ADV}$.

Attack 1 (Measurements Substitution Attack). *Let $\mathcal{ADV}$ be an adversary that has full control of the untrusted part of $\mathcal{P}$. $\mathcal{ADV}$ successfully launches a Measurements Substitution Attack if she manages to substitute the measurements received from TEE by some others of her choice, in a way that is indistinguishable for $\mathcal{V}$.*

Attack 2 (False Result Attack). *Let $\mathcal{ADV}$ be an adversary that overhears the communication between $\mathcal{V}$ and MT. $\mathcal{ADV}$ successfully launches a False Result Attack if she can tamper with the response sent from MT to $\mathcal{V}$.*

While the first two attacks target directly the protocol communication, we also define a third attack that aims at targeting a false positive (FP) case, analyzed further in Sect. 5. An adversary could exploit the FP by substituting $\mathcal{V}$'s application with another of her choice. The resulting trace, even if it comes from a different application, could still pass as valid by $\mathcal{V}$.

Attack 3 (Application Substitution Attack). *Let $\mathcal{ADV}$ be an adversary that overhears the communication between $\mathcal{V}$ and $\mathcal{P}$. $\mathcal{ADV}$ successfully launches an Application Substitution Attack if she manages to replace the trace that $\mathcal{V}$ is* *expecting with another of her choice, with non-negligible advantage, where the advantage of $\mathcal{ADV}$ is defined to be the following conditional probability:*

$$\text{Adv}_{\mathcal{ADV}} = Pr[\mathcal{V} \text{ accepts the trace} \mid \mathcal{ADV} \text{ switched the application}]$$

4.4 Security Analysis

We now prove the security of our protocol in the presence of a malicious adversary $\mathcal{ADV}$ as defined in Sect. 4.3.

Proposition 1 (Measurements Substitution Attack Soundness). *Let $\mathcal{ADV}$ be an adversary that has full control of the untrusted part of $\mathcal{P}$. Then $\mathcal{ADV}$ cannot perform a Measurements Substitution Attack.*

Proof. For $\mathcal{ADV}$ to successfully launch a Measurements Substitution Attack, she needs to replace the measurements μ, with some other measurements μ' of her choice. To do so, $\mathcal{ADV}$ can either generate a fresh μ', or replay an old one. In both cases, $\mathcal{ADV}$ must generate a message $m_5 = \langle r, m_4, H(\tau, A), \text{out}, \sigma_{\mathcal{P}}(H(r||m_4||\text{out})) \rangle$. It is clear from the message structure, that the only component that $\mathcal{P}$ cannot forge, is the message m_4 included in m_5. As m_4 is signed by the TEE, and given the EUF-CMA security of the signature scheme, $\mathcal{ADV}$ can only forge the TEE's signature with negligible probability. Hence, the only alternative for $\mathcal{ADV}$ is to use an older m_4 message that she received from the TEE sometime in the past. Let $m_{4_{old}}$ be the old m_4 message such that $m_{4_{old}} = \langle r_{4_{old}}, \text{Enc}_{pk_{\mathcal{V}}}(\mu), \sigma_{TEE}(H_3) \rangle$, where $H_3 = H(r_{4_{old}}||\mu')$. While this approach solves the problem of forging TEE's signature, $\mathcal{ADV}$ now needs to further tamper with this message by replacing $r_{4_{old}}$, with a fresh random number. This is important because otherwise, $\mathcal{V}$ will not be able to verify the freshness of the message, and will thus abort the protocol. However, $r_{4_{old}}$ is included in the signed hash of the TEE, and given the second preimage resistance of the hash function H we have that $H(r, \mu') \neq H(r', \mu') \; \forall r, r'$ such that $r \neq r'$. Hence, $\mathcal{V}$ realizes that something is wrong and aborts the protocol.

Proposition 2 (False Result Attack Soundness). *Let $\mathcal{ADV}$ be a malicious adversary that overhears the communication between $\mathcal{V}$ and MT. Then $\mathcal{ADV}$ cannot successfully perform a False Result Attack.*

Proof. For $\mathcal{ADV}$ to launch a False Result Attack, she needs to forge the message m_6 sent by MT to $\mathcal{V}$ in a way that $\mathcal{V}$ will not be able to distinguish any difference. To do so, $\mathcal{ADV}$ has two choices: (i) substitute the encrypted bit, with a bit of her choice; (ii) replay an older message.

Substituting the encrypted result is feasible since $\mathcal{V}$'s public key is publicly known. Hence, it is straightforward for $\mathcal{ADV}$ to encrypt a bit under $pk_{\mathcal{V}}$ and replace it with the actual encrypted result. However, since the encrypted bit is also included in the signed hash, $\mathcal{V}$ will be able to ascertain that the integrity of the message has been violated. Thereupon, for $\mathcal{ADV}$ to successfully substitute the encrypted bit, she needs to also forge the MT's signature. Given the EUF-CMA security of the signature scheme, this can only happen with negligible probability and so, the attack fails.

Insomuch as $\mathcal{ADV}$ overhears the communication between $\mathcal{V}$ and MT, she has knowledge of the random numbers used to ensure the freshness of the messages. On that account, $\mathcal{ADV}$ could try to forward to $\mathcal{V}$ an older m_7 message, with a fresh random number. However, just like in the previous case, the random number is also included in the signed hash, and consequently $\mathcal{ADV}$ would once again have to forge the MT's signature, which can only happen with negligible probability.

The above proofs support our claim that in both cases the attack can only succeed with negligible probability. As a result, $\mathcal{ADV}$ cannot successfully launch a False Result Attack.

Proposition 3. *Let n be the total number of traces captured to perform an attestation process. Let p_α be the probability of an attacker obtaining a success result with a single trace derived from another operation, and p_β the honest user success probability, using a single trace coming from the appropriate operation. Assuming that $p_\beta > p_\alpha$, there exists a threshold number of traces, x_{th}, required to pass the attestation process, for which $P(\alpha) = 0$ and $P(\beta) = 1$, using a sufficiently large number n of traces.*

Proof. Let $\{X_i\}$ be a succession of independent random variables that take one of two different results:

$$X_i = \begin{cases} 0, & \text{do not pass the attestation process} \\ 1, & \text{pass the attestation process} \end{cases}$$

Let $x = \sum_{i=1}^{n} X_i$ be the number of times we pass the attestation process. We know, by the strong law of large numbers (SLLN) that:

$$P(\lim_{n \to \infty} \frac{\sum_{i=1}^{n} X_i}{n} = E(X_i)) = 1 \tag{1}$$

where $E(X_i)$ is the expected value of variable X_i. From the binomial distribution formula:

$$P(x) = \binom{n}{x} \cdot p^x \cdot (1-p)^{n-x} \tag{2}$$

Leveraging that, in the binomial distribution, the expected value $E(X_i)$ of a variable matches with its probability p. We can substitute in Eq. 1, yielding:

$$P(\lim_{n \to \infty} \frac{\sum_{i=1}^{n} X_i}{n} = p) = 1 \Rightarrow P(\lim_{n \to \infty} \frac{x}{n} = p) = 1$$

Let us consider now the two different cases of p_α and p_β. For a sufficiently large n, we get that:[2]

---

[2] Notice that "almost surely" is a concept used in probability theory to describe events that occur with probability 1 when the sample space is an infinite set.

$$P(\lim_{n \to \infty} \frac{x_\alpha}{n} = p_\alpha) = 1 \Rightarrow \lim_{n \to \infty} \frac{x_\alpha}{n} = p_\alpha \text{ almost surely}^4 \qquad (3)$$

$$P(\lim_{n \to \infty} \frac{x_\beta}{n} = p_\beta) = 1 \Rightarrow \lim_{n \to \infty} \frac{x_\beta}{n} = p_\beta \text{ almost surely} \qquad (4)$$

Since $p_\beta > p_\alpha$ by assumption (an essential condition to perform a solid attestation), we can select x_{th} defined as the threshold number of traces such that $p_\alpha < \frac{x_{th}}{n} < p_\beta$ for which we need a number $\frac{x}{n} \geq \frac{x_{th}}{n}$ to have a positive result of the attestation process. Then, from Eq. 3 and the fact that $p_\alpha < \frac{x_{th}}{n}$ by definition, we get:

$$P(\alpha) = P(\lim_{n \to \infty} \frac{x_\alpha}{n} \geq \frac{x_{th}}{n}) = 0$$

Analogously, from Eq. 4 and the fact that $p_\beta > \frac{x_{th}}{n}$ by definition, we get:

$$P(\beta) = P(\lim_{n \to \infty} \frac{x_\beta}{n} \geq \frac{x_{th}}{n}) = 1$$

5   Evaluation

With the previous sections explaining how we capture the traces from the ADC and how we establish security between the prover and the verifier system, we are in a position to explain our experiments. We open with a description of our analysis framework, including empirical evaluation (Sect. 5.1). We then close with a security analysis of the different framework parameters (Sect. 5.2), guiding selection when instantiating the Sect. 4 protocols.

5.1   Methodology

Our procedure consists of (i) selecting the traces generated by the ADC that belong to a given program; (ii) generating a template by averaging a large number of traces; and (iii) comparing this template to different traces, some that belong and some that do not to the same given program. Our methodology uses profiling both to build the templates and calculate the correlation threshold that operations should surpass to complete the attestation, both which vary across binaries (see Table 2). As an alternative, non-profiled approaches could be an interesting research direction to potentially improve scalability and agility. We utilize the Pearson correlation for our comparison metric. These, ultimately, will lead to statistics about the true positive (TP), true negative (TN), false negative (FN), and false positive (FP) rates that will allow us to make a concrete analysis concerning the suitability of the traces retrieved by a given sensor or peripheral to perform attestation. From this data, we obtain the following parameters, which are typical in information classification, that give an idea of the accuracy and relevance of our experiments.

$$Precision = \frac{TP}{TP + FP} \qquad Recall = \frac{TP}{TP + FN} \qquad F1 = 2 \cdot \frac{Recall \cdot Precision}{Recall + Precision}$$

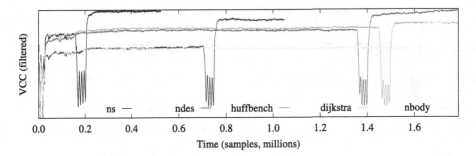

Fig. 5. Several templates selected, with different number of samples.

This way, precision gives a measure of the number of correct results among all the returned results, while recall gives a measure of the number of correct results divided by the number of results that should have been returned. This means that a low result of precision implies that a high number of incorrect results are considered as correct, so our system would be yielding many FP. On the other hand, a low recall implies that we are not considering as correct some results that indeed are correct, leading then, to a high number of FN. Finally, F1 is the harmonic mean between recall and precision, and allows us to give an idea of how good our system is at retrieving results with one single measurement.

Specifically, we utilize the executables in the Bristol Energy Efficiency Benchmark Suite (BEEBS) [23, 24], providing a broad spectrum of programs[3] to profile w.r.t. our methodology. We execute the BEEBS programs and capture their traces from the ADC in order to perform attestation by comparing each trace with templates previously obtained for the other BEEBS programs. The aim is that a trace coming from a certain program only matches (leading to a high correlation value) with the template belonging to its own program and does not match (yielding a low correlation value) with other programs' templates.

To accomplish this, we first capture 1000 traces from each program and generate templates from them. Then, we apply a Savitzky-Golay filter to obtain the final template. Figure 5 depicts the final template of five BEEBS programs, where the trigger operations determine each program operation area (see Fig. 2). It is important to notice that the amplitude shift in the traces is not a reliable differentiator, since it depends on the moment the traces are taken.

One observation from Fig. 5 is that the templates associated to each program take different times, translated into different number of samples, to complete their execution. The program will be running while the ADC is capturing samples between the start and the ending trigger. The rest of the trace after the end trigger is simply noise. Our ADC captures 2^{21} samples for every trace and template, but in order to perform the correlations, each program and its template are separated into different groups according to their lengths ranging from 2^{17} to 2^{21} samples. This way, depending on the length of the different templates, we

---

[3] https://github.com/mageec/beebs.

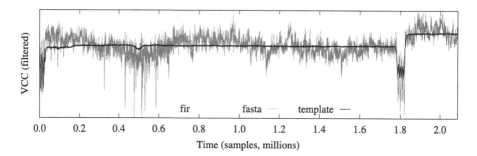

Fig. 6. Matching of the fasta template (black) with two different traces (fasta, fir).

keep the execution part from the traces and templates by selecting a number of samples between 2^{17} to 2^{21} samples, trying to catch the relevant information from said execution. Since the rest of the trace, once the program is executed and finished, is simply noise, we discard it.

After computing all the templates, our experiment consists of capturing 1000 traces for every program and comparing them against their own template. To achieve this, we compute the Pearson correlation between every trace of the program selected and its template. We store this in a correlation vector $corr_{vector} = (corr_1, corr_2, ..., corr_{1000})$, then the components of $corr_{vector}$ are ordered from smallest to largest, in order to compute the 25th percentile. This is to say, we compute a threshold value $corr_{thres}$ from which 750 components of the vector are above it. In practical terms, this means that during the matching stage, a trace that has a correlation value above the threshold will be considered as representative of an honest execution from a certain program, while a trace with a correlation value lower than this threshold cannot certify that the trace belongs to the program related to the template. This matching stage, in practical terms, works as a training set for our correlation system where we select a threshold value that let pass the 75% of the traces from that matching set. When we move to the evaluation stage, the threshold value is the one that we previously selected, but it does not need to pass exactly the 75% of the traces, since the traces from the evaluation stage are not the same as the one from the matching stage. Nonetheless, it should yield a similar ratio of traces that pass the attestation. This way, we ensure that the threshold admits a sufficient number of traces, without allowing a large number coming from other operations. In Fig. 6, it is visible to the naked-eye how a correct trace matches with its template, against a trace that does not belong to the program according to the used template.

After this, we select a template and compute correlations for all the BEEBS executables, with a set of 1000 traces from each program. If traces that do not belong to the program being checked match with the corresponding template, having a correlation value higher than the threshold, we will have a FP. On the contrary, if a trace that belongs to this program does not match with its own template, having a correlation value lower than the threshold, we will have a FN. From these statistics, we compute recall, precision, and F1 score as previously defined. To obtain those statistics, we first trim the traces to have the same number of samples than the template used in each case, in order to be able to compute the Pearson correlation value between the traces and the given template. Figure 7 illustrates the whole process, repeated for the templates obtained from each program. We verified that this process can be carried out even if the templates are generated from a set of data from a given board of a certain model, and the evaluation stage where we compute the correlation of the traces with the templates previously generated are captured from a different board of the same model. This characteristic demonstrates the robustness of our attestation protocol, and its utility in systems where we can have pre-loaded templates for given binaries coming from different devices.

We present the complete statistics in Table 2. It includes the correlation threshold value for each program, the name of the program that yields the highest FP rate, the absolute number out of the 1000 traces that provides a correlation value higher than the threshold (leading to FP), recall, precision, and F1 score metrics. From Table 2, we can see that out of 47 programs, 35 have a precision above 0.90 and 42 above 0.80, while 27 programs have a recall above 0.70 and 44 above 0.60. Thus, our method correctly distinguishes positive results among the total number of traces, having in general a low FPR, and leading to excellent precision values. On the contrary, the recall results are lackluster, meaning that a significant portion of correct results are not retrieved by our system, leading to an improvable FN rate (FNR).

Another concern is the fact that out of 1000 traces, in the worst FP case scenario from a specific benchmark, 82 traces from ndes program are considered as correct results by the nettle-aes template, leading to a FPR of 8.2% from that specific operation. This means that traces coming from a given operation are likely useful to attest others. The consequences, at this point, are clear. To have said 8.2% of FP results, would lead to an inadmissible number of incorrect traces passing the attestation process. This is especially worrying, taking into account that the recall (which is equivalent to TPR, the TP rate) is 69%. With these results, each time we want to use this attestation process, we have roughly a 3/10 probability of failing even if the computations are carried out properly, and around a 1/12 probability of having a correct result in cases where the retrieved trace matches with the template, even if it does not belong to the correct program. This is far from the aimed numbers to perform solid attestation using our proposal.

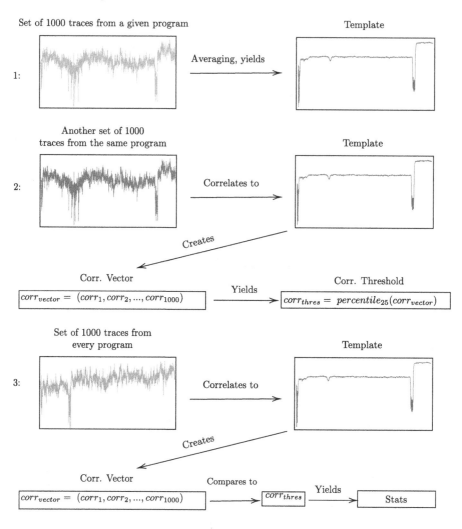

Fig. 7. Process repeated with every template to obtain statistics.

5.2 Parameterization

To overcome these deficiencies, we can use several traces to perform the attestation. We aim to improve these numbers by requiring that out of n traces, a minimum number x_{th} must be above the threshold correlation value. Proposition 3 presents the general case, but now we must assign discrete values to the various parameters.

For our case, and to obtain a good trade-off between the probabilities of having FPs that pass the attestation, and having FNs that are not able to pass even if they belong to the correct template, we consider the following threshold.

It is the midpoint of p_α and p_β, recalling those parameters from Proposition 3.

$$x_{th}, n \in \mathbb{N} : x_{th} = \left\lceil n \cdot \frac{p_\alpha + p_\beta}{2} \right\rceil \land p_\alpha < \frac{x_{th}}{n} < p_\beta$$

It is important to notice that each user can freely select this threshold number of traces by, for example, giving different weights to p_α and p_β or selecting a totally different relation. As previously indicated, we select this threshold to have a good trade-off between an attacker trying to cheat the attestation process with a trace coming from another operation and an honest user.

Table 1. Parameter variations to achieve different security levels.

Security level	n	x_{th}	$P(\alpha)$	$P(\beta)$
32-bit	52	21	$2.39 \cdot 10^{-10} \approx 2^{-32}$	$1 - 5.43 \cdot 10^{-6} \approx 1 - 2^{-17}$
64-bit	114	45	$5.18 \cdot 10^{-20} \approx 2^{-64}$	$1 - 2.22 \cdot 10^{-11} \approx 1 - 2^{-35}$
128-bit	243	94	$3.72 \cdot 10^{-39} \approx 2^{-128}$	$1 - 6.27 \cdot 10^{-23} \approx 1 - 2^{-74}$
256-bit	494	191	$9.83 \cdot 10^{-78} \approx 2^{-256}$	$1 - 4.14 \cdot 10^{-44} \approx 1 - 2^{-144}$

Moreover, the user determines the security level by selecting an appropriate number of total traces n. Here, we understand the security level as a measure of the probability of passing the attestation protocol using traces coming from a different operation, given the number of traces required to be above the correlation threshold and the total number of traces n. Larger values of n tend to minimize the FP probabilities and increase the corresponding TP probabilities (thus, reducing also FNs). For our worst FP scenario coming from a specific benchmark, we have 82 traces out of 1000 coming from the ndes benchmark that yield FP results using the nettle-aes template. On the other hand, the TPR for nettle-aes is 0.69. In this case, we can identify the FPR from the ndes traces, with an attacker's probability to successfully cheat the attestation process of the nettle-aes operation, thus, $p_\alpha = 0.082$. Analogously, the TPR for nettle-aes is the success probability of an honest user, thus $p_\beta = 0.69$. Iterating, we found that for $n = 243$ traces, the threshold needed to pass the attestation is:

$$x_{th} = \left\lceil 243 \cdot \frac{0.69 + 0.082}{2} \right\rceil = 94$$

Combining our results for the obtained threshold with the binomial distribution (Eq. 2) for $n = 243$ and $p_\alpha = 0.082$, we get that the probability to cheat the attestation is:

$$P(\alpha) = P(x \geq 94) = P(94) + P(95) + ... + P(243) \text{ using } p_\alpha = 0.082$$

$$P(\alpha) = 3.72 \cdot 10^{-39} \approx \frac{1}{2^{128}} = 2.94 \cdot 10^{-39}$$

Table 2. Complete statistics for every BEEBS benchmark used.

Benchmark	$corr_{thres}$	Max. FP	Precision	Recall	F1
aha-compress	0.7248	crc32 (23)	0.9617	0.7540	0.8453
bs	0.7096	newlib-sqrt (37)	0.9135	0.7710	0.8362
bubblesort	0.5312	nbody (30)	0.8959	0.7490	0.8159
cnt	0.7112	frac (3)	0.9775	0.6950	0.8124
cover	0.7264	crc (35)	0.9122	0.5820	0.7106
crc32	0.7447	aha-compress (9)	0.9783	0.5410	0.6967
crc	0.7724	duff (4)	0.9947	0.7570	0.8597
ctl-stack	0.6795	sqrt (50)	0.6018	0.8070	0.6895
ctl-vector	0.7070	ns (10)	0.9868	0.8200	0.8957
cubic	0.7232	sqrt (1)	0.9987	0.7890	0.8816
dijkstra	0.5141	nettle-des (1)	0.9986	0.7020	0.8244
duff	0.7318	crc (44)	0.9481	0.8040	0.8701
fasta	0.4935	bs (12)	0.9374	0.7340	0.8233
fibcall	0.6551	newlib-log (73)	0.6986	0.7370	0.7173
fir	0.6268	none	1.0000	0.8010	0.8895
frac	0.7856	crc32, newlib-sqrt (2)	0.9880	0.7420	0.8475
huffbench	0.5608	newlib-log (14)	0.8525	0.6360	0.7285
janne_complex	0.4192	crc (19)	0.8014	0.6860	0.7392
jfdctint	0.7598	nettle-des (48)	0.9360	0.7020	0.8023
lcdnum	0.3827	cnt (38)	0.6283	0.7100	0.6667
levenshtein	0.5909	template (4)	0.9904	0.7250	0.8372
matmult-float	0.7009	none	1.0000	0.6520	0.7893
matmult-int	0.4645	several operations (2)	0.9804	0.7520	0.8511
mergesort	0.7296	sglib-hashtable (44)	0.9058	0.6730	0.7722
nbody	0.5610	bubblesort (30)	0.8066	0.7130	0.7569
ndes	0.6663	nettle-aes (80)	0.8638	0.6340	0.7313
nettle-aes	0.6318	ndes (82)	0.8903	0.6900	0.7775
nettle-des	0.7444	cover (21)	0.9613	0.7690	0.8545
newlib-log	0.5017	dijsktra (78)	0.6399	0.6290	0.6344
newlib-sqrt	0.5191	dijkstra (81)	0.4573	0.7170	0.5584
ns	0.7599	none	1.0000	0.7320	0.8453
nsichneu	0.7869	none	1.0000	0.7210	0.8379
picojpeg	0.6009	st (13)	0.9805	0.6540	0.7846
qrduino	0.5639	sglib-listsort (6)	0.9834	0.4740	0.6397
rijndael	0.6470	ndes (5)	0.9927	0.6800	0.8071
select	0.6120	template (27)	0.9415	0.7880	0.8579
sglib-arrayheapsort	0.6372	bs (2)	0.9912	0.6720	0.8010
sglib-arrayquicksort	0.7020	mergesort (11)	0.9807	0.7110	0.8244
sglib-hashtable	0.6919	mergesort (77)	0.8894	0.6350	0.7410
sglib-listinsertsort	0.6251	various (1)	0.9947	0.7540	0.8578
sglib-listsort	0.5108	qrduino (24)	0.9492	0.6540	0.7744
sqrt	0.5113	rijndael (2)	0.9923	0.6470	0.7833
st	0.5812	picojpeg (24)	0.9644	0.6770	0.7955
stb_perlin	0.6476	template (3)	0.9833	0.6460	0.7797
tarai	0.6927	wikisort (37)	0.9025	0.7500	0.8192
template	0.6654	select (19)	0.9487	0.6840	0.7949
wikisort	0.7092	sglib-listinsertsort (9)	0.9673	0.7090	0.8182

which is equivalent to a 128-bit security level. Using only 243 traces to complete the attestation process is a very promising result, especially since this is only a proof-of-concept of our novel attestation approach.

Considering the TPR, for $n = 243$ traces and $p_\beta = 0.69$, we get that:

$$P(\beta) = P(x \geq 94) = P(94) + P(95) + \ldots + P(243) \text{ using } p_\beta = 0.69$$

$$P(\beta) = 1 - 6.27 \cdot 10^{-23} \approx 1 - \frac{1}{2^{74}}$$

Thus, we achieve an (almost) perfect TPR with the selected number of traces. It is important to notice that these 243 traces are needed in our worst case scenario. Concretely, our worst case scenario is that in which a higher number of traces coming from a different operation passes the attestation process of another binary. For the rest of binaries, the security level achieved will be equal or better than this one. Table 1 show similar results about the number n of traces and the threshold x_{th} required to pass the attestation with various security levels for this worst case scenario.

Ideally, we would achieve a certain security level by isolating the minimum number n of traces and the x_{th} required to find a given $P(\alpha)$. However, this is not possible, since the inverse function of the binomial cumulative distribution does not exist. In other words, there is not an analytical form to find n starting from a given $P(x_{th} \geq x)$. That is the reason why we use the iteration approach, through readily-available numerical methods that are easily and fastly computed by any tool or programming language considering the equation from the binomial distribution.

6 Conclusion

The main contribution of this paper is the proposal of a new method to verify the integrity of a SoC, by natively capturing the side-channel leakage produced during the execution of a given operation. In our case, an ADC present in an FPGA adjacent to the AP carrying out the operation that aims to be verified is suitable to measure the voltage fluctuations caused by the execution itself. These voltage fluctuations are able to characterize the performed operation and to distinguish it from other binaries.

This attestation method does not rely on the request-to-response time, using instead the power signal generated by the program execution, which provides more detailed information about what its proper behavior should be. Additionally, our method does not require an external setup with physical proximity to capture the side-channel vector, rather native components. Thus, it implies no software or hardware overhead to the system, since it simply internally captures a power trace while carrying out executions in a normal operating mode.

To end, our attestation protocol completes the work. It describes not only how our system can capture the power leakage that allows us to characterize a given operation, but also how to manage the resultant power trace to, realistically, verify the integrity of an untrusted system. This achieves our main goal: checking that an untrusted system is executing programs honestly, without the presence of any malware. As far as we are aware, our work is the first constructive application of remote power analysis, identified as an open problem in [19].

Limitations and Future Work. Our proof-of-concept work exhibits a variety of limitations that should be addressed in future related studies. A brief summary follows. (i) TP rates are improvable, especially taking into account that our traces are fairly noisy. Nonetheless, using several power traces we are able to overwhelmingly detect honest users vs. attackers. (ii) Substitution attacks are a real threat, in case the ADC resolution is not sufficient to capture malicious modifications in the instructions from a binary. Future work includes exploring attacker strategies to modify binaries to produce power traces that pass attestation. (iii) The matching between traces and templates are mainly based in the duration of the executed operation, since we use the ending triggers as a distinctive mark in the power traces. However, the fact of using a whole power trace (vectorial data) instead of the classical request-to-response time (scalar data) hardens proxy attacks, because an attacker does not only need to solve a challenge in a given time, but to generate a power trace similar to the template, which is a difficult challenge. (iv) Consulting Fig. 1, a natural observation is that requiring a TEE for dynamic attestation seems paradoxical, in the sense that the target binary could simply be part of the TEE itself. However, a major goal of TEEs is reducing the Trusted Computing Base (TCB); keeping the target binaries outside the immediate TCB significantly narrows the attack surface.

Acknowledgments. (i) This project has received funding from the European Research Council (ERC) under the European Union's Horizon 2020 research and innovation programme (grant agreement No. 804476). (ii) This project has received funding by the ASCLEPIOS: Advanced Secure Cloud Encrypted Platform for Internationally Orchestrated Solutions in Healthcare Project No. 826093 EU research project. (iii) Supported in part by the Cybersecurity Research Award granted by the Technology Innovation Institute (TII). (iv) Supported in part by CSIC's i-LINK+ 2019 "Advancing in cybersecurity technologies" (Ref. LINKA20216). (v) The first author was financially supported in part by HPY Research Foundation. (vi) M. C. Martínez-Rodríguez holds a postdoc that is co-funded by European Social Fund (ESF) and the Andalusian government, through the Andalucia ESF Operational Programme 2014–2020.

References

1. Abera, T., et al.: C-FLAT: control-flow attestation for embedded systems software. In: ACM CCS, pp. 743–754. ACM (2016). https://doi.org/10.1145/2976749.2978358
2. Castelluccia, C., Francillon, A., Perito, D., Soriente, C.: On the difficulty of software-based attestation of embedded devices. In: ACM CCS, pp. 400–409. ACM (2009). https://doi.org/10.1145/1653662.1653711
3. Chen, B., Dong, X., Bai, G., Jauhar, S., Cheng, Y.: Secure and efficient software-based attestation for industrial control devices with ARM processors. In: ACSAC, pp. 425–436. ACM (2017). https://doi.org/10.1145/3134600.3134621

4. de Clercq, R., et al.: SOFIA: software and control flow integrity architecture. In: DATE, pp. 1172–1177. IEEE (2016). http://ieeexplore.ieee.org/document/7459489/

5. Coker, G., et al.: Principles of remote attestation. Int. J. Inf. Sec. **10**(2), 63–81 (2011). https://doi.org/10.1007/s10207-011-0124-7

6. Dessouky, G., et al.: LO-FAT: low-overhead control flow attestation in hardware. In: DAC, pp. 24:1–24:6. ACM (2017). https://doi.org/10.1145/3061639.3062276

7. Dolev, D., Yao, A.C.: On the security of public key protocols. IEEE Trans. Inf. Theory **29**(2), 198–207 (1983). https://doi.org/10.1109/TIT.1983.1056650

8. Gnad, D.R.E., Krautter, J., Tahoori, M.B.: Leaky noise: New side-channel attack vectors in mixed-signal IoT devices. IACR Trans. Cryptogr. Hardw. Embed. Syst. **2019**(3), 305–339 (2019). https://doi.org/10.13154/tches.v2019.i3.305-339

9. Gnad, D.R.E., Krautter, J., Tahoori, M.B., Schellenberg, F., Moradi, A.: Remote electrical-level security threats to multi-tenant FPGAs. IEEE Des. Test **37**(2), 111–119 (2020). https://doi.org/10.1109/MDAT.2020.2968248

10. Goldwasser, S., Micali, S., Rivest, R.L.: A digital signature scheme secure against adaptive chosen-message attacks. SIAM J. Comput. **17**(2), 281–308 (1988). https://doi.org/10.1137/0217017

11. Gravellier, J., Dutertre, J., Teglia, Y., Loubet-Moundi, P.: High-speed ring oscillator based sensors for remote side-channel attacks on FPGAs. In: ReConFig, pp. 1–8. IEEE (2019). https://doi.org/10.1109/ReConFig48160.2019.8994789

12. Gravellier, J., Dutertre, J., Teglia, Y., Loubet-Moundi, P., Olivier, F.: Remote side-channel attacks on heterogeneous SoC. In: CARDIS. LNCS, vol. 11833, pp. 109–125. Springer (2019). https://doi.org/10.1007/978-3-030-42068-0_7

13. Han, Y., Etigowni, S., Liu, H., Zonouz, S.A., Petropulu, A.P.: Watch me, but don't touch me! contactless control flow monitoring via electromagnetic emanations. In: ACM CCS, pp. 1095–1108. ACM (2017). https://doi.org/10.1145/3133956.3134081

14. Lee, D., Kohlbrenner, D., Shinde, S., Asanovic, K., Song, D.: Keystone: an open framework for architecting trusted execution environments. In: EuroSys, pp. 38:1–38:16. ACM (2020). https://doi.org/10.1145/3342195.3387532

15. Li, Y., McCune, J.M., Perrig, A.: VIPER: verifying the integrity of peripherals' firmware. In: ACM CCS, pp. 3–16. ACM (2011). https://doi.org/10.1145/2046707.2046711

16. Lipp, M., et al.: PLATYPUS: Software-based power side-channel attacks on x86. In: IEEE S&P, pp. 1080–1096. IEEE Computer Society (2021). https://doi.ieeecomputersociety.org/10.1109/SP40001.2021.00063

17. Lisovets, O., Knichel, D., Moos, T., Moradi, A.: Let's take it offline: boosting brute-force attacks on iPhone's user authentication through SCA. IACR Trans. Cryptogr. Hardw. Embed. Syst. **2021**(3), 496–519 (2021). https://doi.org/10.46586/tches.v2021.i3.496-519

18. Liu, H., Vasserman, E.Y.: Gray-box software integrity checking via side-channels. In: SecureComm. Lecture Notes of the Institute for Computer Sciences, Social Informatics and Telecommunications Engineering, vol. 238, pp. 3–23. Springer (2017). https://doi.org/10.1007/978-3-319-78813-5_1

19. Martínez-Rodríguez, M.C., Delgado-Lozano, I.M., Brumley, B.B.: SoK: remote power analysis. In: ARES, pp. 7:1–7:12. ACM (2021). https://doi.org/10.1145/3465481.3465773

20. Msgna, M., Markantonakis, K., Naccache, D., Mayes, K.: Verifying software integrity in embedded systems: a side channel approach. In: Prouff, E. (ed.) COSADE 2014. LNCS, vol. 8622, pp. 261–280. Springer, Cham (2014). https://doi.org/10.1007/978-3-319-10175-0_18

21. Nazari, A., Sehatbakhsh, N., Alam, M., Zajic, A.G., Prvulovic, M.: EDDIE: EM-based detection of deviations in program execution. In: ISCA, pp. 333–346. ACM (2017). https://doi.org/10.1145/3079856.3080223

22. O'Flynn, C., Dewar, A.: On-device power analysis across hardware security domains. IACR Trans. Cryptogr. Hardw. Embed. Syst. **2019**(4), 126–153 (2019). https://doi.org/10.13154/tches.v2019.i4.126-153

23. Pallister, J., Hollis, S.J., Bennett, J.: BEEBS: open benchmarks for energy measurements on embedded platforms. CoRR abs/1308.5174 (2013). arXiv: 1308.5174

24. Pallister, J., Hollis, S.J., Bennett, J.: Identifying compiler options to minimize energy consumption for embedded platforms. Comput. J. **58**(1), 95–109 (2015). https://doi.org/10.1093/comjnl/bxt129

25. Ramesh, C., et al.: FPGA side channel attacks without physical access. In: FCCM, pp. 45–52. IEEE Computer Society (2018). https://doi.org/10.1109/FCCM.2018.00016

26. Schellenberg, F., Gnad, D.R.E., Moradi, A., Tahoori, M.B.: An inside job: remote power analysis attacks on FPGAs. In: DATE, pp. 1111–1116. IEEE (2018). https://doi.org/10.23919/DATE.2018.8342177

27. Schellenberg, F., Gnad, D.R.E., Moradi, A., Tahoori, M.B.: Remote inter-chip power analysis side-channel attacks at board-level. In: ICCAD, p. 114. ACM (2018). https://doi.org/10.1145/3240765.3240841

28. Sehatbakhsh, N., Nazari, A., Khan, H.A., Zajic, A.G., Prvulovic, M.: EMMA: hardware/software attestation framework for embedded systems using electromagnetic signals. In: MICRO, pp. 983–995. ACM (2019). https://doi.org/10.1145/3352460.3358261

29. Seshadri, A., Luk, M., Perrig, A., van Doom, L., Khosla, P.K.: Pioneer: verifying code integrity and enforcing untampered code execution on legacy systems. In: Malware Detection, Advances in Information Security, vol. 27, pp. 253–289. Springer (2007). https://doi.org/10.1007/978-0-387-44599-1_12

30. Seshadri, A., Luk, M., Perrig, A., van Doorn, L., Khosla, P.K.: SCUBA: secure code update by attestation in sensor networks. In: WiSe, pp. 85–94. ACM (2006). https://doi.org/10.1145/1161289.1161306

31. Seshadri, A., Perrig, A., van Doorn, L., Khosla, P.K.: SWATT: software-based attestation for embedded devices. In: IEEE S&P, p. 272. IEEE Computer Society (2004). https://doi.org/10.1109/SECPRI.2004.1301329

32. Yang, S., Alaql, A., Hoque, T., Bhunia, S.: Runtime integrity verification in cyber-physical systems using side-channel fingerprint. In: ICCE, pp. 1–6. IEEE (2019). https://doi.org/10.1109/ICCE.2019.8662071

33. Zhao, M., Suh, G.E.: FPGA-based remote power side-channel attacks. In: IEEE S&P, pp. 229–244. IEEE Computer Society (2018). https://doi.org/10.1109/SP.2018.00049

How (not) to Achieve both Coercion Resistance and Cast as Intended Verifiability in Remote eVoting

Tamara Finogina[1], Javier Herranz[2(✉)], and Enrique Larraia[3]

[1] Scytl Election Technologies, Barcelona, Spain
tamara.finogina@scytl.com
[2] Departament de Matemàtiques, Universitat Politècnica de Catalunya,
Barcelona, Spain
javier.herranz@upc.edu
[3] nChain, Zug, Switzerland
e.larraia@nchain.com

Abstract. We consider the problem of achieving, at the same time, cast-as-intended verifiability and coercion resistance, in remote electronic voting systems where there are no secure channels through which voters can receive secret information/credentials before the voting phase.

We discuss why some simple solutions fail to achieve the two desired notions and we propose (a bit) more involved solutions that are satisfactory. Part of the discussion is closely related to the gap "full versus honest-verifier" when defining the zero-knowledge property of cryptographic zero-knowledge systems.

Keywords: Electronic voting · Coercion resistance · Cast as intended verifiability · Zero-knowledge systems

1 Introduction

Consider the following situation, very common in electronic voting. A voter interacts with a voting device VD (which may be a webpage or a voting terminal) to cast its intention m. The result of the interaction is typically a public-key encryption $C = \mathsf{Enc}_{\mathsf{pk}}(m; r)$ of the intention m, computed using randomness r. This ciphertext will be sent to the ballot box of the election, and then it will be decrypted (typically after a privacy-preserving operation, like shuffling). Suppose the voter does not trust the voting device (VD) performing the encryption. Casting a vote consists of two steps: (1) the voter sends its option m to VD, (2) VD prepares a ciphertext C and sends it to the ballot box. How can the voter be sure that C actually contains encryption of its choice m? If the system provides some way for the voter to be convinced, then it achieves the property of cast-as-intended verifiability (CAI, for short). One possibility is that the voter

E. Larraia—Work done while the author was at Scytl Election Technologies.

M. Conti et al. (Eds.): CANS 2021, LNCS 13099, pp. 483–491, 2021.
https://doi.org/10.1007/978-3-030-92548-2_25

obtains a proof that its vote has not been changed, that is that C is indeed correct encryption of m. This proof can be either human-verifiable (e.g. a choice return code, a tracking number, etc.) or require the help of a verification device (such a mobile phone, for instance, to run some mathematical/cryptographic computations). However, in both cases, the sole existence of such proof might open a door to intentional vote selling or coercion.

In this work we focus on the following scenario: there are no secure channels that allow voters to receive some secret information or credential, but each voter has a personal (trusted) device to run mathematical/cryptographic computations, in the voting phase. In such a scenario, is it possible to achieve the two properties, namely CAI verifiability and coercion resistance? The second one means a coercer cannot distinguish a (real) execution of the voting phase between the voter and VD with input m from a (simulated) execution of the voting phase with any other input m^*, possibly chosen by the coercer, even if the coercer forces the voter to use some specific (distribution of) values during the voting phase. Of course, this notion of coercion resistance (CR, for short) makes sense only if one assumes that the coercer cannot control the voter during the execution of the voting phase (otherwise, the coercer becomes the voter, and there is not much to do). Please note, that our informal definition of CR does not account for forced-abstention attacks (i.e. the coercer forces voter not to participate in the election), since their mitigation requires [9] anonymous voting channels, which are hard to achieve in practice.

Contributions and Organization of the Paper. After recalling some necessary cryptographic notions in Sect. 2, we discuss in Sect. 3 possible solutions to the CAI+CR problem that are not satisfactory. Then in Sect. 4 we present two solutions that are satisfactory. The gap between unsatisfactory and satisfactory solutions is closely related to the gap between the honest-verifier and full zero-knowledge property of cryptographic zero-knowledge systems. In particular, we show that a solution with one or two rounds of communication between the voter and the VD cannot be secure. The two solutions of Sect. 4 are generic and could be described for general binary relations, zero-knowledge systems, etc. However, for the sake of clarity and simplicity, we directly describe specific instantiations of the generic solutions, for the particular case where voting options m are encrypted using the ElGamal.

We want to stress that this (short) paper is intentionally written in a not-fully formalized way, without detailed definitions of the security notions and without security proofs at all. Our main goal here is to present the main conclusions of our study in a clear way, to the broadest possible (maybe non-cryptographic) audience. The missing details and formalization will be added in a future extended version of this (ongoing) work.

2   Cryptographic Preliminaries

2.1   ElGamal Public Key Encryption

ElGamal public key encryption scheme [5] works as follows:

- The key generation protocol takes as input a security parameter κ and generates a prime number q and a cyclic group $G = \langle g \rangle$ of order q. The secret key sk is chosen at random from $\mathbb{Z}_q$, the matching public key is $\mathsf{pk} = g^{sk}$.
- The encryption protocol takes as input a public key pk and a message $m \in G$; then a random value $r \in \mathbb{Z}_q$ is chosen, and the ciphertext $C = (c_1, c_2)$ is computed as $c_1 = g^r$ and $c_2 = m \cdot \mathsf{pk}^r$.
- The decryption protocol takes as input the secret key sk and a ciphertext $C = (c_1, c_2) \in G \times G$, and outputs $c_2 / c_1^{sk} = m$.

2.2   Zero-Knowledge Proof Systems

In a zero-knowledge interactive system, a prover P has some secret witness w of the fact that some public element x belongs to some language $\mathcal{L}_{\mathcal{R}}$, where $\mathcal{R} \subset \mathcal{W} \times \mathcal{X}$ is a binary relation and $\mathcal{L}_{\mathcal{R}} = \{x \in \mathcal{X} \mid \exists w \in \mathcal{W} \; s.t. (x, w) \in \mathcal{R}\}$. In an execution of the protocol, such a prover P and a verifier V interact by sending and receiving information through a number of rounds. At the end, the goal is that P convinces V of the fact that P knows a secret witness w such that $(x, w) \in \mathcal{R}$. Typically, three properties are required for such a protocol:

- **Completeness:** if both P and V are honest and $(x, w) \in \mathcal{R}$, then the verifier always accepts the proof as valid.
- **Soundness:** if P is dishonest and $(x, w) \notin \mathcal{R}$, then the verifier does not accept the proof as valid.
- **Zero-Knowledge:** the execution of the protocol does not leak any information about the secret witness w. This is formalized requiring, for every verifier V^*, the existence of a polynomial-time simulator M_{V^*} s.t. $\forall (x, w) \in \mathcal{R}$ the output $\langle P(x, w), V^*(x) \rangle$ is identically distributed to the output $\mathsf{M}_{V^*}(x)$.

If Zero-Knowledge holds for any possible verifier V^*, then we say the protocol achieves *full zero-knowledge*. However, if it only holds for verifiers V^* that correctly follow the prescribed steps of the protocol, then we say the protocol achieves *honest-verifier zero-knowledge*. A Σ-protocol is an example of an interactive system with honest-verifier zero-knowledge; it is a three-move protocol producing transcripts with the form (a, e, z), where the first message a is sent by the prover, e is a value chosen by the verifier uniformly and at random from a suitable challenge space, and z is the answer computed by the prover.

3   CAI+CR: Discussion of Some Unsatisfactory Solutions

Most e-voting systems are designed to provide CAI verifiability by outputting some proof, therefore it is assumed that a coercer is quite limited e.g. the voting or registration is done without a coercer's control, nor can he obtain private voter's data, credentials or impersonate the voter, etc. The only scheme that focuses on full coercion is Civitas [4], however, it does not deal with CAI as VD is assumed to be honest.

One of the simplest ways to provide CAI verifiability is via transferable proofs e.g. QR-codes that store encryption randomness, NIZK proof of encryption randomness knowledge, etc. However CR does not hold when voter is not trusted.

Another approach requires secure channels to deliver some secret information to a voter and assumes that the voter will not share it with anyone. For example, return-code based schemes pre-deliver voting cards with the mapping between choices and return codes to each voter. Similarly, the voter can receive tracking numbers, secret keys, voting cards with vote-codes, pre-computed ballots, etc. However, in the settings without secure channels, this strategy would not work.

It seems the only way to achieve both CAI and CR, without trusting voters to keep CAI proof private or using secure channels, requires interaction. Next we discuss why some strategies fail in providing both CAI and CR.

Solution U_1: Cast-or-Challenge. This technique [3] is used by Helios [2] and its derivatives to achieve the CAI property: the VD sends to the voter the randomness r that was used to produce the ciphertext $C = \mathsf{Enc}_{\mathsf{pk}}(m; r)$. The voter can then use another device to re-encrypt m with r and check that the result is C. This process is repeated a random number k of times, until for the $k+1$-th interaction the voter does not require the randomness and casts the ciphertext.

While this solution is quite popular and enjoys CR, however, it does not provide CAI strictly speaking, since the sent ballot is never audited. True, it gives some chance to detect VD misbehavior, but a malicious VD may guess the last verification attempt and cheat or prepare separate ballots for auditing and sending. Moreover, studies show that users do not understand this verification method and on average only 43% of users are able to verify their votes [1].

Solution U_2: Using Σ-Protocols. A different possibility (not explicitly proposed anywhere, as far as we know) is to consider an interactive Σ protocol between VD and the voter, to let VD convince the voter that C encrypts m.

Unfortunately, the zero-knowledge property of a Σ protocol is honest-verifier only; and in our application, the verifier (the voter) can be under control of a coercer. If the coercer forces the voter to choose the challenge e in a particular way, for instance as $e = \mathsf{Hash}(a)$, where a is the message voter sees before introducing the challenge, then the coercer can easily verify if the voter obeyed and voted for m^* or not. Note that for such e it is computationally infeasible to simulate a valid transcript (a', e', z') for a different voting option $m^* \neq m$ that satisfies the required distribution $e' = \mathsf{Hash}(a')$ (see for instance [10]), thus the voter must cast its vote for m^* in order to satisfy the coercer.

Solution U_3: Using OR-Proofs. There are CAI mechanisms proposed (implicitly or explicitly) in the literature [6,8], based on the idea of designated verification, that deal with the problem of coercion.

In the first round of the protocol, $\mathcal{V}$ generates an instance (public element and trapdoor witness) of a hard relation and sends to $\mathcal{P}$ the public element. For instance, if we consider the Discrete Logarithm relation, $\mathcal{V}$ chooses $x \in \mathbb{Z}_q$ at random, computes $y = g^x$ and sends y to $\mathcal{P}$. In the second round of the protocol, $\mathcal{P}$ computes a non-interactive zero-knowledge proof π for the language: "I know r such that $C = \mathsf{Enc}_{\mathsf{pk}}(m; r)$" OR "I know x such that $y = g^x$". Such a non-interactive (one-shot) proof can be computed by applying the Fiat-Shamir transformation to a Σ-protocol for the OR language above.

CAI verification holds because VD $= \mathcal{P}$ has no way of knowing the trapdoor x, while for CR the voter can use the knowledge of x to generate fake proofs for the coercer. However, CR approach heavily relies on the fact that an (honest) $\mathcal{V}$ actually knows the witness x as clearly stated in [6,8]. Unfortunately this assumption is false in a scenario with strong coercion: the coercer can generate the pair (x, y), give y to $\mathcal{V}$ and force it to run the above protocol with that specific public element y. Since $\mathcal{V}$ does not know x, it cannot simulate proofs and the only valid proof π it can show to the coercer will reveal its vote m.

3.1   On the Necessary Number of Rounds

We omit the rounds where the voter sends its voting option m to the VD and where VD publishes the ciphertext C. Our study starts at the point, where m and C are already known to both $\mathcal{V}$ and $\mathcal{P}$. In some particular protocols (like the ones that we will describe in Sect. 4), the exchange of m, C can be integrated with the rest of the interaction aimed at providing CR and CAI.

One Round is Not Enough. Let us imagine a one-round protocol: it consists of $\mathcal{P}$ sending a single message π to $\mathcal{V}$; for the CR property, it should be impossible for the coercer to distinguish (C, m, π) from (C, m^*, π^*). But the same holds for the voter, who has not participated in the protocol at all, which breaks the CAI property because the voter gets exactly the same conviction for any possible voting option.

Two Rounds are Not Enough. Essentially the same idea extends to CAI mechanisms with two rounds: $\mathcal{V}$ first sends some message a to $\mathcal{P}$, in the first round, and finally $\mathcal{P}$ replies with some message π, in the second round. A coercer may force $\mathcal{V}$ to use a specific $\hat{a}$ as the first message of the protocol, so that only transcripts $(\hat{a}, \pi)$ will be accepted by the coercer. In such a case, as in the previous situation with one round, CR property would imply that the protocol does not provide CAI: if the coercer cannot distinguish if $(m, C) \in \mathcal{L}_\mathcal{R}$ or if $(m^*, C) \in \mathcal{L}_\mathcal{R}$, due to the CR property, then the same holds for $\mathcal{V}$, which breaks the CAI (soundness) property. Here $\mathcal{L}_\mathcal{R} = \{(C, m) \mid C \text{ is an encryption of } m\}$ is the ElGamal language.

Therefore, at least three rounds of communication between $\mathcal{V}$ and $\mathcal{P}$ are needed in order to get both the CR and CAI properties. We have not been able to find a simple solution with three rounds of communication. In the next section we describe two solutions which, when implemented in the ElGamal ciphertext case, involve four rounds of communication.

4   CAI+CR: Two Solutions

We describe in this section two ways of achieving both CAI and CR in our considered setting for remote e-voting (without secure channels). For each of the solutions, we first describe it in a generic and informal way, and then we describe the protocol in detail for the particular case of ElGamal ciphertexts that we are considering as the illustrative example through all this paper.

Solution S_1: Committing to Challenges. The departing point for the solution S_1 is the unsatisfactory solution U_2 (using a Σ-protocol). The problem with solution U_2 was that a Σ-protocol is only honest-verifier zero-knowledge, which opens the door to coercions like the one described when discussing solution U_2. The solution is easy: use an interactive protocol for the ElGamal language $\mathcal{L}_\mathcal{R} = \{(C, m) \mid C \text{ is an encryption of } m\}$ which is full zero-knowledge, and not just honest-verifier zero-knowledge. A way of obtaining such a protocol is to use a well-known technique, described for example in [7]: the verifier $\mathcal{V}$ starts the protocol by committing to the challenge e that he will use later in the Σ-protocol. The prover $\mathcal{P}$ must check that the challenge e is a valid opening of the commitment previously received from $\mathcal{V}$.

There are different possibilities for the commitment scheme employed in this generic solution. For our detailed description in the ElGamal case, we will use Pedersen commitment scheme [11], which needs that an additional generator $h \in G = \langle g \rangle$ of the cyclic group G is published as part of the common public parameters of the election.

Detailed Protocol for ElGamal Ciphertexts. We assume both $\mathcal{P}$ and $\mathcal{V}$ already have access to values q, G, g, h such that $G = \langle g \rangle = \langle h \rangle$ has prime order q. The sending of m from $\mathcal{V}$ to $\mathcal{P}$ and of C from $\mathcal{P}$ to $\mathcal{V}$ can be integrated in the four rounds of the protocol, which works as follows:

1. $\mathcal{V}$ chooses $e, w \in \mathbb{Z}_q$ uniformly at random, computes the commitment $Z = g^e \cdot h^w$ and sends Z and the voting option m to $\mathcal{P}$.
2. $\mathcal{P}$ chooses $r, t \in \mathbb{Z}_q$ uniformly at random, computes $C = (c_1, c_2)$ where $c_1 = g^r$ and $c_2 = m \cdot \mathsf{pk}^r$, and also the pair $a = (A_1, A_2) = (g^t, \mathsf{pk}^t)$. The two pairs C and a are sent to $\mathcal{V}$.
3. $\mathcal{V}$ sends both e and w to $\mathcal{P}$.
4. $\mathcal{P}$ checks if $Z = g^e \cdot h^w$. If this is not the case, $\mathcal{P}$ aborts the protocol. Otherwise, $\mathcal{P}$ computes the value $z = t + e \cdot r \mod q$ and sends it to $\mathcal{V}$.

For the CAI property, the voter will be convinced if the two following equalities hold: $g^z = A_1 \cdot c_1^e$ and $\mathsf{pk}^z = A_2 \cdot \left(\frac{c_2}{m}\right)^e$.

For the CR property, since the value e must be committed before the pair a is obtained, the problem with unsatisfactory solution U_2 does not exist anymore: the only choices of the voter (or the coercer) are those of e, w in step 1. Even if the coercer requires some specific distribution for these two values, the voter can simulate a valid transcript (m^*, e, w, C, a, z) for the real ciphertext C and any option m^* (possibly selected by the coercer), by choosing e, w with the required distribution (by the coercer), then choosing $z \in \mathbb{Z}_q$ at random, computing $A_1 = g^z \cdot c_1^{-e}$ and $A_2 = \mathsf{pk}^z \cdot \left(\frac{c_2}{m^*}\right)^{-e}$ and finally defining $a = (A_1, A_2)$.

Observe that the above simulator also works for instances (m^*, C) not in the language (i.e. when C is not an encryption of m^*): the outputs of P and M are indistinguishable under the DDH assumption. This holds for any language $\mathcal{L} = \{(C, m) \mid C \text{ is an encryption of } m\}$ where the encryption scheme is IND-CPA secure.

Solution S_2: Augmented OR Proofs. The departing point for the solution S_2 is the unsatisfactory solution U_3: a non-interactive proof for the OR language "C is encryption of m OR I know x such that $y = g^x$". We had already discussed that this idea provides full CR as long as the voter $\mathcal{V}$ really knows the trapdoor x, and convinces the VD of this fact. This proof itself must be simulatable (a Σ-protocol), it cannot be a non-interactive (one-shot) proof; otherwise, the coercer could compute in advance the hard instance (x, y) along with a non-interactive proof of knowledge π_1 of x, and give to the voter just y, π_1, and not the trapdoor x (which would forbid the voter from simulating valid transcripts for coerced voting options).

Detailed Protocol for ElGamal Ciphertexts. We assume that both $\mathcal{P}$ and $\mathcal{V}$ have access to values q, G, g such that $G = \langle g \rangle$ has prime order q, and a secure hash function $H : \{0,1\}^* \to \mathbb{Z}_q$. The protocol works as follows:

1. $\mathcal{V}$ chooses the trapdoor $x \in \mathbb{Z}_q$ uniformly at random and computes the associated public element $y = g^x$ on the one hand. Then he chooses $t \in \mathbb{Z}_q$ uniformly at random and computes $a = g^t$ (first message of the Σ-protocol to prove knowledge of x) on the other hand. The voter $\mathcal{V}$ sends y, a and the voting option m to $\mathcal{P}$.
2. $\mathcal{P}$ chooses $r, e \in \mathbb{Z}_q$ uniformly at random, computes $C = (c_1, c_2)$ where $c_1 = g^r$ and $c_2 = m \cdot \mathsf{pk}^r$, and sends ciphertext C and the challenge e to $\mathcal{V}$.
3. $\mathcal{V}$ computes $z = t + x \cdot e \bmod q$ and sends z to $\mathcal{P}$.
4. $\mathcal{P}$ checks if $g^z = a \cdot y^e$. If this is not the case, $\mathcal{P}$ aborts the protocol. Otherwise, $\mathcal{P}$ computes a non-interactive zero-knowledge proof $\pi = (z_1, z_2, h_1, h_2)$ for the OR language, as follows
   - choose $w_1, z_2, h_2 \in \mathbb{Z}_q$ uniformly at random and compute $A_1 = g^{w_1}$, $A_2 = \mathsf{pk}^{w_1}$ and $Z_2 = g^{z_2} \cdot y^{-h_2}$,
   - compute the challenge as the hash value $h = H(C, y, A_1, A_2, Z_2)$,
   - compute $h_1 = h - h_2 \bmod q$ and $z_1 = w_1 + h_1 \cdot r \bmod q$.

For the CAI property, the voter $\mathcal{V}$ accepts the interaction as convincing if the OR proof π is valid; that is, if the following equality holds:

$$h_1 + h_2 \bmod q = H\left(C, y, \ g^{z_1} \cdot c_1^{-h_1}, \ \mathsf{pk}^{z_1} \cdot \left(\frac{c_2}{m}\right)^{-h_1}, \ g^{z_2} \cdot y^{-h_2}\right)$$

For the CR property, the only influence a coercer can have on the voter is in the distribution of the two values x and t of step 1. To simulate an execution of the protocol with the same ciphertext C but for a different voting option m^*, the voter chooses x and t with that distribution. Steps 2 and 3 are performed as in the real protocol. Finally, the voter can simulate the proof π for the OR language by using the knowledge of the trapdoor x, as follows:

- choose $z_1, w_2, h_1 \in \mathbb{Z}_q$ uniformly at random and compute $A_1 = g^{z_1} \cdot c_1^{-h_1}$, $A_2 = \mathsf{pk}^{z_1} \cdot \left(\frac{c_2}{m^*}\right)^{-h_1}$ and $Z_2 = g^{w_2}$,
- compute the challenge as the hash value $h = H(C, y, A_1, A_2, Z_2)$,
- compute $h_2 = h - h_1 \bmod q$ and $z_2 = w_2 + h_2 \cdot x \bmod q$.

5   Conclusion and Remaining Work

This short paper presents the main (positive and negative) results that we have obtained until now when studying the problem of achieving at the same time coercion resistance and cast as intended verifiability. We are currently working on the formalization of these two properties and the formal proof that our solutions in Sect. 4 satisfy them, as well as on post-quantum secure instantiations (based on lattices) of our solutions.

Acknowledgements. The work is partially supported by the Spanish *Ministerio de Ciencia e Innovación (MICINN)*, under Project PID2019-109379RB-I00.

References

1. Acemyan, C.Z., Kortum, P., Byrne, M.D., Wallach, D.S.: Usability of voter verifiable, end-to-end voting systems: baseline data for Helios, Prêt à Voter, and Scantegrity II. In: EVT/WOTE 14 Workshop, San Diego, CA, August 2014. USENIX Association (2014)
2. Adida, B.: Helios: web-based open-audit voting. In: Proceedings of the 17th USENIX Security Symposium, pp. 335–348 (2008)
3. Benaloh, J.: Ballot casting assurance via voter-initiated poll station auditing. In: USENIX/ACCURATE Electronic Voting Technology Workshop, EVT 2007 (2007)
4. Clarkson, M.R., Chong, S., Myers, A.C.: Civitas: toward a secure voting system. In: 2008 IEEE Symposium on Security and Privacy, S&P 2008, pp. 354–368 (2008)
5. El Gamal, T.: A public key cryptosystem and a signature scheme based on discrete logarithms. IEEE Trans. Inf. Theor. **31**(4), 469–472 (1985)
6. Guasch, S., Morillo, P.: How to challenge *and* cast your e-vote. In: Grossklags, J., Preneel, B. (eds.) FC 2016. LNCS, vol. 9603, pp. 130–145. Springer, Heidelberg (2017). https://doi.org/10.1007/978-3-662-54970-4_8

7. Hazay, C., Lindell, Y.: Efficient Secure Two-Party Protocols. Techniques and Constructions. ISC, Springer, Heidelberg (2010). https://doi.org/10.1007/978-3-642-14303-8

8. Jakobsson, M., Sako, K., Impagliazzo, R.: Designated verifier proofs and their applications. In: Maurer, U. (ed.) EUROCRYPT 1996. LNCS, vol. 1070, pp. 143–154. Springer, Heidelberg (1996). https://doi.org/10.1007/3-540-68339-9_13

9. Juels, A., Catalano, D., Jakobsson, M.: Coercion-resistant electronic elections. In: Chaum, D., et al. (eds.) Towards Trustworthy Elections. LNCS, vol. 6000, pp. 37–63. Springer, Heidelberg (2010). https://doi.org/10.1007/978-3-642-12980-3_2

10. Moran, T., Naor, M.: Receipt-free universally-verifiable voting with everlasting privacy. In: Dwork, C. (ed.) CRYPTO 2006. LNCS, vol. 4117, pp. 373–392. Springer, Heidelberg (2006). https://doi.org/10.1007/11818175_22

11. Pedersen, Torben Pryds: Non-interactive and information-theoretic secure verifiable secret sharing. In: Feigenbaum, Joan (ed.) CRYPTO 1991. LNCS, vol. 576, pp. 129–140. Springer, Heidelberg (1992). https://doi.org/10.1007/3-540-46766-1_9

Subversion-Resistant Quasi-adaptive NIZK and Applications to Modular Zk-SNARKs

Behzad Abdolmaleki[1]($\boxtimes$) and Daniel Slamanig[2]

[1] Max Planck Institute for Security and Privacy, Bochum, Germany
`behzad.abdolmaleki@csp.mpg.de`
[2] AIT Austrian Institute of Technology, Vienna, Austria
`daniel.slamanig@ait.ac.at`

Abstract. Quasi-adaptive non-interactive zero-knowledge (QA-NIZK) arguments are NIZK arguments where the common reference string (CRS) is allowed to depend on the language and they can be very efficient for specific languages. Thus, they are for instance used within the modular LegoSNARK toolbox by Campanelli *et al.* (ACM CCS'19) as succinct NIZKs (aka zkSNARKs) for linear subspace languages. Such modular frameworks are interesting, as they provide gadgets for a flexible design of privacy-preserving blockchain applications. Recently, there has been an increasing interest to reduce the trust required in the generator of the CRS. One important line of work in this direction is subversion zero-knowledge by Bellare *et al.* (ASIACRYPT'16), where the zero-knowledge property even holds when the CRS is generated maliciously.

In this paper, we firstly analyze the security of the most efficient QA-NIZK constructions of Kiltz and Wee (EUROCRYPT'15) and the asymmetric QA-NIZKs by González *et al.* (ASIACRYPT'15) when the CRS is subverted and propose subversion versions of them. Secondly, for the first time, we construct unbounded (strong) true-simulation extractable (tSE) variants of them. Thirdly, we show how to integrate our subversion QA-NIZKs into the LegoSNARK toolbox, which so far does not consider subversion resistance. Our results together with existing results on (SE) subversion zk-SNARKS represent an important step towards a subversion variant of the LegoSNARK toolbox.

1 Introduction

Zero-knowledge (ZK) proofs introduced by Goldwasser, Micali and Rackoff [23] are cryptographic protocols between two parties called the prover and the verifier with the purpose that the prover can convince the verifier of the validity of a statement in any language in NP without revealing additional information. Besides this zero-knowledge property, such a system needs to provide soundness, i.e., it must be infeasible for the prover to provide proofs for false statements. While ZK proofs, in general, may require many rounds of interaction, an interesting variant is non-interactive zero-knowledge (NIZK) proofs. They require only a

© Springer Nature Switzerland AG 2021
M. Conti et al. (Eds.): CANS 2021, LNCS 13099, pp. 492–512, 2021.
https://doi.org/10.1007/978-3-030-92548-2_26

single round, i.e., the prover outputs a proof, and this proof can then be verified by anybody. A long line of research [22,26,27,30,31,36,40] has led to efficient pairing-based succinct NIZKs called zero-knowledge Succinct Non-interactive ARguments of Knowledge (zk-SNARKs), which are NIZK arguments with i) a stronger notion of soundness called knowledge soundness and, more importantly, ii) in which proofs, as well as the computation of the verifier, are succinct, i.e., ideally a small constant amount of space and computation respectively. Due to these latter properties, zk-SNARKs are a suitable tool to preserve privacy within cryptocurrencies and distributed ledger technologies, most notably used within Zcash [45] and Ethereum [12], and they increasingly attract interest outside of academia.[1,2] In this paper, we are interested in quasi-adaptive NIZK (QA-NIZK) arguments [33]. These are NIZKs in which the common reference string (CRS) depends on a language parameter and they have many applications and have been intensively studied [1,6,7,9,17,21,24,33,35,37–39,44].

For practical applications of (QA-)NIZKs and zk-SNARKs, an important question is the generation of the CRS. While in theory it is simply assumed that some mutually trusted party will perform the CRS generation, in many real world settings (such as fully decentralized systems) there typically does not exist such a trusted party. Recently, there has been an increasing interest to reduce trust in the generator of the CRS. One of these lines of work is subversion zero-knowledge initiated by Bellare *et al.* in [10], where the zero-knowledge property even holds when the CRS is generated maliciously, i.e., the CRS generator is subverted. Following this initial work, Abdolmaleki *et al.* [2,4] as well as Fuchsbauer [19] investigated subversion zk-SNARKs. More recently, Abdolmaleki *et al.* (ALSZ) in [3] initiated the study of subversion zero-knowledge QA-NIZK (Sub-ZK QA-NIZK for short). While the latter is an important step, it leaves a number of open problems such as weakening the requires assumptions, stronger soundness guarantees and demonstrating impact for real-world applications.

Our Contribution. Our results can be summarized as follows.

Sub-ZK QA-NIZKs. We investigate the most efficient QA-NIZK constructions of Kiltz and Wee (KW) [37] and the asymmetric QA-NIZKs by González *et al.* (GHR) [24] in a subverted setup. We show that for KW we can construct Sub-ZK QA-NIZK arguments for the most efficient their argument Π'_{as} (which requires a witness samplable distribution [33]) by extending the CRS suitably. Thereby, compared to the recent Sub-ZK QA-NIZK based upon KW by ALSZ, we consider a variant where the CRS is subverted, but the language parameter is chosen honestly. We note that latter does not represent a problem for practical applications, as these parameters can typically be obtained in a transparent way such that no trusted setup is needed, e.g., by deriving them using a suitable hash function modelled as a random oracle. In contrast to ALSZ, which

---

[1] ZKProof (https://zkproof.org/) being the most notable industry and academic initiative towards a common framework and standards has been founded in 2018.

[2] Zero-knowledge proofs are *on the rise*, cf. https://www.gartner.com/en/documents/3947373/hype-cycle-for-privacy-2019.

relies on a new non-standard knowledge assumption for their subversion zero-knowledge property, our Sub-ZK QA-NIZK can be shown to have this property under the Bilinear Diffie-Hellman Knowledge of Exponents (BDH-KE) assumption [2,4] (being a simple case of the PKE assumption [16] or viewed differently an asymmetric-pairing version of the KoE assumption [15]). Moreover, we present a Sub-ZK QA-NIZK version of GHR by relying on the same BDH-KE assumption.

Simulation Extractability of Sub-ZK QA-NIZKs. We investigate the construction of Sub-ZK QA-NIZK that satisfies the stronger notions of knowledge soundness and in particular a weakened version of simulation extractability (SE) called true-simulation extractability (tSE) [32]. SE for QA-NIZK has to the best of our knowledge only been used in the independent concurrent work by Baghery et al. [9] in a non-subverted setting. We recall that a (QA-)NIZK is called unbounded SE if knowledge soundness holds even if the adversary is allowed to adaptively see an arbitrary number of simulated proofs (restricted to statements inside the language for tSE). The strong tSE notion of QA-NIZKs is important as, similarly to SE, it guarantees non-malleability of proofs thus prevents man-in-the-middle type of attacks, i.e., where an adversary takes a given proof and alters the proof or proven statement without having access to the full witness anyways. Our work is the first treatment of tSE Sub-ZK QA-NIZK and we present unbounded tSE Sub-ZK QA-NIZKs based on KW (also in the non-subversion setting).

Towards Subversion LegoSNARK. LegoSNARK [13] is a framework for Commit-and-Prove zk-SNARKs (CP-SNARKs) with the aim of constructing a "global" SNARK for some computation C via the linking of "smaller" specialized SNARKs for different subroutines that overall compose to C. The main idea is that by letting each subroutine of C be handled by a different proof system one can choose the one that maximizes a metric (e.g., efficiency) that is important for the concrete application. LegoSNARK uses a knowledge-sound version of the KW QA-NIZK (with succinct proofs) as the zk-SNARKs for linear subspace languages and in particular, they use a knowledge-sound version of the KW QA-NIZK Π'_{as}. We will show how to integrate subversion primitives into LegoSNARK. In particular, we show how to integrate our Sub-ZK QA-NIZKs instead of their non-subversion counterparts. Together with the results on subversion (SE) zk-SNARKs [2,5,8,19,28,41], we thus make an important step towards a complete subversion (SE) variant of the LegoSNARK framework.[3]

2   Preliminaries

Let $\lambda \in \mathbb{N}$ be the security parameter. By $y \leftarrow \mathcal{A}(x; \omega)$ we denote the fact that $\mathcal{A}$, given an input x and random coins ω, outputs y. By $x \leftarrow_\$ \mathcal{D}$ we denote that x is sampled according to distribution $\mathcal{D}$ or uniformly randomly if $\mathcal{D}$ is a set. Let

---

[3] We note that there are some tasks, such as fitting existing subversion (SE) zk-SNARKs into the commit-prove framework remaining that need to be worked out in detail. However, we do not expect that one faces significant problems there.

RND($\mathcal{A}$) denote the random tape of $\mathcal{A}$, and let $\omega \leftarrow\!\!\$\ \mathsf{RND}(\mathcal{A})$ denote the random choice of the random coins ω from $\mathsf{RND}(\mathcal{A})$. We denote by $\mathsf{negl}(\lambda)$ an arbitrary negligible function. We write $a \approx_\lambda b$ if $|a - b| \leq \mathsf{negl}(\lambda)$. For algorithms $\mathcal{A}$ and $\mathsf{Ext}_\mathcal{A}$, we write $(y\|y') \leftarrow (\mathcal{A}\|\mathsf{Ext}_\mathcal{A})(\cdot)$ as a shorthand for $y \leftarrow \mathcal{A}(\cdot)$ and $y' \leftarrow \mathsf{Ext}_\mathcal{A}(\cdot)$. Algorithm $\mathsf{Pgen}(1^\lambda)$ returns $\mathsf{BG} = (p, \mathbb{G}_1, \mathbb{G}_2, \mathbb{G}_T, \hat{e})$, where $\mathbb{G}_1$, $\mathbb{G}_2$, and $\mathbb{G}_T$ are three additive cyclic groups of prime order p, and $\hat{e} : \mathbb{G}_1 \times \mathbb{G}_2 \to \mathbb{G}_T$ is a non-degenerate efficiently computable bilinear map (pairing). We use the implicit bracket notation of [18], that is, we write $[a]_\iota$ to denote ag_ι where g_ι is a fixed generator of $\mathbb{G}_\iota$. We denote $\hat{e}([a]_1, [b]_2)$ as $[a]_1[b]_2$. Thus, $[a]_1[b]_2 = [ab]_T$. We denote $s[a]_\iota = [sa]_\iota$ for $s \in \mathbb{Z}_p$ and $S \cdot [a]_\iota = [Sa]_T$ for $S \in \mathbb{G}_{3-\iota}$ and $\iota \in \{1, 2\}$. We freely use the bracket notation together with matrix notation, e.g., if $\boldsymbol{XY} = \boldsymbol{Z}$ then $[\boldsymbol{X}]_1[\boldsymbol{Y}]_2 = [\boldsymbol{Z}]_T$. Furthermore in our figures, we will not explicitly provide return statements for P and Sim, but output all π elements.

Computational Assumptions. We require the following assumptions.

Definition 1 (BDH-KE Assumption [2,4]). *We say that* BDH-KE *holds relative to* K_0, *if for any PPT adversary* $\mathcal{A}$ *there exists a PPT extractor* $\mathsf{Ext}_\mathcal{A}^{\mathsf{BDH\text{-}KE}}$, *such that*

$$\Pr\left[\begin{array}{l}\mathsf{p} \leftarrow\!\!\$\ \mathsf{K}_0(1^\lambda); \omega_\mathcal{A} \leftarrow\!\!\$\ \mathsf{RND}(\mathcal{A}), \\ ([\alpha_1]_1, [\alpha_2]_2\|a) \leftarrow (\mathcal{A}\|\mathsf{Ext}_\mathcal{A}^{\mathsf{BDH\text{-}KE}})(\mathsf{p}, \omega_\mathcal{A})\end{array} : [\alpha_1]_1[1]_2 = [1]_1[\alpha_2]_2 \wedge a \neq \alpha_1\right] \approx_\lambda 0.$$

Where $\mathsf{aux}_\mathcal{R}$ is the auxiliary information related to the relation generator of $\mathcal{R}$. Note that the BDH-KE assumption can be considered as a simple case of the PKE assumption of [16]. Also, BDH-KE can be seen as an asymmetric-pairing version of the original KoE assumption [15].

In the following let $\mathcal{D}_k$ be a matrix distribution in $\mathbb{Z}_p^{(k+1) \times k}$.

Definition 2 ($\mathcal{D}_k$-Matrix Diffie-Hellman ($\mathcal{D}_k$-MDDH) Assumption [42]). *The* $\mathcal{D}_k$-MDDH *assumption for* $\iota \in \{1, 2\}$ *holds relative to* K_0, *if for any PPT adversary* $\mathcal{A}$, $|\mathsf{Exp}_\mathcal{A}^{\mathsf{MDDH}}(\mathsf{p}) - 1/2| \approx_\lambda 0$, *where* $\mathsf{Exp}_\mathcal{A}^{\mathsf{MDDH}}(\mathsf{p}) :=$

$$\Pr\left[\begin{array}{l}\mathsf{p} \leftarrow\!\!\$\ \mathsf{K}_0(1^\lambda); \boldsymbol{A} \leftarrow\!\!\$\ \mathcal{D}_k; \boldsymbol{v} \leftarrow\!\!\$\ \mathbb{Z}_p^k; \\ \boldsymbol{u} \leftarrow\!\!\$\ \mathbb{Z}_p^{k+1}; b \leftarrow\!\!\$\ \{0,1\}; \\ b^* \leftarrow \mathcal{A}(\mathsf{p}, [\boldsymbol{A}]_\iota, [b \cdot \boldsymbol{Av} + (1 - b) \cdot \boldsymbol{u}]_\iota)\end{array} : b = b^*\right].$$

Definition 3 ($\mathcal{D}_k$-KerMDH Assumption [42]). *The* $\mathcal{D}_k$-KerMDH *assumption for* $\iota \in \{1, 2\}$ *holds relative to* K_0, *if for any PPT* $\mathcal{A}$,

$$\Pr\left[\mathsf{p} \leftarrow \mathsf{K}_0(1^\lambda); \boldsymbol{A} \leftarrow\!\!\$\ \mathcal{D}_k; [\boldsymbol{s}]_{3-\iota} \leftarrow \mathcal{A}(\mathsf{p}, [\boldsymbol{A}]_\iota) : \boldsymbol{s} \neq \boldsymbol{0} \wedge \boldsymbol{A}^\top \boldsymbol{s} = \boldsymbol{0}_k\right] \approx_\lambda 0.$$

Note that as shown in [42], if $\mathcal{D}_k$-MDDH holds then $\mathcal{D}_k$-KerMDH holds.

Definition 4 ($\mathcal{D}_k$-SKerMDH Assumption [24]). *The* $\mathcal{D}_k$-SKerMDH *assumption holds relative to* K_0, *if for any PPT* $\mathcal{A}$,

$$\Pr\left[\begin{array}{l}\mathsf{p} \leftarrow \mathsf{K}_0(1^\lambda); \boldsymbol{A} \leftarrow\!\!\$\ \mathcal{D}_k; ([\boldsymbol{s}_1]_1, [\boldsymbol{s}_2]_2) \leftarrow \mathcal{A}(\mathsf{p}, [\boldsymbol{A}]_1, [\boldsymbol{A}]_2) : \\ \boldsymbol{s}_1 - \boldsymbol{s}_2 \neq \boldsymbol{0} \wedge \boldsymbol{A}^\top(\boldsymbol{s}_1 - \boldsymbol{s}_2) = \boldsymbol{0}_k\end{array}\right] \approx_\lambda 0.$$

Let $\mathcal{D}_{\ell k}$ be a probability distribution over matrices in $\mathbb{Z}_p^{\ell \times k}$, where $\ell > k$. Next, we define five commonly used distributions (see [18] for references), where $a, a_i, a_{ij} \leftarrow\!\!\$\, \mathbb{Z}_p^*$: $\mathcal{U}_k$ (uniform), $\mathcal{L}_k$ (linear), $\mathcal{IL}_k$ (incremental linear), $\mathcal{C}_k$ (cascade), $\mathcal{SC}_k$ (symmetric cascade):

$$\mathcal{U}_k : \mathbf{A} = \begin{pmatrix} a_{11} & \cdots & a_{1k} \\ \cdots & \cdots & \cdots \\ a_{k1} & \cdots & a_{kk} \\ a_{k+1,1} & \cdots & a_{k+1,k} \end{pmatrix}, \quad \mathcal{L}_k : \mathbf{A} = \begin{pmatrix} a_1 & 0 & \cdots & 0 & 0 \\ 0 & a_2 & \cdots & 0 & 0 \\ 0 & 0 & \cdots & 0 & 0 \\ \cdots & \cdots & \cdots & \cdots & \cdots \\ 0 & 0 & \cdots & 0 & a_k \\ 1 & 1 & \cdots & 1 & 1 \end{pmatrix},$$

$$\mathcal{IL}_k : \mathbf{A} = \begin{pmatrix} a & 0 & \cdots & 0 & 0 \\ 0 & a+1 & \cdots & 0 & 0 \\ 0 & 0 & \cdots & 0 & 0 \\ \cdots & \cdots & \cdots & \cdots & \cdots \\ 0 & 0 & \cdots & 0 & a+k-1 \\ 1 & 1 & \cdots & 1 & 1 \end{pmatrix}, \quad \mathcal{C}_k : \mathbf{A} = \begin{pmatrix} a_1 & 0 & \cdots & 0 & 0 \\ 1 & a_2 & \cdots & 0 & 0 \\ 0 & 1 & \cdots & 0 & 0 \\ \cdots & \cdots & \cdots & \cdots & \cdots \\ 0 & 0 & \cdots & 1 & a_k \\ 0 & 0 & \cdots & 0 & 1 \end{pmatrix},$$

$$\mathcal{SC}_k : \mathbf{A} = \begin{pmatrix} a & 0 & \cdots & 0 & 0 \\ 1 & a & \cdots & 0 & 0 \\ 0 & 1 & \cdots & 0 & 0 \\ \cdots & \cdots & \cdots & \cdots & \cdots \\ 0 & 0 & \cdots & 1 & a \\ 0 & 0 & \cdots & 0 & 1 \end{pmatrix}.$$

Assume that $\mathcal{D}_{\ell k}$ outputs matrices $\mathbf{A}$ where the upper $k \times k$ submatrix $\bar{\mathbf{A}}$ is always invertible, i.e., $\mathcal{D}_{\ell k}$ is robust [33]. All the above distributions can be made robust with minimal changes. Denote the lower $(\ell - k) \times k$ submatrix of $\mathbf{A}$ as $\underline{\mathbf{A}}$ and denote $\mathcal{D}_k = \mathcal{D}_{k+1,k}$.

Quasi-adaptive NIZK Arguments. We recall the definition of QA-NIZK arguments of Jutla and Roy [33]. A QA-NIZK argument provides a proof for membership of words x with according witnesses $\mathbf{w}$ in a language $\mathcal{L}_\varrho$ defined by a relation $\mathcal{R}_\varrho$ which is parametrized by some parameter ϱ chosen from a distribution $\mathcal{D}_p$. The distribution $\mathcal{D}_p$ is witness samplable if there exist an efficient algorithm that samples $(\varrho, \mathsf{tc}_\varrho)$ so that the parameter ϱ is distributed according to $\mathcal{D}_p$ and membership of the language parameter ϱ can be efficiently verified with tc_ϱ. The CRS of QA-NIZKs depends on a language parameter ϱ and as mentioned in [33], it has to be chosen from a correct distribution $\mathcal{D}_p$.

A tuple of PPT algorithms $\Pi = (\mathsf{Pgen}, \mathsf{P}, \mathsf{V}, \mathsf{Sim})$ is a QA-NIZK argument in the CRS model for a set of witness-relations $\mathcal{R}_p = \{\mathcal{R}_\varrho\}_{\varrho \in \mathsf{Supp}(\mathcal{D}_p)}$ with ϱ sampled from a distribution $\mathcal{D}_p$ over associated parameter language $\mathcal{L}_p$, if the following properties (i-iii) hold. Here, Pgen is the parameter and the CRS generation algorithm, more precisely, Pgen consists of two algorithms K_0 (generates the the parameter p) and K (generates the CRS), P is the prover, V is the verifier, and Sim is the simulator.

(i) **Completeness.** For any λ, and $(x, \mathbf{w}) \in \mathcal{R}_\varrho$,

$$\Pr\left[\begin{array}{l} \mathsf{p} \leftarrow \mathsf{K}_0(1^\lambda); \varrho \leftarrow\!\!\$\, \mathcal{D}_p; (\mathsf{crs}, \mathsf{tc}) \leftarrow \mathsf{K}(\varrho); \pi \leftarrow \mathsf{P}(\varrho, \mathsf{crs}, x, \mathbf{w}) : \\ \mathsf{V}(\varrho, \mathsf{crs}, x, \pi) = 1 \end{array} \right] = 1.$$

(ii) **Statistical Zero-Knowledge.** For any computationally unbounded adversary $\mathcal{A}$, $|\varepsilon_0^{zk} - \varepsilon_1^{zk}| \approx_\lambda 0$, where $\varepsilon_b^{zk} :=$

$$\Pr\left[\mathsf{p} \leftarrow \mathsf{K}_0(1^\lambda); \varrho \leftarrow\!\!\$\, \mathcal{D}_p; (\mathsf{crs}, \mathsf{tc}) \leftarrow \mathsf{K}(\varrho); b \leftarrow\!\!\$\, \{0, 1\} : \mathcal{A}^{O_b(\cdot)}(\varrho, \mathsf{crs}) = 1 \right].$$

$\mathsf{K}([M]_1)$

- $A \leftarrow_\$ \hat{\mathcal{D}}_k; K \leftarrow_\$ \mathbb{Z}_p^{n \times \hat{k}}; C \leftarrow KA \in \mathbb{Z}_p^{n \times k};$
- $[P]_1 \leftarrow [M]_1^\top K \in \mathbb{Z}_p^{m \times \hat{k}}; \mathsf{crs} \leftarrow ([A, C]_2, [P]_1); \mathsf{tc} \leftarrow K;$
- **return** $(\mathsf{tc}, \mathsf{crs}).$

$\mathsf{P}([M]_1, \mathsf{crs}, [y]_1, w):$	$\mathsf{V}([M]_1, \mathsf{crs}, [y]_1, [\pi]_1):$	$\mathsf{Sim}([M]_1, \mathsf{crs}, \mathsf{tc}, [y]_1):$
- $[\pi]_1 \leftarrow [P]_1^\top w \in \mathbb{G}_1^{\hat{k}};$	- **if** $[y]_1^\top [C]_2 = [\pi]_1^\top [A]_2$ **return** 1;	- $[\pi]_1 \leftarrow K^\top [y]_1 \in \mathbb{G}_1^{\hat{k}}.$

Fig. 1. KW QA-NIZK Π_{as} ($\hat{\mathcal{D}}_k = \mathcal{D}_k$ and $\hat{k} = k + 1$) and Π'_{as} ($\hat{\mathcal{D}}_k = \bar{\mathcal{D}}_k$ and $\hat{k} = k$).

The oracle $\mathsf{O}_0(x, w)$ returns $\bot$ (reject) if $(x, w) \notin \mathcal{R}_\varrho$, and otherwise it returns $\mathsf{P}(\varrho, \mathsf{crs}, x, w)$. Similarly, $\mathsf{O}_1(x, w)$ returns $\bot$ (reject) if $(x, w) \notin \mathcal{R}_\varrho$, and otherwise it returns $\mathsf{Sim}(\varrho, \mathsf{crs}, \mathsf{tc}, x)$.

(iii) **Adaptive Soundness.** For any PPT $\mathcal{A}$,

$$\Pr\left[\begin{array}{l} \mathsf{p} \leftarrow \mathsf{K}_0(1^\lambda); \varrho \leftarrow_\$ \mathcal{D}_\mathsf{p}; (\mathsf{crs}, \mathsf{tc}) \leftarrow \mathsf{K}(\varrho); (x, \pi) \leftarrow \mathcal{A}(\varrho, \mathsf{crs}) : \\ \mathsf{V}(\varrho, \mathsf{crs}, x, \pi) = 1 \wedge \neg(\exists w : (x, w) \in \mathcal{R}_\varrho) \end{array}\right] \approx_\lambda 0.$$

Additionally, we define a stronger soundness version called knowledge soundness.

Computational Knowledge Soundness. For any PPT $\mathcal{A}$ there exists a non-uniform polynomial time extractor $\mathsf{Ext}_\mathcal{A}$ such that,

$$\Pr\left[\begin{array}{l} \mathsf{p} \leftarrow \mathsf{K}_0(1^\lambda); \varrho \leftarrow_\$ \mathcal{D}_\mathsf{p}; (\mathsf{crs}, \mathsf{tc}) \leftarrow \mathsf{K}(\varrho); \omega_\mathcal{A} \leftarrow \mathsf{RND}(\mathcal{A}); \\ ((x, \pi); w) \leftarrow (\mathcal{A}\|\mathsf{Ext}_\mathcal{A})(\omega_\mathcal{A}; \varrho, \mathsf{crs}) : \mathsf{V}(\varrho, \mathsf{crs}, x, \pi) = 1 \wedge (x, w) \notin \mathcal{R}_\varrho \end{array}\right] \approx_\lambda 0.$$

QA-NIZK Argument for Linear Spaces. Now we recall the two constructions of QA-NIZK arguments of membership in linear spaces given by Kiltz and Wee (KW) [37] for the language

$$\mathcal{L}_{[M]_1} = \left\{ [y]_1 \in \mathbb{G}_1^n : \exists w \in \mathbb{Z}_p^m \text{ s.t. } y = Mw \right\}.$$

The corresponding relation is defined as $\mathcal{R}_{[M]_1} = \{([y]_1, w) \in \mathbb{G}_1^n \times \mathbb{Z}_p^m : y = Mw\}$. This language is useful in many applications (cf. [33] and follow up work). We recall the full construction of the Kiltz-Wee QA-NIZK arguments for linear subspaces in the CRS model in Fig. 1. Let $\hat{\mathcal{D}}_k$ and $\bar{\mathcal{D}}_k$ be matrix distributions in $\mathbb{Z}_p^{\hat{k} \times k}$ and $\mathbb{Z}_p^{k \times k}$ respectively. We denote $\hat{\mathcal{D}}_k = \bar{\mathcal{D}}_k$ if $\hat{k} = k$, and $\hat{\mathcal{D}}_k = \mathcal{D}_k$ if $\hat{k} = k + 1$.

Theorem 1 (Theorem 1 of [37]). *If $\hat{\mathcal{D}}_k = \mathcal{D}_k$ and $\hat{k} = k + 1$, Fig. 1 describes a QA-NIZK argument Π_{as} with perfect completeness, computational adaptive soundness based on the $\mathcal{D}_k$-KerMDH assumption, perfect zero-knowledge, and proof size $k + 1$.*

Theorem 2 (Theorem 2 of [37]). *If $\hat{\mathcal{D}}_k = \bar{\mathcal{D}}_k$, $\hat{k} = k$, and $\mathcal{D}_\mathsf{p}$ is a witness samplable distribution, Fig. 1 describes a QA-NIZK argument Π'_{as} with perfect completeness, computational adaptive soundness based on the $\mathcal{D}_k$-KerMDH assumption, perfect zero-knowledge, and proof size k.*

Asymmetric QA-NIZK for Concatenation Languages. We recall the constructions of asymmetric QA-NIZK arguments of membership in different subspace concatenations of $\mathbb{G}_1^{n_1} \times \mathbb{G}_2^{n_2}$ given by Gonzalez *et al.* [24] in the full version.

3 QA-NIZK Arguments in the Subversion Setting

In this section, we investigate QA-NIZK arguments when the CRS is subverted and propose corresponding Sub-ZK QA-NIZK arguments. First we discuss subversion security and then our focus will be on the fundamental and the most efficient QA-NIZK construction Π'_{as} in [37] (cf. Sect. 2). Due to the lack of space we present the subversion versions of the asymmetric QA-NIZK construction Π'_{asy} in [24] (cf. Sect. 2) for linear languages in the full version.

3.1 Security Definitions for Subversion QA-NIZK Arguments

The notion of subversion security for QA-NIZKs in the CRS model was first noted by Jutla and Roy in the full version of [33] (cf. [34]). They have shown that one can obtain both soundness and zero-knowledge (under falsifiable assumptions) when the language parameter ϱ is subverted but the CRS is *generated honestly*. They showed that such a setting can cover a large family of subspace languages. Later Abdolmaleki *et al.* [3] (ALSZ) defined the security of QA-NIZKs in the bare public-key (BPK) model, when both ϱ and the CRS are subverted. More precisely, they obtain a version of the Kiltz-Wee QA-NIZK [37] when both ϱ and CRS are chosen maliciously, but under a new non-falsifiable KWKE knowledge assumption. ALSZ also obtain (knowledge) soundness when only ϱ is chosen maliciously under a new (non-falsifiable) interactive assumptions KerMDH^{dl} and SKerMDH^{dl} (cf. [3]).

In this paper, we investigate the missing direction, namely the security of QA-NIZKs in the CRS model when the CRS is subverted but with *honestly chosen* ϱ. This can be viewed as a dual version of Jutla and Roy's QA-NIZK in [33,34]. Concretely, we define Sub-ZK QA-NIZKs security with some changes in the CRS model. The most important properties are completeness (an honest prover convinces an honest verifier, and an honestly generated CRS passes the CRS checking), computational (knowledge) soundness, and statistical subversion zero-knowledge (given a possibly subverted CRS, a proof generated by the honest prover reveals no information about the witness). We additionally consider introduce a notion of true-simulation extractability (tSE) [32][4]. Therefore, we rely on tag-based QA-NIZKs.

A tuple of PPT algorithms $\Pi = (\text{Pgen}, \text{Vcrs}, \text{P}, \text{V}, \text{Sim})$ is a Sub-ZK QA-NIZK if properties (i-iii) hold and is a tSE Sub-ZK QA-NIZK if properties (i-ii) and vi hold. Here, Vcrs is a new algorithm that checks the well-formedness of the CRS.

---

[4] Compared to the one independently introduced by Baghery *et al.* [9] we use non-black box extraction and guarantee only tSE.

We note that since soundness is proved in the case crs is generated correctly (by the verifier or a trusted third party) and V does not need to run Vcrs, so the computational soundness are similar to the original QA-NIZK definitions. We note that similar to ALSZ by a subversion ZK QA-NIZK argument we mean a *no-auxiliary-string non-black-box zero knowledge subversion ZK QA-NIZK argument*. In this paper for the sake of simplicity we just use subversion ZK QA-NIZK or Sub-ZK QA-NIZK for short. Subsequently, we recall only the properties that differ from the definitions of QA-NIZK in *Sect.* 2 (and in particular we omit (*iii*) adaptive soundness and computational knowledge soundness).

(i) **Completeness.** For any λ, and $(x, \boldsymbol{w}) \in \mathcal{R}_\varrho$,

$$\Pr\left[\begin{array}{l} \mathsf{p} \leftarrow \mathsf{K}_0(1^\lambda); \varrho \leftarrow\!\!\$\, \mathcal{D}_\mathsf{p}; (\mathsf{crs}, \mathsf{tc}) \leftarrow \mathsf{K}(\varrho); \pi \leftarrow \mathsf{P}(\varrho, \mathsf{crs}, x, \boldsymbol{w}) : \\ \mathsf{Vcrs}(\varrho, \mathsf{crs}) = 1 \wedge \mathsf{V}(\varrho, \mathsf{crs}, x, \pi) = 1 \end{array}\right] = 1.$$

(ii) **Statistical Subversion Zero-Knowledge.** For any PPT subverter Z there exists a PPT extractor Ext_Z, such that for any computationally unbounded adversary $\mathcal{A}$, $|\varepsilon_0^{zk} - \varepsilon_1^{zk}| \approx_\lambda 0$, where $\varepsilon_b^{zk} :=$

$$\Pr\left[\begin{array}{l} \mathsf{p} \leftarrow \mathsf{K}_0(1^\lambda); \varrho \leftarrow\!\!\$\, \mathcal{D}_\mathsf{p}; \omega_\mathsf{Z} \leftarrow\!\!\$\, \mathsf{RND}(\mathsf{Z}); (\mathsf{crs}, \mathsf{aux}_\mathsf{Z}) \leftarrow \mathsf{Z}(\varrho; \omega_\mathsf{Z}); \\ \mathsf{tc} \leftarrow \mathsf{Ext}_\mathsf{Z}(\varrho; \omega_\mathsf{Z}); b \leftarrow\!\!\$\, \{0, 1\} : \mathsf{Vcrs}(\varrho, \mathsf{crs}) = 1 \wedge \mathcal{A}^{\mathsf{O}_b(\cdot, \cdot)}(\varrho, \mathsf{crs}, \mathsf{aux}_\mathsf{Z}) = 1 \end{array}\right].$$

The oracle $\mathsf{O}_0(x, \boldsymbol{w})$ returns $\bot$ (reject) if $(x, \boldsymbol{w}) \notin \mathcal{R}_\varrho$, and otherwise it returns $\mathsf{P}(\varrho, \mathsf{crs}, x, \boldsymbol{w})$. Similarly, $\mathsf{O}_1(x, \boldsymbol{w})$ returns $\bot$ (reject) if $(x, \boldsymbol{w}) \notin \mathcal{R}_\varrho$, and otherwise it returns $\mathsf{Sim}(\varrho, \mathsf{crs}, \mathsf{tc}, x)$.

(vi) **True-Simulation Extractability.** For any PPT $\mathcal{A}$ there exists a non-uniform PPT extractor $\mathsf{Ext}_\mathcal{A}$,

$$\Pr\left[\begin{array}{l} \mathsf{p} \leftarrow \mathsf{K}_0(1^\lambda); \varrho \leftarrow\!\!\$\, \mathcal{D}_\mathsf{p}; (\mathsf{crs}, \mathsf{tc}) \leftarrow \mathsf{K}(\varrho); \omega_\mathcal{A} \leftarrow\!\!\$\, \mathsf{RND}(\mathcal{A}); \\ (\tau', x', \pi') \leftarrow \mathcal{A}^{\mathsf{O}(\cdot, \cdot)}(\omega_\mathcal{A}; \varrho, \mathsf{crs}); w \leftarrow \mathsf{Ext}_\mathcal{A}(\omega_\mathcal{A}; \varrho, \mathsf{crs}) : (x', w) \notin \mathcal{R}_\varrho \\ \wedge (\tau', x') \notin Q \wedge \mathsf{V}(\varrho, \mathsf{crs}, \tau', x', \pi') = 1 \end{array}\right] \approx_\lambda 0.$$

where $\mathsf{O}(\tau, (x, \boldsymbol{w}))$ outputs $\mathsf{Sim}(\varrho, \mathsf{crs}, \tau, x, \mathsf{tc})$ if $(x, \boldsymbol{w}) \in \mathcal{R}_\varrho$ and adds (τ, x) to the set Q keeping track of the queries. If $(x, \boldsymbol{w}) \notin \mathcal{R}_\varrho$ it outputs $\bot$. One can also define a stronger variant called strong tSE which changes the winning condition to $(\tau', x', \pi') \notin Q$ and O records (τ, x, π) into Q.

3.2 QA-NIZKs with Subverted Setup

In this part, we construct a Sub-ZK QA-NIZK based on the QA-NIZK from KW [37], where we focus on the most efficient version $\varPi'_\mathsf{as}$. Intuitively, for constructing such a system, one needs two properties. Firstly one needs to make the CRS publicly verifiable, and secondly the trapdoor of the CRS should be extractable under some knowledge assumption (the latter is required to simulate proofs in the subversion zero-knowledge game).

We achieve the first property by defining a Vcrs algorithm which takes the CRS crs and the language parameter ϱ of the QA-NIZK's language and checks

$\mathsf{MATV}([\bar{A}]_2) \; /\!/ \; \mathcal{D}_k \in \{\mathcal{L}_k, \mathcal{IL}_k, \mathcal{C}_k, \mathcal{SC}_k\}$

---

check $[a_{11}]_2 \neq [0]_2 \wedge \ldots \wedge [a_{kk}]_2 \neq [0]_2$;

if $\mathcal{D}_k = \mathcal{L}_k$ **then** check $i \neq j \Rightarrow [a_{i,j}]_2 = [0]_2$;

elseif $\mathcal{D}_k = \mathcal{IL}_k$ **then** check $i \neq j \Rightarrow [a_{ij}]_2 = [0]_2$;

$\forall i, [a_{i,i}]_2 = [a_{1,1}]_2 + [i-1]_2$;

elseif $\mathcal{D}_k = \mathcal{C}_k$ **then** check $i \notin \{j, j+1\} \Rightarrow [a_{ij}]_2 = [0]_2$;

$\forall i, [a_{i+1,i}]_2 = [1]_2$;

elseif $\mathcal{D}_k = \mathcal{SC}_k$ **then** check $i \notin \{j, j+1\} \Rightarrow [a_{ij}]_2 = [0]_2$;

$\quad \forall i \left([a_{i+1,i}]_2 = [1]_2 \wedge [a_{ii}]_2 = [a_{11}]_2\right)$; **fi**

return 1 if all checks pass and 0 otherwise;

Fig. 2. Auxiliary procedure MATV from [3] for $\mathcal{D}_k \in \{\mathcal{L}_k, \mathcal{IL}_k, \mathcal{C}_k, \mathcal{SC}_k\}$.

the well-formedness of the crs. If the possibly maliciously generated crs (from the prover's point of view) passes the Vcrs algorithm, it is guaranteed that there exists a trapdoor tc for crs. Then, by using the BDH-KE assumption, we can extract the trapdoor tc from crs which realizes the second property. As in [2] in context of subversion zk-SNARKs, we also need to add some extra elements $[\bar{A}]_1 \in \mathbb{G}_1^{k \times k}$ and $[C]_1 \in \mathbb{G}_1^{n \times k}$ to the CRS (assume that $\mathcal{D}_k$ outputs matrices A where the upper $k \times k$ submatrix $\bar{A}$ is always invertible). Then, we prove that the new construction is complete, subversion zero-knowledge and adaptive sound in Theorem 3. We note, however, that there are also subversion zk-SNARKs [19] where one can achieve the public verifiability property of the CRS for free, i.e., without adding some extra elements to the CRS. We show that this can also be the case for subversion ZK QA-NIZKs and in particular the asymmetric QA-NIZKs which we discuss in the full version of this paper.

Before describing the full construction of our Sub-ZK QA-NIZK argument Π_{sub}, we recall the definition of an efficiently verifiable distribution $\mathcal{D}_k$ from [3]. This guarantees that for $A \leftarrow_\$ \mathcal{D}_k$ there exists an algorithm $\mathsf{MATV}([\bar{A}]_2)$ that outputs 1 if $\bar{A}$ is invertible (we assume that the matrix distribution is robust) and well-formed with respect to $\mathcal{D}_k$ and otherwise outputs 0. Clearly, the distributions $\mathcal{D}_1, \mathcal{L}_k, \mathcal{IL}_k, \mathcal{C}_k$, and $\mathcal{SC}_k$ (for any k) are verifiable, as can be seen in Fig. 2 that allow one to verify whether $[\bar{A}]_2$ is invertible.

Figure 3 describes Sub-ZK QA-NIZK argument Π_{sub}, which is the subversion ZK version of the KW QA-NIZK argument Π'_{as} [37].

In Lemma 1, we show that from any adversary producing a valid CRS crs it is possible to extract the trapdoor K (simulation trapdoors). We will use it in the proof of subversion zero-knowledge in Theorem 3.

Lemma 1. *Let* BDH-KE *assumption hold and let* $[M]_1 \leftarrow_\$ \mathcal{D}_p$. *Then for any PPT adversary* $\mathcal{A}$ *there exists extractor* $\mathsf{Ext}_{\mathcal{A}}$ *such that the probability that* $\mathcal{A}$ *on input* $[M]_1$ *and randomness* ω *outputs* crs *such that* $\mathsf{Vcrs}([M]_1, \mathsf{crs}) = 1$ *and that* $\mathsf{Ext}_{\mathcal{A}}$ *on the same input, outputs* $\mathsf{tc} = K$, *is overwhelming.*

$\mathsf{K}([M]_1)$

- $A \leftarrow_\$ \mathcal{D}_k; K \leftarrow_\$ \mathbb{Z}_p^{n \times k}; C \leftarrow K\bar{A} \in \mathbb{Z}_p^{n \times k};$
- $[P]_1 \leftarrow [M]_1^\top K \in \mathbb{Z}_p^{m \times k}; \mathsf{crs} \leftarrow ([\bar{A}, C]_2, [P, C, \bar{A}]_1); \mathsf{tc} \leftarrow K;$
- **return** $(\mathsf{tc}, \mathsf{crs})$.

$\mathsf{Vcrs}([M]_1, \mathsf{crs})$:

- **if** $[\bar{A}]_1 \in \mathbb{G}_1^{k \times k} \wedge [P]_1 \in \mathbb{G}_1^{m \times k} \wedge [\bar{A}]_2 \in \mathbb{G}_2^{k \times k}$
  $\wedge [C]_1 \in \mathbb{G}_1^{n \times k} \wedge [C]_2 \in \mathbb{G}_2^{n \times k}$
  $\wedge [\bar{A}]_1[1]_2 = [1]_1[\bar{A}]_2 \wedge [C]_1[1]_2 = [1]_1[C]_2$
  $\wedge [M]_1^\top [C]_2 = [P]_1[\bar{A}]_2 \wedge \mathsf{MATV}([\bar{A}]_2) = 1$ **return** 1;

$\mathsf{P}([M]_1, \mathsf{crs}, [y]_1, w)$:	$\mathsf{V}([M]_1, \mathsf{crs}, [y]_1, [\pi]_1)$:	$\mathsf{Sim}([M]_1, \mathsf{crs}, \mathsf{tc}, [y]_1)$:
- $[\pi]_1 \leftarrow [P]_1^\top w \in \mathbb{G}_1^k$;	- **if** $[y]_1^\top [C]_2 = [\pi]_1^\top [\bar{A}]_2$ **return** 1;	- $[\pi]_1 \leftarrow K^\top [y]_1 \in \mathbb{G}_1^k$;

Fig. 3. Sub-ZK QA-NIZK Π_{sub}: Sub-ZK Π'_{as}.

$\mathcal{A}([M]_1; \omega_\mathcal{A})$	$\mathsf{Ext}_\mathcal{A}([M]_1; \omega_\mathcal{A})$
$(\mathsf{crs}, \mathsf{aux}_\mathcal{A}) \leftarrow \mathcal{A}([M]_1; \omega_\mathcal{A}); \mathbf{return\ crs};$	- $(\bar{A}, C) \leftarrow \mathsf{Ext}^{\mathsf{BDH\text{-}KE}}_{\mathcal{A}_{\mathsf{BDH\text{-}KE}}}([M]_1; \omega_\mathcal{A});$
	Compute $K = C\bar{A}^{-1}$;
	- **return** $\mathsf{tc} = K$;

$\mathcal{A}_{\mathsf{BDH\text{-}KE}}([M]_1; \omega_\mathcal{A})$

$(\mathsf{crs}, \mathsf{aux}_\mathcal{A}) \leftarrow \mathcal{A}([M]_1; \omega_\mathcal{A});$
return $([\bar{A}]_1, [\bar{A}]_2, [C]_1, [C]_2);$

Fig. 4. The extractors and the constructed adversary $\mathcal{A}$ for Lemma 1.

Proof. Let adversary $\mathcal{A}$ output crs such that $\mathsf{Vcrs}([M]_1, \mathsf{crs}) = 1$, which guarantees that elements from P, $\bar{A}$ and C are consistent and in particular that $[M]_1^\top [C]_2 = [P]_1[\bar{A}]_2$ and $\bar{A}$ is invertible. Beside the main $\mathcal{A}$, we use an internal subverter $\mathcal{A}_{\mathsf{BDH\text{-}KE}}$. We note that both the subverter and the adversary are in connection and separating them is just for readability of the proof. Let $\omega_\mathcal{A} = \omega_{\mathcal{A}_{\mathsf{BDH\text{-}KE}}}$. Let $\mathcal{A}_{\mathsf{BDH\text{-}KE}}$ run $\mathcal{A}$ and output $([\bar{A}]_1, [\bar{A}]_2, [C]_1, [C]_2)$. Then under the BDH-KE assumption, there exists an extractor $\mathsf{Ext}^{\mathsf{BDH\text{-}KE}}_{\mathcal{A}_{\mathsf{BDH\text{-}KE}}}$, such that if $\mathsf{Vcrs}([M]_1, \mathsf{crs}) = 1$ then $\mathsf{Ext}^{\mathsf{BDH\text{-}KE}}_{\mathcal{A}_{\mathsf{BDH\text{-}KE}}}([M]_1; \omega_\mathcal{A})$ outputs $(\bar{A}, C)$.

Let $\mathsf{Ext}_\mathcal{A}$ be an extractor that with input $([M]_1; \omega_\mathcal{A})$ and running $\mathsf{Ext}^{\mathsf{BDH\text{-}KE}}_{\mathcal{A}_{\mathsf{BDH\text{-}KE}}}$ as subroutine, extracts $\mathsf{tc} = K$. For the sake of simplicity, the full description of the algorithms is depicted in Theorem 4. More precisely, the extractor $\mathsf{Ext}_\mathcal{A}$ first runs $\mathsf{Ext}^{\mathsf{BDH\text{-}KE}}_{\mathcal{A}_{\mathsf{BDH\text{-}KE}}}([M]_1; \omega_\mathcal{A})$ which outputs $(\bar{A}, C)$. Then, $\mathsf{Ext}_\mathcal{A}$ computes K. Indeed, by having $\bar{A}$, CM, and the fact that A is invertible, the extractor $\mathsf{Ext}_\mathcal{A}$ can compute $K = C\bar{A}^{-1}$.

Theorem 3. *Let Π_{sub} be a Sub-ZK QA-NIZK argument for linear subspaces from Fig. 3. Let $\mathcal{D}_\mathsf{p}$ be a witness samplable distribution. (i) Π_{sub} is subversion complete, (ii) if BDH-KE holds, then Π_{sub} is statistically subversion zero-knowledge, and (iii) if $\mathcal{D}_k$-SKerMDH holds then Π_{sub} is computationally sound.*

Proof. (i: **Completeness**): This is straightforward.

(ii: **Subversion Zero-Knowledge:**) Let the BDH-KE assumption hold. Let $\mathcal{A}$ be an adversary that computes crs so as to break the subversion zero-knowledge property of the Sub-ZK QA-NIZK in Fig. 3. That is, $\mathcal{A}([M]_1; \omega_{\mathcal{A}})$ outputs $(crs^*, aux_{\mathcal{A}})$. Let $\mathcal{A}$ be the adversary from Fig. 4 of Lemma 1. Let $\mathsf{RND}(\mathcal{A}) = \mathsf{RND}(\mathcal{A}_{\mathsf{BDH\text{-}KE}})$ in Lemma 1. Note that the subverter and the adversary are in connection. Underlying Lemma 1, if $\mathsf{Vcrs}([M]_1, crs^*) = 1$ then $\mathsf{Ext}_{\mathcal{A}}([M]_1; \omega_{\mathcal{A}})$ from Fig. 4 outputs K.

Fix concrete values of λ, $p \in \mathsf{im}(\mathsf{K}_0(1^\lambda))$, $[M]_1 \leftarrow_{\$} \mathcal{D}_p$, $([y]_1, w) \in \mathcal{R}_{[M]_1}$, $\omega_{\mathcal{A}} \in \mathsf{RND}(\mathcal{A})$, and run $\mathsf{Ext}_{\mathcal{A}}([M]_1; \omega_{\mathcal{A}})$ to obtain K. Thus, it suffices to show that if $\mathsf{Vcrs}([M]_1, crs^*) = 1$ and $([y]_1, w) \in \mathcal{R}_{[M]_1}$ then

$$\mathsf{O}_0([y]_1, w) = \mathsf{P}([M]_1, crs^*, [y]_1, w) = [P]_1^\top w,$$
$$\mathsf{O}_1([y]_1, w) = \mathsf{Sim}([M]_1, crs^*, [y]_1, K) = K^\top [y]_1$$

have the same distribution. This holds since from $\mathsf{Vcrs}([M]_1, crs^*) = 1$ it follows that $P = M^\top K$ and from $([y]_1; w) \in \mathcal{R}_{[M]_1}$ it follows that $y = Mw$. Thus,

$$\mathsf{O}_0([y]_1, w) = [P]_1^\top w = [K^\top M w]_1 = K^\top [y]_1 = \mathsf{O}_1([y]_1, w).$$

Hence, O_0 and O_1 have the same distribution and thus, Π_{sub} is Sub-ZK under the BDH-KE assumption.

(iii: **Adaptive Soundness:**) The proof is similar to the adaptive soundness proof of Π'_{as} in [3,37] but with some modifications in a way that instead of KerMDH, similar to [3], the adaptive soundness proof of Π'_{as} is based on the $\mathcal{D}_k$-SKerMDH assumption (due to adding $[\bar{A}]_1$ to the CRS). Assume that $\mathcal{A}$ breaks the adaptive soundness of subversion Π'_{as} with probability ε. We will build an adversary $\mathcal{B}$, that breaks $\mathcal{D}_k$-SKerMDH with probability $\geq \varepsilon - 1/p$.

Let $\mathcal{B}([A]_1 \in \mathbb{G}_1^{(k+1)\times k}, [A]_2 \in \mathbb{G}_2^{(k+1)\times k})$ generate $M \leftarrow_{\$} \mathcal{D}'_p$. Note that the $\mathcal{D}'_p$ exists since $\mathcal{D}_p$ is witness sampleable. Let $M^\perp$ be the basis for the kernel of $M^\top$ where $M^\top M^\perp = 0$. Then it computes $[A']_\iota = \begin{pmatrix} [A]_\iota \\ R \cdot [A]_\iota \end{pmatrix} \in \mathbb{Z}_p^{(n-m+k)\times k}$ for $\iota = \{1, 2\}$ where $R \leftarrow_{\$} \mathbb{G}_\iota^{(n-m-1)\times(k+1)}$.

Let $[\bar{A}']_\iota = [\bar{A}]_\iota \in \mathbb{G}_\iota^{k\times k}$. Define implicitly (we do not know this value) $K \leftarrow K' + M^\perp \underline{A}' \bar{A}^{-1} \in \mathbb{Z}_p^{n\times k}$ where $K' \leftarrow_{\$} \mathbb{Z}_p^{n\times k}$. Thus,

$$[C]_\iota = (K' \| M^\perp)[A']_\iota = [K' \bar{A}' + M^\perp \underline{A}']_\iota$$
$$= [(K' + M^\perp \underline{A}' \bar{A}^{-1})\bar{A}]_\iota = [K\bar{A}]_\iota$$

and

$$[P]_1 = [M^\top K']_1 = [M^\top (K - M^\perp \underline{A}' \bar{A}^{-1})]_1 = [M^\top K]_1.$$

Thus, $crs' = ([A, C]_2, [A, C, P]_1)$ has the same distribution as the real crs.

With probability ε, $([\boldsymbol{y}]_1, [\boldsymbol{\pi}]_1) \leftarrow \mathcal{A}([M]_1, \mathsf{crs}')$ is successful, so, for $\boldsymbol{y} \notin \mathrm{span}(M)$ we have that $\boldsymbol{y}^\top M^\perp \neq \boldsymbol{0}_{1\times(n-m)}$. Since $\mathcal{A}$ wins, $\boldsymbol{y}^\top C = \boldsymbol{\pi}^\top \bar{A}$. Thus,

$$\boldsymbol{\pi}^\top \bar{A} - \boldsymbol{y}^\top C = \left(\boldsymbol{\pi}^\top \| \boldsymbol{0}_{n-m}^\top\right) A' - \boldsymbol{y}^\top \left(K' \| M^\perp\right) A'$$
$$= \left((\boldsymbol{\pi}^\top - \boldsymbol{y}^\top K')\| - \boldsymbol{y}^\top M^\perp\right) A' = \boldsymbol{c}^\top A' = 0$$

where $[\boldsymbol{c}]_1^\top \leftarrow [(\boldsymbol{\pi}^\top - \boldsymbol{y}^\top K')\| - \boldsymbol{y}^\top M^\perp]_1$. Define $[\boldsymbol{c}]_1^\top$ as $[\boldsymbol{c}_1^\top \| \boldsymbol{c}_2^\top]_1$ with $[\boldsymbol{c}_1]_1 \in \mathbb{G}_1^{k+1}$ and $[\boldsymbol{c}_2]_1 \in \mathbb{G}_1^{n-m-1}$. Set $\boldsymbol{s}_2 \leftarrow_\$ \mathbb{Z}_p^{k+1}$; $[\boldsymbol{s}_1]_1 \leftarrow [\boldsymbol{c}_1 + R^\top \boldsymbol{c}_2 + \boldsymbol{s}_2]_1$. Clearly, $\boldsymbol{s}_1 - \boldsymbol{s}_2 = \boldsymbol{c}_1 + R^\top \boldsymbol{c}_2$ and

$$(\boldsymbol{s}_1^\top - \boldsymbol{s}_2^\top) A = (\boldsymbol{c}_1^\top + \boldsymbol{c}_2^\top R) A = \boldsymbol{c}^\top A' = \boldsymbol{0}_{1\times k}.$$

Since $\boldsymbol{c} \neq \boldsymbol{0}_{n-m+k}$ and R leaks only through A' as RA,

$$\Pr[\boldsymbol{c}_1 + R^\top \boldsymbol{c}_2 = 0 \mid RA] \leq 1/p,$$

where the probability is over $R \leftarrow_\$ \mathbb{Z}_p^{(n-m-1)\times(k+1)}$. Finally $\mathcal{B}$ outputs the pair $([\boldsymbol{s}_1]_1, [\boldsymbol{s}_2]_2)$ as the answer to the $\mathcal{D}_k$-SKerMDH problem.

4   Subversion True-Simulation Extractable QA-NIZK

In this section, we present an unbounded true-simulation extractable Sub-ZK QA-NIZK (tSE Sub-ZK QA-NIZK) version of the Sub-ZK QA-NIZK. To this aim, we rely on the discrete logarithm assumption, in the algebraic group model (AGM) [20]. Roughly speaking, inspired by [37], we first modify the Sub-ZK QA-NIZK Π'_{as} in Sect. 3.2 to make it unbounded tSE, then we add some new elements in the CRS to make it publicly verifiable. We define a new Vcrs algorithm to check whether the CRS is well-formed. Then by applying the technique from Lemma 1, we show the extractability of the CRS. We present the full construction of unbounded SE Sub-ZK QA-NIZK in Fig. 5. We note that we overcome the problem in [37] of requiring that $n > m$ and the lack of knowledge soundness, which does not make then usable within LegoSNARK. So we avoid the $n > m$ restriction, but for knowledge soundness, the matrix $[M]_1$ must be generated using a witness sampleable distribution $\mathcal{D}_\mathsf{p}$, i.e., there must exist a polynomial time algorithm that samples M in $\mathbb{Z}_p$ such that $[M]_1$ has the same distribution as the one sampled with $\mathcal{D}_p$. However, we note that this is satisfied for the use-case within LegoSNARK where M includes bases of a Pedersen-like commitment schemes (cf. Sect. 5). Finally, we discuss how to obtain strong true-simulation extractability (tSE) for our construction.

In Lemma 2, we show that from any adversary producing a valid CRS crs it is possible to extract the trapdoor K (simulation trapdoors). We will use it in the proof of subversion zero-knowledge in Theorem 4.

Lemma 2. *Let BDH-KE assumption hold and let $[M]_1 \leftarrow_\$ \mathcal{D}_\mathsf{p}$. Then for any PPT adversary $\mathcal{A}$ there exists extractor $\mathsf{Ext}_\mathcal{A}$ such that the probability that $\mathcal{A}$ on input $[M]_1$ and randomness ω outputs crs such that $\mathsf{Vcrs}([M]_1, \mathsf{crs}) = 1$ and that $\mathsf{Ext}_\mathcal{A}$ on the same input, outputs $\mathsf{tc} = K$ is overwhelming.*

$\mathsf{K}([\boldsymbol{M}]_1)$

- $\bar{\boldsymbol{A}}, \boldsymbol{B} \leftarrow_\$ \bar{\mathcal{D}}_k; \boldsymbol{K} \leftarrow_\$ \mathbb{Z}_p^{n \times k}; \boldsymbol{K}_0, \boldsymbol{K}_1 \leftarrow_\$ \mathbb{Z}_p^{k \times k}; \boldsymbol{C} \leftarrow \boldsymbol{K}\bar{\boldsymbol{A}} \in \mathbb{Z}_p^{n \times k};$
- $(\boldsymbol{C}_i)_{i=0}^{i=1} \leftarrow \boldsymbol{K}_i \bar{\boldsymbol{A}} \in \mathbb{Z}_p^{k \times k}; [\boldsymbol{P}]_1 \leftarrow [\boldsymbol{M}]_1^\top \boldsymbol{K} \in \mathbb{G}_1^{m \times k};$
- $[(\boldsymbol{P}_i)_{i=0}^{i=1}]_1 \leftarrow [\boldsymbol{B}]_1 \boldsymbol{K}_i \in \mathbb{G}_1^{k \times k}; \mathsf{crs} \leftarrow ([\bar{\boldsymbol{A}}, \boldsymbol{C}, (\boldsymbol{C}_i)_{i=0}^{i=1}]_2, [\bar{\boldsymbol{A}}, \boldsymbol{C}, \boldsymbol{B}, \boldsymbol{P}, (\boldsymbol{P}_i)_{i=0}^{i=1}]_1); \mathsf{tc} \leftarrow \boldsymbol{K};$
- **return** $(\mathsf{tc}, \mathsf{crs})$.

$\mathsf{Vcrs}([\boldsymbol{M}]_1, \mathsf{crs}):$

- **if** $[\bar{\boldsymbol{A}}]_1 \in \mathbb{G}_1^{k \times k} \wedge [\boldsymbol{B}]_2 \in \mathbb{G}_2^{k \times k} \wedge [\boldsymbol{P}]_1 \in \mathbb{G}_1^{m \times k} \wedge [\bar{\boldsymbol{A}}]_2 \in \mathbb{G}_2^{k \times k} \wedge [\boldsymbol{C}]_1 \in \mathbb{G}_1^{n \times k} \wedge [\boldsymbol{C}]_2 \in \mathbb{G}_2^{n \times k}$
- $\wedge [(\boldsymbol{P}_i)_{i=0}^{i=1}]_1 \in \mathbb{G}_1^{k \times k} \wedge [(\boldsymbol{C}_i)_{i=0}^{i=1}]_2 \in \mathbb{G}_2^{k \times k} \wedge [\bar{\boldsymbol{A}}]_1[1]_2 = [1]_1[\bar{\boldsymbol{A}}]_2 \wedge [\boldsymbol{C}]_1[1]_2 = [1]_1[\boldsymbol{C}]_2$
- $\wedge [\boldsymbol{M}]_1^\top [\boldsymbol{C}]_2 = [\boldsymbol{P}]_1[\bar{\boldsymbol{A}}]_2 \wedge [\boldsymbol{B}]_1^\top [(\boldsymbol{C}_i)_{i=0}^{i=1}]_2 = [(\boldsymbol{P}_i)_{i=0}^{i=1}]_1[\bar{\boldsymbol{A}}]_2 \wedge \mathsf{MATV}(\bar{\boldsymbol{A}}) = 1$ **return** $1;$

$\mathsf{P}(\tau, [\boldsymbol{M}]_1, \mathsf{crs}, [\boldsymbol{y}]_1, \boldsymbol{w}):$

- $\boldsymbol{r} \leftarrow_\$ \mathbb{Z}_p^k; [\boldsymbol{\pi}]_1 \leftarrow ([\boldsymbol{\pi}_1]_1, [\boldsymbol{\pi}_2]_1) \leftarrow ([\boldsymbol{P}]_1^\top \boldsymbol{w} + (\sum_{i=0}^{i=1} \tau^i [\boldsymbol{P}_i]_1^\top) \boldsymbol{r}, [\boldsymbol{B}]_1 \boldsymbol{r}) \in (\mathbb{G}_1^k)^2;$

$\mathsf{V}(\tau, [\boldsymbol{M}]_1, \mathsf{crs}, [\boldsymbol{y}]_1, [\boldsymbol{\pi}]_1):$

- Parse $[\boldsymbol{\pi}]_1 = ([\boldsymbol{\pi}_1]_1, [\boldsymbol{\pi}_2]_1);$ **if** $[\boldsymbol{y}]_1^\top [\boldsymbol{C}]_2 + [\boldsymbol{\pi}_2]_1^\top \sum_{i=0}^{i=1} \tau^i [\boldsymbol{C}_i]_2 = [\boldsymbol{\pi}_1]_1^\top [\bar{\boldsymbol{A}}]_2$ **return** $1.$

$\mathsf{Sim}(\tau, [\boldsymbol{M}]_1, \mathsf{crs}, \mathsf{tc}, [\boldsymbol{y}]_1):$

- $\boldsymbol{r} \leftarrow_\$ \mathbb{Z}_p^k; [\boldsymbol{\pi}]_1 = ([\boldsymbol{\pi}_1]_1, [\boldsymbol{\pi}_2]_1) \leftarrow (\boldsymbol{K}^\top [\boldsymbol{y}]_1 + \sum_{i=0}^{i=1} \tau^i [\boldsymbol{P}_i]_1^\top \boldsymbol{r}, [\boldsymbol{B}]_1 \boldsymbol{r}) \in (\mathbb{G}_1^k)^2.$

Fig. 5. Unbounded true-simulation extractable Sub-ZK QA-NIZK argument $\Pi_{\mathsf{utse\text{-}sub}}$.

Proof. Let adversary $\mathcal{A}$ output crs such that $\mathsf{Vcrs}([\boldsymbol{M}]_1, \mathsf{crs}) = 1$, which guarantees that elements from $\boldsymbol{P}, \boldsymbol{C}$, and $\bar{\boldsymbol{A}}$ are consistent and in particular that $[\boldsymbol{M}]_1^\top [\boldsymbol{C}]_2 = [\boldsymbol{P}]_1[\bar{\boldsymbol{A}}]_2$. Beside the main $\mathcal{A}$, we use an internal subverter $\mathcal{A}_{\mathsf{BDH\text{-}KE}}$. We note that both the subverter and the adversary are in connection and separating them is just for readability of the proof. Let $\omega_{\mathcal{A}} = \omega_{\mathcal{A}_{\mathsf{BDH\text{-}KE}}}$. Let $\mathcal{A}_{\mathsf{BDH\text{-}KE}}$ runs $\mathcal{A}$ and outputs $([\bar{\boldsymbol{A}}]_1, [\bar{\boldsymbol{A}}]_2, [\boldsymbol{C}]_1, [\boldsymbol{C}]_2)$. Then under the BDH-KE assumption, there exists an extractor $\mathsf{Ext}_{\mathcal{A}_{\mathsf{BDH\text{-}KE}}}^{\mathsf{BDH\text{-}KE}}$, such that if $\mathsf{Vcrs}([\boldsymbol{M}]_1, \mathsf{crs}) = 1$ then $\mathsf{Ext}_{\mathcal{A}_{\mathsf{BDH\text{-}KE}}}^{\mathsf{BDH\text{-}KE}}([\boldsymbol{M}]_1; \omega_{\mathcal{A}})$ outputs $(\bar{\boldsymbol{A}}, \boldsymbol{C})$.

Let $\mathsf{Ext}_{\mathcal{A}}$ be an extractor that with input $([\boldsymbol{M}]_1; \omega_{\mathcal{A}})$ and running $\mathsf{Ext}_{\mathcal{A}_{\mathsf{BDH\text{-}KE}}}^{\mathsf{BDH\text{-}KE}}$ as subroutine, extracts $\mathsf{tc} = \boldsymbol{K} = \boldsymbol{C}\bar{\boldsymbol{A}}^{-1}$. Thus, from the Kronecker-Capelli theorem we know that this system has a unique solution. For the sake of simplicity, the full description of the algorithms is depicted in Fig. 6.

Theorem 4. *Let $\Pi_{\mathsf{utse\text{-}sub}}$ be the unbounded tSE Sub-ZK QA-NIZK argument for linear subspaces from Fig. 5. (i) $\Pi_{\mathsf{utse\text{-}sub}}$ is subversion complete, (ii) if BDH-KE holds, then $\Pi_{\mathsf{utse\text{-}sub}}$ is Sub-ZK, and (iii) if the discrete logarithm assumption, in the AGM holds then $\Pi_{\mathsf{utse\text{-}sub}}$ is unbounded true-simulation extractable.*

Proof. Completeness and Sub-ZK proofs are straightforward from Theorem 3 (for the Sub-ZK proof, one first extract tc underlying Lemma 2 and then follows the Sub-ZK proof of Theorem 3).

$\mathcal{A}([M]_1; \omega_{\mathcal{A}})$	$\mathrm{Ext}_{\mathcal{A}}([M]_1; \omega_{\mathcal{A}})$
$(\mathsf{crs}, \mathsf{aux}_{\mathcal{A}}) \leftarrow \mathcal{A}([M]_1; \omega_{\mathcal{A}}); \mathbf{return} \ \mathsf{crs};$	- $(\bar{A}, C) \leftarrow \mathrm{Ext}^{\mathsf{BDH\text{-}KE}}_{\mathcal{A}_{\mathsf{BDH\text{-}KE}}}([M]_1; \omega_{\mathcal{A}});$
	Compute $K = C\bar{A}^{-1};$
	- $\mathbf{return} \ \mathsf{tc} = K;$

$\mathcal{A}_{\mathsf{BDH\text{-}KE}}([M]_1; \omega_{\mathcal{A}})$
$(\mathsf{crs}, \mathsf{aux}_{\mathcal{A}}) \leftarrow \mathcal{A}([M]_1; \omega_{\mathcal{A}});$
$\mathbf{return} \ ([\bar{A}]_1, [\bar{A}]_2, [C]_1, [C]_2);$

Fig. 6. The extractors and the constructed adversary $\mathcal{A}$ for Lemma 2.

(iii: Unbounded True Simulation Extractability:) We show this under the discrete logarithm assumption in asymmetric bilinear groups in the AGM [20]. Without loss of generality, we consider $\Pi_{\mathsf{utse\text{-}sub}}$ for $k = 1$. Assume an algebraic adversary $\mathcal{A}([M]_1, \mathsf{crs}, \mathsf{aux})$ against the simulation extractability of $\Pi_{\mathsf{utse\text{-}sub}}$ where aux is an associated auxiliary input and $\mathsf{crs} = ([a, C, (C_i)_{i=0}^{i=1}]_2, [a, b, C, P, (P_i)_{i=0}^{i=1}]_1$ and she accesses her simulation oracle on the instances $([y_1]_1, \ldots, [y_q]_1)$ to obtain the responses $(([\pi_1]_1, \tau_1), \ldots, ([\pi_q]_1, \tau_q))$. Let $[\zeta]_1$ be a vector that contains M and the portion of aux that has elements from the group $\mathbb{G}_1$ and assume $[\zeta]_1$ includes $[1]_1$. $\mathcal{A}$ returns a tuple $(\tau, [y]_1, [\pi]_1 = ([\pi_1]_1, [\pi_2]_1))$ along with coefficients that explain these elements as linear combinations of its input in the group $\mathbb{G}_1$. Let $r \leftarrow_{\$} \mathbb{Z}_p$ and these coefficients be:

$$[y]_1 = Y_0[P]_1 + Y_1[\zeta]_1 + Y_2[a]_1 + Y_3[b]_1 + Y_{4i}[(P_i)_{i=0}^{i=1}]_1 + Y_5[C]_1 + \sum_{j=0}^{j=q} Y'_j[y_j]_1$$

$$[\pi_1]_1 = Z_0[P]_1 + Z_1[\zeta]_1 + Z_2[a]_1 + Z_3[b]_1 + \sum_{i=0}^{i=1} Z_{4,i}\tau^i[P_i]_1 r + Z_{10}[C]_1 + \sum_{j=0}^{j=q} Z'_j[\pi_{1j}]_1$$

$$[\pi_2]_1 = Z_5[P]_1 + Z_6[\zeta]_1 + Z_7[a]_1 + Z_{8i}[(P_i)_{i=0}^{i=1}]_1 + Z_9[b]_1 r$$

$$+ Z_{11}[C]_1 + \sum_{j=0}^{j=q} Z''_j[\pi_{2j}]_1 \tag{1}$$

Let the extractor $\mathrm{Ext}_{\mathcal{A}}([M]_1, \mathsf{crs}, \mathsf{aux})$ be the algorithm that runs $\mathcal{A}$ and returns $w = Z_0$. Then, we have to show that the probability that the output of $(\mathcal{A}, \mathrm{Ext}_{\mathcal{A}})$ satisfies verification while $y \neq Mw$ is negligible. In other words, assume that the output of $\mathcal{A}$ is such that $[y]_1$ is not queried before, and $[y]_1 \neq [M]_1 Z_0$, and plugged into the verification equation we have:

$$[y^\top K + \pi_2^\top \sum_{i=0}^{i=1} \tau^i K_i - \pi_1^\top]_1 [a]_2 = [0]_T.$$

This means that $y^\top K + \pi_2^\top \sum_{i=0}^{i=1} \tau^i K_i - \pi_1^\top = 0$. If it happens with non-negligible probability, we can construct an algorithm $\mathcal{B}$ that on input

$([\boldsymbol{K}]_1, [\boldsymbol{K}]_2)$ outputs nonzero elements $\boldsymbol{\alpha} \in \mathbb{Z}_p^{n \times n}$, $\boldsymbol{\beta} \in \mathbb{Z}_p^n$, and $\gamma \in \mathbb{Z}_p$ s.t.

$$\boldsymbol{K}^\top \boldsymbol{\alpha} \boldsymbol{K} + \boldsymbol{K}^\top \boldsymbol{\beta} + \gamma = 0$$

and then we can construct an algorithm $\mathcal{C}$ against the discrete logarithm assumption in asymmetric bilinear groups, which given elements $([t]_1, [t]_2)$ returns the exponent $t \in \mathbb{Z}_p$. More precisely $\mathcal{B}([\boldsymbol{K}]_1, [\boldsymbol{K}]_2)$ proceeds as follows:

- Choose $([\boldsymbol{M}]_1, \mathsf{aux})$ from $\mathcal{D}_\mathsf{p}$ along with its $\mathbb{G}_1$ elements (i.e., a vector $\boldsymbol{\zeta}$ of entries in $\mathbb{Z}_p$).
- Sample $a, b \leftarrow_\$ \bar{\mathcal{D}}_k$, $K_0, K_1 \leftarrow_\$ \mathbb{Z}_p$, set $(C_i)_{i=0}^{i=1} \leftarrow a K_i$, and $(P_i)_{i=0}^{i=1} \leftarrow b K_i$. Run $\mathcal{A}([\boldsymbol{\zeta}, \boldsymbol{P}, \boldsymbol{C}, (P_i)_{i=0}^{i=1}, a, b]_1, [a, a\boldsymbol{K}, (C_i)_{i=0}^{i=1}]_2)$. We note that $\mathcal{A}$'s input can be efficiently simulated.
- Once received the output of $\mathcal{A}$, it sets $\boldsymbol{\alpha} := \boldsymbol{Y}_0 \boldsymbol{M}^\top$, $\boldsymbol{\beta} := \boldsymbol{Y}_1 \boldsymbol{\zeta} + \boldsymbol{Y}_2 a + \boldsymbol{Y}_3 b + \boldsymbol{Y}_{4i}(P_i)_{i=0}^{i=1} + \boldsymbol{Y}_5 \boldsymbol{C} + \sum_{j=0}^{j=q} \boldsymbol{Y}_j' \boldsymbol{y}_j - \boldsymbol{M} \boldsymbol{Z}_0$ and $\gamma := -(\boldsymbol{Z}_1 \boldsymbol{\zeta} + \boldsymbol{Z}_2 a + \boldsymbol{Z}_3 b + \sum_{i=0}^{i=1} \boldsymbol{Z}_{4,i} \tau^i P_i r + \boldsymbol{Z}_{10} \boldsymbol{C} + \sum_{j=0}^{j=q} \boldsymbol{Z}_j' \pi_{1j}) + \sum_{i=0}^{i=1} \tau^i K_i (\boldsymbol{Z}_5 \boldsymbol{P} + \boldsymbol{Z}_6 \boldsymbol{\zeta} + \boldsymbol{Z}_7 a + \boldsymbol{Z}_{8i}(P_i)_{i=0}^{i=1} + \boldsymbol{Z}_9 br + \boldsymbol{Z}_{11} \boldsymbol{C} + \sum_{j=0}^{j=q} \boldsymbol{Y}_j'' \pi_{2j})$

Notice that $\boldsymbol{K}^\top \boldsymbol{\alpha} \boldsymbol{K} + \boldsymbol{K}^\top \boldsymbol{\beta} + \gamma$

$$= \boldsymbol{K}^\top \boldsymbol{Y}_0 \boldsymbol{M}^\top \boldsymbol{K} + \boldsymbol{K}^\top \boldsymbol{Y}_1 \boldsymbol{\zeta} + \boldsymbol{K}^\top \boldsymbol{Y}_2 a + \boldsymbol{K}^\top \boldsymbol{Y}_3 b + \boldsymbol{K}^\top \boldsymbol{Y}_{4i}(P_i)_{i=0}^{i=1} + \boldsymbol{K}^\top \boldsymbol{Y}_5 \boldsymbol{C}$$

$$+ \boldsymbol{K}^\top \sum_{j=0}^{j=q} \boldsymbol{Y}_j' \boldsymbol{y}_j - \boldsymbol{K}^\top \boldsymbol{M} \boldsymbol{Z}_0 - (\boldsymbol{Z}_1 \boldsymbol{\zeta} + \boldsymbol{Z}_2 a + \boldsymbol{Z}_3 b + \sum_{i=0}^{i=1} \boldsymbol{Z}_{4,i} \tau^i P_i r + \boldsymbol{Z}_{10} \boldsymbol{C} + \sum_{j=0}^{j=q} \boldsymbol{Z}_j' \pi_{1j})$$

$$+ \sum_{i=0}^{i=1} \tau^i K_i (\boldsymbol{Z}_5 \boldsymbol{P} + \boldsymbol{Z}_6 \boldsymbol{\zeta} + \boldsymbol{Z}_7 a + \boldsymbol{Z}_{8i}(P_i)_{i=0}^{i=1} + \boldsymbol{Z}_9 br + \boldsymbol{Z}_{11} \boldsymbol{C} + \sum_{j=0}^{j=q} \boldsymbol{Y}_j'' \pi_{2j})$$

$$= \boldsymbol{K}^\top (\boldsymbol{Y}_0 \boldsymbol{M}^\top \boldsymbol{K} + \boldsymbol{Y}_1 \boldsymbol{\zeta} + \boldsymbol{Y}_2 a + \boldsymbol{Y}_3 b + \boldsymbol{Y}_{4i}(P_i^\top)_{i=0}^{i=1} + \boldsymbol{Y}_5 \boldsymbol{C} + \sum_{j=0}^{j=q} \boldsymbol{Y}_j' \boldsymbol{y}_j) - \pi_1$$

$$+ \sum_{i=0}^{i=1} \tau^i K_i \pi_2 = \boldsymbol{K}^\top \boldsymbol{y} - \pi_1 + \sum_{i=0}^{i=1} \tau^i K_i \pi_2 = 0.$$

Note that, one among $\boldsymbol{\alpha}$, $\boldsymbol{\beta}$, and γ must be nonzero. Indeed, if they are all zero then $\boldsymbol{Y}_0 = \boldsymbol{0}$ and also $\boldsymbol{Y}_1 \boldsymbol{\zeta} + \boldsymbol{Y}_2 a + \boldsymbol{Y}_3 b + \boldsymbol{Y}_{4i}(P_i)_{i=0}^{i=1} + \boldsymbol{Y}_5 \boldsymbol{C} + \sum_{j=0}^{j=q} \boldsymbol{Y}_j' \boldsymbol{y}_j - \boldsymbol{M} \boldsymbol{Z}_0 = \boldsymbol{0}$, thus from Eq. (1), we have $\boldsymbol{y} = \boldsymbol{M} \boldsymbol{Z}_0$, which contradicts our assumption on $\mathcal{A}$'s output. If $\gamma = 0$ then from Eq. (1), we have $\pi_1 = \boldsymbol{Z}_0 \boldsymbol{P} + \sum_{i=0}^{i=1} \tau^i K_i \pi_2$ which means the adversary has output one of the simulated proofs and so the queried τ, and contradicts our assumption on $\mathcal{A}$'s output.

Finally we show how the above problem can be reduced to discrete logarithm problem, i.e., the adversary $\mathcal{C}$ on input $([t]_1, [t]_2)$ returns t. Indeed $\mathcal{C}$ samples $\boldsymbol{r}, \boldsymbol{s} \in \mathbb{Z}_p^n$ and implicitly sets $\boldsymbol{K} = t \boldsymbol{r} + \boldsymbol{s}$. We see that $([\boldsymbol{K}]_1, [\boldsymbol{K}]_2)$ can be efficiently simulated with a distribution identical to the one expected by $\mathcal{B}$. Next, given a solution $(\boldsymbol{\alpha}, \boldsymbol{\beta}, \gamma)$ such that $\boldsymbol{K}^\top \boldsymbol{\alpha} + \boldsymbol{K}^\top \boldsymbol{\beta} + \gamma = 0$, one can find $e_1, e_2, e_3 \in \mathbb{Z}_p$ such that:

$$0 = (t\boldsymbol{r} + \boldsymbol{s})^\top \boldsymbol{\alpha}(t\boldsymbol{r} + \boldsymbol{s}) + (t\boldsymbol{r} + \boldsymbol{s})^\top \boldsymbol{\beta} + \gamma = t^2(\boldsymbol{r}^\top \boldsymbol{\alpha} \boldsymbol{r}) + t(\boldsymbol{r}^\top \boldsymbol{\alpha} \boldsymbol{s} + \boldsymbol{s}^\top \boldsymbol{\alpha} \boldsymbol{r} + \boldsymbol{r}^\top \boldsymbol{\beta})$$
$$+ (\boldsymbol{s}^\top \boldsymbol{\alpha} \boldsymbol{s} + \boldsymbol{s}^\top \boldsymbol{\beta} + \gamma) = e_1 t^2 + e_2 t + e_3$$

In particular, with overwhelming probability (over the choice of s that is information theoretically hidden from $\mathcal{B}$'s view) $e_3 \neq 0$. From this solution, $\mathcal{C}$ can solve the system and extract t.

On Achieving Strong True-Simulation Extractability. We recall that for strong tSE we additionally require non-malleability on the proofs π in that our winning condition is changed to $(\tau', x', \pi') \notin Q$. Now to achieve this we can use the generic compiler from [32] and in particular we additionally use a strongly unforgeable (sEUF-CMA-secure) one-time signature (sOTS) scheme (e.g., Groth's sOTS [25] or Boneh-Boyen signatures [11]). The prover P is now changed so that in addition to computing the proof of the tSE Sub-ZK QA-NIZK it samples a key pair of the sOTS and signs the proof, where the signature and the verification key are attached to the proof. Moreover, instead of randomly choosing the tag τ, P uses a collision-resistant hash function and computes the tag as the hash of the verification key of the sOTS and the word x. Verification is then straightforward.

5 Integrating Sub-ZK QA-NIZK into LegoSNARK

5.1 The LegoSNARK Framework

We recall that LegoSNARK [13] is a framework for Commit-and-Prove zk-SNARKs (CP-SNARKs) with the aim of constructing a "global" SNARK for some computation C via the linking of "smaller" specialized SNARKs for different subroutines that overall compose to C. LegoSNARK denotes these specialized SNARKs by proof gadgets which form the basic building blocks that can be reused and composed as required. The main idea is that by letting each subroutine of C be handled by a different proof system chosen such that one that maximizes a metric (e.g., efficiency) important for the concrete application.

Therefore, LegoSNARK relies on the commit-and-prove (CP) methodology [14], i.e., one proves statements of the form *commitment* $c_{\mathsf{ck}}(x)$ *contains* x *such that* $\mathcal{R}(x, \boldsymbol{w}) = 1$. LegoSNARK considers new CP-SNARKs for several basic relations, where the main one is $\mathsf{CP}_{\mathsf{link}}$ for proving that two different commitments (i.e., Pedersen-like commitments) open to the same vector. More precisely, $\mathsf{CP}_{\mathsf{link}}$ proves that a linear relation $\boldsymbol{F}\boldsymbol{u} = x$ holds for a committed vector $\boldsymbol{u}$, a public matrix $\boldsymbol{F}$ and public vector x.

Using $\mathsf{CP}_{\mathsf{link}}$ LegoSNARK obtains CP versions of popular efficient zkSNARKs, such as Groth's [27], and zkSNARKs for linear subspaces (QA-NZIKs) [37], latter which can prove statements about data committed using the Pedersen scheme for vectors [43]. Such commit-and-prove schemes are useful in applications where one needs to commit before the SNARK keys for a relation are created, e.g., to post commitments on a blockchain so that one can later prove statements about the committed data.

5.2 Integration of Sub-ZK QA-NIZK into LegoSNARK

We now show how to integrate our Sub-ZK QA-NIZK (as well as unbounded tSE Sub-ZK QA-NIZK discussed in Sect. 4) into the LegoSNARK framework of CP-SNARKs [13]. LegoSNARK uses a knowledge-sound version of the Kiltz-Wee QA-NIZK Π'_{as}. They show how to use this QA-NIZK to construct CP-SNARKs that work for any commitment scheme whose verification algorithm is the same as the generalized Pedersen commitment and present two schemes. The first scheme $\mathsf{CP}^{\mathsf{Ped}}_{\mathsf{link}}$ allows proving that commitments under different keys open to the same vector and the second more general scheme $\mathsf{CP}^{\mathsf{Ped}}_{\mathsf{lin}}$ allows proving the correctness of a linear function of a committed vector.

Subsequently, we will show how to transform our Sub-ZK QA-NIZK and (strong) tSE Sub-ZK QA-NIZK into Sub-CP-SNARKs and (strong) tSE Sub-CP-SNARKs. Then, we will construct subversion variants of the more general $\mathsf{CP}^{\mathsf{Ped}}_{\mathsf{lin}}$ which we denote Sub-$\mathsf{CP}^{\mathsf{Ped}}_{\mathsf{lin}}$ and tSE Sub-$\mathsf{CP}^{\mathsf{Ped}}_{\mathsf{lin}}$ respectively. For the Sub-$\mathsf{CP}^{\mathsf{Ped}}_{\mathsf{lin}}$ version, we note that our result can be applied equivalently to the more specific first scheme. Technically, we, therefore, need to show that our Π_{sub} based on Π'_{as} is knowledge-sound. With regard to the potentially malicious generation of the respective commitment keys, as mentioned in [13], for Pedersen commitments they can easily be sampled in a transparent way such that no trusted setup is needed, e.g., by deriving them using a suitable hash function modelled as a random oracle. Consequently, we obtain a subversion variant of LegoSNARK for the QA-NIZK part and stress that using other recent results on subversion zk-SNARKs in [5,8,29,41], one can further extend the toolbox of a subversion variant of the LegoSNARK framework.

We now demonstrate how to construct a Sub-$\mathsf{CP}^{\mathsf{Ped}}_{\mathsf{lin}}$ and (strong) tSE Sub-$\mathsf{CP}^{\mathsf{Ped}}_{\mathsf{lin}}$ for the linear relation $\mathcal{R}^{\mathsf{Lin}}$, which checks linear properties of some committed vectors: for a fixed public matrix $M \in \mathbb{Z}_p^{n \times m}$, relation $\mathcal{R}^{\mathsf{Lin}}_M$ over public input $[y]_1 \in \mathbb{G}_1^n$ and witness $w \in \mathbb{Z}_p^m$, with $w := (w_j)_{j \in [\ell]}$ and $w_j \in \mathbb{Z}_p^{n_j}$, holds iff $[y]_1 = [M]_1 w$.

For simplicity, we mostly use the notation in [13]. Let Com be a commitment scheme such that $\mathsf{Com.VerCommit} = \mathsf{Ped.VerCommit}$. Let $\mathsf{pk} = [h]_1 \in \mathbb{G}_1^{n+1}$ be the key of the global commitment Com. In our subversion $\mathsf{CP}^{\mathsf{Ped}}_{\mathsf{lin}}$, the public inputs of the prover are ℓ commitments $(c_j)_{j \in [\ell]}$ and another commitment c'; the witness is a set of openings $((w_j)_{j \in [\ell]}; (o_j)_{j \in [\ell]})$ for commitments $(c_j)_{j \in [\ell]}$ and $[y]_1$. In particular, the prover must prove: $\mathcal{R}^{\mathsf{lin}}_{\mathsf{ped}}(y, (c_j)_{j=1}^\ell, (w_j)_{j=1}^\ell, (o_j)_{j=1}^\ell) = 1 \iff$

$$\bigwedge_{j=1}^\ell c_j = (o_j, w_j) \cdot [h_{[0 \ldots n_j]}]_\iota \wedge y = [M]_\iota \cdot (w_1, \ldots, w_\ell).$$

Our scheme, called subversion Commit-and-Prove (Sub-$\mathsf{CP}^{\mathsf{Ped}}_{\mathsf{lin}}$), is quite similar to $\mathsf{CP}^{\mathsf{Ped}}_{\mathsf{lin}}$ of [13] but it uses a Sub-ZK QA-NIZK in the prove phase. The Sub-$\mathsf{CP}^{\mathsf{Ped}}_{\mathsf{lin}}$ essentially consists of the following algorithms:

$\mathsf{CP}^{\mathsf{Ped}}_{\mathsf{lin}}.\mathsf{K}(\mathcal{R}^{Lin}_M, \mathsf{pk})$: parse $\mathsf{pk} = [h]_1 \in \mathbb{G}_1^{m+1}$. Use $[h]_1$ and $\mathcal{R}^{Lin}_M$ to construct $[M^*]_1$ as in Eq. 2. Run $(\mathsf{crs}, \mathsf{tc}) \leftarrow \Pi_{\mathsf{sub}}.\mathsf{K}([M^*]_1)$. Return $(\mathsf{crs}, \mathsf{tc})$.

$\mathsf{CP}^{\mathsf{Ped}}_{\mathsf{lin}}.\mathsf{Vcrs}([M^*]_1, \mathsf{crs})$: return $\Pi_{\mathsf{sub}}.\mathsf{Vcrs}([M^*]_1, \mathsf{crs})$.

$\mathsf{CP}^{\mathsf{Ped}}_{\mathsf{lin}}.\mathsf{P}([M^*]_1, \mathsf{crs}, [y^*]_1, w^*)$: return $\pi \leftarrow \Pi_{\mathsf{sub}}.\mathsf{P}(M^*, \mathsf{crs}, [y^*]_1, w^*)$.

$\mathsf{CP}^{\mathsf{Ped}}_{\mathsf{lin}}.\mathsf{V}([M^*]_1, \mathsf{crs}, [y^*]_1, \pi)$: return $\Pi_{\mathsf{sub}}.\mathsf{V}([M^*]_1, \mathsf{crs}, y^*, \pi)$.

Notice that the scheme Sub-$\mathsf{CP}^{\mathsf{Ped}}_{\mathsf{lin}}$ considers each w_j to be committed using a Pedersen commitment scheme whose key is $\mathsf{pk} = [h]_1 \in \mathbb{G}_1^{m+1}$. The general idea is to express such a commit-prove relation with the linear subspace relation $\mathcal{R}_{[M^*]_1}(x^*, w^*)$ that holds iff $[y^*]_1 = [M^*]_1 w^*$, where $[y^*]_1 \in \mathbb{G}_1^l$, $[M^*]_1 \in \mathbb{G}_1^{l \times t}$, and $w^* \in \mathbb{Z}_p^t$ can be built from the inputs of $\mathcal{R}_F^{Lin}$ for $l = \ell + n$ and $t = m + \ell$, as follows:

$$
\overbrace{\begin{pmatrix} c_1 \\ \vdots \\ c_\ell \\ y \end{pmatrix}}^{y^*} = \overbrace{\begin{pmatrix} h_0 & 0 & \cdots & 0 & h_{[1,n_1]} & 0 & \cdots & 0 \\ 0 & h_0 & \cdots & 0 & 0 & h_{[1,n_2]} & \cdots & 0 \\ \vdots & & \ddots & \vdots & \vdots & & \ddots & \vdots \\ 0 & 0 & \cdots & h_0 & 0 & 0 & \cdots & h_{[1,n_\ell]} \\ 0 & 0 & \cdots & 0 & M & M & \cdots & M \end{pmatrix}}^{M^*} \overbrace{\begin{pmatrix} o_1 \\ \vdots \\ o_\ell \\ w \end{pmatrix}}^{w^*} \quad (2)
$$

Subsequently, we show that we can obtain a Sub-CP-SNARK suitable for LegoSNARK when using a suitable knowledge-sound Sub-ZK QA-NIZK Π_{sub}.

Theorem 5. *Let $M \in \mathbb{Z}_p^{n \times m}$ be a matrix from a distribution $\mathcal{D}_p$, and aux be an auxiliary input distribution. If Π_{sub} is subversion zero-knowledge and knowledge sound, then the Sub-CP-SNARK construction Sub-$\mathsf{CP}^{\mathsf{Ped}}_{\mathsf{lin}}$ given above is (i) subversion zero-knowledge and (ii) knowledge sound.*

We present the proof in the full version. Additionally, we show that we can obtain a (strong) tSE Sub-CP-SNARK suitable for LegoSNARK when using a (strong) tSE Sub-ZK QA-NIZK $\Pi_{\mathsf{utse\text{-}sub}}$.

Theorem 6. *Let $M \in \mathbb{Z}_p^{n \times m}$ be a matrix from a distribution $\mathcal{D}_p$, and aux be an auxiliary input distribution. If Π_{sub} is subversion zero-knowledge and knowledge sound, then the tSE Sub-CP-SNARK construction is tSE Sub-$\mathsf{CP}^{\mathsf{Ped}}_{\mathsf{lin}}$ given above is (i) subversion zero-knowledge and (ii) unbounded true-simulation extractable.*

Proof. The proof is straightforward from subversion zero-knowledge and unbounded true-simulation extractability of $\Pi_{\mathsf{utse\text{-}sub}}$ in Theorem 4.

Remark. LegoSNARK does not consider the integration of the asymmetric QA-NIZK (Π'_{asy}) by González et al. [24]. We note, however, that this can be done analogously to Π'_{as}, which further helps to increase the expressiveness for languages supported by QA-NIZKs in LegoSNARK. Furthermore, we want to remark that our subversion version of Π'_{asy} can be integrated into LegoSNARK analogously to the integration of the subversion version of Π'_{as}.

Acknowledgements. We would like to thank Antonio Faonio for helpful discussion. This work received funding from the European Union's Horizon 2020 ECSEL Joint Undertaking under grant agreement n° 783119 (SECREDAS), from the European Union's Horizon 2020 research and innovation programme under grant agreement n°871473 (KRAKEN), and by the Austrian Science Fund (FWF) and netidee SCIENCE under grant agreement P31621-N38 (PROFET). This work is supported by the German Federal Ministry of Education and Research BMBF (grant 16K15K042, project 6GEM).

References

1. Abdalla, M., Benhamouda, F., Pointcheval, D.: Disjunctions for Hash proof systems: new constructions and applications. In: Oswald, E., Fischlin, M. (eds.) EUROCRYPT 2015. LNCS, vol. 9057, pp. 69–100. Springer, Heidelberg (2015). https://doi.org/10.1007/978-3-662-46803-6_3

2. Abdolmaleki, B., Baghery, K., Lipmaa, H., Zając, M.: A subversion-resistant SNARK. In: Takagi, T., Peyrin, T. (eds.) ASIACRYPT 2017. LNCS, vol. 10626, pp. 3–33. Springer, Cham (2017). https://doi.org/10.1007/978-3-319-70700-6_1

3. Abdolmaleki, B., Lipmaa, H., Siim, J., Zając, M.: On QA-NIZK in the BPK model. In: Kiayias, A., Kohlweiss, M., Wallden, P., Zikas, V. (eds.) PKC 2020. LNCS, vol. 12110, pp. 590–620. Springer, Cham (2020). https://doi.org/10.1007/978-3-030-45374-9_20

4. Abdolmaleki, B., Lipmaa, H., Siim, J., Zając, M.: On Subversion-Resistant SNARKs. J. Cryptol. **34**(3), 1–42 (2021). https://doi.org/10.1007/s00145-021-09379-y

5. Abdolmaleki, B., Ramacher, S., Slamanig, D.: Lift-and-shift: obtaining simulation extractable subversion and updatable SNARKs generically. In: ACM CCS 2020 (2020)

6. Abe, M., Jutla, C.S., Ohkubo, M., Pan, J., Roy, A., Wang, Y.: Shorter QA-NIZK and SPS with tighter security. In: Galbraith, S.D., Moriai, S. (eds.) ASIACRYPT 2019. LNCS, vol. 11923, pp. 669–699. Springer, Cham (2019). https://doi.org/10.1007/978-3-030-34618-8_23

7. Abe, M., Jutla, C.S., Ohkubo, M., Roy, A.: Improved (almost) tightly-secure simulation-sound QA-NIZK with applications. In: Peyrin, T., Galbraith, S. (eds.) ASIACRYPT 2018. LNCS, vol. 11272, pp. 627–656. Springer, Cham (2018). https://doi.org/10.1007/978-3-030-03326-2_21

8. Baghery, K.: Subversion-resistant simulation (knowledge) sound NIZKs. In: Albrecht, M. (ed.) IMACC 2019. LNCS, vol. 11929, pp. 42–63. Springer, Cham (2019). https://doi.org/10.1007/978-3-030-35199-1_3

9. Baghery, K., González, A., Pindado, Z., Ràfols, C.: Signatures of knowledge for Boolean circuits under standard assumptions. In: Nitaj, A., Youssef, A. (eds.) AFRICACRYPT 2020. LNCS, vol. 12174, pp. 24–44. Springer, Cham (2020). https://doi.org/10.1007/978-3-030-51938-4_2

10. Bellare, M., Fuchsbauer, G., Scafuro, A.: NIZKs with an untrusted CRS: security in the face of parameter subversion. In: Cheon, J.H., Takagi, T. (eds.) ASIACRYPT 2016. LNCS, vol. 10032, pp. 777–804. Springer, Heidelberg (2016). https://doi.org/10.1007/978-3-662-53890-6_26

11. Boneh, D., Boyen, X.: Short signatures without random oracles. In: Cachin, C., Camenisch, J.L. (eds.) EUROCRYPT 2004. LNCS, vol. 3027, pp. 56–73. Springer, Heidelberg (2004). https://doi.org/10.1007/978-3-540-24676-3_4

12. Buck, J.: Ethereum upgrade byzantium is live, verifes'first zk-snark proof
13. Campanelli, M., Fiore, D., Querol, A.: LegoSNARK: modular design and composition of succinct zero-knowledge proofs. In: ACM CCS 2019 (2019)
14. Canetti, R., Lindell, Y., Ostrovsky, R., Sahai, A.: Universally composable two-party and multi-party secure computation. In: 34th ACM STOC (2002)
15. Damgård, I.: Towards practical public key systems secure against chosen ciphertext attacks. In: Feigenbaum, J. (ed.) CRYPTO 1991. LNCS, vol. 576, pp. 445–456. Springer, Heidelberg (1992). https://doi.org/10.1007/3-540-46766-1_36
16. Danezis, G., Fournet, C., Groth, J., Kohlweiss, M.: Square span programs with applications to succinct NIZK arguments. In: Sarkar, P., Iwata, T. (eds.) ASIACRYPT 2014. LNCS, vol. 8873, pp. 532–550. Springer, Heidelberg (2014). https://doi.org/10.1007/978-3-662-45611-8_28
17. Daza, V., González, A., Pindado, Z., Ràfols, C., Silva, J.: Shorter quadratic QA-NIZK proofs. In: Lin, D., Sako, K. (eds.) PKC 2019. LNCS, vol. 11442, pp. 314–343. Springer, Cham (2019). https://doi.org/10.1007/978-3-030-17253-4_11
18. Escala, A., Herold, G., Kiltz, E., Ràfols, C., Villar, J.: An algebraic framework for Diffie-Hellman assumptions. In: CRYPTO 2013, Part II (2013). https://doi.org/10.1007/s00145-015-9220-6
19. Fuchsbauer, G.: Subversion-zero-knowledge SNARKs. In: Abdalla, M., Dahab, R. (eds.) PKC 2018. LNCS, vol. 10769, pp. 315–347. Springer, Cham (2018). https://doi.org/10.1007/978-3-319-76578-5_11
20. Fuchsbauer, G., Kiltz, E., Loss, J.: The algebraic group model and its applications. In: Shacham, H., Boldyreva, A. (eds.) CRYPTO 2018. LNCS, vol. 10992, pp. 33–62. Springer, Cham (2018). https://doi.org/10.1007/978-3-319-96881-0_2
21. Gay, R., Hofheinz, D., Kiltz, E., Wee, H.: Tightly CCA-secure encryption without pairings. In: Fischlin, M., Coron, J.-S. (eds.) EUROCRYPT 2016. LNCS, vol. 9665, pp. 1–27. Springer, Heidelberg (2016). https://doi.org/10.1007/978-3-662-49890-3_1
22. Gennaro, R., Gentry, C., Parno, B., Raykova, M.: Quadratic span programs and Succinct NIZKs without PCPs. In: Johansson, T., Nguyen, P.Q. (eds.) EUROCRYPT 2013. LNCS, vol. 7881, pp. 626–645. Springer, Heidelberg (2013). https://doi.org/10.1007/978-3-642-38348-9_37
23. Goldwasser, S., Micali, S., Rackoff, C.: The knowledge complexity of interactive proof systems. SIAM J. Comput. 18, 186–208 (1989)
24. González, A., Hevia, A., Ràfols, C.: QA-NIZK arguments in asymmetric groups: new tools and new constructions. In: Iwata, T., Cheon, J.H. (eds.) ASIACRYPT 2015. LNCS, vol. 9452, pp. 605–629. Springer, Heidelberg (2015). https://doi.org/10.1007/978-3-662-48797-6_25
25. Groth, J.: Simulation-sound NIZK proofs for a practical language and constant size group signatures. In: Lai, X., Chen, K. (eds.) ASIACRYPT 2006. LNCS, vol. 4284, pp. 444–459. Springer, Heidelberg (2006). https://doi.org/10.1007/11935230_29
26. Groth, J.: Short pairing-based non-interactive zero-knowledge arguments. In: Abe, M. (ed.) ASIACRYPT 2010. LNCS, vol. 6477, pp. 321–340. Springer, Heidelberg (2010). https://doi.org/10.1007/978-3-642-17373-8_19
27. Groth, J.: On the size of pairing-based non-interactive arguments. In: Fischlin, M., Coron, J.-S. (eds.) EUROCRYPT 2016. LNCS, vol. 9666, pp. 305–326. Springer, Heidelberg (2016). https://doi.org/10.1007/978-3-662-49896-5_11
28. Groth, J., Maller, M.: Snarky signatures: Minimal signatures of knowledge from simulation-extractable SNARKs. Cryptology ePrint Archive, Report 2017/540

29. Groth, J., Maller, M.: Snarky signatures: minimal signatures of knowledge from simulation-extractable SNARKs. In: Katz, J., Shacham, H. (eds.) CRYPTO 2017. LNCS, vol. 10402, pp. 581–612. Springer, Cham (2017). https://doi.org/10.1007/978-3-319-63715-0_20

30. Groth, J., Ostrovsky, R., Sahai, A.: Perfect non-interactive zero knowledge for NP. In: Vaudenay, S. (ed.) EUROCRYPT 2006. LNCS, vol. 4004, pp. 339–358. Springer, Heidelberg (2006). https://doi.org/10.1007/11761679_21

31. Groth, J., Sahai, A.: Efficient non-interactive proof systems for bilinear groups. In: Smart, N. (ed.) EUROCRYPT 2008. LNCS, vol. 4965, pp. 415–432. Springer, Heidelberg (2008). https://doi.org/10.1007/978-3-540-78967-3_24

32. Haralambiev, K.: Efficient Cryptographic Primitives for Non-Interactive Zero-Knowledge Proofs and Applications. Ph.D. thesis, New York University

33. Jutla, C.S., Roy, A.: Shorter quasi-adaptive NIZK proofs for linear subspaces. J. Cryptol. **30**(4), 1116–1156 (2016). https://doi.org/10.1007/s00145-016-9243-7

34. Jutla, C.S., Roy, A.: Shorter quasi-adaptive NIZK proofs for linear subspaces. Cryptology ePrint Archive, Report 2013/109

35. Jutla, C.S., Roy, A.: Switching lemma for bilinear tests and constant-size NIZK proofs for linear subspaces. In: Garay, J.A., Gennaro, R. (eds.) CRYPTO 2014. LNCS, vol. 8617, pp. 295–312. Springer, Heidelberg (2014). https://doi.org/10.1007/978-3-662-44381-1_17

36. Kilian, J.: A note on efficient zero-knowledge proofs and arguments (extended abstract). In: 24th ACM STOC (1992)

37. Kiltz, E., Wee, H.: Quasi-adaptive NIZK for linear subspaces revisited. In: Oswald, E., Fischlin, M. (eds.) EUROCRYPT 2015. LNCS, vol. 9057, pp. 101–128. Springer, Heidelberg (2015). https://doi.org/10.1007/978-3-662-46803-6_4

38. Libert, B., Peters, T., Joye, M., Yung, M.: Non-malleability from malleability: simulation-sound quasi-adaptive NIZK proofs and CCA2-secure encryption from homomorphic signatures. In: Nguyen, P.Q., Oswald, E. (eds.) EUROCRYPT 2014. LNCS, vol. 8441, pp. 514–532. Springer, Heidelberg (2014). https://doi.org/10.1007/978-3-642-55220-5_29

39. Libert, B., Peters, T., Joye, M., Yung, M.: Compactly hiding linear spans. In: Iwata, T., Cheon, J.H. (eds.) ASIACRYPT 2015. LNCS, vol. 9452, pp. 681–707. Springer, Heidelberg (2015). https://doi.org/10.1007/978-3-662-48797-6_28

40. Lipmaa, H.: Progression-free sets and sublinear pairing-based non-interactive zero-knowledge arguments. In: Cramer, R. (ed.) TCC 2012. LNCS, vol. 7194, pp. 169–189. Springer, Heidelberg (2012). https://doi.org/10.1007/978-3-642-28914-9_10

41. Lipmaa, H.: Simulation-extractable snarks revisited. Cryptology ePrint Archive, Report 2019/612

42. Morillo, P., Ràfols, C., Villar, J.L.: The Kernel matrix Diffie-Hellman assumption. In: Cheon, J.H., Takagi, T. (eds.) ASIACRYPT 2016. LNCS, vol. 10031, pp. 729–758. Springer, Heidelberg (2016). https://doi.org/10.1007/978-3-662-53887-6_27

43. Pedersen, T.P.: Non-interactive and information-theoretic secure verifiable secret sharing. In: Feigenbaum, J. (ed.) CRYPTO 1991. LNCS, vol. 576, pp. 129–140. Springer, Heidelberg (1992). https://doi.org/10.1007/3-540-46766-1_9

44. Ràfols, C., Silva, J.: QA-NIZK arguments of same opening for bilateral commitments. In: Nitaj, A., Youssef, A. (eds.) AFRICACRYPT 2020. LNCS, vol. 12174, pp. 3–23. Springer, Cham (2020). https://doi.org/10.1007/978-3-030-51938-4_1

45. Sasson, E.B., et al.: Zerocash: decentralized anonymous payments from bitcoin. In: 2014 IEEE Symposium on Security and Privacy. IEEE (2014)

THC: Practical and Cost-Effective Verification of Delegated Computation

Pablo Rauzy$^{(\boxtimes)}$ and Ali Nehme

Université Paris 8, Saint-Denis, France
`pr@up8.edu`

Abstract. Homomorphic cryptography is used when computations are delegated to an untrusted third-party. However, there is a discrepancy between the untrustworthiness of the third-party and the silent assumption that it will perform the expected computations on the encrypted data. This may raise serious privacy concerns, for example when homomorphic cryptography is used to outsource resource-greedy computations on personal data (e.g., from an IoT device to the cloud). In this paper we show how to cost-effectively verify that the delegated computation corresponds to the expected sequence of operations, thus drastically reducing the necessary level of trust in the third-party. Our approach is based on the well-known *modular extension* scheme: it is transparent for the third-party and it is not tied to a particular homomorphic cryptosystem nor depends on newly introduced (and thus less-studied) cryptographic constructions. We provide a proof-of-concept implementation, THC (for *trustable homomorphic computation*), which we use to perform security and performance analyses. We then demonstrate its practical usability, in the case of a toy electronic voting system.

Keywords: Data and computation integrity · Security and privacy in the cloud · Usable security

1 Introduction

Delegating computation to a third-party is pretty common nowadays, with the proliferation of small devices like smartphones and tablets which are mostly terminal interfaces for cloud services. This tendency is even accelerating with the so-called *Internet of Things*. Indeed, a lot of low-power and low-performance devices are now getting connected together and, most of the time, to centralized and proprietary cloud services. Most of these devices are supposedly made to make people's life better, but part of the process is the monitoring of personal user data, for example smartwatches may collect the location and the level of physical activities of their wearer.

Hence, serious privacy concerns need to be addressed. When data only need to be stored or transmitted from the device to the cloud or from a user to another, classical cryptography (symmetric and asymmetric) can solve the problem. However, most of the time users' data have to be processed, e.g., to generate statistics or

© Springer Nature Switzerland AG 2021
M. Conti et al. (Eds.): CANS 2021, LNCS 13099, pp. 513–530, 2021.
https://doi.org/10.1007/978-3-030-92548-2_27

to compute quantities that are more informational than the raw values collected by the devices. Homomorphic cryptography allows users to encrypt their data before they are sent to the cloud for further processing. Computations can then be performed on the encrypted values, and the result can be sent back to the users, who are able to decrypt it.

While this may seem to be enough to solve the privacy issue (depending on the definition of privacy), it is not enough for users to be able to fully trust the third-party performing the computation on their homomorphically encrypted data. Indeed, there is no reason to trust the third-party with the execution of the expected sequence of operations.

For the sake of simplicity, consider this dummy example: an insurance company offers multiple options (at different prices) to their clients depending (among other things) on how well they want to be covered for weight-related diseases. In order to help their clients to choose the option that better suit their need, the insurance company offers a service that watches their body mass index (BMI $= \frac{mass}{height^2}$) over time. However, people do not want their private data such as mass and height to be sent in clear over the network, *nor to be revealed to their insurance company*. This is where homomorphic cryptography can help. Here, the user's device would send $\mathcal{E}(mass)$ and $\mathcal{E}(height)$ the homomorphically encrypted values of the user' mass and height to the insurance's cloud service, which would perform the BMI computation on the encrypted values and return it to the user, who would decrypt it and use the information to decide which insurance plan to choose. In this scenario, the user does not trust the insurance company with their personal data, but we still assume that the BMI computation is performed correctly, i.e., *the insurance company is trusted with the computation even if it is not considered trustworthy*. Yet, it is in the interest of the insurance company to sell their more expensive plans, so maybe their service would instead compute BMI$' = \frac{\mathcal{E}(mass)+20}{\mathcal{E}(height)^2}$ to influence the user's choice...

From this dummy example, we understand that in order to be able to delegate computation to an untrusted third-party, we need to have a way to verify the integrity of the delegated computation results[1].

Related Works. There are existing works on the subject [9,10,13,14]. However, these attempts at verifiable delegation of homomorphic computation are either impractical and/or introduce complex cryptographic constructions and rely on them. They also require the collaboration of the untrusted third-party, which our method does not. For example, the work of Lai et al. [10], which is the closest to what we want to achieve ourselves, introduces a new cryptographic primitive called "homomorphic encrypted authenticator", and stays at a theoretical level (it does not provide an implementation). The lack of practical and usable implementations of related work to benchmark THC against (for both security and

---

[1] Note that in a real-world IoT situation dealing with e.g., complex health or position data, it is important for the verification to be cost-effective.

performance) is a real concern. We believe our implementation[2] is an important contribution in this regard.

Contributions. In this paper we present THC, a method to practically and cost-effectively implement *trustable homomorphic computation*. Our goal is to provide a way to verify the integrity of delegated computations generically, in order to let as much freedom as possible in the choice of the homomorphic cryptosystem to use. We provide a proof-of-concept implementation (See footnote 2) in Python that we use to analyze the security and performance of the proposed method. For demonstration purpose, we also used our THC implementation to build an electronic voting system that lets a group of agents organize a secret vote using an untrusted third-party server.

Organization of the Paper. In the next section, we detail modular extension, the technique on which THC is based. After that, we present our proof-of-concept implementation in Sect. 3. We then use it to study the security and performance of the proposed method respectively in Sect. 4 and Sect. 5. In Sect. 6, we demonstrate THC in a practical use case by building an electronic voting system. Finally, we draw conclusions and think of perspectives in Sect. 7.

2 Modular Extension

Our goal is to be able to verify the integrity of a computation $\mathcal{C}$ performed on our behalf by an untrusted third-party. Of course, the verification has to be inexpensive compared to carrying out the computation $\mathcal{C}$ by ourselves.

There is another area of cryptography where the same problem with the same constraint exists: implementation security against physical attacks. One kind of physical attacks consists in injecting fault during the cryptographic computation (e.g., using an electromagnetic impulse targeted at the processor performing the computation) in the hope that the intermediate values that are tampered with (e.g., the content of a register that gets randomized) will influence the final result of the computation in such a way that will help breaking the cryptography. Such attacks have been demonstrated to be feasible since 1997 when Boneh *et al.* presented the BellCoRe[3] attack [3] which essentially reduces the complexity of retrieving an RSA private key to computing a gcd instead of solving an integer factorization problem.

In 1999, Shamir presented a countermeasure [18] to the BellCoRe attack. Shamir's idea is based on the principle of *modular extension* (see Fig. 1). It consists in lifting the computation into an over-structure (e.g., an overring $\mathbb{Z}_{pr}$) which allows to quotient the result of the computation back to the original structure (e.g., $\mathbb{F}_p$), as well as quotienting a "checksum" of the computation to a

---

[2] THC is available at https://code.up8.edu/pablo/thc. It can also be installed directly with `pip3 install thc`.

[3] The attack is named after the *Bell Communication Research* labs, where it was discovered.

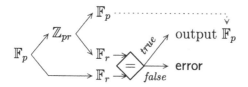

Fig. 1. Sketch of the principle of *modular extension*.

smaller structure (e.g., $\mathbb{F}_r$). What has just been described is the *direct product* of the underlying algebraic structures. If an equivalent computation is performed in parallel in the smaller structure, its result can be compared with the checksum of the main computation. If they are the same, we have a high confidence in the integrity of the main computation.

Although it was originally designed to protect CRT-RSA[4], the modular extension scheme has been successfully ported to elliptic curve scalar multiplication [1,2], and has been formally studied in both settings [6,15,16]: the cost of the countermeasure is minimal, and the non-detection probability is provably inversely proportional to the security parameter r (the size of the small structure).

Getting back to our concerns, a nice property of the modular extension scheme that, to the best of our knowledge, has not been taken advantage of yet, is that the "small computation" over $\mathbb{F}_r$ can be carried out independently from the "big computation" over $\mathbb{Z}_{pr}$, and can thus be performed on another machine entirely.

Hence our main idea: leveraging modular extension to verify the integrity of delegated homomorphic computations. By doing so, we rely on a well-established tried-and-tested method rather than introducing novel cryptographic construction that would still have to withstand the test of time. Implementation is straightforward: delegate the "big computation" over $\mathbb{Z}_{pr}$, locally perform the "small computation" over $\mathbb{F}_r$, compare the results modulo r and either return the verified result of the delegated computation modulo p, or signal an error, according to the modular extension scheme.

3   THC Implementation

In this section, we present our proof-of-concept implementation of THC. We have multiple goals with this implementation:

- show that THC is *generic*: the implementation should be able to work with any homomorphic cryptosystem as long as its ciphertexts live in a modular structure such as a field or a ring;

---

[4] CRT-RSA is an optimization of RSA using the Chinese Remainder Theorem, which makes it vulnerable to the BellCoRe attack but is indispensable on low-end devices such as credit cards (it provides an almost 4× speed-up and allows for security parameters 2× bigger).

- show that THC is *secure*: the probability of not detecting an error in the delegated computation is inversely proportional to the security parameter;
- show that THC is *cost-effective*: the verification of delegated computations using THC should be nearly free;
- show that THC is *practical*: it should be easy to use in a realistic system.

3.1   The Core

The core of the implementation consists of three classes: the THC implementation itself, and two interfaces[5]: HomomorphicCryptosystem and Computation. We will first present these interfaces and then the THC class.

HomomorphicCryptosystem. This interface requires five methods:

- a constructor, to setup the cryptosystem;
- encrypt, which takes a plaintext as argument and returns a ciphertext;
- decrypt, which does the opposite;
- get_modulus, which returns the characteristic of the ring in which the ciphertexts live; and
- mod, which applies a modulus to a ciphertext[6].

Computation. This interface requires two methods:

- local, which takes a modulus and an array of arguments, performs a computation with them and returns the result modulo the given modulus; and
- remote, which is supposed to query the untrusted third-party to perform the same computation.

THC. This class is where the modular extension scheme is implemented. Apart from its constructor, where it is given an HomomorphicCryptosystem instance $\mathcal{H}$ a Computation instance $\mathcal{C}$, and the security parameter r, it has two methods:

- compute, which takes a list of arguments $\langle a_i \rangle$ and
  1. encrypts its arguments:
     $\langle c_i \rangle \leftarrow \mathcal{H}.\text{encrypt}(\langle a_i \rangle)$,
  2. does the remote computation in $\mathbb{Z}_{Nr}$ (where N is obtained using the $\mathcal{H}.\text{get\_modulus}()$):
     $\text{result}_{Nr} \leftarrow \mathcal{C}.\text{remote}(Nr, \langle c_i \rangle)$,
  3. does the local computation in $\mathbb{F}_r$:
     $\text{result}_r \leftarrow \mathcal{C}.\text{local}(r, \langle c_i \bmod r \rangle)$,
  4. verifies the result using the second method:
- verify, which takes result_{Nr} and result_r as arguments and, as per the modular extension scheme presented in Sect. 2: compares $\text{result}_{Nr} \bmod r$ and result_r for equality, then returns $\mathcal{H}.\text{decrypt}(\text{result}_{Nr} \bmod N)$ if the comparison succeeds, or returns $\perp$ (i.e., False) otherwise.

---

[5] We use the abc Python lib (see https://docs.python.org/3/library/abc.html) for that, as Python object-model does not natively support abstract classes or interfaces.

[6] This is necessary because some cryptosystems have ciphertexts that are not plain numbers, e.g., ElGamal uses pairs and the modulus needs to be applied to both elements independently.

A Trivial Example. To explain more clearly how everything interacts and how THC is used, here is an example of `HomomorphicCryptosystem` implementation, which does not actually do any encryption[7], followed by an example of `Computation` implementation, which allows to instantiate linear polynomials:

```
class Field (HomomorphicCryptosystem):
    def __init__ (self, p):
        self._p = p
    def get_modulus (self):
        return self._p
    def encrypt (self, m):
        return m % self._p
    def decrypt (self, c):
        return c % self._p
    def mod (self, c, mod):
        return c % mod

class Linear (Computation):
    def __init__ (self, a, b):
        self.a = a
        self.b = b
    def local (self, mod, args):
        return (self.a * args[0] + self.b) % mod
    def remote (self, mod, args):
        c = Cloud.PolynomialAPI() # imaginary
        c.compute_in_ring(mod)
        return c.linear([self.a, self.b], args[0])
```

Given these implementations, the THC class could be used like this, with the security parameter $r = 17$:

```
>>> thc = THC(Field(p=59233), Linear(42, 51), 17)
>>> y = thc.compute([2021])
```

Here, y should be $(42 \times 2021 + 51) \bmod 59233$, that is 25700. According to what was explained in Sect. 2, THC will call the `Linear.remote` method with 59233×17 as `mod` and the "encrypted" value of 2021 in `args`, while the `Linear.local` method is called with 17 as `mod` and the "encrypted" value of 2021 modulo 17 (i.e., 15) in `args`.

We know that the local computation will return $(42 \times 15 + 51) \bmod 17 = 1$. If our imaginary Cloud Polynomial API gives a wrong result, its comparison with the local computation modulo 17 will most likely fail[8], and THC will return `False`. Otherwise the server returns the expected 84933 which satisfies $84933 \equiv 1 \bmod 17$, so THC will return the results modulo 59233 to give the expected answer: 25700.

3.2   Homomorphic Cryptosystems

For a given homomorphic cryptosystem to work with THC, the condition is that its ciphertexts live in a field or ring structure. This constraint still leaves a lot of choices on the table. To demonstrate the genericity of THC, we chose to implement four different homomorphic cryptosystems (in addition to the trivial one we already presented), mostly chosen for their simplicity of implementation:

---

[7] Remark that it is quite homomorphic nonetheless ;).

[8] In real settings, much bigger security parameters are used.

RSA, ElGamal, Paillier, and HE1. For illustration purpose, we will present the first two in details, including their implementation code.

RSA. The first cryptosystem we implemented is RSA [17], which is homomorphic for multiplications when used without padding (which should really never be the case when any level of security is required). The implementation of textbook RSA is quite straightforward (`modinv` is the modular inverse):

```
class RSA (HomomorphicCryptosystem):
    def __init__ (self, p, q, e):
        self._N = p * q
        self._e = e
        self._d = modinv(e, (p - 1) * (q - 1))
    def get_modulus (self):
        return self._N
    def encrypt (self, m):
        return pow(m, self._e, self._N)
    def decrypt (self, c):
        return pow(c, self._d, self._N)
```

We do not need to implement the `mod` method as the trivial version is actually already provided by the `HomomorphicCryptosystem` base class. We can test RSA's homomorphic property in a Python interpreter where `rsa` is a properly instantiated RSA object:

```
>>> c1, c2 = rsa.encrypt(43), rsa.encrypt(47)
>>> rsa.decrypt(c1 * c2)
2021 # 43 * 47 is 2021
```

ElGamal. The ElGamal cryptosystem [8] is also homomorphic for multiplications. In addition to be able to multiply ciphertext, ElGamal can also do scalar multiplication homomorphically thanks to its malleability. Its implementation is more complex than that of RSA, but this is an occasion to show that an `HomomorphicCryptosystem` implementation can consist of glue code that calls an existing external cryptographic library (namely PyCryptodome[9]):

```
import Crypto.PublicKey.ElGamal as EG
from Crypto.Random.random import StrongRandom as SR
class ElGamal (HomomorphicCryptosystem):
    def __init__ (self, p, g, y, x):
        self._p = p
        self._eg = EG.construct((p, g, y, x))
    def get_modulus (self):
        return self._p
    def encrypt (self, m):
        r = SR.randint(1, self._p - 1)
        return self._eg.encrypt(m, r)
    def decrypt (self, c):
        return self._eg.decrypt(c)
    def mod (self, c, mod):
        return (c[0] % mod, c[1] % mod)
```

Since ElGamal ciphertexts are pairs, we also have an example of how the `mod` method is used. Again, given a properly instantiated `ElGamal` object `elg` in a Python interpreter, we can test the homomorphic properties of ElGamal:

---

[9] Python Cryptography Toolkit, https://www.pycryptodome.org/.

```
>>> def scalar_mul (c, k):
...     return (c[0], c[1] * k)
>>> def mul (a, b):
...     return (a[0] * b[0], a[1] * c[1])
>>> c1, c2 = elg.encrypt(43), elg.encrypt(47)
>>> elg.decrypt(mul(c1, c2))
2021 # the value of 43 * 47 hasn't changed
>>> elg.decrypt(scalar_mul(c1, 10))
430
```

Paillier. The Paillier cryptosystem [12] can do homomorphic additions (the product of ciphertexts corresponds to the addition of plaintexts) and thus scalar multiplication. We will use it in Sect. 6 to build an electronic voting system.

```
>>> def add (a, b):
...     return a * b
>>> def scalar_mul (c, k):
...     return c ** k
>>> ten = pai.encrypt(10)
>>> three = pai.encrypt(3)
>>> pai.decrypt(add(ten, three))
13
>>> pai.decrypt(scalar_mul(ten, 3))
30
```

HE1. In their 2017 paper [7], Dyer et al. present several variants of their homomorphic encryption over the integers. From the initially proposed version HE1, they derive variants allowing to mitigate brute force guessing attack even if the inputs distribution has insufficient entropy, and then variants where they add dimensions to the ciphertexts to enhance security. For our testing purpose, we chose to implement the initial version presented in the paper, as it is easy to code and yet allows for homomorphic additions and multiplications at the same time, enabling to compute any polynomials homomorphically.

```
>>> a, b = he1.encrypt(11), he1.encrypt(3)
>>> c, d = he1.encrypt(2), he1.encrypt(9)
>>> he1.decrypt(a * b + c * d)
51
```

4   Security Analysis of THC

Before looking at experimental data, we start with some theoretical background. In the following, we call *delegated computation* the one we ask the third-party to perform, and *remote computation* the one the third-party actually performs.

4.1   Theoretical Background

The goal of THC is to verify the integrity of a delegated computation. As such, its level of security can be defined as its probability of detecting that the remote computation has been tampered with. This probability is equal to $1 - \mathbb{P}_{nd}$, where $\mathbb{P}_{nd}$ is the probability of non-detection.

The formal study of $\mathbb{P}_{nd}$ is carried out in the third section of Dugardin et al.'s paper [6] in the case of single and multiple faults in the computation. The precise value of $\mathbb{P}_{nd}$ depends on the specific computation that is delegated, but it is shown that $\mathbb{P}_{nd} \approx \frac{1}{r}$ where r is the chosen security parameter. In the appendices of the same paper the authors predict a theoretical upper-bound of $\frac{57}{r}$ in practical cases. We will not repeat the full proof here but we are still going to sketch it below.

Computations that concern us are polynomials (i.e., we can do additions and multiplications) of the input variables (the ciphertexts that we send to the third-party). We call $P(x_1, x_2, ..., x_n)$ the polynomial corresponding to the delegated computation, where the x_i are the input variables. We give the formal name P' to the remote computation, i.e., the computation of P that might have been tampered with. The polynomials P and P' can differ on everything: constant terms, like terms, and degree.

Let N be the modulus of the homomorphic cryptosystem we are using. Let r be our security parameter. Let $c_1, c_2, ..., c_n$ be the ciphertexts that we send to the third-party we delegate the computation P to. THC will detect an error if $P'(c_1, c_2, ..., c_n) \not\equiv P(c_1, c_2, ..., c_n) \bmod r$. That is, errors will not be detected if and only if: $P'(c_1, c_2, ..., c_n) \equiv P(c_1, c_2, ..., c_n) \bmod r$, while $P'(c_1, c_2, ..., c_n) \not\equiv P(c_1, c_2, ..., c_n) \bmod N$. Note that if the second condition is not fulfilled, there is actually no errors in the result of the computation. Hence, $\mathbb{P}_{nd}$ is the probability of having $P(c_1, c_2, ..., c_n) - P'(c_1, c_2, ..., c_n) \equiv 0 \bmod r$. We call ΔP the polynomial $P - P'$. For random tampering with the remote computation, we have $\mathbb{P}_{nd} = \frac{\#\text{roots}(\Delta P)}{r}$, where #roots gives the number of roots of a given polynomial in $\mathbb{F}_r$.

One could argue that a malicious third-party may not *randomly* tamper with our computation. However, we recall that due to the modular reduction by r, the inputs and coefficients of ΔP are effectively randomized. Thus, it is actually reasonable to consider ΔP's coefficients and its inputs to be random and evenly distributed over $\mathbb{F}_r$, which allows us to conclude that **the probability of non-detection of errors $\mathbb{P}_{nd}$ is indeed inversely proportional to the security parameter r**.

Moreover, in his 2006 paper [11], Leont'ev demonstrates that *"the number of zeros of a random polynomial lying inside the field $\mathbb{F}_q$ has, asymptotically as $q \to \infty$, a Poisson distribution with parameter $\lambda = 1$. In particular, a random polynomial over $\mathbb{F}_q$ has "on the average", as q increases, exactly one root in $\mathbb{F}_q$"*. This means that the proportionality constant #roots(ΔP) of $\mathbb{P}_{nd}$ is such that $\mathbb{P}_{nd} \approx \frac{1}{r}$. In particular, when r is a random 32-bit prime number as it would be the case in most practical situations, we have that $\mathbb{P}_{nd} \approx 10^{-9}$.

Nevertheless, a malicious third-party could retrieve the value of r, e.g., because in some cases we might need to provide it with the value of Nr, so that the result of the computation of P does not grow too large, and they obtain r from that by factorizing Nr. In practice, N is either prime (e.g., in ElGamal) or the product of two big primes (e.g., in RSA, Paillier, and HE1), and r is prime, but potentially much smaller, typically it is a randomly chosen 32-bit prime number, so obtaining r this way is realistic.

In such cases, a malicious third-party could easily tamper with our computation in an undetected manner. However, it would be limited to adding multiples of r to the final result of the computation. Indeed, only multiples of r can be added in P^t to bypass THC's verification. Moreover, we recall that this tampering happens on homomorphically encrypted values. This means that there is no way for a malicious third-party to perform a precise attack on the actual (i.e., decrypted) result of the computation without breaking the homomorphic encryption scheme. In practice, a malicious third-party is thus limited to vandalism. In cases where this vandalism is not obvious once the results are decrypted (e.g., a proposition getting billions of billions of votes when there are only a few dozen of participants in the vote), it is still possible to detect it by delegating the same computation twice using different values for r. If both computation do not return the same seemingly valid result, vandalism is detected. Note that this strategy requires to retrieve the result of the delegated computation a first time before delegating the same computation again using a different value for r. Otherwise, the malicious third-party can tamper with both computations in the same way by adding a multiple of the product of the two r values (which is admittedly even more constraining).

Remark that with extremely malleable homomorphic cryptosystems like HE1 which supports scalar additions and multiplications (besides additions and multiplications between ciphertexts), the decrypted result of an erroneous remote computation will keep the property of being the actual result of the computation added to a multiple of r, i.e., $\exists k \in \mathbb{Z}$ such that $\mathcal{D}(P^t(c_1, ..., c_n)) = \mathcal{D}(P(c_1, ..., c_n)) + kr$, where $\mathcal{D}$ is our homomorphic decryption function. In such situations, if r is chosen large enough to be bigger than the biggest expected result, it is possible to detect errors that bypassed THC's verification and even to get the correct result back by reducing the erroneous result modulo r.

4.2   Experimental Study

For our experimental study of THC's security, we wrote several implementations of `Computation` specifically for testing and analysis purposes[10]. These implementations' `remote` method do not actually query a third-party, but rather perform the same computation as the `local` method does, except that in order to simulate a misbehaving third-party, it inserts a random fault in the computation. Three of these have been used to test the probability of non-detection:

- `Product` computes the product of its arguments (for RSA, Paillier, HE1);
- `PairProduct` does the same thing but element-wise on pairs (for ElGamal);
- `RandomBinaryPolynomial` takes a degree at instantiation and generates a random binary polynomial of this degree, that we used with HE1.

---

[10] Scripts used to produce and analyze our experimental data are available in our Python package repository at https://code.up8.edu/pablo/thc.

Each of these computations were tested with random numbers and using randomly chosen r on 2, 4, 8, 16, and 32 bits.

The results are presented in Table 1a. In all cases, the number of missed error quickly drops as r size increases until it reaches a satisfying 0 when r is a 32-bit prime. However, we remark that for small r sizes, only the configuration where the HE1 homomorphic cryptosystem is used to perform a `RandomBinaryPolynomial` computation (called `HE1-poly` in the table) corresponds to the theoretically predicted probability of non-detection (i.e., $\mathbb{P}_{nd} \approx \frac{1}{r}$, as per Sect. 4.1). This is actually not so surprising. Indeed, Leont'ev's result [11] concerns the number of roots for a *random* polynomial, which is exactly what we have in HE1-poly. Moreover, Leont'ev's result is valid in $\mathbb{F}_r$ when $r \to \infty$, so it is expected that it does not hold for very small r. These experimental results confirm the predicted influence of the security parameter.

Table 1. Experimental results.

Experiment	r size (bits)	#runs	#missed	Ratio	Mean time (µs) in $\mathbb{Z}_N$	in $\mathbb{Z}_{Nr}$	in $\mathbb{F}_r$	Cost
RSA–prod	2	1000	810	0.81	77.144 ± 2.54	79.036 ± 2.65	0.485 ± 0.03	3.08%
	4	1000	269	0.269	76.575 ± 2.34	78.550 ± 2.27	0.495 ± 0.04	3.22%
	8	1000	30	0.03	76.465 ± 2.72	78.570 ± 2.42	0.561 ± 0.05	3.49%
	16	50000	6	0.00012	76.580 ± 2.96	79.052 ± 3.03	0.655 ± 0.06	4.08%
	32	**100000**	**0**	**0.0**	77.382 ± 3.49	79.349 ± 3.26	0.752 ± 0.07	3.51%
ElGamal–prod	2	1000	897	0.897	107.400 ± 5.09	108.705 ± 4.74	1.257 ± 0.14	2.39%
	4	1000	372	0.372	107.320 ± 2.49	107.686 ± 2.77	1.236 ± 0.09	1.49%
	8	1000	56	0.056	107.885 ± 3.74	108.948 ± 3.63	1.416 ± 0.18	2.30%
	16	50000	8	0.00016	107.666 ± 4.24	108.709 ± 4.64	1.563 ± 0.20	2.42%
	32	**100000**	**0**	**0.0**	109.061 ± 6.07	110.778 ± 6.13	2.164 ± 0.28	3.56%
Paillier–prod	2	1000	896	0.896	308.094 ± 68.99	307.876 ± 67.74	0.519 ± 0.12	0.10%
	4	1000	395	0.395	268.897 ± 16.11	269.238 ± 15.29	0.466 ± 0.05	0.30%
	8	1000	19	0.019	269.308 ± 8.96	269.641 ± 8.44	0.533 ± 0.07	0.32%
	16	50000	6	0.00012	270.559 ± 12.48	271.879 ± 12.02	0.608 ± 0.08	0.71%
	32	**100000**	**0**	**0.0**	271.324 ± 13.06	272.549 ± 13.66	0.717 ± 0.10	0.72%
HE1–prod	2	1000	904	0.904	117.082 ± 20.80	117.053 ± 20.85	0.661 ± 0.12	0.54%
	4	1000	383	0.383	114.053 ± 22.38	114.033 ± 22.80	0.660 ± 0.13	0.56%
	8	1000	31	0.031	118.745 ± 20.47	118.617 ± 20.33	0.773 ± 0.14	0.54%
	16	50000	7	0.00014	122.356 ± 16.44	122.459 ± 16.88	0.923 ± 0.13	0.84%
	32	**100000**	**0**	**0.0**	120.954 ± 17.10	121.104 ± 17.20	1.066 ± 0.15	1.01%
HE1–poly	2	1000	376	0.376	520.025 ± 16.46	518.606 ± 17.36	3.538 ± 0.25	0.41%
	4	1000	57	0.057	515.870 ± 4.64	516.368 ± 5.57	3.666 ± 0.20	0.81%
	8	1000	4	0.004	517.472 ± 9.81	516.168 ± 11.18	4.137 ± 0.29	0.55%
	16	50000	1	0.00005	532.335 ± 35.14	531.020 ± 35.19	5.140 ± 0.70	0.72%
	32	**100000**	**0**	**0.0**	531.379 ± 25.29	531.682 ± 23.52	6.345 ± 0.82	1.25%

(a) Experimentally observed security of THC.   (b) Experimentally observed time-cost of THC.

5   Performance Analysis of THC

Using THC costs both in additional memory usage and computation time. The additional memory usage strongly depends on the specific application, but is precisely predictable. Indeed, for each homomorphically encrypted number, THC needs to keep its residue modulo r, so the additional memory used correspond to the number of sensible information that are needed for the delegated computation multiplied by the size of r.

The additional computation time also depends on r. It is possible to get a sense of it by observing random computations, using the same settings as in Sect. 4.2, except that the "remote" computation does not insert errors[11].

The results are presented in Table 1b. For all configurations, N is a 2048-bit number. Times are expressed in microseconds and are means computed over 1000×1000 runs, that is 1000 random computations that are executed 1000 times each in a loop to get something measurable and averaged. Each mean is accompanied by its standard deviation. These computations were executed on an Intel® Core™ i5-6300U CPU @ 2.40 GHz, with Python version 3.7.3.

The *cost* is defined as the additional time it takes to compute in $\mathbb{Z}_{Nr}$ instead of $\mathbb{Z}_N$ added to the time it takes to perform the local computation in $\mathbb{F}_r$. It is expressed in percentage of the computation time in $\mathbb{Z}_N$.

Note that in most applications, the local computation in $\mathbb{F}_r$ can actually be performed in parallel to the remote computation in $\mathbb{Z}_{Nr}$, meaning the time cost we present is largely overestimated. Indeed, as can be seen in Table 1b, most of the cost comes from the local computation in $\mathbb{F}_r$. This can be explained by the fact that the size of N (2048 bits) and Nr (between 2050 and 2080 bits) are very similar. So much in fact that the standard deviation of the experimental cost is sometimes bigger than their difference.

These results show that **the cost of verifying a delegated computation using THC is minimal**. Indeed, the cost in additional computation time is on the order of a percent of the unverified computation time, and the cost in additional memory usage is linear with regard to the number of inputs of the delegated computation, with a constant factor depending on the size of the security parameter (typically 4 bytes). This is particularly encouraging, as computations delegated on homomorphically encrypted data tend to be expensive, owing to the size of the ciphertexts.

6   Use Case: Electronic Voting

In this section we sketch an example of THC use case[12] to help readers get a better grasp of both its utility and usability. We start by presenting a scenario, then a "naive" solution without THC, then we show how to use THC to improve

---

[11]   Scripts used to produce and analyze our experimental data are available in our Python package repository at https://code.up8.edu/pablo/thc.

[12]   The demo voting client and server are included in the THC Python package available at https://code.up8.edu/pablo/thc.

over this solution. Some explanations are doubled with Python code for clarity. Note that although the presented code was written for this sole purpose and is thus extremely simplified, it should still work as expected when executed.

Scenario. A group of agents wants to organize a vote to make some decisions. It can be a group of people (e.g., an association or a political group) or it can be some kind of sensor network that need to make a centralized decision. These agents have secure means of communication between them so they can securely exchange information or share a common secret. However, the vote has to be secret in order to avoid influence bias in the case of a group of people, or to avoid privacy concerns with regard to the data collected by the sensors (which may be owned by different people).

To keep each vote secret for all participants, votes are cast to a third-party. This third-party is an untrusted service provider, typically a voting platform in the cloud. It should not be made aware of any participant's choice, and is not trusted with the counting of votes either. In addition, participants should be able to verify that others votes are valid (no cheating).

We will use homomorphic cryptography to ensure that the voting platform can store all the votes and count the result without being able to snoop on any participant's vote nor on the final result. We will use our proposed *trustable homomorphic computation* scheme to ensure the validity of each vote as well as the integrity of the vote count.

We will see how to implement a *cumulative voting* system, where each participant has a given number of points and freely assign them to each proposition (or candidates). Cumulative voting is frequently used in federated organizations to take decision at a federal level, as each of the federated groups usually has a number of votes that depends non-linearly on its size. We remark that *plurality voting* is a particular case of cumulative voting where each participant has a single point and thus can vote for a single proposition.

Note that a *score voting* system, where each participant gives a score chosen among a finite number of possibilities (e.g., an integer between 0 and 10) to each proposition, can be implemented as an overlay on cumulative voting: it is equivalent to have a plurality vote between the possible scores for each propositions. Also remark that *approval voting* is a particular case of score voting where the score is either 0 or 1.

Threat Model. The third-party (1) should not be able to learn about any of the participants' vote, (2) should not be able to learn about the result of the votes, and (3) should not be able to manipulate the votes. Participants can securely exchange the secret keys that have to be kept secret from the third-party.

Please note that we are not actually trying to build a production-ready electronic voting system and that we disregard a lot of security details that would be mandatory for such an application (e.g., making sure it is not possible to vote twice, or to vote on behalf of someone else without their consent, etc.).

Initial Solution. We need to be able to count votes, so a natural choice is to use the Paillier cryptosystem, which can perform additions homomorphically, to encrypt the votes. We call $\mathcal{P}_{enc}$ and $\mathcal{P}_{dec}$ the encryption and decryption functions of the Paillier cryptosystem. We have that $\mathcal{P}_{dec}(\mathcal{P}_{enc}(m_1) \times \mathcal{P}_{enc}(m_2)) = m_1 + m_2$ (for easier reading, we omit the private and public key arguments to these functions). We also use a symmetric encryption scheme $(\mathcal{E}, \mathcal{D})$, such that $\mathcal{D}(\mathcal{E}(m)) = m$ (again, we omit the secret key).

We call $p_1, ..., p_n$ the propositions for a given vote. A ballot is a pair of the form $((b_1, ..., b_n), id)$ where b_i corresponds to the number of votes for p_i, and id uniquely identifies the agent of which it is the ballot. The sum $\sum_{i=1}^n b_i$ must be less than or equal to the number of votes V_{id} that the agent id has. For example, if there are 3 propositions, both $([0, 0, 7], a)$ and $([1, 2, 3], a)$ are valid ballots for a if a has 7 votes, but $([3, 4, 5], a)$, $([3, 4], a)$, or $([2, 2, 2, 1], a)$ are not. The encrypted version of the ballot (b, id) that is sent to the third-party is the pair $((c_1, ..., c_n), hid)$ where $c_i = \mathcal{P}_{enc}(b_i)$ and $hid = \mathcal{E}(id)$.

For each ballot (c, hid), the third-party can compute the product $C_{hid} = \prod_{i=1}^n c_i$ and make it public so that each participant can verify that $\mathcal{P}_{dec}(C_{hid})$ is at most equal to the number of votes that the agents identified by $id = \mathcal{D}(hid)$ is supposed to have.

Given the list of all submitted ballots $\mathcal{B}$, the encrypted results of the vote $(r_1, r_2, ..., r_n)$ can be computed by the third-party such that $r_i = \prod_{j=1}^{\#\mathcal{B}} \mathcal{B}_{j,i}$, where $\mathcal{B}_{j,i}$ is the c_i of the jth ballot in $\mathcal{B}$. The participants can retrieve the results of the vote $(P_1, ..., P_n)$ by computing each $P_i = \mathcal{P}_{dec}(r_i)$.

Problem. The presented solution is almost sufficient: threats (1) and (2) are covered by the Paillier cryptosystem. However, threat (3) is still a problem. Consider the following scenario. A group of people organize a secret vote on the platform provided by the third-party T. The question is "Should we move away from T to organize our votes?", the propositions are "yes" and "no", and each participant has one vote. In practice, people who want to chose another voting platform vote "yes", i.e. $(1, 0)$, those who want to continue using T vote "no", i.e., $(0, 1)$, and those who do not care about the platform either submit a blank vote, i.e., $(0, 0)$, or do not participate at all.

```
from thc.crypto.paillier import Paillier
from thc.utils import prime
paillier = Paillier(prime(1024), prime(1024))
mod = paillier.get_modulus()
ballots = []
def cast_vote (choice):
    if choice == 'yes':
        y, n = paillier.encrypt(1), paillier.encrypt(0)
    elif choice == 'no':
        y, n = paillier.encrypt(0), paillier.encrypt(1)
    else:
        y, n = paillier.encrypt(0), paillier.encrypt(0)
    ballots.append((y, n))
```

Initially, most people do not really care about the voting platform and many do not participate in the vote. At some point one person decides to dig into the subject and discovers that T makes use of analytics and advertisements trackers on their web interface. This person then decides to loudly campaign in favor of the "yes", explaining why using trackers is wrong and how it violates users privacy. Soon enough, more people participate in the vote.

```
cast_vote('yes'), cast_vote('no'), cast_vote('blank')
cast_vote('no'), cast_vote('yes'), cast_vote('no')
# here the campaign for the "yes" happens
cast_vote('yes'), cast_vote('yes'), cast_vote('no')
cast_vote('yes'), cast_vote('blank'), cast_vote('yes')
```

Of course it is not possible to know if the campaign convinced them or merely reminded them about the vote, before it is counted. When the vote is closed the platform should compute the result on the encrypted data and return it.

```
from functools import reduce
def result (votes, m):
    return reduce(lambda a, b: (a * b) % m, votes)
res_y = result([b[0] for b in ballots], mod)
res_n = result([b[1] for b in ballots], mod)
```

Then, the participants can retrieve the results and decrypt them.

```
yes, no = paillier.decrypt(res_y), paillier.decrypt(res_n)
```

In our example, yes is 6 and no is 4: the group decided to move away from T. However, T heard about the campaign against them and because T is clearly an evil company, they decide to manipulate the vote to have a better chance of keeping their users. Instead of taking the all the vote into account as they are, T replaces all the ballots with copies of ballots randomly chosen among those they received before the campaign against them happened.

```
from random import randint
for i in range(len(ballots)):
    forged_ballots.append(ballots[randint(0,5)])
res_y = result([b[0] for b in forged_ballots], mod)
res_n = result([b[1] for b in forged_ballots], mod)
```

The number of votes stays the same, the C_{hid} for each ballot seems okay (i.e., it is either 0 or 1 when decrypted). For the participants, there are no particular reasons to suspect a manipulation of the vote. Indeed, T cannot know the vote of any specific person nor the final result thanks to the homomorphic encryption. However, at least if the campaign for the "yes" was convincing enough, their manipulation probably biased the results in their favor.

This time, when decrypted by the participants, yes could be 4 and no could be 7, for example, thereby changing the vote result and the group decision in favor of T. These results, while manipulated, look totally legit: as explained before, the campaign for the "yes" may have reminded people to vote without convincing them.

Using THC. In a parallel universe, the same events happen, except the participants of the vote decide to use THC to verify the integrity of the vote count. At the beginning they choose a small random prime r that they keep along the other secrets (i.e., the two big primes used for Paillier), then they adapt the modulus given to T, and they create an instance of THC[13].

---

[13] Here we will only use the verify method of THC, so a Computation instance is not necessary. See Sect. 3.1.

```
r = prime(32)                             # new
mod = paillier.get_modulus() * r          # modified
thc = THC(paillier, None, r)              # new
```

They keep track of the residue modulo r of the votes. These are shared among participants so that any one of them can verify the results.

```
ballots_r = []                            # new
def cast_vote(choice):
    # ...
    ballots_r.append((y % r, n % r))      # new
```

When the vote is closed, participants compute the results modulo r on their side.

```
res_y_r = result([b[0] for b in ballots_r], r)  # new
res_n_r = result([b[1] for b in ballots_r], r)  # new
```

And when they receive the results from T, they use THC to verify the integrity of the delegated vote count.

```
yes, no = thc.verify(res_y, res_y_r), thc.verify(res_n, res_n_r)  # modified
```

This time, if T manipulates the vote, `yes` and `no` will be `False`, otherwise they will contain the actual result of the vote: threat (3) is no longer a problem.

Note that we do not dwell on it here, but THC could also be used to verify the integrity of each C_{hid} if thought necessary. More importantly, **remark the practical usability of THC**: it only requires a few lines of code on the client side, and is entirely transparent on the server side.

More Problems. Using THC, we significantly reduced the necessary trust in third-parties to which computations are delegated. However, we are still far from having removed the necessity of the trust entirely: THC can only verify the integrity of computational aspects of the delegated data processing. Logical aspects are left unverified (e.g., in our scenario, if T publishes the list of ballots, the secrecy of the vote is broken as any participants can decrypt the ballots[14]).

7   Conclusions and Perspectives

In this paper, we presented a method for verifying the integrity of delegated computations, targeted in particular at delegated computations on homomorphically encrypted data. We provide an implementation of this method called THC (for *trustable homomorphic computation*) that we used to assess the genericity, the security, and the cost of the method. We also detailed a practical use case.

We showed both in theory and in practice that THC is secure, cost-effective, and practically usable. Our implementation itself, or any implementation of the modular extension, can be used in existing code at minimal cost both in terms of development and run-time resources, thereby reducing the necessary trust in third-parties to which computations on sensible data are delegated (e.g., cloud service providers).

---

[14] Again, we never intended to design a production-ready electronic voting system This particular problem could be mitigated using the right cryptographic tools, but is still relevant to illustrate our point here.

Nonetheless, we did not achieve the goal of not having to trust the third-party *at all*. Indeed, logical aspects that must be ensured by the third-party cannot be verified using THC. In the scenario we develop in Sect. 6 for example, if the voting platform publishes the encrypted vote count incrementally after each vote rather than only when the vote is closed, it becomes possible to break the vote secrecy for anyone who knows when someone else voted.

A state-of-the-art implementation of homomorphic encryption, TFHE [5], has been used by the CEA-LIST crypto team to build Cingulata [4], a compiler that translate arbitrary C++ programs into Boolean circuits that are homomorphically evaluated using TFHE. With Cingulata, the logic of the program is protected by design, as it is embedded into the homomorphically encrypted circuit to be evaluated by a third-party. However, the third-party could still mess with the evaluation. Since TFHE ciphertexts live on a torus, which should share the properties necessary for modular extension, it would be interesting to study the feasibility of using the THC method to verify the integrity of the evaluation of delegated Cingulata circuits.

References

1. Baek, Y.-J., Vasyltsov, I.: How to prevent DPA and fault attack in a unified way for ECC scalar multiplication – ring extension method. In: Dawson, E., Wong, D.S. (eds.) ISPEC 2007. LNCS, vol. 4464, pp. 225–237. Springer, Heidelberg (2007). https://doi.org/10.1007/978-3-540-72163-5_18
2. Blömer, J., Otto, M., Seifert, J.-P.: Sign change fault attacks on elliptic curve cryptosystems. In: Breveglieri, L., Koren, I., Naccache, D., Seifert, J.-P. (eds.) FDTC 2006. LNCS, vol. 4236, pp. 36–52. Springer, Heidelberg (2006). https://doi.org/10.1007/11889700_4
3. Boneh, D., DeMillo, R.A., Lipton, R.J.: On the importance of checking cryptographic protocols for faults. In: Fumy, W. (ed.) EUROCRYPT 1997. LNCS, vol. 1233, pp. 37–51. Springer, Heidelberg (1997). https://doi.org/10.1007/3-540-69053-0_4
4. CEA-LIST Crypto Team: Cingulata: a compiler toolchain and RTE for running C++ programs over encrypted data by means of fully homomorphic encryption techniques (2018). https://github.com/CEA-LIST/Cingulata
5. Chillotti, I., Gama, N., Georgieva, M., Izabachène, M.: TFHE: fast fully homomorphic encryption library (2016). https://tfhe.github.io/tfhe/
6. Dugardin, M., Guilley, S., Moreau, M., Najm, Z., Rauzy, P.: Using modular extension to provably protect Edwards curves against fault attacks. Cryptology ePrint Archive, Report 2015/882 (2015). https://eprint.iacr.org/2015/882
7. Dyer, J., Dyer, M.E., Xu, J.: Practical homomorphic encryption over the integers. Int. J. Inf. Secur. **18**, 549–579 (2017). https://doi.org/10.1007/s10207-019-00427-0. https://arxiv.org/abs/1702.07588
8. ElGamal, T.: A public key cryptosystem and a signature scheme based on discrete logarithms. In: Blakley, G.R., Chaum, D. (eds.) CRYPTO 1984. LNCS, vol. 196, pp. 10–18. Springer, Heidelberg (1985). https://doi.org/10.1007/3-540-39568-7_2
9. Fiore, D., Gennaro, R., Pastro, V.: Efficiently verifiable computation on encrypted data. Cryptology ePrint Archive, Report 2014/202 (2014). https://eprint.iacr.org/2014/202

10. Lai, J., Deng, R.H., Pang, H., Weng, J.: Verifiable computation on outsourced encrypted data. In: Kutyłowski, M., Vaidya, J. (eds.) ESORICS 2014. LNCS, vol. 8712, pp. 273–291. Springer, Cham (2014). https://doi.org/10.1007/978-3-319-11203-9_16

11. Leont'ev, V.: Roots of random polynomials over a finite field. Math. Notes **80**(1–2), 300–304 (2006) https://doi.org/10.1007/s11006-006-0139-y

12. Paillier, P.: Public-key cryptosystems based on composite degree residuosity classes. In: Stern, J. (ed.) EUROCRYPT 1999. LNCS, vol. 1592, pp. 223–238. Springer, Heidelberg (1999). https://doi.org/10.1007/3-540-48910-X_16

13. Parno, B., Gentry, C., Howell, J., Raykova, M.: Pinocchio: nearly practical verifiable computation. Cryptology ePrint Archive, Report 2013/279 (2013). https://eprint.iacr.org/2013/279

14. Parno, B., Raykova, M., Vaikuntanathan, V.: How to delegate and verify in public: verifiable computation from attribute-based encryption. Cryptology ePrint Archive, Report 2011/597 (2011). https://eprint.iacr.org/2011/597

15. Rauzy, P., Guilley, S.: A formal proof of countermeasures against fault injection attacks on CRT-RSA. J. Cryptograph. Eng. **4**, 173–185 (2014). https://doi.org/10.1007/s13389-013-0065-3. https://eprint.iacr.org/2013/506

16. Rauzy, P., Guilley, S.: Countermeasures against high-order fault-injection attacks on CRT-RSA. In: IACR Workshop on Fault Diagnosis and Tolerance in Cryptography (2014). https://eprint.iacr.org/2014/559

17. Rivest, R.L., Shamir, A., Adleman, L.: A method for obtaining digital signatures and public-key cryptosystems. Commun. ACM **21**, 120–126 (1978). https://people.csail.mit.edu/rivest/Rsapaper.pdf

18. Shamir, A.: Method and apparatus for protecting public key schemes from timing and fault attacks. US Patent Number 5,991,415 (1999). https://www.google.com/patents/US5991415

TIRAMISU: Black-Box Simulation Extractable NIZKs in the Updatable CRS Model

Karim Baghery$^{(\boxtimes)}$ and Mahdi Sedaghat

imec-COSIC, KU Leuven, Leuven, Belgium
`karim.baghery@kuleuven.be, ssedagha@esat.kuleuven.be`

Abstract. Zk-SNARKs, as the most efficient NIZK arguments in terms of proof size and verification, are ubiquitously deployed in practice. In applications like Hawk [S&P'16], Gyges [CCS'16], Ouroboros Crypsinous [S&P'19], the underlying zk-SNARK is lifted to achieve Black-Box Simulation Extractability (BB-SE) under a trusted setup phase. To mitigate the trust in such systems, we propose TIRAMISU (In Italian, TIRAMISU literally means "lift me up"), as a construction to build NIZK arguments that can achieve *updatable BB-SE*, which we define as a new variant of BB-SE. This new variant allows *updating* the public parameters, therefore eliminating the need for a trusted third party, while unavoidably relies on a *non-black-box* extraction algorithm in the setup phase. In the cost of one-time individual CRS update by the parties, this gets around a known impossibility result by Bellare et al. from ASIACRYPT'16, which shows that BB extractability cannot be achieved with subversion ZK (ZK without trusting a third party). TIRAMISU uses an efficient public-key encryption with updatable keys which may be of independent interest. We instantiate TIRAMISU, implement the overhead and present efficient BB-SE zk-SNARKs with updatable parameters that can be used in various applications while allowing the end-users to update the parameters and eliminate the needed trust.

Keywords: zk-SNARKs · Updatable crs · Black-box simulation extractability · C∅C∅ framework

1 Introduction

Zero-Knowledge (ZK) [34] proof systems, particularly Non-Interactive Zero-Knowledge (NIZK) arguments [18] are one of the elegant tools in modern cryptography that due to their impressive advantages and practical efficiency, they are ubiquitously deployed in practical applications [15, 41, 42, 44]. A NIZK proof system allows a party P (called prover) to non-interactively prove the truth of a statement to another party V (called verifier) without leaking any information about his/her secret inputs. For instance, they allow a prover P to convince a verifier V that for a (public) statement x, he/she knows a (secret) witness w that satisfies a relation $\mathbf{R}$, $(x, w) \in \mathbf{R}$, without leaking any information about w.

© Springer Nature Switzerland AG 2021
M. Conti et al. (Eds.): CANS 2021, LNCS 13099, pp. 531–551, 2021.
https://doi.org/10.1007/978-3-030-92548-2_28

Typically, a NIZK argument is expected to satisfy, (i) *Completeness*, which implies that an honest prover always convinces an honest verifier (ii) *Soundness*, which ensures that an adversarial prover cannot convince an honest verifier except with negligible probability. (iii) *Zero-Knowledge* (ZK), which guarantees that an honestly generated proof does not reveal any information about the (secret) witness w. In practice, it is shown that bare *soundness* is not sufficient and it needs either to be amplified [44] or the protocol needs to be supported by other cryptographic primitives [15]. To deal with such concerns, different constructions are proposed that either satisfy one of the following notions, one of which is an amplified variation of soundness. (iv) *Simulation Soundness* (SS), which ensures that an adversarial prover cannot convince an honest verifier, even if he has seen polynomially many simulated proofs (generated by Sim), except with negligible probability. (v) *Knowledge Soundness* (KS), which guarantees that an adversarial prover cannot convince an honest verifier, unless he *knows* a witness w for statement x such that $(x, w) \in \mathbf{R}$. (vi) *Simulation Extractability* (SE) (a.k.a. *Simulation Knowledge Soundness*), which guarantees that an adversarial prover cannot convince an honest verifier, even if he has seen polynomially time simulated proofs, unless he *knows* a witness w for statement x.

The term *"knowledge"* in KS (in item v) and SE (in item vi) means that a successful prover should *know* a w. *knowing* is formalized by showing that there exists an algorithm Ext, which can extract the witness w (from the prover or proof) in either *non-Black-Box* (nBB) or *Black-Box* (BB) manner. Typically, nBB extraction can result in more efficient constructions, as it allows Ext_A to get access to the source-code and random coins of the adversary $\mathcal{A}$. Although the constructions that obtain BB extractability are less efficient, they provide stronger security guarantees, as it allows us to have a universal extractor Ext for *any* $\mathcal{A}$. The term *"simulation"* in notions SS (in item iv) and SE (in item vi) guarantees that the proofs are non-malleable and an adversary cannot change an old (simulated) proof to a new one such that V accepts it. The notion SE provides the strongest security and also implies non-malleability of proofs as defined in [27]. Moreover, it is shown [35] that SE is a sufficient requirement for a NIZK argument to be deployed in a Universally Composable (UC) protocol [22].

zk-SNARKs. In the Common Reference String (CRS) model [18], NIZK arguments require a trusted setup phase. Based on the underlying assumptions, they are constructed either using falsifiable or non-falsifiable assumptions [49]. At the beginning of the last decade, a line of research initiated that focused on constructing NIZK arguments with succinct proofs, which finally led to an efficient family of NIZK arguments, called zero-knowledge Succinct Non-interactive ARgument of Knowledge (zk-SNARK) [10,17,19,36,37,39,46,47,50]. zk-SNARKs are constructed based on knowledge assumptions [24] that allow *succinct* proofs and nBB extractability. Gentry and Wichs's impossibility result [33] confirmed that *succinct* proofs cannot be built based on falsifiable assumptions. Beside *succinct* proofs, all initial zk-SNARKs were designed to achieve completeness, ZK and KS (in item v) [17,36,37,46,50]. KS proofs are malleable, thus in practice users needed to make extra efforts to guarantee the non-malleability of proofs [15]. Following this concern, in 2017, Groth and Maller [39] presented a zk-SNARK that can achieve SE (in item vi) with nBB extractability, consequently generates non-malleable proofs. Recent works in this direction have led to more efficient schemes with the same security guarantees [9,10,19,47].

Mitigating the Trust in the Setup Phase of zk-SNARKs. In 2016, Bellare et al. [13] studied the security of NIZK arguments in the face of subverted CRS. They defined (vii) *Subversion-Soundness* (Sub-SND), which ensures that the protocol guarantees soundness even if $\mathcal{A}$ has generated the CRS, and (viii) *Subversion-ZK* (Sub-ZK), which ensures that the scheme achieves ZK even if $\mathcal{A}$ has generated the CRS. Then, they showed that Sub-SND is not achievable with (standard) ZK, and also we cannot achieve Sub-ZK along with BB extractability. Two follow-up works [1,31] showed that most of zk-SNARKs can be lifted to achieve Sub-ZK (in item viii) and KS with *nBB* extraction (nBB-KS). Baghery [8] showed that using the folklore OR technique [14] any Sub-ZK SNARK can be lifted to achieve Sub-ZK and SE (in item vi) with nBB extraction (nBB-SE). Meanwhile, as an extension to the MPC approach [16] and subversion security, in 2018 Groth et al. [38] introduced a new variation of the CRS model, called *updatable* CRS model which allows both prover and verifier to update the CRS and bypass the needed trust in a third party. Groth et al. first defined, (ix) *Updatable KS* (U-KS), which ensures that the protocol guarantees KS (in item 1) as long as the initial CRS generation or one of CRS updates is executed honestly, and (x) *Updatable ZK* (U-ZK), which ensures that the protocol guarantees ZK as long as the initial CRS generation or one of CRS updates is done by an honest party[1]. Then, they presented a zk-SNARK that can achieve Sub-ZK and U-KS with nBB extraction (U-nBB-KS). Namely, the prover achieves ZK without trusting the CRS generator and the verifier achieves nBB-KS without trusting the CRS generator but by one-time CRS updating. Recent constructions in this direction have better efficiency [32,48]. Recently, Abdolmaleki, Ramacher, and Slamanig [2] presented a construction, called LAMASSU, and showed that using a similar folklore OR technique [8,14,28] any zk-SNARK that satisfies Sub-ZK and U-nBB-KS can be lifted to achieve Sub-ZK and U-nBB-SE. (xi) *Updatable nBB-SE (U-nBB-SE)*, which ensures that the protocol achieves SE with nBB extraction as long as the initial CRS generation or one of CRS updates is done honestly. Recently, it is shown that two efficient updatable universal zk-SNARKs Plonk [32] and Sonic [48] can also achieve U-nBB-SE [43]. Considering the impossibility of achieving Sub-ZK along with BB extraction [13], such schemes [2,32,48] achieve the strongest notion with nBB extraction.

Using zk-SNARKs in UC-Protocols. A UC protocol [22] does not interfere with other protocols and can be arbitrarily composed with other protocols. In 2006, Groth [35] showed that a NIZK argument that can achieve BB-SE can realize the ideal NIZK-functionality $\mathcal{F}_{\mathsf{NIZK}}$ [40]. In 2015 Kosba et al. [45] proposed

---

[1] Sub-ZK is a stronger notion than U-ZK, as in Sub-ZK $\mathcal{A}$ has generated the CRS, while the later achieves ZK if at least one of CRS updates is done honestly.

a framework called CØCØ along with several constructions that allows lifting a sound NIZK argument to a BB-SE NIZK argument, such that the lifted version can be deployed in UC-protocols. In summary, given a sound NIZK argument for language $\mathbf{L}$, the CØCØ defines a new extended language $\hat{\mathbf{L}}$ appended with some primitives and returns a NIZK argument that can achieve BB-SE. We review the strongest construction of the CØCØ in the full version [11].

Unfortunately, the default security of zk-SNARKs is insufficient to be directly deployed in UC protocols. The reason is that zk-SNARK achieves nBB extraction and the extractor $\mathsf{Ext}_{\mathcal{A}}$ requires access to the source code and random coins of $\mathcal{A}$, while in UC-secure NIZK arguments, the simulator of *ideal-world* should be able to simulate corrupted parties. To do so, the simulator needs to extract witnesses without getting access to the source code of the environment's algorithm. Due to this fact, all those UC-secure applications that use zk-SNARKs [41,42,44], use CØCØ to lift the underlying zk-SNARK to achieve BB-SE, equivalently UC-security [35]. Note that the lifted zk-SNARKs that achieve BB-SE are not *witness* succinct any more, but they still are *circuit* succinct.

Our Contributions. The core of our results is presenting TIRAMISU as an alternative to the CØCØ framework but in the *updatable* CRS model. Technically speaking, TIRAMISU allows one to build simulation extractable NIZK arguments with updatable parameters that satisfies a variant of black-box extractability which we define in this work. In the NIZK arguments built with TIRAMISU the parties can update the CRS themselves instead of trusting a third party. The construction is suitable for modular use in larger cryptographic protocols, which aim to build SE NIZK arguments with BB extractability, while avoiding to trust a third party.

To construct TIRAMISU, we start with the CØCØ's construction and lift it to a construction that works in the updatable CRS model. Meanwhile, to attain fast practical performance, we consider the state-of-the-art constructions in the updatable CRS model and show that we can simplify the construction of CØCØ and achieve the same goal, particularly in the updatable CRS model. Technically speaking, the strongest construction of the CØCØ gets a sound NIZK argument for the language $\mathbf{L}$ and lifts it to a new NIZK argument for the extended language $\hat{\mathbf{L}}$, that can achieve BB-SE. The language $\hat{\mathbf{L}}$ is an extension of $\mathbf{L}$ appended with some necessary and sufficient primitives, including an encryption scheme to encrypt the witness and a Pseudo-Random Function (PRF) along with a commitment scheme that commits to the secret key of the PRF (more details in the full version [11] and Sect. 4). In composing TIRAMISU, we show that considering recent developments in building NIZK arguments with updatable CRS, namely due to the existence of nBB-SE NIZK arguments with updatable CRS (with a two-phase updatable CRS [9,10,19,20,37] or with a universal updatable string [2,32,38,48]) we can simplify the definition of $\hat{\mathbf{L}}$ by removing the commitment and PRF and construct more efficient SE NIZK arguments with (a variant of) BB extractability that also have *updatable* CRS. We show that, TIRAMISU also can be added as a layer on top of the construction proposed in [2], called LAMASSU, and together act as a generic compiler in the updatable CRS model to lift any sound NIZK argument to a SE NIZK

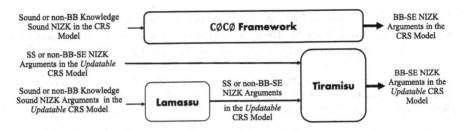

Fig. 1. Using CØCØ and TIRAMISU to build BB-SE NIZK arguments in the *standard* and *updatable* CRS models.

argument with a variant of black-box extractability. But, we show that the schemes built with this approach are less efficient than the ones built with only TIRAMISU. Figure 1 illustrates how one can use CØCØ and TIRAMISU to build BB-SE NIZKs in the *standard* and *updatable* CRS models, respectively. Similar to CØCØ framework, TIRAMISU results in NIZK arguments whose proof size and verification time are (quasi-)linear in the *witness* size, that is an unavoidable requirement for UC security [22], but still are independent of the size of the circuit, which encodes $\hat{\mathbf{L}}$.

Bellare et al.'s Negative Result. In [13], Bellare et al. observed that achieving Sub-ZK and BB extractability is impossible at the same time. As BB extractability requires the simulator create a CRS with a trapdoor it withholds, then it can extract the witness from a valid proof. But Sub-ZK requires that even if $\mathcal{A}$ generates the CRS, it should not be able to learn about the witnesses from the proof. However, if a NIZK argument achieves BB extractability, an adversary can generate the CRS like the simulator. So it has the trapdoor and can also extract the witness and break Sub-ZK. Therefore TIRAMISU achieves the best possible combination with downgrading Sub-ZK (in item viii) to U-ZK (in item x) while achieving *updatable* BB extractability, either U-BB-SE or U-BB-KS. U-BB-SE and U-BB-KS does not need a trusted third party, therefore from the trust point of view, they are stronger definitions than *standard* BB-SE and BB-KS, respectively, which require a trusted setup phase. But, in definitions of U-BB-SE and U-BB-KS, to bypass the needed trust, we rely on the existence of a nBB extraction algorithm in the setup phase that can extract the trapdoors from the (malicious) parameter generator or updaters. This seems to be unavoidable fact to achieve updatability and BB extractability at the same time.

Key-Updatable Public-Key Cryptosystems. TIRAMISU uses a semantically secure cryptosystem with *updatable keys* that we define here. We show that such cryptosystems can be built either in a generic manner from key-homomorphic encryption schemes [4], or via an ad-hoc approach. Using both generic and ad-hoc approaches, we present two variations of El-Gamal cryptosystem [29] instantiated in the pairing-based groups which fulfill the requirements of a cryptosystem with updatable keys. Efficiency of both constructions are evaluated with a prototype implementation in the Charm-Crypto framework [3], and seem to be practical. The new syntax and constructions can be interesting in their own right, particularly for building other primitives in the updatable CRS model [21,26].

There are some related definitions for encryption schemes that support updating the keys [23,30], however their definitions do not fit our requirements for distributing trust across multiple updaters in the updatable CRS model.

Table 1. A comparison of TIRAMISU with related works. ZK: Zero-knowledge, SE: Simulation Extractable, U: Updatable, S: Subversion, nBB: non-Black-Box, BB: Black-Box. ✓: Achieves, ×: Does not achieve.

	Zero-Knowledge			Simulation Extractability			
	ZK	U-ZK	S-ZK	nBB-SE	BB-SE	U-nBB-SE	U-BB-SE
TIRAMISU	✓	✓	×	✓	✓	✓	✓
CØCØ [7,45]	✓	×	×	✓	✓	×	×
[5,19,39]	✓	×	×	✓	×	×	×
[8,10,47]	✓	✓	✓	✓	×	×	×
[2,19,20]	✓	✓	✓*	✓	×	✓	×

*Theorem 4 in [2] states LAMASSU, can achieve U-ZK and U-nBB-SE, but it can be shown that it can achieve Sub-ZK along with U-nBB-SE which is a stronger combination.

Table 1 compares NIZK arguments built with TIRAMISU with existing schemes that can achieve a flavour of SE and ZK. Schemes built with CØCØ achieve BB extractability, thus they cannot achieve S-ZK, and the constructions that achieve Sub-ZK [2,8,47] can achieve (U-)nBB-SE in the best case.

Road-Map. The rest of the paper is organized as follows; Sect. 2 presents necessary preliminaries. Section 3 defines the syntax of a key-updatable cryptosystems and presents efficient variations of the El-Gamal cryptosystem as an instantiation. Our construction, TIRAMISU, and its security proofs are described in Sect. 4. In Sect. 5, we present U-BB-SE NIZK arguments built with TIRAMISU.

2   Notations

Throughout, we suppose the security parameter of the scheme be λ and $\mathsf{negl}(\lambda)$ denotes a negligible function. We use $x \leftarrow_\$ X$ to denote x sampled uniformly according to the distribution X. Also, we use $[1 \ldots n]$ to denote the set of integers in range of 1 to n. Let PPT and NUPPT denote probabilistic polynomial-time and non-uniform probabilistic polynomial-time, respectively. For an algorithm $\mathcal{A}$, let $\mathsf{im}(\mathcal{A})$ be the image of $\mathcal{A}$, i.e., the set of valid outputs of $\mathcal{A}$. Moreover, assume $\mathsf{RND}(\mathcal{A})$ denotes the random tape of $\mathcal{A}$, and $r \leftarrow_\$ \mathsf{RND}(\mathcal{A})$ denotes sampling of a randomizer r of sufficient length for $\mathcal{A}$'s needs. By $y \leftarrow \mathcal{A}(x; r)$ we mean given an input x and a randomizer r, $\mathcal{A}$ outputs y. For algorithms $\mathcal{A}$ and $\mathsf{Ext}_\mathcal{A}$, we write $(y \, \| \, y') \leftarrow (\mathcal{A} \, \| \, \mathsf{Ext}_\mathcal{A})(x; r)$ as a shorthand for "$y \leftarrow \mathcal{A}(x; r)$, $y' \leftarrow \mathsf{Ext}_\mathcal{A}(x; r)$". Two computationally IND distributions A and B are shown with $A \approx_c B$.

We use additive and the bracket notation, i.e., in group $\mathbb{G}_\mu$, $[a]_\mu = a \, [1]_\mu$, where $[1]_\mu$ is a generator of $\mathbb{G}_\mu$. A *bilinear group generator* $\mathsf{BGgen}(1^\lambda)$ returns

$(p, \mathbb{G}_1, \mathbb{G}_2, \mathbb{G}_T, \hat{e}, [1]_1, [1]_2)$, where p (a large prime) is the order of cyclic abelian groups $\mathbb{G}_1$, $\mathbb{G}_2$, and $\mathbb{G}_T$. Finally, $\hat{e} : \mathbb{G}_1 \times \mathbb{G}_2 \to \mathbb{G}_T$ is an efficient non-degenerate bilinear pairing, s.t. $\hat{e}([a]_1, [b]_2) = [ab]_T$. Denote $[a]_1 \bullet [b]_2 = \hat{e}([a]_1, [b]_2)$.

3   Public-Key Cryptosystems with Updatable Keys

As briefly discussed in Sect. 1, one of the key building blocks used in TIRAMISU is a cryptosystem with updatable keys that we define next. Similar definitions are proposed for zk-SNARKs [38], and signatures [2], but considering previous definitions in [23,30], to the best of our knowledge this is the first time that this notion is defined for the public-key cryptosystems. In contrast to subversion-resilient encryption schemes [6] that the key-generation phase might be subverted, here we consider the case that the output of the key-generation phase is updatable and parties can update the keys. We aim to achieve the standard security requirements of a cryptosystem as long as either the original key generation or at least one of the updates was done honestly. Similar to the case on paring-based subversion resistant NIZK arguments [13], we assume that the group generator is a deterministic polynomial time algorithm, which given the security parameter, it can be run by every entity without the need for a trusted third party.

3.1   Definition and Security Requirements

Definition 1 (Cryptosystems with Updatable Keys). *A public-key cryptosystem* Ψ_{Enc} *with updatable keys over the message space* $\mathcal{M}$ *and ciphertext space* $\mathcal{C}$, *consists of five PPT algorithms* $(\mathsf{KG}, \mathsf{KU}, \mathsf{KV}, \mathsf{Enc}, \mathsf{Dec})$, *defined as follows,*

- $(\mathsf{pk}_0, \Pi_{\mathsf{pk}_0}, \mathsf{sk}_0) \leftarrow \mathsf{KG}(1^\lambda)$: *Given the security parameter* 1^λ *returns the corresponding key pair* $(\mathsf{pk}_0, \mathsf{sk}_0)$ *and* Π_{pk_0} *as a proof of correctness.*
- $(\mathsf{pk}_i, \Pi_{\mathsf{pk}_i}) \leftarrow \mathsf{KU}(\mathsf{pk}_{i-1})$: *Given a valid (possibly updated) public key* pk_{i-1} *outputs* $(\mathsf{pk}_i, \Pi_{\mathsf{pk}_i})$, *where* pk_i *denotes the updated public-key and* Π_{pk_i} *is a proof for the correctness of the updating process.*
- $(1, \perp) \leftarrow \mathsf{KV}(\mathsf{pk}_i, \Pi_{\mathsf{pk}_i})$: *Given a potentially updated* pk_i *and* Π_{pk_i}, *checks the validity of the updated key. It returns either* $\perp$ *if* pk_i *is incorrectly formed (and updated), otherwise it outputs* 1.
- $(c) \leftarrow \mathsf{Enc}(\mathsf{pk}_i, m)$: *Given a (potentially updated) public key* pk_i *and a message* $m \in \mathcal{M}$, *it outputs a ciphertext* $c \in \mathcal{C}$.
- $(\perp, m') \leftarrow \mathsf{Dec}(\mathsf{sk}_i, c)$: *Given* $c \in \mathcal{C}$ *and the secret key* sk_i, *returns either* $\perp$ *(reject) or* $m' \in \mathcal{M}$ *(successful). Note that in the standard public-key cryptosystems (and in this definition before any updating)* $sk_i = sk_0$.

Primary requirements for a public-key cryptosystem with updatable keys, $\Psi_{\mathsf{Enc}} := (\mathsf{KG}, \mathsf{KU}, \mathsf{KV}, \mathsf{Enc}, \mathsf{Dec})$, can be summarized as follows,

Definition 2 (Perfect Updatable Correctness). *A cryptosystem* Ψ_{Enc} *with updatable keys is perfect updatable correct, if we have,*

$$
\Pr\left[
\begin{array}{l}
(\mathsf{pk}_0, \Pi_{\mathsf{pk}_0}, \mathsf{sk}_0 := \mathsf{sk}_0') \leftarrow \mathsf{KG}(1^\lambda), r_s \leftarrow_\$ \mathsf{RND}(\mathsf{Sub}), \\
((\{\mathsf{pk}_j, \Pi_{\mathsf{pk}_j}\}_{j=1}^i, \xi_{\mathsf{Sub}}) \| \{\mathsf{sk}_j'\}_{j=1}^i) \leftarrow (\mathsf{Sub} \| \mathit{Ext}_{\mathsf{Sub}})(\mathsf{pk}_0, \Pi_{\mathsf{pk}_0}, r_s), \\
\{\mathsf{KV}(\mathsf{pk}_j, \Pi_{\mathsf{pk}_j}) = 1\}_{j=0}^i : \mathsf{Dec}(\mathsf{sk}_i := \{\mathsf{sk}_j'\}_{j=0}^i, \mathsf{Enc}(\mathsf{pk}_i, m)) = m
\end{array}
\right] = 1 \ .
$$

where sk_j' *is the individual secret-key of each party and* pk_i *is the final public-key.*

Definition 3 (Updatable Key Hiding). *In a cryptosystem* Ψ_{Enc} *with updatable keys, for* $(\mathsf{pk}_0, \Pi_{\mathsf{pk}_0}, \mathsf{sk}_0 := \mathsf{sk}_0') \leftarrow \mathsf{KG}(1^\lambda)$ *and* $(\mathsf{pk}_i, \Pi_{\mathsf{pk}_i}) \leftarrow \mathsf{KU}(\mathsf{pk}_{i-1})$, *we say that* Π_{Enc} *is updatable key hiding, if one of the following cases holds,*

- *the original* pk_0 *was honestly generated and* KV *algorithm returns 1, namely* $(\mathsf{pk}_0, \Pi_{\mathsf{pk}_0}, \mathsf{sk}_0) \leftarrow \mathsf{KG}(1^\lambda)$ *and* $\mathsf{KV}(\mathsf{pk}_0, \Pi_{\mathsf{pk}_0}) = 1$,
- *the original* pk_0 *verifies successfully with* KV *and the key-update was generated honestly once, namely* $\mathsf{KV}(\mathsf{pk}_0, \Pi_{\mathsf{pk}_0}) = 1$ *and* $(\{\mathsf{pk}_j, \Pi_{\mathsf{pk}_j}\}_{j=1}^i) \leftarrow \mathsf{KU}(\mathsf{pk}_0)$ *such that* $\{\mathsf{KV}(\mathsf{pk}_j, \Pi_{\mathsf{pk}_j}) = 1\}_{j=1}^i$.

Definition 4 (Updatable IND-CPA). *A public-key cryptosystem* Ψ_{Enc} *with updatable keys satisfies updatable IND-CPA, if for all PPT subvertor* Sub, *for all* λ, *and for all PPT adversaries* $\mathcal{A}$,

$$
\Pr\left[
\begin{array}{l}
(\mathsf{pk}_0, \Pi_{\mathsf{pk}_0}, \mathsf{sk}_0 := \mathsf{sk}_0') \leftarrow \mathsf{KG}(1^\lambda), r_s \leftarrow_\$ \mathsf{RND}(\mathsf{Sub}), \\
(\{\mathsf{pk}_j, \Pi_{\mathsf{pk}_j}\}_{j=1}^i, \xi_{\mathsf{Sub}}) \leftarrow \mathsf{Sub}(\mathsf{pk}_0, \Pi_{\mathsf{pk}_0}, r_s), b \leftarrow_\$ \{0,1\}, (m_0, m_1) \leftarrow \\
\mathcal{A}(\mathsf{pk}_i, \xi_{\mathsf{Sub}}), b' \leftarrow \mathcal{A}(\mathsf{Enc}(\mathsf{pk}_i, m_b)) : \{\mathsf{KV}(\mathsf{pk}_j, \Pi_{\mathsf{pk}_j}) = 1\}_{j=0}^i \wedge b' = b
\end{array}
\right] \approx_\lambda \frac{1}{2} \ .
$$

where ξ_{Sub} *is the auxiliary information which is returned by the subvertor* Sub. *Note that* Sub *can also generate the initial* pk_0 *and then an honest key updater* KU *updates it and outputs* pk_i *and the proof* Π_{pk_i}.

3.2 Building Key-Updatable Cryptosystems

We first prove a theorem that gives a generic approach for building a cryptosystem with updatable keys using the key-homomorphic cryptosystems. Then, we use the generic approach and present the first key-updatable cryptosystem.

Theorem 1 (Key-Updatable Encryptions). *Every correct, IND-CPA secure, and key-homomorphic scheme* Ψ_{Enc} *with an efficient extractor* $\mathsf{Ext}_{\mathsf{Sub}}$, *satisfies updatable correctness, updatable key hiding and updatable IND-CPA security.*

The proof is provided in the full version of paper [11].

A Key-Updatable Cryptosystem from Key-Homomorphic Cryptosystems.

Next, we show that the El-Gamal cryptosystem [29] instantiated in a bilinear group $(p, \mathbb{G}_1, \mathbb{G}_2, \mathbb{G}_T, \hat{e}, [1]_1, [1]_2)$ can be represented as a key-updatable encryption scheme constructed from key-homomorphic encryptions. In bilinear group based instantiation, in contrast to the standard El-Gamal encryption (reviewed in the full version [11]), the public key consists of a pair $([x]_1, [x]_2)$. Consequently, the algorithms of new variation can be expressed as follows,

- $(\mathsf{pk}_0, \Pi_{\mathsf{pk}_0}, \mathsf{sk}_0 := \mathsf{sk}_0') \leftarrow \mathsf{KG}(1^\lambda)$: Given 1^λ, obtain $(p, \mathbb{G}_1, \mathbb{G}_2, \mathbb{G}_T, \hat{e}, [1]_1, [1]_2) \leftarrow \mathsf{BGgen}(1^\lambda)$; sample $\mathsf{sk}_0' \leftarrow_\$ \mathbb{Z}_p^*$ and return the key pair $(\mathsf{pk}_0, \mathsf{sk}_0) := ((\mathsf{pk}_0^1, \mathsf{pk}_0^2), \mathsf{sk}_0) := (([\mathsf{sk}_0']_1, [\mathsf{sk}_0']_2), \mathsf{sk}_0')$ and $\Pi_{\mathsf{pk}_0} := (\Pi_{\mathsf{pk}_0}^1, \Pi_{\mathsf{pk}_0}^2) := ([\mathsf{sk}_0']_1, [\mathsf{sk}_0']_2)$ as a proof of correctness (a.k.a. well-formedness).
- $(\mathsf{pk}_i, \Pi_{\mathsf{pk}_i}) \leftarrow \mathsf{KU}(\mathsf{pk}_{i-1})$: Obtain $(p, \mathbb{G}_1, \mathbb{G}_2, \mathbb{G}_T, \hat{e}, [1]_1, [1]_2) \leftarrow \mathsf{BGgen}(1^\lambda)$; then for a given $\mathsf{pk}_{i-1} := (\mathsf{pk}_{i-1}^1, \mathsf{pk}_{i-1}^2) := ([\mathsf{sk}_{i-1}]_1, [\mathsf{sk}_{i-1}]_2)$, for $i \geq 1$, sample $\mathsf{sk}_i' \leftarrow_\$ \mathbb{Z}_p^*$ and output: $(\mathsf{pk}_i, \Pi_{\mathsf{pk}_i}) := (([\mathsf{sk}_{i-1} + \mathsf{sk}_i']_1, [\mathsf{sk}_{i-1} + \mathsf{sk}_i']_2), ([\mathsf{sk}_i']_1, [\mathsf{sk}_i']_2))$, where $\mathsf{pk}_i := (\mathsf{pk}_i^1, \mathsf{pk}_i^2)$ denotes the updated public-key associated with the secret key $\mathsf{sk}_i := \mathsf{sk}_{i-1} + \mathsf{sk}_i'$ and $\Pi_{\mathsf{pk}_i} := (\Pi_{\mathsf{pk}_i}^1, \Pi_{\mathsf{pk}_i}^2) := ([\mathsf{sk}_i']_1, [\mathsf{sk}_i']_2)$ is the proof for correctness of the update.
- $(1, \perp) \leftarrow \mathsf{KV}(\{\mathsf{pk}_j\}_{j=0}^i, \Pi_{\mathsf{pk}_i})$: Obtain $(p, \mathbb{G}_1, \mathbb{G}_2, \mathbb{G}_T, \hat{e}, [1]_1, [1]_2) \leftarrow \mathsf{BGgen}(1^\lambda)$, and then,
  - for $i = j = 0$, given $\mathsf{pk}_0 := (\mathsf{pk}_0^1, \mathsf{pk}_0^2) := ([\mathsf{sk}_0]_1, [\mathsf{sk}_0]_2)$, and the proof $\Pi_{\mathsf{pk}_0} := (\Pi_{\mathsf{pk}_0}^1, \Pi_{\mathsf{pk}_0}^2) := ([\mathsf{sk}_0']_1, [\mathsf{sk}_0']_2)$, checks $\Pi_{\mathsf{pk}_0}^1 \bullet [1]_2 \overset{?}{=} [1]_1 \bullet \mathsf{pk}_0^2$, $[1]_1 \bullet \Pi_{\mathsf{pk}_0}^2 \overset{?}{=} \mathsf{pk}_0^1 \bullet [1]_2$, $[1]_1 \bullet \Pi_{\mathsf{pk}_0}^2 \overset{?}{=} \Pi_{\mathsf{pk}_0}^1 \bullet [1]_2$.
  - for $i \geq 1$, given $\mathsf{pk}_{i-1} := (\mathsf{pk}_{i-1}^1, \mathsf{pk}_{i-1}^2) := ([\mathsf{sk}_{i-1}]_1, [\mathsf{sk}_{i-1}]_2)$, a potentially updated $\mathsf{pk}_i := (\mathsf{pk}_i^1, \mathsf{pk}_i^2) := ([\mathsf{sk}_{i-1} + \mathsf{sk}_i']_1, [\mathsf{sk}_{i-1} + \mathsf{sk}_i']_2)$, and $\Pi_{\mathsf{pk}_i} := (\Pi_{\mathsf{pk}_i}^1, \Pi_{\mathsf{pk}_i}^2) := ([\mathsf{sk}_i']_1, [\mathsf{sk}_i']_2)$, checks $(\mathsf{pk}_{i-1}^1 + \Pi_{\mathsf{pk}_i}^1) \bullet [1]_2 \overset{?}{=} [1]_1 \bullet \mathsf{pk}_i^2$, $[1]_1 \bullet (\mathsf{pk}_{i-1}^2 + \Pi_{\mathsf{pk}_i}^2) \overset{?}{=} \mathsf{pk}_i^1 \bullet [1]_2$ and $[1]_1 \bullet \Pi_{\mathsf{pk}_i}^2 \overset{?}{=} \Pi_{\mathsf{pk}_i}^1 \bullet [1]_2$.
  in each case, if all the checks pass, it returns 1, otherwise $\perp$.
- $(c) \leftarrow \mathsf{Enc}(\mathsf{pk}_i, m)$: Obtain $(p, \mathbb{G}_1, \mathbb{G}_2, \mathbb{G}_T, \hat{e}, [1]_1, [1]_2) \leftarrow \mathsf{BGgen}(1^\lambda)$ and then given a (potentially updated) public key $\mathsf{pk}_i := ([\mathsf{sk}_i]_1, [\mathsf{sk}_i]_2)$, such that $\mathsf{sk}_i := \mathsf{sk}_{i-1} + \mathsf{sk}_i'$, and a message $m \in \mathcal{M}$, samples a randomness $r \leftarrow_\$ \mathbb{Z}_p^*$ and outputs $c := (c_1, c_2) := (m \cdot [r\mathsf{sk}_i]_T, [r]_T)$.
- $(\perp, m) \leftarrow \mathsf{Dec}(\mathsf{sk}_i, c)$: Obtain $(p, \mathbb{G}_1, \mathbb{G}_2, \mathbb{G}_T, \hat{e}, [1]_1, [1]_2) \leftarrow \mathsf{BGgen}(1^\lambda)$ and then given a ciphertext $c \in \mathcal{C}$ and a potentially updated secret key $\mathsf{sk}_i = \mathsf{sk}_{i-1} + \mathsf{sk}_i'$ it returns, $\frac{c_1}{c_2^{\mathsf{sk}}} = \frac{m \cdot [r\mathsf{sk}_i]_T}{[r\mathsf{sk}_i]_T} = m$.

In the proposed construction, for the case that $\{\mathsf{KV}(\{\mathsf{pk}_j\}_{j=0}^i, \Pi_{\mathsf{pk}_i}) = 1\}_{j=0}^i$, under the BDH-KE knowledge assumption (See the full version [11]) with checking $[1]_1 \bullet \Pi_{\mathsf{pk}_j}^2 \overset{?}{=} \Pi_{\mathsf{pk}_j}^1 \bullet [1]_2$ for $0 \leq j \leq i$, there exists an efficient nBB extractor

Ext$_{\mathsf{Sub}}$ that can extract all sk'_j from the subvertor Sub_j. Note that here we considered the standard version of the El-Gamal cryptosystem, but we could also take its *lifted* version, which encrypts g^m instead of m.

A More Efficient Key-Updatable Cryptosystem. The technique proposed in Theorem 1, acts as a generic approach but might lead to inefficient constructions. We present a more efficient key-updatable variant of El-Gamal cryptosystem.

Hash-Based El-Gamal Cryptosystem in Bilinear Groups. The hash-based variation of El-Gamal cryptosystem [29], is proven to achieve IND-CPA in the random oracle model. In the rest, we present a new variation of it, instantiated with bilinear groups, and show that the proposed variation can be represented as a secure key-updatable encryption scheme. The PPT algorithms $(\mathsf{KG}, \mathsf{KU}, \mathsf{KV})$ in the new variation are identical to those in the first variation, while the encryption and decryption algorithms $(\mathsf{Enc}, \mathsf{Dec})$ behave as follows:

- $(c) \leftarrow \mathsf{Enc}(\mathsf{H}, \mathsf{pk}_i, m)$: Given the one-way hash function H, a public key $\mathsf{pk}_i :=$ $(\mathsf{pk}_i^1, \mathsf{pk}_i^2)$ and a message $m \in \{0,1\}^n$ as inputs. It samples $r \leftarrow_{\$} \mathbb{Z}_p^*$ and returns $c := (c_1, c_2) := (m \oplus \mathsf{H}((\mathsf{pk}_i^1)^r), [r]_1)$.
- $(\perp, m) \leftarrow \mathsf{Dec}(\mathsf{H}, \mathsf{sk}_i, c)$: Given the hash function H, the secret key sk_i, corresponding to pk_i, and a ciphertext $c := (c_1, c_2)$, decrypts c by calculating $m := c_1 \oplus \mathsf{H}(c_2^{\mathsf{sk}_i})$.

Theorem 2 (Hashed El-Gamal Cryptosystem with Updatable Keys). *The proposed variation of Hashed El-Gamal encryption satisfies updatable correctness, updatable key hiding and updatable IND-CPA if BDH-KE and Extended asymmetric Computational Diffie-Hellman assumptions hold in $(\mathbb{G}_1, \mathbb{G}_2)$, and the hash function H is a random oracle.*

The proof is provided in the full version of paper [11].

3.3 Performance of the Proposed Key-Updatable Cryptosystems

We evaluate practical efficiency of both the proposed key-updatable cryptosystems using the Charm-Crypto framework [3], a Python library for pairing-based cryptography[2]. We apply Barreto-Naehrig (BN254) curve, $y^2 = x^3 + b$ with embedding curve degree 12 [12] as an SNARK-friendly curve. Benchmarks are done on a laptop with Ubuntu 20.04.2 LTS equipped with an Intel Core i7-9850H CPU @2.60 GHz and 16 GB of memory. As we observed in Sect. 3.2, both the pairing-based and hash-based constructions have the same $(\mathsf{KG}, \mathsf{KU}, \mathsf{KV})$ algorithms. In Fig. 2, we plot the running time of key-updating, KU, key-verification, KV, and the transcript size versus the number of key updates, where *transcript* refers to all the keys as well as the proofs generated with all updaters.

---

[2] The source code is publicly available on https://github.com/Baghery/Tiramisu

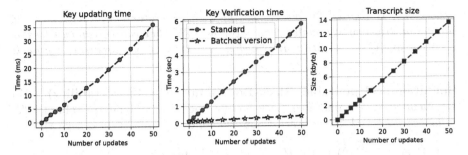

Fig. 2. Key updating, key verification (standard & batched versions) and transcript size for both the proposed key-updatable cryptosystems.

As it is illustrated in Fig. 2, in both constructions, the key updating, key verification times and the transcript size are practical and grow linearly with the number of updates. One time key updating along with generating the underlying proof requires ≈ 1 millisecond (ms), while to update a key 50 times and provide proof of correctness only takes ≈ 36 ms. To verify the validity of a key that is updated 50 times, a verifier requires ≈ 6 s in the standard form of KV algorithm, however, using the standard batching techniques [1] this can be done $12\times$ faster, in ≈ 0.5 s. In terms of the transcript size, for a key that is updated 10 times, the verifier requires to store ≈ 3 Kbytes.

Our experiments confirm that the time required for running the encryption algorithm is constant and takes about ≈ 32 ms and ≈ 1.2 ms in the pairing-based and hash-based constructions independent of the number of updates, respectively. While the running time for the decryption algorithm are equal to ≈ 4.5 ms and ≈ 1 ms, respectively. One may notice that the ciphertext size remains constant in our setting they are equal to 1028 and 46 bytes in the paring-based and Hash-based encryption schemes, respectively.

4   TIRAMISU: BB-SE NIZK in Updatable CRS Model

We present TIRAMISU, as a protocol that allows one to generically build NIZK arguments in the updatable CRS model, which achieve U-ZK [38] along with either Updatable Black-Box Simulation Extractability (U-BB-SE) or Updatable Black-Box Knowledge Soundness (U-BB-KS) which we define next. We first define Updatable Simulation Soundness (U-SS) that is used in TIRAMISU.

Definition 5 (Updatable Simulation Soundness). *A non-interactive argument Ψ_{NIZK} is updatable simulation soundness for $\mathcal{R}$, if for any subvertor* Sub, *and every PPT $\mathcal{A}$, the following probability is* $\mathsf{negl}(\lambda)$,

$$
\Pr \left[
\begin{array}{l}
(\mathbf{R}, \xi_{\mathbf{R}}) \leftarrow \mathcal{R}(1^{\lambda}), ((\mathsf{crs}_0, \Pi_{\mathsf{crs}_0}) \,\|\, \mathsf{ts}_0 := \mathsf{ts}_0') \leftarrow \mathsf{K}_{\mathsf{crs}}(\mathbf{R}, \xi_{\mathbf{R}}), r_s \leftarrow_{\$} \mathsf{RND}(\mathsf{Sub}), \\
((\{\mathsf{crs}_j, \Pi_{\mathsf{crs}_j}\}_{j=1}^i, \xi_{\mathsf{Sub}}) \,\|\, \{\mathsf{ts}_j'\}_{j=1}^i) \leftarrow (\mathsf{Sub} \,\|\, Ext_{\mathsf{Sub}})(\mathsf{crs}_0, \Pi_{\mathsf{crs}_0}, r_s), \\
\{\mathsf{CV}(\mathsf{crs}_j, \Pi_{\mathsf{crs}_j}) = 1\}_{j=0}^i, (\mathsf{x}, \pi) \leftarrow \mathcal{A}^{\mathsf{O}(\mathsf{ts}_i, \cdots)}(\mathbf{R}, \xi_{\mathbf{R}}, \mathsf{crs}_i, \xi_{\mathsf{Sub}}) : \\
(\mathsf{x}, \pi) \notin Q \wedge \mathsf{x} \notin \mathbf{L} \wedge \mathsf{V}(\mathbf{R}, \xi_{\mathbf{R}}, \mathsf{crs}_i, \mathsf{x}, \pi) = 1
\end{array}
\right] ,
$$

where Π_{crs} is a proof for correctness of CRS generation/updating, ts_i is the simulation trapdoor associated with the final CRS that can be computed using $\{ts'_j\}^i_{j=0}$, and Q is the set of simulated statement-proof pairs returned by oracle $O(.)$.

Definition 6 (Updatable Black-Box Simulation Extractability). *An argument Ψ_{NIZK} is updatable black-box (strong) simulation-extractable for $\mathcal{R}$, if for every PPT $\mathcal{A}$ and subvertor Sub, the following probability is negl(λ),*

$$\Pr\left[\begin{array}{l} (\mathbf{R}, \xi_{\mathbf{R}}) \leftarrow \mathcal{R}(1^\lambda), ((crs_0, \Pi_{crs_0}) \parallel ts_0 := ts'_0 \parallel te_0 := te'_0) \leftarrow K_{crs}(\mathbf{R}, \xi_{\mathbf{R}}), \\ r_s \leftarrow_\$ \mathsf{RND}(\mathsf{Sub}), ((\{crs_j, \Pi_{crs_j}\}^i_{j=1}, \xi_{\mathsf{Sub}}) \parallel \{ts'_j\}^i_{j=1} \parallel \{te'_j\}^i_{j=1}) \leftarrow ... \\ ...(\mathsf{Sub} \parallel \mathit{Ext}_{\mathsf{Sub}})(crs_0, \Pi_{crs_0}, r_s), \{\mathsf{CV}(crs_j, \Pi_{crs_j}) = 1\}^i_{j=0}, r_\mathcal{A} \leftarrow_\$ \mathsf{RND}(\mathcal{A}), \\ (x, \pi) \leftarrow \mathcal{A}^{O(ts_i, ...)}(\mathbf{R}, \xi_{\mathbf{R}}, crs_i, \xi_{\mathsf{Sub}}; r_\mathcal{A}), w \leftarrow \mathit{Ext}(\mathbf{R}, \xi_{\mathbf{R}}, crs_i; te_i) : \\ (x, \pi) \notin Q \wedge (x, w) \notin \mathbf{R} \wedge V(\mathbf{R}, \xi_{\mathbf{R}}, crs_i, x, \pi) = 1 \end{array}\right].$$

where $\mathit{Ext}_{\mathsf{Sub}}$ in a nBB PPT extractor (e.g. based of rewinding or knowledge assumption), Ext is a black-box PPT extractor (e.g. using a decryption algorithm), Π_{crs} is a proof for correctness of CRS generation/updating, and ts_i, te_i are the simulation and extraction trapdoors associated with the final CRS that can be computed using $\{ts'_j\}^i_{j=0}$ and $\{te'_j\}^i_{j=0}$, respectively. Here, $\mathsf{RND}(\mathcal{A}) = \mathsf{RND}(\mathsf{Sub})$ and Q is the set of the statement and simulated proofs returned by oracle $O(.)$.

Intuitively, the definition implies that under the existence of a nBB extractor in the he *setup phase*, the protocol achieves SE with BB extraction, as long as the initial CRS generation or one of CRS updates is done by an honest party. Our definition of U-BB-SE is inspired from the standard definition (realized under a trusted setup) presented by Groth [35], which considers two extractors, one for the setup phase and the other for the rest of argument. However, our definition uses a non-black-box extractor in the setup phase, which seems a *unavoidable* requirement for building U-BB-SE NIZK argument *without a trusted third party* [13]. Indeed, using some arguments or assumptions with non-black box extraction techniques, e.g. by rewinding [25] or knowledge assumptions [1,13,38], is a common and practical way to mitigate or eliminate the trust on the parameters of various cryptographic protocols. We also consider building NIZK arguments that can achieve U-BB-KS which is a weaker version of U-BB-SE, where in the former, $\mathcal{A}$ would not have access to oracle $O(\cdot)$. Note that in Definition 5 and Definition 6, it is equivalent for the adversary to batch all its updates and then think of one honest update. This requires that the trapdoor contributions of setup and update commute. This is true of known constructions in the updatable CRS model [48]. Therefore, in the underlying NIZK and key-updatable cryptosystem, we expect that they both satisfy the property that trapdoors combine and commute.

Our main goal is to construct an alternative to the C∅C∅ framework [45] but in the *updatable* CRS model, such that in new constructions the end-users can bypass the blind trust in the setup phase by one-time updating the shared parameters. Our starting point is the strongest construction of the C∅C∅ framework (reviewed in the full version [11]) that gets a sound NIZK argument and lifts it to a BB-SE NIZK argument. To do so, given a language $\mathbf{L}$ with the corresponding $\mathbf{NP}$ relation $\mathbf{R_L}$, the C∅C∅ framework defines a new language $\hat{\mathbf{L}}$ such that $((\mathsf{x}, c, \mu, \mathsf{pk}_s, \mathsf{pk}_e, \rho), (r, r_0, \mathsf{w}, s_0)) \in \mathbf{R}_{\hat{\mathbf{L}}}$ iff,

$$c = \mathsf{Enc}(\mathsf{pk}_e, \mathsf{w}; r) \wedge ((\mathsf{x}, \mathsf{w}) \in \mathbf{R_L} \vee (\mu = f_{s_0}(\mathsf{pk}_s) \wedge \rho = \mathsf{Com}(s_0; r_0))),$$

where $\{f_s : \{0,1\}^* \rightarrow \{0,1\}^\lambda\}_{s \in \{0,1\}^\lambda}$ is a pseudo-random function family, $(\mathsf{KG}_e, \mathsf{Enc}, \mathsf{Dec})$ is a set of algorithms for a semantically secure encryption scheme, $(\mathsf{KG}_s, \mathsf{Sig}_s, \mathsf{Vfy}_s)$ is a one-time signature scheme and $(\mathsf{Com}, \mathsf{Vfy})$ is a perfectly binding commitment scheme.

As a result, given a sound NIZK argument Ψ_{NIZK} for $\mathcal{R}$ constructed from PPT algorithms $(\mathsf{K_{crs}}, \mathsf{P}, \mathsf{V}, \mathsf{Sim}, \mathsf{Ext})$, the C∅C∅ framework returns a BB-SE NIZK argument $\hat{\Psi}_{\mathsf{NIZK}}$ with PPT algorithms $(\hat{\mathsf{K}}_{\mathsf{crs}}, \hat{\mathsf{P}}, \hat{\mathsf{V}}, \hat{\mathsf{Sim}}, \hat{\mathsf{Ext}})$, where $\hat{\mathsf{K}}_{\mathsf{crs}}$ is the CRS generator for new construction and acts as follows,

- $(\hat{\mathsf{crs}} \| \hat{\mathsf{ts}} \| \hat{\mathsf{te}}) \leftarrow \hat{\mathsf{K}}_{\mathsf{crs}}(\mathbf{R_L}, \xi_{\mathbf{R_L}})$: Given $(\mathbf{R_L}, \xi_{\mathbf{R_L}})$, sample $(\mathsf{crs} \| \mathsf{ts}) \leftarrow \mathsf{K}_{\mathsf{crs}}(\mathbf{R}_{\hat{\mathbf{L}}}, \xi_{\mathbf{R}_{\hat{\mathbf{L}}}})$; $(\mathsf{pk}_e, \mathsf{sk}_e) \leftarrow \mathsf{KG}_{\hat{e}}(1^\lambda)$; $s_0, r_0 \leftarrow_\$ \{0,1\}^\lambda$; $\rho := \mathsf{Com}(s_0; r_0)$; and output $(\hat{\mathsf{crs}} \| \hat{\mathsf{ts}} \| \hat{\mathsf{te}}) := ((\mathsf{crs}, \mathsf{pk}_e, \rho) \| (s_0, r_0) \| \mathsf{sk}_e)$, where $\hat{\mathsf{crs}}$ is the CRS of $\hat{\Psi}_{\mathsf{NIZK}}$ and $\hat{\mathsf{ts}}$ and $\hat{\mathsf{te}}$, respectively, are the simulation trapdoor and extraction trapdoor associated with $\hat{\mathsf{crs}}$.

Considering the description of algorithm $\hat{\mathsf{K}}_{\mathsf{crs}}$, to construct an alternative to the C∅C∅ framework but in the *updatable* CRS model, a naive solution is to construct the three primitives above (with *gray* background) in the *updatable* CRS model, and then define a similar language but using the primitives constructed in the updatable CRS model. But, considering the state-of-the-art ad-hoc constructions and generic compilers to build NIZK arguments with updatable CRS model, a more efficient solution is to simplify the language $\hat{\mathbf{L}}$ and construct more efficient BB-SE NIZK arguments with updatable parameters.

Continuing the second solution, since currently there exist some ad-hoc constructions that allow two-phase updating (e.g. [9,10,19,20]) or even a lifting construction to build nBB-SE zk-SNARKs with universal CRS in the updatable CRS model (e.g. [2]), therefore we simplify the original language $\hat{\mathbf{L}}$ defined in C∅C∅ and show that given a simulation sound NIZK argument with *updatable* CRS we can construct U-BB-SE NIZK arguments in a more efficient manner than the mentioned naive way. To this end, we use the key-updatable cryptosystems, defined and built in Sect. 3.

Let $\Psi_{\mathsf{Enc}} := (\mathsf{KG}, \mathsf{KU}, \mathsf{KV}, \mathsf{Enc}, \mathsf{Dec})$ be a set of algorithms for a semantically secure cryptosystem with updatable keys $(\mathsf{pk}_i, \mathsf{sk}_i)$. Similar to C∅C∅ framework, we define a new language $\hat{\mathbf{L}}$ based on the main language $\mathbf{L}$ corresponding to the input updatable nBB-SE NIZK $\Psi_{\mathsf{NIZK}} := (\mathsf{K_{crs}}, \mathsf{CU}, \mathsf{CV}, \mathsf{P}, \mathsf{V}, \mathsf{Sim}, \mathsf{Ext})$. The language $\hat{\mathbf{L}}$ is embedded with the encryption of witness with the *potentially updated* public key pk_i given in the CRS. Namely, given a language $\mathbf{L}$ with the corresponding **NP** relation $\mathbf{R_L}$, we define $\hat{\mathbf{L}}$ for a given random element $r \leftarrow_\$ \mathbb{F}_p$, such that $((\mathsf{x}, c, \mathsf{pk}_i), (\mathsf{w}, r)) \in \mathbf{R}_{\hat{\mathbf{L}}}$ iff, $c = \mathsf{Enc}(\mathsf{pk}_i, \mathsf{w}; r) \wedge (\mathsf{x}, \mathsf{w}) \in \mathbf{R_L}$.

The intuition behind $\hat{\mathbf{L}}$ is to enforce the P to encrypt its witness with a potentially updated public key pk_i, given in the CRS, and send the ciphertext c along with a *simulation sound* proof. Consequently, in proving BB-SE, the updated sk_i of the defined cryptosystem Ψ_{Enc} is given to the Ext, which makes it possible to extract the witness in a *black-box* manner. By sending the encryption of witnesses, the proof will not be *witness* succinct anymore, but still, it is succinct in the size of the circuit that encodes $\hat{\mathbf{L}}$.

CRS and trapdoor generation, $(\hat{\mathsf{crs}}_0, \hat{\Pi}_{\hat{\mathsf{crs}}_0}) \leftarrow \hat{\mathsf{K}}_{\mathsf{crs}}(\mathbf{R_L}, \xi_{\mathbf{R_L}})$: Given $(\mathbf{R_L}, \xi_{\mathbf{R_L}})$ acts as follows: execute key generation of Ψ_{Enc} as $(\mathsf{pk}_0, \Pi_{\mathsf{pk}_0}, \mathsf{sk}_0 := \mathsf{sk}_0') \leftarrow \mathsf{KG}(1^\lambda)$; run CRS generator of NIZK argument Ψ_{NIZK} and sample $(\mathsf{crs}_0, \Pi_{\mathsf{crs}_0}, \mathsf{ts}_0 := \mathsf{ts}_0') \leftarrow \mathsf{K}_{\mathsf{crs}}(\mathbf{R}_{\hat{\mathbf{L}}}, \xi_{\mathbf{R}_{\hat{\mathbf{L}}}})$, where ts_0 is the simulation trapdoor associated with crs_0; set $(\hat{\mathsf{crs}}_0 \| \hat{\Pi}_{\hat{\mathsf{crs}}_0} \| \hat{\mathsf{ts}}_0 \| \hat{\mathsf{te}}_0) := ((\mathsf{crs}_0, \mathsf{pk}_0) \| (\Pi_{\mathsf{crs}_0}, \Pi_{\mathsf{pk}_0}) \| \mathsf{ts}_0 \| \mathsf{sk}_0)$; where $\hat{\Pi}_{\hat{\mathsf{crs}}_0}$ is the proof of well-formedness of $\hat{\mathsf{crs}}_0$, $\hat{\mathsf{ts}}_0$ is the simulation trapdoor associated with $\hat{\mathsf{crs}}_0$, and $\hat{\mathsf{te}}_0$ is the extraction trapdoor associated with $\hat{\mathsf{crs}}_0$; Return $(\hat{\mathsf{crs}}_0, \hat{\Pi}_{\hat{\mathsf{crs}}_0})$.

CRS Updating, $(\hat{\mathsf{crs}}_i, \hat{\Pi}_{\hat{\mathsf{crs}}_i}) \leftarrow \hat{\mathsf{CU}}(\mathbf{R_L}, \xi_{\mathbf{R_L}}, \hat{\mathsf{crs}}_{i-1})$: Given $(\mathbf{R_L}, \xi_{\mathbf{R_L}}) \in \mathrm{im}(\mathcal{R}(1^\lambda))$, and $\hat{\mathsf{crs}}_{i-1}$ as an input CRS, act as follows: Parse $\hat{\mathsf{crs}}_{i-1} := (\mathsf{crs}_{i-1}, \mathsf{pk}_{i-1})$; execute $(\mathsf{crs}_i, \Pi_{\mathsf{crs}_i}) \leftarrow \mathsf{CU}(\mathbf{R_L}, \xi_{\mathbf{R_L}}, \mathsf{crs}_{i-1})$; run $(\mathsf{pk}_i, \Pi_{\mathsf{pk}_i}) \leftarrow \mathsf{KU}(\mathsf{pk}_{i-1})$; set $(\hat{\mathsf{crs}}_i \| \hat{\Pi}_{\hat{\mathsf{crs}}_i}) := ((\mathsf{crs}_i, \mathsf{pk}_i) \| (\Pi_{\mathsf{crs}_i}, \Pi_{\mathsf{pk}_i}))$, where $\hat{\Pi}_{\hat{\mathsf{crs}}_i}$ is the proof of well-formedness of $\hat{\mathsf{crs}}_i$; Return $(\hat{\mathsf{crs}}_i, \hat{\Pi}_{\hat{\mathsf{crs}}_i})$. Note that after each update, the simulation and extraction trapdoors are updated, for instance $\hat{\mathsf{ts}}_i := \mathsf{ts}_i = \mathsf{ts}_{i-1} + \mathsf{ts}_i'$, and $\hat{\mathsf{te}}_i := \mathsf{te}_i = \mathsf{te}_{i-1} + \mathsf{te}_i' := \mathsf{sk}_{i-1} + \mathsf{sk}_i'$, where ts_i' and te_i' are individual (simulation and extraction) trapdoors of the updater i, and ts_i and te_i are the trapdoors of the CRS after updating by i-th updater.

CRS Verify, $(\bot, 1) \leftarrow \hat{\mathsf{CV}}(\hat{\mathsf{crs}}_i, \hat{\Pi}_{\hat{\mathsf{crs}}_i})$: Given $\hat{\mathsf{crs}}_i := (\mathsf{crs}_i, \mathsf{pk}_i)$, and $\hat{\Pi}_{\hat{\mathsf{crs}}_i} := (\Pi_{\mathsf{crs}_i}, \Pi_{\mathsf{pk}_i})$ act as follows: if $\mathsf{CV}(\mathsf{crs}_i, \Pi_{\mathsf{crs}_i}) = 1$ and $\mathsf{KV}(\mathsf{pk}_i, \Pi_{\mathsf{pk}_i}) = 1$ return 1 (i.e., the updated $\hat{\mathsf{crs}}_i$ is correctly formed), otherwise $\bot$.

Prover, $(\hat{\pi}, \bot) \leftarrow \hat{\mathsf{P}}(\mathbf{R_L}, \xi_{\mathbf{R_L}}, \hat{\mathsf{crs}}_i, \mathsf{x}, \mathsf{w})$: Parse $\hat{\mathsf{crs}}_i := (\mathsf{crs}_i, \mathsf{pk}_i)$; Return $\bot$ if $(\mathsf{x}, \mathsf{w}) \notin \mathbf{R_L}$; sample $r \leftarrow_\$ \{0,1\}^\lambda$; compute encryption of witnesses $c = \mathsf{Enc}(\mathsf{pk}_i, \mathsf{w}; r)$. Then execute prover P of the input NIZK argument Ψ_{NIZK} and generate $\pi \leftarrow \mathsf{P}(\mathbf{R}_{\hat{\mathbf{L}}}, \xi_{\mathbf{R}_{\hat{\mathbf{L}}}}, \mathsf{crs}_i, (\mathsf{x}, c, \mathsf{pk}_i), (\mathsf{w}, r))$; and output $\hat{\pi} := (c, \pi)$.

Verifier, $(0, 1) \leftarrow \hat{\mathsf{V}}(\mathbf{R_L}, \xi_{\mathbf{R_L}}, \hat{\mathsf{crs}}_i, \mathsf{x}, \hat{\pi})$: Parse $\hat{\mathsf{crs}}_i := (\mathsf{crs}_i, \mathsf{pk}_i)$ and $\hat{\pi} := (c, \pi)$; call verifier of the input NIZK argument Ψ_{NIZK} as $\mathsf{V}(\mathbf{R}_{\hat{\mathbf{L}}}, \xi_{\mathbf{R}_{\hat{\mathbf{L}}}}, \mathsf{crs}_i, (\mathsf{x}, c, \mathsf{pk}_i), \pi)$ and returns 1 if $((\mathsf{x}, c, \mathsf{pk}_i), (\mathsf{w}, r)) \in \mathbf{R}_{\hat{\mathbf{L}}}$, otherwise it responses by 0.

Simulator, $(\hat{\pi}) \leftarrow \hat{\mathsf{Sim}}(\mathbf{R_L}, \xi_{\mathbf{R_L}}, \hat{\mathsf{crs}}_i, \mathsf{x}, \hat{\mathsf{ts}}_i)$: Parse $\hat{\mathsf{crs}}_i := (\mathsf{crs}_i, \mathsf{pk}_i)$ and $\hat{\mathsf{ts}}_i := \mathsf{ts}_i$; sample $z, r \leftarrow_\$ \{0,1\}^\lambda$; compute $c = \mathsf{Enc}(\mathsf{pk}_i, z; r)$; execute simulator of the input NIZK argument Ψ_{NIZK} and generate $\pi \leftarrow \mathsf{Sim}(\mathbf{R}_{\hat{\mathbf{L}}}, \xi_{\mathbf{R}_{\hat{\mathbf{L}}}}, \mathsf{crs}_i, (\mathsf{x}, c, \mathsf{pk}_i), \mathsf{ts}_i)$; and output $\hat{\pi} := (c, \pi)$.

Extractor, $(\mathsf{w}) \leftarrow \hat{\mathsf{Ext}}(\mathbf{R_L}, \xi_{\mathbf{R_L}}, \hat{\mathsf{crs}}_i, \hat{\mathsf{te}}_i, \mathsf{x}, \hat{\pi})$: Parse $\hat{\pi} := (c, \pi)$ and $\hat{\mathsf{te}}_i := \mathsf{sk}_i$; extract $\mathsf{w} \leftarrow \mathsf{Dec}(\mathsf{sk}_i, c)$; output w.

Fig. 3. TIRAMISU, a construction for building BB-SE NIZK argument $\hat{\Psi}_{\mathsf{NIZK}}$ with updatable CRS.

In security proofs, we show that due to updatable simulation soundness (in Definition 5) of the underlying NIZK argument Ψ_{NIZK}, the *updatable IND-CPA* security (in Definition 4) and perfect *updatable completeness* (in Definition 2) of Ψ_{Enc} is sufficient to achieve BB-SE in the updatable NIZK argument $\hat{\Psi}_{NIZK}$ for the language $\hat{L}$. By considering new language $\hat{L}$, the modified construction $\hat{\Psi}_{NIZK} := (\hat{K}_{crs}, \hat{CU}, \hat{CV}, \hat{P}, \hat{V}, \hat{Sim}, \hat{Ext})$ for $\hat{L}$ can be written as in Fig. 3.

Efficiency. Considering new language $\hat{L}$, in new argument $\hat{\Psi}_{NIZK}$ the CRS generation (CRS updating and CRS verification) of the input argument Ψ_{NIZK} will be done for a larger instance, and one also needs to generate (update and verify) the key pairs of the updatable public-key cryptosystem. The corresponding circuit of the newly defined language $\hat{L}$, expands by the number of constraints needed for the encryption function. Recall that the language $\hat{L}$ is an appended form of language L by encryption of witnesses. However, due to our simplifications in defining language $\hat{L}$, the overhead in Tiramisu will be less than the case one uses the C∅C∅ framework. Meanwhile, as we later show in Sect. 5 the efficiency of final constructions severely depends on the input NIZK argument.

The prover of the new construction $\hat{\Psi}_{NIZK}$ needs to generate a proof for new language $\hat{L}$ that would require extra computations. The proofs will be the proof of input nBB-SE updatable NIZK argument Ψ_{NIZK} appended with the ciphertext c which leads to having proofs linear in *witness* size but still succinct in the *circuit* size. It is a known result that having proofs linear in witness size is an undeniable fact to achieve BB extraction and UC-security [22,33].

As the verifier is unchanged, so the verification of new constructions will be the same as NIZK Ψ_{NIZK} but for a larger statement.

The proof of Theorems 3–5, are provided in the full version of paper [11].

Theorem 3 (Perfect Updatable Completeness). *If the input NIZK argument Ψ_{NIZK} guarantees perfect updatable completeness for the language L, and the public-key cryptosystem Ψ_{Enc} be perfectly updatable correct, then the NIZK argument constructed in Fig. 3 for language $\hat{L}$, is perfectly updatable complete.*

Theorem 4 (Computationally Updatable Zero-Knowledge). *If the input NIZK argument Ψ_{NIZK} guarantees ZK, and the public-key cryptosystem Ψ_{Enc} is updatable IND-CPA and satisfies updatable key hiding, then the NIZK argument constructed in Fig. 3 for $\hat{L}$ satisfies computational updatable ZK.*

Theorem 5 (Updatable Black-Box Simulation Extractability). *If the input NIZK argument Ψ_{NIZK} guarantees updatable correctness, updatable simulation soundness and updatable zero-knowledge, and the public-key cryptosystem Ψ_{Enc} satisfies updatable perfect correctness, updatable key hiding, and updatable IND-CPA, then the NIZK argument constructed in Fig. 3 for language $\hat{L}$ satisfies updatable BB simulation extractability.*

Note that to bypass the impossibility of achieving Sub-ZK and BB extractability in NIZKs [13], one-time honest key generation/updating on pk_i is a crucial requirement which does not allow an adversary to obtain the trapdoors associated with final updated CRS, particularly the extraction keys.

Building U-BB-KS NIZKs with Tiramisu. The primary goal of TIRAMISU is constructing BB-SE NIZK arguments in the updatable CRS model. However, due to some efficiency reasons, in practice one might need to build an Updatable Black-Box Knowledge Sound (U-BB-KS) NIZK argument. In such cases, starting from either an updatable sound NIZK or an U-nBB-KS NIZK (e.g. Groth et al.'s updatable zk-SNARK [38]), the same language $\hat{L}$ defined in TIRAMISU along with our constructed updatable public-key cryptosystem allows one to build an U-BB-KS NIZK argument. Namely, given an updatable cryptosystem $\Psi_{Enc} :=$ (KG, KU, KV, Enc, Dec) with updatable keys (pk_i, sk_i), and an *updatable sound* NIZK $\Psi_{NIZK} := (K_{crs}, CU, CV, P, V, Sim)$ for language L with the corresponding **NP** relation R_L, we define the language $\hat{L}$ for a given random element $r \leftarrow_\$ \mathbb{F}_p$, such that $((x, c, pk_i), (w, r)) \in R_{\hat{L}}$ iff, $(c = Enc(pk_i, w; r)) \wedge ((x, w) \in R_L)$.

Corollary 1. *If the input Ψ_{NIZK} for R_L guarantees updatable correctness, updatable soundness and updatable zero-knowledge, and the public-key cryptosystem Ψ_{Enc} satisfies updatable perfect correctness, updatable key hiding, and updatable IND-CPA, then the NIZK argument for language $\hat{L}$ satisfies updatable correctness, updatable knowledge soundness and updatable zero-knowledge.*

The proof can be done similar to the proof of Theorem 5, without providing the simulation oracle to the adversaries $\mathcal{A}$ and $\mathcal{B}$.

Table 2. A comparison of BB-SE NIZK arguments built with the C∅C∅ and TIRAMISU. n': Number of constraints used to encode language $\hat{L}$, $|pk|$: Size of the public key of Ψ_{Enc}, λ: Security parameter, E_i: Exponentiation in $\mathbb{G}_i$, P : Paring, l': the size of statement in new language $\hat{L}$, w : the witness for $R_{\hat{L}}$.

	C∅C∅ (with [37])	TIRAMISU (with [2,38])	TIRAMISU (with [19,20])
Trusted Setup	Yes	No	No
CRS Updatability	No	One-phase (Universal)	Two-phase
CRS Size	$\approx 3n'\mathbb{G}_1 + n'\mathbb{G}_2$	$\approx 30n'^2\mathbb{G}_1 + 9n'^2\mathbb{G}_2$	$\approx 3n'\mathbb{G}_1 + n'\mathbb{G}_2$
CRS Verifier	—	$\approx 78n'^2 P$	$14n'P$ (batchable)
CRS Updater	—	$\approx 30n'^2 E_1 + 9n'^2 E_2$	$\approx 6n'E_1 + n'E_2$
Prover	$\approx 4n'E_1 + n'E_2$	$\approx 4n'E_1 + n'E_2$	$\approx 4n'E_1 + n'E_2$
Proof Size	$o(w) + 3\mathbb{G}_1 + 2\mathbb{G}_2 + \lambda$	$o(w) + 4\mathbb{G}_1 + 3\mathbb{G}_2$	$o(w) + 3\mathbb{G}_1 + 2\mathbb{G}_2$
Verifier	$4P + l'E_1$	$6P + l'E_1$	$5P + l'E_1$

5   Building U-BB-SE NIZK Arguments with TIRAMISU

To build an U-BB-SE NIZK argument with TIRAMISU, one needs (1) a key-updatable cryptosystem Ψ_{Enc} that satisfies *perfect updatable correctness, updatable key hiding*, and *updatable IND-CPA*, and (2) a NIZK argument Ψ_{NIZK} that guarantees *updatable simulation soundness* or *U-nBB-SE*. Next, we instantiate

$\Psi_{\sf Enc}$ and $\Psi_{\sf NIZK}$, and obtain two U-BB-SE NIZK arguments. For $\Psi_{\sf Enc}$, one can use either of the proposed variations of El-Gamal cryptosystem in Sect. 3. Whereas for $\Psi_{\sf NIZK}$, one can either use an ad-hoc construction (e.g. [32,48] with universal CRS, or [9,10,19] when their CRS is generated with [20], which will have a two-phase updating), or a construction lifted with LAMASSU [2] (e.g. using [38]).

In BB-SE NIZK arguments built with TIRAMISU, the parties have to update the shared parameters individually once and check the validity of the previous updates. This is basically the computational cost that the end-users need to pay to bypass the trust in the standard CRS model. As an important practical optimization, it can be shown that the prover can only update the CRS $\hat{\sf crs}_i := (\sf crs_i, \sf pk_i)$ partially, namely only $\sf pk_i$. Table 2 summarizes the efficiency of two BB-SE NIZK arguments built with TIRAMISU and compares them with a construction lifted by the CØCØ framework in the standard CRS model. We instantiate CØCØ with the state-of-the-art zk-SNARK [37] and instantiate TIRAMISU with 1) the lifted version of [38] with LAMASSU [2], and 2) one of the constructions proposed in [10] when their CRS is sampled using the two-phase protocol proposed in [20]. As we observed in Sect. 3.3, in the resulting U-BB-SE zk-SNARKs, the overhead added by the key updateable encryption schemes add very little overhead to the CU and CV algorithms.

Both CØCØ and TIRAMISU constructions result a linear proof in the witness size, but they keep the asymptotic efficiency of other algorithms in the input NIZK. Consequently, instantiating TIRAMISU with a more efficient nBB-SE NIZK argument will result in a more efficient BB-SE NIZK argument. Therefore, as also is shown in Table 2, suitable ad-hoc constructions result in more efficient U-BB-SE NIZK arguments. We found constructing more efficient updatable nBB-SE zk-SNARKs as an interesting future research direction. Following, the impossibility result of Gentry and Wichs [33], it is undeniable that achieving BB extraction will result in non-succinct proof. Consequently, in all the schemes in Table 2, the proof size is dominated with the size of c which is a ciphertext of IND-CPA cryptosystem and is $o(\sf w)$.

Acknowledgements. This work has been supported in part by ERC Advanced Grant ERC-2015-AdG-IMPaCT, by the Defense Advanced Research Projects Agency (DARPA) under contract No. HR001120C0085, by the Research Council KU Leuven C1 on Security and Privacy for Cyber-Physical Systems and the Internet of Things with contract number C16/15/058, and by CyberSecurity Research Flanders with reference number VR20192203.

Any opinions, findings and conclusions or recommendations expressed in this material are those of the author(s) and do not necessarily reflect the views of the DARPA, the US Government, or Cyber Security Research Flanders. The U.S. Government is authorized to reproduce and distribute reprints for governmental purposes notwithstanding any copyright annotation therein.

References

1. Abdolmaleki, B., Baghery, K., Lipmaa, H., Zając, M.: A subversion-resistant SNARK. In: Takagi, T., Peyrin, T. (eds.) ASIACRYPT 2017. LNCS, vol. 10626, pp. 3–33. Springer, Cham (2017). https://doi.org/10.1007/978-3-319-70700-6_1
2. Abdolmaleki, B., Ramacher, S., Slamanig, D.: Lift-and-shift: obtaining simulation extractable subversion and updatable snarks generically. In: Proceedings of the 2020 ACM SIGSAC Conference on Computer and Communications Security, CCS 2020, pp. 1987–2005, New York, NY, USA. Association for Computing Machinery (2020)
3. Akinyele, J.A., et al.: Charm: a framework for rapidly prototyping cryptosystems. J. Cryptogr. Eng. 3(2), 111–128 (2013). https://doi.org/10.1007/s13389-013-0057-3
4. Applebaum, B., Harnik, D., Ishai, Y.: Semantic security under related-key attacks and applications. In: Chazelle, B. (ed.) ICS 2011, pp. 45–60. Tsinghua University Press (January 2011)
5. Atapoor, S., Baghery, K.: Simulation extractability in Groth's zk-SNARK. In: Pérez-Solà, C., Navarro-Arribas, G., Biryukov, A., Garcia-Alfaro, J. (eds.) DPM/CBT -2019. LNCS, vol. 11737, pp. 336–354. Springer, Cham (2019). https://doi.org/10.1007/978-3-030-31500-9_22
6. Auerbach, B., Bellare, M., Kiltz, E.: Public-key encryption resistant to parameter subversion and its realization from efficiently-embeddable groups. In: Abdalla, M., Dahab, R. (eds.) PKC 2018. LNCS, vol. 10769, pp. 348–377. Springer, Cham (2018). https://doi.org/10.1007/978-3-319-76578-5_12
7. Baghery, K.: On the efficiency of privacy-preserving smart contract systems. In: Buchmann, J., Nitaj, A., Rachidi, T. (eds.) AFRICACRYPT 2019. LNCS, vol. 11627, pp. 118–136. Springer, Cham (2019). https://doi.org/10.1007/978-3-030-23696-0_7
8. Baghery, K.: Subversion-resistant simulation (knowledge) sound NIZKs. In: Albrecht, M. (ed.) IMACC 2019. LNCS, vol. 11929, pp. 42–63. Springer, Cham (2019). https://doi.org/10.1007/978-3-030-35199-1_3
9. Baghery, K., Kohlweiss, M., Siim, J., Volkhov, M.: Another look at extraction and randomization of Groth's zk-SNARK. Cryptology ePrint Archive, Report 2020/811 (2020). https://eprint.iacr.org/2020/811
10. Baghery, K., Pindado, Z., Ràfols, C.: Simulation extractable versions of Groth's zk-SNARK revisited. In: Krenn, S., Shulman, H., Vaudenay, S. (eds.) CANS 2020. LNCS, vol. 12579, pp. 453–461. Springer, Cham (2020). https://doi.org/10.1007/978-3-030-65411-5_22
11. Baghery, K., Sedaghat, M.: Tiramisu: black-box simulation extractable NIZKs in the updatable CRS model. Cryptology ePrint Archive, Report 2020/474 (2020). https://eprint.iacr.org/2020/474
12. Barreto, P.S.L.M., Naehrig, M.: Pairing-friendly elliptic curves of prime order. In: Preneel, B., Tavares, S. (eds.) SAC 2005. LNCS, vol. 3897, pp. 319–331. Springer, Heidelberg (2006). https://doi.org/10.1007/11693383_22
13. Bellare, M., Fuchsbauer, G., Scafuro, A.: NIZKs with an untrusted CRS: security in the face of parameter subversion. In: Cheon, J.H., Takagi, T. (eds.) ASIACRYPT 2016. LNCS, vol. 10032, pp. 777–804. Springer, Heidelberg (2016). https://doi.org/10.1007/978-3-662-53890-6_26
14. Bellare, M., Goldwasser, S.: New paradigms for digital signatures and message authentication based on non-interactive zero knowledge proofs. In: Brassard, G. (ed.) CRYPTO'89. LNCS, vol. 435, pp. 194–211. Springer, Heidelberg (1990). https://doi.org/10.1007/0-387-34805-0_19

15. Ben-Sasson, E., et al.: Zerocash: decentralized anonymous payments from bitcoin. In: 2014 IEEE Symposium on Security and Privacy, pp. 459–474. IEEE Computer Society Press (May 2014)

16. Ben-Sasson, E., Chiesa, A., Green, M., Tromer, E., Virza, M.: Secure sampling of public parameters for succinct zero knowledge proofs. In: 2015 IEEE Symposium on Security and Privacy, pp. 287–304. IEEE Computer Society Press (May 2015)

17. Ben-Sasson, E., Chiesa, A., Tromer, E., Virza, M.: Succinct non-interactive arguments for a von Neumann architecture. Cryptology ePrint Archive, Report 2013/879 (2013). http://eprint.iacr.org/2013/879

18. Blum, M., Feldman, P., Micali, S.: Non-interactive zero-knowledge and its applications. In: Proceedings of the 20th Annual ACM Symposium on Theory of Computing, pp. 103–112. ACM (1988)

19. Bowe, S., Gabizon, A.: Making Groth's zk-SNARK simulation extractable in the random oracle model. Cryptology ePrint Archive, Report 2018/187 (2018). https://eprint.iacr.org/2018/187

20. Bowe, S., Gabizon, A., Miers, I.: Scalable multi-party computation for zk-SNARK parameters in the random beacon model. Technical Report 2017/1050, IACR, 26 October 2017

21. Campanelli, M., Fiore, D., Querol, A.: LegoSNARK: modular design and composition of succinct zero-knowledge proofs. In: Proceedings of the 2019 ACM SIGSAC Conference on Computer and Communications Security, pp. 2075–2092 (2019)

22. Canetti, R.: Universally composable security: a new paradigm for cryptographic protocols. In: 42nd FOCS, pp. 136–145. IEEE Computer Society Press (October 2001)

23. Canetti, R., Halevi, S., Katz, J.: A forward-secure public-key encryption scheme. In: Biham, E. (ed.) EUROCRYPT 2003. LNCS, vol. 2656, pp. 255–271. Springer, Heidelberg (2003). https://doi.org/10.1007/3-540-39200-9_16

24. Damgård, I.: Towards practical public key systems secure against chosen ciphertext attacks. In: Feigenbaum, J. (ed.) CRYPTO 1991. LNCS, vol. 576, pp. 445–456. Springer, Heidelberg (1992). https://doi.org/10.1007/3-540-46766-1_36

25. Damgård, I., Pastro, V., Smart, N., Zakarias, S.: Multiparty computation from somewhat homomorphic encryption. In: Safavi-Naini, R., Canetti, R. (eds.) CRYPTO 2012. LNCS, vol. 7417, pp. 643–662. Springer, Heidelberg (2012). https://doi.org/10.1007/978-3-642-32009-5_38

26. Daza, V., González, A., Pindado, Z., Ràfols, C., Silva, J.: Shorter quadratic QA-NIZK proofs. In: Lin, D., Sako, K. (eds.) PKC 2019. LNCS, vol. 11442, pp. 314–343. Springer, Cham (2019). https://doi.org/10.1007/978-3-030-17253-4_11

27. De Santis, A., Di Crescenzo, G., Ostrovsky, R., Persiano, G., Sahai, A.: Robust non-interactive zero knowledge. In: Kilian, J. (ed.) CRYPTO 2001. LNCS, vol. 2139, pp. 566–598. Springer, Heidelberg (2001). https://doi.org/10.1007/3-540-44647-8_33

28. Derler, D., Slamanig, D.: Key-homomorphic signatures and applications to multiparty signatures. Cryptology ePrint Archive, Report 2016/792 (2016). http://eprint.iacr.org/2016/792

29. ElGamal, T.: A public key cryptosystem and a signature scheme based on discrete logarithms. In: Blakley, G.R., Chaum, D. (eds.) CRYPTO 1984. LNCS, vol. 196, pp. 10–18. Springer, Heidelberg (1985). https://doi.org/10.1007/3-540-39568-7_2

30. Fauzi, P., Meiklejohn, S., Mercer, R., Orlandi, C.: Quisquis: a new design for anonymous cryptocurrencies. In: Galbraith, S.D., Moriai, S. (eds.) ASIACRYPT 2019. LNCS, vol. 11921, pp. 649–678. Springer, Cham (2019). https://doi.org/10.1007/978-3-030-34578-5_23

31. Fuchsbauer, G.: Subversion-zero-knowledge SNARKs. In: Abdalla, M., Dahab, R. (eds.) PKC 2018. LNCS, vol. 10769, pp. 315–347. Springer, Cham (2018). https://doi.org/10.1007/978-3-319-76578-5_11

32. Gabizon, A., Williamson, Z.J., Ciobotaru, O.: PLONK: permutations over Lagrange-bases for Oecumenical Noninteractive arguments of knowledge. Cryptology ePrint Archive, Report 2019/953 (2019). https://eprint.iacr.org/2019/953

33. Gentry, C., Wichs, D.: Separating succinct non-interactive arguments from all falsifiable assumptions. In: Fortnow, L., Vadhan, S.P. (eds.) 43rd ACM STOC, pp. 99–108. ACM Press (June 2011)

34. Goldwasser, S., Micali, S., Rackoff, C.: The knowledge complexity of interactive proof systems. SIAM J. Comput. **18**(1), 186–208 (1989)

35. Groth, J.: Simulation-sound NIZK proofs for a practical language and constant size group signatures. In: Lai, X., Chen, K. (eds.) ASIACRYPT 2006. LNCS, vol. 4284, pp. 444–459. Springer, Heidelberg (2006). https://doi.org/10.1007/11935230_29

36. Groth, J.: Short pairing-based non-interactive zero-knowledge arguments. In: Abe, M. (ed.) ASIACRYPT 2010. LNCS, vol. 6477, pp. 321–340. Springer, Heidelberg (2010). https://doi.org/10.1007/978-3-642-17373-8_19

37. Groth, J.: On the size of pairing-based non-interactive arguments. In: Fischlin, M., Coron, J.-S. (eds.) EUROCRYPT 2016. LNCS, vol. 9666, pp. 305–326. Springer, Heidelberg (2016). https://doi.org/10.1007/978-3-662-49896-5_11

38. Groth, J., Kohlweiss, M., Maller, M., Meiklejohn, S., Miers, I.: Updatable and universal common reference strings with applications to zk-SNARKs. In: Shacham, H., Boldyreva, A. (eds.) CRYPTO 2018. Part III, volume 10993 of LNCS, pp. 698–728. Springer, Heidelberg (2018)

39. Groth, J., Maller, M.: Snarky signatures: minimal signatures of knowledge from simulation-extractable SNARKs. In: Katz, J., Shacham, H. (eds.) CRYPTO 2017. LNCS, vol. 10402, pp. 581–612. Springer, Cham (2017). https://doi.org/10.1007/978-3-319-63715-0_20

40. Groth, J., Ostrovsky, R., Sahai, A.: Perfect non-interactive zero knowledge for NP. In: Vaudenay, S. (ed.) EUROCRYPT 2006. LNCS, vol. 4004, pp. 339–358. Springer, Heidelberg (2006). https://doi.org/10.1007/11761679_21

41. Juels, A., Kosba, A.E., Shi, E.: The ring of Gyges: investigating the future of criminal smart contracts. In: Weippl, E.R., Katzenbeisser, S., Kruegel, C., Myers, A.C., Halevi, S. (eds.) ACM CCS 2016, pp. 283–295. ACM Press (October 2016)

42. Kerber, T., Kiayias, A., Kohlweiss, M., Zikas, V.: Ouroboros Crypsinous: privacy-preserving proof-of-stake. In: 2019 IEEE Symposium on Security and Privacy, pp. 157–174. IEEE Computer Society Press (May 2019)

43. Kohlweiss, M., Zajac, M.: On simulation-extractability of universal zkSNARKs. IACR Cryptol. ePrint Arch. (2021)

44. Kosba, A.E., Miller, A., Shi, E., Wen, Z., Papamanthou, C.: Hawk: the blockchain model of cryptography and privacy-preserving smart contracts. In: 2016 IEEE Symposium on Security and Privacy, pp. 839–858. IEEE Computer Society Press (May 2016)

45. Kosba, A.E., et al.: C∅C∅: a framework for building composable zero-knowledge proofs. Technical Report 2015/1093, IACR, 10 November 2015

46. Lipmaa, H.: Progression-free sets and sublinear pairing-based non-interactive zero-knowledge arguments. In: Cramer, R. (ed.) TCC 2012. LNCS, vol. 7194, pp. 169–189. Springer, Heidelberg (2012). https://doi.org/10.1007/978-3-642-28914-9_10

47. Lipmaa, H.: Simulation-extractable SNARKs revisited. Cryptology ePrint Archive, Report 2019/612 (2019)

48. Maller, M., Bowe, S., Kohlweiss, M., Meiklejohn, S.: Sonic: zero-knowledge SNARKs from linear-size universal and updatable structured reference strings. In: Cavallaro, L., Kinder, J., Wang, X.F., Katz, J. (eds.) ACM CCS 2019, pp. 2111–2128. ACM Press, November 2019
49. Naor, M.: On cryptographic assumptions and challenges. In: Boneh, D. (ed.) CRYPTO 2003. LNCS, vol. 2729, pp. 96–109. Springer, Heidelberg (2003). https://doi.org/10.1007/978-3-540-45146-4_6
50. Parno, B., Howell, J., Gentry, C., Raykova, M.: Pinocchio: nearly practical verifiable computation. In: 2013 IEEE Symposium on Security and Privacy, pp. 238–252. IEEE Computer Society Press (May 2013)

Author Index

Printed in the United States
by Baker & Taylor Publisher Services

Printed in the United States
by Baker & Taylor Publisher Services